To Butch — In memory of the three years we spent together in the war against the European Axis — with warm regard.

Dwight D Eisenhower

My Three Years with Eisenhower

.The Personal Diary of

CAPTAIN HARRY C. BUTCHER, USNR

Naval Aide to General Eisenhower, 1942 to 1945

SIMON AND SCHUSTER NEW YORK, 1946

MANUFACTURED IN THE UNITED STATES OF AMERICA
BY H. WOLFF BOOK MFG. CO., INC.
NEW YORK, N. Y.

To
General Eisenhower
and the spirit of understanding
which he inspired

GLOSSARY

AA—antiaircraft
AAF—American Air Force
A/C—aircraft carrier
AEF—Allied Expeditionary Force
AEAF—Allied Expeditionary Air Force
AFHQ—Allied Force Headquarters
AG—adjutant general
AMG—Allied Military Government
ARC—American Red Cross
ANVIL—invasion of southern France
AT—antitank
ATC—Air Transport Command
AVALANCHE—attack at Salerno
AWOL—absent without official leave
BOLERO—build-up of U. S. strength in
    United Kingdom
BUTTRESS—attack on toe of Italy across
    Strait of Messina
CCS—Combined Chiefs of Staff
CG—commanding general
CIC—Counter-Intelligence Corps
CIGS—Chief of Imperial General Staff
C-in-C—Commander-in-Chief
Com Z—Communications Zone
CORKSCREW—seizure of Pantelleria
CP—command post
C/S—Chief of Staff
CTF—Central Task Force
DFC—Distinguished Flying Cross
DP—displaced persons
DRAGOON—invasion of southern France
    (formerly ANVIL)
DSC—Distinguished Service Cross
DSM—Distinguished Service Medal
ETF—Eastern Task Force
ETOUSA—European Theater of Op-
    erations, U. S. Army
FABIUS—amphibious landing exercise
fumtu—fouled up more than usual
FUSAG—First U. S. Army Group
G-2—Intelligence
GHQ—general headquarters
GYMNAST—invasion of French North
    Africa (changed to TORCH)
HIRES—invasion of Sardinia
HUSKY—invasion of Sicily

JUGGLER—bombing of fighter factories
    near Vienna
JUPITER—invasion of Norway
LCI—landing craft for infantry
LCT—landing craft for tanks
LCVP—landing craft for vehicles and
    personnel
LST—landing ship tank
MOI—Ministry of Information
MP—military police
MT—military transport
MTB—motor torpedo boat
OM—Order of Merit
OSS—Office of Strategic Services
OVERLORD—cross-Channel invasion of
    France
OWI—Office of War Information
PLUTO—pipe line from England to
    France
PM—Prime Minister
POINTBLANK—all-out bombing against
    Germany
PRO—Public Relations Office or Officer
PRD—Public Relations Division
PT—patrol torpedo boat
PWD—Psychological Warfare Division
RCT—regimental combat team
RDF—radio direction finder
ROUNDUP—1943 plan for cross-Channel
    invasion of France
SC—Supreme Commander
SHINGLE—end run to Anzio
SIW—self-inflicted wound
SLEDGEHAMMER—invasion of French
    channel coast to gain toehold
snafu—situation normal, all fouled up
SOS—Services of Supply
tarfu—things are really fouled up
TORCH—invasion of North Africa
U. K.—United Kingdom
VGDIP—very God-damned important
    personage
VIP—very important personage
VIPI—very important personage indeed
WD—War Department

I RAISE MY GLASS

So many persons have helped me in one way or another to compile this book I'm apprehensive that I may fail to mention all of them. First, for her untiring and loyal assistance, I wish to pay my thanks to Miss Gladys Hall, formerly my secretary for nearly ten years before I joined the Navy, and who was graciously loaned to me for this work by CBS. Helen Harper Shultz, a former CBS employee, typed until her fingers were sore. Jeanne Butler Dixon chased such detail as initials and proper rank until she was dizzy. During the three years when I dictated diary entries the notes were taken down chiefly by Mary Alice Jaqua and Warrant Officer Margaret Chick, both of whom were conscientious and cheerful helpers to whom I again express my thanks.

Jack Goodman, editorial chief of S&S, and I spent weeks making many cuts and writing headings. Then we cut some more. Quincy Howe, who in addition to his work as news analyst for CBS is on the editorial staff of Simon and Schuster, indicated cuts and suggested headings. To both I extend my thanks as well as appreciation of their consideration in my first and probably only attempt at writing a book.

Max Schuster's encouragement inspired me to meet my contract date on the nose but when I did, he said S&S have numerous real authors who have missed their D-Days by months. One, who was seven years overdue, claimed he was plot-locked. Max said I was "big with book." He insisted at every meeting I not forget the story I told him about "the highest." I haven't. I dress my ship to all the S&S gang, but in particular to Bart Winer, who read copy and among other things valiantly but unsuccessfully tried to change Oujda to Ujda because his map said so; Tom Bevans, formerly sergeant, who enthusiastically did all sorts of mysterious things with the printers; Peter Schwed, former artillery officer, who arranged the maps; and Beverly Harmon, Jack Goodman's secretary, who got so involved with my stuff she nearly flunked her own English examination.

Among those at the War Department who have helped me chink in or check facts overlooked or partly recorded while in the field are, in addition to those mentioned in the foreword: Colonels R. Ernest Dupuy, H. V. Roberts, Charles Boehnke, Dan Gilmer, and Stewart Beach; Lieutenant Colonel Gordon Carruth; Captain Eugene Healy, liaison officer, and Lieutenant A. Schwartzmann, who assisted Colonel Monaghan in preparing the summaries of global warfare which are inserted at monthly intervals with the hope of helping orient the reader.

To Ed Klauber and Casey Jones, managing editor of the Washington Post, both of whom, among others, sort of nudged me into preparing the book, and then gave me good advice as to procedure, I can only say that at times during its preparation I wouldn't have thanked them for the nudge, but now that I have struggled through the word marathon I can thank them with all sincerity.

To the British Army—and to Colonel V. E. Scott-Bailey particularly— to the Royal Navy, and to the RAF, as well as to the French Embassy, I give my hand for their wholehearted assistance on numerous details.

To the U. S. Navy I give a salute and say thanks for the help and repeat my gratitude for one of the most interesting assignments any naval officer could have had in the war.

Probably not a single entry was made in the diary without the aid of one or more cigars. These came from a variety of sources including friends at home, such as Jerry Brandon, Steve Early, Harry Hopkins, Sidney Weinberg, Harold Smith, George Allen, C. R. Smith, Earl Gammons, Duke Patrick, John Pelley, Ralph Brunton, Sol Taishoff, Edgar Bill, John Patt, Ann Gillis Slocum, Bob Trout, and John Baer. Because of the generosity and thoughtfulness of these friends—and I'm certain I've overlooked someone—I seldom was out of my favorite Burns Panatelas and a new box seemed always to turn up just in time to keep me going. It seemed like Christmas every time a box arrived.

And last, and therefore of greatest importance, my thanks and gratitude to General Ike for the pleasant and exciting assignment to which he called me. It was an honor to be in his service.

H.C.B.

TABLE OF CONTENTS

PART FOUR: Overture to Liberation 471

PART FIVE: Cross-Channel Invasion 565

PART SIX: The Destruction of German Might   757

PART SEVEN: "This War Was a Holy War"   851

INDEX   877

"OPERATION DOORSTOP"

WHEN I started to put this diary into book form in July, 1945, I ran across an article in the London Express of the same month headed, "At 83 He Still Writes World War I History." The Express story related that Brigadier General Sir James E. Edmonds was dipping into the last of 25,000 boxes of documents he has had to study as official historian of the 1914-1918 war. He began his writing in 1919 and although several volumes of his work have been published, World War II has come and gone before his meticulous record of the First World War has been completed.

Mine is no such meticulous record. Such a carefully prepared history is necessary, but useful primarily for students of history and of military strategy. My hope is that by giving a running account of what I saw I can telescope for the reader the most important developments of the war in Europe. I should emphasize, however, that General Eisenhower has often himself said that no one, including the Supreme Commander, can possibly know everything going on in such a vast struggle of free peoples against tyranny.

When General Ike told me to keep a diary, he had in mind that it would be principally a catalogue showing dates, places, and reminders of interesting events, official and personal. Because I had the privilege of living with him much of the three years, the diary became an intermingling of almost daily entries about the war lives of us both, but necessarily from my point of view, not his. In fairness to General Ike, I hope the reader will keep this distinctly in mind.

As this book took shape, I debated with myself the advisability of asking General Ike to read it. We corresponded on the subject and we came to the conclusion that it would be inadvisable for him to treat my effort any differently from that of other reporters. Consequently, he has not seen the manuscript and I wish to make clear to the reader that this book is my responsibility and not General Eisenhower's. Yet, although I wrote this book, I like to think General Eisenhower lived it. Nor does he share in any income that may come from the book. I will send him an autographed copy but have written him that when the material is published, I should not only go to Tahiti (as we had frequently hoped to do when opportunity permitted us to sit by an open fire and make postwar plans), but will dig myself a deep foxhole and crawl in. Nevertheless, I would like to be a mouse hiding behind a stack of the Westerns on his night table when and if he ever finds time to read this stuff.

I first met Dwight D. Eisenhower in Washington at the home of Sam and Francke Pickard (landlords of his younger brother, Milton) at their home in Chevy Chase, D. C., nineteen years ago. He was then a major. One of the few things that stick in my mind about that evening was that all of us did various parlor tricks. Ike had one none of us could do; he stood stiffly erect, slowly fell forward without moving a muscle, but, at the last instant just before it seemed he would break his nose on the floor, his strong hands and muscular arms quickly broke the fall. He can still do the trick and does on appropriate occasions.

At that time he was on duty at Fort Benning, Georgia, and was coaching an Army football team. He was in Washington on a trip with the team. I also remember that he lamented the fact that he probably would be called to Washington for service in the War Department, as he greatly preferred to stay with troops in the field.

Sure enough, Major Eisenhower came to Washington, where he became assistant to the Chief of Staff and to the Assistant Secretary of War. As a staff officer, he prepared important reports on raw materials, such as rubber, tin, and manganese, essential for any war in which our country might become engaged.

We became friends over the course of the years. He had an assignment for a year in France, serving again briefly in Washington, and subsequently spent several years in the Philippines. We had not corresponded, but one day during the fall of 1941, I read a glowing account of his work as Chief of Staff of the Third Army, which had just finished, in Louisiana, the largest peacetime maneuvers in the history of the Army. In a few weeks I met him again in Washington, he having just been called to understudy Major General Leonard T. Gerow as Chief of the Operations Division of the War Department.

When General Ike received his appointment as Commanding General, European Theater of Operations, he asked permission of Admiral King for assignment of a reserve officer from the Navy to him as an aide. Admiral King not only consented but said Ike could name the reservist. This was me. I recall that our wives, foreseeing that an aide would need formal calling cards, phoned an officer in the Navy Department, an authority on protocol, and asked how the card should be printed; should I be described as "Naval Aide," "Aide-de-Camp," or what? The protocol specialist said there was absolutely no precedent for the assignment and that I could make my own precedent. General Ike liked the idea of an officer in naval uniform on his staff as a sort of symbol of unity of command of the Armed

Services. I had no responsibility for naval matters and, indeed, at first had the title of personal assistant, but because of my uniform, soon became known as the Naval Aide. This title stuck. As the war went on, other Army officers under Ike's command followed suit and had naval aides, and at least one Admiral—Alan G. Kirk—had an Army aide. The Navy paid my salary and the Army furnished transportation and billets (there was a good deal of both of the latter, as you will see).

I had been keeping the diary for a couple of months when General Ike asked to see it—one of the few times in the three years that he ever took the trouble even to scan through it. His comment, when he first saw it, was that I was keeping it in too great detail and that I could accomplish the purpose by using a single loose-leaf sheet to note each day's entry, using the top half of the page for official and the bottom for personal events. I replied that I was entranced by the flow of history-making messages, as well as events and conversations, and, liking to think that I have something of a nose for news, couldn't refrain from writing the story as I saw it develop. I felt myself fortunate in my position. I had a ringside seat for a big show and I knew how lucky I was to be a firsthand witness to world history in the making. I had something of a feeling that I was a reporter for the general public, but at that time I had no clear idea as to whether or how the material ever would be used.

General Ike had no objection to my way of doing it but, so far as he was concerned, he was interested primarily in reminders; when and if he ever undertook to write about the war, he would have access to all the official messages in his files and those of the War Department. I thought that the mere mechanics of assembling messages would not only delay the process of writing, but some might be lost or sent to the archives. For my part, if I ever tried to write a book, I wanted to avoid the tedious task of poring over hundreds of messages. I would prefer to keep a running account of the most significant items as they came to my attention. I suggested that I thought he eventually might wish to write, probably not until the war was over, but he would be aided by having a convenient record in one set of binders to which he could refer to enliven his memory.

When we were on the move, I generally carried a portable typewriter and fortunately remembered some typing which I had partly learned in high school. When it wasn't convenient to carry one, I occasionally wrote longhand, particularly when working aboard the General's Fortress while traveling. Each day I tried to remember what to me was news of the previous day and to write or dictate it at the earliest opportunity.

I had many chores to do for the General. My duties were never spelled out by him. He never thought a good staff officer needed to have explicit instructions on how to solve a problem. In addition to the normal duties of an aide, which run all the way from "baggage smashing" (as General Ike called the management of the office, arrangement for cars for trips and for living accommodations) to buffer and confidant. As the months passed, I found myself dealing largely with the press, taking their reports of good or bad situations in Ike's command, relaying them to him and, in turn, as opportunity permitted, giving the correspondents information in which they expressed an interest. Sometimes I missed contributing to the diary for several days at a stretch. That's why the reader will find an occasional date missing here and there in the diary.

The original diary is on 8½ x 11-inch loose-leaf sheets—typed on one side; on many of the reverse sides are pasted or stapled messages of current interest—in binders, some leather, others cloth-covered cardboard. Because of the fear that our headquarters might be bombed, I had made two sets of microfilms of the sheets after they accumulated. Insofar as it was possible, the original and two microfilms were kept in separate safes.

I returned from Europe with General Eisenhower on June 18, 1945. At that time I had no firm notion of writing a book. I discovered that some war correspondents returning from overseas during the three years had spread the word to their editors and publishers that I had kept a voluminous diary. This word-of-mouth publicity had developed, I judged, largely from the correspondents who had come to me from time to time for information or background for their stories. Quite frequently I had to get out the diary to give details of past events. This apparently intrigued some of the writers. So I decided to whip the diary into book shape.

General Ike had no objection to my writing about what I saw, heard, or observed. I told him I would use the human-interest and personal portions of the diary and would leave to him, if he chose, and to others, the task of writing about strategy and tactics. But I soon found, after he had returned to Europe, that information about development of strategy and tactics was interwoven in the diary to such an extent that inevitably I was bound to poach on the military experts' field.

During the war, many reporters came to me for personal information about General Ike's travels, how he spent his day or just for background about him. I always talked as freely to reporters as my job would permit, and usually the stories were submitted to me for checking before dispatched. If I had a story on my desk about General Ike, he would not look at it. He felt that if the story was complimentary to him, he would be in the position of endorsing praise about himself, and if it was uncomplimentary, he had no desire to get involved. General Ike always told the correspondents and so instructed the censors that no stories critical of him

or his operations should ever be stopped. They were free to write about
him in any way they wished, so long as military security was not violated.
He followed the same rule with respect to my writing this book.

As I had been on a special assignment for the last nine months of the
war and was with General Eisenhower only part of that time, I did not
then have the time or the facilities to write many entries. However, I
kept notes and with the aid of occasional contributions of official messages
and correspondence kept in the diary by Colonel Ernest R. Lee, the General's American military aide, and reports of the General's trips by Colonel
James F. Gault, the British military assistant, I subsequently dictated
entries to cover the latter period. Fortunately for me, I was present when
several of the historic events took place and made extensive notes.

The diary eventually reached about a million words—a monumental
number of small words (I don't know many big ones)—on which I had to
be the city editor, cutting and selecting from the entries to make this book.

In less than three months of daily effort, I had edited from the diary
and had written a total of 640,000 words. By this time I had given the
project the code name, "Operation DOORSTOP."

I found myself continually in a dilemma while editing the diary. Some
of the entries, made while under pressure of the campaigns, appeared too
brutally frank for publication. And I did not want to stir up any discord
among our Allies, but, after all, Allies are like families and occasionally
there are differences which can be settled only by frank discussion. Yet I
wanted to give the reader an honest report and I tried to do so.

I deleted many details about inspection trips, week-by-week casualty
records, routine official events, and repetitions in the day-to-day planning.
Occasionally I have digested or compressed material which seemed too
long or too technical for the interest of the civilian reader. As some of the
information in the diary came from private gatherings, where I was either
a guest or an aide to the host, I have tried hard to be a gentleman about
cutting things that were interesting at the time but were not said for publication. I suppose anybody who keeps a diary and subsequently goes over
it for publication has a tremendous temptation to second-guess and make
himself look like an oracle. I have tried to resist this temptation. The
reader will find that I am no prophet, and any second-guessing done in this
book will be found in the footnotes.

I had the good fortune to have the help of a number of officers who
read the manuscript. Colonel V. E. Scott-Bailey, Military Adviser to
British Information Services and attached to the Embassy, and formerly
our chief censor in the Mediterranean, read the copy from a British point
of view. From a historical standpoint from OVERLORD on, it was checked

by Major Duncan Emrich, Chief American Historian of SHAEF. Lieutenant Colonel Frank Monaghan, Chief of the News Analysis Branch, War Department, and formerly professor of history at Yale, read it with the idea of providing month-by-month summaries of the current state of the global war.

I am pleased that the Armed Services Edition have accepted the offer of Simon and Schuster and myself to print Three Years With Eisenhower for free distribution to members of the forces overseas even prior to commercial publication of the book in the United States. It makes me feel good because I have a notion that there are thousands of GIs and officers still overseas who served under General Ike who would like to know something of what went on in the ivory tower.

I have not attempted to give any biographical information about General Ike or his family, as this has been done by others who are specialists. And professional writers.

January, 1946   H.C.B.

Margaret Bourke-White made this picture for *Life* magazine in General Eisenhower's office at 20 Grosvenor Square in the summer of 1942. Because the war
news was so grim and all of the faces of the General's so-called personal family
were smiling for the photographer, it was withheld from publication. In addition, the General's British driver, Kay Summersby, who knew London and
the signless English roads, had her tongue out at the moment, and Mary Alice
Jaqua, who helped me in writing the diary, was caught in a particularly fetching
pose. From left to right, "Lord" Gilbey, veteran of World War I and driver for
the General; Sergeant Mickey; Kay; Colonel (then Captain) Tex Lee; General
Mark Clark; the writer; the then three-star General; Beetle; T. J.; Miss Jaqua,
and Warrant Officer Marshall, the expert stenographer.

MOST IMMEDIATE

GIB W/T PASS TO
          U.S. UNIT SRK/A   FROM ALGIERS W/

DARLAN   LAN   WISHES   —   TO

NEGOTIATE   —   —   —   IMMEDIATE

          WITHIN   HOURS

HE   REVERTS   NOT   DEAL

WITH   ANY   —   FRENCHMAN   @

MUR   PHY   TO BE PRESENT   BY

MY   DEMAND   ©   RECOMMEND THAT

ARRANGEMENTS FOR DEMANDED ALGIERS   BE

PRESENT   ED   ©   PARTICULARS OF

NAVY   —   —

This is a signal through channels of the Royal Navy from General Clark at Algiers to the Allied Commander at Gibraltar, giving the welcome news that Darlan, whom we thought would be helpful in stopping the fighting, wished to negotiate. You may have to be something of a cryptographer to make out the message, but this semigarbled signal at least illustrates the difficulties of communications in the early days of TORCH. I retained it because it was the first offer of capitulation received by General Ike.

Admiral Darlan, General Eisenhower, Admiral Sir Andrew Browne Cunningham, and General Giraud at a ceremony in Algiers soon after the French capitulated and joined hands to fight the Axis. Tribute was paid to the French, British, and American soldiers who gave their lives in the invasion of North Africa.

Sometimes General Ike doodled a figure quite true to life. I took this from his desk after he had had a long session with General Henri Giraud in Algiers.

Shortly before the German counterthrust which ended at Kasserine Pass, this photograph was taken at the headquarters of II Corps, then in command of Lieutenant General Lloyd Fredendall, center. General Lucian Truscott, then in charge of General Ike's Advance Command Post, wears the two stars.

Lieutenant General F. N. Mason-MacFarlane, Governor of Gibraltar, and General Ike discuss the ticklish Spanish situation, at the St. George in Algiers.

After the fighting was finished in Tunisia, General Giraud expressed the gratitude of the French people by giving General Ike his own Grand Cordon of the Legion of Honor, which he had refused to wear until he again could march down the streets of Metz. General Ike accepted the honor and said he, too, would not wear the decoration until Metz was liberated, hoping they could parade down the streets together. He didn't like being photographed as he was kissed, consequently the picture was withheld at that time.

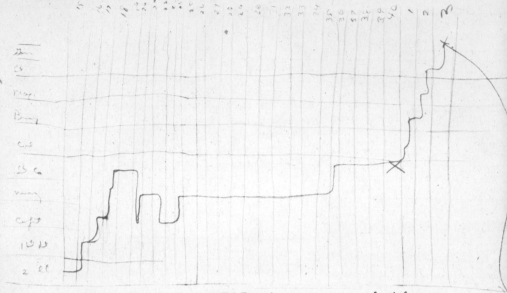

One day at the St. George, Ed Beattie came to see me for information about General Ike's promotions in the Army. I thought the
Allied Commander was a proper authority on this subject and, as he
was free at the moment, asked him to give Ed the facts. He drew this
graph to indicate his rank each year, from Second Lieutenant in 1915
to four-star General in February, 1943. I drew the line showing him
hitting the skids after reaching the fourth star and he drew the
fishing pole to indicate his postwar ambition.

General Patton got his third star in Tunisia, where he commanded the II
Corps while its mission was to help Montgomery get through the Mareth line.

I took this picture at the headquarters of General Alexander (center) in Tunisia when the Germans were undergoing what General Ike called "their inevitable Tunisia." General Omar N. Bradley (right) then had command of the II Corps, having succeeded Patton, who, in turn, had succeeded Fredendall.

The bridge foursome in which the luck of the Naval Aide and General Mark Clark sometimes balanced the skill of the Allied Commander and Major General Al Gruenther, Fifth Army Chief of Staff. Taken at the airfield near Oujda where Clark was training the Fifth Army and itching for action. He and the Army got action, a long siege of it, after the landings in Salerno Bay.

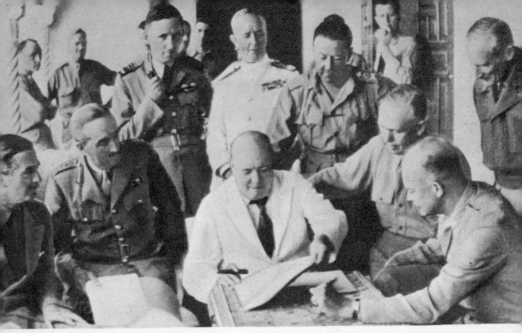

On the veranda of General Eisenhower's villa when the Prime Minister, accompanied by General Marshall, visited Algiers to discuss strategy. Seated, left to right, the Foreign Minister, Mr. Anthony Eden; the CIGS, Sir Alan Brooke; the Prime Minister; General Marshall, and General Ike. Standing, left to right, in the background, Colonel Frank McCarthy; General Tom Handy; Air Chief Marshal Tedder; Admiral of the Fleet Sir Andrew Cunningham; General Alexander; the writer, with a cigar; and General Montgomery.

I took this aboard the Aurora when she led the parade of Royal Navy warships which bombarded Pantelleria to determine the number of shore batteries still functioning after heavy air attacks. Commodore Roy Dick (left), Executive Officer to Admiral Cunningham, and General Ike, quite happy about the test.

General Marshall was a master at conducting a press conference. This photograph was taken after he talked with correspondents at the St. George. In the background are the inquisitive Naval Aide and Brigadier General Robert A. McClure, Chief of Information Services of AFHQ, who was startled when General Ike took all the correspondents into his confidence and told them weeks in advance that we would attack in Sicily. The confidence was not broken. His main purpose was to prevent correspondents known to be close to AFHQ from speculating about the next Allied blow in the Mediterranean.

President Roosevelt, General Eisenhower, and General Patton (left), in Sicily, fall of 1943. As usual the secret-service men were very much in evidence, protecting the Commander-in-Chief, presumably from the United States Army.

Generals Ike and Montgomery (left) look across the two-mile Strait of Messina to the toe of Italy, where the latter would soon attack. Monty commented that it would be a pleasure to return to the Continent, as the last time he had been there, he and many of his compatriots had been somewhat rudely evicted at Dunkirk. General Ike is studying the terrain on which our artillery shells are falling. The attack across the strait came a few days after this picture was taken, on the fourth anniversary of the start of the war.

The Allied Commander visited personnel of the 101st Airborne Division the evening before D-Day for OVERLORD. This widely printed photograph is, to me, a reminder of one of the toughest decisions of the war that the Supreme Commander had to make. Air Chief Marshal Leigh-Mallory had earnestly advised the Supreme Commander against the American airborne operation which was intended to help the ground troops get ashore and stay there. The Air Marshal feared that from 70 to 80 per cent of the effectives in the operation would be lost. General Ike ruled otherwise. The airborne operation was successful and Leigh-Mallory was the first to say that fortunately he was wrong.

The Prime Minister was a frequent visitor at General Ike's Command Post in the woods near Portsmouth. This was taken on one of the occasions when Mr. Churchill ardently sought to dissuade General Ike against the southern invasion of France. Standing, left to right, are Commander Thompson, the Prime Minister's Naval Aide; T. J.; Colonel James Gault; the so-called Naval Aide; Beetle, and Brigadier L. C. Hollis, Secretary, British Chiefs of Staff.

Our landings in the
Cherbourg — Havre area
have failed to gain a
satisfactory foothold and
~~I have withdrawn~~
the troops. ~~~~~
~~condition.~~ ~~This particular~~
~~Junction~~ | My decision to
attack at this time and place
was based upon the best
information available, ~~and~~
If the troops, the air and the
navy did all that ~~possibly~~
Bravery and devotion to duty
could do. If any blame
or fault attaches to the attempt
it is mine alone.

If the cross-Channel operation had failed, General Ike intended to issue a communiqué and he rough-drafted it the day before the landings. He stuck the draft in his wallet and forgot about it until several weeks later, when he found it. I asked him for it as I thought it of interest, since it showed how he instinctively assumed responsibility, particularly if anything went wrong.

Major General R. S. McLain, Commander of the XIX Corps, only American Corps Commander who was a National Guardsman, General Ike, and Lieutenant General William H. Simpson, commanding the Ninth Army, at the citadel at Jülich, former German strong point on the Roer River which was well beaten up by the Ninth Army when it started its offensive to the Rhine.

The Supreme Commander's inspection trips seemed almost unending. He kept a careful eye on the flow of supply—and how it flowed. Here he is shown visiting rear-line facilities at Cherbourg and talking with PFC T. L. Honeycup about quantity of ammunition his crew could unload in one day. Sergeant Jules Grad, *Stars and Stripes* pool reporter, is shown behind the General.

General Ike's rapid departure from the status of a relatively unknown staff officer to that of an important world figure is shown by this casual crowd that quickly gathered at the Scribe in Paris as he departed after a press conference. Many GIs carried cameras, and the Supreme Commander, whenever time permitted, would stop briefly to permit the amateur photographers to get shots.

Discussing the surrender terms at Rheims, while in another room representatives of the German Doenitz regime examined the terms of unconditional surrender: left to right, Major General Kenneth Strong, G-2 of SHAEF; Major General Pinky Bull, G-3; Admiral Burrough, C-in-C Allied Naval Expeditionary Forces; General Spaatz, and General Morgan, Deputy Chief of Staff. Nearly hidden by Morgan is Air Marshal J. M. Robb, head of SHAEF air staff.

This marks the day and the event that all the world had been waiting for. General Gustav Jodl, the German Chief of Staff under Doenitz, with his back to the camera, in the center, signing the document under which all remaining forces of the German Army were bound to lay down their arms in unconditional surrender. The scene is the war room of Supreme Headquarters at Rheims which Beetle complained was a Hollywood setting. On General Jodl's left is Admiral von Friedeburg of the German Navy and, on his right, is Major Wilhelm Oxenius of the German General Staff. Allied officers across the table are, left to right, Lieutenant General Sir Fred E. Morgan, Deputy Chief of Staff; General François Sevez, representative of General Alphonse Juin, French Chief of Staff; Admiral Sir Harold Burrough, C-in-C Allied Naval Expeditionary Forces; Beetle; Lieutenant Ivan Chermiaev, interpreter; Major General Ivan Susloparov, Russian representative; General Carl A. Spaatz, Commanding General, USSTAF; Air Marshal J. M. Robb; Major General H. R. Bull, and Senior Lieutenant Colonel Ivan Zenkovitch, interpreter. The naval officer in the background is on a special mission re: fountain pens.

Field Marshal Keitel at the Berlin ratification of the Rheims unconditional surrender. The photographer caught this expression of Prussian and Nazi arrogance, which I, and all others who saw it, will forever carry in our minds. Left to right, Colonel General P. F. Stumpf, commanding the Luftwaffe; Keitel, wearing Hitler's highest decoration; and Admiral von Friedeburg, Commander-in-Chief of the German Fleet, who later committed suicide.

From where I sat at the banquet, these three—Tedder, Zhukov, and Spaatz— were prominent amongst those at the head table who bobbed up like jacks-in-the-box proposing toast after toast with Russia's secret weapon—vodka.

PART ONE

Preparation for Invasion

JULY TO NOVEMBER, 1942

The Battle of the Social Front

LONDON, WEDNESDAY, JULY 8, 1942

Ike says I'm to keep a diary. Have never kept one, so this is a new job. But everything is new, including dictation into a dictaphone, so might as well get started.

Ike is striving to get quarters outside of London, to eliminate many of the distractions which now bother him and interfere with general efficiency of the headquarters staff. In the meantime, we are operating in the apartment building, called "flats," at 20 Grosvenor Square, quite an address for military headquarters. There's a Marine mess in the basement, from which arises the odor of boiled cabbage and Brussels sprouts.

Captain Ernest (Tex) Lee, the General's Aide-de-camp, Miss Theg, the General's stenographer, and I are crowded into a 10x12 office adjacent to Ike's. So many persons come and go, and as these notes are both personal and secret, I felt it wise to get a dictaphone in my room at the Dorchester. We had been waiting several days for this one to become available. Then Ike's own machine arrived from Washington by air and he released his old one to me. Didn't expect to fight a war with a dictaphone.

Now to catch up to date:

Around the middle of June, I was at the CBS office one evening, giving Earl Gammons, my successor as head of the Washington office, a fill-in on the background for his new job. I had gone into the Navy June 1. Ruth * called from Fort Myer, where she was having dinner with Mamie † and Ike. Ike had just come home from the War Department and was full of news, and what news! General Marshall had designated him Commanding General of the European Theater. Further, Ruth said, Ike wanted *Butch to go with him.*

Later Ike asked me to lunch, to discuss arrangements. What he wanted was an old friend around to whom he could talk eye to eye, without having to worry about subservience. I said I was complimented even to be considered for the job, sure wanted to go, and would do my darndest.

He obtained Admiral King's assent to the principle of assigning a Naval Reserve officer as one of his aides. However, my immediate superiors in the Communications Division of the Navy first thought the Army was proselytizing Navy men and were not too happy.

Had just begun to handle my job under them. However, they turned out to be darned good sports, especially after Ike called on one of my chiefs, Captain Joseph Redman, and I received my Navy orders to report to General Eisenhower in Washington. There was no precedent for it. General Eisenhower then endorsed the Navy orders, which was a bit unusual, and instructed me to report to him further at London. Meanwhile I was to bone up in the War Department on plans for European operations, so I wouldn't be too much of a civilian lunkhead.

Ike, Captain Lee, and Sergeant Michael McKeogh, of the Corona McKeoghs, left Bolling Field by Stratoliner Tuesday, June 23. As Ike is the junior major general, or at least was, of the several major generals over here, he was in the position of being their Commanding General with a slightly junior rank. Also, the British were beginning to wonder: was General Eisenhower merely an interim commanding general, after all?

Incidentally, upon advice of Captain Dillon, Secretary Knox's confi-

* Mrs. Butcher.
† Mrs. Eisenhower.

dential aide, I brought along two sets of aiguillettes (chicken guts, some say), each with three strands to match the three stars of a lieutenant general. When the Senate confirms Ike, it will also validate my three-strand aiguillette, but neither of us gives a damn about them—they are a bit too flashy for Ike's taste and will be worn only on formal occasions, when absolutely necessary.

Everyone congratulated me on my good fortune in being selected aide to General Eisenhower. I even congratulated myself. There were some very pleasant and typical farewell parties—one at Joe Davies', one at Burning Tree, and another at "Uncle" Jesse Jones'. I just happened to be the current excuse for poker games. The Burning Tree party, engineered by Steve Early, naturally enough developed into a poker game, in which they took me to the well-known cleaners. I lost the limit under our "poverty" rule. Made up for this at the other two, however, even though they did say I had to cheat to beat Frank Page out of a big pot at Joe Davies' house. Uncle Jesse was very gracious also. He got first prize at his party and I got the second. At least he and I enjoyed it.

Ike had given instructions that I was to come with Colonel T. J. (Thomas Jefferson) Davis.* His crony, Ralph Pulsifer, a lieutenant colonel, and I finally got off from Washington by train Tuesday afternoon at 6, to take the Clipper from LaGuardia Field. T. J. and I left the Pan American Clipper at Foynes, in Eire. Both of us had brought a civilian suit, which we wore during our brief stay in Southern Ireland. We were driven about forty miles to an airfield, where a British Overseas Air Command plane, with all windows blacked out, flew us to Bristol. There we boarded a train for the last leg of the journey. We were met at the station by none less than the great George Allen † and Captain Ernest Lee.

Ike was going out of town on an inspection trip that night, but wanted to see us first, and George came along. If a war could be made happy, George could do it. He was a good tonic for Ike. General Ike had asked me to see him in suite 408 at Claridge's. Ike said he was glad to see me. He complained about his ornate gold-walled suite and said he was going to

---

* Colonel T. J. Davis is to be Ike's Adjutant General. Colonel Davis had been aide to MacArthur and closely associated with General Eisenhower in the Philippines. He is roly-poly, with bright, flashing brown eyes, and comes from Columbia, S. C. In general the AG keeps the record for the headquarters, the roster of personnel, and issues orders for and upon authority of the commander.

† George Ed Allen had been Commissioner of the District of Columbia by appointment of President Roosevelt and was recalled by the President for further duty in this position on what the President termed "short-term loan" from the Home Insurance Company; a fine storyteller with the butt of the joke often himself; an enthusiastic but frequently dejected follower of the ponies; a tight poker player, and a noisy but companionable golfer. George and I had become fast friends in Washington.

move as soon as possible to a less pretentious apartment. Ike said he had told Tex Lee to fix a desk for me in his outer office, but space was limited, and I would find myself in cramped quarters.

Ike had been very busy and was seeking ways and means to combat what we have come to call "the Social Front." He was having to decide on numerous invitations to lunch and dinner, and already had a heavy schedule. He won't fight the war over a teacup. Yet, he didn't want to offend either the British or the Americans, all of whom wished to be nice to him. He was also having difficulty in determining who was important and who was not, who should be seen and who could be put off. Later I got Ed Murrow * to help us on this. However, meanwhile, we—or rather Ike— settled his social policy: no functions involving purely civil activities, only military.

The existing headquarters staff was the outgrowth of a special observer's mission assigned to London while America still was neutral, and the transition from Special Observer to Commanding General, one being essentially a reporting job and the other an action responsibility, had left American General Headquarters a bit slow on its feet. Ike instituted the seven-day work week that prevailed in the War Department and groused a good deal over the lackadaisical attitude.

"After all," he said, "it is a war and we're here to fight, and not to be wined and dined."

Ike arrived in London the evening of June 24. Next morning he started a day filled with staff conferences. He stressed to the staff that each section must bear its share of responsibility and push incessantly toward the attainment of the objective, which is to have an army in the field, ready to attack, by early spring of 1943.

What concerned the Commanding General most was the cultivation of determined enthusiasm and optimism in every member of his staff and every subordinate commander. He refused to tolerate pessimism or defeatism and urged anyone who could not rise above the recognized obstacles to ask for instant release from this theater. He urged the greatest informality in the staff work, put himself at the disposition of his subordinates, but told them they are free to solve their own problems and not get into the habit of passing the buck to him.

All staff work was to be characterized by an absence of formality, and, as he put it, "we are not operating or writing for the record, but to win the war."

The staff was further informed that all policy-making applying to this theater lay with this headquarters. It was emphasized that no set scheme

* Chief of the Columbia Broadcasting System's European news service.

of organization, training, or concept of command was to prevail over common sense and in adjusting our means to meet our needs. Absolute freedom in planning to meet our requirements has been granted this headquarters. This imposes a corresponding responsibility to act decisively and promptly and with no alibis.

During the next few days, the new CG held almost constant sessions with his staff officers. One of the toughest problems was the organization of the headquarters of the theater (ETOUSA, European Theater of Operations, United States Army) and the Services of Supply (SOS), headed by General John C. H. Lee.

Ike pointed out to me that the same issue kept coming up throughout the last war and remains a tough one. There is no perfect solution, but in General Lee Ike felt he had one of the finest officers in the Army and a man who had the best possible qualifications for a job that requires a high degree of human understanding.

Ike had already announced his intention of moving General Headquarters outside London, where all hands could live together like a football team and think, plan, and execute war all our waking hours. He has had the Headquarters Command, Colonel P. B. Rogers, in charge, scouring the countryside.

I reported at headquarters Friday morning, July 3. Had lunch with Ed Murrow, General Robert A. McClure, and George Allen at Claridge's. I had hamburger. It tasted sweet. Ed said it was horsemeat and I hoped he was kidding. Ed will be a great help. He is on intimate terms with Winant, Churchill, and many others.

Understand General McClure, Military Attaché at the Embassy, is to be Ike's head of G-2 (Intelligence). He knows his stuff.

Had dinner with Ike and George Friday night. Ike told a story on himself about his visit at Lord Louis Mountbatten's ancestral estate. After an official dinner in London, Lord Louis, Ike, and Captain Lee set out for Lord Louis' ancestral castle, somewhere south of London. Lord Louis had taken one of his cars that had not been used much, and it broke down. They reached the castle about 2 A.M. Ike had told his orderly, Mickey McKeogh, to pack him "light." He was assigned to the most dignified suite, in which many of the world's great dignitaries doubtless had preceded him. One room had Chinese wallpaper dating from 1760. Most of the younger servants had gone to war, and some old retainers had been called back to domestic service. One was attending Ike. His nose was turned up to start with, but when he unpacked the American General's brief case, with its one pair of pajamas, one toothbrush, razor, and small items, the nose rivaled a barrage balloon at full height. Being a Kansas country boy at large,

Ike noticed this disdain, felt self-conscious, and, even as you and I, left a handsome tip when he departed at 6 A.M.

During dinner George was not averse to giving some military advice. With Rommel pushing toward Cairo, George envisioned the loss of the Suez, plus a join-up with the northern prong of the giant German pincers through Russia and into Turkey. This would close the Mediterranean, and give Hitler a tremendous advantage. George then foresaw Hitler quickly taking Eire, then sitting back and saying: "All right, boys—I'll starve out England." George had this all down, chapter and verse. To reply, Ike said he was forced to tell a story. He said there are only two professions in the world in which the amateur excels the professional. One, military strategy and, two, prostitution.

The next morning, I got together a little piece for Ike to consider for his remarks at the acceptance of the Washington Club. Ike took my 150 words or so, added a line or two, and this became our first press release covering a public speech for the Commanding General. The Press Relations Office put it out as a handout, and the General, Lee, and I were driven by "Lord" Gilbee, the English chauffeur, to the club. About 500 were present: Red Cross workers, Lady This-and-That and So-and-So, plus a snappy Army orchestra. The speakers were Ambassador Winant, presented by Mr. William Stevenson, the head of the American Red Cross in Great Britain, Admiral Harold Stark, and Ike. The General had decided not to read his stuff, and I could tell that beneath his outward pleasantness, the "ladeda" of the occasion was getting under his skin. True enough, when he got up, the red blood was rising up his neck. He was darned close to mad. He delivered the little speech from memory, substantially as written. It was probably his soldierly and belligerent attitude more than what he actually said which caused the whacking ovation when he finished.

Later, Ike told me an old Englishwoman had come to him and said she had lost her husband and a son in the war. She had been despondent and dejected, but said Ike's speech had cheered her up and given her the first real confidence in the war. She had been waiting for toughness.

Also, two American Red Cross nurses had been cheered up. Their group of sixty American girls in the Harvard Unit had been in England a year and had never been visited by an American officer from headquarters. They felt somewhat neglected, and Ike promised that he and General Clark, who will be stationed in south England, would visit their hospital. They tried to get him to promise to attend a dance at Salisbury the nurses were giving that night, and Ike, wanting to cheer them up, halfway promised. (He never dances, anyway, except under duress.)

That evening, being somewhat concerned about his half promise and fearing that the nurses might become so discouraged they would pull up and go home, their year of voluntary service having just terminated, he gave me my first Army assignment—to pay a visit to the nurses, with George and Captain Lee. When we arrived, we found they were not short of men. They were just short of American men. We met the heads of the hospital, shared in the fun, and visited until the dance was over.

The dedication occurred on the morning of the Fourth, and Ike had promised Ambassador Winant to attend the Fourth of July reception for the American colony. This was given from 4 to 6 at the home of the Ambassador, which had been donated by John Pierpont Morgan. Winant had not been living there, and the place had to be opened for this occasion. Ike didn't realize what he was getting into. He was placed in the receiving line and shook hands with most of 2630 persons who passed through. Although his appearance there probably did some good, we all felt it was a hell of a way to fight a war. However, it was the first reception in three years, and probably his last for the duration.

I was standing by in a side room while Ike was doing the glad-handing, when Brigadier General Charles L. Bolte telephoned to say that details of the first American air raid on German airfields in Holland had been received. We already knew that two of the six planes were lost. General Bolte came over with the report, which Ike stepped out of the line to read, then decided, as soon as the reception should be over, to return to headquarters to check over a press release which Lieutenant Colonel Harold Hinton, the PRO,* was preparing. One of the American fliers, Captain Charles C. Kegelman, after his plane had been struck by flak while flying at fifty feet, putting out one motor, righted his plane, turned against an enemy flak nest, and gave it his guns, silencing the opposition. Ike decided immediately to give this man a DSC (Distinguished Service Cross), announcement of which he included in Lieutenant Colonel Hinton's draft of the press release. In this he was heartily supported by Generals Spaatz and Eaker. Subsequently, DFCs (Distinguished Flying Crosses) were awarded to Kegelman's crew.

The Fourth of July, 1942, had been a busy day, but Ike was liberating himself from social distractions.

Ike was at the office early Sunday and was raising hell because the Chief of Staff and section heads were not in the office by 10 o'clock. Butcher, having been on special detail at Salisbury the night before, rolled in at 3:30 P.M. That evening, Ike, accompanied by General Clark, and under

---

* Public Relations Officer. Not to be confused with Prophylactic Station, also labeled PRO in Army abbreviations.

the guiding hand of Gilbee, went to Chequers, formal residence of the King's First Minister, to spend the night with Mr. Churchill.

George and I went out to Tony Biddle's country house in Sunningdale for dinner. Had a delightful time. Mrs. Biddle is a gracious and "easy" hostess. Present were Ed Beattie, of UP; Quentin Reynolds, of *Collier's*; Jack Kelly, of Pan American; Helen Kirkpatrick, of the *Chicago Daily News*; Mr. and Mrs. Winslowe-Brown, of Newcastle, and one or two others. Quent Reynolds had just returned from an uneventful mission in a medium bomber over France. He was lamenting the lack of action, and also the loss of a few dollars at gin rummy en route.

Although the opening of the diary may read like a social calendar, the Commanding General actually is hard at work.

On Thursday, July 2, and after a siege of 245 days, Sevastopol, last Russian stronghold in the Crimea, fell to the Axis. Russia's peril had not appeared so grave since the general offensive had reached the Moscow suburbs. The Red Army is carrying the brunt of the battle. The papers at home and in England are filled with demands for a second front.

Rommel finally has been stopped by the British some seventy miles from the Delta. Much of the American and British production, and a large proportion of British manpower, are being rushed to help Auchinleck, not merely to hold but to drive back Rommel. Both the Russian and desert situations are causing grave concern.

President Roosevelt and the American Joint Chiefs of Staff * insist that we help Russia stay in the war. How long Russia can last is the query in everyone's mind. While familiarizing myself with plans in the War Department, I learned that the Combined Chiefs of Staff, representing British and American land, sea, air, and production power, have been considering a quick thrust across the Channel during the summer of 1942, on the assumption that if a toehold can be obtained on the French coast, some of Germany's strength will be diverted from the Russian front. This projected operation goes by the code word, SLEDGEHAMMER. Its purpose is to serve as lifesaver to a drowning ally. But the main project in this theater

---

* The American Joint Chiefs of Staff together with the British Chiefs of Staff comprised the Combined Chiefs of Staff, which was the top military authority charged with directing the prosecution of the war. The Combined Chiefs were General Ike's bosses. The British Chiefs of Staff were represented on the Combined Chiefs by a British Joint Staff Mission in Washington and through this Staff Mission, the British Chiefs of Staff, headquartered in London, expressed the views of and acted for the British Chiefs. From time to time during the war, meetings were held of the Combined Chiefs with both the American and British Chiefs of Staff in attendance, such as at Washington, London, Casablanca, Quebec, and Malta. The roster of the Com-

is to plan, build up, and execute a major all-out effort across the Channel in the spring or summer of 1943. This much larger projected operation goes by the code word, ROUNDUP. The build-up of American strength in the U.K. (United Kingdom) is called BOLERO.

After many conferences with the British during his first three weeks as Theater Commander, General Ike reported to General Marshall in Washington that the British Chiefs of Staff and the Prime Minister had decided that the SLEDGEHAMMER operation could not be successfully executed in 1942 if our invading force was expected to retain its beachhead. (It must be borne in mind that the United States is relatively new in this war and we are perhaps inclined to take more chances. The British by now have had nearly three years of it, and have suffered a succession of defeats in ground operation. Understandably, they are cautious and realistic.) Lack of suitable landing craft (only enough for one division) is the principal material reason given by the British. They feel that, psychologically, a failure would cause almost disastrous results and even a partial success would cost more in adverse effect on ROUNDUP—the 1943 big-league operation. Instead of trying to get a toehold in France this year, the British Chiefs propose deception of the enemy by assembly of shipping. They also urge Commando raids on an increasing scale both in size and intensity to keep the enemy upset. They count, too, on an accelerated air offensive.

British military authorities are fearful, in reaching this decision, that General Marshall may feel that they have let him down. Yet the British Chiefs state that no other person in the military world commands such universal respect and confidence as the American Chief of Staff.

---

bined Chiefs of Staff, the American and British Chiefs of Staff, and the British Joint Staff Mission, as of July, 1942, follows:

General of the Army George C. Marshall	American Joint Chiefs of Staff	
General of the Army Henry H. Arnold		
Fleet Admiral William D. Leahy		
Fleet Admiral Ernest King		COMBINED
Admiral of the Fleet Sir Dudley Pound	British Chiefs of Staff (in England)	
General Sir Alan Brooke		
Air Chief Marshal Sir Charles Portal		
Field Marshal Sir John Dill	British Joint Staff Mission (headquartered in Washington)	
Admiral Sir Andrew Cunningham [1]		
Rear Admiral W. R. Patterson [1]		
Lt. General G. N. Macready		
Air Marshal Douglas C. S. Evill		

[1] Cunningham served during early part of month but was replaced in July by Patterson.

The British appear to be favoring an attack in North Africa—"to get on Rommel's tail"; in fact, the PM has said that President Roosevelt suggested such an operation before the United States entered the war. Ike, however, feels that if he were ordered to conduct an offensive in 1942, he would prefer to cross the Channel rather than open a new front in North Africa, which he fears would not materially assist the Russians in time to save them.

The British would like an early appointment of a Supreme Commander, and some British officers have been outspoken to Ike in favor of General Marshall, even if he had to operate from Washington.

War in the Pacific seems quite removed from London, at least in British papers. Good news today, however, which made page 1. American sub sinks four Jap destroyers. Good enough.

Ike works late and doesn't like his staff to disperse until "the Old Man" has gone. When we got back to the Dorchester Monday evening, General Clark, Ike, and I sat around and gassed until it was time for them to go to the Ambassador's dinner. Ike said he thought he had been Chief of Staff for more years than any other officer of his age, and that he had never left the office until his "Old Man" had departed. This headquarters, he thought, is not clicking the way it should.

While Ike was "ambassadoring," George and I had dinner at Claridge's and were en route to a newsreel theater—cinema, I suppose I should say—when we walked into George's friends, Dr. Daniel P. O'Brien and Dr. Hugh H. Smith, former Johns Hopkins men long with the Rockefeller Foundation in Europe. They insisted that we accompany them to their apartment to try some old port. We did. Three bottles until one o'clock. These men know many things and well. Dr. O'Brien says there is a spectacular development in medicine coming along that will be a greater benefit to mankind than sulfanilamide, cures certain infections that even sulfanilamide won't touch. Called penicillin and derived from bread mold. Takes eleven acres of mold to cure the scorched face of one flier. The doctors are going to America to arrange mass production by commercial producers.

Dr. Smith hoped the Supreme Commander would be an American. Said he felt the British people, having some lack of regard for British generals at the moment, probably because of Tobruk, would welcome a hard-hitting American general as King Bee. Dr. O'Brien shared this opinion. I told them this bridge was not being crossed at the moment.

When we were throwing the bull in Ike's room, as he was getting dressed for a private dinner at the Dorchester, Ike lamented the fact that British generals do not have aides in London; only in the field. This means that when he's invited to a meeting, of which there are many important ones going on, no one suggests he bring an aide. He would like to take me, so I will know what is going on and report it in the official or personal diary. Takes too much of Ike's time to try to tell me everything that has happened. I get a lot of it by helping read proof on messages to Washington, watching the outgoing letters, and by general curiosity.

Walking back from lunch on Audley Street this afternoon, for the first time noticed a woman street sweeper. Uniformed, plump, and cheerful, she was gingerly brushing accumulated horse manure into her dustpan on wheels, and humming a tune.

With this, I will close the prelude, and try to take up the diary day by day henceforth.

LONDON, THURSDAY, JULY 9, 1942

This was not a particularly exciting day. As usual, there were no bombs in London, although hit-and-run (the British say "tip-and-run") Jerry planes frequently sneak into southern and eastern England. Much desk work until late in the day, when Ike, Chief of Staff General Bolte, Colonel Rogers and his British counterpart, with a black beret, looking very snappy with a swagger stick, and another officer or two and I visited one of the outlying places where the American GHQ might be established—Hounslow Barracks. This place is about forty-five minutes by automobile from Grosvenor Square. We had high hopes for it.

As we approached we could see sewer pipes outside the brick and stone walls. We looked over the barracks carefully, returned many salutes, but the newest building we saw had a cornerstone marked 1860—would be too cold for officers to work at desks. Wouldn't be hard to fix if we were in America, but lack of shipping space weighs against importing material to make the barracks usable. When the CG poked his head into one of the barracks, several English soldiers in their underwear stood stiffly at attention.

Ike, having no formal dinner tonight, was in a good mood for George and me, and particularly George, to discuss possibilities for the evening, mostly bridge. George tried hard to get a fourth. Among the persons he phoned was a lady of the peerage, and she said, after explaining to him that she was engaged for the evening, "Isn't it too bad that the most important man in England simply cannot find a fourth at bridge!"

After a very fine dinner, George insisted that we walk up Piccadilly to our hotel, if for no other reason than for the CG to know the morality conditions on Piccadilly. It may be well to say that George said that we would see at least "three combat divisions of ladies of the street" on our way back to the Dorchester. When the first one approached, she looked straight at George and purred:

"Hello, fat boy. Does your mother know you're out?"

Ed Murrow calls 'em the bravest in London; stayed on the street in the heaviest raids.

Today, at the request of the press through PRO, a great many photographs were taken of General Eisenhower. Captain Lee, who runs the appointments, set aside a full hour this morning. First there was a specialist in color, Robert Capa, accompanied by Quent Reynolds. A color picture is supposed to be on the cover of *Collier's*. Ike doesn't care when or if they use any picture, because he thinks the less he's in the papers, the better. The still photographers got many shots, at least—there was a full hour of same—and I will say that no one but a Sunday-school teacher with a class of nice girls could have been as obliging as Ike. After one hour and a hundred or more bulbs, we finally got the crowd away, with satisfactory grace.

The General strongly advocates the arrangement suggested by a British lady that the British open their homes for American soldiers. He feels, in company with General Mark Wayne Clark, whom he describes as one of the really coming officers of the American Army, that if an American soldier has the opportunity of living, say for a week end, in the home of a British family, possibly helping them to wash the dishes, tending the garden, and becoming a handy-andy around the house, there could be developed a much greater degree of friendliness and companionship than if both are standoffish. Few can quarrel with that principle. I should add that I'd had lunch in company with Mr. Stevenson, head of the American Red Cross, and that he had said this was impossible because he had lived in England for three years and he knew how difficult it was for the British to accept any stranger into their homes when they would take two or three years before a stranger would be invited.

But Ike and General Clark had discussed it; they know their British, they know their soldiers, and they say that is the way to do it. So, if the Red Cross doesn't want to push the idea, already advanced most vigorously by British women, some fourteen thousand strong, then Mr. Stevenson will turn out to be quite wrong.

Let this go down as a note: "singleness of purpose"—this is the phrase I have heard about Ike on many sides during my first week in London. They, and I mean the British as well as the Americans who are involved, mean we shall have under Ike a singleness of purpose to pursue our invasion plans until Hitler is forced to fight where we want and forced to yield.

Another note: General Eisenhower has reached these isles at a moment when the morale of the British is at its extreme low. Their sons and husbands and brothers and fathers were at Tobruk. How or whether they have come through, these proud wives, mothers, and sisters do not know.

The New Three-Star General

LONDON, FRIDAY, JULY 10, 1942

Sat down with Captain Lee for breakfast at the officers' mess this morning. He said, nonchalantly: "I see by the morning paper that the General's promotion as Lieutenant General has been confirmed by the Senate."

When we reached the office, an official message to this effect had come through from General Marshall.

Friday being a lucky day in my book, I suggested that Ike be sworn in immediately and arranged for T. J. to do so, despite the fact that he doesn't take over as Adjutant General until tomorrow.

George took us to a celebration lunch at Claridge's. Not all of the same persons, however. There was the new three-star General, also General Clark, T. J., Lee, Jack Kelly of Pan Air, and I. There were four "short-snorters" present. Three of us, General Clark, Lee, and I, could not produce the qualifying American dollar bills, and each was fined a pound, but was admitted to the sacred but prolific order of "short-snorters." This netted the others nearly a pound apiece. We have a chance to get our money back if we can find others without American dollar bills. Ike took a special delight in soaking his aides.

For the record: I had arranged for a Signal Corps photographer to make a picture of the swearing-in exercise, but so many pictures of Ike had been made on Tuesday that no publicity was given to the swearing-in. Also, Ike's hand, raised to take the oath, unfortunately covered the third star in the picture.

Airborne Demonstration

LONDON, SATURDAY, JULY 11, 1942

Ike asked me to accompany him and General Clark to see an airborne demonstration at Silkhill near Salisbury, about two hours' drive southwest of London. We were driven in General Clark's car.

The Silkhill demonstration, under the command of Major General F.

A. M. Browning, was to show the development of technique for seizing an enemy airport. The demonstration consisted of parts of the various operations not at this time made completely consecutive. For instance, a smoke screen laid by aircraft to conceal the landing of airborne equipment and troops was deferred until late in the demonstration, so as not to mar the view of the four or five hundred spectators, including Air Chief Marshal Portal and various other high officials. Most interesting was the use of gliders. Carrying seven men and equipment for each, two gliders to a plane, the gliders would cut loose, swoop low over the field, and keep gliding, close to the ground, for a mile. They had no brakes, but were skillfully handled by regular RAF pilots. When the training of glider pilots progresses sufficiently, such high-class pilots will not be needed. One exceptionally large glider, capable of carrying, I think, twenty-three armed soldiers, landed behind trees about a mile from the observers, and we could not tell whether it was so intended or not. The paratroops jumped from 600-800 feet, and each one made a good landing. Even carrier pigeons were dropped by parachute, not to mention motorcycles, cannon, and bicycles. Jeeps came by glider. When the affair was finished, I asked General Clark if he thought our American paratroopers' work had reached this stage, and he said it had not, but was coming on rapidly. Glider production in States advancing rapidly.

Royal Story

LONDON, SUNDAY, JULY 12, 1942

As every day is a workday, we were all at the office fairly early. The four American members of the bombing crew that made the daylight raid on Nazi airdromes in Holland, celebrating the Fourth of July, came in to pay their respects to the CG. Captain Kegelman in the meantime had become a Major, not because of his exploit, but, as he said, "it was on the way." George came in while they were waiting and, much to his delight, discovered that the rear gunner was from his home town, Tupelo, Mississippi —Sergeant Cunningham. The boys were a joy; extremely modest. I told Kegelman of the story about his wife in Oklahoma when she heard the news of his exploit and his DSC from Ike from a newspaper reporter on the telephone. Her comment had been quoted as: "Read it again and then I'll faint."

I stepped into Ike's office when the boys were presented. Ike didn't ask them to review their adventure, as he figured they were tired of talking about it. During a lull in the conversation I mentioned to Ike that the fliers had discovered what appeared to be a store of naval ammunition and that they were going back to get it. When the fliers were leaving the office, going down the corridor, I overheard Sergeant Cunningham say, "Who was that guy who said we were going back to get it?"

Have neglected so far to record what I think is a classic story about the King and Queen. Incidentally, when I gave a reporter for *Time* a verbal list of Ike's appointments and activities for the week, so much had happened that I forgot even to mention his duty call on the King on Wednesday.

Ike has been having a steady grind of appointments each day, and when we arrive at flat 314 in the Dorchester, he frequently is so tired that I hesitate to ask him many questions, knowing that when and if he is ready to talk, he will. I feel it part of my job not to raise problems, particularly concerning the war, during the hours when the Commanding General should be getting some diversion and relaxation. Consequently, while I was curious about his visit with King George VI, I didn't ask him anything about it. But yesterday, Ike told some details of his forty-five-minute conversation with the King, whom he found to be most personable and very much "in the know" as to current and prospective plans for Allied operations.

The King told of an incident that had occurred at Windsor Castle, the residence of the King and Queen and their lovely family. About six weeks ago, the King had related, he and the Queen had been informed by Baron Clive Wigram, custodian of the ancient property, that two high-ranking American officers would like to visit the castle on Sunday afternoon. The castle normally was closed to visitors then, but the King and Queen had readily assented to the visit and volunteered to stay in their quarters to avoid embarrassment to the American sightseers. However, by the time Sunday afternoon rolled around, it was such a beautiful day, they found themselves sitting in a small, secluded garden in the area where Baron Wigram ordinarily brought distinguished visitors. While enjoying the sunshine, they suddenly heard Baron Wigram's voice. He was saying, as he touched a flower with the cane, "A lusty little fellow" and "Here's a bright little chap." Remembering their promise not to be in the garden and fearing their royal presence, if discovered by the Americans, might embarrass them and cause Baron Wigram to shorten the tour of the castle, the King and Queen quickly stooped behind a hedge and escaped from the small garden through a low opening in the wall, under which they had to crawl on their hands and knees. Both the King and Queen had a good laugh. His Majesty relived the incident as he described the visitors as one very tall and the other simply tall. Ike completed the King's story by identifying the generals—one was Mark Clark and the other, of course, was Ike. They had visited the castle while on a quick mission to England several weeks before Ike had orders to go to Europe as CG.

The General Meets the Press

LONDON, MONDAY, JULY 13, 1942

Accompanied Ike to the London Clinic at 5:30, where he received a new type of injection for the neuritis in his shoulder. The treatment proved more rigorous than either of us had anticipated, and I certainly hope it works. On my recommendation, he has been having an osteopath rub him, and the shoulder has shown some progress, but not fast enough. He didn't want to take the time to go through the rigmarole of a complete laboratory checkup, which he was certain would be required if he reported his ailment to the Army doctors. The doctor seemed quite hopeful of success for the treatment, which required insertion of the needle in several places in a small area and forcing a flow of novocain through the joint where the fourth rib joins the backbone.

General McClure joined us for dinner at Ike's apartment. In conversation after we had left Ike for the evening, McClure was not too sure about the advisability of moving headquarters out of London, because of the need of maintaining close contact with British war establishments in town. Also said that so much reliance is placed on radio, to give directions to aircraft and ships, that the British are fearful of jamming by the Nazis. Apparently, this was done by the Germans when they succeeded in running the *Scharnhorst* through the Strait of Dover. By jamming, so much confusion was caused that the best offensive could not be carried out by the British. Apparently there are several radio stations on the French coast especially equipped for jamming.

McClure pleased at change in attitude and effectiveness of General Staff since Ike has arrived, but says there are a lot of difficulties yet to be met, particularly in exercising complete command of American forces. (This seemed to me to have been straightened out by Ike. Maybe not.)

LONDON, TUESDAY, JULY 14, 1942

Generals Marshall and Eisenhower exchanged cables, reviewing the prospect of an agreement with the British for offensive operations this year. General Ike reported to Marshall that he had repeated the American view of the transcendent importance of keeping Russia in the war, and that British and Americans should do whatever may best assist to that end. The CG had explained to the British—as a matter of personal opinion —that the collapse of Russia would force the United States to go on the defensive throughout the Atlantic and to build up offensive operations against Japan.

However, the British position continues conservatively along the line that a moderately successful invasion in 1942 probably would have little or no effect on the Russian front, while a disaster, resulting from a premature attempt to invade, would adversely affect the Russians. The CG cautioned, however, that this opinion was not unanimous among all the British, but was generally held and was the conclusion of the Prime Minister.

General Ike added that, within the past few days, the feasibility of continuing convoys to Murmansk has been brought into serious consideration and, if these should be stopped, he believes that the British probably will consider some 1942 operation mandatory. CG constantly urges the view that no matter what the nature of future decisions, there should be no slackening of intensive effort to build up and train our forces for a supreme effort at whatever moment they may be called upon to fight.

I had run onto a statement by one of our public-relations officers, in connection with the release of pictures taken of Ike, Lee, and myself last week, which indicated that newsmen and others had the impression that no names of American officers in the British Isles could be printed or broadcast except those of General Eisenhower and General Spaatz. Upon checking the facts, I found that a censorship directive had been issued prior to Ike's arrival, creating such a limitation, and prohibiting mention of the names of any officers above the rank of major, to prevent identification of commanders and hence of units of armed forces with which the officers have been identified. However, this has left Ike in a bad light. It means his and Spaatz's are the only names which can be printed. I was anxious to have it corrected.

Ike called a press conference, or rather a "conference with the press," as he put it, for this afternoon at 4 o'clock. It was an effective meeting. Ray Daniell, head of the London Bureau of *The New York Times*, and President of the Association of American Correspondents in London, presented a memorandum of complaints about censorship and our public-relations officers, upon behalf of the association's executive committee. Among other things, it charged that certain personnel of the Public Relations Office looked with "disdain" upon newspapermen and their work. There are, of course, two sides to the story, but something is wrong.

Ike took up the complaints one by one and, insofar as he could, took action on them on the spot. The censorship rules will be revised to give newspapermen more freedom and clearer understanding, yet retain desired security.

After the group departed, some twenty-five or thirty of them, Ike had the Chief of Staff make immediate arrangements to add some additional censors to complement the force of two now covering a twenty-four-hour day. He also called Mr. Daniell on the phone and suggested that he, as President of the Association of Correspondents, have a small committee draw up their own proposed plan of censorship for Ike's personal consideration. If this is satisfactory, he made clear that he wanted to work with the newspaper and radio men on a basis of complete frankness and trust. He said he had been double-crossed by only one newspaperman in his life, yet had dealt with the press for many years. This attitude, as might be expected, was well received.

He also gave out a story, mimeographed, setting forth the names of five senior subordinate commanders in this theater, permitting their names to be used hereafter in stories. This also served to make clear that he is the boss. After all, he told the newsmen, it is his neck that is on the block, and it is his policies which will succeed or fail. He also said that every effort would be made to satisfy the complaints of the press. He asked me to be an ex parte student of the problem and to be in a position to advise him as to the recommendations and suggestions which will come to him from the correspondents. After watching Ike deal with the press, I don't think he needs a public-relations adviser. He is tops.

Incidentally, he told them a story (intended primarily for background, but because the press would like to use parts of it, he permitted them to do so) about the invitation of some fourteen or fifteen thousand British women to take American soldiers into British homes when they are on leave. This story supplemented his off-the-record suggestion that as stories that had news interest developed, they could successfully combat the Axis propaganda that the RAF and American Air Force were not getting along well together and that British and Americans were not mixing well. This may be a major problem and he asked the press, as patriotic Americans, to tell the good stories—aggressively, not defensively. The press also asked if they could see the colored troops. Ike said he saw no reason why they couldn't and would fix it. As background, he told them his policy for handling colored troops would be absolute equality of treatment, but there would be segregation where facilities afforded. The colored troops are to have everything as good as the white.

Ed Murrow was at the conference and called me afterward to say that

Ike had made a grand impression and that he (Ed) had been a member of the executive committee which drafted the bill of complaint. Said he wanted to spend some Columbia money on me, so accepted a date for lunch Wednesday.

LONDON, WEDNESDAY, JULY 15, 1942

Lunch at the Connaught Hotel with Ed Murrow, Bob Trout, and Charles Collingwood, all former CBS associates. Helped train Bob from a pup at WJSV. Much radio talk with the three of them, and as might be expected from good radio reporters—I might have been doing it myself, had I still been on the other side of the fence—they phrased questions to get an expression from me as to when and if there would be a second front. For instance, Bob was wondering whether he ought to plan to stay in London or return home. My answers were of necessity evasive and indefinite, but I did indicate to Bob that all of us thought this theater would be the scene of action at some time. Referred them to Mrs. Winston Churchill's public statement, which appeared in the press yesterday, that there would be a second front. Am afraid they thought CBS lunch money was wasted.

Terrific difficulties working in small office with Lee, who bellows like a bull; with two typewriters, not noiseless; with frequent interruptions by callers coming and going. Particularly so, as I need a private place to dictate my stuff, which, after all, is secret and, no doubt, would make good listening and good reading to many who are not known enemies. Incidentally, these notes are kept in the safe unless I am working on them and are replaced in the safe if I am called from the desk.

Second Front in 1942?

LONDON, THURSDAY, JULY 16, 1942

Big things today. Moved into a new office this morning, sharing with Captain R. C. Booth, assistant to the Chief of Staff. No typists and much less confusion, plus more space. Also, chairs for visitors. Two cloth-covered windows which let in the breezes. (Practically no glass available to replace bombed-out panes.) Have abandoned the dictaphone.

Captain Lee came in before noon and said the General was canceling all appointments for a week. He was in the dark as to the reason. I assumed it was some extraordinary inspection trip.

Didn't see Ike until late this afternoon, when he called for me. We

hashed over some ideas for improving public relations, including the
wisdom of removing the Public Relations Office from the supervision
of G-2, which is also the censoring agency. A division of this sort would
be parallel to that already in effect in Washington, where Byron Price
runs censorship and Elmer Davis war information. In the War Department, also, General Alexander D. Surles, the chief Public Relations Officer, reports to the Secretary of War, not to G-2 (Intelligence, including
censorship). Censorship is negative and publicity is positive; one is re-
pressive, the other promotional and service. The two do not mix well
when administered together. Ike also received a letter, which he had sent
on to me during the day, from Mr. Daniell, cleverly ducking the responsibility for getting up proposed rules of censorship, but making a number of
useful suggestions.

For the first time since we have been here, Ike suggested we leave the
office "early"—6 o'clock. We had hardly sat down in Ike's apartment
when he received an important message. It turned out to be from General
Marshall and involved immediate consideration of a second front in
Europe in 1942. This the British had been opposing, and Ike had so
reported to Washington.

Important visitors are on their way from Washington tonight—General
Marshall, Admiral King, Harry Hopkins, and others. It is obvious they
are going to try to argue the British, particularly the Prime Minister, into
making a quick move for at least a toehold on the Continent, with the
hope of helping the Russians, who have been falling away fast the last few
days. Ike has been greatly concerned over the Russian position and last
night described it as "desperate."

The Marshall message to Ike required immediate assembly of data and
views as to when and where and with what such a drive could be made
this summer or early fall. Take a look at the date. Remember the Channel
and that an invasion requires fairly good weather. The "season" for invasion is late May to September 15; in other months weather is too
unreliable and waves are too high. Also, the British military have been
promised a two-month notice from the PM before starting an invasion.

Ike immediately set me to calling for the senior generals. In short order
came General Lee, head of Service of Supply; Colonel Ray Barker, Assistant Chief of Staff for Plans; General Tooey Spaatz, Air Force; and by
10 o'clock from Salisbury, General Clark.

Ike outlined the facts and views they are to assemble. The Washington
visitors are due late Friday afternoon, and General Marshall requested
Ike, by personal message, to have all the dope ready.

Ike says that, oddly enough, a second front on the Continent depends primarily on the British, who, so far, have not wanted to do it this year; yet the Americans favor it. A drive on North Africa to hit Rommel's rear depends primarily on American troops brought from the United States with costly and scarce shipping facilities, yet is desired by the PM and not by the American military leaders.

Opening of a second front on the Continent soon is regarded as helpful to Russia only if it will cause Germany to withdraw troops and flying forces from the Russian front. And even with a second front in the next two or three months, would it be too late? Germany is thought to have enough forces in France to repel any attack which can be made by the British and Americans, now or in the very near future. All present were extremely doubtful of any relief coming to the Russians, yet it appears necessary to do something immediately to help them. At the same time, it is difficult to help Russia or to appraise her situation when "Uncle Joe" does not give us any information.

Today I read three editorials from American newspapers, all urging a second front. Judging from what I heard tonight, I believe the editorial writers and others, except those closely familiar with the facts, little know what a cost, probably what a futile cost, is involved in a second front now.

If Germany rolls up Russia's armies and gains the rich oil fields that seem to be easily in her grasp, will the United States then concentrate on licking Japan first and leaving Germany until later? How much later, it is impossible to tell. With Japan and Germany, with their highly industrialized systems, then having the vast resources of Burma, the Dutch East Indies, the Malayan peninsula, and all their raw materials, the British Empire, as we have known it, would be gone, and the United States would find itself in a defensive position, substantially alone in the world. Plans already have been made for removal, if necessary, of the seat of the British government from London to Canada. Upon the discussions to take place in the next few days may rest the future history of the world.

LONDON, FRIDAY, JULY 17, 1942

At 11:30 this morning Ike called me into his office, where he was having a meeting with Generals Clark and Lee and a number of other staff officers. He tossed me a message just received. It served notice that the Honorable Stephen Early had been added to the group coming from Washington. What a surprise! I immediately asked if I could meet him at Prestwick (Scotland) and was given a prompt go-ahead. Steve was an old friend of the days before he became press secretary to Roosevelt, when he represented Paramount newsreel and I CBS.

The TWA Stratoliner bearing the Washington party was due at Prestwick at 5:20 P.M. We had time for "high tea," which we were glad to get,
as we had missed lunch. Discussing the virtues of high tea, Commander
Thompson was reminded of an incident which occurred on the last flight
the PM and his party had made to Washington. Members of the party
discussed the advisability of having lunch or high tea before arrival. The
question was put to the Prime Minister. He settled it with the flat statement that it was time for "high whisky."

The TWA plane came in at 5:19. In the party were: General Marshall,
Admiral King, Harry Hopkins, Steve, Brigadier General Charles P. Gross,
Brigadier General W. B. Smith, Colonel Hoyt Vandenberg, Commander
Ruthven Libbey, Major Frank McCarthy, and Commander J. R. Fulton,
Harry Hopkins' doctor.

Since the weather was bad, it was decided the party would not continue
its flight to an airport near London, as originally planned. The PM had
sent his own train to stand by for this contingency. We boarded the train
at the town of Prestwick at 6 o'clock.The train trip gave opportunity for
extended visiting. Harry Hopkins, Steve, and I were apparently the last to
bed. Harry and Steve played gin rummy. I bet on Steve, unfortunately.

We breakfasted aboard and left the train at Euston Station, where the
party was met by Ike, the Ambassador, and some British officers, both
Army and Navy.

Steve and I had dinner in the CG's apartment with Ike and General
Clark, with much friendly and big talk. Since Thursday, Ike has been
working night and day, preparing reports for General Marshall's use, and
has frequently been closeted with Marshall, Admiral King, and others of
the party. They are preparing the case for a second front this year, to be
presented to the British. Harry Hopkins has gone to Chequers for the
week end.

Ike Recommends the Second Front in '42

LONDON, SUNDAY, JULY 19, 1942

Ike worked hard all day. Kept two stenographers busy, writing a proposal
to be used by General Marshall and Admiral King with the British.

Ike, Clark, and I had lunch with Steve at Claridge's. Steve was much
taken by both the CG and Clark. Incidentally, the PM calls the tall,
lanky, sharp-nosed Clark "the American Eagle." Don't know what he
calls Ike.

Steve told me after lunch that the PM had raised holy hell with Harry
because the precise protocol of calling upon the Prime Minister first had

for some reason not been followed, and discussion had started informally among General Marshall, Admiral King, and various members of the British General Staff. The PM had declared in most vigorous language, as he strode up and down the room at Chequers, that he was the man to see first, that he was the man America should deal with, and that the British Army-Navy staffs were under his command. And to emphasize his authority, he read from a British book of war laws, and, as Steve put it, as he read each page, tore it from the book and threw it on the floor!

The PM had said that the party should have been handled so that he personally met the American delegation at the railway station. Anyway, all this apparently didn't faze Harry, who can give as well as take. Harry regarded this as primarily a continuance of the previous meeting in Washington. They had a verbal slugging match, as seems to be customary between the two. But they are deep and respectful friends. Seems the PM has the quality of getting off his chest what he has to say.

Late in the day, Ike finished the draft of the basic proposals for Marshall and King to present to the British, and we waited at the apartment during the evening for word from Marshall if there were to be any changes. Presently, an officer came with the proposal, as slightly revised by Marshall and King, and with a handwritten note from Marshall to Ike to take a look at their changes and to polish the language if necessary. There had been no change in the meaning, but some of the fire of Ike's pungent language had been toned down. General Clark was with us. Ike phoned Marshall to say that he had no further suggestions. The proposal was for a second front in France by October of this year, to help the Russians. These are momentous days!

Nearly forgot to mention that Ike, Clark, and I listened at the office to Ed Murrow's broadcast on the BBC Home Service from 6:30 to 6:40 this afternoon. Ed painted Ike as representative of the "great American middle class." Ike got a chuckle out of Ed's line, "I don't know whether Eisenhower is a good general or not."

LONDON, MONDAY, JULY 20, 1942

As soon as General Marshall arrived in London on Saturday morning, he held a conference at the Claridge with Admiral King, General Ike, and our other top military and naval commanders over here. They discussed a possible attack on western Europe this year, taking into account British as well as American findings, and giving primary consideration to the help such an operation would give the Russians. This means assessing, first, the real situation on the Russian front and, second, the prospects for a

second front in the west. By Sunday morning, opinion crystallized in favor
of an attack on the Cherbourg peninsula. General Marshall is to see the
British war leaders today and recommend immediate preparations for an
attack in September, if conditions then appear favorable. This project
calls for intensive training and changes in present shipping schedules.
Only a final decision concerning this year's operations can relieve the
present tense atmosphere.

After work, General Clark and I returned to the apartment. Ike had
to stand by for a call from Marshall, so Clark and I had dinner at the
officers' mess. He returned to stand by Ike, and I took a walk.

Met a Canadian Scot on leave from Aldershot and discovered he had
no place to sleep; invited him to use my spare bed. He was Lance-Corporal
Dick Lawrence of Truro, Nova Scotia, a machine gunner with the Toronto
Scottish outfit. He was wearing kilts. He was a big fellow, and apparently
hadn't slept in such a comfortable bed for a long time. He sprawled all
over the bed and was still sleeping soundly when I left in the morning.

Still trying to find location for headquarters outside London, but not
much progress.

The Bombed Areas

I had asked T. J. to get Steve and me passes to see the bombed areas which
ordinarily are not shown. Instead of a pass, we got the personal services
of none less than Admiral Sir Edward Evans, whom I discovered later is
known as Evans of the *Broke*, a name attached to him during the last war.
As Commander of three British destroyers, he had bobbed up against a
lot of German cruisers and destroyers on a dark night in the Channel and
had sunk all the German ships without loss of a destroyer.

The Admiral and his driver, Margaret, spent two hours showing us
damage, particularly the East End and the Surrey Commercial Docks.

The Admiral was especially active during the blitz. He gave us some
unpublished figures. Casualties from the London boroughs, 17,000 dead,
40,000 wounded; 1,300,000 buildings, roughly eight out of ten, hit. One
out of eight houses was ruined—300,000 in all.

He took us to what had been the Morley School, where night classes
had been held. Four hundred had been in this building when it received
a direct hit. Broken water mains flooded the basement, drowning many.
Escaping gas asphyxiated others. Margaret had worked in a rescue squad
and had assisted in the extrication of forty-five persons. For this she had

received a medal. Said this was the first time she had been back to the site of the Morley School since the disaster. All the debris had been cleared away.

Despite the diversions occasioned by Steve's presence, I managed to get some work done. Consulted with Colonel Case, G-2, on his proposed reply to the official complaint of the Association of American Correspondents in London. A letter had been drafted for signature of the Chief of Staff, but Ike had handled the conference with the press himself, so I told Colonel Case the CG should handle the letter and sign it himself. Case and Colonel Hinton, the PRO, have worked out a statement covering the liberalized press-relations policy outlined by Ike at his conference. This is being widely circulated to press and all officers concerned in this theater. Steve saw this and said it was a splendid job, and he ought to know. I didn't know at the time that Ike had required Case to redraft it four times before it met approval.

Steve also saw Ike's draft of an identical letter, to be addressed to each of his five senior commanders—i.e., Clark, Lee, and Spaatz (all in England), Russell P. Hartle (in Northern Ireland), and Charles H. Bonesteel (in Iceland). The letter was long and covered a variety of the CG's desires for attention in his command. One in particular brought emphasis to the desirability of facilitating friendly commingling of American and British soldiers—a point that Ike has pressed every day.

When I got back to the Dorchester I saw a strange pair of shoes at my door. Inside I found my Scotsman of the night before, sound asleep. How he got in, I don't know. He didn't awaken then or at 7:30, when I left for work. Apparently, he liked my hospitality—certainly the bed. Got a note from him on Wednesday, via Mickey, full of thanks.

No Second Front in 1942

LONDON, WEDNESDAY, JULY 22, 1942

Ike had been busy dictating various documents for the use of General Marshall and Admiral King. Also in numerous conferences with them and the staff. Knowing I was not in a position to keep intimately in touch with events these stirring days, the CG dictated a memo for me, too.

The gist of his comment was that the British have repeatedly gone on record against the proposed SLEDGEHAMMER attack because they believe it will not relieve Russia's situation and will expose us to the risk of a tactical disaster—partly because of superior German strength in the west; partly because of bad weather conditions. The Americans had assumed that the British could mount an attack on Cherbourg within sixty days, but it now appears that they need at least three months—preferably four. This would mean postponing the operation until mid-October. And by that time the Russians will get less benefit and the weather will become much worse.

The American point of view, expressed by the CG and General Clark, was that the Russians' situation may become so desperate as to make even an unsuccessful attack worth while, especially if it could be launched soon. Everyone recognized the risks; everyone also believed that the British and American military leaders and the British and American people wanted to see something positive attempted. In any case, agreement at the military level should be reached today by General Marshall and Admiral King, for the United States, and the British Chiefs of Staff. The Americans hoped to provide two divisions, some auxiliary troops, and a reserve armored division, all under the field command of General Clark.

Archibald MacLeish, James Warburg, and Murray Brophy, formerly with CBS on the West Coast, were in London and came in today to confer with Ike. Sat in with them. They are setting up a London Bureau for the Office of War Information, as headed by Elmer Davis at home. Have plans for propaganda leaflets, both "black" and "overt." "Black" means those printed and distributed over Europe by us, but intended to indicate they are published surreptitiously in the occupied countries. "Overt" classifies those openly identified with the United Nations' effort. This will be Jim Warburg's main job. MacLeish will leave after setting up the bureau. Brophy is arranging radio broadcasts for American soldiers in England.

Lunched with Steve and Dr. Fulton. Steve mentioned privately that British are going along on second front this year. Figured Marshall-King mission a success. His comment based on dope from Harry Hopkins.

Ike left for important meeting of Combined Chiefs of Staff with Marshall and King about 6. This continued into formal dinner until nearly 11.

Steve said the barometer had gone down, and the British had refused to go along on the American proposal for a second front this year but had made alternate proposals. This I had known from Ike, but this job makes me tongue-tied.

Almost as important as the second-front discussions has seemed the arrival of my trunk, which came today. Ike's still is missing; supply people under General Lee burning the cables to find the Commanding General's trunk, apparently feeling this personal example of their efficiency will affect his appraisal of all their service. They shouldn't worry too much, but boy, are they busy!

LONDON, THURSDAY, JULY 23, 1942

Saw a report today that telephone calls handled through the American Forces switchboard here in 20 Grosvenor have increased from 2000 to 6000 a day in six weeks. There are twenty-one girls and four more are being added. Most of these need training, but are the best available. Phone service is the one and practically only source of irritation.

Saw Ike and General Clark at breakfast. The proposal for a second front this year has definitely been turned down by the British as too risky and too unlikely really to help the Russians.

"Well, I hardly know where to start the day," Ike said. "I'm right back to December fifteenth." He added that he was worried that circumstances now will cause further dispersal of the Allied forces, particularly American. He and Clark were deeply disappointed. Ike thought that Wednesday, July 22, 1942, could well go down as the "blackest day in history," particularly if Russia is defeated in the big Boche drive now so alarmingly under way.

During the day, Ike got his gang together at the office and they settled down to assemble pieces of the wreckage of their plans. Briefly, the British wanted to attack on a new front in Africa, but to accelerate heavy bombings on the Germans, harass with Commando raids on the Continental shore, and wait for a break in German morale.

On this day, Ike completed and submitted to General Marshall, at the latter's request, plans for preparation and action. This met with approval of Marshall and King and contents were summarized by them in a message to the President. Its major strategy was to prevent the Germans and Japs from joining forces, by their giant pincers movement, in the Middle East. Rommel can almost smell the Suez and the Japs are knocking at the door of India. If the Middle East should be lost, additional important resources, particularly oil in Iran and Iraq and the fabulous riches of India, would be in the hands of the Axis. The war would be prolonged many years.

Ike and I went back to the hotel about 7. He had had no lunch, having worked straight through and delivered his proposal to Marshall late in the afternoon. Steve had seen Ike and Clark at Claridge's and given them a cocktail. I undertook to stew up some of the noodle soup, but found that the electric water heater, by misapplication of the plug, had burned out.

Then I tried the alcohol heater. All this in Ike's bedroom, while Ike and Clark chatted in the living room. The alcohol burned black and sooty, and we had to shut it off. With hurt pride over my poor results, I had humbly to ask room service to prepare our soup. About this time, General Smith (Beadle) came in and we increased the ration of dehydrated noodles to four portions. This, with bread and butter, was all we had for dinner, but it was probably the best we've had in London.

While we were enjoying this dinner, a call came from General Marshall that he and the Admiral had transmitted the essence of Ike's recommendations to the President. Ike said, during dinner, that Napoleon had written that the most difficult thing for a commanding general is, after making a plan like ROUNDUP (which Ike was fearful would now be abandoned by the British), to await the development of the plan and not allow himself to become impatient and diverted from the main plan by starting inconsequential side shows. Napoleon had learned that such distractions weaken the effect of the major plan and, in fact, interfere seriously with its execution. Ike is fearful that just this is happening now.

Both Beadle and Clark were doubtful that ROUNDUP (invasion of Europe in 1943) would be junked by the British. Beadle said, "We should carry out ROUNDUP if we have to wait three years."

Tonight marks the end of seven days and nights of what Ike calls a "blitz." It was just a week ago that we learned of the delegation coming from Washington. Ike has worked eighteen hours a day every day, and tonight is the first relaxation—and this on noodle soup. And this is not the end of the blitz, by any means.

(Steve told me something today, by way of wanting to make a bet, that when repeated by me to Ike, we decided to leave in our subconscious minds—but it's big!)*

The New Decision—TORCH

LONDON, FRIDAY, JULY 24, 1942

Got in a good day's work today. Saw very little of Steve, as he lunched with the Prime Minister and the guests.

A private railway car has been refinished by one of the British railway companies for Ike's use. He was asked to see it this afternoon, but was in conference with Marshall and gang. Captain Lee was tied to his desk, so the "dog's body" † undertook the inspection. It is a beautiful car. It is finished in teakwood, with a dining room that seats eight normally and ten if desired; also serves as an office with a desk for the CG. The car sleeps six individuals in separate compartments.

General Clark returned to his headquarters in southern England today,

* See February 15, 1943 entry.
† Term frequently used by the British to describe an aide: something always under foot and easy to kick.

but first got a haircut at a "hairdresser's" (barbershop) recommended by General Bolte, who said it was not only good but was patronized by the King. Clark had a haircut, shampoo, and tonic. He gave the cashier a pound note, expecting change, but she said: "It's one pound, four, sir."

The General thought $4.80 was high. We told him it must be worth something to sit in the King's chair.

Ike spent much of the day with Marshall, King, Hopkins. Indications of getting together with the British, not on a second front for '42, but with the prospect of substantial agreement.

Stopped at Claridge's for cocktails at a party given by MacLeish, Warburg, and Brophy in honor of Steve and for the American press and radio. Someone told me a new name for Grosvenor Square—"Eisenhowerplatz" —and for the Air Force—"Spaatzwaffe."

Met Ike at his apartment later. We spent a quiet evening, standing by for any calls from Marshall.

(Actually, the decision of the Combined Chiefs had been made this day, Friday, subject to the approval of Churchill and Roosevelt. It was to clean up North Africa and Rommel. New code name selected— TORCH.)

LONDON, SATURDAY, JULY 25, 1942

General Clark had invited Steve to visit his II Corps headquarters near Salisbury and asked me to take him there. All plans had been made to spend the afternoon and evening, which would have been very enjoyable. Then Steve phoned me to cancel all plans, to get to the Claridge right away, and he would tell me why. I hurried the two blocks.

The delegation was going home that night. Steve said: "By God, you can't go back to the office any more today. Harry and I are having a luncheon, and I'm calling your boss to command his attendance. You're going to pour me on the train tonight."

Lunched in Harry's suite, other guests being Mrs. Randolph Churchill, Miss Kathleen Harriman, her father, Minister Harriman, and Ike, who came in from Marshall's suite for a quick lunch. Found Kathleen had forgotten her "short-snorter" bill, so she was penalized five shillings for each short-snorter present. We discovered Harry hadn't been made a short-snorter, and he joined with pleasure and cash. He was happy to be going home, as his wedding with Louise Macy is set for the 30th at the White House. The Prime Minister and Mrs. Churchill and the Harrimans sent lovely silver gifts to be carried home. Other short-snorters made and hooked were Tony Biddle, William Bullitt, and Lew Douglas. The luncheon and afternoon were not without uncertainty. Harry talked with the President by telephone and found that the President hadn't received the last message from Marshall and King which covered the proposed agreement and the actual tentative agreement among the Combined Chiefs of Staff, and each was subject to approval by Roosevelt and the Prime Minister. Since the Prime Minister was understood to be in agreement, the question was up to the President.

Finally, the President received the message at Washington. He wanted immediately to have a meeting of his advisers—just who, we didn't know. If he had disagreed, the party could not have left London as planned. Finally another call came from Washington, and about 6 o'clock, Harry, who had been receiving numerous callers, and had been ducking in and out of parlor and bedroom doors, and trying to be host while conducting an international negotiation via transoceanic telephone, poked his head out of a bedroom door and said:

"O.K., boys, we're going home."

Poured Steve on the train and he poured me off.

Rode home from the station with Ike about midnight. When we got to his rooms, he told me that the proposed agreement provided that Marshall would be Supreme Commander of American and British Forces, and that he (Ike) would be Deputy Supreme Commander under certain conditions or Supreme Commander under others, with prospect for action in Africa. In other words, Ike would be given still higher responsibility. He said he had been told by Marshall (while taking a bath at Claridge's) that while discussing in the Combined Chiefs of Staff meeting the selection of a Supreme Commander for the North African operation, Admiral King had said:

"The best man you can possibly get is right here and available—General Eisenhower."

Ike had no idea King appraised him thus. The British had insisted the top commander should be an American and the expedition be led by American troops (though many troops would also be British) because of their hope that Americans would meet less resistance from the French.

The agreement is, however, complicated. It makes a considerable change in plans and may result, Ike suspects, in the abandonment of the second-front idea even in 1943. Plans and training for a Continental invasion are, however, to be pressed hard. The new plan is for an offensive against northern and western Africa. This is partly to encircle the Axis, not only to attempt to save the Middle East, but to clear North Africa of the Axis and to put more pressure on Japan in the Pacific. This amounts to a policy of the two great English-speaking nations doing something now, while awaiting the inevitable preponderance of production. In addition, the defense of the British Isles remains a paramount consideration. The islands afford the best base for air operations against Germany and for invasion of the Continent. Ultimate object is invasion through France, but this must wait, possibly until the Germans crack. A great deal, perhaps the final outcome of the war, depends on Russia.

General Eisenhower Explains the Strategy for 1942

LONDON, SUNDAY, JULY 26, 1942
General Clark and I breakfasted with Ike, who undertook to explain the new agreement in all of its ramifications. These are some of the main points he made.

On July 22, the British Chiefs of Staff and the Prime Minister rejected the American proposal for an attack on Cherbourg in 1942. This means that the Allies can do nothing to help the Russians this year and must prepare for the possibility of a Russian collapse. But the President insists that American troops must be in action against Germany some place during 1942.

It therefore appears that ROUNDUP—the major invasion of western Europe—must wait until the whole German position deteriorates badly. Meanwhile, the problem is to determine the proper action for Allied forces during the remainder of 1942. The old GYMNAST operation * seemed to have more to recommend it than the dispatch of American troops to the Middle East. It was decided to start preparing for GYMNAST—now TORCH—at once. The British do not share the American view that TORCH rules out ROUNDUP.

As a result of these decisions, one individual will have charge of preparing for both TORCH and ROUNDUP. This commander will have a deputy in Britain who will subsequently command TORCH, and General Marshall wants General Eisenhower to have that responsibility. General Eisenhower remains commander of the American Armed Forces in Europe; he continues to prepare for the major invasion of Europe from the west, including a possible preliminary attack on the Cherbourg peninsula; and he has full Allied command of the projected invasion of North Africa.

These operations require three separate staffs, plus General Clark's

---

* GYMNAST was the code name for an Allied operation in French North Africa, planned on the assumption the French would not resist. When the Combined Chiefs decided to send an expedition into North Africa, the old name GYMNAST was changed to TORCH and will be referred to hereafter in these pages as TORCH.

II Corps staff: one for the present European theater, another for the projected North African invasion, a third for the invasion of Europe from the
west. The British regard these arrangements as final, but secret. General
Eisenhower expects to receive a directive to this effect within a week,
giving him the necessary authority to put these plans through.

Diplomatic Interlude

LONDON, MONDAY, JULY 27, 1942
We spent the night at Clark's headquarters after Ike had kept his promise
to visit the American Red Cross Hospital, Harvard Unit, at Salisbury. At
6 A.M. an MP aroused all occupants of the officers' quarters and requested
us to go to the air-raid shelter, as a raid was on. Apparently, I was the last
one out, for I had stopped to shave and to put on my stiff collar. We had
coffee—so-called—and tea in the shelter, but saw no planes, although we
heard thumps in the distance.

Reached London at 10:30 A.M. Ike had a busy schedule. He dealt with
a variety of problems during the day. We had luncheon at the flat for
Lady Stella Reading, head of the Women's Voluntary Service. Lady
Reading had been described by Mrs. Churchill as one British woman who
would be qualified to serve in the Cabinet. The pride of British women,
who are keenly anxious to be of service to American soldiers and sailors, has
been hurt by the ruling of the American Red Cross that British women
who volunteer for work in the American Red Cross must take off their
hard-won British uniforms and wear those of the American Red Cross.
The British women are proud of their uniforms. They rightfully feel they
have earned them through service in the blitzes, and this certainly is true.

It was evident that there was opportunity for the creation of much bad
feeling, because of the clash of the Red Cross policy and the understandable and commendable pride of the British women. If the situation were
reversed, what would an American woman do? You know damned well.

Ike decided to call in all the responsible heads, discuss the full problem,
outline his views, and get a clear-cut understanding and policy immediately, in order to avoid any further growth of ill-feeling.

MacLeish and Warburg were in to discuss with Ike and Colonel Case,
head of G-2, with me sitting by, the best method by which the London
Bureau of OWI at Washington could integrate with the military in this
theater. Ike outlined an organizational setup for them so they could work
efficiently and in harmony with military objectives as they developed. He
specified that Colonel Case shall co-ordinate their activities with our staff.

They are to meet once a week. Political warfare is important, even if new, and Ike's position was that he or his staff would outline problems in this field as they arise, and leave the detail, psychology, and execution to those best qualified to function along these lines. He made clear, however, that the London Bureau of OWI (and there was no disagreement whatsoever by MacLeish and Warburg) should make sure that all its efforts were integrated and in co-operation with those of the British, as it would be silly for the Americans to be telling the people of the occupied countries one story, and the British another. Likewise, the propaganda effort in this theater, from an OWI standpoint, must be made to fit with the world-wide policy of the OWI in Washington.

Left Ike conferring with General Ismay. His day ended after 11. No wonder he slept through the first air-raid alarm I heard or was in, with AA cracking away in Hyde Park just across the street.

LONDON, TUESDAY, JULY 28, 1942

After luncheon with Lady Reading yesterday, Ike had instructed me to see Ambassador Winant and ask him to arrange a meeting as promptly as possible in his office. Had walked across the Square to see Mr. Winant, talked to him briefly, and before I could reach my office again, he phoned to say the meeting had been arranged for 3 o'clock Tuesday. Nice work. At the meeting today, those present were the Ambassador, Brendan Bracken, Stevenson, General Lee, Colonel Sawbridge, Lieutenant Colonel G. E. Ramey, head of the Special Services, and myself.

Lasted more than an hour, and all of the points raised by Lady Reading were discussed, particularly the ARC prohibition of non-Red Cross uniforms in the Service Club. Every use of voluntary British women's organizations is to be made. The question of uniforms is to be settled, possibly by a distinctive Red Cross frock that will permit modest display of British identity, or a simple Red Cross arm band on the British uniform.

This arrangement is logical. The British organizations are especially to be used in areas where the ARC is not yet organized, and every effort will be made to avoid duplication.

LONDON, WEDNESDAY, JULY 29, 1942

The CG was growling today about the staff. An example arose recently when a message from Washington disclosed that the Ambassador wanted to create a committee to select targets for strategic bombing—something that is obviously a military operation. All this had developed with the staff and without Ike's knowledge. It was straightened out by him with good feeling, as Ike and the Ambassador see eye to eye and get along well.

Dined with Ike and T. J. Had fun and talk. To bed early. Only heard the air raid slightly. Just turned over and went back to sleep.

LONDON, THURSDAY, JULY 30, 1942

Ike is waiting for President Roosevelt and the Prime Minister formally to approve plans for the new setup. Said to start thinking about light summer clothes, as we may need them in a few weeks re TORCH.

We had dinner in the apartment and are getting damn tired of looking at those walls. After General Clark, who had shared Ike's flat, had moved to his own headquarters, Ike had asked me to move in with him. There are three rooms—living room and two bedrooms with baths. The flat faces Park Lane and we look into Hyde Park, when curtains aren't drawn for blackout.

Torch Begins to Glow

LONDON, FRIDAY, JULY 31, 1942

Without my knowledge, Ike has given instructions that hereafter when there are conferences in his office, Captain Lee is to arrange for me to be present so I can keep more closely in touch with the news.

In anticipation of soon receiving official governmental approval, from both the Prime Minister and the President, for the TORCH operation, the CG had an hour-and-a-half meeting in his office this morning. Those present were: Brigadier G. M. Stewart, Director of Plans, British War Office; Captain C. E. Lambe, Director of Plans, Admiralty; Air Commodore W. Elliott, Director of Plans, Royal Air Force; Major General R. H. Dewing; and from this headquarters, General Spaatz, Colonel Ray Barker, and Colonel Howard A. "Pinky" Craig, and Captain Ralph S. Wentworth, representing the United States Navy. I sat in.

The CG opened with a general statement. He assumed that all present were familiar with the basic plans agreed to by the Combined Chiefs of Staff last week (the plan on which governmental approval is awaited), that everything said is to be completely tentative while awaiting the formal directive. Therefore, no decisions could be made at this conference, but, as time is of the essence, he did not want to linger. Every effort must be put forth on plans for TORCH.

The CG said that his discussions with General Marshall indicated that the PM looked upon the African assault as an American operation to or around Casablanca on the west coast, and as primarily a British operation on the north coast—but to be led, at the time of the landing operations, by American troops for such psychological advantages as might be gained from the French. Regardless of any misgivings about the operation that staff planners or officers on this level might have had while other opportunities for attack were under consideration, they must now focus their minds on the fact that decision has been made by the Combined Chiefs of Staff, *and soon*, to launch TORCH.

Brigadier Stewart said the essence of the North African operation in the Mediterranean is to take Tunisia in twenty-eight days—this being the time estimated necessary for the Germans to move troops, probably from France, to combat the invasion. He estimated that eleven divisions and forty squadrons of aircraft would be needed for the North African operation.

The CG called attention to his understanding of the intention of General Marshall and the Combined Chiefs to make the two assaults; namely, for Casablanca and for ports within the Mediterranean, simultaneously. Captain Lambe, for the British Navy, said there was insufficient naval escort to move convoys simultaneously to both points and that this would mean that the operation inside the Mediterranean would have to precede the Casablanca operation on the Atlantic by at least two or three weeks. As many as four airplane carriers, eight auxiliary carriers, and three battleships would be required for the Mediterranean assault, assuming there would be two major landings and the accompanying fleet split to cover both landings. The CG said his message to Marshall of yesterday would require amplification and explanation in view of the inability to provide naval escort for both missions simultaneously.

General Spaatz suggested that all the American Air Force now in the British Isles should be used for TORCH. He also anticipated that German bombers would harass the convoys en route through the Strait of Gibraltar and in the Mediterranean. Air Commodore W. Elliott said that the British would not expect more air opposition from the Germans in the Mediterranean than was experienced in the Battle of Britain, when British convoys continued to move through the English Channel despite the presence and activity of practically all of the Luftwaffe on the French mainland. The Air Commodore emphasized, as did General Dewing, the absolute necessity for establishing air bases step by step in Africa for satisfactory operations. Seizure of Oran was of primary importance for this purpose. The Air Commodore estimated that about 140 German bombers would be encountered.

General Eisenhower, seeking to recapitulate, asked what do the British now conceive of as the primary military objectives to be attained by the TORCH operation. Brigadier Stewart and Captain Lambe discussed the objectives and concluded: (1) to open the Mediterranean; (2) to prevent the Italian and French fleets from becoming free to join as a large naval force, possibly at Casablanca or Dakar, which would require United States and British naval forces in comparable strength to be stationed possibly at the Shannon River in Eire—this to protect convoys, U. S. to Britain, and to fend the threat of the combined enemy navy; and (3) to pull German forces from Russia.

The CG continued: "When you have taken North and West Africa, where do we go from there? For morale of our troops it will be necessary to do something more than merely sit after the seizure. Is it feasible to take Sicily?"

Brigadier Stewart said Sardinia was much better, that it would afford air bases for bombing attacks as far away as the Danube and would bring all Italian objectives within range.

Although October 1 is the date set in the American plan so far, the British are aiming at September 10, primarily because of favorable moon conditions and other weather considerations.

The concept of the entire plan seems to be changed from that originally understood by Eisenhower from Marshall. It now appears to be a concentration in the Mediterranean rather than, as General Eisenhower put it, "a sock with the right to Casablanca and with the left through the north coast of Africa." The British emphasized that the key is Tunisia. Its seizure would disrupt Rommel's supply lines and make his situation difficult, if not untenable.

The big defects for the entire attack are shortage of naval support and landing craft and the surf conditions on the west coast, where heavy swells from the Atlantic make landing difficult, if not impossible, in the late fall.

The CG summarized the conference, saying he would explain the changes in concept to General Marshall, so that the over-all plan could be reconsidered.

Planning officers are en route from Washington, and every effort is to be expended to shake down all aspects of TORCH. The American planners are to have access to the British studies and are to co-ordinate and consult with the British, but are to operate under the Commanding General. The probability has been indicated that General Marshall will be named Supreme Commander and that General Eisenhower will be the Deputy Supreme Commander for TORCH, SLEDGEHAMMER, and ROUNDUP, and also Commander-in-Chief of the Allied Expeditionary Force for TORCH. The

General said privately to the British that he was in an embarrassing position until his formal orders came, but was not going to let a little embarrassment stand in the way of getting on with the plans.

JULY, 1942: *The fight for Egypt took the pattern of attack and counter, air power playing a more decisive role as both sides dug in at El Alamein. In their dogged defense the British sustained heavy losses. U. S. tanks first tried out in Libya. Allied bombers hit Tobruk and Matruh, which were also bombarded by the Royal Navy. In Russia the Nazis, moving forward, crossed the Don, took Voroshilovgrad and Rostov, approached Stalingrad, and advanced in the Caucasus. RAF and a slowly growing number of U. S. bombers hit hard and constantly at North Sea shipping and ports. German subs struck costly blows at Allied shipping off the American coast. The Jap steam roller in China moved forward along key railways, but the U. S. Air Force, replacing the AVG, helped Chinese make local gains and destroyed many Jap planes. Jap garrisons in the Aleutians were strengthened to ten thousand. (Still could have used some real good news.—H.C.B.)*

LONDON, SATURDAY, AUGUST 1, 1942

Spent an hour with Paul Manning, of Newspaper Enterprise Association, who wants to spend a day with the CG to get a story for his 700 or so papers. Has already done this on General Spaatz and is booked for other senior commanders. As usual, the CG, constitutionally disinclined to personal publicity, put him off.

The CG returned about 5:30 P.M. from an inspection trip to air bases and immediately plunged into the draft of an answer to General Marshall's query re TORCH which arrived this morning. With Colonel Ray W. Barker, he drafted a four-and-a-half-page cable, summarizing the whole situation.

The CG had cut short the trip arranged by the Air Force when this message arrived.

General Marshall's inquiry had raised several questions which had been prompted by the CG's report that the British felt that the unavailability of a sufficient number of warships would prevent simultaneous landings on the Mediterranean shore and on the west coast of Africa. Asked if the movement of four divisions through the Strait of Gibraltar could be accomplished without eliminating all chances of surprise. Asked what measures the CG would propose to prevent cutting of communications through the Strait by German or Spanish action. Admitting difficulties of landing in the Casablanca areas, which Ike had mentioned, would it not be necessary quickly to seize this area and establish a secure line of com-

munications? How will quick seizures be accomplished if weather is
unfavorable on west coast? Other questions were: Have you figured on
United States escorts? Where would two United States divisions for
initial landings depart from? Where do the six to eight divisions in the
follow-up depart from, and how many of these are United States divisions?
Will it be necessary to send combat loaders to the United Kingdom, and
if so, how many? Also, previous concept indicated need of seven divisions,
and now ante has been raised to ten or twelve divisions. Why? All these
questions were answered insofar as information at hand would permit.
But, of course, many of the questions required study by the planners.

While drafting the reply, a memorandum came to Ike from the Combined Chiefs of Staff. It included the significant statement that he is
assigned the tough job of Acting American Supreme Commander for
TORCH. Some job! The "acting" needs clarification, to give him a free hand
to plan and prepare, but he is going ahead in the interest of time, which
seems to press and press.

The President is insistent on attack by Allied forces somewhere *this
year*. Marshall's message included a request for Ike's estimate of earliest
date of attack in Africa. Ike will have to exert vigorous leadership to direct
the co-ordination of planning by both British and Americans. He badly
needs help on planning. Colonel Barker has been swell, but is worked to
death. Ike suggested a meeting of British Chiefs of Staff Sunday afternoon, to get going. He is now responsible, at least "acting," for Allied
Supreme Command of TORCH and for planning SLEDGEHAMMER (what remains) and ROUNDUP, which, by reason of TORCH, seems to be pushed
further into the future. His first choice is to concentrate on ROUNDUP, but
he is a soldier and must take orders. So TORCH apparently will be the first
big job—one that involves tremendous risks, with the principal objectives,
from the British point of view, of reopening the Mediterranean, with all
of the advantages, particularly for shipping, that would probably follow.

About 8 o'clock, after the message to Marshall had been dispatched,
Mickey drove us "somewhere in England" to have a quiet night in the
country, but the CG didn't get the rest to which he is entitled and so
thoroughly needs. The weight of the three monumental tasks being placed
on his shoulders prevents him from returning to sleep after he has had a
normal night's rest—normal to him is about five hours and frequently less.

LONDON, SUNDAY, AUGUST 2, 1942
Someone sent Ike *Time* for July 27, and the *Washington Times-Herald*
for July 29, and they certainly had a fast passage. Noticed in the *Times-*

Herald the Scottie story: "Wounded 'Eagle,' Last of 19, Promised U.S. Air Transfer." The text of the story is as follows:

LONDON, July 28 (CTPS). Lying in a Cambridge hospital with his back broken in three places, 33-year-old Scottie Cooke, former Hollywood scenario writer, has received a letter from Lieutenant General Dwight D. Eisenhower, it was reported today, promising to facilitate his transfer from the Royal Air Force to the United States air arm.

"I'm delighted to secure for the American Army men of your unusual experience, qualifications and gallantry," Eisenhower wrote after hearing Cooke desired to join the United States Corps. "The instant you come out of the hospital, please come to my office personally and I will see that all necessary steps are instituted forthwith," Eisenhower added.

Cooke is the last alive of a group of 19 Americans who threw up their jobs two and a half years ago and paid their own passage to join the RAF here.

In August, 1941, he married an English girl and the following month limped home in a badly shattered plane after a raid on Frankfort and has been hospitalized ever since.

The doctors, according to Cooke, are still not sure of his recovery, but he is convinced he can regain the use of his legs. "If they would only strap me into some old crate and let me back over Germany," he said, "I could still show them something."

His wife declared he was thrilled by Eisenhower's letter and "full of plans to keep the appointment with the General."

It illustrates to me the impossibility of trying to keep his name out of the press if what he does is newsworthy. This is the story Bill Downs of the UP first broke. Bill then came to see me. The dying condition of Gunner Cooke, lying in a Cambridge hospital, had touched this reporter deeply. Downs had said that the one big thing that Cooke wanted was to transfer, after he left the hospital, to the American Air Force. Ike had readily consented to send a letter promising this, but instructed me to ask Bill Downs to handle it without mention of Ike's name, merely attributing it to Theater Headquarters. The CG wanted no personal publicity, especially at the expense of this unfortunate flier. Downs handled it in this manner, but when a London paper followed up on his story, its English reporter found Cooke not only elated, but displaying the letter. Thus the story, including Ike's name, broke in the London papers and was picked up by the CTPS. It's a hard life in this war for any general who wants to avoid publicity. Also hard on the aide.

Colonel Al Gruenther, C/S in Ike's old spot with the Third Army, under Major General Walter Krueger, at Fort Sam Houston, arrived tonight after a twenty-seven-hour flight from Washington. Gruenther reported to Ike at the apartment while we were at dinner.

I neglected to mention that during the day the July 27 issue of *Life* arrived by hand of some other transatlantic passenger. I discovered in it a

big frontispiece of Ike and, further along, a smaller picture of his brother
Milton. When I showed these to Ike, I first opened the magazine at Milton's smiling mug, which gave Ike a great kick. Then I said, "Here's
another fellow you might be interested in." Leafed back to the full-page
picture of Ike. He nearly fell out of his chair.

The Anglo-American Team Takes Shape

LONDON, MONDAY, AUGUST 3, 1942

Saturday I had a long talk with Major General R. H. Dewing, British
liaison officer assigned to the CG. I know that Ike highly respects his
ability and integrity. We will have much in common. He can help me
keep in touch with rapidly unfolding developments, and possibly I can
assist him occasionally. He has had Washington indoctrination, and I
expect we will get along swell. He will go to certain conferences with the
British which I will not attend, and I probably will know of some developments with which he is unacquainted. We will exchange information.

Dewing wanted Lieutenant General H. Willans, head of the Welfare
Service for the British Army, to meet Ike, to make known to him that the
British service (comparable to our Special Services) is available for the
needs of our troops. Arranged for General Willans to come in today and
the conference was satisfactory.

Ike had a twelve-hour day at the office, starting with a conference at 8:45
with Admiral Stark, Captain Wentworth, Generals Clark and Dewing,
and Colonels Barker and Craig. Others calling during the day were Major
General George V. Strong, Lord Louis Mountbatten, Stevenson of the
Red Cross, and at 6:15, another conference with the planners—Captain
Lambe of the Royal Navy, Air Commodore Elliott, Colonel Ted Curtis,
their secretary, Generals Clark and Dewing. Butcher in a corner.

Their spokesman, Captain Lambe, presented their organizational
scheme of planning for TORCH. The British are to put at Ike's disposal
practically all of their experienced planners who can draw on any ministry or source of information. They are creating an Executive Planning
Section of the Joint Planners, to deal exclusively with TORCH. The personnel of this group will include several officers who have mounted all of the
British expeditions. Ike told them he was making Colonel Gruenther his
Deputy Chief of Staff to be in charge of TORCH planning, and Gruenther
would serve to keep him intimately and regularly in touch with problems
as they develop. Ike asked me to get Gruenther to meet him at the apartment this evening.

Ike had interrupted Captain Lambe with the query: "With TORCH to be our immediate assault, when do you figure ROUNDUP can be done, if ever?" Captain Lambe answered to the effect that if Russia holds out, if the Middle East stays safe, and if Turkey is still neutral, or at least not actively with the Axis, then the Germans will be locked in Russia for another winter. (A lot of "ifs"!) This will give time to decide on ROUNDUP. It may be accomplished late in 1943, but probably not until 1944. Planning for it would continue.

"In other words," Ike said, "ROUNDUP may be described in aviators' language as 'ticking without load.' " * Ike had gone on to say that since SLEDGEHAMMER is out and ROUNDUP is on the shelf, then his mind could clarify the organization for TORCH. Ike suggested that ROUNDUP planning could best be handled by Lord Louis' group because of Commando experience, leaving other planners free to proceed with plans for the African expedition.

Gruenther got his assignment at the apartment this evening. It is all new to him, but he acts as if he can pick up the ball and carry it.

LONDON, TUESDAY, AUGUST 4, 1942

Ike had General Sir Harold R. L. G. Alexander to lunch at the apartment alone. He has been designated by the British as ground commander for the push for Tunisia after the landings are made in the Mediterranean. General George Patton is to command the operation against the west coast, now aimed at Casablanca. This was an important luncheon, for with Ike junior to General Alexander in rank, with no actual battle experience, with his appointment as C-in-C not yet confirmed by the President, with Alexander having commanded at Dunkirk during the evacuation and more recently in Burma, there was the touchy question of how acceptable Ike might be to Alexander. I was in Ike's office, visiting with Colonel William Stirling, of the Secretariat, British Chiefs of Staff, when Ike returned from lunch. His first comment was, "That guy's good! He ought to be Commander-in-Chief instead of me!"

This evening I asked Ike how he felt they could click.

"Fine," he said. "The last thing Alexander said as we were going out of the door after lunch was, 'You're off to a good start.' "

Ike construed this as approval of him, which is important.

Ike proceeded to cast his organization, despite absence of explicit orders to himself as C-in-C, AEF. But everyone here who knows anything about the prospective operation of TORCH takes it for granted that Ike is "it." In

* Air Force expression describing an idling propeller.

any event, he is not hesitating; going ahead full speed. Date of attack tentatively set today—sh-sh-sh . . . October 7!

LONDON, WEDNESDAY, AUGUST 5, 1942

British asking Washington to send ten American submarines and a tender to help cut Rommel's supply line in the Mediterranean. They suggest basing them on Gibraltar. State that whatever stir may be caused by their arrival at Gibraltar will have died down before TORCH, if they are sent promptly. This request was passed to Ike by General L. C. Hollis, Office of the War Cabinet, with a personal note reminding Ike he had promised to help through Marshall to get the subs and asked him to "put in a word."

Movements of a Dog's Body

LONDON, THURSDAY, AUGUST 6, 1942

Margaret Biddle called yesterday to invite me to a luncheon to meet King Haakon, Crown Prince Olaf, and Crown Princess Martha of Norway. Said it would be a very small luncheon, entirely private in their apartment, completely informal and short. I accepted, and then she wondered if by any chance General Eisenhower might like to come. I put it up to Ike, and although he abominates luncheons, he said that this one sounded interesting and since Margaret Biddle was the hostess he would be glad to go. The Norwegians were pleasant and interesting. The King was democratic and sociable; chipper at seventy. Instead of six or seven guests, there were about twenty, and instead of the luncheon being short, we had, of course, to observe the rule about not leaving before the King. As a result, we didn't get away until 3:15, although in enjoyable company. En route back to the office, Ike growled at the time lost. Gave me hell.

All the Norwegians showed a determination to win, but they were concerned with the psychological letdown of their people because no second front had been opened on the Continent.

After Ike got to bed tonight, reasonably early, Colonel Gruenther had a great desire to see him, and I refused—asked him to come around to breakfast. Gruenther still wasn't satisfied and made a personal call on me to induce me to awaken Ike. He said that there was a war on, but I noticed it was still going on when he did awaken. After all, a man who works from fifteen to eighteen hours a day, and whose problems frequently keep him awake at night, should not be roused unless absolutely necessary. No hard feelings, just protecting Ike.

"For General Eisenhower's Eyes Only"

LONDON, FRIDAY, AUGUST 7, 1942

Colonel Gruenther in for breakfast, with a message from Washington indicating further shortage in shipping. This worried him, for it bears directly on capabilities for TORCH. Seems the British have ships available for one division only; their available ships already carrying troops and supplies from America to Britain.

Gruenther indicated that the British are opposing the CG's desire for a Supreme Naval Commander and a Supreme Air Commander both responsible to him for TORCH. Ike said that as long as he is to be C-in-C (assuming he will be formally notified) he will have the kind of organization *he* wants. October 7 as date for TORCH operation questioned by Gruenther. Ike said that this date had been set with a feeling on his part that it is better to make an early deadline, as Ike put it, "to make 'em get down the road!" T. J. also in during breakfast, fussed by uncertainty of routine for getting cables to the message center. The officer handling routine messages for General Bolte, C/S, had sent to T. J., as Adjutant General, an outgoing cable in a sealed envelope the night before. It had lain overnight in a folder when it should have gone promptly to Washington. It was not T. J.'s fault, for messages should go through the message center, with copies from there to the Adjutant General for the permanent record. T. J.'s brown eyes sparkled when he said, "I'm going to clear up that situation."

This day—another Friday, incidentally—Ike received a message, "for General Eisenhower's eyes only," from General Marshall. It informed him that General Eisenhower was acceptable as C-in-C for the TORCH operations to the United States Chiefs of Staff and to the President, who would so inform the Prime Minister. The communication went on to say that the formal directive for General Eisenhower's guidance, submitted by the British Chiefs of Staff, is being studied and will be reported upon shortly. Admiral Leahy was requested by the President to give General Eisenhower orders to proceed with the development of his staff and planning. This is just what Ike has been doing. No announcement, however, until the operation is under way.

Incidentally, Ike got a note from General Archibald Nye, dated August 7, expressing "distress at the necessity to transfer General Alexander from the command of a task force under your orders to take over a new command in the Near East." It was General Alexander with whom Ike had lunched at the apartment on Tuesday, and with whom he had been so

impressed. Apparently, something hot in the Middle East. General Montgomery, assigned for the job with Ike, is described by Nye as "a very able
soldier but also an excellent co-operator." Hope he is good.

Ruses

LONDON, SATURDAY, AUGUST 8, 1942

Just a day at work. Nothing very exciting. Ike still pounding away at plans,
spending hours with Colonels Gruenther and Barker, polishing up the
outline of TORCH to be submitted to the British Chiefs of Staff.

Ike sent a letter today to Major General Sir Hastings L. Ismay, Secretary of the British Chiefs of Staff, so there would be "no misunderstanding" about the method of handling the cover plan for TORCH. "Cover," I
find, means deception. The purpose is to make the enemy believe we are
striking at another point, and is designed to gain every advantage of surprise.

Correspondents frequently come to me with their "inside" information in the hope of obtaining corroboration so that when their stories
are printed they will not be denied as untrue. In this way I hear of a
variety of ruses, including a current one brought in today by Ed Beattie,
of UP, that we are going to invade Norway. (Another one is that we are
going into Dakar.) To encourage this idea I have some heavy GI shoes,
suitable for arctic wear, in a corner of my small office. I also have a heavy
box, nicely lined with waterproof cloth, which to the observing reporters
may be regarded as suitable for use in a cold climate.

Now General Montgomery is out. Seems Gott's death in desert means
he must go there. (Lieutenant General W. H. D. Gott had commanded
the British Eighth Army and had been killed in an aircraft accident.)
A Scotsman named Anderson has been assigned to Ike. Fine reputation.

Enter General Patton

LONDON, SUNDAY, AUGUST 9, 1942

Double summer time vanished today for the season. Not only did we have
the extra hour to sleep, but slept later than usual, Ike getting an unusually
good early morning "second sleep," the period that really relaxes. At the
office by 10. After extended discussion with Colonels Gruenther and
Barker, Ike got off a long personal letter by bomber pouch to General

Marshall, relative TORCH. Outlined his plan of attack on both West and North Africa. Ike wondering what to do with requests from the War Department for recommendations for Legion of Merit in this theater. Some doubt cast by Marshall on sparing Beadle to Ike for his C/S. Needed badly. Also question of promotions of half a dozen colonels to brigadiers. Promotions must go hand in hand with present needs of the expanding operations, particularly planning for TORCH. I notice Ike is most worried when he is uncertain about an organizational pattern. Once the pattern clarifies in his mind, his brow unwrinkles.

Back to apartment. No comings or goings planned, so started to fix some dehydrated chicken noodle soup. This was interrupted by a call from General Patton, who is to lead the American forces into West Africa. Ike invited him to come right over. Had room service fix the soup. General Patton joined us for a drink and dinner. He and Ike agreed on various personnel assignments. Patton worried because G-2 indicates about 8000 more enemy troops on west coast, near landing place, than he will have. Also worried about heavy swells, which sometimes run to fifty feet, and scarcity of suitable beaches for landings. He had an ironic note in his voice when he said someone had suggested he be sure to have a good second man because he might be drowned. Patton is a good fellow, curses like a trooper, and boasts that while he is stupid in many particulars (his own description) there is one quality he knows he has—the ability to exercise mass hypnotism.

"In a week's time," he said, "I can spur any outfit to a high state of morale."

General Patton is senior in rank in the regular Army to Ike. The CG had hoped to get Patton for this task, but because of the difference in rank hesitated to ask for him. He was delighted when General Marshall sent him.

Interesting to hear Ike and Patton talk Army personalities. General Ike dislikes officers who feel they have fulfilled their responsibility when they simply report a problem to a superior and do not bring the proposed solution with them. Patton says he doesn't necessarily want a smart staff; he wants a loyal one. He says he has a sixth sense and can guess the intentions of the enemy better than a staff of G-2. So on until 12:15, which was 1:15 by yesterday's time, and Ike to bed; I an hour before.

Major General George V. Strong, G-2 in Washington, in town this week. Ike thinks very highly of him. Says he is the best G-2 the WD has ever had. Hard worker and knows his stuff.

Forgot to say that walking to the office this morning, Ike told me to have Lee take the day off. It was a beautiful day. I told Lee three times,

warned him that it was an order, and endeavored to convince him that not
to follow it would incur vigorous, if only momentary, wrath. Lee's loyalty
is so superb that he insisted on staying, ignoring the order. He carried
something into the General's office and was hit by a ton of bricks. Came
out like a puppy with its tail between its legs.

"My God, the General hopped all over me!"

Reluctantly, he stole away from the building into the beautiful sunshine, but telephoned an hour later to see if everything was going all right.
Next morning he told me he had never spent such a miserable day. He was
away from the scene of action and not with the boss.

LONDON, MONDAY, AUGUST 10, 1942

Ike concerned about anti-British sentiment at home. A story which broke
in the U. S. that our airmen were not getting co-operation from the RAF
is all wet. Probably will need press conference to deny effectively. Ike's
information all to the contrary. RAF is practically wet-nursing American
fliers in sweeps over France. Our fliers learn quickly, but much more rapidly when flying in company with experienced British. They are very
cocky when they first come over, thinking their methods and equipment
the best in the world. Apparently this isn't always true. That they need
actual fighting experience is to be expected; there is also a big question
mark on American-built fighter planes vs. the Me 109 and the F-W 190.
Our boys like the Spitfire after they learn to get it off the ground. Vision
for taxiing is bad, but they like to fly it. Heard they cracked up nineteen
on the ground at one airfield.

Ike received the outline of TORCH from Brigadier Generals Gruenther
and Barker (promoted). After seeing numerous visitors on a variety of
subjects this morning, he carried it down to the British Chiefs of Staff
at 12:15.

Social invitations still pouring in. Lady Astor phoned Lee a day or two
ago to invite Ike down for dinner and an evening. George Bernard Shaw
was to be present, whom I would like very much to meet. But Ike said,
"To hell with it; I've work to do."

Brigadier General Lucian K. Truscott, in charge of our Rangers, who
are training with the Commandos, came to the apartment tonight to
inform Ike that the Commando planners had some criticism of the TORCH
plan. They questioned timing and landing at Casablanca. Ike already had
received constructive criticism from Lord Louis, as prepared by his Vice-
Chief, General Hayden. It approved the operations plan in general, but
insisted that more centralized direction of planning was required, *and*

now. Ike had told me to prepare a letter to Lord Louis to say, "I agree with practically every word." He's calling General Clark to take charge of plans. Apparently, criticism from Commandos aimed at facilitating co-ordination of British planning. American planning has proceeded under General Gruenther. Ike intends Clark to develop a new kind of Allied staff, with both nationalities working together, side by side.

Ike had a gripe against the Navy. Had cabled Marshall to ask King for assignment of two of the Navy's most capable officers to assist in planning. When the officers sat in with General Gruenther's planning gang, they were welcomed with the statement that there were a thousand questions which the Navy could help answer. The Navy said, "We are here only to listen."

Ike's comment was that apparently some in our Navy are jealous of the British Navy; that if Admiral King himself were here, or he could talk with him, there would be no difficulty.

The Navies Join TORCH

LONDON, TUESDAY, AUGUST 11, 1942

T. J. in during breakfast. Ike said T. J. could go to Africa as Executive in Charge of Headquarters and to supervise records. Not as big a job as Adjutant General for the whole theater. But T. J. says he has already had Colonel Ralph Pulsifer, his deputy, running the Adjutant's office for a week. Got a laugh when Ike indicated there might be some doubt about T. J.'s wanting to go. T. J. already has his shorts on order at the tailor and his heart would be broken if he couldn't.

To help orient our Navy to TORCH and to get its active co-operation to bear on the immediate problem, the CG had a meeting this morning. Those present were: Admirals Stark, Alan G. Kirk, Robert Bieri, and Andrew C. Bennett; Captains Frank P. Thomas (representing Admiral Royal E. Ingersoll, C-in-C Atlantic Fleet), Ralph S. Wentworth, Edward A. Mitchell, and Jerauld Wright; Generals Patton, Bolte, Gruenther, Barker; Colonel Craig; and Lieutenant Colonel Horne L. Litzenberg of the Marines.

Captain Thomas did most of the talking for the Navy. Said TORCH, on Casablanca side, will require greatest armada of all times—from 200 to 400 transports and 200 warships; emphasized difficulties; need of watching German fleet, which he said includes at least one aircraft carrier, perhaps two. Said our Navy feels Mediterranean operation of TORCH should be primarily British Navy, with American Navy substituting one or two battleships at Scapa Flow to watch the Germans, thus to release equivalent number British battleships.

Planners have had difficulty getting exact statement of British capabilities. Will be necessary for American Navy to weigh its capabilities for creation second supply line (in addition to the one from U. S. to Iceland and British Isles) against world-wide deployment of our warships. Admiral Stark interposed that a year ago the Navy doubted its capabilities to handle one supply line across the Atlantic. This has been accomplished, and now there is to be a second.

The CG stressed need of co-operating with British; that it is a partnership venture; that the two navies must work together, and that, above all, both Army and Navy are under orders to carry out this important mission. Captain Thomas wanted to know where the orders would come from. The CG explained they would come from the Combined Chiefs of Staff, and that he had been asked to consult on the preparation of a directive. This work is under way, and the proposed outline was submitted to the U. S. Chiefs of Staff yesterday.

"It's sort of a shuttlecock," he said.

Captain Thomas asked where does control of C-in-C of TORCH begin and end with respect to the Navy. Answer was promptly given that it is up to the Navy to land the troops on the shore; thereafter, it is the responsibility of the Army, but the Navy will have to maintain supply line and give protection; also requested Navy establish and maintain harbor defense at Casablanca and Oran.

General Eisenhower stated and restated that TORCH is an order from their Commander-in-Chief, the President of the United States, and the Prime Minister; whether we like it or not, it has to be carried out, despite any obstacles. If there isn't a single protective warship, his orders call for moving into West and North Africa and he is going to do it, warships or not—"and if I have to go alone in a rowboat."

Recited that, in diplomatic correspondence shown to him by General Ismay, the President had suggested months before we got into the war that the British undertake an offensive in Africa, such as that now ordered. Consequently, the Prime Minister refers to the President's "suggestion." Although this operation highly favored by British, particularly as compared to SLEDGEHAMMER, he emphasized difficulty of British supplying replacement on account of extraordinary demand for protective home forces. TORCH upsets and causes at least six months' hiatus in plans and preparation for ROUNDUP.

The Russian question mark lurks behind all discussion of major strategy. The CG emphasizes that the decision for TORCH had been made with the guess that Russia might not be able to hold out, and its purpose is to "contain" the large German forces now engaged there. The TORCH operation is sufficiently removed to cause the Germans further to disperse their forces, regardless of the outcome in Russia, which, incidentally, looks worse.

The meeting concluded with understanding that Navy is to consult Admiralty on details and endeavor to crystallize what is now a deep haze as to capabilities on both sides.

Last words of CG to meeting were that his door was always open; that he could be called on the phone; and that whenever questions arose which the Navy wanted to ask him, there should be no hesitation; that he was here and on the job all the time.

Around 4 o'clock, Ike called me in. Found he'd lunched at his desk on peanuts and raisins. Said he was getting "damned tired of looking at these four walls. Let's take a drive in the country." He had some time to spare because the British Chiefs of Staff were meeting at 6 o'clock to consider further the outline of TORCH, submitted by Ike today. The answer will probably not be available until Wednesday morning at the earliest. Ike much bothered by necessity of getting approval of several Chiefs of Staff, which means delay. Every minute counts, especially now. If British Chiefs of Staff approve plan, it goes to U. S. Chiefs and finally to the Combined Chiefs of Staff in Washington for consideration and approval.

Had a quiet dinner and went early to bed, the General much refreshed. He really needs a week end away from the crowd, to break the continual pounding. He's been hitting this pace since December 14.

LONDON, WEDNESDAY, AUGUST 12, 1942

Deception and cover plans have been submitted with two main alternatives, Norway and Dakar. Suggest troops embarking for Africa from U. S. and U. K. be told they are en route to reinforce the Middle East, with possibility of a stop at Dakar. This would explain light clothes for tropics.

The President and American Chiefs of Staff have notified the British Chiefs of Staff of approval of the draft directive for TORCH. However, it's not yet approved by British Chiefs. Notice the objective has stretched a bit; purpose now, in concert with desert forces, is to "gain complete control of North Africa, from Atlantic to Red Sea." Previously was only to Suez. But suppose they mean about the same. General Ismay's comment, in transmitting the American approval of the directive, was that, "It may, I fear, want one or two amendments."

Trying to follow the evolution of TORCH is like trying to find the pea in a three-shell game. Now it develops that the American and British Navies cannot jointly provide escort for simultaneous attack on Casablanca and objectives inside the Mediterranean. Current talk is to have General Patton's task force land inside the Mediterranean and proceed southwestward, taking Casablanca from the rear. This would also avoid the heavy swells of the Atlantic which make landing at Casablanca so precarious. This proposal leaves Ike in the middle with General Marshall, who has insisted on Casablanca as a protection to communication on the one hand, and on the other the Navies, who say they simply haven't got the warships to do both jobs. Casablanca could follow the Mediterranean operation by two weeks to a month.

Supplies, vulnerability of Gibraltar if Spain hops in, and forty-day turn-around of convoys from America are among the ever-increasing problems. Not to mention the worry of the British over depleting the defense strength of the British Isles, thus making Hitler a present of an easy target for, say, spring, '43.

Limitation on shipping continues to harass our planners. Gruenther found only nine combat loaders (cargo ships converted to carry troops and small landing craft, and so forth, for quick unloading offshore—takes at least ninety days to convert them). Some of those now on hand urgently needed for training. Ike said he would be glad if someone would give him some good news, as every step in planning disclosed further obstacles.

"But," he said, "I don't know where I'd rather be."

Gruenther says white cloth is greatly needed by Arabs; seems they insist on white cloth to bury their dead and will kill to get it. North Africa tightly rationed on gasoline, sugar, and God knows what. General Patton figures on living on fat of land until supplies reach him, having noticed in his studies that there's a rich agricultural region easily accessible. Might not be so rich when he gets there.

LONDON, THURSDAY, AUGUST 13, 1942

Relatively quiet today, although Ike got off a three-page cable to General Marshall outlining changed status of TORCH. Both Navies insist it's impossible to escort two expeditions for two assaults inside the Mediterranean and one at Casablanca at the same time.

News of Axis attack on British convoy in Mediterranean is bad. The converted aircraft carrier *Eagle*, earmarked for TORCH, has been torpedoed and sunk. Other news respect convoy is bad, according to the word of

General Gruenther. He saw Admiral Sir Bertram H. Ramsay this afternoon, who was doleful since a battleship, still another aircraft carrier, two or three cruisers, and God knows what else may be lost. This on top of the *Eagle* not too cheerful a prospect for TORCH. But attitude of all our fellows only grimmer and more determined.

General Dewing, the British liaison officer, in this morning. Concerned over depletion of reserves in British Isles. Also pictured weakness and vulnerability of Gibraltar, especially the airfield, which lies between "the Rock" and the Spanish-controlled mainland. Seems airfield is on so-called international ground and is exposed to machine-gun and artillery fire of Spanish. Dewing is considerably less than optimistic about the Gibraltar situation.

Eisenhower Secretly Becomes Allied Commander-in-Chief

LONDON, FRIDAY, AUGUST 14, 1942

Important events seem to be developing a habit of occurring on Fridays. Today Ike's directive arrived. It makes him the Allied Commander-in-Chief of the Allied Expeditionary Force. So now he's Allied C-in-C instead of simply CG of ETO. In fact, he now is both.

During the day Ike dispatched a message to the Operations Division of the War Department, strongly recommending that the first fifteen landing craft for infantry (LCIs) be completed in the U. S. and sent to this theater as early as practicable. This is important to facilitate training while good weather lasts; also to be available for combat, especially for SLEDGEHAMMER in case this operation should be resurrected. Also insisted they be equipped with suitable antiaircraft armament and that as a matter of first priority this be installed as soon as possible after the vessels are launched.

Planners discovered that equipment for 1st Division will not reach U. K. until long after August 20. The data available from SOS indicate that some of the equipment for the 1st Division is en route, but the bulk still remains at home. In the missing equipment is most of the artillery, including 105-mm. howitzers. Information at hand shows that this and other necessary equipment cannot be made available here by stealing from the 34th Infantry Division and arming 1st Division with British 25-pounders. Apparently, only recourse will be to use two combat teams of the 34th Division as spearheads of British attack in Algiers, instead of 1st Division units.

Another message sent to the Operations Division at Washington today

gave the better news that, according to "current" information (and I use
current quoted, since it may change tomorrow; it has before), the British
can provide combat loaders and landing craft for all units participating
in the Algiers and Bône assaults. In other words, the two American regimental combat teams which will lead the assault in the British sector will
be on British vessels. This frees the combat loaders and landing craft now
being prepared in America for use in transporting the expedition which
is to depart from there for Casablanca.

The purpose of this cable was to give information to planners at home
so that they could set earliest date at which expedition would be able to
sail from U. S. On the basis of the data, the CG requested the War Department's estimate of date when U. S. expedition could land on the
African coast. It also requested General Marshall's answer respect modified conception of TORCH operations. This major question, i.e., General
Marshall's feeling about inability of combined Navies to escort two expeditions at the same time, is unanswered.

Last night noticed an intelligence report saying reinforcements of two
Italian and two German divisions had supposedly reached Rommel. As
I'm now attempting to save Ike's time by reading and marking for his
attention newspapers, mimeographed radio news bulletins, intelligence
reports, and so forth, I pointed this out to him. He said, "The way things
are going the war will be over before we get in it!"

General Clark in to dinner, with a mixture of war talk and light chat
until 10:30. Clark has problems of molding his planning organization
with British and American personnel. Ike is insistent that his idea of
complete integration of both nationalities will work. He told Clark that
some changes would have to be made until the right personalities are
found.

Then to bed for a good night's rest.

Dim View from Washington

This morning a message from General Marshall awaited Ike. Marshall
and staff had been studying Ike's long cable of August 13, relating expressed inability of Navies to provide escorts for the desired simultaneous
assaults on Casablanca and Mediterranean objectives. Same cable to Marshall had also given detailed review of planning to date.

Marshall stated that there was a unanimity of opinion of Army officials in Washington that the proposed operation (referring to entire TORCH) appeared hazardous, with less than a fifty per cent chance for success. This was modified slightly by his statement that this was an immediate and superficial view. However, as the British might say, the prospect for success is somewhat less than consoling.

Navy at Washington, however, had unofficially, and despite the critical situation in the Pacific, estimated they could provide escort for the Oran forces, including the aircraft carrier *Ranger*, and probably, "although not certainly," one converted carrier, recently commissioned, with thirty-fighter capacity, for the expedition sailing from home on October 1. Also stated that escort for two convoys to follow up first expedition can be provided in time to have them on the water when initial landing is being made. Two more converted carriers with fighters probably available to sail from home by the end of October.

Marshall also said that Ike's request for troops can be met with the possible exception of antiaircraft for second convoy and part of the ground echelons for Air Force.

The pessimistic note of the less than fifty per cent chance of success arose partly from lack of detailed information at WD of extent of British carrier support. In this connection Marshall and staff also queried to what extent Ike would be prepared to meet possible German air assaults launched from Spain and Spanish Morocco. Wanted Ike's completely frank view. Also wants him to get similar frank expression from General Patton. Wonder if General Marshall, in view of repeated obstacles reported by Ike, is thinking of canvassing with the President the advisability of canceling the operation. Would be a letdown if TORCH is called off. But it's foolhardy and wasteful to rush in where analysis of operation shows there is less than a fifty-fifty chance of success.

A. J. Liebling, correspondent for *The New Yorker*, investigating handling of the colored troops in this theater, saw Ike in my office since a heavy conference was going on in his own. Liebling interested in possible ways of dealing with colored problem in this theater; rightly feels it will cast long shadows into the future race relationships, particularly at home. Ike said colored troops were being given equality of treatment with such segregation as the situation permits. Said he would be interested to have Liebling's report of conditions after he completes a prospective tour of camps where colored troops are posted. The CG said that so far both the British and Americans have been concerned more with the anticipation of trouble than with its actual existence. We know of only one or two incidents, and these between white and colored Americans.

The directive policy with respect to Negro troops was sent to the

Amcross* in London, July 16, in a letter from the Adjutant General's office. It said:

Negro troops are to be allowed the same pass and furlough privileges as white troops—consequently Negro soldiers will come to London and other cities.

They will expect to use the facilities of Red Cross Clubs. While obviously desirable that wherever possible, separate sleeping accommodations be provided for Negro soldiers; whenever that is not possible, Negro soldiers properly on pass or furlough should be given accommodations in the Red Cross Clubs on the same basis as other soldiers.

It is believed that to avoid friction between white and Negro soldiers, care should be taken so that men of the two races are not needlessly intermingled in the same dormitory or at the same table in dining halls.

Yesterday, the CG cabled General Marshall that there appeared to be some doubt in the minds of the British Chiefs of Staff that the tentative agreement reached in London during his visit makes Ike responsible for planning of SLEDGEHAMMER-ROUNDUP. Their doubt arises because the agreement has so far not officially been confirmed by the U. S. Chiefs of Staff, and Ike asks for this confirmation. General Marshall replied today in an ultra-secret message not to be distributed to the staff. Says he intended Ike to be responsible for SLEDGEHAMMER-ROUNDUP.

Another message from Washington says the War Department is pushing preparations to meet October as earliest practicable date for expedition to leave U. S. This is the convoy that Captain Frank Thomas, USN, has called the greatest armada ever to sail. Also informed us that the U. S. combat loaders, now partially converted, will be unsuitable for landing the assault units if there should be resistance. The reason given is that the crews will be untrained for initial assault, but ships and crews will be suitable to transport reserve and auxiliary troops which follow the assault troops.

Value of General Clark as Deputy C-in-C strikingly shown by his memorandum to General Eisenhower dated today, summarizing the conferences and resulting decisions reached in a single day, August 14. Purpose of the memo was to complete the CG's information of current plans, all of course made by Clark under general understanding and specific authorization given him by Ike as the unannounced C-in-C, AEF.

A condensed paraphrasing of this memorandum follows:

Air Vice-Marshal Welsh will head the Air Staff of TORCH. After initial landings, seizure of airdromes will get first priority. Three tank landing craft will proceed to Gibraltar; a large number would impair the security

---

* American Red Cross.

of the whole invasion. The British state that their ships could handle all American troops leaving their ports, but it was impossible to answer General Patton when he asked if he could expect to have assigned to him all "combat loaders"—ships that carry smaller landing craft and combat personnel—that arrive from the United States. Naval authorities will have command of all troop movements from embarkation to landing.

General Patton's mission will be to land at Oran and establish a beach-head to secure an airdrome. General Doolittle's fliers will support General Patton's ground forces under Patton's command. Antiaircraft units will come with first convoy from the United States. Railway engineers may be deferred to second echelon. The role of General Terry Allen's 1st Division also came up for discussion, with special reference to delays in the arrival of its equipment.

At a general discussion of air operations, General Doolittle made clear that the U. S. Air Forces would provide sufficient cover for American troops landing at Oran but that there would be no surplus to cover British landings at Bône in initial stages. General Anderson called attention to this British deficiency, and British resources will try to meet it. Generals Patton and Doolittle double-checked on their air requirements, fearing diversion of air power to the British area. But this, in turn, hinges on General Anderson getting together with Air Vice-Marshal Welsh.

Navy plans are progressing, too. Admiral Bieri has submitted to Ike a schematic diagram of the Chain of Command, picturing the organizational setup. Ike's "box" is titled the naval "Supreme Commander." I assume this means C-in-C, AEF. The chart shows Cinclant (which stands for C-in-C, Atlantic Fleet) and Admiralty boxed on a level parallel with Ike and also indicates that a flag officer to act as naval adviser will be attached directly to him.

Cinclant will provide covering forces for central and south Atlantic, escorts from U. S. to Mediterranean and Casablanca, and logistic support of the U. S. naval forces.

The C-in-C of the naval forces in the Mediterranean is to be British. Chart indicates there will be British covering forces, escort forces, and two amphibious forces, plus one American amphibious force for the operations inside the Mediterranean. Must be borne in mind that naval plan is subject to change. For example, present idea is to land Patton's gang inside the Mediterranean and work back overland to Casablanca.

Yesterday Ike had received the forecast of General Marshall, who had requested him to give the frank opinions of himself and General Patton, concerning the whole project of TORCH. Today, Ike completed and cabled to General Marshall a detailed estimate of the chances for success or failure of TORCH. A summary of General Eisenhower's views—in which Generals Patton and Doolittle concurred—follows:

Tentatively, the British plan to have one carrier with twenty fighters and twenty torpedo planes east of Gibraltar, another carrier with sixty-six fighters and eighteen torpedo planes at Algiers, and an old carrier with thirteen planes may also be available.

The French have about 500 planes in Africa. None is modern, but land-based fighters are faster than our carrier-based planes. Total Allied carrier-based fighters are estimated at 166, with only twenty or thirty in the eastern Mediterranean.

After the first landing fields have been secured in North Africa, we must be able to land, assemble, and dispatch from Gibraltar airfields at least thirty fighter planes a day. If the Spaniards take hostile action shortly after our landings, it will become almost impossible to get these fighters through because Gibraltar lies wide open to Spanish attack. A spell of bad weather could also seriously weaken air support during the early stages of the invasion.

Fourteen poorly equipped, moderately well-trained, and professionally commanded French divisions occupy North Africa. If these divisions offer united, co-ordinated opposition to the invasion, the Axis will have time to rush substantial reinforcements to North Africa before we have seized the major seacoast objectives. There is no indication yet that Spain plans to enter the war, but the Germans might force the Spanish Army to attack Gibraltar, which the Allied forces could not hold under such circumstances. It is also possible that the Germans might transfer some of their air forces in western Europe to Spain. But the fact that the Germans have not yet made any moves toward Spain suggests they do not care to take the risks of occupation. They also have good fields in Sicily. The prospects of the North African invasion depend on continued Spanish neutrality—at any rate, during the early stages—and nothing more than token resistance from the French forces in North Africa. Profound secrecy will tend to keep Spain neutral. The French near Algiers are likely to welcome the invasion; those between Oran and Casablanca and those near Tunis are more likely to resist. The chances of making successful initial landings look better than even. The chances of capturing Tunis before Axis reinforcements arrive look considerably less than fifty per cent. Building up a land-based air force presents great difficulties. Poor port facilities will delay heavy concentration of ground troops. Communications between Oran and Casablanca are long and uncertain. The attitude of the French remains problematical. Any sign of failure or hesitancy might lead the Axis to occupy Spain at once, with serious results to the whole course of the war.

Ike said on the way to the hotel late this afternoon that this had all been extremely difficult to work out. I asked him if General Marshall might decide to recommend to the President the abandonment of TORCH. Seems evident this is in the General's mind. Ike indicated this is a possibility.

Had chiefs of radio and press bureaus, principal staff officers of PRO, and editor of *Stars and Stripes* for a buffet luncheon today. Ike spoke off the record for nearly an hour.

The press asked that his vigorous but off-the-record affirmation of the co-operation between the RAF and American fliers be released so it could be printed. To this he agreed. Considerable talk about the color problem. A correspondent expressed concern that at least one "irresponsible and biased" reporter was about to send troublemaking articles back home on the color question. Someone raised the point that existent censorship rules bar Negro stories of this type. Ike said, "Take it off!" Later he was importuned by a small group of first-rate correspondents to reconsider his decision, but he stuck to it. Said in the long run it would be better for the news, good or bad, to flow freely. Might just as well let the American public know what the problems are and our success or failure in meeting them.

Psychological Warfare

LONDON, SUNDAY, AUGUST 16, 1942

Relatively leisurely day at the office. Ike called for the diaries and spent an hour going through them. It has become increasingly apparent to me that the official and personal diaries are merging into a single journal. We're keeping copies of all pertinent documents relative to TORCH in a "black" file, and that constitutes an official record. Ike agreed we should keep the one diary covering both official and personal sides. Consequently will incorporate into the personal diary the official notes kept by the General and Lee until I took over, plus such additional items of an official nature as have been dictated and laid aside for inclusion in the official diary. This settles a problem which has been bothering me. I have found it difficult to separate the activities as originally intended. Pleased to note that Ike's comment was, "Fine!"

Read a report today from Lieutenant General Sir F. Mason-MacFarlane,

Governor and Commander-in-Chief of Gibraltar. He says that any unusual activity at Gibraltar is known to Berlin within twenty-four hours. Says that if as a result of TORCH activity Spain should become a belligerent against the Allies, both the naval base and the air station at Gibraltar would go out of commission at once. Advises that we must conceal objective, and reassure the Spanish government "convincingly and rapidly," should their suspicions be aroused. Ike felt this information should be known to General Marshall, so summarized it in a dispatch. Just another "if."

Bombing policy of the United States and Britain is set out in an agreement signed by General Sir C. T. Paget, C-in-C Home Forces; Air Chief Marshal W. S. Douglas, Commander of Fighter Command; and General Eisenhower as CG, ETO. Policy is to bomb German industrial centers, submarine plants and bases, and transportation, without priority as to the three classifications. Choice of targets will depend upon flying conditions.

Political warfare, particularly that to be associated with TORCH, is to be co-ordinated by a directive which Ike has asked his deputy, General Clark, to prepare. Will be under Mr. W. H. B. Mack of British Foreign Office, who will be on General Eisenhower's staff under General Clark.

Accompanied Ike to Norfolk House this afternoon to see General Clark, who is taking hold firmly and reassuringly of the planning operations. Great relief to Ike finally to get such good help. T. J. also there as military secretary. General Gruenther working under Clark. Much secrecy, many guards, and general atmosphere of stern business. "Cover" plan discussed. Ike gave general approval to plan.

Solo one, described by General Clark, is intended to deceive the enemy into believing we are to attack through Norway.

Solo two is to mislead our own troops so that any leaks, which are inevitable, will not disclose the true objective. They are to be told that their uniforms and equipment for use in the Middle East will be aboard ship; that they will probably stop off for action at Dakar. Clark recommended to Ike one modification of the proposed plan; i.e., the troop commanders down to the regimental level should be informed of the true objective. Ike agreed this was necessary and advisable. Numerous personnel questions discussed and agreed upon.

Am frequently amazed at the detail in which plans must be made. Clark brought up the point that General Anderson will need transportation from Gibraltar, his initial operating base, to the Mediterranean shore; probably a destroyer. Jokingly discussed assignment of submarine for escape from Africa in case everything goes haywire.

We returned to the office to dispatch the message relative Gibraltar's exposed position and consequent weakness. Reassuring to find the Chief of Staff, Brigadier General John E. Dahlquist, on the job and waiting to handle the message. General Bolte and Colonel Case are to start home today, Bolte to get a division and Colonel Case an AA outfit. Both have been in to say their farewell. Dahlquist is to be Acting C/S until the possibility of Beadle Smith's coming is finally settled. General Marshall has already served notice of the doubt of sparing Beadle. This is a disappointment because practically from the moment he knew of his assignment as CG, Ike planned to have Beadle as his C/S. In general, the organization is taking hold and Ike feels relieved, though not entirely satisfied yet.

LONDON, MONDAY, AUGUST 17, 1942

General Clark in for breakfast this morning with some items to be checked by the CG. Seems the Commandos can't train as many landing troops as has been expected, but Clark has worked out alternative with General Anderson, who is to lead the British assault in the Mediterranean.

Both Ike and Clark gratified at crystallization of plans. Beginning to see daylight.

Discussed the recommendations for Legion of Merit, the CG growling because most of the proposed recommendations submitted to him for forwarding to the WD are for officers, with relatively few for privates, corporals, sergeants, or warrant officers. Felt men who had been in the ranks should be recognized.

Clark emphasized shortage of landing craft. Only eighteen of one type and about eighty of another, which he thought was a pitiful trickle from the much ballyhooed American production. Both he and Ike wondered where all this production is going.

Ike's shoulder kicking up again. Had made a date with the London Clinic for 6:30 Tuesday. May have to use the needle again.

Daily report of General Clark's conferences, covering August 16, has been submitted to the CG. In it he summarized numerous details of planning, including statement that the British figure three weeks are needed to load the vessels for the expedition. The substance of Clark's report was that General Lemnitzer has joined TORCH headquarters at Norfolk House, and will be AA officer and temporary C/S without designation, assisting General Gruenther.

Clark also reported that General Patton will have General Doolittle under him as commander of the United States Air Forces for TORCH, and that General Patton is responsible to the C-in-C for both air and ground operations of the U. S. forces. Patton will need 346th Engineers Regiment from England. No difficulty about this anticipated. Patton advised he proposed to bring only light tanks with the assault forces, believing no armored resistance will be met prior to D+30 (thirty days after day of initial attack). Clark mentioned to him the possibility of mined beaches. May be necessary for Clark to return to Washington for consultation with Patton before the "great armada" sails. Patton returning home; leaves General Truscott to represent him here.

Mr. Mack of the British Foreign Office, who is to be political officer for TORCH, gave as his opinion that Vichy would order French in North Africa to fight and they "would undoubtedly do so."

No landing craft now available in Northern Ireland.

While waiting for dinner, Ike received a phone message from General Spaatz that the first American daylight bombing raid over France had been successful. Twelve Flying Fortresses, escorted by seventy-five Spitfires, bombed the railway yard and a locomotive repair plant with a capacity of 250 locomotives at Rouen, with no losses. Don't know yet whether Spitfires were piloted by Americans or British. Raid had been led by Major General Ira C. Eaker. Ike much worried about this, for he regards Eaker as an extremely valuable man.

We are experimenting with our ideas on bombing operations—high level, principally daylight. If our conception works, British can bomb at night and we in the daytime, or both. Fact that all twelve got back safely, despite attack by German fighters, including Focke-Wulfs, indicates American ideas on this subject may not be so haywire as has been indicated. Our bombing tactics call for close formation flying. Each bomber has tremendous fire power in virtually every direction, even from the belly, where there is a revolving turret only big enough for a small-sized gunner.

Discussion centered on aircraft. Ike said that one thing that has been learned is that fire power from planes is greatly increased, or at least is more effective, if guns are close together on ship, such as through propeller. Apparently, fire from guns along wings set to concentrate the bullet stream in a small pattern 300 or so yards away is not as effective as a parallel stream of bullets in a small pattern. New American fighter now in production said to be a humdinger. Hope so! So far all members of the British and even American press comment adversely on American fighter planes especially, and also on bombers.

Had a good chuckle with General Patton. He told us he already had drafted his proposed demand for surrender of Casablanca. His pronouncement said that as much as it hurts for two former Allies to be fighting each other, the vicissitudes of war have required him to attack the French, and unless Casablanca surrenders within ten minutes, he will have the Navy shoot the hell out of 'em. Being in a Navy uniform, I couldn't help mentioning this call on the sister service to back up his demand.

Patton is a rugged man. Don't doubt his statement made some days ago that he can mesmerize troops into a high state of morale. His language is salty, to the point, and colorful. His swear words are frequent and expressive. No wonder Ike's so pleased to have him.

As General Patton said good night he added, "I just want you to know, Ike, that after studying my job in Africa my mind is at ease."

To bed by eleven.

A Leak

LONDON, TUESDAY, AUGUST 18, 1942

General Ike's staff at Norfolk House is working on all sorts of schemes in the hope of confusing the Axis by feints in numerous directions. One is a plan to invade Norway.

Incidentally, I noticed a feature article in one of London's papers today that elaborated a suggestion made in America by Air Vice-Marshal Hugh Pughe Lloyd, formerly in command at Malta, advocating an Allied attack on French Morocco.

Message late today from the British Chiefs of Staff gives the more alarming information that the enemy may be hot on the scent of the TORCH plan. The CG received a formal message from the British Chiefs of Staff stating flatly that a French official, according to a member of the French staff in Washington, had said that the Americans are working on plans for operation in French Morocco. This French official stated further that he had heard the same thing in London.

In transmitting this disquieting news to General Strong, G-2 in Washington, the CG emphasized the danger and reported that the British Secretary of State had taken the matter up via the Ambassador in Washington and requested that General Marshall be advised. The CG insisted that drastic measures be instituted to insure secrecy.

Didn't take General Marshall long to act on Ike's suggestion that the boundary lines of the European Theater be pushed out. New boundaries now go to hell 'n' gone, extending "to the south to include all land and adjacent sea area east of 20 degrees west longitude; north of the Tropic of Cancer; and west of 15 degrees east longitude." The eastern boundary takes in Tripoli. The western boundary goes beyond the coast line of Africa and includes Madeira and the Canary Islands, among others. The southeast corner would seem to be near the end of a railway line at a town called Tedjerri. Wonder if we'll ever be there. Theater is to be divided when mission is accomplished, as suggested.

Leo Dolan and Charles Smith, of INS, in first thing this morning. Walloped censorship, citing cases which tended to emphasize the domination of the British in censorship matters. Ike immediately telephoned Brendan Bracken, Director of the MOI, and told him that the existing situation is unsatisfactory; that if he wanted to he could send any information he desired to the WD, including news stories, and let the WD decide what should be made public. This would plug leaks in British censorship and illustrates the necessity for close co-operation. Arranged to have General McClure, G-2, meet Bracken later in the day to work out a more satisfactory operation.

Failed to report hitherto that after last Saturday's lunch-press conference, Ike ordered removal of censorship concerning color problem. Admiral Stark came in Monday, much concerned. Navy had censored a story by Frederick Kuh, of the *Chicago Sun,* of incident which had occurred around July 1, in Londonderry. Seems there had been a near riot of a few white and colored men in the Navy. Admiral fearful Ike's liberal policy would leave the Navy behind the censorship eight-ball. Ike supplemented his verbal statement of policy on this question by a letter to Daniell, in which he said, of course, if a story arbitrarily emphasized relatively unimportant incidents and made them appear typical, the censor would be justified in suppressing such a story. In other words, writers seeking merely to make headlines and trouble would not be passed, although stories of an objective nature, relating incidents in their proper perspective, would be passed as announced. This satisfied Stark, and he okayed the letter.

LONDON, WEDNESDAY, AUGUST 19, 1942

James Warburg, of OWI, in first thing this morning to see me regarding various factors preventing desired partnership between Americans and British. Warburg worried over the difference between American and British Army rations. Ike having considerable difficulty with this problem. Still isn't settled and may never be because the American Army prides itself on having the best-fed soldiers in the world. When the British were in France, their ration was better than that of the poilu.

Like that geyser in Yellowstone that gathers steam and spouts only at irregular intervals, Ike has been accumulating different reasons for having the staff, some twenty of them, into his office for what he later termed a "lecture." It was called on the spur of the moment, and I didn't hear of it until it was half finished. Apparently, before I arrived, he'd instructed the C/S to put out a memo making clear that any orders issued by him, through the two aides, Major Lee or Lieutenant Commander Butcher, were to be considered as if actually given by him. General also criticized laxness in saluting. (Returning to hotel last night in the big black car with three stars front and back and an American flag on the radiator cap, down Audley Street, past the officers' mess, met some fifteen officers and only one saluted: and he a British officer.) Said if he observed any further laxities in saluting—not that he cared for himself, but it was an index to discipline, training, and alertness—he would ask the name of the offender, the name of the outfit or section, and would hold the commander or section head responsible.

Also cited a story related by Warburg. One of his men had seen an American officer enter the Mt. Royal Hotel dining room for breakfast, juggling two grapefruit. (British also patronized this hotel; they scarcely ever saw a grapefruit.) He ostentatiously had them cut, pulled a sack of sugar from his pocket, and lavishly sprayed it over the grapefruit and the tablecloth. The CG condemned such display as ungentlemanly, and just the kind of thing which will impede progress toward mutual respect. Said if he had been present, he would immediately have ordered the officer home by slow boat, preferably unescorted.

To judge from information previously furnished by War Department, the American expedition might sail from U. S. about October 1. This would allow establishment of D-Day on about October 15. This date bad on account of phase of the moon, and it seems unwise to risk delay merely in the hope of utilizing team from 1st Division rather than from 34th.

"Each day that passes," Ike said, "is a day of additional risk with regard to secrecy, and secrecy is vital to success."

Personally, have never possessed so many secrets, but, fortunately, they don't press to get out. Now, however, no one around this job, except Ike, knows of projected Commando raids, such as yesterday's on Dieppe.

How the Dieppe Raid Looked from London

LONDON, THURSDAY, AUGUST 20, 1942

News of first American bombing raid on Rouen, followed by twenty-four Flying Fortresses' raid on Abbeville yesterday, plus participation of one detachment of Rangers' battalion in Commando raids on Dieppe early this morning, has been played hard at home, with overemphasis on extent of American participation. Notice in London *Daily Telegraph* this morning a facsimile of headlines from New York evening papers—splash streamers from three of them say: "U. S. and British Invade France!" "Tanks and U. S. Troops Smash at French Coast!" "U. S. Troops Land with Commandos in Biggest Raid!" With this overplay of American participation, it isn't surprising that one of the messages received by CG last night was from General Marshall, questioning advisability of so much publicity regarding U. S. raids and personalities. Advised conservative handling of references to U. S. in Dieppe.

Personally, think we're making a mountain out of a molehill. After all, these are "firsts" and become news even though only a few American troops or fliers take part. Probably will be one or two-day play, and then American press will subside to more objective handling of news.

If anyone has been conservative as to personal publicity, it has been the CG. It was partly to avoid having stories repeatedly carrying his own name that he changed the censorship rules early in July to permit mention of the senior commanders. Other names have cleared censorship from time to time. Naturally, news of air activity and the personalities involved is interesting to home readers and radio listeners, and is vigorously sought by the correspondents. In addition, the Commandos and Rangers afford particularly good copy. At least two ex-Hollywood film personalities are in publicity capacities with air and Commando-Ranger outfits.

General Truscott, commander of our Ranger operations, returned from the Dieppe show but had no further significant details to add. He had been on a destroyer, had picked up some of the survivors of the ill-fated assault force.

The CG's message yesterday relative to leaks received a prompt reply from General Marshall last night. Apparently, best curative for unfortunate disclosure is the hope that the Germans can be led to assume that the leaks are naïve and deliberate attempts on our part to mislead them. Continuation of daily air reconnaissance from Ostend northward, to keep the Germans guessing, would probably lead them to think our real intention is Norway. If this idea is accepted and continued, and air activity in France is supplemented by a moderate number of naval and ground troops preparing for amphibious operations for the north, then the disclosure re TORCH may be neutralized. Message further indicated that Marshall and staff in Washington fully expect the German General Staff to have knowledge of the TORCH operation, except possibly the date and composition. General Strong added in the same cable that the Chief was much disturbed about the leak and was investigating it. Drastic measures were contemplated to prevent future ones.

The third message received last night was a brief note from Mount-batten's headquarters about the Dieppe raid. Said there were 500 fighter sorties. Loss to enemy was seventy planes destroyed, thirty-two probably destroyed, and ninety-two damaged. Of our own (mostly British), there are sixty-eight missing, of which nine pilots are known safe. Commandos were mainly Canadian, with a detachment of U. S. Rangers (fifty) and a small unit of British Special Service Troops and of the Fighting French.

General Patton off to Washington. He is keyed to a pitch as high as his falsetto voice and his go-to-hell attitude emphasizes his energy and ambition to succeed. Wonder where I'll see him next? Volunteered to send cigars to replace mine he had smoked.

LONDON, FRIDAY, AUGUST 21, 1942

Lord Louis in late today with a report on the Commando raid at Dieppe Wednesday. There were about 6000 troops involved, and 2000 were lost or captured. We knew that only fifty Americans were in the assault, of which our own reports show thirteen killed or missing. Colonel Loren B. Helsinger lost a foot when a shell hit the destroyer he was in. Lord Louis recommended that four Americans be decorated by the CG. They were sharpshooters stationed on the second floor of a house from which much of the foundation was shot away. All miraculously escaped and took part in a successful assault on a battery in which some 160 Germans were killed in hand-to-hand fighting and the battery was silenced. Lord Louis full of praise of the conduct of Americans who participated. The CG said he wouldn't bestow medals on the Americans until after the Canadians, British, and Fighting French had been decorated. He said, "The tail shouldn't wag the dog."

CG had said to me that the raid was a fiasco. He felt a little better about it after talking to Lord Louis. Outstanding to my mind is the ill-luck which ran the raiding ships blindly into a German convoy along the

French coast. E boats and flak ships turned loose and raised hell. Wouldn't happen once in a hundred times, but it did this time.

During the day a cable prepared by the staff under Clark's direction, with approval of the C-in-C (synonymous with "CG" and Ike), was sent the WD, requesting that troops actually to be engaged in TORCH be led to believe they are bound for the Pacific, possibly Australia. The desirability of issuing maps, instructions concerning currency, customs of the country, and so forth was mentioned.

General Eisenhower cabled the WD requesting selection of a civilian administrator to govern in French Morocco after it had been seized. He wants the administrator on his staff as soon as practicable for preparation of plans and suggested that Mr. Bullitt might make a suitable recommendation. Made clear, however, that the individual will be a member of his staff and will have no independent avenue of official communication to any individual or official in the U. S. The individual should bring with him key military and civilian personnel.

Medicos messaging Washington for three hospital ships for TORCH.

The CG, with Generals Clark and Handy, had dinner with Field Marshal Sir John Dill, who is enthusiastic over TORCH. Some other British generals, however, look upon it as an "adventure."

Ike Summarizes the Situation

                                            LONDON, SATURDAY, AUGUST 22, 1942

The CG tied up most of the day in conferences with General Handy, General Clark, and others. Busy drafting a letter to the Combined Chiefs of Staff, to be submitted through General Ismay and to apply to the outline plan for TORCH. Planners and advisers to the CG insisted that he make clear to the Combined Chiefs the inadequacy of the assault force. This weakness comes, presumably, from the inability of the two Navies, particularly our own, to supply escort vessels for follow-up convoys to maintain the expedition.

The vulnerability of the airdrome at Gibraltar likewise is a No. 1 worry.

Ike torn between desire to go ahead and do the job with the tools available and the necessity of stating his military belief that the assignment is ultra-risky without the ships and planes and other equipment which they seem to expect him to have but which actually have not been made available. What was to have been a major assault, with tremendous resources of the two great nations behind it, has now deteriorated into an attack on the northern coast of Africa, the original intention of simultaneously attacking Casablanca having been cast aside because of the shortage of naval escort and the dangerous surf. With Gibraltar, long the trade-mark symbolizing security, actually extraordinarily vulnerable in the two particulars most important to us—i.e., airdrome and harbor—an assault entirely within the Mediterranean leaves our forces in a position to be cut off from the springboard for planes and from the main source of supply through the Strait. Casablanca would afford a supply line under the present plan, but would have to be captured by back-tracking from Oran.

The C-in-C is left in a position of having honestly to appraise the chances of success and report back to his bosses, knowing full well that such a report may be regarded as either an attempt to make a written record for "I told you so" use in the event the great mission fails, or whimpering, a practice he strongly dislikes, for more equipment. Yet he is keyed to put the job over; if only political reactions of Vichy and Spain could be ascertained as definitely as can purely military questions!

The letter was drafted and redrafted a half-dozen times and finally Ike stuck it in his desk drawer, to let it rest until morning.

LONDON, SUNDAY, AUGUST 23, 1942

I had awakened early and had made my Nescafé when the door opened and Ike poked his head in, saying, "I thought you would have some coffee." He had been unable to sleep late as planned: was still puzzling over the letter to the Combined Chiefs of Staff. Breakfasted on it and got to the office by 10. Ike went to work on the letter again. He read a draft to me, and I suggested removal of a word—"hasty"—as it was used to apply to the consideration given to the planning of TORCH, which I thought had been anything but hasty, and to the contrary, thorough. Suggestion accepted. Great contribution to the war effort by Butcher.

After one more revision, the CG signed the letter and sent it to the Combined Chiefs of Staff. He made it clear that the submission of the letter did not indicate any unreadiness on his part, or of any of his subordinates, to undertake TORCH determinedly and wholeheartedly and that he desired to express to the Combined Chiefs his entire satisfaction with the designations to principal command and staff positions.

He said it was his opinion that this expedition is not sufficiently powerful to accomplish its purpose against the potential opposition in the general theater, the purpose prescribed by the Combined Chiefs of Staff. Determined resistance from the French forces would virtually eliminate hope of gaining Tunisia ahead of Axis troops, which could then be built up more rapidly than our own forces. Use of the Spanish Army and the elimination of Gibraltar as an air and naval base would create difficulties of the most serious kind. This means that success must depend more upon political than upon military factors. The apparent inability of the combined navies to provide escorts for an attack at Casablanca, along with those planned inside the Mediterranean, has distinctly decreased the opportunity for creating throughout North Africa the impression of overwhelming attack, so essential to producing a readiness to accept Allied occupation without material resistance.

He said that he felt that the most favorable situation we can reasonably hope to find in North Africa is continued neutrality on the part of the Spanish and submission on the part of the French. Under these conditions the expedition, assuming that initial and follow-up forces arrive as planned, should succeed. Positive French assistance can scarcely be anticipated in view of the tremendous pressure that the enemy can exert, in France, on the friends, families, and interests of the North African inhabitants. Moreover, it would appear that once French territory has been invaded by us, whatever military assets remain to the French in Europe will become almost instantly available to the Germans.

He pointed out that there was no need to dwell upon the inescapable costs of this expedition measured in terms of its adverse effects on other Allied ventures throughout the world. Every other theater will have to be cut to the bone in order to provide the strength necessary to attain the prescribed object. This situation will persist for a number of months, no matter what the degree of initial success.

He added that his naval advisers had expressed grave doubts as to the ability of the combined navies to provide the continuous escorting and covering resources that will be essential. They believe that additional losses, commitments throughout the world, and increased enemy reaction, particularly by air and submarine, will make the naval aspects of this operation one of increasing hazard and difficulty. Finally, he pointed out that there will always remain the threatening possibility of Axis reaction through the Iberian peninsula. When and if sufficient Axis forces are released from the Russian theater to be available for a deliberate campaign in that direction, there would appear to be little that the Allies could do to escape the inevitable effects of an Axis occupation of Spain.

He expressed the personal opinion that if the two governments could find the naval, air, and ground forces, with the shipping, to carry out, simultaneously with the attack planned inside the Mediterranean, a strong assault at Casablanca, the chances for success would be greatly increased. The advantages to be gained would be in reducing the hazard of either Spanish or French hostile reaction, in more quickly establishing an auxiliary line of communications by land, and in increasing the port capacity of the occupied zone. Such simultaneous attacks could not be made before November 7 at the earliest.

The Vulnerability of Gibraltar

LONDON, MONDAY, AUGUST 24, 1942

Sat in on a long conference in Ike's office on the vulnerability and strength of Gibraltar, if any, for our purposes. General Mason-MacFarlane, the Governor General of Gibraltar, was present. He had arrived in England by a Catalina yesterday. He reiterated the warning in his written report. Every movement at Gib is seen by the enemy. There is danger of the Spaniards making the airdrome unusable immediately activity starts. The airfield is small; there will be 180-200 Spitfires closely assembled on the field when and if TORCH gets under way—an easy target for bombing by the Germans and Italians; also for the Spanish machine guns set up along the barbed-wire entanglement, some only twenty feet from the edge of the field. MacFarlane says a million gallons of gasoline in four-gallon tins have been cached on, about, in, over, and through the crevices of Gibraltar. Much of this gasoline already stored in dumps, likewise a good target for incendiaries. Feared the whole damn Rock would blaze if this gasoline is ignited. Wants no more tins; instead wants a tanker anchored in the commercial harbor, with gasoline to be lightered or hosed to the field. Tanker would be a small target for high-altitude bombing. AA would keep enemy planes well up.

Will need to get rid of a battalion garrisoned on the Rock, to make room for additional personnel, if our headquarters established on Gib, and emphasized most vigorously that any unusual movement (certainly, the presence of big shots) was quickly noticed by enemy agents. Reported there is already much talk of British-American forces going into French Morocco, although Casablanca is thought to be the target. American officers visiting Gibraltar, to make arrangements for signals, headquarters, and so forth, should go in Canadian or British uniform. This already done —three U. S. signal officers went in British uniform. Wonder if they would be shot as spies if caught by Jerry?

Another problem is water. Gib's supply is adequate, barely, for normal use, but insufficient to meet unusual demand. Warships will have to be well stocked with water when they leave U. S. and U. K., but many will need to stop there for refueling; especially true of the British covering forces to shadow the French and Italian fleets. They will need full fuel tanks for emergency.

Danger so far as airdrome is concerned concentrated in three-day period after D-1. If Oran airfield quickly captured, then Spitfires can be flown from Gib to Oran and based there. If things go badly and there is a holdup, Spain will probably be high-pressured by Hitler into belligerence against U. S. and U. K. However, MacFarlane said, Spain desires to stay neutral, and strong assurances on our part that we have no intentions against Spanish Morocco probably would keep her quiet. Thinks likely Spain would resist German invasion of Iberian peninsula, but doubts ability of Spanish to do much effective fighting.

MacFarlane said that the French in Morocco could be expected to fight unless there is overwhelming show of force on our part. French planes have attacked stray British craft, but the French could probably not continue defensive operations long because of shortage of gasoline and ammunition. Emphasized that move toward Tunisia should be at the speed of a *Blitzkrieg* rather than over the relatively long interval of three weeks from the initial assault date, as planned. General Clark pointed out that this estimate was based on the presence of strong and persistent opposition, but if defense is weak or quickly dissipated, it should take no more than seven days to reach Tunisia from Bône. Planners had figured the Germans and/or Italians could get into Tunisia in strength in twenty-eight days.

Churchill "out of town." Where—Russia? Must be, for through General Ismay of the British Chiefs of Staff, he has sent several queries about TORCH. Wants it "lit" as soon as possible, to ease not only the military but also the political situation in Russia.

Ike went off to a meeting of the British Chiefs, to discuss with them, at their request, his critical comment of TORCH. When he returned, he said he was in a hell of a pickle. Chiefs had respected his letter, but now want him to go back to the original plan to include Casablanca and also to add an assault on Philippeville, so that the show of strength will be so overwhelming that resistance will be frightened into ineffectiveness. (As I am dictating this to Miss Jaqua, there is an air raid on. We have our secret papers in the safe, as required by the rules. We have just heard three explosions and, both of us being greenhorns at air raids, don't know whether they are AA or bombs. Miss Jaqua thinks they are not bombs, as she didn't hear a screech. Whatever is going on outside doesn't seem to faze the traffic. There are low clouds and, apparently, some German raiders slipped into the London area. Our barrage balloon in Grosvenor Square is nestling close to the ground, among the trees. Various officers are walking up and down the street, intent on personal or official business, seeming not to care about the raid.)

In the conference with the Combined Chiefs of Staff, the first Sea Lord, Admiral Sir Dudley Pound, had referred to a conversation of the President in which he was reported to have said that TORCH and the maintenance of a sea line to Murmansk were to be the No. 1 priorities in the U. S. war effort this year. Certainly, Sir Dudley had said, the British are putting into TORCH everything they have available. They have even pulled two aircraft carriers from the Indian Ocean, where they are badly needed. Admiral Pound insisted to Ike that U. S. put up more naval escort.

While I was with Ike, Clark came in, as did Handy, and the three of them went into a deep-brown study as to what the hell to do next. Ike had already dictated the first draft of a long message to General Marshall, which he read to the other two. The whole question revolves around the amount of naval escort, for both the original armada and the continuing escort of convoys for supplies.

What Goes on in the Mind of a C-in-C

LONDON, TUESDAY, AUGUST 25, 1942

The harassed Ike, mulling over his troubles as Allied Commander dealing with America and Britain, not to mention the land, sea, and air services of each, nor the variety of high political problems involved with Spain and France, has always to consider not only the purely military matters, but international politics and personalities. He was realizing the former could be treated with more precision than the latter. The War Department reaction to Ike's appraisal of success in TORCH is to curtail the objectives to fit the naval forces available. The President insists on ground action for American troops in 1942—the sooner the better. American Chiefs of Staff now propose to limit the landings merely to Casablanca and Oran, omitting Algiers. The British preferred to land as far east on the north shore of Africa as Philippeville or Bône. The Prime Minister and the British insist that to make the campaign a strategic success Tunisia must be taken, and quickly; consequently: landings as far to the east as possible are to our advantage. No one advocated landing as far east as Bizerte because of enemy air strength on near-by Sardinia and Sicily. Philippeville and Bône were risky enough, bearing in mind that a recent convoy of thirteen supply ships to Malta had all been sunk but one—and later it was sunk in a Malta harbor.

Yet the American point of view has to be considered: if we don't land at Casablanca and thus have no alternative line of supply to that through the Strait of Gibraltar, the expedition risks being cut off. And then wouldn't the two great countries look like amateurs? The Strait is only eight miles wide; if the Spanish opposed us, or are overrun by the Germans, the coastal guns on either side of the Strait, both under Spanish rule, can stop our convoys carrying supplies. The limiting factor is naval escort, and as the British are putting in all they can find, even to stripping their fleet in the Indian Ocean, they feel the U. S. will have to assign more warships to TORCH. The U. S. Navy is hard pressed to meet all the demands placed upon it: escort of convoys, active fighting in the Pacific (a naval battle is even now raging in the Solomons). Increasing demand for warships of all kinds for a variety of urgent duties makes the ever-rising production of ships in America seem as if it is only moving at a snail's pace —yet it's prodigious.

By limiting the extent of the initial invasion, Ike feels, we give up before we start in the race against time and the Germans to capture Tunisia. If the Germans or the Italians get entrenched in Tunisia, we will simply have large American and British forces anchored in French Morocco, where it will be difficult to extract them for accomplishing the real and ultimate objectives—striking at the heart of Germany through France. The limitation of the invasion defeats its own purpose.

Churchill After His Visit to Moscow

LONDON, WEDNESDAY, AUGUST 26, 1942

Ike was at the PM's for dinner last night with General Clark. Got back about 1:30. Having failed to sleep much the night before, left word he was going to "sleep in." But despite his good intention was up as usual at 7.

Averell Harriman, just back from Moscow, had called on the CG Tuesday afternoon late and had told Ike that Stalin and Churchill, with Harriman present, had minced no words; had put all their cards on the table, so far as he could tell. Had appraised the military situation most frankly and deliberately. Harriman said that it was his belief that the Russians could hold out; that they have twenty-five divisions in the southern Caucasus; that they are still making 2000 tanks a month, but have great need for trucks.

Stalin appeared confident, but the bad news of the danger of Stalingrad had developed since the party had left Moscow. Apparently, the Germans have found a way to make the Rumanians and Hungarians fight more like Germans. Divisions of these nationalities have been giving much stronger accounts of themselves than hitherto. Same is true of the Italians in Egypt.

Ike and Clark had dined alone with the PM. He was in good form as usual, but was insistent that the TORCH operation proceed. Said rather than forego TORCH, he would hop on a plane and see the President in Washington.

Having no better place to go and no brilliant ideas, we lunched alone at the flat. Had some cold grouse that Major Lee had brought last night. Flavor was *high*. We had soup. The PM, it developed, had been angry because of disagreement with some of the British generals who had sided with General Ike and against the Prime, who showed his temper by fighting his soup. Since the PM is short and blockily built, his chin isn't very much above the soup plate. He crouched over the plate, almost had his nose in the soup, wielded the spoon rapidly. The soup disappeared to the accompaniment of loud gurglings.

The PM is perfectly nonchalant while entertaining guests. General Clark reported that the PM had inadvertently pushed a highball glass off a side table, but went right on talking, not even glancing around to see where the glass and contents had fallen. During the evening, he asked a servant to bring him his change of socks—he took off his shoes, the socks he was wearing, put on the other pair, and replaced his shoes, without the slightest embarrassment. Later he walked to the open door, put his back to its edge, vigorously rubbed his shoulder blades against it, and said, "Guess I picked 'em up in Egypt."

Asked if the PM drank as much as is reputed. Was told he had only a glass of sherry. He smokes a terrifically long and big cigar, but plays with it more than he smokes. After dinner, he lit one of these, and during the evening, it burned about an inch, dying out frequently. Ike had the impression that the PM rather relishes his reputation as a heavy smoker and drinker, but actually is much more moderate than rumor would indicate.

Ike and Clark are to spend the night with the PM either Thursday or Friday of this week. The PM, undoubtedly, will deal directly with the President and attempt to keep TORCH lit. Ike has at no time expressed an unwillingness to go forward with the assault and is somewhat fearful that his honest appraisal of the dangers may be misconstrued as a fear rather than as a deliberation.

During Churchill's recent visit to Moscow, the reasons for his (the PM's) objection to SLEDGEHAMMER had been explained, but, apparently, without completely convincing Stalin of the military soundness of his views. The PM had then outlined TORCH, and awakened great interest in

Stalin. Before leaving Moscow, the PM was told, "May God prosper that operation." As a result of these conversations, the "former naval person," as Roosevelt addresses him, feels completely committed to launching TORCH at the earliest possible date, on as grand a scale as possible.

Looked at a house for a "hideout" to escape the four forbidding walls of the Dorchester, as directed by Ike. Will still live here, but need a place to retreat. Went out to see the house this afternoon with Lieutenant Colonel Bussey, British billeting officer, and Captain A. E. Stewart of our headquarters. It is called Telegraph Cottage. Small, unpretentious, remotely situated on a ten-acre wooded tract, with a lawn in back and rose garden. Between Coombe Hill and Little Coombe golf courses. House rents for about $32 a week. The owner will keep up the garden, including vegetables, and all we have to supply are bed linen, food, and two colored boys to cook and keep house. Mickey will be in charge. Has five small bedrooms—a bit more than we need—but only one bath. Fireplace for heat. I decided to take it and told Ike later that he is in a position of being able to say, whenever anything goes wrong at the house, "your judgment was lousy." *

Sometime after 6 o'clock, three short buzzes on my buzzer called me into the boss's office, where he and General Clark wanted to get away from the uncertainties and imponderables which press upon them every minute of the day.

"Let's go down to Wayne's and have some of his sausage for dinner."

Off we went. Sausage nearly ready by the hand of Clark's Negro orderly, Chaney, when a message came that the PM would like to see Ike immediately unless he was in a meeting. Ike departed promptly and was away about an hour; had dinner on a tray.

All Ike said about the talk with the PM was that it had been hinted quite definitely that the PM wants to go to Washington and take Ike.

More Doubts About TORCH

                                          LONDON, THURSDAY, AUGUST 27, 1942
In General Clark's report of his conferences and decisions, as Deputy C-in-C, during August 26, he relates that just prior to General Handy's

---

* I later discovered that with his usual perspicacity the Naval Aide had selected a residence only a half mile from one of the important British decoys for enemy aircraft. The existence of these decoys was at that time a military secret. The decoys automatically flared into flame when enemy bombers came within six miles and frequently successfully diverted attack from important industrial or military establishments to relatively unpopulated areas.

departure for Washington he summarized the conference with the PM
of Tuesday night, making a point of Churchill's insistence upon action
by mid-October; how he took immediate steps to aid the project by ordering the First Sea Lord to cut down the sailing time from the U. K.
to the Mediterranean to about ten days. Clark emphasized to Handy,
who was already most appreciative of the CG's difficulties, the need of
furnishing a definite directive without a moment's unavoidable delay.
Handy also aware that we are ready to go ahead just as soon as we get
the basic decision.

General K. A. N. Anderson, British Task Force Commander for TORCH,
was to be called by the PM, so Clark gave him a "fill-in" on the PM's
views (an American officer helping guide a British officer as to the views
of the Britishers' own Prime Minister). Other British officers, primarily
those dealing with supply problems, joined the conference and, judging
from the report, are having one hell of a time. These British officers
agree that the plan, as now set up, cannot be logistically supported.
General Anderson feels that landings inside the Mediterranean are feasible but doubts his ability to advance in time to forestall Axis occupation
of Tunisia. Feels this will be true regardless of date finally set for initial
assault. Clark, the essence of patience, apparently got tired of hearing
reasons why the job couldn't be done. He reported: "I broke up this conference with the comment that the operation was definitely on and that
ways and means to make it successful would have to be found."

Message from Marshall today advises that the "former naval person"
is pressing the President to agree to proceed with the North African
assault with whatever forces and equipment are available and at the
earliest date.

LONDON, FRIDAY, AUGUST 28, 1942

Had invited Bill Paley, CBS president, who has just arrived in London,
to lunch today and found that Ike and General Spaatz were available,
so the four of us ate at the flat. Bill much thrilled by the opportunity
to talk war shop with the generals. Later said much impressed by Ike
and Tooey. The two of them, my ex- and current bosses, took turns
ribbing me.

Ike and General Clark went to Chequers for the night. Both said they
hated to go; that their position in relation to the United States Chiefs of
Staff, the British Chiefs of Staff, the President of the U. S., and the PM
made discussion of the expedition difficult, and left them open to quotation by the PM to the President—quotes which, without being completed,

might distort the original meaning. Further, they are both getting tired of talking. Ike said he would be ready to start on this expedition instantly, if he could only get through this period of tedious, tiresome rehash.

In General Clark's report covering August 27, he informed the CG that Admiral Ramsay, during a meeting at the Admiralty, had announced that the Royal Navy couldn't do the Philippeville landing, much to the distress of General Anderson; Clark had soothed Anderson with the information that the PM had indicated that additional naval forces might be made available from the Indian Ocean; that certain ships now in the U. K. and the U. S. will have to remain here, as they will be needed for the North African troops, and will not have to return to the U. S.; and "that," and "that," and "that"—all indicating that a million details are needed to plan and arrange an expedition like TORCH. How Clark keeps his good humor, I don't know. Of course, he consults on policy and on many individual decisions with the CG. However, at the moment, he's taking a tremendous load off Ike's shoulders.

Lots of Quarterbacks

LONDON, SATURDAY, AUGUST 29, 1942
In General Clark's report today on the activities of August 28, he relates that he has discussed with the Air Force planners the possibilities of various devices to prepare the way for the American landings in North Africa: skywriting, American flags dropped by parachutes, and leaflets. Generals Arnold, Doolittle, and Hansell, according to Colonel Vandenberg's statement to Clark, "all agree with him [Vandenberg] that we have no more than about one-fourth the air strength supporting the American attack that might be profitably put to use."

Clark had discussed with Admiral Ramsay the possibility of including in the plan a feint at Casablanca. Ramsay likes it. Navy people don't care for the risk involved in bringing a large convoy into the vicinity of Casablanca without strong naval support—by *strong* they mean one or more battleships and cruisers and at least one carrier.

Just finishing lunch at the flat with guests of my own, when the door burst open. Here was the Commanding General, ETOUSA, closely followed by General Clark. All surprised. He'd returned early to draft and dispatch an important message to Washington and had intended to talk over its phraseology with Clark and others while lunching at the flat. Unfortunately, the Aide had taken over, and the Commanding General obligingly found lunch at General Clark's.

What had happened at Chequers was that the PM had pressed further for quick action on TORCH; was striving valiantly to resolve the differences of opinion between the U. S. Chiefs of Staff and the British Chiefs. There had even been a meeting of the British Chiefs of Staff at Chequers during the morning.

At the PM's request, the CG outlined the plan as it stood. The British Chiefs had laid great stress on forestalling the Germans in Tunisia, and for this reason it had been decided to push the initial landings as far east as possible. The line-up, in brief, was this: the British Chiefs had their eyes mainly on occupying Algeria and pushing on to Tunisia at the earliest date, while the American forces insisted on getting Casablanca, even at the cost of some postponement in the initial assault.

Subsequent discussion revolved around the point as to whether the Bône and Philippeville landings, inside the Mediterranean, should be abandoned. British felt that if they were abandoned it might be possible to meet the U. S. Chiefs of Staff's insistence for Casablanca.

LONDON, SUNDAY, AUGUST 30, 1942

The President wants to cut the suit to fit the cloth and land only at Casablanca and Oran, with Americans only, but using many British ships and naval escort.

Clark's daily communiqué to Ike, covering August 29, advised that the headquarters staff for TORCH had been started to work on the new Roosevelt all-American assault plan—all-American except for the British Navy and probably some British air support. This football team of planners must be dizzy trying to follow all the signals for the play called by the several quarterbacks.

Meanwhile, training is going along; officer personnel is being assigned; supplies and equipment are being assembled and earmarked, and efforts to bolster the naval support continue.

LONDON, MONDAY, AUGUST 31, 1942

British Chiefs had a meeting today to which the CG and General Clark were invited. Ike is of opinion that the PM's reply to the President will give in detail exact British naval force that can be made available to Americans for the attack. British Chiefs had even considered, but had discarded, the idea of using a British division in American uniforms. Figured it might lay them open to charge of bad faith.

The Allied C-in-C reiterated that there is no hope of the 1st Division taking part in a major expedition from the U. K. to attack before October 30, and this is absolutely the most optimistic date. Both he and Clark think Algiers should be included in the first attack, but repeated their conviction that this can be done only with some additional naval strength from the U. S.

The CG got to bed the earliest of any night since he has been in London—10:30—all set for a good night's sleep, of which he has had but few lately. About 11 he was already sound asleep when my phone rang. It was the secretary of the PM, wanting to know if the General could go to 10 Downing later "that evening" if the PM so desired. Had to alert Ike and, of course, he said "yes." Secretary said he would call back later. I don't know what time it was—probably around midnight—when the phone rang again; secretary saying would it be more convenient for the General to come at 10:30 the next morning? It would, but in the meantime, Ike was awakened again. At 5 A.M., Ike poked his head in my door. "Did you leave word with the switchboard operator to call me at five o'clock? She's on the phone and says it's time for me to get up." It was a mistake, as I later found; the switchboard operator had merely confused extension numbers. Ike was good-natured about it and, fortunately, went back to sleep promptly, something unusual for him these days.

AUGUST, 1942: *In Russia Nazi offensives threatened Astrakhan, captured Maikop and Grozny oil fields, assaulted Stalingrad with a million men. Chinese, attacking in Kiangsi, recaptured nine Jap bases and one hundred miles of Hangchow-Nanchang railroad and reached bomber range of Jap home islands. Italian ships shelled Yugoslavia as guerrilla uprisings there killed 3000 Axis soldiers. Yank marines hit the dense Solomon Islands, opened the battle of Guadalcanal, closed on Tulagi, destroyed Jap seaplane base on Makin. Naval forces repulsed two Jap Navy counterattacks in the Solomons. Decimated Allied troops studied lessons learned during abortive Commando raid at Dieppe. First mass United States air raids against French targets were carried out. Brazil declared war against Axis after Nazi submarines sank five of her ships near her coast. In North Africa Rommel attacked the British flank. (British valiantly trying to get convoys to Malta. The price in ships and men emphasizes the importance of Malta as a sea and air base from which Rommel's line of supply can be attacked.—H.C.B.)*

Footnote on Air War

Message from General Marshall called the CG's attention to an article in *Time*—issue of August 31—saying that American pilots who fly Spitfires prefer them to American pursuits. Article said American impression that our aircraft are the best in the world might be—in fact, probably was—wrong.

The CG arranged for General Spaatz, Brigadier General Frank O. Hunter of Fighter Command, and four or five squadron leaders to come in for a talk. Sat in on part of the conversation today.

While the Air Force is training its pilots to learn this vicious game by experience, this being the "big league" of the world's air fighting, some American pilots have been assigned Spitfires. Others are being trained in P-38s (Lightnings) and P-39s (Airacobras). When the Americans flew Spitfires, they became sold on their performance, particularly their speed and agility. Our fighting planes, according to General Hunter, have been weighted down with gadgets—most of these items have been added at the suggestion of the British advisers in America, though over here the British dispense with many of them on their own planes. Our P-38s are having to be deweighted, but Hunter confidently expects them to perform satisfactorily against the German F-W 190, which he claims outflies the old-model Spitfire. It is only natural that American pilots flying Spitfires speak highly of them when interviewed by American newspapermen. The test of the pudding is in the eating—as General Spaatz pointed out, the test of the Flying Fortress was in its performance, though there had been much criticism of the early models. Criticism, even by the British, has turned to praise, since the Fortresses have demonstrated quite satisfactorily that they can take care of themselves to a remarkable degree, while making accurate daylight raids on enemy objectives. The five squadrons of P-38s will go into action in the near future and not until then will we know the real truth. Certainly, Generals Spaatz and Hunter didn't want to be forced to press our fliers, inexperienced in actual combat, into contact with the cream of the Luftwaffe until they had gained the necessary experience and the planes had been "adjusted." It was felt that the effectiveness of the P-38 at high levels, and the P-39 up to 12,000 feet, was substantially equal, if not actually superior, to that of the F-W 190. The deciding factors in a battle are the ability and courage of the pilots.

Ike and I left the office early today—about 4:30—to stretch our legs at Telegraph Cottage. The two colored soldiers—Hunt, of Petersburg, Virginia, the cook; Moaney, of Cambridge, Maryland, on the Eastern Shore, the waiter, house boy, and "handy-andy"—got dinner, and it tasted like home. Had corn on the cob. Will have to do more of this, for it affords relaxation and change of scenery. The unending days of keeping everlastingly at it are beginning to tell, especially on Ike. He enjoyed the change. Back to town about 11.

Evolution of TORCH

LONDON, WEDNESDAY, SEPTEMBER 2, 1942
The changing considerations which have affected TORCH leave me confused, so last night I asked Ike to review the background so I could keep the record straight.

General agreement was reached by the Combined Chiefs on July 24 to undertake operation TORCH. General Marshall agreed to it, understanding there was available to the Allies sufficient air, ground, and naval strength to execute strong attacks simultaneously at Casablanca, Oran, and Algiers. Originally it was calculated the attack could not be mounted until December 1.

The President approved TORCH tentatively before General Marshall and Harry Hopkins left London on July 26, but insisted that we attack not later than October 30. All of the agreements provided that General Eisenhower was to be Commander-in-Chief of the operation and that the expedition would consist of combined British and American land, sea, and air forces.

Some time elapsed before official word was received from Washington confirming command arrangements, and for a period of about ten days the decision of the Combined Chiefs to attack in North Africa was kept so secret that not even the various commanders-in-chief in the British services were informed. As a result, General Ike and his staff could do nothing but make discreet studies of a G-2 nature. Finally his formal authorization was received. Planning was started formally with organization of a combined British and American staff in Norfolk House. Admiral King sent members of his planning group, but these representatives were not authorized to make any commitments from the American naval strength. At this time—September 2—the exact amount of American naval strength that can be counted upon is not known.

The planners soon discovered there was not in sight sufficient naval strength to support three major landings simultaneously. Numerous alternatives were studied and General Ike finally decided, in view of the ambitious objectives prescribed by the Combined Chiefs, to make the entire attack inside the Mediterranean. This would hasten a rapid push into Tunisia. The Casablanca attack was abandoned because of reports showing that very bad surf (waves sometimes are as high as fifty feet) would endanger landings on the Atlantic Coast line and because of shortage of naval escort.

When General Ike's solution of the dilemma was communicated to the

War Department, grave anxiety was expressed. Study by his planners had shown conclusively that it was impossible to build up a force of sufficient strength to make tactical considerations the governing ones in undertaking the operation. Capacity of ports and consequent slowness of build-up made clear that if French forces in North Africa oppose the landings as a unit and with their full strength, there will be little hope of achieving the great purpose of sweeping to the eastward quickly to gain control of the whole of North Africa. Consequently, the whole campaign had to be considered as depending entirely on political factors. All depends on the accuracy with which our political leaders can foresee correctly the reactions of French and Spanish forces in North Africa to the landings.

Measured purely from a military standpoint, the risks of the operation were considered so great as to condemn it if military factors alone are considered.

About the middle of August, the U. S. Chiefs of Staff proposed to the British Chiefs that the directive to General Ike be rewritten on the basis of attacking only at Casablanca and Oran. The U. S. Chiefs were apprehensive that the Strait of Gibraltar would be closed and consequently desired an alternative land line of communications running from Casablanca to Oran, thus decreasing dependence of the expedition upon the hazardous route through the strait. General Ike felt that the alternate supply route was desirable, but the fact remains that if the French resist, the damage that could be caused the long and insecure line of communication between Casablanca and Oran would be sufficiently ineffective to prevent its use for some months because of needs of rehabilitation and new construction. Again this emphasizes the dependence of the expedition upon the nonresistance of the French forces, particularly Army.

The transatlantic essay contest then proceeded apace between General Ike's headquarters and the U. S. and British Chiefs of Staff. The President and the Prime Minister likewise corresponded. The general result of all this was that no firm plan could be made. It became necessary to prepare for a number of contingencies, hoping that not too much time would be lost, no matter what the nature of the final decision. Both the Prime Minister and the President were pressing for an early attack, apparently not realizing that failure to reach firm decisions between themselves and between the two Chiefs of Staff made impossible definite preparation.

On August 29 the President proposed that no British land forces be used, that the attacks be directed at Casablanca and Oran, and that the entire project be entirely American except for supporting naval forces and shipping and, possibly, also some air. This plan contemplated preparation of an American force in the United Kingdom for the attack on Oran.

This force required a vast amount of hurried training, improvisation of units, and resorts to expedients of various kinds, inevitably requiring more time. Because of the relatively favorable conditions for landing inside the Mediterranean and the unfavorable conditions caused by the heavy Atlantic swell at Casablanca, we might find ourselves ashore at Oran but unable to land on the west coast. This would be most undesirable. However, the President manifestly has been swayed by two considerations which he considers conclusive; one, if the attack is wholly American, the French probably will not resist and, two, the desire to secure Casablanca as a base and a line of communication from there to Oran. If the President is correct in his assumption the French will not resist, no other factors are important because the first great prize—possession of the three principal French ports—will come about automatically.

The British studied the President's proposal and announced themselves ready to go along with him on any plan he approves since, under his proposal, the U. S. is shouldering the responsibility exclusively. However, they consider the failure to go into Algiers simultaneously with the attacks at the other two points a very great error. The British contend that almost certainly weather will permit an attack on Oran and Algiers on any given day and that the attack at Casablanca must be flexible as to time and probably will have to wait for a considerable period to find a suitable surf. This is where the matter stands at the moment.

From General Ike's standpoint, we are undertaking an operation of a quite desperate nature which depends only in minor degree upon professional preparation or on the wisdom of military decisions. He is reminded of the return of Napoleon from Elba—if the guess as to psychological reaction is correct, we may gain a tremendous advantage in this war; if the guess is wrong, it will be almost as certain that we will gain nothing and lose a lot. The unfavorable potentialities are vast, including not only the chance of a bloody repulse, but of inciting into the ranks of our active enemies both France and Spain, which are now classed as neutrals. If we can take into North Africa such a strong land, sea, and air force that resistance rapidly can be crushed, TORCH unquestionably would be a good operation so long as the Allies now have practically abandoned hope for a cross-Channel operation in 1943. However, since such a strong force cannot be provided by Britain and America at this time, General Ike feels we are sailing a dangerous political sea and this particular sea is one in which military skill and ability can do little in charting a safe course.

Ike and I went to a private dinner at Claridge's given by Dick Allen of the Red Cross for Harvey Gibson, the new Red Cross chief. Stevenson, to be the second man, was there, as were the Ambassador and Colonel

Ramey. Confident Gibson won't let little things bother him, but will handle problems in statesmanlike manner. Much talk of the colored question, which seems to come up from a variety of angles. Red Cross to provide clubs and customary service for Negro troops.

Home to bed early. Hope it really isn't bedbugs that have given me some twenty-five bites. May be a supermosquito. Mickey has looked through the bed, especially the mattress, and pronounced no bugs present. Whatever it is, the Air Force could use it.

Had just gone to sleep when Major Lee phoned that he had a long message for the boss. Came to my room and, after reading it, we decided not to awaken him; that it would keep until morning. Ike and I were going to church at 8:30 A.M., the CG having to live up to his own proclamation of National Day of Prayer.

When I told Ike about the message in the morning, he growled: "There'll be something impossible in it." Message said President had communicated to the PM his proposal for his all-American assault, and specified troops and equipment to leave U. S. about October 20. Apparently, British-American views at last coming together.

The Transatlantic Essay Contest Draws to a Conclusion

LONDON, THURSDAY, SEPTEMBER 3, 1942

The U. S. Joint Chiefs have figured a way of meeting the desires of both the President and the Prime Minister. They recommend simultaneous landings in Casablanca, Oran, and Algiers. For Casablanca, there would be 34,000 U. S. troops for assault, 24,000 in immediate follow-up to land at a port (as distinguished from scrambling ashore from landing craft over the beach); for Oran, 25,000 U. S. troops for assault, 20,000 to follow-up at a port; for Algiers, the U. S. contingent in the assault would be 10,000 troops. British for the assault and follow-up to be determined by the C-in-C.

One of the "details" yet to be settled is the number of American naval units to be committed in the operation.

Thus the transatlantic essay contest seems to be drawing to a peaceful conclusion, with the master minds on both sides of the Atlantic having put forth their best efforts to arrive at a sound and strong plan of attack within the limitations of the available resources of the two great countries. Many details remain to be settled.

Either Ike or Clark, or both, may have to go to Washington, but Ike is seeking to avoid it, at least for himself.

The probabilities, as given to the CG by Lord Louis, are four *bad* days to one *good* day *against* finding practicable landing conditions on the Atlantic Coast side; and four *good* days to one *bad* in *favor* of finding such conditions inside the Mediterranean.

The PM is sending a message to the President, asking for further information as to naval forces the U. S. will be able to supply. He also proposed to place Admiral Sir Andrew Browne Cunningham in naval command under Ike. Wants to reduce the Casablanca force to strengthen the assault on Algiers.

Churchill is itching to get the expedition under way; he has ordered full speed ahead, on assumption Roosevelt will approve compromise.

LONDON, FRIDAY, SEPTEMBER 4, 1942

Roosevelt willing to reduce Casablanca force and hopes to cable the Prime Minister a list of U. S. naval craft that can be spared for TORCH. Feels he and the PM are getting close together.

Ike happy as a child because he didn't have to waste time going to Washington immediately, and because understanding between the two governments seems about to be achieved at last.

Ike had a transatlantic phone call from General Handy in Washington.

After receiving the phone call, and knowing the President actually was giving the green light to Churchill, the CG called me and said we were going to get the hell out of here and go to the cottage. Mickey had assembled duplicate sets of shaving equipment, pajamas, clean clothes, and so forth, so we were prepared for the night. Had time before dark to roam the garden and to enjoy the change of scenery.

LONDON, SATURDAY, SEPTEMBER 5, 1942

Churchill agrees to the military layout "as you propose it." He volunteered that since the British have troops already trained for landing, he would be willing that they wear the American uniform and added, "they will be proud to do so."

General Patton, my cigar-smoking friend, sent me a box from the Army and Navy Club. He had inscribed on the cover, "partial payment." He wrote the CG that his plan for taking Casablanca calls for seizure of two harbors immediately north of the initial objective. Patton doesn't know yet that the compromise between Roosevelt and Churchill reduces the size of his force by one regimental combat team (about 5000 men), which is to be used for the Algiers assault.

Because of the great flow of supplies from the U. S. to the U. K., there has been insufficient time to catalogue all the equipment, spare parts, etc., which have been dumped in the British ports. It is exceedingly difficult for the SOS to find out exactly what we have. Consequently, when it comes to mounting an expedition like TORCH, much time is lost and worry caused because the SOS people can't immediately lay their hands on what is needed. It is known that certain items, such as spare parts for tanks and some calibers of ammunition, are not available here.

Ike is worrying about the weather for D-Day. He wrote to Patton today, "I am searching the Army to find the most capable chaplain to assure a fairly decent break in the weather when the big day comes."

The American Fifth Column

LONDON, SUNDAY, SEPTEMBER 6, 1942

The first directive given Ike as C-in-C for operations of the Allied Expeditionary Force in North Africa ordered him and his forces to clear the northern portion of Africa of all Axis forces. It was intended for a quick clean-up of Rommel. However, when the differences of opinion developed between the Americans and the British, the first directive became inapplicable and had to be modified to conform to the compromise. He and General Clark approved today the proposed language of a new directive. It leaves the date of the attack to be set by the C-in-C as early as practicable. The initial, intermediate, and ultimate objectives are: landings in the Casablanca, Oran, and Algiers areas, to be simultaneous, if practicable; ports to be seized for landing of follow-up forces and for supply; beachheads to be rapidly expanded with a view toward exploitation to acquire complete control of French Morocco and western Algeria, to afford bases and airfields for extensive air and ground operations to the eastward; and combined air, ground, and sea operations with a view toward assuring complete control by the United Nations of the entire North African area from Río de Oro to Tunisia, inclusive, and to facilitate air operations against the enemy forces and installations in the Mediterranean area.

Mr. Robert Murphy, under the *nom de guerre* of "Lieutenant Colonel McGowan," is to visit us in London, most secretly. He is the hot shot on relationships with the French in Morocco; while his official title is Head of Civil Affairs Section for TORCH, he might be described as the head of the American fifth-column setup there. Murphy's visit to London is to be kept a closely guarded secret both in Washington and here and be known only to a minimum number of persons. Absolutely essential to travel so he will meet no Frenchmen. Suggested that safest method is to travel by Ferry Command from U. S. to England and return to U. S. by the same means, thereafter to return to his post in French Morocco by the normal route via Lisbon. Inconvenience to Murphy regretted, but security considerations demand it.

Clark reported that Colonel Hughes (our old friend, Everett), "who apparently has the best over-all picture of the supply situation," estimates that the SOS-ETO can meet food and, in general, ammunition requirements in the theater of operations for a period of forty days. This estimate is based on a force of 112,000 men. In addition, up to twenty days of supply can be furnished in many other categories. However, due to unbalanced stores in the SOS, some serious deficiencies have appeared, notably in spare parts for weapons and motor vehicles, and these must be obtained from the U. S.

Line of communication for supplies to support U. S. forces at Oran and Algiers must be maintained between U. K. and Mediterranean until a line is opened direct from the U. S. to the Mediterranean ports.

Left the office early in the afternoon for the cottage. I borrowed a set of left-handed golf clubs from Ed Murrow. Ike and I played two holes twice for a bob each. My score was 7-7-9-4, the 4 resulting from a 30-foot putt that curled into the hole, to take a bob from Ike, he having been on the green in the orthodox two, but three-putted. Ike's score is a military secret. Early dinner and early to bed. No trouble to sleep in the country.

Somewhere in these notes should be recorded an explanation General Spaatz gave during a conference the other day as to the difference between the British and the American theories of air attack. The British have sent great numbers of fighter squadrons to sweep France during the day, hoping, by attacking trains and small objectives, to entice the Luftwaffe into the air to fight and thus to reduce their number, even at the cost of uneven exchanges, while the night bombers make their depredations on the industrial centers of Germany and enemy-occupied territory.

The American Air Force discounts the value of these sweeps over France; they waste planes and personnel and do not contribute much to the demoralization and destruction in the heart of Germany. Our bombing operations are concentrated on primary military objectives, in line with Ike's directive to hit the submarine-construction yards, industrial plants, and railway centers.

Spaatz thinks the British are making little progress toward winning the war by sending spectacular but rather inconclusive sweeps of Spitfires and light bombers over France, although he speaks highly of the British night-bombing tactics. Accuracy of night bombing leaves much to be desired, however. Fortunately, daylight bombing by Flying Fortresses is substantially more accurate, but with the British bombing at night and the Americans by day the Germans will feel an increasing effect, physically and psychologically.

A Vital Page Is Lost and Beadle Smith Arrives

LONDON, MONDAY, SEPTEMBER 7, 1942
Refreshed and reinvigorated by three nights of good rest at the cottage (me, too), the CG today cabled the Operations Division, WD, that with substantial agreements reached, all preparations can proceed "unhampered by the uncertainties and changing conceptions" that have been perplexing the planners.

The planners may be perplexed, but no more than I, and I'm worried as well. A page of the diary is missing; *it's the page of the first* TORCH *directive to Ike to clean up the North African coast.* If some enemy spy has managed to get that sheet, all our hope of attaining surprise is already in vain. In merging the official and personal items into one set of pages, many pages had to be recopied and renumbered. This the faithful Miss Jaqua has been doing for many long days. The loss was discovered during the process of microfilming. I had sent Miss Jaqua, Corporal Marshall (General Ike's personal stenographer), and Mickey, with side arms, to the Army's film laboratory to do the job. In the process, page 117 was discovered missing—just wasn't there.

Although there seems no other conceivable way for the sheet to get out of our offices, which are guarded not only by the Marines at the entrances, but by guards in the Commanding General's outer office day and night, the darn page is gone. We have searched and re-searched, but no page 117. It must have been discarded and burned in the secret stuff Miss Jaqua had finished copying, but that's not definite.

Had to tell Ike today, though I hated like poison having to add to his worries. He was considerably upset but was so considerate I could have wept. Said not to tell anyone outside the office, as there is no need of alarming the whole headquarters, but to continue the search. After all, I'm responsible and probably should be sent home on a slow boat, unescorted, to use one of Ike's favorite expressions.

First loss of B-17s operating over enemy territory occurred Sunday.*

---

* There was a loss previously before General Ike assumed command. Fortresses of early design bombed submarine pens on the French coast and we suffered a high percentage of loss. From this trial some British writers as well as professional airmen be-

Forty-two Fortresses, in two groups, took off to attack an airplane factory near Albert. Enemy fighters were encountered in mid-Channel on the way to the target, and thereafter the B-17s were under continuous attack, but most of them pushed through to the target and are reported to have bombed accurately and destructively. Of the two lost, one of them was seen to be gliding down near the target, followed by three enemy fighters.

Ike feels that the Albert action may be of considerable significance. It is possible that the enemy is beginning to feel the effects of daylight precision bombing and is bringing his fighters into the air, in the hope of defeating our effort. There always has been some doubt that the enemy would pay any attention to bombing action in this area. If the ratio of losses reported in this action is any index of what we may expect when under continuous fighter attack, then we have taken another long step in proving the case for the heavily defended, high-altitude bomber, operating on a precision basis in daylight. If both these assumptions are proved to be correct, then the inevitable result will be the withdrawal of enemy air forces from other points to combat the American effort here. Ike emphasized to Washington his belief that the purpose of building up quickly a strong U. S. force of B-17s in the U. K. should remain a priority feature in all our future plans, and that the mounting of TORCH tends to emphasize rather than diminish the importance of developing and maintaining such a bombing force in England.

Beadle Smith is here at last. His square jaw and deeply dimpled chin indicate his character: tough in action with the staff, but delightfully informal off duty. Ike had been expecting him, sometimes despairingly, for two months, but he was so valuable to General Marshall as U. S. Secretary of the Combined Chiefs of Staff committee in Washington that Ike almost gave up hope of getting him. Ike suggested that we go immediately to the cottage, for there was much news to exchange. Beadle had been intimately familiar with the ins and outs of the TORCH operation in the WD, in the Combined Chiefs meetings, and in the White House, during the six or seven weeks when indecision reigned.

Ike and Beadle both concerned with the necessity for crystallizing the direction the grand military strategy of the U. S. and G. B. will take, once the TORCH operation is completed. A meeting of minds of the President, the PM, and the Staffs at an early date is essential. In democracies plans are frequently changed to meet the strong current of political opinion;

---

came skeptical of the widely heralded American bomber and the idea of daylight precision bombing. But from this experience, the belly turret was developed and fire power of the B-17 generally increased.

these must be weighed against the greater value of understanding and pursuit of a clear-cut objective toward which all effort would be unremittingly applied.

Beadle said that it was clear that the President will handle the political angles of TORCH with the French, and he's a master. The American fifth column in French Morocco is expected to be effective, for important French leaders, both military and civil, will actively support the American invasion. Beadle thinks it "will be a pushover."

While the WD shared with Ike the feeling of frustration caused by the continued delay of the U. S. Navy to specify the number and type of escort vessels it could supply for TORCH, Beadle said there were some good reasons why this had not been done earlier. Admiral King was confronted with broad and insistent demands from the President for naval escorts. Recently the President had called in the Admiral and instructed him to provide escorts for convoys carrying bauxite from Brazil to America. Bauxite is essential for aluminum for planes and thus important. Brazil has recently become a belligerent. Another of the President's requests was to reinstitute the convoys to Murmansk, quite a chore in itself, judging from the beating we took in the last one we escorted about two months ago. On top of these orders, our Navy has been having its troubles in the Pacific.

The Navy had taken a walloping at Tulagi—four cruisers, three of them American and one Australian, the *Canberra*, had been surprised by the Japs in a night action. According to Beadle's information, because the shore line blotted the enemy ships from the usual radar screen, our cruisers did not know of the presence of the Jap ships (several cruisers and destroyers) until star flares were dropped behind the American ships by the enemy, thus silhouetting our ships to the Japs, who opened fire at 3000 yards, making effective hits on the first round.

Beadle said it was an action of the kind naval commanders spend years to study and plan: involved surprise, at night, under conditions which permitted close-range fire, with opportunity for destroyers to dodge in close to their objectives, to launch torpedoes. The Navy side of the story hasn't been completely told. Beadle said that the Japanese are massing their naval strength again and our Navy will have a tough time to hold the ground gained in the Solomons.

Other Navy troubles include the so-far-unannounced loss of another modern aircraft carrier in the Pacific. Beadle wasn't sure of its name; as again the information was hush-hush. Seems we had eleven aircraft carriers when the war started, some old and some modern. In the Midway action we knocked off four Jap carriers, and in the Coral Sea battle we lost one and the Japs one. Since then we have lost one or two more, but without compensating damage to the Japs. At the moment, there are two American and seven Jap carriers in the Pacific, so we cannot afford to have further losses. The Japs had more carriers at the start of the war than the Navy had estimated—started with something like thirteen.

Unfortunately, also, our carrier-construction program is slow. One or two carriers that have been damaged will require at least six months for repair; another carrier is supposed to be off the way in January, and still another one available late in '43. The shortage of carriers and the lack of a building program of this sort of ship are all the more embarrassing since naval activity in this type of warfare proves conclusively the need of a maximum number of good carriers.

Despite all these difficulties, Admiral King has not recanted on his commitment to furnish the *Ranger*, one of our most modern carriers, and two converted carriers for the Casablanca assault. The Admiral had been enabled to press the TORCH case effectively with the President when Ike's message demanding the fulfillment of previous commitments had been received. Beadle said that Admiral King welcomed the message, for it made it possible to get a firm decision from the President. Certainly, the President has tough decisions to make, involving untold numbers of world-shaking problems, such as Brazilian bauxite on one hand and the Russian convoys on the other; the Japs behind him, geographically, and the North African offensive ahead.

As we sat before the open fire, the CG and his new Chief of Staff philosophized on many things. There was General Marshall's tough job. He had handled with patience and firmness the divergence of views which finally led to the agreement on TORCH.

Ike said, "Come hell or high water," that once the plan for TORCH is set, he is going ahead with the equipment available and is not going to whine to the War Department.

Beadle discussed Marshall's amusing little eccentricities. Frequently, Beadle said, the General would ask him to get so-and-so, "You know who I mean, 'red eyes,'" and from this Beadle would have to figure out who best fitted that description. The General persisted in calling his confidential assistant McCartney, although the name is McCarthy; his secretary he calls Mason, though her name is Nason.

The importance of an ability to express oneself lucidly and succinctly when presenting a proposal or problem to the U. S. Chief of Staff was cited as the reason for the failure of some high officers to make good with him. Those who speak slowly and haltingly and seem to fumble are soon passed by in the rush to get things done.

Ike left to Beadle his choice of jobs. It had been planned that he would be C/S for the theater. Then the TORCH operation had been set, and Ike wanted him as C/S for the expedition. It was mutually agreed that General Smith should start as C/S of the theater, shake the looseness from the staff, get it running as Ike would like to have it, and then work into the TORCH job at Norfolk House. Beadle is expected to get a second star soon.

During part of this talk, we had taken a stroll over the golf course and, oddly enough, walked right to the green, where I had sunk a 30-foot putt the day before. The CG gave a highly colored description of how his superior golf had been wasted by the luck of an aide. "You are always wanting lucky generals," I reminded him. "You ought not to object to a lucky aide."

LONDON, TUESDAY, SEPTEMBER 8, 1942

Beadle was up at 4 this morning after having flown the Atlantic the previous night with virtually no sleep. Said he'd heard a cock pheasant crowing. Roamed through the pine trees and rhododendrons of the ten acres and came in at 7 o'clock as I was fixing the coffee. Beadle has been an ardent hunter most of his life and the lure of game was more attractive than much-needed sleep.

Ike, Beadle, and I went back to the cottage for lunch; tossed the handball for five minutes and felt fine. Ike and Beadle spent most of the day together, discussing plans.

Meanwhile I've had queries from PRO, saying that the press, always with its nose to the wind, is smelling activity. The news hounds have noted the comings and goings of officers to and from the United States, some of them with one-way tickets for home. There seem to be even more rumors in England than we had at home; they keep cropping up in a variety of places. Most of these have been checked and found to be pure fabrication.*

General Clark's report for the day indicates that, as usual, he is going ahead with the detailed plans for TORCH. Air plans again discussed.

There is to be no over-all air commander for the operation. There will be two air commanders: General Doolittle for the U. S. and an undesignated RAF officer for the British. These two will be under direct control

* Lord Haw-Haw was credited in the pubs and elsewhere with an intelligence system throughout the United Kingdom that permitted him, for instance, to state that Big Ben was five minutes fast, or that the Germans knew that General Lee had just moved his headquarters to Cheltenham and that the Luftwaffe would pay a call on the place the first night. Actually, Cheltenham had a day raid some time after Lord Haw-Haw was reported to have broadcast his prediction. An analysis of his broadcasts generally disproved that such predictions had actually been made.

of Headquarters, and after the C-in-C has made broad decisions as to objectives and distribution of flying forces, Air Marshal Welsh will execute these directions through the two (American and British) commanders.

Welsh questions the advisability of using air-transport squadrons for movement of paratroops to Oran. It may be of the greatest importance to use these air transports later for rapid movement of ground forces to Tunis to beat the Axis. Use of transports for paratroops at Oran should be carefully weighed against the possibility that many transports might be lost, thus limiting ability to move forces by air east of Algiers.

Discussion of paratroops at Oran with Colonel Edson D. Raff and Major William P. Yarborough, of the parachute battalion, and Colonel W. Bentley, of troop carriers, revealed that three squadrons of transports will be used; that 520 men will jump, and that it is understood by all concerned that Colonel Bentley's "command of the paratroops will terminate as soon as that unit has jumped."

Colonel Bentley recommends that the attack be launched on a Sunday morning because, while in North Africa, he had observed that the French officers and many of the enlisted personnel habitually leave their stations on Saturday afternoon and don't return until late Sunday. Perhaps the French haven't heard of Pearl Harbor.

Operations of the U. S. Air Force based in England will have to be curtailed, if not stopped entirely, as the time approaches for their move to North Africa; although aircraft are highly mobile, their bases and ground crews are relatively immobile. When the Germans notice the absence of B-17s over the Continent, they may smell a rat.

The CG and Clark went to 10 Downing Street for dinner with the PM. Beadle, T. J., and I visited at the flat. Beadle to bed early, while T. J. and I listened to the radio account of the PM's speech he had given during the day at the House of Commons. Followed the "fireside" given last night (Labor Day) by the President, in which he said that during the July conferences, which he made no longer secret, certain vital military decisions had been made. Incidentally, the presence of Steve Early in this theater, not to mention General Marshall, Admiral King, and Harry Hopkins, was disclosed by the PM during his address. Said Steve was here for informal discussions of problems with Bracken. President had said something, in speaking of the four main theaters of American operations, that appeared especially significant to me, in view of the discussion Ike and Beadle had had Monday, relative to the need for crystallizing the efforts of the two governments upon a great central objective. Of course, they had agreed that we should continue to pierce at the heart of Germany, and

felt that the TORCH operation would delay this vital thrust, although bene-
fits from the North African occupation are likely to be extraordinarily
great. The President, speaking of the European area, said:

Here the aim is an offensive against Germany. There are at least a dozen
different points at which attacks can be launched. You, of course, do not expect
me to give details of future plans, but you can rest assured that preparations
are being made here and in Britain toward this purpose. *The power of Germany must be broken on the battlefields of Europe.* In due time you will
know what these decisions are and so will our enemies. I can say now that all
of these decisions are directed toward taking the offensive.

The President's declaration that the power of Germany must be broken
on the battlefields of Europe seemed a strong indication that he has not
succumbed to the popular demand for an all-out cleanup of Japan to
"tidy up" the Pacific, leaving the European squabbles to an indeterminate future action.

The report of the PM was of double significance to me, not only for
what he said, but for the integrity of his statements as well. There is at
least one field of operations of this war in which I feel sufficiently informed
to justify passing judgment on that portion of the PM's speech affecting
our prospective expedition. Everything he said rang true; he stopped short
only when discretion was necessary for security reasons. No other single
action of the PM has stirred my appreciation of his qualities more than to
know that what he said was true insofar as my information permits me
to judge.

"O.K. Let's Go"

LONDON, WEDNESDAY, SEPTEMBER 9, 1942
Ike returned from the dinner about midnight. I was sound asleep when he
came in to give me the dope. I asked him if the President had transmitted
to the PM the U. S. Navy's commitment for escort vessels for the Casablanca junket, and he said "yes." Ike said that the PM told him the final
exchange with the President on TORCH had been from Roosevelt, "Hurrah"; to which the PM had replied, "O.K. Let's go."

As Ike and Clark had anticipated, the PM now is insistent upon settling
a date for the attack. When the PM questioned him, Ike declared,
"November 8—sixty days from today." The PM was disappointed; he is
so anxious to see the operation under way (planners still aiming at November 4). Ike had made clear to the PM that with the plan now set for use
of American Regimental Combat Teams from the U. K., it is necessary

to equip them so that the units will be appropriately balanced. This takes time and the men must be trained. The PM, seeking haste, again suggested that British soldiers, more advanced in their training than Americans, be used in American uniforms and reiterated that he would be "proud to have 'em wear 'em." But Ike said that the sham would soon be discovered and would undermine confidence in the whole American operation. Thought the PM was disappointed at his decision.

Asked Ike if the PM had mentioned the fine reportorial job he had done in speaking in Commons during the day.

"Did he? He read most of it to us."

While the PM was directing his dinner conversation for a moment to General Clark, Ike seized the opportunity to release a suppressed yawn, only to have the PM turn suddenly toward him and catch him at it. Not for this reason, but because the PM wanted to talk foreign affairs with Mr. Eden, who came in at 11, the two Americans were released much earlier than anticipated. Seems there is a long hallway from the drawing room to the front door, along which guards are stationed. At past dinners, the PM had followed his two guests to the door, and, as each new thought struck him, held his guests until it was completely discussed, mostly by the Prime Minister. Anticipating that some such afterthoughts might hold them again (not that they dislike talking with the PM—in fact, their comments have all been to the contrary—but both were anxious to get home to bed and not become drawn into a regurgitation of TORCH), Clark, with his long strides, paced the escape down the narrow corridor. They felt as if they'd almost run out of 10 Downing.

The CG had discussed with General Spaatz the effect of termination of American air offensive against Germany and today sent a message on this subject for General Marshall. Said he was seeking means to conceal from the enemy, insofar as possible, the withdrawal of our air units for active operations. We will continue bluff attacks as incidents of the training of our new units arriving here this month, and in this way can keep up some deception. In addition, he believes it will be possible to carry out an occasional raid with the older units earmarked for TORCH. The British will furnish heavy fighter protection to carry out these efforts, so they can be accomplished without undue loss.

In General Clark's report covering activities for September 8, so many plans are humming that five single-spaced, typewritten pages are required for the Deputy to keep the CG current.

The supply problem is certainly a big one. Apropos of this, I had seen a list which had been cabled to Washington. It consisted of some 3000 words, many of which were abbreviated. It specified a requisition of supplies of a type intended to afford a forty-five-day reserve for the expedition. Even medals for heroic actions were requested: Medal of Honor, 10; DSC, 25; DFC, 50; DSM, 25; Purple Heart, 250; Soldiers' Medal, 100; Silver Star, 100.

Another item that struck me was $500,000 worth of tea, sugar, and cotton goods for payment of native laborers to be employed for various construction jobs such as airports. Beadle had said that Patton's force alone would require 5000 tons of .45-caliber ammunition, for tommy guns, etc. This is a shipload.

Beadle said one night that once we have Tunisia, Rommel won't last a month; that his supply lines will be in great jeopardy. Note in the press a story that Rommel is ill and, therefore, may have been relieved, or it may be just another propaganda story.

Good aerial photographs have been made of Algiers, but those of Oran and Casablanca are only fair. Appropriate maps are being printed for distribution to the troops at the appropriate time—probably down to platoons. Clark said excellent models of the beaches in Algiers area have been completed. One of Oran is to be ready at the end of the month, and models of Casablanca area are being made in the U. S.

Clark has in mind that Algiers will be the best place for the General Headquarters. Brigadier Mockler-Ferryman, G-2, had said there was nothing to be gained by disguising U. S. pilots or other personnel or by concealing their presence at Gibraltar. He recommends that U. S. markings be placed on British aircraft any time after the pilots arrive at Gib, and it would be well to have a limited number of visits by U. S. air transports prior to D-Day, so that the heavy concentration on and around D-Day will not be so noticeable.

Ike, Beadle, T. J., and I had dinner at the cottage. Ike hit the hay early, leaving the three of us to settle the war. Beadle said that the Germans were using many second-class troops in Russia and that some of their crack divisions hadn't been located by our intelligence service. Thinks they might be somewhere in France, available to move through Spain. Has a notion Hitler has something up his sleeve.

We agreed this is one expedition in which the diplomats will be in the front rank, preceding the soldiers. Some are already there, encouraging our friends to help us help them to freedom. I asked Beadle why we had so assiduously avoided de Gaulle of the Fighting French in this operation. His answer made sense: "If you take de Gaulle and his people into this operation, we would be simply adding to our existing complications all of the additional hatreds that are inherent in civil war," he said. "In our civil war, it was brother against brother, and father against son. The civil wars are the bitterest, so we are purposely keeping the de Gaullists out of this picture."

I reminded Beadle of Lord Louis' statement that days on which weather and surf would permit landings at Casablanca were four bad to one good, and one bad to four good inside the Med. He said, "Well, we have a long-range weather forecaster who has been working in Alaska; he has made predictions four months in advance which have been remarkably accurate. We are bringing him into this operation."

More Problems of Diplomacy and Supply

LONDON, THURSDAY, SEPTEMBER 10, 1942

General Clark's report covering the activities at Norfolk House for September 9 relates that Colonel Stirling, of the Secretariat of the British Chiefs of Staff, had called and reiterated that the PM is pressing the Chiefs for early action, and wanted to know the limiting factors that prevent D-Day from being set earlier than the first week of November. In answering his query, Clark cited the nonarrival of equipment for the 1st Division, lack of maintenance supplies, unbalanced stocks, the date of arrival of the combat teams from the U. S., conversion of combat loaders, and completion of auxiliary carriers in the U. S. Clark also added that the schedule for amphibious training for the two RCTs of the 1st Division indicated they would be finished about October 8. Emphasized that we must have rehearsals, and again stated that we are unwilling to put British soldiers into American uniforms.

Staff recommendations for supplies, estimated ammunition expenditures, gas and oil consumption, and hospitalization had been approved by Clark. All classes of supplies are to be built progressively for the total forces ashore to not less than the following levels: By D plus 30—fourteen-day reserve; D plus 60—thirty days; D plus 90—forty-five days.

Colonel "Wild Bill" Donovan, Director of the Office of Strategic Services, is coming to London to get prepared for the campaign. The CG received a message from General Strong, G-2 in Washington, today, asking him to inform Donovan, upon his arrival, of a number of decisions reached by the Joint Chiefs of Staff at Washington. These indicate the line of activity Donovan will direct, under the supervision of the C-in-C. Apparently, Donovan had submitted a number of proposals, some of which were approved and others disapproved after he had departed. Under the approved items were: the acquisition of forty million francs, disbursements to be controlled by supreme and local commanders after arrival 'in area; OSS radio transmitters to be placed under complete control of the Supreme Commander; stores to be supplied guerrilla groups, subject to control by C-in-C; project for broadcast by important French officer or official, again subject to approval of C-in-C, such broadcasts carried out from aboard ship in each area of assault; leaflets desirable, but under C-in-C. Urged British to expedite completion of powerful broadcasting station in U. K. to cover North Africa; two agents to be assigned duty with Task Force Commander. Recommends OSS representative (former Ambassador Phillips) be at the disposition of the C-in-C.

Among the items disapproved by the Joint Chiefs are: staff talks with separatists; promises to pay salaries and pensions to personnel; forays against Italian objectives; change in tempo of present economic assistance.

Now that the decision is made, the heat is on to advance the attack of D-Day. November 4 has been selected for planning operations, and this represents the *most* optimistic date, as fixed by arrival of shipments from the United States. Conditions here are equally restrictive and may cause delay to as late as November 8 (the date Ike gave the PM).

Message from General Arnold for the CG and General Spaatz indicated considerable concern over the stopping of American air operations in England in order to prepare for the move to North Africa. Arnold is particularly desirous of getting the P-38s in action so that a prompt test of their performance in actual combat will be available for guides in further production of fighters. Urged continuance of intensive air operations until the last possible moment, as the Eighth Air Force is now accomplishing the purpose for which it was intended; namely, to draw German fighters from other fronts, force attention of the German air force, and reduce their war effort by bombing important targets. A continuation of the present action provides the best possible preparation for TORCH. Feels a large reduction in the present air effort in the U. K. would be a lost opportunity to strike a severe blow against Germany and might give the tipoff that preparations are under way for operations elsewhere.

Ike answered this, saying that the ground elements of our air squadron setup for service with the Expeditionary Force are compelled to begin packing of equipment immediately. However, provision is being made to carry on at least two U. S. bombing missions per week, with from twenty-four to thirty B-17s on each mission, and we will be able to do some actual combat work with the P-38 group. (Ike has frequently mentioned in conversation with me that we ordinarily think that a flying force is extremely mobile, but actually it is one of the least mobile of any fighting units. The repair and service facilities have to be moved to the new location, and it isn't merely a question of flying a plane from one scene of action to another.)

General Marshall queried the CG today about the phraseology of the revamped directive. He feels that the British will offer strenuous objections to the elimination of the eastward movement to get on Rommel's tail and wants Ike's judgment before today's meeting of the Joint Chiefs of Staff in Washington.

Ike answered that the maximum objective that can reasonably be considered as obtainable with the resources that can be made available for the initial stages had influenced his acceptance of the directive previously submitted to him by General Marshall. Ike did not object to the inclusion of the questioned paragraph which implied continuance of the assault to the eastward. When and if Tunisia is seized, he would not "under any circumstances undertake an ill-advised, understrength, reckless advance toward the border of Libya." He would accept the paragraph as the British want it rather than raise the issue at this time involving the Atlantic versus the Pacific, or of militating against the early success of TORCH.

How Commitments to Russia Affect TORCH

LONDON, FRIDAY, SEPTEMBER 11, 1942

Al Jolson was in this afternoon, having completed a triumphant tour with Patricia Morison, Merle Oberon, and some others to American military centers in Northern Ireland and England. Says our soldiers, as well as the British, laugh at anything. Heard him tonight at the *Stars and Stripes* cocktail party. One of his gags may not be a contribution to Anglo-American friendship, but it certainly got a laugh. He said he had found many things to like in England, but the beer is lousy. "Why don't they put it back in the horse?"

General Clark's report covering his activities of yesterday is again voluminous. Some of the highlights are:

Air Marshal Welsh has been ordered by the Air Ministry to command the RAF units supporting the eastern task force and Air Commodore A. P. M. Sanders is to be the Chief Air Adviser on the staff of the C-in-C. Capacity of the Gib airdrome has been considered again. Under our present plan, 250 fighters must leave from Gibraltar during the first three days; in addition, three fighter squadrons will be based on Gib for local defense, and some aircraft for submarine patrol will be based there. Some reduction will be required; how much remains to be determined. About twenty of the crated Spitfires can be erected at Gib per day, meaning that work on them must start not later than D minus 12. The Air Marshal thinks that the Axis will be strongly tempted to bomb before the force is ready to operate. (Notice some increase of enemy bombers in southern France already.) Welsh suggested that a small detachment of pilots already there test the newly assembled aircraft, although 168 American pilots are due in Gib by special convoy on D minus 14.

American Air Force participation still requires attention. Clark had instructed Colonel Vandenberg to draft a cable to the WD stating that final decisions as to employment of air forces in North Africa would be made here. Flexibility is still being sought, for it may be necessary to mass our air effort to the east, where eventually the strongest hostile air force probably will be met. The plan at the moment seems to allot disproportionate numbers of aircraft to Casablanca, where the opposition, once a landing is made, is likely to be less than on the Mediterranean side.

New medium tanks arriving in the U. K. are M-3s rather than M-4s, as expected, so if no M-4s are received in later shipments, only light tanks will be available for use.

Clark had discussed the tonnage that could be put ashore on the beaches at Oran in the four or five days the leading convoys can remain. There is a possibility of using "coasters" (small coastwise vessels), each of which would carry in the neighborhood of 1000 tons with balanced loads.

Commodore T. H. Troubridge, RN, called. He has had much experience in the Mediterranean and brings the good news that heavy air attacks are not expected outside a radius of 200 miles from Sardinia (just measured this distance on a map with my pencil; notice that the radius comes close to Algiers, our prospective headquarters).

The CG replied today to General Marshall's message of September 9. Ike said that the plan suggested for eventually designating part of the U. S. forces in North Africa as the American Fifth Army is "concurred in." Suggests that it not be done, however, until the Oran and Casablanca forces have joined, at which time appropriate recommendations will be made directly to General Marshall.

In the message today, Ike requests the WD approval that all Axis prisoners of European origin be sent direct to the U. S., in U. S. ships, and be held there, the U. S. acting as the detaining power. This would mean the British will turn over to the U. S. forces any Axis prisoners captured by them, and the U. S. will treat such prisoners the same as those captured by the American forces. Disclosed that all prisoners captured by the British normally are sent to Canada, and facilities there are fully utilized for the prisoners from the U. K. and the Middle East. It is desirable to avoid retaining prisoners in the U. K., for their food simply adds to the strain on shipping.

LONDON, SATURDAY, SEPTEMBER 12, 1942

CG returned after lunch. The conversations at Chequers on September 11 and 12, 1942, with the Prime Minister and several top British commanders concentrated on the date for launching TORCH. The Prime Minister has accepted November 4 as the earliest possible date and is now chiefly concerned about the latest possible date, which appears to be the fourteenth. General Ike's own guess remains November 8. They also discussed securing some P-39 fighter planes now in the United Kingdom on consignment to Russia. The United States will replace them with others sent via the Alaskan route. Ike was most impressed with the undemonstrative heroism of Britain's merchant sailors.

General Clark's report for activities of September 11 mentioned that Mr. C. B. Clobet, who has worked with Colonel Eddy in Tangier and previously at Casablanca for twelve years, had called to discuss French defense in North Africa. At Casablanca, he estimated that unfavorable surf conditions would permit landings only one day out of seven, and attempts on other days might result in disaster. He suggested direct attack at small ports along the coast. They are weak and could easily be overcome. Defenses of Casablanca itself are particularly strong against attack by sea. There are eight French submarines, fourteen destroyers, and a battleship based at Oran and ready for action, although the battleship probably would operate at reduced speed.

Air Marshal Welsh has checked the capacity of the Gib airdrome, finding it will permit 175 fighters to depart on D-Day, 220 by D plus 4, and 250 very soon thereafter.

Brigadier General Lyman L. Lemnitzer and Brigadier F. W. Vogel have studied the request of General Anderson for additional forces, and recommend that he be allotted a total of 51,000 troops (7000 less than requested), which Clark approved. The distribution of troops in the area at the time of arrival of the third convoy will be: Algiers 110,000; Oran 70,000. General Gale is now to check with shipping authorities and the Admiralty to determine if necessary vessels and naval escort can be provided.

The CG got quick action on the recapturing of the P-39s. Cabling to Marshall today, he reported that orders have already been issued to stop the shipment of P-39s to Russia, on personal intervention by the PM, who had been assured by Ike that the U. S. would replace these planes to Russia via the Alaskan route. The PM had directed that motor trucks be substituted for P-39s in the next convoy, trucks being especially desired by the Russians. While the exact number of P-39s to become available to us is not yet determined, it will be shortly. The next convoy from the U. K. to Murmansk is already fifty per cent loaded, but only by actual inventory can it be determined how many planes have been irrevocably committed to the shipment. We may get the full 200.

The experience of a convoy now en route to Murmansk may completely eliminate any possibility for a later Russia convoy, and thus relieve the PM of making a very tough decision (thirteen out of forty ships lost, last report to date).

British concerned that if a convoy to Russia has to be run too late in the fall, it may get locked there by ice; even temporary loss of a half million tons of shipping would be a catastrophe.

Preparations for Robert Murphy

LONDON, MONDAY, SEPTEMBER 14, 1942
The CG had Mockler-Ferryman and Mack, Generals Clark and Smith, and myself to the flat for dinner.

We talked of plans for the reception of Murphy, who is to come from the U. S. in a day or two, probably Wednesday. It was decided he should be met at Hendon by General Smith and brought direct to Telegraph Cottage. This was Beadle's suggestion, and the CG agreed to it only because of the necessity for complete secrecy. Nothing short of this sort of need could force Ike to violate the seclusion of the cottage. We would feed eight at the cottage and bring Ambassador Winant, Mr. Harriman, and Dr. H. Freeman Matthews, the councilor, in after dinner. Murphy would spend the night at the cottage and go directly to Hendon airfield in the morning; take a waiting plane there for Prestwick, and thence by a waiting plane to the U. S.

Beetle (who, I have now discovered, spells his name this way, though his name is Bedell; henceforth I shall spell it Beetle) had talked with Murphy in Washington and undertook to give our dinner group an advance "fill-in." Murphy, it seems, has eighteen months' experience as distributor of U. S. relief supplies in North Africa. He had made firm contact with the C/S of the French Army in Algeria. He had been told that under certain conditions, French opposition would fade. Beetle had said that much would depend, at the forthcoming meeting, upon the instant appraisal of Mack and Mockler-Ferryman, not only of the facts and opinions presented by Murphy in the forthcoming dinner meeting, but also of Murphy himself, as to whether the whole plan, places, dates, etc., should be made known to him. The President, as director of the political maneuvers, has consulted fully with Murphy for a couple of weeks in Washington. Beetle has a high opinion of Murphy but doesn't want the British officials to take his word for it; wants them to wait until they can see Murphy, hear his story, and then make their own appraisal of him and his stories.

As Deputy C-in-C, General Clark has accepted, in a courier-borne letter, the invitation of Lieutenant General F. N. Mason-MacFarlane for Ike and him, and either two aides or two other staff officers, to stay at the Governor's House in Gibraltar. Noted Clark is due to arrive there D minus 2, or D minus 3, by air, followed two days later by the CG. Message also told MacFarlane the target date has now been set as November 4. (This is a date for the planners; November 8 the more likely one.)

To bed by midnight.

                                            LONDON, TUESDAY, SEPTEMBER 15, 1942

Ike had a skull session today with some of the generals most concerned with TORCH.

He told them that the success or failure of TORCH will measure the value of each commander. The commanders, in turn, will judge their subordinate officers in the same fashion. This is not an ordinary task but a major crisis, and all commanders expressed full understanding of their separate missions and of the supreme importance of whole TORCH operation. Also stressed importance of elementary discipline and military courtesy and need for bringing all units up to standard. No time for dilly-dallying. We must demand satisfactory performance.

The presence of Beetle continues to be a great satisfaction to Ike. It relieves him from many of the details of staff direction he's been forced to handle ever since his arrival in London. In addition, Ike now feels a sense of security, so he can leave the office to make short visits to bomber and fighter commands and other near-by units. Today he visited the bomber command in Bushy Park, returning to the cottage for lunch.

Ike and I went to the cottage for dinner and were joined afterward by Beetle, who had been licking his chops in anticipation of some bean soup and baked beans, which he had engineered with the colored cook and house boy. Although Beetle had attended an official dinner in town, he still had an appetite for the beans. When he arrived, I broke the bad news to him: the bean soup and baked beans, ham bone and all, had been eaten by the two boys "for fear they would spoil." Apparently, the boys couldn't withstand the temptation, though bean soup and baked beans must keep a week. All of us were greatly disappointed when we learned this news, and I was somewhat at a loss to know what disciplinary action to take. Overnight, the thought occurred to me to get the boys to write a report to the Chief of Staff, European Theater of Operations, United States Army. I ordered this done. The report was headed: STATUS OF BAKED BEANS AND BEAN SOUP AS OF SEPTEMBER 14, 1942, and was formally prepared in longhand on tablet paper by Private Hunt, the cook. It was submitted to me, and I gave it to the Chief of Staff, who said he would prepare an appropriate reply. Somehow the paper was moved from his desk and got into the channels for attention of the staff. When the Chief of Staff was ready to write his answer, he couldn't locate the document. Apparently it had gone the way of many documents that sink into the quicksands of the staff. The C/S ordered a thorough search, but, so far, the report on the beans is missing.*

Something I had never thought about is the frequency with which a paratroop battalion can repeat its jump in actual operation. Generally about a two-week interval for recovery is required because of the high rate of loss of equipment. Ordinarily, fifty per cent of the parachutes are ruined or lost. Time is also required to dry and repack those still serviceable.

Terrific pressure for shipping for TORCH is indicated by General Gruenther, who stated that every bit of space in the convoys has now been allotted. That for every ton added, a ton belonging to some other unit must be left behind.

"Colonel McGowan" Arrives

LONDON, WEDNESDAY, SEPTEMBER 16, 1942

Clark had informed Major Joe Phillips, the former editor of *Newsweek*, that he would be Public Relations Officer of the Allied Force Headquarters, and had requested him to outline and submit a complete plan of what personnel he would need, officers and enlisted men, to set up his office, first in Norfolk House, second at Gibraltar, and, third, at Algiers. He is to begin work on this immediately.

I attended a luncheon given by Ed Murrow for Bill Paley at the Savoy. While it was under way, I received an urgent call from Ike, so left im-

---

* Think G-2 is investigating.

mediately, to the accompaniment of jibes that "it must be the start of the second front."

Ike's word to me was that Beetle had had word that the "most secret" guest from the U. S., Mr. Murphy, was arriving somewhat earlier than expected and had hurried off to Hendon airport to meet him. I was to pick up General Clark, Brigadier Mockler-Ferryman, and Mr. Mack at Norfolk House and take them to the cottage, for Beetle would bring Murphy directly there from Hendon. Ike was going direct from the office to the cottage. At 7:30 I was to return to London to call for Ambassador Winant, Mr. Harriman, and Mr. Matthews at the Embassy. There would be eight for dinner, including myself, but we didn't have the facilities to feed eleven.

When I reached the cottage with my charges, I found Ike and "Colonel McGowan," in Army uniform, already hard at it, sitting under the big pine tree on our lawn. Murphy, I saw, was tall, slightly stoop-shouldered, and talked more like an American businessman canvassing the ins and outs of a prospective merger than either a diplomat or a soldier. Beetle had returned to clean up C/S matters on his desk. All of us sat on the lawn for a couple of hours, enjoying the sun and hearing from Murphy detailed information on the situation in Algeria and French Morocco and the plans for French co-operation. Murphy impressed all of us as an honest reporter who delivered his story objectively. If all that he anticipates in the way of French co-operation comes to pass, many of our worries will have been needless. However, he couldn't answer the two big questions: 1. Would the Spaniards fight, especially in Spanish Morocco, and would they attempt to close the Strait of Gibraltar or attack Gib airdrome and harbor? 2. What would happen in France itself?

Grew chilly at sunset, so we moved into the living room before a bright coal fire. Colonel Julius Holmes, who had returned with Beetle, was designated secretary, and the conference continued until dinnertime. I had soup and then skedaddled to pick up Winant, Harriman, and Matthews. Since they didn't know the location of the cottage and I returned with them after dark, I doubt if they could retrace the route; although there would be no particular objection to these gentlemen knowing the location.

On the drive, Mr. Harriman said he'd told his daughter, Kathleen, that he was being taken by the Ambassador to see some new airplane gadgets being manufactured in an outlying factory, and had said, "You know how crazy he is about gadgets." All this, of course, to avoid disclosure of his real purpose. Harriman had recently returned from the U. S. and, having spent considerable time with the President, had been requested by him to see Murphy while he was in London.

The session continued in a room that was more smoke-filled because of the blackout than any smoke-filled room in which the presidential selections are reputedly made at national conventions. I served in my usual role of kibitzer, water boy, cigarette girl, and flunky.

The operation and the numbers of the forces involved were explained to Mr. Murphy. He expressed great pleasure and said that the figures were exactly what his French friends in North Africa had been hoping for. They had feared that it might be the intention, if and when the time came, to send a small force of one or two divisions and leave it to the French to do the rest. They would be greatly encouraged by the size of the expedition.

Mr. Murphy explained that so far he had not been authorized to make any specific proposals to his friends and the talks he had had were on very general lines. He had had many conversations with General Mast, Chief of Staff to General Koeltz, who commands the corps near Algiers, and he was sure that he could be relied on. The officer (Tostin) commanding the airfield at Oran was friendly, and Mr. Murphy was confident that if a message were conveyed to him in time, he would arrange for the airfield (Maison Blanche) to be at the disposal of the American forces without opposition. Mr. Murphy had also great hopes of General Béthouart, who commands the division near Casablanca, and he thought that something could be done with General Mendigal, who commands the French Air Force.

Mr. Murphy had been in close touch with Colonel van Heck, the head of the youth organization known as the Chantiers de la Jeunesse. This is a well-organized body, the members of which can be helpful, when the time comes, for preventing the destruction of, and for taking over, various key points. The difficulties of transportation and communication had, however, to be considered. The members of this organization are scattered and cannot be assembled for specific tasks at a moment's notice. It takes time to get messages to them, and transportation is exceedingly difficult.

On the whole, Mr. Murphy was confident that he would be able to do a great deal to help the landing forces.

Discussion took place on the directive which authorizes Mr. Murphy to inform those French nationals whom he considered reliable that the United States contemplated landing troops at an early date and that our friends would be given at least twenty-four hours' notice of the place and time of landing. General Eisenhower explained the dangers involved in the disclosure of plans and in giving any indication that American forces would arrive at an early date. Mr. Murphy suggested that he might tell his friends that the date contemplated was early next year—say February; it would be a simple matter to move forward the date later on and cite Axis provocation or some other reason for the change. In considering what should be said to the French, he hoped it would be kept in mind that his friends wanted North Africa to be saved from the Axis as much as we did.

The latest news from General Giraud was a message that General Mast received in August. This message was to the effect that we could count on the French Army being with us and that the best time for action would be the spring of 1943, when landings could be effected by the Allies in France and in French North Africa, this being subject to provocation by the Axis in North Africa. Mr. Murphy suggested that, on his return to North Africa, he might suggest to Mast (who had, incidentally, through the French intelligence service, the Deuxième Bureau, been partly responsible for arranging General Giraud's escape from Germany) that he send a message to General Giraud to the effect that the United States was now in a position to take action on a substantial scale and inquire whether he was willing to act at this moment. Mr. Murphy said that there would be no physical difficulty in getting General Giraud out of France if he decided to come. He had a praetorian guard of his friends around him, and they would arrange for him to leave by air. Mr. Murphy could not express a definite opinion on General Giraud's reaction to such a message. His staff had hitherto thought that the Allies were too weak for a large operation of the nature contemplated, but if General Giraud knew we were strong enough, he might be willing to come out.

If General Giraud decided to come, the question of French command in North Africa would have to be settled. His friends had always made the point that the command in North Africa must be French. On this point, General Eisenhower said that the question of command must wait. It could not be settled at once. The French forces would be supplied in due course with arms and equipment, but this would take time. A little could perhaps be supplied at once as an earnest of our good intentions, but until we were satisfied that the French forces in North ·Africa were able to defend the territory on their own after they had been supplied with the necessary equipment, it was essential that we should retain the command. The Allied force in North Africa would, within a short time, amount to half a million men, and it could not be contemplated that a force of this size could be placed under a French general. We could say, however, that the French troops would remain under the command of a French general, but they would have to give the fullest and most whole-hearted co-operation to the Allied Commander-in-Chief.

In regard to the messages to be addressed by the President to the leading French officials on D-Day, Mr. Murphy said that he had already submitted drafts in Washington. General Eisenhower said that he would send to Washington a list of the points which he thought should be incorporated in the President's messages. Mr. Murphy said that it was contemplated that the President would send messages to Marshal Pétain, Mr. Yves Chatel (Civil Governor of Algeria), General Alphonse Juin, General Charles Noguès (Resident General in Morocco), Admiral Jean Pierre Esteva (Resident General in Tunisia), and to the Sultan of Morocco and the Bey of Tunis. In regard to the Pasha of Marrakech, Mr. Murphy thought that a personal and oral message would be adequate.

(Ambassador Winant, who even outsmoked me with his big Coronas, signaled me he heard a noise outside the window; taking a flashlight, I cautiously investigated. Found only Mickey on his assigned duty of patrolling around the house, our only guard. He'd stubbed his toe in the gravel path. All was well.)

It was suggested to Mr. Murphy that after delivering the messages, he and all United States officials might be confined to house arrest and that he should take any steps open to him to render this impossible and to insure that he would be in continued communication with the Allied Commander.

It was agreed that nonco-operating Frenchmen should be left to the friendly French to deal with and that the Supreme Commander should limit his interference to preventing private acts of vengeance.

General Eisenhower laid stress on the importance of instructions regarding the attitude of French and Allied forces in the vicinity of the frontier of Spanish Morocco being drawn up with the greatest care, in order to avoid any sign which could be interpreted by the Spanish as in the slightest degree provocative.

General Eisenhower impressed on Mr. Murphy the importance of the text of the President's messages and proclamations being available to this headquarters at the earliest date possible. The propaganda and leaflet lines depended on knowledge of drafts and terms. The task-force commanders should also be aware of the terms.

Ike, Murphy, and I stayed at the cottage all night, our conversation continuing considerably after our guests had departed and resuming again during and after breakfast. Ike authorized Murphy to tell his French co-operators that there would be an initial force of 150,000 men, and a buildup to a half million as rapidly as port facilities would permit. Murphy was anxious to have certain goods for the French, particularly those needed by the Arabs, available as soon as possible. It was suggested that those French cargo ships lying in port when our forces begin the assault, and probably amounting to some 212,000 tons, could be used to transport goods from the U. S., the French ships to join the regular American convoys. This would be an inducement to the French not to scuttle their ships. Only those with a shallow draft can be used, for port facilities to accommodate deep-draft vessels will be needed for our cargo ships, whereas the small vessels can unload in small river harbors.

Murphy said that he felt humbled by the weight of responsibility placed on his shoulders. He disclaimed any knowledge of military operations (although he shows considerable) and suggested that Ike send an authorized officer of some standing to guide French co-operators on fifth-column activities at strategic points; e.g., the designation of coast artillery to be silenced by the French from the rear, the signaling to the convoys by lights or otherwise as to whether opposition would be expected, the seizure of radio stations and newspapers, and especially of airdromes, the protection of hydroelectric power in French Morocco, and various other military actions from within needing expert handling.

The case against such an assignment was that if an American officer went into French Morocco in the near future, it might be a tipoff to the enemy. Ike and Murphy discussed a plan of landing such an officer (probably Beetle) by submarine, but left the decision until later. It may be that if Murphy's message to his collaborators, Charles Mast and Giraud, accomplishes the desired purpose of full collaboration, the French will know best how to do these things and the specific points of operation can be sent by courier. Don't think Beetle knows that Ike contemplates putting the finger on him, but he won't mind, I'm sure.

"Colonel McGowan" was taken to Hendon about 9 A.M. by Colonel Holmes. A waiting plane was to whisk him to Prestwick, where the TWA Stratoliner would carry him to Washington. After a few days in Washington, he would again fly the Atlantic, this time to Lisbon and thence to French Morocco.

LONDON, THURSDAY, SEPTEMBER 17, 1942

General Clark's report of conferences and decisions of September 16 again emphasized the problem of supply and indicated his growing impatience. Captain Jerry Wright, USN, had submitted a report showing length of time the Casablanca convoys could remain at sea without refueling if landing conditions at Casablanca are unfavorable. He had discussed also the possible effect of German action to close the Strait of Gibraltar. The Captain had said that the Strait cannot be kept open if we hold only the Gibraltar side. Clark recalled that Sir Dudley Pound had said some convoys could be put through under these conditions. However, if the Gibraltar airfield and harbor are bombed early in the operation, before we have developed enough force to move into Spanish Morocco, the Strait, which is only some eight miles wide, will be closed and we will be dependent for our communications upon the overland route from Casablanca to Oran.

(In the discussion with Murphy last night and this morning, I had asked him about this route. He said there is a sixteen-foot macadam road from Oran to Casablanca. He had driven it in ten hours without pressing. The railway is antiquated and could move only 1500 tons a day—about enough to supply one division. The railway can be rehabilitated by our engineers. It is standard gauge. Murphy said that he had caused an inspection of the roadbed and found it satisfactory. Our engineers can install sidings to permit more frequent passing of trains. Probably locomotives and even box and flat cars will have to be sent from home.)

Messages back and forth from London to Washington in considerable length and detail continue to point the finger to the almost insurmountable problem of supply. Word of submarine attack on a convoy en route from the U. S. to the U. K. also is disquieting. After all, at least two ships that set out from home with 105-mm. howitzers failed to reach here. One went aground, and the second, carrying replacements for the first, had to put in at Bermuda because of shifting cargo.

The Tempo Quickens

LONDON, FRIDAY, SEPTEMBER 18, 1942

Plans for advising General Franco of the purpose of our expedition to French Morocco have been suggested by the British Foreign Office and were communicated today by the CG to General Marshall. The suggestion had come through Dr. H. Freeman Matthews, who has been assigned to Ike as political adviser and deputy for Murphy. It is to be presented to the President as representing the on-the-spot approach of the British Ambassador at Madrid, Sir Samuel Hoare. Both governments would send notes to General Franco via the Ambassadors, who would present them either individually or together, depending upon circumstances at the time. The main points of the message proposed for the U. S., after giving Franco an explanation of the character and purpose of the operation, are: (1) we realize the Spanish interest in North Africa and do not threaten Spanish territory, metropolitan or ´overseas; (2) our action is unavoidable, as General Franco, with his military knowledge, will realize, since the Allies cannot allow French territory to be used as a base by Axis forces; (3) act will not complicate the trade agreement and exchange of goods between the U. S. or His Majesty's government and Spain; (4) Allied control of the North African coast will reduce risk of Spanish ships being sunk by Axis submarines; (5) Franco need have no fear as to our intentions, for we desire, along with him, to save the Iberian peninsula from the evils of war and to see Spain given an opportunity to recover from its civil war and take its due place in the "reconstructed Europe of the future."

Ike agreed to the general character of the proposed communication, but recommended that precautions be taken to prevent and avoid premature action, and that the President be informed of this proposal as soon as possible. Ike growled to me that military necessity requires dealing with Franco, whose dealings with Hitler and Mussolini and the despotism he stands for Ike thoroughly dislikes.

General Doolittle reported today and was brought up to date on the air plans. The absolute necessity for teamwork and co-operation with the British was impressed upon him, and Doolittle said, "I understand exactly." Doolittle also said that there would have to be some "house-cleaning in his personnel." He is to let Clark know about this later, and Clark will present the report to the CG for approval.

Vice-Admiral A. L. St. G. Lyster, commander of all aircraft carriers in the Home Fleet, had a discussion with Clark on various air-fleet matters. There are seven British carriers for this operation inside the Mediterranean. The Admiral made three suggestions: first, that at least a dozen Spitfires be detailed to be flying over Oran when our troops land, so that they can land on the airports immediately upon seizure. These planes would have two and a half hours of fuel, and the Admiral thought it wiser to risk losing twelve Spits than an aircraft carrier. Second, he suggested that to enlarge the space for planes, we take steps to procure the eighteen-acre graveyard on Gibraltar, mentioned by General Mason-MacFarlane. Thirdly, he pounded on the theory that we should be ready at all costs to exploit our landings and drive eastward at the greatest possible speed.

The Admiral also recommended the use of dummy parachutists and said he would have eighteen planes for this purpose, if desired. Also believed that troops at Malta, possible 4000-5000, supported by fighters, should move from Malta simultaneously to attack Tunis, when our troops attack Oran and Algiers. Also suggested we might strip some of our bombers and "stuff" them with soldiers, so that the eastward drive could be expedited.

On the personal side today, Major Phillips had called to ask me to lunch, to discuss plans and facilities for handling press and radio for TORCH. The limitation of space at Gib seemingly compels adoption of the system already set up for use on Commando operations for one-for-all news coverage. The Commandos likewise are limited in space, and only one American correspondent or radio man can be taken on each raid. The press and radio representatives have agreed to this heretofore and have their list set up for rotation.

If only one American writer covers our operation from Gibraltar, he will serve virtually the entire world with news for a period of about five days. Some job. Two American correspondents can go with each task force, but, as previously decided, all communiqués will issue from the Gibraltar HQ. There will be a British Reuter's man at Gib, for one is permanently stationed there. An allotment of 7500 words a day on the cable from Gib to London has been assigned for news. I discussed these problems with Ike this evening, and he felt that the responsibility for one man was terrifying—what if he should become sick or be out of action?

Clark wants to lead his own task force rather than be Ike's Deputy, and Beetle agrees with Clark. Pointed out that there is no particular precedent for a deputy. Ike's reasoning is that something might happen to him and that the Deputy should be able to assume immediate command when and if Ike should be knocked out. Beetle strongly disagreed in principle—says Ike always should be one rank above his deputy or any other American officer in his theater.

Beetle stayed for dinner, and Ike and I reluctantly slept in the flat, wishing we were at the cottage.

LONDON, SATURDAY, SEPTEMBER 19, 194-

Late last evening, while Ike, Beetle, and I were having dinner at the flat, Captain W. Abbott, of our G-2, called with an important message from the British Chiefs of Staff relating that a news editor of the UP in London had sent a message to Lyle Wilson, UP bureau manager in Washington, which had been "intercepted" by the WD. This message said, in plain language, that the UP should prepare for coverage not at Dakar but at Casablanca, and elsewhere in French Morocco, as this is where the American forces are striking. The information at hand did not disclose to us whether the message had been sent by cable, which would have made it relatively secure, or by radio, from which it could certainly have been copied by the enemy. It was, unfortunately, in plain language, but the fact that any members of the press had the poor judgment to transmit it gave rise to serious brow-wrinkling. (And I have lost that damned page from the diary; it gives all the assault areas.)

In the Deputy C-in-C's report of the operations at Norfolk House for September 18, he informed the CG that Air Commodore Sanders had considered the suggestion of Admiral Lyster that twelve Spitfires be in the air over Oran, ready to land as soon as the airport is seized. Sanders said that this plan must be carefully timed and that, since the attack plan calls for an assault at 1 A.M., it would be impossible for the planes to land before dawn. General Clark reported that this would be taken into account, but added that we should be willing to sacrifice the Spitfires if necessary to strengthen the weak, carrier-borne fighter support.

Sanders also reviewed the use of paratroops and said that if the troop transports were flown back to Gib, great confusion would result. Clark's answer was that the transports that cannot return to Gib would just have to land in the desert. Dummy paratroops aren't practicable, since the eighteen planes required for this purpose can be used more profitably elsewhere.

Periscopic reconnaissance of the Mediterranean shore is regarded as practicable by General Gruenther. Crews can make sketches and get valuable photographs. The alternative plan, to use General Patton's forces inside the Med if anything goes wrong at Casablanca, is to be prepared in time for General Clark to carry it to Washington by the middle of next week.

General Patton's G-2 had advised that the Moslem religion of the Arabs prohibits warfare during the eleventh and twelfth months. If the war starts before the eleventh month it's O.K. He recommended November 9 as the final date to open a campaign without offending the Moslems. The Moslem calendar starts the eleventh month on our November 10. Believed the Axis would propagandize our violation of Moslem customs if we attacked later. Also, we must be careful of the sacred cities, Rabat and Salé. Policy re Arabs should be consistent for all task forces. . . . General Patton had sent word that French prisoners should not be sent to the U. S. This matter already handled and only European Axis prisoners are to be sent to America. . . .

Doolittle had okayed the Air Plan and "has no argument."

A Day in the Life of an Aide

LONDON, SUNDAY, SEPTEMBER 20, 1942

This has been a leisurely day and gives an opportunity to think back over the week and, perhaps, to recount some items of interest that may have been omitted or, at least, to emphasize some already mentioned.

This morning, I spent an hour with Lincoln Barnett, a writer for *Life* magazine, which wants a piece on the CG and also wants Margaret Bourke-White to do a photographic study of the boss. Had Barnett meet him, and in response to the request for the photograph, Ike said that he had long wanted a picture, for personal reasons if nothing else, of the immediate circle of friends with whom he works and is in close daily contact—Clark, Beetle, Major Lee, T. J., Warrant Officer Marshall, Miss Jaqua, the three drivers, Mickey, Gilbee, Mrs. Summersby, and me. Barnett readily agreed.

Bill Paley came on a hurry-up call from Claridge's, to get a word in with the CG before leaving for America today. Bill expressed to me later his growing conviction that he is going to get in a uniform, no matter how important other people think the broadcasting business. I remember how disconcerted Bill was when I quit to join the Navy. Informed him of Ike's repeated statement that an Army fights just as hard as the pressure of public opinion behind it, and that his work in directing broadcasting activities of a coast-to-coast medium is important, although I recognize that when the war is over, few people will appreciate the service he has performed. Unfortunately, public opinion still regards the wearing of a uniform as the highest demonstration of patriotism.

I have some additional impressions of the meeting at the cottage with Mr. Murphy Wednesday evening which I feel might well be recorded. First of all, we are banking on the complete good faith of the French officer, General Giraud. He is the General who escaped from a German prison by climbing down an improvised ladder some 150 feet. Quite a feat for a man of his age, as I understand him to be somewhere in his late sixties. The whole scheme of dealing with General Mast, the C/S in Algeria, and through him with General Giraud, presents the question as to whether these men can be trusted. While an aide is supposed to be seen and not heard, I couldn't refrain, while sitting on the lawn at the cottage, from inquiring of Murphy, during a momentary lull in the conversation, as to what there is to prevent the Germans from taking General Giraud any time they wish, having in mind that they may have let him escape from Germany in anticipation of his usefulness at some time.

Murphy answered this by saying that Giraud is surrounded by his close friends, most of whom are officers and are armed. They had engineered his escape. In addition, French public opinion would be highly offended if the Germans manhandled this French officer, who not only in France but in French North Africa is reputedly a great hero. Murphy also pointed out that Giraud had escaped from a German prison camp in the First World War; that he knew him personally and hadn't the slightest doubt as to his integrity. This question was raised by others during the evening, and there was nothing to do but rest on the wholehearted endorsement of Murphy, and we simply have to hope that Murphy is absolutely right.

Even though Mast and Giraud are able to swing the French Army in Africa to the support of the Americans, and if all this goes as advertised by Murphy, there has been no intimation that the French fleet will follow the French Army. In fact, just the opposite is indicated. It is likely there will be quick and vigorous opposition from the French Navy. The enmity toward the British (because of the shelling of the French fleet at Oran), which Murphy described as running rampant throughout French Morocco, is even keener and more bitter in the French Navy.

There also remains the tremendous question mark of Spanish Morocco. We do not know to what extent the Germans and Italians, as a natural follow-up of their aid to General Franco during the civil war, may have infiltrated their own officers and equipment, especially planes, into both Spain proper and Spanish Morocco, ready to fight off any such move as we are prepared to make. The German-Italian Armistice Commissions surely have not been idle in French Morocco, Algeria, and Tunisia, and they have free access to Spanish Morocco.

Little things: Ike's favorite expression, still unwittingly used, is "Now let me tell you something." . . . Won a hole of golf with an eleven; Ike sixteen. . . . Instructed Private Hunt, our cook at the cottage, to cut down on the food, for our waistlines are increasing. . . . I'm in the middle between BBC and Navy's London PRO. Mr. J. B. Clark, director of overseas broadcasting, claims to have been rudely treated by the PRO. Clark was in to ask me to help out, since I know the Navy side of the story. Think I will get the two of them together, eye to eye, and step aside before I get hit. . . . Cottage so peaceful you'd never know there is a war if it weren't for occasional Spitfires and trainers practicing overhead. And the bomb holes on the golf course. . . . When we talk of public relations, I have a feeling that I will gain a reputation as an expert in this field. I'll be getting the credit for Ike's good sense, for he is the keenest in dealing with the press I've ever seen, and I have met a lot of them, many of whom are phonies. I question whether Ike is still on a publicity honeymoon, and so does he. He wonders when they will start calling him "paper general" because he has never been in a battle.

Ike has gone to the cottage, probably to cheat on me by playing a round of golf in my absence, but I am being a martyr today by staying at the office a couple of hours longer, to keep abreast. He, Clark, and Beetle driving to Chequers this evening and will meet with the British Chiefs of Staff and the PM tomorrow morning. It means a long night for them, and these country boys always say how they hate it. When the PM's secretary phones to inquire if the CG can visit the PM at Chequers, he always adds that the CG is free to bring others whom he might wish to take part in the discussions. While Ike could hog the show, he has always suggested that Clark go and, now that Beetle is here, makes it a three-some. This permits integration of firsthand information within the organization and again symbolizes team play at the top.

General Clark's report for September 19 indicates that various aspects of the major plan are beginning to be "buttoned up." Troops will not get equipment in time to start loading on October 8, and Washington is to be informed bluntly. . . . Probability of extending D-Day from November 4 to November 8 made known to staff workers, who cheered, as it gives a few more days for assembling matériel, "marrying up" equipment with troops, and loading of convoys. Meanwhile training is proceeding. Various units moving into the amphibious training ground on prearranged dates for intensive training with combat loaders. . . . Same old story re supplies. Major General N. G. Holmes, the British director of movements, had consulted with General Clark and his associates, to be oriented before he sees the PM at 6 P.M., Sunday. Said extension of the date still makes the loading situation "tight" and that it is difficult to plan the convoys until he knows the movement of ships coming from the States to join the first follow-up convoy. All agreed that U. S. Navy must be asked to enlarge the first fast follow-up convoy, which it has limited to twenty vessels (from the U. S. direct to Oran), and that we must take the risk of using relatively few escort vessels for a large number of combat loaders and supply ships.

General Marshall apparently shared the CG's alarm over the UP leak re French Morocco, as he replied today that on receipt of the CG's message, an investigation was initiated and action taken. First, the British authorities had been requested to take necessary steps to censor "on your side" any cabled message referring to specific operations. The British had also been informed of American concern of the published story in the London *Daily Mail* of September 15, and copied in American papers of the same date. This story speculated all too accurately. Second, the heads of UP, AP, and INS have agreed that they will not distribute any stories of similar content which they might receive from England. Third, American censors are instructed not to pass to addressee any matter tending to focus attention on any one area. In any stories speculating as to future offensive action by the Allies, the press associations have agreed to include at least two possibilities without emphasizing one above the other. The OWI has agreed not to release information dealing with prospective operations without specific approval of the Bureau of Public Relations, WD.

Visit to Chequers

LONDON, MONDAY, SEPTEMBER 21, 1942

Drove out to Chequers this morning to return with Ike and Generals Clark and Smith. Visited in the "grand hall" with Commander Thompson, the PM's Naval Aide. First time I had seen Chequers. Noticed over the entrance the Latin words, *Pro Patria Omnia*—Ike's free translation given later was "All for the Fatherland." Over a gate leading to a formal garden are the words, "All care abandon ye who enter here." On the reception desk in the great hall is a reproduction in red, white, and blue of the Longfellow verse sent to the PM by Mr. Roosevelt. It reads:

> *Sail on, O Ship of State!*
> *Sail on, O Union, strong and great!*
> *Humanity with all its fears,*
> *With all the hopes of future years*
> *Is hanging breathless on thy fate!*

Harry Hopkins, according to Thompson, hates Chequers more than the devil hates holy water, to use one of Ike's most common phrases. When Hopkins was there a couple of years ago in the winter, Thompson found him huddled in an overcoat, seated on the edge of a piece of bathroom furniture, reading the morning paper and trying to keep warm.

The house is unusually difficult to heat, has no central heating, and architects have despaired of installing modern heating because of their fear of injuring the exquisite paneling, some of which is four or five hundred years old. Thompson claims this is the bunk and says that last winter he had to twist sheets to stuff the windows in his room to keep out the snow.

In a guest book, we found the signatures of Wendell Willkie, John

Cowles, and Joe Barnes, to mark Willkie's foray in England after the 1940 presidential campaign. This hall is covered with rare paintings, each of which is described in detail in a catalogue reposing on the big central desk. The room seemed haunted with bulging English noses, on which I was sufficiently American to comment, but was topped by the Commander, who asked if I had also noticed that most paintings showed the royalty with dirty necks.

While we were thus settling minor matters, the meeting with the PM broke up; Ike came striding down the great hall, greeting us and commenting that he had to sign the "big book" again. As he was doing this, he said to me, "Discouraging, discouraging," but didn't, at that time, elaborate. What he meant was that the PM had just begun to take into account the risks involved in TORCH and the probability of delay for a real invasion of the Continent. All of this had been pointed out to him in the various memoranda prepared by Ike and submitted to the British Chiefs by General Marshall last July. At the moment, the PM has the itch to do something "big and grand" on the Continent, but doesn't seem to get hep to the fact that establishing some thirteen divisions, nine American and four British, in North Africa—with all this means in commitments and supply, especially ships and escort vessels—would, of course, delay the vital push at Hitler.

Conferences and decisions held by General Clark on September 20 disclose that Brigadier General Thomas B. Larkin, in charge of supplies for TORCH, will return to Washington with General Clark to see how the ships are being loaded. There have been frequent complaints that the manifests of these ships, as transmitted to us, do not give sufficient information.

Contingency plans for use in the event that Patton's primary plan is upset by unfavorable surf are in the making, any one of which can be used by direction of the C-in-C. One might be to mill around off the coast, in the hope the weather will clear within seven days; another would be to proceed to Oran and land over the beaches, running some of the convoy into Gibraltar and other portions into the U. K.; still another would be to push on to Philippeville, Bône, or Bougie or any other available port. However, Frederic Paul Culbert, General Patton's "onshore" man at Casablanca, had been in and ventured the opinion that surf conditions would not be too severe for landing at Casablanca. Feared our great trouble would be the French Navy, which has vessels in the Casablanca-Dakar region, and that they will fight unless there is some change in the political setup.

Difficulty of getting paratroops into the theater was considered. Our convoys are now filled; air transport is also largely committed to the movement on Oran and Casablanca for carrying maintenance personnel for the air units. Shuttle service between North Africa and the U. K., using these transport squadrons, is impracticable because of the gasoline supply in North Africa.

The supply situation still uncertain. The SOS still doesn't know in detail what it has on hand in the U. K. Guns are here, but the fire-control mechanisms have not arrived, and it is reported that a supply ship sunk in the Atlantic last week was carrying sight mechanisms.

The General and the Press

LONDON, WEDNESDAY, SEPTEMBER 23, 1942
The luncheon in honor of the CG given by the Association of American Correspondents in London was held today at the Savoy. Ike made a short, but customarily pointed speech "off the record," thanking the press and radio for excellent co-operation. He asked them not to speculate as to when and where future action would take place, but emphasized "we are going to fight." About a hundred there. Ray Daniell, as President of the Association, when presenting Ike, said that the press was trying to be helpful (which we have found to be true) and would do anything necessary, within the bounds of truth and accuracy, to help win the war. Ike responded that he didn't agree; so far as he was concerned, he would lie, cheat, and steal to beat the Hun. He declared that good sportsmanship wasn't part of this war and that we had to recognize we were fighting tough and vicious enemies who would stoop to any type of warfare to win. He added that he expected fair play and good sportsmanship from his associates and allies, and would practice it with them, but so far as the enemy was concerned, no holds are barred. In his opinion, he said, now is the time to mind the words of Stephen Decatur (see *Chicago Tribune* masthead).

Later heard from various sources that the speech hit the bull's-eye with the press, but, as it was off the record, was unreportable.

Left the lunch early and drove to High Wycombe to visit Fighter Command Headquarters under General Frank O. "Monk" Hunter. I have heard cross-examinations of witnesses, but the way the CG asked questions of Hunter as to the current and prospective operations of the command would be the envy of most lawyers. Among the questions asked was whether the Fighter Command had any plans for meeting the competition of the German fighter that has been known to have reached

43,000 feet over England, but was unreachable by a Spitfire. Hunter said that they had stripped a P-38 of about 1000 pounds of excess weight, reached the altitude, and fired at one of the German planes, but without effect. Ike asked to see the soldiers' mess and their quarters. They are living in tents, which, unfortunately, have to be placed under trees where the sun doesn't reach them. I looked at some and they seemed damp, although the sun was shining.

Top-Level Planning

LONDON, THURSDAY, SEPTEMBER 24, 1942

Although General Clark left for Washington yesterday, his report covering the previous day's activities and decisions came in today as usual. Clark had instructions to try to eliminate whatever necessity may have been felt for General Eisenhower to make a trip to Washington. Many of the supply difficulties are being cleared up, and, in all probability, the November 8 date will be met.

The CG met with the planning staff at Norfolk House at noon today.

General Ike informed the staff that since there is a possibility that PQ-19 (convoy from U. K. to Murmansk) may not sail, it is probable that some of the ships which are already loaded with supplies might be used in our operation and, if so, immediate steps must be taken to prevent unloading. As soon as possible, the manifests are to be available to the staff.

Security, especially by American personnel, was emphasized by the General, and all commanders and section chiefs were enjoined to make certain that their subordinates are properly instructed. (That damned paper.) Officers found under the influence of liquor are to be dealt with drastically.

General de Gaulle has some information about American intentions in French Morocco, Mr. Mack related at the meeting, and the problem of relations with General de Gaulle after the initiation of TORCH was discussed by the CG. (The plan favored by the CG has been for de Gaulle to be notified after the beginning of TORCH of the reasons he couldn't be taken into the operation without jeopardizing its success. The CG felt that he should be associated with ROUNDUP, the plan for the major assault on the Continent.)

Chain of command was discussed by General Smith, the C/S, and the C-in-C spoke briefly on the importance of co-operation and teamwork. He said that while lines of demarcation and chains of command are important, the best results come from mutual understanding and confidence.

Air Commodore Sanders posed the question of what to do with any junior French air officers who might wish to join the Allies when hostilities begin. Could they join by landing on a Spanish airdrome by prearrangement, or would our planes or AA shoot them down while attempting to come to our side? Necessity for a well-defined policy emphasized. General Ryder said that matters of this kind would be clarified before activities begin, and Mr. Murphy could be relied on to help with such problems.

Admiral Cunningham stressed the need of definite policy governing Allied actions in case of attack by French naval units and aircraft. Draft of a proposed policy read by General Smith is to be studied further by G-3 (Operations and Plans).

Ernie Pyle, human-interest columnist, with a string of about eighty papers, whose style reminds me of the late Odd McIntyre, was in today. We gassed for a couple of hours, Ike coming to my cubbyhole for a chat with him.

LONDON, FRIDAY, SEPTEMBER 25, 1942

In the afternoon, I accompanied Ike on a visit to Bomber Command, where General Eaker and his staff were Johnnies-on-the-spot with information, hospitality, and general alertness. Bomber Command is in the buildings of a famous old school for girls. The British had tried to commandeer the place for their own use, but had failed. When the Americans arrived, the British poured on the heat and got it for us. It was here that the famous story about the bells originated. The men moved into the girls' dormitory, and after they had retired the first night, the officers heard buzzes and bells ringing in their quarters, they being in the old administrative offices. They roused themselves and traced the calls until they found their origin, which was in the sleeping rooms formerly occupied by the girl students. In these rooms were little signs above the push-buttons, reading, "If mistress is desired, ring bell."

The General was shown aerial photographs of targets that had been bombed in the occupied countries and in Germany, chiefly submarine nests. The effect of the operations was shown, some of them indicating extraordinary accuracy, but there is much yet to be destroyed.

A large flight of Flying Fortresses had been awaiting good weather for a mission over Germany. Unfortunately, high-level bombing requires practically cloudless sky up to 25,000 feet or thereabouts, to get a good sight on the target. Such weather is rare in the fall, winter, and spring, and gives rise to doubt of the applicability of our bombing policy to air activity in this theater, where really favorable weather and cloud conditions prevail for perhaps only sixty to ninety days out of the 365. This is insufficient to keep the enemy on the run and causes Ike worry as to the ultimate effect of our bombing policy, although the British system of blanketing an area with bombs at night seems effective, if not accurate.

General Eaker gave the CG the results of ten missions. There have been 194 sorties (a sortie is the flight of one plane over enemy territory). There have been 352.2 tons of bombs dropped on the targets; a quarter of a million rounds of ammunition fired, with forty American casualties, three of whom were killed, eighteen injured, and nineteen missing. Claims on enemy aircraft number ninety-five—eighteen destroyed, thirty-six probables, and forty-one damaged. The aircraft losses to the U. S. numbered only two.

When we returned to 20 Grosvenor late in the afternoon, there was a message for the CG from General Marshall that cheered Ike considerably. It said, "I do not think you will be called to the United States and will try to save you the trip."

LONDON, SATURDAY, SEPTEMBER 26, 1942

Our reception room looked like the Hall of Fame this morning. Brigadier General Davis, the highest-ranking Negro officer in the U. S. Army, had arrived from America at the CG's request; Captain Eddie Rickenbacker was also waiting, not to mention half a dozen others.

I had arranged a retake of the group picture for *Life*, the first one having shown Kay Summersby, the Irish driver, with her tongue sticking out impudently, and Miss Jaqua, the slave to these notes, shown seemingly eye-flirting with the General. In addition, the General had been caught in a pose too jovial for these stern times, and the rest of us had been snapped in similarly jovial expressions. Most of my morning was spent getting this on and off and over with. Margaret Bourke-White also took numerous close-ups of Ike standing with his cap on, by the mantel, before the American flag and the flag of a lieutenant general.

This morning Ike had received a message from Clark in Washington, who related that he had had long and satisfactory talks with General Marshall, and subsequently with Admiral Leahy and "Colonel Mc-Gowan." This was followed by a luncheon conference with Harry Hopkins. All seemed pleased with the progress of TORCH to date. Clark brought up the dissatisfaction of the U. S. Navy with the command relationship. The Navy had apparently understood that Admiral Cunningham was to be a staff officer instead of Naval Commander. The Navy was also concerned as to what official action it should take against French forces, with the onset of hostilities.

The British Chiefs of Staff adopted code names, at the Prime Minister's request, for the four principal assault points in North Africa. These will be used by the PM in communications relative to TORCH. Ike was fretting today because Casablanca, which already is causing him enough worry, thus has been rechristened *Dunkirk*.

Ike, Beetle, T. J., and I settled the war around a fire at the cottage, where we had dinner.

LONDON, SUNDAY, SEPTEMBER 27, 1942

Beetle has been feeling badly; his old ulcer is kicking up, and we are worried for fear our crackerjack C/S will be laid up. Ike has been trying his damnedest to get him to take medical treatment or, at least, to be seen by a doctor, and said he would have any specialist needed flown over from home. Beetle was afraid the medicos would rulebook him out of the war. Beetle is on a milk diet, and we are trying to force him to rest. Probably nothing short of orders from the CG will make Beetle take proper care of himself.

Later in the day, General Clark cabled the C-in-C that Admiral Cunningham had submitted to Admiral King a proposed draft directive to our naval task-force commanders, covering the action to be taken if the French Navy resists. This has been expanded by the USN to cover French Air Forces as well. The conference at Washington deferred agreement subject to the C-in-C's approval, which was asked promptly so that his views could be presented to the Combined Chiefs of Staff meeting on Monday. The outline of the proposed directive said that no offensive action would be taken unless the French indicate hostile intentions by act or disposition.

LONDON, MONDAY, SEPTEMBER 28, 1942

A letter written by General Clark (see page 104) to the Governor General of Gibraltar and carried on the person of R. N. Turner, a Royal Navy officer, by air, had been found on Turner's body, which was washed ashore at Cádiz (Spain). His plane had crashed. In this letter, Clark had given General MacFarlane the time of D-Day when it was November 4. Fortunately, the envelope had been sent to Madrid by the Spanish but ulti- mately reached the British. Apparently, it hadn't been opened. Whether any other secret papers were on the ship and picked up by salvagers isn't known. Another worry for Ike, only this time the Prime Minister is the chief worrier.

Each soldier in TORCH is to wear a five-inch arm band showing a U. S. flag.

The CG went to a meeting he had called of the planners at Norfolk House. Numerous questions were discussed, including: the supply of air transport; the alternate plans in case no landing is possible at Casablanca; the status of naval command; and air operations.

Ike and Beetle went to 10 Downing to have dinner with the PM and, if history gives a damn, I went to bed.

LONDON, TUESDAY, SEPTEMBER 29, 1942

The General and Beetle were at 10 Downing Street for dinner last night, Ike returning to the flat "early" for a PM session—1:30 A.M. The plans for TORCH, as well as consideration of other aid to Russia, such as JUPITER (invasion in Norway), had been discussed by the guests, but the chief news was the concern of the PM and other Britishers for Beetle. The PM had taken Ike into a separate room, to counsel that medical attention should be given Beetle at once. The British are fond of him and are dis- tressed to see him looking so pale and wan.

Ike told me he would have to order Beetle to bed, and instructed me to arrange with Harvey Gibson, Commissioner of the American Red Cross, to assign a nurse to him. She is one of the Harvard unit—Ethel Wester- man. During the forenoon, he ordered Beetle to bed in his flat at the Dorchester. Beetle's illness is a hard blow, particularly at this time. Beetle's absence will throw additional work on Ike. Clark is still in Washington.

The Problem of Naval Command

LONDON, WEDNESDAY, SEPTEMBER 30, 1942

Apparently, the President will make a radio speech or some kind of an- nouncement to add to the impression that the TORCH operation is exclu- sively an American effort, according to a message received by the C-in-C from General Marshall today. Marshall added that it appears "that the best possible announcement (upon which the American press can expand as much as it likes) will be that emanating from the Germans and from Vichy on D-Day, flowing from their knowledge of you as C-in-C of the

forces which have made the landings. Furthermore, Roosevelt will probably include your name and position in his broadcast."

No announcement of the formation of the Allied Force Headquarters
will be made until after D-Day.

Beetle's condition is worse, and upon advice of General Hawley, Surgeon General, whom Ike had called in, a verbal order was issued to Beetle,
sending him to the American General Hospital at Oxford. Beetle cajoled
Ike into promising that he would be permitted to leave the hospital and
return to work just as soon as he gave his word that he felt O.K. A British
ambulance carried Beetle to the hospital and had two blowouts on the
way. His stomach condition had so weakened him that the doctors ordered
a blood transfusion.

Ike met General Clark at Hendon airport around 6 o'clock; accompanied him to town and got the lowdown on various subjects discussed
by Clark in Washington. Admiral King's objection to permitting the
U. S. naval task forces to be under the command of Admiral Cunningham, RN, was one of the main subjects. Ike has indicated that because of
King's feeling, he will accept the arrangement advocated by the U. S.
Navy. This, however, will give Ike a senior commander for the American
Navy, one for the British Navy, another for the American Air Forces, and
still another for the British Air Forces, not to mention the ground forces.
It looks as if he will be trying to do a circus stunt of riding about six horses
at the same time.

I had a session at Norfolk House today, at Major Phillips' request, with
General Matejka, Brigadier Mockler-Ferryman, and Brigadier W. A. Scott,
regarding communication facilities available for the press and radio.
Appears advisable to use Radio Algiers after we establish our headquarters, transmit to BBC and thence across to New York for retransmissions
by the networks and for voice-casts to the press associations. If the station
is captured without too much damage and isn't too essential for purely
military communications, and if the PWE and OWI don't grab too much
time for their propaganda, then the British-American public may hear
radio reports direct from our headquarters. This is a goal I hope we can
achieve.

In a previous discussion with Phillips, supported by Ike, I suggested
the enlargement of the press contingent permitted to accompany the
task forces. As I have recorded, there was to have been only one reporter
set up for Gib to supply news to the entire world for the first five days.
This seemed to us a tremendous burden for one man to bear. Phillips has
arranged for additional space so that each of the three major American
press associations may be represented, not only at Gibraltar, but with the

task forces on the mainland, where radio, movie, and photographic personnel will accompany them.

SEPTEMBER, 1942: *The battle for Stalingrad seesawed, with initial German successes halted by Russian counterattacks. Moscow radio calls upon Red soldiers to defend every house, every stone in embattled city. German and Rumanian troops joined in Caucasus advances. Initial Jap advances toward Moresby offset by later Allied counterattacks. Marines in Solomons continued their battles of annihilation despite Jap reinforcements much hampered by Yank naval and air action. Rommel attack in Libya stalled by air attacks on his communications and daring patrol raids deep into his territory. In Madagascar British advanced steadily. American heavy bombers blast Kiska. Chinese advances continued at reduced pace. The air war on the Western Front continued with heavy raids against widely separated targets located in Crete, Düsseldorf, the Ruhr, and North Africa. Attrition against Axis supply lines continued, especially by British subs in the Mediterranean. (But enemy planes based on Sardinia, Sicily, and Italian mainland play havoc with convoys passing from Gibraltar to Malta.— H.C.B.)*

ROVER

LONDON, THURSDAY, OCTOBER 1, 1942

A message from "Colonel McGowan" from Washington today confirmed that he is now returning to his post in Algiers.

Lord Louis ("Dickie," as Ike calls him) Mountbatten is distressed to think that the Royal Marines assigned to TORCH might be used for ordinary infantry operations, since they are picked troops and, with the number of casualties expected, replacements would be difficult. He has written a long letter to Ike, expressing his hope that they will be used in amphibious assault either at the outset or in subsequent operations such as might be attempted against Sardinia or Sicily. Ike responded that he had no intention of using them as ordinary infantry.

Ike was busy at 20 Grosvenor Square and also at Norfolk House, but took time to drive two hours each way to Oxford to visit Beetle. Found him in good spirit but itching to get out. Ulcer still bothering, so he has to stay, but it is a continual fight to keep him quiet; he's so anxious to be on the job and his conscience is so smitten by what he calls "letting Ike down" at this time. Ike, on the other hand, is trying to get Beetle well so he will be useful when the big moment comes, although he is badly missed now.

Have been carrying a tremendous secret in my bosom these several days.

I refer to nothing less than the fact that Mrs. Roosevelt is to pay our theater a visit, arriving here about October 15. The Ambassador conveyed this information, very hush-hush, to the CG. I suggested a code name, ROVER, violating the general rule requiring designation of a name entirely foreign and disassociated with the subject, but everyone in on the secret seems delighted with the name, especially Mr. Winant, who laughed when I told him.

Beetle had been anxious to have me assigned as ROVER's aide, but the Navy uniform saved me, for Ike thought it inappropriate for me to be telling her about the Army. (Not only would it have been inappropriate, but I would have had a hell of a time telling her anything much about the Navy, not to mention the Army.) Major Richards Vidmer, the former sports writer of the *New York Herald Tribune*, now attached to our G-2, is to have this assignment. She is to spend two weeks here—the first two days at Buckingham Palace, and the last two with her cousin, Minister Gray, in Dublin, and will have a rigorous itinerary in the intervening days and nights.

LONDON, FRIDAY, OCTOBER 2, 1942

General Marshall wired Ike today that word had been received from Colonel Eddy at Tangier that the chief harbor pilot of Port Lyautey had been smuggled out of Morocco, and is now en route to London and Washington. As this action changes the tempo of operations in North Africa and will cause widespread comment tending to rivet attention on this particular area, information is requested as to whether or not Ike was consulted by the OSS and whether such action had his approval.

To this Ike replied that he had not been consulted by OSS or any other authority concerning the project mentioned. His orders to OSS representatives have been to do nothing in that area without his approval and that nothing unusual is to take place there.*

Major Phillips was in today with a less consequential bellyache about OSS/OWI—we all have difficulty differentiating the two. Seems Percy Winner is representative of OWI in Mack's policy-planning group and is full of hope. Wants political propaganda to take precedence over press and radio communications. Phillips wanted me to do something about it, but I expect Mr. Mack will handle it, as I do not like to attempt to intervene.

Today the General accompanied General Anderson, who will be the commander of the Eastern British Assault Forces in TORCH, to an "exer-

* Later was informed by OSS that General Patton had requested removal of the pilot.

cise" near Brighton, the purpose of which was to demonstrate the laying
of a barrage with close follow-up by infantry. Two divisions were engaged.
The British infantry showed plenty guts following the barrage, their line
of advance being generally only fifty yards from exploding shells. Ike said
that there were four wounded. One infantryman lost a leg when a smoke-
bomb canister hit the ground and bounced obliquely. The other three were
less seriously wounded. Ike was full of praise for the bravery of the infantrymen. However, he said that if he had been running the show, he felt
he would have used some different tactics. Thought use of live ammunition as well as mines, which were purposely exploded close to the visiting
officers, to afford realism, well worth while. (Papers said an officer was
killed.)

Someone mailed Ike a clipping, which he handed me today, grinning
broadly. It said: "Our trusty reporter was scouring around a Midwest state
recently, looking for a town named MacArthur. 'You're in the right burg,
but you've got the wrong name, buddy,' said a local native. 'They changed
the name to Eisenhower last week.'"

The Navy outline plan for TORCH has been completed, mimeographed,
and distributed to a restricted list of commanders involved in the operation. This lists the assignments, routing, and timing, and other pertinent
details of covering naval forces in the Mediterranean, another off the
Azores, an escort force based on Gibraltar, and assault convoys. There are
Western (Casablanca), Central (Oran), and Eastern (Algiers) Naval
Task Forces, the Western being the USN.

In the covering group for the Western Force will be: the sixteen-inch
battleship, *Massachusetts*; two eight-inch cruisers, the *Wichita* and *Tuscaloosa*; and five destroyers. In the flag group of this force will be one
eight-inch cruiser, the *Augusta*, as flagship, two destroyers, and four submarines. Labeled "Fire-support group" is one fourteen-inch battleship,
the *New York*; three six-inch cruisers, the *Philadelphia*, *Savannah*, and
Brooklyn, and six destroyers. In the aircraft-carrier group are the *Ranger*
and three auxiliary craft, the *Santee*, *Sangamon*, and *Charger*. There are
also five fast and three slow mine sweepers.

The Central Naval Task Force for the assault on Oran includes one
HQ ship, *Largo*; the battleship *Rodney*, when detached from covering
force in the Med; the aircraft carrier *Furious*; the auxiliary carrier *Biter*;
two six-inch cruisers, *Jamaica* and *Aurora*. One antiaircraft ship, *Curaçao*;
one auxiliary AA ship, the *Alynbank*; thirteen destroyers; eight mine
sweepers, two sloops, six corvettes, two cutters, eight trawlers, and eight
mine layers.

The Eastern Naval Task Force is the Algiers assault group. It has the

HQ ship, the *Bulolo*; two six-inch cruisers, the *Sheffield* and *Bermuda*; air-craft carrier *Argonaut*; the auxiliary A/C *Avenger*; two cruisers, *Scylla* and *Charybdis*; two AA ships, and destroyers, sloops, corvettes, mine layers, and mine sweepers in about the same proportion as for the Central Force.

The covering force labeled "Force H" will be responsible for covering the assault from interference by Vichy and Italian Mediterranean fleets; the Azores covering force will provide cover for the Casablanca assault.

The plan delegates responsibility and makes assignments in minute detail. The responsibility for operation of the captured ports will be British at Algiers and all ports east into Tunisia, and at Oran will be British in the assault phase, with the USN to assume responsibility as soon as possible; and USN at Casablanca and other ports in French Morocco.

Some 173 ships of war, from battleships to corvettes, are listed for the enterprise, not counting assault loaders and cargo vessels, hospital ships, landing craft, and so forth.

Force H will have three modern battleships, the *Duke of York* as flag-ship, the *Renown* and the *Rodney*. Two A/C, *Victorious* and *Formi-dable*; four cruisers, *Bermuda*, *Argos*, *Cerius*, *Phoebe*; and fifteen fleet destroyers. It also will have at its disposal, for oiling inside the Mediter-ranean, the oilers *Brown Ranger* and *Dingledale*, escorted by one corvette and antisubmarine trawlers.

Report from Patton

LONDON, SATURDAY, OCTOBER 3, 1942

Policy regarding offensive action against French forces is being set. In a message from the C-in-C to General Marshall today, the definition of policy was submitted for action by the Combined Chiefs of Staff, with the request that it be considered speedily, as early publication by the AFH to commanders should proceed. The proposed policy is to be incorporated in orders for naval, air, and ground forces.

Definite allocation of nine U. S. divisions for TORCH was requested in a cable from the CG to General Marshall today. The best estimate made here indicates that this number of U. S. divisions can be built up in the new theater as rapidly as, if not faster than, six British divisions. It was requested that the nine divisions be equipped, appropriate training be initiated, and shipping requirements definitely set up.

Things currently worrying the Allied C-in-C: (1) selection of air officer who can quickly supervise the building and maintenance of airfields in North Africa, a job not as glamorous but as important as command of the combat fliers; (2) designation of a commander for the Central Task Force to attack Oran; (3) desirability of retaining an American deputy to himself; (4) necessity of avoiding friction between ourselves and the British and between the Army and Navy; (5) promotion of officers after TORCH is launched; and (6) the naval command, which disturbed him for a while apparently, is sorting itself out, largely because of the personality and co-operative attitude of Admiral Sir Andrew Cunningham and the development of team play by U. S. Navy.

Despite his worries, Ike has expressed himself several times recently as to the splendid support and backing he is receiving, not only from the American and British Chiefs of Staff, but from his own staff. Everyone is keen to get on with the job.

Although the major decisions relative to planning have been made by Ike, there are numerous details General Clark and staff are striving to clarify.

The great strategic importance of Malta as a naval and air base situated astride Rommel's supply line forces the enemy to resist every effort of the British to supply the beleaguered island. Since the enemy appears obsessed with the idea that we will make a desperate effort to assist Malta, our strategists are hopeful that the Germans and Italians will expect us to attack in that area, perhaps in Sicily or even Italy. Clark favors encouraging this idea, thinking it will help keep the French fleet at Toulon.

Forces leaving the U. K. and those leaving the U. S. are being told that they are going around the Cape of Good Hope.

General Patton, Commander of the Western Task Force, has reported from his headquarters in the U. S. his plan of attack. After expressing his opinion that the picture is "gloomy," he said:

"However, you can rest assured that when we start for the beach we shall stay there, whether dead or alive, and if alive, we will not surrender. When I have made everyone else share this opinion, as I shall certainly do before we start, I shall have complete confidence in the success of the operation."

As to the alternative, if weather and surf conditions prevent a landing in the region of the three points, namely, Safi, Fedala, and Port Lyautey, Patton advised the alternative of directly storming the harbor at Casablanca. The Navy should, he said, use at least one old battleship and could storm the harbor in one day, supported by ground forces to be disembarked as rapidly as a foothold could be gained in the harbor. He ventured the opinion that the losses would be less than would be suffered by risky attempts at beach landings under unfavorable weather conditions.

Furthermore, he doesn't want to be held up if the Central and Eastern forces are delayed because of bad weather inside the Med. If the weather is appropriate at Casablanca on D minus 1, he wants to shoot the works and not wait for simultaneous attacks. After the three beachheads have been established, he plans to start armored elements from Safi to the north. The troops in Fedala, supported by air from Port Lyautey (assuming the airport has been captured), will move to the south, possibly also supported by air from a field north of Rabat. The two expeditions will converge on Casablanca. Patton proposes to give a thirty-minute ultimatum to the Governor of Casablanca "stating that I will accept his surrender and give him all honors of war and parole his troops; or that I will bombard him from the sea, bomb him from the air, and attack him on the ground. It is my belief this bluff will work."

General Patton thanked Ike for the "opportunity with which you presented me of getting into this." Patton said, "If our G-2 estimate of the enemy is correct, we will have quite a fight. Just how hard it will be will depend upon the amount of earnestness the French put into it. It does, however, seem to me very desirable from a political point of view to make this seem a very serious resistance, in order to put them right at home, because if we admitted that they made only a token resistance, we are apt to get their families in metropolitan and occupied France in trouble. Perhaps it isn't necessary to worry about this as they may fight like hell anyway."

Ike's First Day Off

LONDON, SUNDAY, OCTOBER 4, 1942

This is a red-letter day, for it is the first one since at least December 14 that Ike hasn't gone to the office. We loitered around the cottage, engaged in target practice with a .22 pistol, and took life easy.

Ike had planned to drive to Oxford to see Beetle, but when I phoned the hospital, found he had flown the coop. When we reached the hotel late in the afternoon, where Ike changed clothes preparatory to driving to Chequers for overnight, we found Beetle in his bed, fast asleep, so we didn't disturb him. By leaving the hospital, he had violated Ike's orders, but Ike couldn't scold him.

General Clark's report of October 3 indicates that the transportation of officers to Gibraltar by air prior to D-Day had been planned more in detail. Instead of C-47s it has been decided to use Flying Fortresses, each of which will carry ten passengers per trip. Each plane will carry combat crews. Clark reports that two "will go down" on D-5, four on D-1 or 2, with two of the B-17s to remain in Gibraltar for use of the C-in-C and head-quarters officers. Passengers will be allowed fifty pounds each, additional baggage to go by air transport. Planes will leave England before 11 P.M., to arrive at Gibraltar just after dawn. Generals are to be distributed among several planes so that if one or more is lost we will still have some generals.

It has also been decided that the C-in-C and five others, including Major Lee, Warrant Officer Marshall, Mickey, myself, and probably T. J. will "go down" on D minus 5. It had been planned that we would reach Gibraltar on D-Day, but two chief reasons influenced the change: (1) a convoy will pass through the Gib Strait on D minus 3, and a decision dependent on weather will have to be made by the C-in-C, who should be on the spot; and (2) we might hit bad flying weather on D minus 1, and by shifting to D minus 5 we should have satisfactory weather, at least one out of the five days before D-Day.

Fifth-column activities to be undertaken prior to D-Day have been discussed. These instructions have been sent directly to "Colonel McGowan" (Murphy), who has now, presumably, returned to Algiers and is to let us know what he can and cannot accomplish.

General Clark was informed that there are 443,000 rounds of 105-mm. ammunition available in the United Kingdom, which is 120,000 rounds in excess of the amount needed aboard the convoys scheduled to arrive on D-Day and D plus 3.

The shipping situation looks better. General Larkin reported that the loading schedule would be met and that so far nothing has developed since his return from the U. S. to make the SOS situation look any worse.

General Everett Hughes has been on a tour of supply depots in the U. K. and has returned more optimistic.

Directive on the French Fleet

LONDON, MONDAY, OCTOBER 5, 1942

Drove to Chequers this morning to meet Ike and Clark. Arrived a few minutes after ten and found them walking to the gate. The discussion with the Prime Minister the night before had lasted until 2:30 A.M., although a part of the evening was devoted to a movie that Ike had already seen twice. The PM and Mrs. Churchill wore heavy overcoats. Ike and Clark weren't so fortunate, so they shivered. The PM had been in fine form. He frequently paces as he talks; sometimes he walks into the huge fireplace, turns around, walks out again, emphasizing a point by waving his huge cigar like a baton.

Today the C-in-C received from General Marshall the directive regarding the French fleet and air forces which had been approved by the C/S and the President. It is also being sent by the British in Washington to the Prime Minister, through the British Chiefs of Staff in London, with the request that the PM inform Ike directly of his approval. No offensive action is to be taken against French forces unless they first take definite hostile action against us. Action contrary to this spirit may have repercussions far-reaching in their effect. Every precaution is to be taken to avoid unnecessary damage to ships and harbor installations. Detailed instructions are given with respect to French surface ships, submarines, and aircraft. We're to go in as friends, but ready to fight.

From a list of names offered by General Marshall to command the Central Task Force, the C-in-C accepted that of General Fredendall, who is on his way.

General Marshall has invited Ike to deal with him on all matters on the frankest possible basis; if Ike disagrees on any question, he is to express himself without reserve. General Marshall also has expressed his complete confidence in Ike's management of the expedition and will support him in every way practicable.

We dined with Beetle tonight. This was his birthday, and we helped him celebrate. There was a moderate crap game, instigated by General Clark, who had returned from the U. S. bearing two of these mischievous devices, although he was unable to make them perform as advertised. Ike didn't participate.

Beetle was bragging about his quart of blood; announced that he had had his batteries charged and was ready to electrify the world. He will work a few hours each day until he is ready to be back in full swing. Ike fearful he is rushing to work too soon.

Slept at the hotel.

A Naval Aide's Invasion Preparations

LONDON, TUESDAY, OCTOBER 6, 1942

The message from General Marshall stating that ten U. S. divisions (instead of the nine requested) had been allocated for TORCH was quickly followed by another one qualifying the first. While the divisions have been allocated, this should not be construed as a definite commitment of this number of divisions. The U. S. is now committed to furnish up to seven divisions and will furnish two more, if necessary, to replace British divisions. The U. S. will still have an additional division available in the immediate future, provided it is required in TORCH and provided the situation elsewhere permits its use in this theater.

Leaflets announcing the purpose of the attack will be dropped by British coastal planes, which will then continue their antisubmarine patrols. (Noticed in an intelligence report that some fifteen or twenty German submarines are operating in the Med at this time.)

Major Phillips was in a couple of times, checking over some of his difficulties in getting the proper representatives of the press, radio, photographers, OWI, and OSS in his PRO setup for TORCH. Advised him to commandeer, if necessary, a portable recording outfit, not only for use of the broadcasters to be run by the Signal Corps, but for potential use with the French. It may be that some of the French leaders will have words of welcome to be broadcast, and it would seem safer to record these first, so we can be sure what is being said before they go on the air.

Arranged with Sir Cecil Graves of the BBC to supply a machine for an unknown purpose, together with an operator "for an indefinite time." The equipment and the operator are to go with the Eastern Task Force into Algiers for use at our headquarters.

Ike Looks Beyond TORCH

LONDON, WEDNESDAY, OCTOBER 7, 1942

Ike, Clark, and Beetle spent a good deal of time together at Norfolk House today, and Ike had several callers at ETO Headquarters. In addition, he attended a secret session at the Embassy, called by Ambassador Winant, so the CG could talk with Myron Taylor, the President's emissary to the Vatican, now en route to Washington via London. Ike thinks the Pope is on our side and says that Taylor reported the Italians are warweary.

Ike, Clark, Beetle, and I had dinner at the cottage and spent the night. I rode out with Clark. He said that there was no doubt that the Germans knew of TORCH and that the only question in his mind is what they are doing to meet it. Expect he will know around about D-Day.

General MacFarlane, the Governor General of Gibraltar, had called on General Clark. The paratroop route over Spain was discussed. Agreed it was advisable for the transport planes over Spain to fly at 10,000 feet. The Spaniards have only a few night fighters, and MacFarlane thought the Germans wouldn't come over Spain to intercept them, although the Spanish would undoubtedly inform Berlin of this unusual air activity. To provide against the contingency of one or more of the planes crashing in

Spain, MacFarlane advised that each plane carry an order telling where it is bound and what its mission is, so Spain will know she is not the object of the attack.

Capacity of the Gibraltar airdrome is now 350 planes. It is greatly congested. Crated aircraft are being assembled upon arrival.

Dealing with the French, even in General Anderson's British force moving toward Tunisia, will have to be handled by Americans if we are to maintain the appearance that this is an all-American attack. Appropriate American officers are being assigned for this purpose.

Desirability of issuing arms to the French was discussed. We have a list of personnel to whom arms should be distributed, but General Clark has been advised that the youth in French North Africa are with us, no matter what happens.

Delivery of aircraft from the U. S. to Russia by the Alaskan route seems to be in a rather uncertain state, judging from a cable today from General Marshall to Ike, answering the query raised by the PM. The query dates from the reacquisition of some 200 Airacobras from the Russian convoy for use in TORCH. Seems the Siberian route had been closed by the Soviets. Russians have requested that ferrying continue on the original basis of fifty A-20s, twelve B-25s, and eighty fighters each month, via Fairbanks. At the moment, there are fourteen A-20s and thirty P-40s at that point.

Although Ike's mind is figuring out problems of TORCH, he subconsciously thinks ahead to ROUNDUP, that momentous cross-Channel push which someday must be done to destroy the Nazis. As U. S. strength in the United Kingdom is diverted to North Africa, he wants to replenish that strength with about six divisions, to be concentrated and trained in southern England. In order to furnish manpower for the North African expedition, the British have greatly depleted their normal armed strength in their homeland. Consequently, additional American troops would give assurance that while we are busy in North Africa, England herself will remain safe.

England is becoming a great base for air operations. In his frequent discussions with General Spaatz and other air officers, Ike is finding that daylight bombing, the efficacy of which we are now undertaking to demonstrate in growing strength, has developed only one real weakness, and that's the necessity of good weather. On a recent mission we had forty-eight planes over enemy-occupied territory, but the entire mission had to return without making the attack and had to jettison all bombs. In this operation, apparently due to the weather, an entire squadron of Spitfires was lost, yet the pilots were experienced men. Ike advocates heavy build-up of U. S. Air

Force in England with every effort and device that will enable us to find and bomb targets even in bad weather. American development of night fighters likewise is needed.

LONDON, THURSDAY, OCTOBER 8, 1942

Ike went to Cheltenham today to see the SOS headquarters. General Lee went with him. When Ike returned he called me into his office. He had a grin as wide as a slice of watermelon. "I'm going to get a dog," he said. This surprised me, for I didn't have the slightest idea he wanted a dog, and rather thought I was fulfilling that mission as "dog's body." But I was delighted. The SOS is looking for the dog, which Ike thinks should be a Scottie. I tried to sell him on a Dandie Dinmont because of our old Danny at home, but Ike likes the attitude of independence struck by a strutting Scottie.

The Pattern of Command

LONDON, FRIDAY, OCTOBER 9, 1942

Ike's creation of a new type of Allied command in which American and British officers work side by side, thus applying their brains and the resources of their respective countries to a complete unity, is now coming into conflict with tradition. The British War Office currently has the problem of writing a directive for General Anderson, commanding the First British Army, assigning him and his forces to General Ike.

In World War I, Allied command consisted of a small headquarters staff under Marshal Foch, with separate British, American, and French commands, which received general instructions from the Marshal, or, at least, came to general understandings as to prospective action under him. The commander of each nationality had certain rights to appeal to his own government if ordered to undertake an attack which would unduly imperil his troops. In trying to draft a directive to General Anderson, some officers in the War Office followed the tradition set by the directive to General Haig in World War I. This, in Ike's opinion, violates the unity of command inherent in assignment of an over-all Allied command by the Combined Chiefs of Staff, which is the directing force representative of both great governments and which, incidentally, is his only boss as Allied Commander. The pattern of command in World War I has long been discussed; Ike feels that the essence of unified command requires daily and intimate contact amongst staff officers of both nationalities and that there should be no doubt as to the responsibility and authority of the Allied Commander.

In trying to help his friends at the War Office write language to depart from tradition and to be harmonious with the unity sought in the new Allied command, he suggests that instead of directing the command officer of the British First Army to report direct to the War Office if any of his troops are imperiled by an order of the Allied Commander, the General should first consult fully with the Allied Commander and then, if still dissatisfied, appeal to the War Office. To Ike, the principle of unity of command is almost holy; he also feels that no time should be lost during a battle by waiting for approval or disapproval of his orders by either the War Office or the War Department.

General Fredendall, who is to command the Center Task Force, arrived by air today, and promptly reported to the CG.

Ike had lunch with Admiral Ramsay in the flat, and dinner as guest of the CIGS.* The dinner broke up early. One of the world-shaking items of discussion was the prospective dog of the Commanding General of the European Theater of Operations, U. S. A. General Ismay, whom Ike now calls "Pug," suggested a simple announcement that the American Commanding General would like a dog would bring a deluge of canines from the public. But Ike didn't want his dog this way.

A new point given to General Clark by Colonel Stirling today is that the British are prepared to have the Allied Commander-in-Chief head up military control of Gibraltar itself during the assault, but such an unprecedented move requires Cabinet approval.

Colonel Stirling had also shown General Clark a Joint Intelligence Committee paper dated October 6, indicating that no particular attention is being paid to Allied preparations by the Axis. Clark describes this as "quite encouraging."

Clark, with two or three officers, plans to leave Gibraltar as soon as practicable after D-Day for Oran, going thence to Algiers and later backtracking to Casablanca, to "tie up both ends of the American effort." (I don't think General Ike could be successfully tied to the Rock of Gibraltar after the assault is under way. My guess is that he will be on the heels of the assault force. He has constantly grumbled at being cooped up in a "cave" on Gibraltar, and has tried to establish his headquarters on a cruiser. Unfortunately, the critical need of communications and the limitations of receiving and sending messages from a cruiser bar such an arrangement. Gibraltar is satisfactory as a communications center.)

* Chief of the Imperial General Staff; roughly equivalent to the position of Chief of Staff of the U. S. Army.

It was a tough day. In the midst of numerous appointments Ike asked me to ring up General Fredendall and invite him to dinner at the flat. Unfortunately, the General had just made another dinner appointment, which Ike wouldn't permit him to cancel, as invitations of the Allied Commander-in-Chief are not "commands." So we dined alone and enjoyed the company.

Packing the field desks, one with my cigars, for the move is under way. The middle office looked like a combination cigar store and supply depot this afternoon, Saturday being considered a good day for these domestic operations. Various correspondents have dropped in and can't help noticing the activity. They also slyly glance at the map of Norway on my wall. I say nothing.

A story that the War Department has directed Ike to make a trip to the U. S. may slip out, thus explaining his absence from London when he goes to the scene of TORCH.

A matter that has concerned Anderson is his feeling that the inhabitants of Algiers may rightly feel that they have been deliberately double-crossed, by public statements, by leaflets, broadcasts, and in the press, into thinking the eastern assault is an all-American operation. Actually, as the inhabitants will see by looking around, there will be British troops in the Algiers region. The CG directed General Clark to study the matter and arrange for the preparation and distribution of a separate leaflet, to be given out some hours after the landing is effected, explaining the nature of the British participation.

Had a leisurely forenoon, arriving at the office at 9:30. Got rid of an accumulation of little things. Ike had conferences with the Chief of Staff, and with Generals Clark, Ryder, and Porter.

Ike and I lunched at the flat and, after checking to find things quiet at the office, decided to respond to the call of the out-of-doors. It was a beautiful day and the two of us went to the cottage. We put on our makeshift golf clothes. As our back gate opens on the thirteenth hole and as we have never had time to go to the first tee at the clubhouse, about a half mile away, we of necessity have been breaking in on the thirteenth hole. Usually there are so few playing there is no difficulty, but the fine weather had brought out numbers of golfers. So, after playing a hole or two, and finding ourselves more or less in the way—the General, particularly, feeling very self-conscious about it—we decided to call off the game.

Engaged in some target practice with the .22, and baked in front of the
fire. Were joined for Sunday supper by Generals Clark and Smith. Ike
and I stayed at the cottage for the night.

General Clark's report dated October 11, covering the activities of the
previous day, summarizes several new problems.

Creation of the North African Shipping Board to handle shipping after
D-Day has been considered. General Ryder had reported that he was
satisfied with the progress of training of the 39th Regimental Combat
Team, and indicated optimism. However, he expects resistance at the
beaches and thinks it not unlikely there may be Germans.

Lieutenant Colonel Elliott Roosevelt, commander of the 3rd Photographic Reconnaissance Group, had requested permission to take an active
part in the operation. Doolittle and Spaatz were agreeable, and Clark
approved the request.

Field Marshal Smuts

LONDON, TUESDAY, OCTOBER 13, 1942

We are having a birthday party for Ike tomorrow night and intended as
a surprise to present him with a Scottie. Beetle is arranging it. But Ike had
put the heat on Major Lee to get a dog, and the delay required explanation. So Beetle and I had to disclose the secret. This afternoon I heard
three sharp buzzes—the General's signal to his so-called Naval Aide. I
went promptly. I found the assembled office people looking at two Scottie
puppies—one four months old, and the other twelve. Ike selected the
younger pup and dubbed Mickey as the "Sergeant Dog Walker," or
"Master of the Hound." Formal presentation will be at the cottage tomorrow night. Tonight, sitting by the fire at the flat, Ike picked a name
for his dog—Telek, this being something of a contraction of Telegraph
Cottage. I told him it sounded like some synthetic name for a toothbrush, and he said, "Well, his tail looks like a toothbrush."

Ike, Clark, and Beetle left around 8 o'clock for 10 Downing Street.
General Smuts was there, and an exhaustive review of the war and current strategy took place. Ike apparently held the floor for some time,
elucidating on the principle that unity of command means just that, and
when there is divided responsibility, the principle is destroyed.

I asked Ike if the PM had become reconciled that delay in ROUNDUP
is the inevitable result of TORCH. Said he had.

Ike had enjoyed the session. I was still up when he returned and found
him in a buoyant mood. Ike had taken a strong liking to Field Marshal

Jan Smuts, whose long and distinguished record was well known to him. Smuts had said, "If you succeed in this operation your name will go down in big letters in military history." He didn't say what should happen if it failed, but he didn't need to.

Around headquarters it has been difficult at times to maintain a proper attitude of confidence and optimism because preparations for assembly of matériel and men for shipping give rise to so many seemingly unsolvable problems that occasionally it seems that the expedition will never get launched. However, so far as General Ike's attitude is concerned, he is displaying a buoyant optimism to the staff. Despite the rush, shipping schedules are being met by and large, with some minor disappointments. Ike now believes that if nothing untoward happens, the play for TORCH will develop almost perfectly up to the point of departure.

He is not even allowing to bother him unduly some rather alarming information about enemy movement of planes, vehicles, and other equipment into the vital area and reports of the reinforcement of their air force in Sicily. He hopes these moves are inspired by nervousness and uncertainty as to our intentions rather than any definite knowledge by the enemy of what we intend to do.

Ike's Birthday

LONDON, WEDNESDAY, OCTOBER 14, 1942

General Marshall sent Ike the draft of a proclamation to be issued in each of the North African territories to be occupied. These have been prepared by joint action of the Treasury, State, and War Departments. Marshall asks for Ike's consideration and concurrence. This puts into effect the arrangement for standard practice in monetary exchange which has been previously discussed.

The plans worked out at Norfolk House for distributing the leaflets and the handling of the President's broadcast on D-Day were summarized in a message for the Operations Division and General Patton. A leaflet containing the President's message to the people of North Africa, issued in the name of the Commander-in-Chief of the Allied Expeditionary Force, will be dropped by planes dispatched from Gibraltar, flying over Casablanca, Oran, and Algiers at approximately H-Hour of the first attack on D-Day. It will carry a colored imprint of the United States flag and a likeness of the President.

A second leaflet is being prepared to forestall the impression by the French that they are being double-crossed by the use of British troops at Algiers. This will be dropped in Algiers and in the area to the east, timed with the entrance of British troops.

The recordings of the President's message must be in London by November 1, and Washington was advised by Ike's staff that the text of his message should not contain any reference to the specific areas where landings will take place. The broadcast will be over the new, secret British high-powered station which is to be ready by that time and which, it is claimed, will reach all of French North Africa. The President's message on transcriptions will be repeated throughout D-Day and succeeding days if necessary.

Admiral Cunningham is back from Washington and brought word to Ike that General Patton's most favored alternative plan in the event of bad weather on the west coast is to threaten bombardment of Casablanca from the sea in an effort to gain entrance to the port without resistance. Ike gave his approval, with the admonition that no bombardment be executed without prior authority from him.

General Marshall informed the Commander-in-Chief that the only statement of American policy desired by the President regarding TORCH is the defeat of the Axis powers and the preservation of French administration in the colonies. The President does not want to make any statement of policy that would involve an attitude either favorable or unfavorable toward the Vichy government. He wants the Axis kicked out of the area and assurance that the colonies will be administered by the French.

By letter to Major General Sir Hastings Ismay, Ike informed the War Cabinet of alternatives for the Western Task Force. It could lie off in the Atlantic while fuel lasts and wait for the weather to clear. If short of fuel, the fleet could go to Gibraltar, ten ships at a time, refuel, and again lie off in the Atlantic. Or, an assault echelon could land in the Oran area. Plans for such a landing have been prepared. Plans have also been prepared so the Western Task Force could land in the Tangier-Ceuta area, or in Algeciras, seize the port, airdromes, and coastal defenses. The last two plans, of course, would be undertaken only in the event of Spanish hostility.

Our old friend "Gee"* came in today. It was grand to see him. He is looking fit and full of vitality; has his 29th Division in the Tidworth area in southern England.

Ike had a full calendar of callers, starting at 8:45 and ending at 5:15.

---

* Major General Leonard T. Gerow, whom General Eisenhower succeeded as Chief of the Operations Division, War Department. They had been associated, on and off duty, for many years.

Even the chaplain was in. I took Gee's aides to lunch at the officers' mess, and Gee, Ike, Beetle, and Everett Hughes celebrated Ike's birthday by luncheon at our flat.

Clark, Beetle, T. J., Major Lee, Mickey, and I had a so-called "surprise" birthday party at Da-de-da.* The puppy was officially presented. The air people had sent miniature parachute and harness for him.

We'd made up parodies on well-known tunes suitable to the occasion, the best being by Lieutenant Colonel E. C. Boehnke, one of T. J.'s right-hand men.

Mickey had arranged for a cake with three stars and three candles. He lit the candles before we'd finished our preliminaries, and as they were unavoidably tiny they were practically burned into the frosting before we sat down. Moaney and John did their stuff nobly as usual. Stayed at the cottage, somewhat awash.

During the day Ike had received a cable:

> MY PRAYERS, BEST WISHES AND COMPLETE
> CONFIDENCE TO YOU ON YOUR BIRTHDAY.
>
> MARSHALL

LONDON, THURSDAY, OCTOBER 15, 1942

The functions of OWI Psychological Warfare, and PWE (British), which have been under Mr. Mack as Chief of the Political Section for the AFHQ (Allied Forces Headquarters), are being combined with the Civil Affairs section. Mr. Matthews, from the American Embassy, has been put at the head of the organization until Murphy, now in North Africa, can take active charge. Mack, because he is British, has gracefully stepped aside after most of the hard work has been done, so that an American front may be given to the political activities. He will, however, be with Ike at Gibraltar as political and civil adviser.

The War Cabinet has delegated military command at Gibraltar during the TORCH operation to Ike, as Commander-in-Chief, without disturbing the civil functions of Mason-MacFarlane as governor, and providing for military operations in Gibraltar under orders originated by the Commander-in-Chief but to be carried out by the government. The paper states, "We shall impress on General Eisenhower the importance of providing adequately for the air defense of Gibraltar throughout the operation."

When we are finished with Gibraltar as a staging point, command will revert to the present system.

---

* Then current code name for Telegraph Cottage.

General Clark has been concerned with monetary arrangements in the new theater. The question was raised in a discussion with Generals Smith and Gruenther, Colonel Holmes, and Mr. Matthews whether civilians in the area would be allowed to exchange American dollars they have on hand for the yellow-seal variety supplied American troops by the U. S. government. A decision on this matter will await a survey of local conditions, i.e., an appraisal of the dangers of counterfeit money and the creation of a black market.

For reasons of security it has been decided every effort should be made to have the printing of the proclamation to be distributed by the Western Task Force done in London. This proclamation is to be in Arabic; it must be printed and in General Patton's hands (in the U. S.) by October 22.

It has been decided that Mr. Mack will be the Supreme Commander's personal adviser on political matters, and at his own suggestion, his title will be British Civil Liaison Officer. Murphy is to head up civil affairs, with Matthews as his deputy. Mr. Mack will advise both the CG and Murphy in matters relating to his particular field.

LONDON, FRIDAY, OCTOBER 16, 1942

Today there was a lot of talk about the dodge concerning General Eisenhower's disappearance from ETO headquarters early in November. It has been proposed that the story might filter through the press or through neutral diplomatic channels that the Commanding General has been recalled to Washington for consultation with the War Department. Ike is concerned that Mamie will really think he's coming home.

General Clark's Rendezvous Is Arranged

LONDON, SATURDAY, OCTOBER 17, 1942

Ike's private car, Bayonet, which he hasn't seen, is being hooked on General Lee's train for the inspection trip in western Scotland. I looked over the train layout today. Unfortunately, Ike's car is built for operation on a line that apparently doesn't speak to the London, Midland, and Scottish, on which we are traveling to Scotland, so the couplings don't fit. Special ones have been made, and when I suggested that the train be reshuffled a bit to give Ike some privacy by avoiding the use of his car as a runway from the three cars in the rear to the dining room ahead, found this couldn't be done in time.

Today a succession of messages from "Colonel McGowan," relayed via General Marshall, came tumbling in, the news both good and bad. Good, in that Darlan apparently wants to play ball, which means the French Navy as well as the Army may be self-neutralized. Ike has been trying to develop a formula for dealing with the nationalistic interests of the French leaders, particularly Giraud.

Representatives of Darlan have informed Murphy most secretly that the French government at Vichy has learned from both German and Japanese sources that the U. S. plans military operations soon against Dakar or Casablanca, or both. Vichy has been urged to prepare for all-out opposition and the Axis indicates it will occupy French North Africa. In fact, messages to this effect have been intercepted. In addition, the French General Staff is convinced Axis aggression is imminent. Darlan, apparently, is willing to join the Allies and bring the French fleet, assuming he would be made commander-in-chief of the French armed forces in North Africa and could be assured of U. S. willingness and ability to furnish material and economic aid on a large scale. Axis supposedly already has massed 100,000 troops on Tunisian border and has prepared for offensive air operation.

Murphy recommends that Darlan be encouraged on the basis of securing his co-operation with Giraud. Darlan expected in Algiers within a week.

General Mast favors dealing with Giraud instead of Darlan, who is suspected of hoping to climb on the band wagon. Mast states that the Army prefers to be commanded by Giraud rather than Darlan, and the Navy, despite being under Darlan's command, would go along with the Army.

Germans with French passports reported to be infiltrating into North Africa—some have already arrived, and other Germans were recently given 500 blank French passports. Americans in North Africa must be ready to protect themselves against assassination by Axis spies. General Mast proposed a unified command with Giraud in top command and Eisenhower to retain complete command of American forces. American submarine desired to pick up Giraud and his party at night somewhere on the southern coast of France.

Mast wants a secret rendezvous of five American officers from Eisenhower's staff at a point west of Algiers—these officers to be thoroughly familiar with the prospective operation. Information as to shore batteries and disposition of French troops and naval units will be sought by this American mission.

General Ike is responding through General Marshall that General Clark and four staff officers will be sent via Gibraltar, as requested, to keep the rendezvous—exact timing to be given by the French in ultra-secret message from Gibraltar. He is informing General Marshall of a formula for command which he will present almost simultaneously to the British Chiefs and the Prime Minister. At this late date, neither the British nor the American government, acting through the Combined Chiefs, wishes to change the Allied Commander-in-Chief, as only American and British forces are involved in TORCH. A new commander selected now would not be familiar with all the meticulous planning. General Ike's formula would make Giraud governor of all of French North Africa, responsible for all French civil and military affairs, under the protection of Allied forces; with Darlan 'to be accepted by Giraud as commander of French military and naval forces in North Africa, so the French forces could co-operate immediately under the general direction of the Allied Commander-in-Chief. Once ashore, and with the French liberated and North Africa becoming a base for further Allied military operations, Darlan could be made Deputy Allied Commander-in-Chief in relief of Clark when he takes command of the American Fifth Army. The question is whether the French can get together under the combination of Giraud and Darlan—the interest in the latter being his influence over the French fleet.

Ike submitted his proposals to the PM and the British Chiefs, who gave them their blessing. The PM congratulated him on his sagacity.

Ike, Clark, Beetle, and I had dinner at the cottage—almost a farewell, as Clark was going on a great adventure, via plane to Gibraltar and submarine to the rendezvous spot off Algiers, to meet "Colonel McGowan" and his French friends. Ike had wanted desperately to make the trip himself, but as Commander-in-Chief he has to be quickly available at headquarters to make decisions. Since Clark is thoroughly familiar with the whole operation, has appropriate rank, and, in fact, has planned most of the detail under policies and decisions laid down by Ike, it was appropriate to assign him. Clark was as happy as a boy with a new knife. Ike won't breathe easily until Clark is back, for he is a close friend of twenty-five years' standing, and if anything should happen to him Ike would be desperate.

Because of the deluge of messages relative to the conflict of French ideas of self-help in North Africa necessitating replies and decisions, most of which needed concurrence by Washington and London, it was impossible for Ike to determine whether he could leave to witness pre-TORCH maneuvers in Scotland. Both Ike and Clark felt it was necessary for one of them to be present during these exercises, to show the men and officers in the field that the topside is interested. In the end Ike responded to his duty to go north for a routine inspection, while Clark obtained the more adventurous and interesting assignment to the south.

Clark left the cottage before midnight with Beetle, and Ike and I stayed all night.

Maneuvers in Scotland

LONDON, SUNDAY, OCTOBER 18, 1942

Left the cottage early to catch the train at 8:30 for the sixteen-hour ride to Kentallen in western Scotland—north of Inveraray—taking Mickey with us. Reached there at midnight; had a skull session on the exercise. Troops of the 1st Division, lying in combat loaders in the lochs—some as far as five or six miles from shore; others within a mile—were to disembark from landing craft at numerous points, under cover of darkness, with the objective of taking "enemy" airdromes, coastal batteries, and in general practicing the kind of operation that lies ahead in TORCH.

In a caravan of ten cars, led by ours, in which were Ike, Colonel Price of the British Army as guide, the driver, and I, we drove from point to point where landings were being made. At each place Ike would leave the cars to slosh through the mud to the beach, talk to the soldiers and officers, observe the operation, and then back to the cars to continue to another point. In all we drove some ninety miles from 1 A.M. to 9 A.M. Monday. It was raining most of the time; our driver was tired out, so I took the wheel for some thirty-five miles. It was my first effort at driving in England; the blackout and left-hand driving were new to me, but I was told later that the cars following me in the caravan had some difficulty keeping up.

LONDON, MONDAY, OCTOBER 19, 1942

We were guests of Admiral Hewitt, RN, at the Admiralty House in Inveraray for breakfast around 9. After breakfast we witnessed from the beach in front of the Admiralty the landing of several LCVPs,* disembarking troops from five American combat loaders lying in the loch. The troops looked fine—full of spirit, agile, and in good physical condition. But Ike was bothered at the lack of experience of the lieutenant, captain, and major grades, who did not seem to know what to do after the troops got on the beach. This was a criticism applicable to most of the landings we saw during the night. When the LCVP disgorges its fighting

---

* Landing craft for vehicles and personnel.

men in an actual operation, particularly with enemy aircraft right overhead, they should disperse as quickly as possible. While Ike was talking over this weakness with Admiral Hewitt, the latter made an apt comment: "Why, those men should fade like stink."

During the early-morning hours we had been stopped by Brigadier General Theodore Roosevelt, who gave us a glowing account of the exercise; said that the troops had captured the "airdrome," bypassed an "enemy" position, and had all but choked Hitler. Having seen most of the operation, Ike was inclined to discount the report. As a matter of fact, the whole demonstration was disappointing, and Ike felt pretty low on the return trip. We boarded the train at 1:30 and departed at 4, to return to London via Edinburgh.

LONDON, TUESDAY, OCTOBER 20, 1942

Returned to London at 7:30 A.M. and reached the office at the normal time. Having been up all night in the rain, sloshing through the mud, Ike was beginning to catch a cold, and Mickey definitely had one. But so far I had escaped.

The unsatisfactory showing of the maneuver, added to the more important worries of Ike, contributed to what he described as a "state of jitters." He called me into his office, said he couldn't concentrate. The thing bothering him most was Clark's secret conference. He had word that Clark had reached Gibraltar safely and had proceeded by submarine Monday evening, ready to be at the rendezvous Tuesday evening at 9. This was to be at a desolate spot on the coast in a lonely house, with no other houses within five or six miles. Its location was to be flashed to the ship from shore by a white light. If there were treachery, Clark and his party might put ashore, never to return. If the conference accomplished its purpose, the whole operation could virtually be assured of success. If it did not, we will have one hell of a fight on our hands.

The increase of German and Italian strength, particularly along the Tunisian border; the infiltration of German fifth columnists; and the knowledge that there are at least thirty clandestine German radios in Morocco and Algiers—all contributed to the uncertainty. Ike's state of mind was just a reflection of continued nervous strain over a period of months. In any event, he had "customers" from 8:55 to 5:50, and probably no one but Beetle and I had been told of his worry.

An idea of playing up American participation in the forthcoming renewal of Alexander's operations to throw Rommel back from Egypt has been rejected by Ike after consultation with the War Cabinet. The fighting will be at close quarters and the sparseness of American forces will soon be evident to the enemy. Consequently, it would not be worth while to try to fool them in this manner.*

If the enemy is as befuddled as the various correspondents in London with regard to places and time, our secret plans are secure. The newspapermen are guessing Norway, southern Russia, and the Middle East; most are hazarding North Africa, but meaning Dakar. The landing of American troops, mostly Negroes, in Liberia has helped focus attention on Dakar and West Africa. The Liberian operation is one set up by Ike while still head of the Operations Division.

From all the rumors we have heard and known opportunities of leakage, current intelligence reports give some assurance that we have perhaps worried unduly. We'll know more on D-Day or shortly thereafter. (No trace of the missing page.)

Ike and Beetle had their regular Tuesday-night dinner and talk with the Prime Minister at 10 Downing Street. Beetle took along some vitamins in accordance with his diet, so he wouldn't have to eat nonregulation food.

General Ike's Directive to General Anderson

LONDON, WEDNESDAY, OCTOBER 21, 1942

The Allied Commander-in-Chief, General McClure, Beetle, Colonel Krum, and I have been kicking back and forth a press release we wanted to get out about a week ago. This story is ostensibly to answer the German claims that several heavily laden troop transports had been torpedoed, but is actually intended to create the impression of continued heavy flow of troops into the United Kingdom, to take the eyes of the Axis away from North Africa. The truth is that not a single American soldier had been lost on the Atlantic at the time of the German claims. In fact, none has been lost to date by enemy action in crossing the Atlantic. But in telling the story, which will be so avidly received at home, Ike was afraid of flaunting fate, for as soon as we issue such a statement it would be just our luck to get a torpedo. Yet there is a military advantage to be gained.

Arrangements have been made to furnish the submarine for Giraud to get from France to Morocco. He was disinclined to fly, except as a last resort.

* American and British supply, plus Royal Navy and Royal Air Force daring to cut Rommel's line of communication, counted heavily in the success of Montgomery.

I had waited up for Ike to return from the Prime Minister's. He got back early—at 1 o'clock. Found nothing very world-shaking had happened and that Ike and the Prime Minister had gotten into a discussion on history, each apparently trying to outdo the other with his knowledge. Beetle said Ike ran rings around the Prime Minister, throwing dates and events around like AA fire in a London blitz.

There was a mess-up in the time for Clark's rendezvous. Colonel McGowan and the party had been at the secret meeting place a night too soon, and they are supposed to meet tonight or tomorrow night. This means Clark has to lie around in a sub. I know he has his dice, for they are his good-luck pieces. He probably will have the crew's money.

The attempt of our Flying Fortresses to deal a heavy blow to the submarine base at Lorient was only partially successful. We lost three aircraft, although we got nine enemy fighters. Only one group of twenty Fortresses found the target because of heavy clouds. Vichy is crying heavy casualties. Direct hits were reported, but these submarine cradles have roofs of some sixteen feet solid concrete and it takes more than one direct hit to do any appreciable damage.

The War Cabinet has approved Ike's idea of the wording for the directive of General Anderson and his British First Army. It makes that army an integral part of the Allied force. If any order is received from the Allied Commander-in-Chief which in General Anderson's view would give rise to a grave and exceptional situation, appeal may be taken to the War Office, provided the time required does not mean the missing of an opportunity to progress or the endangering of any part of the Allied force. Also, the Allied Commander-in-Chief must first be informed of the intent of, as well as the reason for, the appeal. Ike feels that monumental progress now has been made in organization for warfare by Allies. He sent a copy to the War Department in the hope that it would serve as a model.

Wednesday night Ike and I spent at the cottage. Ike quietly concerned about Clark. The mix-up on the time for the rendezvous had not added to his peace of mind.

News from Madrid and Washington

LONDON, THURSDAY, OCTOBER 22, 1942

During the day Ike approved the final draft of the brief news announcement that our troop ships on the Atlantic at the time of the German propaganda claims of the sinking of heavily laden vessels have now landed safely in the United Kingdom. It was released at 8 o'clock tonight. We are knocking on wood!

Ike greatly concerned about Clark. A further message from "Colonel McGowan" had indicated the meeting would take place tonight—namely, October 21/22.

In a list of colonels who have been active in mounting the TORCH expedition and who are holding responsible positions, Ike recommends that General Marshall approve the promotion to Brigadier of our good friend, Colonel Thomas Jefferson Davis. He is the Adjutant General and Executive Officer for Allied Forces Headquarters. He is one of the most capable officers I have met, and does not seek promotion.

LONDON, FRIDAY, OCTOBER 23, 1942

Ike conferred at length today with General Spaatz about plans for Air Force objectives in the Bay of Biscay region and elsewhere to upset the U-boat bases. He had a schedule of conferences, but slipped out with Admiral Stark and Beetle at 4 o'clock to join the small group to welcome Mrs. Roosevelt at Paddington Station.

The King and Queen were there, and His Majesty spotted the American CG and took him aside for a talk. The King knew the latest details of the TORCH story. Wanted to know of Ike if he had heard from Clark and asked for Ike's opinion of the reliability of "D," and also of "G." Ike said later that he had to think quickly, as he hadn't been accustomed to using those initials for Darlan and Giraud. Ike is fond of the King. He is democratic, and certainly is not aloof from military matters. Not being familiar with the British form, Ike merely addressed the King as "Sir." He noticed Beetle standing stiffly at attention, so called him over and introduced him to the King as informally as a traveling salesman.

On the 9 o'clock news tonight, the announcer, describing the arrival, said that Mrs. Roosevelt had been affably meeting the assembled welcomers, but when she spoke to General Eisenhower she had laughed heartily. Apparently, the result of a plain Kansas welcome.

Went out to the cottage for dinner and the evening. Mickey had a bad cold and after he had gone to bed early I took him a hot toddy. He described it to Miss Jaqua: said I knocked on his door, brought in a great steaming pitcher. He took one glass and drank it; poured another and downed that; reached for a third, but doesn't remember a thing from then on. Says he's well today.

LONDON, SATURDAY, OCTOBER 24, 1942

Ike said that he was going to drive himself, alone, to the cottage, principally to prove to himself he could remember the route, but also to escape routine. When last seen he was going down the middle of the road, veering a little bit to the right and a bit uncertain. He has no driver's permit, isn't sure of the way, but doesn't care. Mickey and I will follow after we have done some packing at the flat.

Ike reached the cottage without incident and felt proud of himself. Spent a quiet afternoon and evening, Beetle coming out about 6 o'clock for dinner.

Clark Returns and Tells the Story

LONDON, SUNDAY, OCTOBER 25, 1942

Around midnight Saturday, General Gruenther called to say that the anxiously awaited message from General Clark had arrived. It had been sent from Gibraltar and gave the alarming news that the meeting had been broken up by the police and that the party had had to take refuge in a wine cellar. In relating this incident, Clark cabled, the cellar had been "empty, repeat empty." He was flying from Gibraltar to London.

We spent Sunday forenoon at the office, and around 1 o'clock Ike was ready for the country. He was as pleased as a boy that Clark was safe and about to return. On the way to the cottage, Ike said that he was going to recommend Clark for a DSM. It wasn't long until Clark and Beetle arrived, Clark looking fit, despite his seven days of hard travel—although he did look a little red around the eyes from sleepless nights. He and his party had flown to Gibraltar by B-17; had taken a British submarine from there to the rendezvous point off Algiers, to a place appropriately termed Cherchel Light. In addition to Clark, the party consisted of General L. L. Lemnitzer, Colonels Hamblen and Holmes, and Captain Wright of the United States Navy.

Three British Commandos, two of them captains, were sent along to handle the landing. They stowed four collapsible canvas boats in torpedo tubes, but the subs still had nine torpedoes aboard. En route to the rendezvous, the submarine stopped to permit a drill with the canvas boats. One of the Commando captains gave the instructions in "one, two, three" fashion; "one, grab the rails; two, put your feet in; three, let your fanny down." After the first trial, which was in broad daylight on the sunny Mediterranean, Clark asked the Commando captain—a big, rotund, boyish fellow—to tell him frankly how well they had done. "Very badly," he said, and announced that he would give them another lesson by personal demonstration at the next opportunity. This didn't come until they were actually ready to embark for the shore, having lain thirty-six hours watching through the periscope for the white light to show from the secret house. Finally, the light came; the five members of the party and the three Commandos gathered on the stern fin, prepared to board their canvas boats. The Commando captain said, "Now, watch me"; he grabbed the rail, got his feet in, and did *not* let his fanny down, and promptly tumbled overboard. They fished him out and thanked him for the exhibition. Although the waves were high, they made the landing successfully.

General Mast and some of his staff officers were there, accompanied by "Colonel McGowan." Mast had detailed plans for landings and capture of the ports and airdromes. Clark said that he was interested to note how closely the French plans, independently made, jibed with the Allied plans, which Clark, of course, did not disclose. Neither did he at any time indicate the D-Day. The French had thought an assault landing on the west coast to take Casablanca too risky. Their plan for capture of Casablanca was similar to the one we had at one time favored. That is, the landing of an assault force near Oran and then backtrack to Casablanca. Generally, there would be no difficulty about neutralizing airdromes, because Mast said, if Giraud approved, he will issue appropriate orders. There would be difficulty with the French Navy, and Mast and his secret group did not trust Darlan and advised against any dealings with him. However, Colonel McGowan was to have a meeting with Darlan's agent in the next day or two, at Darlan's request. Mast and his associates thought that the French Navy would put up a fight at the outset, which would soon diminish, and the Navy would acquiesce to the Allies. Whether we would gain such ships of the French Navy as were in African ports, and what would happen to French warships in Toulon and Alexandria, were questions left unsettled.

The formula developed by Ike for satisfying the demands of Giraud and Mast for Supreme Command seemed to be acceptable to Mast, except for Darlan. Giraud would be Governor and Mast, Deputy Chief of Staff of the Allied Expeditionary Force. Clark felt the situation did not permit complete disclosure of the part the British are to play, although the French acquiesced to the scheme of the British coming in to Algiers "in transit," to move quickly eastward to Tunisia.

The conference had started at 10 P.M., and at 7 A.M., while Clark was in the lavatory, Colonel McGowan had mysteriously received word that the local police were suspicious and that two of them were on their way to the rendezvous. When Clark returned to the meeting room he said he saw Frenchmen jumping in all directions. One of the more dignified generals, who had been in a bemedaled uniform with high leather boots, had already unclothed as far as his underwear, had his uniform in a valise, and was stepping through the window into the great out-of-doors. Because of the difference in language and the excitement, it took Clark some moments to discover the reason for all this. The Americans and Commandos were hurried into an empty wine cellar and sat there very quietly while the owner of the house, one of the secret French group, patiently assured the police nothing was wrong. As time passed, the cellar became a bit close. The Commando who had demonstrated boarding a canoe from the sub, was seized with a fit of coughing. Clark said that he didn't know whether to choke him or shoot him. Clark asked him if he would have some gum, but the Commando said that he had never chewed any. However, Clark took his own wad of gum from his mouth, handed it to the Commando, who chewed it gingerly and fortunately stopped coughing. Presently the novice gum-chewer asked Clark if he had another piece. "Why?" whispered Clark. "Because this one has no flavor."

I am not altogether clear as to what happened to the police, but during the time the landlord was reassuring the "law," the wine-cellar contingent stealthily made its way to the beach. The surf was high and launching of the light canvas boats difficult. Clark, completely disrobed except for his overseas cap with the two stars, got into one of the boats and sat on his clothes. They got off the beach, but hadn't gone far when a high wave overturned them, end for end, and all of Clark's clothes were lost. He and the others had to swim, but everyone got back on the beach; there stood Clark, naked as God made him, except for his overseas cap, and shivering. (He came back with his lucky dice—where he kept them, I don't know—maybe they're "floaters.") He went back to the house, but was not greeted hospitably by the owner, who feared the police were watching. However, Clark had a carbine* and succeeded in creating a satisfactory air of hospitality. Found a fancy silk French tablecloth in the house, dried, and draped the embroidery about himself like a sheik. A pair of trousers was found and he was partly clothed. It was too dangerous to stay at the house, so the whole party adjourned into the woods, to await a more favorable surf. Eventually, the surf calmed somewhat, but in the meantime Clark, McGowan, and party spent the day in the woods. When they got hungry, Colonel McGowan volunteered to return

* While going over this passage, Jack Goodman of Simon and Schuster asked me, "How did Clark keep that overseas cap, the dice, and the carbine?" My reply was and is, "I don't know."

to the rendezvous house to get a loaf of bread. Peering out of the woods, he jumped back suddenly and said that two Arabs were coming along the beach. He changed his course and detoured through the woods to seek the bread. Clark posted General Lemnitzer with a carbine to stand watch.

When the surf calmed somewhat, the three boats were launched and the party set out for the sub, now only a quarter of a mile offshore. The cockleshell in which Colonel Holmes was precariously perched was overturned. He was carrying some papers given him by McGowan; they were lost, but were properly in a weighted bag. The important information as to location of coastal batteries, airdromes, and other defenses was saved.

The submarine commander had maneuvered his craft so skillfully and had been such a fine officer throughout that Clark is recommending him for an appropriate American decoration. The torpedo men were frantic because en route they had seen several enemy ships, but the skipper would not permit attack because of the importance of his prime assignment. They broke radio silence long enough for Clark to get off the message asking for a Sunderland flying boat to meet them and take them into Gibraltar. The meeting place was quickly arranged; the flying boat arrived and the transfer was made. As Clark and party left the submarine, all hands were on deck and at attention. They gave three rousing "Hip, hip, hoorays." Clark carried back a list of names given him by the crew of persons to be telephoned in and about London, with appropriate messages appended to each name. Clark couldn't speak too highly of the quality and bravery of the skipper and his crew.

After arranging for some 2000 rifles to be sent immediately to Mast, as requested, Governor MacFarlane had shown him all over the Rock, and many details of the forthcoming event were discussed. He found the Rock peppered with innumerable caches of gasoline in cans, which if set afire by bombing would make the place hotter than hell and rather more uninhabitable. However, he found the legendary monkeys in fine fettle, but couldn't restrain the thought of roast monkey.

I asked Clark how he managed to put his long carcass to sleep on the sub. He said that there were five of them in a small compartment and he had had his feet in Lemnitzer's face. Also asked him what motivated the Frenchmen he met: were they fighting for national liberty, or were they merely scheming for personal position? "Well," he said, "until the police came, all I heard was *l'honneur, l'honneur, l'honneur*."

The Prime Minister and his office had been on the phone frequently to get a report from Clark. After he had finished reporting to his commander, Clark returned to headquarters to talk to the Prime Minister on the scrambler. The Prime Minister was so interested he asked Ike, Clark, and Beetle for luncheon Monday to get all the details.

During the evening we listened to the radio news and found practically all of it much more encouraging than at any other time since we have been here. The El Alamein battle has been launched, with General Montgomery announcing initial successes. Ike says that if quality and quantity of matériel and men can count in desert warfare against the wily Rommel, then Montgomery should win. He has 300 new Sherman tanks with 75s in completely revolving turrets. The obnoxious German 88s, which raised havoc with the British at Tobruk and through the retreat to El Alamein, will be countered by mobile 105s. Everything is being put into this operation, and it should succeed. Desert warfare, however, is difficult —as if any warfare were easy. Under the light cover of sand there is limestone, in which slit trenches are cut. It takes almost a direct hit to knock out such a trench. The British are laying a heavy barrage just as in World War I, with infantry to follow to neutralize mine fields and especially to cut through a path over which tanks and artillery may follow. With air superiority for the Allies, the equipment, men, and the will to win, we should turn the tide at last.

Ike had announced to Clark that on D-Day, or shortly thereafter, he would recommend Clark for the DSM. Clark had merely grinned and gone on with his story. Ike also said that he ought to write up this trip into a story. "It could be printed in a month, and I bet you someone would pay you a $1000 for it." My guess would be, if movie rights were included, $10,000. No one can estimate the value of the mission as yet— it has possibilities of having been of critical importance. The work of Colonel McGowan in arranging the contacts in North Africa has been sterling. However, the proof of the pudding is in the eating, and we will know on or about November 8.

Mast had insisted that if Giraud gives a favorable answer on Tuesday, as expected, that an American rather than a British submarine transport him from the south coast of France to Algiers. Also, he must be in North Africa by at least four days before D-Day, in order that appropriate orders can be given to neutralize defense points. Arrangements were made for either an American or a British submarine, and if the latter, under the nominal command of an American naval officer and carrying the American flag, to take Giraud from France to North Africa.

While the French Army seems to be friendly for this operation, the Navy is still a big question mark. We await news of McGowan's conference with Darlan's agent.

The Last Week in London Begins

LONDON, MONDAY, OCTOBER 26, 1942

A week from today we fly off to Gibraltar. The General was busy on numerous clean-up jobs regarding TORCH, but spent considerable time with Generals Spaatz, Eaker, and Hansell on plans for bombing the submarine bases in the Bay of Biscay, and the over-all strategy for operations in this theater.

Ike, Clark, and Beetle lunched with the Prime Minister, and Clark repeated his story of the submarine trip to Algiers, which the Prime Minister was delighted to hear.

LONDON, WEDNESDAY, OCTOBER 28, 1942

General Marshall sent a reply to the Commander-in-Chief's formal message summarizing Clark's secret trip. Naturally, the high-level officials "in the know" in Washington, particularly in the War Department, are following with great interest and considerable suspense the negotiations with respect to Mast and Giraud. General Marshall feels that if the results hoped for are obtained, it will make an interesting page in history. He is in complete accord with General Eisenhower as to decorating Clark and his party and asked that they be given his thanks for their courageous and able performance of a hazardous task.

Possibility of hostilities between French and Spanish Morocco might be precipitated by overenthusiasm of the French. The Commander-in-Chief cabled to the War Department today that such an eventuality would have a seriously adverse effect on our plans and requested that General Mast be advised through Murphy to instruct French commanders that incidents, however provocative, must not be permitted to lead to hostile action on the part of the French. Also, no development in this area, including even an advance by Spanish forces into French Morocco, will justify action by the French forces that might bring Spain into active collaboration with the Axis at this time. Arrangements are being effected here for representations to be made by the American diplomats, followed by the British Ambassador, to Franco on D-Day.

Captain Jerry Wright, USN, is to be flown to Gibraltar to await final instructions from General Ike relative to picking up General Giraud from the southern coast of France via submarine.

General Clark held a meeting with Air Vice-Marshal Sanders, Generals Doolittle, Gruenther, and Lemnitzer, Colonels Raff and Bentley, and

Major Yarborough to discuss means of getting parachute forces into Bône as rapidly as possible. Two plans are necessary: one in case resistance is expected; the second in the event none is expected. The first has been prepared; the second will be prepared at once. The latter will call for a landing by loaded air transports at La Senis (Oran) airport. No jump will be made at Bône unless conditions require it. If possible, it is desirable to conserve the parachute battalion for the operation to seize the airport near Tunis.

The decision as to which plan is to be put into effect will be made at Gibraltar and signaled to Bentley before he takes off.

Spent the night at the cottage. Telek is growing rapidly. He can now leap up the stairs, which he at first took only by one negotiated jump at a time.

LONDON, THURSDAY, OCTOBER 29, 1942

Ike made his farewell visit to the King today, and took Clark and Telek with him, but Telek stayed in the car. The King wanted to be brought up to date on developments, but most of all to wish the Allied Commander-in-Chief every success.

Ike also had a meeting with the British Chiefs of Staff. There is a British force being assembled either for striking where needed or as reserve for TORCH. It is made up of units that were originally intended for TORCH at the time we figured on six American divisions and six British. Now, however, we have nine American and four British, so, at Ike's request, the British are creating this reserve force of units originally assigned to TORCH. As usual, there are shipping difficulties. It will be called the Northern Task Force and will consist of one Army tank brigade and five infantry brigades. Ships will have to be made available from the TORCH convoys. As the Middle East is already short 100,000 men for the big battle with Rommel, shipping having been diverted to TORCH, ways and means of overcoming this perpetual shortage will have to be found.

The submarine under the nominal command of Captain Wright has left Gibraltar to pick up General Giraud at a point somewhere on the Gulf of Lyon.

Major Phillips has completed his arrangements for the thirty-odd war correspondents who are to accompany the various expeditions. Four of them will go to Gibraltar. It was suggested that the names of the principal commanders be released just prior to H-Hour, when news will be scarce.

No Comment

Today had my first experience with "cover" as it sometimes works. A story transmitted back from Washington today said: "General Eisenhower will return to Washington for consultation." Colonel Krum, PRO, came running; wanted to know what to tell newspapermen. Wishing to retain some aspect of integrity even with our PRO, I put him back in channel by taking him to the Chief of Staff and let Beetle give the official answer. He said that he was greatly disappointed that the story was out; it was supposed to be a secret, and so far as headquarters is concerned, the answer to inquiring newsmen is "no comment." Since then I have had personal visits from Ed Beattie, UP, and telephone calls from Bill Downs, CBS, and Ray Daniell, *New York Times*, each saying AP had carried the story and what is the truth? Simply repeated that I had heard the Chief of Staff tell the PRO thus and so—so my conscience is clear.

The Prime Minister called and wants Ike to lunch on Monday for a final check-up on detail and, no doubt, to wish him well.

The Eisenhower recall to Washington is still front-page news. According to a story in the papers this morning, a reporter asked about it at the President's press conference yesterday. The President had replied he would not like to comment on the movements of Army officers, and thought it inappropriate to print stories about the travels of officers, as such information is of value to the enemy.

This doesn't relieve concern both Ike and I feel for our wives, who are being duped, too. This morning Ike dictated a cable to General Marshall, asking him to tell Mrs. Eisenhower in strictest confidence, at an appropriate time, that he will be in Gibraltar, not in Washington. (He decided not to send it; was fearful of disclosure; didn't want even the code clerks to know the story is a phony.)

We are in a hectic transition: General Hartle and his staff are moving in, and General Eisenhower and his staff are moving out. Beetle is to have the cottage until he leaves for Algiers in two or three weeks. Then General Hartle is to have it.

Major Lee took me across the street almost on tiptoe this morning to see the scout car that is to be modified for use of the Allied Commander and associates in Africa. Lee's imagination is running away, but in the right direction. The scout car will also be fitted to pull a trailer to carry provisions, cooking equipment, a tent, and probably an artificial oasis. It will even have a motorcycle suspended from the rear, "unless the handle bars stick over the back so far they will gouge the General in the ribs."

We are gathering at the cottage tonight for a farewell dinner. Present will be Clark, Beetle, T. J., Ike, and myself.

I am leaving these notes for microfilming in the custody of Lieutenant Craig Campbell, who will be rear-echelon aide to Ike, and under the guardianship of Miss Jaqua. The original pages and one set of microfilm will be kept in a special safe at headquarters of the European Theater, with only Campbell having the combination here. One set of microfilm will be kept in another safe. Both Ike and I feel the notes are running too long—these will be cut to particularly interesting happenings. If nothing special happens on a given day, we will just pass it by. I have felt that someday some professional writer might take these notes and make a book of readable interest. While the original documents which are summarized here will be available to properly qualified researchers and writers at the War Department, I have attempted to make this chronicle sufficiently detailed to afford the essential information needed by any real writer to put together a book on rather short notice. If it is never published, I will have had my fun because it has kept me busy and, as Ike would say, out of mischief. Certainly Ike and I will someday (I hope) have fun going back over the pages telling of trying and absorbing days. Maybe in retrospect they will seem less trying than at the time we lived through them.

OCTOBER, 1942: *The tremendous battle for Stalingrad continued with both sides withdrawing and advancing in bitter, costly fighting. Stalin declared Stalingrad will be "twilight of the German Army." Elsewhere in Russia Germans steadily gained. After taking German strong points to straighten the El Alamein line, Alexander's forces with Eighth Army under Montgomery set off a frontal attack against the Axis, scoring several break-throughs. Heavy convoy losses in the Mediterranean forced Axis to use air cover, with loss of thirty-seven planes over Malta alone in one day. Attacks against Malta ceased when Axis lost 116 planes in one week. Record air raids on European targets continued to shatter Nazi production and supply lines. On Guadalcanal Japs succeeded in landing reinforcements despite heavy losses to naval and air attacks. After sharp naval engagements which cost the United States several units, including the carrier* Wasp, *the Jap Navy abandoned the southern Solomons.*

LONDON, SUNDAY AND MONDAY, NOVEMBER 1 AND 2, 1942
While Ike and I were at a private showing of *The Magnificent Dupe,* Sunday evening, two messages came in from Murphy via General Mar-

shall. Although we had told General Smith where we would be, Beetle had gone to dinner and forgotten to leave word where he could be reached, so by the time we got to the cottage to spend our last night there for some time, the telephone wires were hot. The Commanding General, who was supposed to be in Washington, was being paged at all the public theaters in town.

The more important message said that information coming to him from Giraud indicated a desire for at least two weeks' time for planning by Giraud after he got to North Africa. This, of course, Ike disapproved, since we have hundreds of ships on the high seas, headed for North Africa, and they can't be held at *statu quo* because of submarines and waning fuel supply. The exact D-Day, and the name of the Allied Commander-in-Chief, apparently, have not been disclosed. The other message from McGowan indicated that Darlan had told high French officials in North Africa before he returned to France that there was no immediate danger of any attack on North Africa. While the German and Italian Armistice Commissions have been active enforcing the terms of the French surrender, some of their personnel are planning to leave North Africa on November 4, according to information. It looks as if Giraud can leave France by November 4, and he knows the submarine nominally commanded by Captain Wright, USN, is waiting for him.

Guesses on plans were coming from every direction. The Germans were so sure the Allies were going to hit Crete that they had withdrawn troops by air from the Egyptian front prior to the recent attack by the Eighth Army. Drew Middleton, now of *The New York Times*, said that he had absolutely reliable information that the attack would be in Norway. This was before he left on an early convoy for TORCH. Another newspaperman, ordinarily "in the know," said that he had absolutely reliable information that General Eisenhower is returning to Washington and that General Marshall is already here. He has been seen coming out of the War Office. Said it was too bad General Eisenhower is to go back and hoped he would be returning to England in some new capacity.

Monday forenoon, the General had a staff conference of the theater generals.

This ends the notes for the time being, as we leave Monday night by train for Bournemouth and then by a squadron of seven Flying Fortresses for Gibraltar. (Weather was unfavorable for flying. Air-raid authorities wouldn't permit the train to stay in Bournemouth during the day, so the entire party returned to London and were ordered by General Ike to disperse, not to go to their offices. We spent the day at the cottage and in the evening went to a private showing of *The Road to Morocco*. Train again departed from London night of November 4.)

Arrival in Gibraltar

GIBRALTAR, FRIDAY, NOVEMBER 6, 1942

Leading a flight of six Flying Fortresses, left Hurn Airdrome, near Bournemouth, Thursday, 8:20 A.M., wave-hopped through bad weather and low ceiling three hours, then ceiling lifted, sun shone part of the time, and we reached Gibraltar at 4:20, circled for an hour, then landed. Crosscurrents around Rock and congestion in the runway imperiled landing. While we circled, three other Fortresses landed. There was an enemy plane around, Clark's Fortress having received word (never learned if ours did, even though listening on the intercom), and Clark's was alerted, with all guns manned. Probably a Ju-88 on reconnaissance. There were three Spitfires around. The fifth Fortress landed, too, but we learned later that the sixth, bearing T. J. and Doolittle, had not taken off because of some mechanical difficulty. It is supposedly on the way today.

Ike had to make a command decision at the English airdrome whether we would risk the flight, as the weather was abominable—rain, fog, and practically ceiling zero. Major Paul Tibbets,* piloting our *Red Gremlin*, was wary, but Ike said that we *had* to go.

We are guests of Governor Mason-MacFarlane at the Government House, once a convent; that is, Ike and I, but Lee is elsewhere, near by. Mickey is with the enlisted personnel, also in GH. Officers mess with the Governor, breakfast 8-9, come when ready; lunch 1:15, the same; but dinner all together and more formal. Easy atmosphere and efficient arrangements. Major Anthony Quayle, the Governor's Aide, has shown me the ropes, including air-raid shelter for occupants of this house. It is in a building a half block away, with heavily concreted roof, once heavily hit by French during retaliatory bombings (200 planes) for the Oran naval scrap. Our assignment is in the broadcasting studio, from which Gibraltar is served by both wired-radio and intermittent broadcasting. Quayle said enemy bombers generally come at 9 A.M., 12 noon, and 6 P.M.

Today Ike had what amounted to a staff conference. Present were Governor Mac, Admirals Cunningham and Bieri, Commodore Dick; Generals Clark and Anderson, and Brigadier C. V. O'N. McNabb, C/S for Eastern Task Force; Brigadier Mockler-Ferryman; Air Marshal Welsh and Air Vice-Marshal Sanders; Colonel Le Count H. Slocum and Colonel

---

* Rising to colonel, Paul Tibbets survived many thrills in air operations, the climax probably being the dropping of the first atomic bomb on Japan.

William Stirling; Lieutenant Jack Beardwood, Clark's Aide, and myself.

First topic was what to do about the Spanish if they start a fight with the French, or vice versa. Spain may seize the opportunity to expand their Moroccan territory to the Sebu; the French, feeling they now have strong allies, may get chesty and resist the Spanish.

This Ike does not want. He had issued instructions to the French, through Murphy, intended to prevent it. Meanwhile messages sent from Washington to London while we were en route from England to Gibraltar indicate Washington wants us to bluff the Spaniards.

Since diplomatic dealings of the Allies with Spain were set at the outset for the British, just as those with the French were made American, and since neither the British nor Ike's real boss, the Combined Chiefs of Staff, have issued him any instructions to the contrary, he is making his own decision: don't pick and don't permit, if at all possible, a fight with the Spaniards now.

Later, if we are strong enough to cope, O.K., but at the moment a bluffing game would be won by the Axis, for the Spaniards know well that German divisions can come into Spain through the Pyrenees and by air.

Because Giraud would ask for the moon if Ike saw him before the operation, Ike is considering sending him a letter setting forth again the declaration that the French will retain their territory, that Giraud can be civil and military leader of the French in Africa, and that when the French military forces there are sufficiently strong to defend their own country from the Axis, then Giraud can have complete control, except that we will wish to use French Africa as a base for going after Rommel's rear, or elsewhere. It is obvious that Murphy has had to talk very encouragingly as to French leadership.

How to hurry Giraud into Algiers was discussed. Ike wanted to fly an amphibian to the sub, marked with the French Tricolor, donate it to Giraud, have the proposed letter delivered, then fly him into the Maison Blanche airdrome near Algiers, to save time. But probably no amphibs available. May have to fly him to Gibraltar, give him an appropriate American-made plane like that French now using, Tricolor it, and fly him to Algiers from here. Or, Murphy might have a French plane at Algiers fly to Gibraltar, pick up Giraud, and return. Both arrangements under way.

Message for Giraud to send to Africa announcing his leadership and alliance with Allies to liberate French Africa will be prepared, sent to Giraud on the sub, let him approve, then sub can radio the O.K. back to Gibraltar, so it may be printed and dropped from planes over Morocco and Algiers. Meanwhile, the sub can't surface in that area in the daytime to signal whether Giraud is aboard, but we should know after dark tonight.

To complicate our situation, Ike discovered this morning that for recent messages coming from Murphy a cipher of poor quality has been used. It could be broken by the enemy in two hours. It is a dangerous departure from the prearranged code and route via Washington and London to Gibraltar. Then a high-grade code was used on one of Murphy's messages. As we had no key to the cipher, three messages from him had to be broken by analytical methods just as would be used on enemy messages. One was broken by our expert in nineteen hours. Washington, London, or Gibraltar didn't have the key. The slightly hysterical content of one advocated most strenuously simultaneous attacks by the Allies on D-Day at several points over the world, which we are unable to do, of course. Said Norway, France itself, and several points on the Continent should be assaulted at the same hour we move into North Africa.

At the conference Ike announced his intention of sending Clark promptly to Algiers to open headquarters and initiate dealings with French. This decision was against his personal desire, but two things force it. First, communications out of Algiers will be inadequate for the Commander-in-Chief to keep control of this widespread operation and keep in touch with London and Washington officials. Gibraltar is the spot for this. Second, Clark can make or defer decisions as deputy, depending on the situations that arise at Algiers, giving him the opportunity to say to the French that the Commander-in-Chief will have to pass on this or that.

Question of the French Navy was discussed. Nothing new; it is expected to be hostile, and only encouraging word was that from Mast via Clark that if Army acquiesced, Navy, as Ike put it, "would have no place to go but out and no place to come but in." As Navy controls coast artillery, and if its radio direction finders are working (Mast had planned to cut the wires), it can shoot the hell out of us at 14,000 yards. Cunningham proposed to "smother out" any opposition, but French Navy will have to start the shooting, as per directive, before we shoot. Ike concurred.

So far no reported losses, or even attacks, on any of our convoys, but Ike announced that word has been received that one is being shadowed. It is about 900 miles northwest of Gibraltar, en route from United Kingdom.

Conference again tomorrow, same time, 11 A.M.

While Ike is in his room, dictating a letter to Giraud, I might say the headquarters for this operation are damned well protected. They are about a half mile inside the Rock, about at ground level, and have only recently been completed. Everything cut out of solid rock. Large operations room is thirty feet high, big map on the wall, just like the movie *Coastal Command*. Office space very cramped; Ike and Clark share one small room; seven of us, aides and the assistant secretary, general staff, are in one room, two doors from Ike.

Living quarters are, however, good targets, and as we are on the second floor of the house, which is the top floor, if the Germans try real hard they can drive us to cover. British say that they don't bother about the Italian bombings; they miss and kill Spaniards. Everything reported heretofore about the Spanish defenses and guns adjacent to and overlooking the airdrome is absolutely true, as anyone could see, flying around as we did yesterday. If the Spaniards hop into this fight, we'll have to get in the Rock. Meanwhile, nearly Florida weather, or should I say Pinehurst?

Since writing the above, the Commander-in-Chief has completed the draft of his letter to Giraud, but it wasn't sent, since Giraud is not to be flown from the sub to Algiers but to Gibraltar.

D Minus 1

GIBRALTAR, SATURDAY, NOVEMBER 7, 1942

The landings, at least inside the Med, start at 1 A.M. in the morning. This is being hand-pecked at 2:15 P.M. H-Hour is just twelve hours, as TORCH is on Greenwich time and Gib has "summer time" the same as Britain and U. S.

Last evening Ike, Clark, and I left the Fortress HQ at 6:30. We sat in Ike's room at Government House and gassed until dinner, at 8:15, with the Governor and other guests. Ike and Clark were "opining" in our bull session that it wouldn't be long until they were either lions or lice. Yet, Ike said, he would rather be leading an invasion directly into France than this one; both lamented the necessity of dealing in such high matters politic as they had been compelled since this operation was started. Both said that they would be happier running divisions. Ike did say that they should be thankful for the opportunity offered them to make some mark in history, as few men ever even have the chance. Clark, who is to fly to Algiers with the advanced headquarters setup, said that if things go badly, he might just keep on flying into Central Africa, land or parachute, and keep the gobs of gold he is carrying for any contingency, including bribes to natives, if necessary. Will be a gentleman, however, and let Ike know where he is, but he'd better bring his own share of the gold swag with him. After dinner, General

Gruenther, my roommate, and Ike beat Clark and me at bridge, they holding all the cards.

The news was not too good this morning. At the 11 o'clock conference, Ike referred to the torpedoing of one of the American combat loaders (the *Thomas Stone*) inside the Med, carrying 1398 men, 52 officers, and important equipment. This cleared favorable, for by lunchtime another message said that it had been hit in the stern (rudder and propeller) and was in tow, probably making its landing, but late.

Ike wanted to be certain this headquarters would be advised affirmatively by the task forces when they land. The orders previously issued to the Naval Task Force Commanders are designed to avoid the breaking of radio silence, which, if broken, permits radio direction finders of the Axis to "pin-point" the sender, as Admiral Cunningham put it, "within ten yards." So the task leaders decide by 1530 today, or 3:30 this afternoon. If they decide to proceed to land, they say nothing to headquarters, and we, therefore, assume they will land, unless otherwise instructed by the C-in-C by 1630, or 4:30 this afternoon. If they hear nothing from Ike, the party is on. The first word we will get, if plans don't go awry, is when the parties actually get on shore.

The air transports carrying paratroopers from England to Oran, numbering some thirty-nine, are to be alerted to take off around 4 this afternoon, to reach Oran, flying over Spain, by dawn.

The real worry was the absence of word from the sub. We still don't know if Giraud was aboard, for no radio message was received during the night. Is the sub sunk? And was Giraud actually aboard? These questions seemed to be answered by a message from a Catalina dispatched to find the sub, ordered to follow a given course and on the surface, which indicated it is Gib-bound with Giraud aboard. But the uncertainty arises from garbled transmission. Message says, "Task gone. P219 [the sub] transmitter out." If G is on the Cat, it should arrive about 4 P.M. Civilian and military advisers think Ike has made a mistake in deciding not personally to see Giraud, feeling the story that he has been detained in London will leave a lasting impression of deception. Meantime, "time's a-wastin'."

Ike had heard that anyone visiting the Rock should see the monkeys because they are supposed to bring good luck. In addition, there is a British saying that as long as there are monkeys on the Rock, it will remain British domain. This afternoon, General Ike and I took a Ford staff car and, with Private Kronke driving, found the monkeys. Ike patted one on the head—not wanting to miss any opportunity for good luck.

Then he took me on a drive around narrow roads on ledges, with sheer drops of hundreds of feet. I sat on the outside and found myself leaning toward Ike. He noticed this, too, and enjoyed my discomfiture. I don't mind heights in an airplane, but I dislike driving along a cliff and looking straight down. I'm afraid I shall never hear the end of this.

At the conference Ike is meeting the press to background them on the operation. The four accredited correspondents, Wes Gallagher (AP), Chris Cunningham (UP), Nixon (INS), and Ure (London *Times* and Reuter's), got background material in Gruenther's and my room at Government House. Seemed content with press arrangements, but sorry they brought Arctic clothing.

After Ike's press roundup, the gang hung around with me after Ike left and expressed their complete satisfaction with arrangements and especially of the frank manner in which the C-in-C had given them extremely helpful guidance. Ike had taken his customary position: the press fellows know their job; the public needs to know all the facts, with only information helpful to the enemy to be withheld; the reporters want to win the war as quickly as anyone, so pitch in and help in your way; don't try to spy on us; you are part of the family and we expect to talk freely; if you violate the faith, "I'll shoot you, if I can catch you."

Communiqué, already drafted, awaits release in Washington and London, the former getting an hour's advance release ahead of London on account of feeling at home that London breaks all the good stories re American operations.

Going back to the conference, Admiral Cunningham said that his information indicates Axis is getting set to wallop us at Sicily, which shows our appraisal of the enemy's deduction as to our intentions was pretty good. The Admiral is sending cruiser considerably eastward in Med which will radio that it has intercepted a French merchant ship. Said French ship (cruiser transmitting) will let out a long squeal of enemy action against her. This will be heard by enemy and should fool him enough to give an hour or so more time before enemy planes on Sicily look for us off Algiers or Oran. Tricks to all trades.

Another item talked at the powwow was Murphy's fanciful suggestions, indicating he is nervous. On the other hand, Ike said that it may be that he is having trouble consoling the French, who may have become jittery because of the continued delay of Giraud. So perhaps Murphy is writing and showing messages to the French, thus trying to quiet their fears. After all, if the job's a failure, they're traitors to Vichy; if it succeeds, they're liberators.

If G doesn't show up, what to do? Have Mast act in his name? Issue proclamations in Giraud's name from here, so they can be broadcast to North Africa? Commodore Roy Dick, the Admiral's Chief of Staff, wisely pointed out that Mast, despite his previous commitment to carry on even if Giraud didn't get there, might change his mind when he learned that Giraud wasn't coming or was lost, for if Giraud were still in France, either Vichy or the Boche, or both, would immediately order him shot. But the sub had been radioed by the Royal Navy to surface at 2 o'clock and send a message, regardless of its own safety. Meanwhile Ike leaned toward having Mast go through with the promise, as he has gone too far to turn back.

General Anderson, to speed his eastern advance, wants to fly in to-morrow. Clark planning fly tomorrow, too. Will have fighter escort.

At lunch, with the press affair intervening before, Clark reported receipt of the message, heretofore given, indicating that Giraud was on the Cat.

If this thing reads as crazily as I think it must, it's because I started to write it at Government House, then picked up the portable and trundled back to the cavernous headquarters because I was sure I was missing something. Sure was—Giraud was being brought direct into headquarters from the seaplane base and Ike would see him here. Then G and the three other French officers presumably will hop to Algiers tomorrow. They're in Ike's office now, Lee standing guard, having just escorted them in. I have just arranged with Major Quayle at GH to move Al Gruenther's and my stuff out of our big room, which has an unused cot, add another cot, and, if necessary, shanghai Clark's room next door for the anxiously awaited G. We won't use our beds tonight, anyway. Mickey's getting out the Scotch, but do they drink it?

While the powwow is parlez-vooing, I should record that the Fortress that didn't get off when we did (brakes didn't work, which disclosed batteries had run down) finally got off yesterday and arrived O.K., except it had been attacked by three or four Ju-88s 200 miles off Cape Finisterre. Copilot hit in the arm, and a few bulletholes in the ship. One Ju is sworn by two of the gunners to have been seen smoking and plunging into the ocean. T. J. said that his reaction was one of complete anger, the more he thought of it, and also that since they had not heard of the safe arrival of but two of the five other Fortresses, this explains the silence, and so he was worried to death. General Jimmy Doolittle was aboard that one, as were the PRO, Major Phillips, Mr. Mack, Dr. Matthews, General Lemnitzer. T. J. wanted to get in the fighting and he surely did. Full of pep today; proud an adjutant general got shot at.

Ike got a cable from the Prime Minister saying that he felt "the Rock of Gibraltar is safe in your hands."

Beetle came through this P.M. with a message that the Prime Minister was hard to hold during Ike's plane trip here. Called Beetle and others at ten-minute intervals after the plane appeared overdue. When message finally arrived that plane had landed, General Ismay and Beetle took it to him. The PM exclaimed: "Don't tell me he's drowned!" Then Beetle assured the "former naval person" Ike was safe, and the PM said, "I never had the slightest idea that it would be otherwise."

Naval commander of ETF reports the *Thomas Stone*, the U. S. combat loader that was hit, is being left with antiaircraft and/or antisubmarine protection, but the convoy must go on if TORCH is to succeed. He asked instructions. Don't suppose his decision will be countermanded.

Captain Jerry Wright, USN, who was the nominal skipper of the P219, has just been in. Said he got Giraud off two days ago. The garbled message was sent, "Task done." How it got into "gone" the cryptos will have to answer, as if it matters now. Had good growth of beard, clothes were greasy, white shirt no longer the same. The sub's radio had gone haywire.

Forgot to mention some really good news. The PM had Beetle cable that General Montgomery had reported the Eighth Army's recapitulation. It was 350 tanks destroyed or captured; 20,000 prisoners; 400 guns, and thousands of vehicles, etc. Army is south of Mersa Matruh—and advancing. This ties in with the intercept of message from Rommel to German General Staff in which Rommel begged for aid immediately or his force would be annihilated. Seems to be coming true, and the truer the better.

Hubbub and bustle around the place like Election Eve.

Murphy hollering, "Where is Giraud?" by radio. Didn't bother Ike after talking with General Gruenther, who said he was handling the answer from "soup to nuts."

We're definitely going in as planned. A message from Ike to TORCH forces at 5:20 P.M., "Warning order. H-Hour confirmed November 8. For East and Center 1 A.M. For West about 4:30 A.M." Find weather and surf, about which we have worried so long, are much better than anticipated.

What's happening in the conference comes in a message Ike sent to the Combined Chiefs of Staff. Sent at 6:42 P.M. Says still conferring, and that Giraud will not broadcast statement until after he reaches North Africa. Details for transporting him there not completed.

This reversed the earlier outlook, when London was advised that a statement was anticipated from Giraud and would be cabled to London for broadcasting from there, in the hope it might do some good. As

Giraud will not make a statement now, no need to hold the broadcast people.

Rumor around our madhouse of a hot message just in that French Chief of Staff at Oran has been placed under virtual arrest. •

The text of the weather report re Atlantic indicates that Providence or one of Ike's lucky charms is effective. The high swells from the Atlantic, crashing against the shores on and around Casablanca, have been considerably nullified by ten-foot waves going southward from area of the entrance to the Strait of Gib. That's the reason for the new estimate of three- to five-foot swells at Mehedia and Fedala, and of four to six at Safi, but with choppy sea.

Message from Beetle in London reports that success in Egypt is having beneficial effect for Allies in Spanish Morocco. Also that the Moors are pleased.

I rather abruptly broke into the conference, announced the presence of the escort to take General Giraud to dinner at Government House. It was clear the discussions were, as Ike had figured, long, tedious, and demanding. Haven't the details yet, except G isn't issuing a statement for broadcast tonight, that Ike was red-faced from talk, and the whole thing looked a mess. G has brought out two of his sons and a captain who speaks English. The French General does not, and Colonel Julius Holmes is interpreting.

A message has just been shown to me before it went to the mimeographers for distribution to the staff. It is an SOS to all ships from the S.S. *Janine*, claiming a bomb attack and specifying latitude and longitude. This is Admiral Cunningham's pet scheme to fool the enemy long enough to give our convoys off Oran and Algiers an hour or more before being snooped by enemy planes.

Ike and Clark went to dinner at The Mount, Admiralty mess, as guests of the Royal Navy. Ike came back about 10:30 and Giraud returned from Government House. On a letter he had been preparing for General Marshall summarizing events of recent days, and on which he had already placed one P.S., to the effect that Giraud had just arrived, tonight he added another in pen that G insists that he be the Allied Commander-in-Chief. In other words, Giraud won't help now. What a disappointment!

Meantime, Major Laurence B. Meacham, General Clark's aide, who had been sent to bring G from the seaplane base, related that Captain André Beaufré, who was one of the three accompanying the General, claimed we had told them the assault wouldn't take place for another month.

Lee was just in the sanctum to get a letter signed and overheard Clark phrasing a statement to Colonel Holmes, as interpreter, something like this: "We would like the Honorable General to know that the time of his usefulness to the Americans for the restoration of the glory that once was France is *now*. We do not need you after tonight." Cold turkey, Lee thought. No point in sending him to North Africa if he doesn't play ball now.

The text of the communiqué released for 1 A.M. GMT Sunday morning announces that landings are taking place at "numerous points" on the shores of French North Africa and, for the first time publicly, the long-held secret that Lieutenant General Dwight D. Eisenhower is C-in-C of the Allied forces. But at Ike's insistence, the communiqué is not datelined with his name.

11:25 P.M. Eastern Task Force is told that "our friends report probably impossible to light red flares. Guides will be waiting near Deux Moulins, Algiers, at White light. . . . Good luck."

The thirty-nine transport planes carrying paratroopers were ordered this afternoon to do their stuff, taking off about now, provided, in the judgment of the commanding officer, the weather is satisfactory for the long and hazardous trip to Oran from the U. K.

Giraud has left Ike's office. Lee strapped on his trusty six-shooter and is escorting him out to the fresh air.

After G left, an outgoing message, signed "Giraud," to Mast in French indicated that if the proclamations weren't satisfactory, not to publish them. The original looked suspiciously like Ike's hand-printing, and presumably was sent at Giraud's request. Transmission may be somewhat slow—perhaps publication will have already occurred.

Lieutenant Jack Beardwood, Clark's aide, who is likewise keeping a running account for Clark's diary, has just been told by his boss that the last thing he asked interpreter Holmes to say to G was: "Old gentleman, I hope you know that from now on your ass is out in the snow."

Clark has just been out to the aides' bull pen and given us an up-to-the-minute "fill-in." Said Ike would argue for an hour with Giraud, then he'd rest while Clark took over. Offered him the governorship, virtually the kingship, of North Africa, with finances to build an army and all national defenses, plus all kinds of support to make an effective fighting force of the French, but the old General declined in seven languages, each meaning "Prestige!" Wanted to know what people would think of him, what of his family, if he didn't become the Allied Commander-in-Chief within forty-eight hours. Clark said G had nothing to offer, and wasn't actively helping at this crucial hour. Butcher says if the fellow doesn't contribute now, and by his failure more American and British lives are lost than need be, why in hell should we ever do anything for him? If he doesn't love his France enough to take the kind of leadership and support that are offered, we go on without him. It's true his name is being used on proclamations in Africa tonight and the "stop" message probably won't get there in time to take his name off them. After all, Giraud and Mast have been encouraging this operation.

"I am General Giraud," he would say. "I'm like Joffre. My prestige! My family!"

Clark ventured that G would sit on the fence for forty-eight hours, see how the assaults go, and then make up his mind. Meanwhile Ike is dictating complete report for the Combined Chiefs of Staff.

PART TWO

The Invasion of North Africa

NOVEMBER, 1942 TO JULY, 1943

TORCH—at Last

It's now 12:40 A.M. Sunday, twenty minutes from H-Hour, GMT. I'm going to join Mickey at Government House and listen to the broadcasts starting at 1. Both the President's proclamation and guarantee and the C-in-C's, spoken in French, are on the program. Ike's voice isn't really Ike's; it's Colonel Holmes'. I don't want to miss my favorite radio hour.

Enemy and Giraud take note of the latest report from the *Thomas Stone*. Twenty-four landing craft, carrying the 39th U. S. Infantry, left the vessel and are moving under their own power, escorted by a destroyer, 140 miles to make the attack.

"Landing successful, A, B, and C Beaches, Eastern Task Force," Commodore Dick reported to Ike, just as I delivered to Mr. Mack and Dr. Matthews, sitting in his office, a quart of gin for the former and a bottle of Scotch for the latter. Since they were a bit sleepy, I had asked Major Tony Quayle to send some down from Government House. Just a bootlegger. But the news is welcome. Admiral Cunningham, in turtleneck sweater and wide braces (suspenders, as the Americans say), followed Dick to Ike's office to add his good word. (2:40)

3:15 A.M.—The radio stuff didn't get started, so far as I could find on the dial, until 1:20, but then it was on in several spots, with transcriptions of the President's voice, Ike's via Holmes', and a spokesman for the Allied C-in-C giving instructions to the French and other citizens of North Africa. Ought to be a good story for Sunday A.M.s at home.

While listening, heard planes, probably Spits, in the air, testing their guns with quick vigorous bursts; getting ready for dawn, which is only three hours away. Searchlights sweep the skies over Gib. Partly cloudy, stars showing here and there, balmy as Florida in April.

Our news of progress coming from intercepts of radio messages back and forth from ships to assaulting parties.

At 3:22 the Center Task Force (Oran) reported landings at two beaches, identified as Y and Z, the latter being unopposed. At 3:32 report of successful landing at X beach, with ships going inshore for unloading.

Garbled intercept from Center Force: "Landings unopposed. Broken xxx shooting began. Do not start a fight unless you have to xxx."

Ike completed earlier a long message to the Combined Chiefs of Staff, reporting his unsatisfactory conference with Giraud.

The news is good from the two Mediterranean forces, where the seas are quite smooth, and General Gruenther is authorized by Ike to let the press use this news.

Had an air alert about 4:30, but we wouldn't have known in the Rock except for word carried in by Major Quayle, who accompanied the Governor and General Anderson on a visit to Ike. Big tunnel was alive with people seeking shelter. The two hashed over with Ike the Giraud situation while we were having coffee. He had been placid as a lamb at the dinner, also appeared reasonable, but he had not referred to his talk with Ike and Clark. Ike doesn't want G in Africa if he won't help, although G wants to go as a spectator. Perhaps he will soften when he finds how well the operation is going (knock wood—haven't heard from Patton, who was due to start landing at 4:30).

Ike and Clark got their cots in, to get some sleep. I had an hour around 3:30, under the table.

De Gaulle will be told the whole story today by the Prime Minister. Will deal a little more liberally on Madagascar, to alleviate hurt feelings. Giraud said de Gaulle was egotist. Pot calling kettle black.

Percy Winner, once a CBS newscaster, now in political-warfare activity on this staff, just dropped by with a note that the transmitter for broadcasting softening stuff along the west coast has been heard at Gib. Station is aboard ship and using wave length of the Rabat transmitter, without interference, playing the *Marseillaise, The Star-Spangled Banner,* and calling: "Hallo, Maroc."

5:45—Fredendall radioes: "Landing continues unopposed."

6:58—Winner reports Paris radio did not mention TORCH in regular 6:45 newscast.

Trouble in Algiers harbor. What's holding up Patton's report? And what about the paratroopers due at dawn at the Oran airdrome?

Lee sleeping like a big Indian, arms crossed, atop two tables. Air in here pretty punko.

Message from Admiral H. K. Hewitt, Naval Commander, Patton's force, just in, says operation proceeding on schedule. Good news.

Vichy radio passed up TORCH. Probably don't know what to say.

Went down to the lavatory and shaved. Cold water. Ike came in, did the same. Wondered what the American papers would look like this morning. Both relieved that indications of strategic surprise found the missing page of the diary was burned. Glad the gals at home know where we are now . . . approximately . . . at least what we are doing. Clark off for Algiers soon.

Three of the thirty-nine paratroop planes down . . . two force-landed, presumably in Spain, third thought at Gib airdrome.

Vichy has now broadcast that Darlan and Juin are in Algiers, directing Navy and Army. Pétain will reply to President. Obvious Axis dictation. Claim heavy bombardment of Oran and Algiers, with attempted landing in Algiers harbor, but all repulsed. Attempt to stir French to defend. Fredendall still doing O.K.—Center Task Force. Still waiting to hear from Patton . . . and paratroopers. Time—8:10 A.M. Royal Navy message says "unknown" vessel twelve miles away from reporting ship. . . . While French Navy seemed to lay quiet during night, looks like there will be some naval scrapping today.

Cunningham wants fifty Spitfires on Maison Blanche airdrome today to meet expected 100 German-Italian bombers that will attack ETF ships.

8:30—Four hours since Western Task Force was due to go in—but Patton's orders did say "about."

Ike cabled Combined Chiefs of Staff at 7:40 that Admiral Hewitt had started Plan A on schedule. But assaults on Algiers and Oran harbors meeting resistance. No reports of captured airdromes yet.

9—MAISON BLANCHE AIRDROME CAPTURED. Hooray.

Merchant ship, apparently loaded with troops, caught trying to escape from Oran. Escorted to harbor by British warship.

Darlan grabbed by Ryder, T. J. just informs me.

Ike has decided to have another talk with Giraud; meeting at Government House at 10:30.

Darlan not actually grabbed (dammit), but expected to be taken into protective custody. Message from Beetle from Murphy. Wants Ike's concurrence. Cripes, get him.

Coastal batteries causing trouble—French Navy controls them.

Had to knock off a French destroyer at Algiers.

Oran airport reported on fire. What becomes of thirty-six paratroop planes?

Ike and Clark off to see Giraud. Lee freshening up.

Rodney, with her sixteen-inch guns, gives notice "intends to engage target, main armament." Meaning the coastal batteries at Oran.

H.M.S. Aurora reports two French destroyers stopped and damaged; another stopped and returning Oran.

Blida airdrome (thirty miles northwest of Algiers) has been captured.

Indirect news from Patton is conveyed from fairly reliable French sources, saying they have lost their 75- to 105-mm. guns around the perimeter of Safi, south of Casablanca, to the Americans. But nothing direct, as yet.

Fate of paratroops in doubt. Colonel Vandenberg, 12th Air Force C/S, whom I just met in the hall, says reports are contradictory and they don't know heads from tails at the moment. One is that Maison Rouge and Blida fields were mined and couldn't be used. Awaiting improved communications.

French warship (cruiser?) sorties and attacked U. S. escort vessels in Western Force, message just received states.

Pétain has replied to Roosevelt, and it is being repeated periodically by Vichy radio. Most important thing he said was: "France and her honor are at stake. We are attacked and we will defend ourselves. That is the order I give."

Indirect word from Patton has reached HQ through Admiral Hewitt, although only two reports since H-Hour. At 7:30 A.M. he said he was being opposed in all areas. Later said landing effected at Fedala with little resistance and that batteries at Chirqui Point had been silenced.

Safi landing party at least partially ashore and meeting resistance at airport.

Three squadrons Hurricanes and Spitfires dispatched to Blida and Maison Blanche airdromes. Tafaroua airdrome, near Oran, also captured and ready for use. Twenty-four Spits of 12th Air Force have left for Tafaroua.

After his conference with G today, Ike sent a message to the Combined Chiefs. Said he had just concluded gentleman's agreement with Giraud that is entirely acceptable to him and is fully compatible with his direct subordination to the Combined Chiefs of Staff. The basis of the agreement is exactly that offered Giraud throughout the long conference of yesterday. Giraud is recognized as leader of the effort to prevent the Axis aggression in North Africa, the Commander-in-Chief of all the French forces in the region, and the Governor of the area. As Commander-in-Chief of the Allied American and British Forces, Ike will co-operate with him to the fullest possible extent and will work in closest collaboration with him.

Giraud will go to Africa to do his utmost to stop all resistance to us and to begin organizing the French forces for employment against the Axis. While there will undoubtedly be future difficulties, Ike is confident that this agreement represents a great step in advancing our interests here and is truly delighted that we were able to bring it about. Present at the conference were General Clark, Admiral Cunningham, General Mason-MacFarlane, and the Commander-in-Chief.

Ike was tired but happy. Took an hour's nap on a field cot in his office-cave until Giraud, now in most co-operative spirit, came to call on him. Then it became a matter of satisfying G's need for a super-radio-equipped plane for personal use, modern fighters to train his pilots, and of rationalizing his insistence for an onslaught of southern France in sixty days.

Just in to answer Ike's bell, and here's what he handed me, in his own hand:

Worries of a Commander

1. Spain is so ominously quiet that Gov. of Gib. reports himself uneasy. No word from any agent or Ambassador.

2. No news from Task Forces. Reports few and unsatisfactory.

3. Defensive fighting, which seemed halfhearted and spiritless this morning, has blazed up, and in many places resistance is stubborn.

4. No Frenchman immediately available, no matter how friendly toward us, seems able to stop the fighting. (Mast, et al.)

5. Giraud is in Gibraltar, manifestly unwilling to enter the theater so long as fighting is going on.

6. Giraud is difficult to deal with—wants much in power, equipment, etc., but seems little disposed to do his part to stop fighting.

7. Giraud wants plants, radios.

8. We are slowed up in eastern sector when we should be getting toward Bône-Bizerte at once.

9. We don't know whereabouts or conditions of airborne force.

10. We cannot find out anything.

Colonel William Stirling, the boss's British Military Assistant, but who spends most of his time assisting General Gruenther, and who has a touch for protocol, thought I ought to advise Government House if the General plans to have dinner there this evening. Busted in, General Doolittle as well as Clark present, but before we could settle this matter of state, in came Admiral Cunningham with a message he thought possibly the C-in-C would want to see. Said DARLAN WANTS TO NEGOTIATE. And wants to know where they can meet. Ike spluttered. Then, what to do with Giraud? Will they work together now?

Cunningham said to remember what the Prime Minister had said: "Kiss Darlan's stern if you have to, but get the French Navy."

Now Ike has one hell of a headache, and Darlan in his message refuses to deal with any other Frenchman.

Neglected to say U. S. Navy reports that Patton's force has taken Safi, has landed practically all of its first stuff, and is generally doing O.K. But French Navy has been pesterin' and a naval battle is under way.

All this when Ike and I had sort of got our minds together on making some noodle soup in our room, if we could get it boiled without offending our host, and then to bed. He needs a rest damned badly.

Darlan Offers to Negotiate

GIBRALTAR, MONDAY, NOVEMBER 9, 1942
(D plus 1)—Probably yesterday's notes should have included the comment of the Combined Chiefs of Staff about Giraud, based on Ike's report of their first meetings on December 7. In the rush I missed it. The Chiefs say that regardless of the outcome of negotiations with Giraud, "we wish you to know that the stand you have taken meets with our complete approval." They only regret that the C-in-C has been forced to devote so much time to this purpose at this critical time.

The day after D-Day for TORCH, I retrieved a memorandum from General Ike's cavern-office written in his own hand, part of which is reproduced on the following page. The full text follows:

> Inconsequential thoughts of a commander
> during one of the interminable "waiting periods."

War brings about strange, sometimes ridiculous situations. In my service I've often thought or dreamed of commands of various types that I might one day hold—war commands, peace commands, battle commands, administrative commands, etc. One I now have could never, under any conditions, have entered my mind even fleetingly. *I have operational command of Gibraltar!!* The symbol of the solidity of the British Empire—the hallmark of safety and security at home—the jealously guarded rock that has played a tremendous part in the trade development of the English race! An American is in charge and I am he. Hundreds of feet within the bowels of the Rock itself I have my CP. I simply *must* have a grandchild or I'll never have the fun of telling this when I'm fishing, grey-bearded, on the banks of a quiet bayou in the deep south.

Again—what soldier ever took the trouble to contemplate the possibility of holding an *Allied* Command. And of all things, an Allied Command of ground, air and Naval Forces? Usually we pity the soldier of history that had to work with Allies. But we don't now, and through months of work we've rather successfully integrated the forces and the commands and staffs of British and American contingents—now we have to get together with the North African French!! Just how the French angle will develop only the future can tell, but I am proud of this British-U.S. command! The final result I don't know—but I do know that every element of my command—all U.S. and British services are working together beautifully and harmoniously! That's something.

How I'd like a few reports. I'm anxiously waiting word of:

> West Coast operations.
> Oran operations.
> Giraud's movements and intentions.
> Darlan's proposals.
> Movements of Italian air.
> Intentions of Spain.

Inconsequential thoughts of
a commander during one of
the interminable "waiting periods"

War brings about strange,
sometimes ridiculous situations.
In my service I've often thought
or dreamed of commands ~~that I might one day hold~~ —
various types — war com... etc
force commands, battle commands,
administrative com... do, etc —
One I now have could never,
under any conditions, have
entered my mind even
fleetingly. I have greater!
command of Gibraltar!!
The symbol of ~~totality of the~~ the British
Empire — the hallmark
of safety & security at home—

Giraud and his three associates got off by Hudson bomber for Algiers around 11 this morning. G is supposed to broadcast from Algiers tonight.

Clark and party, to open the advance base, got off for Algiers in another plane, about the same time. Of course Algiers surrendered last evening at 7. Clark will talk to Darlan when he gets to Algiers.

Captain Jerry Wright, USN, who was sent in British sub P219 to retrieve G, handed me his personal notes, "Log of Getaway," which I am keeping in our safe. When G was being transferred from boat to the sub, he slipped, fell into the Med, was damned nearly drowned, but some sailor caught him by the coat collar.

A signal came from Patton, who said all resistance to the assault at the beaches has been overcome. Confirmed capture of port and town of Safi, but air opposition continues. Silenced batteries at Safi, Cape Blondin, and Cape Fedala. Four bombers destroyed on ground at Rabat. AA fire silenced Fedala. One enemy destroyer sunk, one cruiser damaged.

So there would be no misunderstanding of Clark's authority, Ike had sent a letter with Clark to General Giraud. It confirmed the decision to set up the advance echelon of Allied Force Headquarters in Algiers on November 9, with Clark and a small nucleus of the staff.

General Clark is empowered to make any necessary decision in the name of the Allied Commander, particularly with a view to speeding the movement of our troops to the east in the hope of occupying Tunisia before the Axis. Any arrangements that Giraud desires to take up with Allied headquarters should be conducted through Clark.

Ike asked Giraud to keep Clark constantly informed as to steps Giraud is taking to stop French resistance, so that we can devote our full attention to meeting Axis threats.

To Murphy at Algiers, Ike also sent a letter via Clark, advising Colonel McGowan, who can now drop his *nom de guerre*, that as Civil Affairs Officer of Allied Headquarters he is to report for instructions to Clark.

Spain apparently will remain neutral, judging from a message from Ambassador Hayes to Secretary Hull, and relayed to Ike. Further information from British diplomatic sources was more explicit but of same intent.

Jean Bart, French cruiser, and several destroyers badly damaged at Casablanca harbor. Cruiser burned out. Fear blocking of narrow entrance for Casablanca harbor, which would mess up the follow-up convoys.

The Du Santon battery near Oran is so situated that the first bombardment of the *Rodney,* with its sixteen-inch shells, apparently did no particular good. Trajectory of fire too low. CTF calling for bombers. None at Gib; trying to get some Flying Fortresses down from U. K. Congestion at Gibraltar airdrome sufficiently relieved now to accommodate about five B-17s. Message from Naval Commander Troubridge, Center Task Force, advises that "Unloading over beaches proceeds but is retarded by heavy swell and delayed in arrival of LCTs. *Aurora* and *Jamaica* engaging two destroyers escaping from Oran at 11. One badly damaged anchored inshore under batteries. The others returned damaged to Oran covered by shore batteries. Enemy shore batteries active and accurate up to 24,000 yards. H.M.S. *Ferndale* giving support fire at Mostaganem, where enemy giving trouble to battalion of U. S. troops on eastern flank. H.M.S. *Gardenia* sunk. Survivors in H.M.S. *Vetch*. No further details. Will send aircraft carrier homeward when Spitfire squadron arrives from Gib to give cover."

If 24,000 yards is correct, that figures out to about fourteen miles. It's the toughest battery we have encountered, so far as we have heard. Ike wonders if Fredendall isn't sending infantry with mortars to blow 'em up from the rear. As target the battery is well hidden.

Ike radioed his thanks to Commander at Malta for his support of sending, as prearranged, bombers from Malta to attack the Elmas airdrome on Sardinia.

Talked to Mr. Mack at dinner. He thinks French leaked on time of assault. Ike doesn't, because we achieved tactical and actual surprise; Gruenther thinks the greatest in all military history re entire operation.

To bed about midnight, but got word before retiring that both G and Clark had landed safely.

Oran Surrenders

GIBRALTAR, TUESDAY, NOVEMBER 10, 1942

(D plus 2)—Two French cruisers reported left Toulon. They'll get sunk if they come nosing about. Final assault to take Oran planned for today. Force H, the large covering fleet, will bombard Du Santon, that effective coastal battery near Oran. Reports from CTF are that civilians are very friendly to American troops; captured French soldiers only obeying orders of superior officers, many are pro-Vichy, and only grievance is over lost comrades.

Vichy claims we have landed at Philippeville, but untrue. Weather delayed this eastern movement, but will get under way soon as weather permits beach landings again.

Damaged Italian cruiser has returned to Palermo "without forty feet of its bow."

French appear to be attempting block dredged channel into Bizerte port. We need it.

Vichy has broken off relations with U. S. Tut, tut. Ike has notified his commanders in the field.

He also radioed Fredendall, CTF, of progress of WTF and ETF. Resistance ceased Algiers area. Ike told Fredendall that his mission is at a critical point. "Clean up that situation today and write your own ticket."

But bad news came from General Anderson, who was trying to get his forces eastward from Algiers, to reach and take Tunisia ahead of the Germans. The news was from a French Colonel, René G. Cerardot, apparently in command of El Aouina airfield at Tunis. He and three other officers had flown to Algiers and reported that forty German bombers had landed at his field the morning of the ninth. Even more disturbing is that after Pétain's broadcast denunciation of Darlan, Admiral Jean Pierre Esteva, the Governor General of Tunisia, had ordered a "friendly reception" of the German planes.

ORAN SURRENDERS, Lee laconically announces. Thought he'd bring back some mail. We had just heard two pouches were in, and we all want some news from home. Oh, yes, Oran quits. Would like to see that tough battery; must have been blown to hell. Will someday. Just congratulated Ike. Said good news coming fast. British sub has just hit an Italian cruiser. Ike's grin wide.

Our first news of Oran surrender comes from Vichy, Gruenther tells me. Have arranged for press fellows to see Ike at 3:30. He has already sent flash cable to Combined Chiefs announcing Oran's fall. Naval units coming along, too. Hope they are usable, also docks and harbor. *Aurelius* on way into harbor to see if it has been blocked.

British have lost large destroyer *Martin*; blew up; another destroyer detailed hunt for survivors until sundown. Looks grim.

Ike penciled a short directive to "Georgie" Patton to hurry up and take Casablanca—"the only tough nut left is in your hands." Algiers in bag for two days; Oran now in.

Message from War Office, London, advises that it has received no indication as to date unusual German or Italian troop movements. Jerries bombed and sank the *Leedstown*, transport, no troops aboard, at Algiers today. American ship.

Clark has reported from Algiers that he has forced Darlan to sign what amounts to an armistice, or else be taken into custody. Darlan has signed orders to all land, air, and sea forces in North Africa to stop fighting. These are being dispatched by air, telephoned, and in general hurried to beat hell. Press conference O.K. Ike asked press to play down extent of

fighting at Oran. Job now is to reorganize our forces and get after the
real enemy—the Axis. Paid highest possible tribute to U. S. and Royal
Navies, operating under the great Admiral Cunningham.

Casablanca Surrenders

GIBRALTAR, WEDNESDAY, NOVEMBER 11, 1942
(D plus 3)—Also Armistice Day. Gruenther was on C/S duty all night
and came to Government House early this morning to give the C-in-C
the news. Patton's force had reached the outskirts of Casablanca, and
had just got an airdrome. U. S. Navy had obtained command of the air.
Reports still fragmentary from Western Task Force, but Al had discovered
they had failed to classify their messages as urgent, so when received by
the Navy at Gib were naturally placed at the bottom of the pile in the
deciphering room. Thus there were reports but they were simply not completely processed, owing to tremendous rush. Meanwhile, Army has
established its own radio channels from Patton's force to Gibraltar.

But there was much more important news. Darlan's order to stop fighting had gone out. Then Pétain fired Darlan. Darlan then sought to
rescind the order. Clark had said, "Damned if you do." Darlan then said,
"Then I must consider myself a prisoner." Clark said, "That's O.K. by
me." Guard was set, and Darlan gave his word as a gentleman that he
wouldn't seek to communicate outside or to escape. Meanwhile, Giraud
had become incensed at our dealing with Darlan, who, incidentally, in
his order had assumed command of all French forces in North Africa, a
job which we had publicly committed to Giraud. Then came news that
the Germans were moving into unoccupied France. Clark then succeeded
in getting Darlan and Giraud and their respective leaders together. "The
time has come for Frenchmen to get together," Giraud had said dramati-
cally. Fate of the French fleet was discussed. Darlan said that he would
order fleet out of Toulon, it being ready to sail, if it is true Germans
have started into unoccupied France. But this movement was not confirmed, and Clark doubted effectiveness of Darlan order to fleet. Nevertheless, is inquiring where fleet should be sent, if we get it.

Clark had wanted to know if Darlan's order to stop shooting had
caused cessation of hostilities at Oran. Was advised by Fredendall that
French commander at Oran had not sought the capitulation talks, so
the order was not effective. Oran was taken by hard fighting, not by
Darlan's order.

Fredendall had reported armistice came at 12:30, with French troops ordered to remain in barracks and prisoners exchanged. They had 600 Americans. Ike said, "Why did they ever surrender?" Worst news was that seven ships and a floating drydock had been sunk in Oran harbor. Didn't say whether scuttled or shot up by our fire. Anyway, entrance to harbor partially if not completely blocked, and we have the first follow-up convoy for Oran due in there today. It will have to mill around in the Med, imperiled by sub and enemy aircraft, until we find if it can go into harbor. Admiral Cunningham has sent a salvage ship from Gib to Oran to blast passage or raise sunken vessels.

Clark and staff are staying at the St. George Hotel in Algiers, where we someday expect to be. . . . Allies have taken over Radio Algiers and a commercial point-to-point transmitter—should improve our communications. Had been hoping that Gib to Malta cable, cut by Italians, might be spliced and connected into Algiers, so we could have such added security a cable affords. But will take at least six weeks, and British have to decide if mission is worth risking a cable ship. We are now tied to Gibraltar for communications reasons, Ike having to keep Combined Chiefs rapidly informed. Also direct movements of task forces in the field. This is especially important now as every effort is being expended to move east into Tunisia. The inadequacy of signal service out of Algiers must be remedied before the main headquarters of AFHQ can be moved there.

WORD JUST RECEIVED OF SURRENDER OF FRENCH AT CASABLANCA. (Arrived 7:38 this morning—Armistice Day.)

Axis is moving planes and men into Tunisian airfields as rapidly as they can. One report received this morning indicated that 200 planes had come into Tunis airdrome. Shuttle service between Tunis and Sicily.

Hitler moving into unoccupied France. We have information he intends to try to establish bridgehead in Tunis for contact from ports of southern France.

Ike irritated at French garrisons for failure to step in and fight Huns in Tunisia. "They don't seem to know which side of the bread is buttered."

London papers for November 9 came in today. Made a big story, or rather several stories, in each paper. Stately *Times* noted on the front-page ear that Americans land in North Africa. *Sketch* had Ike surrounded by big headlines and picture covering top quarter of page.

General Anderson's troops have landed at Bougie, but the landing couldn't be made at Djidjelli because of heavy swell.

Ike took time to read the headlines. He was sitting in his underpants. Had spilled ink on his trousers, and Lee was trying to get the spot out, but no gasoline.

Rommel presumably was in Tunis yesterday, trying to arrange for defense bridgehead, offensive bombing. Not much left of his Afrika Korps, according to London papers, twenty-eight tanks and 20,000 men. Six Italian divisions had been deserted by the Nazis and were captured with equipment.

Tablada airdrome, wherever that is, has received instructions to send all available Junkers motors and spare parts to Italian Africa today.

Beetle wires Ike that today is Patton's birthday. Isn't Casablanca enough of a present?

Somervell cables 10,000,000 gallons gas being shipped. . . . Three hundred officers and staff of German Armistice Commission trying escape from Casa. . . . Ike relayed intelligence to Patton, hoping to catch 'em.

Re Tunis: Report has it that on El Aouina airdrome, Tunis, there are 100 aircraft, gliders, and ten aircraft carrying tanks. Five hundred German troops deployed. Sidi Ahmed also occupied. . . . Algiers-Tunis railway cut. . . . Ike told Anderson better plan sea-borne reinforcements when he gets to Tunis—when and if.

New Zealand, another returning transport, torpedoed.

Pétain reported as having "disappeared."

At Algiers we got the books, records, and money of the German Armistice Commission. Also got their codes and ciphers. May be very helpful.

Bône Captured, and the Germans Occupy All of France

GIBRALTAR, THURSDAY, NOVEMBER 12, 1942

Overnight news from Clark at Algiers hopeful but not conclusive. Darlan has issued a mild order, more in the nature of an invitation, to the French fleet at Toulon to come to North Africa, and Giraud and Darlan both have been contacting French military and civilian leaders in Tunisia, encouraging them actively to fight the Axis invasion there, which has begun. Clark had, at least for the moment, achieved working harmony between the two rival would-be French leaders, making Darlan the King Bee (title not known yet) to head civilian affairs, and Giraud to head military.

Meanwhile we learned during the late evening that German occupation of unoccupied France has proceeded apace, with Nazis expected to reach Toulon this morning. What, then, becomes of the French fleet, the biggest prize of the war? Will it join us in North Africa or will it play ostrich and let Hitler have it by default? Personnel of the fleet hate the British and don't think the Americans are so hot, either.

Doc Matthews, civilian adviser at headquarters, was to fly to Algiers this morning, as requested by Clark. Ike told him to tell Clark that he approved everything he has done with the French, and if there is anything Clark thinks Ike could contribute, to let him know. Also, for Pete's sake, to acknowledge receipt of the various messages we have tried to get through to him; also that Ike had requested General Marshall to make Clark Lieutenant General now. (This all happened at Government House at breakfast.) When we reached the office, there was a late message from Marshall saying that the nomination of Clark for Lieutenant General had gone to the Senate.

Ike had concluded overnight to fly to Algiers if the news from Clark wasn't reasonably decisive this morning, in the hope that his presence as C-in-C might add sufficient weight and influence to get the fleet and resistance in Tunisia. Where Clark is suave and diplomatic, Ike is frank and direct, so there might be an advantage. The weather this morning was, as the British say, "pouring with rain," thunder, lightning, and practically ceiling zero. Flying looked out for the day.

Also, no further information from Patton or Hewitt.

British had lost two destroyers by torpedoes during the night—*Hecla,* abandoned; *Marne* still afloat, 2:21 A.M., 12th.

Neglected to record that Pétain had appointed General Noguës Resident General of French Morocco, as North African leader, in place of Darlan. Guard over Darlan has been released.

Ike has ideas that would be helpful in dealing with the French. This morning he suggested to Matthews that French take their fleet to Dakar or to Oran, be given a sector, and let them run it. They have about forty useful submarines alone. This French fleet is important.

The Prime Minister had cabled through Beetle in London that de Gaulle wants to send a mission here to co-operate with the North African French leaders, and has also communicated this recommendation to the President. This will be one more complication, but may be helpful.

Failure to get answers to two questions put to Patton thirty-six hours ago is bad. Where are his headquarters, and what is condition of the port at Casablanca? Neither do we know result of naval action in west. Supply people in London calling for port information. Convoy sailings, loadings, timings, everything dependent upon information. Maybe it's communications, but Patton has planes that could fly couriers with complete dope to Gib. Incidentally, outside of Navy, particularly Royal Navy, our signals have been far from satisfactory. Biggest failure of the expedition, except Patton's silence.

Wireless communication between Algiers and England reported satisfactory, but no official links open yet to Oran or Casablanca.

Glimmer of hope out of Tunisia: the three French services decided to obey Darlan's order not to resist the Americans and British and warned Germans that French cannot guarantee their safety, which doesn't quite make sense to me. Why don't the French start tossing the Huns out? Also reported Germans have installed large ack-ack guns at Tunis airdrome.

Weather bad for flying in whole area of our operations today.

Germans thought to be moving about 5000 troops from Tripoli into Tunis, and because of short water haul from Sicily, to be prepared to move in from there. But there are indications Germans believed to be nervous about their status in Tunisia.

Ike radioed * Patton last night, asking if he wanted the squadron of twenty-seven P-38s of 14th Fighter Group now at Gib. If so, to which airdrome, and what is its condition? If not, they will be sent to Oran.

All last night a message from the Allied Commander was broadcast in French through Navy channels:

"Hitler has denounced the armistice. I invited the French fleet to join the United Nations in the fight for freedom. So hasten the day of France's liberation. Hitler has taken your country. Now he wants your ships. Do not let him take them. The enemy is close upon you. So hasten the day of France's liberation. Hitler has taken your country. Now he wants your ships. Do not let him take them. The enemy is close upon you. Sail at once for Gibraltar. Join us."

Reports of casualties have come in slowly; incomplete report made to London office today lists for 39th Combat Team two killed, ten wounded; 168th Combat Team, ten killed, thirty-eight wounded in Oran operation. There was one group of Commandos and Rangers, numbering 600, that apparently got caught in accurate, effective shore-battery fire while ramming into Oran harbor to protect its facilities. Only 120 lived through it. Nothing from Patton on casualties, either.

Casualties are considered light. Only air and headquarters personnel

---

* From Gibraltar to the forces at Casablanca, Oran, and Algiers communications were by wireless telegraphy. The Mediterranean area is notably bad for radio communication because of atmospheric and "skipping" effects. Because of the fear the Germans would detect any signs of unusual activity at Gibraltar, the existing RAF, Royal Navy, and British Army transmitters were used, and the great volume of traffic taxed both facilities and operators. Gibraltar was the head of a submarine cable, however, and General Ike had excellent contact by this means with London and Washington, via London.

will be hospitalized at Gib; remainder on hospital ships, as originally planned.

Intelligence report from Malta says significant movements in Sicily. Nineteen Ju-52s arrived at Catania and one Merseburg six-engined plane, presumably for towing transport gliders, had arrived at Catania, too. Malta's bomb raid on the Elmas airdrome on Sardinia, for which Ike thanked the Malta governor a couple of days ago, did some good: ammunition dump blown up, two hangars and seaplane wharf damaged, and three bombers and one fighter destroyed on ground.

This morning the Eastern Task Force is moving from Bougie eastward, and paratroopers will drop on Duzzerville airdrome. Forces hitting out for Bône fast as possible and protecting right flank to the south with one motorized brigade.

Haven't mentioned, as I recall, that our paratroop (U. S.) effort was sour. Of thirty-nine transports flown from U. K. over Spain, only twenty are now serviceable. They didn't land on the airport at Oran, as planned; some of them set down on a dry lake bed. Some in Spanish Morocco. Consul advises there are sixty-one paratroops there. True, weather wasn't too good, but navigators were green. Better next time.

Ike just buzzed for me, and as I went in I grabbed a late message from Fredendall. It said he had established headquarters at the Grand Hotel, had got one ship out of the channel yesterday, another today, and the convoy could come in. Good work. Also has thirty-eight German prisoners and queried disposition. Ike said tell him to send the s.o.b.s to U. S. in returning convoy, and if any get torpedoed by U-boats, hope it's the one they're on.

Message from Marshall said that President Roosevelt wanted to send his message of congratulations two days ago, but Marshall recommended he wait until Ike on African soil. Speaks of "perfection of the performance of our forces up to the present time."

Enemy seems apprehensive that another American force will soon consolidate our position in North Africa by taking Dakar. This may keep hostile subs away. Hope it does.

Report received from RAF that night of November 10/11 nine Beaufighters attacked at dusk Tunis airdrome and left in flames ten German aircraft and damaged sixteen others, including two large gliders.

Absent voters' election supplies just arrived. Election was, I believe, November 2.

Bône captured. Message was timed 11:18 A.M.

Ike had press conference in which he elaborated on Clark's fine job in the rendezvous before D-Day.

At lunch at GH heard BBC news. Describes 1500-mile flight U. S. paratroops to Oran as longest in history, but didn't say whether they achieved result, although understand troopers helped generally at Oran.

Phillips handed me copy of Kirkpatrick's story from Oran to *Chicago Daily News*, describing riotous welcome of 400,000 French people in Oran to American entry. Said she was in leading car upon entry. Americans are superwelcome in North Africa. Also AP story from there re picturesque and bumptious celebration of Armistice Day, with Oran mayor taking lead.

Learn that *Hecla* is bad loss; *Marne* being towed; both outside Med. *Ibis* hit by aerial torpedo ten miles north of Algiers and sunk. *Viceroy of India* and *New Zealand* had been returning Algiers to Gib, routed independently, when were torpedoed and sunk.

Admiral Bieri, USN, with small staff, has been sent by Ike to deliver dispatches and collect information from Admiral Hewitt, who is to get Patton to rendezvous. Aboard H.M.S. *Welshman*, fast mine layer, makes thirty-seven knots, 3000 tons, due there 8 P.M. Maybe we'll finally find out what's going on with "Lost WTF." Radio communication has been hopeless; for some reason our set of codebooks and Patton's don't jibe.* Patton informed to avoid all interference in existing methods of control of tribes. He is to hire labor freely and repair airfields. Hewitt is to take all necessary measures to protect convoys against subs. Suggested placing enough force in Casablanca to control searchlight, which is suspected as guide to enemy subs. If this is impracticable, notify French you will shoot at it if they attempt to turn it on.

Another to Patton said inability this headquarters to establish signal channel to Patton ashore is critical. Our station has heard Hewitt's ship radio repeatedly with strong signal, but it neither receives nor transmits messages. Ordered to take immediate action to establish channels prescribed and report through Hewitt cipher system which you can now operate.

Three Italian battleships, large number of destroyers, have left Taranto, but cruisers have not left harbor, Royal Navy reports. Something brewing?

Sub attack at Casablanca last night. We lost one transport, with two others damaged. The previous reference to searchlight followed fact that these lights were turned on and silhouetted our ships, apparently deliberately.

---

* Later I was told Patton's codebooks were stowed at the bottom of an as-yet-unloaded ship.

Bône ours without opposition. Commandos and paratroops British. Told Joe Phillips time that British were getting credit for this eastern push.

Germans and Italians have moved quickly to occupy southern France. Eyeties got Cannes and environs.

We have taken an aerial shellacking at Bougie at dusk. Dive bombers and just plain bombers, unhampered by fighter opposition from us, knocked hell out of convoy of transports in harbor. Four ships badly damaged or destroyed. Fighter aid being rushed for that area, but this heavy loss due primarily to failure to make landing at Djidjelli and to capture adjacent airdrome, where we could probably have had fighters operative during the day.

My Royal Navy friends hope that the two Italian battleships and some fourteen destroyers steaming toward Naples from Taranto may be intercepted by a British sub, set on its trail. Some mystery about a third battleship which was in this group when recced * earlier today. Maybe sub has knocked off one. Could use some good news.

Two American Navy fighters of Western Force shot down a British Hudson yesterday. It was seeking information we couldn't get by radio from Patton or Hewitt. Mistaken identity or nervous trigger fingers. Ike has instructed C/S to redouble efforts to force knowledge of identification of planes by all personnel.

Now 7 P.M. "tunnel time," or 8 Gib. Ike still hard at it, and so are we satellites, but we don't have to make the decisions. He's iron. I've seen a lot of top-flight executives doing supposedly important things under considerable stress. Despite the pressure on Ike and the irritation caused by the current confusion on political problems, he operates just as coolly as during the planning. But he would be a lot happier if this was simply a military job.

Germans are moving into Tunisia pretty fast. Photo recce † shows six E boats at Bizerte and sea-borne reinforcements believed at sea. Two motor vessels and five destroyers sighted at 5:30 A.M., destination probably Bizerte. From this point looks like a tough fight. Anderson has messaged us, cautioning against publicity of places taken, such as Bône, since it gives enemy aid for bombing attacks. British troops, including Commandos, have reached Djidjelli by road. Gasoline put ashore. Airdrome should be serviceable soon. Need it badly.

Just tried to pry Ike loose from his desk, where he is drafting something. Isn't ready. Gruenther's making a try. I'm hungry.

---

* Reconnaissance made.
† Pronounced "recky."

The Deal with Darlan

GIBRALTAR, FRIDAY, NOVEMBER 13, 1942

Early this morning Ike received a radio from Clark at Algiers saying an early visit there by the Allied Commander would be beneficial. Said he could explain better, eye to eye, the involved political setup and tactical situation. He had concluded shortly before midnight of Thursday a long powwow with Darlan, Giraud, Murphy, and Noguès, but no peace pipe was smoked. Noguès, whom Pétain had appointed as his prime representative in French Africa, had upset Clark's plan. Clark had flatly told Noguès that the Allies would not recognize him as Pétain's supreme military and political boss. After this ultimatum had been delivered, Darlan and Giraud outlined a plan to get all the French leaders together, which sounded like news. Clark thought this was the answer, but wanted his boss to come and see and hear for himself.

So Ike, Admiral Cunningham, his flag lieutenant, Dampier (Dampy), Colonel William Stirling, the General's British Military Assistant, and I flew off from Gib's pinched and still crowded field. Three P-38s, with their twin fuselages twisting in and out of the clouds above, under, and on either side of us, looked out for Jerries, who had been around. But we saw none. Arrived Maison Blanche about noon. Will finish, or pick up from here, tomorrow. Too darned tired tonight.

GIBRALTAR, SUNDAY, NOVEMBER 15, 1942

(My birthday)—No time to type yesterday. In Algiers Ike transacted business quickly and effectively, reboarded Fortress around 3:30, back at Gib at 7, only to discover we had air and other officers nuts because visibility practically nil for landing. Rain, low-hanging mist. Didn't get scared, Ike said, until about 10 that night, so we took a toast to our safe landing.

Well, what happened? Ike had sent Thursday afternoon late his ultimatum for Clark to read to the French. It was received by Clark at 3 A.M. Friday, too late for the Thursday meeting, but Clark had stressed the same obvious theme of the need of French unity, and quickly, if we were to win the race for Tunisia.

When we got off the plane, Clark and aides were there to meet us, having commandeered two private automobiles that had been in storage for two years account gasoline shortage. Needed batteries, and tires were so thin we had to drive slowly the eight miles from airdrome into the city. Algiers looked enchanting; an architectural mixture of the old and new worlds. Clark was all smiles re Ike's arrival; said he was at the end of his rope, had served an ultimatum that they had to get together today because the C-in-C was coming.

When we reached the St. George Hotel, Clark's headquarters, there was a brief meeting preliminary to the session with the French, which Ike had radioed should be arranged so he could accomplish his objective speedily and return to Gibraltar the same day. At this preliminary meeting, Murphy arrived, somewhat breathless, and reported that Darlan and Giraud had just reached agreement to be offered to General Eisenhower. This provided: (1) Darlan to be Governor, or equivalent title, of French North Africa; (2) Giraud to form French Army of volunteers, and in three days to have some forces active against Germans and Italians in Tunisia; (3) Darlan to dispatch an emissary to try to induce Admiral Louis Edmond Collinet, the Dakar naval commander, to active collaboration; (4) Noguès to remain as Governor of French Morocco, where he reputedly can control the skittish and troublesome Arabs; (5) distribution of gasoline, sugar, tea, and other necessary supplies to be begun promptly (this was included in the original plans for the entire operation, and each convoy carried one or more ships to meet this need, but Ike had emphasized it should be given primarily to those who will "work and fight" with us); and (6) the French fleet. (My notes read "still messing around." Later Admiral Cunningham related that he had Darlan's promise to send a message to the Admiral controlling that portion of the French fleet at Toulon, warning him an Italian fleet was steaming toward Toulon, hoping this would jar him loose.) On the subject of supplying foodstuffs, Murphy said primary need was gasoline, so that food grown in Algiers could be transported to population centers.

At the 2 o'clock meeting, Darlan, Giraud, Noguès, and Juin came to the St. George to meet Ike.

Ike said (through Murphy and Holmes as interpreters) that he had heard that an agreement had been reached, which is acceptable to him, and he would acknowledge Admiral Darlan as Head of State. In this attitude he was representing Great Britain and the United States. Many details remained to be worked out, to assure that co-operation in the future could be complete.

General Clark, as his Deputy Commander-in-Chief, spoke for him. The C-in-C said that if the details of the agreement worked out amongst the French leaders received the approval of General Clark, this approval would be backed by himself and the Allied force.

Ike demanded most of all one thing: signing the agreement must mean they would attack the Germans; the immediate task is to get on to Tunisia.

Darlan replied, stating that the French leaders would respect the agreement scrupulously. He heartily agreed with the objective of beating Germany, but offered an additional objective: the reconstruction of France, which Ike enthusiastically endorsed, but asserted the French themselves would have to "get in and pitch."

Didn't go to the luncheon, as I was busy discussing future quarters for us with the hotel owner, so just got in on tail end of Ike's extremely short confab, just in time for Ike to introduce me all around. He had first ordered me to stay in Algiers for twenty-four hours to find quarters for future use, but when I returned with the party to airdrome to take my bag off the Fortress, he changed his mind, and told me to come along. (Left my cap at the St. George, so went bareheaded twenty-four hours until Commodore Dick, RN, who really had lost his when the wind swirled it out the waist gunner's window, returned to Gibraltar, wearing mine.)

The point of honor made by the French placed something of an unpatriotic stigma against Giraud for having conferred with the enemy, and this had been stated to his face by the other French. Consequently, they preferred, and he agreed, to defer any announcement of his participation; meanwhile he was too busy himself organizing French resistance, probably guerrilla, to the Axis in Tunisia. Mast, who had been an active collaborator with us and a disciple of G, was in hiding, for fear he'd be shot. General Béthouart in French Morocco, another Allied sympathizer, was in the jug, on order of Noguës. Others were being held for trial or court-martial.

Ike discovered that they still felt a loyalty for Marshal Pétain. The group even preferred to send word to Pétain as to their action, so as not to feel in their own consciences that they had completely broken away from him. The strength of the French leaders with the populace of North Africa seemed to depend on the closeness of any leader with the Marshal. Darlan had been able to stop some fighting, especially in Casablanca.

But the recognition of Darlan, made public by Darlan himself over the radio at Algiers Friday evening, and carrying with it the assertion that Pétain had given the group a fatherly blessing, had created raised eyebrows in London, where Darlan was commonly regarded as a "stinking skunk." Further, the British government had been co-operating with de Gaulle, and de Gaulle was not happy with Darlan, but would go along with Giraud. De Gaulle was recognized leader of Madagascar and other French colonies taken by the British for safekeeping.

Anyway, by Saturday morning Ike had a cable from Beetle in London.

saying the deal was being coolly received. There are no objections from U. S. A. so far. Ike had to explain the deal, primarily because of the non-announcement of Giraud's participation—he being the guy Ike had previously blessed. Six pages of his crisp English were required to tell the British his American point of view re French, shared by the British as well as Americans on our staff, and most certainly regarded as an achievement by Murphy, who has been living with the French for many, many months.

The American acceptance was not explicitly given, but we knew we were all right with the homefolk when a swell message of congratulations for Ike and the forces of TORCH was received from the President this morning. Ike sent it on to all commanders, so they and all their men would know of the pat on the back.

At lunch we learned through diplomatic channels that Hitler has demanded of Franco free passage for his forces through Spain, which probably is a diplomatic counterattack against Franco's friendly exchange with the President. But if Hitler's hordes come through Spain, and there may or may not be Spanish opposition, old Gibraltar will be the recipient of heavy cannonading from the mainland, which half encircles this fortress. We would have to spread our fire from the center to the edges of the half-circle, while their dispersed batteries could concentrate on the center, which is us.

After lunch we had a radio from General Clark (confirmed by Senate as Lieutenant General yesterday and notified today) that Darlan was about to release his slate, including Giraud, which is good, but intends to announce no traffic with de Gaulle. This would be unpleasant for the British, would indicate a split in French opposition to the Axis, as well as among themselves, and in general would raise hell. So Ike is getting off a fast radio (slow motion at best) to Algiers to get Clark to delete reference to de Gaulle. Meanwhile Ike has written Noguès today, expressing co-operation and kindred things and demanding the release of our friends from their jails. Copy to Darlan, with note that he realizes he will take up matters affecting French North Africa in a regular manner through Darlan, but had some things especially to say to Noguès. Has ordered Americans salute French officers.

GIBRALTAR, MONDAY, NOVEMBER 16, 1942

Photo recce of Toulon, impossible account weather for several days, shows the *Strasbourg* has been left its customary mooring. Does this have any significance?

We didn't get the text of the Darlan announcement from Clark, signals being what they are, but this morning's Gibraltar *Chronicle* front-pages only that "Darlan has approached the admirals commanding portions of the French fleet at Dakar and Martinique to come along. Wants machinery parts of French warships at Casablanca transported to Martinique. May get some help along this line." No mention of de Gaulle.

Ike has written Beetle at length, and is tossing off a small book to General Marshall. Itching to get to Algiers, impatiently awaiting improvement of signals, but this took a backward turn when Clark's reply to Ike's urgent message re Darlan's statement arrived eighteen hours after dispatched by radio from Algiers. Some dumb cluck marked it routine instead of urgent. Says he is sending me to Algiers soon to get quarters properly set. Contrary to his personal feeling for small, unpretentious living quarters, thinks advisable to throw a little dog to impress the natives, so I'll find a villa.

Maison Blanche airdrome and docks bombed last night. Axis has about 150 aircraft at Bizerte and Tunis, mainly fighters, but some dive bombers.

Warning sent to task forces that our cipher may be "compromised." Message received from Western Task Force aroused suspicion it was planted by enemy. Wanted to get dope on next convoy, but gave itself away.

General Patton sent in a letter giving Ike a chronological account of his operation. Ike issued special communiqué to give Patton some deserved but delayed credit. Communications had failed both ways and in between.

Message from General Marshall reports President approves Ike's dealing with French as reported, and merely asked that he be consulted in future. The PM was fearful it was all a giant plot and that the French leaders would conspire to escape. Wanted them watched. Ike had cabled the PM he had sat at the "former naval person's" feet too long to be fooled.

One of our American pilots flying a P-38 from U. K. to Gib landed at Lisbon for gas, having lost one spare belly tank, was told he was thereby interned. Told the airdrome official he wanted to clear his supercharger, or something, got back in plane, started motor, and dashed away, leaving his jacket with identification papers. Fearful of a diplomatic upset for thus flaunting Portugal, which has been friendly, and of indicating a "mightier than thou" attitude, Ike had Gruenther radio our Ambassador at Lisbon the story and to be prepared to answer questions frankly. Consideration would be given to return the lad and plane for internment. Recently an American paratroop plane came down at sea off Portugal, the crew was rescued, taken ashore in Portugal, and allowed to depart as "experienced seamen."

Ike trying to get tanks and other armored units to General Anderson, who is tentatively planning attack Bizerte and city of Tunis Saturday or Sunday, when he can get his support in order. Ike asking British Chiefs of Staff to activate a small attack with forces from Malta on far coast of Tunisia at Sousse. Anderson wants this to divert and upset Axis defenders. No opposition expected at Sousse. Awaiting approval of British Chiefs. Will probably put that operation under Ike as well. Malta forces "rarin' to go." Ike radioed Malta Governor (Gort) relative to their bombing assistance that "it is our devout hope to repay you at an early date."

Should mention that the *Laconia,* the ship bearing wives and children of French officers from Dakar, instead of being royally received at Casablanca, as desired, was seeking to come out of harbor during naval engagement and bombardment, against orders, and was dive-bombed by the USN. Not sunk, but messy. . . . Giving them special care now. Ship failed to obey the rules.

Trial of pro-American French, such as General Béthouart in Morocco, will be "deferred indefinitely" to permit charges of treason to die out. Meanwhile they are still at least technically in hoosegow, but in comfort. Noguès is handling this, but Ike has cabled Clark to get Darlan to issue general order of amnesty.

Casualties so far will run about 570 killed, 300 wounded, 200 missing, T. J. estimates from reports, but not final.

Clark radioes Darlan just decided appoint Admiral Emile H. Muselier as Naval Commander-in-Chief, Giraud already being announced as Commander-in-Chief of Army and Air.

Took a good big drink for my birthday, wrote a letter home, and to bed.

ASDIC * at First Hand

Flew to Algiers to house-hunt on Tuesday, November 17. Hitchhiked a ride from Maison Blanche to Algiers in a jeep. Called on General Clark, who was at the St. George. He assigned congenial Major Laurence B.

---

* Device for detecting submarines under water by sending a sound—a "ping"—from the ship. If there is an echo returned, it may be a U-boat, a sunken ship or something else.

Meacham, his other aide, as his rental agent. Meach already had tabbed two or three villas, and we set out to look at them. The first one seemed ideal, but representatives of General Giraud already had staked a claim to it. Meach was for jumping the claim, but I didn't think General Ike would wish to be in a position of outranking or evicting any tenant, especially Giraud. Spent the day jeeping to other villas, only to find that because of the extreme shortage of housing in Algiers, it having accumulated thousands of refugees from Europe, we made but little progress.

I noticed two lovely white villas on the hillside that had not been on our list. In trying to find our way to them, we got lost. Eventually the jeep sputtered and died—for even these mounts will not run without gas. By this time it was dark, and after borrowing some gas, returned to the St. George for the night.

Dined with General Clark and associates in the Army mess in the St. George, served by the French staff of the hotel, with mess sergeants and GIs supervising in the kitchen, particularly to watch the food supply, which has a habit of disappearing out the kitchen door. Algerian red wine, 18% alcohol, gives a pleasant glow, but a bad head.

Next morning we still couldn't find the apparently hidden entrance to the two villas where we hoped to house both Eisenhower and Clark. We learned, however, that they were owned by a rich wine merchant and wholesaler who was described by the CIC (Counter-Intelligence Corps) as pro-German. Also discovered they had not been requisitioned, so without further ado, Headquarters Command filed appropriate papers with the French, we having come as liberators, not as conquerors.

Ike expected me to return to Gib by air, but not only was the weather bad, but practically all the aircraft were in use to supply Anderson's rush for Tunisia. Thinking I could return overnight by surface craft, I obtained permission from the Royal Navy to ride on one of its corvettes, leaving Algiers for Gibraltar that evening.

I found the corvette, H.M.S. *Starwort*, taking on oil in the busy harbor. The skipper, officers, and ratings were most hospitable and cordial. Asked the skipper when I went aboard if they had had any luck against U-boats. The reply was quite nonchalant, "Oh, yes, we got one only yesterday."

As we pulled out of Algiers harbor at dusk, there was a red alert, meaning enemy aircraft around, and all hands were called to action stations. I stayed on the bridge. Nothing showed up.

As I visited the officers, the normal British reticence gradually gave way. The U-boat, sunk the day before, was off Oran, and the *Starwort*, after some competition with a Royal Navy destroyer, managed to take all of the German crew; but couldn't prevent scuttling.

The *Starwort*, a year old, had been on the Murmansk run and had dropped pattern after pattern of depth charges but until the day before had never had the good luck to get a U-boat. When the ASDIC had detected the U-boat off Oran, the *Starwort* made its run, dropped its charges, took a good jarring, turned to repeat, when suddenly the starboard lookout shouted, "Hurrah, we got the bahstahrd." Sure enough, off the bow stuck half the U-boat, almost vertical. The crew was taken aboard and put ashore at Algiers. They had been thoroughly arrogant.

The skipper spent hours preparing a report of the incident for the Admiralty. He told me, "The Admiralty is a bit sticky about its language, and I have been trying to find appropriate words to describe the condition of three of the prisoners. They were brought aboard with their trousers very unclean, indeed."

Reporting to Ike at Gib, found him fidgeting to get his headquarters staff and himself moved to Algiers, but still tied to the cable head at Gibraltar by messages from Washington and London that required prompt and extensive replies.

While I was away, London informed us that negotiations with Admiral Georges Robert, at Martinique, had been initiated—six Fortresses had attacked Bizerte in daylight on the sixteenth—450 paratroops dropped near Souk-el-Arba—German bombers pounding our advanced port at Bône; Spits gave protection, but lost three, although two pilots saved; six enemy planes downed, others damaged. . . . G-3 report indicated Axis buildup in bridgehead Bizerte-Tunis now 6000-8000 troops, with main strength at Bizerte, where heavy defense in antitank and antiaircraft guns installed. Some French troops active for us in Tunisia and eastern Algeria, but weak in transport, AA, and AT. Bulk of returning convoys now west of Gibraltar. Many attacked by air and sub, but losses not regarded as excessive. . . . Some losses have occurred off our unloading ports because congested harbors unable to accommodate all ships; these have to mill about in open sea with sparse protection. Harbors being cleared. . . . Thirty-eight members Italian-German Armistice Commission being shipped to U. K. . . . Forty-four officers and men captured from U-boat in Mediterranean being sent direct to U. S. (must be the *Starwort*'s haul). . . . Word from reliable source that Admiral Platon sent by Laval at Vichy to urge Esteva in Tunisia to resist Allies. Report indicates Laval has urged military alliance with Germany. Pétain and Weygand refused. Weygand plugging for our side. . . . De Gaulle has publicly declared that Fighting French have nothing to do with

present African situation. . . . Gratified that Combined Chiefs have
approved everything General Ike has done in regard to political situation
in Africa (this has caused him more headaches than any tactical phase
of the entire operation). . . . 503rd Paratroop Battalion landed successfully at Youks-les-Bains and is ready for action. . . . Eighth Army coming along in the desert. . . . Monty's men have taken Benghazi. . . .
American tanks and armor moving through Algiers, headed east, to help
Anderson. . . . Twenty more Axis commissioners captured by French
at Gabès. German patrollers west of Mateur driven off by French. . . .
Ju-52s trying to land at Gabès fired on by French AA. . . . French fleet
still at Toulon and no indication of their joining us.

Fortress bringing Brigadier General Asa N. Duncan, from England,
last week seen by other aircraft in the formation flying to Gibraltar with
number-three motor smoking badly; turned to return to England. While
170 miles off English coast, it was lost. General Spaatz and party were in
other aircraft. We will miss General Duncan, because he was not only an
able officer, but well liked and respected by all.

We Move to Algiers

ALGIERS, TUESDAY, NOVEMBER 24, 1942

Yesterday flew with General Ike and party in Fortress from Gibraltar to
Tafaroua, the airfield near Oran, en route to Algiers, to which we have
now moved permanently—so far as one can say permanent these days.
At Tafaroua, a blanket of sticky mud, we burst a tire on the tail wheel
on landing.

General Ike and I were guests of Major General Fredendall and staff
at lunch in Oran. French co-operating in this area, but much needs to be
done. Fredendall's force, which took the city, now being drawn upon for
men and matériel rushing to the east.

The port is clogged with sunken ships, but Navy salvage crews busy
clearing it; some cranes in order. Have number of crews and hordes of
badly clothed, half-starved Arabs at work unloading. (They are so under-
fed they can work only six hours a day.) Drove in the neighborhood of
that tough shore battery Du Santon, but couldn't see much except many
evidences of our shell fire.

The tire on the Fortress having been repaired, we flew on to Maison
Blanche and proceeded to the St. George.

A corner suite of three bedrooms and parlor that I had tabbed for
General Ike and personal staff has become both working and sleeping

quarters. Most of the night the Jerries were over. With the ack-ack from our ships in the harbor and from the guns on the shore, plus occasional thumps from bombs, the old St. George quivered and shook. No one slept much. Ike was in the corner bedroom and I in the one next to him. In the morning, he was fuming about the effect of the bombing and what he thought of our inadequate defense, particularly absence of night fighters. Worried about effect psychologically on French and Arabs. Little damage to shipping.

Today we are installed in one of the two rented villas. General Clark and Major Meacham are temporarily living with us. The bombing destroyed water and gas mains serving the villa. Nor is there heat. Our breakfast this morning was cooked by Sergeant Chaney, Clark's orderly, over a wood fire in the dining-room fireplace. Somewhere he had found some eggs and had Army bacon. The house was as big as a barn, with only two proper bedrooms and baths in the whole house. However, there are four servant bedrooms and plenty of floor space for bedding rolls if needed.

At the St. George, they had cleared out the beds, acquired some desks, had some telephones rigged, and we are almost in business. Everyone is shivering from cold. There is no heat in the St. George except here and there a small fireplace. Fortunately, there is one in Ike's office. Soldiers sleep in the hallways, cold, but out of the rain. Corridors gritty with mud, which becomes dust when the barefooted Arab women wield their brooms.

Reaction to Darlan

ALGIERS, THURSDAY, NOVEMBER 26, 1942 (THANKSGIVING DAY)
The furor which arose in America over Ike's recognition of Darlan, following the initial flare-up in Britain, has now died away, so far as the immediate impact from our rear is concerned. The President's statement that this was a military recognition and would not necessarily be a continuing political setup quieted things but has left Darlan in a weakened position with the French factions.

In the meantime, Darlan has virtually delivered Dakar to the Allies, and the officials at Dakar are asking to deal with the Americans. Conference set for Algiers on Saturday. The modern battleship *Richelieu* probably will be sent from Dakar to U. S. by French for completion. Now at Dakar with three or four cruisers, several destroyers, and about eight subs. Darlan also holds out hope for a turnover of the several important French warships at Alexandria, barnacled though they are, to come into the big show.

Every effort being made to keep the push going eastward, but we are having difficulties. Rain the past two days again has muddied our airdromes, particularly parking spaces, so B-17s have to be propped under wings to keep from sinking hopelessly into quagmire. It's the African rainy season. The Boche, on the other hand, has well-prepared, hard-surfaced landing fields on Sardinia and Sicily, as well at Tunis and Bizerte. Our advanced fields for fighters and light bombers in Anderson's territory are bogged down, except at Bône, and there only the runway itself, 150 yards wide, may be used for parking. Planes very close together on ground and too good targets. Have lost heavily in Spitfires on the ground. Germans have their Me-109s in action from Tunis and/or Bizerte. Of eighty P-38s, fifty are operational. Weather bad for high-level bombing. Today P-38s and A-20s being sent to bomb airdromes in Tunis, one of which now has eighty Stukas, newly arrived, said to be packed almost wing to wing. If weather permits our boys to get through, they should raise hell.

Anderson started his ground push yesterday, expecting air cover, but weather prevented. Stukas free to attack when we can't get our fighters off the ground.

Admiral Cunningham has lost most of shipping sent east of Bougie, and is disinclined to send more there until Air Marshal Welsh can assure air cover. This held up by mud. So the use of water transportation to hasten move eastward is greatly impaired. Ike had Welsh, Doolittle, and White-ley, the Deputy Chief of Staff, for an after-dinner talk at the villa last night, and tried to bring order out of fumbling. One thing bothering all is the inadequate defense against night bombing on shipping and on Maison Blanche airdrome at Algiers. Shipping people and Royal Navy up in arms. Night fighters cannot work effectively account delay by British of installing radio directors, called ground-controlled interception, which guide our night fighters to within 300 yards of enemy planes. This purportedly installed, but location was bad and had to be moved. Also, British had declined to ship with invasion force its hush-hush radio-direction device that guides night fighter the remaining 300 yards and tells fighter pilot by a white light on control panel when to press the trigger. Reason was it might fall into enemy hands. This restraint now overcome and equipment being sent by plane, although British originally said would only send in weighted parcels in a ship, to be thrown overboard if endangered. Beau-fighters, used for night fighting, only six to start, reduced to three, after raid on Maison Blanche, by own AA fire and by enemy bombs on air-drome. Reinforcements en route. But quite evident Ike has to take British by the horns to make them overcome their traditional "co-operation" among land, sea, and air services and impel recognition of single command for actual operations as well as planning. The whole thing in Algiers and to the east needs vigorous co-ordination only Ike himself can arrange.

Beetle flew to Gib from London and spent a couple of days bringing Ike up to date on the backlash created in British official circles re recognition of Darlan, especially by the Prime, who had come around very well, Beetle deserving of fine commendation for fighting the rear-guard action of diplomacy.

When Beetle returned to London, he carried numerous problems that needed to be trouble-shot: more night fighters were needed; more planes generally were needed—these he was to take up with Air Chief Marshal Portal. Then he had problems of procurement of supplies, particularly to hasten foodstuffs for North African civilian population, which had to be pressed personally at Washington. He advised that he thought best to catch a plane for the U. S. and get everything in apple-pie order. Ike agreed to this decision in a cable, but reminded him that when talking with people in Washington that "I have no complaints."

Ike has had a satisfying military victory to date, regardless of the outcome of the hot fight expected for Tunisia, but all this good work has been, unfortunately, so far as we can judge, obscured by the political reaction of the recognition of Darlan. While this was a deal negotiated by Clark, promptly affirmed by the Allied C-in-C at the famous Friday-the-thirteenth meeting in Algiers, Ike has had to take the rap for it publicly. Not that he minds, as that is his burden, but the effect has been to pour cold water on what appears to have been an extraordinarily skillful military feat. One, incidentally, in which the fighting and casualties were much harder and greater than the public was purposely led by Allied Headquarters to believe, because we did not want the French to remain embittered against us for having to club them into submission, at least until Darlan stopped the French from fighting.

So hot had become the American reaction to Darlan, aided by disgruntled or disillusioned de Gaullists, that General Marshall had cabled Ike for consent to make public the casualty figures. This indicated that Marshall was really having his troubles, so Ike said O.K., even if the next of kin hadn't been notified. There were about 500 dead, 900 wounded, and 300 missing, totaling nearly 1800. These should be compared to the casualties expected by the planners, who had placed the figure around 18,000. At least the recognition of Darlan had the result of theoretically saving the difference between 18,000 and 1800 casualties. Not to mention the advantages, from a military standpoint, of prosecution of our drive for Tunisia, the release of thousands of soldiers who would be needed to police the country if we hadn't accepted the leadership offered by the French, and the tidbits of the French fleet expected to fall to the Allies through Darlan's influence. Of course, Darlan has been billed by propaganda and publicity for two years as pro-Nazi, and for the public to swallow him as a patriotic and earnest Frenchman is a bit difficult.

Ike Gets into Harness

Since getting into harness at Algiers yesterday morning, Ike has galvanized the staff and the widely separated commanders into co-ordination. The aerial defense of Algeria was so bad, particularly on Sunday and Monday nights (there was bad weather Tuesday night), that grave fears were held that the French and Arabian population would revolt from the bombings.

Today (Thursday) Ike has had in for conferences and decisions the following: Air Marshal Arthur Tedder, of the Middle East Command of RAF; Air Vice-Marshal Keith Park, of Malta; Admiral Cunningham; Colonel Uzal Ent, Acting Chief of Staff to Lieutenant General Frank M. Andrews, Theater Commander for the Middle East, USA; and Jimmy Doolittle, to mention the key figures. Amongst other things, he has air and naval agreement for defense of Algiers and other ports where our shipping is vulnerable to enemy air attacks. It won't be complete, however, until the equipment for night fighting comes in from England.

On another point action has been taken. All the smart operators said that it would be very bad, indeed, to send under their own power the motorized portions that couldn't be shipped by train eastward to Tunisia. The half-track vehicles (armored) would dissipate a third of the life of their treads just to get to the battle area. (Half-tracks are personnel carriers and are lightly armored and carry machine guns. Some have antitank guns.) Ike's decision was to hell with the life of the half-tracks. What are we saving them for? Now's the time to use them, before the German can further reinforce his rapidly mounting forces. In addition, he ordered that officers should accompany each train eastward and see to it they got through, or know the reason why. They are to assemble on November 27 (Saturday) near Constantine, and join in on Anderson's First Army offensive, which began in the rain yesterday morning. Meanwhile, they had been waiting for trains to carry the combat team eastward. Hell, Ike wanted them to march, as that's the way wars are won and have been throughout history.

Policy on bombing, too, is being straightened. There will be co-ordination of attacks against shipping and airdromes from Malta, Middle East, and French North Africa. Airdromes get the immediate attention.

While the loss of ready communication back to London and Washington, which was so essential while at Gibraltar, seemed overpowering as a reason against moving headquarters and himself to Algiers, two or three days here have justified Ike's decision. We are now getting on with the war, and he is on the spot where he can command direct rather than through a subordinate, who is always considered a subordinate, no matter how efficient he is.

News tonight indicates that General Anderson has pushed within twenty-four miles of Tunis, and Major General Lunsford E. Oliver's Combat Team B may be used effectively pushing farther east to cut off Eyeties and Huns coming into Tunisia from Tripolitania.

The French Fleet

ALGIERS, FRIDAY, NOVEMBER 27, 1942

Ike and Clark are going in the semiarmored Cadillac to the front tomorrow. Principal danger is air attack. There will be a jeep or scout car in front and plenty of machine guns. Exclusive trip. No aides. Too precious.

Percy Winner, of Psychological Warfare Section, just came running into the outer office with a hot message, saying he had to see the General pronto as the French fleet has just scuttled itself. Took him right in. Ike was dictating from a chair by the fire, and Winner read the dope, which was a report from a French news agency received in Algiers by radio.

Essence of it was that Hitler had publicly declared that since the French officers, admirals, and public officials in North Africa, "most of which discarded," had aided the Allies to take North Africa, he was taking Toulon by force, if necessary. Then the *Strasbourg* and perhaps other vessels (Winner had heard "a large part of the fleet") had scuttled.

Ike took it calmly, trying to foresee just what it would mean, immediately appraised it as beneficial so far as keeping the scuttled units from the Germans, but wondered why in the world the French naval officers haven't responded to the call to join the Allies immediately after D-Day. Told me to take it to Admiral Cunningham immediately, which I did, Winner accompanying, to read the French. Found the Admiral had a brief signal via Darlan around noon, indicating *Strasbourg* had scuttled, and that Pétain had ordered the crew to abandon ship. Cunningham thought the news good, said he wanted to talk to General Eisenhower. Darlan had issued the order, while still in the Vichy government, for the fleet to scuttle if likely to fall into German hands.

When Admiral Cunningham arrived at our office, Ike had assembled G-2 (Mockler-Ferryman), G-3 (Lemnitzer), Gruenther, and Clark. After recital of the gist of the news, even though unconfirmed, the Admiral expressed the feeling that some of the fleet would seek to escape, especially destroyers. Thought the French people would be angry; that Hitler had pulled a political bull; that we might get seven or eight cruisers, numerous destroyers, and some subs. As destroyers seeking refuge from Toulon will be forced into Algiers for want of a better place to go, he told Ike, in response to the question as to how they might be protected and/or welcomed, that he had sent a "welcoming committee" of two battleships, two aircraft carriers, and an appropriate number of cruisers and destroyers to protect any fleeing vessels from German aircraft and submarines, which, no doubt, were stationed strategically off Toulon to try to bag any "scampering rabbits."

The Admiralty, becoming impatient, had cabled the British admiral at Alexandria to tell Admiral Godfroy that the British Exchequer could no longer keep a hesitant French fleet; that it was high time the Alexandria units came into the fold. It appeared to Cunningham, as well as to Ike, that we have more to be thankful for from Hitler's action than we have to be mourned. Incidentally, learned that scuttling of all the French units at Alexandria (if accomplished) wouldn't hurt much because British have seen to it that the ships were anchored in such shallow water that after six-foot drop they would be on bottom, except for one battleship.

This should help our efforts to get other remnants, mostly large remnants, of the fleet, and sunken French warships can't do us any harm. It would take the Germans at least a year to raise and refurbish the scuttled vessels. Salt water plays hob with intricate electrical wirings and fire control and damages machinery.

A Letter from Darlan

ALGIERS, SUNDAY, NOVEMBER 29, 1942

Thirty-eight B-17s got off for the hastily arranged bombing of the Bizerte harbor and airdrome, and results are reported as very good. Two were lost, but some ten enemy aircraft were destroyed, several others damaged.

Ike and Clark got off about 6:30 yesterday morning on what Clark described as a Boy Scout trip. They were in the semiarmored Cadillac, with Mickey and Chaney, the sergeant "bat boys," in a quarter-ton truck.

A jeep and a scout car were leading. The rear was protected by another scout car. Plenty of .50-caliber guns, but elevation for antiaircraft guns for defense against enemy aircraft, from which principal danger might be expected, was disquietingly low.

The forward movement of the First Army has continued, according to reports this morning. The squeeze is being put on Bizerte. Colonel Raff, whom Ike made a colonel on the spot two days ago because of his excellent paratroop direction and general leadership of French, Senegalese, and American forces in area around Gafsa in Tunisia, was reinforced and resupplied by nineteen transport planes yesterday. Anderson's army is meeting annoying defensive action from the Germans as they retreat; booby traps, road mines, sniping, and harassment from the air. It was for the last reason that Anderson shouted for quick and smothering air action against enemy airdromes. Welsh, of the RAF, and Doolittle were not seeing eye to eye on tactics, but after Ike had them on the carpet again Friday evening, they "laid on" the offensive operation above mentioned. Welsh came into our office after the conference to phone orders and, when connections were slow, used naughty words. Doolittle inspires his men. They have worked and fought like dogs. Little rest, sleeping in their planes or close by, using emergency rations, they have risen to heights of endurance and courage. Transport pilots, "unheralded and unsung," likewise have done a marvelous job.

The defense of Algiers from night bombing has been improved. Six RAF Beaufighters, equipped with the latest secret gadgets * for this work, have been flown in from the Middle East. Ground equipment has been flown in from U. K. Additional Beaufighters are ready to be "collected" in U. K. as soon as pilots from here can go get them. Additional and similar protection being provided at Bône, which has continued to catch brunt of enemy air action. Although we had a clear night over Algiers last night, there were no alarms. Perhaps weather at Sardinia was too bad for the Hun and Eyetie.

Clark phoned to headquarters last night to say that he and Ike were well beyond Constantine and reported no "untoward incidents." Expect to be flown back Monday forenoon by Beaufighters.

Telek, Ike's dog, is with us, having been brought from Gib by Mickey in the transport plane that also brought Lee, Private Secretary and Warrant Officer Marshall, and Stenographer and Sergeant Kolman, as well as

---

* First Jerry raid of twelve planes after arrival of the night fighters with their secret devices for finding enemy planes in the darkness resulted in nine being shot down and the other three hit so badly they probably didn't get back to base. News of this remarkable score got through French censorship, greatly distressing the RAF, which wanted the Jerries to keep coming.

office gear. The Scottie is growing rapidly but seems just a bit lonesome amidst the cold stone and tile floors and walls of Villa dar el Ouard (Arabic), meaning "Villa of the Family." He's reached the age of enjoying chasing his own tail. He's hard to housebreak; no one has the heart to punish him.

The Governor General of West Africa (Dakar), M. Pierre Boisson, has arrived in Algiers. U. S. wants an American commission to negotiate final terms, aided by Army and civilian personnel from Algiers. Wants port facilities, airdrome, and battle wagons at Dakar for our use.

Today, Ike received a most heartening message from Secretary Stimson, which should cheer him when he returns. With the military victory obscured by the Darlan recognition, a good word from Henry L. is satisfying. Apparently, we haven't been disowned yet.

Beetle wired from London this morning that the PM was most glowing in his praise of the way things are going, and particularly of Ike. Beetle off by plane for U. S. A. this morning. Expects to be gone ten days.

Several days ago, Darlan wrote a rather pathetic letter to General Ike, in which he meditates on the premature letdown of his regime by the President's "military necessity" statement, in which it was indicated Darlan was only temporary. I have saved a copy of Darlan's letter, which had been transmitted to the President and Prime Minister. On it, I have noted that the PM said this was "pathetic and dignified."

Darlan wrote:

                                              Alger, November 21st, 1942

My Dear General:
      Information coming from various parts tends to give credit to the opinion that "I am but a lemon which the Americans will drop after it is crushed."
      In the line of conduct I have taken out of pure French patriotic sense in spite of the heavy inconveniences which are to result for me from it, though it would have been extremely easy for me to let events develop without my intervention, I, as a person, do not count.
      I did what I did only because the American government took the solemn engagement to restore French sovereignty in its integrity as it existed in 1939 and because the armistice between the Axis Powers and France was broken by the occupation of the whole of French metropolitan territory, against which Marshal Pétain has solemnly protested.
      I have acted neither through pride, nor ambition nor intrigue, but because the place I held in my country made it my duty to act.
      When French sovereignty in its integrity is an accomplished fact—and I hope it will be in the least possible time—I firmly intend to go back to civilian life and retire to end a life during which I have eagerly served my country. If this is the way I can interpret the declarations attributed to President Roosevelt, according to which an agreement with me can be but a tem-

porary one, I completely agree. But I have the perhaps excessive pretension of thinking that under present circumstances it is around my name, in association with those of such men as General GIRAUD, General NOGUES, Governor General BOISSON, Admiral MUSELIER, that Africans can unite for a loyal and confident co-operation with the armies, allies of French forces and the people, union which forms an essential part of the United States' success in Africa.

Things being thus, the work of reuniting all Frenchmen, which I am undertaking for a common aim, would be very difficult for me if France's allies were themselves to spread doubts among Frenchmen concerning the interest and the scope of that work.

I hope I can trust the United States government will realize that, and, were it only in view of the result to be expected in the struggle into which enters back French Africa, will not give Frenchmen the impression that the authority of the Chief who makes it struggle again is a diminished one.

With kind regards, I am, very sincerely yours,

[Signed] *Admiral Darlan*

When this was sent by Ike to the two governments, the PM appeared to be touched, as he directed that a most friendly reply be made. The reply of the U. S. for the President, sent to Ike by Marshall, was much more "hold-backish." Ike was to write a letter expressing appreciation of what Darlan has done "thus far," or words to that effect, but was not to indicate he conveys anything more than his own appreciation. Meanwhile, Beetle reported the scuttling of French ships had raised Darlan's stock in England. The evening paper of Algiers, oddly out on Sunday, *Le Soir*, has a piece on the front page this evening that all the world revolts at Hitler's oppression, which caused the scuttling.

Ike Returns from the Front

ALGIERS, MONDAY, NOVEMBER 30, 1942

Ike and Clark, with retinue incomplete, arrived about midnight. Tired and sore. Little things went wrong on the trip, but they accomplished their mission, which was to go over terrain and to discuss the whole situation with General Anderson with a view to expediting all possible aid to his effort.

A twelve-year Arab boy had rushed across the road in front of the scout car immediately preceding the car in which Ike and Wayne were riding. The lad was struck by the car and killed. A French lieutenant who happened to see the accident held the poor lad entirely at fault.

Driving in blackout toward Anderson's flitting headquarters, one of the scout cars, perhaps the same one, skidded into a deep ditch, flinging five soldiers against an embankment, banging them badly.

When they reached Guelma, the last known address of Anderson, he had just moved his headquarters forward. They were put up for the night by the American consul, were up at 5 Sunday morning, finally through good luck located the secret headquarters, but not before they had encountered an excited American colonel who was angry because of lack of air support and claimed British soldiers were being murdered. Said the Germans dive-bombed Beja and there was nothing left. Anderson did not re-echo this situation, if true, but he was informed that both the RAF and the 12th Air Force had been placed under his direct call for support of his ground operations.

Today, Ike had a miserable cold, practically flu. He was feeling badly when he started on the trip Saturday morning. Today he is at the house, conferring, dictating, but getting a good rest. Has read messages from the constant flow, some important, some routine, which Lee and I have selected. The lieutenant doctor, in charge of headquarters dispensary, has prescribed rest, paregoric, and customary treatment for colds. Ike wrote a long review of the operation to date to General Marshall and had Major General Jimmy Doolittle in for a talk. Sunshiny and crisp today.

Ike received a long message from General Marshall conveying the wish of Secretary Hull that civil matters in North Africa be turned over to the State Department gradually, as military operations dictate. Marshall cabled that the last sentence had been written in by the Secretary (Hull) himself. It expressed the thought that the Allied Commander may encounter a transition period during which he might wish to divest himself of certain responsibilities and that the civilian group under Murphy's direction will be able to undertake them as Ike sees fit and in accordance with his judgment. Ike responded that he agreed with every word.

Just now Murphy is knee-deep in conferences with Darlan and Boisson relative to the manner and method of Dakar joining the Allies. Boisson wants to come in under Darlan and wants to do business here pronto. Since Marshall, Hull, and the President want an American commission, probably headed by an admiral, USN, from the U. S. to handle, this embarrasses Ike, who has cabled his situation to the Chief of Staff, with recommendation to conclude principles here and details at Dakar later by the commission.

NOVEMBER, 1942: *American-British expeditionary forces, landing in Morocco and Algeria, met scattered French resistance. Rommel's Afrika Korps, abandoning Italian allies, fled through battered Libya to dig in at El Agheila. Admiral Darlan took over chief French political responsibility in North Africa, while General Giraud became military chief. Germans take over "unoccupied"*

France. Laval named "Chief of Government." French fleet scuttled in Toulon harbor when threatened by German seizure. French troops battled Germans in Tunisia. Siege of Stalingrad became first major Nazi disaster as Russians launched successful offensive while also gaining in the Caucasus. Picture of Axis defeats was repeated in the Pacific: Australians recaptured Kokoda and Gona; Americans destroyed Jap troops and planes on Guadalcanal; Allied planes blasted Mandalay, Bangkok, and Burmese installations. Alcan highway formally opened. Allied diplomatic victories included acquisition of some of Vichy fleet, agreement with Martinique, and alliance with French West Africa. (The forces seeking to preserve and protect the rights of the common man, aroused and showing their democratic might, at last were on the offensive.—H.C.B.)

The Opposition Stiffens

ALGIERS, TUESDAY, DECEMBER 1, 1942

Generals Patton and Spaatz arrived today, the former from Casablanca, the latter from London.

This afternoon Ike, who was feeling much better from the day of rest, although far from cured of his cold, accompanied General Ryder to visit American soldiers and a few officers who were wounded in action, requiring hospitalization, and therefore entitled to the Purple Heart. There were some eighty-seven in all on whom General Ryder pinned medals (Ike declined the honor for himself; said that they were Ryder's men and the Allied C-in-C shouldn't steal the glory), and Ike talked with some fifty at four hospitals and headquarters of the 39th Infantry of the 34th Division. Many were from Iowa and Minnesota. Ike would shake hands with each one, ask him where he was hit, how he felt, and if he expected to get out soon. One replied he had been hit "in the butt."

The cable to Gib has been repaired, and a direct radio circuit has been opened to the U. S.; British did a swell job. A cable-repair ship had been sent from Gibraltar by Admiral Cunningham with a sloop, the only available escort, to protect it. Sardinia, bristling with the might of the Luftwaffe, was within range. In twenty-four hours the cable ship searched, found, and spliced the cable, giving AFHQ reliable service from Algiers to Gibraltar, and hence to London and Washington.*

"Sitrep," situation report, indicates Anderson is meeting stiffer opposition in the east. British planes from Malta have hit the important north quay, where troop disembarkation and unloading of German supplies

---

* Within a few days, when a storm caused ships in Algiers bay to drag their anchors, the cable was broken again and the cable ship had to return to repair it. This disruption occurred while General Ike was in another transatlantic essay contest.

take place, with a 4000-pound bomb and scored other hits there and on airdromes. Air Marshal Tedder, of the Middle East, will come temporarily, at Ike's request, to apply his experience to our problems. Spaatz was requested by Ike to come here for the same reason.

I have reconnoitered the mechanics of placing a wreath on the Monument aux Morts in downtown Algiers which Ike will have to do in the morning. It has been arranged by Darlan, and Ike and Admiral Cunningham will place wreaths. Purpose is to commemorate the dead of all three nations in the North African fighting.

Failed to mention another function of the day. This morning at 10:30, Ike pinned the DSM on General Clark on the portico outside our offices. Movies, stills, and press were on the job.

After the details were made tidy, returned to my desk and found Ike had sent a radio to General Marshall, advising that Clark would head the Fifth Army.

ALGIERS, THURSDAY, DECEMBER 3, 1942

Yesterday was a long one. Started early, included wreath-laying with Darlan and Cunningham, luncheon as guest of Darlan at the Palais d'Etat in honor of Boisson, a reception given by Ike (upon urgent advice of Clark) in honor of Darlan, Boisson, Giraud, and numerous other French officers, including skippers of the two French subs that escaped from Toulon. The day ended, so far as the office was concerned, at 9:15 with an extended conference about affairs in Tunis.

General Anderson has just returned from his headquarters and, with Cunningham, Welsh, Doolittle, Clark, Whiteley, Spaatz, and various and sundry, is at this moment in Ike's office, seeing what can be done. Our Eastern Task Force has reached, at least for the moment, what may be its point of "diminishing power," being at the end of a long and tortuous line of supply. Axis dive bombers, strafers, tanks, mines, and sabotage have stopped the advance within twenty-five miles of Tunis and Bizerte. Our air forces have worked themselves into a state of exhaustion. So much so, that notice was served on Ike they could not keep the pace. Anderson was notified. Overnight it looked to Ike as if we would be stalemated and would have to begin the slow process of methodically building up, just as Generals Alexander and Montgomery had to do at El Alamein.

One piece of good news was from the Royal Navy, which sent a task force of cruisers and destroyers to intercept an enemy convoy en route to Bizerte. Got two troop-laden transports, two merchantmen with supplies, three destroyers (Italian), and a tanker. The last really was sunk by the RAF, and Cunningham was lamenting this morning that the airmen beat him to it. The Admiral is a great "soldier."

Our line of communication from Casablanca has been threatened by reports that the Spaniards are moving troops, intending to occupy the territory in French Morocco to the Sebu. Ike has informed the Combined Chiefs of Staff that he intends to move American troops into this area of French Morocco, to remove the temptation from the Spaniards. General Noguës, in town re powwows with Boisson, et al., had advised this. Combined Chiefs concurred, so this move will proceed soon.

The attack intended to result in capture of Tunis, and first set for yesterday morning but deferred when a German counterattack threw our forces off balance, will be delayed until around December 8, to give time for proper assembly of supplies and reinforcements. Anderson's army has gone so fast and so far, its line of communication has been stretched thin. The time can be used to good advantage also for consolidating control over units now of necessity widely scattered. The attrition of enemy supply will continue, and if naval and air attacks can hit a few more times like night before last, the enemy will be badly off. Essentially it's a race for supply. The Axis now has around 11,550 German troops and 3500 Italians in the Tunis-Bizerte area.

The enemy's handling of planes makes it difficult now for us to damage him much on the ground. He uses the airdromes at Tunis, Bizerte, and elsewhere in Tunisia from dawn to dusk, then flies some of his planes back to the Italian island of Pantelleria or to Sicily, or perhaps Sardinia, thus avoiding the additional risk of leaving them on the fields at night. His aircraft operate from bases within twenty-five to one hundred miles of their front line and can dive-bomb and sweep frequently, whereas our airdromes are back so far, at least the usable ones, that the fighters reach almost their extreme range in getting to the front, then can't stay long, account of fuel.

The boss is getting off some super-duper messages to General Marshall and the Combined Chiefs of Staff re Dakar and Darlan, who insists on negotiating exclusively with Americans, not with the British. Thus Ike is making arrangements with the frank understanding that although ostensibly American, the terms will be equally applicable to the British and other United Nations allies. Boisson says he can't go home unless he has something to popularize his deal.

General Spaatz is to be Deputy C-in-C to co-ordinate all air activities. Spaatz's experience and judgment should relieve Ike of the almost daily task of co-ordinating air activities himself.

ALGIERS, FRIDAY, DECEMBER 4, 1942

We are waiting for the French to sign the agreement giving the Allies carte blanche and active military and naval support. Ike has complete approval from the Combined Chiefs of Staff, concurred in by the Foreign Office and the State Department, to release a press statement from here, so if the signatures are affixed today, we will probably have a press conference in the morning.

One point that rankled in Boisson's breast was the activities of Free French in Equatorial Africa, bordering Dakar and Togoland, where occasional border clashes of Free French and so-called Regular French have resulted in about 300 of Boisson's French officers and other adherents being imprisoned. Boisson wants these freed simultaneously with release of British and other internees now held in Dakar. Says the British can control French National Committee, the de Gaullist group, and insists he can't face his homefolk without gaining amnesty for his own officers. Ike has backed him in this demand, but the point has been at the moment dropped from the main agreement and awaits further negotiation. British are likely to work this out with de Gaulle.

Jimmy Doolittle at lunch today told Ike the American fliers took a pasting yesterday over Bizerte. Eighteen B-17s, bent on daylight bombing of the docks and shipping, flying at 20,000 feet, and escorted by sixteen (two had to return account engine trouble) P-38s, at 25,000 feet, were attacked from above by F-W 190s and Me-109s. Seven P-38s were lost and two more failed to return, but all Fortresses dropped their forty-five tons of 500-pound bombs on the harbor targets, hitting two ships. Heretofore we have been getting four for one, and this licking disturbed Jimmy. Felt the F-W is the most modern and, therefore, best fighter of any country. Engine failures signalize inadequate maintenance. Analyzed also the Germans, who have avoided air fights until yesterday, are now feeling our attacks on their supply lines, and are air-fighting with determination. Thinks also Germans may have their radar installed. Another point discussed was necessity of Fortresses being over target about 11 each morning, which gives enemy chance to have his fighters air-borne and waiting. From Oran (Tafaroua) the distance requires early start to reach objective and return to base and still have daylight for landing. Need to be over target before noon because heavy cloud gathers from then on nearly every day. Jimmy was pouring out this and related troubles to Ike, who became somewhat exasperated, and said:

"Those are your troubles—go and cure them. Don't you think I've a lot of troubles, too?"

Jimmy replied: "I'm sorry I can't give you good news every day—I gave you some yesterday."

Five of us (Beetle, T. J., and I—forget the other two) have bets of ten dollars apiece with Ike that he will get his fourth star by December 25, Christmas. My hunch is that Beetle, who is returning from U. S. via London, may have an inkling of this, but Ike thinks his bet is a cinch. Says if he were General Marshall, damned if he'd make another four-star general, but admits it would be nice to be numbered with Grant, Sherman, Sheridan, and Pershing, who were made four-star generals on the field of battle. In this Allied Command are a full admiral, a full general, and an air marshal, yet as Lieutenant General, Ike, although outranked, gets along fine. No one seems to care about metal stars on shoulders so long as the battle is on.

There seems to be a fear in some quarters that the French may suck us in, our arms and supplies, and then if things should go badly in Tunisia, turn on us. They could raise a lot of hell, particularly with our lines of supply, but I can't subscribe to this view.

We have about 7000 troops at the front line. About 10,000 in the concentration are well back. Our front line somewhat this side (west) of Mateur and Tebourba, but we have a height which commands Tebourba. Right now our forces are "consolidating." All efforts plus ingenuity being mustered to hurry transportation, particularly from trains (which pack sidings) onto trucks to dumps.

ALGIERS, SATURDAY, DECEMBER 5, 1942

Last evening, when General Ike was ready to leave the St. George for the villa, it was "pouring with rain." I walked with him to the front door, where the driver usually waited with the car. To my astonishment and Ike's disgust, we found the car had been ordered by Major Lee to stand by under a portico on the other side of the building so that the Allied Commander wouldn't get wet. The lobby was packed with officers and men waiting for transportation and, of course, they came respectfully to attention when General Ike entered, I at his heels. Ike spluttered and said loudly, "I'm going to fire an aide." I thought he meant me.

After our guests had arrived at the villa and refreshments were poured, I proposed a toast to the new aide. General Ike looked up quickly and said, "What new aide?" I said, "My replacement." His retort was, "Who ever said you were an aide?" Subject closed.

News from the eastern front is bad. Ike has sent a long personal message to the PM to keep him up to date—this through "Pug" Ismay.

If only the Combined Chiefs would sound off. re the Dakar deal, Ike could give out a prepared statement at a press conference, then clear up the misconceptions and rumors of the newspapermen by an off-the-record talk. Things ain't a-breakin' right, says I.

But Brigadier General C. R. Smith, just over from U. S., says that the Darlan recognition has caused no appreciable reaction at home, that the victory was the important thing. If anything, we have left the impression the job is too easy, probably account our effort to minimize extent of fighting, to keep from wrenching French feelings. Yesterday the French, fighting under Colonel Raff, took a town in southern Tunisia, killing some fifty Germans, wounding too few, and capturing nearly 100. At least some of the French are fighting.

In England we were harassed on the Negro question by liberty-loving provocateurs. In Africa we, apparently, are supposed by these same gentlemen to have a general election of Arabs, Jews, and French to elect a Congress and President, and then go on with the war.

General Smith has comprehensive plans for widespread air service for all of Africa. Dakar a great help to him. He was out of cigars, so gave him a box and thereby established another line of communication for future shipments direct from Washington, via southern all-weather route.

We Lose the First Race for Tunis

ALGIERS, SUNDAY, DECEMBER 6, 1942

Ike said this morning while we were shaving that we may have to retreat in Tunisia. Tough. Axis has built up to around 31,000 men in all of Tunisia, and is using dive bombers, tanks, and sabotage effectively. Our D-Day for the all-out attack to take Tunis and isolate Bizerte is set for December 9 and has been approved by Combined Chiefs. They express the wish, however, that everything be thrown in to clean up the situation so that we will not be engaged in a long battle of attrition. Want western Mediterranean cleared from our side of the water.

Mr. Murphy phoned, wanted to see me, and when he arrived I found he really should see Ike. His worry was that Boisson is growing suspicious, that his governors of various colonies under his jurisdiction are fearful we are making him a dupe, that we really are planning an attack, and that he wants to go home today with some sort of letter from General Eisenhower showing the general arrangement is satisfactory. All this because we have not heard from the Combined Chiefs. Looks as if the question of approval or disapproval got to "higher levels," meaning Roosevelt and the PM, and they are exchanging transatlantic messages, leaving Dakar in mid-air.

Upshot is that Ike is going to have the press in at 2:30 to clarify the situation for them and to correct the several misapprehensions under which I know and have informed Ike they are laboring. Murphy supplemented these views.

As the reputation for anti-Semitism and for policies akin to the Nazis is attached to Darlan and the Vichy regime with which he was associated, we have attributed the adverse public reaction at home and in England to the fear such policies would be perpetuated in North Africa under the Darlan regime. To help allay such fears, Murphy has talked with Darlan, who proposes to deal liberally with the problem as rapidly as complicated age-old hates and prejudices of Arabs and Jews will permit. Murphy has dispatched a message through the War Department for Secretary Hull concerning the welfare of both Jewish and Spanish refugees. Darlan has promised informally to alleviate the condition of the Jews by restoring them their property, which was sequestered under post-armistice legislation enacted under Axis pressure, and also returning to them the right to practice certain professions, such as medicine and law. The message went on that Darlan and many other French officials state that if sensational steps to improve the lot of the Jews are taken, there will inevitably follow a violent Moslem reaction which, in the present uncertain state of public affairs, would be most untimely and unwelcome.

Murphy called Hull's attention to the special situation prevailing in French North Africa, where there are approximately a total of only 300,000 Jews as compared with 11,000,000 Moslems. The latter do not occupy an equal status in many respects, such as normal right of franchise, right to hold public office, etc., for the reason that the comparatively small European population of 1,500,000 for years has protected its status in this area by special legislation.

Murphy continued that the military situation prevents the immediate release of several thousand European refugees now interned until the military operation is farther advanced and transport is available for their eventual repatriation or other disposition. It is also wished to avoid at this time an adverse Spanish reaction, as many of the internees are Spanish Loyalists and, if arbitrarily returned to Spain, fear Franco would order them shot.

Report from G-3 just in from Anderson: "We are attacked."

This was followed by a courier with a personal and most secret letter from General Anderson for the Allied Commander. While General Anderson was at Algiers conferring with Ike, he reported that his forces had had a "nasty setback." Heavy losses had been suffered by his Infantry

Brigade Group, several U. S. medium tanks were knocked out, and a large number of guns, mainly six-pounder antitank and Bofors, were lost. Anderson said that this action, coming on top of previous heavy fighting and the prolonged strain caused by four weeks of ceaseless effort and hard living, has exhausted the fighting value of the Infantry Brigade until it can be rested, reinforced, and refitted. He said that Surreys and Northamptons are down to only about 330 all ranks, the Lancashire Fusiliers is about 450 strong, while two Hampshires, sent ahead with the I Guards Brigade, have been wiped out—only ninety all ranks remaining. The defeat has been caused by heavy dive-bombing attacks. Our field artillery too dispersed in small packets. Faulty handling of U. S. medium tanks, which advanced to counterattack by themselves, without support from field artillery and tank-destroyer guns, whereas Germans, when supporting field artillery is unavailable, help their tanks by heavy dive bombing.

Anderson was sorry to report that because of the reverse, any major attack on December 9 or for several days after is out of the question. His troops have been dive-bombed so much that mental and moral strain was considerable and the matériel losses were heavy. While it was too early to decide for certain, he anticipated withdrawal to the Medjez-el-Bab or Teboursouk-Beja-Dj. Aviod area will be necessary if he fails soon to knock out Tunis. He would hold this line until he could launch a big attack after proper preparation. In the Tunis-Bizerte area, the Hun has definitely daylight mastery of the air.

Supply lubricants, special octane gasoline, ammunition of all kinds, and spare parts are needed for U. S. tanks and guns. The supply is precarious. He needs reinforcements and wants to know when the remainder of the 1st U. S. Armored Division will arrive from Oran. He closed with a statement that the troops were very far from downhearted, but, for the moment, he must be prudent, as nothing but harm would come from rushing in recklessly now when he is unready.

(It is obvious we have lost the race for Tunis.)

"Dakar Is with Us"

ALGIERS, MONDAY, DECEMBER 7, 1942

Tunis seems far away, but Dakar is in the bag, with the string tied in a pretty bow just as directed by the Combined Chiefs of Staff, with the President holding his finger on the knot and the Prime Minister tying it.

Ike's actual message, sent at 12:55, merely said, "Dakar is with us."

An American commission, headed by Rear Admiral William Glassford, USN, is to go from U. S. to Dakar to thresh out details, but in meantime Boisson says American planes can pass through Dakar as soon as he returns, which will be promptly. General Clark is back from reconnoitering his headquarters. Expects to go east soon.

This morning the PM came through with a rah-rah message to Ike that would have done credit to a sales manager seeking to pep up one of his star salesmen who was having hard going. The Prime Minister is not discouraged. He is filled with admiration for the brilliant advances and is not at all disappointed by the check our vanguards have received in their audacious attempt to seize the maximum territory possible before enemy resistance solidified. He said that the Allied Commander was absolutely right to run all risks and the opposite policy would have denied us invaluable gains. He felt that the protracted fighting in Tunis must be very costly for the Axis and pledged himself to do everything in human power to support the operations. He regretted that in the midst of fighting battles, General Ike had to be bothered by all the Darlan business. He asked General Ike to think of him as a solid fortification covering his rear, so the Allied force could go for the swine in front with a blithe heart.

Addenda

ALGIERS, TUESDAY, DECEMBER 8, 1942

Items I've failed to record: Charles Bedaux, the stretch-out promoter with whom American labor leaders raised hell when he was discovered as the advance man for the Duke and Duchess of Windsor's visit to U. S., has been arrested here by the French on charges of being a Nazi agent. They have photostats of certain letters appointing him as an industrial agent by the Germans. . . . Message today reports good news that Milton, Ike's brother, en route London with Beetle, and coming this theater—OWI business. . . . Giraud sent message this morning he had heard General Anderson planned a "withdrawal" of about twenty miles. Just when we have been moving heaven and earth to get reinforcements and supplies to him for an attack December 9, but that is temporarily off. . . . Ike had session with air people this morning, with much talk heard through the door. Seeking to confirm just what Anderson intends to do. . . . General Clark and Meach off to the front this morning. Clark will see Anderson. . . . Ike was intent on getting more American armor up east last night, but supply people were kicking it couldn't be maintained. . . . General Gale, British Allied Supply Chief, was at the villa for dinner, and immediately afterwards got busy to accomplish what his subordinates had said was "the impossible." Ike's view is it takes the impossible to win wars, and is trying to instill this spirit.

Censorship

ALGIERS, WEDNESDAY, DECEMBER 9, 1942

D-Day for assault to take Tunis and pen up Bizerte was postponed "for a week or ten days" by General Anderson. Disappointing to Ike, who is irritated at any delays. If he ever gets Tunisia, he'll be a changed man; now he's like a caged tiger, snarling and clawing to get things done.

There was a meeting at 5 yesterday afternoon on HIRES,* the project of attacking Sardinia. Brigadier Sugden outlined to those assembled (Ike, Cunningham, Whiteley, Gruenther, and smaller fry, especially me). Broadly, could be attempted, with port of Cagliari the principal objective, as it is the main and largest port of the island. Attack would be made by two British brigades and one U. S. division. Could not be attempted, however, until we have mastery of the air, Tunisia has been taken, and our "build-up" of personnel and supplies, except maintenance, has been completed for TORCH. Inflow of troops and equipment expected by end of January, thereafter it's question of maintenance, which is set up by shipping authorities. Ships, including combat loaders, now in use for build-up would be assigned to movement for HIRES, with one division, probably U. S. 45th, to be trained in U. S. A. for amphibious operations. Element of surprise to be sought, so training in landing craft has to be done elsewhere than in Med. There are as usual, Ike pointed out, a great number of "ifs and whens" involved, and we doubt if the suggested target date of March 30 can be made, but it is being set up tentatively for that date.

A "paper" will now be drafted by Sugden and, if approved, will be submitted to the Combined Chiefs of Staff. But our eyes, and especially Ike's, are on Tunisia. It's hard to give much thought to such future operations while our immediate battle is absorbing constant attention.

All this came along after Ike had received a most glowing message from General Marshall, but ending with a strong criticism of censorship at Algiers as well as London.

General Surles has echoed the complaint received here from London that the press stories announcing Ike's deal for Dakar were twenty-five hours in transmission and that CBS and NBC had got their stories through by short-wave promptly. Press associations asking to buy time on

---

* Code name for the proposed operation.

Radio Algiers to send their news, which made sense to me, and I so advised PRO Phillips, but he says Signal Corps, being jammed with military traffic, is using the station and can't spare any more time. Suggested then that one of the two daily broadcasts of the networks be shared with the press associations, but Phillips says they would holler like hell.*

Met General Patton, his aide and sergeant, at the airport. They were dressed like parachutists, but only special tank regalia. Patton en route to east front to see for himself. Patton's transport plane had arrived during an air-raid alarm and was fired on by AA. Probably failed to give proper signal. Patton full of usual pep, and spent the night with us.

The General and the "Politicians"

ALGIERS, THURSDAY, DECEMBER 10, 1942

Last night we had a two-ring conference after dinner at the villa, and I shuttled between both. Ike was with Murphy and Colonel Holmes in the dining room. These he calls the "politicians." In the improvised sitting room where we gather before dinner sat General Patton and the British General Morgan and Brigadier General Robert C. Candee, of the Air Force. The British had come for conferences about Spanish Morocco, and Morgan had especially wanted to see Patton, whose Western Task Force would be used along with British troops from U. K. if the Spaniards became hostile in their part of Morocco. Patton's forces had moved into the controverted Sebu river area and had actually got two miles into the International Zone because, by Patton's own admission, he had directed the force to go to a certain town he indicated on the map. This happened to be inside the zone, where troops are definitely not supposed to go. "Neglected to put the calipers on it," said Patton. Force had backtracked outside the twenty-mile zone.

Murphy and Holmes had been sent by Ike to perk up Darlan on his liberalization of Nazi-inspired decrees in the form of a new ordinance, which is supposedly being rewritten. Darlan had shown Murphy and Holmes a letter from a rabbi in Constantine, urging that reform of the hard and unjust laws against the Jews in Africa be modified slowly. If done too rapidly, the rabbi feared reprisals against Jews by the Arabs. Ike had heard from London that it would be helpful to have the revised ordinance there before the secret debate re Darlan comes up in the Commons Thursday. Ike also wanted cleared and available for publication what-

* But time was found on Radio Algiers to voicecast news to the press associations.

ever "liberalization" might have been accomplished to date. Murphy and Holmes came in late, direct from a conference with Darlan, and had what was wanted, as far as it went. Ike dictated to me a message to General Marshall for the President. Revised ordinance was cabled overnight to Mack at Foreign Office. So all bases touched.

What tickled me was shuttling between the two groups: in one we were liberating the Jews, at least as far as the Moslems would permit; in the other, General Patton was figuratively racing through Spanish Morocco like a gay *caballero* on the back of a tank.

The two-ring circus at the house last night brings to mind that one of the things General Ike is learning, and occasionally speaks about, is that waiting for other people to produce is one of the hardest things a commander has to do. Another thing is that in the higher positions of a modern army, navy, and air force, rich organizational experience and an orderly, logical mind are absolutely essential to success. He is finding that the flashy, publicity-seeking type of adventurer can grab the headlines and be a hero in the eyes of the public, but this evidence of ambition makes it difficult for him to deliver the goods in high command. The slow, methodical, ritualistic person is absolutely valueless in a key position. Between the two types the Commander must manage to get a balance. Above all, the Commander must have an inexhaustible fund of nervous energy. He is called upon day and night to absorb the disappointments and discouragements and the doubts of his subordinates and to force them on to accomplishments which they regard as impossible. He must indoctrinate them with the spirit of unity and pass the word along. To find the kinds of officers for the ideal balance is the real job of the Commander.

As a kibitzer of the political and military doings of AFHQ and particularly of General Ike, I am becoming increasingly impressed with the development of this man. I have had the privilege of knowing many of Washington's important people, with slight acquaintance and some observation of Presidents, from Coolidge to Roosevelt, and I should guess this fellow Eisenhower can hold his own with any man I ever met. And he talks the same language to the GI, the Tommy, the sailor, the British, and the French. His ability to bring services and nationalities together seems to flow from his frankness and honesty. They trust him, and, fortunately, he has a gift from the Lord to express himself lucidly, a quality sometimes lacking in military men. Also, Ike has a friendly and magnetic personality. It draws people not only to *him*, but closer together as teammates. And his teammates surely realize that if they do their jobs well, he will give them the credit.

Didn't have time to write yesterday. Ike's brother Milton and Beetle are
staying at the villa, having flown in yesterday from Gibraltar. I'm sleeping
in Mickey's bed, the one I high-graded from the St. George, in the downstairs cloakroom, and being Telek's roommate as well. This morning I
stepped out of bed, mentally recoiling from the dreaded cold tile floor,
and my foot landed in the middle of Telek's puddle. This war is hell.

Ike has had an off-and-on two-day conference with Air Marshal Tedder,
top airman for the Middle East. Spaatz, Major General Louis H. Brereton, Cunningham, Beetle, Welsh, and assorted brains, on plans for
mutual prosecution of the pinch on Rommel. General Anderson also was
here yesterday to see Ike and the staff. Major Lee just commented: "The
boss has laughed a couple of times today—his cold must be breaking up."
My guess is that he's beginning to see daylight through all the talk and
banging to get things done.

Milton is getting into the news problems. Radio Maroc, which has
been beating the world on news of our operations, has been a prime
source of trouble in U. S. because press picks up items, allegedly twisted
by Maroc. He has found one or more of his OWI men has been in charge
of directing Maroc's operations. What he already has done is to reflect
the miserable press situation we apparently have at home, where a hand-
ful of columnists, commentators, and other newspaper people have thrown
a lot of sand over the Darlan deal. Also, the fact that Ike has tossed bouquets to subordinates, and has been magnanimous in giving them public
credit for his efforts, has given an impression at home, at least in the War
Department, that the Allied C-in-C is not the actual boss of this show.

General Marshall has criticized direct quotations of officers, particularly high-ranking ones, and indicated that Ike had been quoted from
Gibraltar in ways tending to cheapen himself. . . . Ike is the best han-
dler of the press when he does it his own way—makes them soldiers along
with the rest—but the rebuff threw him off stride. Another press conference scheduled tomorrow, which I hope will be a regular procedure
again. Just now poor Joe Phillips is getting blamed for bad public relations, when of course the Darlan arrangement was bound to cause criticism. With the French helping as they are, and in position to hurt if
they merely stop helping, it is dangerous to rock the boat.

On Joe's recommendation, and passed on to the boss with my nickel's
worth, General McClure, our G-2 in London, is to come here pronto
to co-ordinate censorship, public relations, OWI, Civilian Affairs, and
Psychological Warfare—that is, on their public statements, etc.

Incidentally, Ike told some dinner guests the other night of his worry over the famous missing page from this book—the page that caused me some sleepless nights and caused Miss Jaqua such anguish. . . . Yet the TORCH operation has been acclaimed as one of the world's greatest military surprises. Ike said that he felt a great relief when the landings had been made successfully, as the missing paper thereby must have been burned, as we thought; certainly it wasn't in enemy hands.

T. J. has got his first star, and we are all happy. . . . Beetle got his second. . . . T. J. is coming to dinner tonight to celebrate. We have from two to six guests (British and American, usually fifty-fifty) from the staff every night . . . work keeps on this way, although semisocially.

Of all things, a nice word for Ike. The British government sent word today through General Marshall that it thanks Eisenhower for getting the release of internees, mostly British, in French West Africa. This was accomplished by Ike's letter to Boisson, and the Free French having released their internees or prisoners of the so-called Regular French Forces. Apparently, Ike's letter did a good job—and Dakar radio announces French in West Africa will actively fight against the Axis. But the big news of the day, in my estimation for many days to come, is Darlan's endorsement of liberal policies—not necessarily "liberal," but a step forward. The people at home should see that the military, especially Ike, is more enlightened than they have seemed to feel.

ALGIERS, WEDNESDAY, DECEMBER 16, 1942

The Darlan "liberalization" statement has been transmitted to America, with favorable comment by the local American correspondents.

The date tentatively set for the continuation of the eastward drive into Tunisia is December 22. Our ground forces in the battle now number about 20,000 British, 11,000 Americans, and 30,000 French, although the latter are poorly equipped and couldn't withstand tank attacks. A U-boat was rammed by a Royal Navy destroyer and sunk in some seventy fathoms near Bône. Divers are being sent to try to get out the secret ciphers, which would be helpful.

The estimate of enemy strength as of December 14 shows about 19,500 German and 11,250 Italian combat troops, with about 2500 German Air Force and 5000 service troops, total about 38,500. Fighting value of German armor described as high, morale of remainder of ground forces not high.

French forces are actively protecting the south flank of the Allied

Army and co-operating wholeheartedly. Considerable French forces have been transferred to Tunisia from Oran and Casablanca.

Lieutenant N. L. A. Jewell, RN, the captain of Sub 219, which took Clark in and out, was a guest for dinner night before last. Captain Barney Fawkes, of the *Maidstone*, sub mother ship, was there, too. Jewell had just torpedoed four enemy merchant ships, landed a Commando party on Italian coast that destroyed a railroad train, and contributed exceptional reconnaissance. Fawkes said that thirteen of the Italians who had placed "limpets," five-pound mines, on ships in Algiers harbor recently were captives on his ship. They succeeded in sinking one ship and damaging two, which were run ashore. Seems they came from a sub, four miles off shore, wore light diving suits, rode astride torpedolike, self-propelled devices with just their heads showing above water, and slipped through to the ships without being observed. Submerging, they quietly fastened their mines to the ships, preferably along the "backbone." One was detected, hauled on deck, and, when he refused to tell just where he had fastened his mine, was hung by the neck over the side until he confessed. This is a rather widely practiced form of sea warfare in the Med, it appears from Fawkes, who cited numerous instances of such attempts and some successes at Gibraltar. Worst thing is it tends to drive ships into small inner harbor at night, making the closely moored vessels an ideal bombing target. Best way to prevent is to keep propellers of ships turning sufficiently to create current. This is too much for limpet men to buck and so can't fasten their mines. Lookouts aboard ships frequently grow lax after a nerve-straining three-week journey through submarine-infested waters.

Repercussions on Darlan

ALGIERS, THURSDAY, DECEMBER 17, 1942

Ike is being buffeted by a succession of tough decisions. Today General Giraud demanded complete control of our Tunisian campaign.

Last night Percy Winner and Jay Allen, OWI, having business with Milton, came to dinner, and directly and indirectly lambasted the Darlan deal to Ike. Dwelt on fact that the French who risked their lives to help the invasion have been disgraced in the eyes of pro-German French, particularly in Morocco, while officeholders under Noguës, who were notoriously pro-Nazi, still hold their jobs. Also, anti-American and anti-Ally literature may be had publicly for the asking, and samples of this were produced. . . .

"Dampy," the congenial young flag lieutenant to Admiral Cunningham, has been in to say, as politely as only the British can diplomatically reach the point, "Would it be possible for the guards at headquarters to recognize the Admiral without requiring him to show his pass each time he enters and departs?" Seems the Admiral entrusts his pass to Dampy, but this morning the lieutenant didn't accompany him. The guard held the Admiral by the arm—this after the guard at the twin villas had insisted on inspecting the Admiral's outgoing car. The good Admiral declared he must have thought someone was trying to steal the General's rug.

Going back to the opinions of Winner and Allen, Mr. Murphy, whom Allen hailed as the best man in his field, sees Ike at least twice a day, and repeatedly has assured him that the SOL and the Legion, both former French groups, are behaving under Darlan. And what is more, Giraud had brought a French division out of Morocco just the day before, which indicated the French want to fight the Axis. In fact, Giraud issued the order moving them toward Tunisia without consulting the C-in-C, and it was embarrassing logistically, because we have all the soldiers we can supply up there. Nor do they have sufficient equipment. This on top of another French move to bring 40,000 Senegalese from Dakar in the Fighting French merchant ships. These ships are needed to bring AA guns, AT guns, rifles, m.g.s,* and other equipment for French from America, so the 40,000, who are poorly equipped for modern war, are another cause of trouble. Now Giraud, realizing Ike's need for him both militarily and politically, is putting on the heat to defend his native soil by leading the Allied forces in Tunisia. How can an Allied Commander-in-Chief, under orders from the Combined Chiefs of Staff, relinquish or delegate his authority to Giraud? Or even replace Anderson, or supersede him, with the French General?

With these perplexing questions before him, Ike told Milton and me when we started for lunch, "If I could just get command of a battalion and get into a bullet battle, it would all be so simple."

Clark went west today and expected to see Patton, and among other things to discuss the alarming report of Jay Allen re distrust of Noguës, dissatisfaction of pro-Ally French, and possible removal of the smart pro-German staff of Noguës (one by one). The police chief is reported as another bad egg.

The War Department offered battalion of Japanese-Americans to Ike, and he accepted.† Glad to have anyone who wants to fight, but just now his worry is to get supplies to the east.

---

* Usual abbreviations for antiaircraft, antitank, and machine guns.
† This was the 100th Battalion. It made an excellent combat record.

ALGIERS, FRIDAY, DECEMBER 18, 1942

D-Day for assault up east set, rather uncertainly, for night of Dec. 22-23.

Admiral Cunningham allows as how we have sunk twenty-six enemy subs since TORCH was lit.

Admiral Godfroy won't bring over his portion of the French fleet at Alexandria unless Darlan is assured of recognition by both governments for duration of the war, but agrees French leaders should be selected by the people immediately after the war. The "temporary expedient" statement of the President, plus Eden's cool statement, made Godfroy extremely distrustful of the tenure of office to be enjoyed by Darlan, yet Godfroy insists he will serve only under Darlan, the man who has helped Ike and the Allied forces militarily at every opportunity.

The General and the French

ALGIERS, SUNDAY, DECEMBER 20, 1942

Mail and packages came through yesterday for all. Ike hit the jackpot. Newspapers, mimeographs, and a variety of stuff from London. They indicate the reaction to Darlan is savage, but we don't know what effect, if any, Darlan's "liberalization" statement may have had—perhaps none, as the press, particularly British, is skeptical.

Ike is surrounded by the French, at the moment, and this could have been said yesterday afternoon and all forenoon today. He is seeking better understanding, and removal of "bad eggs"—probably Noguës, and certainly Chatel, and efforts are being made to bring Marcel Peyrouton from Argentina to succeed Chatel. But where to find a qualified Frenchman who is a good administrator, well enough known to the public, to take over? Just now Ike has Mr. Murphy and General François d'Astier de la Vigerie, an emissary from the Fighting French, going over the whole mess.

Colonel Stirling and Mr. Mack, Ike's emissaries to London, who were to tell the reasons for accepting Darlan, have returned and seem more impressed with London's animosity to Darlan than with the reasons which dictated the action. Stirling and Mack feel Darlan must be junked soon after Tunis is taken. Before going to London, both of them, especially Mack, who represents the Foreign Office, had told Ike his reasons for accepting Darlan were "unanswerable." Apparently their knees are weak, or perhaps the savageness of opposition is irresistible.

Some of the London papers speak of the act, by Eisenhower, as "revolting" and "disgusting."

Speaking of d'Astier, by some slip-up he wasn't met at the airdrome when he arrived yesterday, which offended him. Then Mr. Murphy, that much-harassed man, had overlooked mentioning to Darlan the prospective arrival of this Free Frenchman. When Darlan and his people heard of d'Astier's presence in Algiers, they wanted to arrest him. Then d'Astier got mad, and was refusing even to speak to the Darlan crowd. This is where the matter stood last night, when Beetle came to the house around 10 to give the round-by-round account. On Ike's authority, Beetle had dispatched General McClure and Mr. Murphy to do two things: (1) get Darlan not to arrest d'Astier; (2) get d'Astier to converse with Darlan.

Darlan and Giraud came to the villa about midnight to urge that d'Astier be sent out of Africa; they feared trouble. Ike maintained this was a French problem and the French should work it out together.

During the forenoon, while d'Astier and Murphy were talking within the office, loud talk came through the door—mostly Ike's.

During lunch Ike said that d'Astier was reluctant to see Darlan, but wanted to have carte blanche, and expected to have it from the Allied C-in-C, to visit and talk with de Gaullists all over French Africa, North and West. This was too much. Ike reviewed the whole circumstances, and arranged, after much parlez-vooing, that d'Astier talk unofficially with Darlan this afternoon. If d'Astier travels over Africa, this being French administration, it's up to Darlan. The possibilities of something that would lead to a reconciliation of de Gaullists and Darlanists, out of d'Astier's mission, were almost smothered by the bad start.

ALGIERS, TUESDAY, DECEMBER 22, 1942

We are off to the front tomorrow at 6 A.M., the Allied Commander-in-Chief preferring to make it a Christmas at the front. Expected back here Saturday evening. I am going along, Brigadier Whiteley, Assistant C/S, going. Taking Cadillac, a Packard in case the Cadillac breaks down, a scout car fore and aft, and will pick up one of the signal mobile units at Constantine.

Failed to mention that Patton sent two live turkeys for Christmas, the crates being so large that Captain Arnold had to send for Mickey and jeep to haul them from the airdrome.

Well, we're off to the front. All the aides are jealous, and I am glad. This is written for their benefit, as they are privileged, especially Lee, to torture themselves by reading this stuff.

General Mud—and the Assassination of Darlan

ALGIERS, SATURDAY, DECEMBER 26, 1942

Well, we're back from our Christmas at the front. General Clark had phoned Ike at Souk-el-Khemis, guardedly indicating there was serious trouble in Algiers and that he should return immediately. It was just before dinner, which we were to have with the officers of the British V Corps. Their headquarters are in a farmhouse. The machinery for farming is skillfully used to camouflage the presence of the headquarters staff and troops—hay rakes cover slit trenches, strawstacks are tunneled for soldiers' quarters, and no cars are allowed in the barnyard because the tracks would disclose to aerial reconnaissance the presence of things "nonagricultural."

We left Algiers at 6:15 Wednesday morning and reached Souk-el-Khemis around 2 Thursday afternoon. General Lunsford E. Oliver guided Ike and General Anderson to a near-by farmhouse, through deep mud, to meet and talk with the officers of Combat Team B. Ike visited a number of GIs in pup tents pitched in mud. It was raining hard all the time. As there was to be a conference of Ike, Anderson, and the Corps Commander, Lieutenant General C. W. Allfrey, as well as Brigadier Whiteley, we returned to the V headquarters at Souk-el-Khemis.

We had learned at the British line-of-communication headquarters at Constantine that Anderson's attack, which had been set for the night of Christmas Eve, had been postponed for forty-eight hours. This was to have been the all-out push on Tunis. It was called off because of the absolute impossibility of moving vehicles in the mud.

At the conference, General Anderson said that he had ordered trials of moving various sizes of equipment, just to be completely satisfied. Nothing could be moved satisfactorily. We had seen four men trying to push a motorcycle from the airdrome at Souk-el-Khemis. Anderson felt that the attack would have to be postponed until there was a good chance of continuing favorable weather. If the attack were launched after as much as a four- or five-day dry spell, there might come another heavy rainy period, and then the vehicles would be lost if the enemy counterattacked with infantry, which undoubtedly he would do. Anderson had consulted the natives on weather characteristics of the region, and they said that the rains would get worse through January and much of February. Anderson said that discretion ruled against attempting an attack for probably six weeks. This was a bitter disappointment to Ike.

Despite the mud, Ike wanted to keep on the offensive, so the enemy couldn't get too well set. Had been exploring the possibilities of supplying a force to push from the south to cut the enemy's supply line from Tunis to Tripoli, possibly at Sfax or Gabès. Out of the conference came the idea of shifting Combat Team B to Tebessa, there to begin setting up a garrison, and to be joined by the rest of the 1st Armored Division. The game was to have a hard-hitting and mobile force that could rush into Gabès, Sousse, or Sfax, play hell with the supplies and lines, and then retire to Tebessa, or whatever point ultimately would be selected for the garrison. This was regarded as a good move, assuming there could be virtually no tank operations in the north and that the texture of the soil and climate would permit movement of heavy armor in the south. There also remained the troublesome problem of how to supply such a large outfit. One suggestion was to run coasters in from Malta, or around the Tunisian elbow, but the Navy probably would frown on such a gamble. This was pretty well buttoned up as a project, dependent upon staff studies of the logistics, which had been under way but remained unfinished.

As to the drive for Tunis, Ike agreed with General Anderson and the V Corps General Allfrey that if the bad weather persisted, the attack would have to be methodical shelling of enemy positions with artillery, infantry moving up, tanks for infantry support coming along to break through; when the infantry had reached the limit of range of artillery, move the guns, and repeat methodically until Tunis is taken.

Then the question of command, repeatedly raised by Giraud, was brought up by Ike. The French wouldn't serve under him, General Anderson freely admitted, although co-operation with General Juin was harmonious and satisfactory. Yet the British First Army was supposed to keep on to Tripoli after Tunis was taken. Anderson offered to quit and go back to England, was most sporting in his efforts personally to find a solution, but fact was the French simply would not go under British command. A solution might be found if Ike himself were to take active personal command at the front, leaving Anderson in charge of the First Army in the north, the French with their own forces in the center of hilly terrain, and possibly under General Juin but leading to Giraud's ultimate control, and the American force in the south. Ike arranged to discuss this possibility and others with General Juin that evening, preliminary to talking again with Giraud when we returned to Algiers.

Ike was talking with Juin when the message came via telephone from General Clark, and it was put in terms so guarded that Ike suspected, but wasn't sure, that Darlan had been shot. Clark said to return to Algiers immediately, which in itself meant bad news.

Within the hour we were packed up and left the farmhouse around 10 Christmas Eve, drove all night and Christmas Day, stopping only for gas, breakfasted in Constantine (where the news of Darlan's death was confirmed), lunched from emergency rations along the road, and reached Algiers around 6 P.M. on Christmas Day.

Ike immediately conferred at the office with the staff people, found things had been handled satisfactorily, and gave some discreet pushing to influence the selection of Giraud as the best man available. Ike's comment while en route home from the east was that Darlan's death ended one problem, but no doubt created many more.

Ike pressed for following through on his decision, while at the front, to create the southern front to cut the supply lines to Tripoli. He had also to straighten the command problem.

I read the swell leather-bound book of Christmas letters from old friends at home promoted by Ruth and arranged by Miss Hall.

First News of Casablanca

ALGIERS, WEDNESDAY, DECEMBER 30, 1942
This noon Ike went home to bed, having caught the flu bug. To-night he has to get up, by his own insistence, to have dinner at the villa in honor of Admiral Cunningham, to whom Ike delivered on Christmas evening a Distinguished Service Medal, by authority of the President.

The command arrangement has been worked out, Ike taking personal command of the front, leaving Anderson still in direction of the First Army in the north, the French and Americans in the center and south under General Clark. Ike's Advance Command Post for the Allied Headquarters will be at Constantine, and Ike will have to shuttle back and forth from Algiers to the forward spot, and from there try to co-ordinate the British, French, and Americans. There will be some 45,000 to 50,000 French troops.

The Darlan thing passed over very quietly. There was an appropriate funeral service, which Ike and others attended. Giraud knelt at the bier and shed a tear.

Ike had paid tribute to Darlan at the press conference, but made it apply only to the six weeks or so that Darlan had been in our picture. He had kept his promises, sometimes with embarrassment, and had thus dealt some blows against the Axis. He also spoke highly of Giraud, who had then been selected. Nogués had come into Ike's office and made clear he did not want the job, possibly fearing a fate similar to Darlan's.

Giraud accepted office, somewhat reluctantly, being a military man, and promptly put the bee on Ike to change the exchange rate of franc to dollar, which is seventy-five francs to one dollar in North Africa, and citing the ratio in Madagascar, where there are thirty-eight to the dollar, and set by the British. So Ike has had to start to get this rectified. U. S. Treasury had insisted on the present rate for North Africa, although British had been willing to be more liberal.

Clark and Spaatz are tickled about southern push and today have flown in punko weather to the east to look over the situation. Conditions favor co-operation between Army and air, which Clark hopes to demonstrate.

Haven't recorded the really amazing news. I won't say "good," because if things were otherwise it might lead to a visit to Washington and home. But the fact is that Washington, as well as London, are coming to us. The President, the Prime Minister, General Marshall, Admiral King, and various bigwigs are going to powwow at a place already recommended after investigation near Casablanca, sometime in January. The President's winter vacation? Imagine it will be ultra-secret, and the press at home will be amazed when they eventually are told where the President has been sojourning.

We had hardly started this operation, only seven turbulent weeks ago, when the Prime Minister sent Ike an urgent suggestion for a meeting, preferably in Washington, to consider global or at least European strategy.

The Prime Minister had even suggested equipping forty-five Turkish divisions with all sorts of modern implements, much of which too scarce even to finish the North African job. It was clear that the Prime Minister is anxious to keep the Axis on the run, foresaw Rommel out of Africa, Mussolini virtually absconded from the war, and the Turks, if supplied, would help the Allies slash away at the "soft underbelly" of Herr Hitler. All this died away in the fighting, so far as we were concerned, except as a thought that someday, perhaps when Tunis is in the bag, there would be a "meeting."

With Ike in "personal command" of the front, and riding British, French, and American forces, he will have his hands full helping to dope out the grand strategy of the war at Casablanca.

Murphy, Bergeret, and Giraud are on the "death list" of an assassin's ring here in Algiers, according to the report of a trusted French agent who gained the confidence of the conspirators. Murphy heads the assassin's list. He is more than casually interested in the effort to round up the ring.

(Sometime later, Murphy and his Civil Affairs people moved into an office building on Rue Michelet, where Murphy had an office on the top floor. One evening, while working late, a bullet whizzed through his window. Thought of the assassination plot rushed to his mind as he ducked for cover. It seems a French air-raid warden had remonstrated with the MPs in French, which they couldn't understand, that certain windows had not been blacked out. The MPs didn't get the idea, so the Frenchman shot through the window. The MPs took the Frenchman to the guardhouse, kept him overnight while a complete investigation was made. The next morning, they told him he could go home.

("I won't go home without an escort—you must send me in a jeep with an MP," he said.

("Why?" he was asked.

("Because my wife would never believe me.")

DECEMBER, 1942: *Air activity in Tunisia increased as lengthened supply lines slowed down Allied ground advances. The German high command was reorganized. British drove Rommel out of El Agheila across Libya toward Tripoli; Mussolini admitted losses of 400,000 men in Africa. Darlan, assassinated shortly after assuming post as Chief of State in French Africa, replaced by Giraud. British and U. S. fliers bombed Turin, Naples, Bizerte, Tunis, Sousse, Taranto, Sfax. Allied bombers hit Japs in India and Burma, where activity became greater after starting with patrol actions. Japanese attempts to reinforce Buna-Gona area cost them heavily. Vandegrift announced Guadalcanal action in mop-up stage. Airfields on Bougainville and New Georgia Islands bombed by Allies. Red offensives before Stalingrad and in Caucasus ground forward against stiff opposition. Heavy raids pounded German transport centers on Continent. Allies obtained use of Dakar; French Somaliland joined Fighting French. (This was a tough month. Guadalcanal and Stalingrad seemed out of our world. We were looking forlornly at Tunis and cursing the mud.—H.C.B.)*

ALGIERS, FRIDAY, JANUARY 1, 1943

I could use some of Mamie's suggested aspirin today. Just after midnight last night, Ike opened, bid, and made seven hearts, a good omen for the coming year.

Fredendall, not Clark, is to command the southern sector in Tunisia. Clark will devote himself to training the Fifth Army.

Message from the Prime Minister today expressed worry over our situation in Tunisia, and tells Ike that Alexander thinks he can take

Tripoli by or in February. Rommel will probably come into Tunisia, where he will be on our hands. Prime Minister worried about the sea flank of Tunisia, too.

Expect the grand strategy meeting at Casablanca, January 12.

Special Services in London has cabled this headquarters, in the midst of our troubles, inquiring if a pianist and a drummer are available as accompanists for the Kay Francis troupe.

Staff Note from F. D. R.

ALGIERS, MONDAY, JANUARY 4, 1943

The President has sent a stiff message to the PM, retransmitted in part by the British Foreign Office to Ike, setting forth the thesis that this is a "military occupation" and that Giraud must do what Eisenhower dictates, both politically and militarily, and if there is any doubt as to Eisenhower's ability to handle, the President will "soon find it out."

The intent of whole operation in North Africa, starting with the directives, especially those relating to not shooting at Frenchmen until they shot at us, as issued by the respective governments through the Combined Chiefs of Staff, was to make the French active, fighting allies. This Ike and the staff have done, and an old ally, laid low by the German drive through France in June of 1940, has been re-created with spirit and will to fight. All they need is equipment and time to train in order to be of considerable effect.

Ike is worried for fear the insistence of the President that this is a "military occupation," regardless of whatever sideline political fight it may represent as between the United States and Britain, may force him to say to Giraud, "Do this, or else." Then if Giraud replied: "I don't choose to do this—what are you going to do about it?" Ike would be up against the man-wasting job of taking over the civil administration of the country, which General Patton reported, soon after the assault was completed, would require 60,000 soldiers in Morocco alone. The French who are guarding our line of communication to the front would be withdrawn, those actually fighting at the front would be called back to their billets around Algiers, Oran, and Casablanca and elsewhere, and we would have to more than offset their strength with Allied troops, and instead of active help from our re-created ally we would have little help, probably passive resistance à la Gandhi, or possibly resumption of French fighting Americans and British *pour l'honneur*.

Perhaps Ike is worrying needlessly, but if the threat, "I will soon find out," of the President develops into some request that Ike is ordered to make on Giraud, Ike feels he will have to take five days before issuing the instruction to Giraud to withdraw forces up front to some line near Constantine that can be defended, and kiss Tunis good-by until we can build up with troops and equipment, not only to pursue the Tunisian objective, but to police the great expanse of French North Africa.

It may be, as Murphy seems to feel, that the President doesn't want the French to create a single, well-established central government before the French people themselves can elect one of their own choice. Certainly, the President's message indicated a desire to deal with a local French government, provisional until after the war, in each of the bits of French territory taken by the Allies.

In any event, the succession of political difficulties, the setback in Tunis, the bombing of Bône, where the cruiser *Ajax* took a dive bomb down her funnel and got her guts strewn around sufficiently to require four or five months for repair, the loss of four supply ships in one day, the apparent ability of German air to hit us effectively and our air's apparent inability to hit commensurately hard with its proportionately larger forces —all these, plus the repetition of monotony of office to house and vice versa, contributed to Ike's foul frame of mind last evening.

Of course, this kind of inner-family growling I don't take seriously, and as I pointed out to Ike, in just eight days, at the PM's and the President's secret meeting he will have the opportunity to make clear the implications of such an extreme position as the President has indicated. None of these lamentations of a private nature shows in the official acts at the office. Just good old American grousing.

Shortly after Ike had me in to lunch to read a message, and we were trying to clear the deck so he could get out of this place for an hour's ride on the fine Sunday afternoon, who should pop in but General Giraud himself, concerned about a local walloping the French had taken at Pichon, but lo and behold, most co-operative and understanding.

Plans for Casablanca

ALGIERS, TUESDAY, JANUARY 5, 1943

Push on the southern front to cut Rommel's supply lines set for January 30.

General Marshall late yesterday sent Ike a long, detailed message giving the plans for the meeting. There are to be three "echelons." The President will fly there in a Navy seaplane. Among those to attend from the American side are General Marshall and Admirals Leahy and King.

Not to overlook Harry Hopkins. George Durno, now a captain in the Army Air Transport Service, seems to be booked to handle press arrangements. The President may decide to see the press at Casablanca. Neither Steve nor Pa Watson mentioned among those to attend. Will be plenty secret-service men. Various places where planes will land are being reconnoitered by the secret service and the military.

The British Foreign Office has furnished a copy of its suggestion for solution of the French provisional-government problem to its Resident Minister in Algeria, Mr. Macmillan, who has passed copies to Ike and Murphy. Looks toward amalgamation of Fighting French under de Gaulle and of Giraud's forces, with view of co-ordinating French effort everywhere in their fight against the Axis. Headquarters of the world-wide French provisional government would be in Algiers. Getting the seat of such a government on French colonial soil may have some attraction.

However, the British suggestion for one centralized, world-wide French government, omitting, of course, occupied France, seems 180 degrees opposed to the notions expressed by the President to the PM. The President indicated a preference to deal with local French groups in each of the "occupied territories." Of course, both ideas are predicated upon the French choosing their own government and officials after the war.

                                    ALGIERS, THURSDAY, JANUARY 7, 1943

Daylight movement by water of supplies and men from Sicily to Tunisia is giving the enemy reinforcements that are difficult to stop. There seems to be a channel between the two places, flanked with enemy mine fields, through which Axis ships move under strong air cover. The Navy has been unable satisfactorily to get at them. We are calling for Mosquitoes from England, to see if we can get in some wallops.

After a solid month of colds, sniffles, and general below-par physical condition, Ike laid up in bed until lunch, then got up and sat by the fire. Had lunch with him at the house, and he feels punk and looks the same. Carpetbags under his eyes. He got worried about Mamie yesterday, slipped down to the signals operating room, and tried out the new two-way teleprinter circuit to Washington. Asked duty officer at Washington to phone Columbia 2000, Apt. 208-H, and ask Mrs. Eisenhower if the absence of recent mail from her indicated illness. Within ten minutes back came a chipper answer that not only was she all right but had been writing regularly and itemized the various officers with whom she had sent mail. So he felt better.

General Ike Fights Two Wars

ALGIERS, TUESDAY, JANUARY 12, 1943

General Everett Hughes carried the diary for December 1 to January 7, inclusive, to London, and has reported his safe arrival with the document.

Ike went to bed the same day with a severe head cold and general grippy condition. Had been persisting in keeping on ever since it first struck him shortly after we arrived here "permanently," November 23. Imagine he caught it in the damp caves of the Rock. Then he and General Clark had made the Boy Scout trip frontward when Ike really should have been in bed. The succession of events kept him from stopping even one day to give his system a chance to throw off the cold, and the accumulated lack of rest for many months finally compelled him to give himself unto the doctors. In between there also was the hectic all-night and all-day ride back from Souk-el-Khemis starting Christmas Eve and ending last Christmas Day at Algiers, where Darlan awaited burial.

His absence from the office has disrupted the normal routine, and I have written nothing since January 7 until now. There has been a lot to write.

The twelve Frenchmen who were arrested after Darlan's assassination are still in custody, and one, the Chief of Police of Algiers, has entered a confession that is dynamite. There will be a public trial, on insistence of Allied Headquarters, but the French claim to have the goods on the ringleaders of the conspiracy. It will be recalled we had information from the French that Murphy, Giraud, and Bergeret were on this group's list for assassination. The Police Chief, according to the official reports furnished headquarters by the French, has confessed—some claim under duress—that about $38,000 in American money was passed in his presence by d'Astier, the de Gaulle emissary sent down from London to Algiers, to his brother, who is one of the dozen.

The trial, if held, will be something of a miniature of the Moscow trials, although the French think it will clarify the atmosphere.

Ike has been hoping to be up and going again by the time of the Casablanca conference, which was to have been Friday. Reports today state there will be a twenty-four-hour delay in arrival. Weather, no doubt. Doctors expected to let Ike come to the office tomorrow forenoon.

General Alexander and Air Marshal Tedder, who recently lost his wife in Egypt in an airplane crash, are expected here, both en route for the Casablanca gathering. They have been expected since yesterday by plane from Egypt, but weather also has delayed them.

On the fighting side (Arthur Krock, in *The New York Times*, wrote recently that high authorities in Washington lament the fact that General Eisenhower is having to fight two wars at once—a political and a military—when one war ought to be enough for any man at one time), we are preparing for the offensive in southern Tunisia between January 20 and 24, with Fredendall hoping, if all goes well, to take Gabès and then Sfax in ten days from the start. Ike's advance headquarters at Constantine are being set up by General Truscott, who will serve there as Deputy Chief of Staff, and, as previously noted, Ike will be in personal command of the whole Tunisian operation, although is being careful not to interfere with Anderson, Juin, or Fredendall in any of the decisions that must be made in the field.

Fredendall's plan (so called by Ike) is on the daring side. It calls for a quick armored thrust to Gabès, sowing of mine fields to help protect his right flank on the south in case Rommel tries for a quick dash northward from Tripolitania. Then the American force pushes northward to take Sfax. The hope is that this southern operation will cause Nehring to redistribute his forces, weaken his front in the north, and give Anderson a chance to spring forward and grab Tunis. If the plan works, we may clean up Tunisia in six weeks. At least Rommel's supply line to Tripoli will be disrupted and Montgomery's Eighth Army will be benefited.

There is considerable debate going on as to whether Rommel will defend or give up Tripoli. Some say it is undefendable; others say to give it up will be a dangerous psychological blow to the Italians. He may give it up and stand against the Eighth Army at the Mareth fortified line at the Tunisian border. Or he may come a-hellin' toward Tunisia to try to hold the bridgehead.

Ike has written General Marshall a personal note, to be delivered when he arrives, to inform him that he is ready to go to Casablanca whenever wanted by the Chief of Staff.

Doctors took Ike's blood pressure yesterday and again today, and it was 168 both times, but they claim this isn't at all unusual for any man who has been and is going through what he is.

The Casablanca Conference

ALGIERS, SUNDAY, JANUARY 17, 1943

A bit behind on my homework and a lot to report.

General Marshall called for Ike to attend the military and high political convention at Casablanca. Went over Friday morning, the fifteenth, in his Flying Fortress, stopping briefly at Oujda, where Ike had fifteen minutes with General Clark, closeted in a sedan parked beside the Fortress at the airdrome.

En route from there to Casablanca the No. 4 motor acted up, and out, but wouldn't quit. Ike was the first to show me the oil spewing from the motor and running off the rear edge of the wing. It was a first-class leak. Crew made us put on our parachutes, indicated where we were to jump, and left for us to decide whether to go out in an old swimmin'-'ole type of dive or simply feet or fanny first. Another motor was conking out when we finally glided into the airport, ending a hundred miles of misery. The propeller shaft had broken, preventing feathering and thus stopping the twirl of the propeller, and causing danger of disintegration.

As we came to the landing, Ike, in removing his parachute, dislodged the pin of one of his stars and asked me to fix it on his shoulder. My hands shook so badly I had great difficulty. He said: "Haven't you ever fastened a star before?"

"Yes, sir," I said, "but never with a parachute on, sir."

The big shots were quartered and guarded in suburb of Casablanca. It was named Anfa Camp, the Hotel Anfa being the headquarters; President Roosevelt and the Prime Minister were put up in near-by villas.

General Patton had met us at the airport and drove us to Anfa Camp.

Ike immediately went into conference with General Marshall and Admiral King. In fact, they had lunch in the General's room.

This was the first of a series of unending conferences for Ike. He kept on with them until after midnight, then had another in his bedroom, where he was waylaid by General Patton, his host. Got to bed around 2 o'clock.

General Patton had asked me to visit his office downtown in the Shell Oil building. I found not only that Casablanca is more modern than Algiers, although of the same type of architecture, but the horses I saw on the streets were relatively sleek and fat, as compared with the skinny nags I see around Algiers.

The Arabs are about the same in both places—in fact, everywhere I have been in Africa there isn't much difference—and the drivers beat their horses in one place as viciously as in the other. Seems to be a way of showing the Arab's superiority over something, even if over only a poor bedraggled horse.

The General said that Ike would have no time to be shown around the city, so I should constitute his eyes and ears and report to Ike. Took me to see the harbor, still partially blocked with sunken ships. The *Jean Bart* had, as advertised, been shot up "proper," although the French had since got her afloat. Patton only permitted the quickest of glances at her, as he didn't want the car driver to stop more than momentarily, for fear of offending the pride of the French. This illustrates the sensitive feeling General Patton has shown to the French, and, according to his reports, the policy has worked for mutual confidence and helpfulness.

Patton's bailiwick around Casablanca has become one vast storehouse. He has in well-spaced dumps strewn over thousands of acres 18,000,000 gallons of aviation gas and some 70,000,000 gallons of lower-octane rating, not to mention a million burlap covers to make sandbags, heaps of Lend-Lease stuff of every description (I had heard this latter category included lipstick, rouge, face powder, and even Mum).

I had taken lunch with Commander Libbey, Admiral King's flag secretary, and we were joined at the table by Sir Dudley Pound, the First Sea Lord, and by Captain Lambe, RN, one of the excellent naval planners whom I had met in London. Then Captain R. P. Pim, the Royal Naval officer who gives the PM the latest intelligence reports each morning, took me by to see the PM's villa, and especially the war room. Charts in this room were set up especially to afford the PM, the President, and others a clear view of submarine concentrations, convoy movements, and location of war vessels of the United Nations.

The most impressive fact in the war room was the number of subs. I tried to count. There were easily a hundred, and no telling how many were in ports for servicing. Most in operation in the Atlantic (and there was a large pack along the northern route from U. S. A. to England and another in the South Atlantic) were, Captain Pim said, based on Lorient or other points along the Atlantic coast of France, mostly in the Bay of Biscay.

Pim said that the President had spent considerable time in the war room the night before, going over all ship movements, analyzing the probabilities of success or failure in the vicious submarine war.

Later I met Major General Eaker, who is commanding American air operations in the U. K. while Spaatz is Allied Commander-in-Chief for air in the North African fracas. Eaker had been called to the sessions by Ike because the bombing policy had been challenged. Eaker had arrived that day but hadn't yet seen Ike, and wanted him to know that he was fearful the British would want to emulate Ike's policy of a unified command in North Africa for air by having the same in England, but under Air Marshal Harris. Eaker said that he could work very happily under Harris, but the change was much more fundamental. Our daylight pinpoint bombing was at stake. The British would insist on night bombing by the Americans, and our crews, Eaker explained, were not trained for night flying sufficiently to find their home bases in crosspatch England in darkness. Said he wanted to keep the Americans bombing by day, let the British continue by night, and smack the enemy on a twenty-four basis.

Parenthetical note: I suppose when I first went to England I had as many inborn prejudices as anyone born, reared, and educated in the Middle West. American officers and men who became acquainted with the British in England before TORCH had found that the lessons all Americans learn in their history books aren't true of the present day; believe it or not, the British are really not red-coated devils. GIs and officers who have come direct from America to North Africa don't understand the British as well and occasionally are heard to say things which, upon acquaintance with the British, they would never say. Beneath the Englishman's exterior, which seems cold to many Americans, are a warmth and a sense of humor in which I find a particular delight. But this comes to mind because of a story recently told me by Colonel Bill Stirling, who is a regular officer in the British Army and who has an unusually strong English accent. He told me that when he went to Casablanca at General Ike's request to help make arrangements for the big conference, he had sought to "make his number" (pay a courtesy call) with General Patton. When he spoke to Patton's aide, and explained that he would like to see General Patton, the aide turned and said loudly to others in the office: "Is there anyone here who understands French?"

It seems pertinent to record what Sir Dudley Pound had told us at lunch. The night before there had been a dinner attended by the President, the PM, and the high-ranking military and naval officials. The President had commented that regardless of criticism of this secret rendezvous, he would hold office for three more years. Sir Dudley had then chimed in with the comment: "That's more than any other person sitting at this table can say."

Sir Dudley had been fearful the Prime Minister hadn't appreciated the remark, but later conversation gave him assurance no offense was taken.

Ike had been on the move so rapidly that his poor aide lost track of him. When I went by Villa No. 2 (the PM's was No. 3) to send word to Harry Hopkins that I was around and would like to say hello, I found Ike was in with the President and with Harry. Ike stayed there until the PM and Combined Chiefs came, met with them extendedly, and then was reported to me as having been seen walking with the Prime Minister in the direction of Villa No. 2.

General Patton had invited guests to his sumptuous but cold villa to be with Ike—General Marshall, Sir John Dill, Admiral King, Lord Louis

Mountbatten—but then Ike was invited to the President's for dinner. I attended Patton's.

Harry Hopkins asked me to breakfast the next morning. Heard Ike come in about midnight, delivered a message or two to him, saw he was caged by Georgie, and went back to bed, only to have a nightmare that the harbor was being bombed and that the Germans were after the Anfa Camp and all of its distinguished and undistinguished occupants.

Ike told me before breakfast that the Eighth Army had progressed much more rapidly than we had been informed. Tripoli was scheduled for capture within ten days. This might alter his plans for the American thrust in southern Tunisia under General Fredendall. Rommel was being driven our way much faster than even the Combined Chiefs had expected. The only question mark was the condition in which the harbor at Tripoli would be found. If the Germans and Italians had time, before evacuating the city, effectively to block the port and damage the moles, derricks, etc., at least ten days and perhaps more would be needed by the engineers to make the port serviceable. Yet the port was absolutely indispensable to further westward movement of Alexander's forces.

A Talk with Harry Hopkins

Harry was still in bed when I arrived at the President's villa at 8. He came downstairs sleepy-eyed, explaining that he had spent the previous evening, after the dinner and a late session at the PM's, in reunion with Elliott and Franklin Roosevelt, Jr. The former is now holder of the DFC from General Doolittle for good and daring reconnaissance by air, and Franklin is a lieutenant in the U. S. Navy. I told Harry that the Signal Corps had ordered his son from his photographic unit operating at the front to get official pictures at Casablanca. But his son was so far advanced along the line that he had not been located so his orders could be delivered. (His orders reached him. Came to see me at Algiers after hitchhiking from the front. Had five-day beard, a Commando knife, needed a haircut, his uniform was dirty, and showed every sign of having roughed it. Sent him Monday morning, with the aid of Beetle, by plane to Casablanca, Beetle having put him up for the night and arranged an overdue bath.)

Talked with Harry an hour and a half. Told me how this meeting originated.

Said that soon after the North African campaign had been successfully launched under Ike, he had advised the President that Joe Stalin should be in on the next meeting. The President agreed, and sent a message to

Joe, who promptly replied that he saw no need of attending a meeting, that all the Allies had to make up their minds to do was to cross the Channel into France "as you promised." So the meeting had to be held without Joe.

Harry said that it had become evident that the Allies had to pick a suitable place to fight after the African campaign was completed. I told him Ike had favored the massing of Allied strength in the United Kingdom and using that as a base to launch a powerful invasion of the Continent across the Channel. Shipping had been the limiting factor, and the Channel afforded repeated use and reuse of the same ships on short hauls. Harry said that he hadn't been certain of Ike's position personally on this question and was glad to know it.

Harry said that Ike had made a fine presentation of his story, including Darlan, Giraud, the assassination, as well as the military aspects of our situation in Tunisia, and had very modestly taken the blame personally for anything that had gone wrong.

Hopkins said that the President was driving his family, General Marshall, and Admiral King simply wild by suggesting that after the meeting he would visit this or that place in Africa. Said F. D. R. would mention the name of some place he'd like to visit without knowing whether any such place existed. This was his way of having fun. The secret-service men, the military, and the Navy would frantically seek to discourage him from unwarrantedly exposing himself to Darlan's fate. But the President loved it. Harry said that he thought the President would at least review some troops.

When I told Harry we live in a vacuum so far as our knowledge of political opinion at home is concerned, and that I had wondered just how badly Ike had been pummeled on the Darlan business, Harry said that Ike had nothing to worry about, that if he wanted to experience bad publicity and general hell-raising by the press, just let him step into the Hopkins shoes for a few days.

At the moment the press, especially Eleanor Patterson's *Times-Herald* and the *Chicago Tribune*, and also the isolationist Senators and Congressmen, were giving him hell because of a long-promised wedding dinner given to him and Mrs. Hopkins by Bernard Baruch. It was thrown at the Carlton and cost forty dollars a plate—unfortunately, just as nationwide rationing was being put into effect. About the same time the story leaked out that Lord Beaverbrook, the British publisher, had sent Mrs. Hopkins an expensive set of emeralds as a wedding present, and Harry the Lend-Lease administrator. . . . Well, maybe Darlan isn't such a burden, after all.

Harry permitted me to say hello to the President, and the hello turned into a ten-minute conversation. The President was in bed, eating his breakfast from a tray, and was in fine spirit. Signed my short-snorter card, which I can't show promiscuously until secrecy is lifted. The President said that he was something of a father confessor to all the boys, and hoped to help Ike out of some of his political troubles while here by having Giraud and, if possible, de Gaulle in for a unity talk. Said that the thing to do now is to keep the political situation on an even keel, do nothing important to disturb it, and get on with the war. I asked him how long he might stay. He said that there were no bills passed by Congress which required his presence for signing, and he was in no hurry to get back. He seemed greatly to enjoy the whole affair. He wanted to know what I thought the sentiment was for de Gaulle. Told him apparently considerable among the civilians, but not so much by the French armed services. Darlan had been their man, now Giraud was it. Told him the French felt there was legality in their action of following Darlan and subsequently Giraud, but the President denied the legality, said that it wasn't true, and gave some reasons, which now escape me, as does a lot of this French stuff. I told him, however, that regardless of legal or illegal, the French armed services *think* it's legal. I got out when the President's naval aide, Captain John L. McCrea, and Admiral Ross McIntire came in. Not only outranked, but outstayed. But all in all I had stayed with Hopkins and F. D. R. an hour and forty minutes and enjoyed every minute.

Did I say that Hopkins had said that if Ike takes Tunisia he will be one of the world's greatest generals? Well, he did. I asked what would happen if he didn't. Didn't get much of a direct answer, so I anticipated Harry's reaction. The governments can't be wrong, and it's the General's neck that comes off, and I told him Ike knew that just as well as anyone.

Ike and I started home in General Eaker's Flying Fortress about noon. Ike's plane required a complete installation of four new motors, the old ones having gone more than 400 hours—more, said Captain Jack Reedy, "than any other Fortress operating in this theater." The trip home was uneventful as to flying, but gave us a chance to exchange information— lopsided, I admit.

Ike had recommended that the European Theater now be taken from him, as originally envisioned, the two theaters split, and attention for the moment in England be given to co-ordinated bombing attacks. Lieutenant General Frank M. Andrews, Air Commander of American Flying Forces in the Middle East, would be given the job, and Ike had so recommended.

Air Marshal Tedder would become the air commander for the whole Mediterranean, but in the North African Theater would be under the Allied Commander-in-Chief. Spaatz would operate the Air Force in North Africa, but Tedder, a brilliant air strategist, would tie together all air operations along the Mediterranean to make the best use of our forces. This is also what Ike wanted.

He had arranged with General Alexander, who had flown to Casablanca from Cairo, to stop at Algiers for a general conference on their plans to tetch up Rommel fore and rear when Tripoli is taken and said Rommel has dug in at the Mareth line.

Ike would have to go to Constantine quickly, to change the plans for the push to Gabès and Sfax, for such a drive would unnecessarily endanger Fredendall's force and would be premature, in view of the acceleration of retreat by Rommel under the persistent pressure of the Eighth Army.

He had found that his work and leadership had been taken rather for granted. His bosses hadn't been at all effusive in praise. Of course, I had heard a lot of good words for him and his forces from the so-called lower levels, but it seemed to me clear that the absence of clear-cut words of thanks from the President or the Prime Minister showed they had their noses to the political winds, and weren't going to be caught holding the bag for a general who had made an unpopular decision and hadn't yet got Tunisia. I told him his neck is in a noose, and he knows it. But such is the life of generals. Then they have tossed out awards and promotions to Ike's subordinates (or rather Ike has), Murphy has been made a minister, and (as this is written) Admiral Cunningham has been made Admiral of the Fleet, topped only by the First Sea Lord, and they are giving him a full Marshal (Tedder) as another subordinate, yet Ike remains a lieutenant general, with his three stars dimmed by the four- and five-star subordinates. . . . These things made me wonder, but the fact is that by force of his own personality, the good sportsmanship about rank shown by his subcommanders, and his general ability to get things done by reason and logic, he is accomplishing as much as if he had a dozen stars. It would be helpful, what with the press and the radio growling at him, directly and indirectly, to have the President send to Congress his nomination as a full general, and then let the Senate confirm it. This would give the necessary governmental support to Ike that would be very helpful, especially with the French. Incidentally, I failed to mention amongst those who outrank him, Giraud, who has a constellation of French stars denoting him a full general.

Philosophizing as to why we hadn't got Tunis when we were so close in those early days, Ike said that it was Anderson's decision that he could

not use all of the 1st Armored Division because he couldn't get supplies
sufficient for more than Combat Team B. If, ventured Ike, Anderson had
been willing to gamble a bit more on his logistics and had accepted the
entire American armored division, as Ike had wanted him to do, then
we would have had the necessary wallop to take Tunis and eventually
Bizerte. This means Tunisia. But that is hindsight, and Ike wasn't complaining, merely chewing his mental cud.

Plans to Trap Rommel

ALGIERS, MONDAY, JANUARY 18, 1943
Flew with Ike to Tulergma airfield and drove an hour into Constantine
to attend meeting at the Advance Command Post operating under the
Deputy Chief of Staff, General Truscott.

The headquarters are in an orphanage.

The Allied C-in-C outlined the necessity of changing the plans for
cutting Rommel's supply lines at Gabès and Sfax, as previously approved,
because of the information obtained at the Casablanca meeting from
General Alexander as to the rapidity of the Axis retreat. Tripoli would
fall by January 26, and if the harbor isn't too badly damaged so supplies
can come through it, the Eighth Army will be at the Mareth line the first
week of March.

Since this is true, it is inadvisable, said the C-in-C, to risk our presently
smaller force to flank attacks from Rommel's Afrika Korps on the south
and the von Arnim force on the north. The Fredendall force must be held
as a mobile reserve, with occasional pokes at the enemy to keep him upset
and guessing, but must not jeopardize itself by undue risk until the Eighth
Army has chased Rommel into the Mareth line and begins its assault
there. In other words, the two Allied forces must be carefully co-ordinated,
which was being accomplished between Eisenhower and Alexander.

General Juin listened and agreed.

As to equipment for the French, the Allies will "scrape the bottom of
the barrel," Ike said, and this was agreed to at the Casablanca meeting.

Fredendall was to conduct raids, to take vantage points, but not Sfax
or Gabès. He should retain a strong concentration of mobile force. He
could take Pont-du-Fahs, or try.

The French are to be more active against the paratroops. Sten guns,
machine guns, 37-mm. guns with armor-piercing ammunition to be furnished. Some .50-caliber machine guns are available for the French, but
they lack mounts. French to help get material so ordnance shops at Algiers

can make mounts. General Juin said that he needed wireless sets for contact between his patrols on line of communications and the outposts. Truscott and Anderson to do their utmost to supply.

More Criticism from Home

ALGIERS, SATURDAY, JANUARY 23, 1943

Seven months ago today Ike landed in England to take up the job of Commanding General, European Theater of Operations. Today he's Allied Commander-in-Chief in North Africa, a theater that is now being divorced from England, and there is talk in the editorials in England and America that indicates some would like to get Ike to Tahiti. We are receiving roundups of adverse editorial comment that the OWI is sending us—daily now—arranged by Milton, at my request, to give us a picture of the feeling at home. The *Daily Oklahoman* has one that is quoted as saying: "Mud is a silly alibi" for "failure of the Allied forces to deliver a knockout blow." There are fierce cries of senseless censorship of political matters, when censorship has been so greatly liberalized on political matters that some of the correspondents assigned here say they have never worked in such a free and easy theater. Admittedly it *was* bad.

Murphy seems to be the main target of criticism, on the ground that he is a Vichyite and has been giving bum advice to the "brilliant" General. (Not all use that adjective.) Colonel Julius Holmes, who has lived and breathed in this French muddle since the Clark submarine exploit, has prepared a summary of the local situation for the information of Elmer Davis, Chief of OWI at home, who had cried desperately for constructive material with which to beat off the critical columnists, radio commentators, and even respectable people. To this, which Ike had held until I could read it, I have made a humble suggestion that has been accepted. It is Murphy's summary, but he was empowered to say that the Commander-in-Chief would welcome a representative group of editors and columnists, both press and radio, to come here themselves, with air transport provided, see what they want, and go home to write their stories without whatever imaginary restrictions might exist within this theater. At least this should let the wolves know we aren't afraid to let them have a look around and find out for themselves, and may have the desired effect of giving our friends a chance to write favorable comment, having this as a peg. I am enthusiastic about it and think it will help. While the offer of the invitation was left to Elmer Davis to make or not, as local conditions there might dictate, I can just see old Elmer, with his dry

Hoosier manner, telling the boys they have an open invitation to go to Africa to find out for themselves.

Have been otherwise occupied of recent and have not recorded the bad news that the French, after weeks of hardship and valiant effort, were forced back on their front when some fifty German tanks moved down the road of a valley in the area of Pont-du-Fahs. This required some readjustments, which Ike personally had to handle, as he still was (until day before yesterday, when he had made another quick trip to the Advance Command Post at Constantine) in charge of the front sectors. Whether the French approved or not, he put Anderson in complete charge, directly under himself, and issued instructions to pull the French back and for the British and Americans to take parts of the French sector. The French were practically powerless to meet tanks with their inadequate weapons, and will have to be held in reserve until they can be properly equipped.

A Visit from General Marshall and Admiral King

ALGIERS, TUESDAY, JANUARY 26, 1943

General Marshall got off today; Admiral King yesterday. Both stayed at the villa. They were accompanied by Lieutenant Colonel Frank McCarthy, the General's assistant, and Commander Libbey, the Admiral's aide.

When I was working in the Navy Department in Washington, the gang in the Communications Division held Admiral King in great awe. He ran a "tight ship" * and had been quoted, when he took over as Naval Commander-in-Chief, as saying that "When conditions get bad, they always call in a s.o.b., so I guess that's the reason they picked me." So all of us were afraid of him. But after visiting with him at the house and observing his gracious consideration of those about him, I formed a different impression.

Of course, Libbey did ask me the latitude of Algiers, and when I said "about the same as Washington," he said he didn't follow me, he being a regular naval officer, trained as a navigator. Said he meant "east and west." I gave this some thought and eventually came up with an answer: "Five to ten degrees east, sir." (Am now going to look at a map and see if I'm right; but I never could keep straight whether longitude is east or west or north or south.) The map says three degrees.

---

* Navy slang for ship whose skipper is a rigid disciplinarian.

General Marshall likewise was an easy guest to accommodate. Mickey looked after him and was deservedly complimented by the Chief of Staff for the efficiency and grace of our hospitality and especially for the "home-like" atmosphere.

Of course, there was one incident that may be classified as "homelike." The Allied Commander-in-Chief was giving up his spacious bedroom to the eminent Chief of Staff of the United States Army. This generosity was earnestly protested by General Marshall. He didn't want Ike to inconvenience himself or to fail to get needed rest. But Ike took General Marshall to the bedroom, accompanied by Telek, who nipped at their heels as they went up the stairs. The bed is double, and has a maroon silk cover. Ike was extolling the virtue of the soft, luxuriant bed when Telek jumped on it, let go on the foot of the bed, and, before Ike could recover from his shock, had quickly changed position to the pillow, where he demonstrated to the two great American generals the astounding capacity of one little Scotch terrier.

I gave up my room to Admiral King, who said he had the best night's sleep in ages. There were no alerts while either of the high officers was here. I think they were disappointed.

When Admiral King was departing yesterday morning, he told Ike (without reference to his early advocacy of him) that he had done a great job, that not only the Navy but the country was behind him, that he should keep up the good work. This was good for Ike; helped his morale. It has seemed to me that so far as recognition is concerned, Ike has always been the bridesmaid, never the bride, but time will correct this.

General Marshall's whole attitude toward Ike was that of father to son. This morning at breakfast (Ike had already eaten and gone to the office) General Marshall gave me "orders" to take care of Ike, keep him out of the office as much as possible, get him home early, get a masseur, have him rubbed down every evening before dinner, make him take a little nap before dinner, make him get a place where he can ride horseback or get some form of exercise, and, in general, do things that relax his mind and body, so he can have a fresh point of view while meeting ever-pressing decisions.

"He may think he has had troubles so far, including Darlan, but he will have so many before this war is over that Darlan will be nothing," General Marshall told me. "You must look after him. He is too valuable an officer to overwork himself.

"When I brought him to head the Operations Division after Pearl Harbor, I put him in the place of a good officer" (I knew it was Gerow) "who had been in that job two years. I felt he was growing stale from overwork, and I don't like to keep any man on a job so long that his ideas and forethoughts go no further than mine. When I find an officer isn't fresh, he doesn't add much to my fund of knowledge, and, worst of all, doesn't contribute to the ideas and enterprising push that are so essential to winning the war. General Eisenhower had a refreshing approach to problems. He was most helpful. But he began to work sixteen or eighteen hours a day and before he left, I was beginning to worry about him, just as I did his predecessor. You must keep him refreshed, but knowing him as we do, it will take ingenuity. It is your job in the war to make him take care of his health and keep that alert brain from overworking, particularly on things his staff can do for him. You must get a masseur. That will give him exercise and, most of all, relaxation."

So today I have found a masseur of four years' experience, whom I am taking to the house tonight, only Ike doesn't know it.

Have just told Ike it's time to go home—5:15—that the masseur is waiting to accompany him.

"Holy smoke," he said, "a masseur?"

"Yes, sir, my orders from your superior, sir, General Marshall."

"Well," said Ike, "send a message to McCarthy for the Big Boss [meaning Marshall] that the masseur has been obtained by you as per instructions and is already at work."

The News Breaks from Casablanca

ALGIERS, WEDNESDAY, JANUARY, 27, 1943

The story of the President's and Prime Minister's meetings at Casablanca was released at 2 A.M. Algiers time this morning. The local French papers were at first restrained by French censorship officials from mentioning the Giraud-de Gaulle meeting, arranged by the President and the PM but only after considerable personal persuasion by Churchill to induce de Gaulle to attend.

Photographs of the two (G and D) were taken, shaking hands. The statement they issued was brief, but said they were agreed to fight the Axis. In this morning's Algerian paper, the heading is "Roosevelt, Churchill, and Giraud Confer." De Gaulle comes in the second line. General McClure said that he had to use persistent persuasion to get the French censorship lifted re mention of de Gaulle. American officers also were placed in the French newspapers, to make certain they did not break the release date.

Appointment of Peyrouton as Governor General of Algeria, in place of Chatel, had drawn severe criticism in U. S. and U. K. His record shows him a capable administrator but once in the Vichy government.

A German plane dropped a note on an American airdrome up forward one afternoon. It said: "Why don't the Americans come out and fight?"

That night Brigadier General Paul Robinett's attack to regain points lost when the German tanks ran through the French was launched, and it was successful. This was at or near Maknassy and Sened. Total prisoners taken were 150, about twenty-five enemy killed. Our casualties were two killed, three wounded, and two tanks lost. The Americans came out to fight, all right.

Had one of our hardest bombing attacks on Algiers about 5 this morning, with the moon shining brightly. About twenty planes came over at 17,000 feet, some dropped to 5000. We got two. Bombs struck a trio of gas trucks, causing a bright blaze that lasted for an hour. Several hits along the Rue Michelet. One hit the *Strasbourg*, a transport, near the outer mole, already damaged by an aerial torpedo. The German Consulate was hit. I was watching out my bedroom window, Mickey at his, and Ike came trundling in to see the fireworks. Thought perhaps he had withdrawn too much light flak from Algiers for use at Bône and Philippeville, but for all the noise and bomb screeches, the damage is not at all serious. General Marshall and Admiral King will be sorry they missed it.

Ike is contemplating moving an operational staff, including himself, to Constantine. General Somervell had strongly advocated that Ike spend more time at or near the front, so he would get "credit." This called for a thorough analysis by Ike to me at the bedroom conference this morning. Too many people are looking for credit, Ike felt, and, after all, just what is the job he's supposed to do? The way he sees it, he can be most effective at Algiers, commuting to Constantine. He has battle-front commanders. But he could operate from Constantine and, as Commander-in-Chief, he would, of course, have living and office conveniences, but this would not be so easy for the staff officers, for that ancient city already has Spaatz's headquarters staff and is overcrowded. Communiqués could be issued from the Advance Command Post, and not at Algiers.

Night before last, when General Marshall, Admiral King, and Ike went to Admiral Cunningham's to dine, I had an "aides' night," with Tex Lee, Robbie Robinson, Lieutenant Craig Campbell, and Lieutenant Colonel Frank McCarthy in for dinner. A story was told on Beetle. Seems the Chief of Staff was walking home after dark and the MP guarding his villa challenged him, made him place his identification card on the ground, retreat ten paces, and lie flat on his belly until the suspicious MP was satisfied Beetle wasn't an enemy paratrooper.

"The Answer Is Yes"

ALGIERS, THURSDAY, JANUARY 28, 1943

General Clark came yesterday, flying from Oujda in his B-25 in an hour and a half. He returned to Oujda this morning.

Clark talked of a lot of things. Ike finally told him frankly that when the "lost his pants" story broke, Marshall was greatly upset. Clark thinks Marshall is mistaken in believing the story "done him wrong," but Marshall's views (and it's only my laziness that has made me inadvertently omit "General," which I don't mean to do with respect to our illustrious Chief of Staff any further) are worth recording, as, indeed, I wish I could do completely.

I have neglected to record General Marshall's views on publicity for generals, expressed to Colonel McCarthy and me the morning I also received orders for care of General Ike. While General Marshall was here, I was privileged to hear him talk for hours. His phraseology is entrancingly superb, his thoughts are well put and frequently pointed up by a pat illustration. But the reason he thinks the "lost his pants" story was bad Army publicity: American fathers and mothers want to feel their boys are being led into battle by sober-minded, serious, conscientious, and forthright generals. General Marshall's reasoning is that while one general might get by with a good story that temporarily makes him a national hero, other generals may follow that example. With an Army of publicity-minded generals, the news-interest points about them, some of which would be silly or, at least, unofficerlike, would spread a feeling of lack of respect.

So Ike takes a personal delight in pointing out to me that normal and natural publicity is the best, and, of course, he is right. Every man likes his publicity, and any man in Ike's position can get it by rather simple and well-known expedients, but the officer who indulges in it digs his own grave.

The Berlin radio predicts that Ike will be transferred back to London and Alexander will take charge in North Africa. It comes at a time when the critics in Britain and at home are needling Ike and hinting that he should be replaced because he hasn't implanted the Four Freedoms into the government here overnight. The German attack comes on the heels of an American rebuff (in the press) to the British press that had suggested that Ike be relieved, because he had offended the liberal's ideals. So he is the center of a controversy, and every day that passes adds some more evidence (especially Giraud and de Gaulle having started to have a "meeting of the minds" publicly under the fatherly tutelage of F. D. R. and the PM) that he made wise decisions, at least militarily.

General Marshall is about the only one who doesn't call Ike Ike. Calls him "Eisenhower." Admiral King calls him "General." The President and the PM and almost everyone I've ever heard of call him Ike.

After Admiral King left Monday, Ike wanted a special convoy run to bring us trucks from the U. S. He radioed the Admiral (caught him at Dakar) if he could possibly supply necessary and scarce naval escorts. Much to his satisfaction, Ike got an answer back the same day. It said: "The answer is yes." This means we will get 5000 trucks, barring losses en route, which will be of inestimable help in the battles ahead.

Must amplify in this soggy log the fact that General Eisenhower complied with General Marshall's health rules, as issued personally to me, on the first morning after the C/S departed. Also had me get a couple of baseball gloves and a regulation $1.25 horsehide ball. Stayed in bed until 9:30, ate breakfast there, thumbed his nose at the office, and said hereafter he would get down about 10, conduct business of importance only, leave at noon, exercise at lunch, maybe get a rubdown, have lunch, take a nap, and get back to the office around 3, dust off some items of world importance, go home around 5, rest, and divert his mind.

"After all," General Marshall had said, "four or four and a half hours with the staff ought to be enough."

How did it work the second day? You guessed it. 'Twas hell on the aide who liked the idea. But this morning the subject was up at 7, ate breakfast with General Clark, arrived at the office in a swirl of dust at 8:15, growling that the charwomen should get their dusty sweeping done earlier, so a man could breathe some fresh air.

JANUARY, 1943: *Russian offensives continued to roll on all fronts as Reds advanced in Caucasus, broke siege at Leningrad, approached Kharkov and Rostov. German force in central Stalingrad, including General Field Marshal von Paulus, surrendered. Air attacks pounded sub pens of Saint-Nazaire and Lorient, port facilities at Cherbourg. First all-U. S. force bombed Wilhelmshaven and Emden in daylight; raid by Mosquito bombers, hitting Berlin in daylight, forced cancelation of Göring 10th Nazi Anniversary speech. German fighters and bombers struck back at London in scattered raids. North African gains continue. Successful seizure of Faid Pass by Rommel disrupted planned Allied advance. British drove Rommel thirty miles beyond Tripoli. Air activity over New Guinea disrupted Jap supply routes. All Jap resistance in Sanananda area of New Guinea ceased. Roosevelt, Churchill, and Combined Chiefs of Staff at Casablanca demanded "unconditional surrender." U. S. announced war budget of 109 billions for coming fiscal year. Stimson announced U. S. casualties in Tunisia totaled 1258. Score in aircraft for 1942*

*announced as 309 American planes lost against 987 enemy aircraft destroyed
and 362 damaged. Iraq joined Allies; Chile broke off Axis diplomatic relations. (When the Russians won their glorious victory at Stalingrad we knew
they still had the necessary punch.—H.C.B.)*

Conference Around an Automobile Hood

ALGIERS, TUESDAY, FEBRUARY 2, 1943

Went to Tulergma airdrome with Ike yesterday, where he held a stand-
up conference on the field around an automobile hood with General
Anderson and those immediately concerned.

The French have been hit again by the Germans in our center. The
French have lost some 2500 men in recent actions, and since the Germans started punching there, some eighteen battalions of French have
been lost. Poor equipment was the trouble at first, but now morale is low,
and both cause weak resistance. The French have a hard time forgetting
the beating they took from the Germans in May and June of 1940.

From a tactical standpoint, General Anderson pointed out to Ike that
with the British moving into the central part of the line from the north,
and the Americans closing in from the south, the whole line is thin and
we are not accomplishing Ike's objective: to build up a striking force on
a small front in the north where the Axis can be hit with overwhelming
force that will carry us through to Tunis.

General Anderson said that he and Fredendall, who is now under his
command, are getting along fine. Fredendall had a force trying to take
Maknassy Monday. It had started the attack the day before, and met
more opposition than had been expected, but Fredendall had reported
to Anderson he expected to take Maknassy during the day, and was
launching his attack at 6:30 Monday morning. I've not yet heard any
conclusive results of this operation, and I have seen the incoming messages. This is being written on Tuesday at 5:15 P.M.

If Fredendall succeeds in taking Maknassy he will so threaten the rear
of the Germans that they may lighten their pressure on the French, who
momentarily were saved at Ousselat valley by Robinett's force. If the
attack fails, Fredendall will have to get back into his shell and conserve
his forces, as Ike is insistent that there must be a large, central, and powerful reserve, mobile so it can strike in any direction on short notice, held
in the central part of Tunisia.

Ike wants General Alexander (appointed at Casablanca as Ike's deputy
for ground forces) to get himself and his staff here as soon as possible,

as tactical decisions, while primarily Anderson's responsibility, come to Ike for scrutiny and approval. Ike's view is that the battle to clear the Axis out of Africa is now one giant battle, needing close and intimate co-ordination and understanding among Anderson, Montgomery, and Alexander. The Eighth Army has followed Rommel some fifty miles west of Tripoli, and the pursuit will continue, dependent upon the clearance of the Tripoli harbor. (Message today from Alexander said no ships could enter the harbor yet.)

Ike concurred in Anderson's plan to withdraw from Faid, Maknassy, and similar exposed points if this will permit the desired concentration and prevent dissipation of forces where commensurate results are unlikely to be obtained. He was fearful that Fredendall would get too exposed with his small detachments and use up men and matériel needed when the two ends of the pincers are pressed on Rommel and von Arnim. But decisions were difficult to make until we knew more definitely Alexander's prospect of advance.

ALGIERS, THURSDAY, FEBRUARY 4, 1943

The Prime Minister is coming our way, due tomorrow. He disappeared from Casablanca; then I heard from Colonel Bill Stirling, Ike's British Military Assistant, that "Winston" had gone to Cairo. Then came an announcement he had called on the President of Turkey.

I assume the Prime Minister was pursuing his long-held conviction that Turkey, with her forty-five divisions, can be drawn into the war against the Axis, provided we can equip her. The Prime Minister put this grand strategy to Ike within a day or two after the TORCH-Day. We then were contemplating an eventual dagger thrust through France into Hitler's industrial Ruhr Valley, so the business of wooing Turkey seemed far, far away. Now, however, with the amazing victory of the Russians at Stalingrad, the Eighth Army's successes, and the occupation of North Africa, and the prospect of pushing the Huns and Eyeties plumb out of Africa, with the improvement of water transport through the Mediterranean, it seems we do have some substantial trading stock with which to induce the Turks to come on in.

This Turk business became Allied policy at the Casablanca conference. It will be interesting to learn the extent of progress made by Britain's star salesman. Grand strategy is to take Sicily soon after Tunis is cleared, hoping to knock Italy out of the war. Then plan for the Turks to join our side.

Meanwhile, the President has returned home, and has had a press conference, in which he approved wholeheartedly the political arrangements over here, and spoke highly of Giraud. Didn't give de Gaulle so much, but some.

Shipping is being found for French equipment, as the President has apparently put on the heat with the homefolk. This comes at a timely moment, what with Giraud distraught over the loss of his French soldiers on the central front. He told Ike a couple of days ago that lack of equipment for his soldiers had resulted in "butchery."

"Our attack on Faid was unsuccessful" is a line from the communiqué of AFHQ, which was a refreshingly frank statement of a fact. Notice, too, that those reporters who have spent considerable time at the front are writing home that the public should not expect an easy victory and that it will be a hell of a battle, or series of them, before the Hun is pushed off his African front porch.

The thrust at Maknassy was called back, because Ike didn't want our mobile reserve in southern Tunisia dissipated by futile rushing around. Hereafter they are to hit only when they know that they have heavy superiority. The mobile reserve will get its chance when Rommel's retreaters come their way. Ike wants Fredendall to let the Americans fight enough so they get "blooded." One such operation is now on. That is the capture of Faid, the first attack, noted above, having been unsuccessful.

Nine of the thirteen or fifteen alleged conspirators in the Darlan murder were released yesterday, and considerably more of run-of-mine prisoners are being let out of concentration camps.

General Patton is to command the American assault force in HUSKY (Sicily) and General Clark is to handle training through the Fifth Army, which becomes a replacement outfit as well. Patton is much set up at his assignment, and will, no doubt, lead his troops à la Teddy Roosevelt at San Juan Hill. Assault will be directly under Alexander, as ground commander, under the Allied Commander-in-Chief.

Generals Clark and Patton flew in from Oujda yesterday, came to the house for lunch, transacted their business, got their instructions, and were off again by air without even going to the headquarters.

The Man Who Came to Dinner

ALGIERS, SUNDAY, FEBRUARY 7, 1943

Our "big company" has been here and left, thank the Lord.

The PM and the CIGS, Sir Alan Brooke, and entourage, arrived Friday, the fifth, in two Liberators after an overnight flight from Tripoli.

The PM was taken to Admiral Cunningham's house, a stone's throw from ours and within the same enclosure, and the CIGS and Sir Alexander Cadogan, of the British Foreign Office, were guests in our house.

On Friday, Ike had a luncheon for twelve, to wit: the PM, de Gaulle, Giraud, Boisson, Noguës, Peyrouton, Sir Alan Brooke, General Anderson, Admiral Cunningham, Murphy, Macmillan, and Sir Alexander Cadogan. It was at our villa and I was house mother. Fixed the seating arrangement myself, and it received approval of Colonel Julius Holmes, who knows the State Department protocol. Solved some diplomatic problems by making General Ike and the PM cohosts, with Giraud on Ike's right and de Gaulle on the right of the Prime Minister. As the British would say, we had quite a flap on.

Ike had dinner at the Admiral's and a long talk with the Prime. Meanwhile, I was participating in a "cover" plan to make a show that the PM was leaving Algiers as originally planned—2:30 P.M. There was word from the War Office that the Germans or somebody were going to assassinate the Big Cigar Man while in Algiers. The presence of hot water for a good bath, the Admiral's soft bed with a radio alongside, and a nice sunshiny day made the PM want to stay more than the three or four hours first "laid on." So when Beetle went to see him that morning, to make an inquiry upon Ike's behalf as to whether Peyrouton and Noguës would be welcome at lunch, the PM not only said O.K. but worked out with Beetle how he could stay longer. Beetle had come back to our house full of hopes as to the bright plan he had conceived. Ike hit the ceiling. He wanted the PM out of town as soon as possible. Safe in London, the PM was worth an army; in Algiers he was a target and therefore a heavy responsibility. The War Office warning should be respected. Every minute he stayed added to Ike's responsibilities.

But the "cover" plan had to be executed. Beetle took Ike's B-17, had it readied for flight to Gibraltar, as planned for the PM's plane, and a caravan of cars was to leave our villas at the proper time. On invitation of Commander Thompson, the PM's aide, I was sitting in the semi-armored car of the General's, alongside the Commander, making out I was the Prime Minister. As the line of cars was forming, with the General's red-leather-cushioned scout car in front, armed with one .50- and one .30-caliber machine gun, and with Major Lee in charge, there was a short burst of machine-gun fire. The Commander jumped when the shots were heard. I told him Lee was merely testing the gun.

We drove through town, my rear being not particularly complimented to sit in the PM's seat at this particular time, especially when an Arab traffic jam stopped us in a narrow street, eventually reached the B-17, made signs of loading people aboard, watched it take off, waving farewells as it zoomed, actually with only the crew aboard.

As we returned to the villa, Lee took me by the arm and whispered that he wanted me to know that when the machine gun went off, the plaster on the house had been "chipped." He took me to look. Instead of mere chipping, there were three lusty bulletholes. As Major Arnold said: "You didn't get a very good pattern, Lee." Of course, it was just a casual thing. There wasn't a soul inside the house except the Allied C-in-C, the Chief of the Imperial General Staff, and the Prime Minister of the Empire on which the sun never sets. Lee was greatly abashed.

So much for the cover plan, except to say that the B-17 was met by the Governor General at Gibraltar with his aides. All this for the benefit of the spies thought always to be lurking thereabout. There was to be a leak of information that the PM was at the Rock, but I didn't see anything printed. Perhaps the spies were fooled, anyway.

We accompanied the real "caravan" that took the PM to Maison Blanche over a circuitous route prescribed by G-2. The farewells were said and resaid. The PM and Ike strolled up and down the rubble runway, indulging in last-minute mutual admiration. Then we left for home. This was around 11 o'clock.

At 1:30 A.M. I heard my phone, found Captain Shaw asking if we again could accommodate our recently departed house guests, CIGS and Cadogan. By the time I could get Mickey awakened, a room cleared, and downstairs, our guests were there, tired and unhappy. Theirs was the second Liberator in the PM's party and it had followed its big, black-bottomed twin down the dark runway for the take-off. But the No. 1 plane, bearing the PM, just revved and revved its motors, without attempting flight. While waiting, the No. 2 plane's four engines had overheated. Eventually the PM was trundled off into a car, and back the party went to the Admiral's. A magneto circuit had failed, and though these planes have two separate ignition systems, the pilot wouldn't risk his precious cargo with only one system working.

I put Sir Alan Brooke in my bed without changing sheets, he being dead tired from sleep lost the previous night, when they flew from Tripoli. My bedsheets were still warm. I took to one of the servant-guest rooms, as did Sir Alexander Cadogan.

Hadn't bothered to waken Ike to tell him the car was back, but did so the next morning, unfortunately spoiling one of the rare occasions when he had planned to relax in bed for a couple of hours, and should have done so, as he had a sore chest and was generally wheezy with cold. So with the familiar battle cry, "This world and then the fireworks," he hopped out of bed, declared he had to get to the office, catch up on yesterday's work, do today's, and be ready to talk some more to the Prime Minister.

One member of the party hadn't returned from the airfield: the Prime Minister's personal doctor, Sir Charles Wilson. Seems when he is confronted with an overnight plane trip, he takes some sleeping pills. This he had done at Maison Blanche. He was sound asleep when the trip was abandoned. The crew left, locking the plane. The next morning the good doctor awakened and found he was on the ground, but where? He found no one in the plane and the door locked. Eventually he was rescued, but he had had a good night's sleep.

Ike came back to the house around noon, in time to learn that the PM was walking down for a visit with him. We didn't wait lunch, as our two house guests were flying to Gib in the afternoon, expecting to take off from there for an overnight hop to England. The PM planned to fly direct from Algiers to England that night.

So Ike had a succession of talks with the PM, all beneficial and conducive to complete probing of minds. Ike returned to the Admiral's for dinner that evening and accompanied the party to the airdrome, where they actually got off.

At the Admiral's house, the PM was called "The Man Who Came to Dinner." Captain Shaw, the Admiral's flag secretary, told me he was convinced the PM was determined to stay in quiet, peaceful (to him) Algiers for a rest. When his staff exhausted their arguments, among other things pointing out to him that perfect flying weather prevailed for the hop to England, the Prime Minister (Captain Shaw maintained) had secretly sent one of his personal detectives to the Liberator and removed a magneto wire, and was perfectly willing to undergo the thirty-mile ride to and from the field just to enjoy his trick. Shaw swore the PM had made a comment that afternoon that had completely confirmed his suspicion.

I asked Ike what had been gained by the visit. Ike thought it was the fact that the PM had come to learn, see, and feel the situation at first hand. Then there was the opportunity afforded for complete discussion of problems. The PM had told Ike he must take care of himself, that he was doing a magnificent job, that he should be careful that nothing should happen to him, all because the PM didn't see a man in sight, except General Marshall, and he couldn't be spared from his present job, to be Allied Commander. He emphasized that the Allied Command was held together by dint of personality of the Commander-in-Chief, that he was very happy with Ike, etc., etc.

The PM said that he would announce Ike's absorption of the Eighth Army on Thursday of this week.

According to the PRO, Joe Phillips, who has just returned from London, where he personally delivered the copy covering the Anfa affair, there is a surprising amount of bitterness between Americans and British in London. The news and radio men reflect it. The two countries have been pushed apart by something. There is no realization that this is an Allied Command, with very little, if any, thought given to nationalism or to national interests: the thought and aspirations are to get on with the war.

Joe had seen the latest impact sheets, showing headlines of American papers. The *Chicago Tribune* and the New York *Daily News*, as well as other isolationist papers, have been saying that Ike is to be elevated to a figurehead job, with the actual command to be handled by three British officers, Tedder for air, Cunningham for sea, and Alexander for ground.

ALGIERS, WEDNESDAY, FEBRUARY 10, 1943

We have had that penetrating kind of cold that goes through your wool uniform, wool sweater, and long underwear, yet the sun has been shining, except for a brief rain this forenoon that cleared before 11.

Ike had a press conference today, to tell the correspondents about the new command setup as background for the information they will be expected to supply authoritatively as soon as the official announcement is made. This presumably will be done by the Prime Minister before the House of Commons tomorrow. Ike thinks it appropriate for the PM to make the announcement, as it amounts to publication of the fact that the Eighth Army is being placed under the Allied Command. The stories written here are to be released when and if the announcement is made. By this handling, we are hopeful the principle of unity of command under Allied auspices will be better understood and appreciated at home.

Ike has put an excellent front on the whole command setup, but actually he has been burning inside to the staff because two weeks ago he found that the Combined Chiefs were attempting to issue directions as to how and what his subordinates were to do. He has written General Marshall. The point is this: an Allied Commander must not have his subordinates subject to orders for operation in his theater from anyone except himself. He, in turn, is responsible to the Combined Chiefs. When duties of Alexander or Tedder are specified by the Combined Chiefs as they come under the C-in-C, the principle of unity of command is violated. Ike requested the services of both of them, as well as Cunningham, and termed them at the press conference "three of England's stars, so far as I know British commanders."

Ike says that the Axis is massing for an attack at Pichon. I asked him if he had enough there to hold. He said that we had "bits and pieces." Seems to me we have stretched out (and this isn't original) so far, and von Arnim and Rommel's forces have begun to consolidate so much that they are pressing out of the ring, or trying to, and our ring is all too thin. The French are being taken to the line of communication for guard purposes, with the Americans moving in to take over in the long line. Will still be some French battalions in the front.

The Germans Lash Out

ALGIERS, MONDAY, FEBRUARY 15, 1943

Ike is at the Advance Command Post at Constantine. Just talked with him on the phone, and because of a more-than-ordinary clash of armor in the American sector, he is standing by there, where battle news is most quickly available.

Ike left Algiers Friday morning, by car, for a three- or four-day trip to the front.

Lee phoned me from the office last Wednesday evening to say that Captain Barney Fawkes, of the *Maidstone*, submarine mother ship, had phoned to offer congratulations on Ike becoming a full general. I phoned Fawkes to check and to cross-examine. Barney said that he had called to add his congratulations and assumed we knew. Had heard it on the BBC. So when Ike walked into the room as I was replacing the receiver, I offered him my hand and said, "Congratulations!"

"What for?" he asked, not putting out his hand.

"On being a full general."

"How do you know?"

As I related the source, he stuck out his hand, but almost simultaneously burst out: "I'm made a full general, the tops of my profession, and I'm not told officially. Well, maybe it isn't true. How did you say you heard it?"

I told him again.

Then the phone rang. It was the message center with a quick teletype from Mamie: "Congratulations on your fourth star."

Then he believed it, but was still grousing because he hadn't been informed officially.

General Ike called into the living room Mickey and the house boys—Hunt, the cook; Moaney, the house boy and handy-andy; and Henry Clay Williams and Foster, waiters. On the spot he promoted them each one grade. Turning to me, he said: "And you can get yourself an aide of your own."

Everett Hughes came to dinner. We sat around the fire, drinking to the full General and listening to the phonograph, on which Ike insisted on repetition of his favorite record, *One Dozen Roses*. He sang all the words and let out all stops when he came to "Give me one dozen roses, put my heart in beside them, and send them to the girl I love."

Mamie's ears must have burned.

The next morning, official and formal word came from the WD's Adjutant General and a warm personal one from General Marshall, who had phoned Mamie at 10 o'clock that morning to tell her first. Another came from the Prime.

The new four-star General drove off early the next morning for the front.

General Clark, one of our expected house guests, couldn't come, after all, as he suffered a severe attack of ptomaine poisoning. General Patton came on schedule, and I accompanied him Saturday night to dinner at Admiral Cunningham's. We returned to our house in mid-evening, feeling the effect of British hospitality, which none can exhibit better than the Royal Navy, and sat by the fire for a bull session. This put us to bed around 1 o'clock, Patton being a charming conversationalist, and full of admiration for Ike, also some warnings re people who would like to cut his throat, but this is strictly private. Anyone who has risen as fast as has Ike passes a lot of brother officers and naturally some of them resent it. Patton flew to Tripoli next morning for a conference on HUSKY and a discussion of desert warfare with General Montgomery.

We took a lacing on the central front last night. One of the combat teams is calling for replacements of fifty Sherman tanks. Ike was worried at breakfast this morning, but in a phone call from him this afternoon, he was much more cheerful, for the news from the fighting had turned better. Seems he had driven in a jeep during the night from Bou Chebka toward Gafsa, which was ordered evacuated the night of 14/15, and the Axis now has it. Didn't want to expend vital strength holding a place not important in our scheme of things, and withdrawal was in line with the decision made by Ike after the Casablanca meeting to regroup the armored forces into a strong mobile reserve without risking small units in unimportant forays. But we have taken a licking. Don't know details of our recovery yet, but apparently there has been some.

Beetle has flown to Tripoli today, and AFHQ has been a morgue, wondering what is going on on the battle line.

We learned that the hostile attack developed against our Faid position the morning of the fourth succeeded through outflanking operations, supported by 90 to 130 tanks, in breaking on to the plain west of the ridge. During that day there was confused fighting west of Faid and east of Sbeitla. As the 10th Panzer Division was not yet engaged in this battle, General Anderson held a strong mobile reserve west of Pichon. He released, however, one battalion of medium tanks belonging to the American Combat Command B, and today we are counterattacking in an effort to clear the valley between Sbeitla and Faid and to permit orderly withdrawal of two infantry battalions from Faid toward Sbeitla.

Lack of adequate reserves made it impossible to hold as long a line as heretofore, so we are shortening the line to keep the enemy pinned into the narrowest possible corridor and to be in good position for later offensives.

We evacuated Gafsa last evening, and the American II Corps is taking up position in defense of the general line Feriana-Sbeitla. There is concern that any further contraction of this line will lose us Thelepte airfields, which are of great importance to current and future operations.

The rush to grab Tunisia for practically nothing resulted in splitting up divisions and other units into small outfits, and, as I know from meetings I have attended with Ike and General Anderson, they were working hard to regroup these units to re-establish divisional organizations both among U. S. and British formations. However, this has not been accomplished, but was in process when the French, owing to their outmoded and scanty equipment, began to deteriorate under German attacks with tanks in the central mountainous area. This was about January 17. To fill in the weak spot, the bulk of the U. S. 1st and 34th Divisions were absorbed, although they had been sent forward to provide general reserves and permit attack.

Obviously, Rommel has struck out to make elbow room for his forces, the better to fight off the British Eighth Army when they try to crack the Mareth line.

Later Ike spoke of the magnificent spirit displayed everywhere by the American enlisted men. He had encountered troops who had been living for many days on C-rations or its equivalent in the British ration. He hadn't heard a complaint, although some spoke with delight at the prospect of white bread and some other items now becoming available. The troops seem to realize that difficulty with transport made motor fuel and ammunition take precedence over bulky rations. He is confident that our soldiers are learning rapidly and, although he believes that many of the lessons we are forced to learn at the cost of lives could be learned in training at home, he is confident that the troops who come out of this campaign will be battle-wise and tactically efficient.

ALGIERS, TUESDAY, FEBRUARY 16, 1943

Ike is supposedly en route here from Constantine by car, having apparently decided against flying. When he flies in less than a Fortress, the Air Force boys insist on "laying on" an escort. Such fighters are badly needed at the front in the current battle. So Ike chose the long, hard, and twisty road back—an eight-hour drive.

Good editorial reaction at home on Ike's being made a full General as well as on the Allied Commander-in-Chief assignment. Papers in from London for as late as February 12, covering Churchill's speech to Commons, and his announcement of Ike's job, seem favorable, but haven't read all.

Admiral Cunningham had his press conference today and said he was "content" with the command arrangement, that he had been happy to serve under Ike from the outset, and that a happy family had been built at AFHQ.

As to the current battle around Faid and Gafsa, orders had been given American troops to evacuate Gafsa, but the fighting around Faid seemed pretty bad for us yesterday. Ike was somewhat blue on the phone when I talked to him last night. This morning he was more cheerful. Will know more this evening.

General Marshall wanted a teletype talk with Ike last night, but, when he found Ike not at AFHQ, decided to postpone it.

Received a great batch of American magazines yesterday: *Life, Time, SEP, Fortune, Newsweek, Collier's,* and the fiery *New Republic,* which on the cover urges in large type that now is the time to "Recall Robert Murphy," the latter being dubbed pro-Vichy and leading the somewhat bewildered Ike into unknown and dangerous political pattern for the resurrection of the downtrodden. I sent this batch, with a note of "Valentine Greetings," to poor Mr. Murphy, who invited me to lunch.

Alexander is due here tomorrow. At his press conference at Cairo when he said he would be deputy to Ike, in response to a question he said he supposed it was "a demotion," but he welcomed the opportunity to work under the American commander. The victory of the British in clearing the Hun from the highly and long-contested portions of Africa, and of driving him into our bailiwick, will make all British a bit peevish, at least under the skin, at the idea of Alexander coming under Ike, who hasn't yet thrown the Hun out of Tunisia.

Setback at Sidi-bou-Zid

ALGIERS, WEDNESDAY, FEBRUARY 17, 1943

We have taken a severe licking in the battle for Sidi-bou-Zid in central Tunisia. Ike fears we may have lost as many as four or five thousand men and considerable equipment, including tanks (fifty Sherman replacements were requested), self-propelled artillery, numerous trucks, half-tracks, and guns. It's the worst walloping we have taken in this fight, and perhaps the stiffest setback of our ground forces in the war.

Ike returned by car from the Advance Command Post last evening about 7, came directly to the office, and started conferring with the Deputy Chief of Staff, Brigadier Whiteley. C/S Smith was at Tripoli. Ike hadn't eaten since breakfast, was tired after the eight-hour trip, but insisted on starting help frontward before eating his supper.

After supper he cautioned me about speaking of "business" when I undertook to ask a question or two about the battle. He said he had a bellyful of such talk, having done nothing else for five days.

He retired early, but I had to awaken him from a sound sleep shortly after 11 to talk with Whiteley, who conveyed the bad news that Anderson was insisting that good tactics required withdrawal to the general lines he had suggested in the airdrome conference at Tulergma a few days ago. Ike concurred. Later, after I had gone to bed again, he called Whiteley and added some notions of his own, the nature of which I do not know. This morning, he is pounding the table with staff members, insisting that everything possible be done to rush help to the front.

In the midst of these military worries, the Giraud troubles come back on his lap. According to a report from Colonel Paddy Flint, of the Liaison Mission, G is upset because when the Americans evacuated Gafsa, a bridge was blown that prevented the French from taking a large quantity of railway rolling stock, including ten engines, some eighty phosphate cars, numerous coaches and flats, from the city. While many were destroyed by the Americans in evacuating, the loss is decried. But more important, Giraud is worried over the Arabs in that area, who may become active against us now that we have retreated from Gafsa and have taken the licking farther north.

ALGIERS, THURSDAY, FEBRUARY 18, 1943

General Alexander and his "PA" (personal assistant) arrived late yesterday and spent the night at our "hotel." Dinner was laid on for fourteen, the limit of our seating capacity (we never stop at thirteen—British superstitious), and I dined at the Admiral's.

Present at Ike's dinner were Admiral Cunningham, General Alexander, Air Marshal Tedder, Vice-Air Marshal Coningham, General Spaatz, General Gale, Admiral Kirk, USN, General Rooks, Brigadier Whiteley, Major General McCreery (C/S to Alexander), Captain Clarke (the PA), Commodore Dick, and Beetle.

General Alexander had hopped over from Tripoli and was anxious to talk with his new Allied C-in-C, and get off for Constantine, which he did at the crack of dawn this morning.

The talk with Ike, and vice versa, came at breakfast. Ike told him he could write his own orders at the front, that he was proud to have Alex serve under him and to let him know what was needed at the front in men, supplies, or whatever, and the C-in-C would do his best to get it from the rear, from the U. K., or from the U. S.

General Alex said that he had been disappointed when his first assignment under Ike for TORCH had been canceled only twenty-four hours after he had received it, that he had wanted to work under Ike, that this was an American sphere, and he fully recognized it was not only necessary but a privilege to come under the American C-in-C.

Ike made clear to him his great satisfaction at the job done in chasing Rommel as Alex and "Monty" had done so splendidly and that he realized that with the succession of victories under their belts, many would have expected Alex to be the boss. But Alex was thoroughly content, and anxious to get at the front to see for himself "the lay of the land."

Alex ventured the firm opinion that the Hun in the present drive, which has been tough and has cost the Americans at least eighty tanks to date, was headed for Tebessa. Ike told him General Anderson had been influenced not to send reserves to Fredendall because of intercept of enemy radio messages, that this was to be merely a diversionary move, and that the real one was coming farther north. So, the information proved to be wrong and made me wonder if we have been listening to something the Germans have purposely been using to build us up for a grand letdown at deception.

Alex was afraid our units had been dispersed too much, and that the Hun would gobble them up one by one, about what is happening.

Said he thought it would be best to give Anderson one sector, as the long front is too much for one man to handle, give Fredendall a part, and then there would be Montgomery coming along from Tripoli.

Ike Takes the Rap

The battle that began at Sidi-bou-Zid has become stabilized, with the American line now running southwest instead of north and south. We have lost some 112 medium tanks, five light tanks, a dozen 155s, eighty half-tracks, ten 75-mm. self-propelled tank destroyers, eleven 105s, five 75 self-propelled howitzers, twenty-two 37s, fifteen scout cars, seventy-seven quarter-ton trucks, four ten-ton wreckers, fifty-three one-ton trailers, sixty-four two-and-one-half-ton trucks, twelve four-ton prime movers, and small numbers of such things as submachine guns, mortars, rifles, pistols, telescopes, twenty-nine binoculars, and even forty watches.

The casualties will run from 1500 to 2000, but the complete count is not available.

Neither do we have any more than guesses as to the amount of enemy equipment destroyed or their casualties. Someone estimated sixty tanks.

The defeat has made all hands realize the toughness of the enemy and the need of battle experience for our own troops. In fact, the correspondents have played up the so-called "greenness" of American troops. This, however, is an erroneous understanding of the professional soldiers' meaning of "green." The professional means "lacking in battle experience" or "blooding."

The loss of the airfields at Thelepte is especially hard to take. These were the best fields in that area.

This morning Ike had a press conference in which he discussed the military situation at the front entirely off the record, permitting only mention that General Alexander had reported to him and had gone to the front to take charge. To the newsmen, Ike assumed full responsibility for the defeat. He ascribed it principally to the miscalculation which "he" had made as to the ability of the French troops, with their poor equipment, to hold the central front. When the French caved in a couple of weeks ago and their sixty-mile front had to be taken over by British and Americans, the line could only be thinly held. American armor was in small packets, which permitted the concentration of German armor to overwhelm them. However, the Americans showed great fighting spirit. He did not mention the real reason I suspect we got caught: the misinterpretation of a previously reliable intelligence from the Germans which indicated that the attack in the Sidi-bou-Zid area was to be merely a feint and that the real blow was to be struck farther north against the British. This information influenced General Anderson to hold armor in reserve while the main punch actually came in the Sidi-bou-Zid sector. When Ike was on his recent trip up front, he found that our own reconnaissance knew of the German build-up. The top man must take the rap for the G-2 error in judgment.

Kasserine Pass

ALGIERS, SUNDAY, FEBRUARY 21, 1943

The Hun made a stab through the Kasserine Gap toward Thala, and it had Ike worried last night. Not because he feared our ability to handle the newest break-through so much, as he did that the forces behind the line were doing everything possible to get armor, supplies, and men to the front. Alexander officially took over yesterday, and Ike has told him, as he has all the others in responsibility at the front, that he would scrape the barrel, rob the Fifth Army, Casablanca, and Oran and send home for more if necessary.

Editorial reaction from home is reported by the OWI. About the only consolation found by the editorialists in the "disaster" is that censorship was sufficiently light to permit the facts to be known to the public, for which commendation was given. But the grimness of war, the casualty lists (when they appear), and the loss of equipment are having a sobering effect upon the wishful thinkers at home who have had us practically storming Rome, and some even Berlin, by now.

Beetle mentioned to me this morning that his hair stood on end with anger when he was shown one of our intelligence reports after the defeat that began at Sidi-bou-Zid early this week. The Germans seemed to be reporting to higher-ups that as the Americans had put up a very weak fight, the push would be continued. Shades of George Washington, John Paul Jones, Robert E. Lee, and the D.A.R.! Well, we shouldn't let such disparaging remarks of the veteran, professional marauders depress us unduly. Perhaps it is just as well they get a bit overconfident. The war isn't over yet.

Brigadier General Barnwell R. Legge, the military attaché in Berne, Switzerland, has reported (apparently before the retreat of this week) from his post that "contacts among German Army officers state that the German General Staff at present esteems General Eisenhower since he did not fall into the dangerous trap which was set for him at Bizerte and

Tunis." If he had attempted the remaining thirty-five kilometers when he had long and insecure supply lines, a great number of unreliable French scattered throughout responsible positions in North Africa, and inadequate reserves in Morocco, to order General Anderson and his weak army to attack in strength, the result might have been disastrous for the Allied nations in northwest Africa.

Therefore, at this time the German General Staff is worried, considering that General Eisenhower employed the intervening time to overcome the early weaknesses and at present is able and does dictate strategy in North Africa. On the other hand, the Germans have not given up hope of retaining the Tunisian bridgehead. It is considered by conservative staff officers that the German "investment" in the Tunisian bridgehead is already excessive.

Ike may have been this far-seeing, but when he concurred with General Anderson at the V Corps headquarters on Christmas Eve that Old Man Mud had him stymied from the all-out attack then planned for the night of December 26, he was ready to make the gamble, trap or no trap. My guess this is pretty punk gossip, and may have been put out to soften us psychologically in our attitude toward the German General Staff. Wonder, could this be a sign of weakness and are they trying in this adroit way to gain some favor, to be cashed in when and if the German people really crack? Time will tell.

Second Guessing

CONSTANTINE, TUESDAY, FEBRUARY 23, 1943

The failure to hold the Kasserine Pass comes from improper placement of two battalions of infantry, one on each side of the two-mile cut through the mountains, according to Colonel Don E. Carleton, C/S at Advance CP, who visited the gap soon after dispositions had been made. They were placed too far out, and German infantry, under cover of darkness, got around them, infiltrating to the ground higher up and behind them. This operation succeeded in opening the pass, through which the Germans, ever resourceful to exploit a victory, sent some seventy tanks and all that go with them, including infantry.

When our forces lost Sidi-bou-Zid, and then made a good stand at Sbeitla, directly west of Zid, there was a disengagement about twilight at the latter place, and a successful evacuation made through the pass and into the valley. Mines were laid at the entrance of the pass, but according to Colonel Carleton, they were marked by mounds of earth, red flags, and simply plain flags, and clearly outlined by barbed wire. While this marking was probably intended to facilitate the evacuation, it served the Germans even better.

Fortunately, the news this morning indicates that we did not lose more ground yesterday, but then again the German wasn't very active, although he periodically dive-bombed Thala.

Indications of stiffer resistance of the American are about the only encouragement to date. These give rise to the hope that as our boys get blooded they become better and more skillful fighters.

According to the off-the-record dope I get around this Command Post, the first of a series of "defeatist" orders was issued to the troops two or three weeks ago. This called for immediate evacuation of Gafsa if the Germans and/or Italians attacked that place in strength.

This was one of the orders which were to carry out Ike's general strategy of regrouping all units and of creating a strong, mobile reserve. He didn't want to dissipate strength by having little, meaningless actions. His idea was not to attack except at points where we had known superiority. He was holding the mobile reserve for its full offensive when the Eighth Army hit its enemy from the south. But the manner in which the orders were issued apparently caused the lower echelons to get fainthearted.

To make matters worse, the weather has been too bad to permit continual strafing and bombing of the enemy, which presents a fairly concentrated target in the Kasserine Valley (although a broad plain), but an especially good one where the valley narrows into the pass. Today, however, the weather seems propitious for strafing. In fact, here at Constantine the sky is cloudless.

One possibility to achieve victory is to close the gap behind Rommel's forces in the valley. Whether it was possible for this to be achieved by Fredendall isn't known at the Advance CP, but all we kibitzers from this safe distance are figuratively yelling at Fredendall from the grandstand, "Tag that guy, he's off base."

The outstanding fact to me is that the proud and cocky Americans today stand humiliated by one of the greatest defeats in our history. This is particularly embarrassing to us with the British, who are courteous and understanding. But there is a definite hangheadedness. Fortunately, this is being followed by a determination to profit by our mistakes, to make definite suggestions to the War Department to improve and intensify training, and to get in there and beat the hell out of the Axis. Those around this CP who know of the intelligence reports from the Germans that the American troops have shown poor fighting quality, which reflect also on all the officers, wish they could be made known to every one of our men and officers at the front. The information chagrins the Americans and should make the troops and their officers fighting mad.

Report in this morning said that seven German military police were captured near Tebessa. They said that they were ordered into the city to direct traffic, as their commander thought the Germans already had Tebessa. Far from it, and I hope they don't get it, certainly while Ike is in that vicinity. Looks as if we have the German stopped in the valley, and we have a lot of power to throw against him, if we ever can only get it massed into the proper places.

Observations at the front brought forth two things of outstanding importance to the American forces. The first is that we have lost a considerable quantity of equipment, which must be made good as rapidly as possible. The second is that from top rank to the GI, all those concerned with the fighting, either in actual combat or behind the lines with supply, have learned now that this is not a child's game. The President's desire for American troops to get experience in North Africa for perhaps greater battles to come is showing results. They are ready and eager to get down to profit by the lessons they have learned and are seeking methods and means of perfecting battlefield efficiency. The American M-3 tank, called the Grant, is outmoded by German developments but, fortunately, no longer is being made, and is being rapidly supplanted by the M-4, the Sherman. The 75-mm. half-track has developed a surprising vulnerability because it is so difficult to conceal that when a German tank or 88 opens up, it is knocked out very quickly. Our 37-mm. antitank gun proved to be ineffective against the German M-3, M-4, and M-6, but 57-mm. guns are now on the way from the U. S. At General Alexander's suggestion we have asked the British for 100 of their six-pounders. We also need mine detectors in growing numbers in each division and, so far as we have heard, we have not made antipersonnel mines in the U. S., and these are needed. Despite all their adversity, the troops are of good heart and have developed a deep anger. This replaces a certain softness that was characteristic of all units before the attack.

Comeback

ALGIERS, SUNDAY, FEBRUARY 28, 1943

Since returning from the Advance Command Post at Constantine Wednesday evening, I have had little opportunity to keep up to date with the diary. General Marshall should see Ike resting in the sun at the villa this

Sunday afternoon. Meanwhile, I hope to catch up on various odds and ends of events.

Rommel apparently had not been hit by a bomb, or otherwise injured, as various rumors had it, but was personally in charge of the Axis thrust starting at Sidi-bou-Zid and ending with the enemy's retreat out of Kasserine Pass. This information comes from an intelligence report that states a letter was taken from a captured German prisoner south of Thala. The letter had one sentence, "Yesterday we were again visited by General Rommel, who is commanding here." It was dated February 22.

Spirit around AFHQ has regained its buoyancy with the recent turn of events. The withdrawal of Rommel's forces through Kasserine Pass and their pursuit by the Allies on the plain have led to resumption of confidence. I hope it does not again lead to overconfidence. Yesterday, Rommel and/or von Arnim laid practically simultaneous attacks at five points along the north and central fronts. This was judged by General Alexander to prevent further reinforcements to the Allied force following Rommel's retreaters out of the Kasserine Gap.

Ike flew to Constantine yesterday morning and conferred with General Alexander for an hour. Principal purpose was to determine where and how Alexander plans to regroup American units. Beetle went along and is continuing from the Advance Command Post to the II Corps headquarters and will be away several days. When Ike returned yesterday, I asked him how the situation was at the front. His answer was "fair."

FEBRUARY, 1943: *British mopped up last Axis resistance in Libya; tank, infantry, and air forces drove into Tunisia. Rommel's offensive seized Kasserine Pass, but stalled at Thala. Allies recaptured Kasserine Pass; von Arnim lost savage thrust for Beja. German supply ships sunk in Mediterranean by British subs and planes. Russian drives periled entire German front in south, recaptured Kharkov, Azov; last German resistance ended at Stalingrad. Bombers hit Cologne, Naples, Lorient, Messina, Wilhelmshaven, Saint-Nazaire, Brest, Dunkirk, and points in Belgium and the Netherlands. Jap attempt to regain the Solomons failed, with heavy sea and air losses; all resistance ended on Guadalcanal. Japs retire toward Mudo, near Salamaua. Planes hit Jap bases at Munda and Kolombangara. U.S.S. Chicago lost in Solomons, submarine Argonaut reported lost. Eisenhower made full general, put in command of all Allied forces in North Africa. Lieutenant General Walter Krueger named Commanding General of U. S. Sixth Army in Australia and New Guinea. (It was from a Tiger tank in the Beja attack that I took a seven-foot copper whip antenna while on shore patrol, a bit inshore. Sent it to Admiral King for the naval archive. He sent word, "Would Butcher like a mast from a German corvette we captured recently?" Never got it.—H.C.B.)*

Semihappy Ending

ALGIERS, MONDAY, MARCH 1, 1943

Late Sunday afternoon Major General Ernest N. Harmon returned from the front and wanted to see General Eisenhower. Upon my phone call, Ike came to the office immediately. In the meantime, General Harmon told me something of his part in the successful action in the Kasserine Valley.

General Harmon, who commands the II Armored Division stationed at Casablanca, had been ordered by Ike, after it became apparent from reports that some officers were suffering from fatigue, to go forward and lend such advice and leadership as he could.

He had an active and, no doubt, effective part in winning a battle that gave at least a semihappy ending to a large-scale American retreat. At least the battle resulted in Rommel's withdrawal from Kasserine Gap, with the Americans and British in pursuit as rapidly as they could lift mines or get around heavily mined portions of roads and blown-out bridges.

He said he had been unable to follow up the Germans and Italians as rapidly as he had hoped, because of the heavy mining. More than one armored reconnaissance car sent to check on the withdrawing Germans was blown up by unseen mines, although the most experienced British engineers had tediously scoured the roads and removed all they could find.

It was his opinion that Rommel would withdraw his forces to the Grand Dorsal, leaving the great plain the Americans had been forced to evacuate as a no man's land, outposted by both sides, with both sides engaging in sporadic raids and general reconnaissance. He thought Rommel was moving troops from north to south to reinforce his units, awaiting the attack of the Eighth Army, probably at Gabès Gap.

I asked him why it had not been possible to close the Kasserine Gap, to pen the Huns and Eyeties into the valley so they could be massacred at leisure. He said he simply did not have sufficient forces. In fact, so many guns had been lost, he had been worried as to the outcome if the Germans had chosen to make a determined attack at the northwest end of the valley. He felt a sense of satisfaction at the job he had done and hoped he could return to the front with his own outfit.

General Harmon's brief command of the successful battle has not been made known.

ALGIERS, THURSDAY, MARCH 4, 1943
Yesterday, Drew Middleton, of *The New York Times*, was in to report
to me the existence of bitter feeling of Americans against British because
of the recent American defeat. He thinks the cause of such feeling comes
from a desire to find an alibi for the defeat. Some of the Americans—both
men and officers—with whom he has talked claimed Nicholson's task force
on the northeast side of the Kasserine Valley failed to be of aggressive
assistance to Robinett's Combat Team in stopping the Axis advance,
nor had the British been sufficiently active in pressing after Rommel
started his withdrawal. If the British had been more active, the story goes,
we could have inflicted a much more decisive retreat on the retreating
enemy. (This story is not true, judging from the statements of General
Harmon, who was temporarily in command of both units.) Middleton
said certain members of the newspaper corps are taking up the criticism
and the feeling generally is bad. Thinks Ike should do something about it.
I told him the file of outgoing press stories did not indicate any such danger signals. He said that his correspondents knew that any story they wrote
which reflected bad feeling between British and Americans would not
be passed by the censors and, consequently, they had not written the
story. He was hoping something could be done to allay the bad feeling.
I told him I would suggest to Ike that he cover the subject again in his
next press conference.

Patton Takes Over

ALGIERS, SUNDAY, MARCH 7, 1943
Ike concluded Thursday to place the tank expert, General Patton, in
command of the II Corps, relieving General Fredendall so that his
ability in training troops, especially after his recent battle experience,
might be employed at home. General Marshall had asked for him. General Patton had been assigned by Ike the task of planning and leading
the amphibious operation against Sicily (HUSKY) as ordered by the Combined Chiefs when they met at Casablanca. Ike had been loath to spare
Patton from that important work.
    Meanwhile General Patton had been "alerted" at Rabat to meet Ike
at Algiers. The two met Friday afternoon at Maison Blanche, Ike
flying in from the east and Patton from the west. Patton was aware
of his assignment, and Ike made clear to him certain specific instructions.

I was standing by. General Ike insisted that there be created in our Army a feeling of partnership between ourselves and the British. Patton's corps will take orders as an American unit direct from the 18th Army Group, commanded by General Alexander.

Patton's first and big task will be to assist the British Eighth Army get through the Mareth line. His force is to tie up as much German strength as possible and secure Gafsa as a forward supply base for Montgomery's army. Care will have to be exercised in moving toward the sea to avoid cutting across Montgomery's line of advance. He is to rehabilitate, re-equip, and train his troops to take advantage of lessons so far learned. The technique of discovery and removal of mines is *not* to be confined to engineer units; additional mine detectors are needed and these are being obtained from the U. S. General Omar N. Bradley has been made Ike's deputy to cover the entire front as his eyes and ears. Patton will find Bradley most co-operative and available for any duty desired. Don't be discouraged about the 37-mm. antitank gun about which we had bad reports because recent tests with the latest ammunition show it will pierce the German M-4 at 800 yards, except for a very small band around the middle, but at close range will pierce any part.

Patton was cautioned against personal recklessness. He doesn't need to prove his courage; General Ike wants him as a corps commander, not as a casualty. Although he must see every portion of his troops and the positions they occupy, he shouldn't forget that, in actual battle, a commander can best direct his outfit from a command post where he can be in touch with all of his staff and subordinates. He is to be cold-blooded about removal of inefficient officers. If a man fails, send him back to General Ike and let him worry about it. Ike would take the responsibility. Success for the rest of the Tunisian campaign will have far-reaching effect on the progress of the war.

Ike and Patton, together with Brigadier General Hugh J. Gaffey, who was to be Patton's Chief of Staff, and Beetle, conferred standing up for half an hour at the airfield. Patton, who normally hates the Hun—as Ike says, like the devil hates holy water—and who now is all the more embittered because his son-in-law, Johnnie Waters, is reported missing in action—damned the Germans so violently and emotionally that tears came to his eyes three times during the short conference. Incidentally, he had brought me a .45 Colt revolver with a sawed-off barrel. There was also a shoulder holster, which fits unobtrusively under my coat, so now I am equipped as a real gunman.

While Ike was away at the front about three weeks ago, General Patton had stayed at the house and he and I had talked until late in the evening.

He had told me of his keen disappointment when Ike had not given him the assignment he has now been given. He felt he was the logical man to chase Rommel, had a great desire personally to shoot Rommel, and had all the spirit that goes with the job. Now he has the opportunity to chase Rommel to his heart's content, and all of us wish him luck.

Today the weather permitted Ike to make a quick flight to see Alexander at the headquarters of the 18th Army Group at Constantine. I accompanied him. His job was to emphasize to General Alexander the need of the British respecting Americans and of preventing loose critical talk. The conference required about an hour.

In his current efforts to improve British and American relationships, I see in Ike something akin to a fireman atop an observation tower watching a forest for smoke or flame. He has put out some fires by logical argument that to win the war the Allies must stick together. As part of his "prevention of fire" campaign, he visited with General Alexander, having already dealt with the question on the American side. Incidentally, it is now "Ike" and "Alex." Ike emphasized his thorough belief that to create the proper atmosphere for development of friendly relations, the top commanders must at all times preach it and also police it. Any American officer spreading anti-British sentiment is likely to be sent home. On the other hand, there have been instances where certain British officers have spoken unwisely. General Alex will undertake to deal with this type.

I have observed that GIs, Tommies, and French soldiers in combat or even in the forward area find upon close association a great deal in common. This is especially true of American troops who have been in the British Isles. At AFHQ, where Americans and British work and live together, the same is true. Brigadier Sugden, AFHQ's chief planner, who lives with a delightful group of British and Americans, has taken to chewing gum and says, "Now we're cooking with gas [long *a*]—and on the front burner."

But between the troops in the forward area and AFHQ, there is a wide spread of nationalistic feeling, frequently expressed by irresponsible junior or higher officers on both sides. I agree with Ike that we have at AFHQ a crucible for forming an effective method of achieving Anglo-American co-operation. This may well spread to other theaters and perhaps even to our respective home peoples. It is possible Ike's effort here may well be regarded as the shining example to accomplish world organization for peace.

Although in the midst of policing loose tongues and of guiding and taking the responsibility for the Tunisian campaign, Ike is pressing for planning for HUSKY. He has been counseling the planners practically to throw away the book in an effort to follow the Tunisian campaign with a quick grab of Sicily, on what the British call an *ad hoc* basis. However, the old bugaboo of shortage of landing craft and of shipping may make impossible such a bold and daring follow-up. Ike says that when he is buried, his coffin should be in the shape of a landing craft, as they are practically killing him with worry.

Assistant Secretary of War, John J. McCloy, and Colonel Donald C. Swatland were at the villa, awaiting our return, to have luncheon. Secretary McCloy with his party of six is returning to the United States via Gibraltar, Marrakech, Accra, and thence across the South Atlantic, starting Tuesday morning. This happens to be important to me, as Ike has decided to send me home for a brief trip, intended to be a week en route, a week there, and a week to return. The purpose is to see and hear how the home front feels and also to contact the Signal Corps and possibly the War Communications Board in an effort to get an American company to install a commercial short-wave radio transmitter in Algiers to operate to the U. S. The press is unhappy with the free service it is getting from the Signal Corps, which feels unnecessarily burdened by the continuous flow of nonmilitary traffic.

Archbishop Spellman Arrives

ALGIERS, MONDAY, MARCH 8, 1943
Archbishop Spellman of New York called on Ike today, bearing a letter of introduction from the President. It didn't seem to be necessary.

At lunch today Ike said he had emphasized his own view to the Archbishop that all churches and other welfare agencies should extend help along humanitarian lines to any comers, regardless of nationality, race, creed, or color. Ike had put this in his own vigorous language. The Archbishop answered that the Pope had said the same thing, only "not quite in the same language." I asked Ike if he had been careful to avoid his usual adjectives and he said he had done his best. He was greatly impressed by the visitor.

The German Nuremberg laws, so far as they apply to French territory in North Africa, are to be repealed by public proclamation tomorrow, by dictum of General Giraud. Ike has wanted both the Nuremberg and all Vichy laws of oppressive character repealed, but this particular step is heartening and may serve to lessen the complaint in the two home countries. Assistant Secretary of War McCloy said yesterday that it was the Nuremberg laws to which Secretary Morgenthau and his associates directed their greatest complaint. Abolition of the laws should permit the Jews to return to their places in the professions without hindrance of quota, which is the present modified basis.

Ike had a press conference today. Bill Stoneman, of the *Chicago Daily News*, sought Ike's help to get a clear and concise outline of the battle that is considered finished with the withdrawal of the Germans out of Kasserine Pass. Ike delivered his Lecture A on necessity of allies working together. He insisted that anyone who sought to dwell upon differences was small. However, he thought it would be reasonable for G-3 to work up a statement of the facts concerning the location and action of all units in that battle. He declared, however, he would not permit to be passed any stories that would create disunity. He would permit the censors to pass any constructive stories that built unity. To do otherwise would simply play into the hands of the Axis.

Today being March 8, the creation of the American sector becomes effective and General Patton reports direct to General Alexander.

Weather permitting, I am taking off with McCloy's party in a C-54 for a roundabout and, I fear, too much of a tourist trip home. I am carrying letters galore and long lists, prepared by Lee and Mickey, of things we need, including a sewing machine. I have had my hair cut, my teeth cleaned, and a big night's sleep in preparation for the event.

MARCH, 1943: *After repelling several German attacks the British Eighth Army opened the assault which broke the Mareth line in North Africa. Americans, under command of General Patton, advanced in Tunisia. Allied bombers hit Rommel's supply ships between Sicily and Tunisia. In Russia reinforced German troops first scored gains then took losses around Smolensk and in the Donets Basin. Heavy bombing of production centers on the Continent, coupled with growing French guerrilla activities, harassed Nazi communications. Heavy raids plastered Berlin, Duisburg, Munich, Essen, Vegesack, Wilhelmshaven, the Ruhr, and Saint-Nazaire. Chinese troops scored gains in Yunnan. Air action near New Guinea destroyed large Jap convoys and scored heavily against Jap air fleets. Jap planes over Darwin are destroyed. General Giraud restored republican form of government in French North Africa. (These summaries were compiled from news reports which necessarily do not give the whole story of our casualties and losses of planes, ships, and matériel. This information would be helpful to the enemy and had to be withheld, but the price of such censorship inevitably is overoptimism on the home front. —H.C.B)*

What It Looked Like at Home

ALGIERS, THURSDAY, APRIL 8, 1943

I left with McCloy's party in a C-54 from Maison Blanche Tuesday morning, March 9, and, via Gibraltar, Marrakech, Accra, Natal, Puerto Rico, and Charleston, S. C., with some sight-seeing en route, reached Washington early Wednesday morning, March 17. Despite my impatience, I had been only a week en route and had traveled 10,000 miles.

Not knowing when I would arrive home, I did not telegraph ahead to advise Ruth and Bev, so I knocked on the door of the Wardman Park Hotel at 7:15 in the morning. The door was opened cautiously. Casually I said to the two gals, "Good morning," as if I had simply returned from a short overnight trip to New York, as I had so frequently done before the war. The next day Ruth said her knees had quaked so vigorously that she had two Charley horses. Bev cried.

Returning to civilization, I had picked up a bug, and on advice of Navy doctor I was kept in bed for two and a half days and given sulfathiazol. On the third day I was permitted up two hours. With the numerous visitors and many things to do, this stretched beyond the permitted time. The result was that I never completely recovered while at home.

On the first day home, Steve Early came out from the White House for lunch. I gave him the ancient, rusty Arabian gun with its grotesquely long barrel that I had carried all the way from Algiers. Steve carried the gun back to the White House and at 5 o'clock returned to the bedside, claiming that I had 'always gotten him in trouble and had repeated after the long absence. He had shown the gun to the President, who had insisted that Steve had to shoot it and in the President's presence.

When I recovered sufficiently to visit the War Department Friday afternoon, Lieutenant Colonel Frank McCarthy, who had accompanied General Marshall to Algiers, informed the General that I was there, and to my surprise I found that the Chief of Staff wanted to see me. I spent a fruitful hour with him. The General was especially interested in Ike's welfare. He wanted to know whether the provisions for horseback riding had been made and, if so, whether "Eisenhower" was finding time to ride. I told him this had been "laid on," with horses due March 15, and that, no doubt, I would find him riding when I returned to Algiers. I had to confess my failure to provide a satisfactory masseur because of the impatience of the patient.

General Marshall had requested that I see him before I returned to North Africa. He had one principal message to be delivered to "Eisenhower"—in which the General persists. The Chief of Staff wanted Ike reminded again not to worry about any of the political machinations and, above all, not to waste time and effort to defend any of his past actions. He should not get into any arguments or debates with the visiting firemen who take his time. He should merely listen politely, yes them if necessary, but, above all, was not to waste his brain power.

The General said that Ike's rise or fall depended on the outcome of the Tunisian battle. If Rommel & Co. are tossed into the sea, all quibbling, political or otherwise, will be lost in the shouting of the major victory.

I visited Ike's son, John, at West Point and found him healthy and happy. Had lunch with him at the cadets' mess. John's principal message to his dad was that West Point was more appealing now that the tennis season is open.

When I returned from New York to Washington after West Point, I received a message from Ike asking me to obtain an automatic bridge-playing machine with advanced lessons. Thought he was lonesome.

Interview with F. D. R.

Wednesday and Thursday—March 24 and 25—I spent in Washington, following up on numerous errands for Ike and the War Department. When I phoned Steve Thursday afternoon that I was leaving Friday noon for Africa, he said it was impossible, as I was booked to see the President, and *not* before Saturday. This caused me to cancel my Friday plane. Friday afternoon I spent in "conference" with Harry Hopkins, Steve, and George Allen in Harry's room at the White House, Steve having arranged for me to see the President at 4:30 for ten minutes. When my ten minutes had elapsed, I stood up, but the President kept talking for twenty-five more minutes, so I had really had thirty-five delightful minutes with him.

The President greeted me with the exclamation that nothing pleased him more than to realize that the Navy was taking care of a general.

He wanted to know how things were going over here—as if he didn't know from official reports—but was inquisitive about commanders at the front, the retreat of the Americans naturally being in his mind. I explained to him the reluctance Ike had in relieving Fredendall, and his hope that with the change to Patton, Fredendall's fine qualities, particularly for training, would not be lost to the Army. The President also wanted to know the circumstances that caused our G-2 to predict that the main thrust of the Germans would come in the north rather than as far south as Sidi-bou-Zid.

I answered his questions as best I could and took the liberty of telling the President in detail of the visit of the Prime Minister in Algiers, including the scare of the War Office in London that there would be an attempt to assassinate the PM while he was here. I told him of Beetle's cover plan to indicate that the Prime Minister had left Algiers on schedule, ending with the three machine-gun bullets in the wall of Ike's villa. All this seemed both to startle and to please the President. He especially liked the thought of Sir Charles Wilson lying asleep in the PM's plane at Maison Blanche after the PM had abandoned the trip for that night because of motor trouble.

The President spoke highly of the method of handling the Casablanca conference. He said that for the first time all participants were enabled to explore each other's minds, get all the cards on the table, and reach decisions without distractions. These distractions, he said, are caused by newspapermen gaining small segments of the complete story and printing them under headlines that frequently mislead the public and fail to portray the complete story. The President felt that in most conferences, particularly where newspapermen have access to the conferees, almost every participant has a pet newspaperman. By buttonholing a participant the newspapermen can get a part of the story, and the whole issue becomes tried in the press on the basis of only a small part of all the facts. The result is distortion to the public and disruption to conferences. Casablanca was a secluded spot, well guarded, and relatively free from the press, where the leaders were able to talk freely without feeling someone would start promoting his point of view in the press by means of contact with his favorite reporter.

The result of Casablanca was so good that the President said he was having a food conference at the Hot Springs Hotel in West Virginia. The grounds would be guarded by military police, no press would be permitted to see the conferees for the duration of the conference, but a brief communiqué would be issued once daily to keep the people intelligently informed. The President thought the press would cry out against this arrangement, but for the public good he felt we need to provide conditions for conferees so they thoroughly can study the problems confronting them, without the distractions of headlines that tell only part of the story.

The President also told me of the U-boat attack against one of our large convoys in the vicinity of the Azores. His son, Franklin, was on one of the escorting destroyers. After the attack got hot—and this he particularly wanted me to tell Ike—the Admiral in charge of the escort broke radio silence to ask Casablanca to send air cover quickly. The

President thought this was an admission by the Navy that the air was useful, after all. (Over here everyone in the Navy whom I know admits not only that air cover is desirable, but that convoys demand it, i.e., Algiers to Bône or Bougie as well as Gibraltar to Algiers and vice versa.)

The principal message the President asked me to convey—and he spoke repeatedly of the General as "Ike"—was: "Tell Ike that not only I, but the whole country is proud of the job he has done. We have every confidence in his success."

I learned Saturday that I was booked to leave the U. S. Tuesday afternoon, so arranged to fly to San Antonio Sunday and back to Washington Monday. Steve and about twenty of the poker-playing gang had a party at Stewart McDonald's apartment in the Carlton. It started with lunch Saturday, continued through dinner, and ended around 5 A.M. I was a contributor. Over my objection, Steve took up a collection to buy a gift for the General. I thought a letter signed by all those present would be sufficient, but he insisted. I brought back a handsome Longines gold wrist watch on which the General's name and the date of the party were engraved. This was tendered by a letter of glowing praise of his work and signed by all present. The signatories were: Stephen Early, George Allen, Ellsworth Alvord, Raymond Beebe, Otis Bryan, Louis Caldwell, Norman Davis, Jesse Jones, Scott Lucas, Stewart McDonald, Frank Page, John Pelley, Robert Smith, Holly Stover, and Merle Thorpe. Curiously, the cost of the watch and the sum I lost were almost the same.

I had about an hour's sleep without removing my clothes when Ruth and Bev awakened me to take me to the airport for the trip to San Antonio starting at 8:30 A.M. I reached my destination at 1 A.M. Monday morning and was met by Mrs. Eisenhower and Mrs. Doud. Mamie and I talked *all night*. They took me to the airport for the 9:30 plane that morning, and I returned to Washington at 10 P.M., having gone two nights with virtually no sleep.

Ruth and Bev took me to the War Department and to the Washington airport Tuesday forenoon. I bade them farewell and was off again for Africa, which, oddly enough, I had found myself referring to as "home." I was going back to the so-called battle front to get some rest. I couldn't stand the pace of the home front.

Return to Algiers

The Eighth Army's success in breaking through the Mareth line made big headlines in the latter days of my stay home. Naturally, I was anxious to get back to Africa for the kill. Reached Algiers Sunday evening after five days and one night of flying—Washington to Miami, to Puerto Rico, to Georgetown, to Natal, to Dakar, to Marrakech, all in a C-54, and from Marrakech to Algiers in a Fortress furnished by Colonel Robert T. Zane, commanding officer of the Marrakech airport. The crew wasn't familiar with the route, so I functioned briefly as navigator to help find Maison Blanche through the clouds. I had 664 pounds of baggage, with packages and mail from practically all of the war widows in Washington who knew I was returning. I even had a wife for Telek, purchased in Washington, walked by Bev, and named by Ruth and Bev Caacie, meaning to them, "Canine Auxiliary Air Corps," but pronounced khaki. She was the best traveler of the lot. General Ike brought Telek to meet Caacie at the field. It was love at first sight.

Upon my return I found to my sorrow that not only had one of our brother aides—Craig Campbell—been temporarily assigned to the 9th Division, then inactive behind the lines, for a refresher course in combat life, but his unit had suddenly been ordered into active combat and his third of the battalion (Company E, 47th Infantry), including Craig, had been reported missing.

Whether Craig might be amongst a group of stragglers feeling their way back from the battleground, whether he had been killed, or whether he is a prisoner, no one has yet reported. At Craig's request I had telephoned his mother at Austin, Texas, to inform her that he was well and happy. I made this call from San Antonio while I was visiting Mrs. Eisenhower on Sunday, March 27. It was likely my report was false at the time —but, of course, I did not know it.

Ike had sought merely to give Craig two or three weeks of life with the troops, to benefit him. Ike had Craig's absence from the office prominently in his mind and was planning to recall Craig as soon as his trip to visit Montgomery was completed.

I found Ike refreshed by riding, which he had taken up in earnest. As the battle progressed satisfactorily in Tunisia, he had gained unexpected leisure and was "disciplining" himself to stay away from the office as much as possible. Beetle's staff had taken even more of the load, so Ike could run his job with much less time than when I left. However, when troubles develop, his hours are unending. His mind rarely stops trying to puzzle out the questions always arising in the great unexplored field that marks a modern-day Allied Command.

"It's when things aren't going well that I catch hell," he said. He had returned during the week from a flying visit to General Montgomery.

It was Ike's first meeting with General Montgomery since London.

They talked of co-ordination of the two Allied forces, pressing the Germans and Eyeties back into the Tunisian corner.

I reported my observations to Ike in detail. Most of the critics assume we have "won the war" and are now quivering for fear we are "losing the peace"; that we will push Rommel & Co. out of Tunisia and thus clear Africa of the Axis is taken for granted. The hardships of our combat troops, the quality of the Axis fighters in Tunisia, and the supreme effort that will be required finally to shove Rommel into the sea are lost in the swirl of wishful thinking that an early victory is inevitable. The American public seems more interested in activities in the Pacific, perhaps because hardships have been dramatized and victories, no matter how small or large, thoroughly exploited in newspapers, magazines, and radio, and not only through normal news coverage, but by public-relations men who returned from the Pacific to broadcast and to lecture. I told Ike I thought we, as Americans, had associated so intimately with the British that we had inadvertently absorbed one of their virtues, namely, reticence. However, this reticence should not prevent our telling the American public of the hardships and good work in this theater. Unless we do make the public more intimately aware of our difficulties, public opinion is likely to succumb to the wooing of the salesmanship of the Pacific. We must recognize that our theater is in competition with every other theater for equipment and attention. If our activities are permitted to be submerged in the minds of the public, we automatically soften our push against Hitler and increase that against the Japs, which to my mind means the lengthening, if not the loss, of the war.

As to Ike personally, Milton told me he was close to being labeled a Fascist during the Darlan and Peyrouton screamings. Ike's true feelings about democracy and the Four Freedoms should be made known to the public as opportunity permits. The abolition by Giraud of the Nuremberg laws and many of the Vichy decrees, which became public while I was en route to Washington, had a wholesome effect, but still did not satisfy many, who felt there was still discrimination against Jews. Milton said at home that Ike had been on thin ice, and this was evident to me, too, from conversations, but he has now weathered that storm. He can grow in stature by simply making known his thoroughly American views.

In the Tunisian battle, while I have not caught up with the detail, some facts are outstanding at this moment. While Patton's forces did not break through the pass to Maknassy, to cut off Rommel's supply line or to harass the Axis troops as they retreated from the Mareth line to their new positions at Wadi Akarit, the Americans nevertheless performed a great military service. They contained two German divisions

so they could not be used in their defense in the Mareth line or in succeeding fighting. This facilitated the Eighth Army's break-through of
the line, but of course was not as glamorous as if the Americans had
succeeded in reaching the sea or of even reaching positions from which
they could shell Rommel in retreat. When I had the interview with the
President, he looked at his map and said he thought Patton should be
able to get through soon to a point where he could shell the coastal
road. Incidentally, the President also said that General Patton had told
him at Casablanca at least five times that he hoped to die with his
boots on, and the President seemed delighted Patton had been given
this assignment. Another point is that Italians are surrendering freely,
some by whole companies, and there is at least one instance of a truck-
load of Italian officers dressed in their finest military gear, including
helmets with plumes, riding gaily to our prison camp. On the other
hand, the Germans we capture—and they are relatively few, compared
to the Italians—are truculent and mean. Rommel must be having his
troubles.

ALGIERS, SATURDAY, APRIL 10, 1943

Today the Royal Navy brought in the good news that our advanced elements of the Eighth Army had moved into Sfax and that warships of the
Royal Navy had gone into the Sfax harbor last night. There had been
considerable of a "flap on" on efforts to prevent the Germans from sinking
a ship across the mouth of the harbor at Sfax. Alexander plans that two
of Patton's four divisions are now to be brought quietly to the far north of
the front along the sea to prepare for the assault on Bizerte. Our Allied
forces are maintaining pressure and all along the line we are on the offensive. There are some 1400 Axis trucks bumper to bumper on the road
leading north from Sousse to Enfidaville, and other concentrations are
being steadily shot up by Allied planes.

But to our rear, the ever-present threat of Spain or of a German break-
through into Spain and attempt to neutralize Gibraltar and strangle our
line of communication through the Strait again breaks into our conscious-
ness with a report from General Clark that General Yague, of the Spanish
Army in Spanish Morocco, has been attempting to create an "incident"
on the border. I mention this because while at home I found the fear
expressed by several military persons that the logical move of Hitler was
to send some of his many divisions through Spain and jeopardize our line
of communications. One report while I was visiting Colonel Claude B.
Ferenbaugh in the Operations Division was that 500 trains had been

loaded with German soldier equipment in France and were moving to the Spanish frontier. So, while the picture in Tunisia looks good, we have always to cast anxious glances over our shoulders at the Strait.

We have caught a "Tiger." In other words, a Mark-6 tank has finally been captured. Americans this time.

General Giraud has made good his promise to create a committee on legislative revision which he mentioned in his speech of March 14, announcing abolition of many pro-Vichy laws. This committee met April 8 to examine all Vichy legislation with a view to its adaption to the principles and laws of the French Republic. General Giraud reviewed to the committee the progress already made in the re-establishment of the elected assemblies in Algeria, Morocco, and French West Africa and reported that 213 of the 308 municipal councils of Algeria have been reinstated and that the *conseils généraux* have been convoked for April 19.

He stated that Jewish children have regained complete freedom to attend schools, Jewish property will be restored ten days after inventory, instructions have been sent to the courts to permit reinstatement of lawyers, Jewish doctors are reopening their offices, and that measures by which Jews will re-acquire their citizenship will shortly be placed in effect.

The Pit and the Pendulum

ALGIERS, MONDAY, APRIL 12, 1943

Robert Sherwood of the OWI has concluded his visit to North Africa and reports fine co-operation and understanding with General McClure. Charles Douglas Jackson of *Time* is being sent by the OWI to North Africa. In a farewell note to Ike today, Sherwood says, "Believe me, sir, my hopes and my prayers are with you—and so are those of some 135 million of your fellow countrymen."

General Alexander sent a congratulatory message to General Patton for publication to his troops.

Sunday was a good day in the air. We shot down fifty-eight enemy planes, mostly transports, and lost three of our own. Two American divisions are being moved from the central sector to the extreme north near the Med coast for eventual storming of Bizerte.

The First Army continued its pressure and has reached a point northeast of Beja. If I were writing the story covering Rommel's situation now, I think I would draw a parallel from Edgar Allan Poe's poem *The Pit and the Pendulum*, the pendulum our air force, the ever-closing walls of the pit the ground and sea forces.

Bradley Relieves Patton

ALGIERS, SATURDAY, APRIL 17, 1943

Ike and I returned from the front Thursday afternoon, April 15, where he conferred with Generals Alexander, Anderson, Spaatz; Patton, II Corps Commander; Allen, 1st Division (who flew up with us); Eddy, 9th Division; and Ryder, 34th Division. We did not see General Harmon, who recently has been assigned to command the 1st Armored Division.

Mindful of American public opinion—an opinion, undoubtedly built up from wishful thinking, that the Americans under Patton should have pushed through to the sea and cut off Rommel as he was retreating in front of the Eighth Army—Ike insisted that General Alexander give the Americans their own sector in the forthcoming and, we hope, final phase of the Tunisian battle. Alexander's plan, previously approved by Ike, called merely for use of the 1st and 9th Divisions in the sector in the north near the sea, to be in the final push, and these under the British First Army. Ike insisted that the Americans have the opportunity to take Bizerte, difficult though the terrain and the objective undoubtedly are, and that they also should have all four divisions.

Ike explained to Alexander the home front in America. Ike emphasized the danger to Britain and America if Americans were given to feel that they had not taken an effective part in the conclusion of the Tunisian campaign. Much of our choice equipment, Sherman tanks, as well as ammunition and food, had gone to the British for their use. If the Americans feel we have not played a substantial part they will be even more intent upon prosecution of the war against the Japs and commensurately less interested in the grand strategy of beating Hitler first and Japan second. Alexander was quick to realize this possibility—actually approaching a probability—and readily acceded to the suggestion. So Americans will have their own front and a chance to take a more conspicuous part in the final push. The II Corps was to be moved quietly and quickly from southern Tunisia to the north, facing the vital port of Bizerte. But it's awful terrain.

There will be monumental problems of supplying four instead of two divisions.

General Patton was to be relieved of command of the II Corps, so that he could continue in the ever-pressing plans for HUSKY. Major General Omar Bradley was to relieve Patton.

In relieving General Patton, Ike made it clear that old "Blood and Guts" had "done his stuff" and that his relief should not be regarded by him, his

Corps, or the public as indicative of failure. For reasons of security, however, Patton's return to Casablanca and Bradley's assumption of command are not to be passed by the censors. Ike dictated at the Advance Command Post a brief letter to Patton, its contents to be made known to his Corps because Ike was fearful that the changes from Fredendall to Patton to Bradley would give rise to a feeling amongst the troops that they had done badly and their commander was paying the penalty.

Actually, the II Corps had not only carried out its various missions assigned it by General Alexander, but in El Guettar sector Patton's forces had broken through and had reached a point twenty miles beyond the line which was their objective. Consequently, Patton was ordered back by Alexander. If his forces remained there, the roads would be jammed with advancing elements of Montgomery's Eighth Army. Unfortunately, the public was not aware that Patton had such a limited objective—one that was dictated by Montgomery's need to have a clear path for the Eighth Army after it had broken through the Mareth line and the Wadi Akarit. Patton also had to secure Gafsa as a supply base for Montgomery. Armchair strategists have looked at the map and determined that Patton should push to the sea to cut off Rommel. However, this was corrected in part by an on-the-record press conference by Ike today in which he made clear the mission of the II Corps.

On Thursday morning left Ike's tented Advance CP, Generals Ike and Tooey in one car, General Porter and I in another, with jeeps and their .50's fore and aft, on roads dusty with the rapid movement of elements of II Corps from its old sector to its new battleground in the north. Ike was intent on calling on General Anderson of the First Army, whom he had not seen for several weeks, as his dealings had been with Alexander since the latter had been given command of the battle front. After thorough exploration of the situation with General Anderson, Ike accepted his invitation to drive fifteen miles north of Beja to see three Mark-6, or Tiger, tanks. These were three of twenty-seven destroyed by the British when the Germans made a push March 26. While Ike was interested in seeing the tanks, he was more concerned with familiarizing himself with the terrain over which American troops soon would operate.

We changed from staff cars to jeeps at Beja, the road eastward being subject to strafing and bombing.

General Anderson himself drove the jeep for Ike. I rode in another and "manned" the .50-caliber gun. Captain Samuelson, one of Anderson's aides, sat in the front seat to guide. We were told that if we were strafed, we had the choice of staying in the jeeps or dashing off the road into the fields, many of which still had mines left by the Germans. When we reached the scene of destruction of twenty-seven tanks, many of which could still be seen on the hillsides, we had to take a one-way dirt track across a field. The track was marked by white tape and along it were signs, "Mines—Verges." Because of possible presence of booby traps, there was a noticeable reluctance to prod into the innards of the Tiger tanks or to touch the articles lying around them. We could hear artillery fire, judged by the experts to be about 2000 yards away. There had been no enemy aircraft that we had seen, although we had seen antiaircraft bursts above and to the right of us. I filled my pockets with burned-out machine-gun cartridges from one of the tanks, pilfered a seven-foot copper whip antenna from another, and got away with an 88-mm. projectile. The size of the Tiger, its armament, and especially its 88 gun were impressive. General Anderson said the British had laid a heavy pattern of artillery fire on this turn of the road when the tanks came charging along. The barrage was so heavy, and so many tanks were hit, that the crews of the Tigers abandoned their mobile fortresses. Clothing was still strewn about and, no doubt, there had been many killed.

On the return trip from inspection of the Tiger, General Spaatz got in the jeep with me, saying that he wanted the extra safety he was assured with a naval gunner manning the .50. He didn't seem to mind when I told him that I had never fired one.

General "Tooey" did not tell Ike, but he told me that he had been on a Flying Fortress raid of Palermo and Sicily the day before. Some forty-eight Fortresses took part, but three had been lost, two by fighters and one by flak. Tooey had seen eight of the crew of one Fortress bail out close to the Sicilian coast but over water. He said it wasn't a pleasant sight.

Tooey's trip on the bombers (it wasn't the first by any means) brings to mind that I haven't seen any criticism of American general officers failing to take risks with their men. Quite the contrary. Patton is a notorious front-line kibitzer, Eaker and Doolittle have flown innumerable missions with their crews, and General Ike has not sought the safety of Algiers, nor has he stayed there from choice. But every time he wants to get where the shooting is, every front-line officer tries to discourage him. Then if he insists, so much protection is thrown around him, the party becomes too large and too many lives are needlessly endangered. So most of the time he just growls at his job in this war.

General Patton was a welcome visitor at our house last night.

While Ike and Patton discoursed on the need of the toughness to build and run an effective army, they agreed that utter ruthlessness, even to their best friends, was mandatory. Troops had a right to good leadership, and it was up to top commanders to relieve any officer who failed to provide it. I could not help but comment that both gave every exterior indication of toughness but actually were chickenhearted underneath. Scarcely had I made this comment when Patton recalled that before leaving the II Corps headquarters, he had taken time to pick some wild flowers and place them on the grave of his aide. As he recalled the incident, he said: "I guess I really am a Goddam old fool." His voice quivered, tears ran down his cheeks.

Yet Patton had exposed himself to enemy fire numerous times to be an encouraging example to our own troops. He had dismissed ineffective and incapable officers and had gained reputation as a ruthless disciplinarian. Ike, too, had on occasion been required to call in old classmates of West Point and lifelong associates in the Army to tell them they were not up to the job and would have to go home. Patton had said that our Army needs bravery plus brains.

Ike went to bed early, and Patton and I discussed the effect on him of his relief. I told him I felt it inevitable that his failure to go to the sea would bring him criticism, but he said so long as he was doing his job, he could take whatever opprobrium was involved. He was satisfied if Ike was satisfied.

This morning at breakfast, Major Lee phoned that General Marshall had sent a message to Patton, saying in effect, "You have done a fine job and have justified our confidence in you."

When I relayed this to General Patton, he said emotionally: "I owe this to you, Ike."

"The hell you do," Ike said.

                                                    ALGIERS, FRIDAY, APRIL 23, 1943
Accompanied Ike yesterday on a flying visit via Flying Fortress and jeep to General Alexander's headquarters, where Ike met General Giraud. Then we jeeped to II Corps headquarters of General Bradley, northwest of Beja, who explained the American attack which was to start last night. General Bradley took us to the headquarters of the 1st Division, where we had the good fortune to find General Terry Allen conducting a last-minute session with his staff on plans for a dawn attack the next morning.

We reached General Bradley's headquarters at 10. It is in tents lying in a heavily wooded ravine around a farmhouse. We were detoured in Beja because certain roads had been declared "out of bounds" with signs "typhus."

While at the front we heard one particularly good bit of news: twenty-one six-engined German transports, each capable of carrying 120 troops, were shot down yesterday morning by our fighters over the Bay of Tunis. The air people thought they were loaded with troops. Apparently the Axis is sending replacements by air, and supplies in the mine-protected channel from Sicily by light-draft vessels heavily armed with ack-ack. Also the First Army got in a wallop on German tanks when they attacked day before yesterday. Some thirty were knocked out, including Tigers.

The Eighth Army took Enfidaville, which was evacuated, and the desert army now is up against mountainous terrain. Alexander's over-all tactics at this phase are to push the greatly reinforced First Army, with its four American divisions in II Corps, in the direction of Bizerte and Tunis, to meet Montgomery's forces hammering northward from Enfidaville, again with the hope of trapping a large block of the enemy. Our G-2, incidentally, informs us that the Axis command in Tunisia has been turned over to von Arnim by Rommel, who supposedly has returned from Italy to Germany.

ALGIERS, SUNDAY, APRIL 25, 1943 (EASTER SUNDAY)
Ike's position just now is something like that of a hen setting on a batch of eggs. He is waiting for the eggs to hatch, and is in the mental state of wondering if they will ever break the shell.

He is waiting as patiently as possible for news of a break-through. He has the equivalent of some thirteen divisions pounding at the Axis' strongly dug-in and mountainous positions. He is shooting the wad. If they can't break through, then he may be on his way home, defeated.

Pressure is on the Axis like nobody's business, but so far no real encouraging gains have been made. However, the Americans in the north apparently have done well, having taken their objectives up until yesterday. Alexander has issued an order of the day commending them for the efficiency and secrecy that marked their great move from El Guettar to the northern sector. Not only did the 1st Division do its stuff, presumably in accordance with the plans we heard discussed at the staff meeting at their headquarters on Tuesday, but the 9th Division, which Ike didn't have time to visit that day, likewise has done well. It is on the extreme north side of the sector, next to the sea, and, looking at the pins on the map, it appears to have made the greatest advance. But you can't tell too well from maps. The terrain is so different in the several sectors.

The action going on now is costly in lives. Even Lieutenant General

"Whitey" McNair, War Department head of the ground forces, has been wounded at the front while visiting the 1st Division. "Serious but not dangerous," the report said. He is in a field hospital, with shrapnel through his shoulder and some head wounds. Ike plans to visit him while on his next trip, which at the moment is "laid on" for Tuesday. Also will make some side trips from the old command post at Constantine. Has never visited the bases at Bône or Philippeville, so hopes to do so this week, after seeing some more of II Corps headquarters. Hope we can see the 9th Division, too.

"Gee" and General Hartle were in town this week, on a quick visit from England. They had dinner with us, including General Hughes, Thursday evening. Gee was his same energetic and courteous self. Ike, answering their questions, emphasized most strongly that scouting patrols and discipline need improvement. I sense a feeling that not much is doing in England re invasion of Europe, except a lot of newspaper talk.

Julius Holmes is back from U. S. A., filled with the same misgivings I had about American public opinion. It is still veering, both naturally and by campaign, to lick the Japs first, and let Hitler wait. He says there is now a well-organized campaign under way, based on fear that the Japs are concentrating for another attack on Australia. Public is being told those running the war for U. S. A. are too complacent about Japan, and giving too much attention to a master plan of global warfare that is based on beating Hitler first.

The beat-the-Japs-first school of thought would bypass the opportunity we now have, and perhaps will never have again, to lick Germany while we can get at her from three sides, with three nations pressing her on all sides and from the air and sea. If we lose this opportunity, the Lord only knows when the job can be done, if ever.

I notice that the President's plan of keeping the press excluded from the food conference, as he told me would be done when I saw him in Washington, has raised a great storm of protest. One Congressman has introduced a resolution to permit customary and complete press coverage of all the sessions. It appears to me that a lot of political partisans at home are thinking more of discrediting or defeating Roosevelt than of winning the war; but, of course, a lot of the same people think we have already won the war.

In our bailiwick, we are getting complaints from front-line commanders on the number of official visitors they have to look after while fighting the campaign. Ike is trying to cut down the number being sent from Washington, but realizes the lessons learned in Tunisia will be useful for the future. Trying to strike a balance, as usual.

Hill 609

ALGIERS, FRIDAY, APRIL 30, 1943

Returned this forenoon by Flying Fortress from Constantine, where we stayed overnight following an interesting visit at the front. Ike called first at the II Corps headquarters, near Beja; conferred with General Bradley, and after lunch "jeeped" to headquarters of the 34th Division to see General Ryder. However, Ryder was at his Advance Command Post some thirty-five minutes away by bumpy road, so Ike talked briefly with Colonel Norman E. Hendrickson, Chief of Staff, and then proceeded toward the front, where the party went by jeep to a hilltop. From this hill we had a good view of No. 609, this being the immediate and most formidable obstacle confronting the 34th Division.

Since Ike visited the 1st Division headquarters a week ago on the eve of its attack, that Division has gone forward successfully, and the 34th has come alongside on the left. Hill 609 is the highest promontory of many high hills, almost mountains, and is being used effectively by the Germans for defense and observation. From here and elsewhere movement of our troops can be watched by the Germans and their artillery fire directed accurately against them. The forward movement of the 1st Division has been held up because of the danger to its left flank by the German position on 609. The 34th Division drew the difficult task of clearing this hill. The 34th had already made a considerable advance, and at the moment we were watching our artillery shell 609, which it had been doing for four days; infantry was cautiously but steadily advancing toward this slope. Around the II Corps headquarters there was a feeling of pride in the 34th because after its bad luck at Fondouk, it was now accounting for itself commendably, another indication that after "greenness" is overcome by actual battle experience, our American troops fight very well. In fact, if No. 609 is taken, which it may be today, we will then be in a position to pass part of the 1st Armored Division onto the coastal plain, where it can be effective. British armor is likewise waiting farther south for infantry to open the "gate."

The 9th Division was farther north and was making good progress. Ike had hoped to visit its CO, General Eddy, but the headquarters were too remote to be reached in the limited time at Ike's disposal.

It was said that from the top of 609 Tunis could be seen. From our hilltop it was interesting to see the burst of American artillery fire on the side of the great bald knob and return fire on American positions to our right. It is not quite accurate to say "return fire," but the Germans

held other hill positions from which their artillery could operate, and
frequently the 34th Division found itself under artillery or machine-gun
fire from German-held hills almost at their rear on the left flanks. Probably no more difficult fighting will be experienced in the African Theater
than that under way in Tunisia now.

Ike then visited General Anderson at headquarters of the First Army.
Anderson said there had been some 3500 British casualties passed back
to hospitals. Allowing for one dead to four wounded, deaths were then
about 900. The comparable American figure was about 2000 wounded
and 500 dead. These apply to the current operation of the First Army,
which had been proceeding about a week.

Flying from Souk-el-Arba to Constantine, I asked Ike if he would state
his outstanding impression. He said it was that the troops were tired.
He repeated that we are throwing at the Germans everything we have
and we must break through. The progress has been slow but steady. Our
weakness is that we have no large pool of reserves. Three of the four
American divisions are now in action. Parts of the 1st Armored Division
are awaiting their chance. The American sector, however, is well supported in depth, and their fronts are relatively narrow. For general reserve the 3rd Division has been alerted to move from Port Lyautey to the
front.

Incidentally, I was told a story by Colonel V. E. Scott Bailey about an
air raid in Bône. He was up there to meet Major James Taylor, who was
in the G-2 section of First Army. They were both late for their meeting,
due to the raid, and, as neither had tin hats, they had stood in a doorway,
taking shelter from the heavy flak, fragments from which were falling
like great hunks of hail. A British Tommy, wearing a tin hat, came down
the alleyway, his hobnailed boots clanking against the stone pavement.
He was carrying two large bottles of beer. The Tommy said to Taylor:

"This is a fine thing. All this stuff coming down and me sent to get a
beer for my chums."

Taylor agreed and suggested he should wait a few minutes. The
Tommy stood in the doorway for two or three minutes, but felt that the
beer was more important than the flak, so left saying:

"Well, I can't help it. Bless* 'em all."

He walked slowly down the street—holding his tin hat over the two
bottles of beer.

On Tuesday, April 27, we had driven to Constantine, the weather
being unsuitable for flying. Our departure from Algiers was delayed because overnight messages had come to AFHQ indicating desire for a

* This was not precisely the word used.

meeting of General Alexander and Montgomery with Admiral Cunningham and Air Marshal Tedder, to be held in Algiers on Tuesday. The
reason for the meeting was a dispute between Montgomery and Cunningham and Tedder, the latter two being in agreement as to the plan
for HUSKY, but "Monty" not satisfied. Essence of his objections was that
his part in HUSKY had to be so strong his risk of defeat would be nil.
Tedder and Cunningham want to take airfields first for air cover.
"Monty" wants them left for attack about D plus 3 or D plus 4. Ike will
have to referee the interservice British scrap.

While this concerned the British primarily, it also affected plans for
the American landings. Ike felt a responsibility and so postponed his
trip until he learned that, because of bad flying weather, the meeting
had been put off, Montgomery having gone to Cairo, where his attendance at an Easter church service was widely publicized.

I spent Tuesday and Thursday evenings in Constantine in serious
poker sessions with General Spaatz, Colonel Ted Curtis, his Chief of
Staff, Lieutenant Colonel Everett Cook, and Major General Idwal H.
Edwards, War Department G-3. I suffered a reverse the first night, but
counterattacked the second and not only regained all lost ground but
drove deep into enemy territory. For the second session Ike had re-
arranged his return trip to afford me an opportunity to recoup. He even
loaned me his wallet of lucky coins. I carried them in my hip pocket
and rubbed every time I got into a crisis. They are useful.

"Tooey" says the Allied Air Force now has 3000 planes in Tunisia,
200 of which are Flying Fortresses. The air is really coming into its own;
nearly a thousand sorties a day are being flown, and medium and heavy
bombers are socking everything from gun frontiers to barges, with good
effect.

The air officers live in close comradeship in Constantine. Air Marshal
Robb and his associates mess with Spaatz and his gang. They play exciting games of darts for ten francs, but when the Americans get together
in a poker game, the British fade away, and I don't blame them, because
the stakes are high. However, "Tooey," "Ted," and "Cookie"—all in the
same fighter outfit in the last war—take in each other's washing and keep
their winnings and losings on the book. Actually, very little cash changes
hands, but I imagine they resent a foreigner like myself moving in and
taking first place, even if only for one night and that as a redemption
for a bad night. However, I have left my winnings "on the book" for a
return engagement when another trip takes us through Constantine, the
general understanding being to settle accounts "ten years after the war."

Over all there was an air of confidence at headquarters of both the

II Corps and the First Army. Some optimistic bits of information were given me by G-2 and G-3 at II Corps. One was that the Germans had left the Italians in the northern sector near Bizerte, which was construed as a sign of expected evacuation from that area. Another was that sixty per cent of the artillery shells that hit American positions in a recent engagement had been duds. This was taken as a sign that munition workers were engaging in sabotage. I had noticed in a "sitrep" that one hilltop held by the Germans and assailed by the British had been surrendered. I mentioned this to Colonel Robert A. Hewitt of the G-3 staff, and he said it had been an encouraging sign, but the Germans had persisted in fighting stubbornly since and so the occasion had to be discounted.

Most significant of all to me was that the Americans had settled down to hard fighting, which they were doing well; that the Eighth Army had found the mountains greatly different from the desert, and its fame might be tempered now by having to fight under conditions that made the successes of the British, French, and American forces in Tunisia seem relatively weak as compared to those of the Eighth Army.

APRIL, 1943: *Allied North African advances continued with capture of thousands of Axis troops and destruction of vast quantities of matériel. Flying Fortresses hit ports and airfields in the Mediterranean. Russian troops advanced on all sectors after yielding in Donets area. Heavy raids continued on Continental production centers, with heaviest raids on Hitler's birthday. Chinese drove Japs out of Yunnan into Burma. Japs lost heavily in planes at Guadalcanal and Milne Bay. Two hundred thousand Japs massed north of Australia as MacArthur's forces occupied Funafuti Island. War Department announced Jap air losses seven times greater than Allies'. General Spaatz reported ratio almost fifteen to one in North Africa. Kiska raided by Canadian and U. S. fliers. Tokyo admitted that some of captured Doolittle fliers had been executed. (This revelation made a lot of our lads want to fight the Japs, too.—H.C.B.)*

We Begin to Get Good News

ALGIERS, SATURDAY, MAY 1, 1943

Beetle phoned Ike at the villa last night before dinner. From Ike's end of the conversation I knew the news was good.

Through interceptions of low-grade ciphers used at the front, we had discovered that some German units were calling frantically for ammunition. From other sources it was learned that three ships loaded with ammunition were en route to fill the urgent demand. The three ships are at the bottom of the sea, thanks to the Navy.

Beetle also reported that of two enemy destroyers bound for Tunisia with some 1600 replacements on each, one had been sunk and the other was burning from stem to stern.

Ike felt the failure of the Axis to get through its badly needed ammunition and the replacements would be a serious blow to their morale.

News from the front shows no important progress, but steady and hard fighting. No news about Hill 609.

Ike has received a message from General Marshall this morning, questioning the timing of HUSKY operation, insisting it should be done as soon as possible and emphasizing that boldness and surprise may have great beneficial effect.

Ike is pondering an answer while sitting alone at the house this afternoon, awaiting my return. We will go to the farm to ride or to play tennis, the latter being preferred by yours truly.

Incidentally, today is May 1, the date on which I am supposed to be a commander, but as I have no official notice, I am still a lieutenant commander. When, as, and if the promotion comes through, I will still have to wait for the scrambled eggs on my cap. Ike now wants scrambled eggs as well, and I have accused him of jealousy.

More News—the Naval Aide Boards a Battleship

ALGIERS, WEDNESDAY, MAY 5, 1943

News that we had finally dislodged the Hun from 609 was followed by capture of Mateur, marking an advance of some fifteen miles. Farther north French and American forces had made good progress, and it was thought that as many as half a dozen German battalions had been surrounded.

There are now fourteen Allied divisions at the front, five of which are American, the 3rd Division having gone up this week as a reserve and for such seasoning as the remaining days of the campaign will afford. Possibly it will relieve our 1st Infantry Division, a crackerjack outfit.

Smiles permeate through AFHQ. The British are telling funny stories, RAF lads saying "good show, good show."

Today I accompanied Ike on a quick Fortress trip to Oujda, to visit the headquarters of General Mark Clark's Fifth Army. We were met by the lanky General and Major General Al Gruenther, his Chief of Staff. We were whisked to town behind ten white-helmeted and otherwise snappy MPs, and Wayne, as Ike calls him, had his men so trained and/or alerted that everyone we saw saluted. My arm got tired. So there could be no mistake, a large four-starred red flag was flown on the car in which Ike and Clark rode.

Ike wanted to talk over some major questions with Clark, whose ideas and judgment on strategy and tactics Ike greatly respects.

Yesterday I went with Ike to have lunch as guests of Admiral Willis, commanding officer of Force H, Royal Navy. It was on H.M.S. *Nelson,* sister ship of the *Rodney,* which was lying near by.

Anticipating the formalities, Ike had asked a couple of days ago that I check to find out just what a general in his position should do when he goes aboard a battleship. Not ever having been on one myself, and me an alleged naval aide, I told him I would simply ask some of my Royal Navy friends to tell me just in what respect the British "piping aboard" ceremony differs from the American. Ike asked what the hell would I say if asked to describe the American custom. He had me. But I said I'd go to my friend Captain Jerry Wright, USN, and ask him how the American service differed from the British. But I was vulnerable there, too, if cross-examined. Finally decided to make a full breast of my ignorance to Jerry. Before I could act, along came Flag Lieutenant Dampier, Admiral Cunningham's aide, who gave me the lowdown. So I prepared Ike. All he had to do when he came up the gangplank was to salute straight ahead, just as he stepped over the rail. Then he would be conducted on a review of the guard that would be assembled to man the rail.

Later I heard through the thin door to Ike's office some loud laughter after the morning conference. Heard Ike telling Admiral Cunningham how he had asked his "naval aide" to get the dope. As I was the topic of conversation, I poked my head in and remarked that "Dampy" was my authority. To this the Admiral quickly warned, "Don't take Dampy's word—he doesn't know, either."

Scratched the back of my hand getting out of the car when we pulled up to the dock to board the barge that was to take us to the *Nelson.* Discovered the blood en route, and claimed a Purple Heart from the Royal Navy, it seeming I had been wounded in action. No sympathy. But when I saluted as I crossed the rail, tagging after Ike, Cunningham, and Hewitt, the USN Admiral, the back of my saluting hand was bloody.

Anyway, everything went off well, and I have now been aboard a battleship.

Getting back to the war, General Marshall is urging Ike to reconsider the "orthodox" plans of his planners and attack Sicily pronto just as the Huns and Eyeties are being finally killed off in Tunisia. Emphasizes the value of surprise, citing Lee, Grant, and Sherman. But they didn't have to wait on ships, some coming from the U. S., combat-loaded, others from the U. K., similarly loaded, and all sorts of logistical problems. But Ike appreciates General Marshall's idea—in fact, has been pushing for the same objective. Now he is in a mental stew trying to figure out how an early attack can be improvised. Loves boldness, and not afraid of the risks, and told Clark today he thought he had it worked out.

Death of Lieutenant General Frank M. Andrews, Theater Commander in England, and of most of his party, including my particular friend, Colonel Morrow Krum, in a plane crash in Iceland was given to us at the house before breakfast just as we were fixing to fly to Oujda. As we left the house Mickey said quietly to Ike:

"I will pray you have a safe trip, sir."

Andrews' death perked again thoughts of major strategy. Would we resume ROUNDUP? Ike thinks we must. We're only nibbling at the edges when we peck off Sicily (and some think that too costly), and if Russia should be knocked out this summer, we'd be in a poor way toward winning the war. Insists we must put not just divisions but armies (mentioned this to Clark's staff officers today) ashore on the Continent. Who would succeed Andrews?

The Prime Minister is always cheering. He's a joy. Today he sent a cable of congratulations to General Alexander for the British First Army, hoping thus to balance the glory earned by the British Eighth Army, which already has won so much praise.

General Marshall also has felt the need of rushing to Sicily and has made some suggestions along this line and advised Ike not to be bound by unorthodox methods of planners. However, although commanders occasionally are inclined to kick the planners out the window and decide risks of an operation themselves, in this instance both planners and commanders are confronted by something neither can cure—shortage of landing craft and of shipping generally. In addition, the Sicilian show will be some weeks in starting because we are throwing so much of our resources and energy into the current battle, and there will be time required for training of some of these same troops for amphibious operations.

To jump over to a matter which may seem detail but actually is extremely important, Ike has been impressed by the virtual impossibility of American officers and soldiers appearing neat and snappy in their field uniforms. Ike thinks we should have a neater and smarter-looking field uniform. He has suggested to General Marshall that the Quartermaster begin now to have designed another winter uniform for next winter's wear. He thought the material should be rough wool because it wouldn't show the dirt and is more easily kept presentable. He liked the appearance of the British battle dress, but thought Americans should design something distinctive for themselves. He thought our head covering was not too good—the helmet is splendid, and its stocking cap interlining is suitable for wear outside the combat zone. While on pass, or working at rear headquarters, the overseas cap is acceptable. He thinks that sloppy fatigue hats and mechanics' caps should be abolished, as most GIs seem to prefer them to more soldierly headgear. He has issued an order prohibiting the wearing of fatigue hats in North Africa.

ALGIERS, SATURDAY, MAY 8, 1943

On Friday I accompanied Ike on a flying visit to the headquarters of the II Corps and from there to divisional command posts of the 34th and 1st.

General Bradley explained the military situation in his sector from the maps in his tent, both generals having to use their spectacles in the dim light. Ike was enthusiastic over the progress of the II Corps, whose Combat Team B, part of the 1st U. S. Armored Division, and the 9th Division, with the Corps d'Afrique close to the rear, were pinching Ferryville from south and north and threatening Bizerte—the most important naval base for our use in the Mediterranean, the capture of which marks the beginning of the end of Mussolini's attempt to make the Mediterranean an Italian lake.

Ernie Pyle had called on Ike some time ago; Ike had told him that when he went up front again he should "go and discover Bradley." Pyle had written almost exclusively of GIs and junior officers, not caring much for the brass hats. He really discovered Bradley, though, and when the lid was off, five or six of his columns were devoted to him.

At the 1st Division headquarters, General Terry Allen was roused from a sleep in midafternoon to tell his story to the General. Allen had been out front most of the night on his duties. Obviously he was very tired. His discussion of the situation was given in a monosyllabic monotone. Said some of his companies were reduced to the size of platoons, casualties amongst the combat troops having been extremely high. His men were tired. They had attacked daily for weeks.

Ike accidentally met Major General Truscott, again CO of the 3rd Division, who was en route to II Corps headquarters. Ike told him arrangements had been made for the 3rd Division to relieve the 1st, starting possibly that night. Truscott was elated, and Ike expressed his hope the 3rd would get into action in the current battle.

When we reached the villa in Algiers, General Tom Handy, Ike's successor as head of the Operations Division, and General Bull were there by invitation for dinner, in tow of Major Lee, who informed us of a message announcing General Devers' appointment as Theater Commander in London.

During dinner we heard the news that American forces had taken Bizerte and the British Tunis. The 9th Division had spurted to the goal. This had come to pass since we had had lunch with Bradley at his headquarters. Surprisingly, there was no jubilation. I had to emphasize that I, for one, was impressed, but Ike said he wasn't interested in the capture of mere geographical locations—he would be satisfied only when all the Axis forces were cleared from Africa. What he feared now was a long-drawn-out affair in the Bon peninsula, which would be costly to us, especially in time. He was hopeful that Alexander would keep the enemy upset and on the run, so they could not reorganize to furnish opposition. He especially wanted the Cape Bon peninsula cut, from Tunis southward. There still was fighting on the Eighth Army front in the Enfidaville area.

Another message came in, saying that a German wireless message had been intercepted. It contained the "good-bys" of the 15th Panzer Division to the homeland. Still another intercept indicated a plan to evacuate 33,000 Germans and 30,000 Italians. This would leave a job for our Navy and the Air Force, which are actively patrolling the sea. Someone, in another message, had recalled Churchill's statement at the time of the threatened invasion of Britain: "We are ready: so are the fishes."

Victory in North Africa

ALGIERS, MONDAY, MAY 10, 1943

Bill Stoneman wrote for the *Chicago Daily News:* "We came into North Africa on a shoestring when we waded ashore at Algiers six months ago tonight. We entered Tunis on the tail of an avalanche."

So much news of the crumbling of the Axis forces has broken upon us that I, for one, am overjoyed. Ike is nonchalant. For him this battle was finished some time ago; now his thoughts are on the next job against Hitler —Sicily. We don't seem to think much about the Eyeties any more, although I heard up front that they were still fighting well with artillery in well-dug-in positions.

There still is hard fighting ahead, particularly on the Eighth Army front in the Enfidaville area. British 6th and 7th Armored Divisions, which broke through to Tunis, have continued southward, hoping to prevent a German retreat into the Bon peninsula. They are still meeting resistance and yesterday called for infantry support.

General Bradley told the story, in the north, in a brief message I took on the phone late last night. He said simply, "Mission completed."

We had spent Sunday at the farm, but I came to the office in the afternoon to pick up the congratulatory messages. I found that General Bradley's II Corps had reported as of noon yesterday (May 9) that General Klauser had "unconditionally surrendered" German troops to General Harmon. His forces included elements of the 10th and 15th German Panzer Divisions, the former having led the German break-through to France in May of 1940, and the 15th having been a distinguished division of the Afrika Korps. General Bradley also reported that from Bizerte to the tip of the peninsula, the mouth of the Mejerda River was being mopped up. Ike was hopeful that the 3rd U. S. Division, which was to relieve the 1st, would get some battle experience.

This morning Ike is dictating answers to congratulatory messages. He just asked me to read his drafts of replies to General Marshall and Secretary Stimson. I thought they were perfect. "I've got to cable the King," he said, as he buzzed for Warrant Officer Marshall, his prize stenographer.

I suggested he start it "Dear Kingy."

Or "Dear Georgie," Ike said.

Marshall ventured: "Dear Rex."

General Smith and his aide, Lieutenant Robinson, were flown in Ike's Fortress to Marrakech yesterday morning, where Beetle boarded a Liberator, the motors of which, I am told by Captain Reedy, our pilot, have already run 575 hours.

I am also sending on Beetle's plane to Admiral King, for the Navy Department collection of war trophies, the copper whip antenna I took from a Tiger. I explained in a note to the Admiral that the tank marked the farthest advance of the Germans in Tunisia on the northern front and its antenna might be of interest to the Navy Department as a trophy taken by a naval officer on shore patrol.

Saturday, after having sweated out his dread of the ceremony, Ike formally transferred the rearmament for the French to General Giraud in a snappy military function at the Foyer Civique. The affair was broadcast widely, including America.

Ike had been reluctant to take part in the ceremony, but finally gave way to the advice of his staff, including me, that it should be done. He is still filled with misgivings, but yesterday while he was riding, numerous French officers and soldiers, who had been letting him pass unnoticed,

were quick to salute. They recognized him for the first time, having seen
him at the ceremony. I thought the affair would do a lot of good, and
so far indications justify that feeling. This morning there is an ardent
letter of congratulations from Giraud about Tunisia. I note particularly
that he expresses his appreciation to Ike for publicly recognizing the fighting qualities of the French Army in Africa. (Same is true privately.)

I wanted Ike to have a press conference Saturday morning. At first he
was reluctant because he feared he might thus take unto himself credit
for victory, but finally consented. He had a fine conference, stressing
the perfection of co-ordination developed amongst the Allies in North
Africa.

Ike also permitted formal announcement that General Omar Bradley
had been in command of the II Corps during the current operations, having relieved General Patton, the former being infantry trained and therefore more suitable for mountainous fighting, whereas Patton, whom he
described as the best armored-force officer in the Army, had been in command while the terrain permitted use of armor.

Then, off the record, Ike explained that General Patton would take
part in the next operation and had to be free to plan his attack. No speculation on future moves is being permitted by the censors, and Ike's announcement was regarded with some dismay by General McClure, the
information director, who was hopeful that after the Tunisian campaign
a considerable number of the correspondents would go home. McClure
was planning to play down the possibility of any future operations spring-
ing from North Africa, but Ike let the cat out of the bag, if indeed it
wasn't already out. He told the correspondents they would be informed
in due time of the future operations, just as he had done at Gibraltar.

Ike had hoped to review fully with Beetle his ideas for conduct of the
war for the next six or nine months, so his Chief of Staff could reflect
them to the Combined Chiefs' meeting in Washington. Ike got this done
between other jobs, but at the moment I am not clear just what he has
recommended. If he had been sure the Tunisian affair would disintegrate
so quickly, Ike probably would have made the trip himself. I think it
would have been good for him, and there still is the chance that General
Marshall again will send for him. But Ike's thoughts now are to get away
from the daily stint at the office and get a change of atmosphere, just as
soon as the fighting ends. He has informed General Marshall that when
it is over he intends to take a "twenty-four-hour leave, where no one can
find me."

At 3 Saturday afternoon, Ike received the Chinese Mission, all of whom
spoke English. They presented him with an autographed picture sent per-

sonally by Chiang Kai-shek. Of course, they wanted Ike's opinion on conduct of the war. He gave them Lecture A, on the need of Allies sticking together—for twenty minutes.

Tag Ends of the Victory

ALGIERS, WEDNESDAY, MAY 12, 1943

Ike intends to take Pantelleria before Sicily. HOBGOBLIN is the code name for the island of Pantelleria, but the operation itself is called CORKSCREW. Pantelleria has valuable airfields, from which we can supply some air cover for landings in Sicily.

Yesterday, I accompanied Ike on a "flying" visit to 18th Army Group headquarters near Le Kef, where Ike conferred with General Alexander at his camouflaged tent camp. I "sat in" on the morning situation report given by three of Alexander's staff officers.

In the north, in the II Corps sector, the Americans had counted at that time some 30,000 prisoners, of which less than 5000 were Italians, so it was a rare bag. Germans and Italians alike were seeking the prisoner-of-war pens, to give themselves up. They came in their trucks, staff cars, and even on motorcycles, one of which carried five Krauts. The "unconditional surrender" had been accompanied by a further stipulation that no stores or equipment were to be destroyed by the Germans. Consequently, in that sector alone we have garnered booty in great quantity. Even new uniforms and shoes were taken, much of which will be used for underclothed prisoners. Fighting had been stopped for the second day in the northern sector.

In the Cape Bon sector, British Armored units quickly had cut the neck of the peninsula so that the number of escaping Axis units was virtually nil. Consequently, Ike's worry that a quick victory would be frustrated by another "Bataan" on the peninsula fortunately was unnecessary. Likewise, with seas too rough for small boats and with eighteen Royal Navy destroyers and numerous motor torpedo boats, some American, continually patrolling around the peninsula, little could escape. Indeed, every sign indicated that the Germans and Italians had even given up hope of this means of escape.

Only one enemy aircraft—an F-W 190—had been seen by the Allied fliers the previous day. It was flying low, apparently seeking escape, and was shot down near Cape Bon.

Our air, during the active fighting, had flown as many as 2700 sorties in one day—probably a world's record. The Cape Bon peninsula has been searched and, where there were targets, strafed. Numerous fires had been seen on the peninsula, as the Nazis sought to destroy their own supplies. Meanwhile the Strategic Air Force had been active bombing targets on Pantelleria and Sicily.

In front of the Eighth Army, however, there was a pocket of Axis resistance estimated conservatively at 27,000 Germans and 10,000 Italians, with the possibility of a total of 60,000. This group was encircled but still fighting.

Last-minute farewell messages sent in the clear from German radio operators in Tunisia to the homeland had been heard. Some of these are described by the British Intelligence Officer as "crude and gross." Both Hitler and Mussolini have sent messages glowing with praise for the valiant fight of the Axis. These came after the wholesale surrender to the Americans. Hitler had ended with the word "astonishing," which the British officer read with appropriate sarcasm.

We had taken along Brigadier Sugden, one of the best British planners, in the Fortress. Through his natural reticence, he glowed with satisfaction.

I asked him if the bag of prisoners in Tunisia would be greater than that taken by Montgomery at El Alamein. He said, "Most definitely. It is unfortunate for the British we have not had many prisoners to trade to the Germans and, consequently, could not effectively combat their threat or practice of chaining. Now we have ample trading stock."

(As I dictate words that indicate the African campaign is approaching the end, the sound of rapid antiaircraft fire comes through the window in Algiers, signifying that enemy air raids still may be expected.)

Returning to Algiers in time for a late lunch, Ike found several additional messages of congratulation, including one of ardent praise from the Prime Minister, who emphasized Ike's genius at promotion of harmony amongst the Allies.

(While dictating the paragraph immediately above, Ike burst into my office, said he was going riding and didn't I want to go with him. I told him history would suffer and begged off, he knowing damned well that I don't like to ride a horse, especially with an English-type saddle.)

Beetle reached Washington last night—departed Sunday morning, arriving there about 7 Tuesday evening—one of the quickest trips by the southern route.

The meeting of the Combined Chiefs of Staff was to have begun yesterday morning. It was announced in Washington by Steve Early that Winston Churchill had arrived. Ike should be there.

Just now Ike is fretting that the ever-present limitation of shipping and the scarcity of landing craft have prevented a quick follow-up of a new blow against the Axis by immediately attacking Sicily while the enemy is disorganized in Tunisia. But despite all his attempts to attain an early attack date, it simply hasn't been accomplished. Bogged by logistics, he is making every effort to speed plans and activation for the attack.

Ike is taking some justifiable pride in his prediction made first in a letter to General Marshall, under date of March 29, that he "guessed" the Tunisian campaign would be finished by May 15. Alexander yesterday reminded him of this prediction and complimented him on it, recalling, too, that his own guess had been June 15. Alexander promised to have the pocket cleared by the fifteenth, to make Ike's forecast come precisely true. That would be Saturday. Incidentally, Ike has won from General Patton three bets of five dollars each made only early last week. Ike bet we would have the Bon peninsula cleared out by May 15—"Blood and Guts" said not until June 15. The third bet, likewise, indicated pessimism by Patton and optimism by Ike. I've forgotten what it was, but, anyway, Ike says he's won it.

Took some good pictures at Alexander's headquarters yesterday—one of Ike, Alexander, and Bradley that the Signal Corps is wirephotoing to U. S. One of Ike has been thoroughly censored by the highest authority, for it shows the Allied Commander-in-Chief in an action indicating need of delousing. The Signal Corps think I am getting pretty good on action pictures, but Ike has reason to regard me as perhaps not sufficiently discreet as to the poses I catch him in.

Major Ramsey, American Aide to General Alexander, had been on a trip to Tunis, and General Bradley had just returned from a look-see at Bizerte. Their story plainly showed that the Germans had been caught more quickly than they expected. At one airdrome near Bizerte several serviceable fighting planes were captured intact; some were in repair shops —wrenches and working gear lying close by. Many planes had been shot up or burned by our effective air. Few had been destroyed by the enemy. The advance in the northern sector had been so rapid, there were virtually no mine fields or booby traps. One German general who was captured said his division, the 10th Panzer, had suffered heavy casualties from which it had never regained during the retreat from Kasserine Pass, because they overran mine fields sown by other German divisions. It has been discovered that the Germans have another ingenious mine—one that is chucked into munition dumps, railway cars, and storage piles. It is an explosive with a time clock that may be set to go off any time up to twenty-one days. Captured dumps are being carefully searched. The Germans do not seem to be short of ammunition, as there were huge dumps captured, although they may have been short in some categories and definitely short of transport. Amongst the booty was Argentine beef, presumably captured from the British in the desert.

A colonel of II headquarters said that Germans and Italians had to be placed in separate barbed-wire enclosures because of their strong animosity. Likewise, the personnel of the Luftwaffe and of the German ground troops obviously do not fraternize. He said he had seen prisoners of these categories in one enclosure, but they separated into groups and showed bitterness. He deduced that the Luftwaffe had been unable to furnish the air coverage to which the German ground troops were accustomed and, consequently, there were hard feelings. This is reminiscent of our own experience during the winter months, when our muddy airfields and relatively great distance from fields to front prevented adequate air coverage for our own troops.

"It will take four months to evacuate all of the prisoners we have taken," Ike said today at lunch. Italians may be used here for labor, as relatively few guards will be needed for them, but as the Germans will require a proportionately higher number of guards, their use as labor battalions becomes too expensive for us. So the Germans, at least, will be sent to the U. S. We have "captured" two Italian hospital ships, which, of course, must be released, but Ike is hopeful of using them to transfer to their homelands permanently disabled Germans and Italians here as prisoners.

Just strolled down to General Whiteley's office to get the latest news to carry home to Ike. He said it had really been very quiet today, startlingly little to report, and didn't quite know if there was anything to see. However, it might interest the General to know that the First Army has reported capture of General von Arnim. He also might like to know that "bush wireless," the Royal Navy source of information, that has consistently been first and right in its relay of information, says that the big pocket of resistance encircled in front of the Eighth Army has capitulated. Just an average day—everything quiet, nothing much to cheer about.

Von Arnim Captured

ALGIERS, THURSDAY, MAY 13, 1943

After the news of von Arnim's capture came confirmation, while we were at dinner last night, that the whole show was over in Tunisia except for sporadic opposition in isolated small pockets.

As if to express his anger, Hitler sent some bombers on an early evening raid of Algiers, our antiaircraft putting up the best barrage yet. One oil tanker hit and possibly will sink, some mines were dropped in the harbor, and there was a near miss on a merchant vessel. Also thirty-one Arabs were killed by panic in an air-raid shelter. Ike and I watched the raid from the front porch, the roof of which protects against falling shrapnel. We saw three of Admiral Cunningham's barrage balloons shot down by our own AA fire. We could imagine how the Admiral was cursing. Later we learned that a heavy piece of shrapnel had crashed through the roof of the Admiral's kitchen. Our smoke-screen devices worked excellently, the city being blanketed by an oily smudge within five minutes after the shooting started.

Ike had a press conference, intended to orient the correspondents on the final phases of the campaign. He commented on General Alexander's brilliant tactic of swinging the sledgehammer blow through the First Army sector rather than the Eighth. He said Alexander figured the Germans would anticipate that the Eighth Army, with its great reputation, would be used for the big attack and, consequently, had kept large forces in front of the Enfidaville position, awaiting what they confidently expected ultimately must come. By quickly moving three divisions of the Eighth Army to support the First Army, the German was caught off guard.

Ike paid tribute to all the commanders and again cited the victory as an example of Allied co-operation at its best.

Most of his talk was "off the record," but he permitted mention of a story from German prisoners that he repeated. It was to the effect that German and Italian soldiers in Tunisia had been told by their commanders that as many as a million Allied soldiers faced them. Ike said no army feels comfortable fighting with its back to the sea, with no possibility of retreat by land. Undoubtedly, the German and Italian soldiers were uneasy in the Tunisian pocket, and this must have deteriorated their morale. He mentioned this partially to emphasize the mass surrender of large units, particularly of Germans. He cited the fact that the U. S. II Corps had counted some 33,000 prisoners, of which less than 5000 were Italians.

Von Arnim and the other German generals are being flown promptly to England for expert examination and then will be sent to America, as will most of the German prisoners, but the bulk of the Italians will be kept in Africa for appropriate labor.

General Ike is sending our G-2, Ken Strong, to interview von Arnim when the C-47 bearing him stops at Maison Blanche. Ike refuses to see von Arnim, his hatred of the Germans, and particularly of the Nazi ideology, being so strong that he does not trust his own reactions before a representative of the Prussian and Nazi regime.

One newsman recalled that the Allies had dropped leaflets on the Italians during the battle, saying that if they surrendered, they would get free passage to America. Ike's answer was, "I hope it wasn't signed." He added, "The Italians would be happy in Africa with proper food and modest pay." A request has come from the U. K. for 30,000 Italians for labor, but Ike didn't think we could fill the order.

Although last night we celebrated mildly von Arnim's capture and the conclusion of hostilities, Ike has not been what I could call jubilant over the result, he having satisfied himself victory would come by May 15 — a confidence that grew after the British took Tripoli and he found the port could pass 3000 tons a day of supplies, which would permit the Eighth Army to keep coming. A questioner at the press conference this morning asked what he regarded as the most critical period of the campaign. Ike said, "From Christmas through January."

General Marshall is feeling enthusiastic, too, judging from a story he passed on to General Ike. He said he had a letter from a man in New York State in which General Marshall's staff had found a suggestion that might "strengthen you in your current battles."

The writer had "just learned that one of our most important men, General Eisenhower, takes cold water with his meals." He counseled that "many nations and armies have gone down to defeat on just such an insignificant point and we cannot afford to let a brilliant mind like Eisenhower's be hampered by his stomach."

Asking General Marshall to forward the letter quickly, it ended, "Rommel would not have been the successful desert fox if he were caught with a cylinder or two missing in his brain by bad indigestion."

Ike's disposition doesn't permit relaxation. He scarcely ever has a feeling of self-satisfaction. He anticipates and discounts current accomplishment because his mind is racing ahead to the next campaign. Thinking ahead about Pantelleria and Sicily, he has been left utterly cold by the Tunisian victory. He becomes impatient and irritated because of the slowness with which the next phase can unfold. He makes himself quite unhappy. He is convinced that if he could undertake the Sicilian operation immediately with only two divisions, he could gain a bridgehead and an advantage that would make the further conquest of the island a simple affair. He suffered almost physically during January, February, and March while the enemy was fortifying its positions in Tunisia and now he resents every day we give the Hun and Eyetie to strengthen Pantelleria and Sicily. There will be a great load off his shoulders when he finally gets to a place where the next operation does not have to be amphibious, with all the inflexibility and delay of across-the-water attacks.

I notice, too, that he has developed a habit of waking about 4 or 4:30 and, as he finds himself sufficiently rested, his mind begins wrestling with his problems. Sometimes he manages to put himself back to sleep, but rarely.

He is hopeful that our efforts to capture Pantelleria may be a test of the effect of concentrated heavy bombing. He expects to concentrate our maximum air power on the island, which is another Gibraltar, to see whether damage to matériel, personnel, and morale can be made so serious as to make the amphibious landing inexpensive in lives.

As to grand strategy, he is hopeful that the current meetings of the Combined Chiefs in Washington will develop an arrow that will give guidance and meaning to all the strategic and tactical effort of the Allies. He still believes that the correct line is a straight, short, and simple one, but has occasionally repeated the old adage, "a poor plan vigorously carried out is better than a perfect plan indifferently executed."

The intimacy of the understanding and friendship amongst Generals Ike, Alexander, Montgomery, and Anderson, to speak only of the ground forces, is shown in their personal longhand congratulatory notes. General Anderson says that one of the proudest memories of his life is to have been so intimately connected with the U. S. Army.

From a message received from the front during the grand collapse of the enemy, I gleaned a few items of some interest. On May 12 the War Office reported it had heard a radio message: "I report the order to defend Tunisia to the last cartridge has been carried out. Signed Arnim." To this the radio operator had added: "Everything destroyed. We are closing down forever. Signed Possel."

Another item concerned a British division, a new unit in the Eighth Army that is going through the same growing pains as did our new divisions. It had attacked in the Enfidaville area but failed to capture its objective and was thrown back to its original line, suffering severe casualties from machine-gun and mortar fire. This seems a bit incongruous amongst all the items of surrender. However, the action happened May 9-10.

The last tank battle was fought with twelve enemy tanks at Grombalia the morning of May 12, General Alexander's headquarters reported, and added that since May 5, 100,000 prisoners are accounted for and it is believed there are 30,000 more to come. (Later estimates give the prisoner bag at about 150,000.) Another item in General Alexander's situation report disclosed that when General Graf von Sponeck, commander of the 90th Light Division—the German outfit that successfully fought rearguard actions during the entire desert chase—was "invited" to surrender, he replied to the New Zealand outfit which made the offer that he "appreciated their sentiment" but that he would resist to the last. Then he surrendered yesterday afternoon.

Vast quantities of war materials of all kinds were captured, including 1200 guns of all types, with at least 150 88-mm., not to mention 200 tanks, mostly German, and aircraft in serviceable condition. In the II Corps area there were huge dumps of ammunition, as well as a million rations of food.

A message from Alexander's headquarters says, "War in Africa should finish tonight." That was last night.

ALGIERS, FRIDAY, MAY 14, 1943

Hitler is still mad. He sent bombers over Algiers again last night and there was a hell of a racket for an hour and a half. Mickey has picked up a dozen pieces of shrapnel from our roof. Plaster is cracked from the vibration.

These calls the last two nights are noisy but grim reminders that the war isn't over, even for those in what may be called "the back area."

Ike has gone to ride, and I am going to visit Wes Gallagher, who, I am surprised to find, is more seriously injured than I had first heard. I hear he has a fractured vertebra and will be in a cast for several months. A jeep turned over with him while entering Bizerte under fire.

Aftermath of Victory

ALGIERS, MONDAY, MAY 24, 1943

In our headquarters, I am noticing officers definitely showing signs of continuing strain; they are planners who make plans for almost any eventuality or attack. Many are at work on HUSKY, which, being amphibious, requires painstaking, detailed planning. Ike is constantly appalled by the number of headquarters and staff officers required to run this sprawling theater and its several tactical efforts. From every side, he is importuned for assignment of more trained staff officers, secretaries, and stenographers.

With respect to this theater, he thinks we should use more WAACs, as he is finding it almost impossible to find enough satisfactory clerks or

stenographers among the enlisted men; besides, men should be released
for heavier duty, especially for combat.

Suggestions for improvement of training combat troops come from
numerous sources and none is passed up. A long letter recently came from
a private in the 34th Division, which has just finished its arduous campaign, including the capture of Hill 609. This private writes from experience and earnestly advocates more thorough training for battle discipline and development of proper mental attitude. Ike has sent his letter
to the Army ground forces in Washington as well as to General Marshall
and has marked portions especially to be read.

In off moments, the Allied Commander is growling about his military
education. None of the schools, including Leavenworth, where every
effort was made to pound into his head military erudition, ever gave him
a hint of what a headache would come out of a quarter million prisoners
of war, especially when transportation facilities are clogged and evacuation
from the theater can be at the rate of only about 30,000 a month. Currently he has one division, the 36th Infantry, practically down to nothing
because the outfit has been stripped to provide static guards and escorts.
So much rail transportation is being used for prisoners, he can't move the
1st Armored Division from Tunisia to Morocco for protection of his rear.

Ikus Africanus

ALGIERS, TUESDAY, MAY 25, 1943

A group of Ike's West Point classmates gathered in China and celebrated the Tunisian victory. They cabled Ike a new name for him, "Ikus
Africanus."

Fresh from a good night's sleep and recuperated from nine sets of
tennis Sunday, I will undertake to catch up this morning.

Things of current interest to me:

1. French unity. Giraud has sent another message by General Catroux
to General de Gaulle in London. It emphasizes establishment of collec-
tive control for the trusteeship of French interests until the war is over
and free choice by the French of their permanent government. The control would be in a committee of nine with both de Gaulle and Giraud
serving on it, the former to preside on civil questions, the latter on military. The union may be rendered more complicated by the news from
official sources that de Gaulle has been requiring a personal oath of alle-
giance to him, so that his followers would be required to follow him, even
blindly or against their own will, on any move he might choose for estab-

lishment of a government after the war. For this and other reasons a feeling has grown that de Gaulle has ambitions to be dictator of France. Giraud regards himself more of a trustee rather than a crusader and wants the responsibility for trusteeship broadened into control by a committee, with assurances to the French people that they shall have the right to form their own government by free choice.

2. New attacks on Italian islands are being planned and activated. In the next month there will be three. An operation to take Pantelleria has received Ike's approval over fears raised by the Staff that this miniature Gibraltar, which is important as an air base for succeeding operations, may be a very tough nut. There are heavy fortifications cut in rock. The island has no beaches on which landings can be properly made. Its shores are virtually all cliffs. The attack must be made in its only harbor and it is small. Intensive air bombardment, supported by naval gunfire, will precede the attempted landing. We don't know whether Germans are on the island. Ike has expressed an interest in going on the mission aboard a destroyer, to see the naval bombardment. Of course, he will need his Naval Aide, I hope.

The next operation is to take Lampedusa, to be followed by the assault on Sicily itself. Lampedusa may "fall in" for us if we take Pantelleria O.K. We have been preparing for the latter task for weeks. The air is pounding away. Amphibious training has begun.

The regrouping of both American and British units has caused difficulty, not so much as to the former, but considerable with regard to the latter. In the British plan of reallocation of forces for the attack on Sicily, the First Army is to be disbanded. Brigadier Sugden, one of our most capable planners, accompanied Ike on our trip to Tunis, where Ike reviewed the Victory Parade. When informed definitely that the First Army, as such, would lose its identity, General Anderson was heartbroken. He said to Ike after the parade that it was both a happy and a sad day for him.

3. Decisions taken in Washington by the Combined Chiefs of Staff: The PM is there and made a whopper of a speech to a Joint Session of Congress. We heard a rebroadcast amidst the flies while at the General's tent camp near Sidi Athman, between Tunis and Bizerte, while awaiting the review. The PM paid Ike a high compliment, saying he didn't know where a more capable officer could have been found to perform the duties of Allied Commander. This compliment came after he had devoted minutes to extolling the fine co-operation evidenced in this Allied Command. The PM also expressed most effectively Britain's interest in the Pacific. I was interested particularly to note how the trend

of public opinion to redirect the war against Japan and more or less abandon that against Germany had risen to a crescendo. It reached a pitch which required a careful answer by the Prime Minister, who pledged that the British would stay in and fight until the Japs likewise unconditionally surrendered.

Now to pick up, somewhat chronologically, what has happened since May 14:

Ike had hoped to spend three or four days in Tunisia, looking over the battlefield. He had planned to leave AFHQ the afternoon of Tuesday, May 18, review the Victory Parade on Thursday, and to return to Algiers Saturday. However, the usual pressure destroyed the plan and he didn't get away until Wednesday morning, May 19.

Among the congratulatory messages continuing to come was one in which Ike took both pleasure and pride. It was from the Chief of Staff of the Red Army.

The General took with him in the Flying Fortress Brigadier Sugden, the British planner, T. J., Colonel Julius Holmes, Mickey, and myself. Our caravan of cars in command of Major Lee had started Monday morning. It had reached the camp near Sidi Athman late Tuesday and met us at the landing strip only three miles from the camp.

When Ike and the remainder of the party visited General Ryder's headquarters of the 34th Division near by, and subsequently toured the Mateur and Bizerte areas, I reconnoitered at the First Army headquarters at Carthage the plan of the parade for Thursday.

Ike abhorred the idea of a Victory Parade. He has asked that it be laid on as a combination of victory and commemoration of those who sacrificed their lives, but it turned out to be just a Victory Parade.

The parade itself ran an hour overtime, as almost all parades do, and Ike, who as Allied Commander-in-Chief "took" the review in company with General Giraud, had to stand all this time at or close to attention, gaining relaxation only when there was a delay. The Goums, those stealthy, throat-slitting Moroccan mountaineers, who had become legendary, attracted the most applause. The MPs got some boos from their brother soldiers. After the parade, we learned that the Giraudist French had greatly exceeded their allotment of troops in the parade, it being obvious that Giraud and Juin, not without good reason, wished to impress the Arabs and the Tunisian population with their strength.

After the parade Ike had lunch with General Juin and was given a decoration by the new Bey of Tunis. So were Giraud, Cunningham,

Alexander, Tedder, and Anderson, in a colorful ceremony complete with gold throne, eunuchs, and native Tunisian troops.

Two letters came Saturday which have given us a good deal of fun. One is to Ike from a New York publisher, inviting him to place himself under contract to write a book, or books, now or in the future. The other is from another publisher suggesting that I write a biography of Ike—a suggestion prompted by Colonel Jock Lawrence of Lord Louis Mountbatten's staff in London. I told Ike his offer came from a firm of only slight reputation, whereas mine was from one of the most famous. He has now declined with thanks his offer, but has kept the door open in case he might wish to go literary after the war, which I sincerely hope he will do. As for myself, the General said he had no objection to my writing a book if I can pay off the mortgage on my home.

Differences at the Top

ALGIERS, THURSDAY, MAY 27, 1943

Met Beetle and party at Casablanca Tuesday evening. Colonel Holmes, head of AFHQ's Liaison Section, went with me in the Flying Fortress. Saw Captain John Boettiger, son-in-law of the President, who is joining the planning and operational group of Military-Civilian Administrators now secretly studying and preparing for HUSKY at Chrea, a secluded mountaintop south of Blida.

General Smith invited Colonel Holmes and me to visit him after dinner, to tell us the score of the Washington meetings.

Throughout the sessions, there had been earnest discussion between the two great Allies. Differences were evident. The British have now won a big victory and their national pride is again showing itself. Our Americans have been subjected to public and political pressure to engage more heavily against the Japs and, apparently, have been showing their teeth to the British. All this is disheartening, although it makes Ike's job as Allied Commander stand out.

Plans approved in Washington call for operations in North Africa to continue as already laid on, with Ike to exploit whatever success is attained, in an attempt to knock Italy out of the war as quickly as possible. His plans will be subject to approval of the Combined Chiefs.

Beetle explained that there had been a thorough discussion with the British again on the question of striking the dagger blow directly into Germany's heart by invading from England across the Channel. The

Americans still want this, but the British remain to be convinced that it can be done.

This question was settled by agreement for a sufficient attack to gain a foothold on the Continent to be launched by May 1, 1944, with the possibility that Ike would be the Allied Commander-in-Chief. General F. E. Morgan, the British officer who had charge of the reserve for TORCH, has been named the chief planner for across-the-Channel operations. Unless the attack is in great strength, the President himself is fearful of defeat, and seems disturbed by events at home. The Prime Minister had been rather critical of Ike and the Allied Command here for failing to be prepared to follow up quickly on our Tunisian victory with the invasion of Sicily. Beetle said he seemed completely to overlook our continued shortage of landing craft.

When we reached Algiers Wednesday noon, May 26, we learned that General Marshall had joined the Prime Minister's party, and with Colonel Frank McCarthy, now secretary of the General Staff, the entire group would be here late this afternoon—Thursday. We have set up General Marshall and Sir Alan Brooke at our house, together with McCarthy and Brooke's aide, Lieutenant Colonel A. B. Boyle, filling all beds and over-crowding bathroom facilities. The PM, traveling as "Air Commodore," again is stopping with Admiral Cunningham next door. In a message he sent this morning to Ike, he said he planned to be in Algiers a day or two and then wished to visit the battleground and troops in Tunisia.

I asked Beetle particularly for the Washington appraisal of the Russian situation. He said that the Germans were teed up for an attack on a monstrous scale on the Russian front, but the Russians were prepared with defensive positions in great depth. He said it was figured the Germans would lose a million men and there was confidence the Russians would win the battle. This great German offensive is intended to knock Russia out of the war or to so paralyze the Red Army that further resistance will be weak or futile, letting Hitler turn his hordes to the defense of his European citadel or to offensives in another direction. The big war is still being fought in Russia.

Beetle said that the Tunisian victory had been greatly cheered at home, but that Ike personally had been sort of overlooked in the publicity. So much so that General Marshall had asked General Surles, Director of the Bureau of Public Relations, that attention be directed so that Ike would be given his proper credit. Marshall declared in his memorandum that it was a "damned outrage" that Ike was virtually ignored and that his modesty and self-effacement as Allied Commander should not be permitted to let his great work go unappreciated by the public.

It is not unlikely, Beetle thought, that Ike would be back in England soon after November 1, either as Allied Commander-in-Chief or as Commander of the American attack. Actually Ike would much prefer the latter, frequently saying he is fed up with operating an Allied Command and wishing to be closer to actual battle-front operations. In any event, Beetle said, the record of this Allied Headquarters is so highly appreciated that inevitably it will be kept intact. To my mind, this means that Ike definitely will be the Allied Commander-in-Chief.

The feeling of discord lurking between the two countries which I had sensed while at home in late March has increased rather than decreased. It is disheartening and disconcerting. However, Ike merely shrugged it off with his usual comment: how can the Allies expect to win a war if they don't co-operate? His mind and his actions are entirely devoted to bringing to bear every atom of strength of the two nations to win the war. He is not so concerned now with where the pressure is applied, but greatly impressed by the need of the Allies for adopting some concerted plan and then pouring their combined strength into its execution.

Beetle said that another meeting of the Combined Chiefs will be held after HUSKY is completed, probably in July or August. Beetle felt most strongly that Ike should attend. The meeting probably will be in Washington.

Beetle said that Montgomery is the national hero in America. The film *Desert Victory* had greatly contributed to his popularity. I learned that Beetle, fortunately, also was aware of the lack of co-ordinated American moving-picture coverage in our operations, of the diverse groups now fumbling in this field, and is prepared promptly to get it co-ordinated.

The Man Who Came to Dinner Comes Again

ALGIERS, SATURDAY, MAY 29, 1943

The PM, General Marshall, Sir Alan Brooke, General Ismay, and entourage arrived at Maison Blanche Friday afternoon, May 28, about 4:30. They had flown from Botwood, New Brunswick, direct to Gibraltar in a C-54—the first time it has been done—distance, 2700 miles. They stopped overnight with Governor General Mason-MacFarlane. It was General Marshall's first visit to Gibraltar. He was greatly impressed. All the anti-aircraft guns were turned loose to give them a show.

Ike had arrived with the Admiral, and the Prime Minister was to ride with the Admiral from the airdrome to the two adjoining villas. Ike planned to bring General Marshall. However, the PM had other notions.

He wanted to ride with Ike. Consequently, the Admiral accompanied General Marshall and I rode in the front seat. The General said that his trip had been ordered by the President so unexpectedly that he and McCarthy had only a few hours to prepare.

Although Ike had the Prime Minister driven to the Admiral's house, the PM didn't even stop there to rest. He immediately trundled with Ike down the driveway to our house. There, with General Marshall and the Admiral, they gathered on the front porch, the PM finding a comfortable chair and seeming settled for the duration. An informal conference, pleasant to kibitz upon, continued until time to get ready for dinner.

General Marshall has taken Ike's room again, this time with only a mild protest. He has inquired as to the welfare and manners of Telek. I have informed him that Telek is about to become a father but is bearing up well. The General seems pleased that Ike has at least partly followed his instructions on care and refreshment of the human mind. The Chief of Staff expects to be at our house a few days and will visit American units from Tunis back to Port Lyautey, time permitting. The Prime Minister, still known as "the man who came to dinner," is going to stay for numerous dinners, his visit being expected to run a week or ten days.

General Marshall is accompanying the Prime Minister this far, at the PM's request to the President, because the PM openly and avowedly is seeking to influence Ike to pursue the campaign in the Mediterranean area until the Italians are out of the war. Presumably, he then wants the Allied effort to continue in the Mediterranean area rather than across the Channel as already agreed by the Combined Chiefs at their Washington meeting. He makes no bones of his point of view and apparently regards the decision already taken as quite open to review and change. The Prime Minister had told the President he felt it only fair for General Marshall, as the representative of the American point of view to the contrary, to be present. During the trip, especially at Gibraltar, the PM has shown every courtesy to General Marshall, making certain that he was accorded all honors meant for the PM, and, in general, looking after the little details of courtesy.

The PM recited his story three different times in three different ways last night. He talks persistently until he has worn down the last shred of opposition. Ike is glad to have General Marshall on hand. A meeting in our dining room is laid on, starting at 5 this afternoon.

This morning at 9 General Giraud hung around Ike's neck his personal Grand Cordon of the Legion of Honor, the highest military award of France, founded by Napoleon. There was a colorful and sentimental ceremony. American, British, and French troops, including colorful Spahis on their white horses, were first inspected by Ike while standing in review and then paraded in front of him.

In accepting the decoration, Ike briefly declared that he did so, not so much personally, as in behalf of the Allied Command, and that he would emulate Giraud's example by not wearing this decoration until France is free and the two again are in Metz. Ike was definitely impressed by this ceremony, thought the award was well meant, and was deeply touched when Giraud said that the Grand Cordon was his personal decoration received for action on the battlefield.

Big-Shot Shop Talk

ALGIERS, SUNDAY, MAY 30, 1943

Our house guests dispersed, General Marshall and Colonel McCarthy flying in Ike's B-17 to our advanced camp between Tunis and Bizerte.

Before dinner, I received a call from Commander Thompson, the PM's aide, inquiring if the General could see the Prime Minister at our house at 10:45 that night. Of course, Ike could, although the date jolted the free and easy lounging he needed so badly.

We returned to the villa in town in time for the PM's late visit. Ike and I sat reminiscing while waiting for the Prime Minister. Ike was growling because of the necessity of spending another night, probably until 1:30, going over the same ground, i.e., "Keep on until you get Italy," which the PM had already covered, recovered, and uncovered—and there were really no serious questions of difference between the two.

"Would you ever have thought a year ago or, certainly, two years ago that you would be in Algiers, in far-off Africa, the Allied Commander of a great and victorious army, sitting in a villa, waiting a late night call from the Prime Minister of His Majesty's government and growling because the PM was fifteen minutes late?" I asked.

Ike enjoyed the picture, upon which he elaborated, going back to his boyhood days when he had been variously a cowboy, a boiler stoker in a creamery, and a semipro ballplayer.

The Prime Minister arrived at the house alone and soon was engaged in a "repeat" of various factors relating to the prospective collapse of Italy and the necessity, in his view, of vigorous prosecution of our campaign after we have taken Sicily.

The PM said that he had "sensed" at home a strong feeling by the Americans that he and the British generally were more desirous of prosecuting the war in the Mediterranean, possibly because of its strategic value for Britain's commerce, than in making a cross-Channel attack. This was incorrect, he felt, as the only difference between them was the matter of "emphasis." The Prime Minister felt we should exploit our advantage in the Mediterranean to knock Italy out of the war while we have the chance.

Ike pointed out that his opportunity for exploitation was somewhat limited by the string the Chief of Staff had placed on seven divisions that are being required to be available for return to the U. K. from November 1 onward. But he would be able to determine early in the campaign for Sicily the attitude and defensive strength of the Italians on the mainland. If Sicily proved to be relatively easy, this would be an index which would dictate an immediate follow-up of a bridgehead on the toe of Italy·across the Messina Strait. If the Italians fought stubbornly in Sicily, as they have done when they were in good defensive positions in Tunisia, then we would be confronted with a long campaign, fighting for each hilltop. This would tie down our forces. It was simply too early, he emphasized, to make a firm commitment now, but, like the PM, he didn't want to lose any opportunity for exploitation that presented itself.

The PM is so persistent in his desire to knock out Italy that he said that the British people would be proud to halve their already short rations for a month if the shipping thus released would contribute to cure the supply difficulty inherent in the conquest of Italy. The PM said that he confidently looked forward to having Christmas dinner with Ike in Rome.

The PM told Ike he had managed to get General Alphonse Georges, a French military leader of standing prior to the fall of his country, "flown out of France." General Georges would be in Algiers for the conferences and seemed to have the Prime Minister's backing for a place in the theater. The PM said that he didn't agree with de Gaulle on requiring Giraud to be off the committee if he were to be Commander-in-Chief of the French armed forces. Ike said that both governments had recognized in Giraud a capable leader of the French Army and since Giraud had demonstrated that he could whip together a fighting outfit which had contributed to the victory in Tunisia, he would continue to back Giraud as C-in-C of French armed forces and would expect the governments to do the same.

The PM spoke of de Gaulle. He supported the view transmitted to me by Mr. Murphy during the day, which was contained in a message from Ambassador Winant from London, to the effect that the British expected an unhappy and impermanent union of the two leaders.

(The BBC is very de Gaulle-conscious. In a broadcast recorded here, I noted that an item announced that the portion of the French fleet at Alexandria under Admiral Godfroy had joined the Allies through Giraud. This statement was followed by another, saying that de Gaulle had arrived the same day in Algiers—implying that the latter was responsible for the former event. Actually, de Gaulle wasn't entitled to the credit. The fleet is to move to Dakar via Suez and the Cape. How useful it will be is problematical, as much modification, no doubt, is required, but the significant point is that the fleet finally came to the Allies under Giraud.)

I have used a variety of schemes to hustle visitors away at night. On occasions, I have yawned openly and loudly. On others, I have paraded in my bathrobe before the lingering guest or guests. Neither of these seemed appropriate for this occasion, so I found my flashlight and walked in front of the door. This was at 1 o'clock. The PM left at 1:10, trudging up the driveway to the Admiral's house with a Scotland Yard man who, I found, had waited outside our front door.

ALGIERS, MONDAY, MAY 31, 1943

The Prime Minister came to our house for dinner tonight. The guests numbered thirteen, so I became fourteen in deference to the British superstition.

Ike and General Marshall were cohosts. Present were none less than the British Foreign Minister, Mr. Anthony Eden, General Brooke, and General Ismay.

Sometime during the dinner-table conversation, the question of diaries came up. The Prime Minister said that it was foolish to keep a day-by-day diary because it would simply reflect the change of opinion or decision of the writer, which, when and if published, makes one appear indecisive and foolish. He cited the diary of a British general who had written in his diary one day, "There will be no war." On the next day war was declared. The diary was published posthumously and, consequently, the general was made to appear foolish. For his part, the Prime Minister said, he would much prefer to wait until the war is over and then write impressions, so that, if necessary, he could correct or bury his mistakes.

Eden is here obviously in connection with de Gaulle's visit. When de Gaulle arrived Sunday, he promptly had a press conference. I had a fill-in today on it from Major Martin Sommers, of the PRO, who said de Gaulle was both sardonic and caustic in references to any other French leaders, particularly Giraud. He said it had been noticeable that no announcement had been made in Algiers that he was to arrive, but that word was now being spread by word of mouth and the correspondents would notice an increasing public acclaim for him.

A general who will have an important part in the attempt to take Pantelleria has raised grave questions as to the success of the operation—

thinks casualties will be awful. Ike doesn't think so and has made the "command decision" to carry on.

MAY, 1943: *Axis surrender in Tunisia allowed Allies to concentrate activities against Pantelleria, Sicily, and Italy. The air raids against Nazi-held Europe attained fantastic proportions and frequency. Production centers, communication lines, and harbors continued to be favorite targets. Sabotage, strikes, and riots flared up in Nazi-held territory. Lieutenant General Devers became Theater Commander in Europe after death of Lieutenant General Andrews. Americans bypassed Kiska to invade Attu. Halsey and MacArthur held conferences on the Pacific war as Japs advanced toward Chungking, west of Ichang. Stalin dissolved the Comintern. James F. Byrnes was appointed War Mobilizer. Germans launched retaliatory air raids against London as the RAF continued to hammer Berlin. (Our Tunisian victory, together with the Russian victory at Stalingrad and the British victory at El Alamein, destroyed the myth, built up since Hitler's drive into Poland in 1939, that the Wehrmacht was invincible.—H.C.B.)*

A Little Lesson on Modesty

ALGIERS, TUESDAY, JUNE 1, 1943

The Prime Minister and party left for Tunis this morning to see the battlefield and review troops. He insisted that General Marshall go along, although the General had just been there yesterday. For the second time he has had to borrow a pair of my pants. The first were khaki. The ones today were Palm Beach. It seems his orderly had failed to pack field trousers for him. He expressed satisfaction at being able to get into my waistband.

Today Commander Tracy D. Kittredge, American Liaison Officer between Admiral Stark in London and de Gaulle, visited me to give me his latest information. It was that some 3000 enlisted men and officers of de Larminat's Fighting French who had accompanied the Eighth Army in its march into Tunisia have been infiltrated into Algiers. I asked Kittredge if he thought their purpose was to create a *Putsch* to take control of the government. He said no, that they seemed to be here for the purpose of lobbying their point of view with Giraud's French troops and officers. Local French police had carefully herded these visitors into places where they could be watched; consequently, de Gaulle has had them quietly leave for homes of friends outside Algiers. It is possible these Fighting French are AWOL, as their Commander is under orders to return his outfit to the Eighth Army in Tripoli because of the fuss created in Tunisia by offering attractive promises to the French Giraudists. One Fighting French officer boasted at dinner in Kittredge's presence last night that there were enough Fighting French troops in Tunisia to take control from the acting Governor, Juin. This officer, apparently, didn't count strongly on the presence of the American 34th Division and the numerous British troops still here, nor on the loyalty to Giraud of the French troops who have fought so valiantly with the Americans and the British First Army throughout the Tunisian campaign.

When I related this report to Ike, he called in the Deputy Chief of Staff, without disclosing his reason, to determine the number of American and British troops available for combat in this area. The number isn't large, but there happened to be two Royal Navy battleships and an aircraft carrier in the harbor today. Then, of course, there is the air. There are a lot of hotheads in the de Gaulle-Giraud camps, and we wouldn't be surprised if there is at least an attempted assassination.

Kittredge said de Gaulle respected Ike and laid to Murphy the recognition of Darlan and subsequently of Giraud; that de Gaulle had frequently told him of his admiration of Ike's military ability.

After our company left last night, Ike said, "Let's sit down and chew the fat." I expressed two views which had been developing in my mind. One, that de Gaulle is running away with the show so far as Giraud is concerned and, two, that the British, by the presence of the Prime Minister, Eden, and at least one other important personage to follow, are consciously or unconsciously impressing the French and the natives by their traditional method of pomp and pageantry. So far the Americans have not met the competition. Secretary Stimson is coming, but I thought Secretary Hull and possibly the Vice-President might attract attention.

Ike's view, probably sounder than mine, is that modesty in victory is as good a virtue for a nation as it is for a person. It is just as becoming for America, he believes, to show this quality as it has been for him to be the retiring and modest commander who has tossed bouquets to all senior subordinates. He isn't concerned about impressions; he is concerned about winning the war. He said, however, it was true the British have gained prestige, but he attributed it to a wider knowledge of French by British officers and men than Americans have, leading to more frequent and extended exchange of views and development of mutual understanding.

"After all, the French know where their equipment is coming from," he said.

Admiral Cunningham has invited Ike to accompany him on a destroyer or a cruiser during the bombardment of Pantelleria, set for June 8. I don't see how the Allied Commander-in-Chief can possibly go to sea without his Naval Aide, but, nevertheless, I have not yet been invited. I am eagerly awaiting instruction. The Prime Minister also wants to get in this show and may cast all discretion to the winds to take part in it. It now seems that he will not worry about the Lampedusa Islands, figuring they will follow if we take Pantelleria, as they will be virtually cut off from Italy.

Caacie is going to be a mother soon. I have bet Ike there will be four pups, and will pay him one dollar for each less than four, dead or alive. He will pay me one dollar for each more than four. Telek, the nonchalant father, has had combat with a scorpion and now has a slit in his tongue, "V for Victory."

Love Fest

ALGIERS, THURSDAY, JUNE 3, 1943

The final meeting with the Prime Minister was held at 5 yesterday afternoon at our house. Present on the American side were Generals Marshall and Eisenhower, Major Generals Tom Handy and W. B. Smith (Beetle), and Brigadier General Lowell Rooks. On the British: the Prime Minister, Eden, Cunningham, Brooke, Tedder, Montgomery, Ismay, Sugden, and Dick.

These meetings were for clarification of the decisions taken by the Combined Chiefs of Staff at the meetings in Washington insofar as they affected our operations or impinged on future plans, particularly ROUND-HAMMER, the current name for the cross-Channel operation to be undertaken by May 1, 1944.

Bombing of the railway yards, called "marshaling yards" by the British, on the outskirts of Rome was agreed as essential in the air campaign to break up Italian communications. The recommendation that such bombings be laid on is being carried by the Prime Minister to the British War Cabinet and by General Marshall to the United States Chiefs of Staff, with a view of getting authority from the U. S. and British governments authorizing Ike to order the bombings. In this connection, Anthony Eden said at the meeting that Rome, like Naples, is on the supply line to Sicily. As the marshaling yards are on the opposite side of the river from Vatican City, and as the accuracy of our daylight bombing has been demonstrated, it was felt the Vatican would be safe from damage. Naturally, all are concerned with the possible political repercussions. There likewise is a possibility of reprisal bombings against Cairo, but the Prime Minister felt that if Cairo were bombed, Egypt might declare war. The Prime Minister had assured the President, after seeing Archbishop Spellman, that we would not bomb Rome for the present, but the Prime Minister now felt there was no tenable objection, as the marshaling yards are proper military objectives.

In closing the meeting, the Prime Minister said that he had been most solidly encouraged and he would take home a feeling of confidence and comradeship which characterized actions in this theater. He had never received so strong an impression of co-operation and control as during his visit here. It would be impossible to embark on an undertaking under better augury. He should not like to go away without reaffirming his full confidence in General Eisenhower and without expressing his admiration of the manner in which the General had handled his many great problems.

To this Ike replied that any praise which might be given belonged to the officers around the table and stated that, while there might be differences of opinion and discussion in his headquarters, these were never based upon national differences.

General Marshall said that the U. S. Chiefs of Staff concurred in the Prime Minister's statement of the accomplishments and success of General Eisenhower and his officers. The fine support given to General Eisenhower by the British and especially by Admiral Cunningham, General Alexander, Air Chief Marshal Tedder, General Montgomery, and General Anderson was deeply appreciated. General Marshall added that he felt the greatest discomfort the Germans must have experienced came not so much from their loss of troops as from the fact that the United States and Great Britain have worked so well as a team.

An incident occurred last evening. I got my foot in it properly.

A major of the French Army, who serves as aide to General Georges, came to the villa while the meeting was in progress and said he was seeking to determine if General Eisenhower and the Prime Minister could have lunch with General Giraud on Friday—the next day. From long training I have subconsciously developed an excuse for avoiding a luncheon for Ike, thinking up an appropriate one even as the invitation is being spoken to me. I promptly told the major the General expected to be away and that the Prime Minister was going out of town. The major requested that I convey his invitation to the Prime Minister after the meeting broke up. I suggested that he tender it to Commander Thompson, the Prime Minister's aide, at the Admiral's house, but he said that the Commander was not there and that he had been sent by the Admiral's aide, Dampier, to see me. So I agreed to put the question.

I had ushered the major in to see the Prime Minister during a previous meeting at our house and the Prime Minister had greeted the major—an emissary of General Georges—most affectionately. Thus I assumed the major to be a real friend and confidant of the Prime Minister.

When I informed the Prime Minister of the invitation and told him I had offered the excuse that he was going out of town, he immediately figured I had violated security of his prospective flight homeward. He discussed the situation with Ike and asked that I phone the major and tell him it would be impossible "because of prior commitments" to accept any further engagements for the next couple of days.

I communicated this to General Giraud's aide, who then asked if Monday would suit instead of Friday. I told him that would have to be checked with Commander Thompson at the Admiral's house. In a few minutes, I learned from Dampier that the Prime Minister, who had by then returned to the Admiral's villa, had decided to have all seven members of the new French Committee for Liberation for luncheon himself.

I had been made out a liar very neatly.

At the urgent request of the press, General Marshall had a conference with them yesterday afternoon, mostly off the record. General Marshall is an expert at talking to the press, opens by soliciting questions, which he then takes up in turn, directing his answer to the correspondent who asked the question. His memory is uncanny.

General Marshall makes a practice of emphasizing the hardships of soldiers in other theaters. He does this to prevent what he calls "localitis"— his term for a local instead of a global view of the war. Over here he talked of Americans fighting in water to their waists in the swamps of Guadalcanal and New Guinea. After a day or two at Washington, he will fly to the southwest Pacific, where he will probably emphasize our tough going in the mountains of Tunisia.

Of interest to me was a statement he made at breakfast this morning. More than 100 officers have been made generals and only one on the list has been placed there by political pressure, and this one, oddly, happened to turn out well. He said that the Prime Minister had criticized the President for not taking Congress more completely into his confidence. The Prime Minister had found that by telling Parliament frankly and honestly the facts of the war, both good and bad, he had developed a confidence in his leadership and in the efforts of the military. The Prime Minister felt that if the President would do similarly, a better understanding would prevail in Congress. General Marshall had explained to the Prime Minister that the President does this very thing, but not in quite the same manner as the Prime Minister. While the President does not address Congress except at the openings, he talks privately with the leaders. General Marshall said that he found patriotic support from members of

Congress when he gave them all the facts; then he relied upon them to make use of those facts to combat the "screwballs."

During General Marshall's visit, he told me of one important improvement in our tanks. We have one almost ready now to combat the Tiger. It is lower than the Sherman, weighs only thirty-two tons, and carries numerous improvements which would make it our most outstanding contribution in this line.

Mickey, who sees all and knows all at the Admiral's household because of his close friendship with the staff there, reported during the week that the Prime Minister's breakfast one morning consisted of one bottle of white wine, one bottle of soda water, and one dish of ice.

ALGIERS, MONDAY, JUNE 7, 1943

Caacie had her pups today. She chose their birthplace under a bed in one of the servant-guest rooms. There were three in the litter, and the largest, coal black, died. The remaining boy and girl seem O.K. I lost a dollar to Ike.

Moaney discovered the arrival while we were at the villa for lunch. After Ike and I had visited Caacie and looked at her new family, I phoned Major Lee at the office. Always seeking to be helpful on any occasion, when I told him the big news, he said: "Anything I can do?"

Bombardment of Pantelleria

ALGIERS, WEDNESDAY, JUNE 9, 1943

A four-star general and a full admiral yesterday used themselves as "bait" to draw enemy fire.

Tuesday afternoon at 6, Ike, Admiral Cunningham, Commodore Dick, Commander Henderson, a naval gunnery officer, Flag Lieutenant Dampier, and I left Maison Blanche in the Fortress, landing at Bône, whence we were quickly whisked to H.M.S. *Aurora*, which was to take the party to bombard Pantelleria, miniature Gibraltar of the Sicilian Strait.

Slipping from the Bône harbor at 1 A.M., we glided quietly at twenty-eight knots toward our objective, picking up a lone destroyer escort, the *Troubridge*, off Bizerte. The captain of our cruiser, Commodore W. G. Agnew, was careful to keep her well within the narrow mile-wide channel which had been swept clear of mines from Bizerte to Tripoli. Somewhat off this unswept path lay Pantelleria.

When we boarded the *Aurora*, I discovered that while the crew had an electric intensity of anticipation of an impending mission on which they were to be accompanied by distinguished guests, they had not been informed of the nature of their mission. It was not until 5 the next morning, as dawn was breaking, that Commodore Agnew, the skipper, authorized an announcement over the ship's loudspeaker that "We are on a mission to *witness* aerial and naval bombardment of Pantelleria in which four cruisers and eight destroyers will take part."

I was on the bridge at the time, having arisen at 4, when I heard over the loudspeaker in my small quarters the dawn call to "action stations." Fearing I would miss something, I hastily shaved, dressed, and made my way through the darkness to the bridge. The reason for the alarm was that the RDF * had detected several ships a few miles away, identity then undisclosed. They might be enemy. Shortly, however, they were identified as friendly and tension lifted.

I had asked the mess boy to call Ike at 7, so at that time I went aft to his stateroom in the Commodore's quarters to see if he was up and about. He had arisen at 6, after a restless night, and was looking for me. At breakfast I mentioned to Admiral Cunningham that our cruiser was to "witness" the bombardment.

"I don't think we are," the Admiral responded emphatically. "I'll see about that."

He immediately ordered his executive officer, Commodore Dick, to "make a signal," the effect of which was to remove the *Aurora* from the role of witness to that of participant.

We reached Pantelleria promptly on schedule, at 10:30. It had been planned that the Air Force would make some 600 sorties on the island fortress during the day, and in between their bombings, the cruisers would let go with their six-inch guns; under this fire the destroyers would creep to 2500 yards of the shore and bang away. The MTBs as they are called in the Royal Navy, or PTs as they are called in the U. S. Navy, then would dash toward the harbor entrance to draw such fire of light defense weapons as might be forthcoming.

The first objective, however, was to determine the location and number of shore batteries known to be six-inchers and one suspected of being nine-inch, each of these known six-inchers having a range of well above 20,000 yards. The Admiral, having removed the *Aurora* from the role of witness, had speeded her so she would lead the pack. Our cruiser and its escort reached to within 7000 yards of shore batteries while we could still see the other four cruisers and eight destroyers coming up. The shore batteries were silent. We sailed along shore at this distance, zigzagging,

* Radio direction finder—British radar.

made a turn, and came back again. Still no action. We were withholding our fire until an expected wave of our bombers laid its eggs.

The A-20s had already been in, and dust and smoke drifted slowly toward us, covering our target, which was the dock area around the harbor and the shore batteries emplaced on the escarpment, probably in solid rock and concrete.

Then the Lightnings came and their dive bombing was thrilling to see. They dropped their belly tanks before diving. One of the ships mistook the tanks for bombs and sounded an alert. Later, while we were waiting on the bridge with cotton in our ears for the first salvo from the *Aurora*, all were startled by the sounds of sharp machine-gun fire from our stern. The gunners were firing at a partly submerged belly tank standing with its tail in the air which, on first impression, seemed like a periscope to the alert gunners. On order from Commodore Agnew, fire was quickly stopped, but everyone was excited by the incident.

Shortly after 11, each cruiser with its two destroyer escorts was in proper position, each approached the targets on separate courses, much as the spokes of a wheel lead to the hub, with each cruiser and its two escorting destroyers sailing diagonally to expected return fire. By sailing in this manner, a minimum of opportunity for "crossing the T" was given to the shore gunners.

When we opened with a broadside of nine six-inch guns, the ship quivered. We were thankful for the cotton in our ears, but the more experienced mariners said that the six-inch made less noise than the fours on the destroyers and corvettes. We shot first at the mole, which could be recognized because through the dust and smoke we could see a high crane. Then our fire was directed to the right * of the crane some 200 or 300 yards, where the docks were located.

After our bombardment had been under way for fifteen minutes, one of the lookouts who was observing the shore with powerful mounted binoculars called out that a signal flag was being run up in the signal tower on the island. It was difficult to make out the meaning of the signal through the smoke and haze. Had we been so fortunate as to be on hand for a formal surrender? We waited expectantly, wondering if the signal flag would be white. Finally, the answer came from the lookout, indicating, appropriately enough, "Alarm."

Frequently we couldn't tell where our shells burst because of the dust and smoke over the harbor. The harbor area was an inferno of TNT. In approximately an hour of intermittent firing, the *Aurora* had let go 150

---

* Admiral Cunningham occasionally directed the fire, saying "more to the right" or "try a bit to the left." It wasn't starboard and port with him.

rounds. Probably the other cruisers did the same. In the course of our bombardment, we made two runs toward the shore, firing as we got to 7000 yards.

As the cruisers were finishing their salvos, the destroyers slid within 2000 yards of the shore. By then two shore batteries had been working fitfully, some thirty shells having been seen to burst in the water. So far as we know, there were no hits on the bombarding vessels. One burst about 300 yards astern of the *Aurora,* but the splash couldn't be seen from the bridge. However, just as this news was relayed to the bridge by the lookout, I saw another flash from the shore battery and waited expectantly. The cruiser had not changed course. As it takes some twenty seconds for a shell to travel the distance, I waited in suspense, expecting at least a near miss. Suddenly there was a terrific roar. I ducked. It was another salvo from the *Aurora.*

The shore batteries seemed to bother the destroyers a bit, so after letting go their four-inchers at close range, they spread heavy smoke screens and sped away to join the now departing cruisers.

While the destroyers had been in close, three MTBs dashed toward the mole at full speed. When they came within perhaps a half mile of the mole, they turned suddenly away, leaving smoke bombs on the water. They had encountered light fire from machine guns and perhaps 20-mm.s.

We were maneuvering in water which had been swept for mines, but the Admiral did not feel too happy. The Axis had been using a new device on mines which, by a small explosion, destroys the line attaching the paravane to the mine sweeper. Frequently, mines are partly dislodged and drift under water, not being completely free to float to the top. Finally, we reached the one-mile channel and proceeded, full steam, to Bizerte.

En route the results of the mission were appraised. The Admiral felt it was obvious that the fire-control mechanism of the shore batteries was not working, as the firing of the two active batteries was inaccurate. He felt we could have taken the harbor if we had had about eighteen landing craft with infantry. Ike felt that with the bombing and the bombardment, and with bombing to be sustained until Friday, June 11, the morale of the defenders would be so cracked that when the big assault actually commences, and with the knowledge we have obtained of the number and location of the two active shore batteries, we should have no difficulty in taking the island.

I reminded them of the defense of Wake Island. The Marines had held out one four-inch gun, undamaged under repeated bombings by the Japs. This gun they carefully hid until finally a Jap cruiser, its officers assuming all shore batteries had been silenced, came within two or three thousand yards of the hidden battery and the waiting Marines. This lone gun had succeeded in sinking the cruiser before the Marines were themselves extinguished by dive bombers.

Ike felt that while it might have been possible for the Italians to have been so sagacious as to realize our bombardment force had been merely a bluff at a landing (which, of course, it was), they would never have better targets. He felt confident of success.

Our trip to Bizerte was uneventful. We went direct to the airdrome, where Captain Reedy and crew were waiting with the Flying Fortress. We were at Maison Blanche by 7:15, after some twenty-five hours away from Algiers—a day and an hour packed with interest and action.

When we returned we learned that some of the other cruisers and the destroyers of the bombardment force were attacked by enemy bombers after we left, but no damage was reported. Twelve enemy aircraft had been shot down over Pantelleria during the day's aerial activity.

The only casualties in our immediate party were a set of decorative ribbons on Admiral Cunningham's manful chest which came unfastened and fell overboard, and my four-star aiguillette, which lost its fastener and had to be stowed in my side pocket.

Surrender of Pantelleria

ALGIERS, FRIDAY, JUNE 11, 1943

Today was D-Day for the attack on Pantelleria, with H-Hour at 12 noon. Shortly after 12 o'clock, word was received here by Ike through Admiral Cunningham: "Pantelleria surrenders: says account lack of water."

Eleven thousand Italians on the island, commanded by an admiral, hadn't been bluffing, after all. They had been pounded into submission and no doubt gave up when they saw the formidable armada of cruisers, destroyers, a monitor, MTBs, and landing craft carrying infantry approaching the island. A white cross had been placed on the airdrome and a white flag run up Semaphore Hill, which presumably is the same visual signal station where, during Tuesday's bombardment, we observed the flag for "Alarm."

Ike is elated. There were those who insisted to Ike the expedition be canceled because of the possible heavy toll of lives. The air people had been strong for capture of Pantelleria because of its airdrome, which would be useful for the next operation and a bad nest of opposition if left in enemy hands. Even sage Admiral Cunningham had vouchsafed some warnings on the conservative side. The ground troops didn't like the idea, either. So Ike had decided with air and, as usual, had taken the responsibility on himself to order the attack.

For the past few days, he has been going through the same type of jitters and worries which marked the days immediately preceding our landings in North Africa. He slept fitfully last night. This morning at breakfast, he said he couldn't wait for H-Hour, but wait he did, and good news it was. As the word of surrender came in, plans for immediate capture of Lampedusa were arranged. Admiral Cunningham is sending a cruiser with its Marines to take the island, which recently received much favorable publicity from the Axis for allegedly having turned back a Commando raid. The Admiral wanted to move just as quickly as news of surrender of Pantelleria will have soaked in at Lampedusa. Ike has decided the attack will start first thing tomorrow, and through Air Marshal Tedder the air attacks laid on for Pantelleria were switched to Lampedusa, with bombs dropping thereon within an hour and a half after the order was issued by Ike. The island is important in that it has a radar station by which the Italians have been observing and reporting movements of our vessels and planes. Its defenders will be given an opportunity to surrender tomorrow evening. If this is declined, all hell will visit them throughout Sunday, then it will be left alone, awaiting inevitable surrender because of lack of food and water. It isn't a sufficient nuisance to tie up our forces, and the bombings should neutralize it, anyway.

Surrender of Pantelleria marks the end of an important experiment for the Air Force. While the incessant bombing of the island has been frequently supported by naval bombardment, it is true that air has done the major job. In addition, it has used all types of bombs to test their effectiveness. These have been dropped carefully on certain objectives and records meticulously kept of type of bomb and place dropped. The results will now be investigated.[*]

Surrender before the first assault boats got to the shore was a personal satisfaction to Ike, who predicted an easy landing despite the doleful hesitance of the commander of the assault troops.

While Ike was anxiously awaiting news from CORKSCREW this forenoon, real troubles and additional responsibilities were piling on him. The President sent two messages, each insisting Ike deal with a firm hand, first to keep Boisson as Governor of West Africa and, second, to keep Giraud as Commander-in-Chief of the French Armed Forces. This fol-

---

[*] Later learned that of fifty-four shore batteries on the island, only two were completely knocked out. The central control system for aiming the guns had been hit.

lowed information, received by the President through Ike's report to the Combined Chiefs yesterday, which disclosed that de Gaulle, upon finding that he could not control the French National Committee for Liberation which he helped create, particularly on the issue of military control of French forces, had sent a letter to Giraud, resigning from the Committee.

Ike had frequent conferences yesterday with Mr. Murphy and Colonel Holmes. Ike's well-wishing friends and bosses advise him to get out of the political machinations, yet the President plunges him back into them. And since the President wishes a firm hand to be applied, he must deal through the military, meaning Ike, rather than through his own personal representative, Mr. Murphy.

Although our messages indicate that Ike's responsibility has now been extended to include the Mediterranean, I have not yet seen an amended directive from the Combined Chiefs giving him a new title or extending the boundary of this theater. I presume these messages merely mean that he has "operational control" of additional British units in the Mediterranean for use as he sees fit. Ike not only has not sought, but has advised against widening of his theater because of complications which would arise by absorbing the Middle East, both organizationally and logistically, on the eve of HUSKY.

Britannicus Rex

ALGIERS, SATURDAY, JUNE 12, 1943

"General Lyon," the Lion of the British Empire, flew into Maison Blanche today—our latest and most distinguished visitor. Although he landed incognito, he really is the King.

This has been and still is a whopper of a secret, although a meeting of British brains is in progress this afternoon to determine when announcement of the King's visit to North Africa should be made. Advisers in London fear a letdown to the British people if they should first learn of the King's visit to North Africa over the Axis radio. The British, understandably, don't like the idea of their King's visit having to remain a secret or to be scooped by the Germans, but the security people are tearing their hair, not wishing to advertise his presence here.

Ike is to have dinner alone with the King tonight and again tomorrow night, but tomorrow the three senior commanders, Cunningham, Tedder, and Alexander, as well as Beetle, are to be there, too.

For the past several days there has been a considerable "flap" amongst the British. Although normally quiet, matter-of-fact, and staid, they have planned enthusiastically for the arrival and the tour of the King.

In order not to attract undue attention, the Allied Commander-in-Chief's car would make its way to Maison Blanche alone and the General would bring the King to General Gale's villa, taken over for the visit. Others allotted to the General's car were the driver, Kay Summersby, and me.

The giant converted Lancaster bomber circled the field twice, made a neat landing, and immediately followed a snappy jeep with a yellow flag to the rendezvous meant to be far from curious eyes. As the plane swung into its parking space, a great swirl of dust engulfed the greeters. As the motors died away, the door opened and out stepped the King in the uniform of whatever rank he chose to give General Lyon.

Ike, Admiral Cunningham, and Air Marshal Tedder saluted and shook hands with him. Selected movie cameramen from the British Army and the U. S. Army Pictorial Service recorded the event. Soon the King and Ike were stepping briskly to the car where the driver and I waited. I saluted in my most military manner; he returned the salute, hopped in the car on the right at Ike's request, I closed the door, and Ike walked briskly around the car to enter by the opposite door.

The King was in fine spirit. He confided in Ike that while this was supposedly an official inspection trip for him, it really was a holiday. He said it gets very boring to live virtually in only one room. After three and a half years of war, it felt good to be on a trip where he could get to the beach in the afternoon and be free from the exacting rigors of the King's business.

He asked many questions as to climate, the natives, and operations. He apparently had received news aboard the plane of the quick surrender of Pantelleria. More surprising to me, as a kibitzer in the front seat, appearing not to listen but actually doing a good job of it, he was up to date on both military and political situations.

The King was recognized by many soldiers as he drove along and there were many salutes to be returned. As we drove along, I queried myself as to whether it was appropriate for me to return salutes meant for the King, but I decided my question in conformity with naval regulations, so I was busy saluting all the way. Later I learned Ike had been bothered by the same question. He had resolved that since he was an Allied Commander, he should defer to the British custom of letting the superior officer return all salutes, but after having made his decision, he could not restrain his normal impulse automatically to return each salute.

After we had dropped the King, we agreed we had done our bit without a hitch, with the possible exception of having intruded on the King's right to answer his own salutes, Ike being only mildly concerned but fearing the King had never been told the difference between the American and British customs.

Ike had a press conference at 3:30 this afternoon at which he took the correspondents into his confidence, trusting them implicitly. (They don't know the King is in town.) Told them the next operation would be against Sicily, "sometime next month." He explained to them our intention of giving Lampedusa the opportunity to surrender today. If the defenders refuse, we will give them a heavy aerial bombardment tomorrow in the hope of neutralizing the radar station and then let time have its inevitable effect on their food and water supply. (They did.)

Again we have more prisoners than G-2 had counted as combatants. We thought there were 11,000 troops on Pantelleria, but a hasty count of those already in hand indicates 15,000. Ike asked the press to say that "more than 10,000" had been hastily accounted for, but didn't doubt the 15,000 figure. He doesn't want to be in the position of permitting the Axis to say we were guilty of exaggerations.

General McClure, the Director of Information, had recommended to Ike that he brief the correspondents as to our future plans. When Ike boldly stated to them our objective is Sicily, McClure was shocked. After Ike left the conference, McClure cautioned the correspondents that many officers of AFHQ were not privy to our next operations, so they should feel more keenly the enjoinder imposed upon them by the C-in-C not even to discuss amongst themselves the next objective. Of course, Ike had already emphasized the secrecy of his disclosure to them, but he made the startling disclosure to "sew them up" against speculation.

Last evening, Mr. Murphy phoned to give me an extended report for the General of his experience in delivering the President's messages to Giraud and de Gaulle. Because Ike didn't speak French, he had asked Murphy to deliver their content. Giraud had merely said, *"Très bien."* De Gaulle expounded for an hour and a quarter, Murphy said, explaining why French sovereignty was being challenged by attempted intrusion by the British and the United States into their "purely nationalistic affairs." At the suggestion to keep Boisson and to retain Giraud as C-in-C of the French Armed Forces, he said that to do so upon suggestion from the U. S., the new French Committee for National Liberation would forsake the sovereignty of France. This was de Gaulle's position. He said, however, that the advice should be placed before the Committee.

De Gaulle also said that it had been unfortunate that the aspirations of the Fighting French, as led by him, had never been understood by America. But he said that he had never anticipated the Americans would let France down. He waved the Tricolor into shreds. He was trying to make an issue. (Incidentally, an issue that will appeal to the liberal press in both countries.)

ALGIERS, SATURDAY, JUNE 19, 1943

During the week, the Combined Chiefs of Staff sent a directive to Ike authorizing him to bomb the marshaling yards in Rome near Vatican City but with admonition that the bombing crews be carefully briefed to avoid dropping any bombs on the Holy City.

Presence of the King in our midst was officially announced on Wednesday, June 16. He is now in Tripoli and on Sunday, June 20, will visit Malta. The announcement included the statement that he had come to North Africa to invest Ike with the Grand Cross of the Most Honorable Order of the Bath—makes Ike a "GCB" but not a "Sir." The ceremony was simple. Shortly after dinner at General Gale's villa given by the King Saturday night, June 12, first intended for Ike alone, but fortunately broadened to include the senior commanders, thus avoiding the second dinner originally laid on—the King stepped quietly to another room and returned with the broad maroon ribbon to which was attached the attractive medallion. With the senior commanders looking on as gratified witnesses, the King soberly and with dignity "invested" our Kansas farm boy with the highest military honor within the power of the British government to bestow. I tried it on later at our house and was satisfied.

By the way, I noticed in a clipping from the *Chicago Tribune* that Colonel McCormick smelled a rat when General MacArthur was given the GCB, claiming it was a typically dirty British trick intended to embarrass him when he runs for President.

On Tuesday, Wednesday, and Thursday (June 15, 16, 17) I accompanied Ike on an inspection trip, often postponed, to the Fifth Army, where Generals Clark and Gruenther, and the entire staff, showed us soldiers in hard training for battle. I could elaborate for several pages in detail of the things we saw, such as: a school for detection and removal of land mines and booby traps; a grand show put on by three artillery batteries of the 82nd Airborne; Ike's magnificent talks to the troops everywhere and the magnificence of the troops themselves; the three Cubs, used by Ike, Clark, and myself, which flew in formation, landing that way in order of rank, with me last; inspections of hospitals; a trip in the new amphibious truck called the "duck" when Ike kidded me about my being the ranking officer; the training show for HUSKY at Arzeu, where we saw a grappling hook fired from a mortar at a strip of barbed wire, then pulled in, uprooting a space of barbed wire several yards wide; the dangerously realistic pattern of the training in general and the realization that, though it does cost lives, it saves many more.

De Gaulle Walks Out

ALGIERS, MONDAY, JUNE 21, 1943

We returned to Algiers Friday evening to find the French political situation in a new turmoil.

The President had become increasingly alarmed over the efforts of de Gaulle and feared that if Giraud lost command of the French Army our rear would be imperiled. He likewise objected to de Gaulle's efforts to replace Boisson in French West Africa. Secretary Hull expressed concern that Ike was away from Algiers during his newest French crisis.

It became necessary for Ike to make known the position of the two governments directly to General Giraud and General de Gaulle; Giraud must be kept in command of the French Army.

To do this he had the two generals 'meet him at the villa Saturday morning at 10. Beetle and Major Leon Dostert, our interpreter, were the only ones present during the conference. Mr. Macmillan, the British Minister, Mr. Murphy, Mr. Massigli, one of the members of the French Committee for Liberation, and I sat on the front porch, awaiting the outcome of the conference. We could hear faintly the rumbling of conversation beyond the screen door that separated veranda and living room—the same room in which Darlan, Giraud, and associates had gathered late one night in December to express their fears that the presence in Algiers of d'Astier, a de Gaullist, would lead to trouble. Their fears had proven correct. Within a few days Darlan had been assassinated.

After an hour, General de Gaulle left the room. Mr. Macmillan walked out of the house with him and, when he returned, reported that de Gaulle had "walked out." Ike continued the conversation with General Giraud for several minutes and then joined our party to tell us the news. It was, briefly, that de Gaulle claimed that any suggestion by the Allies as to the identity of the French Commander-in-Chief constituted an intrusion of the sovereignty of France. De Gaulle had insisted the request should be put in writing to the Committee itself rather than to individuals.

As Giraud had launched into a discussion of French problems, de

Gaulle had excused himself to Ike, saying he had heard "all this before," and although he was gracious to his host, the effect was that he walked out of the meeting of the Allied Commander-in-Chief. Ike had agreed to submit in writing to the French Committee the "suggestions" for Monday's session.

It seemed probable that de Gaulle, through his press agents, would spread the story to the press. We learned that de Gaulle had immediately given an interview to Helen Kirkpatrick of the *Chicago Daily News,* which she promptly filed. In this, she said that Eisenhower had delivered an "ultimatum" that Giraud must continue as Commander-in-Chief. Consequently, Ike agreed to have a press conference Saturday afternoon at 3:30 to give the background off the record. At the conference, the political writers who accompanied de Gaulle from London were present, some of whom plainly showed their partisanship for de Gaulle and their distaste for the position Ike has taken to preserve Giraud on insistent instructions from the President and supported by the PM. However, the conference had the effect of giving straight dope to the writers and, according to reports later received from General McClure and Colonel Phillips, his conference served to stop the writing of erroneous and self-serving stories.

Now Ike is in position of carrying out orders by the President but representing the desires of both governments, which will cause a new outburst of criticism of him, reminiscent of the Darlan reaction. The President is insistent that de Gaulle not have control, yet the propaganda policy of Britain, followed by America's liberal press, has made de Gaulle the symbol of French resistance. Now it is left to Ike to tell him where to get off. It is a tough spot.

The PM has been a bit more understanding of the need of giving the Allied Commander-in-Chief considerable latitude to deal with de Gaulle, but the President has been adamant.

Just now we are waiting to learn the reaction of the French Committee to the written proposal. There have been rumors of revolt of the French Army against Giraud and of a *Putsch* by de Gaullist forces. The Security people laid on a small guard at the farm Saturday night and last night. Ike said at breakfast that perhaps he should carry a pistol, but I think he forgot it.

Too bad de Gaulle can't be used as the traveling salesman of French resistance, giving him some appropriate high-sounding title without disturbing the military command under Giraud, who, after all, is a five-star general as against de Gaulle's two stars, and, while inept as to politics, has been sincere and forthright on military matters.

Preparations for HUSKY

ALGIERS, WEDNESDAY, JUNE 23, 1943

A year ago today Ike, Lee, and Mickey landed in England. If as much can be accomplished in the coming year as has been in the last, we should by then soon see the end of the war.

Final conferences have been held this week at the headquarters of 141, equivalent of Norfolk House in TORCH, but this time operated more secretly so far as my knowledge is concerned than were those at Norfolk House from which General Clark reported daily to the Commander-in-Chief by brief memorandum.

More than 1000 ocean-going vessels—transport and escort—will be in HUSKY, the invasion of Sicily. This will be more by 250 than were in the North African landings. The thousand figure does not include small landing craft, small escort vessels and coasters. We will have 149,000 men in the first wave—10,000 more than landed in the Casablanca, Oran, and Algiers attacks. We will attack on an eighty-mile front.

Ike, Mickey, and I probably will leave for Malta July 6 or 8, where the only decision Ike could be called upon to make is to stop the operation. But he wishes to be close to Alexander and Cunningham, ground and sea chiefs. Tedder, presumably, will be at the more permanent base, near Carthage, La Marsa.

Meantime the French situation seems to have taken a turn for the better. Last night Beetle called to say that Murphy and Macmillan had brought him a report of the Committee's action. It had decided unanimously to make Giraud Commander-in-Chief for North and West African forces, with de Gaulle a similar title for forces outside of this area. Both would be part of but responsible to a war committee which would be directly under the French Committee.

Tonight Ike dines with the King at Admiral Cunningham's house. Yesterday, Ike met him again at Maison Blanche. His Majesty had been due to arrive at 5:30 P.M., but surprised everyone by arriving at 3. He had been on the ground five minutes when Ike reached there. The King had enjoyed a memorable visit to the Tunisian battlegrounds, Malta, and Tripoli.

Today a sizable armada of landing ships, troop carriers, and escort vessels of the U. S. Navy has assembled in Algiers harbor for landing exercises to take place tonight on the beaches just west of Sidi Ferruch, which is about fifteen miles west of Algiers. We will probably see some of this operation late tonight or early tomorrow morning. It was good to see the United States Navy and so many American flags.

We lost two landing ships last night. Both were torpedoed east of Algiers, indicating enemy subs are still active in the Mediterranean. LSTs are precious. Yesterday, General Patton told me the American landings on Sicily will be "nasty." We will have against us marine mines, land mines, enemy aircraft, shore batteries, searchlights, flares, and small arms' fire. Yet Patton expects to have a beachhead three or four thousand yards long by daylight.

ALGIERS, SATURDAY, JUNE 26, 1943

The President has apparently become more resigned to the vicissitudes of French politics than his earlier messages have indicated. He is now leaving to Ike greater discretion to deal with the day-by-day French crises, but is keeping before Ike the main objective, i.e., friendly non-de Gaullist control of Dakar and West Africa because of its importance to South Atlantic operations and to South America, and, of course, the general proposition that we have peace and quiet in our North African base for future operations.

While the President was insisting to Ike that Boisson be retained as Governor General of French West Africa, what did the old boy do but up and secretly resign to Giraud. The latter, fearing Boisson may have emulated Peyrouton by sending a similar resignation to de Gaulle, and not wanting to be outfoxed, immediately sent a telegram to Boisson accepting the resignation.

Meantime de Gaulle, judging from piecemeal reports, is rapidly gaining popularity with the public in North Africa. His propaganda machine is well oiled. Major Lee attended a French movie and found de Gaulle overshadowing Giraud in all the news shorts. De Gaulle even took credit for the Tunisian victory by the film's emphasis of Le Clerc's Fighting French and by his own presence in the film and by the absence of Giraud.

On Thursday, June 24, we visited the 1st Division during its operations immediately following the trial landing west of Algiers. Two main difficulties had been developing in the landing. The first was the failure of the Navy to hit the proper beaches in the darkness. The second was lack of communication during the transition of command from Navy to Army. Upon Ike's suggestion, General Terry Allen curtailed the land maneuvers of the 1st Division to give time for practice on communications and on landings.

The principal cause of the Navy's failure to land its craft and its precious cargo of soldiers and equipment at the proper beaches was searchlights on the shore, which were "defended" by the British. This made it impossible for the skippers of the landing craft to see the dim red lights that mark the landing place. This, however, is not a worry, according to General Patton, because searchlights would be shot out in an actual attack within a minute or two after lighting. The radio communications were weak because much of the division's equipment had already been stowed aboard ships for the HUSKY operation.

I thought the 1st Division was operating smoothly. General Patton was in the office yesterday, having spent most of the night watching the exercises, and sought my help to relay a message to Ike to get Admiral Hewitt, Commander-in-Chief of the U. S. Naval forces in HUSKY, to agree that any damaged landing craft or ships carrying Army personnel or equipment should be beached so some of the equipment could be salvaged rather than to attempt to save the vessels themselves by withdrawing them to safer waters. General Patton was also insistent that the identity of the divisions and their regiments and battalions, and even companies, be disclosed to the press as early as five days after the operation.

JUNE, 1943: *De Gaulle became governor of Algeria as head of French Committee of National Liberation. Allied air action concentrated on Pantelleria, Lampedusa, and Linosa. Heavy attacks pulverized Italian and German bases. General Marshall accompanied Prime Minister Churchill on tour of Tunisia. President Roosevelt threatened retaliation if Axis should use gas. Shuttle bombing heavily damaged Italian and German bases. Heavy raids hit French, Belgian, and Netherlands coasts. Military revolt overthrew Castillo's Argentine government. Russians started new Caucasian advances after repulsing German offensive thrusts. Britain closed Syrian-Turkish border as invasion tension increased. In the Pacific Jap aerial attacks were repulsed with heavy Jap losses. MacArthur's forces landed on Rendova Island, near Munda, in New Georgia group. Yank air attacks upon Kiska continued, with all resistance on Attu ended. (We watched the Russian effort with great interest. We kept a map of their progress and placed the pins from news by radio and Stars and Stripes, but we had little or no official information from our ally.—H.C.B.)*

ALGIERS, THURSDAY, JULY 1, 1943

Yesterday marked the first anniversary of my departure with T. J. from Washington. At my invitation, he came to dinner last night so we could celebrate.

Ray Clapper called to see me yesterday afternoon. Fortunately, Ike

wasn't busy and spent an hour and a half reviewing the campaign for
Ray. When he finished, Clapper was "on air." Said he had never before
been excited in an interview. Ended his conversation by practically nomi-
nating Ike for President. Ike and I have picked up this theme and are
already forming our cabinet. Beetle will be head of the Gestapo, as he
likes to cut throats. T. J. will be the Postmaster General, and I am tentatively slated, subject to good behavior, for Secretary of the Navy.

Beetle said that our Intelligence reports from Sardinia indicate a high
state of alert; even householders have shotguns pointed out the windows
in anticipation of our attacking there. Movement of the British Mediterranean fleet through the Sicilian narrows into the eastern Med tonight
is a feint to make the Germans and Italians worry about Crete and the
Dodecanese. While the enemy has Sicily as number-one priority for
defense and has recently shipped the Hermann Göring Division to the
island, they are also working feverishly to build defense at Sardinia and
no doubt also at Crete and in the Dodecanese.

General Ike visited the 3rd Division at Tunisia and was impressed by
it and other units attached. He thinks highly of Truscott. Ike also feels
that Admiral King has sent three very capable naval officers for HUSKY,
Admirals Kirk and Hall, in addition to Conolly. Ike acts like a football
coach who is pleased that his team is keyed up for a big game.

This noon Ike was wondering if he could arrange to get a Beaufighter
at Malta to fly him over the beaches two or three hours after the landings, about daylight. I told him that as this was over the sea it was naval,
consequently he would need his Naval Aide, but unfortunately, the carrying capacity of a Beaufighter is limited to one passenger. I doubted if he
would be permitted to engage in this risky inspection. I suggested that
good photographs from high altitude taken shortly after dawn would
serve the same purpose.

Colonel Phillips, the PRO, is sending two reporters to Malta to cover
Generals Ike and Alexander for all British and American media. E. J.
Gilling will represent the British; John Gunther, the American.

I have urged Ike to have an off-the-record press conference Tuesday
morning before we leave Algiers, to tell the correspondents about the
toughness of the HUSKY operation. I have urged that we do not permit
ourselves to let the public believe this is an easy attack. The difficulty
should be emphasized. If we get licked, the public will know it was hard.
If we win, the public will give the forces credit for overcoming strenuous
opposition. General Ike agrees on the principle, for we don't want to
have an overbuilt confidence at home such as arose during General
Anderson's rapid rush to Tunisia in November.

ALGIERS, SATURDAY, JULY 3, 1943

Flying seven hours and covering 1500 miles yesterday, we visited seven airdromes and various units in Tunisia.

We had two extraordinarily good breaks during the day. The first unit we saw was the 52nd Fighter Group located at Sebala Airdrome between Tunis and Bizerte. This is a coastal-defense unit with Spitfires. It has just passed its hundred mark of enemy planes shot down.

The other was a fortunate timing of Ike's visit to the 99th Fighter Squadron—the all-Negro unit. One of its members, Lieutenant Hall of Brazil, Indiana, had just shot down the first enemy plane for the group. It is probably the first time in history that a Negro in a pursuit plane has shot down an enemy in aerial combat.

Yesterday was a quiet day so far as air action was concerned, and consequently we saw no action. It was, however, the lull before the storm, because today—D minus 7—marks the beginning of the aerial assault against Sicily, with some on Sardinia. This air attack against Sicily will rise in growing crescendo of sorties, just as was true at Pantelleria. It will reach 3000 sorties on D-Day. Targets will be airdromes, communications, shipping, docks, and particularly the ferry service across the two-mile-wide Messina Strait, to hinder, if not prevent, reinforcement from the mainland to the island.

We were met at El Aouïna, north of Tunis, at 10 A.M. by Air Chief Marshal Tedder, Lieutenant General Spaatz, Air Vice-Marshal Coningham, Major General Jimmy Doolittle, Major General "Uncle Joe" Cannon, and Brigadier General Ted Curtis.

General Ted Curtis told me we now have about 5000 combat airplanes in the theater, of which eighty per cent, or 4000, are operational. Going into the HUSKY battle we have a numerical superiority of at least two to one, although our bases will, of course, be considerably removed, especially at the outset, from the battle line. This condition will improve when, as, and if we capture some or all of the eleven airdromes in the southeast corner of Sicily.

While visiting the 99th Fighter Squadron—the Negro fliers—I was told of a radio conversation overheard during the air assault on Pantelleria. One of the P-40s with a colored pilot had been badly shot up. His buddy flew alongside to appraise the damage. Over the radio he told the occupant of the battered plane to bail out. "I ain't gonna bail out. I hear there's shark in these waters. I'm goin' home." He landed safely.

I notice the British Chiefs of Staff have approved the suggestion that a rumor be broadcast, timed with the attack on Sicily, that Italy has asked for an armistice. The result will be interesting to observe. Certainly all our home papers will pick it up as true. The British Chiefs are prepared to meet the kickback from this as a ruse, being merely a necessity for war, and hope the editors will be forgiving.

The Germans have moved some heavy bombers into their side of the Mediterranean. Some forty-five attacked Bône one night this week. Only eight bombs were dropped, doing little damage, but with the great concentration of shipping, particularly of landing craft, in all our harbors, we can expect attack any night.

The British Help Us Celebrate the Fourth

ALGIERS, SUNDAY, JULY 4, 1943

A couple of days ago, Captain Tim Shaw poked his handsome and smiling countenance into my small office and said that the good Admiral was wondering what the Royal Navy might do to help the Americans celebrate their independence from the British. The Admiral wanted to know if it would be appropriate for the ships of the Royal Navy in Algiers harbor to "dress ship" on July 4—which means formal display of flags. I told Tim I hadn't given a thought to the approaching of Independence Day—that it was pleasing that our ex-oppressors had thought of it—and that when opportunity permitted, I would discuss it with the Boss.

Ike was delighted the Admiral had made the suggestion and immediately elaborated on the idea. We could arrange for British, French, and American representation at an appropriate formation in front of the St. George; we would have the flags of the three countries; a French band, the U. S. Army Band, and the troops of each nation and service. This would be at high noon. At that time, the Royal Navy could fire a forty-eight-gun salute, this being appropriate for the Fourth of July and a recognized Army salute—one gun for each state.

I then went up to Tim's office and gave him the news. He wasn't shocked. He was amused. He said, "It will break every rule in the 'big book,' " meaning the Royal Navy's book of regulations, which, apparently, is as big as that of the U. S. Navy. Tim said that ships of the Royal Navy were not permitted to fire any salute in wartime. It seems that in the last war some enthusiastic skipper fired a salute while in a neutral port and nearly had a new war on his hands. As no saluting was permitted, the ships carry no blanks and would have to use live ammunition. Anyway, he would put it to the Admiral and let me know.

Soon Tim was back in my office—the Admiral had said O.K. "We'll do it if it breaks every rule in the book." A quick study had shown that it would break at least seven.

Anyway, the ceremony was held at noon today. It was a simple but touching ceremony—characteristic of the co-operation at AFHQ. I could scarcely stand at attention as I could picture Captain Barney Fawkcs, skipper of the *Maidstone*, the submarine mother ship in the harbor, supervising the firing of the forty-eight-gun salute. We could hear the sound of the shot and, in a few seconds, could hear and see the burst about 5000 feet in the air.

After the ceremony, I spoke to Brigadier Whiteley, our good-natured and efficient British Deputy Chief of Staff, about the significance of the day, and chided him about America being a "lost colony." Whiteley's reply was, in effect, that the British Empire would not have become an Empire if it had had to drag along the United States. It's this kind of kidding that makes this outfit click. This line of talk flows from Ike himself. Many times I've heard him talking to the British, joking about our different pronunciations of words. Often he asks them how they account for their pronunciation of "gas mawsk" with first the short and then the long *a*. Occasionally he says, "Someday I'll take time off and teach you English English." They love it.

Later I learned from the U. S. naval contingent that because the Royal Navy broke its rules to celebrate our Fourth, the U. S. Navy ships in the harbor had to follow suit and break some of their own.

The count of troops captured on Pantelleria has reached 11,000. The PM owes General Ike fifty francs on a bet,* the basis being one centime for every Italian over and above the PM's estimate of 6000 men.

The African "Pip"

ALGIERS, TUESDAY, JULY 6, 1943

Ike describes his feelings before the battle "as if my stomach were a clenched fist." Both of us are suffering from the African "pip."

Ike's feeling is akin to that which he experienced in the pre-TORCH days. It came again just before the big clean-up battle in Tunisia. Then again on D-Day for Pantelleria. That each of these operations has come off as advertised has not relieved Ike's anxiety. It is no small event, even in his life, to be sending 150,000 men on a highly dangerous landing on an enemy coast highly fortified with mines in the water and on land, shore batteries, U-boats, and worst of all, close air bases for havoc-wreaking

* Paid in full.

fighter bombers. I haven't mentioned the Italian Navy—but should I?

Yesterday General "Jumbo" Wilson, British Commander-in-Chief in the Middle East, arrived and is our house guest, with his aide, Major Chapman-Walker. Last night we had the two for dinner, plus Lord Louis Mountbatten, the Combined Operations Chief, who has arrived from England to observe the operation from Tunisian and Malta headquarters.

Lord Louis still expounds the virtues of de Gaulle, but acquiesces in the recognition of Darlan as a necessity and asserts that de Gaulle undertook to represent an unpopular cause when France fell.

The Commando chief has some new wrinkles in warfare. Reconnaissance of the Channel coast of France indicates that the Germans are heavily defending the ports, realizing that the only way we could maintain a foothold for operations on the Continent would be through a port. Consequently, Lord Louis, who frequently surprises me by his amazing ability for discovery of ingenious devices for war, has consulted with scientists and has come up with three types of "false ports," the use of which would make unnecessary, for a time, at least, occupation of an established port. One of these possibilities utilizes the principle that bubbles in water transmit energy. One scientist has proposed the laying of a perforated pipe line on the floor of the sea on the invasion coast through which a great volume of air would be released. The heavy upward flow of bubbles would absorb the force of the waves. Another scheme was to have huge canvas bags moored to form a floating mole. Another is to float across the Channel a huge artificial harbor and to sink a large number of old merchant ships to form a breakwater. Other ideas are in the works—anything that will create an artificial harbor will help an invasion. The guy is a Rube Goldberg—and an efficient one—at war.

He and his associates also have developed a new type of assault craft for landings. It is like a landing craft, but is heavily armed with hundreds of rocket guns. When perfected, it would lay down a barrage on the shore that would blast a path through the enemy. The force of one rocket is described by Lord Louis as greater than a six-inch shell, and salvoes are unloosed almost simultaneously. The carpet of fire is devastating. Five of the rocket craft have been completed on an experimental basis, and have been sent for use in HUSKY, but our staff, without Ike's knowledge, has rejected them as being unready. Lord Louis is pressing his desire to have them used, to test their effectiveness in actual battle. He claims there is everything to gain and nothing to lose, with a chance of proving a super-weapon useful for the grand assault on the Continent when, as, and if.

Incidentally, the use of "black radio"—the broadcast of a false story to Italy on D-Day, or thereabouts, claiming an armistice had been granted —has been ruled out by the Prime Minister. Perhaps it is just as well, as faith in our news would be jarred.

After two hours of animated conversation, led chiefly by Ike, General Wilson, and Lord Louis, the last suddenly called me into a corner, whispering he would have to leave as he had promised to visit Admiral Hewitt, but inquired if I would arrange to get General. Ike to sign his short-snorter bill.

The President has accepted the French Committee's arrangement for separate civil and military authorities in French West Africa, but he instructed Ike to inform the French Committee that because of North and South America's interest in Dakar for its value as a base for protection of convoys and operations in the South Atlantic, we must insist that every co-operation is expected from the new regime, and if it is not forthcoming, a change of our own selection will be dictated.

While I am away the diary is to be microfilmed in duplicate from January 8 to date. This task has been awaiting installation in Algiers of proper equipment, which is now available. I live in fear that with just one copy of the diary in our office safe in the St. George Hotel, a bomb could spoil a lot of effort, whether it be good or bad.

Softening Up Sicily

SIDI ATHMAN, TUNISIA (FAIRFIELD REAR), THURSDAY, JULY 8, 1943 Over all, our air offensive against Sicily is going according to schedule. The airdromes in the northwestern part of Sicily have been heavily and · frequently bombed, but until D minus 1 there will be no concentrated bombings and other air operations in southern Sicily which would definitely indicate to the enemy that our landings are to take place in that area. Every effort is being made to obtain tactical surprise.

One U-boat got two of the ships in a Canadian convoy coming from the U. K., somewhere between Algiers and Bizerte. How heavy the casualties are we don't know, as our routine intelligence reports do not reach us quickly at this remote camp.

Meantime Force H of the Royal Navy has attempted to decoy German and Italian air strength to the eastern Mediterranean. In this force are now six battleships and attendant cruisers and destroyers. They are making a show of themselves in the neighborhood of Crete, where Commando landings have been made in the last few days. It is hoped the enemy will spot Force H and be left guessing as to our real intentions. This is one time the Royal Navy really wishes to be seen by the enemy—not that the "silent service" isn't usually looking for a scrap. But this time this diversionary move of Force H is being deliberately undertaken to be "snooped" by enemy aircraft which ordinarily flit high over the Sicilian Strait.

Tedder hopes to lay on a shuttle bombing from England over Italy to Africa and return to England, with the U. K. bombers to drop bombs on Italian cities coming and going. These would be timed with bombings from North African and Middle East bases so that at least three cities— Turin, Naples, and perhaps the marshaling yards at Rome—would be struck heavily during the same night.

Fairfield Rear is not too well located for our convenience. It is an hour's ride over roads congested with Arabs, trucks, and other types of vehicles, many of which are carrying bombs and gasoline to the numerous airfields on the plain over which we look from the knoll where the camp is located. Directly in front of us at the Sidi Athman field are squadrons of Beau-fighters, equipped to carry torpedoes, on the lookout for shipping over the strait and around the Italian coastline. Toward the south are two large fields for medium bombers. Overhead are Lightnings, Spitfires, and various aircraft coming and going—a scene which is reminiscent of the descriptions given by observers from the cliffs of Dover during the battle of Britain. Only we don't see dogfights overhead. They take place over Sicily or the strait. Seldom can we know whether a returning formation has lost any of its planes. As I write I can see through the trees two squadrons of B-26s which have just risen from one of the fields south of us. They will be met by their fighter escort. It was from one of these fields last Friday when Ike visited the combat crews that he was told that in thirty missions not a single bomber had been lost. The bomber crews were proud of their fighter escort, who, in turn, claimed they had never lost a bomber by enemy fighter while under their protective custody. Grand spirit and co-operation.

The great difference to me between operations TORCH and HUSKY is that in the former Ike had direct control of all operations. He was the focal point from which decisions as to operations flowed. In this operation the responsibility rests with General Alexander, as Deputy Allied Commander for ground operations, Admiral Cunningham, and Tedder, with Ike sitting as referee to settle contrary desires of the services. For a time it will be virtually under control of Admiral Cunningham while the Navy is escorting its precious cargo to the shore. The only major decision Ike can make in this operation is to call it off. The rest is left to his subordinates. But all he can do is to hope and pray for the best. Meanwhile he is doing his best to keep from becoming irritable, at which he has been doing a fine job.

We really have two places to live—one at Amilcar, on the Bay of Tunis, near Carthage, where Ike's Advance Command Post is located, known as Fairfield, and this remote camp some thirty miles from that point where we are now, called Fairfield Rear. Commuting between the two will be tedious, if not dangerous, because of the heavy traffic in supply for our airfields which abound in this area.

D Minus 1, Sicily

MALTA, FRIDAY, JULY 9, 1943, 4:05 P.M.

Tomorrow is D-Day. H-Hour is 2:45 Saturday morning. Paratroopers begin dropping and gliders going in before midnight tonight.

We arrived in Malta on schedule at 5 o'clock yesterday afternoon, Ike being met by Alexander, Cunningham, Tedder, Air Vice-Marshal Park, and a representative of the Governor, Field Marshal Viscount Gort, to whose summer palace, the Verdala, we were quickly driven to meet Gort himself. Most amiable. Tea, and Ike and General Whiteley were off to the Admiral's headquarters for an hour-and-a-half conference on the latest developments.

Three ships bound for HUSKY have been sunk in the western Mediterranean, each happening to carry equipment for the Canadian division which operates with General Montgomery's forces. Bad luck for the fighting Canucks. Another ship was sunk, but in the eastern Med. It was an MT and about 200 of 900 troops were lost. It was coming from Alexandria. So far no bad or good news, and absence of bad is regarded as good news from the U. S. Navy or its vessels. But the necessarily imposed radio silence may not be golden.

Verdala Palace, where we are living with the Governor and his staff, was built by a don of the Knights of Malta about 1500. It is square, with four-sided towers at each corner, and surrounded by a now dry moat. Ike has the reception room on the second floor as an office, but likely won't use it. His bedroom adjoins, and has a side stairway leading down to a dungeon, walls of which still have carved niches in the heavy stone where prisoners could be chained. British, who have occupied the island since the Napoleonic wars, 1814, have whitewashed the stairway and chamber so they don't appear so gruesome as might be expected. I have a room in one of the towers, reached by a spiral stairway, steps of which are deeply worn. Am out of breath when I reach my landing. Have a water pitcher, washbasin, fancy soap dish, and a thundermug. Ike has the same, plus a lavatory and a bathtub.

The two correspondents will file direct from Malta, by arrangements completed this afternoon, and will be a ready and quick link between Ike and his senior subordinates on one side and world public on the other. They have been spoken to this afternoon by Ike, at my request, so they understand the necessity of retaining balance between the efforts, as reported, of the two nations. Ike's thesis was that Americans like to feel they are doing something important and are making a substantial contribution to the war effort. If they feel Americans are doing well over here—hoping we do—then they will be less inclined to want to sack the grand strategy of beating Germany first.

So these two correspondents have the picture: if they report their portion of the operation properly, America can keep her head and concentrate on beating first the one enemy that the three major Allies—England, America, and Russia—can get at together. Then they can gang up on Japan. The writers left here determined to help in every way, but will need some proper information to base their "situationers" * on. Ike said he especially wanted to give due credit to the American Navy for its part in this show—"if everything goes O.K."

Visited Admiral Cunningham's headquarters with Ike and Whiteley. The mind reader, Captain Shaw, and I had a cup of cheer while the "higher level" considered the situation. The main thing before them was the wind, which was blowing a gale (5.6 on the Royal Navy's scale; top is 8). Driving from the Navy's subterranean headquarters the several miles to the palace, Ike noticed the windmills, of which there are many, familiar to Iowa and Kansas, twirling rapidly and therefore ominously. He wondered if his luck was running out. To soften the anxiety, I suggested it might go down with the sunset.

During dinner, at which Lord Louis was present, there was further discussion of the gale. "To be perfectly honest," he said, "it doesn't look too good."

Unfortunately, the wind is blowing from the west, and therefore rolls the high waves onto the shore on which the Americans are to land—and it's too late now to stop the approach of more than 2000 vessels from west and east. This afternoon all ships were shown by the Navy to be in their proper places and no further losses reported, although the slow convoy including Canadians was attacked by air with as many as 100 sorties during the day. Not a single hit was reported, interpreted here-

---

* Thumbsuckers concerning the military situation.

abouts as indicative the enemy aviators were disinclined to press home
their missions against heavy ack-ack. Are they caving in?

The Germans had moved most of the planes from the airdromes in
southeastern Sicily bombed during the day, so we didn't get many on
the ground, according to Major General Clarence R. Huebner, an American member of Alexander's operations staff. He was in my cubbyhole
portion of the cave twice today to visit and to hope the planning was
going to turn out O.K. He quietly had the jitters and wanted to talk
unofficially—thinks the Americans have the best-equipped and best-
manned, especially best-higher-level-officered, army in the world.

There has been little enemy air opposition over Sicily, and little ack-
ack except around the ports.

Tonight after dinner we skedaddled down to the southeastern end of
the island, hoping to catch a glimpse in the moonlight of the 264 C-47s
carrying paratroops or pulling British gliders—a combat team to be let
loose off Syracuse and to glide in to attack important bridges and road
centers. This is the first time the Allies have used gliders in an actual
operation. They are used in this particular effort to avoid probable loss
of C-47s by ack-ack because there is so much of it around this port.
The C-47s will simply let loose their charges before the ack-ack gets
heavy and turn for home—near Kairouan, in Tunisia, where we visited
just a week ago.

Ike, Lord Louis, who said he would be the guide, Whiteley, and Captain Clark, RN, who is Governor Gort's C/S, went in the staff car, Jim
Gault and I bumping along behind—far behind—in a jeep.

I was detained to take a message, through Captain Shaw of the Royal
Navy, from General Marshall to Ike asking to be notified four hours
before H-Hour if the party was on or off. So I was too late to see any of
the gliders pass over the end of the island. They were beaming on the
lighthouse on the tip of the small point. But saw Admiral Cunningham
and Commodore Dick as they were returning from the lighthouse. They
said they had seen some sixty planes and gliders. When we reached the
point, the next wave wasn't due for forty minutes, so I hurried back to
the cave office to give Ike his message. He had just returned and had
seen some of the transport planes bucking the high side wind. He had
murmured a prayer for their safety and success.

He got his answer off almost exactly four hours before H-Hour—said
all had gone according to plan so far, that a westerly wind was making
the American part of the job difficult, but he hoped to have good news
to report in the morning.

Tonight we are carrying our Army cots and blankets over to the

Admiral's headquarters to sit in on the "wake." That is the spot where news comes quickest. Wind has "receded" to twenty to twenty-five miles an hour. Fortunately, we haven't the heavy Atlantic swells in the Mediterranean, but, unfortunately, we don't have the saving south wind that blew up from the Strait of Gibraltar to wash out the adverse waves, as had happened at almost the last minute at Casablanca. The Mediterranean waves, according to Lord Louis, may not be too bad for landing craft, even if the wind is strong, because they are deep and steep. Today he had gone aboard a fast Royal Navy mine layer which cruised amongst the British landing craft all during the daylight hours, and reported not an enemy plane in sight and that everything was O.K. But I bet there are a lot of seasick as well as homesick kids on the high Mediterranean seas tonight.

Speaking of having not seen any enemy aircraft during the day, Captain Shaw said Vice-Admiral A. U. Willis of Force H had apparently slipped up in his operation "so far." This is the battleship task force sent east in the Mediterranean to make the Germans think we would attack Crete or Greece, and it was hoped the "snoopers" (reconnaissance aircraft) would spot them going through the Sicilian Strait. But although four saw them, our own aircraft were so alert they shot down every damned one of them—a strange irony of warfare. Finally, when the forerunners of the fleet got to Alexandria, they were "snooped" while in port, so maybe the Germans got fooled, after all. Admiral Willis had written a note to Ike, hoping his force would not have to remain idle. If the Italian fleet would only come out of its hole, it would see more than its shadow.

Meant to relate that during a lull this P.M. Ike called me in to outline his idea of a book he would like to do after the war; had jotted down twenty-four names of important persons he had worked for or with, not political, and including every big name I ever heard of. Said he was of a mind to write his experiences with and impressions of each. Said he would paint each one's character, and around each tell some stories which would make the book useful as a history. Told him that truth wouldn't prevent him from being sued for libel and he might have a merry time defending himself in court after the war if he pursued his fancy. Urged him to come down to earth and consider a practical question: the two reporters, Gunther and Gilling, who should be carefully backgrounded as to the need of balance in reporting on an Allied Command. Which he did. Tore up his notes. But not a bad idea.

PART THREE

The Conquest of Italy

JULY, 1943 TO JANUARY, 1944

D-Day, Sicily

MALTA, SATURDAY, JULY 10, 1943, D-DAY, 9 A.M.

After our wild-goose chase to see the gliders cross the island, we returned to the AFHQ advance command post last evening about 10:30. Ike tended to a quick reply to General Marshall, and sent a more complete one to be transmitted over the C-in-C's private radio channel to the command post at Tunis and the AFHQ proper at Algiers. This wireless, set up by our Signal Corps, could not open for security reasons until H-Hour, 2:45 this morning. It will continue to perk, we hope, so Ike can be in quick communication with the home fronts.

These chores dispatched, Ike, General Whiteley, and I went over to Admiral Cunningham's headquarters to await the returns. As nothing was expected until around .3 o'clock, I left word for a "shake" at 2. Whiteley and I were sleeping on light cots in the office of the U. S. Naval Liaison Officer, Commander Boit. I dressed at 2, went to the war room, found there was no news, so went back to my cot. Commander Henderson, on duty in the war room, and my friend of the Pantelleria bombardment, said he would call me when any news of importance came along. Didn't want to awaken Ike, who was sleeping soundly in the adjoining room, unless the news warranted (all this was in the cavern, but this one has air-conditioning). About 4:30 Henderson rang up to say there had been intercepts of radio signals of the American landing parties to the west, indicating our parties were ashore on Red and Orange beaches, but this didn't mean much. So didn't bother Ike. No news from the American side. Did learn, however, that the wind, which had been reported as about twenty miles per hour at midnight, had gone down some more, thank God, and seemed to have swung more northerly, which also was helpful. Dozed again, picturing the seasick lads in landing craft and some possibly ashore, and wishing them luck. Ike had rubbed his lucky coins before retiring.

FLASH—General Whiteley has just had a call from the Navy war room that a signal just in from the U. S. Naval Task Force, presumably from the command ship, *Monrovia*, and still only partially deciphered, indicated that landings seemed to be going all right with the Americans. They had definitely got ashore at Gela, about halfway up the coast in our sector. This is the first news of any consequence we have had from the American side.

The flash has broken the sequence of events I had wandered along with, so I will abandon same, being not too good anyway, and capsule the "situation" as of 9:15 A.M.

Most paratroopers had landed within one mile of their designated spot. One group hit about ten miles off the target, but even this may further distract the enemy. No report from the gliders, except that six from one were rescued at sea, having failed to glide to land.

No report of any losses of ships.

Getting their information from intercepts of the landing parties' wireless messages, the Royal Navy had numerous fragmentary reports around 5 this morning. The Canadians apparently had not only got ashore, but had their landing craft for tanks beached for unloading. Ships were riding at anchor. The swell had receded.

First fighter sweep from Malta had returned about the time we stirred, and had shot down two Ju-88s.

While en route to the palace this morning, Ike expressed the fear that the Germans would breathe a sigh of relief to realize that we were only going after Sicily. They could destroy the airfields, the ports, and let us sweat out the slow approach to their Continental "fortress." They could wear us down, absorb our forces, and proceed with their attempt to annihilate Russia's armies. All this by way of looking on the pessimistic side. At that time we had no solid news from the U. S. forces, and it is important that the good old U. S. A. do well . . . but hell, we were eager for information.

Nothing is so agonizing as to sit and wait. Now we know how our wives feel when we are late getting home and they don't know where in hell we are.

Since I typed the above, the Royal Navy Signal Officer, Commander L. G. Durlacher, phoned me to say he had a signal from Admiral Hewitt. It said landings at Gela (1st Division) had been made at 2:45, on schedule, followed by succeeding waves of landings. No enemy action of surface ships. No enemy air action. No mines. Slight opposition from the shore. As they approached they could see from the *Monrovia* that there were many fires in and around Gela, presumably the result of our bombing. The 1st Division has two airdromes to take near Gela, one close by to the east and another perhaps ten miles inland. They have taken Gela, Hewitt indicated. Good work. When I told Ike, he was elated, but quickly he asked what had happened at the two other spots where Americans were to make landings . . . but no news yet as to those. The 45th Division, under Major General Troy Middleton, never in action before, is on the right flank of the 1st Division, and the 3rd, under Truscott, is shooting for Licata, perhaps the toughest of all.

While Ike is watching current operations like a hawk, he has had to think of grand strategy. He had to answer last night the query of General Marshall, presumably prompted by the President's and the PM's desire to get air bases in the Azores. We need air patrol in that area to combat U-boats.

At 10 this morning he has a session with the Commanders-in-Chief at the Admiral's dugout, but in the part that conveniently opens onto the harbor.

Shortly after he left, and as the two special correspondents with the censor, Captain C. G. Duncan-Clark, sat down in my office, Jimmie Gault brought the news that the Seventh Army, meaning Patton's command, had made all their initial landings by 6 A.M. Swell news. Now Jim must get all his tacks on the map he keeps in Ike's room. Says he will give me his lecture on Switzerland when and if the Allies reach the Mt. Etna area of Sicily.

Captain Dorling, the Royal Navy PRO, has hinted darkly of a scheme of the Admiral's and Ike's to take a warship to visit the western task force. This apparently developed while Ike was attending the conference, and he isn't back yet. Of course he will want his Naval Aide, I hope, but doubt, dammit. Ike has had the urge for days to get into this thing. Wanted to take a Beaufighter early this morning to go see for himself, but the air people said they wouldn't give him a plane and the Navy vowed if he got one they'd shoot him down, so that was that. They simply don't want to have him take unnecessary risks.

While waiting to go to his conference, Ike asked if he could read this stuff, so I knew he was desperate for something to do in the waiting period. I hadn't read it over myself since hurriedly typing it, and believe it or not, I, who am not easily embarrassed, found myself so. It's so darned jumpy and quick-on-the-trigger, as well as rambly. But he handed the first seven pages back a little later, and damned if he didn't say, "Not bad, not bad." Or did I mishear him? Did he say, "Too bad, too bad"?

Message just in from General Marshall asking Ike to "be prepared" to release to the Italian people a joint message from the President and the Prime Minister. They give old Musso and the Fascists hell. Offer the Italian people dignity and proper government in accordance with their best traditions. But they must overthrow Musso & Co. Another also just in, giving text of message sent by the President to the Pope. Piously poignant.

Things are quiet, chilly, and so damp my seat stays wet—"an air of quiet confidence pervades the Advance Command Post of Allied Force Headquarters."

A Sunday at War

MALTA, SUNDAY, JULY 11, 1943

All had a big night's sleep. Ike hit the hay right after dinner—as soon as he could politely disengage himself from conversation with our gracious and hospitable Lord Gort and assembled messmates—and didn't awaken until 5:30.

Attack on Sicily went well during the day, but news of losses have started to come in. Last evening we learned that the American destroyer *Maddox* had been dive-bombed and sunk in two minutes with heavy loss of life. Two other U. S. destroyers limped into port at Malta, one towed by a tug.

This morning I learned that one of our hospital ships, brightly lighted and properly marked with glaring red crosses, was dive-bombed by the enemy and sunk during the night, indicative of the barbarous war we are fighting. Nearly all the crew and patients, totaling 400, were saved. Now most of the wounded from the west side of Sicily will have to be evacuated in landing craft—uncomfortable.

Lord Louis returned to the palace before I retired last night and told those assembled that he had sailed with Admiral Cunningham in the *Abigail*, the thirty-knot mine layer, some sixty miles along the American, Canadian, and British landing beaches. Said he saw only a few wrecked landing craft and never so many ships of all kinds and descriptions. Said the whole show looked like a rehearsal. One American beach had been bombed while his ship was offshore.

Ike is hopeful the Admiral will permit him to go in the *Abigail* or some other ship tomorrow to visit Patton and Montgomery, who moved over to Sicily today.

Yesterday Ike couldn't go with the Admiral because he had to be at the Advance Command Post to answer to General Marshall the question of timing the proclamation to the Italians which the President and the PM propose to issue. Ike doesn't want to get too cocky by issuance of a message for all Italy before we have a larger foothold in relatively small Sicily. Will advise them when he thinks time is ripe. Meantime is having pamphlets printed, broadcasts prepared, etc., by the staff at AFHQ.

The Germans apparently expected the attack in the west but not in the east of the island, so their mobile reserve, around Palermo, is going after our Seventh Army under Patton, and heavy fighting is reported. Tonight we are laying on a diversionary attack by sea—empty MTs, escort vessels, etc.—on the northwest corner of the island, to keep the enemy upset. Just now he seems to be moving forces to meet Montgomery's Army on the east. Syracuse fell to us at 9 last night. Haven't heard the condition of the harbor, nor that of the one at Gela, taken by our 1st Division, and these ports are vital. Hear that Germans already are destroying port at Palermo, as if our bombers hadn't done so already.

Major General Joseph M. Swing, American paratroop specialist over here from home, has been in this morning to give a detailed report of his knowledge of the paratroop action thus far. Some 364 aircraft, mostly American-piloted and C-47s, took off from Kairouan the evening before D-Day. Of these 127 towed gliders, the remainder carrying paratroops. Gliders were British, paratroops American. All but eight planes had returned to their base at Kairouan yesterday when General Swing visited them. Three had been shot down by ack-ack after dropping their paratroops. Some of the remaining five may be on remote beaches, or airfields, forced down for lack of gas or other reasons. Most of the paratroops were landed at a crossroad, about four miles northeast of the airdrome at Gela behind a fortified center, which they took. All the remaining 356 planes were at Kairouan, ready to take off with new loads to new objectives when signaled by Patton. Expected to go last night, but Patton, who apparently is still aboard the command ship *Monrovia,* didn't ask for them.

The glider effort remains somewhat obscure. Were to have been released from the east side of Sicily into the headwind. They were to have been turned loose at 1000 feet altitude, 3000 yards offshore from their objective, but the high wind against them forced some into the sea, perhaps five or six. Whether those who made land accomplished their mission, I don't know.

Accompanied Ike to the naval caves at 6 yesterday, where he attended the twice-daily conference. I left there on invitation of Captain J. A. Grindle, RN, to talk with returning skippers of LCI (L) craft, back from Monty's landings on the east coast. Talked to four of them. Had no air, sea, or shore opposition on their beaches. Had heard machine-gun fire ashore. Busted their unloading ramps on the rocks. Seas had been heavy. Were to be ready in nine and a half hours for return with another load of 200 soldiers each. One young skipper—and they all were—was greatly distressed that a soldier, British, who had gone ashore, only to return seemingly ill after a short time, had been treated for seasickness on the return journey, but had been found dead in his bunk as the craft pulled into harbor. Captain Grindle gave his skippers hell for breaking their ramps, said they were hard to replace in North Africa and they had hereafter to fight harder to preserve their equipment. "Hell," he said. "You'll have to make perhaps two hundred trips to Sicily in your craft and you must fight hard to keep them in shape."

A Royal Navy commander whom I met at the Navy headquarters had just returned from the landing operation on the east side. Said lack of air attack was surprising and predicted they would catch plenty from the air today or soon. His reasoning was that Germans had used today to satisfy themselves as to the size and location of our attack on the many vulnerable targets. He perhaps isn't in a position to know the whole picture. It would appear that we have so heavily bombarded the enemy's airfields in Sicily, Sardinia, and on the toe and heel of Italy that he hasn't many proper airdromes from which to operate any aircraft, no matter how many or how rapidly he might choose to move his air reserve.

In this operation, differing from Gibraltar days, we don't get the individual messages from navy, air, and ground. Consequently, we have to go on verbal reports, which are quicker but not so detailed—and sometimes erroneous.

Should mention that Ike, Whiteley, Jimmie Gault, and I slipped down to a sandy beach for an hour in sea and sun. Beach was barred to soldiers account swell and undertow. Ike stayed on the sand, saying damned if he wanted to swim in "sand mixed with water." Rest of us enjoyed it. Ike had the fidgets. Lay on sand awhile, then got up and dug holes in the sand with a stick. Anxious to get back to headquarters to receive reports. Has some tough decisions to make—as to recommendations to Combined Chiefs for exploitation of whatever success we have in Sicily. Also the Azores plans.

Russian fighting seems hard. Thousand tanks reportedly launched by Germans in one attack, preceded by aerial and heavy artillery fire. Wouldn't we be in a mess if the Red Army should fold or give way? Our efforts, however, must be giving the enemy great concern. If we only had the ships, LCs, and troops equipped to start invading from across the English Channel, then he'd really have his hands full. We are only nibbling at the navel of the underbelly. As someone said yesterday, when we get Italy the Germans will know that a great deal of our shipping will be required to feed the Italians and to give them coal to keep from freezing, as we are the great humanitarians. Such absorption of shipping would delay purely military movements.

"We" Visit Sicily

MALTA, SUNDAY AFTERNOON, JULY 11, 1943

"We" are going on a destroyer to visit Patton on the west and Montgomery on the east, starting sometime tonight, details of time and place of embarkation to come from the Royal Navy. Have just been over to the good old RN and consulted with my friends as to detail, but they say the trip has been arranged on such "high level"—between the General and the Admiral—that certain items such as time of departure, place, and expected time of return have not leaked down to "our level." Anyway, I learn from my side of the high level we will go aboard after dinner, get away around 2 in the morning, will contact the *Monrovia* to find Patton's headquarters, and then try to get him to a convenient point where Ike can talk to him. Same idea re Montgomery.

Because of their urgent request, I have arranged for the two newspapermen to go along. They will get a good story out of it, especially if they can get the chance to record the first step of the Allied C-in-C on Continental territory captured from the Axis.

Losses during the landing operations—the assault phase—numbered 256, according to Admiral Cunningham's statement to Lord Gort at this morning's meeting. . . . Flitting Spitfires coming and going in droves . . . they return from Sicily over the northwest corner of Malta and go out over the southeast, traveling over a big race circuit, only counter-clockwise.

SIDI ATHMAN, TUNISIA (FAIRFIELD REAR), TUESDAY, JULY 13, 1943
General Ike, General Whiteley, W/O Marshall, Mickey, Corporal Love —Whiteley's batman—and I arrived from Malta last evening behind Captain Jack Reedy's capable piloting. In the preceding eighteen hours we visited Sicily.

Our party for the Sicilian trip kept growing. It finally totaled eleven, some of whom were to stay. They were the Allied C-in-C, Commodore Dick, Major General Swing of the Paratroop Command, his aide, Lieutenant Colonel Douglas P. Quandt, Major General Huebner, who operates in the G-3 of General Alexander's headquarters, Colonel Abraham of the British "Q," Colonel Gault, the two newspapermen, John Gunther and E. J. Gilling, and I.

We were driven to the Customs House, where we were met by an ancient barge of the Royal Navy. This resplendent craft had a brightly polished brass smokestack not unlike that of our old-time American fire wagon. But it was propelled by a gasoline motor. In this we were taken across the Valletta harbor to one of its many "deep creeks," which make it one of the finest natural harbors and naval bases in the world, to the large destroyer H.M.S. *Petard*. She was lying alongside a tanker, taking on oil, and had just come away from Force H and en route to Malta had picked up a crew of a German plane which had been in a rubber boat ninety hours. After this crew had been revived they were taken on deck and shown the mighty fleet wallowing in the Mediterranean. They couldn't believe their eyes. Axis propaganda had repeatedly assured them the bulk of the Royal Navy long ago had been sunk.

Lieutenant Commander R. C. Egan, RN, amiable skipper of the *Petard*, made us comfortable, gave us beer, and prepared for sailing at 2 A.M., which, at twenty-six knots, would put us offshore at Licata about sunrise.

Ike had the skipper's cabin. I had a cot in the skipper's mess room adjoining Ike. Both of us were over the screws. From the frequent changes of speed during the night it was obvious that the *Petard* was passing many LSTs and other craft going to and coming from Sicily. These she had to duck in the darkness and still stay within the narrow channel swept free from mines.

We had left orders for a "shake" at 5. Breakfast was at 5:30. I had already been on the bridge, but after breakfast Ike and I mounted the bridge just as the sun was coming over the hills of Sicily. During the night Commander Egan, who had been on the bridge throughout, had been advised that the U. S. Navy had laid a large mine field to protect its ships from submarine and surface action from the north and west.

We had received a signal that General Patton would be aboard Admiral Hewitt's command ship, the *Monrovia*, so after a glimpse of Licata, which was covered by haze and smoke, we cruised parallel to the coast in a southeasterly direction to meet the *Monrovia* off Gela. As we approached her we saw a black column of smoke rising from the water. As we neared it we found it to be a merchant ship and later learned it had been skip-bombed by the Germans the day before, had caught fire, and had been hastily abandoned by the crew. After several hours her heavy load of ammunition had thunderously blown up, sending pieces of metal several miles to the south amongst the 45th Division, but did no damage to the many surrounding craft in the broad crescent of beach in which our ships were anchored.

The shore-landing craft from the *Monrovia* had difficulty coming alongside the *Petard*, which gave us proof of the effect of the heavy swell which had to be overcome during the landing and subsequent unloading to the beach.

Aboard the *Monrovia* we found General Patton in good spirits. He had been unable to move his headquarters ashore, but all of its equipment had been landed and he expected to establish his command post ashore for the Seventh Army during the day. He had been ashore the previous day and, while overlooking the progress of the 1st Division, which had met a stiff counterattack from the German mobile reserve, had been machine-gunned by Italians. Fortunately, none of his party was hit.

Ten enemy tanks had been knocked out during the counterattack the previous day. One of them within 300 yards of General Patton. While we visited, the U. S. cruiser *Savannah* was giving artillery support to the 1st Division's attack east and north of Gela. It had started at 4:30 A.M. Both the new 4.2 mortar and the long-range but accurate fire from the *Savannah* were given credit for destroying the tanks. We could see her shells bursting several miles back from the beach. No word had been received from the 1st Division as to the progress of its attack.

Taking us to his "war room," which also was his cabin, he showed on a map that the American invasion was well up to, if not ahead of, the schedule in all sectors, except that of the 1st Division at Gela, where stiff opposition had been met. General Truscott, with his promising 3rd Division, had lived up to expectations. His was on the left flank, including Licata. On the right flank—Gela being the center—the 45th Division, under General Middleton, likewise had taken its objectives, and a union with its right flank with the Canadians who had landed in the southern tip was momentarily expected.

Ike spoke vigorously to Patton about the inadequacy of his reports of progress reaching headquarters at Malta. Because of our inability to know at headquarters of even his impressions of progress, we were unable to determine just what assistance, particularly in the air, he needed. It had been obvious after a few hours that the Axis had expected any landings in Sicily to come on the western side and thus were better prepared to meet the Americans than the British on the east. In addition, the enemy apparently was concentrating its air attack on the west. We had found that the fighter squadrons from Pantelleria which were assigned to give air cover for the Americans could not get off at dawn because of ground fog prevailing each morning on its hastily rebuilt airdrome. Consequently, five fighter squadrons from Malta had been assigned to give protection to the Americans.

Communications from the ship were heavily burdened. I was told even operational messages were running seven hours behind. I didn't have a chance to check the accuracy of this statement.

My old friend, Captain Jerry Wright, told me that they had had an hour-and-a-half air raid the night before, with two or three low-flying bombers coming in at a time. Nothing was hit, but there was much low antiaircraft fire, with bullets and shell fragments skipping off the waves in all directions. The beach parties had been subjected to fighter-bomber attack with bombs and machine-gun fire. These devils flew low through the valleys and just over the treetops to avoid detection by our radars. They had delayed the shore operations and had given our troops the "trigger fingers," making them touchy when even friendly craft, so easily identifiable as the Spitfire, came overhead. There have been complaints of our troops firing on Spitfires. It seems they will never learn.

When we left General Patton I thought he was angry. Ike had stepped on him hard. There was an air of tenseness.

Ike hoped to get ashore at Gela, but when told by General Patton that it took an hour and a half in a landing craft simply to get to the beach, this project had to be canceled. He had been especially hopeful of visiting

Bradley and his II Corps headquarters then pin-pointed on the map near Vittoria, some fifteen miles south of Gela and well inland.

Jerry Wright told me that all but one of the four seaplanes carried by the cruisers had been shot down. These slow-flying planes have little chance against the swift Messerschmitts when attacked. All they can do is twist and turn while seeking to reach the "protective" antiaircraft fire of the warships. Jerry told me, too, that we had lost two LSTs, with heavy casualties, by dive bombers.

From the *Monrovia* we sped about five miles offshore toward the landing party of the 45th Division, where Ike "made a signal" to Admiral Kirk aboard his command ship, the *Ancon*, "Congratulations and good luck," but we didn't have time to board her.

We continued watching the shore line and occasionally saw columns of smoke well inland, indicating a battle in progress. We found the H.M.S. *Hilleary*, the command ship for the Canadian-British landings off the southern flat tip of Sicily. Ike was most anxious to get ashore, particularly to see the Canadian commander if he were available close by, or at least to visit some Canadian troops. He wanted personally to express to them his gratitude in having Canadians under his command and to wish them good luck.

We were taken ashore in a "duck," passing through a hundred naked soldiers bathing along the beach. Ike met a Canadian Captain J. E. Moore of Vancouver, British Columbia, an artilleryman. After learning that the commanding general of the Canadians was well inland at his headquarters and that considerable time would be required to reach him, Ike asked Captain Moore to convey his message of good wishes to the Canadians. Ike then was driven by the British beach master, a colonel, in a jeep about a mile inland over a narrow road cloaked in four inches of light silt dust, hoping to find the assembly center for Canadian personnel. However, the Canadians had moved on.

Others of the party, in a duck, had followed Ike's jeep—particularly the two newspapermen, who had encouraged Ike to go ashore as they thought there was great historic significance in the Allied Commander's first visit to territory captured from the Axis. After about an hour ashore, we "ducked" to the *Hilleary*, where Ike conferred with the Admiral while the press, Gault, and I enjoyed a long, tall gin drink by courtesy of the *Hilleary*'s captain.

I neglected to say that while dashing at twenty-eight knots along the coast, after passing the *Ancon* and en route to the *Hilleary*, we saw two large splashes like bomb bursts some 400 yards astern the *Petard*. I was on the bridge at the time. There was an immediate call to battle stations, as the first impression was that we were under air attack. We searched the sky but couldn't see a plane. There were no more shots. Ike and the other officers were on the quarter-deck. Apparently, the call to battle stations sounded much more exciting over the loudspeaker system than it appeared to me on the bridge. One of the naval officers had insisted that Ike wear a tin helmet. The only one quickly available sat on his head like Happy Hooligan's hat.

On the *Hilleary*, Ike had the good fortune to see the Chief of Staff to General Montgomery, and as the time was rapidly slipping away and as he had already seen Montgomery in Malta, he decided not to go farther along the coast. Consequently, we sped back to Malta, reaching Valletta harbor at 2:30, where the party was taken off by the brass-smokestacked barge. Admiral Cunningham—faithful, loyal, and courageous soul that he is—was waiting at the Customs House to meet Ike.

When we reached our Advance Command Post headquarters in Pinto tunnel, Ike learned to his great chagrin and consternation of a report that twenty-three of our air troop carriers, while engaged in operations during the night, had been shot down over American lines in Sicily. Immediately he dispatched a hot message to General Patton, demanding a quick report. This tragedy cast a pall of gloom over an otherwise interesting and fruitful day.*

My over-all observation of the trip was that I had gained an optimistic impression at Malta because the landings were easy. After seeing the difficulties, particularly the swell of the sea and the hubbub and turmoil of the beaches and learning of the darting attacks of enemy fighter-bombers on our beaches, I became much more realistic. We have a difficult job ahead of us in Sicily. How long it will take depends largely on our clean-up of the enemy's mobile reserve. Mere movement will be slow. Fortunately, we have most of the 2nd Armored Division ashore and should do well. However, on the eastern side the British were making good progress, being at the moment favored by the enemy concentration against the Americans on the west. Before we left headquarters last night we learned that the Eighth Army had taken Augusta and we understand its port is in good shape. This, with Syracuse, whose port also is virtually undamaged, gives us two good ports. That at Licata had been partially demolished by the Italians but still was capable of taking four or five LSTs at a time. There is no real harbor at Gela.

---

* Later information disclosed that the incoming planes carrying paratroopers were mistaken by U. S. and Royal Navy ships as enemy planes, the friendly aircraft unfortunately having arrived in darkness during or immediately following a raid by German planes.

SIDI ATHMAN, TUNISIA (FAIRFIELD REAR), THURSDAY, JULY 15, 1943
Returned from Algiers in the Fortress with General Whiteley last evening, having flown there Wednesday afternoon, on Ike's request, to get the "lay of the land" and to look after various odd bits and, incidentally, to see the pups.

Those in Algiers feel quite remote from the battle front, as indeed they are. The large corps of correspondents felt scooped by our two Malta correspondents and at first there had been considerable lag in the flow of news from Alexander's 15th Army Group headquarters at Malta through Tunis and thence to Algiers.

The French situation was still of interest to the correspondents and a bother to Beetle, who told me that Juin again was threatening to resign and that Giraud had, as Beetle anticipated, sold his "bill of goods" to the President, who had committed 300,000 tons of equipment to be delivered to the French in North Africa in August, provided we could allocate sufficient port facilities to handle it. Beetle said we were already short 30,000 tons of shipping space for our own military operations and the port facilities were already embarrassingly clogged. On Ike's request Beetle had attempted to forestall such a high-level commitment by the President, advising General Marshall of the tightness of our shipping situation, but apparently this had not accomplished its purpose.

Interviewed by press correspondents at Amilcar on Tuesday (among them Dick Wilson, my old friend of the *Des Moines Register-Tribune,* and Ray Clapper), and when asked for a prediction as to when Sicily would be "ours," the Commander-in-Chief said, after inserting appropriate "ifs," that provided everything goes satisfactorily, we should have Sicily in two weeks. That would make July 27 Ike's "cave-in" day.

During the conference I got in my nickel's worth for the U. S. Navy by reminding Ike of Admiral Cunningham's glowing tribute to our Navy's skillful handling of landings in the heavy swell. He then repeated the Admiral's statement that the United States Navy had been magnificent in seamanship and in all respects. Don't know if this was printed, but hope so.

AMILCAR, TUNISIA (AFHQ, ADVANCE CP), FRIDAY, JULY 16, 1943
The command setup for the Sicilian operation is badly disjointed by reason of need of Navy headquarters at Malta, of air communications at La Marsa, on the Tunisian coast, some miles northward of our Advance Command Post, and the uncertainty of just where Alexander of the ground forces finally will light. At the moment Cunningham and Alexander are at Malta; Tedder and Eisenhower in Tunisia.

To illustrate the confusion arising from the separated headquarters and commanders, Beetle has phoned from AFHQ at Algiers this afternoon to General Whiteley to say that an order to move Commandos from Gibraltar to Tunis, to be ready for quick call for an operation in Sicily, has been in effect countermanded by a message direct from Malta. Just what is wanted is not known. When Whiteley put this up to Ike, he found Ike knew nothing of it, had not known such an order had been issued, and was put out at the lack of co-ordination.

If the battle weren't going so well, the separation of commanders would be most serious. But it is going very well, indeed. So much so—and this irked me a bit—a colonel of the Operations Division, WD, said, while waiting to see Ike this morning, that he had been to Sicily and had a peek at our easy war. He had gone from Bizerte to Licata on an LST, stepped ashore while they unloaded, and returned on the same LST. However, he was much impressed with the rapidity of unloading.

Yesterday Air Marshal Tedder and Lieutenant General Spaatz had lunch with Ike, Whiteley and I also being present. Our Air Force has almost complete domination of Sicily in the air, according to the conversation of Tedder and Spaatz. They were bellyaching because more targets could not be found. Spaatz said we have four airdromes operating in Sicily. Comiso was taken so quickly that dishes of food were left in the mess halls, and there had been no time for enemy sabotage.

Yesterday afternoon Lord Louis, just back from Sicily and Malta, came in to see Ike and Tedder and spent a couple of hours giving them his impressions of operations in Sicily. His is an unorthodox mind as judged by the British military, particularly that of the ground forces, but Ike thinks he frequently comes up with an interesting idea. The Italian General Achille d'Havet, commanding Coastal Division 206, which had surrendered to the British, had been on Lord Louis' ship returning to Malta. The Italian said that about 200 ships had been spotted on Friday afternoon on the eve of D-Day, but as the Italians had seen large convoys before, they were not particularly alarmed. Then six-foot waves on the west coast of Sicily gave them additional assurance. The first news the Italians and Germans on the island had of an attack—and this was delayed—came from the presence of our paratroopers. There also was aboard an Italian naval liaison officer, likewise a prisoner, who said he was greatly disappointed that the Italian fleet did not live up to the understanding of all Italians that when and if the homeland were attacked, the fleet would immediately give battle, which, of course, it didn't.

This morning we had an interesting report from Italian sources in Sicily that Italians and Germans were becoming more bitter against each other "hourly" and there were instances in which the two had actively fought. The report went on to say that Sicilian civilians and some soldiers were co-operating with the Allies, some going so far as to give information as to location and size of the Italian and/or German dispositions. Our latest report says some 15,000 prisoners have been taken by the Americans. British, Canadian, and American forces are making steady progress. It now appears there were seven enemy divisions in Sicily, of which three Italian divisions have already been destroyed or captured. Judging from movement of enemy vehicles reported by our pilots, our G-2 calculates a determined stand will be made in the northeast corner of Sicily in the hope of preventing our movement across the Strait of Messina to the "toe." Montgomery's Eighth Army is moving on Catania, which, when taken, should give us another good port if not too badly damaged. The port of Augusta has been found to be practically intact, so with that of Syracuse we have already two good terminals for our line of communications on the east.

British Minister Macmillan consulted with Ike here today and advocated that the Allied Commander-in-Chief ask the two governments promptly to grant recognition to the French Committee for National Liberation. He maintains that the volume of queries on French affairs coming from the home governments will become impersonal, which would tend to remove Ike as the personal target of the critics.

AMILCAR, TUNISIA (AFHQ, ADVANCE CP), SATURDAY, JULY 17, 1943
Ike's bothered about the Air Command. In the current operations against Sicily, Air Marshal Tedder, who is in charge of all Mediterranean air operations, has taken active charge because the targets are outside North Africa, beyond the province of General Spaatz as commander of the Northwest African Air Force.

This situation has resulted in Spaatz being virtually squeezed out of his job, yet the vast majority of all aircraft in the operation is American. Ike is keenly aware that there may be American reaction against the current arrangement. This morning he sought to straighten the command setup. He hoped to make Spaatz Tedder's deputy for all Mediterranean air operations and to succeed Tedder as the chief when the present commander returns to England in September. Whether he will actually return to England was another question Ike had to put to Tedder.

· Yesterday an ammunition ship in the harbor at Algiers exploded and set fire to another ship laden with drummed gasoline and killed and wounded an unestimated but large number of persons, mostly Arabs. Force of the explosion broke the front window in Ike's office in the St. George Hotel and even broke his lamp.

Naval action is perking up. The Royal Navy was shelling Catania last night while the U. S. Navy was giving the same treatment to Empedocle. A U-boat was sunk in the Messina Strait, as was an E-boat, but one of the Royal Navy's "heavy ships" and a cruiser were damaged by torpedoes and have put in at Malta.

The Germans apparently are strengthening their opposition, although the help they are getting from the Italians remains questionable. Ike heard that one Italian battery with a new cannon, on which the oiled protective paper still remained, had been abandoned. Two German artillerymen, presumably sent to show the Eyeties how to shoot their new gun, were found with their throats neatly slit.

Last night Ike received a super "Eyes Only" from the Prime Minister, content of which is still undisclosed to me, and as the information has not been volunteered by Ike it must be an extraordinary secret. The RAF decoding officer who received the message brought it in person, in custody of Major Lee, after we had gone to bed. The first paragraph, Ike did say, was devoted to instruction that the signal be delivered to the Allied Commander-in-Chief in person and to be read only by him and the cipher officer.

After I got Ike out of bed to sign for his hush-hush message he stopped at my room to talk. I told him of my concern about bombing Rome, which is to take place Monday, July 19. Said that while it is confined to the marshaling yards, some four or five miles from the Vatican, it is closer to some ancient churches, particularly the Basilica of St. John's.

It is true the marshaling yards are a bottleneck of extreme military importance and constitute an excellent target, the ruin of which would greatly impair supply to southern Italy. This afternoon—in fact, in one hour—we start a similar heavy concentration of bombs on the marshaling yards in Naples, but the air people think it necessary to couple the Naples attack with one on Rome, so that the marshaling yards at two important centers will be completely wrecked

Some British Military Diplomacy

AMILCAR, TUNISIA (AFHQ, ADVANCE CP), SUNDAY, JULY 18, 1943
Last evening we went to General George Clark's villa, the "White House," for a swim. Lieutenant General A. G. L. McNaughton, the Canadian

Commander-in-Chief, was there. He spoke to Ike about the refusal of General Alexander to permit him and his immediate staff to visit the Canadian division in Sicily. Ike had already arranged for McNaughton to go as far as Malta but had told him he would have to get permission of the 15th Army Group to proceed to Sicily. When this permission was firmly declined by Alexander, McNaughton's pride obviously was hurt and he claimed that no matter how quiet he kept the affair it was bound eventually to come out and had already reached the importance of a "governmental matter," between Britain and Canada. Ike had no authority over the British commanders in such matters, which are classed as "operational."

When Ike related this conversation to me on the beach I told him I thought it was a gross insult to Canada, that he would get the blame, that the affront to Canada would be picked up by the anti-British press in America and there would be all hell to pay. I suggested that we get Mc-Naughton a C-47, load a jeep in it, and send him to the American sector and let him make his way to the Canadians, telling Alexander and Montgomery what we are doing. They have control of who comes and goes in their sector, just as Americans have the same control in our sector. Further, he felt it was an issue between the British Empire and one of its Commonwealths. He felt disinclined to intrude in such a family matter. However, General Alexander appeared for a swim and Ike immediately swam out to discuss with him the incipient revolution. He found Alexander adamant. Said McNaughton had no business coming here during an operation and that while he had treated McNaughton politely, if he had been a junior officer he would have placed him under arrest. Said that when he was ashore in Sicily there was no transportation, that he had thumbed a ride on a lorry carrying rations, and that he knew Montgomery's Eighth Army headquarters had only one car. In view of the critical shortage of transportation and the nuisance to busy staff officers to look after the Canadian Commander-in-Chief, he positively would not grant McNaughton's request.

Ike pointed out the danger involved, the importance of Canada in the war, and cited the incident of Prime Minister Mackenzie King making a public statement to the House of Commons in Ottawa, claiming the British government and Ike had intended to prevent release of the fact the Canadians were in the Sicilian invasion, indicative of a chip-on-the-shoulder attitude. But since Alexander was so insistent, Ike felt constrained to support his subordinate commander, who with Montgomery has the final say-so on entry into Eighth Army area.

Consequently, he trundled up the long steps to the villa and informed

McNaughton that his intervention in behalf of the Canadians had been of no avail, repeating Alexander's reasons in diplomatic language.

Last night with General Whiteley we discussed this ominous situation. I had already made clear my fear about the psychological reaction of the bombing of the Rome marshaling yards near the Vatican, which is to start Monday at 11 A.M. I told Ike that when he recognized Darlan he offended the Jews; now he will be blamed for the "insult" to the Canadians, and is running the grave risk of an unfortunate Italian and world-wide reaction from the bombing of Rome. He is likely to be as unpopular as a skunk at a husking bee.

Whiteley sided with Alexander, but Ike said he felt Alexander was not giving sufficient weight to the problem of a democracy conducting a war. It is obvious, he said, the Canadian public needs inspiration and some means should be worked out for accommodating McNaughton. Said he might be told that we would put him ashore with rations in Sicily on the Canadian beach and let him thumb a ride to the divisional headquarters, now some fifty miles from the beach, but Whiteley thought McNaughton would be just a nuisance. Said the Canadian was being naughty.

I ventured the query as to how the British had ever succeeded in holding together an empire when they treat the respected military representative of its most important Commonwealth so rudely. Whiteley replied that if McNaughton is the military figure he is supposed to be, he will understand the situation and will accept the inevitable like a soldier.

General Patton made a quick trip to La Marsa in a B-25 yesterday. He wanted to see General Alexander, to clarify the order to the Seventh Army. He was mad as a wet hen because the order said the Seventh Army would protect the rear and flank of the Eighth Army and left the Americans in an inferior position. Alexander clarified the difficulty and said the American Army has the definite objective of joining in the attack on Enna, the important rail and road junction in central Sicily, and then will proceed northward to the coastline to cut western from eastern Sicily.

Patton told Ike his casualties number 5600, of which 500 were killed, 1900 missing, and the remainder wounded. To me this seems heavy in view of our impressions that the fighting had been relatively easy. However, Patton said that now they were meeting northern Italians as well as Germans, and it is well known the northern Italian is a better fighter than the Sicilian. They are meeting no Sicilian troops, which leads to the assumption Mussolini had removed them to other scenes of Italian operations. Ike was disappointed in this, for he had in mind permitting

Sicilian prisoners to be returned to their farms in line with the suggestion of General "Jumbo" Wilson, who had said that this scheme had worked so well for the Germans in Greece.

At yesterday's meeting Admiral Cunningham disclosed that the "heavy ship" which had been torpedoed was an aircraft carrier. It will have to be returned to the U. K. for repairs.

The question of location of headquarters doesn't seem to have been settled by yesterday's meeting, although another meeting is laid on for Monday, July 26. Neither has the command setup with Tedder been clarified, so far as I know, although Ike seemed optimistic after his session with Tedder yesterday, but mentioned this morning it still remained to be settled.

The Allied Commander-in-Chief has to return to Algiers to decide accumulated questions as to the American theater which have been assembled by the Deputy Theater Commander, General Hughes.

As a result of yesterday's meeting Ike has had drafted a recommendation to the Combined Chiefs of Staff that as soon as we take Messina we proceed across the strait to the toe of Italy. The gist of his recommendation is that we carry the war to the mainland and the attack on the toe and ball would be accomplished by other landings and perhaps an attack on Naples.

It is likely Ike will attend the meeting of the Combined Chiefs of Staff when it is held in London, possibly late this month or early August. I have not learned the content of the Prime's ultra-secret message, but I assume it has to do with the prospective meeting.

The Naval Aide Is Wrong Again

ALGIERS, SUNDAY, JULY 25, 1943

I haven't contributed to the diary during the week but can summarize the events briefly.

The Seventh Army under General Patton has swept into Palermo, meeting moderate resistance, and is rapidly clearing the western half of the island. In the meantime, General Montgomery's Eighth Army is stymied at Catania. Ike had a fear that terrain and ease of reinforcement by the Germans in the Mt. Etna-Catania area would cause Montgomery trouble, but both Alex and Monty had not regarded these factors as very important. Now the scheme of attack has been altered to swing the American 45th Division, after it hits the northern coast, westward toward Messina along the coast road, the 1st Division parallel but on interior roads, and the Canadian 1st Division likewise eastward but on an interior road, farther south, all three to hit Germans and Italians and to ease Montgomery's situation. Montgomery is building up a force and will be ready to deliver a wallop no doubt simultaneously with or shortly after the attack of the Americans and Canadians.

The meeting of the Combined Chiefs will not be held in London, after all, but in Quebec around August 7—a time when Ike will be busy with the exploitation of HUSKY, which now seems to point toward the project BUTTRESS, the attack on the toe of Italy from across the Strait of Messina. Consequently, Ike will be unable to attend the Quebec conference, where it would have been grand to have had Mamie meet him. He yearned for this opportunity.

Officers coming from Washington to this headquarters have told me of the possibility of General Marshall being chosen to head the Allied invasion of France from England, already decided to be undertaken early next spring. The duties of the office of Chief of Staff would be separated, leaving General Marshall the ranking field commander, but the Chief of Staff to be in charge of the home front and of central administration for all theaters. The person mentioned for this home job is Ike. If he has to return to Washington to take this backbreaking job, his heart will be practically broken. But he's a soldier.

During the week Ike had a hot message from President Roosevelt saying it had been "rumored" in London that the Allied C-in-C had "recognized" the French Committee for Liberation and pronounced, in effect, that such recognition can be given only by the two governments. All this Ike knew and felt chagrined that the President would even take the trouble to act on a rumor. Ike has, however, upon recommendation of Mr. Macmillan and of Mr. Murphy, notified the President that recognition of the Committee would facilitate our operations. But the President has elected to announce at a press conference that since there is no sovereignty of France, the membership of this Committee will not be recognized. Obviously he doesn't like de Gaulle.

Ike has been busy this week with a full schedule on callers. He has had many accumulated problems to settle with the Deputy Theater Commander, General Hughes, and the Judge Advocate, General Adam Richmond. The latter reported on some serious cases of rape and killings by American soldiers. Discipline in the Algiers area has been made a task of the Military Police of the Mediterranean base area under General Art Wilson, but General Hughes himself is responsible. They are cracking down hard and grumbling is heard on all sides, but the results seem to justify the severity of the measures. I walked from the St. George to our villa one evening this week and was saluted so much that after three blocks my arm was tired.

The pups are fine, although the little lady has weak hindquarters. I am feeding her vitamin pills.

Despite my misgivings on the bombing of Rome, I am pleased to say that the only severe outcries have been the expected ones from Rome and Berlin. However, the Pope issued a statement saying, in effect, that he had hoped Rome would not be bombed, but now that it has, hoped it wouldn't be again. I didn't regard the pronouncement as helpful to us. Actually, we don't know what effect the bombing had on the Italian people. It doesn't seem to have retarded the celerity of surrender in western Sicily, where the Americans now have some 90,000 prisoners of the total of 110,000 taken to date.

General Mark Clark and his Fifth Army will have their chance in AVALANCHE, another amphibious job, this time at Salerno, south of Naples, the object being to get the good port at Naples as quickly as possible.

Exit Il Duce

ALGIERS, TUESDAY, JULY 27, 1943
(Beverly's birthday)—Flew with Ike to La Marsa late Sunday afternoon for the conference of senior commanders Monday morning. Before breakfast Ike received a message relayed from Algiers that Mussolini had quit and the King had announced his direct command of the military forces and appointment of Marshal Badoglio as Commander-in-Chief.

This was extraordinarily good news. The British Minister, Mr. Macmillan, arrived after breakfast to discuss the situation. It was agreed that immediately a message should be sent to the Combined Chiefs of Staff, asking authority to pursue a line of propaganda by broadcast and pamphlet from North Africa which would give the House of Savoy and the Italian people their obviously much-wanted "white alley" to get out of the war.

Everyone wondered what had happened between Hitler and Mussolini at the conference which was disclosed by the bombing of Rome to have taken place on that very day—July 19. Had Hitler dictated to the original dictator that defense of Italy should be placed under control of the Germans? Had Mussolini agreed, and then when he reported at Rome found his cabinet and advisers to the King unwilling to permit Italian forces to be "sacrificed"? Whatever history may show to be the answer, the fact was Mussolini was out and Allied forces under Ike had overthrown their first dictator.

Ike regretted existence of rapid communications. If we were still in the day of sailing ships, he thought he could deal more quickly and advantageously with the Italians than is possible when he has to communicate to both Washington and London and wait for the two capitals to concur or direct. Ike is for building public opinion amongst the Italians which would encourage King Victor Emmanuel to send an emissary to negotiate quickly for peace. He is for offering them peace with honor, including repatriation of Italian prisoners as rapidly as possible, provided, of course, they will complete the overthrow of Fascism and turn and fight the eight to ten German divisions on the Italian mainland. He would ask them to guarantee safe use of certain airfields and strategic points from which the Germans could be dealt with. His objective is to give the Italians the opportunity they seek of getting out of the war as quickly and as honorably as possible, but they must have a good excuse to act.

Macmillan was instructed to draft these thoughts into a message, submit it to Ike while at the conference, with the commanders, and if agreeable, it would be sent immediately to the Combined Chiefs of Staff.

Beetle had been spending several days at the Advance CP and met us at the airfield. Beetle had been to Sicily with Alexander for a conference with Montgomery and Patton at Syracuse. He was pessimistic about quick victory in Sicily. Montgomery said it would take another month. Ike was irritated at the delay; couldn't see why, with overwhelming air support, naval bombardment from the sea, and the power that lay in British, Canadian, and American forces, the issue couldn't be settled much more quickly. Felt inclined toward rushing a division into Naples area for capture of an airdrome three miles from the beach. Felt this was a time to take great risks, as the enemy is upset, off balance, and excited. So little to be gained by pursuing BUTTRESS, which means merely getting a toehold on Italy, when a bold kick in the shins might cause Italy to give up the fight. But Beetle was all caution, reflecting the conservative view of Alexander and Montgomery. From the conversation, I judged the British commanders had become so schooled in conservatism—possibly arising from some bad experience in the desert —that they were not as bold as might be desired.

The next morning after news of the end of Mussolini's twenty-year career as dictator, and after Macmillan had departed to write Ike's message, Brigadier Sugden, one of our most capable planners, came along with the news that after consulting with other planners, he regretted to say that because of the lack of landing craft and commitment of these craft to supply the beaches in Sicily, it would be impossible to launch an attack even on the toe of Italy until September 7. Ike was let down by

the cold appraisal of a shrewd planner, yet Ike knows how seriously the
Prime Minister and the President will be pounding for a quick follow-up
now that Mussolini is out. No movement to either the toe or the shin of
Italy could be made without landing craft.

With this unpromising set of facts confronting him, Ike went to the
meeting, which lasted for nearly three hours, and, as usual, the planners, backed by stern reality, won the day. Naples cannot be attacked
immediately, neither can the toe of Italy, but Ike did get the date advanced somewhat before September 7. It was agreed it is necessary to
control all of Sicily, the Strait of Messina, and the toe before directly
assaulting Naples. In the meantime, civil war may break out in Italy
between Fascists and anti-Fascists, as well as battles between the Italians
and the Germans. Ike obviously was disappointed at the inability to
move ahead. If Italy can be taken out of the war by offer of an honorable
peace or by a quick blow in a vital spot, such as Naples, the war might
be shortened by many months and certainly the build-up for cross-
Channel operations from England could be greatly hastened.

Enter Mr. Secretary Stimson

We flew back Monday afternoon to Algiers, where Secretary Stimson,
Major General "Day" Surles, Mr. Harvey H. Bundy, the Secretary's
special assistant, and Lieutenant Colonel William H. S. Wright, the
Secretary's aide, had arrived, the first three housed in our villa.

We sat on the veranda, Ike answering questions of the Secretary and
expounding at length on the current Italian situation.

While the Secretary was vitally interested in the current development,
he was more concerned about commitment of American participation
in post-HUSKY plans. He had just arrived from London, where he had
conferred off and on for a week with the Prime Minister. He felt that
the Prime Minister was obsessed with the idea of proving to history that
invasion of the Continent by way of the Balkans was wise strategy and
would repair whatever damage history now records for Churchill's misfortune at the Dardanelles in the last war. The Secretary seemed apprehensive lest the PM would seek to avoid the commitment of the British
and American governments to invade France next spring. The PM had
repeatedly referred to corpses floating in the Channel. What the Secretary wanted from Ike was his opinion because he had to hurry home to
express not only Ike's but his own views to General Marshall and the
President before the next meeting of the Combined Chiefs at Quebec.

Ike was confronted with a difficult situation: if he fails to exploit what now appears to be a rapidly approaching victory over Italy, history will say that he "missed the boat," yet our own government seems to want to slam on the brake just when the going gets good!

Mr. Stimson was apprehensive because the American people seem to favor an all-out fight against Japan after the Mediterranean is cleared.

Ike's answers to Stimson's questions were about the same as those he had made to the PM, who had come to Algiers to high-pressure him into an early commitment for post-HUSKY, except now the campaign was much farther along and Ike had a firmer basis for his statements. But even now he could not foretell when and how Italy would capitulate. He had always been for ROUNDUP or SLEDGEHAMMER, provided the British would support it wholeheartedly, but there was much to be said, he thought, for exploiting our anticipated victory over Italy. By causing withdrawal of Italian troops from the Balkans, where there are said to be some thirty divisions, and others from France, we embarrass the Germans greatly because they will have to substitute troops for the arduous policing tasks. Mr. Macmillan had told us that commanders of five Italian divisions in Yugoslavia had informed British secret-service agents that they wished to surrender. And, over all, loss of Italy to the Axis would be a psychological shock to the Germans and an uplift to the peoples of the occupied countries.

Tomorrow I am taking the Secretary on a flying trip to La Marsa, in Tunisia, where we will be met by Generals Spaatz, Doolittle, and Cannon for a short visit with some of the air units, returning the same day. Plans are flexible because the Secretary's physique requires him to rest frequently. He is approaching seventy-six and is truly "America's Elder Statesman." He has been right in calling the turn against aggressors since Japan moved into Manchuria. He has lived to see how right he was.

JULY, 1943: *Mediterranean tense with anticipation of possible Allied invasion effort as British Commandos raided Crete and Allied aerial might continued to hammer military installations in Sicily and Italy. Axis radio described invasion threat "another Allied bluff" and declared that any invaders "would be tossed back into the sea." Allies invaded Sicily in twin series of landings against disintegrating Italian resistance; Germans fought bitterly to slow Allied advances which, in seventeen days, conquered most of island. Badoglio appointed Italian premier following "forced" resignation and arrest of Mussolini. Allied leaders warned Italy of continued bombing until acceptance of peace terms. Over Germany Allied planes continued heavy attacks against selected targets. First air raid on military objectives in Rome, hitherto inviolate, shook Italian will to resist. Starting with invasion of Rendova General*

MacArthur took personal direction of advance on Salamaua. U. S. naval forces inflicted heavy losses on Jap fleet in Kula Gulf and elsewhere in Pacific continued systematic decimation of Jap shipping. Russians opened Orel drive and made significant, if limited, gains as each side daily sent thousands to bloody oblivion. (It's hard to believe that just a year ago this month we were doubtful if the Russians could hold out.—H.C.B.)

ALGIERS, MONDAY, AUGUST 2, 1943

Following the shelving of Mussolini and the quick denunciation of Fascism within Italy, the Prime Minister and the President on succeeding days called for "unconditional surrender." After they had spoken to their publics, the proposed message to the Italians which Ike caused to be sent on Monday, July 26—intended to give the Italians their "white alley"—was approved by the Combined Chiefs. The Prime Minister had insisted on insertion of a saving clause demanding the Italians not turn over British or American prisoners to the Nazis to be taken away to Germany. The message was broadcast to Italy, starting Friday noon, July 30. Immediately there was a murmur in the press corps because the message indicated permission to retain the House of Savoy.

We left Maison Blanche by Fortress Saturday morning, and flew first to Tunis so that Ike could fulfill Air Marshal Tedder's request for an immediate conference. The Air Marshal had word that Badoglio was actively trending to the Germans and wanted permission to resume the heavy aerial bombardment of Italy, particularly of Naples and of the marshaling yards at Rome. Ike gave his assent.

General Patton met us at the Boccadifalco airfield, which is nestled amongst the mountains bordering Palermo. He was in fine form and felt proud of the accomplishment of the Seventh Army. He said it is the best group of fighting men in the world. It is true their accomplishments are remarkable, although their opposition has been less than that of the British Eighth Army on the east. However, the Americans claimed that if Montgomery's army had moved as rapidly as our Seventh, the Germans could not have concentrated at Catania to stop them. Now the 45th Division, moving eastward along the northern coast road of Sicily, and the 1st Division, moving on its right, were making steady but slow progress. Mere marching over the terrain is difficult. Gun emplacements have to be spotted during the daytime, then mortars and artillery—such as can be transported and emplaced in the precipitous mountains—are carefully sighted on these strong points and break loose with their concentrated fire after darkness, while our infantry surrounds and mops up the blown-up enemy positions. This makes for slow going, but the progress has been steady.

Patton said they would continue this type of attack persistently so the enemy would never have a chance to regroup. In order to keep the pressure persistently applied to the enemy, he was relieving the 1st Division with the 9th, and the 45th with the 3rd. One of the difficulties encountered, particularly along the coast road, was effective enemy demolition of the road bed. On one side was the sea, on the other sheer cliffs, sometimes reaching mountain-high. A demolition would tumble the base of the road into the sea and make the work of the Army Engineers most difficult. Incidentally, General Patton paid a high tribute to their excellence.

General Patton is living in the palace of the king of Sicily, who had been overthrown in 1861, after Garibaldi had taken Sicily with 1000 men. Major General Terry Allen, commander of the 1st Division, and Brigadier General Theodore Roosevelt, his assistant, had been relieved by Patton, the decision confirmed by Ike. The former for "war weariness," and to be returned to America, without discredit, under our rotation policy. There he could rest and take another division, as he's an excellent commander. His men love him. General Huebner is taking his place. General Roosevelt had proved to be a gallant leader of inexperienced troops. He is battle-wise and extremely courageous. Likewise, he has "had it." Ike thought eventually his good qualities could be utilized by later assigning him to an inexperienced division about to go into battle. Awaiting such an assignment, he will be given another in the North African Theater where his qualities will be useful. The 1st Division has been in more fighting than any other outfit in this operation, and General Allen simply became fatigued to such a low ebb that he was unable to afford the inspiration and the leadership, as well as the imagination and discipline, that are necessary for a divisional commander.

We saw the effect of bombing in Palermo. It was devastating but satisfactory. When I saw the effect of bombing at Bizerte I felt sad, but at Palermo my feeling was the Eyeties asked for it and they got it.

Two ships of about 125 feet in length had been lifted, by the force of an explosion, entirely out of the water and onto the quay—a scene that would make a cartoon for Ripley's "Believe It or Not." Apparently, an ammunition ship that had been bombed blew up, created a tidal wave, and washed the ships onto the quay ten feet above the normal level of the water.

The first thing the Americans had to do at Palermo was to organize Italian workers with GI bulldozers to clear the streets, particularly those in the vicinity of the docks. Now most of them are clear. The port had reached a level of 2000 tons' discharge, with rapid increase in prospect. American destroyers and PT boats were lying in the harbor.

General Patton had called on the Cardinal of the Palermo arch-diocese, Lavitrona, and the Cardinal had promptly returned his call. They had become fine friends. The Cardinal had shown Patton some of the ancient cathedrals. He had also given the General a message to be transmitted to the Pope, a copy of which I carried back with me and dispatched from Malta, at Ike's direction, to the Combined Chiefs, so it could be sent by proper channels representative of both governments. In it the Cardinal said he and his people were being treated with the "utmost courtesy" and that the occupation had occurred without any "unpleasant incidents." The message had come through the former Lieu-tenant Governor of New York State, Charles Poletti, who is now a colonel in the Allied Military Government. I asked General Patton how Poletti was doing and he said, "Beautifully, but I think he is electioneering for Roosevelt among the Sicilians."

After a Spam luncheon in the palace, we took off for Syracuse to meet General Alexander. The two Generals conferred under an olive tree, back-grounded by a mule grudgingly affording the power which drew water from a deep and cool well. When the mule stopped, he was beaten with a long lash by an Italian farmer—an ex-soldier of the last war—who expressed his friendship for the Allies in this one by freely giving of his Chianti and Marsala.

Ike was anxious that there be no misunderstanding between Alexander and Patton as to plans for the attack scheduled to start the next day—August 2—today. Patton was to continue his methodical and steady ad-vance; Montgomery was to lay on all he had and try to break through. Incidentally, Monty has 400 big guns and his attack at Catania will be reminiscent of El Alamein. It should be reported, too, that members of the Secretary of War's party, who had just come from London, said the slowness of Monty in taking Catania had given the British public a let-down. The Prime Minister had expressed to Secretary Stimson his pro-found gratitude at Ike's statement at having undertaken publicly to balance the progress between the stalled British Eighth Army and the rapidly advancing American Seventh Army. Ike had told the press the Seventh Army had relatively easy going and the Eighth very difficult. Actually, the Eighth Army has been getting a great deal of publicity for any kind of movement and the Seventh Army, which has been going great guns, is still somewhat under the cloud of the great reputation of the Eighth.

Returning to Malta, we stayed overnight at Verdala Palace, again the guests of Field Marshal Lord Gort and his friendly assistants. Ike had a meeting of the senior commanders Sunday forenoon during which the entire Italian situation was discussed, plans were refined for attacking the toe of Italy, and consideration was given to helping General Wayne Clark and his Fifth Army plan its attack on Naples, probably September 9, with the BUTTRESS (on the toe) to come September 2.

Ike was itching this morning to know the result of the long-planned bombing of the Ploeşti oil fields in Rumania. More than 150 B-24s of the 9th Air Force were to take off from the Tripoli area and seek to damage this important source of oil to the enemy. Losses would be great. Ike hoped that they wouldn't be greater than twenty per cent, but by the investment of whatever the loss, if the oil fields could be substantially damaged, the Germans' supply of oil would be seriously curtailed. The planes are going in files of three each so that if the first or second hits a barrage balloon, the third would probably get through to the target. This indicates the desperation of the attempt. As I was reaching the office earlier than Ike this morning, he asked that I check with the air people and phone him at the farm as to results. I found 177 bombers had taken part, at least a third of which had not reported in two hours after due, but some of these would probably be found at various airfields along our side of the Mediterranean. According to an early report, the mission was successful, five of the seven refineries having been hit.

Alexander figures it will take another month to clean up Sicily, and Montgomery is less optimistic than he. But at an off-the-record press conference at Palermo yesterday, Ike said that while he was wavering on August 5, particularly after seeing the terrain which was described by General Patton as "making El Guettar look like a plain," he said he still would stick with his date. Quent Reynolds, whom we last saw in London, was there, fresh from four months in Russia.

This morning Ike received authority to prescribe conditions for an armistice with Italy, agreed to by the President and the PM and transmitted for Ike's "eyes only" by General Marshall. I note that the President is of the same opinion as Butcher—namely, that Italy is more likely to negotiate for peace through neutral diplomatic channels than directly with Eisenhower, only I have said it would be the Vatican.

Price of Ploesti

ALGIERS, TUESDAY, AUGUST 3, 1943

We spent last night at the farm. About midnight Beetle phoned me to tell Ike that a message for his "eyes only" from General Marshall had just arrived. It reported that through the Vatican the Italian government is asking for our conditions for making Rome an "open city." This meant immediate cancellation of the second bombing of Rome, which was to have taken place within a few hours. Beetle had already set the wheels in motion to stop it. I tiptoed down the hallway, found Ike was sleeping soundly, so decided to tell him in the morning. But around 2 A.M., Ike was prowling around the house and I heard him. He had gone to bed early and had slept his five hours. I told him the story. By 7, he had phoned Beetle to make certain all ends were tied together, and found there had been additional exchanges of messages during the night from the British Chiefs of Staff, reflecting the Prime Minister's view that we should proceed with the bombing, but finally one from the Combined Chiefs of Staff leaving the question to Ike's discretion. Conditions suggested, among other things, that Rome must be stripped of military personnel, equipment, and all military movement through the city must be stopped. It also would require the seat of government to be removed from Rome.

These conditions are being forwarded to the Italian government through the Vatican, but in the meantime, Ike is authorizing the bombing of outlying airfields if they show enemy activity.

Bombing of the Ploesti oil fields seems to have been reasonably successful. Five of the seven refineries were confirmed as hit, according to RAF Intelligence. Of 177 B-24s of the 9th Air Force, whose crews were specially trained for this job, some 120 reached the target and did their stuff from low level (100 to 700 feet) with incendiary and delayed-action bombs. Our first report yesterday morning said that fifty had not returned.*

Ike's request for temporary assignment of four heavy-bomber groups from the 8th Air Force to North Africa for concentrated bombing of military targets in northern Italy has been rejected by the Combined Chiefs. A suggestion from General Marshall that four medium-bomber groups might be sent if they would be useful has met opposition from General Devers of ETO. So it looks as if we are getting nothing more to help give Italy her final blow, and to hasten the acquisition of advanced air bases from which Germany may be hit more frequently. Ike had transmitted the request originated by Air Marshal Tedder and General Spaatz with the thought that since the over-all objective of bombing operations is to reach industrial targets useful to Germany and since many of these targets, particularly fighter factories in and near Vienna,

* American Air Force officers in the Mediterranean felt the loss was excessive. They favored high-level bombing.

can best be reached from this theater, then the heavy bombers could operate for six or eight weeks from our bases. Ike is furious. He feels that the much-flaunted mobility of our Air Force has been exposed as talk rather than action. We have the bases and the crews for maintenance for a short period, but others feel the cross-Channel aerial bombardment would be seriously impaired by this temporary diversion of either the heavy or the mediums.

Yesterday General Montgomery started his Eighth Army attack at Catania, and while we knew the attack date, the first word we had that the attack actually was in progress came from the BBC. The corps of some fifty or sixty correspondents supposedly covering these operations from AFHQ insisted on a communiqué, so they could write their stories, but AFHQ had no information, Monty being tight of mouth while attacking.

Today, I accepted an invitation from Colonel Phillips to give background information to the correspondents about operations in Malta. There were about fifty correspondents, British and American. Charlie Daly, of CBS, whose *nom de guerre* on the air is John, soberly asked me if I had heard at Malta any news of the illustrious and elusive British Colonel, J. Hamilton Forby.* I replied equally soberly that although I had not actually seen him, I had heard of his good work and that he had been very helpful in getting certain advance information about Sicily which had required personal reconnaissance behind enemy lines. Some British correspondent then inquired if Forby's name might be released for publication, and I replied that he would have to consult the censors.

It is now 4:45 P.M. and, so far as I have been able to determine, no one in AFHQ has any news of the progress of Montgomery's attack.

The meeting of the Combined Chiefs, no doubt attended by the Prime Minister and the President, is scheduled for Quebec, August 17. General Marshall realized that Ike couldn't attend while we are still

---

* This is a mythical character, created in the lively imaginations of several correspondents, including Helen Kirkpatrick; Charlie Daly; Red Mueller; Drew Middleton; Quent Reynolds; Ed Beattie; the PRO, Lieutenant Colonel Joe Phillips; the likable Chief Censor, Lieutenant Colonel Scott-Bailey; and Lord knows who else. Forby's exploits grew with every meeting of all or any of the correspondents. He was reported having been seen at the Alette Hotel, where many of the correspondents lived; lurking at the Agrico, which housed the information services, and occasionally was reported in and out of the St. George, AFHQ. He turned up in London, Cairo, Moscow, and Zeralda, the press men's "rest camp" on the beach north of Algiers. He was the Paul Bunyan of the Mediterranean. I later learned that after the press conference, a new correspondent had asked the censors for release of Forby's name but he was told solemnly that Forby was on the "hush-hush" list.

fighting to get Sicily and, indeed, while we are still sitting with our hands open to catch the remains of Mussolini's messed-up Italian empire.

While we were at the Governor's Palace in Malta, listening to the BBC Sunday morning, we heard that General Giraud had been made Commander-in-Chief of the French forces including an expeditionary force, thus straightening the dual commandership previously shared with de Gaulle. The latter is to be in charge of "Civil Defense" and to devote himself primarily to civil affairs. The development seems satisfactory from our point of view. North Africa has become an immense base from which future operations can be mounted, and any evidence of security and stability in this area gives Ike satisfaction.

Disturbances of the Peace

ALGIERS, WEDNESDAY, AUGUST 4, 1943

Tomorrow is the day Ike predicted to his press conference a couple of weeks ago that we would have Sicily cleaned up. It now looks as if he was a bit optimistic, but he did receive from Alexander last evening a message indicating withdrawal of Germans and Italians in front of Montgomery, whose attack started August 2. If this withdrawal develops into a rout, Ike still may be substantially correct.

Two incidents have occurred in the past twenty-four hours which disturb the peace.

The first is the slowness of the arrival of situation reports from the 15th Army Group to AFHQ. This delay was magnified yesterday when the Prime Minister announced on the floor, and the BBC quickly carried the news, that we had taken three cities in Sicily—an advance that AFHQ had not been authorized to release because the communiqués are written by the 15th Army Group and the names of these places had not been included. On investigation we found that the 15th Army Group had a radio transmitter working direct with London. The PM got his information from a "sitrep" which reached there long before ours arrived, and probably assumed the information had been given to the press. While we recognize that the PM has consistently scooped his British generals on giving news to the public of even their own advances, this is the most flagrant incident that has occurred during our operation. On investigation, we find that transmission of this particular "sitrep" from 15th Army Group to AFHQ took eleven hours. Our correspondents again were beaten when Mr. Patterson, the Under-Secretary of War, announced in New York last week that Americans had taken San Stefano.

The second is much more serious. The Prime has complained to Harry Hopkins, with the hope that Harry will lay his complaint before the President, that a proclamation of the AFHQ broadcast to the Italians last Saturday while we were in Sicily and Malta, and to which Eisenhower's name was attached, tended to commit the two governments without prior approval of the President or the PM. The Prime construed the propaganda statement as emphasizing that the Allied forces had purposely laid off bombing of Italy after Mussolini's fall while Badoglio was forming his new government. The Prime Minister stated that the politicos should make the public announcements. The generals should provide the action.

The proclamation in question was originated by political-warfare people of AFHQ and actually was proposed by one of the British politicalwarfare officers. It was approved in Ike's absence by the Board on Political Warfare, on which sat both the British and American ministers, Macmillan and Murphy. Macmillan is the PM's personal representative. It was approved by our British Chief of Staff, General Whiteley.

That it has had a good result in Italy is indicated by the reports of wholesale evacuation of certain of the big cities we have bombed and where the Italians would expect additional bombings after the lull was terminated. In other words, "Eisenhower's proclamation" that bombing would be renewed seemed to have the desired effect.

As propaganda is an essential element of modern warfare, the Combined Chiefs have given AFHQ the implements for its use, such as highpowered radio stations, portable facilities for printing pamphlets, and numerous and assorted experts. It would seem the PM is anxious to keep within his and the President's hands such public announcements to the enemy. This is understandable, but his complaint indicates a better understanding is needed so that the general in the field may use this new implement without having to wait for specific approval from the home offices of each manifesto. This waiting process takes about three days, during which the President and the PM exchange views and attempt to reach an understanding. In the meantime, the psychological moment for an effective statement to the enemy may have passed. It is as if we had to wait for specific approval of the PM and the President for opening on the enemy with our heavy guns, only these guns happen to be aimed at the mind rather than at the body. Ike has not yet answered the complaint, which also is of interest because it is the first time within my knowledge that the PM has complained to the President of Ike's operation. Heretofore, the PM had registered any bellyaches direct with Ike. Something is irritating the old boy.

Both incidents add to a feeling that I think is ominous of suspicion between Americans and British. Questions are being asked: Why should 15th Army Group report direct to London and bypass AFHQ? Why should the PM, as it was reported by Colonel MacDonald of the Air Force, in company with General Spaatz yesterday, go out of his way in speaking to the House of Commons to say that the attack in Sicily is under the personal command of General Alexander? The last question is understandable, but may indicate some lurking irritation of the PM. All of which again gives rise to the question: Can Allies fight together in victory as we did in adversity in Tunisia? If we cannot, then there is little hope of working together successfully after the war.

Going home to lunch, I could see that Ike was angry. He had dictated an answer to General Marshall relative to the Prime Minister's message. This he would let cool until after lunch and then take another look at it. We had played a game of ping-pong to clear the mental processes.

One glorious quality of AFHQ is the way its decisions or actions are defended by both British and American personnel whenever questions are raised by the home governments. Now Minister Macmillan, believing the Prime Minister has not had all the facts, has stepped to the wicket and "knocked 'im for six," as the British say.

Our statement to the Italians had encouraged civilians to evacuate cities during the lull of our bombing. Its purpose was to bring Italian public opinion to bear against the Badoglio government in an effort to hasten Italian decision and to save lives. It also afforded a means of covering up an enforced lull of air operations. Because our fliers had worked full out so long, a three-day rest was essential. I think the tiff is one of the growing pains of psychological warfare, which is becoming an increasingly important weapon, and we are only just now beginning to use it effectively. Ike is more interested in getting the two home governments, through the Combined Chiefs, to give a broad outline of propaganda policy under which his staff for psychological warfare can operate. This will avoid undesired actual or virtual commitment of the home governments beyond the terms of the directive. He has sent this suggestion to General Marshall for the information of the President.

ALGIERS, FRIDAY, AUGUST 6, 1943

The Sicilian operation didn't cave in by August 5 as Ike optimistically guessed, but Montgomery got Catania and this morning Patton wired that the 1st Division was in Troina at 8:30.

To the latter hangs a tale. The Prime Minister announced three days ago to the House of Commons that Troina had been captured. He had used information sent him privately by General Alexander. Just what Alexander told the PM that caused the premature and untrue claim that Troina was ours, we don't know, but, in any event, the PM and the BBC had it on the air, even if erroneously, long before we had similar information at AFHQ. Yet when the BBC news came out, General Alexander's 15th Army Group quickly sent a signal to AFHQ demanding an investigation to discover the source of the leak and intimating that it must have come from London, but that if it had come from London, then the Allied Commander-in-Chief should instigate a query and reprimand to the BBC. Yet it is a bit difficult to reprimand the real source, which is the Prime Minister.

Ike has taken this situation in hand politely but firmly in a message to General Alexander and also sent Beetle to 15th Army Group to help straighten out this and other affairs. Alexander has suggested that he will send a similar personal message to Ike each day, giving not only factual information, but his impressions of the progress.

Ike has communicated with the CIGS relative to a complaint from the Seventh Army that a recent broadcast of the BBC said that on the Seventh Army front the going was so easy that the troops were eating grapes and indulging in swimming, while the impression was given that the Eighth Army was confronted with severe opposition. Ike's point was that in an Allied Command credit must be skillfully balanced and he made it clear that the Seventh Army has made remarkable gains against stubborn resistance. As the BBC is the principal radio service heard in this area, it bears a tremendous responsibility in handling its news.

ALGIERS, SUNDAY, AUGUST 8, 1943

Everywhere I happen to go, I find the American Red Cross doing a grand job. The gratitude of the GIs for the service and even the companionship of the Red Cross girls is unbounding. I have a hunch that the good work of the so-called little people in the Red Cross will make many fine reputations for those at the top.

One example of the kind of assistance rendered by Red Cross personnel which could be described "over and beyond the call of duty" has come to my attention and I have been trying to assist. Mollie Ford, who runs the Information Desk in the enlisted men's Red Cross Club downtown, called to get information as to the location of an American officer, claimed by a French girl to be the father of her expected baby. The daughter of highly respected parents who live in Oran, she had become acquainted with an officer in our railroad service. The officer had not answered any of the girl's fervent pleas for help.

Through T. J., I got the Adjutant General's Office to trace the officer and found him in a replacement depot near New York. I found the new address and passed it along. Miss Ford had got a job for the jilted girl at the Red Cross, found her a place to live with a French family who could help to care for the baby, obtained services of a doctor, and, in general, had become a big sister to the girl much in need of help. The Army would bring the alleged father back for a wedding if the prospective mother would make an affidavit that the man named was the father.

The girl said she loved the American and if he didn't choose to return voluntarily, she would sign no paper. No paper was signed.

Ike Bucks for Colonel

ALGIERS, THURSDAY, AUGUST 12, 1943

Ike went to the dispensary Tuesday, August 10, to take a physical examination for promotion in the regular Army to the rank of colonel. The doctors insisted he go to bed for a rest. This he has been trying to do, but succeeds in fits and starts.

On the military front the Seventh and Eighth Armies are slogging along in Sicily, finding progress slow. It is a tedious race for Messina. The roads and bridges are demolished by the slowly retreating enemy. Mines are everywhere. Truscott's 3rd Division has made successful amphibious landings behind the enemy's lines on the north coast, the first one resulting in 1500 prisoners, 300 of which were German. We haven't the details on the second yet, but were told it was successful. This morning General Patton sent a personal radio to Ike saying that Colonel H. A. "Paddy" Flint's 39th was entering Randazzo, key traffic center of the Mt. Etna area. It has been a prize to which our eyes have been fixed.

Admiral Cunningham has advocated to Ike a bold landing at Rome, which is relatively lightly defended. This would have effective psychological reactions in Italy, but the harbor at Rome is not nearly as useful as that at Naples. Unfortunately, Rome is far beyond the effective range of our nimblest fighters—the Spitfires. Flying from our closest airfields on Sicily, they can go only as far as Salerno, where the landings are to be made to take Naples, give air cover for only twenty minutes, and then must return to Sicily to refuel. Without air cover any landing would be a juicy target for the Jerry.

From a cable from General Marshall this morning to Ike it now appears that we will go as far as we can in Italy, give up the seven U. S. divisions beginning November 1, and be prepared for an invasion of southern France as a diversionary move when the twenty-nine divisions move into northern France from the U. K. next spring. This means we will probably spend our fall and winter in Italy.

What had appeared to be a quick collapse of Italy has disappeared into uncertainty, with the definite knowledge that the Italians are solidifying their opposition to us and are really fighting. Around headquarters, we are inclined to attribute this to the hard-boiled attitude of the Prime Minister and the President, who publicly insisted upon "unconditional surrender" as soon as Mussolini was out. No surrender ever was made without some conditions; the main need is to have the Italians realize, admit, and act as if they've been defeated.

Ike's message offering an honorable peace was well received at home and may still have some effect with the Italian people, whose pressure on Badoglio and the King may be overwhelming, but the extent of this we were unable to determine. It appears that the Germans are rushing reassignments to Italy and that we will have very tough fighting.

When General McClure returned from visiting the 15th Army Group, where he sought to bring order out of chaos on the handling of communiqués, he called me to say that, contrary to General Alexander's impression, the Prime Minister had received, by direct radio message from General Montgomery, the information that Troina had been captured. Apparently the Prime is too impatient to wait on even the Army Group Commander for inside information, and Montgomery is pressed to supply the PM with news. This item was not fulfilled until four days after the PM's public pronouncement. I have told Ike, and he agrees that the system of special reports to the Prime Minister occasionally causes confusion. However, the system indicates the intense interest and zeal of the Prime Minister to get on with the war.

BBC: Fumtu

ALGIERS, SATURDAY, AUGUST 14, 1943

Ike is still in bed, as much as his nervous temperament will permit. He is getting a good rest and is rapidly responding to it. I had to tell him yesterday morning in his bedroom while we were having our coffee—after he had hopped in and out of bed, pranced around the room, and lectured me vigorously on what history would call "his mistake"—that, after all, he was only talking to me, that I didn't have to be sold, and that he would profit by slipping out of high gear back to intermediate and expounding more leisurely. But he has only one speed and that is superhigh.

He mentioned two "mistakes"—the landing at Casablanca and our supercautious approach to Italy. On the latter Ike now thinks we should have made simultaneous landings on both sides of the Messina Strait, thus cutting off all Sicily and obtaining wholesale surrender and saving time and equipment, particularly landing craft, which would have permitted a rapid rush on the mainland itself. The trouble with Ike trying to rest is that he has no harness for his brain cells; they keep poring over problems both real and imaginary as ants swarm over an anthill.

News from the battle front continues impressively favorable, particularly from the American side, although Monty and his Eighth Army have got as far as Mascali, north of Catania, about two thirds of the distance of the coast road along Mt. Etna. On the American side the second "end run" worked very well. The big effect of the end run is to deprive the German of sufficient time to lay his customary mine fields and to demolish bridges. Patton's cryptic announcement that Paddy Flint had reached Randazzo didn't come true until 9 A.M. yesterday, but the Americans were first in the town and are pressing onward toward Francavilla. In the central area between Mt. Etna and the north coast, Patton's Seventh Army has nearly reached Montalbano and reconnaissance elements are in Patti on the north coast. So at this moment we are practically surrounding Mt. Etna.

As of August 13 the Seventh Army had taken 96,000 prisoners and had inflicted on the enemy 10,650 dead and wounded. Our losses are estimated as: killed—1135; wounded—4250; missing—1000; total—6385.

Patton's great progress gives Ike a warm glow, as there are many Army officers who could not see through Patton's showmanship and boisterousness to discern his fine qualities of leadership, on which Ike banked so strongly. In addition, the success of the Seventh Army lets Americans hold their heads high amongst the British and other Allies who may have been a bit skeptical after the Kasserine affair.

One of the hardest things to rationalize or harmonize with troops of two nationalities is that circumstances require them to be fighting under the coverage of one principal source of broadcasts, the BBC, which, naturally, emphasizes British news. To the GI as well as to the officers in the Seventh Army in Sicily, the BBC seems always to be emphasizing the accomplishment of the British Eighth Army. Yet the British themselves are frequently critical of BBC. I recall that General Montgomery threatened to postpone his attack on the Mareth line because he claimed the BBC disclosed prematurely that he would use his "famous left hook." I have heard RAF officers claim that inadequate credit is given to the

British fliers. The officers of the Royal Navy occasionally grumble quietly; they truly are the "silent service."

No service or nationality ever seems to be quite satisfied with the credit given it by the BBC. It seems to be radio's sad lot in life never to be thought fair, try as hard as it does. To an American lad who has piloted a B-25 from Tunisia to some target in Italy, to the crew of a B-17 which, with seventy or eighty other planes, makes a long flight to bomb aircraft factories near Vienna, fighting off enemy fighters and flying through intense flak, the omission of their exploits by BBC is almost unforgivable, particularly if some minor RAF activity gets mentioned. The crew may not realize that news of their operation had not yet been released when they listened to the radio.

It is perfectly natural for the American press and radio to play up the news of American battle action; likewise natural and to be expected that the British press and radio play up news of British nationals.

Since news of combat in this theater is heard almost exclusively from the BBC, and we get practically no quick news from other sources, a first-rate problem is created. If it is not corrected, Ike's efforts to instill Allied unity from top to bottom are stymied. He has struggled to obtain complete unification; it became the theme of the integrated team which he created at Norfolk House and it has been the guiding precept of his operations in the Mediterranean. He carries the idea into all of his press conferences, communiqués, and into every contact with the people. He regards unity as important, not only from the standpoint of our particular military operations, but from that of providing the spirit of comrades-in-arms among our fighting men in Europe, which is absolutely essential if we are to develop full-out enthusiasm for the policy of licking Germany first.

The recent broadcast by the BBC was reported by officers of the American Seventh Army as saying that the Seventh was lucky to be in the undefended western part of Sicily, eating grapes. Information from our Intelligence sources shows that during the early stages of the Sicilian invasion, the Americans faced at least two thirds of the German strength on the island; that the only serious counterthrust made by the Germans was directly at the Seventh Army, and that all or practically all of the German tanks were employed in the Seventh Army area. In spite of all of this, by both communiqués and press conferences, Ike has been most careful to preserve a balance of presentation that would do full credit to everybody. Yet the statement alleged to have been made by BBC has very much annoyed the Seventh Army. The American soldier finds difficulty in differentiating between the BBC, which is well known to be operating under government charter, and the British government itself. The British troops in the field likewise have perpetual mads on the BBC. So far as I can see, it's fumtu.*

Ike has occasionally discussed this problem with General Alexander, Admiral Cunningham, and Air Chief Marshal Tedder, and they have always seen eye to eye with him. Ike is appealing to the Prime Minister to use the influence of his high office to make clear to the BBC the effect of one-sided broadcasting and has suggested that, in the interest of accuracy and unity, scripts for newscasting should be scrutinized in advance by some qualified representative of the British Chiefs of Staff, which he feels is imbued with the same ideas concerning unification as he. He is not seeking aggrandizement or overplay of America's part, simply balanced reporting in the interests of winning the war.

Yesterday we bombed Rome for the second time, and of course the BBC gave the operation liberal credit as American. What the repercussions will be from home we don't know. From England and from the Middle East we hit Milan, Turin, Genoa, and Berlin on the same day. The Italians must know we aren't joking.

The operation JUGGLER, the bombing of fighter factories near Vienna, is scheduled for today or tomorrow. It will be another raid like that on Ploesti—expensive in craft and personnel, but a good investment if targets are hit a wallop. This mission is a result of intelligence which indicates the Germans are building relatively few bombers and many more fighters.

Ike is concerned about the heavy losses of Flying Fortresses in daytime raids on German factories. Of 181 sent from England to bomb a synthetic-gasoline plant in Germany, twenty-five were lost. We are already suffering a shortage of crews. He anticipates that we may reach a point of destitution amongst the operational crews, who must know that their chances of coming through are slim. They are promised relief to go home after twenty-five missions, but with nearly eleven per cent of losses, no flier can look forward with any satisfaction to the likelihood of his actually getting home. Ike wondering if our bombing policy in England may have to be changed to follow that of the British, i.e., night bombing of areas, forsaking the accuracy of daytime operation.

Complete Victory in Sicily

ALGIERS, TUESDAY, AUGUST 17, 1943

Truscott's 3rd Division entered Messina at 8 o'clock last night. Yesterday at the meeting of the Commanders-in-Chief at La Marsa, one of the

* Fouled up more than usual.

British officers—Brigadier Sugden—said he knew jolly well that Patton, after driving his Seventh Army all over Sicily, would be the first into Messina and, he said, "He's got the Eighth Army bloody well surrounded." Sugden was right.

Ike received orders from the Combined Chiefs to lay off bombing of Rome, pending settlement of the question of its becoming declared an "open city."

Mr. Macmillan, the British Minister, is back from his visit in London, but missed the PM, who had already gone to Canada. His brother ministers of the Cabinet, particularly Sir Stafford Cripps, felt AMGOT could do more for democracy if it immediately held free and open elections in the territory we occupy in Sicily. According to Bob Murphy, Macmillan felt dejected. The British public, he reported, seems rather tired of the war but, oddly, is insistent on "unconditional surrender." The two simply do not fit. We can shorten the war by giving Italy honorable terms, not to mention the lives that would be saved.

Decisions were reached at Ike's Commanders-in-Chief meeting to go across the Messina Strait early in September as soon as landing craft and guns can be assembled and for the attack for Naples to be made September 9.

Naval and air headquarters are to be re-established in Algiers, which will aid co-ordination. Our headquarters presumably will stay here until we move to the Italian mainland, probably Naples.

Ike has been to the dispensary today for another checkup. Such rest as he has been able to get has helped considerably.

I have received the official certificate making me *Le Quatrième Rang Officier de l'Ordre du Ouissam Alaouite Chérifien* from the Sultan of Morocco. The certificate makes me a commandant in the order, generally referred to by Patton as that of "Lion Tamers." I thus am a junior lion tamer.

This forenoon T. J.—General T. J. Davis, the AG—phoned me to get on the interoffice phone so he could talk confidentially. When I did, he said that Brigadier General Fred Blesse, the Surgeon General, had received a report from one of his medical officers in Sicily which was most alarming and implicated General Patton. T. J. thought General Ike should see Blesse as soon as possible, to get the full story, rather than to have it go through lower levels and create a great deal of talk. Blesse came in around noon and showed Ike the report, the gist of which was that Patton had visited evacuation hospitals and had routed out certain patients by the "scruff of the neck," presumably suspicious they were laggards. Whatever the cause, Ike said afterward he would have to give Patton a jacking up. I added my nickel's worth that regardless of method, Patton had done a swell job. Ike added that the medical report showed that many American soldiers had marched over the rough terrain until they had literally worn the skin off their feet.

The fighter factories near Vienna were successfully bombed on the fifteenth. But only sixty-one of the Liberators of the Middle East actually found the targets. However, they claimed to have destroyed some 400 fighters on the ground as well as hit the factory.

Victory in Sicily and Peace Feeler from Italy

ALGIERS, WEDNESDAY, AUGUST 18, 1943
I had dictated my piece for August 17 before lunch, but the big news broke later in the day. It was about a peace feeler from Italy which seems bona fide and indicates that Italy not only will get out of the war, but will fight on our side. A General Castellano had arrived at Madrid, traveling in plain clothes. He had a false passport under the name of Raimond Imas and ostensibly was a member of an Italian mission en route to Lisbon to meet the Italian Ambassador to Chile returning from his post. This ruse was necessary, he had told the British Ambassador at Madrid, because if the Germans heard of his real mission, he would be summarily shot when he returned to Italy. He would have to return starting August 20 because that is the date on which the Italian Ambassador from Chile is due to land at Lisbon.

General Castellano brought a letter of introduction from the British Minister to the Holy See. He said that he came officially from Marshal Badoglio with full authority to make a specific and very urgent proposal. Italy, he said, is in a terrible position; peace is desired by practically everyone in the country; the Italian Army is badly armed; Italian aviation is practically nonexistent, and German troops are streaming into Italy through the Brenner Pass and by way of the Riviera. The Italian feeling against the Germans, he said, is intense. Badoglio's government, carefully watched by the Germans, felt powerless to act until supported by strong Allied landings on the mainland. When this happened, Italy was prepared to fight the Germans. Badoglio regarded every hour as important because of the constant arrival of more German units. There were thirteen divisions already there. The German plan was to hold the line over the Apennines and Ravenna.

Ike immediately called Brigadier Strong, the G-2, and the British Minister, Mr. Macmillan. Ike then sent a message to the War Department to be retransmitted to the Combined Chiefs of Staff at Quebec. Ike informed the Combined Chiefs he is prepared to send one or more staff officers to deal directly with General Castellano at Lisbon and proposed general instructions to the effect that as much information as possible be obtained; that the Allies make no promises in advance, but if the Italian Army is really anxious to speed up the Allied landings in Italy, it immediately should engage in widespread sabotage, particularly against means of transportation, airfields, and any public utilities useful to the Germans. The Italian government would have no recourse but to rely on the decency and sense of justice of the Allied governments once they have signed the terms of the unconditional surrender.

This morning Ike received from the Combined Chiefs of Staff, on approval of the President and the Prime Minister, instructions to send immediately two staff officers to meet with General Castellano now at Lisbon and prescribed quite precisely the terms that should be discussed. Unconditional surrender still is insisted upon, but some modification seems intended. One American and one British officer should go to Lisbon to deal with Castellano and should present him the Allies' terms already drafted. The two emissaries should present to Castellano the terms of the statement of the unconditional surrender which Italy must accept, but these do not visualize the active assistance of Italy in fighting the Germans. The extent to which such participation will be permitted depends on how far the Italian government and people aid the United Nations against Germany during the remainder of the war. Upon behalf of the United Nations, it is stated, however, that wherever Italians fight Germans, destroy German property, or hamper German movements, they will be given all possible support. Allied bombing will be directed upon targets which affect the movements and operations of German forces. General Eisenhower is to fix the date and hour of cessation of hostilities and the Italians must undertake to proclaim the armistice when it is announced by the Allied Commander. All Allied prisoners in danger of capture by the Germans must be released. The Italian fleet, and merchant shipping, must put to sea for Allied ports. Italian aircraft shall fly to Allied bases; any ships or aircraft likely to fall to the Germans must be destroyed. It is suggested that Badoglio, despite the watchful Germans, can do much to hinder Germans, prior to announcement of the armistice, without open resistance. A secure channel of communications between Badoglio's headquarters and General Eisenhower's should be provided.

Ike is sending Brigadier Strong and General Smith as quickly as Beetle can return from Sicily. He was recalled last night and is due around noon.

He and Strong immediately will be flown to Gibraltar, where arrangements are to be made for a civilian plane to take them in plain clothes to Lisbon for the ultra-secret meeting.

As usual, history is being made, perhaps at a faster tempo than normal. But we have become so accustomed to the unfolding of history on the spot that we are no longer surprised at anything that happens.

Patton in Trouble

ALGIERS, FRIDAY, AUGUST 20, 1943

Admiral Cunningham is re-establishing his naval headquarters at AFHQ and Air Marshal Tedder likewise will move back to the home base. This brings sea, air, and the high command together again, leaving only those ground forces under Alexander at a distant point.

Demarce Bess, of *Satevepost*, came to see me yesterday, carrying a detailed statement of complaint against General Patton's obviously abrupt treatment of a soldier in the 93rd Evacuation Hospital. Bess includes in his report a statement that "if I am correctly informed, General Patton has subjected himself to general court-martial by striking an enlisted man under his command." While Ike had already taken action by sending the Surgeon General, General Blesse, to Sicily to investigate and had written a burning letter to General Patton, the matter is far from being closed. Bess had said that he and his associates who had investigated the case had refrained from writing stories, but it is impossible long to keep such a colorful scene out of the press. Quent Reynolds likewise is back from Sicily and has asserted that there are at least 50,000 American soldiers who would shoot Patton if they had the slightest chance. Charlie Daly, of CBS, had previously given me a detailed report. He thought that Patton had gone temporarily crazy. Ike is in position of having to deal severely with a general who had commanded an army in one of our country's most successful operations and who is the best ground gainer developed so far by the Allies. Just one of the many worries which plague the Allied Commander-in-Chief.

Yesterday Ike stewed because the Combined Chiefs had ordered that the three groups of American bombers sent here to bomb the Ploesti oil fields and the Vienna fighter factories return to England. Ike feels most strongly that because of the higher percentage of good weather for bombing activities in the Mediterranean and because we need the groups here to help take Italy, the Combined Chiefs of Staff have made an unwise decision. He is combating it. General Spaatz said that weather in the

Mediterranean permits more bombing operations in one month than are permitted by the bad flying weather in the U. K. in three months.

Flip-Flop

Beetle and General Strong returned from Lisbon last evening. Beetle immediately reported to Ike at the farm. The scene was reminiscent of the time at Telegraph Cottage when General Mark Clark returned from his secret mission to North Africa, except that Beetle had not lost his pants.

The terms of "unconditional surrender" were presented to General Castellano, who is the chief planner on the Italian General Staff. Beetle had spent all of Thursday night answering questions of Castellano, which were not necessarily in opposition to the terms, but for clarification. The main difference seems to be that the Italian General Staff wants to execute a complete flip-flop and join the Allies to fight the Germans. To this Beetle was not authorized to agree, but he thinks the Italians will insist on collaboration with us. Decision on this point must be given by the President and the Prime Minister, as it affects Italy's position at the peace table, but in my book we should accept them not only as collaborators but as Allies if they will fight the Germans.

Castellano reflected an intense hatred for the Germans. He drew out on a map for Beetle the location of Italian and German divisions in Italy, so the Germans may receive the brunt of our bombing. A radio channel between the Italian General Staff and AFHQ also was arranged, Castellano being given a small transmitter and appropriate cipher. Unfortunately, the ship bringing the Italian Ambassador from Chile was delayed and consequently the delegation of which Castellano is a member as front will not be ready to return to Italy until August 28. A further meeting is in prospect, probably in Sicily, August 31. In the meantime, according to our Intelligence, which Beetle said was substantiated by Castellano's information, there are now fifteen German divisions in Italy and reinforcements continue to flow.

Next Castellano told Beetle how the overthrow of Mussolini was accomplished. Four generals, including Badoglio and Ambrosio, the Chief of Staff, had concluded that Mussolini was a liability, yet they had to gain the support of the ardent Fascist members of the Council in order to get enough votes to throw Mussolini to the dogs.

Grandi, second in Fascist command under Mussolini, was led to believe that when Mussolini was voted out, his mantle would automatically fall on Grandi's shoulders. But after Mussolini was booted, Grandi was the victim of a neat double-cross. The King had been brought into the picture and appointed Badoglio to his present controlling office while Grandi and his brother Fascists were out in the cold. The Fascist party was ordered dissolved. Beetle asked Castellano if he could tell him where Mussolini is at present. The answer was, "Hitler would like to know, too."

Throughout the discussions at Lisbon, Castellano and the other Italians talked loud and long about the "honor" of Italy, yet, as they talked of honor, they unashamedly described how they had given Grandi the double-cross and, more important, aspired to make a complete flip-flop from partners in the Axis to allies in the United Nations.

As to treatment of Italians under the terms headed "unconditional surrender," Beetle had cited the humaneness of our military government in Sicily. Castellano is a Sicilian and he had already heard of the friendship of Sicilians for the Allies as well as the decency of our treatment of them.

I asked Beetle why Badoglio had chosen this method of approach to the Allies, as I had been convinced the Vatican would be the mediator. He answered that because there are so many nationalities represented at the Vatican, leaks are inevitable and, as the Italians fear reprisals by the Germans, they simply could not afford to take the risk.

Castellano wanted to know our military plans with respect to Italy. Beetle had simply answered that we will attack on the mainland, but did not disclose places or dates. Beetle did not doubt that Castellano was the bona fide representative of Badoglio's government.

On the question of Portugal entering the war, Beetle said that the British Ambassador had told him that arrangements had been concluded the day before for this entry in October. The Portuguese insist on adequate fighter and antiaircraft protection before they make the leap and this protection is being supplied. It is anticipated that the Germans will heavily bomb Lisbon because of the importance of the harbor when and if Portugal publicly joins the Allies.

As the Portuguese visa officer at Gibraltar didn't have power to authorize the visa for Beetle's American passport, he was issued, along with Brigadier Strong, a British passport. He went to Portugal in plain clothes as Mr. Walter Smith and stated that he was born in London at 20 Grosvenor Square—the address of our old headquarters. Strong, of course, gave his own address correctly but also dropped his military title.

Had a drink last night with Quent Reynolds and Knickerbocker, both of whom have just returned from Sicily. I heard again the complaint against General Patton. All the press, while not printing the story, are incensed. Ike has already sent Patton the sternest letter reprimand he had ever written an officer and the matter still is not closed. He has demanded that Patton apologize to the "victims." He has sent his special assistant, General Lucas, to look further into the matter and, as he said last night, might have to send Patton home in disgrace. Yet, on Patton's side, he has pushed the Seventh Army by great marches, perhaps unparalleled in history, to the triumphant entry into Messina, completing his part in a campaign which will be a model for study in military schools for decades.

To me Ike cited history to show that great military leaders had practically gone crazy on the battlefield in their zeal to win the fight. Patton is like this. He said that the press probably is construing the normal grousing of the soldiers as the real thing, whereas the truth is that soldiers love and respect a successful leader. Nothing breeds confidence like success, Ike said. Yet despite the good work of Patton, Ike is deeply concerned and has scarcely slept for several nights, trying to figure out the wisest method of handling this dilemma. The United Nations have not developed another battle leader as successful as Patton, Ike thinks. Now, because of Patton's almost unforgivable displays of temperament, should he be tried by court-martial? An officer striking a soldier is a high offense. We haven't sufficient rank in this theater to try a lieutenant general; he would have to be reduced to his permanent rank to be tried here or be sent home for trial.

Incidentally, Quent and Nick ascribed the success of the Seventh Army to the extraordinarily capable division commanders and to General Bradley.

After I had gone to bed last night Ike sat in my room for half an hour, debating the question, not so much with me as with himself. He's sweating it out.

ALGIERS, WEDNESDAY, AUGUST 25, 1943

The Commanders-in-Chief meeting was held at AFHQ, Monday, August 23. It was decided that our headquarters temporarily would be located in Tunisia for the attack on Naples.

The staffs of Admiral Cunningham and General Alexander—and even the two estimable commanders—have been differing, and Ike is being the referee. While the Navy is charged with the responsibility for troops until they are landed on the hostile shore, the Army is interested to know details of just how the Navy plans to accomplish its mission. The Army

commander has a fearful responsibility for the safety of his ground troops
and feels he and his staff are justified in scanning and possibly criticizing
the Navy's plans. The Admiral has always conducted his amphibious landings with skill and bravery and has unfailingly co-operated with AFHQ.
In fact, he has been the model.

We had Generals Alexander and Montgomery, as well as Brigadier
Lemnitzer, who is serving in the 15th Army Group's Plans Section, and
Major General T. W. Richardson, Alexander's Chief of Staff, for lunch
on Monday. Both Alex and Monty said that the Germans are getting
ahead of us on tank design, particularly gun power. Montgomery said that
our tank designers apparently build a tank and then stick a gun in it
rather than design a gun and build a tank around it. He claims we are
outshot by the German tanks. I gathered he did not know of the new
Sherman of which General Marshall spoke so glowingly last spring. I
assume we are to get these new ones.

After lunch, Monty asked Ike to sign his short-snorter bill.

General Bradley came for dinner direct from Sicily. I mixed a couple
of bourbon Old-Fashioneds for him as partial payment for a grand job.
In discussing the campaign, he was matter-of-fact, as usual. He is a man in
whom all, especially Ike, have great confidence. Called Ike's attention to
our worn-out artillery, particularly the Long Toms (155-mm. rifles), and
Ike was flabbergasted that no one had called his attention to this before.
Next morning, Ike called Bradley in his office and went after the ordnance
problem full tilt. Guns have worn out their linings and have to be
relined. Some Long Toms had their insides worn so badly that shells had
exploded just after passing out of the muzzle.

General Alexander's pilot of his C-47 plane, Captain White, phoned
his aide, Major Lloyd Ramsey, who also stopped at our house, to say
that the 500-hour inspection under way at Maison Blanche had disclosed
that the wings were about to fall off. General Alexander had been reluctant
to mention that his plane was not in good condition, so I brought up the
subject with Ike, who immediately ordered me to get Alexander a more
satisfactory plane. Ike didn't want any commanders riding in a fragile
one. This one was called "Patches," as it had been bombed on the
ground twice before Alexander got it and had 400 patches on it.

The meeting of the Combined Chiefs of Staff at Quebec, known as
QUADRANT, has concluded, according to public announcement of the
President and the Prime Minister, in which aid to China and prosecution of the war against Japan were declared to have been thoroughly
canvassed. Over-all decisions for prosecution of the war were not announced but were left for the enemy to discover "on the battle front."

It was broadly hinted that offensives in several war sectors would be launched.

With respect to our operations in the Mediterranean, the zeal with which the Prime Minister, while in Algiers, pressed for exploitation to get Italy out of the war seems to be damped. We asked for retention of the three groups of B-24 bombers which were loaned by the 8th Air Force in England to Africa for operations against the Ploesti oil fields and Vienna fighter factories. This was rejected, with the explanation of General Arnold that the Allies are in an "all-out" air war with Germany from England and that the three bomber groups are considered vital. Yet the use of these bombers in our attack on Italy, particularly against enemy airfields, would have been a tremendous help, not only for our attack on the toe of Italy, but at Naples. On the final message of rejection of his pleas, strongly requested by Tedder and Spaatz, Ike merely wrote "licked."

Then there were ten American landing craft—LSTs—which were passing through the Mediterranean to India. If we could use them for our Italian attacks until September 30 and send them on their way, our margin of safety for the operation would be greatly increased. This request likewise was rejected.

In addition, the Combined Chiefs of Staff reaffirmed their decision to withdraw seven divisions—four American and three British—from this theater starting November 1.

Ike has felt that his bosses have already discounted an Italian victory and, consequently, are stripping his fighting force prematurely and not taking sufficient notice of the rapid build-up of German forces in Italy, which has now reached some fifteen divisions. It is becoming increasingly apparent that the Germans intend to defend their European Citadel as far from Germany as possible and will make Italy a battleground whether the Italians co-operate with them or not.

The Vatican complained bitterly over the second bombing of Rome, claiming another church had been hit. Speaking repeatedly of the Eternal City, the secretary of the Vatican had reported to the American diplomatic representative, Ambassador Harold S. Tittman, that the Holy See had prevailed on the Italians not to bomb Cairo or Athens, yet we had unhesitatingly socked Rome as well as other Italian cities where Catholic churches were being demolished. Significantly, I thought, the Catholic hierarchy emphasized that Italian anger is being aroused by our bombings, particularly of Rome.

Ike is staying at the farm today, as the doctor told him he should rest at least one day this week. He has been hobbling around the office with a bedroom slipper on one foot because he wore an angry blister on the big joint of his big toe while walking without socks.

ALGIERS, FRIDAY, AUGUST 27, 1943

The limited recognition of the French National Committee for Liberation was tendered yesterday with misgivings as to its acceptance, but lo and behold, the French received it with enthusiasm and gratification.

Photographic reconnaissance and other intelligence indicate that the Germans and Italians are withdrawing from the toe in the area where General Montgomery's corps is to attack. Numerous coast-artillery guns have been taken away and others destroyed, judging from the aerial photographs. This would make Montgomery's task appear a pushover, with the prospect of rather quickly getting as far north as the instep on a line east from Corigliano. It appears that the Germans are fearful of being trapped by an Allied landing higher up on the boot. This is just what is hoped will be accomplished by AVALANCHE, the attack at Salerno to take Naples and to cut off or force withdrawal of Germans between Naples and the foot of Italy. But it is a pity that we didn't have the landing craft ready to move the Fifth Army on Naples just as the battle of Sicily was ending. Then, too, we had to let the Air Force build up its striking power from Sicilian bases.

Last night we had our first air raid in Algiers in a couple of months. Some thirty or forty Ju-88s came over and dropped flares but only ten bombs. Most of this was to civilian property and personnel. Flares were dropped near the farm where we stayed for the night, and the enemy planes seemed either to come in or go out of Algiers over the farm, diving as they escaped or entered the flak area. One dropped his stick of three 500-pounders about a mile away, breaking some glass about the place. I was on the front porch, watching the show. Had a grandstand view.

AUGUST, 1943: *Allied fleet shelled Italian ports; planes crumbled objectives in Naples. After Patton's forces took Messina, fighting ended in Sicily with Axis casualties of 167,000 against 25,000 Allied; greater part of Nazi forces had already escaped to Italian mainland. ("He's got the Eighth Army surrounded."—H.C.B.) Sicily-based bombers hit Italian targets with special attention to railheads and ports. Tremendous air raids against German cities continued; Nazis forced to order civilian evacuation of Berlin. Rome bombed again. Churchill and Roosevelt, conferring in Quebec, granted limited recognition to de Gaulle. Russia's armies reached the Sea of Azov, with advances on all other fronts. Lord Louis Mountbatten named Supreme Allied Commander in Southeast Asia. Land fighting in New Georgia and the Solomons marked by Allied advances and heavy Jap losses. Britain warned Spain to adopt neutral attitude. Germany declared state of siege in Denmark as Danish Navy blew up ammunition dumps, scuttled ships unable to flee to Sweden. One of great surprises of war developed as formidable U. S.-Canadian task forces landed on Kiska to engage the little men who were not there; they had been evacuated by submarine: the first Jap failure to resist reconquest of American territory.*

Plans for AVALANCHE

ALGIERS, THURSDAY, SEPTEMBER 2, 1943

Beetle is still in Sicily negotiating for peace with emissaries of the Italian government—a peace which will make Italy a battleground. The Italians present a pathetic picture. They are negotiating for peace with a rope around their neck. Ike said yesterday they are simply frightened to death because the Germans, undoubtedly, will wreak a fearful vengeance. However, they seem intent upon concluding a peace provided we can get our troops and other support to Italy promptly. Last night Ike heard from Beetle that a message had been received via secret radio from Rome that the terms had been accepted. This message is being rechecked to make certain it isn't a phony or a plant. If the acceptance is bona fide, the announcement of the armistice following unconditional surrender is to be made twenty-four to forty-eight hours prior to our landing in Salerno Bay. This will be the signal for all Italian services to turn against the Germans, to seize and protect airdromes, to menace and, if possible, stop movement of German troops, and for the Italian fleet and probably other vessels to seek safety in ports which we control.

D-Day for the Salerno landing is September 9, with American paratroopers and gliders landing north of Naples starting at 9:30 P.M. and the landings of the Fifth Army at Salerno Bay to start at 3:30 A.M. on the ninth. As was true in the North African landings, we are confronted with the uncertainty of the effectiveness and extent of help from the nationals of the invaded country. While there are indications that the shore batteries of Salerno Bay normally are manned by Italians, the Germans may smell the trick and take them over. If so, we are in for a hot time. The landing is at the extreme limit of air protection, which will be provided from Sicily and from aircraft carriers. On D-Day there will be a thousand sorties to form an air umbrella over the landing area. For Spitfires based on Sicily, two and a half hours of flight will be required to afford about twenty-five minutes of protection over the battle area.

Sunday, August 29, Ike and I took off from Maison Blanche at 6:40, landing at Casabile, in Sicily, where we changed to a C-47 with four escorting Spitfires and continued to Catania. Here General Montgomery, accompanied by photographers, met Ike.

After lunch, Monty's photographers were on the job. Monty took Ike in an open car and I followed in a jeep with Monty's aide, Captain "Johnny" Henderson, up the tortuous coastal road to Messina—a drive of nearly two hours. The Italians greeted Monty and General Ike, whom, of course, they did not know, with V signs and expressions of good cheer. At Messina, Ike and Monty stood at the water's edge and carefully surveyed the Italian mainland only two miles away. Here the strait is like the Mississippi River. Our guns were shelling enemy batteries with noisy irregularity, but as the sun was then in the eyes of the enemy and as they apparently did not wish to risk discovery of their locations by opening fire, there was no return fire, although we heard a machine gun. The day before, our road had been strafed by twelve Messerschmitts, but we didn't even see an enemy plane.

Monty had a family dinner—only Ike, his two aides—the other is Captain John Poston—and I. Monty showed he had the soul of a host and although he neither drinks nor smokes, he freely offered those inevitable tokens of hospitality. He enjoyed joshing his two aides as to their escapades at Claridge's at the conclusion of the Tunisian campaign. Seeing Monty at close range, I found I liked him.

Monday morning we were driven at hell-bent-for-election rate through heavy traffic and over numerous "diversions"—the British word for detour —on the coastal road to Catania. I got the impression that the Eighth Army driver and his motorcycle escort wished to impress the General with their mobility. Ike didn't seem to mind, but at least I was impressed.

We were met at Catania by Major "Feller" Ramsey, General Alexander's American aide, with Alexander's C-47.

Ike had his meeting of the Commanders-in-Chief at General Alexander's camp in a black tent pitched near a burned-out Italian truck. The camp is in an olive grove—hot, dusty, and swarming with flies.

While Alexander wanted Ike to stay for lunch, Ike preferred to hurry home. We had rations in the Fortress and reached Maison Blanche about 5:30. Ike immediately went to the office, where he cleaned up accumulated messages.

On Tuesday, August 30, we flew to Nouvion airfield, about an hour's drive south of Mostaganem, where General Wayne Clark met Ike. We were taken to his headquarters for an exposition on the AVALANCHE—

Salerno Bay landings—plan. Air Chief Marshal Tedder went with us. The Air Chief Marshal and I had what was to me a very enjoyable visit. He has a fine sense of humor and also must be an expert judge of men, for he finally said: "Butch, if General Ike ever gives you up as his aide, I just want you to know that I don't want you either."

As to the plan for AVALANCHE, the main thrust on Naples is assigned the X Corps, consisting of the 36th and 46th British Divisions. They are to be landed north of the Foca River in the Salerno Bay. Their objective is to break through the deep defiles or passes that lie between their landing beach and Naples, to get on the plain approaching Naples. The Americans will be on their right, landing on the south side of the Foca River. This will be the 36th Division of the VI Corps, which has the 34th Division in reserve. Its job will be to protect the right flank of the X Corps. As a diversion, the paratroopers and glider troops of the 82nd Airborne Division, it is planned, will be landed north of Naples. Every effort is to be made to capture airdromes and to get them working as quickly as possible. It is hoped that within two or three days we will have four or five airdromes working.

The U. S. Navy carries the load in operation AVALANCHE. There are only three British landing craft and British troops are being transported in American LSTs. Another diversion—this one entirely by the Navy—will be a noise-making operation north of Naples, but will include the capture of some islands, including the isle of Capri, on which we will quickly install radar stations.

From the air point of view, this is the most difficult operation we have given them. Air Chief Marshal Tedder, in an appropriately worded talk, emphasized that AVALANCHE has been under way for ten days or a fortnight. Our bombers have been wrecking Italy's communications system and incessantly pounding military objectives.

On Saturday evening, August 28, Beetle had come to the house to tell Ike in detail of the conversations that already had taken place with a General Zanessa, who had arrived from Italy by way of Spain and Gibraltar, apparently oblivious of the previous approach of General Castellano. Was General Z an emissary of another faction in Italy—perhaps one playing with Germany? Was he seeking to discover for the Nazis the extent and scope of our negotiations? Beetle was having General Z (later referred to in cables as Zebra) for dinner at his villa. Ike instructed Beetle not to disclose that other negotiations were in progress or that an answer was expected by the thirty-first from General Castellano. He should pump General Z and keep him under friendly surveillance until we could make certain by checking via secret radio to Rome whether the emissary is bona fide. We should show no weakness and disclose no desire to hurry the negotiations.

Apparently the question of bona fide was cleared while we were away Sunday and Monday, for Beetle had gone to Sicily to meet the emissaries, who had found ways of flying from Italy to Sicily.

Then last night we got the news that Badoglio had said "yes" to unconditional surrender. We cannot help but have some sympathy with the terrible dilemma in which Italy finds herself.

Ed Kennedy, the local bureau chief for the Associated Press, has just returned from America, where he found the newspapers more concerned about the build-ups of various American generals by the home press and radio. They regarded such build-ups with some misgivings, Kennedy indicated, because of the possibility of some one of them capturing public opinion and becoming a presidential candidate. He felt that news about Ike had been appropriate and modest.

Kennedy had heard from numerous persons, at Marrakech, where he changed planes, a variety of disconcerting stories about General Patton. He was fearful that the stories would appear at home and that the war correspondents assigned to this theater would be regarded as guilty of whitewashing General Patton or of being subjected to rigid censorship that prevented their writing the truth. I found Ike wasn't too busy to see Ed, so the three of us sat and discussed the question at length, Ike having felt that his action of ordering Patton to apologize had been satisfactory, but he was amazed to learn how the stories are snowballing toward home. Kennedy expressed himself as thoroughly satisfied with the action Ike had taken. Ike considered having Patton hold a press conference at which he would state, on the record, what had happened and how he had apologized.

Subsequently Quent Reynolds, Clark Lee, and Red Mueller came to see me, and as the door to Ike's office was open and he had a temporary lull, he had them in and covered the same ground. They all felt that Ike had handled the matter very satisfactorily. He did not ask any of them not to write the story. All seemed to feel, as he did, that Patton's great military record made him so valuable that he was worth saving.

I argued that it would be unwise to have Patton hold a press conference at this time. We should wait to see if the stories will dissipate. Oncoming events will build new headlines and occupy the minds of correspondents with other events. Ike felt, however, that he, at least, should have the Inspector General make a thorough canvass of the situation in Sicily to determine if the troops still have any grievances. This would determine the extent to which Patton's efforts to apologize have corrected the impression of his mistreatment of certain individuals under stress of battle.

Ike had asked General Patton to sit in on the conference at Mostaganem so he could add any suggestions from his experience in Sicily. His only suggestion was quickly to seek the co-operation of the leading Italian—the mayor or ex-mayor in any captured town—because he said they were most helpful in many ways.

On the personal side, General Patton is developing into an ardent lobbyist for me, embarrassingly so. Jokingly, he told Admiral Hewitt that if he wanted to get in good with Ike, he should make me a commodore. Then he spoke to Ike to see if I could be given a leave so I could visit Patton in Sicily. As I have no desire either for a leave or, if I had one, to spend it in Sicily, I rejected the suggestion when it was related to me by Ike.

One of the conditions of armistice desired by General Castellano, who is now at our Advance Command Post—Fairfield—with Beetle, is that Allied military support be given the Italians at Rome to protect their capital city and the Vatican from the Germans when and if the armistice is announced. Ike has arranged for a substantial portion of the 82nd Airborne Division to be dropped near Rome, timed with AVALANCHE, and to be facilitated by detailed arrangements in co-operation with the Italian military authorities. This eliminates the drop north of Naples. This plan has been approved in a personal message today by the President and the Prime Minister, who are together at the White House. The paratroops will be dropped provided the Italians meet the conditions Ike has imposed.

Tomorrow morning at 4:30, Montgomery's British and Canadian troops cross the Messina Strait to attack the mainland of Italy, the first invasion of the Citadel of Europe. When we stood at Messina, looking across the water at the mainland, Montgomery had recalled that he had been driven out of Europe at Dunkirk and his re-entry marks a tremendous change in the fortunes of war for Britain and the Allies. The attack comes on the fourth anniversary of the declaration of war.

I neglected to add an important item of news in Ike's life. When we returned from Mostaganem Tuesday, Major Lee brought to the house a message from General Marshall to Beetle in which it was disclosed that the President was announcing today the nomination of Ike as permanent Major General and the award of the Oak Leaf Cluster for his DSM, with an appropriately worded citation. The permanent promotion was a surprise to Ike and he was thoroughly delighted. However, I did not think the award was commensurate with the job done and said so, but obviously those in the regular service regard a permanent appointment to the highest peacetime rank in our Army as a greatly coveted reward.

Monty Stubs the Toe

ALGIERS, FRIDAY, SEPTEMBER 3, 1943

Late yesterday afternoon, Ike had a message from Generals Alexander and Beetle saying that for "operational reasons" it may be necessary for one of them to sign the armistice agreement and "unconditional surrender" with General Castellano, with whom they have been meeting in Sicily. Ike had previously radioed the two that under the terms by which Russia would approve the proposed agreement, only Ike was directly empowered to affix his signature, although he preferred to delegate the responsibility.

Ike was at the farm when the message came, suggesting a deputized signature be permitted. Whiteley read to Ike the gist of the message over the telephone from my office. I immediately sensed the grave importance of Ike signing the document himself, not only for reasons of history, but because it would be expected of the Allied Commander-in-Chief himself. I called him back to volunteer my view that he should by all means be the signer. Then I drove out to the farm and found that he had ordered the Fortress alerted for an early-morning trip to Sicily. He was obviously peeved at me for butting in. Radio communication with the 15th Army Group had been miserable all day, so he decided to fly there on the chance that Castellano still would be awaiting final approval of his government to affix his own signature.

Ike had agreed to review the 1st British Division near Hammamet on Saturday. I had been handling the arrangements for Lieutenant General Allfrey, the V Corps Commander. Ike instructed me to stay behind, arrange for a C-47, and accompany General Allfrey and party because he had offered to carry them in his Fortress and now it will be unavailable. Major Lee was instructed to accompany Ike to the meeting for affixing the signatures to the historic document—a meeting which I greatly regretted having to miss, but Ike said it was a "crooked deal" and that the document would not become public possibly for ten years after the war. Nevertheless, I felt a sly photograph with my Contax would be invaluable. I asked Lee to bootleg one or several on his camera.

Ike feels that the terms of agreement are unduly harsh. He suspects that our home governments want to make a propaganda Roman holiday by publicizing to the entire world the stern restrictions of the surrender—the terms which will be formalized at a later ceremony. Already London and·Washington have sent messages to the United Nations, asking for their concurrence in the terms. This Ike regarded as extraordinarily risky to AVALANCHE, as the news, undoubtedly, will leak from some capital. The negotiations in Sicily may have set the public announcement of the armistice only five hours before the actual launching of AVALANCHE, scheduled for 3:30 A.M. Tuesday, September 9. A leak in the meantime seems almost inevitable and will probably cost us heavily in lives, as the Germans will begin taking over Italy and certainly will replace Italian coastal units which manned pillboxes and shore batteries with their own German troops. This will make the landing even more hazardous.

The French have authorized Ike or his chief of staff to sign for them but have served notice that they have numerous and detailed interests to safeguard. This is another reason why Ike had hoped to handle the negotiations with Italy as a purely military matter, as he did the Darlan affair, so that his objective would not be complicated with a variety of demands from all the belligerents against Italy. Russia has sent a simple and flat "yes."

ALGIERS, MONDAY, SEPTEMBER 6, 1943

Ike got to Sicily in time to sign the so-called "short-term" agreement with General Castellano, whose own final authority did not reach there until Friday afternoon. But he decided that Beetle should sign, and so the Allied Commander-in-Chief was merely a witness. This document is not to be made public now and will be superseded by the "long-term" document to be signed at a formal and public ceremony some time later. Ike will sign the formal agreement.

General Castellano is executive officer to the Chief of Staff of the Italian Joint Staffs—Army, Navy, and Air—who is General Ambrosio.

It is agreed that the announcement of an armistice will be made simultaneously by the Italians and the Allies in Ike's name at 6:30 P.M. Wednesday evening, September 8.

Whether the King and Badoglio will run out of Italy depends upon the success of our paratroop division which is to be dropped near Rome the same night. There are four Italian divisions in the vicinity of Rome, but the Eyeties simply quake with fear because of the one German Panzer division in that area.

Even General Castellano, according to Ike, thought the Italians had "missed the boat" by not seeking and declaring an armistice immediately after Mussolini was kicked out. This, General Castellano felt, would have had popular support in Italy and would have prevented the Germans from gaining time for the build-up to nineteen divisions which are now in Italy.

Generals Clark and Gruenther had dinner with us last night and we had a farewell bridge game. I had a last-minute desire to go on the Naples show and General Clark offered to take me as his aide, but after Ike had agreed and Clark had phoned Admiral Hewitt, he found there was no space aboard the command ship *Ancon*, which was overcrowded with working personnel. It was lying in Algiers harbor, ready to depart that night.

General Clark was concerned lest the Italians welsh on their agreement. He suggested that Ike listen to the Italian radio to make certain they had announced the armistice terms before he actually confirmed acceptance. As Clark's forces will be under the Italian shore batteries in Salerno Bay, he said he had some interest in the Italians keeping their word. The change of the plan, which first called for dropping a large part of the 82nd Airborne Division north of Naples to a similar drop near Rome, weakens Clark's tactical position, and he made certain that in the event the Italians did not carry out in good faith the armistice which has been signed, he would be empowered to have the paratroops dropped at Naples.

There was another bridge engagement of Eisenhower and Gruenther versus Clark and Butcher, but Clark did not seem to have his mind on the game and we got beat. We took them to the *Ancon* and bade them farewell and good luck.

Ike would like to be directed to try Mussolini himself, that onetime famous gentleman being committed by the agreement to be delivered to the Allies. If Ike had a directive to try the dictator, he said this morning, he certainly would find him guilty and would take great pleasure in seeing him hanged. However, we concluded that any trial of Mussolini would be conducted on a "high level"—with jurists from at least several of the United Nations. I suppose Haile Selassie would like to be the executioner.

A page from the *United States News* of August 13 reached me today. It is headed: OUR LOST CHANCE IN ITALY; A LESSON FOR THE FUTURE—HOW ALLIED FAILURE TO FOLLOW THROUGH GAVE AXIS NEW BREATHING SPELL. This reflects impatience on the home front, but no one seems to emphasize the bitter truth, which is that troops do not have that mysterious power attributed to Jesus when he walked across the water. We still have to rely on landing craft and, unfortunately, we didn't have enough to continue to supply Sicily and conduct two other large-scale operations at the same time.

BAYTOWN, the attack on the toe of Italy across the Strait of Messina, started on schedule and is operating successfully, with a minimum of resistance. The Germans apparently have pulled back. Italians are readily surrendering and their white flags are reported everywhere.

Oddly, we have now been offered more merchant ships than we can use, but we still are short of the landing craft vital for pouring men and matériel onto beaches. If we get suitable ports in Italy, particularly Naples, we can run big ships into port. This will be helpful.

On Friday, I "chaperoned" Lieutenant General Allfrey, Commanding Officer of the British V Corps; Brigadier C. Huxley, his Chief of Staff; Major General H. J. Hayman-Joyce, the new Commanding Officer of the British 4th Division, and their aides, in a C-47 to Tunis, where we joined Ike for the trip to Hammamet Saturday morning to review the British 1st Division.

Next morning we took off in General Ike's Fortress, piloted by Captain Larry Hansen, of Cleveland, Ohio. I am gradually learning that I should not challenge General Eisenhower on any of his statements of fact. On every trip a rather precise schedule is figured out in advance, seldom on paper. From long experience, we know almost to the minute the normal flying time from Maison Blanche to all principal airfields. The other night, while General Ike and I were talking about co-ordination of his and my trips, so our parties could join and fly from El Aouina to Hammamet, I allowed a half-hour flying time between the two airfields. Ike said it would take less than twenty minutes. So we made a bet of five dollars. In some way, Larry Hansen learned about this bet. When we took off from El Aouina, Larry didn't circle the field—just headed straight for Hammamet at low level—not taking time to climb above 500 feet. He found the wind in the proper direction to make a landing at Hammamet without circling and was on the ground in less than fifteen minutes, according to Ike's own timing. I am learning.

The review of the British 1st Division was inspiring. Twelve thousand British troops marched in front of the reviewing stand where Ike stood in the hot sun for two hours at attention. After the review, he spoke briefly to the officers of the division and said it was a remarkable event when an American was privileged to review British troops as an Allied Commander-in-Chief and that the day had been symbolic of the fine co-operation which prevails in the Allied forces.

Ike said this morning that he was thinking of sending me back to Washington to carry all the papers incident to the Italian armistice, but I told him that if I went home, I preferred to go on an Italian warship in the event some are sent to the United States for installation of radar and for other improvements.

After dictating the above for the diary, I was buzzed into the General's office, where I could overhear the robust voice of Admiral Cunningham. I was asked by the General how quickly I could be in Malta to board the *Warspite*. My answer encouraged him to go on and, accompanied by a wide smile from the Admiral, I was told that if I would get to Malta promptly I could go on the *Warspite* to witness the surrender of the Italian fleet when, as, and if it carries out arrangements for slipping out of Italian ports into our custody. It will be the *Warspite's* job to "chaperone" the Italians. It was suggested that I take my camera. I immediately prepared.

Later this afternoon Ike called me in to ask my preference: (1) go home with the Italian armistice papers, or (2) make the trip on the *Warspite*. I immediately voted for Number 2. Beetle remarked that I was "always the sailor." The decision was not hard to make because there are few times in the life of any man when he can witness the surrender of a fleet.

The Surrender of Italy

AMILCAR (AFHQ, ADVANCE CP), TUESDAY, SEPTEMBER 14, 1943
Returned from the *Warspite* trip Saturday evening, the eleventh, bearing four rolls of Contax and eight packs of 16-mm. colored movie film. Spent the night with Ike at the little villa and flew in the Fortress to Algiers Sunday morning to submit to Army Pictorial Service my photographs of the delivery of two battleships, five cruisers, and five destroyers of the Italian fleet. After they were developed, I spent the evening helping Captain Smith of the Pictorial group prepare proper captions. Eight of the pictures were wirephotoed to America, "first and only" visual reports of the historic sea meeting from the *Warspite*. The 800 feet of film were sent by air courier by Pictorial Service to be delivered to the Eastman Company at Rochester, New York, and, after developing, to be made available for newsreel and historical purposes by the War Department.

Colonel Joe Phillips, the PRO, had radioed a request to me aboard the *Warspite* to write the story of the meeting under my own by-line. However, since Clark Lee of INS and David Brown of Reuter's had been assigned to cover General Eisenhower and the senior commanders for the current operation, and as I am on General Ike's personal staff, I thought it more appropriate to give them the information so they could write stories if they wished. I spent Saturday evening giving them the dope in considerable detail.

While I was aboard the *Warspite*, General Ike was having his troubles with the Italians. I am dictating this from information I received when I returned. I have had a fill-in from the General and, with some notes kept by Major Lee, can pick up the gist of the story.

General Maxwell Taylor, Airborne troops, and Colonel Gardner, Air Forces, had been sent to Rome secretly to get detailed information from Badoglio and his staff for the purpose of the American paratroop drop to help the Italian forces protect Rome and the Vatican from the Germans. The Italians were badly frightened of the Germans and claimed they could not prevent the Germans from taking complete possession of Rome for more than twelve hours, and strongly advised against our proposed airborne operation. The Germans had cut supplies of gasoline and ammunition, some Italian units having as little as twenty rounds per gun. The landing of an American paratroop division under such circumstances appeared suicidal.

Marshal Badoglio, at the last minute, was showing alarming signs of not going through with his part of the joint proclamation of the armistice, which was set for 6:30, September 8. In fact, he asked for a postponement. When this state of events became known to Ike, he immediately radioed Badoglio that the Allied Commander intended to broadcast the acceptance of the Allies at the hour originally planned and that if Badoglio, or any part of his armed forces, failed to co-operate as agreed, he would publish to the world a full record of the affair. He flatly told Badoglio that he was expected to do his part, and refused to accept Badoglio's plea for a postponement. General Ike agreed, on the earnest representations of Badoglio, that the airborne operation for Rome be temporarily suspended. Ike told the Italian general that he had sufficient troops near Rome to insure the temporary safety of the city if he would only use them. The Allies had made plans on the assumption that Badoglio was acting in good faith, and if he and his associates did not live up to their commitments, no future actions of his could restore any confidence whatsoever in him or his country. Dissolution of his government and nation inevitably would follow. Badoglio was ordered to send General Taylor and Colonel Gardner to Bizerte at once by aircraft.

The result was that Badoglio broadcast his proclamation as originally agreed.

With the landings at Salerno Bay coming off the next morning, General Ike retired at a reasonable hour and slept until 6:45. The U. S. Navy reported that landings were progressing according to plan and first waves were ashore at 4:11 A.M. Subsequent reports spoke of sporadic resistance from a few coast guns. At the Advance Command Post, there were almost continuous flights of B-17s and B-25s passing overhead to bomb roads leading to Salerno Bay.

Berlin announced creation of a Free Fascist Government.

Picking up the story of my travels and experiences since my last report in the diary, written Monday, September 6: I boarded the *Warspite* at Malta Tuesday afternoon. She is the flagship of the 2nd Division of Force H, which is the Royal Navy's principal fleet of capital ships in the Mediterranean.

When I boarded the *Warspite*, I wondered how much information had been given Admiral Bisset. When I indicated that I knew of his eventual mission and learned from him that he had been given some inkling of this job but his specific instructions were in a sealed envelope not to be opened until later, I kept my mouth shut. He told me that only three officers on the *Warspite* had any idea of the part his division was to play.

When I boarded, the Admiral had me as his guest for lunch and at all times I was treated with the utmost courtesy and consideration.

Force H assembled off the south side of Malta late Tuesday afternoon and steamed toward its position some sixty miles off Naples, reaching our assigned area for patrol late Wednesday afternoon—the eve of D-Day, as the landings were to be made starting at 3:30 Thursday morning.

Knowing that the armistice terms were to be announced at 6:30 P.M. on the radio, I suggested to the Admiral that we be sure to have our receiving sets tuned to the Algiers station. When the time was reached, our radio operators reported difficulty hearing the station, but from below, a British sailor rushed to the bridge and unceremoniously shouted: "Those bloody Eyeties have chucked their hand in!"

The word spread like fire over the ship. I was immediately invited to the wardroom mess for drinks. There was a variety of comment; one naval officer was disgusted. "Now," he said, "we will have to feed the Italians and we never will get spuds aboard ship." (There were no fresh ones aboard—only dried or dehydrated.) As it was clear these officers had not been informed of the heavy reinforcements the Germans had put in Italy, I endeavored to curtail their overenthusiasm, as to them it seemed apparent that Italy was out of it already. The ship's crew, as well as officers, were all smiles.

I retired to my cabin about 9 o'clock, wanting to get a good night's sleep, for I anticipated some activity at dawn next morning and wanted to be on the bridge to see it. I had hardly closed my eyes when the public-address system carried the command "Battle stations," which might mean anything. I quickly slipped my trousers and Army field jacket over my pajamas, put on some bedroom slippers, and, bareheaded, started to the bridge. I was about halfway when there was a terrific roar; we had opened a barrage against an enemy air attack, which later developed to be German torpedo planes—about twenty—which came in singly while the main body hovered outside our antiaircraft range, waiting for a chance to slip close enough either to one of the battleships or to the *Formidable*, to drop torpedoes. The noise of our ack-ack, the four- and the six-inch guns, was deafening. I was given some cotton for my ears. Some lad who was working under cover loaned me his tin hat, as the Admiral's bridge was exposed to falling shrapnel.

I had my movie camera and kept it working, but I wonder how the pictures will look. I shall not know for at least a month.

The raid continued at intervals over three and a half hours. There was bright moonlight, and our ships were silhouetted to the enemy. Admiral Bisset tried to minimize this exposure by keeping his ships headed into the moon or directly away from it, trying to make his turns on his prescribed patrol during a lull. The planes always attacked from the dark quarter, away from the moon. While the *Warspite* had her stern to the moon, one torpedo plane was seen to drop its torpedo about 600 to 800 yards off our port bow. I saw this plane as it turned away scarcely 100 yards from our bow. Our Oerlikon guns let go at it furiously, but, strangely, not one seemed to register. As the plane disappeared, I noticed the wake of the torpedo, which by then was running parallel to the *Warspite* on the port bow between thirty and fifty yards away, the ship having been quickly turned to bring her course parallel to the torpedo. Only by the quick action of Captain Packer on his bridge above had the torpedo missed. I noticed that it was running toward the *Formidable*, but it passed her stern.

When all reports were assembled from the seven destroyers in the screen, the *Valiant*, and the *Formidable*, it appeared that three aircraft had been shot down. We could see heavy ack-ack fire from the 1st Division, so we knew it was under attack, too. The moon set about 2 o'clock in the morning, and I, for one, was thankful for the darkness.

The *Warspite* had used all its guns except the fifteen-inch. The operations office on the Admiral's bridge was a shambles, for, with the first broadside, all of the reference papers, books, and paraphernalia came tumbling from the shelves. Even the glass on a sketch of one of the Admiral's four daughters was broken.

As no one could see an approaching plane, our only method of discovering it was by its self-disclosure on our radar screen. When one came in range, its course was given and heavy barrage extending to 3500 yards was laid in that direction. Sometimes a plane came to the view of some lookout peering through his powerful glasses, and he would yell, "Here comes the bloody blighter—shoot him." Someone would pick up the cry and I could hear the refrain, "Get the bastard"—that is, before the firing started. Afterward you could hear nothing but the guns, which filled the air with tracers. The shells from the six-inchers were set to explode at 3500 yards and all guns were fired only slightly above parallel to the water. One projectile from an Oerlikon gun killed a sailor on the *Faulkner* and two of her ratings were injured. These were the only casualties.

During the evening we had received a signal saying that an Allied reconnaissance plane had reported that the Italian fleet at Spezia had started out of the harbor promptly at 6:30. It said there were three battleships, six cruisers, and about twelve destroyers. This was the packet we were to meet. The course prescribed for this fleet was Spezia, north of Corsica, and thence southward along the west side of Corsica and Sardinia to a point off Cap de Garde near Bône, where we were to meet them at 8 o'clock Friday morning, September 10.

When the officers and crew learned that their division was to meet the Italians they were, of course, greatly exhilarated. We left the *Formidable* with the 1st Division and set off with our two battleships and seven destroyers about midafternoon Saturday, September 11. We fully expected another air attack that evening, as we were certain we had been snooped during the day. However, enemy aircraft apparently concentrated on the 1st Division, which, we heard, had suffered another attack, but we passed unmolested.

As we moved along to our rendezvous, we received a signal that the *Roma*, one of the three Italian battleships, had been hit by a bomb and was afire. Soon there came another signal, originated by Italian authorities in Rome, imploring the Allies to stop bombing their ships, as they had signed an armistice. Subsequently, we picked up a reply made by AFHQ (I presume by Ike) disclaiming our responsibility and insisting that it was the Germans who had done it. We all regretted the diminution of our prize.

Later I learned that an American reconnaissance plane, manned by a British crew, had been keeping an eye on the Italian fleet as it plowed through Mussolini's "Mare Nostrum" and had suddenly seen antiaircraft fire break out from the Italian ships. They were being bombed from high level out of sight of the reconnaissance plane as there were scattered clouds. Suddenly, a flash came from one of the ships and in a moment there was a terrific explosion, indicating a magazine had been hit. The *Roma* had sunk in twenty minutes after one hit, and the Commander-in-Chief of the Italian Navy had been killed.

Off Bône Friday morning, we were boarded by representatives of Admiral Cunningham—Captain T. M. Brownrigg and Lieutenant Seth Smith, RN. Admiral Bisset and I had assumed that the Italian Admiral in command of the remaining ships would be brought aboard the *Warspite*. While Brownrigg was conferring with Bisset, I was endeavoring to get pictures of the Italian fleet, which had finally barely come into view twelve miles distant, at 8:25. We had first picked them up on the radar screen at forty-seven miles. As I was taking my pictures, Brownrigg and Smith had reboarded their motor launch and, as I later discovered, were going aboard the Italian flagship, the cruiser *Savoia*. I could have kicked myself for not having suggested that I go along, but it was too late. (Brownrigg said the next day that he would have refused my request, as he didn't know just what would happen.)

We approached the Italian fleet from the eastward. They were coming from the westward. We kept to the outside, keeping the Italian fleet closer to shore than we. Every officer and rating was at his battle station and our guns were trained on the fleet. While no trouble was expected, Admiral Bisset did not wish to be caught unprepared. As Brownrigg and Smith were seen to board the *Savoia* and all appeared serene, the tension was relaxed, and from gun turrets came smiles and cameras.

Soon we had a signal by blinker from the *Savoia* saying that in the party were two battleships, five cruisers, and five destroyers, one other cruiser and five destroyers having been detached to pick up survivors from the *Roma* and to take them to Majorca, but these would follow as soon as possible. The Admiral instructed the Italian fleet to form behind us and follow. We did not place even a destroyer to their rear; they were "on their own." As a matter of fact, the whole Italian fleet could have turned tail and outrun us, as they had great advantage in speed, one of their cruisers being capable of forty-one knots and the battleships probably thirty knots, whereas the best our battleships could make was about twenty-four knots.

As we passed Bizerte between 5 and 6 P.M., aircraft with photographers flew around us. Admiral Cunningham and Ike, who modestly did not disclose his presence to the British fleet, as he felt it was Admiral Cunningham's party, came by on a destroyer. Admiral Bisset dipped his flag and the destroyer responded.

The Italians were deathly afraid of another air attack, and could not believe, as I later learned from Lieutenant Smith, that they would be in relative safety in Malta. They could scarcely conceive that the Germans dared not fly into the Malta area in the daytime. They had also been frightened of submarines and mines, and were careful to stay precisely behind us in the mile-wide channel from Bône to Bizerte and through the Sicilian Straits. We had our paravanes working to catch any stray mines.

During the night, Admiral Bisset had given instructions for a change of course, which occurred in the middle of a zig. We had resumed zigzagging as soon as we were out of the channel. Our zigzagging seemed strange to the Italians, and they had some difficulty adjusting themselves to it. Consequently, when we changed course around 3 A.M., the Eyeties found themselves "lost," but they were still showing themselves on our radar screen, so they were not lost to us, but, aboard their flagship, Smith said they were frantic. Finally, after an hour and a half, they again got us on their apparently inferior radar system and were happy to have found themselves.

When we reached the harbor of St. Paul's in Malta around 9 A.M. Saturday, we found two other Italian battleships and some cruisers and destroyers which had arrived from Taranto. We parked our contingent alongside, but first had the *Savoia* and the two battleships come abreast the *Warspite*, whose crew came to attention as the bosun's whistle was sounded. The Italians likewise were at attention. Their decks were colorful with their blue uniforms, red lifebelts with water container attached. When they replied to our bosun's whistle, I swear theirs had an operatic trill. The *Warspite* continued into Grand Harbor, where she was made fast to buoys near the Customs House. We learned that Admiral d'Zara, senior officer since the death of their C-in-C, but who had been in the Taranto portion, was to come ashore at 4 o'clock, when he would meet Admiral Cunningham. A guard of honor from the *Warspite* was placed in front of the Customs House landing for the Italian Admiral. I stayed to see this ceremony and to make pictures of it. The Eyetie was brought ashore in the Admiral's brass-stacked barge, from which he stepped briskly, saluting continuously, shook hands with Commodore Dick, who had been sent by Admiral Cunningham to escort him by car to the Admiral's office. The defeated Admiral quickly, and in a businesslike manner, reviewed the guard and soon was whisked away with Commodore Dick in the car which he had been deliberately provided so he could see the damage Italian bombs had done to Malta. He could have been walked sixty feet up a circular and deeply worn staircase to the Admiral's quarters, but "ABC," as I find he is frequently called in the Navy, wanted to impress the Italians with the ruins of Malta, for which they are partly responsible.

Admiral Cunningham sent this signal to the Admiralty in London: BE PLEASED TO INFORM THEIR LORDSHIPS THAT THE ITALIAN BATTLE FLEET IS NOW ANCHORED UNDER THE FORTRESS GUNS OF MALTA.

I returned to Amilcar by RAF courier plane, in time for dinner with Ike. General Spaatz was a guest. I found Ike greatly worried about General Clark's situation at Salerno. The Germans had counterattacked heavily. Clark needed reinforcements quickly. Ike greatly missed the use of the eighteen LSTs which he had requested weeks ago but which the Combined Chiefs of Staff had refused. Ike also lamented the decision of the Combined Chiefs when they rejected his pleas to retain three bomber groups. These, Ike felt, would have greatly aided our efforts to break communications of the Germans. Yesterday, Ike finally got authority to use the eighteen LSTs which were en route to India, but which had stopped in North Africa, but it will take five days to unload and reload them—five precious and vital days.

This morning, the news from General Clark was bad. The British divisions in the X Corps have been pushed back and the 36th Division took a heavy beating yesterday. The situation was critical, and Ike has gone to his daily meeting at the temporary headquarters of 15th Army Group at Bizerte.

While at Algiers, I found reports that New York, particularly the Italians, had gone wild with the news of the armistice. England had a day of prayer. Both countries are in for a serious letdown when they awaken to the hard facts which we have known all along, that a mere armistice does not end fighting in Italy. In fact, it looks as if we will be fighting Germans there all winter.

Also, while in Algiers, I had a call from Mr. Norman Davis, President of the American Red Cross and a good friend. We talked for an hour and a half yesterday morning in Ike's regular office. Before the Quebec meeting, Davis said that the President had asked him to confer with Secretary Hull and Sumner Welles to develop a practical postwar program for policing the world—one which could be agreed to by the British and subsequently submitted to the Russians. He said that the President had approved their proposal, which he, Davis, had proposed. It was for unity of the three countries to provide policing force in the occupied countries while the defeated nations are thoroughly demobilized and their armies reduced. In the meantime, committees representing the three nations could consider reduction of armament for the victorious nations. That there would be an after-the-war superpolicing power supported jointly by the victorious countries was the core of the scheme. He said that the British had approved it and that Hull, Eden, and Molotov would meet soon either in London, where the British wanted it, or in Washington, where he thinks it should be. Subsequently, he said, there will be a meeting of Roosevelt, Churchill, and Stalin. He felt, too, that the Russians would accept this proposal.

Davis said that he had counseled against the current practice of kowtowing to the Russians. He said that we should state our facts and our policies straightforwardly and the Russians would have greater respect for us.

He said that the most influential group in America after the war would be the returning soldiers; that the British had already undertaken to indoctrinate their soldiers by weekly lectures on their responsibility as citizens after the war. He said that he had advocated most earnestly similar indoctrination of our own troops and felt this would be done. Indoctrination would consist of selling the soldiers on the need of America exercising the responsibility which must go with the power she will have when the war is over and must take an active part in adjustment of world affairs. He said that the policing forces would not endeavor to settle every little squabble within or between countries if aggression were not involved, but its primary purpose would be to prevent the small nations being overrun by greedy and larger neighbors.

Mr. Davis told me he had addressed a meeting of several thousand troops in Palermo and was followed by General Patton. Of course, General Patton knew of the comment going around amongst his GIs. Quent Reynolds had reported that 50,000 of them would shoot Patton on sight. So when "Georgie" was introduced, he merely stepped to the front of the platform, saying: "I just thought I'd stand up here and let you soldiers see if I'm as big a s.o.b. as you think I am."

The GIs practically raised the roof with their cheers.

You can't keep a fellow like that down.

Setback at Salerno

AMILCAR (AFHQ, ADVANCE CP), WEDNESDAY, SEPTEMBER 15, 1943
Last night Ike received alarming news. It was dispatched September 14, at 11:48 A.M., via Admiral Cunningham from Admiral Hewitt, USN. Hewitt reported that the Salerno bridgehead is narrowing and our forces are now taking the defensive. He said that our fellows are fatigued and the existing enemy drive toward the beach about two miles wide had

penetrated a deep salient along the Sele River between the British X Corps and the American VI. Naval gunfire was being used to break up an enemy tank offensive reported only three miles from the beach.

Admiral Hewitt suggested that the general situation ashore called for employment of heavy air bombardment and naval bombardment by battleships and other major vessels which could strike behind enemy positions. He asked Admiral Cunningham if such forces were available. In answer to Admiral Hewitt's question, the Commander-in-Chief Mediterranean ordered two battleships and appropriate screening destroyers to Salerno Bay.

General Ike had been required to make a command decision that the landings at Salerno Bay would be made despite the planners' qualms over the shortage of landing craft and denial of our request for temporary use of additional bombers. He had the support of the land, sea, and air commanders, who have striven every possible way to make good the deficiency, but the responsibility still remains his.

Now, with Clark in trouble, Ike is moving heaven and earth to help him and his Fifth Army. He has the Air Force pounding away to disorganize the expected heavy counterattack of the Germans. Even B-17s are making two missions a day. He expects soon to see Montgomery's advance north of the toe have some effect on the enemy near Salerno. Admiral Cunningham had boldly rushed cruisers loaded with British airborne troops into Taranto, and, although one cruiser was mined and lost, the entire British 1st Airborne Division was put ashore. This was to help Montgomery speed his advance. Parts of the U. S. 82nd Airborne Division have been sent to Clark as reinforcements. Landing craft intended to bring up service troops of assault division have been diverted to bring the 3rd Division, resting in Sicily, into the battle of Salerno. The 34th Division, loaded at Oran and expected to go directly into Naples after capture, must go to Salerno and be landed from ordinary transports over the beaches—an awkward performance, but necessary. Eighteen LSTs, en route through the Mediterranean to the Far East, were made available at the last minute by the Combined Chiefs, but they are loaded, some with rails, and have first to be unloaded. The first eight will start picking up the British 78th Division in Sicily further to reinforce Monty at Taranto.

Last evening, General Spaatz saw the General at his villa to discuss the draft of a proposed personal message from Ike to General Marshall in support of Spaatz's plea to General Arnold, Chief of the Air Forces, for a higher percentage of replacements of crews. Because of the heavy demand on them to support the ground battles, in Sicily, in the toe, and now at Salerno, and as weather permits virtually daily operation, the crews are just plain tired out.

General Spaatz related that the air had been "all out" during the day. A particularly lucky hit had been made on an ammunition train in Batti-paglia, a key point near Salerno Bay. The train had blown up and, according to returning fliers, had completely wrecked the center of the town. A tank battle had been noted between Battipaglia and the sea. Also, our service craft were being dive-bombed. The fighting on the ground appeared intense.

Fortunately, the predicted bad weather for flying, which was expected to slow up our operations today, has not materialized and probably will not affect us because the cold front, according to General Spaatz, has moved down our way. This is a great break for ground troops at Salerno, as their situation can only be saved by help from Air and Navy.

As General Spaatz was leaving, Ike recalled that he had disagreed with Spaatz many times on the question of serving a rum ration to hard-working fliers, but if they can save the situation at Salerno, he personally would see that we get rum from the British and if he couldn't pay for it out of his contingent fund, he would be glad to pay for it personally. Would Spaatz pass the word to his boys? (Having tasted British rum aboard ship, I don't think the fliers will be greatly pleased. Some good American beer or Scotch whisky would be appreciated.)

We are awaiting a further report from General Clark. Alexander was to have visited him last night. Ike is tremendously worried but has the satisfaction of having done everything he could think of before, during, and after the landings to make the whole assault a success.

We First Hear of OVERLORD

AMILCAR (AFHQ, ADVANCE CP), THURSDAY, SEPTEMBER 16, 1943
General Alexander signaled Ike last night, after visiting General Clark in the Salerno area, that while he was still not happy, he was happier than he had been twenty-four hours previously. Our ground troops were greatly fatigued but in good spirit, he said. Air and naval bombardment had immeasurably increased their morale.

This, plus our knowledge of our air activity, which has continued on a stupendous scale, raised our spirit.

Visited with Beetle last evening, who said he had become thoroughly alarmed when the German communiqué had announced that our 36th Division was in "headlong flight," as the Germans are reasonably accurate in their official reports, particularly as to ground activity. This is the Texas division which Ike reviewed near Mostaganem and to which I was a witness. As I thought at the time, little did the personnel of that division, whose sunburned faces showed hope and determination as we passed along them, know what the future held for them. Now many are dead, wounded, or officially missing. Apparently, "headlong flight" has been used by the Germans to describe a withdrawal to bring the American front back to that of the British front when its 56th Division was driven out of Battipaglia. But we will know more after today's meeting, when General Alexander will give Ike a complete report.

At breakfast this morning Ike philosophized as to prospective shifts in high command, flowing from the Quebec meeting of President Roosevelt, Prime Minister Churchill, and the Combined Chiefs. So far, we have little fact to go on, except that a grand-scale, cross-Channel invasion of France has been decided for the spring of 1944, and a new code name assigned—OVERLORD, replacing the old one, ROUNDUP.

Ike's views were punctuated by a comment that if the Salerno battle ended in disaster he would probably be out.

As to the current battle at Salerno, Montgomery has a great chance to be a real hero. Yesterday his Eighth Army made good mileage and is now sixty miles from the Fifth Army and has reached a point where two roads may be used rather than one. I wonder what the result would have been in the toe of Italy if Patton had been the commander instead of Montgomery. Patton would have burned shoe leather, as he did in Sicily. I told him I thought Montgomery would be inspired by the competition and the opportunity to "out-Patton" Patton by reaching Clark in record time. My guess was that Monty will move as he has never moved before. He is the potential hero of a grand melodrama and he will be quick to grasp the possibility of adding further luster to his name.

Last night Lieutenant General Mason-MacFarlane, who, with Macmillan and Murphy, constitute our Allied Mission to the Italians at Taranto and Brindisi, submitted a long report. He had seen the King, Badoglio, Ambrosio, Rossi, and the Minister of Marine, who is unnamed. Outside of the acquisition of the Italian fleet we have virtually nothing to gain, certainly, from the Army, except as the soldiers may be used as labor at ports and on our line of communication. He said that they are short of boots and ammunition and have 1918 armor.

After that, the Combined Chiefs, apparently most anxious over our Salerno situation, have now asked for a recapitulation of the various requests from AFHQ which were made over the past several weeks in preparation for AVALANCHE and which had been denied.

Ike had made a penciled note on this message: "Let's be particularly careful to give clean-cut decisive answer."

Yesterday Ike asked for return of the three bomber groups at the earliest possible moment because they are familiar with Italy and could immediately be useful. We await decision of the Combined Chiefs.

There will be a meeting with Badoglio in Tunisia. Ike said that the home governments are anxious to have the long-term agreement signed with appropriate showmanship. He hates the thought, but it must be done.

The whole Italian campaign has been complicated by the conflicting desires of America and Britain. The former does not want to be committed too strongly in Italy for fear of diminishing the strength and scope of OVERLORD. Britain has only reluctantly acceded to OVERLORD, but really has its heart in the Mediterranean and therefore prefers to go all-out in Italy and thence at the so-called "soft underbelly."

I insisted in our discussion that Ike was the logical and inevitable choice for the European command. He thought that while his record as Allied Commander in North Africa would cause his name to be considered, he doubted if anyone except Generals Marshall and Brooke could be assigned. He had begun to hope that he would be left in the Mediterranean because of his semi-independence. He didn't relish the idea of returning to a headquarters in London or Washington.

News from Salerno is much better. Clark has reported that the situation is vastly improved and is getting better hourly. Air and naval support, Clark said, continued to be superb. There are indications that the enemy is withdrawing to the east and northeast and, apparently, is somewhat nervous because of the advance of the Eighth Army, which has now begun to move speedily. A small group of newspapermen of the Eighth Army had preceded the army itself and joined up with a reconnaissance outfit of the American Fifth.

Crawling up the Boot

AMILCAR (AFHQ, ADVANCE CP), SATURDAY, SEPTEMBER 18, 1943
General Ike, with Major Lee, departed from Amilcar early yesterday via plane to Palermo and thence by the cruiser H.M.S. *Charybdis* to the Salerno beachhead to visit General Clark.

As all the trip by cruiser to Salerno was to be in daylight, I was not without misgivings for Ike's safety. My old friend, the *Warspite*, when sent with the *Valiant* to bombard the enemy behind General Clark's lines, was hit in daylight by two glider bombs, with two near misses. Casualties were light, only about eight killed and twenty-five wounded. First we heard the old battle wagon was making four knots toward Malta, but last night the air people said she was in tow of a tug.

The glider bombs are perplexing. The U.S.S. *Philadelphia* and U.S.S. *Savannah* likewise were victims of this new Germanic device. I was at General Spaatz's villa for dinner last night. One of the air men told me that four glider bombs traveling at 600 miles an hour came over the *Warspite* and suddenly dived straight toward her, two hits and two near misses. The glider is propelled by rocket. Jamming, which was used the night I was aboard the *Warspite* when it was attacked, was not effective in this instance. It is guided by radio from a control aircraft hovering outside the flak area. When the gliding bomb comes within a certain distance of a large mass of metal, it is magnetically or otherwise guided directly to its target. What if the Germans use such bombs on London? They are alleged to carry 1500 pounds of explosive, and if they can be controlled similarly from a ground station across the Channel, the Germans could raise hell again in once Merrie England.

Our military progress in Italy is such as to create broad smiles at Advance Command Post. The Eighth Army has made contact with the Fifth, General Clark's VI Corps counterattacking and regaining more than its lost territory. Now the Germans are said to be pulling away from the southern flank of our Salerno beachhead, but are concentrating on the northern side toward Naples, where we have difficult defiles to capture before we can get to the plain leading to the coveted port.

The *Charybdis* brought Ike to Bizerte this morning, where he will attend the usual meeting and return to Amilcar early this afternoon. I was relieved to know he had reached land safely.

AMILCAR (AFHQ, ADVANCE CP), TUESDAY, SEPTEMBER 21, 1943
Ike is recommending to the Combined Chiefs that, from a military standpoint, the Allies should accept and strengthen the legal government of Italy under the King and Badoglio and accept the government as cobelligerent. The only alternative is to sweep the government aside and set up an Allied Military Government of occupied Italy, but this would require a heavy drain on our manpower for policing and administration. He is hopeful that all anti-Fascist elements in Italy will support the new government and that it may make substantial contributions in fighting Germany.

Sardinia has been cleared of Germans, primarily by voluntary withdrawal, and Brigadier General Theodore Roosevelt has been sent to appraise the situation. French and Italians are fighting shoulder to shoulder in Corsica to drive out the Germans, who are now said also to be evacuating.

Ike wishes he had landing craft and troops to land about three divisions in "end runs" back of the Germans along the boot of Italy. This would give us a better chance to destroy the enemy rather than merely follow him northward. Ike also expects Naples to be in our hands within ten days. Cholera and typhus are reported there, and we will have to supply about 100 tons a day of foodstuffs. Incidentally, Bob Murphy said that civilian requirements of food and other supplies for the four southern provinces of Italy, as estimated by the Italians, would be 100,000 tons a month. Taranto was said nearly a week ago to have food for only ten days.

Yesterday a cablegram arrived from Cape Town, South Africa, reading:

I OFFER DONATE TEN THOUSAND POUNDS TOWARD WAR FUNDS IF YOU ARRANGE FOR MUSSOLINI'S PERSONAL APPEARANCE ON THE STAGES OF OUR CAPE TOWN THEATERS. THREE WEEKS' ENGAGEMENT.

—STODEL AFRICAN THEATERS, LTD.

A "TL" and a Blast

AMILCAR (AFHQ, ADVANCE CP), THURSDAY, SEPTEMBER 23, 1943 While Monty is resting his Eighth Army and "winding up its tail"—a process that delays his forward movement for a week or ten days—and General Clark's Fifth Army is both attacking to clear defiles on the road to Naples and collecting its divisions, Ike has received both a "TL" and a blast from the homefolk.

Yesterday he received a personal message from the Prime Minister, who, incidentally, has just made another of his whacking reports to the public via the House of Commons, stating: "I congratulate you on the victorious landing and deployment northwards of our armies. As the Duke of Wellington said of the battle of Waterloo, 'It was a damned close-run thing,' but your policy of running risks has been vindicated."

But today General Marshall took the starch out of Ike. The Chief of Staff feared the enemy would gain great advantage during the time required to take Naples. Could we hold a line before reaching Naples and make an "end-run" dash for Rome? This would make Naples and much more fall like a ripe plum.

At lunch Beetle and I undertook to help Ike frame his reply, some of our assistance being facetious and some serious. When the bad news was breaking from Salerno, the three understrength bomber groups we got from England were temporarily reassigned to AFHQ by the Combined Chiefs. This reversal of its decision indicated that the bosses were concerned and that our home fronts were thoroughly scared. Beetle thought we should have one section at AFHQ whose job would be solely to keep the home front frightened.

I suggested we might complain about the quality of training of the GIs—if they were trained to walk on water, then we wouldn't have had to wait for landing craft. Beetle said that our training taught them to walk on water but not with full packs. Amphibious operations require the dark of the moon—at least part of the outfit. The man in the moon needs to hurry too, but, unfortunately, we have no control over the moon.

Ike had eaten practically no breakfast and passed up his lunch. We were simply trying to cheer him. Ike thinks along the same lines as General Marshall, but he is grieved to think that General Marshall does not give him credit for cracking the whip. In the Salerno operation he had to insist that it be attempted, despite misgivings and moanings from many of his staff.

In Sardinia the Italians have discreetly followed the Germans without making contact. An attack on the evacuation port from which the Germans were speeding to the mainland of Italy was laid on by the Italians for the day after the Germans departed. However, Sardinia is clear of Germans, and Brigadier General Roosevelt, who was sent over there, reports airfields in good order and inhabitants friendly. In Corsica, American Commandos have joined the French, who are hastening the evacuation of the Germans, but Corsica still is not entirely clear.

On the political side, the Prime Minister has unhesitatingly approved and, in fact, amplified Ike's recommendation for acceptance of the Italian forces under Badoglio and the King as cobelligerents, but adds that they must "work their passage."

Mr. Macmillan and I had an interesting discussion yesterday as to whether the President will take the same view. Wes Gallagher, of the Associated Press, freshly returned from the U. S., thinks our dealings with the King will be even more unpopular at home than those with Darlan. Incidentally, the Prime Minister is most anxious to have the King make a broadcast to the Italians to assure them that Badoglio represents the legal government.

Ike's answer to General Marshall, who, with Field Marshal Dill, had complained that Ike was not showing sufficient initiative, caused him a great deal of mental anguish.

We have the paradox of the Prime Minister applauding Ike's willingness to take risks while General Marshall and Sir John Dill, from their global viewpoint in Washington, criticize him for failure to be bold.

AMILCAR (AFHQ, ADVANCE CP), SATURDAY, SEPTEMBER 25, 1943

The President's reply as to policy for dealing with the King and Badoglio arrived night before last. Ike is ordered to withhold the long-term armistice provisions pending further instructions, but on the basis of military necessity Ike is empowered to make recommendations from time to time to lighten the provisions of the military armistice in order to enable the Italians, within the limit of their capacity, to wage war against Germany.

The President went further and said that if the Italian government, as represented by the King and Badoglio, will declare war on Germany, Italy will be treated as a cobelligerent provided there is a clear understanding that this status is not in any way to prejudice the untrammeled right of the people of Italy to decide on the form of government they eventually will have and that no final form of the government of Italy will be decided upon until the Germans are evicted from their territory.

The AMG and the Armistice Control Commission for Italy will be merged in their functions as soon as practicable and as such shall furnish guidance and instructions to the Badoglio government on military, political, and administrative matters.

We are continuing to build up our forces on the mainland. In the Fifth Army, the X Corps has made slow progress because of the high ground held and well fortified by the enemy, but on the right flank the VI Corps, particularly the 3rd Division thereof, is making such rapid progress that it threatens to outflank the Germans in front of the X Corps.

Ike and Beetle are waiting for word from Badoglio via Admiral Cunningham, who is in charge of arrangements for the meeting aboard a warship at Malta, at which the armistice conditions will be discussed. It has been learned that General Castellano has never delivered to his government the text of the long-term agreement and so the King and Badoglio are in the dark. However, they have co-operated beautifully to date under the terms of the military armistice signed by Beetle, September 3, at our tented Advance Command Post near Casabile, in Sicily.

Ike also is halfway expecting a call home for consultation. If he does not receive word from Marshall to visit at home before the end of the month, he has said that I should go. General Spaatz has invited me to fly with him.

We are about to have several important visitors. Secretary of the Navy

Knox is arriving next week. Lord Louis is due any day. Field Marshal
Smuts is coming October 1. General Somervell, Donald Nelson, and
Secretary Morgenthau are also expected. Obviously, this is vacation time
in Washington.

SEPTEMBER, 1943: *British Eighth Army landed in southern Italy five days*
prior to announcement of unconditional surrender of Badoglio government.
Allied landings at Salerno met strong German resistance. Nazis occupied
Rome, fought savagely at Salerno, sacked Naples, fell back to prepared de-
fense lines. Russian troops, advancing on all fronts, retook Donets Basin,
crossed Desna River, took Novorossiisk, Bryansk, Smolensk, crossed Dnieper,
took important rail center of Krichev. Pacific war roared on with capture
of Lae and Salamaua, start of annihilation of Japs at Finschhafen. Heavy
bombing struck German targets including Berlin, with round-the-clock at-
tacks directed against Mannheim-Ludwigshafen, Aachen, and Darmstadt.
Bombers also hit north Italian cities, Brenner Pass control points. Yugoslav
guerrillas fell back but retained general initiative. Kurile Island installations
bombed, Jap ships and planes destroyed. Major General Royce replaced Brere-
ton in command of U. S. Middle East forces. Secretary Hull refused lend-lease
to Argentina. (And we got most of the Italian fleet.—H.C.B.)

VIPs *

ALGIERS, TUESDAY, OCTOBER 5, 1943

The last time I dictated for the diary was September 25 at Amilcar. On
less than a half-hour's notice I was aboard a plane with Beetle, en route
to Algiers, to be Ike's representative to meet the Secretary of the Navy,
Colonel Knox. He arrived in Algiers Monday morning and was the house
guest of Admiral Hall. I attended dinner there that evening and the
next evening accompanied the Secretary and his party aboard H.M.S.
Euryalius for Bizerte. Unfavorable weather for flying meant taking to
the cruiser, which the Secretary regarded with a somewhat skeptical eye,
because while on a recent trip from Scotland to Scapa Flow he had
become violently seasick. The Mediterranean was still rolling from a
heavy storm that had wrecked scores of landing craft on Salerno beaches.

We changed from the cruiser to the Secretary's C-47 at Bizerte, flew
to Palermo, where the party was met by Admiral Hewitt, whose command
ship, the *Ancon*, was in the harbor, and by General Patton. We proceeded that evening to the Gulf of Salerno, Admiral Hewitt, the Secretary,
and his aide, Captain "Pop" Perry, aboard the U.S.S. *Nicholson*, and

---

* VIPs are very important personages, outranked only by VGDIPs.

Captains Leland Lovette, von Heimburg of Admiral Hall's staff, and I aboard the U.S.S. *Mayo*.

Both destroyers had been recalled from Salerno, where they had aided in the landings, and since had been on escort and patrol duty. The *Mayo* had "smelled" a sub en route to Palermo and had dropped all its depth charges but had had no proof of a kill. However, an American mine sweeper, the *Skill*, had been torpedoed and sunk in Salerno Bay the previous day. Not a very healthful place to take the Secretary of the Navy.

The Secretary's party went ashore at Salerno, where we were met by General Wayne Clark, who took us to his Fifth Army headquarters and for a visit to Battipaglia, where the Secretary could see the effect of naval gunfire as well as of bombings.

Went on PT boats to the isle of Capri and spent a couple of pleasant hours. Naples was covered by smoke from numerous fires; it fell the next day. The island seems untouched by war. Like all American tourists, we all bought liberally of the usual trinkets. We were guests of Admiral J. A. V. Morse, RN, formerly port commander at Algiers. His billet was the villa of Edda Ciano, daughter of Mussolini. It was said that she and her children spent their summers at this villa. Her bedroom had a bed eight feet wide. Venetian blinds opened by push button from bedside.

Captain von Heimburg and I separated from the party and engaged a driver with horse and buggy to take us the mile or so to the port. The destroyers put us in at Palermo Friday morning, October 1. The Secretary's C-47 took us to El Aouina, where I had arranged for the Secretary and party to lunch with Ike. I was burning with desire to tell Ike the big news disclosed to me by Colonel Knox: General Marshall had been named Supreme Commander for OVERLORD, and it was "probable" that Ike would be recalled to Washington to be Chief of Staff of the U. S. Army.

From Algiers I got the Secretary off en route to America at 8 o'clock Saturday morning with an Army fife-and-drum corps playing everything except *Anchors Aweigh*, and they would have played this if they had had the necessary instruments.

As Donald Nelson, the War Production chief, was arriving with a special letter from the President to Ike, my next orders were to render honors to him and to arrange for his meeting with Ike. He was with his traveling companion, Jim Landis, former Security Exchange Commissioner, Dean of the Law School at Harvard and Civilian Defense Administrator.

Nelson was optimistic about when the war would end. He said that information given him in England showed that morale of German civilians was very low because of the concentrated bombings of their cities and industrial plants. He said that there had been one stretch of six days of good weather during which Germany got hell from the air. There was so much turmoil within the country that if weather had permitted continuation of the bombings two more days, the Germans would have given in. Ike counseled that this view was overoptimistic; that our troops are in contact with the German soldiers and we will be the first to know when morale really has cracked, although it is possible the German home front may become wobbly. However, judging from all the information we have from prisoners, the Germans are still living in a world of their own created by their propaganda. Nelson was en route to Moscow to confer on production matters.

Lord Louis was passing through en route to his new theater, with directive to fight the Japs in Burma and other places in that part of the world, which will require some study of the map. He had spent Sunday evening with Ike at Amilcar after a hectic series of misadventures by arriving at the wrong airdrome, causing Ike to drive three and a half hours from one place to another, trying to locate his guest. Lord Louis desired to pattern his command after Ike's.

Yesterday I received clippings from America reflecting the tempest which was raised when the *Army and Navy Journal* said that General Marshall was being kicked upstairs because of powerful British interests. Such talk makes no contribution to the winning of the war.

I have tried to figure just what the President will do with Ike under the new setup. The job of Chief of Staff does not appeal to Ike, and he believes he would be a failure in it because he is not a politician. I have told him he would be either the best or the worst Chief of Staff the Army ever had. His forthrightness and abomination of politics could make him so respected even by politicians that he would be a great success. On the other hand, he does not have the patience and diplomacy which made General Marshall such a success at it. Ike would prefer most of all to remain Allied Commander in the Mediterranean and to exploit our victory because there is a real probability that with bombing from our forward airfields and co-ordinated efforts in this area we can contribute immeasurably to an early end of the war. He wants to remain a field commander. If shifted from the Mediterranean he would much prefer to have command of an American group of armies under General Marshall in the cross-Channel push.

Meantime our intelligence indicates that with the Russians keeping red hot after the Germans, our victory in the Mediterranean, and the heavy bombing of German cities, the Germans may be forced to withdraw from France, in which event the cross-Channel attack would be merely to occupy France and to pursue the enemy into Germany.

On Wednesday, September 29, Ike and staff conferred with Badoglio and party aboard H.M.S. *Nelson* in Valletta Harbor at Malta. Ike specified Malta as the meeting place because he wanted the Italians to see some of the damage they had caused. He demanded that the Badoglio government declare war against Germany. Badoglio said he'd take up the matter with the King. Many details were adjusted, looking toward more active assistance from Italians. Badoglio thought that when he could get his troops to Sardinia, he could put eight divisions in the field against the Germans.

Men for the Middle East or Italy?

ALGIERS, FRIDAY, OCTOBER 8, 1943

Ike is currently being pressed by the Prime Minister to send men, equipment, planes, and surface vessels to the aid of the Middle East in its effort to hold islands. They lost the island of Cos to the Germans and are fearful of an attack on Leros. Ike has attempted to aid their situation without diminishing our strength for the major battle to come in Italy this winter. He has again put pressure on Badoglio and the King immediately to declare war against Germany in the hope this will crystallize the resistance of Italians on the islands and elsewhere. The King had preferred not to declare war until Rome had been taken, but last evening we had a signal from General Taylor, who is on the Military Mission to the Italian government, that Badoglio had fully agreed on the necessity and was promptly putting the question to the King. As the latter's approval was anticipated, the only question remaining was the timing of the announcement. All news and propaganda wheels have been greased to carry the news as soon as the announcement may be made, which will probably be tomorrow, October 9. Ike felt that declaration of war by the King would be a great psychological help because certainly some Italian units would be induced to fight, whereas now they are just jellyfish. In addition, he had instructed that the German-occupied airdromes in Greece be smacked by our air. This has been done effectively.

Military operations by both the Fifth and Eighth Armies are proceeding satisfactorily, although the usual demolitions and mines are thickening. Heavy rains have flooded creek and river beds through which detours normally are made around blown-out bridges. Logistics are being straightened, the port of Naples is being cleared, and, as the British say, things are being "tidied" for the big push to Rome.

Ike has a meeting not only of the Commanders-in-Chief but with General "Jumbo" Wilson, Commander-in-Chief Middle East, at La Marsa tomorrow. His entourage is flying there tomorrow morning. Matters affecting the Middle East's fervent pleas for help will be considered. In this issue is wrapped the fundamental difference between Britain and America as to the prosecution of the war. The Prime Minister wants us to exploit our advantages throughout the Mediterranean as rapidly as possible. Ike and his AFHQ staff feel that every atom of our strength will be required to beat the Germans in Italy. The Germans have recently moved in another division, now making a total of twenty, which will just equal our ground strength. The balance in our favor comes in the air, where our superiority is appraised by Ike to be equivalent to ten ground divisions. Every subtraction from our strength makes more difficult our opportunity for destruction of the Germans in the major battle to come.

Naples is in a bad way because its utilities were effectively destroyed by the Germans and at least one monstrous delayed-action mine has exploded. This was in the post office in Naples, and according to reports, everyone on the first floor of the post office was killed, as were most persons within the block. The aqueduct which supplies water has been cut in seven places. Some water remains in the city's reservoir, which is being rationed, but not enough to carry away refuse. Unfortunately, too, the aqueduct carries water from territory still held by the Germans. The telephone exchange was effectively wrecked; the electric system likewise. However, in the port we are getting in some 2500 tons a day, with capacity mounting each day. Three Italian submarines are being put to work generating electricity for lighting the dockyard in Naples.

General Taylor has wired today that Badoglio has informed him confidentially that he expects to be ready to declare war next Monday or Tuesday and that the King probably will make a broadcast if desired. Two presumably liberal ex-members of Parliament are being brought from Naples to take Cabinet posts.

ALGIERS, MONDAY, OCTOBER 11, 1943

Ike left the Advance Command Post at Amilcar this morning for a two-day trip to the front of Italy, stopping tonight with Monty. Major Lee is accompanying him.

The Commanders-in-Chief, at Ike's Sunday meeting at Amilcar, unanimously held to the view that we will need all our strength to beat the

Germans in Italy, our only margin of superiority being in the air, ground forces so far about evenly matched with German divisions, too.

Bob Murphy just came in to introduce his successor—Minister Edwin Wilson, fresh from Panama, who is to serve on the new Mediterranean Commission, with British, French, and Russian membership. Wondered if Bob is being thrown to the wolves because of Darlan. He really has done a swell job, easily and without fuss on his part. Hate to see him go, but there is a chance he may keep on with AFHQ, working on Italian problems. Don't know where the State Department could use him to better advantage.

ALGIERS, TUESDAY, OCTOBER 19, 1943

Ambassador Harriman and his daughter Kathleen arrived on Thursday, October 14. I met them at Maison Blanche and put them up at the General's villa.

Had a bathroom conference with Harriman, who had just returned from the States after a visit of several weeks. He said that the publicity about General Marshall's prospective appointment had possibly upset the intention, but the controversy had given an opportunity for the friends of General Marshall, particularly newspapers, to give him credit for his excellent contribution to the war. While the decision seemed to have been made to make Marshall the Supreme Commander in England as well as for Ike to be Chief of Staff in Washington, Harriman was not at all certain the plan would be consummated.

It appears that Secretary Stimson had insisted to the President that Marshall go to England. The President in turn advanced the notion at the Quebec conference, where the arrangement was agreed to by the Prime Minister. To maintain balance, the Mediterranean command would have to be given to an Englishman and Ike would be Chief of Staff in Washington. However, when Admiral King had an opportunity to register his views he strongly protested the loss of Marshall, who, he emphasized, was a great teammate. King was seeking to influence Stimson and/or the President to keep Marshall in Washington. In all these discussions General Marshall has remained aloof.

Secretary of the Treasury Morgenthau arrived Friday forenoon, so Ike had both Harriman and Morgenthau for lunch. Secretary Hull arrived in the afternoon, so he had Harriman as house guest and the Secretary, with some of his companions, for dinner. Both the Harriman and Hull parties took off that evening for Cairo, en route to Moscow, so Ike's day was spent largely with visiting firemen.

Before dinner Secretary Hull had received Mr. Massigli, of the French Committee for National Liberation, as well as de Gaulle. I gave the Secretary a glass of bourbon and "branch water." Then I left the living room while he talked first to Massigli and then to de Gaulle separately. While standing in the hallway, visiting with Hull's physician, Dr. Perry, I noticed the good doctor seemed agitated. He said he could hear the Secretary speaking much too loudly and would soon wear out his larynx and would be voiceless in Moscow. Later I learned the Secretary had managed to get another snifter—much to the consternation of the doctor.

Secretary Morgenthau was enthusiastic about the opportunity of visiting an active theater and has considerable business here, particularly with respect to the problems of money in occupied territory in Italy, and rate of exchange. Said that he had been called to a meeting of fifty Senators who criticized AMGOT's paper money distributed in Sicily, apparently being worried that we were aping the Germans by using printing-press money. He said that he had asked the Senators not to voice any criticism publicly because it would immediately become propaganda for the enemy. However, on his trip he proposed to learn all about the use of this money. Said that so much of it had to be printed, and the Government Printing Office was so busy on other work, that the Army had found among soldiers many printers who were assigned to run the presses for this job and this job alone.

Mindful that Morgenthau was perhaps our severest critic in the Cabinet when the Darlan deal was made, and knowing that Captain "Piggy" Warburg is not only a stanch supporter of that arrangement but an authority on the economics of North Africa, I suggested that Ike appoint him special aide to Morgenthau. Now the party, under the tutelage of the Deputy Theater Commander, General Hughes, has gone on a tour in this theater, including Malta and probably Sicily and Italy.

Admiral Sir Andrew Cunningham departed Sunday, October 17, to take up his position as First Sea Lord in London. Ike had asked me to have an appropriate ceremony arranged for Saturday at 11 A.M. Soldiers, sailors, and airmen of both Great Britain and the United States formed a guard of honor and the U. S. Army Band furnished the music in a simple but impressive ceremony in front of the St. George. When the Admiral said good-by all round, he had tears in his eyes. He said, "Good-by, old Butch," which I liked. He had just heard the last strains of *Auld Lang Syne*, which was one of the three band numbers personally selected by Ike. The others were *Hail Britannia*, and *Columbia, the Gem of the Ocean*. Ike had written a letter, personal and warm, to the Admiral, which he requested me to give to Captain Shaw to be handed to the Admiral only after the wheels left the ground.

When he returned to the St. George there was a letter from the Admiral awaiting Ike, likewise intended not to be read until after the parting.

The principal cable correspondence with the Combined Chiefs of Staff has to do with a point in the so-called long-term agreement with the Badoglio government. After the document was agreed to at Malta, the Prime Minister had a second thought which had to do with making certain the Italian fleet had completely surrendered. While it had surrendered, the Italians had sought a softening of the phraseology of the terms of "unconditional surrender," and the Prime Minister wanted to make certain that a change to meet this request had been agreed to by the United States, United Kingdom, and Russia and would not serve to let the Italian fleet off the hook.

Military operations are going well but slowly. Heavy rains have hindered effective use of our air and have bogged our ground troops. However, they have crossed the Volturno and are pushing slowly ahead on the road to Rome.

Ike expects to have another meeting of his Commanders-in-Chief at La Marsa after Beetle returns from Washington with the latest information. Ike is anxious to know his status, not merely as a matter of personal curiosity, but to aid him in making plans. It is difficult for him to make plans which may have to be executed by others. He has already spoken to General Alexander about the prospective change, on the assumption that Alexander will inherit his mantle.

Slowdown in Italy

ALGIERS, THURSDAY, OCTOBER 28, 1943

The campaign in Italy has slowed. It is mountain fighting, slow and tedious. The German build-up is proceeding so rapidly that Ike thinks even when and if we take Rome and advance farther up the boot we will not have sufficient strength to risk an all-out battle in the Po River Valley—certainly not until spring, when weather will permit us to apply effectively our superiority in air power. This means an all-winter campaign in Italy, offensively, until we are well past Rome and then the establishment of a defensive line to be held until weather permits an onward push.

Preparation for planning a diversionary attack for OVERLORD in southern

France is under way. Ike is sending General Patton, and four French officers, including General Juin, to Corsica soon to reconnoiter that island as a possible staging area. It is hoped that this will attract the attention of German spies and induce the enemy to keep its forces dispersed. Patton also is to show himself in Cairo. The Seventh Army is only a shell of its former self in Sicily, but we are trying to make the Germans believe it still is a strong fighting force, ready to hit anywhere in the Mediterranean.

Commenting today on the OVERLORD plan as developed to date, Ike said that there's not enough wallop in the initial attack.

Today Ike received a brief letter from George Allen dated October 6, in which he enclosed a clipping from the *Washington Post* reading:

EISENHOWER URGED FOR PRESIDENT

NEW YORK, *Oct. 4 (INS).* Tanks Corps Post No. 715 of the American Legion in New York City is on record last night as determined to boost the candidacy of Gen. Dwight D. Eisenhower for President of the United States.

A resolution to that effect was adopted by the post September 21, but not made public until now. The resolution said the members of the post had "no knowledge or concern as to the political affiliations or beliefs" of General Eisenhower, but considered him presidential timber by reason of his outstanding "leadership qualities."

George had said merely, "How does it feel to be a presidential candidate?" I was in Ike's office when he was considering his reply. He was exasperated. He quickly wrote in pencil on George's letter, which he directed me to stick in an envelope and mail:

> *Baloney! Why can't a simple soldier be left alone to carry out his orders? And I furiously object to the word "candidate"—I ain't and won't.*

On Wednesday, October 20, I flew to Naples to investigate living quarters for Ike, his senior commanders, and the Allied Commander-in-Chief's immediate entourage. I stayed with General Clark at Fifth Army headquarters. I tabbed Roseberry Villa with three substantial residences in one enclosure, the property of Prince Umberto, and an adjoining residence called Villa Emma, where Lady Hamilton did her stuff. I also found a hunting lodge in the hills behind the main palace at Caserta, where the new AFHQ probably will be established. Also tabbed apartments in said palace—one for Ike and another for Beetle.

Ike had visited General Clark while I was in Naples on my special mission. They toured the battle front on Thursday afternoon and Friday, departing from Naples in the Fortress Friday at 3. Ike returned to Tunis, where he attended the marriage of Air Chief Marshal Tedder to Mrs. "Toppy" Black. Ike and Tedder have become buddies.

The wanton destruction in Naples re-creates all my sometimes dormant hatred for the Germans. In addition to destruction of military nature such as the water viaduct, the electric power plant, and the central telephone exchange, and a half dozen de luxe water-front hotels—leaving only the Parko Hotel undisturbed, where the Germans had headquarters and billets—I saw partial destruction of a home for the poor, total ruin of a home for the incurable, and a fire-gutted sanitarium or hospital. In the Parko, a delayed-action mine with 2000 pounds of explosive fortunately had been located by the engineers. In the post office the engineers had gone over the building four times, but the mine was so cleverly hidden it was not discovered.

An Italian college student who conducted me on a visit in the country to find a farmhouse for the General told me that his father, who is a doctor in the hospital, had two patients, boys of twelve and fourteen years, both without legs. They had accepted the apparently friendly beckon of German soldiers to cross the street. They were then met with a hand grenade which sheared their legs. German friendliness.

Another incident he related was that of eighteen Italian *carabinieri* who had undertaken to prevent the Germans from destroying the telephone exchange. They were taken to an open field, ordered to dig a hole, summarily shot, and then buried in their self-dug grave. And these were only a few of scores of similar incidents, not the least of which were sexual murders and wholesale execution of Italian families arbitrarily summoned from their homes and shot down in cold blood.

General Clark had me as a guest at his mess. I asked him about the fighting quality of British and American troops, as the Fifth Army has the X Corps of British and the VI Corps of Americans. He said that the British were bolder than the Americans but were not so adept at maneuver. If the British had a machine-gun nest to capture they were inclined to go after it headlong in frontal attack. If the Americans had a machine-gun nest to capture their normal instinct was to approach from all possible directions like Indians. The result shows in the casualties, of which the British have the greater proportion. The total at that time was 15,000 dead, wounded, or missing for the entire Army, which Clark regarded as relatively light in view of the severity of the fighting and the roughness of the terrain. Clark said that he wanted to do an end run toward Rome, perhaps at Anzio, but doesn't want to risk the seaborne force until his troops have shoved our front farther north, preferably as far as Frosinone.

Early that evening, just after dark, I heard the unmistakable unsynchronized groan of a German plane over the palace of the Duchess d'Aosta in Naples. I was surprised our antiaircraft did not open. In the palace grounds the Fifth Army had its headquarters—a likely target. The plane passed over the palace, dropped a white flare almost directly overhead, and proceeded to the harbor, where it dropped red and green flares which cast a Christmas-tree effect. Soon the harbor was cloaked in a heavy smoke screen. The raid lasted about an hour. The official estimates claimed fifteen to thirty-five enemy aircraft had been over. I had the impression our defense still was disorganized. One bomb struck an antiaircraft battery near the PRO building, killing all sixteen of its crew—one of the rare instances of a direct hit on a battery, particularly at night. I must admit I did not feel comfortable in this raid. I had just learned that General Clark's staff had elected not to put General Eisenhower in the palace where I was because they were still worried that it might have a delayed-action mine. So I had the thought of mines underneath and the bombs overhead. As we move closer again to the war we shall all have to get reaccustomed to air raids.

No shipping was hit, but in a raid the night I left, Friday, a ship loaded with cased gasoline was destroyed.

Ike now is puzzling over one of his many complex problems. Badoglio's government is recognized as a cobelligerent. This government asks for the release of Italian prisoners. They have few, if any, Allied prisoners to exchange. As cobelligerents they have reason to expect all their prisoners. Yet the Italians are contributing to the Allied war effort by their labor in England and America. If they are returned to Italy they become an economic burden not only to Italy, but to the Allies, particularly America, who have the job of supplying essential food and clothing. The Badoglio government is showing its good faith by pressing for inclusion of at least one Italian division in line of combat in addition to supplying troops for labor and guard of lines of communication.

More Criticism

ALGIERS, SATURDAY, OCTOBER 30, 1943

Lieutenant General Somervell, Chief of Army Supply Forces, had dinner with us last night, and a long conference with Ike in the office this forenoon.

We are dismayed by the prospect of a long, tedious, and costly campaign to take Rome—a situation not unlike that which prevailed in Tunisia last winter. The going in Italy is painfully slow.

General Clark is having difficulty getting landing craft to make end runs, as they are needed so badly for our over-all build-up in Italy. General Alexander has decided that ground forces should have first priority in build-up, with heavy bombers second.

This afternoon Ike received another critique from General Marshall, this time pointing the finger at what appears to him improper or inadequate application of our Air Force to prevent the German build-up.

Our Strategic Air Force has been pounding Greece and Yugoslavia, as well as the Middle East, to protect our right flank. In addition, when weather permitted, it has hit the German line of communications.

Another "needle" with General Marshall's name on it today stated that this theater is the only one in which *Yank* is not printed, and why do we give exclusive privileges to *Stars and Stripes*. Being somewhat personally responsible for the present arrangement, in which all of our resources and talent for reporting go into *Stars and Stripes*, which has become an excellent newspaper, with distribution at the front line, I will be interested to know what is said in the official reply. We also have radio stations for service to the armed forces. Shortly after we arrived in Algiers it was decided not to dissipate our meager facilities for printing and manpower by having two publications. There was and still is a critical shortage of paper. At that time North Africa and England were all a part of a single European theater and so we arranged to have *Yank*, as then printed in England, cover North African activities. When the theater was split in two, no one seemed to think whether *Yank* should be published here, as *Stars and Stripes* filled the need for current news.

Admiral Sir John Cunningham, the successor to Sir Andrew, was a guest at dinner last night. He said that the Germans had finally awakened to the desirability of attacking our escort vessels instead of the cargo ships. Their new acoustic torpedo, he said, is now used first against the escort and, if successful, the merchant vessels are then left like ducks in a pond—easy to shoot. The U-boats can then use their ordinary old-style torpedoes on them. He said that the U-boats had been recalled during the summer for refitting and now have better radar and the new torpedoes. They are a great menace. However, the antisub campaign always has gone in cycles, and he expects us to develop competent countermeasures, but we will have to take relatively heavy losses before we again get the upper hand.

Today Ike received the first critical letter from England that I recall. I didn't show it to him, but because it is the first from England, I am recording it in the diary:

DEAR SIR:

Someone once called this war a "phony" war (whatever that may mean). Well, as thousands of Englishmen can see, the only part of this war being "phony" is your being appointed Commander-in-Chief of the Allied Forces in North Africa, when two of the finest generals (Montgomery and Alexander), having cleared the enemy from the Egyptian frontier to Tunis, take second place to someone whose only qualification is that he is an American. You are spoken of as C-in-C North Africa; where does Europe begin, if Italy comes under your command? Don't think I do not give credit for the help through men, materials, and Lend-Lease, but don't forget we have been in this war for four years, twelve months we stood alone, on top of which we have produced some fine leaders who have had "actual" experience of present-day warfare. You promised to look after Gen. de Gaulle while Giraud went to the U. S. A. It wasn't necessary because de Gaulle can look after himself. He is now in his right place, as head of the Provisional Government of France, with millions of supporters in Metropolitan France. De Gaulle is the best-liked Frenchman in England who stood by us when we stood *alone*. *We never forget friends.* Thank God in this war, as in the last, we can afford to hold up our heads. Churchill has said we want nothing out of the war. Well, in any case we shall come out with less than we started, having leased for 99 years, naval bases in exchange for 50 obsolete destroyers. We were grateful for the ships at that time, but as events have proved, they were required for your protection as well as for our own. No, sir, you got the best of that bargain.

With kind regards, I remain,

Yours truly,

(Surrey, England)

We had another critical one yesterday, but from America. It was from some Texan on an RFD route who complained that a man capable of using all of the normal and some of the super-American cusswords, as Clark Lee characterized Ike in a story, was not fit for a general who leads men into battle. Instead he should be proficient at prayer. I recalled to Ike that he had once said to me, "Why, dammit, I *am* a religious man."

OCTOBER, 1943: *Intensity of European bombing increased. Planes, based in North Africa, several times hit Munich. Other targets for Allied bombers included Emden, Frankfurt, Ludwigshafen, Bremen, Hanover, Münster, Koesfeld, Schweinfurt, Düren, plants and airfields in East Prussia, Pomerania, Poland, France, and the Netherlands. In Italy Allies advanced steadily toward Rome, though slowed down by determined Nazi resistance and bad weather. Italian and Greek targets were shattered by Allied bombers. Italy declared war on Germany. Partisans in Yugoslavia took Cherso and completed occupation of all Adriatic islands. U. S. announced sending of 2,289,700 tons of food to Allied fronts in past eight months. Generals Stilwell and Somervell conferred with Mountbatten in India; General Wedemeyer named Chief of*

Staff to Mountbatten. Hull, Harriman, and Eden conferred in Moscow. Russians cleared Germans from Crimean gateway, took Dnepropetrovsk. Allies took Kolombangara base; bombed Burma, Macassar. Rabaul wrecked with loss of many Jap planes; 123 Jap ships sunk. Other landings made in Treasury group. Tokyo announced cabinet changes, with Tojo taking over Ministries of Commerce and Industry. Hitler lectured Nazi chieftains on home-front morale. (We always seemed to want to keep the home front from being too optimistic; perhaps the people at home had a better perspective than those who were in the field.—H.C.B.)

Prelude to Cairo

ALGIERS, TUESDAY, NOVEMBER 2, 1943

When Secretary Morgenthau arrived a couple of weeks ago he brought Ike a personal letter from the President. When Ike handed it to me, he told me to keep it ultra-secret because in the last paragraph the President had indicated that he would be in Africa by the middle of November.

We assumed he would come for the conference to follow that just closed in Moscow and attended by Eden and Hull. Last night, AFHQ received a signal that Colonel Frank McCarthy, staff assistant to General Marshall, and a party of Army and Naval officers are due to arrive in Algiers Saturday, November 6. They represent the President and the Joint Chiefs of Staff and, I assume, are coming here to make arrangements for the trip and the meeting which presumably will be attended by the PM and "Uncle Joe." Whether the meeting will be in Algiers, Cairo, or even Casablanca, we do not yet know. Perhaps that is what McCarthy is to determine.

Announcement of a seven-point peace plan came out of Moscow last night. They cover conduct of the war, organization of the peace, and an international plan for world security and the trial of war criminals. So far the general outline of procedure and of purpose, as stated to me by Norman Davis, are coming through. Not only were the governments of Britain, the United States, and the Soviet Union represented at the Moscow meeting, but China was represented by her Ambassador.

The General is flying to Tunis this afternoon. I am going with him but will continue probably tomorrow with Beetle to Naples.

Italian politics, reminiscent of some of our difficulties with the French, are boiling. Sforza and other professed liberals are insisting that the King abdicate and that his six-year-old grandson be the new King, under a regency. Presumably Badoglio would be the Regent and Sforza, Prime Minister.

Catching up to Date

The last I dictated for the diary was November 2—a lapse of eleven days
—the longest since this compilation was begun. In the meantime, I made
a second trip to Naples to show Beetle the layout for villas for the high-
ranking officers. Headquarters Command had found additional villas
around Caserta, one of which Beetle selected for himself. Arranged for
the Mountain Lodge to be furnished and supplied with hot water in
preparation for the General's arrival. Decision was made firm while Beetle
was there that headquarters would move to the Caserta Palace.

I had left Algiers for Naples on Tuesday, November 2, with brief stop-
over at Palermo, where I picked up General Patton. Traveled in Beetle's
C-47 and carried, at General Ike's request, five cases of cigarettes, gifts to
him from home, which he wanted the Fifth Army to have.

Returned from Naples via Tunis with severe chills. Took to bed at
the guest villa in Tunis Sunday afternoon, the seventh, and took the
usual Butcher cure of pills and hot toddy. These seemed to help, but
aboard the plane next day, en route to Algiers, underwent another succession of chills when the plane flew high to get above bad weather. After
a few hours in the office Monday, hit the hay and have been on a sulfa-
diazene diet all week. Today is the first I've been up—weak as a kitten.

Meantime Lieutenant Colonel McCarthy, of the advance echelon for
the forthcoming meeting of the President, the Prime Minister, and Stalin,
has called to see me. He said that General Marshall and everyone in
Washington are as much at sea as to changes in high command as we are.
Agreed that if General Marshall definitely knew whether he was to have
the Supreme Command in England, he certainly would have advised Ike.

The big party is to arrive between the seventeenth and nineteenth, the
President coming by one of our new battleships—the *Iowa*—to Oran,
making the run through the Strait of Gibraltar in darkness, as the sea
off Oran is a hot spot for enemy torpedo-glider bombers these days, a
recent convoy having lost four ships in that area. The President is to
spend the night at Oran and then fly to Tunis, where he will be put up
at our now abandoned "White House."

The next week should bring some light to the unsettled condition as
to command. Everyone is suffering from the uncertainty, and certainly
not the least is Ike. He has pressing problems, solutions to which cast
their shadows ahead into potential command of another Allied Commander-in-Chief. One such is that of expansion of this theater into the

Balkans. He has made a recommendation that this be done, on the assumption a Britisher will be in command.

On the battle front in Italy the going has become tougher and slower. Apparently the Fifth Army has reached the line the Germans intend to hold for the winter. After having penetrated this line north of Venafro, the VI Corps has had to beat off eight or nine vicious counterattacks, which they did successfully. Mud and rain have slowed progress all along the line. Rome looks farther and farther away. Prospects of a Christmas dinner in Rome seem dim.

Major Lee is now Lieutenant Colonel Lee. I told him the promotion was not only well merited but, in my opinion, tardy. It had been delayed by Ike only because he felt that if Lee were to return to duty with troops, he would have too much rank for his experience and his superiors would find difficulty in placing him.

Ike and Beetle went on a partridge hunt Thursday. They came home with few partridges and were wet to the skin. Today Ike has a cold and I am fearful he is coming down with a bug as virulent as mine and at a time when he will need all his energy and intelligence.

When Eden returned from Moscow he contacted the Turkish Foreign Minister and proposed that Turkey give air bases to the British immediately. As the British have held the Turks in their vest pocket throughout the war and as the trend of the war is now so favorable to the Allies, the Turks seem to have acceded, because Ike has been asked to spare four fighter squadrons for operations from Turkish bases. The big scheme is to give air cover to convoys to Russia through the Aegean and particularly to help the Russians on their southern flank. Additional naval units will be assigned the Aegean run. The Turks probably will not take more than a defensive role and will rely on the British to supply anti-aircraft protection for Istanbul and British bases, in addition to the fighter protection. Turkey, perhaps, would take a more active role if the Allies could spare more equipment for her divisions. However, if the present contemplated arrangement results in shortening the route to Russia, a good deal will have been accomplished.

An Allied Military Commission, with Major General Joyce as its acting Deputy President, has been created, and Lieutenant General Mason-MacFarlane has returned to his post at Gibraltar. Badoglio has decided that the King should not abdicate now, as advocated by Sforza and Croce, who want not only the abdication but the Crown Prince to be passed over, and the crown to go to the son of the Crown Prince. The King himself tried to form a liberal government, but failed. He was in Naples, at Roseberry Villa—earmarked for the General—while we were in Naples.

The present plan is to keep the existing setup intact until we reach Rome, with the hope that a more representative liberal government may be established. PWB workers, whom I saw at Naples, said that Italians filtering through the lines from the north had said that northern Italy would prefer abdication of the King and establishment of a democracy. If this were done, all Italians would have a greater will to fight.

Comment from visitors who have called on me during the week, such as Niles Trammel and John Royal, of NBC, Charles Daly, of CBS, and Chris Cunningham, of United Press, indicate that our home fronts are becoming impatient at the slow progress toward Rome. If our home governments are awaiting the capture of Rome to announce that Ike is to be either Chief of Staff at Washington or Army Group Commander in England, the pronouncement will be somewhat delayed unless we get a better break in the weather.

ALGIERS, WEDNESDAY, NOVEMBER 17, 1943

Monday morning Ike flew direct to Malta in order to keep his rendezvous with the Prime. Then it developed that bad weather prevented the PM from flying from Gibraltar. Instead, the *Renown*, which is carrying the PM and party, accompanied by the heavy cruiser *London* and escort vessels, continued to Algiers, where, under a heavy sky with intermittent rain, the battleships pulled into harbor. There was a terrific flap around headquarters, trying to determine whether the PM should risk the bad flying weather to proceed by air to Malta. It ended, however, with the PM deciding to stay aboard the *Renown* and to continue all the way to Malta by water. Beetle went down to see him and had a long conversation. Afterward he told me that the coming conference will be the "hottest one yet," as the PM and the British are still unconvinced as to the wisdom of OVERLORD and are persistent in their desire to pursue our advantages in the Mediterranean, especially through the Balkans. If the British should carry the day at Cairo, the entire Mediterranean operation will be placed under one command, who would be Ike. If the Americans win out for OVERLORD, the PM was certain that General Marshall would be the Supreme Commander and, according to Beetle, added that Ike would succeed General Marshall as Chief of Staff.

Ike has had an enforced wait at Malta, as the Prime Minister is not due there until this afternoon at 5—too late for Ike to have his conference and return by air today. He has cabled that he will return to Algiers Thursday around noon. In the meantime, he has been confined to his bed by his severe cold.

As to the war itself, the Russians continue to make substantial gains and are reported at one point within eighty miles of the Polish border. In our theater the fighting in Italy has been hampered, if not practically stopped, by heavy rains and consequent mud. Americans in the VI Corps were counterattacked and driven off a hill and have had to withdraw to avoid severe mortar and artillery fire. The build-up of forces continues, with Ike having to referee a competition between the air forces and General Alexander's ground forces for priority, the former wishing to hurry movement of the heavy-bomber group of the 15th Air Force to Foggia and vicinity, and Alexander, of course, with an eye to the difficulties of battle, argues plaintively for heavier movement of reinforcements and supplies.

A Beef About the Secret Service

ALGIERS, THURSDAY, NOVEMBER 18, 1943

After all plans had been perfected in detail for passage of the President's party from Oran to Tunis and onward to Cairo, during the night Beetle received a signal from Admiral King, aboard the *Iowa*, saying that the Germans had discovered from our press and radio news that the meeting place is to be Cairo. The signal suggested, as the alternative, consideration of Khartoum, in Anglo-Egyptian Sudan, at the junction of the white and blue Nile rivers, 1345 miles south of Cairo. All past plans may have to be scrapped to get the President's party of eighty into Khartoum. Possibly the group will have to be flown to Accra, on the west coast, and thence down to Khartoum, via the old air supply route.

Yesterday the secret service strongly objected to General Ike's desire to meet the President at the quay at Mers-el-Kebir, west of Oran, and to drive him to La Senia airdrome and then to accompany him in the plane to Tunis. Their reasons are twofold: (1) Ike's prominence would adversely affect security, and (2) a meeting at the quay would delay the rapid movement from quay to airdrome, which had been organized.

General Art Wilson was sent from Oran to relay the objections of the secret service, but after my conference with him last evening, the secret service has now modified the plan. I cannot forget, and am certain Ike will not, that the secret service mingled with our troops and even patted them on the hips while they were at parade for the President's inspection last January when he was en route from Casablanca to Rabat. The secret service seemed overzealous when it suspected that American soldiers, who have taken the oath to support the President of the United

States—their Commander-in-Chief—might attempt to assassinate him. Just the fact that the secret service failed to take into account the Army's loyalty made Ike furious at that time. Now when they even intimate that it would be unwise for a four-star general, the Theater Commander, to meet the President and accompany him to the airdrome, my blood boils. Fortunately, it has worked out peacefully and General Ike will be "permitted" to meet the President when he comes into our theater. Anything short of a proper welcome to the theater might seem discourteous to the President, and several flunkies have been taking too much authority in their own hands.

VGDIPs

ALGIERS, TUESDAY, NOVEMBER 23, 1943

A year ago today General Ike took up permanent residence in Algiers.

The Prime Minister still is acutely interested in vigorously prosecuting the war in the Mediterranean. He also still exhibits reluctance about pursuing the cross-Channel attack through France, and his attitude is typical of that of the British generally, yet they do not want to place themselves in the position of welshing on the decision already taken at Quebec. Judging from my conversation with Harry Hopkins, I think the question of pursuance of OVERLORD is decidedly open for reconsideration at Cairo. It conceivably could be changed in favor of supplying troops and equipment for exploitation of our position in Italy and in the Balkans. The PM probably will insist on Turkey coming into the war, and, indeed, intelligence transmitted through the American Ambassador Laurence Steinhardt, from Ankara, indicates that the Turks already have decided to enter the war in the near future, provided they have fighter protection against German bomber raids expected against their principal cities—Istanbul, Ankara, and Izmir. We know this fighter support already has been laid on because at least three RAF fighter squadrons have been sent to the Middle East for Turkey.

To pick up chronologically with Ike's travels, he returned to Algiers from Malta Thursday afternoon, November 18, and on Friday flew to Oran. On Saturday morning, November 20, he met the President at the quay and flew with him to El Aouina, at Tunis.

I had endeavored to fly to Tunis Friday morning in General Spaatz's plane, with Brigadier General Booth, Spaatz's supply officer, but weather prevented it. As Colonel Lee was sending the General's own car for use of the President at Tunis, I took General Booth with me for the long drive. We left Maison Blanche at 1 P.M. Friday, and with only an hour's stop at Setif for dinner we reached Tunis at 6 A.M., with only such sleep as we could catch between turns at the wheel.

I had arranged, on instructions, for General Marshall and Admiral King to be taken to the General's little villa, formerly used by General Doolittle and called "Times Square." The flight of C-54s began arriving at El Aouina shortly before 2 A.M. The planes had taken off from La Senia in order 1-2-3-4, with a fifth C-54 traveling empty as a spare. The President and his immediate party were in No. 1, General Marshall in No. 2, and Admiral King in No. 3, and lesser lights of these celestial ranks in No. 4. Because the secret service fears enemy fighters, the order of landing was purposely fixed 2-1-3-4.

Colonel Lee took General Marshall to the White House, where the President was to live, and here he and ten others were to be the President's guests for luncheon, while I waited for Admiral King and General Ike. The President's plane landed smoothly and quickly taxied to its proper stopping place. A crew of soldiers hastily and efficiently assembled a ramp. The first off was General Ike, looking for his car and driver, which were close by. Then the President was wheeled down the ramp and placed in the General's car. Harry Hopkins joined me in the car with Admiral King, and I deposited them at the White House. When Ike drove up with the President, I was standing by the door and heard the President say inside the car, "Hello, Butch."

Later Ike came to me and said that the President wanted to see me. We had a pleasant five-minute visit in which the President spoke of his pleasure at being away from Washington, where he described backbiting as rampant. He said he would willingly change places with me. I told him he had borne many troubles and great responsibilities in his nearly twelve years as President. His answer was, "There are some things you simply have to do." The President mentioned Steve Early. Said he had to leave him home to run the show. Marvin McIntyre had suffered a relapse and would not be at the office until January. The President seemed doubtful that McIntyre ever would recover. A bridge table was placed before the President and a large dossier of accumulated messages spread before him, so I said good-by, wished him "happy landings," and left.

When Ike had told me the President wanted to see me, he said that the President had told him that he had almost taken me from him because Elmer Davis had sought to resign as head of the OWI and, when asked by the President who could carry on his job, Elmer had told the Chief Executive "Harry Butcher." This was news to me, as it was to Ike. However, the President had induced Elmer to stay on, but Harry Hopkins had chimed in that he thought I still would be drafted, as Elmer probably would go out in January. This certainly was not good news. I told Ike that his brother Milton would know much more about the job and probably could be loaned by Kansas State College for the duration.

General Ike was asked to dine with the President, but General Marshall and Admiral King were not. They were delighted to have a free evening and it was my fortunate lot to be their host. Ike dropped in to clean up for his dinner and had time for an hour's visit with the Army and Naval Chiefs. When Ike arose to keep his appointment, Admiral King walked with him to the door and said, "I hate to lose General Marshall as Chief of Staff, but my loss is consoled by the knowledge that I will have you to work with in his job."

General Marshall had not mentioned or indicated anything about Ike's probable assignment and Ike was embarrassed, not only by the warmth of the Admiral's statement, but by the spontaneity of his comment in General Marshall's silent presence.

Ike returned from the President's dinner at about 10:30. During the evening we learned that the President had decided to stay over the next day and to leave Sunday evening for an overnight flight to Cairo. However, General Marshall and Admiral King decided they would adhere to the original schedule and take off Monday morning at 7:30.

Our house guests were airborne without incident. General Ike had offered to show the President battlefields in Tunisia, including Bizerte. However, on reflection, he decided Bizerte was too dangerous because to get into the city the harbor channel had to be crossed in a landing barge. As there is much water traffic on the channel, and the barge might be bumped and overturned, Ike felt there was too much risk involved, so changed the trip simply to go to Medjez-el-Bab on the south side of the Medjerda River and return on the north side, recrossing at Djedeida and thence back to Tunis and the White House.

A Long Talk with Harry Hopkins

While Ike was engaged in this important sight-seeing, I took Harry Hopkins to General Spaatz's caravan headquarters. Harry's questions vividly indicated the scope of reconsideration of the whole war strategy in Europe which is to come at Cairo. With fifteen heavy-bomber groups to be operated from the Foggia airfields by January, 1944, how much help can we give the Russians in their westward advance? Spaatz had a

map of military objectives showing those which could be reached from
Foggia, Sardinia, or the heel, and those which are closer to our bases in
England. In answer to Harry's questions as to possible air assistance to
the Russians—whose progress Harry repeatedly referred to as "amazing"
or "astounding" or "miraculous"—Spaatz cited the Ploesti oil fields and
refineries as the best target to help the Russians. He said that most of the
oil from this important center goes to German air and ground forces
opposing the Russians. Outside of "psychological attacks" on railroad
centers and depots in the Balkans, such as the recent attack on Sofia,
there was little else that could be bombed in the Balkans which would
really help the Russians. Our program for destruction of fighter factories
and other munition plants would be equally helpful to the Russians,
Spaatz pointed out.

In answer to another query from Hopkins, Spaatz said that it would
require 600 heavy bombers and 1800 tons of bombs to wipe out Ploesti.
He based this on the previous attack in which Ploesti was only one-
quarter damaged. He simply multiplied by four the number of planes
and weight of bombs of the previous attack. Later, Brigadier General
Norstad, Spaatz's brilliant operations officer, said he thought this was
too low, that the oil fields should be attacked twice on a similar scale.
Spaatz would go after the objective at high level and, if necessary, use
the newly developed navigational aids for area bombing through the
clouds.

Harry pursued this line of thought: if the Air Force theory that Germany can be forced to capitulate by bombing is correct—which he emphasized has never been accepted by the Combined Chiefs of Staff—
would mounting of OVERLORD be necessary? Should we consider diverting
divisions and supply, and particularly shipping, from OVERLORD to our
Mediterranean operations? How far should we try to push back the
Germans in Italy if we are not going to exploit our advantages beyond
that of using Foggia for continuation of bomber attacks against German
industries?

Without trying to answer these questions or to report in detail the
answers Hopkins received, I can give the outstanding statements which
impressed me. Spaatz said that after the weather clears in the spring, say
in April or early May, so that bombing can be persistent or practically
continuous for operations both from England and from the Mediterranean, he is confident Germany will give up within three months.
Spaatz didn't think OVERLORD was necessary or desirable. He said it would
be a much better investment to build up forces in Italy to push the
Germans across the Po, taking and using airfields as we come to them,

thus shortening the bomb run into Germany. He foresaw the possibility of getting the ground forces into Austria and Vienna, where additional fields would afford shuttle service for bombing attack against the heart of German industry, which has moved into this heretofore practically safe area. Hopkins seemed impressed with this point of view.

Hopkins said it had been a purpose of POINTBLANK—the all-out bombing effort against Germany—to make the Germans rise and fight in the air, thus to destroy the Luftwaffe. There still are 1400 to 1500 fighter planes opposing our bombing efforts in western Germany and France. General Arnold had indicated that OVERLORD would be impossible unless the bulk of 1400 fighters and their replacements were destroyed, so the Allied Air Force in Britain would have command of the skies when the ground forces attempt the invasion.

We were guests of General Spaatz's mess for lunch, at which I met Major General Richard K. Sutherland, Chief of Staff to General MacArthur, who, General Marshall had told me the night before, had been ordered to observe our air operations in England and our battle front in Italy while en route to Cairo, so he would realize there is another war than that in the Southwest Pacific. General Sutherland was placed beside Harry Hopkins at lunch. Over coffee after lunch, Sutherland pursued his nonstop conversation with Harry, who caught my eye and said, "We've got to go." We went out to "Times Square," sat by the fireplace, and enjoyed four hours of talk and speculation.

Harry said it was definite that Marshall would be Supreme Commander in England if the British do not wash out on OVERLORD. He said it was a weakness in the attack to have one partner lukewarm. He thought there must be some nonstated reason why the British sought to have the Cairo conference so soon after the Quebec conference. He thought probably the Russians and the British had gotten together and decided the best strategy now would be to exploit our situation in the Mediterranean, with the objective of opening the Aegean route through the Dardanelles to the Black Sea to hasten delivery of Russian supply. This also envisages inducement of Turkey definitely and actively entering the war.

He said that the question of OVERLORD is paramount at Cairo. Another question arises from American insistence that the Supreme Commander have control over the entire British-American warfare against Germany. I asked him if he thought Russia might be included in this command, and he said, "No."

Harry felt that the Russians' great drive would gain for the Soviets world-wide recognition as having licked Germany, leaving American and British interests at the peace table considerably submerged by the Russians. I pointed out that the Russians had achieved success using great quantities of American and British equipment, which, undoubtedly, had delayed activation of our own divisions. He said that this was true but the Russians say they have 200,000 casualties before breakfast, whereas our casualties in the Mediterranean campaigns have been small in comparison. He thought it possible the Russians might now prefer that our efforts be redoubled in the Mediterranean and that the cross-Channel operation be delayed or abandoned, dependent upon conditions in Germany as the Russians advance and as we theoretically push through Italy into Austria or southern France.

If the conference decides to increase our efforts in the Mediterranean, Ike is to remain the boss. Harry said that the war was too big for consideration of any personality, no matter how big. He said it was logical that General Marshall, having been responsible for the plan to invade Germany through France and having trained the Army to do it, should be the Supreme Commander, particularly as he possessed the appropriate world-wide prestige. I told him I understood that the Prime Minister would feel perfectly content to take either General Marshall or General Eisenhower in that job and that loss of General Marshall as Chief of Staff would be practically a calamity in the midst of the war. Our critical problem on the home front lies in Congress. I pointed out, and emphasized, that General Marshall had displayed remarkable acumen and diplomacy in dealing with all shades of opinion in Congress. Furthermore, no commander can learn the art of applying land, sea, and naval power without actually having done it in a theater or on a battle front. It would take at least six months for General Marshall to get the "feel" of this joint application, whereas General Ike has developed this sense as a result of a year of tremendous activity attended with unusual success. Furthermore, it would take General Ike six months to get the "feel" of the Chief of Staff's job.

Harry said nothing to me about the possibility of my taking Elmer Davis' job, and I did not raise the question because I want the idea to die.

I drove Hopkins back to the White House and returned for an early dinner and to bed. The President's party got off without incident at 10:30 Sunday evening, November 21.

The President instructed Ike to be present at Cairo and told him to have a C-54 return from Cairo to fly him there. Ike is to make the trip overnight on Wednesday, November 24, weather permitting, and has arranged for his commanders-in-chief also to go.

Meanwhile the fighting in Italy is virtually stalemated by torrential rains. The attack laid on for the twentieth was postponed but is due any moment. One signal in today indicates it was to have started on the Eighth Army front during last night, but so far we have no information.

Late yesterday, when we returned to AFHQ, I found to my dismay but not surprise that Drew Pearson had broken the story about General Patton's eccentric activities during the Sicilian campaign. T. J. called to tell me. I also heard it from Red Mueller, of NBC, who had joined Charles Daly, of CBS, and Demaree Bess, of *Satevepost*, in the petition to General Eisenhower many weeks ago. Ike had had several sleepless nights trying to determine how to save the best ground gainer of the United Nations generals and still prevent repetition of the actions. He had written Patton a stern rebuke and then had personally ordered Patton to apologize to each soldier individually, and collectively to the assembled officers of each division. This action had been explained by Ike to these press and radio men, and they, in turn, spread the word to other correspondents that disciplinary action had been taken and they voluntarily co-operated beautifully in not sending stories home about the deplorable affair. However, Charlie Daly phoned me last night to say that the information director had just read to the correspondents a statement of AFHQ saying that General Patton was and still is commanding general of the Seventh Army and that he had not been reprimanded. Charlie took violent exception to the latter, saying the reaction would be hostile in the home press, and it left Ike in the position of "covering" his own effective action. I felt the same and quickly informed Ike. He had approved the first part of the statement, but a statement had been added that Patton had not been reprimanded,* and this without Ike's knowledge.

NOVEMBER, 1943: *Moscow conference closed with agreement of four leading United Nations to fight until unconditional surrender and to continue action for international co-operation and security. Italian campaign moved slowly as British crossed Sangro River and U. S. took La Falconara. Allied drive finally broke German "winter line." Messerschmitt plant at Wiener Neustadt seriously damaged by new 15th U. S. Air Force. Air raids on Continent became heavier with Berlin taking five consecutive saturation raids, one by 775 RAF bombers. Russians gained on all fronts except at Korosten and Zhitomir and advanced to within thirty miles of Poland. Reds took Kiev. In Pacific bombers hit points in New Guinea, Marshalls, and the Gilberts. U. S. Marines landed on Tarawa and Makin atolls, advancing despite heavy losses. Allied forces on New Guinea captured Bongo. Gilberts taken after one hundred hours of fighting. Jap cruiser sunk in Pacific; bombers hit*

---

* General Ike had, of course, sternly reprimanded Patton, but it was a personal blistering and was not formally made a matter of record in Patton's "201" file in the War Department. The 201 file is the personnel record containing all official citations, efficiency reports, and related data.

*Rabaul, New Britain, Wewak, Buka, and Buin. Chinese forces encircled 100,-
000 Japs in Hunan. Stimson revealed Jap losses for month over 550 planes,
seventy-four naval and merchant ships, against Allied losses of ninety-one
planes and one ship. German paratroops and sea-borne invaders recaptured
Leros Island in the Aegean. (The Krauts seemed to have a succession of
"winter lines."—H.C.B.)*

Ike Returns from Cairo

ALGIERS, SATURDAY, DECEMBER 4, 1943
This is the longest period in which I have not dictated for the diary.
General Ike and party have been to Cairo, where Ike presented to the
Combined Chiefs of Staff his picture of the military situation in the
Mediterranean. I had the choice of going on the Cairo trip or to Naples
to visit Fifth Army and attend to details of housing in connection with
the establishment of our Advance CP at Caserta. I chose the latter be-
cause I had had my fill of conventions and had seen and talked with the
American principals who would take part.

Ike returned to Algiers Wednesday morning, December 1, and I flew
back from Naples yesterday.

He told me that Elliott Roosevelt had returned from the meeting of
the President and the Prime Minister with "Uncle Joe" at Teheran and
had said that the Russians insisted that we not only keep the pressure
against the Germans in Italy all winter but launch the cross-Channel
operation not later than May. This dictates that OVERLORD must be done.
He enjoyed the trip, principally for the change of environment, but doesn't
know what decisions have been taken, especially as to his own future.

The presidential party is to return to Tunis Sunday or Monday. Ike
and party, including me, are to meet them. He hopes that the answers
will be given to the questions which have pervaded all our thinking for
three months.

While at Cairo, Ike took time to see the Pyramids, Luxor, and Jerusa-
lem, and now displays the good effect of a change of scenery and at least
momentary relaxation.

As for me, I had an interesting experience on the Fifth Army battle
front. Generals Clark and Gruenther permitted me to accompany them
to an advanced observation post 1500 feet up on a mountainside from
which we could look across a valley two or three miles wide, in which
Mt. Comino loomed like Gibraltar, only larger. It was held by a full
division of Germans, who had strongly fortified it. Clark was determined

to take the mountain, as its possession was essential if we were to make further progress toward Cassino. Nine hundred guns, ranging from 155s down to tank destroyers and antiaircraft guns, were used in a spectacular bombardment that started promptly at 4:30 P.M. Many of the projectiles sailed over our heads. This had been preceded by aerial bombardment —dive and high-level bombing—to the extent of 500 sorties for the day. At 5:15, after this bombardment, the infantry of the 36th American Division and of the 56th British, as well as the American Special Service Force, specially trained for mountain fighting, were to begin their advance. This gave them a night of darkness and, fortunately, there were no clouds and a crescent moon. Since I returned, I have heard the attack succeeded, at least to the extent of taking important enemy positions. Clark told me that after he took this mountain, there were two smaller ones and a larger one to be similarly attacked. When these are taken, he can move his tanks through the valley onto relatively open ground, suitable to employment of mobile armor. But he must have a spell of good weather, as tanks and most vehicles can move only on surfaced roadways now.

ALGIERS, SUNDAY, DECEMBER 5, 1943

I have heard Ike speak of his gratitude to General Marshall, to the President, and to the country for the opportunity he has been given. He regards himself as a fortunate beneficiary of circumstances. If he hadn't told General Marshall while still in the Operations Division that he hated to serve in Washington, that he had no expectation of a promotion and didn't give a damn, perhaps G. C. M. wouldn't have pushed him into the European command in June of 1942. Since he was thoroughly informed of the variety of plans for switching from the defensive to the offensive against Germany, and the promotion of cross-Channel invasion plans, his views were sought by the British military leaders and, particularly, by the Prime Minister. When, in July, 1942, it was decided to launch the North African campaign and an American was needed to be the Allied Commander, Ike was the logical, yet "lucky," choice, as he views it.

I appraise Ike's mental attitude as akin to that of a football quarterback who has been playing an excellent game but who rebels when the coach orders him to the side lines while the game is still at fever pitch.

All will be relieved when the definite answer is forthcoming, and this is expected when the presidential party comes to Tunisia. Ike anticipates that he will have to depart for Washington quite soon because the OVER-

LORD operation will require immediate and personal direction of General Marshall in England.

The news from the Teheran conference with "Uncle Joe," as conveyed to Ike by Elliott Roosevelt, plainly shows that Russia is in the driver's seat. Decisions taken at Cairo by the Anglo-Americans obviously could not be effected until opinion of the Russians was obtained. Whereas the Prime Minister hoped to exploit our Mediterranean situation and, if possible, to avoid the heavy cost of life inherent in the cross-Channel attack, and the Americans were prepared to agree if Russia were willing, when the Russians firmly stated that we should continue the offensive in Italy all winter to contain German troops, and also launch OVERLORD not later than May, the die was cast. Even Churchill's persistent desire to bring Turkey into the war was blackballed by the Russians, who took the practical position that Russia, Britain, and the United States were already using all the equipment and supplies that the United States could produce, and so, reasoned the Russians, why take on another drain on supplies?

ALGIERS, MONDAY, DECEMBER 6, 1943

Oddly, although we have no information and don't expect any until the General sees the President, now expected at Tunis tomorrow evening, we seem to have taken for granted that we are to go back to Washington. While we still put an "if" in our plans, Ike is considering the "round-the-world" route, including a visit to MacArthur and possibly to Lord Louis. This will give him firsthand information of conditions in their theaters, the better to prepare himself for his new job.

The battle for Mt. Comino, which I saw start last Thursday afternoon and early evening, has been generally successful, but some pockets of Germans still remain to be dealt with on the ridge above the monastery.

Apparently our air defense of Bari was not well co-ordinated. There was a failure to "lay on" the red alert when the radar detected enemy planes approaching. In any event, the enemy aircraft found the harbor lighted, the ships closely packed together, and had the good fortune to hit an ammunition ship which blew up, spreading fire to four others, one of which also was an ammunition ship, and when it blew up, a total of seventeen ships were destroyed. This loss will slow the development of Foggia and perhaps the advance of the Eighth Army.

We are preparing to fly from Maison Blanche to El Aouina, starting at 9:30 Tuesday morning, to be on hand to meet the presidential party, which is due from Cairo in the late afternoon.

Ike Is Made Supreme Commander

AMILCAR (AFHQ, ADVANCE CP), FRIDAY, DECEMBER 10, 1943

Ike is to be Supreme Commander of the Allied Expeditionary Force in England!

We got this news direct from General Marshall, whose cable to Ike from Cairo was so vague that it indicated he assumed Ike knew he had been selected for the supreme job. We were awaiting breakfast Tuesday morning, prior to flying from Maison Blanche to meet the returning President. The phone rang, I answered, and Beetle's voice, almost trilling, asked if he still could catch the C-in-C if he came right over.

The message made clear that the Prime Minister still insists that Beetle remain in this theater because of his experience in dealing with the French and Italians.

Immediately Ike declared to Beetle that he would insist that his own Chief of Staff accompany him to his new job. Beetle thought he could easily be spared after the transition period and seemed unmindful that if he stayed in Africa as the proposed Chief of Staff to the new Allied Commander and as American Theater Commander, he would easily be entitled to his third star. General Alexander, incidentally, is to be in charge of the battle in Italy, and General "Jumbo" Wilson, of the Middle East, is to be Allied C-in-C. Why "Alex" did not get the Mediterranean command from the British, we do not know.

The President and his party arrived at El Aouina airfield in midafternoon. Ike took the President in his car to the White House and I had Harry Hopkins and Major John Boettiger with me. When opportunity permitted, Harry took me aside and told me privately that Ike was to be Supreme Commander. Hopkins said he thought the President and others thought General Marshall had come rightly to regard his job as Chief of Staff as more important to the war effort. He could devote his superior qualifications to global warfare, with which he is now intimately familiar. He could deal with Congress. The decision in Ike's favor had been made after very careful consideration of all of the factors, with important weight given to the need of General Marshall's experience in dealing with Congress in his present job and of Ike's battle-front knowledge and success in this theater. Ike's personal appearance before the Combined Chiefs of Staff at Cairo and his demonstration of his grasp of the military situation had added to the good impression already held of him.

The President, with Ike, General Spaatz, and General Smith aboard, as well as Hopkins, Admiral Leahy, Real Admirals Ross T. McIntire and Wilson Brown, and Major General "Pa" Watson, flew to Malta Wednesday morning so the President personally could present Lord Gort an inscribed testimonial from America to brave Malta. From there they flew to an airfield in Sicily, where the President reviewed such American troops as could be assembled on the field. On Ike's recommendation, he also gave the DSC to General Clark for bravery and leadership at Salerno, the Legion of Merit to Beetle (who couldn't be found at the moment) and to a half dozen other officers from colonel to lieutenant who had distinguished themselves in action.

The plan originally was for the President and party to fly from Sicily to Marrakech to spend the night. However, when the big C-54 attempted to land at Luca Field, in Malta, Major Otis Bryan, the pilot, discovered to his dismay that the hydraulic pressure had failed and prevented opening of the wing flaps, which are useful, if not necessary, to the landing. The plane circled twenty minutes until the wing flaps could be lowered. The landing was made successfully, but two hours were required for location and repair of the broken mechanism. Consequently, the party returned to El Aouina and the President stayed overnight. The party departed at 6:30 Thursday morning for direct flight to Dakar, some 2500 miles. So far as I have heard, this is the first direct hop attempted between these points, although the mileage is well within the range of the C-54.

The C-in-C and immediate entourage are now awaiting the return of the Prime Minister from Cairo.

Many incidents of interest to me developed during the presidential visit. The President himself discussed all sorts of problems, ideas, and ambitions with Ike. These were not confined to military subjects, but Ike felt complimented by the President's frankness and indications of complete confidence in him.

I had numerous talks with Harry Hopkins and felt that he was more than happy with what appeared to me from the outset as the logical arrangement. Ike, however, still professed that his primary desire was to remain in the Mediterranean, where he properly had his fingers on the pulse of all operations. But he learned he can take Tedder with him and that Spaatz will have command of the Strategic Air Force, both in England and the Mediterranean—the better to co-ordinate the air attack against German industrial objectives. Spaatz told Ike that the scheme would work best if he were to be immediately subordinate to Ike, so that when the cross-Channel battle starts, all the power of the SAF can be directly under control of the Supreme Commander. General Arnold, apparently, had not envisioned this arrangement and, consequently, another problem with the new command remains to be settled.

In returning to England, Ike expects to make Major General John C. H. Lee Deputy Theater Commander and Commanding General of the Army Service Forces. Plans cannot be crystallized until Ike has overcome the insistence of the PM for Beetle's retention in the Mediterranean. Ike says there will be no argument on this, however, as he plans simply to say "no" and insist that he has a right to take his own Chief of Staff and chief teammate on his new and important job.

This morning Ike received a message from the Combined Chiefs saying the President and Prime Minister had approved their decision that this theater should be expanded to include all of the Mediterranean and Turkey effective today. They gave him formal notice that he is to be Supreme Commander of the Allied Expeditionary Force in England and take his new job when convenient, as soon as possible after January 1, 1944. Public announcement of his appointment and of the new Mediterranean commander is to be made simultaneously.

When the President departed yesterday morning, he asked Ike to consult with the PM as to the wordage of the announcement—Harry Hopkins having insisted to the President that the story must make clear that Ike is to be the Supreme Allied Commander or else the change will appear as a demotion. This morning Ike had a signal from the President, presumably from Dakar, thus indicating that he had arrived safely, requesting that announcement be deferred until he reaches Washington. He also asked if Ike would prefer a delay until Rome is captured.

After Ike read this message at breakfast this morning, he said he didn't care to wait until Rome is taken because once decision has been taken to change your job, everyone has "ants in his pants" to get on with the new one and inevitably loses interest in the old. However, since the transfer isn't effective until January 1, we might get Rome by then, which would make the transition perfect. On the other hand, there is so much work to be done in England and the problem of staff assignments so difficult, particularly since much of the staff has been assigned, he feels he will need every day until the attack. In the meantime, however, he plans to spend a few days in Italy, not only to say farewells, but to have the satisfaction of having established his own Advance Command Post on the continent of Europe.

Amongst pleasures of seeing friends in the presidential party was that of having been a guest at dinner with the President on Tuesday evening. Elliott brought his mess crew of his Photographic Reconnaissance

Unit and served a regular GI meal, using two Italian prisoners as waiters.

At the Teheran meeting the Russians had sided with the Americans on OVERLORD. They insisted the Germans be kept engaged in Italy as actively as possible all during the winter and what they term "a second front" must be started not later than May. Furthermore, Uncle Joe was prepared to fight the Japs when the Germans were licked. My report from Elliott Roosevelt about Teheran said that Stalin and his military staff laid out before Roosevelt and Churchill the Russian plans for a great offensive against Germany, but said that if it was desired, Russia could diminish her attack against Germany to proceed against Japan. However, this offer had not been accepted, as both the Prime Minister and the President wished first to press against Germany as strongly as possible. Obviously, Stalin had preferred to finish off Hitler's hordes first.

Ike is disappointed that General Marshall has decided to proceed from Cairo to Australia rather than to return here for discussion of organization of this theater. I reminded Ike that General Marshall was hopeful, even last May, of visiting MacArthur and that he utilized this opportunity to do so.

For the first time since we learned of the possibility of Ike's transfer, we now feel that we have a definite and concrete mission. This adds zest to living and interest in pursuing the objective. It has already made a remarkable difference in Ike. Now he is back to his old system of incessant planning and thinking out loud of qualifications of this or that man for certain jobs.

Ike Clears Some Personnel Questions with Mr. Churchill

AMILCAR (AFHQ, ADVANCE CP), SUNDAY, DECEMBER 12, 1943
The PM arrived yesterday, and his specially built Lancaster was first landed at a fighter field forty miles beyond El Aouina which was "closed." It was, to all traffic but that particular plane. Air Marshal Tedder quickly sent word for the PM's plane to take off and fly back to El Aouina, where it arrived about 9. All of us had waited from 7.

The PM appeared tired and told Ike twice, while riding from the field to the White House, that he felt very tired, indeed. He hoped to gain several days' rest, but still insisted that he should visit General Alexander in Italy. Last night, however, he agreed to have Alex come here and probably will not visit Sicily, although I imagine his love of troops will entice him to the front when he feels up to it.

While the PM held out for Beetle, Ike says he merely grinned and said that is an undebatable subject; Beetle must stay with him. The PM seemed to acquiesce by saying that he hoped that Beetle would be left at AFHQ sufficiently long to indoctrinate the new Allied Commander. Ike had responded that he would do better than that. If the PM would have his British Allied Commander come soon, he would "teach him himself." The fact is the PM has not made up his mind as to the man. Ike thinks it will probably be General "Jumbo" Wilson, but Alexander is still in the running.

Ike had intended to return to Algiers today, but when the PM decided to have General Alexander come to Tunis and it was found that General Arnold, who was to have met Ike in Algiers today, could be diverted to Tunis, he decided to spend an additional day here, conferring on air with Arnold, Tedder, and Spaatz. There will be another conference with the PM, the CIGS, and General Alexander.

Last evening, Ike, after a preluncheon conference with the CIGS, lunch with the PM and talk for an hour after lunch, then dinner at 8:30 and further talks, was completely whipped down—even his voice was hoarse. He got in eight hours of sleep and today is ready for more.

This morning he phoned Beetle in Algiers to send a recommendation to General Marshall that General Devers be brought from England to become American Theater Commander in the Mediterranean.

Ike clearly misses the opportunity to check his views with General Marshall, particularly as he is now thrown into discussions of problems on highest level without knowing whether his recommendations to G. C. M. will be accepted. However, he is proceeding on the assumption that General Marshall will agree substantially to his recommendations.

Ike had four personnel questions to clear with the PM or the CIGS and jokingly listed them in this order: (1) permission for Telek and family to enter the U. K. without six months' quarantine; (2) retention of Beetle as Chief of Staff; (3) assignment of Lieutenant Colonel James Gault as his British Military Assistant; and (4) at Beetle's request, transfer of Brigadier Strong, our G-2, to the new London headquarters.

Telek and family probably will go to quarantine. Beetle is O.K. The CIGS readily agreed to the new assignment for Jimmie, who in a few days will go to England to get our quarters set. The CIGS suggested, with respect to Strong, that Ike first study the staff already assigned to COSSAC,* General Morgan's planning group for OVERLORD, and then decide whether he wants Strong transferred.

* General Morgan was nominated by the Combined Chiefs of Staff in January, 1943, at the Casablanca Conference to draw up plans for the "return to the Continent." He

CASERTA (AFHQ, ADVANCE CP), SUNDAY, DECEMBER 19, 1943
Ike arrived in Naples yesterday noon by Flying Fortress to "establish" his
Advance CP on the continent of Europe. He was accompanied by
Beetle. A small staff operates a war room, signals, and necessary house-
keeping chores just as was true at Constantine, Amilcar, and Malta,
where we had Advance CPs from time to time as the campaign progressed.

I have been here a week and for several days had the help of Sergeant
Farr and three house boys to establish and make as homelike as possible
a rather ornate villa known as Della Ortensie, overlooking Naples Harbor,
and a hunting lodge of Prince Umberto on the mountain back of the
palace in Caserta which houses our headquarters.

While waiting for the C-in-C's plane to arrive at Pomigliano yesterday, I visited with General Clark, who had flown to meet General Ike.
General Clark was critical of the Air Force for failing to bomb or strafe
roads behind enemy lines after dark. They had not refused to do it, he
said, but simply did not get it done. He thinks the reason is that our
American fliers are not taught night flying. He said the Germans move
a division out of the line and another one in during the night. They even
have headlights on their trucks just beyond the range of our artillery.
If he could get effective air action against road movement at night, his
progress would be facilitated.

Yet the Fifth Army has made good progress in the past two or three
days and Clark was pleased to have an optimistic report for the
C-in-C.

I told him I had heard that the brigade of Italians had done badly. He
said they had in their first attack (in fact, had failed). Their commander
had asked for the brigade to be withdrawn from the line, but Clark had
insisted that they stay and attack with the Americans. The attack was
successful and the Eyeties were given an objective. Now the Italians are
very proud of themselves and have regained, or found, new confidence.

Today Ike and Beetle were escorted by General Clark on a visit to the
American part of the Fifth Army front. Ike flew back to Caserta in a Cub.

---

was given the title of Chief of Staff to the Supreme Allied Commander (designate)
and from the initials christened his organization COSSAC, just as Ike's headquarters
was soon to be known as SHAEF. Although he had been nominated in January and had
early begun work on the plans, General Morgan did not receive a formal directive until
April 27, 1943. The plans which he drew up, with a joint Allied staff, were approved
at the Quebec Quadrant Conference in August, 1943. Although Ike and his commanders were to recommend some changes in them, everyone recognized the basic,
brilliant strategy of General Morgan's work. History will probably know him as the
"planner of OVERLORD."

Just now I handed a message to the General which had been repeated to him from Algiers. It concerned the attitude of the CCS toward operation HERCULES, and sought to make certain that no commitment would be made to the Turks that this operation would be undertaken. It has to do with Greece and the Aegean Islands—just what, I frankly admit I do not know. When Ike undertook to read the message, he said, "I get tired of having to read all these Charlie-Charlies in these messages," Charlie-Charlie meaning CC for Combined Chiefs.

The Supreme Commander Shoots a Rat

CASERTA (AFHQ, ADVANCE CP), MONDAY, DECEMBER 20, 1943
After Ike returned from the front Sunday afternoon, he visited for the first time the hunting lodge, where he took up quarters. I had found this remote and ancient stone building, nestled amongst the hills which make the mountain ridge rising behind Caserta. It is in a high-walled enclosure containing hundreds of acres of woods and miles of trails for riding. I had been enthusiastic about its possibilities as a retreat for Ike where he could sit and contemplate before the fireplace or even warm his backside by an Italian-type high earthen stove in the living room.

I had perhaps oversold the joint to the boss and to myself. In any event, when he arrived at the "dream cottage" he was tired and a bit disgruntled. He had promised to take six of us, including Colonel Elliott Roosevelt, to General Clark's for a specially prepared Italian dinner to be cooked by the downtown restaurant owner, Giacomo, but in Clark's own tent mess. He would have preferred to eat quietly and get to bed early.

So he sat down in the first room he entered—the living room with the Italian stove—which was warm and, I thought, attractive. He wasn't inclined to move to accept my invitation to inspect my "dream cottage."

Presently Mickey came dashing down from Ike's bedroom. He shouted, "There's a rat in the General's bathroom," and added that he was afraid of rats. He carried Telek, who had discovered the rat, and wouldn't let him down.

The rat was sitting on a toilet seat, a perfect target for Ike, who put on his spectacles, growled that the light was bad, and carefully took aim and shot—furrowing the seat under the rat. It jumped to a pipe. Always an advocate of trigger squeeze, he again took careful aim and shot. He clipped its tail. The rat jumped a foot higher, clinging to the pipe. Again Ike shot. The rat tumbled to the floor after a final shot and lay quivering.

Williams was the mobile reserve and was on hand with a large stick of firewood and did the mopping up.

Ike, Beetle, Lee, Mickey, and drivers got away in two cars the next morning for the seven-hour drive to Bari at 7:20, I being left at home to look after some Christmas shopping for the General. It's a tough war. . . . For my own part, I noticed several red welts on my body from some insect. I suspect we have lice as well as rats. But, as Beetle said, the place is not so bad, considering it's only thirty-five miles behind the front lines.

We First Hear of V-1

ALGIERS, TUESDAY, DECEMBER 28, 1943

After stopping for a brief visit with the PM at the White House in Carthage on Christmas Day, the General flew on to Algiers. I returned from Naples December 26, bringing the household staff and equipment.

Yesterday, Ike wired General Devers, advising him that his current tentative plans would place him in the U. K. about January 10 to 12 and regretted that he could not have had a personal talk with him in advance of presentation to General·Marshall of his first impressions of logical command system for OVERLORD and of the American organization. He invited Devers, however, to give him any information he desires on personalities or plans.

Ike is trying to get battle-experienced commanders in OVERLORD. If an untried commander, no matter how high his reputation at home as a trainer or director of maneuvers, failed in battle, Ike would have to relieve him and possibly do so at an inconvenient moment.

We spent Friday at Capri, I having lobbied Ike into taking the day off. He took all of his personal staff.

When we left, I shanghaied my old friend of Washington days, Lieutenant Commander "Ozzie" Roberts. We took him to the so-called "Ridgeway Villa" for Christmas Eve dinner. My mother had sent canned popcorn, which the boys had popped and strung to decorate a small Christmas tree. Other guests were William Giblin, of Red Cross War Relief in North Africa and Italy, Margaret Morin and Mollie Ford, Red Cross girls, and Charlie Daly. We had dinner on GI rations. The house was cold, several of the windows having been broken by a bomb blast, and more than mere Christmas spirit was needed to keep me warm. Ike's principal Christmas present was the formal announcement by the President, which we heard on the Italian radio set, that he was the new

Supreme Commander for the cross-Channel push. There were presents for all the boys, Ike giving each of them an old Roman coin.

Ike and party left Naples in the Fortress Christmas morning at 9. Stopped at Tunis to see the Prime Minister and reached Algiers late on the holiday.

When I returned to Algiers late Sunday, December 26, I found Ike had spent much of the day with his successor, General "Jumbo" Wilson, and had discussed fully with him transfer of the Allied Command. General Jumbo departed for England yesterday and expects to return to Algiers January 8 to take over his command on the tenth.

We are packing to leave Algiers for the U. K. A C-54 will be available for office and household staff and equipment. The General and a small party will go in a Flying Fortress. As we prepare to take up residence in England, I have been interested to note a report from Allied agents at Madrid. It states that the Germans have built cement platforms for the launching of rocket-propelled glider bombs at Barneville, Chantilly, Cramont, Frechun, Gamaches, Neufchâtel, Octeville, Saint-Germain, and Watten. The report states that each platform is built on the slope of a hill so the projectile may be elevated toward its target "somewhere in England," which I would assume to be mainly London. Each platform is 150 to 200 meters in length and breadth. Heavy electrical cables are connected to a catapult on each platform. The rocket bombs are transported in railway dining cars. Each weighs fifteen tons, of which five are liquid air and five phosphorus. This must be Hitler's secret weapon.

While we were in Naples, we had a report of a 1300-plane raid on shore establishments of France, and later I saw a report that several of these rocket installations have been hit. Hitler's surprise and secret weapon thus may prove ineffective.

Ike started Beetle to England today by air. He is to investigate the organizational setup, plan office space and living quarters.

Yesterday Ike had a press conference—his farewell. However, he hopes to have another one on or about January 8 to introduce General Wilson, but will quickly hand over the conference to his successor. At Ike's conference yesterday, he was asked when he thought the war would end. He studied a minute and then answered forthrightly:

"I believe we will win the European war in 1944."

After the meeting, I told him I thought the quotation would add to the overoptimism at home. He added a qualification, making it read:

"It is my conviction that the Allies will win the European war in 1944. The only thing needed for us to win the European war in 1944 is for every man and woman, all the way from the front line to the remotest hamlet of our two countries, to do his or her full duty."

Pattern of Command for OVERLORD

ALGIERS, WEDNESDAY, DECEMBER 29, 1943

This morning, as we were sitting down to breakfast, I commented that I felt today would bring good news. Ike went to the telephone and called Colonel Dan Gilmer, the Secretary of the General Staff, to inquire if there were any messages from General Marshall. A broad smile broke on Ike's face as Gilmer replied: "You got everything you wanted."

The Chief of Staff and he saw eye to eye with Ike on the readjustment of assignment for commanders. In addition, General Marshall requested that he come straight to the U. S. before he goes to England, see his family, and get at least a brief rest.

As soon as possible, General Devers is to take command of the American theater organization in North Africa and be Deputy Allied Commander. The headquarters staff of the Seventh Army, largely dormant since its success in Sicily, is to plan ANVIL—the amphibious assault through southern France—under the supervision of General Clark, who will retain command of the Fifth Army until Rome is captured and then take command of the Seventh Army. General Patton will come to England to command an army, this despite the bad public reaction over the face-slapping incident. General Hodges is to be sent to England, on Ike's call, and eventually is to command an army or be alternate to Bradley as Army Group Commander. General Eaker is to become Commander-in-Chief of Air Forces for the Mediterranean, with Air Chief Marshal Sholto Douglas as his deputy. General Jimmy Doolittle is to command 8th Air Force, based in England, whose headquarters staff is to provide personnel for over-all headquarters for General Spaatz and his Strategic Air Force. Spaatz commands U. S. strategic bombing from both England and the Mediterranean against Germany, so the entire weight of our heavies and long-range fighters can be directed from a single source. Spaatz, however, reports directly to the Combined Chiefs. Theater and SOS organizations, both North Africa and England, are to be consolidated in the interest of efficiency and economy.

Ike sent a message to General Montgomery saying he had heard of Monty's plan to fly from Africa to England in his regularly assigned C-47. Ike begged him not to risk his neck in a two-motored craft on this long trip, particularly with a crew which has not regularly made the run. He offered to give him highest priority on one of the regular C-54s with four motors. Monty is to be in Ike's new command for the long-awaited plunge of the dagger into Germany's heart.

ALGIERS, THURSDAY, DECEMBER 30, 1943

The great uncertainty as to whether Ike would have to or should go home finally crystallized in the message from General Marshall. The kindly Chief of Staff thinks Ike would make a mistake by not coming home first. G. C. M. points out that things have been going ahead in the United Kingdom for a long time and under a wise and aggressive man and that Beetle has already been there. Ike will be under terrific strain from now on. General Marshall is interested that he be fully prepared to bear the strain and he is not interested in the usual rejoinder that Ike can take it. It is of vast importance that the new Supreme Commander be fresh mentally, and he certainly will not be if he goes straight from one great problem to another. As a clincher, General Marshall said: "Now, come on home and see your wife and trust somebody else for twenty minutes in England."

I am arranging with the Air Transport Command for a special C-54 to fly us to the States. Mickey and I will accompany the Chief, and Mickey is really walking on air. Have also arranged for three convalescents and two others to go home with us. The only stipulation Ike placed on selection of the convalescents by the medicos was that two of them must play bridge, as he wanted a foursome.

DECEMBER, 1943: *Pacific Charter, pledging punishment of Jap aggression and expulsion from all except home islands, signed by Roosevelt, Churchill, and Chiang Kai-shek, as Chinese troops seized Changteh. Stalin joined Churchill and Roosevelt in plans against the enemy and further agreement to work for "a world family of democratic nations." Turkish Premier conferred with Churchill and Roosevelt at Cairo. After sustained bombing of Cape Gloucester, MacArthur landed on New Britain, took Gloucester after additional landings by Marines. Other New Guinea bases fell to Allied troops as air action continued against Marshall Islands. Air raids against German bases on Europe got heavier by fleets of three thousand heavies, with Pas de Calais area hit often. Eisenhower named Commander of Anglo-American invasion forces with Air Chief Marshal Tedder as Deputy. British Navy destroyed famed German Scharnhorst. Italian campaign developed into series of stiff battles as Yanks dug Germans out of cellars in Ortona, took Mt. Comino massif. Russians cleared middle Dnieper, broke 185-mile Nazi wall west of Kiev. U. S. bombers, while raiding German port of Emden, shot down 138 Nazi planes while losing only twenty. November reports show fewest sinkings by German U-boats since May, 1940. ("Took Mt. Comino massif"—only four words, and true, but what a sight.—H.C.B.)*

Trip Back Home

20 GROSVENOR SQUARE, LONDON, SUNDAY, JANUARY 16, 1944
Ike, Mickey, and I left Algiers for Marrakech in the Fortress shortly after noon, December 31.

Arriving at Marrakech about 6, Ike was taken immediately to see the Prime Minister. Ike found the PM insistent that the SHINGLE operation, the end run * to Anzio toward Rome with two divisions, be executed. He pressed for his way, despite shortage of landing craft and the great hazard of annihilation to the landing force if Fifth Army should be unable to reach it by land. General Clark had told me he wanted his ground forces at Frosinone before the end run is attempted. Ike felt that the insistence of the PM indicated he had practically taken tactical command in the Mediterranean. This feeling, plus the knowledge that General "Jumbo" Wilson was desirous of keeping Allied Force Headquarters at Algiers, so far behind the lines, left Ike with a rather unsatisfactory impression as he departed from the theater.

We left Marrakech at 4:45 the morning of New Year's Day, in a C-54 piloted by Captain Guy Cain, and reached Terceira, Azores, in six hours. Flying somewhat inside the three-mile limit off San Miguel, one of the Azores, a shore battery opened and fired at us three times. I had seen the flash when the battery fired and immediately went forward to the pilot's compartment. I asked Captain Cain if he knew we were being shot at. He said, "Yes, sir, I have decided to fly away." I later found that these made the fifty-seventh shots fired by the so-called "friendly" Portuguese of that island.

After three hours for refueling—the British gasoline truck has a small hose and we were taking 3100 gallons—we took off for Bermuda, which we reached after eleven hours. After a couple of hours we again were on our way, and in four hours' flying time, reached Washington, Sunday, January 2, at 1:30 A.M. Assuming we were within the three- or even the twelve-mile limit of the United States by midnight, we can say we were in Africa, the Azores, Bermuda, and America on New Year's Day. On Christmas Day, Ike had been in Naples, Tunis, and Algiers.

We had taken Telek and Caacie's family, Junior and Rubev, and they sported fancy Scotch-plaid leashes and collars. Our reception by our wives in our respective apartments across the hall from each other was

---

* The PM, by the way, with his English playing-field and cricket background, had at first had difficulty understanding the term "end run" and had even sent cables from London asking that the term be defined. It had not, so far as he knew, ever been used in traditional military parlance before.

somewhat jarred by the presence of the dogs, which immediately left their marks first on Mrs. Eisenhower's Oriental and then Mrs. Butcher's. As the hotel was a poor place for training, Ike gave Junior to Milton's boy, Buddy, at Manhattan, and Rubev was tearfully presented by Beverly to Paul Porter's daughter with a mortgage on the first boy puppy born, if any.

Life on the home front is quite a story. These dirges of sacrifice at home, coupled with the glamour of the war in the Pacific, and universal hatred of the Japs, leave the returning serviceman from the Mediterranean astonished. The result in my case was largely to make me shut up and to grin and bear the tales of woe.

Ike had cabled General Marshall that in order to see his family he would like to have secrecy on his visit observed for a few days. When he reached Washington the Germans had started propaganda indicating they anticipated a quick winter thrust across the Channel by the Allies to take place within two or three weeks, and consequently General Marshall requested a censorship ban on grounds of military security so that the Germans would not have the benefit of knowing that General Eisenhower was in America, which, of course, would indicate to them that their fear of a "quickie" invasion was groundless. He desired to keep the Germans confused. As a result, Ike's movements were furtive and clandestine. He was in the hands of the War Department throughout. Colonel Frank McCarthy, General Marshall's right-hand man, was assigned to meet him with a car at the back door of the Wardman, reached by a generally unused servants' staircase. With the stars from his overseas cap removed and those on his shoulder covered by his overcoat collar, Ike then was driven to a private entrance to the Pentagon in a black sedan by a soldier in a civilian chauffeur's uniform. No one but the office staff could see him as he entered.

He went there first on Sunday afternoon and used the office of the Secretary of War. When he returned there was company at our apartment. Steve and Helen Early had arrived. Ike asked them to come to his apartment. Steve, upon learning of the General's desire for fresh oysters, drove off to Harvey's and presently returned, not only with a great tray with fifty oysters, but with several thick, juicy steaks. Tom Carson had just returned from his farm and donated two chickens and some dozens of fresh eggs, as well as butter, which really is tightly rationed. The party reached the climax when the president of the hotel company was found in the small kitchen of the apartment with a white apron tied around his neck, busy washing and drying dishes.

On Monday evening, January 3, General Marshall was having a dinner for some of the ranking members of the House and Senate Military Affairs Committee.

Ike spoke for twenty-five minutes about the campaigns in the Mediterranean, and when he finished all stood and drank a toast proposed by General Marshall, first to the President and then to Ike. Ike had ended his military discussion with the statement that he found the most difficult question in the field to be answered was that of "What about the strikes?" He said that he needed an answer to that question and that the troops needed it. This set the pattern already cast by General Marshall, who had recently held an off-the-record press conference in which he said that the railroad strike and the threatened steel strike had given the Germans hope of disintegration of our home front—so much so, that the probability of the war ending within several months had been lost. This statement had first been printed without reference to General Marshall himself, but subsequently the *St. Petersburg* (Fla.) *Times* had identified the anonymous authority as General Marshall. From then on the fat had been in the fire. Labor had been insulted and had publicly replied in a variety of defensive and accusatory press releases.

One question remains unsettled in OVERLORD, i.e., does the Supreme Commander have command of the Allied Air Forces in Britain? General Marshall said that he had intended, if named Supreme Commander, to insist on the point, even to the extent of denouncing in the public press any arrangement short of unification. Ike still has the problem to lick.

In the next eleven days Ike visited John in West Point with Mamie, conferred fully and often with General Marshall, spent several days with Mamie at White Sulphur Springs, and flew to Kansas to see his mother.

On Thursday, January 13, Ike again utilized General Marshall's office for a couple of hours, sandwiching at the desk. He made a three-minute recording for the Fourth War Bond Drive, dictated a number of messages, and conferred with Generals McNarney, Handy, and Somervell. With respect to the latter, a list of questions had been formally presented, to which Ike dictated answers. They had to do with supply organization on the Continent after ANVIL and OVERLORD have joined. He also saw Elmer Davis, director, and Edward Klauber, deputy director, of the OWI and readily agreed that the OWI's representative, George Lyon, should go to London to look out for the "public's interest" in news of the big push.

We took off from National Airport at 7 o'clock in the evening, in a C-54 of which Captain W. G. Golien was chief pilot. He has a tremendous number of flying hours—around 16,000—and later told me had flown former Ambassador Joe Davies on his trip to Moscow.

We reached Bermuda in three and a half hours, thanks to a strong tail wind. Had a late snack with General Strong and his officers in the regular mess, Ike being interrupted repeatedly, as is now usual in a semipublic place, to autograph short-snorter bills. Leaving Bermuda at 1:20 A.M., we arrived at Prestwick in seventeen hours' flying time, stopping only at Terceira, Azores, on the way. There we were met by Lieutenant Colonel James Gault, the General's British Military Assistant, who had General Lee's train with Ike's former car, the "Bayonet," standing by to take the party to London. England was wrapped in fog, and flying from Prestwick would have been impossible. We reached London at 11 P.M. in a dense fog and found that Jim had selected and had furnished an attractive house called Hayes' Lodge on Chesterfield Street near Berkeley Square.

Today Ike has conferred with General Lee, General Bradley, and Lieutenant General Fred E. Morgan, KCB, the British Chief of Staff of COSSAC. Ike is now in the process of checking Beetle's reports on the organization and location of headquarters and soon will be into the plans for the invasion.

According to Lieutenant Colonel R. A. Harris, a Canadian who is the military assistant to General Morgan, and who visited with me for an hour while Morgan was with Ike, the attack is tentatively laid on for the dark period in early May, probably May 5. It is now planned that three divisions will be in the first assault, with two as immediate followups. There are to be thirty-five divisions in all, fifteen of which are British or Canadian and twenty American. The British ground forces are under the 21st Army Group, commanded by General Montgomery, who arrived in England from Italy with a flare of trumpets and inadvertently gave undesired publicity to Norfolk House, which General Morgan had been trying to keep as the secret rendezvous of the chief planners and staff of OVERLORD. At the outset the Americans will be under the 1st Army Group, commanded by General Bradley.

Harris said there probably are a hundred platforms for launching glider bombs on the French coast. Although repeated air attacks have been made against them, only five are known to have been destroyed or damaged. He said there are several theories as to the purpose of the Germans, many believing they have been "sucking us in" with a giant hoax. This school thinks the Germans have built these platforms as decoys in the hope of diverting our bombing from their industrial plants.

This afternoon the announcement of Ike's arrival and assumption of duty as Supreme Commander, Allied Expeditionary Force, has been authorized. In order to accomplish General Marshall's purpose, the wording has purposely been made to indicate that Ike has been here several days. The statement says: "It can now be announced that General Eisenhower has assumed the duties in the U. K. assigned him by the Combined Chiefs of Staff. On his journey from the Mediterranean to the U. K. he had conferences with the President and the Prime Minister."

Today Ike already has instructed General Lee to consolidate all of the Services of Supply activities in this theater and to do it now and not to consider it as merely a plan. He has also told him that he will delegate the primary responsibilities of Theater Commander to him.

PART FOUR

Overture to Liberation

JANUARY TO JUNE, 1944

LONDON, TUESDAY, JANUARY 18, 1944

The most important question confronting Ike at the moment, which, no doubt, will be the subject of unending discussion in planning for days or weeks to come, is the strength of the initial assault wave to hit the beaches across the Channel. In order to assure necessary strength for this vital plunge, most of the planners and commanders who have been working on the problem, including General Montgomery and Beetle, have recommended a serious reduction in ANVIL—the southern France end of the giant pincers.

Ike had had a considerable part in the effort of the U. S. to equip the rebuilt French Army. He feels we have in it a very considerable investment, and the French troops, plus the Americans and British, must be used to obtain a final decision against Germany. Therefore, a gateway for them into France must be obtained or all of our French investment will have been wasted. Unless we have a southern France invasion, a great number of American and other forces would be locked in the Mediterranean. In addition, he feels that a commitment by the British and American staffs was made at Teheran, assuring the Russians that ANVIL would take place.

Again, the principal limiting factor is landing craft. The cross-Channel operation may have to be delayed to await further production—a challenge to the home front which, unfortunately, can't be told.

Allied Family Problems

LONDON, THURSDAY, JANUARY 20, 1944

Ike made his duty call on the King today, visited the CIGS, Sir Alan Brooke; and the First Sea Lord, our old friend Sir Andrew Cunningham, on Tuesday; and met with and spoke to the principal members of the AEF staff at Norfolk House, Wednesday.

The King was pleasant and even asked Ike to autograph a blank card for His Majesty's aunt, who, it seems, collects signatures. Ike didn't remember the name of the relative.

After his meeting with the CIGS Tuesday, Ike said he had been amazed over a complaint voiced by Sir Alan against Beetle—amazed because it was the first complaint Ike ever had heard about Beetle from the British. It seems that Beetle was pressing the CIGS for transfer of Generals Gale, Whiteley, and Strong from AFHQ to SHAEF, and when the CIGS did not readily agree and indicated that Beetle was "raiding" AFHQ of its best talent, Beetle declared that Sir Alan was not being "helpful" and started for the door. This provoked a bit of frank talk, but Beetle obtained consent for transfer of the first two. He was especially regretful that the CIGS would not release General Strong because of his thorough knowledge of Germany and all-around capability as G-2. Ike explained to the CIGS that Beetle fights for what he wants but, win or lose, he means no harm.

I went with Ike to the meeting at Norfolk House Wednesday morning, where 120 of the principal officers assembled to hear his greeting. Ike emphasized that in an Allied Command such as this he expects thoughts and words which indicate nationality to be erased.

Last evening Beetle dropped in for a long visit at Hayes' Lodge on Chesterfield Hill.

SHINGLE, the Prime Minister's pet military project, is to be launched January 22, weather permitting, and will consist of two divisions and possibly part of another landing at Anzio. There will be one British division and one American and the landing will be made on the west coast somewhat ahead of General Clark's Fifth Army, with the hope that ground forces can reach the amphibious assaulting party in time to make the operation successful and especially to help beat off counterattacks.

It seems there is a double about-face on the de Gaulle issue. First de Gaulle has become frightened of the radical and Communistic elements which he has gathered in his coterie of supporters, both in the resistance element in France and in Algiers, and has been sobered by their extreme views. Ike had recognized this before he left Algiers, which accounted for a love fest he had with de Gaulle before leaving for Washington. Now, as we are planning for returning to the Continent through France, we find our own State Department and the Foreign Office, to some extent, unwilling to permit the French Committee of Liberation to take responsibility for setting up a provisional government in areas of France which we liberate. The French National Committee had proposed a scheme which Beetle, Ambassador Wilson, and others in Algiers had thought practicable and fair, so Beetle had dispatched Wilson and Brigadier General Julius Holmes to Washington to attempt to bring the State Department in line.

Yesterday morning the London *Express* played the story that command of the air operations from the U. K. had not been placed under the Supreme Commander. Ike commented that this type of publicity would make more difficult his job of welding a force which would work together harmoniously and enthusiastically, and hoped that the trial of the issue would not be made in the press. Yet the question of air command is unsettled. Air Chief Marshal Tedder is due in today. So far Tedder's appointment as Deputy Supreme Commander makes him merely "an ambassador without portfolio," but both Ike and Beetle expect that Tedder will not be shoved around by the Air Ministry or Air Chief Marshal Harris of RAF Bomber Command, who seems to have been dictating the policy of separate command. At the moment the air operations from U. K. are under a directive from the Combined Chiefs, aimed primarily at destruction of German industry, but operational control of air for OVERLORD is to flow to the Supreme Commander at "an appropriate date." Both Ike and Beetle felt Tedder would help get this straightened. Beetle especially emphasized that Portal would be fair and honest and big-minded, and emphasized as well that Sir Andrew, who also is a member of the Combined Chiefs of Staff, would follow the pattern of application of land, sea, and air power which was developed so successfully under Ike in the Mediterranean. It is important that air operations fit in with the plans for OVERLORD, which will require bombing of communications and strong points for weeks ahead of the actual invasion. The issue will come down to the desirability of continuing the all-out attack against German industry or diversion of all or part of the air power for the invasion.

While both General Arnold and General Spaatz do not like to see the Strategic Forces of the "heavies" used except against POINTBLANK (all-out air attack) targets, they both nevertheless recognize that during the invasion period, at least, they should come under the Supreme Commander's control. This will probably work out all right. Spaatz is in the peculiar position of having in his command control of U. S. Strategic Air Forces in both the U. K. and the Mediterranean. His command, therefore, geographically transcends Ike's. After the invasion period, command of the Strategic Forces should revert to the Combined Chiefs, with Portal and/or Arnold as their agents, who in turn pass execution to Spaatz and Harris. The Strategic Air Forces can thus be free to hit their main objectives without dissipating their strength against tactical targets. Ike can always call upon them, in any case, in an "emergency." Ike and Spaatz see eye to eye on this.

Plans to move AEF Headquarters to Widewing (Bushy Park, near Kingston), the former headquarters of the 8th Air Force, are now firm. Ike hopes that by intermingling of officers in messes and closer contact in living quarters, he will be able to accelerate the welding of an Allied Command.

Beetle was realistic in pointing out last night that Ike again will be the target for those critics who say the British have cleverly accepted an American as Supreme Commander but have infiltrated British commanders for land, sea, and air, even though a majority of the troops are American and the ratio of British to American planes in the U. K. is four to seven. This is something on which we shall be on the defensive, and therefore Beetle was anxious for Ike ultimately to take over the ground operations, particularly after we have two army groups and he can get his advance command post in France. Also, incidentally, there are some 870,000 Americans in our forces in the U. K. at this time. In talking with Beetle, Ike did not fail to bring up the personal complaint of the CIGS, and Beetle expressed regret he had been abrupt. Thought perhaps the war was getting on his nerves. Or his stomach. Or both.

Beetle does not know that General Ike has recommended him for his third star.

Ike Changes the Plan

LONDON, FRIDAY, JANUARY 21, 1944

The new Supreme Commander, moving into his job with an Anglo-American staff already created by General Morgan, is busily engaged in meetings.

The meeting held with Admiral Ramsay, General Montgomery, and Air Marshal Leigh-Mallory today may prove to be one of the most important of the war. Ike wanted the strength of the assault increased from three to five divisions and the area of the attack widened. He also wanted to employ two airborne divisions on the Cotentin (Cherbourg) Peninsula and not to use one against Caen. Leigh-Mallory felt that it would be wrong to use the airborne on the Cotentin Peninsula and that losses will be seventy-five to eighty per cent. Ike believes it should be done to cut the "neck" of the peninsula, and so does Monty. They will still use one airborne near Caen to seize bridges over the Orne and Dives, but will not try to take the city itself from the air. With all these changes, the need for postponing the assault for a month is apparent.

Exchange of Letters with a Hostile Ally

LONDON, SUNDAY, JANUARY 23, 1944

SHINGLE has started well; so well that part of the British press, given the opportunity to boast a bit about a British general, is doing some sly crowing. Infantry got ashore "standing up" without immediate opposition, although land mines were numerous.

Ike has been awaiting the launching of SHINGLE. He sent personal messages to Wilson, Alexander, and Clark.

Today Ike received the following letter—the only one of its kind in recent months and by the same person whose letter is recorded in the diary under October 30, 1943 (I had thrown away the first one—but this one got to the Boss):

Horley, Surrey,
17 - 1 - 44

DEAR SIR:

While I offer you a personal welcome to England, I do not do so as C-in-C of the Allied Forces because I consider that either General Montgomery or Alexander should have held that position. Remember we have been in this war for over four years. Twelve months we stood alone. Our troops have done some very hard fighting, especially in Africa, where we chased

Rommel for over a thousand miles out of Africa. If for some reason a British general was not desired we should have preferred a Russian general to lead the Allied Forces in the same way as they have led their wonderful Army in Russia. We are all very pleased that Mr. Churchill has seen that wonderful Frenchman, General Charles de Gaulle, who is now in his right place as head of all loyal Frenchmen. Perhaps some day your country will recognize his sterling qualities.

> With kind regards
> Yours very truly,
> (Signed ———)

To this Ike personally dictated an answer:

DEAR MR. ———:

I well understand the feelings that prompted you to write your letter of the 17th of January. Moreover, I am the first to agree with you that any one of the generals you suggested, and possibly even any one of a number, would have been a better selection than that actually made for the accomplishment of my task. However, I hope you will agree that as long as this duty has been placed upon me by Great Britain and the United States, I have no recourse except to do my very best to perform it adequately.

I hope also that the mere fact that you do not agree with the two Governments in their selection of the Commander will not prevent you from doing everything that it is possible for you to do to help win this war speedily and conclusively, so that we may have an end of destruction and carnage.

I thank you for your personal welcome, which I well understand is to be distinguished from any thought of official welcome to these islands.

> Sincerely yours,
> DWIGHT D. EISENHOWER

Today Ike received a personal letter from General Arnold in which "Hap" expressed satisfaction that Ike had presented strong views to him that both the U. S. Strategic Air Forces in Europe under Spaatz and the Bomber Command of the RAF under Harris should be placed under the Supreme Commander's direct control for the impending operations. "Hap" wished to be advised when and if Ike presents his recommendation to the Combined Chiefs, and particularly desired to be completely informed in advance so he could support the request. Incidentally, when Beetle visited the Prime Minister at Marrakech, the PM had reiterated that control of all operational aircraft would go under the Supreme Commander for OVERLORD, but subsequently Beetle learned that the Air Ministry had documented statements from the PM that did not jibe with his latest position. However, Ike feels the PM will go "all out" for the proper arrangement when the time is opportune.

It now appears that General Patton will come to the U. K., but we don't know yet who will head the planning and assault of ANVIL. Certainly the tactical surprise achieved against the Germans in the landing south of Rome will give greater heart to those who approach OVERLORD with little faith—not to mention the chagrin which the German General Staff, as well as the German public, must feel in this latest setback to the once mighty Wehrmacht.

We are moving into our old home, Telegraph Cottage, when the new headquarters at Widewing are completed, around February 1. I am delighted.

Yesterday perhaps 150 clippings from American papers reached my desk. All but one hailed Ike's appointment as Supreme Commander and retention of General Marshall as Chief of Staff. The one sour note was from the New York *Daily News*, reprinted by its sister paper, the *Washington Times-Herald*. It did not deal with Ike's new command, but criticized his statement that we will win the European war in 1944 as giving rise to false hopes of early victory, but more specifically lampooned his qualification in the statement which said that every man and woman in every city and hamlet had to do his or her duty if his prediction is to come true. The editorial said that this would be a convenient loophole through which a "talking general" could slide if he did not deliver the goods in 1944—or words to that effect.

The bulk of the editorials emphasized Ike's modesty and self-effacement, of which to me his selection of Telegraph Cottage, a small, old, and badly heated house, is an example. Of course, no announcement has or will be made that he is living in this cottage, but every officer, whether he lives in more or less spacious and comfortable quarters, will know that their Chief is living more modestly than nearly any general officer.

We will probably have to retain Hayes' Lodge as an overnight place in London. Ike will have meetings with the Prime Minister at Downing Street and dinners to attend in London. Occasionally the fog becomes so thick one cannot drive from London to Kingston Hill, or even around London, without a guide walking ahead of the car with a flashlight. He will have certain days in London when he will receive callers at his office, which, it has now been agreed, will be, as General Lee suggests, at 47 Grosvenor Square. This change from 20 has appealed to me from the outset and even more so since I have learned that 20 Grosvenor not only has been publicized as the headquarters building, but the British equivalent of our American *Life* has devoted seven pages of pictures to the building and offices, inside and out.

Beetle, incidentally, has been pressing at every opportunity for Ike to move out of London. Beetle is apprehensive that rocket bombs will be released on London in the near future. Ike thinks we are likely to have them by the middle of February. Our U. S. Air Force again has raided the heavily built "ski" platforms on the French coast. There are said to be 158 of these platforms from which rocket bombs are to be launched. Some of them, but only a few, have been knocked out by our bombs. They are difficult to hit and seem constructed like the virtually indestructible submarine pens at Saint-Nazaire and elsewhere.

Sunday evening Beetle dropped in at Hayes' Lodge to report on his meeting with General Montgomery and planners. As a result, agreement has been reached, subject to Ike's approval, and along lines desired by both Ike and Monty, for a large assault over a wide bridgehead.

The Prime Minister has returned from Marrakech and seems fully recovered from his long siege of pneumonia. As always, once the British are committed to a project, no matter how much they may pick flaws in it before they sign on the dotted line, once they have given their word or signed, they go through with everything they have, heart and soul. The Prime Minister is prepared to scrape the bottom of the barrel to increase the effectiveness of the Allied attacks, and has indicated that the calculations of planners, who are compelled to work within the limitations of an estimated availability of resources, must not be permitted to curtail our strength if we can intensify our production effort.

The week has shown a deep conviction in all military circles here that the Allies are approaching a tremendous crisis and are gambling for incalculable stakes.

For the cross-Channel operation, the limitation of suitable beaches for landing, especially of proper beaches which have roads leading inland to facilitate transport, has dictated that if we are to obtain quick initial success, we must broaden our attack. As Ike pointed out when he first saw the plan in Algiers, long before he knew he was to command the operation, we must take more beaches than the planners originally intended. We must get a force ashore which can take the Cherbourg Peninsula and gain for us the all-important harbor and port of Cherbourg. We will need five divisions assault-loaded, but this means additional assets in several lines, chiefly Navy, with special emphasis on landing craft.

Every effort is being made to preserve a strong ANVIL, with an assault strength of at least two divisions.

It is clear that even at the cost of a month of good campaign weather after we get ashore, OVERLORD must be delayed until the end of May.

We Watch the End Run at Anzio from the Side Lines

LONDON, TUESDAY, JANUARY 25, 1944

Ike is getting into his old line-up of appointments. They seem unending.

The Military Government people already are planning the peace terms with Germany. They are having a meeting today to discuss dismemberment.

The end run of the Fifth Army is proceeding satisfactorily to date, although an Intelligence report just received, and a public statement of General Wilson's in this morning's papers, indicate that a counterattack with the equivalent of two divisions is momentarily expected. The British 1st Division has all its infantry ashore and the U. S. 3rd Division has entirely landed in the assault area. Perhaps the Americans had better beaches to land on. The bridgehead late yesterday was twenty miles wide and seven miles deep. Ike is worried because the bridgehead isn't deeper. The morning papers are optimistic and print a variety of rumors that we have taken Littoria and its airfield and have cut the Appian Way, but our Intelligence reports do not confirm these. We could still get a bad wallop.

Last evening three hospital ships off Anzio were attacked from the air, the *St. David* being sunk, and the *Leinster* was set on fire but it was brought under control and she has now returned to Naples.

When the Supreme Commander had his press conference on Monday, January 17, he was asked if General Montgomery would be the ground Commander-in-Chief. Ike suggested that the writers should not "go off on the end of a limb." A variety of interpretations have been given to the statement, most of which indicate Montgomery as Bradley's opposite number—Bradley being commander of the 1st U. S. Army Group, called by its initials FUSAG. On the previous day General Montgomery had made a speech to the U. S. 29th Division and had flatly stated that he was to be the ground commander.

"I came home the other day from Italy," he said, "to take command of the British Army and the American Army of which General Eisenhower is the Supreme Commander, and he has put one army, the First American Army, under me for the battle. We are going to fight and that is a very great honor for me."

Actually General Montgomery is correct concerning the assault, but when there are sufficient American divisions ashore, Montgomery will command the British group and Bradley the American.

Reunion in a Kennel

LONDON, THURSDAY, JANUARY 27, 1944

Last evening Ike received a message of the British Chiefs of Staff as sent to the British Joint Staff Mission at Washington. Briefly, the British agree with Ike's expansion of OVERLORD from a three-division to a five-division assault and say in general that the resources will be found by hook or crook. Meantime the American Joint Chiefs of Staff are working on Ike's message and have asked a number of questions of our planners.

Yesterday I met General Patton, his aide, and Caacie at Cheddington airfield, about thirty-five miles northwest of London, and took Caacie to the kennel to begin her six months' imprisonment in quarantine. Telek is already there and is definitely not enjoying the confinement.

So much news interest has attached to the dogs, particularly Telek, that any attempt to avoid the strict quarantine law of Britain might have greatly impaired General Ike's standing in the public eye. When Ike appreciated the situation which might develop if he did not comply, he unhesitatingly arranged for Telek to go to quarantine promptly upon arrival in England. General Smith had brought him by plane from Africa. Ike said, however, that the ordeal was equivalent to "locking up a part of my heart." He visited Telek at the Hackbridge Kennels on Monday afternoon and was immediately confronted with a photographer who wanted a picture of the General holding Telek. This was refused, but photographers have taken numerous pictures of Telek alone, some backgrounded with an enlarged photograph of the General which someone had placed in Telek's bare kennel above his pallet of straw. By holding a piece of meat above the General's picture the photographer had cleverly made Telek appear to be licking his master's face. Ike is very fed up on the news interest in his dog and frequently gives me Billy Hell for what he terms overpublicizing the dogs. However, I cannot control news interest and I have assured him that no one has ever been hurt for loving a dog, but he wants his love life with Telek kept private. However, he is rapidly learning that there is little privacy available in the life of *the* Supreme Commander.

General Patton, cloaked in censorship for a few days, came to dinner last night. Ike had seen him during the afternoon at the office and told me before Patton arrived at the house last evening that he had given him a severe bawling out for failing to follow Ike's instruction of counting ten before issuing an order or by taking any abrupt action. Patton had been most contrite, as he was last night. He is a master of flattery and succeeds in turning any difference of views with Ike into a deferential acquiescence to the views of the Supreme Commander. For instance, he told Ike during a lively discussion of history that anyone would be foolish to contest the rightness of the Supreme Commander's views, particularly as he is now— in Patton's words—"the most powerful person in the world." Ike glumly and noncommittally passes off such flattery.

General Patton is to command the Third Army, headquarters of which are now assembling. While censorship has been imposed on Patton's arrival, Ike said last night he does not intend to keep him "under a blanket" for more than a few days, and cited to me the fact that upon arrival he had immediately released the name of General Bradley after it had been bottled for months.

When Patton's name is released we will probably get critical reaction from the press, not only in the U. S. but in the U. K., because of his new assignment. According to General McClure, the British press had keenly resented Patton's action in Sicily. Some American correspondents had felt the incident would ruin Ike. Of course, he was made Supreme Commander after disclosure of Patton's rash action. Incidentally, Patton said last night that hereafter he certainly would be more careful as to the place he has a tantrum and certainly will not choose a hospital.

Ambassador Winant has submitted from the European Advisory Council an advance copy of the points to be made in the terms of surrender of Germany. Beetle has appropriately commented that "This is counting chickens before they are hatched, but it is something that may worry us later." The proposed terms stipulate "unconditional surrender" and itemize various points incidental to complete occupation and subjugation of Germany, including eradication of laws against the Jews, relinquishment of occupied territory, return to the 1938 boundary of Germany, abolition of the German General Staff, and payment by Germany of the cost of occupation. These are only a few of the points. Press and radio in Germany are to be controlled in the interests of military security and peace and order. All we have to do now is to get it signed for Germany. This may still be quite a chore.

Lieutenant Colonel Gault, who is a perpetual pleasure, has reported for me the gist of Ike's trip to the British 79th Armored Division in Suffolk. It is experimenting on mines, mine clearance, and tank obstacles, particularly those which will be encountered across the Channel. Models were built of antitank obstacles and different types of sea and esplanade walls likely to be found on the coast of Normandy and of the Low Countries. The work is ultra-secret. The British have developed a tank on the front of which is a rotor arm, driven by the tank engine. To the rotor arm are attached chains of various lengths which, when the rotor revolves, strike the ground with force, thus detonating mines. Called a Crab, it's speed is about one and a half miles an hour—an improvement on the old Scorpion used in the desert, which was a half mile. (This type of flail was used in the desert with some success, but some of my British friends have told me they considered the Germans not quite sporting when they placed the detonator to a mine some yards ahead of the mine itself, so when the flail hit the detonator, the mine blew up under the tank.)

Another new device is a plow attached to the front of a tank which makes a furrow eighteen inches deep and is intended to dislodge and shove aside the perilous mines. Behind the tank is dragged an ordinary cultivator intended to detonate any remaining mines.

Another tank has been made into a portable ramp. If a high wall has to be crossed by tanks, this ramp is driven up to the wall and then becomes a small bridge over which other tanks may climb to the top and plunge over.

To me, the most exciting new gadget demonstrated is a Sherman tank which has been made amphibious. It is called the DD. To me the fact that a tank, weighing some thirty tons, can be made to float and propel itself in water and emerge on the beach is one of the surprising innovations of the war. Ike went aboard one of these when it was launched and steered it during its amphibious run.

There were numerous other mechanical devices designed primarily to help tanks and infantry through mine fields. The British also have a flame thrower attached to a Churchill tank. It will throw a flame 130 feet, carries 400 gallons of mixture, thereby enabling sixty shots of a second each to be thrown by the tank. This is useful against pillboxes. Its carbon monoxide fumes suffocate the enemy if he isn't already burned to death.

LONDON, FRIDAY, JANUARY 28, 1944

Ike returned from his trip in time for dinner last night.

Today Ike pinned the third star on Beetle at Norfolk House, his nomination having been confirmed by the Senate. Beetle had thought there would be a ruckus, certainly in the Committee, when his name was presented, but so far have heard of none.

Global Sitreps

LONDON, SATURDAY, JANUARY 29, 1944
General Marshall has given Ike what amounts to a free hand to relieve division, corps, and even higher commanders who are already assigned in the ETO and to select others from a long list which has been submitted. Ike assumed that General Marshall wants him to have the right to hire or fire, which is fair enough, the Supreme Commander having to carry the responsibility, anyway.

Weather has cleared for continuation of the aerial bombardment of Germany and today the U. S. Air Force dispatched 930 heavies with more than 600 escorts against Frankfurt, results not being known as this is written, but the 930 represents the largest number of American bombers ever dispatched in one operation.

I have been attending the reports of the situation on all the fronts, given by Intelligence officers in the war room at 20 Grosvenor. The largest convoy ever to proceed from the U. S. to the U. K. is now en route somewhere south of Greenland. In it are eighty-three merchant ships. A pack of sixty or more U-boats is assembled off the western coast of Ireland, lying in wait for this and other convoys. A convoy en route to Murmansk was attacked by six U-boats during the week and seven ships were sunk. However, January may be a record month for low number of losses, the total as of yesterday being eighteen, as against at least triple that number in preceding months. Two U-boats were sunk by our aircraft yesterday. One hundred and sixty-two sea mines were laid by the RAF off Kiel last night. These are more or less normal operations and reflect the intensity of activity against Germany.

The length of the front line in Russia as measured on the map is slightly more than 1900 miles, an increase of 500 miles over the front line as it existed when the Russians started their big offensive in July, 1943. If the Germans retreat to the shortest line from the Baltic to the Black Sea, it is presumed German divisions may be released and the same strength of opposition continued against the Russians. Our Intelligence shows the Russians have 430 divisions and the Germans 200 plus on the Russian front.

The battle at Anzio bridgehead in Italy is going slowly. At lunch Ike wondered what was causing the slowness.

Release of the report of Jap mistreatment of American, British, and Filipino prisoners in the Philippines has caused a furor at home.

London seems slow and unexciting after the activity and travels in the Mediterranean.

Spasmodic Poker Game

LONDON, MONDAY, JANUARY 31, 1944

I spent Saturday evening as guest of Lieutenant General Spaatz, Brigadier General Ted Curtis, and Colonel Everett Cook at Park House, where I took another lesson at poker. Our game was interrupted frequently by telephonic consultation about the communiqué covering the largest daylight air raid of the U. S. Air Force.

During dinner the air-raid siren wailed. Heavy AA guns soon went into action near the house. The windows rattled, reminiscent of Algiers. Dinner went on, with only occasional reference to the raid, but we could hear the German planes overhead. There was a sharp whine of a diving plane and Spaatz said: "There's a night fighter going after one of 'em." After the raid was over, Spaatz said that German fliers who had been overhead must feel very dispirited because of the poor results and the heavy opposition. Later I found that 24,000 shots of AA fire were fired, with three enemy AC shot down. Seems like a lot of ammunition.

This month is closing with the least shipping loss from U-boats of any month in the war. The U-boats off the Cape of Norway have attacked another convoy en route to Russia. In today's report no merchantmen have been lost, but one British destroyer, the *Hardy*, was sunk south of Bear Island.

Our VI Corps in the Anzio bridgehead is attacking and making fair progress, but the Germans now have a formidable force in front of it. Newspaper expressions of hope that Rome would be quickly captured and praise for General Alexander's brilliant maneuver have now given way to explanations by the armchair experts, one of whom today said that, after all, the main purpose of the fighting in Italy was to contain German forces to benefit Russia. Progress on the old line in Italy has been slow, with activity nil on the Eighth Army front, and hard pressure on that of the Fifth Army. The French seem to be doing well, and our 34th again has attacked toward Cassino. As Ike indicated at his final press conference in Algiers, in every campaign there comes a time when slow but vicious slugging becomes inevitable. This certainly is the case in Italy, despite the brilliant end run. But I can't forget that General Clark wanted to be as far as Frosinone before attempting it.

JANUARY, 1944: *Night and day bombing of Germany increased in frequency and tonnage, with plane plants, railyards, and chemical factories chief targets. Italian fighting continued bitter. Allies inched forward around Cassino, established precarious, diversionary beachheads at Anzio and Nettuno; crossed Garigliano River. Russians entered Poland, took important cities in Ukraine and White Russia, approached Estonia. Allied bombers pounded New Guinea and New Ireland targets. MacArthur's troops and Marines annihilated Jap garrisons on opposite sides of New Britain. Successive raids destroyed 256 Jap planes over Rabaul. Navy planes bombed Kusaie Island, 700 miles from Truk, and Wake; supported air raids against Marshall Islands preliminary to invasion. U. S. and RAF unveiled jet fighter plane. Lieutenant General Bradley announced as Senior Commander, U. S. Ground Forces in Britain. U. S. and Great Britain refused recognition of Bolivian revolutionary regime. OWI revealed Bataan and Corregidor atrocities. (It might be said, too, that Jerry paid us some calls, sometimes seeming all too personal, at our new London address.—H.C.B.)*

LONDON, TUESDAY, FEBRUARY 1, 1944

Ike's frank critic, of Surrey, England, who had deplored appointment of him as Supreme Commander, recorded under January 23, 1944, has mellowed a bit. Ike's personal direct-by-mail campaign with his only dissatisfied English customer may be regarded as satisfactorily concluded, and Ike is happy.

LONDON, THURSDAY, FEBRUARY 3, 1944

Last night Ike was a guest at the PM's dinner for the King. The King didn't leave until 1 A.M. and Ike was held for a talk with the PM until 1:30. The PM is not too enthusiastic about the progress in the Anzio beachhead.

Yesterday Ike sent a congratulatory message to Air Chief Marshal Arthur Harris of the RAF Bomber Command and to General Spaatz, in which he said in part, "Every ton of bombs that falls on the enemy's war machine helps to hasten the day of his ultimate defeat."

"Monty" has hit the front pages again with a speech to soldiers in southern England saying he is fed up with the war and hopes, therefore, to get it finished this year. He said he never takes an army into battle until he is certain of victory.

Ike has been made a member of the Athenaeum Club, an exclusive organization for those who have distinguished themselves along intellectual lines. Neither money nor family has any influence with selection. Although Ike does not know yet who nominated him for membership, his name was seconded by the First Sea Lord, Admiral Sir Andrew Cunningham. A special point was made that for the second time in 130 years the book in which nominations and seconds are written was sent out of the club to the Admiralty so Admiral Cunningham could inscribe his name. Ike has accepted, but only after first worrying lest it would lead to an enforced attendance at some dinner. The honor is so unique, however, that he has expressed himself as hoping to visit the club after the war. This afternoon he is making a trip to another club—the Hackbridge Kennel Club—to visit Telek and Caacie.

Move of Supreme Headquarters to Widewing is meeting opposition. Staff officers get entrenched in comfortable living quarters and some like the leisurely luncheon afforded by the London clubs. To remove themselves from easy access to club life seems a hardship and consequently there is much pulling against the new. However, Ike says he is moving if he has to become established in Widewing alone.

Press Relations on OVERLORD

LONDON, SUNDAY, FEBRUARY 6, 1944

The Prime Minister and his War Cabinet are concerned over the security of OVERLORD. It is feared there may be a leak. The press of both countries have been asked not to speculate as to place, dates, or size of the attack.

The Prime Minister felt that despite the precautions taken and the normal control by censors of the flow of stories from the U. K. and the U. S., there still was a possibility that correspondents could gain fragments of information about forthcoming operations and then unwisely exchange their tidbits until a general line of information may be collected by members of neutral embassies and transmitted by them in cipher to their own countries, from which it may easily become known to the enemy. Therefore, a very stringent attitude is recommended for our dealings with the correspondents. We are cautioned particularly not to give background information, either before or after OVERLORD starts.

After consultation with General McClure, General Ike has concluded that correspondents will not be accredited to SHAEF until a short time before the actual operation, but he does not want such an aloof attitude taken by our staff that correspondents will be forced to use spying methods to get legitimate information. He would feel insecure if either he or his public-relations staff here were anything but friends to the press and sees no reason why this relationship should endanger the operation. He has generally found that correspondents can be trusted. However, discretion will be used to avoid telling the press anything which even in the remotest contingency could be dangerous.

In watching the flow of requests for material for OVERLORD, particularly landing craft, and the responses from the War Department, I am more and more impressed that the good old U. S. A. really is fighting two major wars at once. The fighting in the Pacific is absorbing many landing craft during this critical phase of the European war; no telling how much our demands interfere with the prosecution of our effort in the Pacific. Whoever has the task, and I suppose it's the Combined Chiefs', in deciding between the Pacific and European wars must be in a terrible dilemma, but, from our standpoint, we feel that since we are committed to winning the European war first, we should have the primary call on landing craft.

I notice that the British press frequently discusses the command setup for AEF. There is considerable evaluation of personalities and abilities. Generally speaking, the British columnists write that General Ike's contribution to the Mediterranean were administrative accomplishments and "friendliness in welding an Allied team." They apparently dislike to believe that General Ike had anything to do with the military decisions in those campaigns. They don't use the words "initiative" and "boldness" in talking of Ike, but often do in speaking of Alex and Monty. Yet, Ike had to make numerous important military decisions and take the final responsibility for all of them. I should think he would get sour on being written about as "Chairman of the Board," and sometimes labeled as "timid," when he has had to do things which were so risky as to make some of his subordinates think him overbold, if not crazy.

LONDON, MONDAY, FEBRUARY 7, 1944

Leaving from Addison Street Station in the special train, Ike, Lieutenant General Bradley, Major General J. Lawton Collins, Lieutenant Colonel J. F. Gault, and I arrived at Plymouth Friday morning. Ike and party were met by Major General Gerow, Commanding Officer of the U. S. 29th Division. The day was spent traveling by car to inspect that division and to observe its training activities. How good it will be in battle remains to be seen, as is true of any "unblooded" division.

Saturday was spent visiting the 4th Division, one of the regular outfits. This division had just arrived. It is under command of Major General R. O. Barton.

Ike made five informal talks to officers and men during the day. In two of them and particularly the largest group, which was the 8th Infantry, assembled at Heathfield Camp at Honiton, he said he would see them all "east of the Rhine" and would personally make certain they had champagne, "even if I have to buy it myself." Later I suggested he was running up something of a bill, and he said that there would be plenty in the contingent fund to buy champagne and that nothing would please him more.

LONDON, TUESDAY, FEBRUARY 8, 1944

The Italian campaign has bogged down, leaving the armchair strategists who were overenthusiastic when the beachhead landings went so well now equally overpessimistic. Apparently these wiseacres now seek a "goat" on whom to lay the blame for failure to exploit our initial advantage.

Wes Gallagher, our war-correspondent friend since Gibraltar days, has just arrived from North Africa. He said that the reason for failure to exploit the beachhead was fear of the various generals to take responsibility. He said that they missed Ike. Wes declared that if Ike had been there he would have said, "Go ahead, the responsibility is mine."

Beetle has talked on the transatlantic secret telephone with Handy in an effort to impress the War Department with the need of more landing craft and to co-ordinate differences in estimates of planners here and there. Handy then cabled an inventory covering the whole landing-craft situation and gave the welcome news that the combined planners agree there is a lift for at least seven divisions for personnel and eight in motor transport for OVERLORD, still leaving a two-division lift for ANVIL. This statement is predicated on a target date for late May. Many of these craft are built on inland waterways, must be moved to New Orleans, crewed, sailed to Hampton Roads or New York to join convoys, and then proceed to U. K. From New Orleans to the U. K. requires six weeks.

Ribbons and Harbors

LONDON, WEDNESDAY, FEBRUARY 9, 1944

Shuttle bombing between the U. K. and Russia and presumably between Italy and Russia is under consideration. Stalin has approved use of six airfields in Russia to accommodate 105 to 200 bombers. The American Air Force is to send technical representatives to work out details and arrange supply of bombs and gasoline, etc. We are also permitted to fly photographic reconnaissance planes in and out from these or other selected bases.

The Prime Minister has volunteered to Ike that His Majesty would be pleased to wear one of the American service ribbons for North Africa and has put the question to Ike, who in turn has relayed it to General Marshall. The King is titular head of the British armed forces and of course made a prolonged visit in Africa.

On the subject of ribbons, I asked Tedder while on the recent trip why he did not wear the African Star. He said he had started service in Africa after the date prescribed and consequently was not entitled to it. He said that the King had noticed its absence from his row of ribbons and had asked the same question. Whereupon the King had said that the trouble lay in Winston having drafted the rule at 3 o'clock in the morning.

Devices to create an artificial harbor across the Channel, mentioned for the first time in my presence by Lord Louis Mountbatten during the Sicilian campaign, are well under way. Steel breakwaters called Bombardon Units are under construction, 73 of 113 required units to be available by April 18. Concrete units to be floated to the site offshore and sunk to form a breakwater also are being built, employing 19,000 laborers, and are to be completed by April 21. Another scheme is to sink ocean-going ships to form a breakwater. Seventy-one 300-foot vessels would be required. Allied resources are under examination for selection of suitable ships. Naval pontoons to form sunken causeways, to facilitate movement of ducks, amphibious tanks, etc., from the water over the beach, will be required—13,000 of them. Another pontoon called the Braithwaite is under consideration. It is said that 4500 will be needed, but only 1200 can be manufactured by March 31. Apparently the scheme discussed by Lord Louis for blowing air bubbles from pipes laid under the water has not been found practical.

Ike Stands by His Colleagues in the Mediterranean

LONDON, FRIDAY, FEBRUARY 11, 1944

All military and many civilian personnel in London, and indeed in most of England, have been living under the fear of Hitler's widely advertised secret weapon—the rocket glider bomb. Much of our aerial bombardment of the French coast has been directed against more than a hundred ski tracks from which the gliders carrying the rocket-propelled bombs are to be launched. This morning, however, there was a report given by the Intelligence officer in the war room, quoting the G-2 of the theater, General Edwin L. Sibert, that because of our bombings the rocket situation is under control and it was explained that bombings had put most of the ski tracks out of operation for four weeks, but probably continual bombing would be necessary to keep them inoperative. The prospect of wholesale attack on London has influenced Beetle in his desire to get the headquarters, particularly of the Supreme Commander, out of London. Now that the danger seems to be dissipating, the glue which seems to hold much of ou staff in London probably will get stickier.

I referred in the comment of February 8 to Wes Gallagher's gripe about failure of generals in the Med to take responsibility and his feeling that Ike was sorely missed. In yesterday's review of press stories filed from London to the U. S. I noticed Wes had written on this subject. He wrote in general that for the first time since 1942 the campaign in the Mediterranean lacked boldness and frankly criticized Wilson, Alexander, and Clark. Ike had told me several days ago that he was fearful that writers, seeking to alibi for their overenthusiasm when the beachhead landing went so well, would begin to draw comparisons of past successes under him in the Med and the current difficulty. This would be most embarrassing to him and would do no good whatsoever.

Yesterday forenoon I sat through a nonnews interview of Charles J. V. Murphy, correspondent of *Fortune*, and Ike stated, but not for publication, his faith in the generalship and decried the overoptimism followed by overpessimism. Last evening, when I told Ike that his prediction about unfortunate comparisons was beginning to come true and cited Gallagher's criticism of the Mediterranean generals, he said that they convince him that he should send a message of encouragement and of confidence to Alexander and Clark. He drafted it in bed before breakfast this morning.

General Marshall wired today that a mutual understanding appears to have been reached as to the facilities available for OVERLORD and ANVIL, but the U. S. Chiefs of Staff desire that the issue be finally decided in a conference between General Eisenhower, "as the representative of the U. S. Chiefs of Staff," and the British Chiefs of Staff.

Tedder has emphasized to Ike the need of production of superhighoctane gasoline for fighter aircraft. This pepped-up gasoline permits twenty per cent improvement in performance under combat. But a product called xylidine is essential. A thousand tons are needed immediately and another 1500 tons in April. Ike wired General Marshall to lend every effort to get the shipments made promptly.

General Patton has just been in my office and, while visiting, re-emphasized that Ike is on the threshold of becoming "the greatest general of all time—including Napoleon."

LONDON, SUNDAY, FEBRUARY 13, 1944

Ike hollered for xylidine a couple of days ago, and today General Marshall replied that shipments will be made as requested, the first to start March

10. Caution is advised on use of this pepper-upper in some water-cooled engines, five of which failed on test, but apparently the dope works O.K. in other motors.

General John E. Hull, of the Operations Division, Rear Admiral Charles M. Cooke, chief planner for the Navy, and party arrived from Washington last night to discuss the landing-craft problem. Ike met them at Claridge's. He wanted to confer with Hull before the delegation contacted others in London. Hull brought a highly secret letter from General Marshall having to do with co-ordination of air for OVERLORD.

Allocation of areas of Germany and satellite countries to U. S. and British forces is under discussion, particularly in event the Germans cave in quickly or merely withdraw from France. The British want to control northwest Germany, Denmark, and the Low Countries because of their interest in the German naval establishments, ports, and air bases.

LONDON, MONDAY, FEBRUARY 14, 1944

Ike has at last been formally named Supreme Commander and SHAEF has come into being. The Combined Chiefs of Staff cabled to Ike his directive as Supreme Commander, Allied Expeditionary Force, dated February 12, and on the following day Ike issued his first General Order as Supreme Commander, creating his headquarters, SHAEF, and assuming command. He is directed to enter the continent of Europe and, in conjunction with the other Allied nations, to undertake operations aimed at *the heart of Germany and the destruction of her armed forces.* (Italics mine.)

The target date for entering the Continent is May 31, 1944.

Ike met with General Hull, Admiral Cooke, and our planners at Norfolk House this morning. I asked him at lunch if he had scrounged any more landing craft. He said that while we would improvise ships for various services, nothing would take the place of LSTs and they are definitely our limiting factor.

LONDON, THURSDAY, FEBRUARY 17, 1944

This morning's papers carried stories of Alexander's press conference on the beachhead yesterday in which he upbraided the correspondents for irresponsible reporting. He said that he had received a cable from "home" indicating the press had reported overoptimistically at the outset and overpessimistically more recently. He said that Anzio was no Dunkirk or Salerno. He deplores such irresponsibility. The stories also carried news that radio transmission of stories from Anzio had been stopped and that in addition to censorship for military security, that for policy had been added. The stories couple reflection of Alexander's irritation with the cancelation of transmission facilities from Anzio and additional censorship restriction. London papers accompanied their stories from the beachhead, delayed by courier transmission to Algiers, with editorials denouncing the withholding from the public of the "on-the-spot" news.

A number of reports of meetings relating to activities of the Supreme Headquarters have been received in the past few days. The Combined Intelligence Committee, considering the possibility of use of gas by the enemy against OVERLORD, figures the chances are negligible. The Chiefs of Staff Committee suggests that the Supreme Headquarters consult the Air Ministry regarding the probable scale of attack by glider rocket bombs against vulnerable OVERLORD areas. (Considerable opinion amongst air people that the launching platforms for glider bombs are decoys to our bombing effort and that they are successful hoaxes.) . . . It is hoped that by continuing and accelerating air and naval operations affecting Norway the Germans may expect us to attack there, thus keeping these troops out of the actual place of invasion. Every German kept away from the actual scene of battle saves lives of our soldiers and should shorten the war.

LONDON, FRIDAY, FEBRUARY 18, 1944
Light on the question of who shall police what in Europe after hostilities cease is given by a telegram from the President to the Prime Minister on or about February 8 in which F. D. R. says: "I am absolutely unwilling to police France and possibly Italy and the Balkans as well. After all, France is your baby and will take a lot of nursing in order to bring it to the point of walking alone. It would be very difficult to keep in France any military force or management for any length of time." Sir Andrew Cunningham remains adamant that the British assume the responsibility of policing the north German ports, whereas Sir Charles Portal takes the position that because of close co-operation among the RAF and the Belgian and Dutch air forces, the British likewise should police these countries.

The Admiralty has revised the naval requirements for OVERLORD and the Supreme Commander has agreed to their figures. The Royal Navy proposes to have in the landing operation four or five battleships or monitors, eighteen cruisers, seventy-eight fleet destroyers, Hunts, and AA sloops, eighty-eight old destroyers, frigates, and corvettes, and hundreds of other vessels from mine sweepers to motor launches.

Warships for OVERLORD apparently will be entirely British, although, of course, there will be many American landing craft. In order to get this fleet assembled, Admiral Cunningham will have to draw on his Mediterranean fleet, which in turn will have to be reinforced by American warships—a maximum of four cruisers, forty-four destroyers, and one or two escort carriers for ANVIL. In addition, the British would still have in the Med six cruisers, two fighter direction ships, two gunboats, eighty-two destroyers and escorts, in addition to trawlers, coastal, and mine-sweeper forces. In addition, seven escort carriers will be made available from the British resources, if required.

The London *Daily Mail*, published by Viscount Rothermere, recently informed the General that they had acquired an ancient sword owned by King William and on which he had had inscribed the coat of arms of George Washington because he was a great admirer of the father of our country. The *Daily Mail* wishes to present this to General Ike. As a result, Ike accepted an invitation to a private luncheon for February 23. However, today the *Daily Mail*, through General McClure, reported with embarrassment that upon further investigation of the history of the sword, the facts were not as previously stated. In fact, the sword was made forty years after Washington had died. Consequently, the *Daily Mail* has withdrawn its offer but still wants to have the luncheon. Because of the delicate situation Ike is going to the luncheon but insisted that I tell General McClure, who is handling the details, that it must be thoroughly private, with no publicity.

The Question Mark of ANVIL

LONDON, SATURDAY, FEBRUARY 19, 1944

Ike, representing the U. S. Chiefs of Staff, went into the "ifs and ands" of OVERLORD and ANVIL to the British Chiefs of Staff this morning. The fact that he represents the U. S. Chiefs of Staff in dealing with the British Chiefs throws a tremendous weight on his shoulders. It makes him the recipient of all the arguments and pressures which the British, particularly the Prime Minister, may wish to advance for or against any particular project involving the U. S. Joint Chiefs and affecting the European Theater. The Supreme Commander has wrestled continually to keep ANVIL alive, but today it had a bad sinking spell.

LONDON, TUESDAY, FEBRUARY 22, 1944

This morning Ike said he had received, during the evening, word from Beetle that the U. S. Chiefs of Staff had "jacked him up." I asked him why. He said he had been trying to avoid making a decision on ANVIL because he wanted flexibility and had understood from Admiral Cooke that the U. S. Chiefs had once written in his directive a complete carte blanche. Now the U. S. Chiefs are yelling for a decision. Yet the decision hangs largely on the outcome of the Cassino-bridgehead battle. If we should win these battles and reach Rome and the Germans should withdraw gradually to the north, we would have use for only a part of our ground forces in Italy and the remainder, including the French divisions still in Africa, should be employed. He said he would give the U. S. Chiefs an answer today that he was quite certain would not make them happy.

Monty thinks ANVIL should be abandoned. He would rather have plenty of landing craft for the cross-Channel operation. He prefers a strong OVERLORD. He has lunched with the Prime Minister at Chequers and strongly advocates to Ike that the Combined Chiefs be advised that it is better to have two really major campaigns, one in Italy and one in OVERLORD.

I also asked Ike this morning the extent to which the Prime Minister was responsible for the decision to launch SHINGLE, the end run which ended in the first glorious and now somewhat inglorious beachhead. He said that the PM was almost exclusively responsible for the decision to do the end run at the time it was actually executed. True, plans had been made by the staff, as had others, but on this particular project Ike had been conservative, whereas in previous operations he had been bold and had had to overrule the caution of some of his senior subordinates.

Now he envisions the Prime Minister becoming just as het up when Ike tells him that the end run will delay, if not eliminate, ANVIL just as the invasion of North Africa delayed and even threatened to eliminate the cross-Channel invasion. When Ike had made clear to the Prime Minister in the fall of '42 that no cross-Channel attack could be launched in '43 because of the drain on the resources of the two countries by the North African operation, the PM had been greatly upset, although Ike repeatedly had made this prediction clear to the PM on numerous occasions. Now with fighting in Italy draining resources of personnel and particularly of landing craft, the strategic advantage of an invasion of southern France simultaneously with that in the north may be lost.

British Tribute to Ike

LONDON, WEDNESDAY, FEBRUARY 23, 1944

The Prime Minister made his usual thorough and frank report on the war on the floor of the House of Commons yesterday. Beetle had been in Ike's office late in the afternoon after the speech and had jokingly related that when the Prime Minister had stated that General Eisenhower had been selected as Supreme Commander, there were cheers. The Prime Minister had added that Britain had been able to work satisfactorily with him. There were more cheers. Then he added that under his command in the Mediterranean the Allies had made great gains in the war. Still more cheers. He had attained unprecedented unity. Prolonged cheers. Then the Prime Minister announced Tedder as Deputy Supreme Commander. Cheers. Whereupon, as Beetle put it, he mentioned the Chief of Staff, Lieutenant General Walter Bedell Smith. *Period.*

Last night Ike attended a dinner at Claridge's at the invitation of Admiral Sir Andrew Cunningham. The purpose of this small dinner, at which only one other American was present—Beetle—was to permit about a dozen British officers who had been associated with Ike in the Mediterranean to pay the tribute that they intended to give him before he hurriedly left Algiers. They presented him with a silver salver.

Ike was deeply touched by Sir Andrew's remarks, which he said were so sincere and extravagant in their praise that he felt a loss of words to respond.

This morning Ike awakened early. When I went into his room he was still in bed and was carefuly inspecting the silver salver. He found a thumbprint on its face and polished it away with the bedsheet.

Stepped-up Air War

LONDON, THURSDAY & FRIDAY, FEBRUARY 24-25, 1944

Ike left London the evening of February 24 by special train, accompanied by Tedder, Monty, and Bradley, on a two-day inspection trip. He returned Friday evening, having seen the British 51st Division—Highlanders—and the American 2nd and 3rd Armored Divisions.

While Ike was away we had two more sharp bomb raids—the sixth raid in five days, one being merely a daytime reconnaissance plane, the others night attacks. On the night of the twenty-fourth, fifty enemy aircraft were over England, of which a majority were said to have been over London. A 1000-kilo bomb hit St. James Square and riddled the front windows at Norfolk House, disrupting the offices of some of our planners. A smaller bomb has forced T. J. to move from his house up Kingston way. He had a busy night helping extinguish fires, and a poker game in progress at his house had been jarred by something more than T. J.'s customary raise.

I have reconnoitered the neighborhood around Hayes' Lodge to find an appropriate shelter into which Ike might be induced, and have found one which will accommodate all of our household. It is an old wine cellar of a house built by Lord Clive and has beds, blankets, electric heaters, and even a small switchboard and a kitchen. It is only a block from our house. It is operated by the Oxford Group and was built before the war, but probably after the Oxford Group had decided that Hitler wasn't one of their adherents. Now my job is to sell Ike on the fact that two great countries have an incalculable investment in him and stake in his welfare so he will realize the wisdom of taking shelter.

The Allied air offensive against Germany has continued and has reached unprecedented effectiveness, not only in damage to aircraft parks, but to enemy fighters. Some 350 fighters have been destroyed in the last five daytime assaults. Spaatz is visiting Italy, co-ordinating attacks from the Mediterranean against targets in southern Germany and Austria, while the 8th and 9th Air Forces from the United Kingdom continue their now almost daily pounding. We have been favored for this by several days of satisfactory weather. The air people say the battle to destroy the effectiveness of the Luftwaffe has reached the critical stage.

Meantime Hitler, perhaps because we have battered his secret weapon— the rocket launchers on the French coast—has recalled bombers from other fronts to make a grand show to the German people of reprisal raids against London. During the earlier raids over London, our score against enemy planes was light and disappointing. In the raid of February 24, however, some twenty planes have been accounted for, which is about ten per cent—probably more attrition than the enemy can stand. Casualties in the London area have been running about a thousand a night—70 to 100 killed, 250 to 300 seriously wounded, and the remainder with minor wounds. There have been many fires, and blocks of houses of the middle-class and apartment buildings have been wrecked. The public is demanding that deep shelters, which have been held in reserve for refugees, now be opened as havens of safety. The "underground" again has become the most popular shelter.

In a note to Ike acknowledging his thanks for the "mention" on the floor of the House, the Prime Minister invited Ike to lunch Friday and commented that his house had now been made weatherproof again, indicating at least broken windows at 10 Downing Street. On the afternoon of the twenty-fourth, I had tea with Admiral and Lady Cunningham, Captain Tim Shaw, and Mrs. A. V. Alexander, wife of the First Lord of the Admiralty, incidental to my delivery of the film of surrender of the Italian fleet which I had put together for the Admiral under the title *Memento of the Mediterranean*. The windows in the Admiral's office had been blown out and he had escaped cuts from the flying glass by dropping flat on the floor. His desk had been covered with glass. Interrogation of captured German fliers has disclosed that the Germans fully intend to make a concentrated drive and have set up the government buildings as primary targets, although the pattern of bombs dropped over London indicates that the enemy airmen drop their loads willy-nilly, probably due to the heavy flak.

Anvil Is Kept Warm

LONDON, SATURDAY, FEBRUARY 26, 1944

Following Ike's representations to the British Chiefs of Staff as to the need for continued planning for ANVIL, conclusions now have been agreed by the Combined Chiefs of Staff and approved by the President and the Prime Minister.

The Italian battle fronts are to have overriding priority of all existing and future operations in the Mediterranean, but ANVIL is to be planned with hope of launching it shortly after OVERLORD. Another appraisal will be made March 20.

As this action largely meets Ike's wishes, he is satisfied. He does not want to abandon ANVIL unless absolutely necessary, despite the position previously taken by the British Chiefs of Staff, who favored its abandonment in harmony with the views expressed by General Montgomery.

LONDON, TUESDAY, FEBRUARY 29, 1944

Last night Ike and Beetle had dinner with the Prime Minister. They were kept until 1:30. I asked Ike how the Prime Minister felt about the Italian campaign. He said that Churchill was disappointed. I asked if he blamed anyone. Ike replied, "Not so far as I could perceive." I asked if the Prime Minister offered any information about current negotiations between Russia and Finland. The answer was "No."

This morning Colonel Lee had a phone call from the office of the Minister of Works. Lee immediately came to me to ask if the General had spoken of an arrangement by the Prime Minister to provide the Supreme Commander with an appropriate air-raid shelter. I said not as far as I knew; arrangements had been made to use the shelter of the Oxford Group, just a block from our house. Lee then discovered from the General that Beetle had told Churchill that the Supreme Commander was inadequately protected. Ike had merely mentioned that it seemed a bit incongruous for him as a military leader to seek safety in an air-raid shelter run by pacifists. The Prime Minister had ordered the Minister of Works to provide appropriate shelter.

FEBRUARY, 1944: *Pacific war flared up as MacArthur's forces took Eniwetok, Kwajalein, and Roi; Halsey took Nissan Islands. Other actions included landing in Admiralty Islands, continuous raids over Rabaul, task force attacks against Truk, Kavieng, and Saipan. New Guinea and New Ireland punished by planes. Tojo became Jap Chief of Staff. In Italy Allies continued slow, costly advances against heavy weather and desperate Nazis. Abbey at Cassino destroyed by Allied shells and bombs. Germans lost estimated eighty per cent of twin-engine and sixty per cent fighter production in week as bombers concentrated against rail and production centers scattered over Nazi-held Europe. Thunderbolts bombed Netherlands points and invasion coast. German sea raiders sunk by cruisers. Reds bombed Helsinki, entered outskirts of Pskov. U. S. 14th Air Force sank Jap convoy off China. (It always seemed we had German aircraft production about knocked out, but a year later our air people were worried about increasing production of fast jet-propelled fighters.—H.C.B.)*

The PM and the General Differ on Air Command

LONDON, FRIDAY, MARCH 3, 1944

Just when Ike thinks he has the problem of air command licked, as he put it today, "someone else's feelings are hurt and I have another problem to settle."

The Prime Minister had taken the position that either the RAF Bomber Command should be independent of the Supreme Commander's control but to work in conjunction with him and his forces or only a part of Bomber Command would be under his control. The PM wanted to conduct his own private war if he chose. Ike had told the PM at one of the two meetings last week that if the British insisted on this less-than-all-out effort for OVERLORD, then he would "simply have to go home." The Americans, he maintained, now have a much larger air force in the U. K. than even the British, have thrown all their Air Force into the Supreme Command, and he could not face the U. S. Chiefs of Staff if the British hold out this important striking force. Ike did not care if the PM wished to hold Coastal Command under separate control, but he insisted that Bomber Command be directed through the organization of the Supreme Commander, as envisioned by the directive of the Combined Chiefs. However, Marshal of the Air Force, Sir Charles Portal,

Chief of Air Staff of the RAF, had insisted that the Combined Chiefs of Staff had meant that only a part of Bomber Command would fall under control of the Supreme Commander. The PM had then said he would agree to whatever arrangement is found satisfactory by Portal and Eisenhower.

WIDEWING, SATURDAY, MARCH 11, 1944

Owing partly to the move from 20 Grosvenor to Widewing which took place Sunday, March 5, but mostly to the illness of Sergeant Chick, I have not dictated for the diary since March 3.

The principal issue under discussion during this period has been that of the air-command setup. Yesterday this issue finally seemed settled, subject to approval by the Prime Minister and ratification by the Combined Chiefs of Staff, for on the latest proposal, submitted March 9 by Marshal of the RAF Sir Charles Portal, Ike pinned a note, "I told CAS [Chief of Air Staff, Portal] it was exactly what we want." Tedder is to direct the OVERLORD Strategic Air plan as the agent of General Ike.

To me this command arrangement represents an achievement of Ike's, obtained by rational and harmonious discussion.

On Thursday, March 9, both Ike and I were the guests of the First Sea Lord, Admiral Cunningham, at luncheon. Lady Cunningham was the hostess. There was no talk of business but many pleasant reminiscences of happenings in Algiers. The Admiral took particular delight in saying that Telek was spoiled. He said that any dog was spoiled who was fed at the table. Ike said that he reserved the right to spoil his dog and, besides, he liked to feed the dog at the table.

We are settled in our new offices at Bushy Park. I have a private office where I can dictate in peace, although Miss Chick's hands frequently are so cold she has to stop to rub them. My teeth occasionally chatter, yet I wear my heaviest GI underwear. The floors are cement and are damp.

On the Kingston and Teddington side, the park is surrounded by a stone wall eight to ten feet high and the entrances are guarded by white-gloved and white-helmeted MPs, called in the London papers, "Ike's snowballs." The hourly shuttle buses to and from London go through this gate, and the generals and VIPs, coming from London for conferences, use this entrance also. This place looks much like an ordinary Army post—Nissen huts, low PX and mess buildings, tents for the British and American troops—but with the difference that two seeming mounds or low hills are actually two long, one-story buildings, covered with huge nets of dingy camouflage, intended to blend with the brownish ground when seen from the air. Our offices are in one of these buildings, C Building, and down the corridor are Beetle and the Secretary of the general staff and the various Gs.

WIDEWING, TUESDAY, MARCH 14, 1944

There are three main problems of current planning—provision of landing craft, employment of air resources, and political relationship with the French. These were discussed yesterday at a meeting of Ike's Commanders-in-Chief. The problem of landing craft has been restated by Ike to General Marshall, who was relied upon for hastening the final answer, delay of which is causing anxious moments.

Leave for all troops under the Supreme Commander is to be withheld starting April 6. Construction and allocation of temporary facilities for docks for the invasion force are proceeding satisfactorily. OVERLORD will require 200 tugs, of which 196 are in sight.

Today Ike took his train, with about thirty officers from SHAEF, to Salisbury to see demonstrations of the new implements of warfare.

WIDEWING, WEDNESDAY, MARCH 15, 1944

I accompanied Ike to see a new B-29 that had just been flown over from America to Bovingdon Airfield. It has the lines of the B-17 but has some important improvements. It will carry ten tons of bombs 5000 miles and will be used principally in the Pacific, although possibly one group will be sent to this theater. We want the Germans to believe the B-29s will be used against them.

The Air Force had about 350 heavies on a mission to Brunswick. General Curtis, Chief of Staff to Spaatz, had accompanied us to Bovingdon and spoke of the day's operation as a "small raid." We are getting accustomed to 800 to 1000 bombers, and anything less seems unimportant.

Generals Ike and Curtis talked about over-all strategy of bombing Germany. Ike said he thought it would be impossible to get enough planes to saturate German industry with bombs. He would rely upon the advice of the committee of experts as to targets and would not quarrel with them so long as we were hitting Germany hard. After all, targets are rather largely dictated by weather. The issue will have to be settled on the ground, anyway—and Curtis did not disagree. As D-Day approaches, we will have to devote increasing bombing effort against railroad transportation.

Ike has ordered that T. J. go into the Public Relations and Psychological Warfare setup, known as G-6, as deputy to General McClure. T. J., who runs the Adjutant General's job like an eight-day clock, came to me during the day, much distressed. Said he knew so little about public relations that he wanted help and had submitted a memorandum to Beetle asking that I be temporarily assigned to go with him on his new job. As I am not very busy these days, I rather relished the idea, but Ike turned it down on the ground that I have become so closely identified with him in our nearly two years of association that if I were taking an executive position in the public-relations organization, many persons would feel that the Supreme Commander was placing his own man in a key spot for a publicity build-up. Ike said he had no objection, however, to my serving on some advisory committee—not public relations—if I wanted more work to do. T. J. is unhappy at the decision and said he is going to present an argument in person to the General. I have told him it will do no good and that I believe Ike is right. Beetle, however, had strongly seconded T. J.'s request.

Recipe for Cross-Channel Invasion

D-Day is creeping nearer, but all too slowly. Today, Colonel Quentin Brown, Headquarters Commandant, came in to discuss facilities for the General at his Advance Command Post, which is to be located at Southwick, seven miles north of Portsmouth. This is reminiscent of our old days in Africa, where we frequently planned Advance CPs. "Brownie" wanted to know if the General would live in his train or would he like another tent camp like the one we operated adjacent to General Alexander's headquarters. I asked Ike at lunch and he said he definitely wanted the tent camp so he could be "free and independent and not a burden on anyone's headquarters."

The directive of the Supreme Headquarters to naval, ground, and air forces has been issued, dated March 10. An estimate of landing ships and craft which will be available for the assault is given for the benefit of Navy planners. The various types of landing ships and craft have now become so numerous and complex that only an expert can tell the meaning of the abbreviations. I totaled the estimate on one page and it numbered 2023.

Two hundred and twenty-four MT ships will be available for OVERLORD. So will a number of coastal vessels. There are eighty ships of 200 tons, 130 of 450, ninety of 900, and ninety of 1750, having total cargo availability of 313,000 tons.

Estimate of land forces available on May 31 for the U. S.: thirteen infantry divisions, six armored, two airborne, four separate parachute regiments, four armored group (composite), one light armored group, and two Ranger battalions. For the British there will be ten infantry divisions, five armored, two airborne, one line of communication, ten tank and armored brigades, eight Commandos, and one independent infantry brigade.

The summary of units operationally available on May 31 are, for the U. S.—nineteen divisions (one parachute regimental combat team), five armored units, two Ranger battalions, four separate parachute regiments. For the British—seventeen divisions, one line-of-communication division, ten armor or tank brigades, one independent infantry brigade, eight Commandos. In the British force is the specially equipped division to overcome tank obstacles, including a flail brigade.

The estimate of air forces available in the U. K. on June 1 shows for the U. S.: (8th Air Force) bombers, heavy, day—twelve squadrons; fighter, day—twenty-five; photo-recce—twelve; (9th Air Force) bombers, medium—sixteen; bombers, light—sixteen; fighter, day—twenty-five; fighter, night—twelve; fighter, recce—eighteen; photo-recce—twelve; troop carrier—thirteen. For the British: fighter, day—eighteen; fighter, bomber—eighteen; fighter, recce—eighteen; fighter, night—eighteen; bomber, light—thirty-eight; photo-recce—eighteen; bomber, heavy, night —twenty; troop carrier—forty-six, and the British Transport Command with thirty squadrons.

In the U. S. Strategic Air Force, a squadron of heavies normally consists of nine planes and there are three squadrons in a group, with headquarters allotted six additional planes, making thirty-three in the group. However, the 8th Air Force has been strengthened to forty-eight planes per group. American fighter squadrons have twenty-five planes with seventy-five in the group. In the RAF, the fighter squadron is eighteen planes, of which twelve are operational.

The estimate of air lift for airborne forces likely to be available on June 1 is 1384 airplanes for transport and paratroops, and 2000 gliders.

The target date for OVERLORD is May 31, 1944. Will the Channel run red with blood?

WIDEWING, MONDAY, MARCH 20, 1944

The biggest military news still comes from Russia, whose armies have crossed the Dniester into Bessarabia and have the Rumanians in a state of superjitters.

Ike has had a regular conference this morning with the Commanders-in-Chief, and a supplemental one with Tedder, Spaatz, and Leigh-Mallory. Spaatz wanted a ruling from Ike to continue use of long-range fighters to escort our heavies on missions into Germany. The 9th Air Force is under the Allied Expeditionary Air Force, commanded by Leigh-Mallory, who had issued a directive, under date of March 10, saying that the Supreme Commander has decided that the time has now come for the U. S. 9th Air Force to operate exclusively under the Allied Expeditionary Air Force and will be released from its commitment to assist U. S. 8th Air Force POINTBLANK operations under arrangements made by that force.

General Spaatz objected to this and had submitted a memorandum to Ike, dated March 18, saying, "I think this is a matter of utmost importance in our operations. Unless the 8th Air Force operating out of U. K. can be assured of the availability of all the long-range fighters, including P-47s, their deep penetrations will result in greatly increased heavy-bomber losses and we will be losing many opportunities to deal punishing blows to the German Air Force." Ike decided the question by giving priority for the present to the 8th Air Force for its long-range deep penetrations.

The AEAF and the 8th Air Force are to co-ordinate their attacks, the first on targets to help OVERLORD, and the second on POINTBLANK to afford diversions of German fighter strength. The AEAF has destroyed or damaged all but about a dozen of the heavily built rocket launchers on the French coast. They are continuing their assault on these objectives but give a higher priority to railway transportation, particularly in France. Some seventy-eight key targets have been listed.

Anvil Grows Cool

WIDEWING, TUESDAY, MARCH 21, 1944

This morning's papers carried a report from Washington that the President had said at a press conference that co-operation with Frenchmen inside France would be Eisenhower's business and he could deal with the French Committee of National Liberation or not, depending upon conditions. This has caused many inquiries from correspondents today, including Wes Gallagher, of the AP, who saw me this afternoon in an effort to get a story. I checked with the PRO and found the proper answer was "No comment." The PRO also denied a request of Gallagher's to see

General Julius Holmes, Deputy Civilian Affairs Director. To this decision Wes took violent objection, claiming it meant he would have to ask the PRO if he wanted to take an officer of SHAEF to lunch, and that it also was not in harmony with Ike's traditional policy of making correspondents quasi-staff officers.

Ike is trying to get more fire power from warships for OVERLORD.

Because of slow progress in Italy, the diversionary attack of two divisions with ten to follow up in southern France, known as ANVIL, is virtually abandoned, except as a one-division threat.

The Private Life of a Supreme Commander

WIDEWING, WEDNESDAY, MARCH 22, 1944

I am frequently surprised at Ike's inability to recognize his own transition from a relatively unknown staff officer in the United States Army to that of Supreme Commander. It is difficult for him to realize his new position in the world. He likes the friendly attention paid to him, particularly by those who may be considered in his personal entourage, or who have some official duty which normally brings them close to him. For instance, he gets a lift and a smile every time we ride past the one-armed civilian guard at the pole gate across Coombe Lane leading into Kingston Road, the salute always accompanied by a generous smile. The same gateman was there when we first took Telegraph Cottage in 1942. When we returned again to reside in the cottage, the gateman obviously was delighted to see the General.

However, the fact that anything he now does may be news is not only strange but repulsive to him. His personal correspondence to his relatives and friends in the States is something he cherishes and regards as thoroughly private. Recently, an enterprising newspaper syndicate managed to collect a number of such letters, including some to his mother in Abilene. I could readily appreciate the considerable interest in these letters and saw nothing wrong in it. Yet Ike felt he had been intruded upon and bitterly resented the disclosure. He thought he had a legal right to prevent publication of his letters, which he felt were a personal bond between him and the correspondents, many of whom were the kin of soldiers under his command. If such letters are to be made public, the privacy of his relationships with mothers, fathers, and others at home would be jeopardized, he felt. I told him he had no legal means of preventing such publication; he is now a prominent figure and anything he writes is likely to be published. He even called in his Judge Advocate General to see if there wasn't a way to deal with the problem, but the

JAG gave him substantially the same answer. Consequently, Ike's only defense is to make his letters back home more or less *pro forma* whereas, heretofore, he has undertaken to say something reasonably significant. He answers, and, no doubt, will continue to do so, every letter the writer of which indicates a sincere interest in the prosecution of the war. His "fan letters" are about equally divided between the Americans and the British.

A Possible Leak

WIDEWING, THURSDAY, MARCH 23, 1944

Possibility that essential facts of OVERLORD, including D-Day as originally set, may have been "compromised" has stirred the high-level officials of SHAEF and the War Department. The G-2s are excited, particularly in Washington.

A few days ago Ike received a personal message from General Clayton Bissell, the new War Department G-2, saying that a package containing important documents concerning OVERLORD had been intercepted in Chicago. It had been sent from our Ordnance Division, G-4, and erroneously addressed to a private residence in a section of Chicago heavily populated by Germans. The package was poorly wrapped and, according to General Bissell, a casual perusal of the papers was made by four unauthorized persons in the headquarters of the Army's 6th Service Command in Chicago, in addition to at least ten persons in the Chicago post office.

It nows appears that the package was addressed by an American soldier who is of German extraction. He states that his sister, who lives at the Chicago address, has been seriously ill and thinks he simply erred in writing the address on the package because his mind was preoccupied with thoughts of home. Thus he wrote on the package his sister's home address rather than the proper address in the War Department in Washington. The clumsy handling would indicate that no professional spy was involved, but, nevertheless, important facts, including strength, places, equipment, and tentative target date have been disclosed to unauthorized persons—just another worry for the Supreme Commander.

Firsthand Story from Anzio

WIDEWING, FRIDAY, MARCH 24, 1944

Major General Lucas, who was relieved by General Truscott as Commander of the VI Corps in Anzio because of extreme fatigue, gave a talk to the SHAEF staff yesterday afternoon and I attended. It might be called "The End Run that Was Blocked." He spoke of the misgivings of himself and staff when he was given orders by Fifth Army to withdraw from the main line and prepare for Anzio. They were given a date of January 25 as target, which even then allowed insufficient time for proper amphibious training. This date was pushed ahead to January 22 after the meeting of the commanders with the Prime Minister at Marrakech. One night exercise for practice landings demonstrated the woeful lack of experience. Even though the infantry units involved—the British 1st and the American 3rd—had partaken in previous landings, their personnel had been so changed by losses and replacements, particularly among junior officers commanding platoons, companies, and battalions, that they were practically new divisions—amphibiously. A test landing had been held in Salerno and everything had gone wrong.

Nevertheless, by great good luck and by improvement of the Navy in finding the proper beaches, they got ashore at Anzio really better than he expected. The 3rd Division was on schedule all the way and its personnel was entirely ashore before daylight and the landing had started at 3 A.M. The British 1st Division, having a poorer beach, took until the next day to get ashore.

Most significant was the bad luck the Allies had in the movement of German troops which was under way when the landing was made. Two German divisions were en route from the Eighth Army front to the Fifth Army front and were just off the beachhead, and another German division was en route from Rome to the main Fifth Army front. All three were quickly diverted against our beachhead. By rapid mobility, the Germans soon had ten and a half divisions piled against us and surpassed us in strength of combat troops. The port was constantly shelled by long-range 190s and 210s, but at no time was unloading seriously delayed, although merchant ships frequently had to pull out to sea to avoid the shore batteries. Some sixty per cent of the long-range shells were duds, which Lucas thought might be attributable to sabotage. There had never been any doubt in his mind that the beachhead would hold, but when the Germans massed six divisions against the British and Americans on the road from Carroceto to Anzio, they had made a penetration which, if held, would have brought their medium-range guns in the position to wreck our small port. However, Lucas had ordered Harmon to counter-attack with the combat team of the 2nd Armored Division. This stopped the advance, but if the Germans had continued pressure on that sector, they would have caused us great embarrassment. Strangely—and he said you could count on the Germans for making a big mistake at the right time—they chose to shift the attack to the sector held by the 3rd Division. Here they were held, and with the aid of naval gunfire and particularly by air bombardment, the beachhead had become stabilized.

He said German prisoners captured in the beachhead were filled with optimism that Germany would win the war and he had sensed no diminution of morale. He frequently stated he was often in a quandary as to the over-all intentions of the Fifth Army and of General Alexander, but he avoided criticism. He seemed to be simply a soldier carrying out orders with which he was not in sympathy.

Now the battle for Cassino has developed into a small Verdun. The great aerial bombardment of the city, which was hailed publicly by General Eaker as a sample of the destruction the Germans could expect from the Air Force, has not gone well. In fact, the Germans have retaken part of the town.

No one seems to know just what is likely to happen in Italy.

Shall We Bomb Oil or Transportation?

WIDEWING, MONDAY, MARCH 27, 1944
Whether strategic bombers work on oil or transportation as the best means of helping OVERLORD is a question for Ike to determine. General Spaatz has submitted a recommendation strongly advocating concentration of bomber effort on synthetic-oil plants. He claims the Germans will defend these plants with their air force. This will lead to continued destruction of both planes and oil. In comparing the effect of oil vs. transportation, Spaatz insists the weight of attack required to deal with a large marshaling yard is about the same as that required for a synthetic-oil plant and the target areas are relatively the same size. Furthermore, only fourteen synthetic-oil plants produce eighty per cent of all German synthetic gasoline and oil, whereas fourteen marshaling yards comprise only a fraction of the German railway system, which can be readily dispensed with without seriously disrupting German military operations. Spaatz sums his recommendation:

(*a*) Continue the destruction of the German Air Force in being and the industry which supports it, particularly the ball-bearing industry,

(*b*) Attack Axis oil production and,

(*c*) Join with SHAEF, AEAF, and the Air Staff in producing a plan for the direct tactical support of OVERLORD. This plan should provide for attacks in great strength upon communications and military installations of all kinds to assist to the maximum the initial phases of OVERLORD.

To clinch his argument, he attached to his paper a captured order from a German quartermaster general of the High Command insisting that because motor fuel is short, every military unit should economize whenever possible.

Those who advocate bombing the marshaling yards to wreck railway transportation see also an advantage in retarding movement of supplies to the French coastal launching platforms, such as rockets and glider bombs. Air Chief Marshal Tedder favors attacking railway transportation because by disrupting train movement, the Germans will be forced to move by road and there become targets for strafing. He states that the choice lies between the oil plan and the transportation plan. He states that no one can question that the oil plan, in view of the proved ability of the U. S. Strategic Air Force to carry out precision attacks deep in Germany, would ultimately have grave effects on the whole German war effort. It is difficult, however, to see evidence to support the view that it could be expected to take real effect in time for OVERLORD or the land operations following the assault. Moreover, it is not a plan in which the RAF Bomber Command can take any really effective part and it is one in which AEAF would be unable to take any part at all. The oil plan is, in fact, not really an alternative to the transportation plan as regards Bomber Command and the AEAF. He adds that the transportation plan is the only one offering a reasonable prospect of disorganizing enemy movement and supply in the time available, and of preparing the ground for imposing the tactical delays which can be vital once the land battle is joined. He notes that every bomb falling on a railway center pays its way, and that the proportion of ineffective hits for these targets is lower than for any other target. A wide selection of targets to jibe with weather also is afforded. He prefers that POINTBLANK and OVERLORD air operations be covered by a new directive in favor of the transportation plan.

Today Ike had members of the War Cabinet for lunch with the principal members of the SHAEF staff. In the afternoon, he had a meeting with the British Chiefs of Staff. I have not yet heard the decision.

Cassino has been described as a failure, so far, by AFHQ. The Combined Chiefs have designated General Wilson as "Supreme Commander Mediterranean Forces," thus making two Supreme Commanders for the Allies. I suppose MacArthur's and Lord Louis' titles will be similarly changed in due time.

It seems that in Cassino there were ancient hidden tunnels under the city in which the Germans found refuge when Eaker's bombers practically leveled the city. Now the Germans have retaken a substantial part of Cassino.

Ike is delighted with the U. S. Chiefs of Staff decision to forget Rome. He has never been keen for taking the place, particularly as we have the principal airfields at Foggia. His only comment was that he had advocated this strategy weeks ago and would have been much happier if the decision had been made then, a decision still subject to the British assent. The Prime Minister has had his heart set on the capture of Rome. Incidentally, the Prime Minister's speech on the radio last night lacked his usual inspirational vigor. Probably he was tired. The speech had been interpreted in the United States as a forerunner of the invasion. There is growing impatience in America for opening the "second front," a misnomer we all dislike.

Ike conferred with the British Chiefs today about the proposal of the U. S. Chiefs for launching a modified ANVIL by July 10, and abandonment of the quest for Rome. Ike made clear his views to the British Chiefs. They agree that no particular geographical location, including Rome, has in itself any significance from a military viewpoint as compared with the principal mission of the Supreme Commander of the Mediterranean forces, which, as already given him by the Combined Chiefs, is to carry on operations which will give maximum support to the cross-Channel invasion of France. The Prime Minister was not present and he likely will favor the capture of Rome for the psychological effect.

We Decide to Bomb Transportation

WIDEWING, THURSDAY, MARCH 30, 1944

The transportation plan for bombing has won out over the oil plan largely because the oil plan will not seriously affect German military operation for six months, too long for immediate benefit to OVERLORD.

The transportation plan can be tackled immediately, giving General Spaatz's Strategic Air Force proper railway targets in Germany to entice German fighters to battle. The transportation plan really covers secondary targets for the strategic bombers, both British and American, their primary efforts still being to reduce production of enemy aircraft and to destroy as many as possible in the air or on the ground. Ball-bearing plants are included. The AEAF will devote itself primarily to the railway targets.

These decisions were reached at a meeting attended by Ike at the Air Ministry under chairmanship of the Marshal of the Royal Air Force, Sir Charles Portal, and attended by Tedder, Leigh-Mallory, Harris, Spaatz,

Anderson, as well as representatives from the War Office, the Air Ministry, Joint Intelligence Service, and Ministry of Economic Warfare, on Saturday. Tedder won out in his advocacy of the transportation plan, and Spaatz, who strongly urged attacking synthetic-oil plants, has temporarily lost. However, it was decided that after OVERLORD is ashore and firmly established, the strategic bombers can then attack the oil industry. The main objective for OVERLORD is to disrupt railways so the Germans will be hindered as much as possible from quickly moving troops and supplies against our beachhead.

The Supreme Commander's view of the problem was that the first five or six weeks of OVERLORD would be a most critical period for the Allied armies. It was essential that we should take every possible step to ensure that our forces get ashore and stay ashore. The greatest contribution that he could imagine the air forces making to this aim is to hinder enemy movement. Granted that the tactical air plan would aim at achieving this after D-Day, then how much easier would the task be made by a preparatory period in which all the air forces available were used to attack railway targets? This would reduce the over-all efficiency of the enemy railway system, canalize the traffic, destroy repair facilities, and make it harder for the enemy to recover from the blows delivered in the tactical battle.

MARCH, 1944: *First German attacks with remote-controlled tanks were repulsed at Anzio after three days of fighting. Bitter fighting in Italy centered about Cassino, reduced to rubble by continuous air bombing. Planes raided railyards at Rome, made first strike at Florence. General Patton relinquished Seventh Army command for undisclosed assignment. German bomber and fighter bases among targets in southern France hit heavily by Allied bombers. Other targets included factories, railroads, and ports and Pas de Calais coastal area. Berlin hit often, once by 2000 planes. Slight Luftwaffe opposition encountered over Berlin, but heavy British bomber losses incurred over Nuremberg. Great Britain suspended all travel between United Kingdom and Ireland. Allied forces opened action for Burma with capture of Walawbum. Reds captured Black Sea port of Kherson, approached Tartar Pass to Balkans by taking Cernǎuti and Delatyn. In the Pacific Navy bombers hit Paramushiru and Oroluk, joined Army planes in attacking Ponape and Kusaie in the Carolines. Allied air patrols sank ships attempting to reinforce Japs in New Guinea. Kavieng, Rabaul, and Wewak chief targets of Allied bombers. Land forces in Carolines killed 3000 Japs at cost of sixty-one Americans killed. U. S. Marines landed on Talasea Peninsula and approached Jap airport. Marines landed on Emerau Island, eighty-four miles from Kavieng. General Orde C. Wingate, British jungle fighter, died in an air crash in Burma. Germans occupied Hungary. (We cheered for the Red Army.—H.C.B.)*

Just Another Day

WIDEWING, TUESDAY, APRIL 4, 1944
Continuing his effort to see every division to be in the big show, the Supreme Commander inspected the U. S. 29th Division Saturday, April 1, and the U. S. 1st on Sunday. The weather was cold and rainy and he returned to headquarters Monday forenoon with a cold. Ike had spoken to so many soldiers and made so many informal talks that his voice was hoarse.

Yesterday he and Beetle had lunch with the Prime Minister, after which Ike sent a message to General Marshall saying that the British are agreeing to the insistent request of the U. S. Chiefs that the directive to General Wilson specify that ANVIL be prepared with a specific target date. The British Chiefs heretofore had sought to avoid setting a certain date because of the slowness of the Italian campaign. However, the U. S. Navy was loath to divert to ANVIL the additional landing craft and naval units intended for the Pacific if the operation might never be launched. Since the British are now agreeing, Ike added in his message to General Marshall that he hopes Admiral King also will send us some battleships to strengthen our gunfire support in OVERLORD, with the idea that the vessels could return to the Mediterranean in time for the amphibious attack on southern France.

The espionage scare that arose from discovery that secret documents pertaining to OVERLORD had been misaddressed to Chicago has now calmed. Major General Clayton Bissell, War Department G-2, has cabled Ike that nothing derogatory has been discovered to date about the twelve persons known to have had access to the documents. All these persons have been warned and are under observation, but their discretion cannot be guaranteed. He asks whether we have developed motive, accomplices, or espionage connections over here and cautions against publicity.

The unfortunate loss of twenty-three transport aircraft in the Sicilian operation by our own naval gunfire eventually reached the press. When this news broke, it added to the apprehension of the professional public-relations people who think that because of this, the Bari disclosure, and the Patton incident, the public has lost confidence in the armed forces' willingness to release bad news about its operations. Relative to the twenty-three transports, there has been considerable hue and cry at home. As a matter of fact, the story could have been released months ago, but with action developing so fast in the Mediterranean and other problems pressing for attention, this affair was more forgotten than purposely hidden. It is, however, the responsibility of the Public Relations Officer to look after such things and not to leave initiative to the Allied Commander. The PRO should have a "bad news" department, and T. J., who comes to see me often, says he will have one.

The Sicilian tragedy had been thoroughly investigated and the errors and uncontrollable factors which caused it were studied for guidance in future airborne operations. General "Hap" Arnold is now double-checking that we won't let the same thing happen in OVERLORD.

Ike said last night that the PM is supporting the President on the French question—i.e., the Supreme Commander will be left free to deal with the French Committee of Liberation under de Gaulle or any other groups which might be helpful. Ike is fearful that this may create civil war among the Frenchmen, but he is not shirking the responsibility they are placing upon him. Meanwhile, the French at Algiers are the source for all sorts of stories trying to high-pressure the President into complete recognition of the French Committee.

Churchill had strongly defended to Ike his demand that the House of Commons support the coalition government. He had brought this issue on an inconsequential matter of equalization of pay for men and women teachers, the government proposal on this matter having been beaten by one vote, whereupon Churchill had insisted on a vote of confidence on that issue. He got the vote overwhelmingly. Churchill had declared to Ike that, on the eve of the invasion, it would be foolhardy to let people over the world believe that the government of Britain was hanging only by a thread. Ike had felt as I, namely, that a vote of confidence should not be on such a minor matter and I had reflected to Ike reports I had heard from some British friends who thought the PM's insistence was a show of petulance.

A study of the enemy's potential use of rocket bombs and pilotless aircraft against our concentrations and cities in England has been made by the SHAEF staff. It concludes that such an attack will not preclude the launching of the assault from the south coastal ports as now planned and that the probable casualties do not make it necessary to move the assault forces west of Southampton. Some interference with the loading and shipping of craft in the Thames and Southampton areas must be expected, but the danger is not sufficient to justify removal of shipping and craft from these areas.

In the London area, the effect of these projectiles would not be much worse during the first three days' bombardment than the recent aircraft bombing raids. In the Southampton area, the density of hits during the first three days would be about 1.9 hits per square mile. The docks might expect to receive about one hit per day. Vessels 200 feet long would stand a chance of 1 in 100 of being hit if spending three days near the aiming point. Many of the sites for launching these projectiles have been destroyed or damaged by our bombing, and if any ski tracks begin functioning they would immediately become targets for our bombs. This whole question is fogged with the mystery of uncertainty. Many still believe the ski platforms are a giant hoax to detract our main bombing effort from Germany proper, yet the ski tracks are there, have been bombed continuously, and some of them still may operate.

WIDEWING, WEDNESDAY, APRIL 5, 1944

News of the decision to make transportation targets the primary objective in preparation for OVERLORD has reached the British Cabinet and has caused the Prime Minister to inform General Ike that said Cabinet takes a grave and, on the whole, adverse view of the proposal. Reason is: French casualties and resultant ill-will of the French. The British Cabinet's view is not shared by the Supreme Commander, who stands by the decision of the Supreme Headquarters.

No Directive on de Gaulle

WIDEWING, THURSDAY, APRIL 6, 1944

De Gaulle continues to increase his domination of the French Committee of Liberation. In another change, he has become the Commander of all Armed Forces of the French. This action was taken without consultation with Giraud, who is, of course, miffed. He threatened to resign and has even sent word asking if the British will give him haven in England for the duration.

Meantime the British and American governments have not come to a decision as to whether the Supreme Commander should deal with de Gaulle in France or whether he should be left free, as the President desires, to deal with de Gaulle or any groups that might be helpful. This had caused editorial comment reminiscent of Ike's recognition of Darlan.

Now the British government wants to move Le Clerc's French division from North Africa to England to be used in the follow-up in the invasion. The government states that it is politically desirable. Ike can use the force and it will be sent.

Berlin is perhaps the political heart of Germany, but the industrial heart which has always interested Ike is the Ruhr Valley. A current study says that once the Ruhr Valley is taken by the Allies, Germany will lose sixty-five per cent of her productive capacity for crude steel and fifty-six per cent of her total coal production. The percentages are based on total production in all of Europe occupied by the Germans. The report concludes that German policy for the conduct of the campaign in the West will be (a) to avoid evacuating occupied territory until the latest possible moment; (b) to keep the lines as far away from German soil as possible; (c) as an overriding consideration, to keep the Ruhr in production.

I concluded from a recent visit aboard an LST at Plymouth that the minimum of sixty days required for training to permit me to take command of an LST was too long to give me a chance to get into the amphibious assault, even if I made the grade in training. After visiting the LST and concluding that the responsibility involved was beyond my seagoing ability and experience, I saw Admiral Kirk and asked if he had any other job at sea for me during the invasion. He said that if the General would release me, he would put me in an executive job in the Ferry Service of the Navy Task Force Service for ferrying from ship to shore and shore to shore with ducks, LCVPs, and, I assume, a variety of landing craft. Kirk said that in view of my desire, he would stipulate that I be assigned aboard a small command ship for this service and on the invasion coast, to avoid being stuck at a base port in England. I told him my next step was to check with the General to see if I could be detached for the period of the invasion.

I found to my pleasure that he will detach me for sixty to ninety days, starting on Y minus 30, meaning May 1, with the proviso that I return to his service. He wants me back by the time he establishes the Continental CP. When I informed Admiral Kirk of the General's favorable decision, he immediately said "congratulations," and that he would advise me further. It looks as if I will get to sea at last. And not as a kibitzer.

We Inform the Russians of D Date

WIDEWING, SATURDAY, APRIL 8, 1944

The time has come to inform the Russians of the D date for OVERLORD so they can carry through with Stalin's commitment to Roosevelt and Churchill at Teheran to launch a large-scale offensive on the Eastern Front which would contain the maximum number of German troops and thus assist our invasion. It has been agreed to send this information through the U. S. and British Missions at Moscow. It is simply that

D-Day will be two or three days before or after June 1, the margin being allowed for weather and tide. In return, the Prime Minister has suggested that we should expect a similar measure of confidence in the Russians, a reasonable flexibility being expected on either side. The exact beaches under attack are not to be given.

The American diplomatic representative at the Vatican warns that Italian public opinion is turning against the Anglo-Americans because of casualties caused by bombing. He reports the Eyeties feel they must lean on the Russians in the future, as they do little bombing of civilians and are, after all, "winning the war."

Washington has informed Russia that as representatives of the Allied Control Commission deal with the Italians on all phases of economic and political life, and as the Control Commission is the organ through which United Nations policy in Italy is maintained, the U. S. government finds it difficult to concur in the Soviet view that her contacts are limited in Italy. The U. S. takes the position that since the Soviet Union has a representative on the Control Commission, the Russians have the same contact with the Italian government as the British and Americans. Becoming diplomatically blunt, the U. S. says that there would seem to be no basis for the Soviet contention that the U. S. S. R. is in a less favorable position than are Britain and the U. S. Solution of political problems in Italy cannot be found until Rome is liberated. The six opposition parties should be brought into the Italian government, but the whole problem should be worked out in the advisory council. In other words, Russia should not try to play a lone hand in Italy.

Our Ambassador also has information through the Hungarian Minister at Lisbon that, according to German sources, Hungarian troops are surrendering on the Soviet front without fight.

McCloy is here to assist in the French situation, which has grown progressively worse. If we are to get any help from the French for the invasion, Ike must have a directive which will permit him to encourage and direct resistance movements within France. In other words, we must have an effective fifth column. If I am going out on a U. S. naval command ship near the invasion shore when the shooting is hot, I would like to feel that some French patriots will spike at least a few of the shore batteries.

General Alexander plans simultaneous attacks of Eighth and Fifth Armies in Italy with a determined effort to burst from the Anzio bridgehead about four days later. The date is not disclosed, but in an earlier signal, General Alexander was quoted as saying he could not lay it on until about the middle of May.

Visit to Air Stations

WIDEWING, WEDNESDAY, APRIL 12, 1944

Returned this morning from a night-day-night trip to visit air stations. Ike was accompanied by General Spaatz and his Chief of Staff, Brigadier General Ted Curtis, and me. We entrained Monday evening, taking a leisurely route with long stopovers at quiet places.

Our first visit on Tuesday morning was at Upper Dunmow, where we saw American B-26s. While we watched, thirty-nine were dispatched at twenty-second intervals to attack the marshaling yard at Charleroi. We motored to Debden, where the 4th Fighter Group operated. Lunched there and met Colonel Donald J. M. Blakeslee—quite the most colorful airman I have met. He has some twenty planes to his credit and is fudging on his operational hours so he won't be grounded. He appears a born leader. Also met Captain Don S. Gentile, who actually leads Americans in Europe with twenty-three enemy planes shot down in the air and seven shot up on the ground. He is Italian-American. Both were decorated with DSCs by Ike.

Next we stopped at Bassingbourne, from which some sixty B-17s had been airborne that morning for the attack on Germany.

Ike made a thorough inspection of billets, training facilities, and kitchens. As we filed through the kitchen and mess room for the enlisted men, I fell into conversation with a sergeant. I was tagging along and, as usual, worked the other side of the street. He had overheard the mess officer telling Ike what a fine mess he was running and what fine chow the men were getting. My new-found friend, who had battle stars for three campaigns in North Africa, gave me the lowdown. He said the mess stinks, the food is frequently cold, and insisted the mess officer was just putting on a good show.

General Ike dedicated a B-17, named *General Ike*. He met all the crew and wished them the best of luck. The Air Force has stopped painting the B-17s olive drab; the Fortresses seem more slick in their natural aluminum finish. By elimination of the drag of the paint speed is increased by six miles per hour. Some of the pilots told me that in the first missions that the nonpainted planes went on, the German fighters were lured to them like trout to a fly.

General Spaatz had one of the new modified P-38 (Lightning) planes which have been equipped with a bomb sight and a place for a bombardier in the plexiglass nose, which has been extended. In air lingo, the new P-38 is called the "Droop Snoot." Ike inspected one with great interest. The pilot invited him for a ride. He accepted immediately and had about a ten-minute ride, twisting and diving, his first ride in a fighter.

During the evening, General Spaatz received word by telephone that we had lost sixty-four bombers and sixteen fighters. Our fighters had shot down forty-six enemy planes and destroyed forty-six more on the ground. It was not a very good day, although results of the bombing were described as from fair to good. There is a lot more life in the Luftwaffe than previous optimistic reports would indicate. Ike said he would feel better about the loss if he knew they had hit their targets.

Ed Stettinius, Under Secretary of State, called on Ike this morning and stopped in to say hello to me. Ed was most cordial, and when I told him I would be pleased when the damned war was over, he said it ought to be "soon." I'm afraid he is too optimistic.

General Alexander has also arrived from Italy. I met him at the gate. He looks fine and is in good spirit.

General Spaatz has been dealing with the Russian air general sent here to contact his forces and to facilitate arrangements for shuttle bombing between the U. K. and Russia. Spaatz said he had tried to play chess with the Russians, but before each game, the Russian general proposed so many toasts, which Spaatz had to drink to be polite, that he could scarcely differentiate between friendly and enemy chessmen. Anyway, the shuttle bombing is to start soon, Spaatz said. Yesterday, according to the press, about ten of our bombers landed in Sweden after a job in Germany.

While I was supervising arrangements for travel of our party from the train to the first airfield yesterday morning, I noticed a crowd gathering and some persons inquired, "When would Monty leave the train?" As it was time for Ike and Spaatz to depart, I went aboard and announced to them that they should hurry as the crowd was impatient to see Monty. They chuckled.

WIDEWING, THURSDAY, APRIL 13, 1944

Three great questions as to the invasion are bothering Ike, but the final answers cannot possibly be given until after the event. These are: the mine fields in the Channel, the batteries on the coast, and the artificial harbors. However, one headache seems cured. The Air Command setup is working O.K.

The wisdom of bombing targets in thickly populated transportation centers in France, Belgium, and Holland is under discussion with political authorities, but all the questions that arise are being settled on a perfectly reasonable basis and everyone is ready to do anything to further the prospects of success; thanks to the almost magic charm of General Ike's personality and to his frankness. Everyone trusts him.

Last evening, Ike resumed his seemingly unending inspections, taking the train to Scotland, where, among others, he will see a Polish division. Beetle is accompanying him, and a respite from their labors will be afforded by an attempt at salmon fishing.

Can Unconditional Surrender Be Unconditional?

WIDEWING, FRIDAY, APRIL 14, 1944

Ed Stettinius told me the President was far from well and that he is becoming increasingly difficult to deal with because he changed his mind so often.

There have been discussions with him as to the meaning of "unconditional surrender" as applied to Germany. Any military person knows that there are conditions to every surrender. There is a feeling that, at Casablanca, the President and the Prime Minister, more likely the former, seized on Grant's famous term without realizing the full implications to the enemy. Goebbels has made great capital with it to strengthen the morale of the German Army and people. Our psychological experts believe we would be wiser if we created a mood of acceptance of surrender in the German Army which would make possible a collapse of resistance similar to that which took place in Tunisia. They think if a proper mood is created in the German General Staff, there might even be a German Badoglio. To accomplish the proper mood, there would need to be a new American-Anglo-Russian statement to define "unconditional surrender." Then we could tell the German people, by radio and pamphlet, the methods of demilitarization we propose; the fact that we intend to purge Nazis from the government machine; that we maintain the right to seize and try war criminals; that there will be orderly transfers of population, and that there will be restoration of freedom of religion and for trade unions. After the three governments had agreed and announced such definitions, our staff feels that the Supreme Commander should make a declaration after the landings to the German commander in the west, reciting, in soldierly language, the principal points of surrender terms. It is believed this would shorten the war. General Ike strongly advocates this view and asked Ed Stettinius to transmit it to the President, which he did by cable.

Intelligence on German Strength

WIDEWING, MONDAY, APRIL 17, 1944

I asked Ike for details of a complaint about our administration in North Africa. He said it was true that replacements had accumulated and many had been used for purposes other than combat. In North Africa, there had been held in readiness for ANVIL 100,000 service troops. With the "off again, on again, gone again, Finnegan" situation of ANVIL, this pool of troops, including port labor battalions and antiaircraft units, had been held in anticipation of an operation which still is under debate.

I just spoke to Major General Albert C. Wedemeyer, Deputy Allied Commander to Admiral Mountbatten in India, who is en route from Washington to his regular station, where he is to take over the Allied Command Post at Imphal, now under attack by the Japs.

Recalling, but not mentioning, the doleful observation of Stettinius as to the President's health, I asked Wedemeyer's opinion. He said he had seen the President recently at Hyde Park and thought he looked very badly indeed and, in addition, was worried—worried about the political situation at home and the effect of OVERLORD. Wedemeyer said that the OWI and other agencies had been actively endeavoring to "adjust" the public mind for heavy casualties.

I have been to the SHAEF war room this morning and scrutinized again the map showing the beaches on which American forces are to land. The water is shallow for a considerable distance from shore and most suitable for the laying of mine fields. Tedder was there and when he asked me what I was interested in, I told him the depth of the water. I wanted to see how far out I could begin wading to get ashore. He directed me to another map showing gun emplacements, hedgehog defense, barbed wire, mine fields on the beach, and numerous enemy airfields within easy striking distance of the invasion fleet. If the President is worried, why shouldn't I be? Incidentally, I am to be under Rear Admiral Don T. Moon, whom Ike described as "a damned good man."

As usual, at this stage of preparation for an amphibious operation, our problems are seemingly intricate and difficult beyond belief, but Ike said today that as each day passes, there is definite progress and he has not lost any of his confidence that the invasion will be a success.

A weekly review on political matters from the Joint Intelligence Committee reports: pessimism on Finnish-Soviet peace negotiations; Secretary Hull's recent speech seems to have restored optimism on U. S. policy toward the French Committee; announcement by the Italian King that he would quit when the Allies reach Rome and appoint the Prince of Piedmont as Lieutenant of the Realm has met with general approval, but the action was criticized by the liberal press as having been long overdue.

On the U-boat war, the review states that during March, of 7100 ships in the Atlantic, U. K. coastal and Indian Ocean convoys, only five were lost by enemy action. Germans still are keeping 500-ton U-boats in the Bay of Biscay, although their use in the narrow and heavily mined waters of the Channel is considered unlikely. However, they could be used in the western approach to the Channel and in the Bay of Biscay. The Germans have fifty-one divisions identified by us as being in France and the Low Countries, of which eight are Panzer, ten field, and thirty-three "LE" (limited employment or lower establishment) which are described as being below normal German standard required for field divisions.

In Italy there is no evidence of any change in enemy strategy (General Alexander's offensive is scheduled for May 14). Five of the seventeen enemy divisions south of Rome are in reserve for rest and refitting. If Hitler should demand more divisions for the east to stem the Russian advance, which has now taken all the Crimea except Sevastopol, he would have to withdraw troops from Cassino. He has already taken from France one infantry and two Panzer divisions for the eastern front, and a general redistribution of reserves, both Panzer and infantry, is still in progress. In this shift, the Brest Peninsula has been strengthened with a parachute division at the apex and a Panzer division at the base and general reinforcement of the Channel coast, plus build-up of force on the Mediterranean coast of France.

Disposition of German divisions as of April 14, 1944, is estimated by our Intelligence services as follows:

Eastern Front	199
Finland	7
Norway	12
Denmark	5
Poland	3
Germany	4
France and Low Countries	51
S.E. Europe excluding Hungary	21
Hungary	5
Italy	23
Unlocated	6
Grand Total	336

Of additional interest is the latest calculation of disposition and strength of the German Air Force. This is as of April 7, 1944, on the four fronts.

The only recent change of any size is an increase of thirty long-range bombers sent to the Russian front. In addition, the GAF has reinforced the southern Russian front by moving a long-range bomber unit from north Russia. Seventy per cent of the long-range bomber force in Russia is now located 'south and east of Lwow. The strength and disposition of the GAF:

Western Front	2250
S. Germany and Austria	330
Mediterranean and Balkans	810
Russian Front	1680
Total Operational	5070

The headlines and ballyhoo of our air attacks on objectives in Germany, particularly Berlin, plus the overoptimistic statements and attitude of some air officers, have built an over-all picture of the weakness of the Luftwaffe, kept weak by the destruction of aircraft plants. No wonder the public believes the war soon will be over.

Now we have found the Luftwaffe far from dead, although obviously it is weakened. The Intelligence review says that considerable reconstruction and repair work have been carried out at fighter-assembly factories since they have been heavily attacked, notably at Regensburg, Marienburg, Fürth, and Aschersleben. Although Marienburg was almost completely devastated last October, the plant there has come into production again, but once again has been damaged. The G-2s state that the Germans obviously are not abandoning old sites or dispersing to new ones, but every effort is being made to maintain the present organization of the industry and to rebuild damaged factories to keep up at least a minimum output.

Speaking of the effect of Allied bombing on the German war effort, the Intelligence Committee is indirectly quoted as saying that the offensive has resulted in a decline of armament production and a general deterioration in industrial and domestic conditions in Germany which must affect German capacity to sustain a third major war front, but the review cautiously adds, "The measure of this deterioration and its effect upon the capacity of the German armed forces to resist invasion cannot, however, be assessed."

Drop in aircraft production in March was from 1225 to 800 machines, and if production can be kept at the latter level it is considered that by Y-Day (June 1) the strength of the GAF on the Western Front (at present 2320 aircraft) will have been reduced to 1800.

So far there is no sign of any serious failure on the part of the railway system to move vital military and economic traffic. Recent damage caused by our attacks in northern and western France has not been sufficient to affect capacity of the system to handle the enemy's main rail requirements in the west after OVERLORD D-Day. (I wonder if this indicates that Spaatz was correct in advocating oil targets rather than transportation for the heavies?)

Aircraft fitted to carry glider bombs have recently been moved to northern Norway, where there is evidence of a build-up of stocks of glider bombs at airfields in north and west Norway. These may be for anti-invasion or attacks on convoys to Russia.

Do you suppose the Germans really are such suckers as to think we will attack through Norway? They did during the North African invasion, and maybe it will happen again. In accordance with General Ike's diversionary efforts, the Royal Navy is to attack Narvik in the near future and will fly reconnaissance planes across Norway far enough to be seen near Swedish territory. This will probably create headlines in Stockholm and ought to build an atmosphere of apprehension in the northern countries and Germany. The fact that the Germans have shifted aircraft for glider bombs to Norway may indicate their belief that our newspaper talk of a cross-Channel invasion is just talk and attack in Norway is the actual plan. I hope we have this good luck.

The situation across the Channel with respect to launching sites for flying bombs is worse rather than better. The Intelligence people recommend a higher priority for this bombing. Recently there has been an increase from twenty to thirty in the number of ski sites outstanding. In addition, the accuracy of the weapon has been improved and it is now estimated that sixty per cent rather than forty per cent of all successful starters would land in an area the size of greater London, if aimed at that area. The estimated scale of attack is more than double that in the original Air Ministry appreciation. Recent increased activity in the Cherbourg area suggests that these sites may be intended for an all-out attack on the Portsmouth-Southampton area, where we are heavily concentrating ships and landing craft for the cross-Channel push, and it is recommended that these sites should receive particular priority. In addition to ski sites, there are seven large sites which are presumed to be connected with a long-range rocket.

The British COS are sufficiently concerned over the threat to England that Ismay called Ike's attention to the portion of his directive which called for the protection of the British Isles, and Ike has ordered an all-out effort against the Pas de Calais sites. This, of course, diverts some of the heavies from strategic bombing.

Indications that the French railway workers are completely cowed by the Germans is found in a recent discussion with a well-informed Frenchman just out of France. He says the Germans are training their own workers to run the railways, but the French railwaymen will not be likely to help us. All of which makes me wonder if we are hoping too much for French resistance. Will it not be more like the attitude of the French in North Africa? The Combined Chiefs have approved supply of equipment for as many as 170,000 Frenchmen to be organized into battalions for policing liberated areas.

The Intelligence people recommend continuation of bombing in the Balkans, with maximum effort on the Rumanian railway system, because the Russian advance has created a chaotic refugee movement which will seriously impede movement of troops, because the German military position is weakest in Rumania and they are dependent upon Rumanian troops to hold the southward advance of the Russians, and because economic interests are greatest in Rumania, whose government is most shaken of any of the Balkan states.

Lieutenant General M. M. B. Burrows, of the British Military Mission at Moscow, has communicated his conviction that the Russians would never forgive us if OVERLORD were postponed. He has been assured that we intend to stick by the agreement made at Teheran. Actually, the attack will come shortly after the agreed month, namely May, so we can have more LSTs and other landing craft to do the job. General Burrows has been advised to keep his shirt on. He has also been told it is unnecessary to send the heads of his naval and air sections to get the latest dope on OVERLORD; neither is it necessary for him to come. Neither is it advisable, as he wants, to send a marked map to explain the operation. The Chiefs say it is too risky to send it.

Admiral Sir Andrew Cunningham has expressed anxiety lest the progress of construction of Mulberries and Gooseberries—the artificial harbors—should fall behind and fail to meet operational requirements. These include monstrous quays to be floated across the Channel and sunk to make artificial harbors. The Admiral is worried that he will have insufficient tugs to tow the concrete barges, for such they are, from the places where they are manufactured to the assembly points and thence across the Channel, if too many have to be hauled in a short time. In a test, two 1000-HP tugs towed one sample of Phoenix (code name for the concrete barges) in calm water at four knots.

Both Supreme Commanders, Eisenhower and Wilson, are under instructions from the Combined Chiefs of Staff not to give the French any information which might compromise OVERLORD. It was all right for Wilson to tell de Gaulle and Giraud and certain key staff officers about ANVIL and to inform them about the use to which the Le Clerc division will be put, but no dates were mentioned. This division is coming to the U. K. and will be in the follow-up. It is the Free French division that came across Africa under Montgomery.

WIDEWING, TUESDAY, APRIL 18, 1944

Ike had an especially busy day yesterday with numerous callers, a meeting of his Commanders-in-Chief, a luncheon with the Prime Minister, and dropped in on a farewell party for Major General Wedemeyer.

He said at the cottage last night that action must be kept going in the Mediterranean while OVERLORD is in progress. This relates to the refusal of the U. S. Chiefs to divert landing craft from the Pacific to launch ANVIL unless the British agree to a date certain. The British are disinclined to agree on a date certain because of the inability to determine the outcome of the Italian battle. In any event, Ike is in the middle—he feels as if the American Chiefs think he is trying to press for the British view and, at the same time, senses that the British think he is wangling for the American view. As a matter of fact, all he is trying to accomplish is to keep fighting activity in progress in the Mediterranean to contain as much German force as possible. The OVERLORD operation is going to be a very tough one, indeed. As noted in yesterday's diary, the Germans have increased their strength along the coast of France and Lord knows how many mines they have laid in the waters and on the shore.

So far virtually the only additional landing craft we have received for OVERLORD have been at the expense of ANVIL.

I didn't realize until I read a report today that so many parachutes are used to drop provisions and equipment. Some 90,000 have been earmarked for use in OVERLORD, and General Wilson is asking for 5000 a month throughout the summer for the Mediterranean. They are used extensively in India too, but discovery that jute can be used for parachutes has permitted India to become practically self-sustaining in this regard. Incidentally, in meeting General Wilson's request, the British Chiefs have asked Ike to request them from the United States—again he is in the middle.

The RAF Bomber Command is taking steps to reduce its losses from night fighters. A new detector is being installed in bombers and will be used beginning May 1. This device helps bombers detect enemy night fighters.

Lunched as guest of General Sir Humfrey Gale in the Yankee Doodle Room today. He had met last night Congressman William Fulbright, of Arkansas, author of the Fulbright resolution intended to commit the

United States to active participation in policing the world after the war. He was greatly impressed by Fulbright, a one-time Rhodes scholar. And I am, as usual, impressed by General Gale, one of the many intelligent British officers I have met. Most of them, especially Gale, have a delightful sense of humor, or perhaps I should write "humour." I have often thought that the Allied camaraderie at Ike's headquarters is helped a lot by the fact that we have American coffee at our desks around eleven each morning and British tea around five. These interludes afford pleasant opportunities for hashing things out on a friendly basis.

The Air Command Again

WIDEWING, THURSDAY, APRIL 20, 1944
General Ike has finally achieved his end of straightening the command channel of those controlling the heavy bombers in the RAF Bomber Command and the U. S. Strategic Air Force. This great force may now be applied as needed by the Supreme Commander for the battle to get ashore. He feels that the Combined Chiefs, and, indeed, the peoples of both countries, expect all the power of land, sea, and air forces to be applied against German forces in a way that will bring victory quickly and at a minimum cost in lives. He is confident that Germany will never be brought to her knees by air power alone, but that each one of the three great services will contribute to ultimate success. He further believes that air power may devastate Germany's cities, our sea power provide the supplies, yet the plodding doughfoot will have to take the ground and hold it before we actually win the war.

The Bomber Command and the U. S. Strategic Air Forces operate under a directive from the Combined Chiefs of Staff which makes Air Chief Marshal Portal the agent for giving day-to-day instructions as to the nature of targets to be hit. After reaching agreement that the Supreme Commander, through his deputy, Air Chief Marshal Tedder, would control the operations of the heavy bombers in support of OVERLORD as soon as the OVERLORD air plan was formulated, General Ike found that orders still were being issued by Air Chief Marshal Portal. It was discovered that technically this was correct, as the OVERLORD air plan had not been agreed upon, the difficulty being the objection of the War Cabinet to the bombing of railway centers in France. The War Cabinet felt such bombings would involve a heavy loss of French life, although it has been arranged to notify, by pamphlet and other means, the French people in areas to be bombed, so they can scurry to safety. Yet Ike has insisted and demanded

that the ground forces have the benefit of the curtailment of movement
of the enemy, which is inevitable by the destruction of French transportation centers. The coming battleground must be isolated as much as possible. Tedder is a perfect master of the art. Ike wants him to supervise and
direct. Fortunately, the question has been settled as General Ike wants
it and everyone seems happy with the logic of the arrangement.

WIDEWING, SATURDAY, APRIL 22, 1944

Ike returned from an inspection of airfields with Tedder in time for lunch
at the cottage. He is meeting with Spaatz at Park House this afternoon—
the subject not having been mentioned during lunch, but the Boss was
obviously agitated about something.*

During his trip with Tedder, Ike said he had made seven talks to RAF
airmen and one speech at dinner. The trip had been interesting but wearing. He saw a "fog dispeller," another of those British contributions to the
war which show that we Americans have no monopoly on ingenuity. This
contraption consists of a series of gasoline-burning jets placed alongside a
runway. When lighted, these throw a hot flame into the air, clearing the
fog to a height of three or four hundred feet. Consumption of gasoline is
terrific; 60,000 gallons an hour. However, the device is used only in an
emergency.

Contact between the French Military Mission to SHAEF by General
Joseph Pierre Koenig has been established. In an *aide-mémoire* prepared
by Koenig after a conversation with General Smith, on April 19, it is stated,
"It is the Supreme Commander's intention to take the head of the French
Military Mission into his full confidence regarding plans for the employment of French forces in operations in France well in advance of their
being committed to these operations."

In communicating this to the Combined Chiefs, attention was called
to the need of authority to reach agreement on a number of questions,
including provision of goods and services, civilian labor, treatment of
banks and security exchanges, transfer of property, custody of enemy
property and that of the United Nations, matters of public safety, public
health, distribution of civilian supplies, and displaced persons.

WIDEWING, TUESDAY, APRIL 25, 1944

Biggest news today is from Russia. Upon being advised of the approximate D-Day for OVERLORD, the Russian General Staff made no immediate
response but, after a couple of days, firmly stated to our Military Mission,

_____
* See entry of May 12, 1944.

now headed by Major General John R. Deane, that they would start an offensive at the same time.

General Deane said he felt disinclined to press for details as to size or places of attacks.

At a meeting of the Chiefs of Staff committee, attended by the Prime Minister, the slowness of production of harbor devices, coupled with the uncertainty of last-minute weather conditions, was discussed. Ike was present and said he was prepared to order British and American engineer units to pitch in and help finish construction but had been advised of possible labor difficulties. The PM ordered that every effort be made to accelerate the present program and that if it was found that any power was required to achieve the objective, an immediate report should be made to him. The problem is to be reviewed again on Thursday, May 4, with all those concerned to report, showing the precise position, the program forecast, and the acceleration achieved during the past week. This seems to be the PM's method of putting the bee on his subordinates to get things done.

The allotment of warships for naval bombardment also was discussed. A very heavy bombardment will be required for the first twenty-four to thirty-six hours and the majority of ships would be firing simultaneously. There are to be twenty-one cruisers with two held in reserve. Admiral Ramsay will have six battleships. The discussion revealed that the British have at least one battleship, the *Malaya*, laid up due to shortage of manpower.

Now that General Giraud has been ousted by de Gaulle, he and some of his friends are seeking an invitation for his appointment as technical adviser in Italy, in London, or in Washington. Giraud, who has done so much for France, is practically a man without a country.

Exercise TIGER

WIDEWING, FRIDAY, APRIL 28, 1944

The Supreme Commander, Air Chief Marshal Tedder, General Bradley, and party, including myself, returned from witnessing the maneuver of the amphibious landing of the U. S. 4th Division at Slapton Sands, between Dartmouth and Plymouth. The maneuver, the code name for which is TIGER, was intended to simulate conditions of the actual landings on the 4th Division's beach in France. This beach has water behind it and high ground commanding the beach. Our engineers had worked hard and long to copy the scheme of fortifications used on the shore on which the inva-

sion landing is to be made. It had been thought that this large exercise
would attract enemy air attacks or possibly attack by surface vessels, particularly E-boats, but none developed on D-Night or D-Day.

I had gone to the exercise with Lieutenant Commander James Reid,
Admiral Stark's Naval Liaison Officer to SHAEF, and Wing Commander
L. G. Scarman, Personal Assistant to Tedder.

The principal innovation is the use of rockets aboard aircraft. The plane
dives at the target and the rocket is released. The rocket accelerates to a
high speed as the propulsion fluid burns, after which the speed diminishes.
If a target is hit during the high speed, extraordinary effect is obtained.
Several squadrons of Typhoons, which fly 400 miles per hour, already have
been equipped, as have been some American planes.

Ike and his party boarded LCI(L) 495 at 6 in the morning. This craft
was in front of the kibitzers. I had gone aboard LCI(L) 487 with Scarman and Reid, as well as other members of an official party from SHAEF,
including Major Generals Harold R. Bull and Robert W. Crawford. We
reached our observing position as the naval bombardment of strong points
on the shore was begun. H-Hour was to have been at 7:30 A.M. unless the
weather was so bad the aircraft could not participate, in which event it
was to have been at 7 o'clock. As the naval bombardment started on
schedule and the weather seemed perfect, with a smooth sea, we assumed
H-Hour was 7:30 as advertised. The LCTs bearing waterproofed tanks
called DDs were in position to be launched at 7:15. These are the tanks
which, with canvas waterproofing, proceed to shore under their own propulsion. They have propellers.

Then there was a delay in the landing; why, we did not know, although
later we heard that H-Hour had been postponed even after the naval
bombardment had begun for one hour. This left LCTs and their cargoes
of DDs (tanks that float) milling around, waiting. In due time, the DDs
were successfuly launched and slowly made their way toward the beach at
three or four knots an hour. One, I noticed, was smoking. It had proceeded about a mile somewhat parallel to the beach when I saw a yellow
object pushed from the tank. I first thought this was a marker buoy, but
soon realized it was a dinghy and that the tank was in trouble. Soon an
LCVP sped toward it. In a few moments, the tank crew was in the yellow
dinghy and the tank had sunk. This was the only tank casualty and, fortunately, no one was lost. Then the first assault wave of infantry in LCVPs
arrived from the transport vessels eight miles out. They landed either with
or shortly after the amphibious tanks. This landing was preceded by rocket
bombardment, at the postponed H-Hour, from three landing craft that
had crept close to shore and fired diagonally at the obstacles, including

barbed wire, tank ditch, and other prepared positions. The rockets had made usable pathways through the barbed wire.

In this exercise effort was made to get tanks ashore quickly in order to use their fire power. Engineers were brought in as rapidly as possible to demolish obstacles with hand-placed explosives. The tanks had to wait while these operations proceeded. If there had been enemy fire, the tanks, being quite close together, would have been easy targets, as, indeed, would the landing craft.

I came away from the exercise feeling depressed. But frequently the poorest kind of exercise presages the best actual operation because the failures are noticed and corrected.

Later that evening when I joined the General's train at Taunton, I heard Ike, Bradley, Gerow, and Tedder in an earnest discussion of today's problem. They asked me if I had heard the reason for the postponement of H-Hour. I replied I had not and was surprised that they did not know either. Gerow emphasized the principle: never change the time once it is set, because too much confusion arises.

During a discussion of the helpfulness of bombing on the beach, Tedder said an agreement had been reached on OVERLORD that there would be mass aerial bombing of the beachhead just before H-Hour. This bombing would start about 200 yards inland from the beach and continue on for eight or nine hundred yards. There would be shorts and longs. The shorts might explode underwater mines. Indeed, a strike photograph of an operation on the French coast a few days ago showed that a bomb that had hit short and, in the water, had exploded a string of the Germans' underwater mines. It is these mines that Gerow fears the most for his landing on Omaha Beach. He also has on his right flank a cliff 110 feet high on which there are gun emplacements. He has two battalions of Rangers assigned to scale the cliff as quickly as possible after H-Hour. They may shoot grappling hooks with ropes attached to the top of the cliff so the agile Rangers can clamber up. The Commandos have used a fireman's ladder to scale cliffs, and some of these are being obtained and will be mounted on ducks. Ike, Bradley, and Tedder were insistent that an amphibious landing had to be timed delicately and each operation had to be conducted within a margin of one or two minutes from the time set. Gerow said his difficulty was in getting the U. S. Navy to agree to precise timing because of the variables encountered by boats, such as wind, tide, and current. The Navy could figure within three or four minutes but not one or two. For the beach attack of bombers at H-Hour, Tedder said this would strike within forty-five seconds of the time estimated.

Gerow said he feared the underwater obstacles most of all, and to date no completely satisfactory method of disposal had been found. The use of bulldozers to shove away obstacles seemed practical and he proposed to use them. They will bend seventy-five-pound railroad rails but will not bend those of 100 pounds. The European railroads use the lighter rail and the only 100-pound rails in France are those which Americans laid there during the last war. It would, indeed, be irony if the Germans had used American rail for their stubby hedgerows of antitank and antilanding-craft devices.

Gerow seemed a bit pessimistic, and finally Ike said to him that he should be optimistic and cheerful because he has behind him the greatest fire power ever assembled on the face of the earth. For the entire landing, there will be six battleships, two monitors, twenty-one cruisers, and an untold number of destroyers. In addition, there will be the greatest amount of air support ever assembled. Then there are the rocket ships and our own artillery which can be mounted on landing craft.

Pilots of observation aircraft normally flown from American battleships and cruisers are being taught to fly Spitfires from bases in England because their own craft are too vulnerable to the GAF, as we learned in the Sicilian attack. Ike said the battleships would not be with the invasion very long, possibly only twenty-four or forty-eight hours.

Gee said he wasn't pessimistic, he was merely realistic, and he and his staff purposely looked on the worst conditions as being possible so that every preparation that could be thought of would be made.

Ike related that while he and Bradley were watching the bombing demonstration the day before, noting the accuracy with which the bombs fell on the target, he had just said to Bradley that he saw no reason why troops in his leading assault wave had to be 1500 yards short of the bomb area when the blanket bombing of the beach took place. Just as he had advocated that the assault wave move up to within 500 yards, the better to take advantage of the confusion and turmoil created by the bombing, the inevitable happened. One plane dropped its bombs more than 500 yards short of the target. The plan still stands at 1500 yards.

Returning this morning, Ike had to meet with the Prime Minister, whose Cabinet was raising hob because of bad reaction expected from the French by bombing of transportation targets. I understand that the PM has appealed to the President. Meanwhile this is about the eleventh day of reasonably good weather for our air effort, which has gone on apace.

The fact that General Patton is in England was released last week. Another problem on Ike's lap is a kick from General Marshall arising out of an informal talk that Patton privately made to a British service club. In this Patton said that Britain and America would have to rule the world after the war. Our PRO has been busy on his own getting Russia included and to some extent had succeeded, but the Republicans at home construed Patton's remarks as a general's intrusion into political affairs—political on Roosevelt's side—just why, I don't know—but in any event, General Marshall says that practically any hope of Senatorial approval of the permanent promotions for a long list of officers, including Patton and Beetle, is out. While Ike was away, Beetle had answered General Marshall, taking on himself the responsibility for releasing Patton's name and reporting that Ike had steadfastly objected to the release. Patton is a great fighter and also a great talker.

I am concerned over the absence of toughness and alertness of young American officers whom I saw on this trip. They seem to regard the war as one grand maneuver in which they are having a happy time. Many seem as green as growing corn. How will they act in battle and how will they look in three months' time? *

A good many of the full colonels also give me a pain. They are fat, gray, and oldish. Most of them wear the Rainbow Ribbon of the last war and are still fighting it. The 1st U. S. Division is the only experienced American infantry division actually in the assault, although the 9th, which also was in Africa, is in the close follow-up.

On the Navy's side, our crews also are green, but they seem to know how to handle their boats, yet when I dictate this, I recall that in plain daylight, with a smooth sea with our LCI standing still, she nearly had her stern carried away by a landing craft fitted out as an antiaircraft ship. We were missed only by inches—in clear daylight.

As the day closed, I was in Ike's office when Beetle phoned on the intercommunication system to say that by E-boat action last night, we had two LSTs sunk and one damaged in the exercise. This happened off Lyme Bay—just where we had been. Casualties are estimated at 300 to 400. Beetle said this reduces our reserve of LSTs for the big show to zero. Ike told Beetle to get off a cable to the Combined Chiefs advising them of the loss.

Ike's Link with the GI

WIDEWING, SUNDAY, APRIL 30, 1944

At the officers' mess today some of us were talking about Ike's method of talking personally with individual soldiers or to small groups of them. It creates a bond of understanding which quickly spreads by word of

---

* This is one of the passages I was most tempted to delete since history made such a monkey out of me.

mouth to other soldiers who may not have been so fortunate as to talk with him. All sorts of extravagant versions come from these brief talks, but they have the great quality of being thoroughly personal and human. Ike frets when reporters get close enough to hear these conversations because he doesn't want the GIs to feel that he is simply putting on a show by talking with them. He is in a continual battle to retain this privacy. Frequently, the reporters get versions of the conversations from the GIs themselves and I regard this as good, but Ike is so keen on re- taining a personal relationship with his soldiers that he growls every time he sees a story covering any of these affairs. As censorship in Eng- land for British papers and correspondents generally is limited to military security, there is little the censors can do to prevent publication. On three recent occasions, Ike has found his words quoted almost exactly as he spoke them to small groups of soldiers. I try to tell him what makes the mare go, but what happens seems to be more than he can fathom. He simply does not realize that what he says is news. But to him, his personal tie with the GI is virtually sacred.

APRIL, 1944: *Pacific Task Force hit Palau, Woleai, and Yap, sinking twenty- eight Jap ships and destroying 214 planes at cost of twenty-five planes and eighteen men. Advances were scored at Empress Augusta Bay and Bogadjim, sixteen atolls in Marshalls occupied. Three air attacks against Hollandia Bay destroyed 388 Jap planes. Timor bombed. Raids over Wewak found no oppo- sition. Allied fleet hit northwest Sumatra with everything from submarines to battleships. Troops, landing at Aitape and Hollandia, trapped an estimated 30,000 Japs in New Guinea. Paramushiru, Shimushu, and Matsua Islands bombed. Japs on Imphal plain first stopped, then routed by heavy artillery action and bayonet charges. Allies repel German thrusts at Aprilia and Anzio. Badoglio government resigned. 8th Air Force dropped 24,000 tons of bombs, destroyed 1300 Nazi planes in April. Ever-heavier bombing hit Brunswick, Ruhr, northeast Germany, Poland, communications and airfields in France and Belgium. Aircraft plants at Aschersleben, Bernburg, Rostock, Arnims- walde, Augsburg, Oberfaffenhofen, Schweinfurt, and Lechfeld pounded by fleets ranging up to 1000 bombers. Cologne and Paris industrial plants took record of 5040 tons of bombs on one raid. Toulon, Pas de Calais, and Berlin hit on many occasions; 2000 planes raiding plants in Friedrichshafen shot down 103 enemy planes, lost thirty-eight bombers, seventeen fighters. Thou- sand-plane raids became commonplace. Russia drove Nazis back to Czecho- slovakia, approached Sevastopol in Crimea; ninety-two Nazi escape vessels sunk off southern Crimea by Reds. Allied planes bombed Budapest, Bucharest, Ploeşti. U. S. Navy Secretary Knox died of heart attack. Britain suspended diplomatic freedom of communications. (Nothing is quite as thrilling as the sight of hundreds of our bombers flying over London, their silver bodies glisten- ing in the morning sunlight, leaving grotesque trails of vapor, en route to hit the Hun.—H.C.B.)*

WIDEWING, MONDAY, MAY 1, 1944

I am to report to Captain Ernest H. von Heimburg, Chief of Staff to Admiral Hall, aboard the *Ancon*, by noon tomorrow at Portland. I don't know whether my assignment is temporary or whether I should be equipped for the full period of service. I am told, however, that I can return for twenty-four hours to pick up additional clothes and not to carry too much aboard the *Ancon*, which will be the American command ship for FABIUS, the four-division landing exercise, again on Slapton Sands. This exercise is the one really expected to attract major opposition of the enemy as its convoys move far out into the Channel. A counterpropaganda scheme has already been laid on in the event the Germans undertake to tell the world the invasion is on and that since it has not landed in France the Allies have been defeated. The landing, of course, is to be on beaches in southern England, but with the sharp E-boat reaction to TIGER, it looks as if we will see action in FABIUS.

At the General's session with the PM Friday morning at which the grave concern of the British Cabinet over the bombing of transportation centers and resultant death of Frenchmen was the subject, Ike told the PM that the British Chiefs would have to send their views through the Combined Chiefs, who are his bosses, and that so far as he is concerned, military necessity dictates bombing of transportation areas.

Secretary Knox, God bless him, died last week.

Just Another Joy Ride

WIDEWING, TUESDAY, MAY 9, 1944

I spent from Tuesday noon, May 2, until Saturday the sixth aboard the *Ancon*, largely in the operations room, watching the intricate task of direction of the amphibious landing of the U. S. 1st Division.

This was to be preliminary to a period of service in the Navy, presumably in the Far Shore Service Command, as arranged by Admiral Kirk, but when I reported to this command at Plymouth, I found the organization already was well set, and if I were to have a responsible place in it, someone probably more deserving would have been displaced. I saw the organization chart, and every niche had a name in it. I felt that if I squeezed myself in by authority of Admiral Kirk, and as I would soon be discovered as an aide of the Supreme Commander, someone might say or feel favoritism. During the several days on the *Ancon* I suffered somewhat from a guilty conscience. Ike had told me before I left that if I found my temporary employment to be inconsequential or unsatisfactory to let him know and he would send for me at once.

Being assigned to the *Ancon* was simply another joy ride. It made me realize that although I had not been busy for many weeks, the work I was doing for the General and the opportunity for service were decidedly worth while. Consequently, I am back at the old stand and probably will stay here unless my old friend, Commander Bob Melling, Communications Officer of the *Ancon*, requests my services as one of his communications officers for the assault. This would require only about a week of training but would get me in the big party without having to spend thirty days before and after, which would be necessary in the Far Shore job.

Another thing I missed—and missed tremendously—was authentic news of all military operations, which is available at headquarters. The farther one gets away from GHQ the more rumors there are and the less true information is obtained. I never appreciated before how much I live on the day-to-day and even hour-to-hour flow of intelligence and operational news through our headquarters.

Anyway, Ike said he was glad I was back and that while he hadn't objected to my leaving temporarily, he felt I had a real job to do, particularly in dealing with the newspapermen who continually seek information about him.

When I left, Ike had said that he was in the midst of discussions with land, sea, and air commanders, not only as to D-Day but as to H-Hour. Realization that the Germans were placing underwater obstacles on beaches where they consider we are likely to land may change the scheme from landing at high tide to assault at low tide. The obstacles are placed by the Germans during low tide at about the half-tide mark.

Yesterday the Commanders-in-Chief met, and Ike decided that D-Day would be Y plus 4 (Y-Day is June 1). On Y plus 4, 5, 6, and 7 the tides are right and the moon is full. H-Hour is yet to be set and may be staggered for different beaches, depending upon the nature and location of obstacles. The type which apparently will cause the most trouble is called "Element C," which is a gatelike structure of steel angles at the center. Then there is the "Tetrahedra," which consists of a pyramid of steel angles standing about four feet six inches. A more common obstacle is the steel stake which is an I-beam or rail sunk into the sand by water jet. The Commandos have experimented with devices to overrun or remove these obstacles. Most of them will require hand-placed demolitions. In addition, mines undoubtedly are strung in the openings between the obstacles.

The AEAF suggested strafing the beaches where the Germans are fixing the obstacles, to slow down their progress, but Ike decided yesterday there should be no strafing, at least this week, for security reasons.

Ike had lunched with the PM yesterday and found him looking more fit than in months. Only the two had been present, and Ike said the PM had become emotional when they parted. "I am in this thing with you to the end," the PM had said, "and if it fails we will go down together." Ike said Churchill had tears in his eyes.

The British Cabinet is still rather unhappy because of our bombing of transportation targets in France, but the bombing goes on. Despite the pressure, Ike has not revoked his command decision.

Admiral Bieri, USN, who was on Ike's staff for TORCH, has been assigned to Ike's staff again by Admiral King. The wise Admiral has shifted three LSTs from the Mediterranean to Channel forces to replace those lost by E-boats. I found the casualties much higher than first stated; between 750 and 800. Failure of signals prevented a Royal Navy destroyer from accompanying the convoy. There were expressions of concern by Americans and British, both Army and Navy, whom I met on the trip. It was an unfortunate mix-up of orders and a sad fate for many fine lads.

Incidentally, FABIUS developed no enemy reaction, but we did get a heavy gale. There were no fatalities. One GI was hospitalized with pneumonia and a second lieutenant was shot accidentally in the buttock. We were "snooped" by enemy aircraft on at least four occasions and had red alerts. I saw one mine sweeper preceding our convoy damaged by an underwater explosion. It was towed into Portland as the *Ancon* was departing. The Germans had been actively sowing mines in this area. Shipping in Plymouth was attacked with glider bombs, whose "mother" aircraft can stay out of reach of antiaircraft guns on the shore.

The naval force I accompanied is to be Assault Force "O" under Rear Admiral John L. Hall, of North African acquaintance, and will land the U. S. 1st Division.

The number of German Divisions in France has increased from fifty-six to fifty-eight.

Averell Harriman was a dinner guest of Ike's while I was away. He confirmed the fact that the Russians were prepared for a full-out attack simultaneously with our invasion. He brought fresh caviar, which Ike likes, and we have been feasting royally with great gobs on Melba toast. It's a hard war.

Patton Saved Again

Ike told me that the furor raised by the press and in Congress by Patton's recent speech simply emphasized his vulnerability if quoted.

Old "Blood and Guts" is still on the job. Ike had handled the situation, and, as usual, had been stanchly supported by Secretary Stimson. The Secretary said he had followed with intense interest Ike's correspondence in regard to General Patton, and he had seen the message of Ike's decision to retain him in his present command.

Mr. Stimson continued that the judicial poise and good judgment, as well as the great courage, which the Supreme Commander had shown in making this decision had filled him with even greater respect and admiration—high as that has always been.

The Russians have asked, through the head of the British Mission at Moscow, General Burrows, for assistance and consent of the British to stage raids on the Finnish and Norwegian coasts. The British have quickly agreed, but have passed the word to the Russians that because the Norwegians fear Russian occupation, the Norwegian Ambassador at Moscow should be informed that the Russians have no intention of staying in Norway. Ike has been notified of this correspondence. The British judge that activity by the Russians in Norway will help confuse the enemy, but I can't see how the Germans can be fooled into believing that we will land anywhere on the Continent except under an air umbrella of fighter protection. All the Germans need is a pair of calipers to measure the distance from bases in England to the French coast across the Channel and they can guess reasonably well the boundary in which any invasion must take place. However, the most that is thought will come of northern activity is to contain some German divisions which might otherwise be released for fighting us in Normandy.

General Jumbo Wilson, Allied Commander in the Mediterranean, had been at Widewing Friday, May 5, to see General Ike. They discussed possibilities of operations in the Mediterranean, and Ike had been pleased to find there is now little difference in their opinions. Ike is hopeful as a result of the conference that General Wilson may now submit to Combined Chiefs a definite proposal for his summer's operations. Both are seeking to avoid immobilization of the strong Allied forces in the Mediterranean at the very time when they should be fighting full out.

An Aspect of Reverse Lend-Lease

Through a friend in the War Office, Colonel Gault has been informed that one of the mess officers at Headquarters Command has purchased a handsome silver tea service for the Yankee Doodle Room at a cost of some £125, or $600. This is charged to reverse Lend-Lease and may be a good investment, but, unfortunately, the purchase is made in the name of General Eisenhower. It is something about which he, of course, has known nothing. When he was told of this, he blew a fuse. He started an investigation to see if other purchases had been made in his name and discovered that certain furniture taken by the ETO Headquarters Command to equip Hayes' Lodge likewise was charged against him, some of it being antique. He is having this returned, and in due course, the house will be completely abandoned, even though it is a very useful facility for him when fog or other conditions prevent him from returning to the cottage after a late session with the PM at 10 Downing. I have checked with the officer who arranged for the purchase of the furniture for Hayes' Lodge and I find that it can all be turned back at ninety per cent of the purchase price, as furniture in England is hard to get. I have discovered, too, a general feeling amongst our purchasing officers that as long as goods purchased from British concerns are paid for via reverse Lend-Lease, the price we pay is inconsequential. Nevertheless, the Supreme Commander has instructed that no one henceforth shall acquire anything in his name except those of us who are on his personal staff, and then he prefers that his personal approval be first obtained.

The investigation, which was conducted quietly by Major General Everett Hughes, formerly Deputy Theater Commander in North Africa, disclosed that four sofa pillows had been acquired for Telegraph Cottage at a cost of ten dollars each. I was responsible for authorizing this intended improvement to the cold and hard davenport and two overstuffed chairs in our plain living room. If words had been a paddle, I could have used one pillow very handily. The pillows were returned.

We have talked of the headlines that would flow from a Congressional investigation of reverse Lend-Lease when and if a silver tea service was discovered purchased for General Eisenhower at $600, and sofa pillows for a General. What grist for a Congressional investigation. Tahiti, here we come.

Alexander Attacks in Italy

WIDEWING, THURSDAY, MAY 11, 1944
Alexander's all-out attack to join the Fifth Army front and the Anzio bridgehead, with the hope of taking Rome, has been pushed forward from May 14 to midnight tonight.

Today the U. S. Chiefs of Staff have notified General Wilson in the Mediterranean that his plans are satisfactory and the Chiefs have agreed to send him nineteen LSTs each with an LCT aboard, the first to arrive in the Mediterranean June 20 and to be completely delivered in July. The three LSTs moved from the Mediterranean to replace the recent loss in the Channel likewise will be made up.

Yesterday Beetle was fussing with the wording of a proclamation to be issued by Ike to the French when OVERLORD starts. Beetle said he was "walking on eggs" to find language which would be effective yet not create a storm of criticism at home as was true in the Darlan case.

WIDEWING, FRIDAY, MAY 12, 1944

Alexander's big attack in Italy was delayed twenty-four hours but got under way last night. Today the 15th Air Force has two sorties per bomber, including heavies, on communications in Italy. Quite the heaviest all-out attack since the Air Force and the Navy came to the rescue of our beachhead at Salerno. So far there are no reports as to the success or failure of the long-prepared attack of Alexander, Clark, and General Sir Oliver Leese, who relieved Monty in command of the Eighth Army.

Yesterday Beetle had me to lunch at his house. Said he would never be fit to be Chief of Staff for another campaign; this one had worn him down. Beetle said he was damned well going to get out of the Army after the war. He was fed up. Said he had no misgivings about our troops getting ashore, but gave me the alarming prediction that our chances of holding the beachhead, particularly after the Germans get their build-up, is only fifty-fifty. But, he said, the chance is worth taking. Said that there will be a time when we have only three-fourths-of-a-division advantage in strength above the Germans, judging by the study of expected build-up of both sides as made by our staff. Beetle said again that underwater obstacles are our greatest worry. Beetle's professional realism and misgivings rather substantiate the reluctance the British have had about undertaking OVERLORD before we are fully prepared. Our Intelligence indicates the German High Command is divided as to *where* we will strike. Beetle thought this good, but he groused most about the refusal of the British Chiefs of Staff to permit SHAEF to deal more frankly with the French. Ike has spoken very plainly to the Combined Chiefs as to the need of releasing him from the injunction of secrecy in dealing with the French.

Ike has been very close-mouthed about the incident which I referred to under April 22 and probably he would have told me what happened if I had asked him, but I never thought to at the proper time. This is the incident which agitated Ike and caused him to hot-foot it to Spaatz's house: T. J.—now our smiling impresario at public relations, and doing well—said last night that the story is all over town that a major general in the Air Force had offered bets at a cocktail party on the date of the invasion and he had talked too freely. He had been reduced to his permanent rank of lieutenant colonel and sent home.

Ike looks worn and tired. The strain is telling on him. He looks older now than at any time since I have been with him, but fortunately he has the happy faculty of bouncing back after a night of good sleep, or a ride on a horse or some exercise.

Final Review of OVERLORD

WIDEWING, TUESDAY, MAY 16, 1944

Ike spent Monday at the general and final review of plans for OVERLORD held at St. Paul's School, London. Among those present were His Majesty the King, the PM, and Field Marshal Smuts. I kicked myself all over the lot for not having had foresight to ask for permission to attend as well, so I could have recorded the highlights. From what I gathered from Ike and the Secretary of the General Staff, Coloned Ford Trimble, the Supreme Commander made the opening remarks, was followed by General Montgomery, Admiral Ramsay, Air Chief Marshal Leigh-Mallory, and General Bradley. Patton was there, resplendent. The King had made a brief talk, and the Prime Minister let go with a slow-starting but fastending stemwinder. He preached bravery, ingenuity, and persistence as human qualities of greater value than equipment.

Admiral Ramsay had said that after careful study the first landing would be made at low tide, so the obstacles normally underwater at half tide could be dealt with by hand demolitions or under conditions permitting "dry attack." In the half-hour between landing and the rise of the tide the obstacles would have to be destroyed or removed. This is where the combat engineers will come in.

When the King departed, Ike thanked him for his attendance and reminded him that the air people said they would have 11,000 planes overhead on D-Day and that the Navy had said that, to put the Army ashore, it had marshaled the greatest armada of transports, landing craft, and warships the world had ever seen. Now all the ground troops had to do was to land and capture some villas for the hot shots, particularly one to accommodate the King, who would be as welcome in France as he had been in North Africa.

The final review ended in a mood of the grimness of the task, yet with confidence in the soundness of the planning and the quality of the men who will have to live and die through the assault and whatever may come after.

Alexander's attack in Italy has continued, with the morning papers carrying good news of success of the French troops which seem to be assigned the central sector between the Eighth Army at Cassino and the Americans on the west coast. Cassino apparently is being bypassed. Our forces in the Anzio beachhead were supposed to attack four days after the big push on the main line, so we expect to hear news from it any day. Ike said the battle so far was consoling because it indicated the Germans had elected to stand and fight rather than to disengage. If they retreated we would have a slow and tortuous task of following them up the leg of Italy, and the Germans would have more reserves to fight us in France.

The Provisional Government of the French Republic

The French had done so well that General Juin, their CO, sent a special message to de Gaulle which was read to the assembled French Committee in Algiers. There were loud and long cheers. In this atmosphere it was announced the Committee's name would be changed to the Provisional Government of the French Republic, and that the Clark-Darlan agreements were not recognized as binding upon the Committee.

De Gaulle's show of independence makes even more difficult Ike's position as referee among the President (who apparently has overruled Secretary of State Hull's public statement of lenient policy in dealing with de Gaulle), the Prime Minister, the Foreign Office, and de Gaulle himself.

The need of a working arrangement with anyone who has direct influence with the resistance groups in France is apparent from an exchange of messages between General Wilson and Ike. On May 14 General Wilson reported that after D-Day, when loyal Frenchmen seek to aid our efforts by sabotage and open resistance, they will be discovered and will have to flee to the mountains to avoid reprisals by the Germans. Wilson proposed to land selected French officers and enlisted men and French-speaking OSS personnel (Jedburgh teams) to organize and lead native groups. An all-out effort to supply and equip native groups would be undertaken. Prior to D-Day, Wilson proposed to land American and British saboteurs to operate against the Nice-Marseille rail lines and communications in the Rhone Valley and Carcassonne Gap. Wilson had understood from his conversations with Ike here that premature popular uprisings, outside of our attacking area in Normandy, should be dampened. He asked for an expression of views and desires.

Ike responded that resistance in France would take two forms: (1) organized groups under Allied control, and (2) general civilian resistance. He stated that it was the SHAEF policy to restrict general civilian resistance to such covert action as may be possible without inviting mass reprisals against the French from the Germans. Overt action is to be delayed until it can be helpful to tactical operations. Groups organized for resistance throughout France are to do their stuff on receipt of action messages from the BBC which will be issued by SHAEF authority in London. Their action is intended to delay enemy forces moving by rail and road, to sabotage enemy telecommunications, and to carry out general guerrilla tasks.

On May 8 Ike sent to the Combined Chiefs a recommendation originated by the Psychological Warfare Division as to the wording of the initial communiqué for OVERLORD. The recommendation read:

> Allied naval forces supported by strong air forces began landing Allied armies this morning on the northern coast of France.

The Combined Chiefs approved the general wording, with one amendment; they said it should begin "under the command of General Eisenhower."

If any officers above field rank wish to use the public telephone for long-distance calls in the United Kingdom they may simply mention the magic word MARCHWIND to the operator and will be put through.

Today, incidentally, all American officers and enlisted personnel are restricted to quarters from midnight to midnight to facilitate the MPs' search for AWOLs.

Because of enemy mine laying from aircraft in strategic channels through which our assault ships have to move, the Air Commander-in-Chief at Portsmouth has issued orders to antiaircraft batteries and ships to open fire on all unidentified planes flying below 2000 feet at night. This order at first was opposed by the AEAF as being unfair to our own airmen, but an understanding has now been reached and the order will become effective.

Today Ike is signing agreements with Belgian, Dutch, and Norwegian governments providing terms on which liberation will be accomplished when, as, and if we get into those countries. Too bad conditions don't permit of our having one with the French.

Ike has asked that visitors to his theater from home be curtailed to those absolutely needed, and the War Department is co-operating.

"Any Day Now"

WIDEWING, THURSDAY, MAY 18, 1944

Germans are broadcasting that the invasion will come "any day now." Say we have completed concentration of ships and forces in the south-coast harbors. Paquis, a French commentator, says we have fifty divisions ready. The papers report that Rommel, von Rundstedt, and other generals are having a hurried conference today, one which was initially to have taken place a week from today.

The papers today carry stories to the effect that all hospitals are being emptied of patients, except for the seriously ill, in order to make room for second-front casualties. Also hospital linen, etc., is to have top priority in laundries as soon as the front opens.

Ike is still out inspecting, his schedule placing him in Northern Ireland today, and his wing of SHAEF is as quiet as a farmhouse parlor.

On request of the PRO, I have been interviewed by five newspapermen yesterday and today—Howard Whitman, of New York *Daily News*; Wes Gallagher and Hal Boyle, of the Associated Press, who had lunch with me today; and Charles Wertenbaker and Bill White, who are doing an exhaustive story on SHAEF for *Life* and *Time*. Whitman, who has been over here two months, told me that some correspondents believe there will not be an invasion; that talk of one is a giant hoax.

If it's a put-up job, we're fooling a lot of people, including ourselves. The staff has tried to figure out the best day and hour for D-Day and H-Hour, bearing in mind the insistent arguments of land, sea, and air forces.

Looks as if Y plus 4 is D-Day. Tidal and light conditions are main factors. An adequate period after morning twilight must be available for aerial bombing of coast-defense and field batteries and strong points. Similarly, an adequate period after morning twilight must be available for naval bombardment.

Initial assault troops must land with a sufficient interval, before the incoming tide prevents their work, to prepare lanes through the heavy obstacles that are above water only near low tide. For certain beaches (where offshore rocks are present) the depth of water must be such as to permit clearance of these rocks by craft carrying initial assault elements.

Y plus 5 and Y plus 6 are also acceptable in case unsuitable weather makes it necessary to postpone the assault. If adverse weather forces a further postponement, it will be necessary to adopt major changes in the assault plan (which would jeopardize the success of the operation and which are therefore unacceptable) or to await the next favorable tidal period, which begins about Y plus 18. An assault in this tidal period entails acceptance of moonless conditions and loss of good campaigning weather after we are ashore.

The Italian offensive is officially reported in General Alexander's sit-rep for today as making "good progress." The attack out of the beachhead at Anzio has not yet been launched.

General Wilson has sent Ike a long exposition on pros and cons of planning Mediterranean operations to assist OVERLORD. There are so many "ifs" in the Italian situation the planners must be going crazy.

Civilian casualties incidental to our bombing of railway yards in France are proving less than the most conservative estimates, so the heat is taken off General Ike on this question, temporarily at least. The weather has been so bad the past three or four days that our air activity is greatly diminished.

Mamie has wired Ike that John has finally decided to cast his lot with the infantry. His graduation from West Point occurs early next month.

WIDEWING, FRIDAY, MAY 19, 1944

What has become of the worry about the pilotless aircraft and the rocket bombs? The fears we heard expressed when we returned to England in January seem to have dissipated. However, the AEAF has from time to time bombed the sites. The latest report I have seen indicates that only fourteen of the 100 or more may now be considered operational.

Today I have read a large part of the plan of the U. S. Third Army commanded by Patton, which is to go onto the Continent through the Cherbourg port when, as, and if, starting two or three weeks after the invasion. The plan is detailed—the mimeographed pages lay two inches thick—and even prescribes the use of penicillin for the wounded behind the lines. Patton's army is to be on the right flank of the U. S. First Army and is to cut off the Brest Peninsula and eventually capture the port of Brest. Subsequently it is to swing to the east in the general direction of Paris. The British Second Army will be on the left of the U. S. First, moving eastward along the coast. One of the ports Patton is to take is Saint-Malo, where I visited twenty-one years ago. I would like to see it again.

The morning papers carried the news that Cassino had been taken by the British Eighth. The Poles had crawled up the mountain on which Cassino Monastery is located and it, too, had fallen. The French and Americans are making good progress, the latter having taken Formia on the coast, and patrols are still pushing on. Still no big attack by our bridgehead forces, but today's sitrep says the 34th Division had patrols in contact with the enemy all along the line, and the Germans claim an increasing crescendo of artillery fire is erupting from our beachhead.

A Lower-Level Review of OVERLORD

WIDEWING, SATURDAY, MAY 20, 1944

I attended a briefing of OVERLORD put on for Admiral Bieri, who has come to us fresh from Admiral King's planning division to ANCXF, which means Allied Naval Commander, Expeditionary Force, commanded by Admiral Ramsay, under SCAEF.*

I must say that since I have heard the briefing I am not as optimistic about the forthcoming invasion as I was. The Germans now have fifty-eight divisions in France. Since their defeats in Russia, the Germans have reorganized their divisions, cutting from 17,000 to about 13,000. They now have some 750,000 troops of various quality and age in France. Von Rundstedt is the top commander. He has under him two army groups, the one northwest headed by Rommel, the one in southern France by Blaskowitz. Rommel is expected to attack quickly in an effort to drive us back into the sea. The German forces are strung out along the coast, with heaviest disposition in the Pas de Calais and somewhat less in the vicinity of the estuary of the Seine and the base of the Cotentin Peninsula. I was surprised to learn that our Intelligence indicates there are some 200,000 Russians in the German Army in France. They have been brought into the army by various means and are supposed to fight well in protected positions, but give up readily. This is said to have been true of them in the Italian fighting.

The Germans have no general reserve of troops. In other words, to strengthen themselves in France they would have to withdraw forces from Italy, the Balkans, the Russian front, or from Norway, Denmark, and the Low Countries. With the Russians launching a general attack simultaneously with our landings and pressure being maintained in Italy and guerrilla activity in the Balkans, they will be busy on four fronts, not to mention the front in the air.

* Supreme Commander, AEF.

As to grand strategy, our intelligence people report that the Germans "appreciate" that we may invade Norway. Actually, the Germans have added a division there. When we invade west of the Seine, we hope the Germans will believe that this is merely a minor operation and that they may expect the major thrust in Pas de Calais, thus keeping the Germans from shifting troops from the latter place to the coast between the Seine and Cherbourg. Our plan is to get sufficient ports in Normandy and Brittany to supply forces of proper size to continue the drive into Germany. This is supposed to take about ninety days, then troops and matériel will flow through these ports direct from the U. S. and the U. K. By D plus 90 we are due at Paris. It should be a busy summer. In this connection it is interesting to note that we are already putting so much stuff through the British ports that forty ships now en route may not be accommodated or unloaded. Today Ike asked the PM that a special appeal be made to the workers to get the job done.

WIDEWING, SUNDAY, MAY 21, 1944

The question of policing Germany after the war has been discussed by Ike; he favors continuation of SHAEF as the instrument of Allied control without dividing Germany into sectors. We now understand Germany is to be divided into three general sectors for postwar control; the Russians in the east, the Americans "in the middle," headquartering at Berlin, and the British in the north and west portions, where the ports are of particular British naval interest.

Weather—and a Report from Russia

WIDEWING, TUESDAY, MAY 23, 1944

I asked Ike today what he considered ideal weather for the landings. He said clear and with a wind of five or six miles an hour blowing inshore, so the smoke and dust of the battle would blind the enemy and not us.

At yesterday's meeting of Ike's Commanders-in-Chief, as it has been for weeks, weather was the principal topic and arrangements were concluded for the "agreed" report from the various weather experts to be received on Sunday, May 28, and daily for consideration at meetings at the Portsmouth headquarters starting Monday, the twenty-ninth. Starting with June 1, the Commanders-in-Chief will meet daily with Ike to consider the weather report and final decision will have to be made the morning of June 3 if the present D-Day, the fourth, is to be kept.

It is the same old story of gambling on the weather and knowing there is nothing that can be done about it, yet myriads of units will be ready to move or be actually in movement on the high seas when announcement of postponement for twenty-four hours or more might have to be made. This has always been the most anguishing period for Ike and now is no exception. At each Monday meeting for some weeks, he has picked a hypothetical D-Day, and the weathermen have made trial predictions.

Bridge is his most complete momentary escape. Last night, playing against Colonel Elliott Roosevelt and General Ted Curtis, Ike and I held good cards and for nearly three hours his mind was relatively free of his responsibilities. We had played badminton half an hour before our company arrived. With a score of eight to seven in his favor, both of us were out of breath and perspiring, so we stopped.

Ike had lunched with the Prime Minister and said, as usual, he was "in between" the Prime and the President and would have to try to negotiate a settlement. I take it he meant the French question, but when he is relatively free in his mind I don't like to prod him into talking of questions that bothered him all day. If he wants to talk, fine; if not, I give him a rest—maybe he doesn't think so, but at least I *try* to give him a rest. He was talking the other night about the diversion that Tedder and Alexander must obtain by their ability to sketch and paint. Said he might like to try his hand at it if he had the material. I am on a quiet hunt for it, but after D-Day the time he now thinks he has for sketching will disappear.

Elliott Roosevelt had just returned from Moscow, where, with Generals Fred Anderson, Ted Curtis, and others of the 8th Air Force, he had consulted the Russians relative to accommodations on Soviet bases for our photographic reconnaissance aircraft. I asked Elliott if the Russians had paid any particular attention to him because he was the President's son. He said decidedly not; that even Stalin's son had been a private in the Russian Army and recently was killed. The Russians, he said, are primarily interested in technological developments and practically revere Americans because of our great reputation as technicians and scientists.

Elliott said Stalin was a stickler for keeping his word, and the great test for the Russians was whether Britain and the United States would keep their word with respect to the second front. Ike commented that he wasn't certain just what commitments had been made, but was confident that there would be no welshing on the second front.

Elliott said the Russian losses, both military and civilian, were estimated at sixteen million; German losses, all military, at four million. The reason for high civilian losses, in addition to the normal casualties from bombing of cities, Elliott explained, is shown in the record at Sevastopol. When the Russian Army was withdrawn, civilian men and women remained to defend the city and held it three or four weeks so the army could be saved "to fight another day."

He asked the Russian air people about their arrangement for relief of fatigued fliers. There is no relief. A Russian pilot with more than thirty missions to his credit is a rarity. Generally he is dead by the time he has thirty missions. The training scheme used by the Russians is to start the pilot flying in the back areas, gradually working forward until he is training so close to the front line after fifty hours in the air that he is as likely as not to have combat. Neither Russians nor Germans on that front go in for high-altitude flying. Most of them do around 8000 to 12,000 feet or lower. There is intense light flak, but little heavy ack-ack reaching to high altitudes. Practically all the Russian air effort is in tactical support of the ground armies.

Elliott had been a guest at dinner at the Moscow Hotel given by the entire corps of American correspondents in Russia—seven of them. There was no wine or spirits and the meal was plain. The bill was the equivalent of $690. Yet if one wishes to live on the regular Russian ration he may do so satisfactorily on as little as five dollars a month. The purpose is to discourage patronage of restaurants and cabarets.

The system of recognition of merit in scientific, cultural, or military life includes a percentage of reduction in price for purchases. A private in the army will automatically get twenty-five per cent off the regular price; a general seventy-five per cent. A ballet dancer, if she is tops in her profession, and the government says whether she is or not, may also reach the seventy-five per cent level. If the general and the ballet dancer retire honorably, they continue to get the reduction. If the general retires dishonorably he is dead, because he is shot.

Discipline in the Russian Army is absolute. Military discipline, as evidenced by saluting and general demeanor, is on a high plane. He said that as a colonel he was small fry. He also said that the government buildings in Moscow made the Pentagon look like a child's playhouse. He had seen an opera in Moscow which was magnificent in performance and lavish in scenery. Where the Metropolitan spends a dollar for scenery, the Russian opera spends $500.

One of the real worries bothering Ike these days is the forthcoming airborne operations. There is almost universal coverage of the European continent by strong flak. When our aircraft carrying paratroopers go into areas where gliders cannot land at night, we run into almost appalling difficulties due to this fire. He is trying to find special support by fighter bombers to protect the paratroopers and gliders.

So far the Supreme Commander has visited approximately twenty airfields, some twenty divisions, and four ships of the U. S. Navy. He has several more inspections coming, but so far has found our troops, regardless of nationality, tough, well trained, and in good fettle. American training at home has improved miraculously because of the lessons learned in North Africa and in the Pacific.

Another case of loose talk has been reported to Ike. This time it concerns a naval officer who is said to have mentioned at a cocktail party places and date of the assaults. Admiral Stark is investigating and taking appropriate action. Ike said this breach of security is so serious it practically gives him the shakes.

One of the jobs Ike had to try to straighten between the PM and the President involves the inability of British ports to accept forty ships bearing matériel for OVERLORD build-up. Despite the relatively short rations of the British, the Prime Minister is willing to sacrifice current delivery of half a million tons of imports for local consumption if the President will agree to help out on shipping to make up the loss during latter months of the year. Ike has asked General Marshall to seek the President's help. "We have simply developed one of those bottlenecks incident to big operations," Ike cabled, "and the only chance of breaking it is to cut further into the import program. Everyone here has plunged into this problem with the greatest good will and I cannot see where anyone is to blame."

WIDEWING, WEDNESDAY, MAY 24, 1944

Ike has given the staff some of his ideas to study for the herculean job of breaking out of the beachhead once we have become firmly established ashore. He wants the staff to seek ways and means best to apply those factors in which we enjoy superiority over the Germans. These are control of the sea, command of the air, including resources in airborne troops, and armor. Ike visualizes an operation in which we would bring in the initial beachhead great strength in armor and seek an opportunity to punch through with a big armored attack in conjunction with a deep and heavy penetration by airborne troops. He has to think so far ahead, it's little wonder that he's not excited when the final victory comes.

General Ike has ordered that all officers commanding combat troops, but none higher than an army commander, shall be allowed to wear a distinctive narrow green band around the shoulder loop of his uniform. Enlisted men may wear a narrow green stripe just below their chevrons. He wants this distinctive marking to set apart combat officers and men from those officers and enlisted personnel who are on staff duty.

WIDEWING, SUNDAY, MAY 28, 1944

Some weeks ago an emissary of Marshal Tito visited Ike and sought his assistance. Ike wrote General Marshall suggesting use of war-weary bombers to increase the flow of supplies to Tito. Now the Chief of Staff has replied that General Eaker has temporarily assigned an additional troop-carrier group from southern Italy and has seven B-25s, thirty heavies of the RAF, and forty Italian bombers engaged in delivering supplies. He also has at his disposal all of the war-weary heavy and medium bombers, which he can use in the Balkans if he so desires. As soon as practicable, a regular C-47 shuttle service to Yugoslavia will be established on landing grounds controlled by Tito.

Today Ike made recordings of a message to be broadcast shortly after H-Hour. Bill Paley, my old boss, supervised the job.

I have just learned about a clever ruse, intended to mislead, if not to needle, the Germans just before D-Day. A British actor who closely resembles General Montgomery is flying in the General's plane from England to Gibraltar. At Gibraltar he is to be "officially" received by the Governor and entertained with his "staff." Through their spies, the Germans will get wind of this and, because they think General Montgomery is out of England, may be lulled into thinking that D-Day will not come for some time, since they know he is in command of the invasion troops.

WIDEWING, MONDAY, MAY 29, 1944

Ike left Friday evening, May 26, by train to spend Saturday with General Gerow. He returned to Widewing Sunday morning, May 28, and spent a long forenoon at the office. On Sunday afternoon after late lunch he enjoyed lolling in the garden at Telegraph Cottage, which is now gloriously alive with azure, purple, and red rhododendron flowers, not to mention roses, poppies, violets, and what not. We even have cuckoos with echoes. Sound just like those which pop from clocks.

Tried his hand at sketching, but when he finished his first attempt at doing our big pine tree, his enthusiasm for the idea petered out. When he finished, he wrote under it "baloney." Betty Baker, an American Red Cross girl, supplied the material and the brief lesson. Ike's desire to sketch is, to me, just another evidence of his boredom and impatience with the long planning period.

Ike returned with a sore left eye. He has had to consult the doctor and is using hot applications. The doctor says the eye has suffered too much strain. In addition, Ike has had a ringing in one ear for a month, but I only heard about it during the past two or three days.

On Friday the twenty-sixth Ike had taken lunch with the King and Queen at Buckingham Palace. There were only the three. He said he had had a grand time, that the King and Queen are such nice people to be with. Even if they weren't King and Queen you would enjoy visiting with them. The Queen is particularly personable and radiates hospitality. She is more talkative than the King. Ike said he might have been embarrassed when the King mentioned to him that he had dropped his napkin to the floor, but he wasn't. The two had recalled again their discomfiture at Windsor Castle when they were "poaching" on an area where they knew two American officers were being conducted to visit on a certain Sunday afternoon two years ago. The two officers were Generals Eisenhower and Clark. The Queen remembered details of their crawling on their hands and knees which the King had not mentioned. She used British slang with ease—had something or other "taped." *

Service was somewhat cafeteria style—each getting up and delving in the modest array of food on a side table. So far as Ike was concerned, the friendliness and companionship of the threesome was reminiscent of any of friends in Tacoma, San Antonio, Washington, or Abilene.

News from the other fronts indicates that the Germans are getting set for an expected Russian onslaught. In Italy the Eighth and Fifth Armies have been giving Kesselring's Tenth Army a good beating. The main front has joined up with the bridgehead. I saw today for the first time in some days a report of casualties in Italy, but the figure is not broken down to show the losses in the last push. Total casualties to May 25 are 109,054 and for the Allied beachhead force 33,241. These seem alarmingly high.

One Sunday paper had a headline that "Kesselring Faces Tunisian Collapse," but the Germans may find ways of escape through the mountains to the east and north of the now all-important town of Palestrina. Whether the Germans meet their "inevitable Tunisia," to recall a phrase Ike once used a year ago, they have taken a good licking, and the capture

---

* Meaning under control or, perhaps, "in the groove."

of Rome is in sight. This should be an important psychological victory for the Allies and may be helpful to us in our invasion of the Continent. The President doesn't want to call it an invasion; he wants to use "liberation."

The effect of our success in Italy makes impossible withdrawal of German forces to assist their defense against OVERLORD. Our Intelligence reports indicate possibility of a German armored division being moved from France to Italy. Now if we only had the landing craft to launch ANVIL and attack in sizable force on the southern coast of France simultaneously with our big attack across the Channel we really would have the Germans upset, but we have to do the best we can with what we have.

Meantime Ike has had to step into a squabble between the British Chiefs of Staff and Combined Munitions Assignment Board to insist that a reserve of four million barrels of 130-octane aviation fuel be maintained in England for our big push.

Apparently the Munitions Board is trying to reduce the amount. This brings to mind that in the plans for supply to OVERLORD after we get ashore is the laying of one or more pipe lines to carry gasoline across the Channel. Called PLUTO, this in itself would be regarded as a considerable enterprise in normal times. I also am impressed by the fact that some eighty cargo vessels are to be sunk in shallow water during the first days of the operation, to form a protection against high waves. These are to be followed by the installation of various devices for construction of artificial harbors.

The French situation is still Frenchy. The PM made a speech in the House during the past week in which he said he had invited de Gaulle to come to London. The latter has not received the invitation, according to the last report, which presumably the PM will formally send on D-Day. In any event, the French are still haughty. Apparently the Foreign Office is playing with de Gaulle as far as Eden dares, while the PM is following the "hands off" policy of Roosevelt.

Misgivings About the Airborne Operation

WIDEWING, TUESDAY, MAY 30, 1944

Ike had a tough one today; Air Chief Marshal Leigh-Mallory, who has been lukewarm to the paratroop phase of OVERLORD, has "gone on record" in a letter emphasizing his fear of colossal losses in the American paratroop operation.

The Air Chief Marshal felt obliged to notify the Supreme Commander that he was very unhappy about the prospective U. S. airborne operation, in which the 82nd and 101st Airborne Divisions are to be employed. In the American operation, some 915 aircraft, ninety-six of which will be towing gliders, will have to avoid our invasion fleet. They will have to fly across the Cherbourg Peninsula from west to east at less than 1000 feet in full moonlight and over country where ack-ack normally is heavy and in which German troops are now known to be concentrated. The Marshal thought the first aircraft would reach their objectives without severe casualties, but later ones would catch the brunt of searchlights and enemy flak. Losses, Leigh-Mallory feared, would be very heavy, especially as the C-47s used by the Troop Carrier Command are without armor protection or leakproof tanks, which makes them particularly vulnerable to all forms of fire. He thinks a large proportion will be lost.

General Ike replied promptly that Leigh-Mallory was quite right in communicating his convictions as to the hazards, but a strong airborne attack is essential to the whole operation and it must go on. Every effort was to be made to work out the last detail; every single thing that might diminish hazards must be done.

Ike also sent a note to the PM today asking that the ban on diplomatic communications be continued after the invasion. His principal reason for the request is that the lifting of the ban will indicate to the enemy that our main effort has at last been launched, whereas at the moment he has reason to believe that the enemy quite likely thinks there is much more of the bad news coming. If the Germans learn that we have shot our wad, they will be able to collect their reserves and concentrate them against our beachhead, and this is just what we don't want. The enemy apparently thinks there will be at least one more amphibious assault, and this in the Pas de Calais. General Ike hopes they continue to believe this.

Incidentally, I learned from a friend in the Military Attaché's office —Major Robert L. Grosjean, son-in-law of Joe Davies—that Belgian, Dutch, Polish, and other Allied governments represented in London have been deeply offended by the ban. They say they are thus classed as secondary allies. Our flow of intelligence, particularly as to the battle order of the Germans, which comes by diplomatic pouch, has been curtailed because these "secondary allies" simply withhold the content of the pouches in retribution for the prohibition against their sending diplomatic pouches out of England. It seems like a simple-minded way to spite the face by cutting off the nose.

Everybody Talks About the Weather

WIDEWING, WEDNESDAY, MAY 31, 1944

Air operations have continued at record-breaking levels both from England and from the Mediterranean. There were some 3700 sorties from England alone yesterday, and the heavies from Foggia paid another call on Vienna and Wiener Neustadt aircraft factories. The weather has continued warm and balmy, with practically no wind.

I lunched today with Brigadier General Arthur S. Nevins, G-3 expert, and we joked about the term "agreed weather report" which comes from the variety of air, naval, and ground weathermen. He said that Group Captain Stagg, who is chairman of the committee of experts, has telephone conferences via scrambler with all the prophets each morning. He said at the outset of the conversation it would seem that all are talking about a different subject but eventually the weathermen agree on the weather, at least as to what they will predict. Nevins said that current reports were optimistic for D-Day. There would be all sorts of chaos and disappointment if it had to be postponed two or three weeks, yet if Ike has advice from sea and air commanders in the negative he will almost be compelled to postpone it. Nevins felt that Ike could override the recommendations of these commanders, but to do so would be to discount seasoned judgment and to assume terrific risk and responsibility for himself.

Transportation is still a considerable problem, although the Prime Minister has acceded to Ike's request to curtail by a half-million tons the already restricted import program for British sustenance. There are now thirty-eight of our ammunition ships lying off northern British harbors, awaiting opportunity to unload. English railroads are taxed to the limit. Southern ports already are clogged with the invasion fleet and other shipping. To unload them at northern ports means reshipment by railway, which already is jammed. The over-all need will be for ports on the Continent, where some 4000 tons a day are expected to be unloaded by D plus 25.

The PM has actually sent his invitation to de Gaulle, apparently having changed his mind. Once he said he would send it on D-Day. Since de Gaulle is coming here, the effort through General Wilson to get him to prepare an address and make a recording for broadcasting from the U. K. has been postponed until he reaches England. The Foreign Office, in a memorandum, says: "There is little doubt that he will be most eager to broadcast."

A new type of fuse for antiaircraft shell which causes the shell to burst in proximity of aircraft and to destroy itself before reaching the ground has been authorized for use in England, despite the additional risk to life and property because some twenty per cent of them are not self-destructive.

Ike wired the Combined Chiefs of Staff today that since it appears that the Germans still fear we will make more than one major landing, and that the first one will be diversionary, whereas it is to be the one and only, the use of devices for an artificial harbor should be kept secret and the Joint Intelligence Committee be instructed to place a ban on any public mention of Mulberries and Gooseberries, so the Germans won't be told gratuitously that we have created our own harbor.

Tex Lee has just tiptoed into this office and whispered that the security people have advised the General that the Germans are trying to locate his residence. Tex wants to know the condition of our small arms.

My favorite spot on Sunday afternoons is Hyde Park. I love to listen to the orations of those who have made this Temple of Free Speech famous the world over and, to me, a symbol of one of the things we are fighting for. My favorite is a small Cockney, with pince-nez glasses, who stands behind a rostrum on which there is a sign, "The One-Man Brains Trust." He always has a crowd, many of whom delight in asking him difficult, if not silly, questions. I think the Brains Trust has a claque. When in need of a topic, one of his cronies, who, I suspect, develop their ideas at some pub, comes forth with a momentous question. One of these was, "In your opinion, is rhubarb bloodshot celery, or is celery anemic rhubarb?" In reply to this question, the Brains Trust discussed his early life at sea, some experiences in Norway, described the odd shape of Norwegian letters, and explained that he, as a common citizen of England, had the right to enter the House of Commons as a visitor without an invitation whereas the King cannot go inside the House without a formal invitation. He said he started on his career as a Hyde Park lecturer as a shill, standing in a crowd and posing questions for a rather dull preacher. One day a bobbie on the beat asked him if he would like a soapbox of his own and if he could keep his remarks clean and he had replied, "I can certainly keep them as clean as the cinema across the street." The first Sunday he had mounted his own soapbox, he had talked for three hours in what proved to be the most embarrassing experience of his life—for he could not attract a single soul for an audience. Ultimately someone came, the audience grew, and he talked eight hours straight and has been in the profession ever since. This practically settled the celery-rhubarb controversy, so he glanced over his pince-nez glasses at the linc of ambitious orators, each with various sizes of crowds. There were a Socialist, a Communist, a Conservative, an Indian, and an assortment of preachers. Strolling among the crowds was a former civil servant who carried a sign to tell the world he had been discharged unfairly some twenty years ago. He had been trying his case in this manner for years. "The difference between me and the rest of those crackpots," the Brains Trust said, "is that they take themselves seriously and don't know they're cracked. I don't take myself seriously and I know I am." The One-Man Brains Trust would be a hit on the radio in America, despite the competition.

MAY, 1944: *Air raids on Europe reached unprecedented fury as thousand-plane attacks became commonplace. Four thousand bombers struck the Atlantic wall with loss of sixteen planes. Vast raids simultaneously hit as many as fourteen German manufacturing cities. Chief weight of explosives was directed against train concentrations, plane and matériel plants, oil fields, and so-called invasion coast in Pas de Calais area. Planes attacking Berlin and Brunswick destroyed many defending Luftwaffe planes. In the Mediterranean, air opposition was light over all other targets except Ploeşti oil fields, raided by Italy-based bombers. Reds cleared Crimea of Germans, destroyed transports evacuating troops from Sevastopol. Allied drives in Italy made steady gains; Gustav line breached; Cassino, Formia, Esperia, Gaeta, Fondi, Pico, Arce, Frosinone captured; offensive from Anzio beachhead begun. Drive on Rome continued to advance, despite Nazi counterattacks. Chinese and American troops entered Myitkyina, severed Kaimaing-Mogaung road. Burma Road cut after capture of Chefang. Japs took Hankow-Peiping railroad. Chinese encircled Japs at Tantantzu after reaching Shweli River in Hunan drive. Yanks invaded Biak, defeated Japs in first southwest Pacific tank battle. Drive toward Wewak took Bunabun harbor without opposition. James Forrestal named Secretary of Navy, replacing late Frank Knox. Berlin radio declared Nazis "fully prepared" to meet any invasion effort. (We were going to find out pretty soon who was right.—H.C.B.)*

The PM Wants to Go Along

WIDEWING, THURSDAY, JUNE 1, 1944

Medium bombers from England are achieving heretofore unknown success against bridges. They are hitting them from high altitude and, best of all, knocking them out.

Ike said that at the air meeting at Stanmore yesterday the problem of eradicating the two or three high-powered radio stations on the French coast for jamming our radar came up for discussion. He had overheard

Air Chief Marshal Harris turn to an associate and say, "Why can't we take on one of these objectives tonight?" This remark had illustrated to Ike the co-operation now evident amongst the heretofore more or less rival air commands. Harris was thought to be the hard nut to crack, yet here he sat, seeking opportunity to be helpful and volunteering to attack difficult targets.

I've heard that the former major general whom Ike sent home reduced to his regular rank is in the War Department, and if he bore any grudge at all it was against himself for indiscreet talk. Ike said that the naval captain was home, but did not know whether he had been reduced.

Ike received a phone call from Admiral Ramsay at Portsmouth. The PM was insisting that he be permitted to be in the invasion, and Ramsay was seeking advice, counsel, or authority from the Supreme Commander. Ike said he had already told the PM that if the Prime Minister were on a ship which happened to get hit, at least four or five other war vessels would be required to come to its assistance, whereas if he were not aboard, the battle would go on and the ship would look after itself the best it could. In other words, the PM was an added burden in battle.

Ike said that the PM's reasons were logical from the position of Prime Minister; he had been a party to ordering the attack, many British lives probably would be lost, and the fact that the Prime Minister was in the invasion himself would show that he was not afraid to go where he had ordered the troops. The PM had made a point, too, that the Supreme Commander had no control over the complement of a British naval vessel. Furthermore, the Prime Minister, as Minister of Defense, has certain rights and obligations not subject to "yes" or "no" of even an Allied Supreme Commander.

Ike had told Admiral Ramsay to say the request had been disapproved by the Supreme Commander, who would see the Prime Minister at an early date and discuss it with him eye to eye.

The Prime Minister had pointed out to Ike that there were no decisions the Prime Minister had to make which would require him to stay on land, whereas the Supreme Commander might be confronted by an emergency requiring a decision and therefore he could not be absent from the control point on shore. Ike had countered that the Prime Minister in battle would simply be a nuisance and that, if lost, both nations would be minus an almost irreplaceable leader.

After we had discussed the pros and cons of the PM's willfulness, a messenger arrived with a letter from the devil himself. In it he hopped on Ike with both feet because Ike had asked the British government to extend the diplomatic ban indefinitely after D-Day. The PM emphasized in his letter that he had not foreseen that the ban would permit such free travel of Americans to and from England and that he had just learned that an editorial writer of the *Chicago Tribune*, now in England, had been permitted to return to the United States. Why should it be permitted the right withheld from friendly governments?

Another bellyache of the PM—and when he aches he shouts most lucidly and persuasively—was a broadcast to Germans approved by SHAEF through our Psychological Warfare Branch, dated May 9, which he said put the United Nations in a position of begging on the eve of victory.

Ike chuckled as he read the letter and said the old boy was really in good form. After the company left, he phoned Beetle on the scrambler, told him the content of the letter, and Beetle almost tore the telephone from the wall. Ike quieted him. He found that an editor of the *Chicago Tribune* had actually been stopped by routine procedure from leaving the U. K.

Ike has told the air people to give hell to the area of the landings, called Neptune. He thinks we have bombed various points along the French coast so regularly that concentration in the landing area during the next few days will not be particularly noticeable, especially as there are some targets, such as jamming stations, not precisely in our lodgment area.

Meetings to consider the weather will have to be held at Southwick House, near Portsmouth, late at night, probably around 1:30, so as to synchronize with shipping dates. Consequently Ike will probably spend his nights at the Advance Command Post and drive back during the day to main headquarters at Widewing, where he can visit the air headquarters at Stanmore, near London. His personal schedule is the subject of study by the Chief of Staff, bearing in mind that his own movements give rise to rumors.

This morning Colonel R. Ernest Dupuy, the SHAEF PRO, and Lieutenant Colonel Thor Smith, who is assigned as PRO for the Advance CP, came in to see the General, and I sat in with them. There will be four reporters chosen by lot for world-wide coverage. One will represent American press associations, another the British, another the BBC, and still another, Red Mueller, the only one whom we know, the American networks. There will be two Army Pictorial Service photographers—one for stills and another for movies. Ike's principal worry was that they would have little to do and less to report, but after the conference I think he is now satisfied that they will find considerable of interest about which to write. I am to be the liaison between Colonel Smith and the General for arrangements as they may be made. Ike has promised to see the correspondents whenever convenient, especially on the eve of the attack and on D-Day. If he makes a trip to the beachhead he said he had no objection if the pool reporters went along, but he made clear to them they are to cover not merely him but all the principals at the Advance CP.

This morning as we drove to the office there was a slight drizzle which made us cast apprehensive glances at the sky. Later the sun came out and as I write in midafternoon there is low cloud. We are all extremely weather-conscious, yet Ike said there was nothing in the weather report "so far"—meaning as of last night, when he talked with Admiral Ramsay —to be unduly disturbing.

As the big day approaches Ike is bearing his responsibility with remarkable ease. Actually he is fatalistic about it—someone has to make the decision when the time comes and he simply happens to be the one who bears the responsibility and he will not hesitate to take it.

SHAEF ADVANCE (NEAR PORTSMOUTH), SATURDAY, JUNE 3, 1944
Ever since I have been with Ike, I have carefully followed his admonition never to arrange for a showing of a moving picture for him if use of the film deprives soldiers of entertainment. In North Africa, films were hard to get, particularly new ones, and there were many evenings when the General could have seen a film but all were in use for the GIs. Our new office caravan is "wired for sound" and I arranged for a movie last night. I try these days to find something light and humorous, never anything on the war. Special Services had no film at Portsmouth but were bringing one down from main headquarters at Bushy Park. As there had been no arrangement for movies for soldiers at the forward headquarters, Special Services suggested 8 o'clock, which fitted in with Ike's personal schedule. The projector, screen, and operator were driven to the camp during the day and because, as I later learned, the projector was being sent for the General, a later show was laid on for the GIs. However, Ike had some unexpected callers and we entered the caravan about 8:30, just as the GI operator was packing up the projector and the screen. He told the General—whom I had not bothered with the details then—he had another show, one for the GIs of the camp, and he would be too late if he ran the film for the General.

With this, the General was in instantaneous and complete agreement, but turned on me and gave me a good cussing out for arranging a film for him at a time which would cause GIs to see the later show and be kept up late. I knew then he really had the pre-D-Day jitters.

D-Day Is Postponed

SHAEF ADVANCE (NEAR PORTSMOUTH), SUNDAY MORNING, JUNE 4, 1944 D-Day was postponed by Ike for at least twenty-four hours last night. Weather looks very bad for air support, but suited Navy, as wind was from southwest and not expected to be so strong by morning, when the attacks were to have begun shortly after good light.

A large portion of the 4000 ships already were at sea, from landing craft to battleships. They were notified shortly after the 4 A.M. meeting this morning. Each task force was previously instructed what to do in just this possibility.

The good old AP last night pulled the oddest bloomer. A girl typing on a tape in the AP office wrote: "Eisenhower's forces are landing in France," or have. This got out, Moscow repeated it, CBS had it, the Germans gave it circulation, and in twenty-three minutes the AP canceled the story. General Bull phoned me around 6 this morning to give me the dope to hold for Ike, who by then was back in bed after getting up at 3:45 to hustle off to Naval Headquarters at Southwick House for the 4:30 session. Said he had already requested deferment of the "world-press" reporters who were to arrive at SHAEF Advance today. Too much going on here at the moment. Even de Gaulle is coming to this camp today, to see Ike, of course, and Tommy—the PM's aide—told me we could keep him.

But then we have become the favorite calling spot for the Prime Minister and his old crony, Field Marshal Smuts. They are on a special train parked at Southampton from which they set out to see troops loading on Friday, but had bad luck hitting the right loading places at the wrong time, and vice versa, so the PM didn't do so well. In the middle of this hide-and-seek behind energetic motorcycle escort, the PM said to call up Ike and he'd come and see him. It was the only thing that worked O.K. for him, but when he arrived here his mental outlook was described by his aide, Commander Thompson, as "peevish."

They came again last evening, just dropped in. The PM disclosed to Ike, which Tommy told me the previous night, that the King had vetoed Churchill's boat ride in the invasion. Now Winston was pouring the heat on Ike to prevent him from going across on D-Day, saying Ike is too valuable, must be handy for emergency decisions, et cetera.

To pick up where I last dictated to Miss Chick at the SHAEF headquarters at Widewing, which I think was Thursday, June 1, will say a lot of things, mostly little, have happened. Some big.

Ike and Jim Gault drove down in time for Ike to make a 10 A.M. meeting at Southwick House, at which time the weather looked right promising. Most important item from the meeting was Jim's report of side-line gossip, which was the definition of a meteorologist, the old mansion being cluttered with them. The answer is that he's an expert who can look into a girl's eyes and tell whether.

Returning to camp last night, the PM's caravan of cars and dashing cyclists swirled in behind, unexpectedly. Filled their gas tanks and diminished our supply of Scotch, there being some ten or more parched mouths to moisten, and announced that de Gaulle would be sent over here to see the Supreme Commander on Sunday afternoon.

Ike had to take a quick supper and dash over to the 9:30 meeting of Commanders-in-Chief, and there decided that if the weather signs didn't look better by 4:30 in the morning, decision to postpone would be made. Haven't heard from Ike, as he is still resting in his sleeping caravan, surrounded by some new Westerns and Sunday papers. He had but little sleep last night. Gave him the signal of the AP slip. He sort of grunted.

Yesterday afternoon I carried out Ike's request to reconnoiter a trip he hoped to make on Sunday afternoon to see troops loading. All loading for the initial assault in this area is practically finished, except for some British troops boarding LCIs at South Parade Pier until noon. Three LSTs will load Monty's Tactical Headquarters stuff this afternoon, and then everybody and everything for the assault will be afloat.

Arranged for passes (even the Supreme Commander must have one) for Ike and party to go to the pier this morning, but suspect the trip is off. Also looked up airfields from which paratroopers and gliders will take off, so Ike might see some the eve of D-Day, which was to have been tonight, but now is Monday night, unless changed again. Would like to see Ike go to Portland Bill, a large hill sticking into the Channel south of Weymouth, over which the transport planes with paratroops and gliders are to pass around midnight to 2 A.M. of D-Day. He did this in Malta. But here the drive would take five hours, round trip.

Ike's Day Before D-Day

SHAEF ADVANCE (NEAR PORTSMOUTH), MONDAY, JUNE 5, 1944
D-Day is now almost irrevocably set for tomorrow morning, about 6:40, the time varying with tides at different beaches, the idea being to strike before high tide submerges obstacles which have to be cleared away.

"Irrevocable" becomes practically absolute around dusk, Ike said this afternoon while talking to the press and radio men, who heard him explain for more than an hour the "greatest operation we have ever attempted."

This morning Ike went to South Parade Pier in Portsmouth to see the loading of some British soldiers aboard LCILs 600, 601, and 602. He always gets a lift from talking with soldiers. He got one this morning, which partially offset the impatience with which he viewed the cloudy weather which had been predicted clear. While talking to the press he noticed through the tent door a quick flash of sunshine and said: "By George, there *is* some sun."

This evening Ike and a party, including press, are driving to the Newbury area to see the paratroopers of the American 101st Division load for the great flight—one which Leigh-Mallory said would cost so heavily in lives and planes.

About midnight he will have returned and will stop at the Naval Headquarters for a last-minute check on news, and then return to the camp and bed. He expects to return to the Naval Headquarters around 6:30 to get actual news.

The actual decision was confirmed and made final this morning at 4:15 after all the weather dope had been assembled. During yesterday the weather looked as if we might have to postpone for at least two days, until Thursday, with possibility of two weeks. Pockets of "lows" existed all the way from western Canada across the United States and the Atlantic, and were coming our way. What was needed was a benevolent "high" to counteract or divert at least one of the parading lows. During the night, that actually occurred. During the day, Force U, the U. S. task force which started from Falmouth at the western end of the Channel at 6 A.M. Sunday, had become scattered, owing to the galelike wind sweeping southern England and the Channel. But Admiral Kirk had heard some encouraging news that the scattering was not as bad as feared. It was enough better by the early-morning session to warrant the gamble, which only Ike could take, and he did, but with the chance of decent weather in his favor for possibly only two days. After that we hope to be ashore, and while weather will still be vitally important, we will have gotten over the historic hump.

Air Chief Marshal Tedder told me that at the Sunday-night meeting when the decision was made to launch OVERLORD, subject to final review at the 4 A.M. meeting, Monday morning, the weatherman who had spoken for all the weather services, after having given a rather doleful report, was asked, "What will the weather be on D-Day in the Channel and over the French coast?" He hesitated, Tedder said, for two dramatic minutes and finally said, conscientiously and soberly, "To answer that question would make me a guesser, not a meteorologist."

Despite the refusal of the weatherman to be a "guesser," Ike had to take the responsibility of making the decision without satisfactory assurance from the meteorologist—a responsibility which Tedder said Ike took without hesitation.

What does the Supreme Commander do just now? Before lunch he played this aide "Hounds and Fox," he being the hounds, and he won consistently, there being a trick in being a hound. We played a game of crackerbox checkers, and just as I had him cornered with my two kings and his one remaining king, damned if he didn't jump one of my kings and get a draw.

At lunch we talked of old political yarns, he having known my old friend Pat Harrison when he was coming up as a young Congressman. I told the story of the Harrison-Bilbo campaign in which the latter supported Governor Conner for Senator against Pat. One of Pat's supporters told a rally the trouble with Pat was that he was too damned honorable and should use Bilbo's tactics. These he illustrated by the famous yarn of Mama and Papa Skunk and their nine children, which ends with Papa alluding to a new and terrible odor wafting into their nostrils, and adding, "I don't know what it is, Mama Skunk and children dear, but whatever it is, we must get some of it."

So we talked, during the lunch, on Senators and skunks and civet cats.

After lunch I shepherded the press and radio men to our little camp, introducing them all round, especially to Mickey, Hunt, Williams, and the rest. Ike took over in his tent, and as usual held them on the edge of their chairs. The nonchalance with which he announced that we were attacking in the morning and the feigned nonchalance with which the reporters absorbed it was a study in suppressed emotion which would interest any psychologist.

The names, as I recall them, are: Robert Barr, for BBC; Stanley Burch, for Reuter's; Ned Roberts, of UP, and Red Mueller, of NBC, who had been with us before. In the order named, they are covering color and personalities of the high command for British radio, British press agencies, American associations, and American networks. In a word, worldwide coverage for the public. Also two lads from Army Pictorial Service.

Ike has just had a phone call from Beetle at SHAEF Main that de Gaulle, whose visit here yesterday is a story in itself, now says he will not broadcast tomorrow, D-Day, as agreed yesterday. Objects to one paragraph of Ike's broadcast already recorded. De Gaulle's objection has to do with his recognition as the exclusive French authority with which we are to deal in France. Ike said that if he doesn't come through, we'll deal with someone else, another of those last-minute things that worry the devil out of the SC. General "Red" Bull said yesterday that no one in the world could carry the political and military problems as well as Ike. Got to run to dinner.

PART FIVE

Cross-Channel Invasion

JUNE, 1944 TO FEBRUARY, 1945

D-Day for OVERLORD

ADVANCE CP (NEAR PORTSMOUTH), D-DAY, TUESDAY, JUNE 6, 1944
The landings have gone better than expected. Every outfit is ashore, but
we have just had a report that Gee, Major General Gerow, with his V
Corps, can't get off one of its beaches because of hostile mortar and artillery fire. This is Omaha Beach. They called the air for some bombing;
air came back and said pin-point the places, and there the matter rests to
the moment, Ike, however, wondering what the 21st Army Group is doing
about it. That really is the only bad news of the day.

Ike dictated some congratulatory messages to Wilson, Alexander, Clark,
Eaker, and Admiral Sir John Cunningham relative to the fall of Rome.

But to go back. Last night, starting from camp at 6, with Ike and Jim in the lead car; Lieutenant Colonel Thor Smith; Stanley Burch, of Reuter's; Lieutenant Leo Moore, APS picture snapper; his sergeant of the same career, and me in the second; and Red Mueller, NBC; Barr, of BBC; Roberts, of UP, in the third, we hit out for the 101st Airborne Division around Newbury. We saw hundreds of paratroopers, with blackened and grotesque faces, packing up for the big hop and jump. Ike wandered through them, stepping over packs, guns, and a variety of equipment such as only paratroop people can devise, chinning with this and that one. All were put at ease. He was promised a job after the war by a Texan who said he roped, not dallied, his cows, and at least there was enough to eat in the work. Ike has developed or disclosed an informality and friendliness with troopers that almost amazed me, I not having been on many of his inspection trips in England.

We concluded the tour with C-47s growling off the runway, carrying the jumpers and their Major General, Maxwell Taylor, to their uncertain mission—one that Leigh-Mallory went on record against as being too dangerous and costly, and to which Ike also went on record, ordering the deed to be done, as it was necessary to help the foot soldiers get ashore.

We returned to camp about 1:15, sat around the nickel-plated office caravan in courteous silence, each with his own thoughts and trying to borrow by psychological osmosis those of the Supreme Commander, until I became the first to say to hell with it and excused myself to bed. There I expected a phone call from Lieutenant Colonel Hugh Barkley, an Intelligence officer of the 101st, who had said his headquarters would have radio word from the air transports the moment the jump was made, and that he would phone me just as quickly as that. Every half-hour or so during the remainder of the night I awakened, said to myself, have I heard from Barkley, and finding the answer no, went back to the D-Eve sleep. At H-Hour, by coincidence, I was awake, that being 6:40, and was contemplating the underside of the drab tent roof, wondering how come such a quiet night in contrast with other D-Nights, when this was supposed to be the biggest and most superduper of all, when suddenly there came the call.

But it was Leigh-Mallory, himself. Wanted to speak to the boss. No, he wasn't awake, I said, but guessed. Could I take the message? Yes, if you've got a scrambler. Yes; in the other tent. Over my flannel pajamas, I slung Pelley's woolen dressing gown, and with the inevitable cinders of these crunching paths grinding into my slippers, I dashed to the tent with the green handset. Someone having left the gear running all night, it was warmed for secrecy. I told L-M I was ready. He was filled with information, good information. Surprisingly, said the Air Marshal, only twenty-one of the American C-47s out of the 850 were missing. Only four gliders were unaccounted for. On the British, eight C-47s were AWOL out of some 400. Amazing good luck. And an RAF Intruder had seen the British paras drop, and it went off smooth, smooth indeed. Grand, said I, grand, I'll tell the boss as soon as he wakes up. Yes, continued the Air Marshal, our night fighters saw three Huns over the Cherbourg Peninsula while the American chaps were going in to drop, and chased them off. Also, said he, there is evidence the Hun was fooled by our tricks; he had most of his night fighters over the Pas de Calais area.

So I tiptoed down the cinder path to Ike's circus wagon to see if he was asleep and saw him silhouetted in bed behind a Western. Ike grinned as he lit a cigarette. I was almost the first with good news, but Admiral Ramsay was just on the phone, telling him things seemed going by plan, and had no bad news at all.

Then Ike started getting hold of General Bull, to get the communiqué out before the Germans beat us, and after an hour of work we were beaten by only two and a half hours, ours hitting the ether at 9:30 via BBC, the Germans having got theirs out at 7, but not very complete, they must admit. And their news is gratifying to us because they speak of our operations in the Pas de Calais to the east of our real show, indicating they are confused and our plans are still secure.

I gassed with the boss awhile, remembering the first D-Night at Gib, when after a tedious one for him and an hour's lie-down under a table for me, we had met at the salt-water basin of the stinking tunnel lavatory to hoe off our whiskers. Being up bright and early, as is my custom on D-Day only, I skedaddled back to my tent, shaved, dressed, and sauntered nonchalantly in the early-morning sun to the office caravan. Ike had done his D-Day toilet as well, this time with running, soft hot water, and looked in the pink. We stood in front of the caravan, enjoying the beautiful, oh, what a beautiful day. A GI came grinding along with the morning papers from Portsmouth, with headlines of the fall of Rome and the Fifth Army's crashing victory, with personal statement by Wayne Clark. Ike said, "Good morning, *good* morning," to the GI, most cheerfully indeed.

Then he dictated a quick report of the situation to General Marshall, saying it is now 8 in the morning and that he still had no information concerning the actual landings or of our progress through beach obstacles. But he said communiqué could not be issued until we had word that leading ground troops were actually ashore. But he said that all preliminary reports are satisfactory. He transmitted Leigh-Mallory's good news about airborne formations. Preliminary bombings by air went off as scheduled, he said, and added that Navy reports sweeping some mines, but so far as is known, channels are clear and operations proceeding as planned. In early-morning hours, reaction from shore batteries was sufficiently light that some of the naval spotting planes have returned, awaiting call. He told why the weather had forced him to postpone the invasion by one day. Said it looked as if the weather would hold for the next several crucial days. He concluded with a report of his firsthand impression of the enthusiasm, toughness, and obvious fitness of the British and American troops. He closed, saying they had "the light of battle in their eyes."

With message in hand I delivered it to the one-man secretariat and I went off to the war tent to see what I could see; found General Bull on the telephone, trying to force the communiqué through Beetle at SHAEF Main, who was braced against it until the 21st Army Group said O.K., and Monty's people wanted to be sure we were ashore to stay before authorizing any statement. Picking up the latest news, which seemed to be a signal from Admiral Kirk, dated 6:52, that everything was going "according to plan," I hustled back to bask in delivery of the good news, but found Bull beating me to it via Alexander Bell's annoying invention.

About then along came Lieutenant General Morgan, who did much of the hard work on the Great Plan, which Ike reminded him of, and to which Morgan said, modestly, "Well, you finished it." Also present was Major General Ken Strong, the G-2 of G-2s, who allowed as how we had surprisingly surprised the Germans and therefore in the game of war had achieved "tactical surprise," and let them try to prove otherwise. Morgan had told me before he got to Ike that the de Gaulle thing finally was on the right track; at least he would broadcast. Seems the trouble was caused partly by subordinates.

After battering ears with phone calls to this and that, our SHAEF British political officer, whose name is Mr. Peake, phoned General de Gaulle himself at 4 A.M., less than three hours before H-Hour, and said will you or won't you, and he said, sure I'll broadcast, when?

So by that time, Morgan not having had the chance to tell Ike what he told me, Ike was ready to go a-visitin'. To Monty's first, where the sweatered General was wearing the countenance of the day, and pleased about it. I found on this, my first visit to the headquarters of 21st Army Group, that they have American-style handsets, whereas we have British old-style magnetic hand grinders. Monty's aides are smarter than Ike's, and since I'm generalissimo at the camp, and impresario of the movies as well, I guess this means me. But the next camp we have we'll have

American handsets and American switchboard and American operators, preferably professional WACs, I hope.

Monty was getting off late today to set up his headquarters across the Channel, his tactical one, where he likes to be. Ike invited him to see the world-press representatives, to which Monty said a not surprising yes, anytime before 3. So I phoned our PRO from Navy Headquarters at Southwick House, our next stop, as Ike directed, he being careful to see that the press and radio fellows get news from all the commanders hereabouts, not just from him or about himself alone.

At Southwick, Commander T. Harland, RN, took me to the war room, where I was told we had lost two destroyers and one LST, by mines, during the night. The *Cory*, U. S., had got it, at location unreported, and a Norwegian destroyer was the other. The LST also was American, and wasn't sunk but damaged, and on this side of the Channel, presumably from a mine laid from the air. Waves were a bit high for the more delicate stuff, like the harbor devices, but ammunition barges and mine layers were moving to get to the beachheads. All was well with the Navy, and its smiles were as wide as or wider than any, except that they didn't like the bloody wind, which didn't go down as the weathermen had predicted.

To go back to another D-Eve incident, when we returned from the trip, Ike asked Jim to phone Naval Headquarters for the latest dope. To do this on the scrambler.

Jim and cane went off to Ike's personal office tent and placed his call. Strangely, the British phones we have leak. No. 9 in the office caravan where we waited for Jim's report is on the same line as No. 9 in the office tent where Jim was talking to the Navy. Whenever any phone is being used, the voices of the users can be heard plainly coming from the other handsets of this sort of party line, even though the receiver is down.

So Ike and all of us in the office caravan could hear the conversation of Jim and the duty officer, but, of course, it was coming through in glub-glubs and blurp-blurps of scramblese. This went on for a few minutes, and Ike said, "God, this must be bad, it's so long." Then it went on some more, and all of us fidgeted. We looked at one another or at the floor, mostly the latter, in silence. Finally I thought I'd relieve the pressure, at least on myself, so I walked over to where Jim was taking down in red pencil on a pad, and repeating, in deadly seriousness, the latest dope. I tried to signal him to hurry, but he couldn't, the man on the other end was doing his duty, this was for the Supreme Commander, and there couldn't be any mistake. Finally Jim rung off and, with me tagging along, silently and importantly burst into the office caravan. Nothing less than a battleship and a dozen destroyers had been lost, the signs indicated, but as Jim solemnly read his notes I perceived Ike's features relax, for it was only the weather report, and it wasn't bad, said possibly decent weather for several days, and not too bad for bombing.

Now where are we? It's Tuesday afternoon. Ike and Jim have trudged off to the war room to see what's being done about Gerow and V Corps, this news having bothered Ike so much, I could see from his questions he wished he were running the 21st Army Group so he could do something about it himself, but from where he sits he can't just step in.

Neglected to say that tomorrow Ike is to go to France aboard the *Apollo*, a fast mine layer, captained by Captain Grindle, my Malta friend who commanded landing craft for HUSKY.

But I haven't reported on the visit of de Gaulle and the Prime Minister here on Sunday. The Prime had D whisked from Northolt airdrome near London by car to the PM's train, New Southampton, where political luncheon was served. Beetle was called there, and the PM called Ike, saying he wanted ten minutes with Ike before D got there, so he would ask D to stay aboard the train and give Winston a head start. Winston was an hour late getting here, talked quickly to Ike, and along came D, it having been decided in the meantime that Ike had to keep D sufficiently informed so he could broadcast a word of encouragement to the French. So Ike took them all on a Cook's tour of the war room, and de Gaulle lectured on what he would do. Whereupon Ike and D strolled up the shady cinder path in front of the signals tent where there was enough elbow room for D to wave his arms and talk. Ike did some too, and in due course they returned, went into the war room, and we heard Anglo-French dictation to one of Churchill's secretaries. D was to broadcast when called upon, but had wanted Ike to take out of his speech any reference to his, Ike's, control of law and order amongst his, de Gaulle's, Frenchmen. That's where it was left on Sunday evening, the biggest news of the affair being the PM's announcement he and party were going back to London, the twenty-four-hour delay, and possibly longer, for D-Day having kept Churchill too long away from the pressing affairs of state in London. He took de Gaulle with him.

In typical British sporting fashion, Air Chief Marshal Leigh-Mallory has written General Ike to admit that he was wrong about the airborne operation. The Marshal frankly said that it is sometimes difficult in this life to admit that one was wrong, but he has never had a greater pleasure than in doing so on this occasion. He congratulated General Ike on the wisdom of his command decision. You simply can't stay mad at people like this.

We Visit the Beachhead

SHAEF ADVANCE CP (NEAR PORTSMOUTH), THURSDAY, JUNE 8, 1944
Yesterday Ike visited our beachhead along the French coast. He accompanied Admiral Ramsay, who took his Chief Signal Officer, Commander R. T. Paul, and PRO Lieutenant Commander J. C. T. Dillon-Robinson. Ike took his British Military Assistant and his Naval Aide.

We departed at 8 from the "King's Steps" in the Portsmouth naval dockyard, where we boarded the fast mine layer *Apollo*. I had taken helmets and gas masks and cameras in the back compartment of Ike's car. In getting this unlocked and satisfying Jim that I actually had the General's helmet, both of us were delayed momentarily in reaching the dock to board the Admiral's barge. When we reached there the barge was circling to return, having already started with the Supreme Commander and the Admiral but someone missed us. As we rather sheepishly joined the party, Ike said, "If you fellows want to go with me, get aboard these boats ahead of me." No comment from the bleachers.

The trip across the Channel through the mine-swept lane was uneventful except that for a few minutes all of us on the bridge thought the *Apollo* would engage in a rescue at sea. The skipper, Captain Grindle, thought he saw a raft in the distance and we altered course to be heroic. As we approached the object we found it was a barrage balloon partly submerged and so we weren't heroes, after all.

We saw one derelict LCVP and passed numerous LCTs and one squadron of mine sweepers, busily widening the channel.

We headed first for the "U" or Utah Beach, where the 4th Division had been landed by naval forces under Admiral Moon, thinking we were steering for the *Augusta*, Admiral Kirk's flagship for the entire American landing force covering "O" or Omaha Beach as well, where the 1st U. S. Division had gone ashore.

We found the *Augusta* off Omaha Beach, and shortly General Bradley, whom Ike was most anxious to see, and Admirals Kirk and Hall came aboard.

On Omaha Beach the 1st Division had encountered the ill-luck of running into the German 352nd Division, prisoners from which had disclosed that the division happened to be in that area on maneuvers. Landing had been slowed and landing craft sunk or holed by mortar and field artillery fire from well-concealed positions. The established gun emplacements had not caused trouble. The one on the cliff called "Maisy" had been taken by the Rangers as planned, but must have been previously silenced by aerial bombardment. The obstacles were really effective. The Teller mines on the steel posts had been hit by some landing craft, the mine making a hole about a yard across, repairable when our salvage crews get to work. I asked Major C. B. Hansen, aide to Bradley, about casualties, and he said he had seen on the beach during the morning forty dead Americans, with many wounded lying in the bushes. The assault force had been pinned down to the beach until 3:30 P.M. on D-Day. The naval gunfire and help from the air, as well as the landing of some guns, had permitted an advance. Now the division was two or three miles inland, Bradley himself having gone a mile inland during the morning. Admiral Kirk said the unloading was behind schedule by twelve hours but would be made up as weather improved.

Proceeding eastward along the British beaches, we stopped alongside the H.M.S. *Hilleary*. Commodore C. E. Douglas-Pennant and Rear Admiral Sir P. L. Vian came aboard and reported slowness of unloading because of weather, but over-all things on their beaches were going well. Through the glasses we could see British lorries and tanks going up a dusty road over pleasant rolling countryside.

While Ike was talking to these naval officers, General Montgomery came aboard from a destroyer. Ike got a fuller exchange of information with him. Monty was happy. He was establishing the tactical headquarters ashore.

We were sailing close to shore on the Admiral's instructions, but, unfortunately, the *Apollo* hit a sand bar and Captain Grindle quickly elected to try to force her across and consequently did not reduce power. With the mast swaying violently, the entire ship jerking, grinding, and even bouncing like a Flexi-Flier suddenly hitting bare gravel, we eventually swung off the bar and floated free. However, the propellers were bent and possibly also the drive shafts. We returned the several miles at six knots to the *Scylla*, which had been signaled to provide a destroyer for our return to Portsmouth.

I could almost have wept when we hit the bar. Captain Grindle had been so kind and efficient conducting the party and he was so proud to have the Supreme Commander and the ANCXF on his bridge. Everything had gone beautifully to that moment. He had just called through the tube to the navigator's room below for the depth of water and had been told that there were six fathoms under her bottom. Then the Admiral had mentioned that the break of the waves indicated shallow water, as indeed I had just commented to Jim that the water seemed very shallow. I was not surprised when we hit bottom. It seemed so inevitable. The Admiral told Ike later that Grindle should have immediately stopped the engines as this would have lifted the stern and permitted the ship to float over the bar. The Admiral also told Ike that while he would make a kind report on the "incident," Grindle would have to face a court of inquiry and, if lucky, would get off with only a reprimand from the Admiralty. "But," said the Admiral, "most good naval officers have a reprimand or two on their records."

We returned on another new ship, H.M.S. *Undaunted*—a destroyer that had been commissioned in March. We reached Portsmouth at 10 o'clock in the evening. Still and moving pictures and news coverage were provided by Burch of Reuter's, Lieutenant Moore of APS, and an official photographer of the Royal Navy.

They were disappointed we had not actually gone ashore, as was I, but Ike really had a most fruitful day, as he was able to see the principal commanders and get the feel of the whole situation, which can only be done satisfactorily by personal interview. Messages and sitreps frequently are so stilted they lack vital significance. To have gone ashore for the mere fact of setting foot on France would have added to the news value of the occasion and perhaps would have been something of a satisfaction to Ike, but it was not necessary so far as the job was concerned.

Commander Paul, Admiral Ramsay's signal officer, had arranged with Captain Grindle quickly to make a red flag with four white stars to denote the presence aboard of the Supreme Commander. This flag was flown throughout the cruise of the *Apollo* along the coast—during which we wove in and out of hundreds of ships.

We saw several of the giant Phoenixes being towed, as well as Bombardons, the artificial breakwaters, and the merchant ships to be sunk to form additional breakwaters were also there, awaiting their fate as soon as the waves abated. The ships are called Corncobs.

During the afternoon the weather, which had been cloudy and even rainy as we left Portsmouth, had cleared, the sky was blue, and the waves were diminishing. We saw aircraft overhead coming and going. I am not surprised to find there were 9000 tactical sorties yesterday. Cruisers, including the French *Compiègne*, were intermittently bombarding German strong points. We could see some of the explosions. The difficulty was to find targets because the Germans had cleverly concealed their positions. There were four red alerts, indicating presence of enemy aircraft in the area, while we were afloat, but except for testing, not an antiaircraft gun was fired, nor were any enemy planes seen in our vicinity. During the evening, however, there was an air attack against the ships alongshore, the H.M.S. *Lawford* being sunk.

Returning to the camp at the Advance Command Post, Ike was immediately sought by Beetle. Ike had given me an "overlay" showing the position of the American ground forces ashore, which I had delivered to General Bull, G-3, in our war room. I found all the specialists in the war room starving for information and I gave them all I could. General Bull walked with me to the camp to see Ike.

The principal rough spot to be ironed out was slowness of communications between General Bradley and 21st Army Group, which was ascribed to difference in American and British signal procedure. Some of Bradley's messages, which Ike had so eagerly awaited on D-Day, had been inadvertently held up, although Bradley had faithfully sent dispatch after dispatch. Today we have word from General Francis W. de Guingand, Monty's Chief of Staff, that this difficulty has been solved.

Today Ike acceded to the request of the press and radio representatives for an interview. On his way to meet them at the PRO tent he said he hardly knew what to say to them, and I suggested that we should not let news of our landings stir the home publics to a state of overenthusiasm as had been true immediately after the Anzio end run. I suggested that he point to the crucial days in which we now stake everything, and to caution the public against overexpectation.

Ike spoke off the record, calling attention to two counterattacks spearheading into the area around Caen, emphasizing the "accidental" presence of the 352nd German Division in front of the 1st Division's beaches, and emphasizing and re-emphasizing the tremendous stake we have in weather, especially for the next few days. The weather prophets predict that today will be cloudy with rising wind, but after today we should have a spell of good weather. Even with good weather we have a fluid front which makes bombing difficult because of the possibility of hitting our own troops. Thus, although we have a great preponderance of air superiority, particularly with good flying weather, as long as lines are not established we could not apply our air power as efficiently to the front lines as might be supposed from the mere numbers of our aircraft. He mentioned, too, that the Germans seemed still to expect landings elsewhere, which was a desirable appreciation for us because it probably will keep divisions fixed, awaiting these threats. Ike was somber in tone, deliberate in his words, and although he had slept late this morning, he seemed tired and almost listless. He became animated only when he spoke of the possibility of good weather and said, "You fellows pray for it, too."

He said the operation was still "hazardous," but would not permit that word to be quoted because it did not quite reflect his feeling about the situation.

At the PRO Rcd Mueller gave me the digest of the communiqués issued in London. While it was factual, nevertheless I sensed a build-up of overoptimism inherent in its language. I told Beetle I felt the communiqué was leading us into overoptimism at home. Beetle sensed the same thing and said that any accomplishments of the troops henceforth would be merely attainment of the expected rather than the unexpected, which is the proper position for us to seek. I always feel we should follow Knute Rockne's strategy of emphasizing the size of the opposing team, the weakness and injuries of our own, so that when we achieve victory it will appear all the greater. At least this was the side on which to err rather than on that of overoptimism; let the enemy be overoptimistic; it's better to go into the game regarded as the underdog. Beetle brought the press and radio representatives into the war room, where he explained the situation on the beachheads. He wanted them to report faithfully but not paint a false picture of optimism; indeed, the situation is somewhat critical and we are now in the inevitable race for build-up. We are already behind twelve to twenty-four hours in unloading, and our margin of ground superiority over the enemy was all too little if we had been able to meet our schedule. Caen was to have been taken on D-Day, yet we are still fighting for it and at the moment were being pushed back by the German counterattack. However, the German build-up has not been quite as fast as we expected, so perhaps the bad break of weather hasn't been fatal.

The Russian Offensive Starts

SHAEF ADVANCE CP (NEAR PORTSMOUTH), SUNDAY, JUNE 11, 1944 Since dictating to Miss Chick on Friday I haven't had opportunity to write in the diary. Here are some of the highlights of the week end.

General Marshall, Admiral King, and party have arrived in London for meetings of the Combined Chiefs. They have a session this afternoon, and are not coming now to the Advance CP as has been rumored frequently the past two days.

Ike left the camp yesterday morning, alone, to attend the morning session at the 21st Army Group Headquarters at 9, but only picked up a quick fill-in from General de Guingand, and then decided to highball for the Widewing headquarters. He had awakened in a snit . . . no information from Monty, who had agreed to radio every night his latest impression of the way the battle was going. Weather had taken another bad turn. He was without information, and felt accordingly. First we knew he was going to the Main Headquarters was when Lee phoned to say the Boss had arrived there.

On Friday evening, nearly midnight, de Guingand had come over to our war room and given Ike the picture. I happened to be present, and recall the main point, which was that because we had busted most of the bridges across the Seine, the Germans couldn't move reinforcements or reserves from the east direct—they had to go around Paris. So the air people, whose meeting at Stanmore de Guingand had just attended, were laying on more bridge smashing and marshaling-yard destruction in the Paris area, particularly south of Paris. They also spotted ten vital bridges across the Loire River to the south of our battle area, and had laid on attacks to bust them. Over-all, while our build-up was slower by some twenty-four hours than we hoped or planned, so was that of the Jerry. He had up to yesterday got some seventeen divisions against us, whereas we figured on twenty. The plan of bombing transportation targets has paid well; if we had left their railroad yards, their bridges intact, we'd have been pushed off the beaches.

Yesterday Ike conferred with General Marshall, Admiral King, and party, who thoughtfully deferred seeing him on the previous night when they arrived as they didn't want to impose on him. They came to his office at Widewing, as did the PM, who was shown the war room and the headquarters generally. He was in fine form, Ike said, and best of all relayed a message from Uncle Joe that the Russians would start their grand offensive *this* morning in the Leningrad area, and generally spread it all along their long line, until the whole front was ablaze. At least that is the word Ike used, and whether it's his, Winston's, or Joe's, I don't know.

Ike's overnight private signal from Monty had really arrived in camp during the night, but as it was in British cipher on what they call "one-time" pads, it came to Jim, who had deferred handling it until he got up at 8. When Jim tried to unravel it, he found he needed help from a cipher officer. In the meantime Ike had departed, but Jim phoned the gist to Ike around 10, and its content buoyed up Ike. Monty had found things quite well indeed and had laid on an attack all along the line which, if successful, would make our beachhead about thirteen miles deep from the shore. This didn't work as expected, for our latest sitrep gives us only small gains, with the 29th Division the farthest out toward Saint-Lô. This place, incidentally, is the site picked for Monty's camp, with Ike's Advance CP to be alongside.

Jim and I called on 21st Army Group and the Naval Headquarters yesterday, gathering news of the progress. Unloading is improving, and although weather is bad for flying today, and forecast bad until noon tomorrow, it's suitable for the Navy. We have about twenty warships along the beachhead furnishing gunfire on objectives spotted from advanced ground parties or from the air. The chart of the places for which fire is called is one of the most interesting and up-to-date sources of information at Naval Headquarters. The data are obtained by interception of the radio conversations between the spotters and the ships.

In the afternoon we called on Captain Grindle, our tough-luck skipper of the *Apollo*, who was wallowing in remorse over his situation. His ship was in drydock, with both propellers looking like three-petaled flowers which had been serrated at the edges by a cruel hand. One of the struts had been broken, of course both propellers have to be replaced, and the ship will be out of action for two months. Jim and I told Ike about our visit when he returned to camp last night. He volunteered to send a brief note to his old friend, Sir Andrew Cunningham, in Grindle's behalf. Monty's destroyer had run aground the same day, and also was in drydock with broken propellers. This news had cheered Grindle.

This morning at 4 A.M., Monty's signal arrived with a loud knocking on the door of Ike's caravan, waking the SC from a sleep into which he had just thankfully relapsed. The runner is supposed to come to my tent, and I read the signal, decide whether to hold or deliver. But this one went right to God. Have conferred with Colonel Smith-Wyndham, the signal chief, and Lieutenant Colonel Braithwaite, the representative of the secretariat, to get the procedure better understood, and also am having all the runners into camp to show them my tent. Should have done this the first day, but none had missed it so far, until last night, which was bad.

Am running the war alone today, in this particular quiet sector.

General Ike Lands in France

SHAEF ADVANCE CP (NEAR PORTSMOUTH), MONDAY, JUNE 12, 1944
Last evening Beetle called Ike from SHAEF Main to say that the PM was sending an important personal message to Ike, which should be read before he went to bed. It arrived about 2 A.M., and although Ike had waited until midnight, I decided not to awaken him, but to give it to Jim Gault, who was accompanying Ike on another cross-Channel trip starting at 5 A.M. The message said the Germans had sent a message to the southwest area of France asking whether Allied troops carried their gas masks with them or in baggage cars. The PM had been alarmed at this.

Ike called me out of bed at 5 to ask me to see General de Guingand during the morning and tell him to make a quiet check to make certain all the troops were carrying their equipment for gas attacks—didn't want to disclose the content of the message, or rather to let D know that more than just Ike knew it here. When I saw D, he said he had already instituted the check.

Ike thought the message might be significant in that use of gas would be a last-ditch effort of the Germans to stave off final defeat. We have lots on hand for counterattack if they start the bad business. The papers say fighting has started in the Leningrad area.

We got Carentan today, the Germans claiming they evacuated it, but we had practically surrounded the place, despite flooding. The push is going well all along the line, the V Corps with 1st and 29th Divisions now having the widest beachhead. The British and Canadians are trying to bypass Caen.

With George Allen on hand to visit, and how I enjoy him, as does Ike, I got left behind on today's trip to France, which will be described as historic.

Lee accompanied General Marshall, Admiral King, and party on the Alive train, which Ike and Jim met this morning at Cosham at 6.

Lots of air overhead today . . . sun shining, but predictions are for bad weather . . . lost another Phoenix last night by torpedo, but the Mulberries and Gooseberries are all in and working as expected, except on Utah Beach, the most western one, where there still is enemy shell fire. Merchant ships are slow to unload there because of the shell fire, but the battery was silenced, at least for the time, by the Navy yesterday.

About ten U-boats have gotten into the Channel and are being vigorously hunted by air and sea.

SHAEF MAIN (WIDEWING), TUESDAY, JUNE 13, 1944

About twenty-five pilotless aircraft came across the Channel last night and nineteen are known to have hit land, four in the London area.

Ike went ashore in France yesterday for the first time.

He had as guests General Marshall, Admiral King, General Arnold, Major General Kuter, Colonel Frank McCarthy, and Commander Charles C. Kirkpatrick, the redheaded and buoyant aide to Admiral King. Soon they were embarked on the destroyer *Thompson*, in command of Lieutenant Commander A. L. Gebelin, for a fast trip to the far shore. They were met off Omaha Beach by Admiral Kirk, U. S. Naval Force Commander, and by Admiral Hall.

An air strip on a bluff above Omaha Beach was rapidly being bulldozed into usefulness. At General Bradley's headquarters, where they lunched on C and K rations, recent operations were discussed by Bradley and most of his subordinates—General Hodges, understudying Bradley, who is to take command of U. S. First Army when Bradley takes Group; General Gerow, commanding V Corps; Major General J. Lawton Collins, VII Corps; Major General Charles H. Corlett; Brigadier General William M. Hoge, whose combat engineers did such an excellent job of removing obstacles on the beaches; Major General Elwood "Pete" Quesada, Commander of the Tactical Air Force supporting American ground troops; Major General John R. Deane, and Admiral Don T. Moon, USN.

They were found by Clark Lee, Bill Stoneman, and Ernie Pyle, familiar faces of North African days. Ernie Pyle complained they got little news. Ike replied, "You're the people we're expecting news from." General Marshall satisfied their thirst for news by telling them the attack on Guam was to be launched that day.

The party was impressed by the overlapping shell holes from naval gunfire along the coast road from Grandcamp to Isigny, where houses were still burning. A number of German dead were seen.

Lieutenant Colonel Gault, reporting on the trip, was impressed by the calm, confidence, and competency of all commanders; the speed with which artificial harbors had been started; the absence of enemy planes, and the remarks of the troops who saw General Ike, such as "There's Ike," "General Ike," or "The old man himself." When Ike returned last night he was buoyant and inspired by his experience. He said that the whole visit ashore seemed more like a tour of peacetime maneuvers, as they didn't get very near the front.

Most satisfactory to Ike was the improved status of unloading, greatly speeded by the artificial harbors. However, the turn-around of landing craft is not satisfactory and Ike said he proposed getting Lieutenant General John C. H. Lee and visiting the "hards," or cement ramps, where they are loaded, to find first hand how the reloading can be expedited. The fact that landing craft bring wounded on the return journey and have to disembark them at piers different from those at which they are reloaded with matériel and personnel has added to the time required. Average time to reload is seven hours, plans permitted four, and elsewhere we have done it in three and a half.

Ike said that casualties are about 11,000, that Bradley had seen 1000 Americans buried. During the day I had seen in the war room a count, which lags a bit, of 546 Americans killed.

Lieutenant Colonel Lee had gone to Prestwick to meet Ike's son, John, whom General Marshall has sent for a brief time to spend his post-graduation holiday before commencement of his regular service. It is now Second Lieutenant John S. D. Eisenhower.

Ike returned about 8:45 last evening, and after dinner we had a bridge game intended to be one rubber but which ran into two, with George and me eventually winning threepence. In the first hand picked out by George he said, "Here, I have the joker." Ike replied, "That's not the joker, that's the six of clubs." George thought this extremely funny; the Supreme Commander, whom George ardently and loudly proclaims the most popular idol of the world at the moment, having to play bridge with a makeshift deck.

The "cat's" hold on our beachheads has become a panther claw, or to speak in nationalistic terms, a lion's claw or an eagle's claw. In any event, it is considerably larger. Last evening while playing bridge, I received a phone call from the Navy saying the British 7th Armored Division had taken Villers-Bocage, which was gratifying. We are still stuck around Caen, but on the American front and on the right flank of the British front we seem to be going apace. Weather continues unsettled. We had rain at the camp overnight, but when I reached Widewing there was sunshine and I learned that air operations are proceeding today. Day before yesterday we had 1488 heavy U. S. bombers against marshaling yards in France—the largest number ever dispatched. There are now four landing strips in the beachhead and from these the battle front is supported. The policy of disrupting the enemy transports by bombing marshaling yards and bridges has paid dividends in this battle. Some of the air people around Tedder's office are raising their eyebrows and indicating, "I told you so."

Ike said last night that in conversation with General Marshall he had said that when the war is over he expected the younger men to take over the Army. Marshall said that Ike was a young man and, "Why do you think we have been pushing you? You will have ten years of hard work in the Army after the war." All Ike could say then was that he hoped to have a six months' rest.

Another sidelight on yesterday's visit to the Continent: the French, as in North Africa, seemed apathetic. Some gave the V sign, some removed their hats, few cheered. They seemed numbed and disinterested, perhaps because those seen had been so close to the big show and had suffered. Yet our reports of guerrilla activity, particularly by the Maquis in other areas, are encouraging.

The Russian kickoff in the Leningrad area seems to be going well, the Russians having overrun heavily constructed outposts of the famous

Mannerheim Line. It also is significant to me that our British-American military mission has sent us what amounts to a situation report from the Russians, the first I have ever seen. No other action is reported as yet.

SHAEF MAIN (WIDEWING), THURSDAY, JUNE 15, 1944

Last night Ike was concerned that Monty couldn't attack until Saturday. Ike was anxious that the Germans be kept off balance and that our drive never stop. But apparently Monty wants to tidy up his "administrative tail" and get plenty of supplies on hand before he makes a general attack.

Ike also said that yesterday we had made no gains, which he didn't like.

De Gaulle was given permission to go to France yesterday on a French destroyer, but by the time he had reached mid-Channel, he had heard that in some French town which we had liberated they had been cheering for Giraud and in another we had already appointed a mayor—a prerogative that de Gaulle felt was his. He had threatened not to set foot on French soil under these conditions, but the result was merely a late cancellation by him of his luncheon engagement with General Montgomery.

The Germans are still holding strong forces in the Pas de Calais, and resistance by organized groups, particularly in the Brittany Peninsula, is effective. We have landed three groups of Commandos, about fifty in each, in the Brittany Peninsula, and they find the interior practically deserted by the Germans.

Ike has taken John and flown to visit Monty on the beachhead today. He has gone in General Spaatz's plane, which is a B-17 with guns, whereas the new superslick B-17 which General Arnold had specially made for Ike has no guns. Tedder went along. Weather is good for air operations and, fortunately, has been better than predicted during the past three or four days.

Ike had lunch yesterday in the Yankee Doodle Room with Lord Louis' Chief of Staff, Lieutenant General Sir Henry R. Pownall. Pownall told a story attributed to Ike, which Ike repeated last night. Of course it wasn't true, but it seems that in Algiers an American and a British officer got into a severe argument which reached such proportions that General Eisenhower himself sent for the men and talked to them in the interests of unity. After giving both of them a lecture he dismissed the British officer but kept the American for further words:

"I don't mind your airing your differences with this British officer. I don't particularly mind that you engaged in fisticuffs with him. I must say that I think you were right in your position. Ordinarily I don't condone cursing and name-calling, and I forgive you for calling him a son-of-a-bitch. But I cannot forgive you for calling him a *British* son-of-a-bitch. Consequently, I am sending you home on a slow boat, unescorted." That's how the story was being told in Burma.

John arrived Tuesday evening, June 13, having come across on the *Queen Mary*. This is the first opportunity in many months that father and son have had opportunity to talk. On Tuesday evening they sat up until one, chewing the fat. John will return by air in about two weeks and will take up his regular duty in the Infantry Training School at Fort Benning, Georgia.

Ike has frequently said that any young officer would profit greatly if he could be around a principal headquarters to see and sense how the high command is run, before he begins his regular tour of duty on the lower rung of the ladder. John fervently hopes for action in this war and is fearful that his period of infantry training will cause him to miss action on the Continent, but is hopeful he will get in the Japanese war.

More about Montgomery's double: The plan came into being as a result of two separate factors. One of them was the result of a sharp-eyed British Intelligence officer's reaction to a newspaper clipping to the effect that Lieutenant James, a British officer resembling Montgomery, had entered a London theater and had been widely applauded by the audience, which mistook him for the General. He permitted the deception to last for a few minutes before disillusioning the people, and the whole thing was humorously reported in the press. This small event was tied by Intelligence to another event which had occurred in 1943. In midsummer, 1943, a transport plane leaving Gibraltar had been shot down by the Germans before its arrival in England. This plane had carried, among other passengers, the actor, Leslie Howard, but the British learned through secret channels that the Germans had shot the plane down because they believed Prime Minister Churchill was aboard. Just before its take-off from the airport, the enemy had received information to the effect that a heavy-set man, wearing a bowler hat and smoking a big black cigar, had boarded the plane. The enemy, taking no chances, attacked the transport. Since the British Intelligence knew that the Germans were keeping close watch over planes departing from neutral airports, they devised the scheme of sending "General Montgomery" out of the country just before D-Day. From all I could gather, the plan worked to perfection. It was just another example of detailed planning to throw the Germans off balance.

Around SHAEF it is said that General Montgomery was lunching with Tedder and other British bigwigs when someone with tongue in cheek reported the latest bulletin of the progress of the matter of Monty's double, saying, "I hear that that fake Montgomery is swaggering about half drunk in Gibraltar, smoking mammoth cigars like a chimney." Monty, a non-smoking teetotaler, rose to the fly, glaring around angrily and ready to send disciplinary cables at once.

The Flying Bombs

SHAEF MAIN (WIDEWING), FRIDAY, JUNE 16, 1944

Last night about midnight an air alert sounded in London, where I happened to be with George Allen, and it continued until about 9:30 this morning. We have had a succession of alerts during the day, with anti-aircraft guns rumbling in the distance. Some 300 of these pilotless, steel-constructed, rocket-propelled planes have come over. Radar plots show they originate in the Pas de Calais area. Unfortunately, but presumably the Germans counted on this, the weather is so bad we can't even send recce planes to spot the sites in actual operation. The bombs cross the Channel between Dungeness and Beachy Head in parallel lines to the Greater London area. (Our headquarters are on the western side of this path.) Their speed is estimated from 250 to 380 miles per hour, tapering off at the end of the journey. Two are reported shot down by night fighters. They carry high explosive equivalent to a 2000-pound bomb, creating a shallow pit and an extraordinarily heavy blast. I heard one pass overhead last night and it made a sound like a two-cylinder motorcycle engine or the motor of an old Model T Ford, this apparently being from the put-put of the rocket.

The British Chiefs of Staff, after the enemy's tryout of the pilotless aircraft the night of June 12/13, formally asked Ike yesterday to resume bombing the supply sites with everything that can be spared "from the needs of the battle of France."

General Marshall has authorized Ike to cite any unit for unusual service in recent operations, and he requested that this be done at once. Let the paper work follow, Marshall advised, but give the deserving units public credit now.

The Supreme Commander prodded the staff to keep him currently informed on such questions as speeding the arrival of fighting troops and ammunition to the beachhead; how soon can the U. S. Communications Zone be set up in France so it will be on the spot to deal with Bradley and others on supply problems; can divisions to come from the U. S. be hurried ahead of the schedule already set; and he especially wants to be kept currently informed of any progress in straightening out our build-up difficulties, to make certain that proper ships arrive at proper times on the proper beaches.

WIDEWING, SATURDAY, JUNE 17, 1944

The pilotless craft, dubbed "divers" in an Air Force report, continued coming last night. The first alert sounded at the cottage just after dinner, while the General, John, and I were seeing a movie of the assault landings in OVERLORD. There were alerts until after dawn. The Bomber Command was out in strength against sites in the Pas de Calais, the radar disclosing. Now to bomb a new site, we have to destroy the surrounding village, which further impairs our deteriorating relationship with the French.

Around 1 A.M. I was awakened by the siren and went to Ike's room, where I found him still reading. In answer to my suggestion that we go to the shelter, he replied in the negative and said that he would prefer staying in his room rather than shuttling back and forth to the shelter all night, so I went to bed. But before I was asleep, there was a hell of a clatter and bang as one or more pilotless demons came too close for comfort. They say you have two seconds to find shelter when the hiss and put-put stop, because the plane immediately dives to the ground. So I decided that at least Butcher would retire to the shelter. A few minutes later, the General and John joined me, as well as Mickey, Williams, and Hunt, these comprising our entire household for the time.

There was much antiaircraft fire and occasionally we heard the violent thud of a bursting diver. Ike finally decided to lie on his cot; I laid a blanket on the concrete floor, wrapped myself in it, and John decided to sit on the bench. Soon Ike was snoring and, as the firing had tapered off, John sought the warmth of his bed in the cottage. I went to sleep and, except for occasional adjustments of my anatomy to the concrete, slept solidly until 7:40.

Ike awakened with a headache from paint fumes which still permeate the shelter. I am having a fan for ventilation installed today along with more suitable cots, so all can have a place to rest comfortably. Ike is loath to take shelter unless everyone in the house has equal protection. Now all of us, including Williams and Hunt, will have cots in the shelter. On the subject of ventilating system, the first proposal put to me this morning by Lieutenant Colonel Shytle was to chip a hole through the 14-inch concrete wall. This would require two days and many hours. I sought the

General's approval just as he was hastily leaving for the Advance CP and he vetoed it with some positive words to the effect that anything that required two days of work shouldn't be attempted. So the first project was abandoned by Shytle, who returned with a simple idea for installing an electric ventilator, which can be accomplished today during Ike's absence, and I have undertaken the responsibility of ordering it done. I may soon be on a slow boat, unescorted.

General Marshall and party left for North Africa and Italy yesterday, Admiral King going back to America. I saw a signal from General Marshall to the President in which he said there were no new recommendations from the Joint Chiefs, King, Arnold, and himself on the de Gaulle question, which has gotten progressively worse, so far as newspaper reaction is concerned, yet the French resistance groups are performing, as Ike said yesterday in his memorandum to the Chief of Staff, "above his expectations."

The 82nd Airborne and the 9th Infantry Division pushed more than halfway across the Cherbourg Peninsula, taking Saint-Sauveur-le-Vicomte, but on the Allied left flank, we are only holding our own around Caen. Monty had said he could not attack before Saturday, which I presumed meant he would attack today, but so far we have heard nothing. We hear Cherbourg harbor is being blocked and facilities are being demolished. Ike received today a letter from Bradley recommending that at least four more American divisions be hustled into the bridgehead. There are sixteen German divisions in line against the entire bridgehead.

SHAEF MAIN (WIDEWING), SUNDAY, JUNE 18, 1944

Today Ike sent a letter to General Montgomery advising against permitting so many visitors to take up his time in these crucial days. Later today, he received a letter in longhand from Monty from his tactical headquarters, asking for Ike's help to keep visitors away, especially for the next two weeks.

SHAEF MAIN (WIDEWING), TUESDAY, JUNE 20, 1944

Ike and John spent Saturday night at the Advance CP.

During the last three days we have had fairly continuous arrivals of Hitler's secret weapon, variously called "Diver," "Pilotless Aircraft," "Buzz Bomb," "Doodle Bug," or "Robot." Perhaps "Junebug" or "Jitterbug" would be appropriate. Certainly, most of the people I know are semidazed from loss of sleep and have the jitters, which they show when a door bangs or the sounds of motors, from motorcycles to aircraft, are heard.

Beetle has been ominously predicting that the Germans will start using their next secret weapon, the rocket, said to contain ten tons of explosive in a fifty-ton projectile, which is skyrocketed from a hole in the ground like a giant sunken stovepipe and encased by heavy concrete. There are seven known sites for launching rockets, five in the Pas de Calais and two in the Cherbourg Peninsula. Fortunately, the latter either have been or soon will be captured by our rapidly advancing American troops, and crews of experts are awaiting opportunity to examine them. One crew was reported to have been en route to a supply site for the "Junebugs" yesterday, shortly after news reached us that Bradley's army had made a rapid advance northward toward Cherbourg, capturing Bricquebec. Incidentally, Cherbourg was reported under shell fire from the 9th Division yesterday.

The Prime Minister is having daily meetings to consider defense measures against the flying bombs. On Sunday, all antiaircraft fire in the London area was ordered stopped because when they are hit, they plummet to earth and explode. They have to be shot down in relatively nonpopulated areas. Barrage balloons supplemented by kites have been placed along the line of flight and in depth. There is a fifteen-mile band of antiaircraft between London and the coast. The fighters were given one day to show their effectiveness and scored forty-eight per cent knockout of all that crossed the coast, but still leaving a considerable number of them to wreak physical and mental havoc in Greater London. The fighters claim their advantage of speed over that of the flying bomb is so slight that practically all the distance from the Channel to London is required to catch and destroy the winged projectile. Consequently, antiaircraft fire hinders their efforts, so after experimenting, decision was reached to use the fighters without ack-ack in good weather and ack-ack in conditions of poor visibility.

Yesterday the weather over Pas de Calais cleared sufficiently for moderate bombing late in the day and more at night, with eleven targets attacked this morning by 8th Air Force. Only one flying bomb has come our way today—from early morning to 3 o'clock—when one hit near Jim Gault's house, breaking some windows and doors. Oddly, the pattern of hits shows that SHAEF is practically in the center of the heaviest concentration. Last night I counted twenty-five explosions from 7 P.M. until 1 A.M. and another that was close enough to make the shelter shake at 4:20 A.M. The strength of the attack is diminishing. Whether it is from diminution of supply or effectiveness of our bombing, we don't know, but, fortunately, the weather reports indicate improvement sufficient for us to discover and get at the sites.

As to the war on the beachhead, Monty again has delayed attack, largely because of weather, this time for forty-eight hours, making it due Thursday, June 22. General Bradley, however, launched his push yesterday morning and first cut across the Cherbourg Peninsula and is now expanding his thrust north and south, with prospect of capturing as many as 40,000 prisoners. Ken Strong, the G-2, said this morning he thought the Germans had ammunition for ten days in the Cherbourg Fortress, which is said to be in one of the most heavily fortified areas on the Continent. He conservatively estimated it would take two weeks to capture it.

Strong criticized the Intelligence work on Hitler's secret weapon. He said the Intelligence officers had gone to extremes, one group claiming the weapon would create devastating effect against England, and the other calling it a giant hoax or an ARP (Air-Raid Protection) for Germany. Their conflicts failed to develop a sensible middle-of-the-road approach with a thorough analysis of the most likely probability. Thus we were lulled to a feeling of safety by one group, which tended to nullify the cries of "wolf" of the other. Now Strong is taking hold, particularly to anticipate the use of the expected rockets.

Meanwhile Goebbels' press and radio are cackling with glee, the story being so ravenously sought by the German public that newspapers which had been permitted to publish only semiweekly are now given sufficient paper to print daily. They picture London in flames and the people rushing to evacuate the city. Most of which, of course, is untrue. There have been some unpleasant "incidents," one of which was the Guards' Chapel, not far from Buckingham Palace, which was struck during church services Sunday, killing probably 200; one of them, Colonel Ivan Cobbold, Ike's and Beetle's host at salmon fishing sometime back. Yesterday seventy-eight flying bombs were plotted over southeast England, twenty-five of which reached the London area. Fifteen were shot down.

Last evening Ike took Lee and John to the Advance CP, where they expected to take a U. S. destroyer across the Channel today to visit Bradley. However, the Channel was lashed with wind, and all convoys, from LSTs downward, had to be canceled, also all unloading on the eastern flank. Ike expects to return to the camp this evening, where, incidentally, there have been no flying bombs, and try to make the trip tomorrow.

The Germans still are pressing to get at our shipping. They use E-boats at night and the U-boats keep bobbing up, principally around Guernsey, Jersey, and the western end of the Channel. Jerry aircraft drop numerous

mines along our landing beaches. The task of sweeping them is complicated because of the presence of so many ships, the mine sweepers having
to weave in and out and do the best they can. Up to the afternoon of June
17, we had disembarked 589,653 personnel, 89,828 vehicles, and nearly
200,000 tons of stores on the five beaches. As between British and American, the personnel is practically equal, but the British have unloaded
51,000 vehicles against our 38,000, and we have practically a balance on
stores. The American beaches started slower but are now working somewhat more rapidly than the British. Nine of eleven Whales being towed
were sunk by the high seas yesterday, the worst loss we have suffered in
the artificial-harbor devices. The Whales are used to make quays over
which LSTs may discharge cargo. On the whole, however, our makeshift
harbors have worked so well that the capture of Cherbourg, while still
essential, is not of such immediate importance as once thought, but for
the long pull, it and others are absolutely essential. It is hoped that the
Germans do not appreciate the tremendous build-up we have succeeded
in making through these harbors. Their existence may not be mentioned
in press stories, as there is strict censorship, although the Germans, with
their recce planes and frequent bombing attacks, must know of their
existence. We may fool them as to capacity, however.

To go back to the flying bombs, which most of us do nowadays, the
PM called on Ike Sunday afternoon at our headquarters preliminary to
his meeting of the Cabinet to consider defensive measures. Ike, having
control of all air operations for the battle, has a definite but unforeseen
responsibility. He has wholeheartedly agreed, and has so directed Tedder,
who attends the PM's meetings, that these targets, called CROSSBOW, are
to take first priority over everything except the urgent requirements of
battle, and that this priority is to continue until we can be certain that
we definitely have the upper hand over this particular menace.

Recently I had a note from an officer who had been relieved because
his subordinates, both American and British, had complained for a considerable time that he was dictatorial and unnecessarily hard-boiled. Yet
he was an efficient man in his job. The officer was returned to the U. S.,
where his widespread experience in actual operations made him in demand for an important job. He wrote me to ask that the Boss be informed
of his confidence in General Ike's leadership and that he, despite the dis-
missal, was constantly pulling for his success. General Ike replied directly
to him in friendly terms and spoke highly of the officer's efficiency, but
emphasized that one who has only mechanical efficiency may overlook
the fact that all organizations are made up of human beings and that a
sympathetic understanding of the personalities and abilities and, indeed,

their weaknesses, is essential to continuing smoothness in operation.

We have been under the impression that General Wilson has a definite directive from the Combined Chiefs of Staff to launch an attack in southern France at the earliest moment, but today he sent Ike a long message advocating hot pursuit of the Germans up the Italian leg and then across toward Austria.

The Weather Gets Worse

SHAEF MAIN (WIDEWING), WEDNESDAY, JUNE 21, 1944

Today, Ike, John, and Lee returned from the Advance Command Post before lunch, weather again having prevented Ike's trip across the Channel. The weather was not too rough for the U. S. destroyer, but the waves were too high on the other side to permit disembarkation. Ike will make his third try tomorrow. The fruitless delays do not improve his disposition.

The persistence of bad weather is the major worry of headquarters. This is the third day that unloadings on the far shore have practically ceased. Everyone takes more than the usual interest in weather these days because of their intense personal concern in air attacks against the sites of the flying bombs and the rockets. I used "flying bomb" this time because this name seems to be most prevalent. Whatever the name, they give no one satisfactory peace of mind. We have yet to receive the rockets.

Ike had been awakened during the night by an urgent phone message from the Prime Minister, who was upset because Admiral Stark had requested authority to withdraw the *Nevada, Texas,* and *Arkansas,* battleships; the *Tuscaloosa* and *Augusta,* cruisers; twenty-six destroyers, and assorted supporting craft, both transport and antiaircraft generally, by July 1. The purpose of withdrawing the U. S. naval vessels was to send them to the Mediterranean to hasten Wilson's amphibious assault in southern France. Admiral Ramsay, the Naval C-in-C, had reported on the situation and considered that it would be unwise to withdraw the American battleships and heavy cruisers until the Cherbourg Peninsula is captured.

During the day Ike sent a message to General Marshall to cover the general situation but primarily to ask Admiral King not to withdraw his ships at this critical stage.

Once before Admiral King leaped into the breach to help Ike, to which Ike referred in his appeal. That was when King quickly agreed to furnish escort for an extra convoy carrying some 5000 motor vehicles from the U. S. to Africa in January and February, 1943. The arrival of these vehicles permitted Ike to move reinforcements from Casablanca and Oran to the front and, as Ike frequently has said, contributed vitally to the great victory which was to follow.

SHAEF MAIN (WIDEWING), THURSDAY, JUNE 22, 1944

Today Admiral Stark has been notified by telephone that release of the U. S. warships could not be agreed, pending the outcome of conferences with General Wilson's Chief of Staff.

However, we are making good progress in Cherbourg. American troops have reached the outer defenses—at least close enough to hear sounds of demolitions in Cherbourg, where the harbor is being systematically damaged. Despite Ken Strong's conservative guess of two weeks for the fall of Cherbourg, most of us are expecting this critical plum to drop in our hands almost momentarily.

Today Ike again returned from the Advance CP, having for the third time been unable to take the trip across in the destroyer. The northeast wind continues to raise hell with our shipping, has stopped convoys, and is lashing our Mulberries and Gooseberries. Some of the Corncobs are reported breaking up. The weatherman says that a great high, lying north of the U. K. and west of Iceland, is forcing bad weather from the Nordic countries across Germany and the French coast, giving us poor visibility for air operations. He says that the weather records for forty years do not show similar conditions. Apparently, we are in an unlucky streak.

Monty's attack, scheduled for this morning, has not been started, largely because of the delay caused by weather. However, General Bradley was to have kicked off a good attack at dawn at the base of the Cherbourg Peninsula (it was postponed), even while Collins' VII Corps assaults Cherbourg itself.

There were plenty of flying bombs last night. A summary of the week's reception shows that ninety-five per cent of all these bombs have fallen within twelve miles of Streatham, five and a half miles southwest of Telegraph Cottage. The headquarters itself are well within this unpleasant boundary.

Dispersal of headquarters staff to the Advance CP and elsewhere, leaving only the absolutely essential personnel at SHAEF Main, is now seriously considered and probably will take place within a week. Our defense measures against the sites have failed to stop the nuisance, although the total number per day seems to be diminishing. Although the British public is taking the affair outwardly calmly, there is a considerable uneasiness. Yesterday Tooey Spaatz laid on a whopper of a daylight attack on Berlin, just to show the Heinies in terms of force, which is the only language they understand, that their lethal toy hasn't stopped our punch.

This morning *Stars and Stripes* carries a box quoting Dr. Dittmar, one of the top Nazi propagandists, seeming to suggest that if the Allies will stop bombing Germany, the Nazis will stop the flying bombs. Of course, no one pays any attention to this sort of bribe, but at least it indicates that some of the Germans would like to make a trade. He got his answer.

General Koenig has written Ike from London asking that French partisans, particularly technicians, workmen, or employees, remain unmobilized at their posts, in order to reduce the effect of the German policy of scorched earth. He requests that these partisans should not show their hands too prominently, and thus invite reprisals, but should quietly protect the principal sources of power, mines, dams, and waterworks, not only to facilitate the Allied advance but for the benefit of the public and the hastening of eventual re-establishment of public utilities.

Ike passed the letter to the staff with the written comment, "I think this is sensible."

Belief that Germany's defeat should occur before 1945 is expressed by the Joint Intelligence Committee in a report that just reached me, but which was agreed in a meeting of June 12.

Looking Ahead and Backward

SHAEF MAIN (WIDEWING), FRIDAY, JUNE 23, 1944
If the OVERLORD landings had been delayed two weeks, which would have been the necessary period of deferment if Ike hadn't given the word to go, we would have hit the worst weather in twenty years, according to a report of our chief meteorological officer, Group Captain J. M. Stagg. During the period June 17 to 21, into which the two-week postponement would have fallen, the sky was completely overcast, with base about 2000 feet, and the wind was mainly northwest, with a force of four to five on the seventeenth, but six or seven times in the main channel on the eighteenth, when it blew from a northeasterly direction.

On Stagg's memo about the weather situation, Ike wrote in longhand, "Thanks, and thank the gods of war we went when we did!—D. E." We were lucky, even though we are still griping about bad weather.

Characteristically looking ahead, Ike has instructed the staff to begin hard thinking about air operations when winter weather sets in. He figures that by September 20, the weather for flying will have so deteriorated that with our long daylight hours of operation shortened, the impact of our superiority in the air will be much less than during the summer days. He wants the staff to study every type of air operation, including normal close support of ground forces, smashing of enemy communication lines, neutralization of sites for flying bombs and rockets, airborne operations, and supply of troops by air.

He is needling the planners to find ways of capturing more ports to increase the flow of troops and supplies.

To avoid embarrassment, Ike has issued an order to all at SHAEF Main that on sounding of the alarm, "imminent danger," all personnel, officers and enlisted, shall proceed speedily to the best available cover, preferably prepared shelter or slit trenches. He desires that seniors themselves set the example, so that juniors may not suffer under the conviction that they should do their duty but are loath to do so because of the example of their seniors. The headquarters building has around it a number of slit trenches and brick shelters. The shelters are simply covered brick walls—above the surface of the ground—and are protective against blast damage and some debris and flying glass, but would not withstand a direct or near-by hit. As nearly everyone in headquarters is working with secret papers, and these papers must be stowed in a safe and locked whenever we rush to the air-raid shelter, there is a great scurry to get the papers in place and the safe locked in the minute or two that ordinarily elapses between the alarm and the explosion.

With nothing pressing but the flying bombs, I went into the Historical Office of the Secretary of the General Staff, consisting of Captain Douglas F. Price, British, and Captain Duncan Emrich, U. S. The two of them are charged with preparing historical accounts of COSSAC, SHAEF, and the draft of Ike's dispatch to the Combined Chiefs on the whole campaign. Price has been nicknamed "1066" because of his predilection for the past, looking upon the war as an annoying interim between his studies, and Emrich has acquired the name of "Buzz" because of his allergy to the buzz bombs. Buzz will take off for the shelter like a streak when the warning sounds, while "1066" methodically sticks at his desk, rounding out a paragraph.

They told me the story of the SHAEF patch that I had heard only inaccurately before. General Morgan, anticipating the arrival of a Supreme Commander, had directed in the autumn of 1943 that a badge be designed, and the committee which was appointed in turn directed the Royal College of Heralds to produce a sign symbolic of the task ahead. Price said that the design had "some sort of waves, presumably indicating an amphibious operation," and was generally not acceptable, although the "Flaming Sword" was accepted as a base for further development.

The final design was produced by Colonel Lack, with the artistic help of Corporal D. Q. Goodall, an ATS girl. Price called my attention particularly to the fact that the "Flaming Sword" was modeled on that of the 2nd U. S. Division Memorial (1917-18) in Washington. Ike approved the badge when he assumed command, and in March it came into general use as the headquarters shoulder patch and vehicle mark. The flaming sword of freedom cuts the black of the Nazi night over Europe and points the way to the final rainbow of peace and liberty. The rainbow is made up of the colors of the Allied nations.

SHAEF MAIN (WIDEWING), SUNDAY, JUNE 25, 1944

Failure of air-ground co-operation always riles tempers and is one of the things Ike has continually to police with understanding and firmness.

When he talks with the ground commanders, he emphasizes the need of their learning the problems of the Air Force and the limitations and possibilities of air power as applied to ground operations. When he talks with commanders of air units, he emphasizes the problems of the ground commander and asks that the Air Force study every possibility of assisting their compatriots on the ground; preferably without killing them in the effort. Whenever there are failures, such as shorts or longs, our ground troops tend to lose confidence in the air. Ike is combating this in every way and urges that each incident be used as an example for improvement and an incentive to bring about greater efficiency in this highly important phase of our operations.

Fall of Cherbourg

SHAEF MAIN (WIDEWING), TUESDAY, JUNE 27, 1944

Ike finally got over to France on Saturday and visited in the American sector, particularly with General Bradley. John and Colonel Lee accompanied him. They went in a destroyer, the *Thompson*, departing from Portsmouth at 7:30 A.M. and returning that day. There was little time ashore, but Ike wanted to consult with Bradley. Among other things, he wanted to make certain that after the capture of Cherbourg, Bradley would turn the American First Army to the south and smash into the Germans to prevent the peninsula from being sealed.

Monty's attack started on Sunday morning, the twenty-fifth, but so far we have had little concrete information about it. He waited so long that at least two additional Panzer divisions face him. In addition, the ten- or twelve-day delay gave the Germans an opportunity to dig in and get set, whereas Bradley kept his fellows moving and the Germans never had much chance to dig in.

Friday night, George Allen had dinner with us and stayed the night in the air-raid shelter. George and I had gone to bed in the house, but before we could get to sleep, I heard the alarm meaning "imminent danger." Sometimes it is called "intimate danger." I went to George's room to awaken him, but found him partly dressed and ready to go. He claims that we started for the shelter "toe to toe" but that I beat him so badly I was not only on but in a cot by the time he reached it and lifting the eighteen-inch concrete roof with my snores. He stayed again with me on Saturday night, and we had the same foot race, only on this occasion George won by a handsome margin. He claimed that he had learned the track and took the rail.

Sunday, June 25, I was at the office until midafternoon, when I took John to Claridge's to meet George. I took them to visit my public-speaking friends of Hyde Park. John was keenly interested, especially when he heard one denouncing his father by name for his idea of mal-functioning of AMGOT in Italy and indicated it was going to happen in France as well.

Upon request of General Gale, Ike's Chief British Administrative Officer for SHAEF, I am leaving tonight for Cherbourg and vicinity to get informal answers to a number of questions as to the conditions of the port and railroad serving it. Although formal reports from proper authorities will come to headquarters in due time, General Gale and all the logistics people were anxious to have a quick impression based on interviews with Army and Naval officers. Lieutenant Commander James Reid, attached to Admiral Bieri, when he learned I was going, obtained the latter's permission to accompany me.

There has been considerable exchange of comment on the directive for General Wilson, but it simmers down to the fact that the Combined Chiefs of Staff are in the process of answering Ike's insistent recommendation that the attack take place in southern France as soon as possible. Landing craft for a three-division assault are being spared from OVERLORD to supplement those already available in the Mediterranean. Wilson always seems intrigued by the Balkans.

Ike is considerably less than exuberant these days. He didn't even seem to get a kick out of the fall of Cherbourg. The latest communiqué says we captured the German General von Schlieben and Admiral Hennecke. The pool correspondents have been in to see me at the Advance CP and I told them that if I were writing a story on Ike's activity of the past two weeks, I would emphasize his concern in the weather and the fact that he may be looking at one battle but is thinking ahead weeks and months. When Bizerte and Tunis fell, Ike registered practically no personal interest or exultation because it was something he had already counted on weeks before. Just now he is concerned about slowness of Monty's attack, the build-up, and Bradley's attack to the south. Bradley is concerned about getting accurate lists of the cargoes of incoming ships at his beaches. General Ike has troubleshot this difficulty and is trying to simplify and speed the procedure.

SHAEF MAIN (WIDEWING), THURSDAY, JUNE 29, 1944

General Ike has ordered that the bombing of sites of flying bombs and rockets on the French coast continue to receive top priority, but when weather conditions are favorable over Germany and all of the Strategic Forces cannot be used against the launching sites, the priorities then are: (*a*) aircraft industry, (*b*) oil, (*c*) ball bearings, (*d*) vehicular production.

All priorities are waived if the land battle requires use of the Strategic Air Forces.

JUNE, 1944: *Allies invaded French Channel coast after tremendous day and night bombardment of communication centers in Hungary, Rumania, France, and Netherlands. Immediate preparation included midnight-to-dawn blasting of invasion points by 1000 British heavies followed by 1300 Fortresses and Liberators. Blasting for eight-hour period totaled 7500 sorties, 10,000 tons of bombs. Heavy naval guns pounded Atlantic wall. Germans began robot bombing of Britain. In first three weeks of invasion Allies liberated more than 1000 square miles of France, destroyed four Nazi divisions, took 20,000 prisoners, approached Saint-Lô, took Cherbourg, captured two robot launching platforms. Heavy bomber assaults continued against communication lines, oil and plane-production facilities. American planes landed in Russia for first time after "shuttle bombing" of Berlin. Italian drives continued as Rome fell and Allies approached Leghorn and Siena. In Russia the Reds outflanked Minsk above Pripet marshes; broke through Mannerheim Line. Chinese in Burma took Lonkin and Tiangtzup. British seized Sawnching, strategic Burma rail center. Carrier task forces in Pacific destroyed many Jap ships and planes in blows against Guam, Tinian, Saipan, Rota, Bonin, and Volcano Island bases. Three hundred Jap planes downed over Marianas. Fighting on Biak gained Aslito air strip, Boroku and Sorido airfields. 20th Air Force made initial appearance with heavy attacks on Kyushu. Two weeks of Saipan fighting inflicted 9750 American casualties. America broke relations with Finland. Poland, Belgium, Czechoslovakia, and Luxembourg recognized de Gaulle's government. (The aggressors were beginning to find that the freedom-loving peoples, once they were aroused and organized for warfare, packed a mighty wallop all over the world.—H.C.B.)*

Visit to Cherbourg

SHAEF MAIN (WIDEWING), SATURDAY, JULY 1, 1944

Two years ago today I arrived in England.

Late yesterday I arrived by C-47 from Landing Strip No. 1 on the bluff above Omaha Beach after spending Wednesday, Thursday, and most of Friday on the Cherbourg Peninsula.

Departing from Southampton on U. S. Coast Guard Cutter 45, Lieutenant Peter Chase, skipper, at 4:30 A.M., we battled a thirty-mile southwestern wind, with riptide, which made the trip slower than normal. We reached Omaha Beach about 1:30 P.M., stayed aboard for a steak dinner which couldn't be cooked en route because the little eighty-footer was tossing wildly. Then we disembarked on a duck, checked in with the naval officer in command at the beach, and I happened to meet Major Chet Hansen, one of General Bradley's aides, who said he wanted a good excuse to get to Cherbourg himself and offered to drive us there in his jeep. We stopped for a few minutes at General Bradley's headquarters near Grandcamp. As the General had Admiral Wilkes with him, I left a copy of my formal orders for General Bradley and with his aide, Hansen, jeeped off toward Cherbourg. We stopped en route near Brix to see an incomplete construction—a launching ramp for flying bombs. I took numerous photographs. The ramp was covered by sixteen to twenty feet of reinforced concrete. A 12,000-pound bomb will penetrate only fifteen or sixteen feet of such stuff with a direct hit.

At Cherbourg we found that Fort Central and Fort de l'Ouest, along the breakwater, had not capitulated. There were stories of sniping, but my guess is that these were mostly American soldiers affected by a touch of vino, of which there was a great deal about. Seeking to find a place to spend the night, we went to the Hôtel Atlantique, but found troops quartered there. It had been the German Quartermaster's Headquarters and was in disarray. All sorts of empty and partly empty wine bottles, documents, old shoes, leggings, food half consumed, black bread, half links of sausage, cartridges, wallets, identification photographs, gas masks—everything one would normally see around a combined office and quarters was thrown in every direction. It was obvious that there was no place there to stay unless one had a bedding roll, and we did not carry ours.

While pondering the next step, I saw Major General Jim Collins, Commanding General of VII Corps, about to get into an armored car. He immediately invited me to be his guest at VII Corps headquarters, near Valognes, and graciously accepted Jim as well. Collins was going with a party to ask, through a loud hailer, the Germans in the two forts to surrender. The invitation would be preceded by heavy bombardment of the forts by our artillery. The mine sweepers that were to come from Omaha Beach could not approach the harbor because the forts would fire on them. Because of the presence of the mines in the water, we could not approach the forts by proper boat to seek surrender. Consequently, Collins' party would proceed down the mole toward the forts to hailing distance and then call on the loudspeaker for their surrender. This is called "hog calling." We saw the bombardment, which was largely white phosphorus. Collins said he would be gone two or three hours and might be late for dinner. I thought it rather nice to take a couple of forts before dinner.

Hansen drove us to the Valognes headquarters, where Captain Jack Walsh, aide to Collins, had had pitched a tent with two cots for us. We dined with the principal members of the staff and I picked up a considerable amount of information useful to answer the general questions given me by General Gale just before I left. These questions had to do with the condition of the port, the railroads, the availability of labor, the prospective tonnage, and the condition of oil depots.

After dinner, Jim and I visited Jack Thompson, of the *Chicago Tribune,* Knickerbocker, of the *Chicago Sun,* and Tex O'Reilly, of the *New York Herald Tribune,* who were quartered in a near-by farmhouse. Their bureau was covered with bottles, as they had benefited from the capture of Fort du Roule, the principal arsenal in Cherbourg, which overlooks the harbor and commands much of the town. In it was found a tremendous store of thousands of cases of champagne, cognac, and even American whisky, much of it carrying labels "Reserved for the Wehrmacht."

Jack, Nick, and Tex had witnessed the capture of the fort. They said it was built tier on tier with separate cells, some of which had partitions or stairways joining them which had been recently closed, the cement still being fresh. When the Germans in the top of the fortress surrendered, other Germans in midsections were still firing artillery at our troops. The newspapermen had accompanied a party of special demolitionists to the roof of the heavy cement circular turret atop the fortress to watch the effort to dynamite into submission those Germans who still fought in the cells below. Charges of explosive were suspended from the roof alongside the open slits below. Ultimately the fort was cleared. It was from one of the caves of this fort that General von Schlieben and Admiral Hennecke were captured, the former having issued an order to each man to fight to the last.

The correspondents were enthusiastic about the fighting quality and co-ordination of American troops and praised the progress made since earlier campaigns. Yet Tex said there was still room for improvement in air-ground co-operation. He said that in the air bombardment of Cherbourg, our pilots had strafed our own troops, causing casualties. But he sympathized with the pilot who had to select one of two ridges as the boundary line and understood the pilot's great opportunity for error.

General Collins returned to headquarters before midnight and immediately went into conference with his staff. I did not see him until next morning, when I learned that the forts had not surrendered. Instead they had answered by machine-gun fire. Fortunately, no one was hit. (Later I learned that dive-bomber hits put a splinter through an opening in the fort, fatally wounding the commanding officer, who had been adamant against surrender. When he was "out of it," the remainder ran up the white flag—some 180 officers and men.)

General Collins loaned us the command car with driver and we headed back for Cherbourg Thursday morning, June 29. I went to the temporary Naval Headquarters, where I found Captain Norman S. Ives, USN, the port commander, and Commodore William A. Sullivan, USNR, the salvage expert whom I had known in Africa and in Italy. Introducing myself to Ives, he immediately asked if I had orders, obviously suspicious of visitors. I told him I had, offered to show them to him, but he declined with thanks when I told him I had already reported to the First Army. I explained my mission, mentioning the list of questions from General Gale, and he said that the latest news was that the forts had just surrendered and he was about to take a small boat to get the officers.

Just then a lieutenant colonel arrived. He said he wished to accompany the party in order to accept the surrender on behalf of the 4th Division, that he was under orders from Major General Raymond O. Barton to take the surrender. The lieutenant colonel seemed suspicious that the Navy captain intended to take the surrender and was vehement in stating his position. I discovered later the reason the Navy got into it was that the Army couldn't read the flag signals of the surrendering Germans, and the Navy, having received the message, naturally assumed that someone should do the job.

Later I learned that five of the German officers, whom I saw when they were brought ashore for questioning, disclosed the position of the mine fields in the harbor and gave valuable information of great importance to the mine sweepers. This information was sent by wooden sailboat— wooden because it would not detonate magnetic mines and its shallow draft would enable it to ride over others—to the approaching mine sweepers the next day.

Commodore Sullivan was gracious and obliging. I asked him how he compared the condition of the port of Cherbourg with that of Naples. He said that Cherbourg was simpler and easier. There were some sixty or seventy small craft still afloat, for which he was thankful. The blocking of the harbor was not too serious, provided he got floating cranes promptly. In short, he was optimistic.

Before I finished talking with him, I spied Lieutenant Commander James L. Middlebrooks, USNR, who had been our construction engineer on WJSV in Washington. Jim had a group of radio technicians whose job was to establish radio communications for the Navy. This had been achieved, and now Jim's crew was scrounging about the city, collecting gear abandoned by the Germans. He had established his communications headquarters in a bombproof and gasproof building on the water front that had been used by the Germans for headquarters of sea rescue. Middlebrooks offered to take me through the Navy yard. He warned me that one naval officer, a Lieutenant Curley, had gone into the yard with a jeep and driver the day before and was missing. Before I left Cherbourg on Friday, I heard that after a thorough search of the extensive yard, covering perhaps a thousand acres, no trace had been found of Curley. We suspected that some lurking German, seeing an officer alone, had overpowered him, killed him, and taken his uniform in an effort to escape. In the Navy yard, I saw E-boat pens, one of which was badly damaged by our own bombs, the other partly damaged by German demolition. In the latter there was an oil barge burning. The locks to the drydocks had been demolished by explosion. Ships had been sunk at the mouth of the basin. The building in which torpedoes and mines were stored had been blown up. Many buildings in the yard were shambles.

We returned to VII Corps headquarters in time for dinner at 8 o'clock. General Collins told me of his disappointment that the mine sweepers had not entered the harbor that afternoon as scheduled. He said they were kept off by fire from an enemy battery in the northwest corner of the peninsula, where some 4000 Germans had been cornered. They were fighting like rats. The 9th Division had been assigned to get that battery at all costs. We learned during the evening that they had. General Collins also told me that his men had found a construction which presumably was a supply site for the flying bombs. I asked him if I could see it the next day, and he assigned his aide, Captain Jack Walsh, to guide me.

Walsh and I set out early the next morning in his jeep. We found the site in Bricquebec. A standard-gauge railroad track had been built as a spur from the established line. This spur, and others from it, fanned through the development, which consisted of widely dispersed buildings in various stages of completion. Some had only the foundations laid, others were complete. There were many structures obviously for storage. There was another type of building to house aluminum tanks about ten feet high and eight feet in diameter, two of which were still at the site and had not been damaged. I took pictures of everything of interest, especially the tanks. Concrete roads without metal reinforcement had been built throughout the area, following, for the most part, established country roads. Each was doubly camouflaged—that is, by a wire screen and appropriate green material above and branches and leaves strewn over the cement below. I noticed the absence of steel reinforcement in the concrete and in the buildings and later was told that apparently no steel was used for reasons magnetic.

I figured that this was a supply site for loading explosive or propellent fluid into the flying bombs. Then they were to be shipped on railroad cars to the launching site at Brix, which I had seen on Wednesday, Brix being only four or five miles away.

I obtained from Colonel James C. Anding, G-4 of the corps, the answers to a number of the questions given me by General Gale. Briefly, the waterworks in Cherbourg needed repair but would be in working order by July 1; the power plant was somewhat damaged, but not too seriously; the gasworks were O.K. About 300 feet of double-track railroad near the Cherbourg railway station had been damaged and would have to be rebuilt. I was also given a map of the harbor showing the damage and harbor entrances that were blocked.

I sat in on a meeting held by Colonel Sibley, the commanding officer for Cherbourg, and heard an analysis of the situation by both Army and Navy experts. Commodore Sullivan was joyous about finding the gear for underwater repair used by the Germans, but he was not as optimistic about speedily clearing the port as when I first saw him. The mines were a new factor, he said, but, unfortunately, we had obtained information, apparently reliable, as to their disposition and type. Most of them were pressure mines, which would require sweeping over the roadstead at least twelve times.* Army engineers were exercising their customary ingenuity in developing places for the unloading of liberty ships, but first concentrated on landing craft and coasters. A strip of unmined water left by the Germans for their escape from the ports on the outer mole would be used by ducks operating from a space of harbor to be cleared first of mines.

With this fresh information in hand and with four rolls of film, carry-

* These mines are detonated by the increased pressure caused by the passage of a ship overhead. They may be set, I was told, for any from the first to the twelfth ship.

ing thirty-five possibly good pictures on each, we charged off for the Omaha Beach at 2:30, reaching there at 5:30, being somewhat delayed by considerable transport movement on the road to and from Cherbourg. We caught the 6 o'clock C-47, stopped briefly at Thorney Island airfield near Portsmouth, and reached Northolt, near London, by 7:30. I phoned Ike I had arrived and he immediately said he had been waiting for me to "get over there." I said I had to wait for the shuttle car from Head-quarters Command, which wasn't due until 8:20. He insisted I go to the commanding officer of the airfield and ask him for a car.

Notes Between Alerts

I found Ike in fine fettle. He envied my gypsy trips and said I see and hear much more than he, and don't have to worry about causing incon-veniences to my hosts. He was hoping to get over to France again, but was concerned about the effect of the flying bombs on morale, not so much personally as their cumulative damage. The PM had expressed grave concern and had said there had been 1600 to date.

Ike regretted that Bradley had to postpone his big attack to open the base of the peninsula. He had planned to strike Friday, June 30, but I had learned from General Collins that the attack was postponed until Monday.

General Marshall had advised Ike on June 28 that President Roosevelt had concurred completely in the stand of the U. S. Chiefs in favor of the southern invasion of France and is opposed to the proposal to use all our Mediterranean forces to fight on into northern Italy and beyond. He has so notified the Prime Minister and hopes there will not be a deadlock in the Combined Chiefs. He insists that both he and the Prime Minister should support General Ike.

I happened to be in General Ike's office when the PM phoned him. It now appears that Mr. Churchill will cable the President today, agreeing to the southern invasion, and that General Wilson will be given a clear-cut directive to attack as quickly as possible. Ike was delighted with the PM's indicated approval.

In his phone conversation, Ike had insisted that he needed an addi-tional big port into which to pour American divisions now awaiting action at home. By getting another port, such as Marseille, he told the PM, our forces could be augmented by perhaps twelve divisions more than presently scheduled. The PM said it was a fateful decision.

Late today, Ike, Jim Gault, and Mickey flew to France, where Ike will spend two or three days at General Bradley's headquarters. I urged him to go to Cherbourg, see the 101st Airborne Division on the way, and continue to the northwest part of the peninsula to see the 9th Division, which is just completing its cleanup. I also located for him the two flying-bomb sites that I had inspected.

A hard-fought battle around Caen employing tanks has been in progress, one of the reports from Monty saying that some 300 German tanks have been destroyed. There are still indications in the report of censorship cuts in newspaper stories filed from the front which indicate that our tanks are inferior to those of the Germans. On the other hand, we captured a German document indicating that our bombing of German factories, particularly those which make ammunition, made the High Command anticipate that the quality of production would deteriorate. They claim that loss of skilled labor, substitution of materials, and relocation of factories give insufficient time to test ammunition, and, therefore, reports of any weaknesses or failures are especially desired.

While dictating this report, Miss Chick and I have been to the air-raid shelter at least a dozen times and I am completing it on Sunday morning, July 2. Last evening at 7 o'clock, a flying bomb hit within 200 yards of our wing. There were five injured but no fatalities. One pane was sucked out of each office in our wing and the private runway from Beetle's to Ike's office was unroofed.

SHAEF's Forward Headquarters has been opened near Portsmouth in a camp not far from the spot where we have had our Advance Command Post. Ike said that there was considerable reluctance amongst officers, both British and American, to leave the Main Headquarters under conditions which might appear that we are running away from the flying bombs. They needn't worry, as the Portsmouth area has already had seventeen and seems to be the target of at least one launching site. Those who have returned from the assault area in France, as I have, feel we are coming more into the war in London than we were in France. Of course, we were not in the combat line.

SHAEF MAIN (WIDEWING), MONDAY, JULY 3, 1944

General Ike feels a tinge of responsibility for Captain J. A. Grindle's misfortune. He is the Royal Navy officer who was in command of the fast mine layer, *Apollo*, which carried Ike and Admiral Ramsay across the Channel to the beaches on D plus 1 and, unfortunately, ran ashore. Ike wrote a letter to his old friend, now the First Sea Lord, Admiral Sir Andrew Cunningham, sharing some of the responsibility with Grindle.

Admiral Cunningham has replied that he doesn't actually deal with these matters himself but that the letter of the Supreme Commander may have some weight in the case. Captain Grindle does not know of Ike's effort in his behalf.

News That Makes the Flying Bomb Seem More Bearable

SHAEF MAIN (WIDEWING), TUESDAY, JULY 4, 1944

Today, the Fourth of July, is my second one in London.

Yesterday we received the formal directive from the Combined Chiefs of Staff ordering General Wilson to launch ANVIL by August 15.

Bradley started his drive in the base of the Cherbourg Peninsula toward Coutances. First reports indicate satisfactory gains.

Monty has issued a directive saying it is his policy to "contain" German armor around Caen on the left front of the beachhead so the Americans on the right would not be bothered too much while taking Cherbourg.

Moaney was sweeping plaster that dropped from our upstairs ceiling when a flying bomb struck in our neighborhood at 9:15 this morning, half an hour after I left for work. At the headquarters, we have taken to shelter eight times today and probably would have been there more often had the loudspeaker system not been closed for repairs for a couple of hours.

Dr. O'Brien, my friend from the Rockefeller Foundation, visited me today. He said that the Germans were amazed in the early days of the Battle of Britain that Spitfires always seemed to be over their bombers no matter from which direction or directions they approached London. The reason was radar. Subsequently, when the Germans pushed into France, they captured an entire trainload of official documents from the British headquarters. They had been hurriedly gathered on the train, which was to make a special run for safety. O'Brien said that a French scientist later was confronted with a complete dossier of his work for the Allies.

O'Brien said that scientists working for the Allies now are earnestly experimenting on uranium by bombarding its atom. The result would be that forty or fifty pounds of the stuff might destroy a large city. He said this in commenting on photographs I had taken of the launching site in the Cherbourg Peninsula. He said that the massive buildings and thick concrete protection indicated that the Germans had not perfected uranium, which, for those of us who have been ducking the flying bombs for lo, these many days and nights, is a good thing. He said that Swedish scientists had told him recently that they doubted if the Germans had gotten

as far on development of uranium as British and American researchers.*
He also said that he thought the Germans were not as far advanced on
gas as the Allies.

Establishment of our Forward Headquarters has depleted the ranks of
officers and personnel at Main Headquarters. Beetle is working at Forward.
General Morgan, his deputy, stays here. In general, the head of a division
goes to Forward and his deputy remains at Main, or vice versa. Forward
has now become organized to take over operations, and Main is becoming
headquarters for the planners, particularly for postwar occupation.

Ike Flies Over the Enemy Lines

SHAEF MAIN (WIDEWING), FRIDAY, JULY 7, 1944

Ike returned from France on Wednesday, the fifth, having modestly
avoided having his picture taken when Bradley pulled the lanyard on a 155,
signaling the "Fourth of July Salute" at high noon of every American gun
against the Germans. His effort to keep secret that he had flown in a Mus-
tang over the German lines had failed miserably (but rightly). He had
gone to the field only to find "fifty photographers, newsreel men, and
reporters."

During his extended visit to the beachhead, Ike had visited the VII and
VIII Corps and their divisions, trying to catch them during actual operations. These corps had begun attacking southward on July 3 and 4. They
found the going extremely tough for three main reasons: first, the fighting
quality of the German soldiers; second, the nature of the country, and,
third, the weather. Our whole attack has to fight its way out of narrow
bottlenecks flanked by marshes and against the enemy, who has a double
hedgerow and an intervening trench almost every fifty yards as ready-made
strong points. Bad weather limits air support and produces mud, reminiscent to Ike of Tunisia in the wintertime. Location of enemy artillery
targets is difficult, yet we have plenty of guns available to deal with them.
Clear weather would help.

Because of Ike's intense interest in knowing more about the terrain, he
took the flight with Major General Quesada, who carefully provided an
escort of a half-dozen fighters. He was, as usual, surprised at the news
interest in his flight. To him it was just business.

---

* I did not record in the diary occasional warnings received at headquarters from the
War Department, telling us to refrain from speculation concerning atomic energy.
We had very little actual information about the atomic bomb, and I had no idea,
when this entry was made, of the fact that the Allied researchers were so close to
success.

One of the things he learned first hand in France was the inadequacy of fire power of American tanks against Tigers and Panthers. He set all hands to work by a special message to Beetle while he was in Normandy and today had "all hands on deck." The result was a special letter to General Marshall, carried by Brigadier General Joseph A. Holly in person. Holly, a tank expert, said he had made six trips across the Atlantic in the last six months, dealing with this and related problems.

The weather generally has been bad, although yesterday we had considerable air activity and today we have a tremendous amount of air power over Germany. The Prime Minister made a statement at the House of Commons yesterday about the flying bombs, the main point being that for each bomb that had reached England, only one life was lost, the score being some 2500 dead and wounded in three days. America is reported aghast at the revelation, particularly that these bombs have been hitting London.

Monty's confident and eloquent directives first called for an all-out slash on the British front to take Caen. The second said this effort was a holding operation to contain the German Army while the Americans took Cherbourg and resumed their push southward. Ike has been smoldering and today burst out with a letter to Monty which, in effect, urges him to avoid having our forces sealed into the beachhead, take the offensive, and Ike would support him in every way, as if it were necessary to say this. I think Monty is characteristically supercautious, but when he gets everything "tidy" he will hit—and hard.

George Allen has spent considerable time with us since Ike returned. Night before last, George asked Ike to explain his parentage, meaning the state in which he was born. Ike carefully explained that he was born in Texas, at Denison, because his father had to move from Abilene to Denison to find employment in railroad work and subsequently had moved to Tyler, Texas, and then had returned to Abilene, Kansas, when Ike was two years of age.

"A chicken may hatch her eggs in the oven, but they're still not biscuits," Ike said, and George roared.

Yesterday, apparently, was one of our few good days of aerial operation against the flying bomb and rocket sites across the Channel. Last evening and this morning until noon were relatively quiet, although we had four alerts of "imminent danger" while at lunch in the cottage, one flying bomb sailing over the house at about 200 feet but crashing out of our hearing.

The vehicle build-up for OVERLORD is in arrears. On the British side, up to July 2, we are short 23,000 and, on the American account, some 32,000. This is caused by weather, slow turn-around of LST and LCT, and diversion to ferry service of LCT. SHAEF has now asked for thirty-six ship sailings per day up to D plus 60, or August 6, in order to overcome the deficiency of vehicles.

The progress of the Americans in the base of the Cherbourg Peninsula is slow because of mud, the hedgerows, the good terrain for defense, and poor flying weather.

On July 4, Beetle sent over Ike's signature a message to the President that on this Independence Day the millionth Allied soldier had landed in France since D-Day.

Yesterday Ike had a letter from a British civilian complaining that the American press was unfair to the British military effort because Americans play up the efforts of Americans. Since the capture of Cherbourg by Americans, there has been a growing feeling that American papers were tooting our own horns too much. Yet the BBC generally speaks of RAF bombing operations, but if they are U. S. Air Force bombers, the BBC calls them "Allied." This is noticeable to all Americans, most especially to our airmen. The British press, however, was gracious on July 4 in paying tribute to the Americans.

Compared to the spirit of the British and American troops, who fight side by side, that of the newspapers and radio in our respective countries frequently appears to us un-Allied because it is natural for the American press and radio to carry stories of the greatest interest to their readers or listeners, which means playing up American activities. It also is natural for the British press and the BBC to emphasize news of the British accomplishments. As General Ike's campaigns are in the area where the BBC primarily is heard by all troops and London papers reach us more quickly than those from America, the problem thus created always has to be faced. Added to these nationalistic interests of the public-opinion media is the persistent effort of Goebbels to emphasize our differences. Yet General Eisenhower and his Anglo-American staff have developed such non-nationalistic teamwork in the supreme effort to win the war that even these differences are being overcome. In fairness to the press and radio of both countries, this problem is recognized and frequently special effort is made, particularly by war correspondents and broadcasters in the field, to bend over backwards, as far as fairness is concerned, to hold together the two great freedom-loving (and free-speaking) publics.

Discussing this in George Allen's and my presence on the evening of the fifth, and fresh from the front, Ike said he would issue a statement extolling the good work of both nationalities. During yesterday, he completed his message, which was released to the press last evening.

Like all press and radio coverage, some reports are good and some **are** bad, depending upon one's viewpoint. On the evening of the Fourth, I heard an extraordinarily good program on BBC. It consisted of reports from its correspondents on the Normandy beachhead, in Italy, and in the Pacific, telling in detail instances of co-operation between Yank and Tommy. This is good stuff all round. However, yesterday there was a letter in the London *Times* criticizing BBC for carrying, on the Fourth, an American program of the Battle of Bunker Hill. Ike asked Beetle, who in turn asked Colonel Ernest Dupuy, to find out if an American officer arranged this program to be broadcast in England. At lunch today, Ike said he would send the man home if it is within his power.

SHAEF MAIN (WIDEWING), SATURDAY, JULY 8, 1944
Monty attacked northwest of Caen this morning, and early reports indicate progress "according to plan."

Ike has cabled General Marshall his idea for establishment of a unified command for airborne operations.

Admiral King has withdrawn all American warships, and Admiral Ramsay would like to retain eight destroyers to work with Admiral Wilkes at Cherbourg. U. S. naval units are going to the assault job in southern France. Ike has intervened with the Joint Chiefs, through General Marshall, to see if Ramsay's request can be met.

A captured German, aged eighteen, has told our interrogators that V-2 is the rocket we have been expecting. The chemical-filled rocket on explosion will destroy by burning an area of (presumably) twenty-five square kilometers. The V-2s are to be fired at English ports, so our supplies will be destroyed and traffic to the Continent disrupted. The prisoner said that V-2 is Germany's last hope of preventing defeat.

There has been a vigorous attempt in the Channel to sink our shipping by human torpedoes, such as were used at Anzio with some success. Two of our ships have been sunk. Two prisoners were taken, one of whom had taken part in the Anzio operation.

The Prime Minister's report of the seriousness of the damage and casualties from flying bombs, and the disclosure that London itself has been the principal target, have sobered, shocked, and angered the American public, judging from the reports back home. Many had thought the war already over, but now they know the truth.

SHAEF FORWARD (PORTSMOUTH), MONDAY, JULY 10, 1944
The General, Warrant Officer Rae, Mickey, and I arrived at the Advance CP, the camp we used during the D-Day period, yesterday. En route, the General and I stopped at Chequers, where the General had an hour-and-a-

half talk with the PM, who was resting in his bedroom. Ike told me later that the PM gave him hell for insisting on the ANVIL operation, the British Premier still being wedded to pursuit of the Germans in Italy and to possibilities in the Balkans.

I had given Ike one of the German cigars I had picked up in a disheveled headquarters in Cherbourg, and he gave it to the PM. When the PM and Ike came downstairs, the PM thanked me for the cigar and I told him I had the original box with a few more in it, which I gave him. He seemed pleased. Mrs. Churchill and the PM's brother were gracious as hosts. The latter and I talked most of the time that Ike was in a huddle with the PM. His name is John S. Churchill. I told him that even though I follow the news probably more meticulously than most persons, I had never known that the Prime Minister had a brother. He seemed complimented and said he had managed to stay in the background and whenever approached by the press had simply refused to talk.

Late in the evening, I visited the war room at SHAEF Forward to get news for the General. I found that Caen had been practically taken. With this as a nightcap, Ike went off to sleep. Americans on the western flank had taken La Haye-du-Puits, and in the center, the 30th Division of the XIX Corps had gained about a mile and a half. It looks as if we were on the march at last, although the weather still is abominably bad and forecasts give no encouragement for the near future.

Lieutenant Colonel Thor Smith, the PRO who looks after our small pool of correspondents, was after me on the phone the moment we arrived, to get Ike to have a press conference. The correspondents handed me a gift for the General, which I declined to accept, telling them to present it to him personally. This they did at the conference this morning. The spokesman was Roberts, of the UP, who said he and one of his compatriots had sought refuge from a flying bomb in London and thus happened into a shop where there was an assortment of old prints for sale. One of them seemed appropriate as a gift for General Ike. It shows a rocket troop of the British Royal Horse Artillery in review order a couple of hundred years ago. A rocket gun is shown being discharged. Roberts said that the press had described the bare walls of the General's office tent so often that they hoped he would use it appropriately for decoration. Ike thanked them warmly and was intrigued by the rocket.

His discourse to them was largely a review of the improved status of the Allies during the past two years. A question was asked about the military effect of the flying bomb. Here Ike's answer had to be general. By way of negation, he said that, certainly, military leaders, such as he, were not saying that the flying bomb is a nuisance only to civilians and hence the military will get on with its work and pay no attention to it. Quite to the contrary; the flying bomb is a nuisance to all. It is definitely a new weapon and its possibilities in the future are great. If flying bombs can be made to be attracted to heat, or to masses of steel of which military equipment is made, and can be launched in great numbers, even though the size of missiles might be smaller, then the weapon becomes significant. As for himself personally, he said he does not like them and everyone with whom he has talked has shared his feeling.

I should add that Red Mueller, who is working on a story about the General, asked me for some anecdotes. I told the newsmen the story of General Marshall's order to me to make Ike work less and to exercise more. The catch line always gets a chuckle—that after getting Ike on Marshall's road to health, I had reported to Washington and had told the story to one of General Marshall's intimates at the War Department, who had said, "That's what General Marshall's doctor ordered him to do, and he doesn't do it, either."

Beetle brought Lord Halifax, British Ambassador to Washington, to lunch today. Most of the conversation was about fly fishing, of which his lordship said he knew nothing, but Beetle had caught four trout on a private preserve a couple of nights ago and now we know all about fishing.

Turning to serious topics after luncheon, the Ambassador was interested to know the extent to which the battleground in France had been damaged by bombing and sabotage of transportation centers and bridges. Ike said that if we had not had the three months of relatively good weather for attack of these targets, the invasion could not have been launched. However, the bridges on the Seine and the Loire, and other transportation necessities, had been effectively broken and rebroken. He gave first weight of importance in this work to the Air Force and, secondly, to the French resistance groups.

Ike repeated his views that the German General Staff regards this war and the preceding one as merely campaigns in their dogged determination first to dominate Europe and eventually the world. He would exterminate all of the General Staff. Or maybe they could be concentrated on some appropriate St. Helena.

Beetle chimed in that imprisonment would not accomplish anything. It would simply lead to eventual release of the prisoners because in six or eight years our own publics again would grow softhearted and conciliatory. Halifax asked Ike how many officers are on the German General Staff. Ike guessed about 3500. He added he would include for liquidation leaders of the Nazi party from mayors on up and all members of the Gestapo.

There was agreement that extermination could be left to nature if the

Russians had a free hand. Ike added that justice would be done if zones
of influence in Germany could be temporarily assigned to the small nations
overrun by Hitler. He would give Russia the largest portion and other areas
to the Czechs, Yugoslavs, Poles, Danes, Norwegians, Greeks, and the
French.

The Unused Communiqué

SHAEF MAIN (WIDEWING), TUESDAY, JULY 11, 1944

Last night was a rather noisy one at the camp. From midnight on, flying
bombs came over, keeping antiaircraft guns active most of the night. Ike
slept on a cot in the dugout shelter; I slept on a mattress on the floor of
another shelter, with Mickey as shelter mate. The bombs are worse when
accompanied by ack-ack fire. There the heavy ack-ack fire of the Portsmouth defenses shook the earth.

We returned to SHAEF Main at noon. Overnight, Ike had received a
message from Assistant Secretary McCloy for Secretary Stimson, who
reached England this morning from Africa, indicating that the President
and de Gaulle had come to an agreement. The President was ready to
accept the French Committee as the *de facto* authority for civil administration in France, provided that complete authority is reserved for General
Eisenhower to do what he feels necessary to conduct military operations
and that the French people will be given opportunity to make free choice
of their own government.

The Combined Chiefs have agreed to equip patriot forces in the areas
under the Supreme Commander, including southern France, with arms
and equipment for forces formed from manpower liberated by our operations to the extent of 172,000 men. These are to be used for garrisoning
liberated areas and for internal security. The target date is set at D plus
300, which would be March 6, 1945.

This afternoon Ike called me into his office and handed me a sheet of
notepaper on which he had scribbled a message. He said he had found it
in his wallet. After reading it, I told him I wanted it. He reluctantly
assented, saying that he had written one in similar vein for every amphibious operation but had secretly torn up each one. The note:

> Our landings in the Cherbourg-Havre area have failed to
> gain a satisfactory foothold and I have withdrawn the troops.
> My decision to attack at this time and place was based upon
> the best information available. The troops, the air, and the
> Navy did all that bravery and devotion to duty could do. If
> any blame or fault attaches to the attempt it is mine alone.
> —June 5.

SHAEF FORWARD, THURSDAY, JULY 13, 1944

During the night, I had numerous phone calls, one of which informed me of an ultra-secret message in our private cipher from Monty. I arranged to have this brought at 7 o'clock this morning and spent an hour and a half with ATS Subaltern Cavaye while we boned out the message. Monty told Ike that he wanted all-out air support for a big offensive which starts Saturday on the eastern flank and Monday on the west, weather permitting. Said the Normandy battle front would be "aflame." He also asked for a tighter ban on visitors.

Monty wanted to keep pressure on Admiral Ramsay to hot him up on Cherbourg to get it cleared of mines and operating as soon as possible. Lord Leathers had sent word to Ike that an accumulation of ships, intended to be unloaded at Cherbourg, is awaiting attention and said that if Cherbourg could not be opened soon, he would like to resume the build-up of supply for the British Isles. Ike immediately sent word "no," that as long as there was a chance of getting Cherbourg ready soon, he would not spare a pound of tonnage from the battle.

The weatherman says we will have a good week end, he hopes. In any event, we had a good day in the air yesterday and today is relatively free from clouds at the camp and we frequently hear aircraft overhead. About 2300 U. S. heavies hit Munich in two days—Tuesday and Wednesday. Since it was blind bombing on both days, the town where Hitler made his start must have paid heavily. Reports from the German press, reprinted in London papers, emphasize the great dominance of our Air Force in the battle area. Movement of enemy troops and equipment is confined to darkness, with virtually nothing moving in the daytime. One report said that only six vehicles in the enemy territory were seen yesterday. On the other hand, our own reporters relate that after two years the Allies still do not have as good a tank as the Germans, nor have we equaled the effectiveness of the enemy's multiple mortar. Ike told me yesterday that the problem of finding ammunition that will penetrate the Tiger and the Panther is complicated. Tests made by the ordnance people in the United States show that our ammunition does penetrate these tanks, except the Panther in front, which is practically impossible. He felt confident we would lick the problem. Our aircraft knocked out twenty-eight tanks counterattacking day before yesterday, using bombs and rockets.

The Radar Guns

Yesterday an interesting over-all study of the ever-present flying bomb and nervously awaited rockets came to Ike's office from the British Chiefs of Staff. Antiaircraft guns, called static guns, automatically aimed by radar, are now in use in southern England. The report said that the first two flying bombs shot at by the static guns were brought down—a favorable sign, indeed. Another interesting aspect of the report was that of the two experimental sites for the rockets, one of which is Peenemunde and was heavily bombed a year ago, the second, Dupice, is in the path of the Russian advance and may be captured. The PM had radioed Uncle Joe of this possibility and asked that Russian troops preserve the site and that Allied experts be permitted to study it. The explosive charge in the rocket is now spoken of as 12,000 pounds, and what was a possibility of the rocket's actual existence has passed to the stage of probability and now, in this paper, is spoken of as absolutely existent and likely to be used against England any day. Effective bombing of four of the six or seven launching sites in the Calais area, no doubt, has postponed use of V-2, as the Germans dub it.

Ike received word, after this morning's meeting at SHAEF Forward, that General Teddy Roosevelt, assistant commander of the 4th Division, had died in France of a heart attack. Teddy was to have been given command of the 90th Division tomorrow. Ike said he had absolutely vitalized the 4th Division, and the division was crazy about him.

Ike spoke to Beetle about using Bomber Command for area bombing of enemy concentrations in the battle line. If an area half a mile in diameter could be saturated in the RAF manner at night, the infantry in a quick attack could then practically walk through. He said this technique should be pressed and developed. This was in connection with his follow-up on Monty's request that Ike issue an order to the Air Force to give him all-out support for the big attack.

Because of Monty's request, Ike changed his personal plans for the day, and, taking me, motored back to SHAEF Main, where he had asked Tedder to meet him at 4 o'clock. He gave Tedder the story and asked him to present his views in the strongest possible terms at the air meeting at Stanmore Friday morning.

SHAEF FORWARD, FRIDAY, JULY 14, 1944

Around midnight Colonel Gault, phoning from SHAEF Main, awakened me out of a sound sleep to say that Monty had "cracked through," to use one of Monty's own favorite terms. The message had come in Monty's and Ike's personal cipher. This was a joke on Jim because whoever has possession of the cipher has to burn the midnight oil to uncork Monty's messages. I had carried the cipher away from SHAEF Main yesterday afternoon, anticipating that Monty would send another wire to Ike and

I would need it overnight. However, Ike drafted a message to Monty and left it with Jim to transmit and Jim had decided it should be sent in this particular cipher. He sent Sergeant A. Van Ostenbrugge and an officer chasing after us to retrieve the bothersome codebook. Thus Jim got the cipher and lost the sleep.

The message related to air support for Monty's prospective operations. He also wanted every effort made by the Navy and others to get Cherbourg harbor cleared. Ike had been pressing on this and all hands were hard at work. Beetle said we ought to ask Monty if he's short of any supplies.

Four Days in One

SHAEF MAIN (WIDEWING), MONDAY, JULY 17, 1944

To capsule some of the events since I last dictated on July 14:

Ike has congratulated Air Chief Marshal Harris of Bomber Command for continual pressing of the air campaign against German industry and for spectacular support of Monty's ground operations at Caen;

Has sent and said words of praise to General Spaatz for the 8th Air Force;

Has sent a special letter with me to T. J., who is recuperating from a sinus operation in the Army hospital near Cheltenham;

Has not completed the over-all airborne command; but General Brereton is slated to head the 1st Allied Airborne army and General Vandenberg to command the 9th Air Force, which came to England from the desert campaign and has pounded secret sites across the Channel;

Has heard from General Marshall that Devers, whom Ike approved for the job, will head the Army Group in command of ANVIL;

Has conferred with Tedder repeatedly about air support for Monty's offensive, now in its second day, a limited offensive having been started yesterday and a much bigger one due to kick off tomorrow morning, with Bradley's force to hit a six-division punch starting Wednesday the nineteenth, weather permitting; has heard from Admiral King that new frigates have been named for his and Bradley's home towns of Abilene and Moberly, Ike cabling his appreciation and wishing the skipper of the new *Abilene* to know that he has every expectation that she will lick any Axis ship of any size anywhere and anytime;

Has today seen the best weather since May, despite predictions to the contrary on the weather map yesterday, today's weather map showing a large white high covering France, part of Germany, and England, with prediction for tomorrow almost as good, and has relented to Beetle's arguments that he should stay at the Advance CP instead of SHAEF Main. Ike, Captain Pinette, and I are going there this afternoon.

Ike's letter to T. J. was overflowing with warmth and loyalty but did not let T. J. "off the hook" as PRO, as he had written me most fervently to press his case with Ike, but since I am not in sympathy with T. J. on this I am afraid I did not press. The job needs a good man, and T. J. is it. In fact, I told T. J. at the hospital Saturday afternoon that he was most decidedly the man for the job.

General Wilson has asked the Combined Chiefs of Staff to equip three Italian divisions, the Eyeties having shown a commendable record in combat, for he needs the troops now that ANVIL will take a lot.

General McNair has reported here for duty at the request of the Supreme Commander, and his assignment has been announced by the War Department as important but "somewhere overseas." Ike has notified Bradley that he proposes to bring McNair with him on a trip in the near future. McNair's presence in this theater has been widely publicized at home and over the short-wave radio. It is surmised that the Germans suspect that we are building a big force to effect a second cross-Channel operation in the Pas de Calais area. They are sensitive in this area, too, because of their sites for flying bombs. Because General McNair has been head of the Army ground forces in the War Department—a fact well known to the enemy—we hope they will think he commands the second striking force.

Another thing taking Ike's time has been negotiation with the British to get them to agree to release of names and identifications of units and commanders, particularly those who have been cited for effective action in the field. The British always are loath to give out this information, but General Marshall has been insisting that publicity of American armed forces be spread amongst units, commanders, and men as widely as possible. I think the British scheme has resulted in overpublicity of the few names of their generals, and underpublicity, if any at all, to many others. In the past this restrictive policy has usually resulted, as Ike explained this morning to a visitor, in publication of the sum total of the negatives, that is, he has been required to take the objections of the British and those of the Americans, add them together, and the result is the "taboo" list. Now he has reached the point where he thinks he will have to tell General Montgomery that as a matter of administrative policy it is necessary for the Americans to release the names of their units, with the hope that the British likewise will liberalize their policy.

He has frequently discussed differences between American and British censorship policies. The War Office policy has never been quite the same as that of the U. S. War Department with respect to the release of the designation of regiments and of the names of commanding officers within a division that has already been identified on the battle front. Our War Department has always insisted on doing this because, in our country, at least, this produces a personality in the news that brings the war closer to the people. For the past two years he has made a great effort to keep these policies on an absolute level throughout his Allied Commands. He has officially supported the British view, not particularly because he believed in it, but in order to have uniformity even in this detail. But now he feels the time has come when he must fall in with the U. S. demands so far as U. S. troops are concerned.

The Germans have disclosed by a broadcast that for the first time their reconnaissance has detected our Gooseberries and Mulberries, but they conclude that these shelters were a measure forced upon us by the "nor'-easter" of June 19-20 and by our belated realization that their demolitions in Cherbourg would deny us the use of that port for a long time.

Resistance groups in France have stopped considerable rail traffic and three main canals and have blown up 10,000 tons of ammunition and a depot. We are still dropping into France at night special troops with jeeps, armor, and ammunition, not only from England, but from North Africa.

Our threat directed against the Pas de Calais will reach its peak about August 14, just before the landings in Southern France, the Germans apparently being convinced that we intend to make another big assault. Real and dummy landing craft at southeastern ports of England opposite Pas de Calais and a variety of other threats to indicate probability of a quick cross-Channel thrust in the Calais area apparently are tying down German divisions which otherwise might be across the Seine into the present battle area.

We hear through intelligence sources that the Germans figure the southern forces will land in the Gulf of Genoa to help both the attack on the Pisa-Rimini line and ANVIL. They also look for activity on the Adriatic coast and in the Aegean.

SHAEF FORWARD, WEDNESDAY, JULY 19, 1944

Ike, Jim, Mattie Pinette, one of the General's secretaries, and I arrived at the camp Sunday evening, July 16, in time for dinner. Ike was hungry for old-fashioned, Army-style baked beans, and yelped that, having hollered his head off for them for two years, he was going to fire the entire personal staff, meaning me primarily, I thought, if it didn't deliver beans, and soon. In fact, I excused myself before dinner was finished because Red Mueller and Ned Roberts were waiting to see me at the PRO tent.

They had heard that we are starting another Army Group, and had seen General McNair. They wondered if McNair's assignment over here was political, or what. Assured them Ike had asked for him. As they were even more inquisitive about McNair's job I didn't say much, but reported to Ike. The next day Beetle had an off-the-record talk with our small bevy of reporters and told them all about General McNair and his functions. Beetle said that the Germans are getting their intelligence through Madrid, and we had heard from our spies there that the German spies had reported to Berlin that our main and primary effort would be through the Normandy beachhead, with no other landings. He hoped the German General Staff wouldn't believe it—at least, not immediately.

Monty's attack with three armored divisions south and east of Caen got off to a good start yesterday, some seven miles having been gained by noon and the bulk of the enemy's defenses penetrated. The RAF had dropped a concentration of 7000 tons of bombs to help the ground troops break through the German defense ring. Around evening Tedder called Ike and said Monty had, in effect, stopped his armor from going farther. Ike was mad. Monty always wants to wait to draw up his "administrative tail." The Americans got Saint-Lô, taken in fighting from hedgerow to hedgerow and settled in the streets.

During the night I helped decipher a private signal from Monty, which rejoiced on his gains and said that the U. S. First Army would kick off on Friday. This had been set for today. Yesterday was superb for the monstrous air bombardment of German lines in front of the British Second Army, but weathermen predicted bad flying conditions for today, and not too good for tomorrow. In fact, Ike was unable to take off from near-by Thorney Isle airfield this morning in his new B-25, Larry Hansen piloting, because of "cloud which touched the ground," as Larry put it. About the time the trip seemed hopeless today, Monty came through with another signal, which I deciphered. Said he wanted to talk to Ike tomorrow, the twentieth, about the air setup.

Ike has told Monty of his effort to protect Monty from visitors, Ike having had a long discussion with the PM on the secret phone this morning. Ike had sent word yesterday that the PM could go to Cherbourg and the rear area but that he was against the Prime Minister visiting commanders or troops in the forward area because they, particularly Monty, did not want to be distracted from the battle. Ike had told the PM he could motor to Omaha Beach, reboard his ship under Navy care, and sail along the

British beaches. But this got misquoted or misinterpreted by the time the PM got it, and this morning the PM called up, boiling mad, saying it would be a Cabinet issue, this business of Monty trying to tell the PM where he could and could not go. Ike took all the responsibility, and after explaining his desire not to bother Monty, the trip was laid on for tomorrow, with the Old Boy permitted to visit in the rear areas and not to see or bother Monty or other combat officers at all.

Spent until nearly 4:30 this morning deciphering a message from Monty. As Monty had radioed that Bradley's attack was off until Friday, thought this might affect timing of Ike's trip. I read it to Ike, who was sleeping in his dugout, where his snores seemed smothered but steady. Said it wouldn't affect his trip and resumed his serenade.

Ike Referees an Air-Ground Quarrel

SHAEF FORWARD (PORTSMOUTH), THURSDAY, JULY 20, 1944
Last evening about 9 Tedder phoned Ike from SHAEF Main and, reflecting the disappointment of the air at the slowness on the ground, said that the British Chiefs of Staff would support any recommendation that Ike might care to make with respect to Monty for not succeeding in going places with his big three-armored-division push. There were reports from advanced recce units, called Phantom, late yesterday that the British tanks east and south of Caen hit an antitank screen that stopped 'em cold, with heavy casualties. Whereupon the tanks were held back and the Scots' 5th Brigade—infantry—given the lead. The loss of trained tank crews hurts the British badly, as they already are moving heaven and earth for replacements.

Monty had a press conference yesterday at which he said that at least 156,000 Germans had been killed or wounded since D-Day. Yet in the big push east and south of Caen only 2500 prisoners were taken.

Ike said yesterday that with 7000 tons of bombs dropped in the most elaborate bombing of enemy front-line positions ever accomplished, only seven miles were gained—can we afford a thousand tons of bombs per mile? The air people are completely disgusted with the lack of progress.

Anyway, Ike is off today to see Bradley and Monty. Jim and one press man who occupies the third and last seat in the B-25, which I gave up, are going, the press man by an arrangement of mine with Ike's acquiescence.

After Ike had learned definitely that weather barred his trip yesterday, and he had disposed of some picayunish problems, he retired to his caravan, where he dozed or slept much of the day, getting up for dinner. Then he appeared quiet and rested, but blue as indigo over Monty's slowdown. Ike said this morning that he had had a good night, awakening only when the alert sounded around 7 but was followed soon by the all-clear. (Morning papers say London had one of its worst flying-bomb attacks, the buzzards coming over in waves.)

It's now 10. Ike is standing around, crunching the cinders with his heels, impatiently waiting for weather news from Larry Hansen, who is at Thorney Isle airfield, awaiting clearance for the cross-Channel flight. Ike has just said he's got to get across, if he has to swim.

Later: at 10:07, Ike said to hell with waiting, let's go down to the field on the chance the weather clearance will be received—and growled that if he had laid on a destroyer to leave at 7, he could have been ashore in France by 11.

While waiting, Jim and I have been talking about Monty's slowdown. I thought Ike might find that Monty ordered his advancing tanks to hold off and in effect "dig in" until the customary counterattack of the Germans had been met, this Monty planning to knock out by air and artillery, then continue his advance, the worst being over. Jim said Monty has only one tactical style—amass artillery and air and then send tanks and infantry into action. I ventured that Rommel must know this play by heart, and simply plants his guns and armor out of artillery range and hides his tanks and infantry. Our publics, I said, are naturally comparing the slowness of our advance out of our bridgehead with the magnificent gains and results on the Russian front. Jim said a comparison of gains was in order. Public opinion in both America and Britain will foment trouble between us.

(Larry has just phoned that all planes are grounded; Ike is en route to the field; I have started to check with Royal Navy to see if a destroyer or something fast can be laid on.)

Going back to Monty, I told Jim that the reason there is a dearth of publicly acceptable British officers to replace General Montgomery, if there were a question of that, is because of the British system of limiting the number of names of British generals who may be written about in the public prints or publicized on the BBC. This entrenches the well-publicized generals and limits the publicly acceptable ones: we can't replace someone with just anyone. It's really one of those symptoms of the chronic rivalry between the air and the ground, fanned by resentment of many British Army and air officers, particularly those who served in the desert, because Monty has not learned the art of giving credit to all services and commanders for his past victories.

Jim said that the British have a system of taking care of unsuccessful generals—in fact, a number of methods of "kicking a man upstairs." Said Monty could be made a peer and sit in the House of Lords, or even given a governorship, such as Malta, whose governor, Lord Gort, is leaving to take over racial-conscious Palestine.

Anyway, Ike is like a blind dog in a meat house—he can smell it, but he can't find it. How he will handle the situation remains the principal suspended interest of the diary, at the moment.

SHAEF FORWARD (SHARPENER CAMP), SATURDAY, JULY 22, 1944
Bradley's six-division attack under Collins' VII Corps was postponed from the twenty-first to today account of heavy rain, and today we still have rain and have had all night, so presumably that push has to be postponed again. The British attack with three armored divisions east and south of Caen bogged down, first because of the antitank screen and then because of rain.

Ike visited Monty and Bradley late Thursday, spent the night back at Telegraph Cottage, having flown directly from France to Heston Airfield near SHAEF Main, spent most of the day at his main office, and drove down to the camp, reaching here about 7 last evening, Friday.

Yesterday he sent a letter to Monty. It recapitulates to Monty the gist of Ike's talk with him on Thursday. The theme is that military necessity dictates that Montgomery push on with every ounce of strength and zeal. In addition to the purely military need of elbow room for maneuver, there is the political situation to consider. The home fronts of both countries are naturally becoming impatient and querulous; they see the great successes in Russia and less spectacular but steady ones in Italy, which, of course, is a German retreat to the Gothic Line, and the progress in the Pacific, the latest being the landings on Guam, announced by Admiral Nimitz yesterday.

Telek got out of quarantine yesterday, and remembers his old tricks, such as chasing his tail and curling over on his back on the slightest chance that someone would rub his belly. He's thin from his poor rations and needs plucking. Caacie is due out on Wednesday. Kay Summersby got Telek in the forenoon. Ike was busy and probably wouldn't have gone for him anyway, fearing the kennel people would have arranged for photographers and newsmen to be on hand.

Optimism on the Lower Level

Papers are filled with the attempted assassination of Hitler, which has strong earmarks of revolt in Germany, and to me is the most hopeful sign of the beginning of the end. Himmler has been placed in command of all forces in Germany, including the regular Army. Doenitz followed Hitler in broadcasting assurances to the German people. Göring did likewise. But no one spoke for the Army. Former Chief of Staff von Bock, who quit the Army after Munich and strongly opposed rash moves by Hitler until Germany could become prepared, and especially advised against antagonizing or attacking Russia, is charged with leadership of the plot and "lives no more." I'm excited about it, but Ike isn't. Probably he's too wrapped up in his own troubles. SS divisions, some eleven, are in the line against us in Normandy, and prisoners say the Gestapo agents are among them to report dereliction to Berlin, with reprisals leveled against the family of the backsliders.

The bad weather brought London its worst attack of flying bombs. One came near our camp last night, exploding with a hell of a wallop. Flak holes have been found in some of the tents, but none in mine.

Roosevelt has been renominated, with Truman as running mate, Henry Wallace having been sacked. President's acceptance speech was broadcast from a naval base on the West Coast; is he going to the Pacific? And if so, will he continue on around the world and visit us? Seems inevitable that we will have another big powwow—Roosevelt, Churchill, and Stalin.

OWI going to town to exploit bombing of Hitler. . . . More importantly, 8th and 15th Air Forces, plus Bomber Command, have found weather day and night good enough to bomb airplane factories, synthetic- and natural-oil plants, some by visual, some by blind methods. . . . The Russians are still driving; Germans in Estonia and Lithuania may be trapped. Some twenty German generals already taken. Rumors of mutiny among Germans up there. . . . Another interesting thing: forty-six officers and crew of U-boat came ashore in small boats near Start Point on the Channel and gave up. Admiral Ramsay told Ike they were fed up. . . . U-boats seen in drydock at Le Havre. Easy air target when weather clears.

I expect we will be home by Christmas.

After lunch today, Ike had a press conference entirely off the record and refused to permit any reference to his meeting with the press, although they could say that they had seen him around camp. He said the coup against Hitler may have far-reaching effect but just how cannot be guessed at the moment. His G-2, General Strong, had ventured the foregoing opinion but had cautioned that the Germans liked a strong man, and severe action to obtain discipline, even by widespread purge, makes the German feel that he is being led by strong men. In other words, there might be a renascence of fighting spirit in Germany. Ike confirmed to the press that he plans to move himself and some of his personal staff to France during the coming week—assuming all facilities will be available.

Ike expressed in his own way disappointment that the campaign had gone no more rapidly, but said if he had three days of good weather, he would really make a statement. He had previously told me that if he had just twelve hours of good weather, meaning tomorrow particularly, we would get a fine dividend. Bradley's attack again was delayed, with hope of launching it tomorrow, weather permitting. We must have a ceiling of 9000 feet for the bombers to lay a "blanket" for our break-through. Today it rained at the camp, but in the afternoon it began to clear.

Ike said casualties since D-Day had mounted to 110,000, of which 68,000 were American. He figured the Germans had about the same, which is unusual for the defending force and attributable to our superiority in air and artillery. He also thought the Germans would get stretched, in defending their outer defense lines in Russia, Italy, and France, to a point where they could no longer supply reinforcements. Then would come the opportunity for a break-through on a major scale. The defeat of Germany would be military. The Germans would delay defeat in the hope of getting better peace terms. He was inclined to deplore all the talk of postwar plans, such as the monetary conference, as tending to take the mind of the public from the day-to-day battle. Readers at home look only for good news and forget or pass over the qualifications placed on any prediction as to when the war will end. He still thinks it will end this winter but said his previous statement that the European war would end in 1944 was intended more as a challenge than as a prediction. He declined to permit any of his words relating to when the Germans will give up to be printed because the qualifications are overlooked.

General Ike has informed Monty, as the Army Group Commander, that the time has come when the Supreme Commander must, so far as American units are concerned, permit them to be identified for publication. The U. S. War Department and the British War Office systems differ. Under the American system, the regiments in a division do not change, although in a British division the regiments may change even during a campaign. Consequently, the enemy never quite knows, in identifying a regiment, just which British division is involved. After an American regiment or division has been clearly identified by loss of prisoners to the enemy, there is no further security, and there should be no objection to publishing the names and activities of subordinate units. There may be some delay until G-2 is satisfied the enemy has established identities, but the new liberal policy will permit correspondents to write news stories of unusual accomplishments of battalions, regiments, and their commanding officers. The American people have keen interest and a right to know all we can tell them about the action of their boys in battle.

SHAEF FORWARD (SHARPENER CAMP), MONDAY, JULY 24, 1944
Bradley's big attack to break out of the beachhead was set to go off at 1 o'clock this afternoon, but at noon it was canceled because of unsuitable flying weather. Some 1600 planes, many in the air at the time of "scrubbing," had to be stopped.

I went with Ike to a luncheon given him by the Naval Commander in charge of the southeastern ports and operations, Admiral Sir Charles James Colebrooke Little. It was aboard the ancient and famous flagship of Nelson, the *Victory*. Keel laid in 1759, finished in six years, the *Victory* was of 2100 tons, had a complement of 850, and on her Nelson won the battle of Trafalgar in 1805. She had 104 guns, fifty-two on a side, ignited by flintlock or match, delivering a thirty-two-pound explosive shot, range 1000 to 1500 yards. One turret of a modern cruiser has greater fire power.

After lunch and pictures, we went to Southwick House, where Ike wanted to have a word with Monty's Chief of Staff, General de Guingand. The word lasted for an hour. Meanwhile, friends at Naval Headquarters said they felt that Monty, his British Army Commander, Dempsey, the British corps commanders, and even those of the divisions are so conscious of Britain's ebbing manpower that they hesitate to commit an attack where a division may be lost. To replace the division is practically impossible. When it is lost, it's done and finished. Even naval ratings, Air Force personnel, and nondescripts are being "cannibalized" for replacements. In addition, the tank losses, including crews, which are even more precious, have been heavy. A lucky bomb hit by a German air attack the night before the push unfortunately played havoc with a crew-replacement center. This made the officer in charge a bit grim.

Word had been received that Monty had sacked a couple of his officers. Reason: they had served in the desert and had developed the habit of looking over the shoulders, meaning they were overfearful of attack from the flank or rear.

Bradley's attack is now set for tomorrow, weather permitting. The Navy people said at lunch that the weather was "settling" and we might expect good weather, at least from a naval point of view, for two or three days or even longer. The official prediction mentioned by de Guingand also seemed favorable.

When I arrived at camp this forenoon, Ike had just gotten in the jeep, bound for the near-by field where Cubs and L-5 liaison planes come and go all day. He went up in a liaison plane, which carries one passenger, and did some piloting, but hasn't said much about the experience.

The PM Gets to Feel Well

SHAEF FORWARD (SHARPENER CAMP), TUESDAY, JULY 25, 1944
Ike, Jim, Red Mueller, and Lieutenant Leo Moore, the Signal Corps photographer, are taking off at 10 this morning for another of Ike's visits to Monty and Brad. They are due back for dinner.

Last night around 1 o'clock, after Ike and Jim returned from a fishing trip with Beetle, my tent phone rang. It was 10 Downing, wanting to know if the PM could talk to the Supreme Commander, but didn't want to awaken him if he was sleeping. Telling 'em to hold the phone, I reconnoitered Ike's distant caravan, picking up cinders in my bedroom slippers and dew on my bathrobe. Hearing no snores, I judged Ike was awake, but, unfortunately, when I spoke to him I discovered he had been sound asleep. Anyway, he came to the phone in his office tent and when I left for my warm Army blankets, he had just said: "What do your people think about the slowness of the situation over there?"

This morning, Ike said he had talked more than half an hour to the PM and that during the PM's recent trip, Churchill had seen Monty after all and had obviously been impressed with the strength of the military situation. The PM was supremely happy. Then de Guingand phoned Ike, to assure him that Monty had "fattened up" the attack, and that one was on today in the British sector, as well as in the American. Ike said he had started to be alarmed at Monty's hesitance ten days ago, had confided in Tedder his fears, and now Tedder is just reaching the phase of irritation in which Ike found himself several days ago. Before Ike departed, he asked me to phone Beetle and to "get him out of the meeting if he's in it" and caution him against even hinting at "the subject we have been discussing." Beetle readily agreed and said he understood there had been some changes, including the enlargement of the push, not to mention the PM's satisfaction with the situation. My guess is that the PM is jubilant over the turn of events in Germany, where Göring has announced that every German soldier, sailor, airman, and all officers henceforth shall abandon the traditional military salute and substitute the stiff-armed "Heil Hitler." This should offend the sense of every military man, as a salute is traditionally a greeting of men-at-arms and not a sign of sub-servience to a political dictator.

Ike thought this the most striking development of the various signs of breakup. For the first time he seemed enthusiastic, but heretofore he has been most conservative. Think he caught some of the PM's exuberance.

I failed yesterday to write, what with interruptions, that two German fliers in Me-109s had flown into an English airfield and, with wheels and flaps down, landed and surrendered, saying they were fed up. Only a little sign, but on top of the surrender of the forty-six U-boaters who came ashore of their own free will and accord, it adds up to something, and on the good side for us. Bomber Command quickly raided Kiel, the now badly bombed U-boat base, but where crews are kept in rest centers, and gave them a good pasting, by bombs as well as with leaflets. Hope our psychological boys will quickly seize the opportunity of exploiting the "Heil Hitler" salute, as this should be good stuff.

Yesterday I told a story to Colonel Gault, our ingratiating Scots Guards-man and British Military Assistant. It was a story written me by my old secretary, Miss Gladys Hall, and told by that inimitable radio character, Arthur Godfrey. I told this story yesterday to all and sundry who would listen, as laughs have been hard to get these days. Arthur has become a cook, it seems, and has a favorite recipe. Take a good piece of beef for roasting, pour over it a quart of Scotch, then a bottle of Vermouth for flavoring, roast for two hours, and remove from the oven. "The roast may not be any good," said Art, "but oh, baby! What gravy!"

This morning at breakfast Jim said that the best laugh of the current period was my story, the whip line of which he recalled as: "What excel-lent sauce it makes!"

This may be a great day on the battle front. I think a walloping victory there now, what with the Russians within 100 miles of Warsaw and going like the devil, and with the Germans still regurgitating their revolution, would be the *coup de grâce* to the befuddled Germans.

De Guingand called, told Ike that Monty was starting something today.

Tedder phoned Ike this morning, to go back to the opening subject, and was coming down this afternoon to pursue his currently favorite sub-ject, the slowness of Monty. But Ike told him he had talked with the PM and the PM was satisfied and Tedder rather uh-huhed, being not at all satisfied, and implying the PM must have sold Ike a bit of goods. Anyway, Ike said he had had this sort of thing happen before, and he had worked things out satisfactorily all around, and probably would this one in time—to which can be added that there's nothing so wrong a good victory won't cure.

"Border on the Reckless"

SHAEF FORWARD (SHARPENER CAMP), WEDNESDAY, JULY 26, 1944
Ike returned glum from his visit with Monty and Bradley. High-level,
pin-point bombing by American crews had fallen short, killing thirty-six
of our own lads and wounding eighty. During the evening, Bradley phoned
Beetle the further news that General McNair had been killed at a forward
observation post, watching the spectacle, probably by a short. Ike was
visibly depressed.

But the other news Bradley phoned, by prearrangement with Ike, and in
an informal code system they had hastily arranged at the meeting at Bradley's headquarters, brought smiles of satisfaction to both Ike and Beetle,
who happened to be in Ike's caravan when I carried in the information.
It was that the 9th had gained 2300 yards from the starting point; the 4th,
1200, and the 30th, 1300. This didn't seem much, but represented a considerable advance since early afternoon (the attack started at 11 A.M.), so
Ike felt much better. Beetle departed, saying that a slow start or a bad
beginning might be the harbinger of a good ending.

Some 1800 bombers of all sizes, but principally American—Bomber
Command wasn't in this show as it was in that at Caen—had dropped their
eggs in narrow rectangles leading into and across the first defenses of the
Germans, through which our infantry was to advance. Lanes were left un-
pitted for armor to pass through. Mark that we start off with infantry, three
divisions, with two divisions of armor, the 2nd and 4th, and the 1st Infantry to follow and to pass through the initial attackers and all to fan out.
At Caen, Monty had tried thrusting his armor ahead, but suffered heavy
losses of tanks and crews, and stopped until infantry could come up to
deal with the antitank screen.

Weather today is just bordering on rain, but aircraft were heard overhead during the early-morning hours.

After I had got to sleep about 11:30 last night, 10 Downing phoned.
The PM again wanted to speak to Ike "if he weren't asleep." Found Ike
still awake. He told the PM that Monty now saw eye to eye with him and
that he felt satisfied, but the battle was touch and go, with hard fighting
under way and much more in prospect. The PM asked Ike to lunch at 1:30
today, and so he is leaving camp soon after the morning skull session in the
war room, where he is at the moment. Tedder is to see Ike before lunch,
and just now Colonel Lee phoned to say that Leigh-Mallory likewise
wishes to see Ike before lunch. Perhaps the air is ganging up on Ike before
he sees the PM. L-M said he was flying across the Channel this afternoon

and would have to leave Ike's office by 12:30, which sounds as if he wants to get in his words in a timely fashion.

Ike wrote Portal the other day, saying that Leigh-Mallory had developed into a good co-operator and had a fighting heart. Portal replied with similar magnanimity, and so L-M's stock has been improved by his action. Good enough.

McNair's death came as a shock. He had been wounded in Africa while observing in Tunisia. The Germans seemed to have his number, but that doesn't quite make sense either, assuming an American bomb killed him, which is what Ike thinks. At least McNair's number came up. I think he's our first lieutenant general to get it. This morning, a signal from General Marshall, written before he was advised last night that McNair had "bought it," said McNair could be given an Army command, with appropriate release of the news in Washington. Last night, Ike wired Marshall that no release whatsoever of the death should be made until plans could be revised in the light of McNair's death. Marshall replied this morning in agreement. McNair is being buried in France amongst the GIs whose dangers he so constantly shared.

Russians going great guns. . . . Hitler's revolt quieting down, so far as we can see. . . . Nothing very exciting, except that hundreds, if not thousands, of American lads getting killed to create the greatly desired break-through—an attack which, if successful, may trap scads of Germans, in the Russian manner. Ike wired Bradley Monday morning, through Monty, that every chance should be taken to win the battle, to border on the reckless, and not to get stopped.

First Army Smashes Through

SHAEF MAIN (WIDEWING), MONDAY, JULY 31, 1944

News reached SHAEF Main at 11 last night that Bradley's First Army * had reached Avranches, but 21st Army Group was disinclined to permit release in the midnight communiqué. It is announced in the noon report to the public today and may overshadow the British attack in the Caumont area yesterday, which got off to a slow but apparently satisfactory start.

I have not dictated since the twenty-sixth and have been at SHAEF Main since that date, the General, Lee, and Jim being at SHAEF For-

---

* It was Bradley's then; the following day Hodges took command of the First Army, Patton's Third was formally activated, and Bradley took over the 12th Army Group, including both First and Third Armies.

ward. I visited General Davis at a rest home in the Cotswolds, near Oxford, yesterday. T. J. told me of an incident which emphasizes the depth of British feeling now manifesting itself in various ways. It arises from the relatively spectacular success of the Americans in their drive down the Cherbourg Peninsula, and the relative stalemate of the British. So much news has been made by the Americans that the BBC recently has been practically all-American. T. J. said his hostess, who is half-American, had become so irritated at the superabundant mention of American successes and absence of counterbalancing news of the British that while her American officer guests were listening to the late news, she switched off the radio. Later she apologized to T. J., who said he understood her feelings but was quite certain the younger American officers present would not. This shows that while Ike has reasonably good teamwork in the military, his example has not affected deep-seated national instincts and probably never will.

Among comment heard about the current battle is the rumor that Patton must be "in there" because our armor is racing ahead so effectively. Patton, of course, is there personally, though not yet in command, but he may have influenced the battle tactically. His Third Army will be formally activated tomorrow, August 1, but in the interest of security there will be no announcement of this for some time.

In the new setup, the 12th Army Group (American) and the 21st Army Group (British) will report directly to the Supreme Commander, although 21st Army Group will retain direction for a transition period. Just how personally Ike has taken command of the ground forces is not yet clear to me. Each time I have suggested he do it, he has belligerently countered, "Then they will have to get someone to be the Allied Commander." But he is moving to France more or less permanently in the next few days (Jim is over there today to look at a site selected by Headquarters Command), and I hope the future will see Ike more definitely and prominently identified with the ground battle.

Kenneth Davis, formerly on Milton's staff at Kansas Agricultural College, has arrived to get material for a biography of Ike. I arranged for him to have a talk with Ike Friday. While talking with me, Ike walked through the office. The biographer, not recognizing his subject, asked, "Who's that?" Davis will see both British and American officers who have served with Ike. Beetle was nice enough to take him in a car on a trip to SHAEF Forward. The lad got a couple of hours of information. At least, he said he had a thousand words of notes. He is quiet and, I believe, thorough.

Rumors in public as well as in military circles, unfortunately substantiated by our own Intelligence reports, indicate that the German use of its V-2, the giant rocket projectile, may be imminent. A special crew in one of our Flying Fortresses flew to Poland, behind German lines, landed, and picked up pieces of one of the rockets obtained by our agents. Our Intelligence people deduce from these that it really weighs fifty tons and presumably carries some ten tons of explosive which will wreck a five-mile area. This, of course, would play hell in London. Intelligence officers now report that the projectile may be fired from a giant concrete slab and apparently does not require the "hole in the ground." There are said to be four kinds of fuel in the rocket mechanism. These are ignited, the thing swishes off into the air and is then guided to its target area by radio. It is said it may reach an altitude of 106,000 feet. Countermeasures center on jamming of the controlling radio station, but no one seems to have anything more definite.

Intelligence reports indicate that the Germans have now chosen to reinforce their Eastern Front, to stop the Russians. One division has moved toward Russia from France and the Hermann Göring Division from Italy, as well as one or more from Norway.

As the columnists say, "it was predicted by this writer" that pressure would be exerted to alter our ground strategy to take the Pas de Calais at the earliest date because of the damage and inconvenience wrought by the flying bombs launched from that area and the gloomy anticipation of the rockets also nesting along that part of the coast. The British Chiefs of Staff have now suggested that its Joint Planning Staff should be instructed to prepare a report on an operation designed to capture Pas de Calais. This, no doubt, will formally reach SHAEF in due course.

Meanwhile, our successes are leading us in the opposite direction, where we are now in position to cut off the Brittany Peninsula, gain valuable ports, and capture at least two, if not three, important U-boat bases, thus far curtailing U-boat operations. In the Brittany Peninsula, there is an extraordinarily large and, apparently, effective group of French resisters and relatively few German troops, perhaps not more than two divisions. Incidentally, our count of prisoners in the push down the Cherbourg Peninsula, which started Wednesday, July 26, has reached 10,000, with more steadily being taken. We have damaged or destroyed a couple of hundred German tanks and, at least, a thousand vehicles. The fleeing Germans present fine targets to our Air Force, and even Rommel, whose death or injury has been rumored or reported at various places in the past two years, has now apparently definitely "bought it." Our Intelligence states that a "reliable source" reports he was wounded in France—presumably by a strafing plane. He is said to be in a hospital, with one eye gone, concussion of the brain, and bulletholes through a lung. Today the papers print that prisoners say Rommel has died. Good, if true.

A tremendous wave of optimism about early ending of the war has swept America, and damned if I blame them.

Not long ago "Bomber" Harris wrote Ike that while the use of the strategic bombers for helping the ground force break through the German defenses was not only necessary but proper at times, he didn't want to have us get our eyes off the main object for the strategic bombers—industrial Germany. Harris recalled that he had said last winter that if one German armament factory were left untouched by our bombers for five months, production would rapidly rise and approach normal. Now for nearly three and a half months, our strategic bombing of German targets has not been carried on at full tilt.

The report covering the sixth week of flying-bomb activity in the U. K., from July 18-25, gives the grand totals for the entire period. The number reported plotted by radar is 4541, and those reported as having crossed the southeastern coast, 3407. "Incidents" outside London number 1777, and in London, 1594. Casualties: killed, 4175; seriously injured, 12,284. Damage to essential installations and services include: seventy factories, seven railroads, three hospitals, ten schools, eighteen military installations, six docks, and forty-seven utilities. Production and services have not been seriously interfered with because most of the damage results from blast, quickly repairable. London continues to receive the greater number of bombs and has the most casualties and damage. An increasing number of flying bombs have been launched from new sites in Belgium and Holland and reach London along the line of the Thames Estuary.

Saturday night, I played poker with Generals Spaatz, Eaker, Major General James E. Fechet and Major General Fred L. Anderson, Lieutenant Colonel Hal Roach, Captain Matty Fox, and Mr. Morris Guest. It was a fine game, financially and otherwise, but the flying bombs came over in about three salvos of three or four each. Captain Sally Bagby, General Spaatz's delightful and capable aide, in addition to bookkeeping for the game, tending bar, and minding the two black kittens * given Spaatz by Tedder, served as our listener. When the "imminent danger" alarm would ring, she would step to the porch and, if the sound of the approaching bomb appeared too ominous, would call us from the game. We would simply stand in the yard and listen and watch and wait. Once one seemed so close—it was coming directly toward us—that Spaatz

---

* Tooey tried smuggling one of the kittens in his blouse for luck. It didn't work.

and I started running for the bushes as if they would have done us any good. Fortunately, the bomb exploded in the air about 300 yards short of the house.

JULY, 1944: *Allied forces moved steadily ahead, capturing Caen, La Haye-du-Puits, Saint-Lô, and Avranches; took entire Normandy peninsula and trapped thousands of German troops. Planes steadily pounded at robot launching sites. Heavy air raids were directed against oil wells, refineries, railroads, and manufacturing centers. Unsuccessful attempt on Hitler's life reported. First fighter shuttle flight between Italy and Russia was accomplished. Siena, Ancona, Leghorn, and Pisa fell to advancing Allied drives in Italy. Bombers from Italy hit Ploeşti and other Balkan oil fields. Airfields on Numfor Island seized after heavy bombing. Yanks took Garapan and Tanapag, to conquer Saipan; Guam invaded after several carrier-plane attacks. Orote Peninsula fell after hard fighting. Superfortresses pounded Yawata and Sasebo. Eastern fleet raided Jap naval base at Sabang, Sumatra; Yank planes bombed Halmahera. Chinese took Shansi in Yunnan; Liling; Hengyang rail center; Yungfang in Hunan, and Sumkrung in Burma. Entire Tojo cabinet resigned. Minsk, Vilna, Pinsk, Grodno, Lublin, Brest-Litovsk, and Lwow fell to engulfing Soviet advances. (I think this was the most significant month of the war in Europe.—H.C.B.)*

"To Hell and Gone in Brittany"

SHAEF MAIN (WIDEWING), WEDNESDAY, AUGUST 2, 1944

Just before lunch, I met Ike in the hall. He was all smiles.

"If the intercepts are right, we are to hell and gone in Brittany and slicing 'em up in Normandy," he said.

I followed him into the office to see just what was the good news. There wasn't much more to be said except that Ike had just been to the war room and had received the latest report which had come in since I had been there at 10 o'clock.

Patton had taken command yesterday, and it was obvious that he had plunged ahead against little or no resistance. Later I learned that the arrow denoting the location of a Phantom recce team showed we had reached Rennes twelve hours ago which to me sounds very much like Patton has not only taken command but has characteristically taken advantage of the situation. In the war room, I was asked by a cheerful RAF officer as to whether the arrow toward Rennes should be labeled "Patton" and another halfway to Saint-Malo should be marked "Patton's aide."

Yesterday, I read an interesting report of the Home Minister on plans for meeting the threat, now almost real, of the rocket bomb. According to his information, it has not a ten-ton, but a seven-ton war head, but its explosive effect on London would be extremely serious. The report related that in five weeks of "receipt" of the flying bomb, London had experienced 1600 incidents, which he expressed in terms of 1600 x 850 kilograms—principally south of the Thames, in London. The average casualties per bomb were 2.4 in London, with three times as many seriously injured and about the same number slightly injured. What interested me was his estimate that 15,500 homes had been totally destroyed, and that 691,000 needed repairs, of which 502,000 had been repaired. Of further interest was his estimate that 229,000 mothers and children under five had been evacuated from London by organized government assistance and that an additional 500,000 had departed of their own initiative. The Home Minister seemed resentful that the military had not taken more notice of their need of defense, nor had they developed a satisfactory counteraction against the flying bomb and had practically nothing to offer against the rocket bomb.

Meantime, Ike is fretting for more progress, as he pushes on the reins. He is all out for destroying the Germans where they sit or perhaps run.

General Marshall has requested information—a request which anyone who has lived in Washington would realize is necessary to answer questions from press and officials. Ike worked late yesterday, early this morning before breakfast, and this forenoon on a detailed report of his current and future operations.

Hardly had he authorized the final draft of his report to General Marshall when he returned from the war room with the exciting information that we had broken through not only into the Brittany Peninsula but to the east from Avranches, to slice the disorganized German forces.

Shortly thereafter Ike cabled General Marshall to award Bradley something that only a regular officer could fully appreciate—a permanent major generalship.

The aide and pilot of General McNair returned to Washington and frankly told friends McNair had been killed by an American bomb. When Marshall heard of this, he quickly cabled Ike that the news would reach the public prints, and in the light of its relation to military security he wondered why the two officers had not been pledged to secrecy before they returned to the United States. Ike replied, advocating frank release of the news to the American public.

Ike saw the PM early last evening, but before, during, and after dinner, although they had spent three hours together, he had nothing to say as to the conference. It related to the PM's presentation of war news to the House of Commons, which was to occur today. He read most of it to Ike—taking nearly an hour—and Ike readily assented to the PM's desire to mention General Morgan as the British officer who did the early planning of OVERLORD with an Anglo-American staff. The PM had not reported in detail for many months and he properly wanted to emphasize the British participation to his people.

We have "broken all bridges" in front of us by bombing out the rail and road bridges across the Seine and we would have difficulty reaching the Pas de Calais for this reason. The Germans are bringing troops across the Seine by barge at night and camouflaging their landing places so we have difficulty finding them readily from the air in the daylight. Nevertheless, our Air Force has been strafing landing places and barges by day and night.

SHAEF FORWARD (SHARPENER CAMP), FRIDAY, AUGUST 4, 1944

We arrived at the General's camp at SHAEF Forward in time for lunch yesterday, and Ike and Jim flew across the Channel, returning to the camp at 8:45. Ike had seen both Monty and Bradley, the former having told Ike that he had sacked a corps and a division commander.

Beetle also had just returned, preceding Ike by a couple of hours, and immediately sent word that he wished to see Ike "the moment he gets in." Ike excused himself from dinner and talked with Beetle privately.

Beetle said that the collapse of Norway is imminent and that our General Morgan had been sent on a mission to Scotland to plan with the command there on action, this being a matter heretofore left to the British Command in Scotland. Beetle said he didn't know just what we could do about a collapse, as we didn't wish to spare too many troops. There also is difficulty in finding a suitable Norwegian officer to lead an occupying force.

Ike has been impatient, repeat impatient, and I mean impatient. He isn't excited about Patton's armored thrust into the Brittany Peninsula because he figures all that will fall like a ripe apple. The thing he is interested in is bold and continuous attacks against the Germans in the central sector around Vire to destroy them so they can't retreat and fight us again, particularly in the Siegfried Line.

At the SHAEF Forward war room last evening, I learned that the Allies had captured some 78,000 Germans, of which the British got 14,000, the remainder falling into American hands. This was information reported to August 1, since which we have captured an average of 4000 a day.

This morning Ike received a message from the Combined Chiefs directing him to consider plans for pushing our ground forces into the Pas de Calais area. The signal says that the almost continuous attacks by flying bombs and the threat of rockets in London constitute a severe threat to Britain's production and tend to impair her ability to continue the struggle. I asked him in the car driving down to SHAEF Forward yesterday if the PM had put the bee on him in this regard, and he said "no."

Ike attended the morning meeting at the war room at 9 and when he returned did not seem particularly cheerful. There had not been much gain reported overnight, and there were street fighting in Rennes and some opposition encountered by Patton's forces, the British sector making little news, the Canadians some. Effective August 1, Patton had taken command of the Third Army, Hodges the First, and Bradley the 12th Army Group. This morning we had the first situation report from the 12th Army Group, that for the 21st Army Group coming in separately, indicating the separation, but direction still is in Monty's hands for coordination of the ground forces. Tedder too has been after Ike to set up a tactical headquarters for SHAEF in France through which Ike would take charge of the battle.

We Set Up Quarters in France

SHELLBURST (IN NORMANDY), MONDAY, AUGUST 7, 1944
Today, two months after D-Day, Ike set up and took up residence in his personal camp near Tournières and Maisons, and I am dictating to Miss Chick under the canopy of a tent in an apple orchard.

We are surrounded by hedgerows ten feet high, except on the east, where the hedge has been trimmed to permit a view of an adjoining field where liaison planes may land. A couple of acres are thus enclosed. The camp consists of General Ike's caravan, two for the WACs, and a spare which may be used for an office or for overnight guests. The Supreme Commander's regular office is in a tent, possibly twenty by thirty feet, with a board floor. There are few secrets that may be kept by General Ike, for his voice can be heard for rods around as he dictates or telephones. The aides and WACs have a similar tent for office work. Colonel Gault and I—and the enlisted men—live in small tents. There are a number of slit trenches for air-raid protection. We are connected with the various headquarters by telephone, and there is a signal center in another camp a quarter mile away, run by Major Marshall Barr. The correspondents live in tents in the latter camp. MPs patrol the perimeter of the camp twenty-four hours a day. The camp nestles in the general farm scene so neatly our visitors have to be guided to it by small signs, marked "Shell-burst."

There are several items of interest to catch up on. On Saturday, August 5, the Prime Minister came for lunch at the SHAEF Forward Camp and practically stayed for dinner. He had started to fly to France, but his plane had been recalled, owing to weather which had caused a preceding plane to crash and kill all of its occupants at the field in France where the PM had been expected to land.

I first heard from Air Vice-Marshal Wigglesworth on the phone that the PM had been recalled and "Wiggles" thought the PM might land at Thorney Island near our camp or proceed to Northolt, near London. On the General's authority, I immediately took a car to Thorney Island and, sure enough, the PM had landed there. I bundled him, the First Sea Lord, Admiral Cunningham, Brigadier L. C. Hollis, Secretary of the British Chiefs of Staff, and Commander Thompson in cars, the first two and I in one and the latter two in an RAF car. We hadn't left the air-field before Ike arrived in his car and took aboard the PM and the First Sea Lord.

We had expected the Prime Minister for dinner, but lunch was hastily arranged for the entire party, the PM taking delight in feeding milk to the General's black kitten, Shaef, from a saucer on the dinner table at his place.

After lunch, Admirals Ramsay and Tennant arrived. A full-fledged conference then took place under the canopy of the General's office tent.

The Prime Minister had already opened the conference at lunch, telling in phrases which only he can use so easily that history would show that Ike would miss a great opportunity if he didn't have DRAGOON, formerly ANVIL, shifted from the scheduled amphibious attack in the Toulon area to the ports in Brittany, notably Brest, Lorient, and Saint-Nazaire, or indeed through the Channel ports, where he assumed they could walk in like tourists. He had not given much thought to the probable demolitions to these harbors on the southern coast or to the great demand already made on Cherbourg or any other Channel ports we may capture. Such landings would quickly give the now rapidly traveling right flank of the Allied armies a stronger force with which to sweep to France, in the view of Mr. Churchill.

Ike said no, continued saying no all afternoon, and ended saying no in every form of the English language at his command. Ike lost the usual support of his former ally, his great friend Admiral Cunningham, who sided with the PM, but General Ike had ardent backing from Admirals Ramsay and Tennant. Ike's position was that sound strategy called for making the Germans fight on as many fronts as possible. The landings in the Toulon area and advance up the Rhone Valley would further extend the enemy. Also, there were logistical problems of the first magnitude involved in loading and follow-up of the DRAGOON force—three divisions were spoken of—which would handicap the eastward movement from the Brittany Peninsula already planned and, in fact, under way even before the Brittany Peninsula had been completely taken.

Ike argued so long and patiently that he was practically limp when the PM departed and observed that although he had said no in every language, the Prime Minister, undoubtedly, would return to the subject in two or three days and simply regard the issue as unsettled.

Meantime the British Chiefs of Staff had cabled General Wilson, in the Mediterranean, to alert him of the possibility of quick change of plans for ANVIL and to await approval by the Combined Chiefs. The U. S. Chiefs quickly replied, registering their complete disapproval, and this morning General Wilson also reported that to switch the plan at this late date would involve unloading and reloading LCTs and LSTs and other ships. Pointing out that many of the ships for this operation are to sail by August 10 to attack August 15, he said the whole idea of a change appeared most unwise. He also said that the rate of build-up in France would be slower through the Brittany Peninsula than through the Toulon area. Thus the PM also was rebuffed by his British Allied Commander.

Ike had been surprised to find that his own Chief of Staff, Beetle, agreed with the PM. I told him that Admiral Tennant had taken me aside after the conference and said that Ike had been "sound at every step of the argument and thoroughly magnificent." A little later Admiral Ramsay telephoned me to add his appreciation of Ike's stalwartness.

Today's war news is good. Patton's fingerlike thrust through Brittany, with the thumb of the hand punching through Laval toward Le Mans, has gone so rapidly that communications simply can't keep pace. Even the correspondents in the field can't catch the battle front, but they are writing in ecstasy about the speed. Patton's spearheads calling for new maps; say they're running right off the old ones. Wouldn't it be great for Patton if his name could be printed? I suggested to Ike release of his name, this being a good time to prove to Ike's critics that he was right in keeping Patton, but Ike said, "Why should I tell the enemy?"

When we landed at A-9, one of the temporary but metaled landing strips near our camp, we had circled the field three times to permit incoming fighter bombers to land and outgoing ones to speed off. I learned that amongst other targets of the day, 200 German motor vehicles had been pocketed and the fighter bombers had been having a shooting party, coming in and out of the airfield, loading their guns, like bees in a hive. At our camp the fighter bombers are moaning and roaring overhead, some doing aerial doodles while awaiting their turn to land.

Destroy the Enemy Now

SHELLBURST (IN NORMANDY), TUESDAY, AUGUST 8, 1944
Today Ike met General Bradley, toured the rear battle area northeast of Coutances, ate his lunch alongside the road, and stopped at Bradley's 12th Army Group headquarters. Ike was pressing for switch of Patton's forces to the northeast, the better to squeeze the enemy into a great pocket against the Seine River. Ike keeps continually after both Montgomery and Bradley to destroy the enemy now rather than to be content with mere gains of territory. He has instructed that the Brittany Peninsula should be taken with a minimum of forces, none to be wasted, which would be helpful in pulling the noose around the neck of Hitler's still struggling soldiers.

After dinner he drove over to Montgomery's 21st Army Group headquarters to make certain that Monty would continue to press on the British-Canadian front, where the Canadians had started a big attack the night of August 7/8. This attack was preceded by heavy bombardment by Bomber Command around midnight and rapidly followed by flails, tanks, and specially constructed troop carriers with weapons removed to accommodate more "bodies." The attack had been supported by a bombardment by U. S. heavies at 1 o'clock this afternoon. Unfortunately, some of our bombs fell short and killed some Poles in the Polish division which has just gone into action under the Canadian Army. The fact that the Canadians have an army in the field is news as well, this being reported in the British press as the first time in Canada's history that she has had a fighting force in action large enough to call an army, although this one includes Poles and will have Belgian and Dutch elements.

The PM got across the Channel to France by air yesterday, August 7, and Ike saw him off at A-9 airfield just before dinner. The PM had talked to Montgomery and Bradley and seemed happy. Ike is strongly supported by Marshall, King, and Arnold in his position that the invasion through southern France must be made and not diverted elsewhere.

SHELLBURST (IN NORMANDY), WEDNESDAY, AUGUST 9, 1944
This morning Ike phoned Bradley to learn the latest news and found
that elements of Patton's Third Army had taken Le Mans, and that the
four Panzer-division counterattack intended to split the Americans at
Avranches had been defeated, the enemy losing some eighty tanks to our
air attack alone. Then Colonel Gault checked with 21st Army Group
and found the Canadians had made about five miles from the kickoff
in their drive and were still pushing.

Long after I was asleep last night, I was awakened to sign for an "eyes
only" message for Ike from General Marshall. I held it until this morning. It said that on short notice divisions en route to the U. K. could
be shipped directly to ports in Brittany. He wished advice from Ike as
to when ports, such as Saint-Malo, Brest, and Saint-Nazaire, could receive
troops and supplies. These ports seem to be strongly defended by their
garrisons and by troops which have been withdrawn into these strong
points to make last-ditch stands and to deny us the use of the ports as
long as possible. The fighting at Saint-Malo is reported today as particularly fierce, hand to hand and house to house. In Brest, the Germans
have been ordered to fall back in groups of fifty or sixty men at half-hour
intervals. The situation at Saint-Nazaire is obscure.

This afternoon Major General Everett Hughes dropped into our camp
at the Advance CP, hoping to catch Ike. Everett is returning home to
check on the American end of supplies, administration, and what not.
Everett had just returned from a visit with General Patton and had been
in the Saint-Malo area yesterday. He said that Patton was on top of the
world but had not lost his sense of feeling for the human being, at least
completely, for after giving the order to bomb Brest and Saint-Nazaire,
he said, "I have sealed the fate of a lot of French civilians." Everett said
that Patton feels we are attempting to encircle the Germans "doughboy
fashion" rather than in "cavalry style." Apparently, Patton would wing
much farther to the south and then close in on the Germans, the terrain favoring rapid movement of tanks.

Last evening, the correspondents told me that at press conferences held
by General de Guingand, Chief of Staff of 21st Army Group, and Lieutenant General H. D. G. Crerar, CG of the Canadian Army, on Monday,
August 7, statements were flatly made that the war would be over in
"three weeks." They reported that the British generals felt we were deci-
mating the enemy and that all of his Panzer divisions had now been
drawn into battle, even those east of the Seine, where reserves are sparse
and these only troops in training.

They, as well as I, thought this kind of talk most unfortunate. If the

war doesn't end in three weeks—and it probably will *not*—the public
will have been led up a blind alley and naturally will be disappointed. I
told Ike about this superoptimism and he lamented it but said there was
little he could do.

SHELLBURST (IN NORMANDY), THURSDAY, AUGUST 10, 1944
Ike is in England today, reviewing the 82nd and 101st Airborne Divisions.
He left the camp yesterday and flew to Heston to reach SHAEF Main.
The PM was still a bit pouty over ANVIL, favoring diversion into Brittany, despite our absence of satisfactory ports. So Ike went to 10 Downing
Street to have a further talk with him. The Combined Chiefs of Staff
have supported Ike completely. But now the PM was bemoaning the
future of Alexander's campaign in Italy. He saw the Italian front drying up just when such fine opportunity presented itself to enter Jugo-
slavia.

Captain Bill Culver, aide to General de Guingand, came over to our
camp and had drinks and dinner this evening, Ike, of course, being away.
Bill said that Monty has six aides, of whom Culver technically is one but
works for de Guingand. Bill amusingly reported that Monty has been
showing signs of irritation lately. He had abruptly ordered a British
lieutenant general to clear out of his area because "I don't want to see
your face around."

General Calvin De Witt, Jr., and aide, Lieutenant Colonel Thomas
M. McGrail, arrived at T-2 this afternoon, and I met them. I took De Witt
to visit Carentan, the Omaha Beach, and Bayeux. He is here taking the
place of the late General McNair.

At Omaha Beach, Captain Chauncey Camp, USN, standing on the
veranda of his Nissen-hut office on the bluff overlooking the beach and
literally hundreds of ships, commented on the narrow path over which
GIs were streaming inland from the beach. "Up that path have trod a
half-million American soldiers—and Dinah Shore."

"Lay Down the Mantle of My High Office"

SHELLBURST (IN NORMANDY), FRIDAY, AUGUST 11, 1944
This morning I took General De Witt and his aide to Bradley's headquarters and sat in the morning military review. We have a good chance
of catching the Germans in a giant trap if Patton's forces manage to get
around to Argentan, the British-Canadians close in from the north to
Falaise, and the remaining gap of some fifteen or sixteen miles is sealed

off. At the moment the Germans are expected again to counterattack near Mortain, where they had amassed five and a half of their seven Panzer divisions, the remaining one and a half still being opposite the British-Canadians. Some 475 to 500 German tanks were thought to be against us in the Mortain area. The weather for Saturday was to continue good and Bradley and his staff were optimistic as to the result. Hoped to "suck in" more Germans.

Returning to the camp about noon, I met a succession of callers, including Generals Crawford, G-4, and Strong, G-2, who felt quite jubilant at the prospects, although he feared the Germans might find one of the many weak spots in Patton's extended Third Army, which has been hurriedly raced eastward from the Brittany Peninsula to swing back and block the Germans as they retreat. However, Strong thought the war would be over in three months.

Ike and Jim returned to camp in time for supper, Ike having strained his knee and been under considerable pain while taking the hour-long review of the 82nd Airborne Division.

General Ike was impressed by his visit to the 82nd and 101st Airborne Divisions, which had greatly assisted in making the landings a success. The divisions had been taken back to England to refit, to collect and train replacements, and are getting ready for another drop. Their morale is high; they have proved themselves in battle.

Ike has been increasingly concerned about the PM's attitude regarding ANVIL and, above all, the feeling that the questioning and apparent dissension might cause a rift in the unity of the Allies at a time when success is almost in our grasp. The PM is upset over Ike's insistence for the landings in southern France, still set for August 15. Mr. Churchill knows that the American chiefs—Marshall, King, and Arnold—defer all questions in the European Theater to General Ike. Consequently, the Prime Minister unlooses on Ike all his art of persuasion. The other day he went so far as to say, with considerable emotion, that he might have to go to the Monarch and "lay down the mantle of my high office."

SHELLBURST (IN NORMANDY), SATURDAY, AUGUST 12, 1944
I mentioned to Ike last night that the Germans had about 500 tanks against us in the Mortain area, and he said, "We've got 3500; what are we scared of?"

Major Larry Hansen, the General's pilot, discovered a weak tire on the B-25 and desired to return to the U. K. to change it. I rode with him, spent the night at Telegraph, and visited T. J., who is again in the hospital. T. J. has worn himself down as Public Relations chief, and Ike is searching for a replacement. Beetle has suggested sending me to "support" Colonel Dupuy, who has been the acting director of Public Relations in T. J.'s absence. Ike has been toying with the notion of sending me in T. J.'s job. However, I feel that this is unnecessary, although it would involve an almost unprecedented jump in rank. Meantime Beetle had cabled General Surles, asking for Brigadier General Wilton B. Persons, the War Department's liaison man with Congress, or someone of equivalent experience. The matter was in abeyance until Beetle visited Ike on Monday. He hoped in the meantime to have a reply from General Surles.

SHELLBURST (IN NORMANDY), SUNDAY, AUGUST 13, 1944
I returned to the Shellburst Camp yesterday at 6:30, having flown with Larry, who replaced one tire on the B-25 but said he was worried about the other. Apparently Larry can always find some unfinished business in the U. K.

Ike had dined with General Bradley on Saturday evening and Bradley had returned the visit. In fact, Bradley was here playing bridge as calmly and peacefully as if he had just come off the golf course on a Sunday afternoon. He stayed for dinner. Said that General Wharton had been given command of a division and within six hours had been killed by a sniper. Tough luck.

In the war room at SHAEF Main today, I was told that our long-distance weather forecaster had said that there wouldn't be a day in the next three weeks when our fighter-bombers couldn't fly. Apparently (knock on wood) we are finally getting the weather we have been praying for.

The Poles, through General Sosnkowski, sent a message to Ike imploring him to supply arms and ammunition by air to the Polish partisans now fighting in Warsaw. He wanted the airfields near Warsaw, as well as large targets inside the city, bombed. He also wanted Polish parachute troops dropped. Ike had to answer honestly that Warsaw is out of his theater and that the matter should be taken up with the Combined Chiefs of Staff.

Grand Central Station in the Apple Orchard

SHELLBURST (IN NORMANDY), MONDAY, AUGUST 14, 1944
Our Shellburst Camp is becoming a Grand Central Station, but this is true wherever Ike stops. I am dictating at 3:30 and so far we have had

several callers. The first was a divisional commander relieved by General Bradley. The commander was sent back to "Papa" for a talk. Ike sent him back to the U. K. to await further orders and, in the meantime, is getting a full report on all the facts in his case. He makes a practice of talking with commanders who are relieved and personally assumes the responsibility.

Lieutenant General John C. H. Lee arrived for a 10:30 appointment. Lee said that Patton was going great guns and that Lee's supply trucks reaching Third Army were commandeered by Patton, who loaded them with troops and hurried them off to get in position to trap the Germans.

Today the Canadians have another big attack on, four divisions of infantry and two of tanks, in a valiant attempt to take Falaise. This started at 2 o'clock this afternoon, supported by a large attack by our heavy bombers. Patton said that if they would change the boundary, he would take Falaise and close the gap, but with the big attack of the Canadians going southward and Patton coming northward, they must not be allowed to get mixed up and perhaps kill one another. Our air would not have freedom, either.

After Lee came General De Witt and his aide, who will spend the night. De Witt had seen Patton and was glowing in his comment about the rapid movement of the Third Army. He said also that Patton was chafing because he had to stop for forward elements north of Argentan, where they were about to overrun the boundary between the British-Canadians and the Americans.

Next came in a group Lieutenant General Humfrey Gale, the British Chief Administrative Officer, General Crawford, our G-4, and Colonel E. N. Clark, also G-4. We had ten for lunch, during which Ike explained why our heavy bombers have dropped bombs short when breaking the way for a ground attack. Our bombing sight is fixed scientifically to hit targets from high altitude. In this support work, heavies have been bombing from lower altitude, from which the sight is not so accurate. The bombers have come in over our troops and dropped their bombs in a path perpendicular to our lines to clear a pathway through enemy defenses. In bombing normal targets, the sight develops some shorts or bombs may inadvertently fall short when the bomb-bay doors are open, or there may be just simple human error. In any event, Ike has ordered that bombing be done parallel to our own lines.

Yesterday Ike issued an order of the day which was made public today so the BBC and the Allied network could get the message to the troops, most of whom find some opportunity to listen even in the front lines. Ike gave this message to me for prompt transmission and I got our PRO,

Lieutenant Colonel Thor Smith, through on our own circuit to Colonel Dupuy in London, so the message could be dictated and immediately released with the dateline: "SHAEF, Advance Command Post in Normandy." I got my instructions at 10 o'clock, and on the 11 o'clock newscast of the BBC we heard Ike's order of the day.

The best index of the way the battle goes is Ike's disposition, which today is sunny, if not almost jubilant.

Thinking ahead, General Ike has been talking and also has written General Marshall about the enforced hold-up of our advance which eventually must occur while we improve maintenance facilities and prepare for a further offensive that could be sustained for a considerable period. He at first thought the Germans would try to make a stand on a number of the natural defense lines in France, but the decisiveness of our victory west of the Seine has convinced him that we should go all-out and take every risk to continue the drive beyond the German border up to the Rhine before we regroup and refit. However, General Montgomery feels that if his Army Group is given practically all the maintenance available to both Americans and British, his 21st Army Group could rush right on into Berlin. This, however, would mean immobilization of all other divisions, as their transport and supplies would go largely to Montgomery, with some left over for General Hodges and his U. S. First Army. Ike thinks this is impractical. In addition to the supply problem, Montgomery's proposed thrust to Berlin would be on such a narrow front that German attacks on his flanks would be effective. Because of the use of all available transport for Monty's projected rush, no other troops in the whole region would be capable of going to Montgomery's support if he found himself under heavy attack.

Ike intends to hustle all his forces up against the Rhine, including those coming in from southern France. He will build up maintenance and reserves as rapidly as possible and then put on one sustained and unremitting advance against the long-coveted heart of the enemy country —the Ruhr industrial area.*

Ike has already assigned General Montgomery great numbers of trucks, temporarily withdrawn from supplying American divisions, to help him reach the Rhine in the north and to threaten the Ruhr. There will be a great airborne attack of three divisions, the 1st British and the 82nd and 101st American, on next Sunday unless weather prevents. Ike hopes this will carry Monty up to and across the Rhine. Then it will become necessary to capture the approaches to Antwerp, so we can use that port. The

* When the Ruhr industries are mentioned, those of the Saar Valley generally are implied as well.

port facilities are practically undamaged, but ships cannot come up the estuary because the Germans hold the islands to the east. The port of Le Havre is to be developed for the use of U. S. forces.

Ike is thanking his stars that he held out for the forthcoming invasion through southern France because of our great need of the port of Marseille. This is becoming essential in view of the stubborn resistance offered by the Germans in some of the smaller ports of France. They fought like tigers at Saint-Malo and Brest and, in taking Brest, the port probably will be so destroyed it will be futile to try to repair it for our military operations.

Ike thinks that if the Russians continue their pressure on the present scale, we on the Western Front will have to fight one more major battle. This will be to break through the German defenses, including the Siegfried Line, on the border and to get started on the invasion. After we get into Germany proper, he doubts if there will be another full-dress battle.

Some of the air people have suggested the desirability of moving a lot of heavy bombers based in England to France, to shorten the trips to demolish German industry. Ike has ruled this is simply beyond the realm of feasibility because all of our facilities for supply must be used for the ground troops and for the shorter-range tactical air-support units. The heavy bombers can still operate effectively from England.

Items of interest: The first cross-Channel pipe line, called Pluto, was connected between Sandown Bay and Nacqueville on August 12. The engineers were gratified to find that the seventy miles of welded pipe could be rolled on huge drums like wire. . . . The Russians have captured some 300 more places. . . . Yesterday was probably our biggest day in the air, nearly 4000 sorties having been flown by AEAF alone, and we had a report last night that 1100 MTs * had been destroyed during the day. . . . SHAEF wants the Combined Chiefs to ask the Russians to give us access to research centers and experimental stations overrun by the Russians in Germany, the better to prosecute the war against the Japs. . . . A study of air supply to support our rapidly advancing forces shows that 1000 tons a day can be delivered. This would speed our progress by three days and would be especially useful when we are ready to cross the Seine, which is now active in the minds of the planners. . . . Ike had a hole in his sock above his shoe. He and General De Witt were leaving this afternoon to visit a hospital near Carentan. I told Ike he would see some nurses and he'd better change his socks. He didn't.

* Military transports.

D-Day for ANVIL

SHELLBURST (IN NORMANDY), TUESDAY, AUGUST 15, 1944
Beetle, Admiral Ramsay, and Lieutenant General "Pug" Ismay came to dinner last evening, having just flown from SHAEF Forward. General De Witt and his aide already were here, so there were eight for dinner.

Before dinner, Ike told of his discussions with the Prime Minister, Ismay sharing the good humor. Ike said that at his last meeting on Friday the PM had practically wept and, in fact, actually had rolled tears down his cheeks in arguing that the Americans were adopting a "bullying" attitude against the British in failing to accept their, meaning primarily his, ideas as to grand strategy. Both love the Prime, as they frequently speak of him, and their comment about him is like that of two admiring sons discussing a cantankerous yet adorable father.

The PM was seeking Ike's support for reinforcements to Alexander's forces in Italy. Ike has always felt that this is a blind alley and that nothing more than holding forces should be kept in Italy after a suitable stopping place, either at the Pisa-Rimini line or in the Po River valley, is reached. The PM wants Alexander to have enough force not only to hold the line but to continue into the Balkans through the Ljubljana gap, in Yugoslavia, to reach Germany through Austria. Ike said the PM wanted to go through "that gap whose name I can't even pronounce."

Ike maintained that practically all of Alexander's present forces would be required to hold the Po River valley and our force would simply be wasted by sending him replacements, especially when the British are already short of manpower and we need to concentrate our forces to push through France into Germany.

Ike also recalled to the PM that America had accepted the British point of view about going into Africa before invading France—the invasion thereby having to be postponed from the earliest feasible date, in Ike's view, the spring of '43, to June of '44.

General De Witt and aide spent the night, but the other guests departed soon after dinner. Jim called 21st Army Group for a report on the Canadian offensive, and the news was not particularly exciting. The Canadians had made about four kilometers and hadn't gone directly toward Falaise, after all. Instead they had veered to the east toward Trun. His informant at 21st Army Group spoke disparagingly of the air effort, indicating it had laid a giant egg. This time it was the Bomber Command whose bombs fell short, killing 100 and injuring 200 of our lads. In any event, the gap wasn't closed, although our air was active until late in the day and some 200 medium bombers and fighters were over the area at night, shooting up anything they could see moving on the roads.

Late Monday afternoon, Ike took General De Witt on a visit to the 5th General Hospital near Carentan. When he returned, he said he was depressed and he looked it. There were about 1100 SIWs—meaning those with self-inflicted wounds—and numerous cases of psychoneurosis or battle anxiety. He said it was always difficult to prove that a soldier had shot himself. This is usually done through the left hand or the foot. The soldier always will say that it was an accident. One had told him he had accidentally discharged his carbine while climbing aboard a truck; he displayed a bandaged thumb, saying it had been shot off. Ike later said that General Kenner had told him that rarely do you find a case of psychoneurosis amongst wounded men. Although there are a few authentic cases, many such complaints are merely imaginary or faked to avoid battle.

At a press conference this morning Ike vehemently castigated those who think they can measure the end of the war "in a matter of weeks."

Today is D-Day for ANVIL, but while the press conference was in progress, starting at 9:15, we had no word that it actually had taken place, although we were informed that H-Hour was 8 A. M. Ike merely told the reporters to listen to their radios during the day for interesting information. He was asked if he would have command of the invasion in southern France and he said, "eventually," but asked them to "lay off the subject for the time being."

Ike authorized the release of Lieutenant General Patton's name as Commander of the Third Army, along with that of Lieutenant General Courtney H. Hodges as Commander of the First. He asked that General De Witt's visit to him not be publicized until Lieutenant Colonel Thor Smith can check with G-2 to make certain such release will be in harmony with our censorship directives.

As usual, Ike spoke feelingly and earnestly about the co-operation of land, sea, and air forces and emphasized the tremendous importance of the logistics people and the job they had done in this campaign.

One of the duties of a general is to determine the best investment of human lives. If he thinks expenditure of 10,000 lives in the current battle will save 20,000 later, it is up to him to do it. This expresses Ike's feeling about the current effort to close the bag on the Germans.

Returning to the subject of the duration of the war in Europe, Ike said that Hitler and gang had nothing to lose by enforcing prosecution of the war through the Gestapo. Hitler, no doubt, knows he will be hanged, if he doesn't hang himself, which Ike thinks likely, and, consequently, will fight to the bitter end. He thinks the German General Staff or Hitler will soon decide to give up some territory which is least useful to them. Ike thinks this is most likely to happen in Finland, where the Germans might bully their divisions through Sweden into Norway and eventually retrieve the garrisons of both countries.

Ike spoke also of the jubilation of the French at finding the French armored division fighting for their liberty. Because these Frenchmen are dressed in American uniforms and have American equipment, the French citizens were surprised and thrilled when they discovered real Frenchmen under the American OD.

The Prime Minister has been in Italy and will witness the southern invasion. He has cabled Ike congratulations on the brilliant operations in Anjou and Normandy. He said it must have been a magnificent sight and the American "turning movement" will long excite wonder. We have just heard from Major General Alexander M. Patch, veteran of Guadalcanal, who commands the U. S. Seventh Army in the southern landings. He says the operation seems successful.

Our old friend Lucian Truscott is commanding the VI Corps, which is comprised of the 3rd, 36th, and 45th Divisions, which were the assault divisions. These were supported by airborne troops, Rangers, Commandos, French Commandos, and the First Special Service Force under Major General Robert T. Frederick (formerly of Operations Division). All the assault divisions reported successful breaching of beach defenses in target area and the attack was proceeding according to plan.

The German Weatherman

SHELLBURST (IN NORMANDY), THURSDAY, AUGUST 17, 1944
It seems that the Allies were not the only ones who had weather problems on D-Day. Group Captain Stagg had an interesting talk with Major Lettau, the chief German meteorologist, who was captured by U. S. forces while on his way from Paris to Rennes. The German weatherman was anxious to know how our forecast for the Allied invasion was made and why we decided on the night of June 5/6. His job had been to provide the German commanders with forecasts of invasion weather. He had advised his superiors that invasion after June 4 was impracticable because of the stormy weather moving in from the Atlantic. He had told them that bad weather would continue without improvement for several days after the fourth. Group Captain Stagg found that the German meteorologist had failed to grasp the significance of a "weather front" which passed through the Channel early on June 5, with relatively good weather fol-

lowing it. On the basis of the German's weather forecast, many officers of their divisions in Normandy were on local leave and others were on maneuvers. The German major said they were taken completely by surprise when Allied invasion started on the morning of June 6—not only because of their own weather forecast but because the Allied forces went in at low tide, with all the underwater obstacles exposed, whereas the Germans assumed we would attack only at high tide.

General Ike is a bit disappointed that because of the extraordinary defense ring created by the Germans north of Falaise, which has taken so long to break, our total bag of prisoners in the pocket will not be as great as he first thought. However, the beating-up of the enemy along the whole front has greatly weakened them. I hear reports it is a massacre.

Bradley can now spare some troops to clean up the Brittany Peninsula, but only minimum forces are to be allocated, as Ike is most interested in continuing the sweep around "right end" to penetrate the enemy's exposed flank and rear.

The Problem of Command Again

SHELLBURST (IN NORMANDY), FRIDAY, AUGUST 18, 1944

The Prime Minister has come around magnificently and has sent Ike a glowing message, after watching the landings in southern France, that the results of all the Allies' efforts may eclipse the Russian victories.

But General Ike's most immediate worry comes from a cable sent by General Marshall, who relates that tremendous publicity has been given through the U. S. by press and radio, including editorial comment, on the creation of an American Army Group under Bradley. Much attention also has been given to General Ike's personal move to France. A recent statement attributed to General Ike that Monty continues in command of all ground forces has produced, General Marshall pointed out, severe editorial reaction, which he feels is to be deplored. General Marshall states he is confused as to the cause of the announcement and both he and the Secretary are strongly of the opinion that the time has come for General Ike to assume and exercise direct command of the ground forces. General Marshall felt that the astonishing success of the campaign up to the present has evoked emphatic expressions of confidence in both General Ike and General Bradley, but the late announcement has dampened the public enthusiasm.

Ike has been considering further ways of speeding the arrival of divisions from the United States. The British are down to the bottom of their manpower barrel and are about to ship their last readily available division.

Our old friend, General de Gaulle, is causing a great deal of consternation in Allied minds, as he desires to fly from Africa direct to France, using his Lockheed Lodestar. This is an unarmed ship and its fuel capacity does not allow enough margin for safety. General Devers and General Eaker have offered him the use of a Fortress or a C-54, which could rendezvous with a fighter escort over England. However, de Gaulle is adamant and desires to use a French ship and a French crew. It has necessitated a message going out from General Smith informing him—de Gaulle —that if he does not co-ordinate the movement and the escort, we cannot be responsible for his safety—which is one more of the problems facing the Supreme Commander.

SHELLBURST (IN NORMANDY), SATURDAY, AUGUST 19, 1944
The *Stars and Stripes* carried an article on command setup which indicated that General Bradley had taken over the two American armies in the field and would have equal rank with Montgomery. This was a premature statement based on an article by Wes Gallagher (which I have not seen) that had cleared through the censors of MOI, not SHAEF. As it was not time for this announcement, SHAEF contradicted the article and the London *Daily Mirror* picked it up with a rather scathing cartoon, deploring that "Monty" no longer commanded all ground operations of Americans and British.

From the other side of the Atlantic, General Surles reported quite an opposite reaction. Some of the American papers had demanded an apology from certain of the London press for stories that General Montgomery had been "demoted" by being placed on an equal footing with General Bradley, the former commanding the 21st Army Group, consisting of British, Canadian, Polish, Belgian, and Dutch troops, and the latter the 12th Army Group, which included Hodges' First and Patton's Third U. S. Armies. The *Washington Times-Herald* had written about "British dominance" of invasion command.

General Ike has discussed the situation with General Bradley, and both of them are somewhat surprised that the plan for the initial, transitional, and ultimate command system of ground forces apparently is not understood by the War Department, where its Public Relations officers informally could explain it to correspondents, if desired. Ike was peeved that the press and the people, even though given a resounding victory— in fact, a series of them—do not feel satisfied. The question of "how" seems of greater interest. Ike feels that the development of command arrangements in this campaign was as carefully planned as the operation itself. Events have closely followed the plan to which all were agreed. General Ike has always been directly responsible for approving major operational policies and all principal features of all plans of every kind.

As far as the ground forces were concerned, the beachhead and area of operations were very constricted. It was obvious that one commander, who could give his entire attention to day-to-day action and who could be actually and constantly on the spot, had initially to be responsible for such details of co-ordination as timing of attacks, fixing of local objectives, and for establishing boundaries between armies.

Months ago General Ike and the planners concluded that about sixty days after D-Day, an American Army Group would be formed and that soon thereafter the battle in Normandy should be won. Diverging lines of operation would then require that the detailed day-by-day co-ordination of tactical arrangements would then be in the hands of two Group Commanders-in-Chief, Montgomery and Bradley, with broad co-ordination and allocation of supply and personnel determined by the Supreme Commander. They had foreseen that there would be a transition period, pending the movement of General Ike's own headquarters to the Continent, during which time the American Army Group would become fully operational. This period was estimated at thirty days after the first sixty.

So far as Ike was concerned, he was indifferent to the newspaper comment, but would be exceedingly sorry if General Bradley's reputation suffered in the slightest.

The command setup will be announced in due course. I think we probably should have announced it heretofore, but as Montgomery fights one type of battle and Bradley another, the G-2s have felt we would simply be doing the enemy a favor if we announced who commands what. In any event, no major effort takes place, by ground, sea, or air, in this theater, except with General Ike's approval, and no one here presumes to question his supreme authority and responsibility for the whole campaign. Ike has formed the First Allied Air Army, commanded by Lieutenant General Brereton. There has been a lot of discussion on the proper use of this force and the selection of a suitable operation.

Trouble-Shooting Assignment

LONDON, MONDAY, AUGUST 21, 1944

The Wes Gallagher story disclosing the separation of command of American ground forces from those of the British and placing Bradley on a par with Montgomery, each commanding Army Groups, brought to a head the question of Ike's sending me to help Colonel R. Ernest Dupuy, Acting Director of PRD. Beetle had again raised the question.

General Ike talked to me Saturday afternoon, told me of Beetle's insistence, and emphasized the danger of stories such as Wes Gallagher's creating a rupture in Allied relationship. He realized that there may be little that I or anyone could do about it, but so far as he was concerned, he would be a bit happier if I would "support" Colonel Dupuy until T. J.'s physical condition could be ascertained by the doctors. He asked me to let him know if and when T. J. could return to active duty. I was to feel free to report direct to Ike, as he recognized that frequently speed and decision were necessary to deal with a prospective bad situation. The assignment, he said, is a trouble-shooting job and I ought to be finished when T. J.'s status is determined and his successor appointed.

Moaney collected my gear and I caught a ride to London with Tooey Spaatz, who had spent the night at the camp.

I have taken a room at the Dorchester and am moving part of my stuff into it from Telegraph Cottage, where I stayed Saturday and last night. The flying bombs are still a nuisance. I tried sleeping in my old bedroom, but after being awakened by the "imminent alert" I decided I might just as well get a good night's sleep—something to which I had become accustomed in the peace and quiet of the apple orchard—so I spent the rest of the night on a cot in the shelter.

I visited T. J. in the hospital yesterday and found him bright, cheerful, and mending, although he will have to stay in bed for several weeks. I agree with him that the hurly-burly of public relations is no job for him now, and I am prepared to recommend to Ike that T. J. go back to his old position as Adjutant General, which is still open to him.

Colonel Dupuy welcomed me to the PRD and put me in the Policy Section, which, I find, deals with a wide variety of problems, including movement of correspondents from the States to the U. K. and to various press camps operated by the Army Groups, armies, and the 9th Air Force on the Continent. The office is in the Ministry of Information.

There is a waiting list of American and British accredited male and female correspondents, as well as of several from neutral countries, who are pressing to get across the Channel. However, as each press camp on the Continent has tents, cots, mess facilities, and jeeps for thirty-five to fifty correspondents we have to get permission at the camp before we can send a correspondent. The PRO at the camp has the problem also of maintaining a balance of representation, American and British, among the press associations, radio networks, and correspondents of individual newspapers and radio stations.

I find that British pride, which seems to have been hurt by the relative slowness of advance of the British-Canadian front, as compared to the more newsworthy break-through of the Americans at Saint-Lô and subsequent end runs, has been hurt even more by the misunderstanding as to Montgomery's command. Some of the London papers have reflected this feeling. Ike has a first-class problem on his hands. I think he must have a press conference soon, as only a frank statement by him will smooth the ruffled feathers.

Ike may have his problems, but now I have a little one of my own. It has seemed obvious to me that our service for correspondents is unnecessarily complicated. In brief, SHAEF PRD makes a policy and the ETO Public Relations Office, under Colonel Jock Lawrence's direction, provides facilities for movement of correspondents. As I see it, most of the good service rendered them and the credit for it go to the theater PRO, and the blame for policy and the red tape that entwines correspondents become discredit to SHAEF PRD. I think the two should be merged, and I am working on it.

Liberation of Paris

LONDON, FRIDAY, AUGUST 25, 1944
PRD is quite the hottest noncombat spot in the Supreme Headquarters organization. The opportunities for error are very high, indeed.

Today Paris seems finally to have fallen, after a premature announcement to the press by the French some three days ago. Poor Colonel Dupuy has been unable to give the correspondents confirmation that Paris has been liberated. His last several press conferences have been most difficult. SHAEF would not confirm the French announcement, and Colonel Dupuy has been on the battle line with the correspondents, particularly the Americans, who insist that if the French say their capital is liberated, why must SHAEF be so far behind in the news?

He is handicapped by slowness of communications. Telephone connections with SHAEF Forward are hard to get, and once a connection is obtained one has to shout to be heard. Official information about progress on the various battle fronts percolates slowly from company to battalion, to regiment, to division, to corps, to armies, and then to army groups, and finally to SHAEF Forward—each step being slowed by necessary coding and decoding of official messages.

We hear that the rocket, now called V-2, is supposed to be imminent. In fact, there is some talk of moving SHAEF PRD underground. Most of our communication facilities, as well as those for the military, have been underground for months.

Secretary of the Navy Forrestal gave a brief talk to our accredited correspondents this week. While he was talking, a flying bomb came over, drowned out his voice, but everyone tried to be braver than the rest and so no one let on he even heard it—least of all Mr. Forrestal. I spoke to him for a minute. He had just seen Ike at the apple-orchard camp. The Secretary said he had told Ike he had "come over to get me." I don't know what he meant and I didn't ask, as there were others present.

Smoothing the Waters

LONDON, THURSDAY, AUGUST 31, 1944

General Ike flew over from the Continent; saw the Prime Minister and had a heavily attended press conference at the MOI yesterday afternoon.

There must have been a couple of hundred correspondents and the PRD staff. He successfully outlined the command setup in a perfectly honest, straightforward manner and, I think, has corrected the situation. He praised Monty and said that anyone who misinterpreted the transition of command as a demotion for General Montgomery simply did not look facts in the face. He said Montgomery is one of the great soldiers of this or any other war and he would now have the job of handling the battles on his side of the front. It would be most unfortunate if this plan of campaign, which had developed as it was conceived from the start, should be interpreted as a demotion or as a slap at anybody.

The Supreme Commander said there were three ways leading to Germany where our forces must go to defeat the enemy decisively and completely. General Montgomery's forces were expected to beat the Germans on the north; General Bradley's to defeat them in the center, and the Mediterranean forces, under General Devers, to press from the south. (He went over a lot of the ground covered in my diary entries of August 18 and 19.) To the attentive correspondents, he made clear that when the initial beachhead was established, it was very restricted, and since there was only one tactical battle to be conducted, he had put General Montgomery in tactical control of the American land force. Montgomery's control was to exist until we could break out of the base of the Cherbourg Peninsula. The time had come when they had broken out, and General Bradley was taking over his part of the job and reporting directly to SHAEF. Ike described Monty as a "great and personal friend" and emphasized that he had a great admiration for him.

A British correspondent asked a question about the "American parade in Paris." I had noticed some inferences in British papers that any military parade should have included British and French as well as American troops. Paris was in the American sector. General Ike replied instantly that one night he was at General Bradley's headquarters, Paris was about to fall, and he had personally ordered General Le Clerc's French armored division under Bradley be given the honor of being first in the city. In addition, he had asked that a small contingent of British, American, and other Allied nationalities, who might be quickly collected, go into Paris to symbolize Allied unity. The only British people at Bradley's headquarters were a little staff group. Ike then had ordered that only a comparable number of Americans should go in. However, Le Clerc's troops could not get into Paris immediately and Bradley had to call up the American 4th Division to assist and, consequently, there were more American troops than had been intended. Subsequently, the battle front moved to the east gate of Paris and it was found that American forces could march two divisions through Paris to the suburban battle front and thus make a showing of power which would quiet collaborationists, and thus give the city confidence. General de Gaulle had wanted a formal parade to make a show of strength, and General Ike had arranged for him to review the American troops as they actually went through the city to meet the Germans on the eastward outskirts of the town. General Ike had invited General Montgomery; Montgomery was tied up in his own sector and could not get away. General Ike added that he had lived "Allied" for two years and a half and his own bosses were both British and American. He felt he had no right to appear exclusively as American, and nothing at his own headquarters is done on a basis of British vs. American. That answered that.

Touching on another tender spot in the British press, Ike said that the German stand in the Caen area was a "do-or-die" affair and that every foot of ground the Germans lost at Caen was like losing ten miles anywhere else. He deplored British writers apologizing for slow progress at Caen when he thought they should have been bragging, as the Germans had thrown in every Panzer division available to hold that region. Every piece of dust on the Caen front was more than a diamond to them, Ike declared. He elaborated that the Germans' tenacity in maintaining strength against Monty's forces at Caen had been a very fortunate decision, as it helped permit the Americans to break through westward from Saint-Lô and start the end runs which eventually dislodged the Germans west of the Seine.

General Ike made clear his belief that there would certainly be one

major battle before we broke into Germany—this would be through the
Siegfried Line to the Rhine—but he said no defensive line is better than
the men defending it. He hoped that by the time we reached the Siegfried
Line, the German morale would be badly weakened, with most of its
best troops scattered or captured. By reinforcement, possibly by drawing
on garrisons from Denmark and Norway, the Germans could put up a
stiff fight from well-fortified positions. We should not be too optimistic
about an early end of the war, as there is still much fighting to be done
before we get into Germany and get our pincers of steel around the Ruhr
and Saar industries.

He paid another tribute to the Maquis, which he said had been far
more effective than many doubting Thômases thought before D-Day.

He was asked if Devers' forces in southern France would soon come
under his command. Not wanting to answer at this time that Devers
would come under his command, he said it was a question for the Combined Chiefs.

I had met Ike at the entrance to the MOI when he arrived, and when
he left he asked me to ride out to the cottage for lunch. I gave him my
story of the need of reorganization of the Public Relations Division as
advocated by Colonel Jock Lawrence, the theater PRO. I had seen T. J.
Sunday and could report he was making progress. I doubted if T. J. could
return to the rough-and-tumble of PRD, but I anticipated the doctors
would permit him to return to his old job as Adjutant General. Ike was
anxious to know if I thought his press conference had satisfactorily covered
the command setup. I told him I thought he would have a very good
press. He said he had been going over a number of clippings sent him
from Washington, showing the trend of stories and editorial comment
in papers all over America. He had been able to assure the Prime Minister
that reports he has had that British Empire participation in the campaign
is not appreciated in the U. S. are greatly exaggerated. He had found that
the stories praised the Allied accomplishments and stressed again and
again how fortunate it was that the American and British leaders and
men work together so well. So far as the press conference went, he felt
that neither the British nor American newsmen gave him the slightest
impression that any real fears need be entertained concerning the soundness of the Anglo-American military partnership in Europe. He had
found the PM pleased at the recent break-through on the British Second
Army front, which seems already to have pierced the line of the
Somme.

We discussed the cause and possible cure of overoptimism at home.
There had been a succession of victories, heralded by headlines and broad-

casts, that had led to a belief the war soon would be over. I asked him if he thought he would be able to move supply fast and far enough to keep our armies moving until they broke into Germany, and he feared we inevitably would be checked. Port capacity is not what it should be, the roads are already clogged with our transport, bridges are out, signal communications are bad; yet these deterrents are overshadowed by the frequent headlines of victorious battles. Ike had mentioned at the press conference that on D plus 85 we were well in advance of the line the planners had anticipated the front would be by D plus 90.

Ike flew back to Granville, where he has established his personal headquarters with that of SHAEF Forward. He asked me to visit him at the earliest opportunity.

AUGUST, 1944: *Third Army approached to within fifty miles of Belgian border after having swept to Paris suburbs, allowing French resistance forces to liberate capital. Allies established two bridgeheads over the Seine; crossed the Marne and the Somme. Allied troops invaded southern France, occupying Marseille, Grenoble, Arles, Avignon, and Toulon; swift advances trapped thousands of German troops. Historic French cities liberated by onrushing Allies—Rennes, Le Mans, Chartres, Orléans, Lisieux, Paris, Rouen, Rheims, Verdun, Amiens. Heavy air raids continued to blast transportation lines, aircraft and armament plants. Nazi experimental station at Peenemunde destroyed. British sank entire convoy believed to be evacuating Nazis from Saint-Nazaire. Eisenhower moved headquarters to Normandy. Nazis gave up Florence; Allies began attacks against Gothic Line. Allies in India, Burma liquidated nine Jap divisions, killing 42,000. Last Jap driven out of India. Reds seized Kaunas; captured Bucharest and rolled on to Bulgaria's Dobruja border. Pacific air activity stepped up as planes hit Halmahera, Nagasaki, Kyushu, Palembang, Davao, Marcus and Yap Islands, and Amboina. Two-day naval assault on Bonin and Volcano Islands destroyed or damaged forty-six Jap vessels. Conquest of Guam completed; advances were scored on New Guinea. Planes of British eastern fleet hit Sumatra in surprise attack. Turkey broke off relations with Germany; Rumania withdrew from the war; Argentina's gold stocks frozen by Secretary Hull. (Optimism reigned in the Allied Forces—one general thought the war would be finished in three weeks, but that wasn't General Ike.—H.C.B.)*

LONDON, SUNDAY, SEPTEMBER 3, 1944

I saw T. J. today and he is making steady progress.

I talked on the phone with SHAEF Forward and find that there is something wrong with Ike, but Tex Lee didn't go into details over the phone and the connection was faulty. Lee said something about Ike having hurt his leg. I had called to make certain PRD may release the text of a Labor Day message that Ike has recorded for use on the Army Hour. I know Ike is worrying about supply.

The Champagne Atmosphere

LONDON, THURSDAY, SEPTEMBER 7, 1944

PRD expects eventually to move to Paris when communications for press and radio have been satisfactorily established. Colonel Dupuy has been working so hard, so long, and needs a rest or, at least, a change of atmosphere so badly, I have urged him to go to Paris to investigate facilities for the correspondents. He and Brigadier William Turner, his deputy, flew over a couple of days ago. Things in Paris have been in a turmoil, best described as the "champagne atmosphere." A half-dozen correspondents, fortunately evenly divided amongst British and Americans, got into Paris when it fell and broadcast uncensored material over a radio station of the French underground. Even an officer of our Psychological Warfare branch got on the air and broadcast an uncensored message. Colonel Dupuy has ordered the correspondents to London and has suspended them, pending approval by Beetle for sterner punishment. General McClure is dealing with his PWD officer. Fortunately, none of the messages contained any matter the censors would have stricken.

I have been trying to hold down Colonel Dupuy's desk while he is away. In an effort to sober the flow of news, I arranged for Brigadier General T. J. Betts, Deputy G-2 of SHAEF, to brief the correspondents. I briefed him first on our need. I wanted him to tell the correspondents how difficult it will be to get through the Siegfried Line. My reasoning is that if we should get through it easily, the GIs should have appreciation by the public of their victory, and if we get stuck in front of it and have a hell of a fight to get through, then the public won't be so surprised and the GIs will get deserved credit. Otherwise they may fight their hearts out and the public will regard the feat as another easy victory. General Betts quickly saw my point and said his story should dampen some of the ardor of those who think the war soon will be over. He gave a fine talk; in fact, it was so good that when he finished, the correspondents rose and applauded. Then someone asked: "Well, General Betts, sir, do you think we will get the Siegfried Line?"

"Why, of course," said General Betts. "We'll go right through it!"

Rather dejectedly I left the briefing room and went back to my desk, where I found some stories from the pool of correspondents at SHAEF

Forward. They had spent a couple of hours interviewing Beetle and had forwarded the stories to PRD for distribution to all press and radio services. Beetle was quoted as saying "Militarily the war is won." The stories had the approval of Beetle himself.

If the correspondents with the Third Army don't mention Patton, apparently the headline writers at home insert his name. In any event, Patton is getting great publicity and is overshadowing Hodges of the U. S. First Army. I have "made a signal" to the PRO of First Army, suggesting that the correspondents there be encouraged to write of that army as Hodges'. This may balance the credit. But it takes a lot of color in any man to balance Patton.

General Ike has had a standing rule that censors must strike any quotations of Patton. The correspondents with Third Army and elsewhere understand this rule and co-operate. They are permitted to write about Patton, but he is protected from his own flamboyant and sometimes hasty words. Any stories that happen to violate this rule are referred to Colonel Dupuy, who, in turn, must send them to Beetle for his personal approval. Today a batch of stories containing Patton's formal citation for good fighting by certain units in Third Army came to me for attention. They had been referred by the censors because the citations had been quoted. I got Beetle on the phone and he readily agreed that henceforth all official citations by Patton may be quoted without reference to the Chief of Staff. The purpose of citations is to give recognition for good work. When the members of a cited unit read about their deeds in home-town papers— clippings inevitably reach them—they are proud of themselves. It's silly to delay such stories, but this case illustrates how arbitrarily a general rule may be obeyed, particularly if the purpose of the rule isn't understood.

George Lyon, personal representative of Elmer Davis of OWI, has returned to London after a visit to the States. He had helped the PRD before D-Day. He was in today with a letter from Elmer to General Ike, continuing the arrangement. George says that no other single incident had created such a furor in the American press as that which arose at the 9th Air Force press camp in Normandy. I knew something of this case as Captain Frank Mayborn, one of the best officers of PRD and owner of a radio station and newspaper at Temple, Texas, had been sent to Normandy by Colonel Dupuy to trouble-shoot the problem. Certain correspondents assigned to the 9th Air Force camp wrote stories to their home papers in the States about ground operations, and the Air Force PRO insisted they write only about activities of the 9th Air Force and not about ground operations. They naturally felt this was a restriction against the freedom of the press. The poor PRO is the victim of circumstances over which he has little control, but I fear he will have to be supplanted.

V-2

Ike has ordered operational secrecy for Allied forces pushing toward Germany. The British and the Americans are less than twenty miles from the German border. The press calls such secrecy a "blackout" of news, but we are going so rapidly that if he permits prompt dissemination of news, the hard-pressed Germans, with their communications disrupted, can keep their war maps up to date by listening to the BBC.

On the London front, Mr. Duncan Sandys held a press conference in the MOI briefing room and told the whole story of the flying bombs. During eighty days of bombing, 8000 bombs were launched, of which 2300 reached the London area.

Yesterday morning about dawn, I was awakened by a terrific and sustained noise that was sort of like a double harrumph. It wasn't the sound of a flying bomb; I suspected it was a rocket, although during the day word passed around the MOI that a gasworks had blown up. On investigation, I find there were two rockets. One landed north of Epping and one north of Cheswick. They made craters from ten to fourteen feet in depth and from fifteen to twenty-five feet in diameter. Because the rocket practically buries itself before exploding, there is less blast effect than from a flying bomb. Radar gave no warning, but subsequent sound-ranging plots indicated that one rocket was fired from the neighborhood of Rotterdam and another from the Amsterdam area.

First contact has been established between Patton's Third Army and Patch's Seventh coming up from the south.

Bulgaria has quit the war.

Finland's "cease firing" order was issued several days ago.

Ike Has His Problems, Too

I spent the week end at Granville with General Ike, who is confined to his bed by a wrenched knee. He is in a small villa named Montgomery overlooking Mont-Saint-Michel, the ancient abbey on a rock, surrounded by water at high tide but by almost flat sand at low. About a week ago, he had flown off from Granville to meet Generals Bradley and Patton. A broken muffler on his C-47 required a change of planes at Chartres for the return journey. Captain Dick Underwood, copilot to Major Larry Hansen, found a liaison plane, an L-5, and flew the General back to Granville, intending to land near Jullouville, where there is a strip for liaison planes on top of a hill overlooking SHAEF Forward. There was a very high wind and visibility was not too good, so Underwood decided to put the plane down on the beach near Ike's small villa. The landing was O.K., but the tide was rising, and Ike helped Dick push and pull the plane to a spot that would remain dry. Ike said he wondered if this beach had been mined and, if so, if they had been demined. But it wasn't a mine that got him, it was a twist in the soft sand that wrenched his knee. They had walked a mile to the road and flagged a jeep, which took them to Ike's house. General Kenner has the knee in some sort of rubber gadget. Unfortunately, it is the knee he has always called his good one, the right one. He has to sit with his leg straight and is quite uncomfortable. But worst of all, the stiff leg makes difficult his normal movement around the country to see the commanders.

There was considerable time to talk and I caught up on a number of topics, after having given my recommendation for merging the theater and SHAEF public-relations functions and for bringing in a new director for administration, which will permit Colonel Dupuy to devote himself primarily to briefing the correspondents, at which he is a master. T. J. soon will be fit for active duty and can go back to his old position as Adjutant General.

Ike thinks this makes sense and is getting off a message to General Devers, asking him for Brigadier General Frank A. Allen, G-2 of the 6th Army Group, who has been recommended for the PRD job by General Surles. I urged that Colonel Dupuy be recommended for the Legion of Merit in recognition of his superior service. Ike said I shouldn't feel wedded to the PRD, to come back when I felt the reorganization was set and the division was operating smoothly. I chuckled, because I doubt if any public-relations office can operate smoothly. There are a half-dozen crises every day.

The idea of a merger is approved, but actual amalgamation probably will await arrival of a new director. Colonel Jock Lawrence, the theater PRO, expects to return to America now that Paris is in the bag. At Ike's request, I brought the matter back "in channel" by consulting fully with Beetle, who seemed pleased with the solution. He also approved PRD and PWD moving into Paris, but said that except for SHAEF Mission to

France, no other SHAEF divisions or sections would be permitted in the city.

General Koenig, the French Military Governor of Paris, had just telegraphed Beetle that the demand for living quarters in Paris by American Com Z * headquarters exceeded the capacity of all the hotels heretofore used by the Germans and deprived the French military of even its minimum requirement.

I had found Ike grousing about the move of Com Zone, because the headquarters and large number of staff officers and personnel were moving pellmell into Paris.

The Com Zone headquarters had been at Valognes, but when Paris fell, this center of transport, supply, and personnel became the natural location for the large service organization. Ike felt that the combat troops who had taken Paris would look back over their shoulders from the front line and see the supply people living in the luxury of Paris. He thought this very bad psychologically and was in the process of ordering General Lee to abandon Paris completely but found the movement had proceeded so far that stopping it was impossible. So he had instructed General Lee to stop the entry of every individual who was not needed at that spot for essential duty. General Lee is to have an investigation of the American personnel in Paris and is to send away from there everyone whose presence is not necessary. He is to use every type of transport available to get them out, including empty trucks returning to base. He had also heard, as I had, that the dress, discipline, and conduct of American personnel in Paris left much to be desired. Paris was to be used as a recreation center for combat troops and space was to be retained for their comfort.

I was pleased to see the house staff again. Henry Clay Williams, with his wide smile, had carefully nurtured Shaef until he had grown so I hardly knew him. Moaney had kept Caacie in good shape and she still knew me, although she still ran from Mickey and fearfully dodged Henry Clay's number-twelve shoes as she and Telek begged food at the table from General Ike. Telek was a friend of everyone and still delighted himself and others by chasing his tail. His favorite spot is on the General's lap, where he growls if the General fails to scratch his back. Hunt's southern cooking was as good as ever—in fact, it seemed better. I found real milk on the table and Ike said he had achieved an ambition. He now had not only one but two cows, which were kept in a field near by, so

---

* Communications Zone, responsible for all American supply and really the extension of the Army Service Forces into France, commanded by Lieutenant General John C. H. Lee.

there were fresh milk and cream for the mess. They were named Maribell and Lulabell.

Ike's office is in a temporary wooden building—a Dallas hut—whose floors creak. Voices can easily be heard through the thin partitions. Some of the officers are living in caravans, others in tents and the small villas of this one-time resort. There is little damage in Granville and in the immediate surrounding area, but at Avranches there are signs of hard fighting, with German tanks, vehicles, and guns strewn along the road in great profusion.

Ike had been to Paris and had taken part in a ceremony during which a plaque of the SHAEF shield for emplacement on the Arc de Triomphe was presented to the citizens of Paris. He had laid a wreath on the Tomb of the Unknown Soldier and had spoken briefly to the people of Paris.

Ike felt that for some days it had been obvious that our military force could advance almost at will, subject only to supply. He is thinking in terms of advancing on a wide front to take advantage of all existing lines of communication. He expects to go through the Aachen gap in the north and the Metz gap in the south and to bring the Southern Group of Armies (6th) to the Rhine south of Coblenz. Then he thinks he should use his airborne forces to seize crossings over the Rhine, to be in position to thrust deep into the Ruhr and to threaten Berlin itself. Patton had been forced to stand still southeast of Paris while supply went to Montgomery's forces in the north and to Hodges' First Army, which was moving on Monty's right. Ike had wanted to make certain there would be no halt in operations toward Antwerp and Brussels, as he needed the port of the former city for further supply, as indeed he needed any improvement in supply. He re-emphasized his satisfaction that Marseille had been taken and that a good line of supply had thus been established up the Rhone valley, permitting rapid advance to Devers.

Ike also had flown to visit Monty at Brussels and had made still another trip, this time to Brest. Yet his movement was inconvenient because of the leg. However, he never likes to have his battle-front commanders leave their jobs to come to see him. He much prefers to place himself at their convenience.

Ike has decided that a northern thrust toward the Ruhr under Montgomery is not at the moment to have priority over other operations. Monty is fearful this will give the enemy time to organize better defense and heavier resistance, and slower progress must be expected in his sector. His prospective attempt to cross the Rhine may have to be postponed until late September, and as winter approaches the weather will diminish the value of our great weight of air power. Monty is concerned about his supply and seeks priority of transport.

Another instance of Ike as the policeman of Allied unity had occurred. I had seen references to it in the press. General Dempsey, commanding the British Second Army, had told correspondents that because the American Army got in his way, his British Army was delayed in advancing to the Seine, after cleaning up the so-called Falaise pocket. Ike had covered the whole situation with Montgomery. It was a question of the Americans overrunning the Army boundary and was one of those things that can happen in closing a pocket and in rapid pursuit of the enemy. General Bradley had construed Dempsey's statement as a direct criticism of American forces.

Effective Friday, September 15, by the direction of the Combined Chiefs, Ike assumes command of General Devers' forces, comprising the 6th Army Group and the 12th Tactical Air Force, which he has termed the Southern Group of Armies.

A Peek Into the German High Command from D-Day until the Break-through

A journal of enemy telephone conversations captured by the Polish Armored Division and passed on to SHAEF by Canadian Army Intelligence gives a realistic picture of the difficulties of the enemy, starting with D-Day. The journal meticulously lists conversations held by the Commander and the Chief of Staff of the German Seventh Army with both lower and higher formations. Herewith are some extracts from it. Remarks in parentheses did not appear in original text.

6 JUNE 44 (Our D-Day)

0925—Chief of General Staff, Seventh Army, to General Marcks, Commander of LXXXIV Corps.

General Marcks urgently requests mobile reserves for the west of Caen, since 21 Panzer Division is committed to the right of the Orne. He would like to have 12 SS Panzer Division.

1655—Chief of Staff reports situation to Chief of Staff Western Command.

Chief of Staff, Western Command (Rundstedt's HQ) emphasizes the desire

of Supreme Command (Hitler) to have the enemy in the bridgehead annihilated by the evening of 6 June, since there exists a danger of additional sea and airborne landings for support. In accordance with an order by General Jodl, all units will be diverted to the point of penetration in Calvados. The beachhead there must be cleaned up by not later than tonight. The Chief of the General Staff declares that such would be impossible. The Commander of Army Group B (Rommel) states that 21 Panzer Division must attack immediately regardless of whether reinforcements arrive or not.

The Supreme Command has ordered that the bad weather conditions of the night of 6/7 June be utilized for the bringing up of reserves.

2240—Commander of Seventh Army (Dollman) reports to Field Marshal Rommel.

Seventh Army HQ has repeatedly requested air support at Riva-Bella without success. Field Marshal Rommel answers that Air Force units are just on the point of changing location.

2400—Chief of Staff of Army to Commanders 21 Panzer Division and 716 Infantry Division.

716 Infantry Division is still defending itself at strong points. Communications between divisions, regimental and battalion command posts, however, no longer exist, so that nothing is known as to the number of strong points still holding out or of those liquidated. . . . The Chief of Staff gives the orders that the counterattack of 7 June must reach the coast without fail, since the strong-point defenders expect it of us.

8 JUNE 44

0640—Chief of Staff to Army Group B.

An operational order in English has been recovered from the water.

(a) Extracts are given from the operation order of VII American Corps, according to which the following units are committed:

On the right: VII American Corps with four divisions.
Mission: To attack northward from the Carentan-Quinéville bridgehead and to take Cherbourg from the land side.

On the left: V English Corps with four English divisions and two American divisions in the Calvados sector.
Mission: To take Bayeux and join up with the American VII Corps at Carentan.

(b) *Our own situation:* Bayeux in the enemy hands. . . . Attack by 1 SS Panzer Corps, because of the situation in the air, was *not* possible until this morning. Direction of the attack: north and NW of Caen, in the direction of the coast. Field Marshal Rommel interrupts and orders 1 SS Panzer Corps to initiate a point of main effort on the left as quickly as possible, using all three divisions.

8030—Chief of General Staff to Marshal Rommel.

The western coast of Cotentin is clear of the enemy and as a consequence the necessity arises to direct 2 Parachute Corps either toward Bayeux or Cherbourg. Field Marshal Rommel orders that the right wing of 2 Parachute Corps, with two divisions, be advanced, first of all, toward Saint-Lô. On inquiry, the Chief of General Staff makes it known that there still exists no communications with the headquarters of 2 Parachute Corps and the divisions, so that nothing is known as to the present location of the corps units. The corps has been ordered to set up radio communications with Seventh Army headquarters immediately. The establishment of communications appears to have been delayed by air attacks, particularly in the Avranches area.

9 JUNE 44

1730—Conversation of Field Marshal Rommel, in Army HQ, with Commanding General and Chief of Staff.

(1) The Chief of Staff acquaints those present with the situation as just reported by the Commanding General

LXXXIV Corps on the Cotentin Peninsula. The essential point is that the enemy has *not* succeeded, until now, in effecting a junction with the Carentan bridgehead, by means of his attack from Isigny toward the west. 6 Parachute Regiment, which has fought better than expected, has been given the order to hold Carentan to the last man.

(2) Field Marshal Rommel . . . orders that the enemy must be prevented at all costs from:

(a) Getting the fortress of Cherbourg, and harbor, in his hands.

(b) Establishing the connection between both bridgeheads; that west of the Orne and west of the Vire.

(3) The Chief of Staff expresses the opinion that the enemy, because of the increased resistance south of Montebourg, will commit more airborne troops in order to take possession of Cherbourg rapidly. Field Marshal Rommel does *not* share this opinion, since the Supreme Command expects a large landing on the Channel coast within the next few days, and therefore the enemy will *not* have more airborne troops available.

(4) As to future operations, the Commanding General Seventh Army is of the opinion that he will only go over to the attack when 2 Parachute Corps is ready for commitment and when the attack can be co-ordinated with the counterattack of 1 SS Panzer Corps. Field Marshal Rommel concurred with this opinion. However, the defense of Cherbourg is to be conducted independently and started immediately, with the greatest vigor.

2400—General Marcks acquaints the Chief of Staff with the unfavorable development at the Sainte-Mère-Eglise bridgehead.

The enemy has broken out, both to the west, across the inundated land, and also in a northerly direction toward Montebourg. In the west he has reached Pont-l'Abbé. In the north he has crossed the road Montebourg-Quinéville. The Commanding General, LXXXIV Corps, believes that tomorrow will be the decisive day for the battle of the Cherbourg Fortress. He has given strict instructions that the line reached this evening must be held at all costs. General Marcks makes the following demands:

(1) Exceptional reinforcement of our own Air Force, to combat the enemy superiority.

(2) Likewise, the sending in of a large amount of antitank weapons.

He maintains that the units brought up have been most inadequately equipped; and that, particularly the "stovepipes" (bazookas), etc., are effective against enemy tanks only at a few meters' range. . . .

10 JUNE 44

1100—General Meindl, Commander 2 Parachute Corps, reports to Chief of Staff.

3 Parachute Division must be brought forward piecemeal, because of lack of fuel. At the present time one regiment is located approximately east of Saint-Lô. The main body of the division is still in Brittany.

77 Infantry Division is, in the opinion of General Meindl, with its advanced elements already in the area of Valognes and the remainder in the region of Avranches.

1245—Commander, LXXXIV Corps, talks to the Chief of Staff.

The advance units of 17 SS Panzer Grenadier Division are stuck in the Saint-Lô area because of lack of fuel.

The Chief of Staff underlines the fact that it is not only a question of preventing a junction of the two enemy groups in the area of Bayeux and Carentan, but the main task is that of preventing the enemy from cutting off the Cotentin Peninsula by a further advance to the west and southwest.

HQ LXXXIV Corps add their intentions thereto; the object is *not* merely preventing the enemy from taking possession of roadways, but to destroy and wipe out the enemy.

1700—Chief of Staff informs Army Group "B."

Panzer Group West has sustained enemy attack and is now engaged in local counterattacks. It is evident, from reports, that Panzer Group West has been prevented from carrying out its basic mission.

Chief of Staff Army Group B presents the views of the Supreme Commander of the Armed Forces (Hitler) that there should be neither a withdrawal, fighting to the rear, nor disengagements rearward to a new line of resistance, but that every man will fight and fall, where he stands.

2330—Chief of Staff to QMG.

Orders given to draw off 65% of the anti-tank close-defense weapons (Panzerfaust and Panzerschreck), from 265 and 266 and the remaining elements of 275 Infantry Divisions, as well as 5 Parachute Division. These weapons are to be sent, at once, to the Saint-Lô area (Camp Michel) and put at the disposition of LXXXIV Corps.

11 JUNE 44

0520—General Marcks, LXXXIV Corps, to Chief of Staff, Seventh Army.

He asks when 17 SS Panzer Grenadier Division will be ready for commitment, since the situation on the right flank is critical. 352 Infantry Division now only has a very small combat value; gaps between them and their right-flank neighbor become constantly larger. Communications with this division no longer exist.

0920—Chief of Staff informs Army Group "B."

Nothing is known as to whether the enemy has effected a union across the Vire. The Panzer Group West has been knocked out by a direct bomb hit on its headquarters; command has been given to 1 SS Panzer Corps . . . road traffic must be dictatorially governed directly by Seventh Army through the employment of road commanders.

EXTRACTS FROM TELEPHONE CONVERSATION OF FIELD MARSHAL KLUGE

(The following extracts from the telephone conversation of Field Marshal von Kluge, Commander-in-Chief West, dated 31 July 44. They deal with the period

when the Americans were exploiting their success west of Saint-Lô designed to cut off the balance of the Cotentin Peninsula. Having taken Coutances and Granville, they were now proceeding toward Villedieu and Avranches, which finally fell on the night of 31 July. Since D-Day, General Marcks of 84 Corps has been killed and replaced by Lieutenant General von Choltitz, while General Hausser has filled the vacancy as Commander of Seventh Army, created by the death of General Dollman. Field Marshal von Kluge has taken over the unprofitable job of Commander-in-Chief West from his weary predecessor, von Rundstedt.)

0100—With Lieutenant General Speidel, Chief of Staff Army Group "B."

LXXXIV Corps receives orders to withdraw to line Villedieu-Avranches, whether orders are still coming through is questionable.

The High Command is to be informed that the left flank has collapsed.

0145—With General Fahrmbacher, Commander XXV Corps.

Two companies of 266 Division are moving toward area south of Saint-Malo as well as one weak battalion of the Parachute Infantry Training regiments.

General Fahrmbacher requests a most forceful order to the Navy, whose co-operation is insufficient.

He can only carry the responsibility if he can issue orders and does not have to ask for everything.

0920—With Lieutenant General Speidel.

The enemy has reached Avranches; our assault guns were obviously pushed back by the enemy. Intervention by 77 Infantry Division is unknown. LXXXIV Corps has already ordered withdrawal to the line Villedieu-Avranches. Infantry Regiment 957 of 363 Infantry Division has apparently *not* moved, owing to hitherto unprecedented enemy fighter-bomber activity. Enemy tank advances on Granville and Avranches were preceded by an umbrella of enemy fighter-bombers. This made any movement almost impossible.

All in all, the situation in the area Villedieu-Avranches is completely unclear. The troops have suffered high losses in men and equipment by strong air activity and the morale has greatly suffered.

On the left flank of Panzer Group West no clear picture. Situation absolutely unclear. Responsibility for the great crisis, which has occurred here, lies with the order of the Seventh Army to try, against the will of LXXXIV Corps, to break through to the south and SE. 91 Infantry Division has established a thin line of resistance along the line Cérences-Bréhal. As a consequence of the break-through of enemy armored spearheads near Cérences the whole Western Front has been ripped open, the key point Avranches has been taken by the enemy, and Villedieu is threatened. Villedieu, springboard for the east and south, as well as Avranches, is the anchor point for Brittany, has to be held under all circumstances or else has to be recaptured.

To accomplish this, on our own, with the troops in their present condition is impossible. Air reconnaissance has to clarify the situation in the area Villedieu-Avranches immediately. Question: What forces can be thrown in immediately? Answer: 708 Infantry Division can be there in about eight days. This division is therefore out of the question for clarification of the situation. A second regiment of 363 Infantry Division must be brought up immediately with all available transportation. What is important is the sealing off of the roads from Villedieu to the east and south as well as from Avranches to the south. Sealing off in Pontaubault, south of Avranches, is probably possible. The situation must be controlled under all circumstances, because this is the decisive phase. The seriousness of the situation must be explained to the Army High Command.

0935—With Chief of Staff Seventh Army, Colonel von Gersdorff.

Yesterday's heavy fighting was successful for the enemy only because he paralyzed all our movements by employing fighter-bombers on an unprecedented scale.

The greatest worry of the Field Marshal is Villedieu as a key point for enemy operation toward the east and south. Whether or not Villedieu is occupied by the enemy has *not* been established. The Field Marshal therefore agrees to the withdrawal of 2 SS Panzer Division to line Percy-Villedieu. Obviously the enemy is still very weak in Avranches. We are dealing with an advanced armored spearhead there. We have to throw in whatever possible. The intention is to bring up 89 and 84 Infantry Divisions.

1000—With Commander XXV Corps.

Commander-in-Chief West informs General Fahrmbacher about the situation, especially as far as the sector Villedieu-Avranches is concerned. It is necessary, to close the Avranches gap by stripping the area of Saint-Malo of forces as far as possible in order to prohibit the influx of the enemy into Brittany.

General Fahrmbacher mentions that in spite of the weakness of the Army, a great number of troops of the Navy and Air Force remain unemployed within the corps area; a situation which appears unjustifiable. This personnel, however, does *not* come under the jurisdiction of the Commanding General.

1045—*With General Warlimont (Hitler's representative).*

The Commander-in-Chief West given the situation within the XXXXVII Panzer Corps and especially the LXXXIV Army Corps. The enemy is in Avranches and may be also in Villedieu. These key positions for future operations must be held at all costs. Another advance of the enemy out of Avranches into Brittany was sealed off at Pontaubault. All available forces from Saint-Malo were brought up. The idle forces of the Navy and Air Force which are absolutely needed for the decisive fight, the price of which is the future or the end of the situation in the bridgehead, are, according to Commanding General XXV Corps, *not* obtainable. General Warlimont agrees to refer this question to the Führer. Commander-in-Chief West describes the seriousness of the situation with impressive eloquence. Whether the enemy can be stopped at

this point is still questionable. The enemy air superiority is terrific, and smothers almost every one of our movements. Every movement of the enemy, however, is prepared and protected by its air force. Losses in men and equipment are extraordinary. The morale of the troops has suffered very heavily under constant murderous enemy fire, especially, since all infantry units consist only of haphazard groups which do *not* form a strongly co-ordinated force any longer. In the rear areas of the front, terrorists, feeling the end approaching, grow steadily bolder. This fact and the loss of numerous signal installations makes an orderly command extremely difficult. LXXXIV Corps has reached a certain degree of disintegration. Part of the responsibility for the present situation rests with the order of Seventh Army for the northern front to break through toward the south and SE. Commander-in-Chief West has, as soon as he was informed thereof, changed this order to reconstitute the front with the forces at hand. Fresh troops must be brought up from the Fifteenth Army or from somewhere else. Commander-in-Chief West recalls herewith the World War I example, in which Parisian buses were used to bring up troops to the Allied front. Now, as then, all available means must be exhausted. It is, however, still impossible to determine whether it would be possible to stop the enemy.

"The Best General the British Have"

LONDON, SUNDAY, SEPTEMBER 17, 1944

Wes Gallagher, of the AP, has just returned from a long tour covering front-line activities. He told me that officers and personnel of Patton's Third Army are burned up because they feel the British have been favored by General Ike with transport and permitted to advance while the Americans in the Third Army were stalled because of lack of gasoline. He said he had talked with junior officers in Patton's army and some had said, "Eisenhower is the best general the British have."

Today I visited T. J. at the hospital and gave him the welcome news that his eventual return to active duty as Adjutant General had been approved by the Chief of Staff and Supreme Commander. His brown eyes sparkled with pleasure. While I was visiting him, hundreds of aircraft, many towing gliders, passed overhead en route to the big jump to cross the Rhine at Nijmegen.

Colonel Dupuy and Captain Frank Mayborn came to my room at the Dorchester this evening, Dupuy just having returned from Granville. He was wearing the Legion of Merit and was proud to have it. It had been pinned on him by Beetle in his caravan—which Dupuy described as a "gypsy hut." He had the news, too, that Brigadier General Frank A. Allen would become director of PRD. He said good-naturedly that he not only got decorated but got the ax.

PARIS, MONDAY, SEPTEMBER 18, 1944

I arrived at Orly airfield, in the outskirts of Paris, in company with Lieutenant Colonel A. H. Rosenfeld, who is managing the move of SHAEF Main from Bushy Park to Versailles, where it will join up with SHAEF Forward, which is moving over from Granville this week. Ike is still in Granville.

"Rosie" and I were given a French taxi by the always co-operative lads of Air Transport Command and immediately set out for Versailles, where I thought I could quickly learn the score with respect to the Scribe * from the headquarters commandant, Colonel R. Q. Brown. It took longer to drive the few miles from Orly to Versailles than to fly from England to Paris. The main road to Versailles is the Red Ball route with one-way traffic—going the wrong way for us. MPs shooed us off onto side roads and we were a couple of hours making the few kilometers. There were considerable signs of fighting here and there, burned-out German tanks, trucks, and *Volkswagen*. The Orly airfield itself had been well beaten up with our bombs, although a couple of runways had been repaired for use and temporary facilities established for the ATC.

I found the scare about loss of the Scribe was largely a false alarm and that Lady Tedder's requirements for the Allied Club would be taken care of.

I have had a talk with Major W. R. Brown of the Communications Branch of PRD, who reports that in addition to our other troubles, parts

---

* Lady Tedder, as head of the Allied Club, had requested assignment of the Scribe Hotel for personnel, and I had been sent to Paris to save it for the correspondents and help her find another one.

for transmitters crated in boxes for Press Wireless and Mackay have been unloaded over the beaches and some crates lost. Press Wireless' transmitter is now in boxes at Chartres, where, before the fall of Paris, it was thought the transmitter should be erected. Mackay's boxes are at Omaha Beach and some are lost. But the real problem is to find trucks to bring the gear to Paris, as all form of Army transport is engaged in rushing supplies to the front—told in the slogan, "Petrol for Patton."

If communications aren't straightened, anything else done to improve public relations will be of no consequence, as prompt and reliable movement of copy is the first concern of correspondents and their home offices.

Plan to Combat False Rumors of Peace

PARIS, TUESDAY, SEPTEMBER 19, 1944

I had a note from Ike today, written from SHAEF Forward at Granville. He had seen Hugh Baillie, of UP, who had asked through me for an appointment, and will see Lieutenant Colonel Harlan Miller, former writer of the "Over the Coffee Cup" column at home, and his British opposite number, Wing Commander Nickolls. The latter two are bird dogs for information for the official moving picture covering this campaign. They want the Boss himself to tell them about the strategy and tactics.

Ike wrote me that he was hearing some repercussions from the Quebec conference, where his recommendations for continuance of the Allied command for purposes of occupation of Germany have not been accepted and, instead, Germany is to be divided into areas in which the Russians, Americans, and the British are to have control on nationalistic lines. I know from previous talks that Ike has strongly favored the continuation of SHAEF for the occupation, as he believes this arrangement will simplify the executive orders from the three governments. However, his recommendation has been disapproved on the highest level.

He reminded me that SHAEF Forward is moving to Versailles this week and said, "Come over and see us when you can."

While still in London, I had worked out with Beetle an arrangement whereby false rumors of peace could be checked officially through him, so the home publics wouldn't be unduly misled. Through the Will Committee, which represents British newspaper publishers, the Ministry of Information, and Elmer Davis, of OWI, we now have a voluntary agreement with the press associations, publishers, correspondents, and broadcasters that such rumors will first be checked with SHAEF PRD before they are passed on to the public. Elmer's self-typed letter, just received, gives a picture of the state of our home front. He writes:

DEAR HARRY:

Thanks for your letter of the 7th, whose promise is implemented by the statement just in today that SHAEF will take the responsibility of knocking down phony peace rumors at any hour of the day or night. Sorry to put this burden on your outfit, but exploration at the White House, the State Department, and the War Department brought the unanimous verdict that whenever it is true, SHAEF will know it first. (Unless they surrender to the Russians, and even then I suppose Eisenhower would be advised in advance.)

Meanwhile I am getting some public acceptance of my theory that very likely there will be no V-Day, but a gradual disintegration. I don't think there is much danger that the home public, in that case, would stay drunk through a V-week; there seems to be a pretty general realization here that even when the European situation is straightened out we shall still have quite a war on our hands, and enough people have relatives in the Pacific to guarantee that this will not be forgotten. Besides, the churches and others are already starting to discourage such exhibitions as were seen on November 7 and again on November 11, 1918. So far has this movement got that it has even been proposed that if there is a V-Day, the Director of this Office should formally and ceremonially go to church. However, I would not want to upset any man of God by so unexpected an appearance.

Life must be somewhat simpler in London, now that the buzzers no longer buzz. It is simpler in Washington, at least for us, now that members of Congress are mostly fighting each other and take no more than occasional side swipes at OWI. However, enough unexpected crises pop up every day to keep the liver well shaken up and functioning. Why ride horseback? You can get the same results in a swivel chair. Ed Klauber * is taking a few days of well-deserved rest, after the strain of running the show during my five weeks' absence in the Pacific.

I hope my government can afford to provide me with a new typewriter ribbon.

As always,
ELMER DAVIS

Scrounging for Facilities

PARIS, WEDNESDAY, SEPTEMBER 20, 1944

Delighted to find Major Bob Neville, editor of Stars and Stripes in the Mediterranean, and Sergeant Bill Estoff, of his circulation department, in the Scribe. Dined with them last night. They were here to arrange for flow of news from the Stars and Stripes in Paris for their editions in southern France. Printing facilities have been obtained at Dijon. These boys are veterans of Africa and Italy and are very much on the alert. Their ingenuity at keeping Stars and Stripes published where it can be dis-

* Deputy Director OWI, and formerly executive vice-president of CBS.

tributed to the combat troops in the front lines is a pleasure to behold.

My one-day mission to Paris to save the Scribe has been extended by Colonel Dupuy because of the need of getting additional facilities here for the PRD. We need a hotel for the staff and a building for the offices, preferably close to the Scribe because of the scarcity of transportation. I am trying to arrange these facilities within walking distance of each other. Also need billets for enlisted personnel. There is a mad scramble for space. I am dealing with SHAEF Headquarters Command and I suspect my friends who are helping me get what we need are not quite certain whether they are dealing with me as an aide of General Eisenhower or as a temporary staff officer of PRD. In any event, they are most helpful.

I hear that General Allen has reported in at Granville and has gone on to London with instructions to take charge and to complete the merger.

PARIS, SATURDAY, SEPTEMBER 23, 1944

Someday someone will write the proper history of the Scribe Hotel as the working and social center of war correspondents. The Scribe Bar is a chief attraction, but the Army mess in the Scribe—with breakfast at ten francs, or twenty cents; lunch and dinner at twenty francs each, or forty cents— is perhaps even more popular. The food in the Paris cafés is terrifically expensive. Consequently, the correspondents and officers who find old or new friends amongst the French, or former employees of bureaus, are crowding the Scribe's dining room. SHAEF messes are run on the basis of pay-as-you-enter, and the mess officer uses these funds to buy food from the Quartermaster. The mess actually makes a small profit, but we cannot indiscriminately feed everyone whom the correspondents or our own staff wish to bring as a guest.

I Get Brought Up to Date

PARIS, SUNDAY, SEPTEMBER 24, 1944

I went out to Versailles today to bring Ike up to date on affairs at my level. I reported to him the comment from junior officers of the Third Army that "Eisenhower is the best general the British have." This disturbed him.

While he was laid up with his injured knee, he could not visit the troops, although he has made some trips to see the principal subordinates up forward. Now that the knee has improved, he expects to visit troops in the forward areas. I told him that this was badly needed and a new arrangement should be made for coverage of such visits. Although the pool of correspondents is relatively small, he has always been worried about their accompanying him on trips. He worries, first, because he feels a sense of responsibility that they get some news and frequently directs or personally arranges that they see his principal subordinates, such as Tedder, Ramsay, and Beetle as well as the staff. However, when Ike travels, he moves rapidly and hates to be conspicuous. At least two cars ordinarily are required to transport the correspondents, the Signal Corps photographers, and the conducting officer. In addition, Ike always feels self-conscious when he talks with GIs and correspondents or photographers are around because he feels that this violates the privacy of his conversation and may make the soldiers feel that he is visiting with them simply for publicity. For this reason, he has generally had an agreement with the correspondents that they will not quote his conversation with GIs. But this does not prevent them from later talking with the GIs themselves.

I advocated elimination of the pool and its replacement by one correspondent who, with the official photographers, could travel in one car. Ike was quite agreeable to this, as he was anxious to relieve himself of his embarrassment by the presence of the larger pool.

I found Ike living in a comfortable house, previously used by General von Rundstedt, at Saint-Germain, a fifteen-minute drive from his headquarters. It had a large and deep air-raid shelter, which I discovered he had not even seen. Telek and Caacie are in fine form and Shaef is still growing; one of the cows is going dry.

Colonel Gault, his British Military Assistant, is living with him, as at Granville.

Ike and I discussed the variety of un-Allied comment I picked up from American and British correspondents. Ike was shocked to know of the extent of anti-British feeling in American correspondents and was surprised when I reported a somewhat similar feeling in British writers, notably those attached to press camps in Montgomery's sector. I told him I had discovered, while working with the PRD, that I had lived in an ivory tower with him, and that I was beginning to learn the facts of life. Ike said that the information I gave him meant that he and others had to redouble their efforts to spread the gospel of Allied Command. My doleful report drew forth his frequently used comment, "This world and then the fireworks."

On military matters, Ike pointed out there had been two courses of action in strategy: one was to concentrate our resources behind a knifelike and narrow thrust into the center of Germany, hoping that such an advance would bring about capitulation; the other was to drive forward through the enemy's western frontiers to suitable positions on which we could regroup while preparing the maintenance facilities necessary to sustain the great bulk of our forces on a drive into Germany which definitely would force capitulation. He favors the latter, although Monty has been anxious to have the bulk of transport and supply to make the gamble for Berlin.

The Supreme Commander had received from General Pyle, Commander-in-Chief of the Antiaircraft Command in England, a generous thank-you note for American assistance against the flying bombs. He said that American aircraft gunners joined the battle with enthusiasm and reinforced the gun belt with eighty guns. He said that in an astonishingly short time they had got to grips with the unfamiliar target and settled down to some excellent shooting. They had done so well that on occasions his own men complained that Americans were knocking down the bombs before they themselves had an opportunity to have a go at them.

Monty had been in a stew about his supply situation and had taken all of the transport from his 51st Division resting at Le Havre to hasten the movement. Ike had arranged for a daily lift of 500 tons of supply by road, with trucks from Com Zone. Ike also had gotten General Spaatz's bombers to go into the supply business and, weather permitting, another thousand tons a day, principally gasoline and ammunition, could be carried from England to the forward areas, about half of which would go to Monty. He also was worried about the supplies for Hodges' Army on his right flank, but Ike had had this checked up.

The Quebec conference, in addition to deciding that occupation of Germany, once the war is over, would be in sectors on nationalistic lines, had removed from Ike his direct command over the RAF Bomber Command under Air Chief Marshal Harris, and the U. S. Strategic Air Force under Spaatz. Spaatz had been most disturbed by the new arrangement. Ike had written both Harris and Spaatz his thanks upon behalf of SHAEF for the great contributions of their air forces in the progress of the ground battle and hoped that every member of their respective commands would be informed of his personal assurance of his lasting gratitude and that each one would realize their countrymen's indebtedness to them for examples of unexcelled courage, skill, and perfection in co-operation.

Ike thought this was a poor arrangement, but had written General Marshall that the personal relationship among himself, "Bomber" Harris, and Tooey Spaatz was so intimate and understanding that no real harm had been done. Ike is still authorized to call for strategic bombers for direct support of land and naval operations, but their main job is to pound enemy industry, especially oil.

Ike had relayed to one of the air-support commanders that he had heard of a plan to diminish the number of sorties normally flown to support ground operations. When Ike received the full explanation for the need of the temporary reduction, caused by the front line getting beyond the useful range of medium bombers from established airfields, and that the diminution would prevail only until new airfields were constructed farther forward, he sent a reply apologizing for any lack of confidence implied by his message and said that he should have known better.

To Lieutenant General Brereton, commanding the First Allied Airborne Army, whose big jump to capture bridges across the lower Rhine I had seen in flight near London on September 17, Ike had sent congratulations for the initial success of the operation. He congratulated Brereton and his British deputy, General Browning, and all officers and ranks serving under them, for the good start. The fighting for the bridges, particularly in the Arnhem area of the British 1st Airborne Division, is still intense and the Germans are counterattacking constantly.

General Brereton had reported on the twenty-third that there had been no news for thirty-six hours of the British 1st Airborne Division at Arnhem. The division is in a very tight perimeter and the enemy is throwing mortar shells and heavy machine-gun fire, followed by counterattacks, into the British paratroopers, whose casualties run heavy and whose resources are stretched to the utmost. To be saved, they must have relief within twenty-four hours.

I heard that the Queen was visiting the 1st Airborne Division, which was ready to take off for its dangerous and vital effort to seize and hold the bridges at Arnhem. She noticed one of the paratroopers carrying, in addition to all his regular gear, a dart board. This surprised her, and she said to the soldier:

"Whatever are you taking that for?"

"Well, you never can tell, Your Majesty," he replied respectfully. "A dart game always helps to pass away dull evenings."

Tears came to her eyes.

One of the items of information I had reported to Ike concerned a certain amount of griping that two American airborne divisions had been assigned to Monty when their use might have greatly speeded Patton in his wild dash. Ike said that from a military standpoint the assignment was perfectly proper and that anyone who understood military strategy would realize the great advantage that would accrue if the airborne operation succeeded in getting Monty a bridgehead across the Rhine. So far as allotment of American divisions to British command was concerned, he said that in Allied operations, he could and would not miss an opportunity to cash in on a gamble simply to avoid nationalistic sensitiveness. As a matter of fact, he pointed out, the British had voluntarily insisted that their airborne division take the toughest and most advanced assignment. What would be the American reaction if either our 82nd or 101st Airborne had been assigned by Monty to the tough spot given the British airborne?

Monty had been pressing harder for allotment of more transport supplies to the 21st Army Group, and Ike again had gone into the problem in great detail. Ike had informed Monty that he had given preference to the left flank, meaning Monty's 21st Army Group, throughout the campaign, including attachment of the 1st Airborne Force to Monty, and adopting every possible expedient to assure his maintenance. On the other hand, all other forces have been fighting with a halter around their necks with respect to supplies, and he illustrated that for four days straight Patton had been receiving serious counterattacks, yet in seven days, without attempting any real advance, had captured about 9000 prisoners and knocked out 270 tanks.

Congressmen have arrived in England as guests of the British and, of course, want to come to France. Ike has arranged that they be conducted by Com Zone in groups, so they can see anything they want, but he doesn't want individual Congressmen to free-wheel, as he feels everyone has enough work without taking time off to show around single visitors.

Ike had had a conference of his Commanders-in-Chief on the twenty-second, and all attended except Field Marshal Montgomery, who sent his Chief of Staff, General de Guingand. Monty felt that affairs on the long front were in a bad state and advocated that the tactical battle required one ground commander on the spot and recommended that the Supreme Commander hand the job over to him, so he would have operational control over Hodges' First Army. Monty had by now altered his thoughts and was not thinking in terms of a quick rush to Berlin, but now sought capture of the Ruhr Valley, which he felt was impossible unless the 12th Army Group was ordered by Ike to halt and supply support given to his Army Group. Otherwise he felt the Allies would not get the Ruhr. With the change in concept of object, Ike found himself in agreement so far as emphasis to the 21st Army Group was concerned, but not for command. He also wanted 21st Army Group to clear the approaches to Antwerp, so that the port, now blocked by enemy occupation on the north side of the Scheldt, would be available for much needed supplies. Monty's plan of concentration of force in the north was supported by Ike, and Monty's effort is to be the main one. The lines held by the Southern Group of Armies under Devers is to take over frontage from the Central Group of Armies under Bradley, who is to continue offensive operations.

General de Guingand reported to Monty most optimistically about the conference, but said that the command arrangements are still being discussed and he hopes they will be satisfactory.

Ike himself wrote to Monty after the conference and believed that complete understandings had been reached which should hold all the way to the completion of our present bid for the capture of the Ruhr. Ike reminded Monty that when they had visited at 21st Army Group headquarters on September 10, Monty had felt that, with additional maintenance from the U. S., his forces would be sufficient to take care of the job in the north and had ordered Bradley to take over some of the 21st Army Group sector to assist Monty. Now Ike finds that Bradley's forces are getting fearfully stretched south of Aachen and that we may get a nasty little "Kasserine" if the enemy chooses the right place to concentrate his strength. So far as Devers was concerned, his line of communication through Marseille is separated from ours, and his supply situation is adequate to permit his forces to continue to fight, thus making the Germans stretch out all along the line.

PARIS, TUESDAY, SEPTEMBER 26, 1944

I was a guest at dinner last night at the Cercle Interallié of Merrill (Red) Mueller, NBC broadcaster who has been in the pool assigned to SHAEF Forward. Whoever checks expense accounts at NBC will be shocked by the cost. Several of the guests, most of whom were on the personal staff of General Ike, rudely guessed at the cost—the estimates ranging from $200 to $450, reflecting the scarcity of food and the exchange rate between the dollar and the franc.

The General has had the members of the pool in for a talk and has told them of his desire to save manpower to avoid inconvenience by reducing the number to one. I imagine it is one of the few times in history that a leading general has asked for a diminution of news coverage about himself. Red, as well as others with whom I have talked, think the Boss's decision is unusual.

I am to stay in Paris to complete the household arrangements for SHAEF PRD to move into the Scribe. I am amazed to find that British publishers have questioned the advisability of moving the PRD from MOI to Paris. They like the speed of communications from the MOI and are fearful of our communications from Paris. I think SHAEF would look very bad, indeed, if its Public Relations Division still operated in London when the battle front now reaches into Germany. The big need is improvement of communications from Paris and from the Army press camps.

Am moving out of the Scribe, where there is no rest, particularly if correspondents think you can do anything for them, and, apparently, a lot of them think I can. Have been assigned a room at the Raphaël on the Avenue Kléberg, next to the Majestic, which is headquarters for Com Zone. The Raphaël is used by SHAEF for transient visitors and, thankfully, I am classified as a transient.

SEPTEMBER, 1944: *Allied offensives in Europe scored new successes. American troops, driving through Luxembourg, penetrated the Siegfried Line north of Trier. U. S. First Army took Roetgen, sent two columns on to Aachen. U. S. troops entered Belgium; British-American troops took Brussels, advanced into the Netherlands. Moselle advances scored by U. S. Third, which joined Seventh twelve miles from Dijon. Allies occupied Antwerp and Namur. Canadians cleared Channel coast from Zeebrugge to Nieuport. German army of 20,000 surrendered at Orléans; 17,000, at Brest. Notable Russian advances reached to the Gulf of Riga, the Danube, the outskirts of Warsaw, the Yugoslav border, penetrated Transylvania, encircled Cluj, liberated mainland of Estonia, ended four-day war with Bulgaria, occupied Prague. Allied units from Italy joined Tito, drove toward junction with Reds in Yugoslavia. Heavy air raids continued to hit all types of targets; incendiary bombs caused crippling fires: on one day 5000 planes hit Germany with 3000 tons of explosives, 600,000 incendiaries. Italian campaign advanced slowly against stubborn Nazi resistance, capturing Pisa, Pesaro, Pistoia, Rimini, and Futa Pass. In the Pacific bombers continued to pound Celebes and Philippine targets; carrier planes blasted Jap targets in the Kuriles and Palaus. Superforts hit Anshan, in Manchuria. Pacific Fleet planes destroyed 433 planes and eighty-four ships in three-day strike at Panay, Cebu, and Negros, in central Philippines. MacArthur's troops landed on Morotai; Nimitz's Third Amphibious invaded Peleliu. 84th Infantry invaded Palau. Halsey's Third Fleet hit Philippines, destroyed 357 planes at cost of eleven planes, fifteen men. Japs launched assault against Kweilin; took Chekiang port of Wenchow. British troops landed in Greece. Allied forces took Le Havre, Calais, and Boulogne. (We had a severe letdown when the combat troops stretched the line of supply so far they had to slow down.—H.C.B.)*

Setback at Arnhem and Review of Present Situation

PARIS, SUNDAY, OCTOBER 1, 1944

I spent considerable time with Ike today. During the week he had been up forward, primarily to talk to General Bradley and other American top commanders, and as many corps and divisional commanders as could be collected. The main purpose was to inform all commanders of the role they and their troops are playing at present in major strategy. Their role is largely static until we have achieved satisfactory build-up of supplies. He assured them their part was equally important in winning the war as the remarkable advance which they had made since July 25. He wanted all commanders, through junior commanders, to impress the importance of this on all troops. He also had his ear perked to find out their troubles and difficulties, in an effort to see where he could be of help. He had had sessions at Bradley's headquarters at Verdun, Patton's Third Army headquarters at Nancy, and Hodges' First Army headquarters at Liége. He had returned to Rheims in a liaison plane and on Thursday, September 28, had spent his first night at his new Advance Camp a few miles west of Rheims. General Bradley and one of his aides, Major Bridge, stayed overnight.

The British 1st Airborne Division had lost its bridgehead at Arnhem, and out of 7500 paratroopers who landed, only 2000 escaped. They had nine days of unrelenting mortar, machine-gun, artillery, rocket, and small-arms fire from the Germans—not to mention tanks and self-propelled artillery. The objectives of the American 82nd and 101st Airborne Divisions were taken and held, but the British division had the most advanced objective. Infantry and tanks had been unable to reach the marooned paratroopers, but artillery of the British Second Army had been very helpful. Although militarily classified as a failure, the action and tenacity of the British, Ike said, constitute a brilliant page in their history.

Abandonment of the Arnhem bridgehead has caused Monty to alter his plans for crossing the Rhine and taking the Ruhr. Monty wants to award British decorations to American personnel, particularly of the two airborne divisions now under his command.

On the personal side, I found Ike in good health and spirits. His knee has showed steady improvement. He was keenly interested in my progress with the PRD and agreed that I had a bear by the tail and probably would have to stay on longer. I told him General Allen had been in Paris for a day and had asked me to take over planning because of my familiarity with SHAEF operational plans. Ike wanted me to know, "You don't have to stay in PRD forever," but if I was needed there, he was going to cable Admiral King to promote me "because I don't want to see you kicked around." This is gratifying but unnecessary, although a jump in rank may help to get my job done more quickly.

Ike was damning his old enemy, the weather. We drew a parallel between his military situation now and that of Christmas, 1942, and the subsequent period when we were stuck in the mud in Tunisia. Ike strongly upholds his strategy of stretch-out of the Germans. They have a tremendously long front in the east, a considerable one in Italy, and one of about 500 miles in the west.

Ike had only to cast his mind over the accomplishments of SHAEF to realize that despite our optimism for the early end of the war that reached its height almost coincidental with the fall of Paris, his forces had to their credit achievements which, undoubtedly, would stand high in military history. However, they still had problems.

Brest, Le Havre, and Boulogne have been captured, and the only major ports in northern France remaining in enemy hands are Lorient and Saint-Nazaire and, on the north coast, Calais and Dunkirk, all four of which are being, as the General says, "contained." (Calais' big guns, which had bombarded Dover intermittently since 1940, had been silenced on September 27, but the city was not fully occupied until October 1.) The link-up of Devers' Southern Group and Bradley's Central Group of Armies has given us a continuous Allied front from the North Sea to the Mediterranean. The front has been moving eastward, but during September our advance in most sectors was slowed as the enemy's resistance increased.

The enemy has, however, established a relatively stable and cohesive front, approximately on the German frontier except in the Low Countries. The Germans have lost a million men in France and an enormous amount of equipment, yet there are no signs of collapse in morale and in the will to defend Germany.

The Germans are capable of defending the western frontier of the Reich, probably initially along the water obstacles of Holland, the West Wall, the Moselle, the Vosges, and, ultimately, the Rhine itself. The enemy may attempt to attack south of Nancy with his armor, to relieve pressure on the remainder of the front and stabilize the Moselle-Vosges line. It is regarded as likely that the enemy will attempt by counterattack to throw us out of the West Wall in places where we have penetrated.

Logistical support for the fighting continues to depend largely on original bases and on long road and rail lines of communications. These are strained to the utmost and restrict the advance and deployment of divisions. Antwerp must be cleared and developed to serve both the Northern and Central Group of Armies. This is a matter of transcendent importance which, Ike felt, unfortunately, might not be completed before November.

Le Havre, developed primarily as a U. S. port, substantially shortens the line of communication and will relieve congestion in other ports. Coal is being mined and moved by inland waterways from Belgium to large cities. Railways are being developed by repair of damaged lines, development of signal facilities, and importation of rolling stock to relieve over-burdened truck transportation.

Resupply of forward units by air has been on a large scale, with American and British heavy bombers having been used while the transport aircraft have been committed to airborne operations. Air supply, however, is costly. In some instances, the cost is one and a half gallons of 100-octane gasoline to deliver one gallon of 80-octane motor fuel to forward depots.

As to intentions, General Ike's plans remain unaltered, that is, to press on with all speed to destroy the German armed forces and to advance deep into Germany. He has not deviated from his opinion that the best means of destroying the Germans is to strike at the Ruhr and the Saar, throwing the great weight north of the Ruhr. In the present phase of operations, the capture of the Ruhr by Monty's Group and by Hodges' First Army is the main effort. Montgomery's British and Canadian Armies also are responsible for opening the port of Antwerp, which is essential to sustain a drive deep into Germany. To clear the Scheldt, it will be necessary to capture Walcheren and Zuid Beveland Islands, as well as the fortified areas on the mainland opposite Flushing, all of which command the approaches to the vital port. The islands are heavily defended, and to capture them will require a major operation with the use of heavy bombardment by warships and concentrated bombing by Strategic Air Forces, followed by amphibious and overland operations.

Bradley's Central Group of Armies is to thrust as far toward Cologne and Bonn as its current resources permit. General Ike has directed that Bradley also be prepared to seize any favorable opportunity for crossing the Rhine and to attack the Ruhr from the south when maintenance permits.

Devers' Southern Group, consisting of Patch's Seventh and the French First Armies, having a separate line of communications, can continue offensive operations without diversion of supplies from the main effort. It is directed toward Mulhouse and Strasbourg. Plans are in progress for alternative airborne operations to gain bridgeheads across the Rhine to assist Bradley in the vicinity of Coblenz and Cologne.

General Ike is responsible for plans and operations to clear the Channel Islands, which, of course, still are held by the Germans. Except for the possibility of armed parties putting out from the islands to raid the coast, and the nuisance of the shore batteries to the Navy and ack-ack to aircraft, there is little concern about taking the islands, particularly in view of our commitments on the long front. Neither is there any favorable sign that the German garrisons will surrender.

There is concern about the internal security of southwest France, and General Ike has asked General "Jumbo" Wilson to move certain French units from North Africa and Corsica to maintain order, and if the fighting on the Western Front permits, he intends to release additional forces from the First French Army. A zone of interior is to be created at the earliest possible moment, at the request of General de Gaulle, thus turning back to the French the control of the liberated area.

After I left Ike at Versailles, I stopped at the Ritz to visit with Congresswoman Edith Nourse Rogers, of Massachusetts, who had a letter of introduction to me from Admiral Ross T. McIntire, the President's physician and Surgeon General of the Navy. She is visiting hospitals, in which she is keenly interested. I found her reflection of statements on the home front, particularly in the midst of a presidential election, quite foreign to my thoughts and those I hear most frequently expressed over here. She said that one of the campaign charges current in the United States when she left was that Churchill had purposely stopped General Ike in the rush across France to delay a giant victory until the eve of the election, in order to help Roosevelt. I told her I thought this kind of talk was an insult to every officer and GI who had been working and fighting.

PARIS, WEDNESDAY, OCTOBER 4, 1944

The date for the move of PRD to Paris has been set for October 10, and everyone is frantically working on facilities and communications.

Tonight, when I returned to the Raphaël, I found Colonel David Sarnoff sitting alone in the lobby in remote control of a big cigar. He said he recently had seen General Allen in London and had told him that PRD would be a complete flop if adequate communications were not provided on the Continent. He said that this is the thing I ought to look into. He had purchased a large and beautiful assortment of lingerie for his family and was returning to the States, wearing a Legion of Merit awarded him during the day.

PARIS, THURSDAY, OCTOBER 5, 1944

Colonel Ford Trimble, Secretary of the SHAEF General Staff, phoned me from Versailles that a message had been received from the Navy, promoting me to Captain in the reserves effective today, subject to physical examination and formal acceptance. Appointment will terminate when and if I report for permanent duty other than on Ike's staff. I think I will accept.

Pretty VGDIPs

General Marshall, former Justice James F. Byrnes, now Director of War Mobilization, Lieutenant General Tom Handy, Major General "Pinky" Craig, and Colonel Frank McCarthy arrived at Orly airport in a C-54, called *The Sacred Cow*, especially equipped for the use of President Roosevelt. The plane was piloted by Lieutenant Colonel Henry T. (Hank) Myers, and had flown nonstop from Newfoundland—the first publicized flight direct to Paris.

General Ike was on hand to meet the party and soon was in animated conversation with General Marshall. General Bradley and Beetle also were there. General Marshall is to stay at Ike's house, but first, Ike, Marshall, and McCarthy were flying with General Bradley to his headquarters.

Jimmy Byrnes is billeted at Hôtel de Lamballe, at 70 Rue Berton, made available by the French for SHAEF VIPs.

The PRD gang and I met the party with a number of correspondents and broadcasters, at the request of the War Department, which, on the occasion of the first formal flight, wished to have the trip publicized. I permitted the correspondents to inspect the plane and subsequently was jacked up because newsmen, apparently, were not supposed to see the interior of the plane especially fitted for the President. I didn't realize it was the President's plane when it landed—it looked like any other C-54 to me.

More Scrambled Eggs

Captain Frank Mayborn had a small dinner at the Chatham to wet my fourth stripe. Lieutenant Colonel V. E. Scott-Bailey, of the British Army, stood on his head. This is not his only claim to fame: he was formerly our chief censor at AFHQ. I asked to have him transferred to PRD to bolster it with personnel in whom Beetle and General Ike have confidence because of past relationships.

I have no gold braid and have found none in Paris, so will have to wait until some can be sent from London. Captain seems a very unfamiliar title; Commander sounds so much more important, especially to the Army.

Frank Mayborn is no hero-worshiper, but he has been telling me his one ambition in the war is to meet General Ike. Today I took him and Scott-Bailey to Versailles and they met the Supreme Commander. Ike was sitting in a glassed-in sunroom next to his office. I was surprised to find him posing for Cathleen Mann, the Marchioness of Queensberry. He greeted all of us most cordially, as usual, and he was especially pleased to see Scott, for whom he has a high regard. The Marchioness said she was sorry we had interrupted her work; that the serious expression on the General's face had now been changed.

Ike said, "Then draw my uniform while I talk to my old friends."

"But," said the Marchioness, "they're spoiling your face."

I knew he hated to sit for a picture. He had done it only once before, in Algiers. The thought of having to spend fifteen minutes a day for seven days had ruined an equivalent number of breakfasts. A British war artist, Carr, had been commissioned to paint the commanders at AFHQ and Ike had felt that courtesy required him to make his contribution.

So far as I know, the Marchioness was only the second artist who has succeeded in getting him to pose, and this was achieved through the personal request of Air Chief Marshal Tedder.

Ike kidded me about my promotion. He wanted to know how many more scrambled eggs I would have on my cap. I told him more than he.

Jim Gault likewise has been promoted; he is now wearing the red tabs on his lapel and the red band around his cap denoting the rank of a full colonel in the British Army.

PARIS, TUESDAY, OCTOBER 10, 1944

The accredited correspondents were flown over from London today, and we were set for them at the Scribe. Communications are now capable of 150,000 words a day, which should be ample unless there is some tremendous burst of news. However, as the front seems rather stalemated, the flow of copy is relatively low.

Played poker at Tooey's again last night and took first prize.

Also brought General Allen and staff up to date on details of our arrangements for facilities in Paris. Allen wants me to look after communications for a while. I told him my first job will be to find my successor; it will be Lieutenant Colonel Marty Ralph, liaison officer of SHAEF Signals, who deals with PRD, PWD, and SHAEF Mission to France, amongst other things. I will promote and when the promotion is finished, he can operate. O.K. by Allen.

PARIS, WEDNESDAY, OCTOBER 11, 1944

I was out at Versailles and saw General Ike. I told him I thought it would be timely if he had another press conference and that I would like to use him as the guinea pig to test our communications. A picture of GIs in a jeep in Germany, surrounded by German women and appearing very sociable, had created adverse reaction at home. Elmer Davis had been quoted in the home papers as saying that the failure of the British to cross the Rhine in the big paratroop operation at Arnhem had delayed victory by three months. This had created another schism in Allied friendliness. I thought Ike might outline his policy for conduct of Allied troops in Germany and, in general, bring the correspondents up to date. He agreed to come to the Scribe tomorrow.

General Marshall is still quartered at Ike's house, but has been on an extended trip to the forward area.

On the subject of General Marshall, I have been given an onerous job— to publicize the U. S. Army Band. Both Beetle and Colonel Frank McCarthy got after me to carry out General Marshall's request and said that the General wanted the band identified with front-line troops. It should be sent to some German city shortly after its capture. I will have to get some public-relations officer to devote his attention to this problem. General Marshall has almost despaired of bringing the Army Band into the same prominence at home as that enjoyed by the Marine Band. He has been after General Ike and Beetle, since the early days in Africa, to promote the Army Band, but correspondents naturally prefer to write news of actual battles, and stories of the Army Band are lost in the competition.

I found that Monty was still concerned about supply, especially for the First U. S. Army on his right flank. Ike has had Air Chief Marshal Tedder go personally to see Marshal Monty. German reinforcement against Monty's northern flank has stopped his advance. A co-ordinated attack to the Rhine, therefore, must be postponed until Monty can be strengthened, probably by U. S. divisions. General Marshall had visited Monty with Bradley and Hodges.

In addition to other troubles, a gale has reduced the intake at Cherbourg and through the artificial port at Arromanches, again pointing to the need of clearing Antwerp.

Tedder is being made personally responsible for all tactical air operations under SHAEF, as Air Chief Marshal Leigh-Mallory has been assigned to the Southeastern Asia Command under Lord Louis Mountbatten.

PARIS, THURSDAY, OCTOBER 12, 1944

General Ike drove in from Versailles this morning for his press conference at the Scribe. General Allen and I met him at the front door. We had placed MPs on guard and cleared away cars normally parked in front of the Scribe. This, apparently, was the tipoff that something important was going to happen, for a large crowd soon gathered.

When Ike finished his conference, the crowd had grown, yet Ike walked across and down the Rue Scribe a block to the Grand Hôtel to say hello to Lady Tedder and staff of the Allied Club. This side journey had not been planned and was entirely impromptu by Ike. The crowd pressed on him very tightly despite the assistance of the MPs, and some shopwindows were broken.

In the press conference, he made clear that we go into Germany as conquerors and there will be no fraternization. The Germans will be treated justly, in conformity with civilized standards as exemplified by our governments, but we will have nothing else to do with them except the necessary official relationships. He spoke feelingly about the Arnhem operation. He said he felt that tremendous advantages had accrued to us through the operation of the First Allied Airborne Army and that the "British 1st Airborne Division not only gave to all the Allied forces one of the most gallant examples of courage in all this war, but by drawing upon themselves the bulk of the German counterattack, they enabled us to hold important bridges." He described it as a valiant maneuver and "it does not detract in the slightest degree from the excellent work and courage of the U. S. 82nd and 101st Airborne Divisions who came behind them." He said, "They did beautiful work and I am proud of them all."

General Ike told the reporters that the Germans are fighting in desperation. They are facing oblivion and defeat and Hitler and his gang have decided to fight until the end. With a pistol in their back, the German people have no choice but to fight also. Himmler's police, Ike said, are stronger in Germany than ever.

The pause in the forward march into Germany, Ike explained, is inevitable while the Allies re-establish lines of communication after their rapid advance.

No Diversion to Italy

PARIS, SATURDAY, OCTOBER 14, 1944

I drove out to Versailles today to see General R. W. Crawford, G-4 of SHAEF, about equipment for PRD and also to check in at General Ike's office, although he had departed before 8 with General Bradley and Colonel Gault to the headquarters of Hodges' First Army at Liége. Ike

was to meet there His Majesty the King, who was on an official but
secret visit to the Continent.

At headquarters there was an information copy for General Ike from
General Marshall of a cable from the Prime Minister to the President.
On his way to Moscow, the Prime Minister had spent several hours at
Naples, discussing the Italian campaign with Generals Wilson and Alexander. He reported he was much distressed by their story. The fighting
in Italy has been hard, losses have been heavy, the men are tired, and
there are no fresh divisions to put in. The PM feared that so much
strength was taken from the Italian front for the invasion of southern
France that complete victory would be denied in Italy unless fresh troops
were thrown in. He feared also that Hitler might be able to withdraw
German troops from Italy and use them elsewhere, perhaps on the Western Front. Additional British divisions had been sent to Monty, and now
the PM was inquiring if two or possibly three American divisions might
be allotted to General Clark's Fifth Army.

General Marshall had also sent to General Ike the President's reply
that he and the Joint Chiefs of Staff agreed that none of Ike's divisions in
France should be diverted to Italy and gave as reasons that additional
U. S. forces in Italy would not affect that campaign this year, that the
U. S. Chiefs of Staff felt that the Germans are free to transfer five or six
divisions from Italy to General Ike's front whenever the enemy considers
such action more profitable than containing Allied forces south of the
Po in Italy, and that diversion of American divisions to Italy would with-
hold fresh troops needed by General Ike.

PARIS, SUNDAY, OCTOBER 15, 1944

Dined tonight with Colonel Sosthenes Behn, president of International
Telephone and Telegraph, who is over here at the request of Com Zone
to help the military get production started on signal equipment. I met
Monsieur E. N. Deloraine, who has built several of the big transmitters
on the Continent and in England, including one at Rugby and a big
long-wave station at Warsaw. Colonel Behn has asked him to put me in
touch with his technicians.

PARIS, MONDAY, OCTOBER 16, 1944

I am getting thanks from the correspondents for installing a post exchange—the GIs' country store—in the Scribe, where cigarettes, candy,
and a variety of supplies may be conveniently purchased. My real motive
has been to have a convenient source of cigars.

Ike has asked me to spend at least a day a week with him at Versailles, but I am working every day on communications with a grand staff of experts, headed by Lieutenant Colonel A. J. Randall, the ranking British officer, and Major W. R. Brown. I have the help of Captain Matthew Fox, former president of Universal Pictures, who is my chief "bird dog."

We have learned of the existence of a sixty-kilowatt mobile transmitter being built here in Paris by the French Laboratoire Matériel Téléphonique,* which I want Com Z Signals to acquire and to complete for possible use in Berlin. I am also trying to get two airplanes to be radio-equipped for emergency use, particularly for coverage of the fall of Berlin. All of us are apprehensive that Berlin will fall before we are equipped to transmit the story properly.

Recently I had to lunch Mr. Deloraine and Mr. Rabitou, manager of the LMT, as well as Colonel Randall and Brownie. I asked Rabitou what he considered the most powerful mobile transmitter. He said, "Sixty kilowatts," which is ten kilowatts greater than the maximum power permitted broadcasting stations in the States. Brownie's ears perked up like a Scotty's.† I asked where such a powerhouse might be found.

"Just a few blocks from here," he replied.

It was being built for the Luftwaffe for some secret use, but he suspected it was either for blind landings at airfields or for direction of rockets on England. Five of the seven trailers had been completed and if we could supply power units, the remainder could be finished. The Germans had paid seven tenths of the cost, but the French had purposely dilly-dallied on plans and construction for two years. It was the first of an order for seven.

We had also discovered that there existed somewhere in France a unit of two radio-equipped railway cars, capable of receiving and transmitting direct to the States. Matty is trying to locate these, and I would like to have them placed on General Ike's train in event the end of the war occurs aboard it.

---

* While preparing this book, I read the following in one of Robert Heinl's mimeographed news bulletins: "Award of the Army-Navy E pennant was made October 29, 1945, in Paris, France, to Les Matériels Téléphoniques, affiliate of the International Telephone and Telegraph Corporation, for services rendered to the United States Army, Office of the Chief Signal Officer, in the European Theater of Operations during the war. The accomplishments of the Laboratories for which they were honored were made possible through secret preparations undertaken during the German occupation, according to officials of IT&T. The Paris Laboratories designed and assembled the huge sixty-kilowatt mobile radio station 'Sigcircus,' with which General Eisenhower's Supreme Headquarters was able to keep in constant touch with Washington."

† Warning—here's another of those entries of interest only to communications experts.

But our main difficulty is refusal of the War Department to grant more frequencies for use of commercial transmitters to operate direct to the States. SHAEF Signals, through which we deal with the War Department, has been advised that we should use modern multichannel equipment to get greater efficiency and wordage on channels already assigned, but, unfortunately, no such equipment is available and would take six months to be built. In the meantime, commercial transmitters operating from Paris have to sign off part of day and night to permit use of the same wave lengths by the mobile transmitters working at Army press camps up front.

I am busy all day and frequently am at the office before 8 o'clock. This is not entirely due to energy, but to the tactics required to assure a hot bath at the Raphaël. Hot water is available only early in the morning and only the early has a chance for a hot tub.

Paris is as beautiful as ever, but certainly not exciting.

I am hoping to visit the press camps up forward, as I have the itch to get on the road and desire to know more about my new job.

PARIS, FRIDAY, OCTOBER 20, 1944

Ike has had a busy week up forward. He lunched with the King at headquarters of Hodges' First Army at Liége.

From Ike's conferences up front, he found that the one thing worrying everybody is the shortage of artillery ammunition. The shortage was not caused merely by port capacity and distribution, but by too few shipments from the U. S. or by limitation of production at home. He cabled General Marshall of his concern and asked if anything could be done to hurry shipments in the next ninety days. From the beginning of the invasion, all units have been rationed on artillery ammunition, but records indicate that whenever a division is in an active sector, whether or not actually in assault, the War Department allocations do not meet minimum requirements.

Visit to the Forward Press Camps

PARIS, SUNDAY, OCTOBER 29, 1944

I left Paris last Monday for a visit to the press camps in Bradley's 12th Army Group. I wanted to familiarize myself with the communications problems and needs, and took with me George Lyon, Major W. R. Brown, and Captain Frank Mayborn. We constituted a team of medicine men who supposedly could find the cure for almost any PRO problem. The four of us, with the driver, Private Young, filled the Chevrolet. In our trail we had a C & R car, bedding rolls, spare rations, and five-gallon cans of gasoline.

Except for George Lyon, who is regarded as a noncombatant, we were equipped for battle. (The regulations require it.) I had my sawed-off sixshooter in a shoulder holster under my improvised Royal Navy battle dress. General Patton had given me the gun when he took command of II Corps in Africa. Brownie and Frank each had the regulation .45 hanging from their hips. Young had a carbine.

I hadn't seen Ike's camp near Rheims. We stopped there to get my bedding roll, and I found his caravan parked in a sea of mud. He was at SHAEF Main in Versailles.

Driving through Rheims to Verdun, we passed numerous airfields from which our fighters and medium bombers were coming and going. There were many signs of the trench warfare of World War I. At Verdun, the rear and main headquarters of 12th Army Group were housed in French military offices and barracks recently used by the Germans.

In the office of Colonel Fitzgerald, the Director of Public Relations and Psychological Warfare of Bradley's Group, German drawings of Lili Marlene decorated the walls.

Lieutenant Colonel Jack Reeding, Fitz's top man for public relations, spent the evening with us, and I learned from him the primary needs of signal facilities for press and radio for Simpson's Ninth Army, whose press camp is at Maastricht, in Holland, for Hodges' First Army, with headquarters and press camp at Spa, in Belgium, and for Patton's Third Army, with headquarters and press camp at Nancy.

Driving on to Luxembourg, we had lunch on C rations en route, supplemented by Frank finally acquiring a long-sought head of cabbage for which he had been yearning for months. In Luxembourg we were billeted in a comfortable small hotel with electricity, hot water, and, best of all, heat. Colonel Bill Nuckols, PRO of the 9th Air Force, and his staff made us thoroughly welcome. We found, as we left Paris and approached the battle front in the proximity of the coal mines, that we were moving from the Arctic to the Tropic zones, at least so it seemed to us.

Correspondents assigned to his 9th Air Force camp—about fifteen— had a wide front to cover, as 9th Air Force furnishes tactical support to ground forces along the whole front of 12th Army Group. This requires them to travel extensively to get stories at operational airfields, and unless the stories are extraordinary, they frequently are left out of the home papers because of more exciting news.

I checked in with General Bradley in the town and was invited to bring George Lyon to dinner. General Bradley had his senior staff officers present. I unwittingly let myself in for a friendly but hot argument with General Bradley and his coworkers. I had known that Major Goodfriend, editorial director of *Stars and Stripes*, had written an editorial denouncing what he thought was favored treatment for German civilians when Aachen was finally captured. He had gone to a replacement depot ("repple-depple" to the GI) near Le Havre, put on a GI uniform, and had made the same trip in two-and-a-half-ton trucks, to the front. He was assigned to the U. S. 1st Division, then busy fighting house to house in Aachen, had taken part in the battle, and had captured some prisoners. In his editorial he had said that GIs moving up front traveled in open trucks with the rain beating on them and were shown little consideration. He had compared what he termed tender treatment by the American military of civilians in Aachen with the treatment of GIs. I made my mistake when I unwittingly said, more to make conversation than anything else, "Did you see the editorial about Aachen in *Stars and Stripes?*" General Bradley certainly had. Only that day he had endorsed a complaint against *Stars and Stripes* made by 1st Division, approved by the corps, then by the Army, now by the group, and Bradley was sending it directly to General Ike. Bradley maintained that the article was incorrect and undermined the GIs' confidence in their officers. Bradley was joined by several of his staff, who obviously had fun in combating my effort to defend Goodfriend, but I am afraid I was on weak ground, as it became apparent that Goodfriend had not got the Command's side of the story. Anyway, it was a fine dinner, and both George and I enjoyed the rough-and-tumble and good nature of the lively argument. The GIs as well as the staff worship General Bradley, who appears more like a quiet, dignified schoolmaster than a successful military leader.

Next day we inspected Radio Luxembourg, now operating for purposes of psychological warfare. I had been hopeful that we could get an hour's time each day on the station for radio correspondents to broadcast their stories so they could be picked up and broadcast by BBC or be relayed through the BBC in London to the American networks. The station is under the general charge of my old boss, Bill Paley, who would like to help us, but, unfortunately, there has been a shortage of Diesel oil for the station's power plant. At one time the entire station railway system of Luxembourg had to be stopped so power could be supplied the giant 250-kilowatt long-wave transmitter. Its coverage is widespread and goes deep into Germany. We found that an accompanying short-wave transmitter had been used by the Germans to serve their propaganda via directional antennae to German troops on the Russian front. PRD is to have use of this transmitter, but a new directional antenna beaming on New York must be installed.

Driving on to Spa we were billeted in a transient hotel, operated by the First Army near the press headquarters, of which Captain Casey Dempsey is the popular director, working under Lieutenant Colonel Flynn Andrews,* who also has charge of psychological warfare for the Army.

Bill Stoneman, of the *Chicago Daily News*, was on hand. Someone told us that Bill, who is an inveterate fisherman, had forged ahead to find a good trout stream, and after catching several fish, despite flying bombs passing overhead and occasional artillery exchanges, discovered he was in no man's land. He made this discovery when a German lad came scuffing along the path, kicking rocks and making noise. Bill had told the German boy to scram because he was disturbing the fish.

About forty correspondents were assigned to this camp, of which ten served British papers or press associations. Half of these used Press Wireless to transmit to New York for relay to London, only a couple of hundred miles away, as the crow flies. The cost was about fourteen cents a word. The British correspondents are desirous of having transmission facilities direct to London.

We had an evening's conference with the Army's and Public Relations' signal officers and the operators of Press Wireless. The Prewee boys had made radio history when their low-powered transmitter started percolating, shortly after D-Day, from the beachhead direct to New York. They had moved with First Army and had carried hundreds of thousands of words to the home front, and frequently put through live- and recorded-voice broadcasts to the networks. Although they were civilians, they suffered all the hardships and underwent all the danger of their countrymen in uniform. Their great need frequently expressed was for additional frequencies so they could operate without having to share the time with the Press Wireless station in Paris.

The conference broke up just before midnight. During the night I was awakened several times by flying bombs passing overhead en route to England. It is a different sensation to hear them going over and to feel certain that they are not destined for your particular locale.

The next day we drove to headquarters of the U. S. 1st Division, which had just taken Aachen. General Clarence R. Huebner, my friend from the Mediterranean, invited us to lunch, during which I asked him how

* Later killed by enemy action.

he had managed to gain the confidence of his division after his relief of the popular Terry Allen in Sicily. He said it had been simple. He required all of them to practice shooting, and ample ammunition was furnished. He said that there wasn't a man in the division who hadn't improved his shooting. There's nothing the GIs like better than to shoot, particularly if they are not supervised too closely. He said he had the "shootinest" division in the Army. The 1st Division's capture of Aachen, General Huebner said, was methodical, and relatively inexpensive in lives. A great deal of artillery was used and the city was "cleaned up" house by house and block by block. He said his division had lost only 150 men killed and some 1200 wounded in taking the city.

We drove on to Aachen to have a look. The town is really beaten up to complete satisfaction. It has had numerous RAF raids by the heavy bombers, and our artillery and tactical air support had left fires still smoldering. As the front line was still only 3000 yards away, the town was subjected to periodic shelling, and once we took shelter in a bombed-out building.

When I had spoken to General Huebner about General Marshall's desire to have the U. S. Army Band play a concert in the first big German city captured by the Americans, he said he wished this could be done, but the concert would have to be on an occasion such as a ceremony to include General Hodges. He felt it unwise to permit the band to play within 3000 yards of the front line. If the Germans heard the music, there would be a refrain of artillery, and not only members of the band, but General Hodges might be killed. Consequently, he had disapproved the idea. So General Marshall has been defeated.

We visited the headquarters of the Allied Military Government and found German men, women, and children coming and going. They looked whipped. They were coming out of their cellars and gave every evidence of really having "had it." We collected a few souvenirs for Christmas presents, and departed for Maastricht, headquarters of Simpson's Ninth Army and press camp.

Major Barney Oldfield, the PRO, had his camp in a comfortable hotel with all modern conveniences, including heat. We found Wes Gallagher again, as always, the bellwether of the correspondents. The Ninth Army was not yet in an offensive role, so there wasn't much news to write from there, but it is expected to take part in an offensive soon and the worry now is how to get press copy and broadcasts out of Maastricht, which has no proper facilities. The copy now must be jeeped in an hour-and-a-half run to Spa and transmitted via the Press Wireless.

Of the countries I have seen, Holland seems the most devastated. Food is extremely short, but the Dutch have borne their lot stoically, and large numbers of them worked valiantly in their underground.

We drove back to Spa and backtracked southward to Nancy, where Lieutenant Colonel Kent Hunter and his popular second man, Captain Drake, ran the press camp. We slept on cots, George and I being billeted in a butler's pantry of a building which once was the schoolhouse. George didn't realize that at least two layers of a blanket underneath are needed to keep warm. He said he had never been so cold.

Next morning I took George Lyon with me to make a call on General Patton. He took us into his morning briefing and succeeded in embarrassing me by introducing me as Admiral to the assembled staff officers. After the briefing General Patton took us to his office, where he explained on a map his next offensive. He was hopeful of reaching the Rhine. Patton's ordnance had developed an extended flange for tanks, permitting them to move over muddy or soft soil. General Patton called them "duckbills." His ingenious staff had found some undeveloped iron foundries near Nancy, and production was under way at the rate of 200 a day. General Patton said that, a couple of nights before, one of the shells from the German long-range railway guns had hit a house across the street. He had rushed out to see if he could be of help and found some French people under the debris. He and a Frenchman pulled on the legs of an old Frenchman sticking out of the wreckage under which his head and shoulders were confined. The Frenchman was yelling loudly, and the harder Patton and his friend pulled, the less he yelled, yet his body did not budge. Patton decided they must be choking the patient, so they took away the debris and found the edge of a table sticking under his chin—the harder his body was pulled, the nearer the Frenchman came to being strangled. Finally he was extricated safely, but then there was the old gentleman's wife, whose bloody head could just be seen above the bricks. The old Frenchman, who had just been saved, cried to his wife not to despair, for a very famous general, a most valiant and courageous man, in fact, none less than General Patton himself, was about to save her, and to be of good heart and great courage. So the old lady was saved too, and now General Patton has two extraordinarily grateful neighbors.

I told General Patton I had heard some criticism from Third Army that General Ike had unduly favored the British by assigning the First Airborne Army to Monty for the attempt to cross the Rhine. Patton said that militarily this was entirely correct and that he wholeheartedly endorsed the strategy. He said he didn't expect to need the paratroopers to cross the Rhine. He would just have Tooey Spaatz send his heavy bombers over and pulverize the opposite shore and then let his men row across. I told him about the statement attributed to junior officers that "Ike is the best general the British have." He replied that although some may naturally have felt bitter because the Third Army finally had been stopped, not so much by the enemy as by lack of gasoline, this did not represent the true feeling of himself or his Army.

We had our lunch of C rations en route as we rode from Nancy to Paris, but eventually made a brief stop. There was half of an open can of cheese that we had not eaten. Frank offered the cheese to a French boy about fourteen years of age who walked alongside, pushing his bicycle. In saying thank you for his gift, the French boy used perhaps the only English words he knew, doubtless learned from GIs. He said, smilingly, "You are filled with hot air."

At each press camp I have found most of the correspondents boosting their own particular general—Bradley, Patton, Hodges, or Simpson. Each does the biggest job, in the eyes of the correspondents, depending on the camp to which they are assigned. Representatives of British papers and press associations as well as the BBC are conscientiously endeavoring to cover action of the American armies.

PARIS, MONDAY, OCTOBER 30, 1944

General Allen has a staff meeting of PRD on Monday, Wednesday, and Friday mornings at 9. I reported on the communications aspect of our trip and obtained the General's authority to send two signal officers to Washington to try to seek reversal of the position of the War Department so we can get additional frequencies, and another officer to find and expedite the shipment of vital radio equipment to repair old and build new mobile transmitters.

Went out to Versailles and had a session with Ike in his office and went on to lunch with him. He is looking fine, except for a touch of conjunctivitis in his left eye. I gave him a "fill-in" on my trip and emphasized my impression that each press camp is something of a claque for its general and that each public-relations officer likewise is primarily interested in his own general. Ike said that this is a healthy condition; he wants his subordinates to receive publicity, but prefers that accomplishments of junior officers and GIs be given proper credit back home. I told him we had heard rumbles from correspondents and others who had visited press camps in Monty's sector of the need of a Deputy Ground Commander for SHAEF. I interpreted this as indicative of dissatisfaction with the progress of the ground battle and the correspondents covering Monty were hoping he would be placed in charge of the entire battle front.

As I am now a so-called communications specialist, I told him of our plans for improving press and broadcast facilities and spoke of our efforts to develop the short-wave station at Luxembourg. He said this is in the sector where the Germans might relatively easily counterattack in strength, and that I might find myself with a transmitter in German hands. He said we were holding that sector with relatively light forces because we are building up for attack north of the Ardennes, and although the Germans also are lightly holding some ninety miles in the Ardennes, they could swing a punch through that sector, if they chose.

PARIS, TUESDAY, OCTOBER 31, 1944

Spent some time at General Ike's office. He gave me a box of cigars that some friends had mailed him. (He doesn't smoke them.)

I found there had been an exchange of messages between General Marshall and Ike relative to speeding the flow of infantry regiments in harmony with the desire of the Combined Chiefs, possibly to be spelled out in a directive, that SHAEF make an all-out effort to end the war in Europe before 1945. Among the aids for an all-out cleanup of the war would be the release for general use of a new fuse for artillery shells, called VT. This fuse automatically detonates the projectile when it comes in proximity of the earth and may be set for various distances. This is an important development. A shell that explodes above the ground, throwing fragments into foxholes, therefore is more effective than those that burst on contact with the ground.

The Combined Chiefs also had considered redirecting the Strategic Bomber Forces to give support to the ground troops, but General Ike had informed General Marshall that because of the bad weather and consequent poor visibility, there was practically no way under these conditions of using the heavy bombers to help the infantry advance. Although the heavies can bomb through cloud by use of radar, this technique is not suitable for bombing close to our own ground troops. General Ike had reported to General Marshall that the progress of the ground battle seemed to be served best by keeping the heavy bombers constantly hammering the enemy's oil and supply lines, for there has been ample evidence that this bombing has been effective against the enemy's ability to move and supply his ground troops. The time, undoubtedly, will come when weather will permit use of heavy bombers in close support for the ground battle.

Antwerp still remains the key to the logistics problem. Ike is prepared to wage a final all-out battle to cross the Rhine if we have the assurance of supply that Antwerp promises.

General Marshall had replied that several cables from Ike's headquarters had given the impression that because of the rocket attacks on Antwerp, which had added to the serious and sustained attacks by flying bombs, another port or ports should be considered as ultimate unloading points.

General Ike had replied to the Chief of Staff that far from having "all of our eggs in one basket," in Antwerp, every other port capable of producing supplies is being developed to the maximum. An explosion of an ammunition ship, which might be caused in several ways, including hits by rockets or flying bombs, would cause a setback in any port.

As to defense of Antwerp, General Ike and his staff knew that the Germans were seeking to wreck the port by flying bombs and rockets and, with the latter, were about to get the correct range. Heavy concentration of antiaircraft weapons has been made to protect Antwerp and Brussels, and some of the defense setup used to protect London against flying bombs and rockets is being moved to the Continent by consent of the British Chiefs of Staff.

General Ike had issued a new directive for the ground battle. It superseded his last one of September 4, since which the enemy has continued to reinforce in the west, indicating that the Germans intend to make the strongest possible stand on the West Wall in the hope of preventing the war spreading further into Germany. The disposition of German forces thoroughly indicates an intent to protect the Ruhr and Saar, and in front of these areas, particularly the Ruhr, the enemy has made its strongest concentrations. In addition, the Germans are sensitive to our threat against the Belfort approaches to the upper Rhine Valley.

The directive stated that limitations of maintenance and transportation had prevented the Allies overrunning the Siegfried Line before the enemy's resistance stiffened. Now we have to deploy superior forces and furnish them adequate resources for intensive fighting. They cannot be maintained effectively during the winter months without the use of the port of Antwerp. Consequently, the securing and operation of the port for our use is the first and most immediate objective.

Ike declared that his intention continues to be the destruction of the enemy's forces. His general plan, subject always to prior capture of the approaches to Antwerp, is to make the main effort in the north to defeat decisively the enemy west of the Rhine and to secure bridgeheads over the river; then, by converging attacks from the north and the south, to seize the Ruhr and advance deep into Germany.

He has directed that operations be conducted to destroy the enemy in the Saar and there also to secure crossing over the Rhine in preparation for an advance to meet the pincers from the north, thus surrounding the Ruhr. These operations are to be so timed to support the main effort in the north to which they are subsidiary.

In the south, aggressive fighting is to continue until the enemy is overwhelmed west of the Rhine and our forces are to be prepared to advance into Germany.

Three general phases were outlined: (1) the battle west of the Rhine, taking advantage of any opportunity to seize bridgeheads; (2) operations leading to the capture of bridges over the Rhine and deployment of our forces on the east bank, and (3) the advance from the Rhine deep into Germany.

After the President, on advice of the U. S. Chiefs of Staff, had declined to divert American divisions from France to help Generals Alexander and Clark in Italy, General Ike had responded to an urgent request of Alex by agreeing to send him 3000 replacements. For this Alex had been extremely grateful and had written an unusually warm letter, carried to Ike by General Alexander's aide. To this General Ike had replied, likewise warmly, and mentioned that war is such a dirty business and costs everyone so much that occasionally he finds relief by the incidental bright spots in the dreary picture when such evidence as Alex's letter reminds him of the several new and great friendships he has formed during the war.

Of immediate concern, however, to General Ike were the complaints and discontent of American wounded men who are returning to the U. S. General Marshall had found that when some of them reached home they were bitter and voiced many complaints about their treatment. Ike already had heard something of this, but upon receiving word from General Marshall, immediately ordered a small group of competent officers and enlisted men, all of them carrying wounds from this war, to visit hospitals, rehabilitation centers, and replacement depots in France and England to determine the cause of the complaints.

OCTOBER, 1944: *American First Army smashed through West Wall defenses and took half of besieged Aachen. Third Army captured seven towns on twenty-five-mile front between Pont-à-Mousson and Château Salins. Allied bombers smashed industrial and communications targets in twenty cities, including Berlin, Vienna, Cologne, Schweinfurt. Planes from Italy supported*

Red drive on Budapest. Anglo-Canadian troops established two beachheads between Leopold Canal and Scheldt Estuary after surprise landing behind German lines in Belgium; British troops took Netherlands strongholds 's Hertogenbosch and Tilburg. Churchill and Eden conferred with Stalin in Moscow. Bulgarian armistice terms signed in Moscow by Russia, Britain, and U. S. MacArthur's troops landed in Philippines. Spruance's Fifth Fleet made landings east of Leyte and south of Samar. Swift drives took most of Leyte, captured Tacloban in few days. U. S. Navy, in powerful support of invasion forces, destroyed and damaged fifty-one Jap ships, including seven battleships. Second naval battle of Philippines cost Japs twenty-four warships of all types. 24th Division cleared Japs out of Jaro, joined 1st Cavalry to north. Japs in China advanced to take Foochow and Kweiping. 14th Air Force in China abandoned Tanchuk base. Allies scored advances in Italy, with British Eighth Army taking Savignano, Mt. Farneto; U. S. Fifth captured Loiano and Mt. Belmonte. British troops in Greece captured Patras as Greek partisans seized Athens. Fliers in Pacific hit Jap bases at Balik Papan, Netherlands East Indies, Wolfe and Zamboanga fields (in Philippines), Kuriles, Wake and Marcus Islands. Superforts hit targets on Kyushu. In Burma British took Tiddim. Halsey's two-day raid on Formosa destroyed 395 Jap planes and 100 ships. General Wedemeyer took command of Americans in China; General Sultan became commander of Yanks in Burma and India after Stilwell was relieved. (News of landings in the Philippines thrilled us.—H.C.B.)

PARIS, FRIDAY, NOVEMBER 3, 1944

I was at Ike's office today when the good news came in from Monty that the approaches to Antwerp and the Scheldt Estuary are now completely free from enemy interference. Monty said that full and free use of the port of Antwerp is now up to the Navy, which already has mine sweepers at work.

Ike immediately replied and expressed his grateful thanks to Monty personally and asked him to convey his congratulations to General Crerar and his First Canadian Army.

I have seen Ike several times when he has received good news which normally he has discounted in advance, but on this occasion he could not hide his elation, for on the capture of Antwerp depended all of his future plans to end the war.

Tomorrow Ike is starting an extended trip during which he hopes to visit the principal commanders and all the corps and divisions in the First and Ninth U. S. Armies. He hopes to talk with as many GIs as possible. Jules Grad, *Stars and Stripes* pool reporter, has been to see me and is thrilled that he is going with the party. Ike said today he had been practically bound hand and foot to his office because of the number of visitors. Now he would reverse the play and become the visitor himself.

PARIS, SUNDAY, NOVEMBER 5, 1944

George Lyon's opposite number, Jack H. Brebner, representing the Ministry of Information, is at the Scribe. He is here to put a burr under the PRD saddle blanket to improve communications and other facilities for the press, particularly to England. I have gone over with him some of our plans for improving communications to the States, but, unfortunately, little improvement in radio communication from France to England can be expected because of the dearth of frequencies suitable for short distances, these being used almost exclusively by the military services. He said that the British publishers objected to the cost of transmission of stories from U. S. Army press camps via New York to London, and, in addition to the cost, he states there is a question of pride. The British publishers simply don't like to rely on relay via New York of battle-front news originating 200 or 300 miles from England. I told him that American publishers don't like to receive war news with the London dateline, but sometimes it couldn't be helped.

I feel that I have an Allied problem on my hands because if I succeed in getting frequencies suitable to cover the American battle fronts and home fronts, the American press and broadcasters may have better service than the British. I am seeking ways to find a balance, but, unfortunately for the British, there are more wave lengths available for long rather than short distances.

PARIS, WEDNESDAY, NOVEMBER 8, 1944

We put election returns on the loudspeaker last night at the Scribe, but no one seemed particularly interested. A few stayed up, but most seemed primarily absorbed in their jobs of covering the war and of recovering from the effect of the Scribe Bar, where the unending process of swapping of stories goes on—referred to as "picking one another's brains."

PARIS, SATURDAY, NOVEMBER 11, 1944

I telephoned headquarters of Strategic Air Forces today at Saint-Germain to get Brigadier General Ted Curtis, Chief of Staff. I got through to "Oyster," the name of the exchange, and thought I had on the line the Sergeant in General Curtis' office. However, the voice said, "This is Tooey Spaatz. What can I do for you?" I said I wanted two of his war-weary aircraft to be radio-equipped for the rush into Berlin, when, as, and if. Tooey said, "O.K. You can have them. Call General Nehr and tell him I said so."

General Nehr says we can have two Flying Fortresses, classified as war-weary, being held at Burtonwood, in England, among many others intended to be filled with explosives and flown by radio direction into sites of rockets or flying bombs.

Brownie is excited and already is planning to send his crack radio man, Lieutenant N. S. Ponte, to the big air-supply center to supervise installation of the radio equipment. One is to communicate direct to England, the other to the U. S. They are called by the code name "Aphrodite."

Com Z has taken the sixty-kilowatt mobile transmitter and will complete it, ready to roll into Berlin. The vans will be hauled by ten-ton prime movers. I have drafted a letter for General Allen to send to Major General W. S. Rumbough, Chief Signal Officer for Com Z, asking that the equipment be ready by December 15, otherwise we may miss the fall of Berlin.*

Do the Germans Have a Bomb That Freezes?

PARIS, SUNDAY, NOVEMBER 12, 1944

I drove to the Oise River valley, north of Paris, today to see some mushroom caverns enlarged and used by the Germans to assemble and store flying bombs and, possibly, other secret weapons. One of the caves was so large that it completely hid a railway train. My friend who guided me to the place had been in the French underground and said he had given the intelligence which had directed Allied bombers to the principal railway yard adjacent to the caverns. The tracks and entrance to the cavern showed ample evidence of the accuracy and effectiveness of the bombing.

My informant said he had lived in contact with German officials close to Hitler and suspected that in remote parts of the cavern, which had been cemented shut by the Germans, there may be new secret weapons. He spoke vaguely about conversations with Germans who hinted at atomic energy and the "bomb that freezes" and asked that qualified Intelligence officers from SHAEF be sent to investigate. I am putting him in touch with Air Chief Marshal Tedder.

Ike Goes and Looks for Himself

PARIS, MONDAY, NOVEMBER 13, 1944

I told Air Chief Marshal Tedder about the story of the freezing bomb and arranged for my informant to see him direct. Scott-Bailey is taking him out to Versailles.

While I was at the Main Headquarters today, I saw General Crawford,

* Wrong again.

G-4, and explained to him PRD's need for six ordnance trucks in which Mackay, Press Wireless, and RCA may mount new mobile transmitters. He said that ordnance trucks are in short supply, but so far as he could see, the lieutenant generals of SHAEF would have no further need for their sleeping vans and I could have six of them.

Ike is at his camp near Rheims. He has been spending most of his time visiting commanders and troops up front.

He hoped and prayed that there would be a short spell of good weather to bring relief from mud, rain, and snow, so tanks and infantry could take the offensive and could be aided by our great superiority of air power. In spite of difficulties, General Ike found that no one was discouraged and that we will yet make the German wish he had gone completely back to the Rhine at the end of his harried retreat across France.

The Prime in Paris

PARIS, WEDNESDAY, NOVEMBER 15, 1944
The Prime Minister has been General de Gaulle's guest in Paris and has appropriately received the honors of the city, with tremendous crowds cheering him at Arc de Triomphe, on the Champs-Elysées.

Yesterday Churchill arrived in the French presidential train at Rheims, where he was met by French authorities and by General Ike, who took him and his party to the camp near Rheims. They discussed anticipated changes of command which he and the President were considering. One involves Italy.

Late in the afternoon, the Prime Minister flew back to England with his party. This fact was a closely guarded secret, and when announcement of his safe arrival was made at 10 Downing Street, some of our correspondents criticized Colonel Dupuy because the news had not been given out by SHAEF.

Morale, Socks, Weather, and Patton

PARIS, MONDAY, NOVEMBER 20, 1944
At Versailles today I found General Ike tired but extremely well satisfied with his travels. Following his visit to the headquarters of all the divisions and corps of First and Ninth Armies, he had spent considerable time with General Patton and the Third Army units, including ordnance depots and supply points in and around Nancy. He had talked to many soldiers, including the wounded in the 12th Evacuation Hospital in Nancy, and had found their morale extremely high.

Ike was most concerned about trench feet. He found that General Patton had been aggressive in providing extra dry socks daily to his troops in the foxholes.

I mentioned again to Ike that he should feel satisfied that his judgment had been vindicated with regard to General Patton, who has become America's most colorful and highly publicized general, certainly from this theater. I told him the public seems to go along with the soldiers who love to fight under a winner.

Ike said he had chuckled at Patton at luncheon for the King at Liége. General Patton had told the King with gusto, when asked how frequently he used his famous pearl-handled revolvers:

"I personally have killed thirty Germans."

"How many?" said Ike.

Patton replied, "Five."

Ike said he thought the abominable weather was a secret weapon of Hitler's and, as I have heard and seen him do many times before, he paced the living room, pausing now and then to look out the window to judge the weather.

Mickey confided in me today that he is going to get married, that the General has given permission, and that I'm invited to the wedding, set for December 16 at one of the chapels in the Palace of Versailles. The girl is WAC Corporal Pearlie Hargrave, who has been one of General Ike's staff drivers since Algiers days.

Some time ago a correspondent of the New York *Daily News* sought an interview with Mickey. They met in my office. When the correspondent asked Mickey what he hoped to do after the war, Mickey said without hesitation, "Run a saloon." I immediately interjected that this would cause a nice headline: GENERAL IKE'S ORDERLY YEARNS FOR SALOON, but Mickey stuck by his stated ambition. He was only dissuaded when I reminded him that Pearlie would have something to say about his postwar plans and, as she is a respectable ex-history teacher from Minnesota, I didn't think she'd like a saloonkeeper for a husband.

On and Off the Record

PARIS, TUESDAY, NOVEMBER 21, 1944

By reducing rather than increasing the number of MPs, less attention was attracted to the arrival of General Ike at the Scribe today than at his previous conference, when he was mobbed.

The correspondents jammed the briefing room. When General Allen mounted the platform and simply said, "Gentlemen, I present the Suprcme Commander," I winced because I recalled Ike telling me that he would much prefer not to be introduced, as he thought the formality entirely unnecessary. I had intended to speak to General Allen about it but had forgotten to do so.

I have noticed in many of Ike's press conferences that the correspondents refrain from smoking until General Ike himself lights a cigarette. They seem to know that he doesn't go very long between smokes. They haven't long to wait, which was again true today. Ike normally prefers conferences with the press on an informal basis and preferably in his own office, but the inconvenience of transporting a hundred or more bodies to Versailles and back, he figures, is too much. Instead, he takes the time and the trouble to come to the correspondents.

Standing before the huge map by the briefer's rostrum, he reminded the correspondents that he had promised to keep up the pressure on the enemy and this we are doing. He was not going to make any predictions. Nothing had pleased him more, he said, than the fact that the First French Army went in so gallantly at Belfort and then got to the Rhine so quickly. Everyone who is a true friend of France, he said, believes that France must do a tremendous amount of its own rehabilitation. The French victory marks something of a milestone in its own accomplishment, for by its own force it has valiantly, in the traditional French manner, with courage and without regard to obstacles, driven the Germans back.

He praised the British for taking Walcheren Island and clearing the port of Antwerp. He said that the Royal Navy, in support of the attack on the western edges of the island, had put on one of the finest shows of the war. With many unarmored vessels and light guns, they challenged heavier guns in reinforced concrete, and slammed it out until they got our soldiers ashore. Very large losses were sustained. He said that the Navy really deserved great kudos for their work "and it will be one of the great episodes in their history."

Going on the right, the Canadian and British Armies have cleared Holland south of the Maas, and have done splendidly. The bulk of their forces are facing eastward and attacking with the U. S. Ninth Army on the right and the U. S. First Army still farther on the right.

Indicating on the map, he said, along the line, as could be seen, there are three avenues toward the Rhine—Belfort, Metz, and Aachen. It is in these areas in which our strength is concentrated to keep the pressure on the Germans, which, he said, would be kept up to the absolute limit.

The air, he said, has had a tough time because of weather. He had traveled considerably along the front and just couldn't understand why the weather always seemed so much worse up front than it does in the rear. Nevertheless, the Air Forces have done vital and necessary work and have done it extraordinarily well. Bombing in Germany itself has been continued in spite of foul weather. The heavies had put on a great show east of Aachen to pave the way for the First Army assault. They had to take off in weather conditions in England that were very severe and succeeded in landing only by the aid of the most miraculous piloting. They had done their job well and to the complete satisfaction of the ground forces.

Teamwork among the ground, sea, and air forces had continued to develop and had become so effective as to be regarded as conventional. It worked so well no one paid any particular attention to it, but, from the Supreme Commander's point of view, the co-operation is miraculous in its combined striking power.

Turning to the people at home, he believed they are united in their determination that the Germans shall not be given a minute's rest. He believed the people of Great Britain and those of the United States are just as determined as we that the German must be hit with everything we have and he must continue to be hit until he finally collapses. The Russians on the east and "Alex on the south" and we over here continue to hammer the enemy until finally the breaking point is going to come. To achieve that breaking point, the people producing at home must continue to do their utmost, but they should understand that the enemy's morale is not broken and that the pressure must go up and up until it reaches a crescendo. Its highest point must be on the day of surrender. We can achieve that crescendo of power if we are united all the way from the man in the foxhole to the man with the plow handle in his hand.

We are going to use up worlds of tires, ammunition, winter clothing, trucks, and guns before final victory is achieved, and these supplies must be available for the troops to use. There is no question, he said, that our soldiers, airmen, and seamen will do the job.

Stopping to light a cigarette and leaning against the rostrum, he said: "This seems to me like a rather dry press conference."

I am inserting a few of the main questions and answers that followed:

QUESTION: From the German point of view, how would you assess our breaking in at Alsace?

ANSWER: I would say the Germans won't regard it as seriously as one farther north. Put it this way: the position we now occupy is far from the Ruhr and that section of the Rhine does not lead as quickly to the definitely decisive areas as some of the other avenues. But this I believe: no conqueror can view with equanimity the loss of any ground he's conquered. It's a definite concession of weakness, not only of morale but of material value. If the maneuver goes on and the forces in the Alsace area get in position to threaten further north it becomes increasingly serious to the German. I think he would look on it as secondary to a similar advance in the north.

QUESTION: I have just come from the States. The people are too optimistic. Can we do anything to make them less optimistic without engendering pessimism?

ANSWER: I think that is a perfectly sound question. I really wouldn't feel, myself, expert enough in this field of public psychology and public opinion to know the line that a bunch of trained newspaper people could take to combat over-optimism. Unless everybody all the way through the whole nation, including that part of the nation that is on the front and that part of it still in our homelands—unless we keep on this job everlastingly and with a mounting intensity rather than a decreasing one—we are merely postponing the day of victory. But I am convinced that the very maximum effort ought to be on the last day and the curve ought to be going up every single day. To get peace you have got to fight like hell for it—that's all there is to it.

QUESTION: Could you tell us something about the fortifications inside the ring beyond the Rhine—what the Germans built?

ANSWER: There is no question about their defenses around certain vital areas on the western borders that are just inside the line east of the Rhine, but I have never heard described any continuous lines of fortifications east of the Rhine. Of course, their ack-ack defenses and local defenses east of the Ruhr are very, very strong.

QUESTION: Any evidence that the Germans may retreat over the Rhine instead of making a great stand west of the Rhine?

ANSWER: I have seen none, and I should think—and this would be merely the attitude of anyone—that if I had brought that much of my force west of the Rhine with a big river at my back and where there are numerous bridges, with the knowledge that the other fellow had a very powerful air force, I'd say, "This far and no farther." I am not saying they won't retreat over the Rhine if we accomplish some decisive stroke. He would save everything he could, but it looks as if that would be the only sensible thing to do as long as he had brought that much force in front of a big obstacle like the Rhine—fight it out there.

QUESTION: Could you say the picture at the start of the winter looks happier than it would on D-Day?

ANSWER: Well—you know, I hate these "yes" and "no" answers. But on one aspect it's decidedly brighter and that is on this one, and I think I explained this to you before: every Allied soldier, airman, and sailor has the right to be proud that from D-Day our forces have got to the Siegfried Line all along from Switzerland to the North Sea. It is a tribute to their skill and courage that we have got there as quickly as we have done it and we are up there on the Siegfried as strongly as we are. That is a long way, as you people who have traveled from Cherbourg to Metz will know—an awfully long way. Probably there has been no exploitation and pursuit like it in history. A whole country was cleared rapidly after the break-through from the beachhead. Now here is a point on which anybody's judgment is as good as anybody else's. What would you think should have happened when we had men fighting in strong Allied forces so close to Germany? There would be some reason to hope Germany would call it a day. But I think as early as August it became evident all along the front the German was fighting in many instances because the Gestapo made him. The Gestapo's control is as firm as ever as far as we can see, so the German is going to battle it out to the end. I feel that Hitler's leading gang of brigands has nothing to lose, and as long as he has this powerful weapon in his hands to make others fight, he and his gang don't care. They are ready to fight it out to destruction.

QUESTION: To go back to this point about what you hoped on D-Day: you have had evidence there was a decided break in German morale early in September?

ANSWER: Early in September?

QUESTION: Wasn't that when they saw you coming up very close to their frontiers?

ANSWER: No. I think that was a reason to believe there was something wrong with German morale when the attempted assassination of Hitler occurred on July 20. Since then nothing has come to my attention to make me think there's a definite break. You can see that all of us without exception were determined to see that exploitation to the final and complete limit. You may know the story on the right flank with the armored divisions where they transferred their gasoline direct from trucks to tanks and even drained gas from jeeps to keep going. When the tanks ran dry, there they were. On the north . . . what date was that airborne operation . . . September 17 . . . we were still trying to catch that fellow off balance to get the very last atom out of him. I told you before that was a successful operation, but not as successful as it would

have been if that fellow had been in the state of demoralization I had hoped he was. I can recall nothing about that time that would lead me to believe it.

QUESTION: Are the French to get more arms?

ANSWER: So far as I'm concerned, every single thing that can be over and behind the demands of the battle itself will be done to help France get more strength to apply more armed force. I want to tell you this: the French fought under me in Tunisia when they were at the lowest ebb so far as equipment was concerned, when the only things they had were those they succeeded in hiding out from the German Army. Figuratively, they had only sticks and clubs. They merely had what little small arms the Germans allowed them to have. They fought under me in Italy and France, and there are no more gallant troops in this whole world than the French soldiers. They are wonderful, and some of the beatings and kickings around they took in Tunisia when they had almost nothing but rocks with which to fight would excite anybody's admiration. They are anxious to fight. Once I saw a French officer break down and weep because he was taken out of a combat organization and assigned to the rear.

QUESTION: A short time ago it was generally supposed the Germans had little or no reserves inside Germany. Is that picture changed at all?

ANSWER: We know that from everything we have been able to find out, from prisoners, papers, statements of Goebbels and all the rest that they are absolutely stripping the country to make new formations, the so-called *Volkssturm*. Those divisions will be made up certainly of the less fit, less well-trained humans than his divisions have been made up in the past. If we are correct in our estimates that he has been stretched on the Russian front, this front, and the Italian front, then they can't be as well equipped as the older divisions. In other words, the reserves he's building up may be quite effective and we mustn't discount them. They are hard to root out of prepared positions such as those of the Siegfried Line. But they will not be Panzer divisions, Panzer Grenadiers, or paratroopers or SS troops.

QUESTION: I believe on November 7 Marshal Stalin in paying tribute to the Allies in the west said that the Red Army will be in Berlin soon. That was a quotation I saw.

ANSWER: Good for him. He will do a good job there, I think.

QUESTION: As it seems to be a mark of Hitler's supreme control orders for his forces to hang on until disaster, has there been anything on the German tactical situation lately to suggest there has now been a different policy being carried out by the High Command?

ANSWER: The conditions aren't the same. First Hitler had the problem of holding what finally became a hopeless position on the beachhead a long way from Germany. There his communications were not only under attack by our overpowering air force in good weather but they were almost hopelessly attenuated. Ours were relatively short and the best we ever had. That was a different story from his going back to the Siegfried, from which retreat leads him almost to a major national disaster. With the Allied armies all along the Rhine, with the threat everywhere and certain cities of the Rhine squarely under Allied guns, it's a different story. Whether or not the Germans can afford to withdraw further than from positions which cover his vital centers is a thing Hitler's General Staff and his leaders have to decide. I think Hitler's intuition did a great deal

to give us the tremendous victory of the Loire and the Seine. It's a different story now. I suppose any man in Hitler's doomed position would decide to fight it out. It would look that way to me. Of course, never forget this—after he had chosen that line of communications down across the Seine into the beachhead and brought forces and supplies there in the effort to kick us out and he had failed, it's probably quite doubtful if he could have retreated with very much success because our air forces and our ground forces pursued him relentlessly. It was a decision which almost any soldier, having made the first blunder, had only one thing to do, and that was to put his money on the same horse to see if he will win the next time. He would have had an awful time retreating, say after July 3 or 4.

QUESTION: You spoke about the increasing pressure that would necessitate more reinforcements. I am a Canadian and I am interested in conscription and anything you could say to me for the need of increasing.

ANSWER: I'll tell you, Miss Canada. I'm not going to get in Canadian politics any more than French, British, or American. But there is a job here for every man we can bring in.

QUESTION: Are the rocket bombs of any significance on the front?

ANSWER: When I visited the various headquarters they said: "We had seventeen around here in the last day or so." They never say it with any joy. I know there have been unfortunate incidents where quite a number of persons have been killed. But so far as the troops are concerned, I have not yet had reported to me a single instance where a V-2 killed a soldier. There have been a few in numerous places. The Germans are shooting principally at our supply centers and at London.

When Ike finished, he said he would leave the selection of a limited number of quotable sentences to the judgment of General Allen, Colonel Dupuy, and me. The correspondents nominated their own selections. One of those approved was "To get peace, you've got to fight like hell for it," and all the correspondents, of course, wanted to use it. I knew that Ike would wince when he saw himself quoted in the papers as saying "hell," yet it is only one of his normal American cusswords. Whenever anything is printed about him that smacks even lightly of profanity, he receives mail from mothers and fathers of soldiers, particularly American, who seem to dislike to be disillusioned in their belief that General Eisenhower never used such naughty words. I didn't feel up to telling the correspondents that the Supreme Commander of nearly 5,000,000 troops didn't wish to be quoted as saying "hell," so I raised no objection.

PARIS, WEDNESDAY, NOVEMBER 22, 1944

We now have heat at the American Express Building, although the Raphaël stays colder than a refrigerator and my bed is so damp it never seems to dry. But then, it is more comfortable than the foxhole, so why should I complain? . . . Bill Shirer is here. Ed Murrow is also here. Ed said today that he and Janet have been overseas so long they feel their ideas are growing apart from those of the people in the U. S. and plan to go home to live before they become expatriates, but not until after the war.

I have been bawled out by an Army captain of Com Z. He got me on the phone and, obviously, thinking I was an Army captain, gave me a good going over because our PX in the Scribe still sells seven packs of cigarettes a week. Com Z has had to cut down and the good captain was on a spot, saying he has 21,000 American troops in Paris who can't buy cigarettes, yet correspondents and a favored few can buy them at the Scribe. I explained our PX was operated by SHAEF and SHAEF has not yet curtailed and it is up to them.

Here We Go Again

PARIS, THURSDAY, NOVEMBER 23, 1944

SHAEF has received a report of a conference that took place in Strasbourg at the Palace-Hôtel et Maison-Rouge on August 10, 1944, in which principal German industrialists, knowing Germany had lost the war, discussed plans for postwar world-wide revival of the Fatherland's industrial empire. The information is regarded as reliable, for the man from whom it was obtained has worked for the French on German problems since 1916 and has been in close contact with German industrialists during the occupation of France. He was in Germany as late as August, 1944. The report says:

Dr. Scheid, who presided, holding the rank of SS Obergruppenführer for Director of the Hermsdorf Schonberg Co., and other industrialists representing Krupp, Rochling, Messerschmitt, Rheinmetall, Bussing, Volkswagenwerke, and officials of the industrial inspection section of German Naval Ministry, and the Ministry of Armament, were present.

Dr. Scheid stated that all industrial material in France was lost for Germany and now the defense of the Siegfried Line was the main problem. From now on German industry must also realize that the war cannot be won and that it must take steps in preparation for a postwar commercial campaign. Industrialists must make contacts and alliance with foreign firms, but this must be done individually and without attracting any suspicion.

Moreover, the ground would have to be laid on the financial level for borrowing considerable sums from foreign countries after the war. As examples of the kind of penetration which had been useful in the past, Dr. Scheid cited the fact that patents for Stainless Steel belonged to the Chemical Foundation, Inc., of New York and the Krupp Company of Germany, jointly, and that the U. S. Steel Corporation, Carnegie-Illinois, American Steel & Wire, and National Tube, etc., were thereby under an obligation to work with the Krupp concern. He also cited the Zeiss Company, the Leica Company, and the Hamburg American Line as firms which had been especially effective in protecting German interests abroad and gave their New York addresses to the industrialists at this meeting.

After this meeting a smaller one was held, presided over by Dr. Boase of the Armament Industry and attended only by representatives of Hermsdorf Schonberg, Krupp, and Rochling. At this second meeting it was stated that the Nazi party had informed industrialists that *the war was practically lost but it would continue until a guarantee of unity for Germany could be obtained.* German industrialists must, it was said, through their exports, increase the strength of Germany. The industrialists must also prepare to finance the Nazi party, which would go underground as Maquis. From now on the government would allocate large sums to industrialists so that each could establish a secure postwar foundation in foreign countries. Existing financial reserves in foreign countries must be placed at the disposal of the party so that a strong German empire can be created after the defeat. It is also immediately required that the large factories in Germany create small technical offices or reserve bureaus which would be absolutely independent and have no *known* connection with the factory. These bureaus receive plans and drawings of new weapons as well as documents which they need to continue their research and which must not be allowed to fall into the hands of the enemy. These offices are to be established in large cities where they can be most successfully hidden as well as in little villages near sources of hydroelectric power where they can pretend to be studying the development of water resources. The existence of these is to be known only by very few people in each industry and by Chiefs of the Nazi party. Each office will have a liaison or agent with the party. As soon as the party becomes strong enough to re-establish its control over Germany, the industrialists will be paid for their effort and co-operation by concessions and orders.

These meetings seem to indicate that the prohibition against the export of capital which was regularly enforced until now has been completely withdrawn and replaced by a new Nazi policy whereby industrialists, with government assistance, will export as much of their capital as possible.

Previously exports of capital by German industrialists to neutral countries had to be accomplished rather surreptitiously and by means of special influence. Now the Nazi party stands behind the industrialists and urges them to save themselves by getting funds outside Germany and at the same time to advance the party's plans for its postwar operation. This freedom, given to the industrialists, further cements their relations with the party by giving them a measure of protection.

Industrialists are not only buying agricultural property in Germany but are placing their funds abroad, particularly in neutral countries. The two main banks through which this export of capital operates are the Basler Handelsbank and the Schweizerische Kreditanstalt of Zurich. Also there are a number of agencies in Switzerland which for a 5% commission buy property in Switzerland using a Swiss cloak.

After the defeat of Germany the Nazi party recognizes that certain of its best-known leaders will be condemned as war criminals. However, in co-operation with the industrialists it is arranging to place its less conspicuous but most important members in positions with various German factories as technical experts or members of its research and designing offices.

"Fight It Out on This Line"

PARIS, MONDAY, NOVEMBER 27, 1944

There is much high-level consideration being given to the issuance of a joint statement by the President and the Prime Minister which might break the will of the Germans to continue to resist, but, after a considerable exchange of ideas, the conclusion finally was reached, on recommendation of the Supreme Commander, that no such proclamation be issued at this time.

General Ike cabled General Marshall that any such statement preferably should follow some successful military operation. The Supreme Commander felt that the statement at this moment probably would be interpreted as a sign of weakness rather than an honest statement of intent.

The Prime Minister had cabled the President that if he were a German soldier, he would look upon any such statement at this time, when the battle for Cologne is at its peak, as a sign of weakness on our part and as positive proof of the advantages of continued desperate opposition. The General Grant attitude "to fight it out on this line if it takes all summer" is one to which the Prime Minister sees no alternative.

The Prime Minister reasoned that the brilliant success of the French in the south, the capture of Metz by American forces, and the break-through of the American Seventh Army at Strasbourg are important facts which must be added to the increased pressure of the First and Ninth American Armies and the British efforts in the direction of Venlo. Mr. Churchill said that even if we are not successful in reaching Cologne immediately, our forces already have gained enough to make the battle a notable step toward the ultimate objective, and he was certain that words would play no part now. In any event, the Soviets should be parties to any proclamation, as they are holding on their front double the number of divisions which oppose us. In addition, Stalin is considering, after the war, taking several million Nazi youth, Gestapo men, etc., for prolonged work to repair German damage to Russia. The Prime Minister felt that it is difficult to say that Stalin's attitude on this is incorrect.

Consequently, neither the President nor the Prime Minister could give any assurances to the Germans without consultation with Stalin as to the postwar employment of German labor. He reminded the President that the Germans are afraid of occupation by the Russians and fear that a sizable proportion of their population will be transported to Russia (or, as they put it, Siberia) to toil to death. There seemed to Churchill that nothing could be said to eradicate this fear which is deeply rooted in the Germans.

General "Jumbo" Wilson is to take the place of the late Sir John Dill, head of the British Staff Mission in Washington. General Alexander, who has commanded the 15th Army Group in Italy, is to succeed Wilson as Supreme Commander, and General Wayne Clark is to command the group. The American Fifth Army is to be commanded by General Lucian Truscott, whom Ike had hoped to have in France.

PARIS, TUESDAY, NOVEMBER 28, 1944

Played checkers last night with Brigadier General Ted Curtis, Spaatz's Chief of Staff, and beat him. He said he hadn't played in fifteen years and I said I hadn't in twenty, but I noticed he played pretty well, too, both of us, apparently, having lied.*

Our "bird dogs" in Washington have smelled out and have even retrieved the precious frequencies which we need to operate more commercial mobile transmitters, and this is the best news in my line since taking over the communications job. It looks as if the campaign will go through the winter, and we now have little to fear that Berlin will be reached before we have signal facilities to serve the correspondents.

* At least I had.

Matty Fox is having good luck and fine co-operation in getting our equipment in the States—five C-54 loads are coming. I talked with him on the phone in Washington and hinted that he also could bring me some cigars. The allotment of cigarettes at the PX is now down to two packs a week in the rear area, including the Scribe, and five up in front. The ration of cigars is five a week. Had a phone call from Sergeant "Winchell" Moaney today and he excitedly reported that Caacie and Telek have mated before witnesses and we should have additions to our family in due time. He also broke the news that one of the cows is going to have a calf.

PARIS, WEDNESDAY, NOVEMBER 29, 1944

I had a symposium on communications for the correspondents in the briefing room today. There were about forty present, and with Brownie and Lieutenant Colonel A. J. Randall on hand as experts, I told them of our current prospective improvements. They seemed to be satisfied.

Fortunately, Lieutenant Colonel George Warden, our chief censor, stopped them from writing what I had said about the sixty-kilowatt mobile transmitter, because it's a military secret. Its code name is "Sigcircus," but our working title has been "Mobile Radio City." Major Sigmund, Com Z's radio engineer, said it will have seventeen vans, a studio for broadcasting and for telephoto and what not.

Mackay had rushed installation of its new transmitter in one of the vans I got from General Crawford, which formerly was used as living quarters for Lieutenant General Gale, the British administrative officer. I wanted the transmitter displayed in front of the Scribe, so the correspondents could see it after the symposium. Unfortunately, it was not set up in time, as the motor died just as the huge van reached the corner of the Scribe. Some Frenchmen had siphoned out the gasoline.

NOVEMBER, 1944: *Allied ground forces scored advances in bitter fighting with U. S. First Army battling through Hürtgen Forest and Third driving to Merten, then pushing across German frontier toward Saarbrücken after breaking Maginot Line. Ninth destroyed 118 tanks on Cologne plains, took Barmen and Altdorf. Air activity increased in weight and scope, with incessant blows against communications centers, plane and oil plants; air fleets often numbered 3000 planes. Nazis released V-2 rocket bombs against Britain, France, and Belgium. British Navy sank nine of eleven ships in German convoy off Norway. Reds approached Budapest. General Mark Clark became commander of 15th Army Group in Italy, with Field Marshal Alexander as Supreme Commander in Mediterranean. British troops helped Tito and Al-*

banian partisans drive Germans from Yugoslavia and Albania. Bitter fighting on Leyte trapped 3000 Japs; U. S. troops advanced to Limon River. American fliers, hammering Jap convoys, destroyed seven in as many days, to sink many ships and drown thousands of troops. Third Fleet carrier planes destroyed 440 Jap planes, sank or damaged thirty ships. Superforts hit Singapore, targets in Japan and China. Japs lost twenty-six planes in attack upon Saipan Superfort bases in attempt to halt raids upon Tokyo. Stettinius became Secretary of State after Hull's resignation. (Now we knew we were in for a tough winter campaign.—H.C.B.)

PARIS, SATURDAY, DECEMBER 2, 1944

I went to the Folies-Bergère with Bill Giblin, head of the American Red Cross War Relief, Margaret Morin, and Mollie Ford, two of his assistants. The show is on a par with Minsky's best burlesque, but we were so show-hungry we enjoyed it, despite the cold (everyone sat in overcoats). On the stage there were more goose pimples than pulchritude. Had my best laugh in months at a pantomimist who had trouble with his zipper.

I saw Beetle today, and he said we are destroying about three fourths of a German division a day on the long battle front. This is about twenty a month. Beetle said that our best intelligence indicated that the Germans could form a new division at the rate of twelve a month and they can also refit battered divisions near the front at the rate of about five. Consequently, exclusive of other fronts, by our pressure the high rate of attrition is gradually drawing the German supply of manpower.

PARIS, SUNDAY, DECEMBER 3, 1944

Our Air Force has developed at home a Chinese copy of a German flying bomb, I learned today at SHAEF. About 100 have been built and contracts let for 1000, with delivery scheduled at the rate of 200 per month. Launching is still a problem. The question has been raised as to whether we want to use them on the Germans, but so much shipping would be required that SHAEF said no.

Weather, Floods, and Mud

PARIS, TUESDAY, DECEMBER 5, 1944

On request of General Allen, I spoke to General Ike today about doing a Christmas newsreel for the troops. He agreed, and our sound crew will go to his camp at Rheims to make the film next Saturday.

The General seemed interested in what I was doing, although I didn't seem to have anything alarming to report. He had heard from Tooey Spaatz that the demands on my time had not kept me from Tooey's gaming table, and this I admitted. I told him I had occasional need for his lucky coins but was managing fairly well without them.

Ike said he had been rubbing them hard lately. One thing that was bothering him was that although a great deal depends upon the date and scale of the anticipated winter offensive of the Russians, actually he knows nothing definite of their plans.

Newly formed German divisions are arriving on our front and we have attracted several divisions directly from Austria and East Prussia. The enemy on our front is badly stretched and is forced constantly to shift units up and down the line to reinforce our threats or attacks. The Germans seem more apprehensive of our operations in the First and Ninth Army areas than anywhere else. Unfortunately for us, the flooded condition of the Roer River, and the German capability of suddenly producing a rush of water by lowering the floodgates of the dams near Schmidt, make our efforts to move forward difficult and very arduous. General Bradley had about come to the conclusion that the area must be taken by a ground attack from the west and southwest. The effort to bomb the dams failed.

Our continued pressure against the Germans is causing them to throw into the line some divisions with only six weeks' training and, consequently, they are suffering a higher rate of casualties than normal amongst well-trained soldiers.

Ike's problem is to continue his attacks as long as the results are so much in our favor, but, at the same time, to prepare a full-out and heavy offensive when weather conditions become favorable, assuming the enemy still holds out. Ike saw no real evidence of trouble developing within Germany and expected the Germans to maintain a strong defensive front for some time, assisted by weather, floods, and muddy ground.

Back in the Old Groove

PARIS, WEDNESDAY, DECEMBER 6, 1944

I am back in radio and communications generally—as deeply as I ever was with Columbia in Washington. As a matter of fact, our operations here are not unlike those in Washington—particularly as we are always seeking more frequencies and new and better equipment. Fortunately, our plan for expanding telegraph, broadcast, and picture transmission direct from the battle fronts to the U. S. has now been approved in Washington, but only after three officers were sent there personally to prosecute our case. They found everyone in the War Department most co-operative and soon had our program approved by the Federal Communications Commission. I hope this will permit a close tie-in between the battle front and the home front, even when the battle front moves into Berlin.

CBS has had poor luck on broadcasts from Paris to the States. This fact has dispelled all thought that I, as an ex-Columbian, would be pro-Columbia. Oddly enough, Mutual gets the best breaks, the Blue next, then NBC, and poor old Columbia gets all the atmospherics, line breaks, poor switching, and power failures—the majority of which have happened on the American side. Bill Shirer, with all his eggs in one basket, with one broadcast a week, and not permitted by CBS to record his remarks for rebroadcast of his own voice on the air, has been hurting all over—right down to his toes. If CBS would permit him to broadcast from Paris before sunset when transmission conditions are best and record his voice in New York for rendition later in the evening, CBS would have assurance of a broadcastable program and would have a usable program even if Bill's voice is torn asunder by the hell-raising of twilight on the Atlantic when he comes on for his regular Sunday-night period. I have kidded CBS and NBC that Mutual and the Blue are young and enterprising and not hidebound by tradition or bias against recordings. This is my favorite theme, and I plague all CBS people with my wail. Bill Paley knows it by heart and I think Paul Kesten in New York could repeat it in his sleep. Why the networks didn't buy lines to Mackay Telegraph in New York, so they could receive Mackay transmission from Paris, remains a mystery to me. I sent a message to the tops of all networks, asking them to look into switching. When we sweat our hearts out trying to get communications out of a war area into America we simply cannot understand the attitude of the traffic men in the networks.

I am enjoying the revival of my sparse knowledge of communications—such as it was—and haven't had a better time during the war than in the past couple of months as head of communications for the Public Relations Division of SHAEF. Some correspondents have been so kind as to say that the press traffic moves more rapidly now out of Paris than before the war.

PARIS, SATURDAY, DECEMBER 9, 1944

Ike called me on the telephone from his camp near Rheims today. He had some questions about the newsreel, but ended up being his own producer. He had representatives of American, British, and French forces. He talked to them before the camera, just as he talks to GIs at the front. Each national group sent a message to the folk at home, and General Ike told each of them to return to their units and wish their comrades a merry Christmas in his behalf.

He said he had a large party of Congressmen coming for lunch on Sunday and did I want to join them.

I said, "No, thank you, sir."

PARIS, MONDAY, DECEMBER 11, 1944

SHAEF has received information that the condition of Allied prisoners in German hands is definitely not good. It is feared that with the coming of winter there will be insufficient clothing and bedding. There is said to be no fuel for heat in German prison camps. Many of the Red Cross food packages, on which Allied prisoners depend so much, have not reached the camps. Since July the German attitude toward Allied prisoners has undergone a marked change for the worse. This change is generally attributed to Himmler.

Last night Jim Gault phoned me from Shellburst, the camp near Rheims, to discuss a story written by Jules Grad, the *Stars and Stripes* pool reporter. Grad had covered the conference and luncheon of seventeen Congressmen with General Ike during the day. They had been told by General Ike that no blame for the current shortage of artillery shells could be placed in any one quarter, but the main point now is that more shells are needed and should be supplied in the shortest possible time. He also advocated combat pay for medics serving with combat battalions.

But the point of Jim's call was a bottle of liquor. Some of the Congressmen had brought presents—one, a jar of pork sausage, another a box of hominy, and still another a bottle of Kentucky bourbon. Jim was apprehensive that the news of the bourbon might cause a bad reaction in America. I didn't think so, but told him I would call the censor at the Scribe and have the story read to me.

I found the story listed the names of several Congressmen who brought gifts and that it was Andrew May, Chairman of the House Military Affairs Committee, who had brought the Kentucky bourbon. Knowing that General Ike has heretofore given similar gifts to hospitals, for the wounded, I asked the censor to write in the story, and I would take responsibility for it, that "General Eisenhower sent the whisky to a near-by field hospital."

Today Jim phoned and wanted to make certain that I accepted the responsibility for dealing with the bottle of whisky as I had. He said that the General was displeased.

PARIS, TUESDAY, DECEMBER 12, 1944

I had Mickey and Pearlie for dinner at the Raphaël. They are to be married Saturday. I offered them my small flat for their honeymoon and they have accepted. I plan to visit press camps in the 6th Army Group.

Ike hopped me today about the bottle of Kentucky bourbon that I said he sent to a hospital. He said that every member of the Military Affairs Committee would know that part of the story was a lie. They would lose respect for his integrity. The bourbon incident would cause them to say "the fellow is a damned liar."

I told him I thought the Congressmen, being good politicians, would not be bothered by the story and that his reputation for honesty could not be shattered by such a small incident. I still couldn't see why he was so concerned.

"What did happen to the whisky?"

"Why, dammit, the Congressmen drank it before lunch," he replied.

Monty and Ike Differ on Strategy

PARIS, WEDNESDAY, DECEMBER 13, 1944

General Ike has been on the road almost daily since his press conference on November 21. He has seen all the army-group and army commanders and many of the corps and division commanders. He has talked with hundreds of GIs.

A month ago there was a trickle of criticism flowing at my level, principally from correspondents assigned to press camps in Montgomery's area, that a deputy ground commander was needed. The argument has been advanced and stories have been written that the Supreme Commander is too busy taking care of political and economic problems to deal personally and effectively with military problems of the battle front. That trickle has now grown practically to a campaign in at least one London paper to put Montgomery in command of the ground battle.

General Ike had spent the night and conferred with the Field Marshal on Tuesday, November 28. Points discussed at this conference were restated in a letter from Monty to "My dear Ike," dated November 30, in which the Field Marshal said we had definitely failed to implement the plan contained in the SHAEF directive of October 28. This directive ordered the main effort to be made in the north to defeat the enemy west of the Rhine, to gain bridgeheads over the Rhine and the Ijssel Rivers, and to deploy in strength east of the Rhine preparatory to seizing the Ruhr. Monty said we had achieved none of this and we had no hope of doing so. He figured that we had, therefore, failed and that we had suffered a strategic reverse.

Monty said we needed a new plan and this time we must not fail, as the need to get the German war finished early is vital. Monty said in the new plan we must abandon the doctrine of attacking in so many places that nowhere are we strong enough to get decisive results. Strength must be concentrated in the main thrust that is chosen, so that success will be certain. In our present operations, we have failed in this respect.

He reasoned that the front divided itself naturally into two main sectors, one north of the Ardennes, the other south. He wants one commander in full operational control in the north and another south. He had suggested to General Ike that there be a land force commander to work under the Supreme Commander and to run the land battle for him, but General Ike had rejected this idea as not suitable and it had not been discussed further. Monty went on that Bradley and he had made a good team, had worked together in Normandy under General Ike, and had won a great victory, but that things had not been so good since the Supreme Commander had made them of equal importance. Monty wanted the objectives spelled out for the spring campaign and requested that a decision be made now. He wanted a further meeting, on the sixth or seventh of December, with the Supreme Commander and General Bradley. Monty suggested that no one else need come to the meeting except Chiefs of Staff, "who must not speak."

Monty's letter made Ike hot under the collar. He replied promptly that he didn't know what Monty meant by strategic reverse; so far as General Ike was concerned, he realized that we had failed to achieve all that had been hoped, but hopes and plans are based on conditions as we know them or can estimate them when the plans are made. He said that the Ruhr is important, but we should not lose sight of the primary objective, which is to defeat the German forces that are barring our way into Germany. The Ruhr itself always has been a geographical objective, not only for its importance to Germany, but because of the German forces largely concentrated to guard the Ruhr to meet our attacks.

General Ike agreed that we must determine how much profit there is in continuation of our current attacks in the 12th Army Group and whether they give real promise of reaching the Rhine. He said further that general plans must be recast in the light of conditions as they now exist. The best line of attack to assure success must be chosen, including the maintenance of deception. General Ike did not agree that things had gone badly since Normandy merely because all we had hoped for had not been attained. He felt that the current situation is analogous to that which existed in Normandy for so long. There our line, as late as D plus 60, was not greatly different than that we had hoped to hold in the first week after the landings, but he had never looked upon the situation then existing as a strategic reverse, even though the long confinement on the narrow beachhead had caused our greatest later difficulties. He pointed out that if we had advanced from the beachhead from the beginning as we had hoped, congestion would have been avoided and our maintenance services would have been in a position to furnish supplies during the critical September days when we actually reached the limit of our resources.

General Ike did not agree that more strength could have been thrown to Monty in the north than was actually maintained there during early September. In the north, the lines of communication were so stretched that even delivery of 500 tons a day to Monty at Brussels cost Bradley three divisions in Patton's army which, had they received benefit of the transport given to Monty, might easily have reached the Rhine in the Worms area.

The Supreme Commander said that, after all, we had gained a great victory in Normandy. Bradley's brilliant break-through made possible the rapid exploitation by all forces which had cleared France and Belgium and had almost carried us across the Rhine. If we had not advanced on a relatively broad front, we would now have a long, narrow line of communication constantly threatened on the right flank and weakened by detachments of large fighting formations. In the south we would have had a similar picture stretching all the way from Marseille to Dijon. Fortunately, we now have a rear that is cleared of the enemy and we can look at the front.

General Ike declared he had no intentions of stopping Devers' and Bradley's operations as long as they are cleaning up our right flank and giving us what he described as "capability of concentration." He did not, on the other hand, plan to push these attacks senselessly.

Later on, the Supreme Commander continued, it will be important to us to have two strings to our bow. He reminded Monty of his two strings at Mareth, where the alternatives had paid off.

Whether or not Monty's or Bradley's Chiefs of Staff attend the meeting, which Ike agreed should be held Thursday, December 7, at Maastricht, he would bring his Chief of Staff and would not by any means insult him by telling him that he should remain mute at any conference.

He told the Field Marshal that he appreciated the frankness of his statements and the usual friendly way to which they were put, but he begged him not to continue to look upon the past performances of this great fighting force as a failure merely because we have not achieved all that we could have hoped. The Supreme Commander was confident that Montgomery, Bradley, and he could remain masters of the situation and that the victory all of them want will certainly be achieved, but all must look at the whole picture stretching from Marseille to the lower Rhine as one great operation, and that when our next attack starts, we will obtain maximum results from all our forces.

As usual, his salutation had been "Dear Monty" and his signature, "Ike."

Supplementing his letter to Monty, General Ike sent him a further message from the headquarters of Bradley's 12th Army Group. He said that on checking figures, he found that Patton's Third Army, since the start of its offensive November 8, had captured more than 25,000 prisoners and that Hodges' First and Simpson's Ninth, from November 16, had captured 15,000—the total exceeding 40,000. In addition, the enemy had suffered other losses, of course, but General Ike pointed out to Monty that the operations seemed well worth while, regardless of positions gained, and the enemy's losses had vastly exceeded our own.

The Field Marshal responded in a letter dated December 2 and said he was disturbed by General Ike's request that Monty "not continue to look upon the past performances of this great fighting force as a failure." Monty said he had never done anything of the sort and had never said anything that could convey that impression. He had written about the SHAEF directive of October 28, which Monty had declared we had failed to carry out. He said that anyone who reads the directive would admit the truth of his statement, but he would be sorry, indeed, if General Ike thought he had said or implied anything else.

The Supreme Commander immediately replied to the Field Marshal and tendered his prompt and sincere apologies for misreading Monty's letter of November 30. General Ike said that in his haste to answer, he had read into Monty's letter a far more pessimistic statement than was justified. General Ike was sorry if his letter gave offense and certainly did not want to give an erroneous meaning to Monty's words or to do anything to upset their close relationship. General Ike sent with the letter a report of General Ken Strong, SHAEF's G-2, which indicated the great damage being done the Germans by current operations. Ike assured

Monty, too, that prospects for U. S. ammunition are brightening as allocations from home have been increased and shipments stepped up. He supposed Monty knew that the RAF was going to take a shot at the Schwammanuel Dam near Schmidt—one of the important dams, controlled by the Germans, that regulate the flow of the Roer River. Ike hoped it would be successful because, as it is now, Hodges' First and Simpson's Ninth stop at the Roer to avoid risk of artificial flooding. If the Schmidt dam is bombed out, Hodges and Simpson thought they could get their troops over the river and then take on the Panzer divisions and chew them up.

From the Prime Minister, General Ike had received a request for the loan of some U. S. engineers who are in England awaiting movement to the front. Churchill said that the British were trying hard to keep ahead on rocket-bomb damage in London and have 120,000 additional civilians working, as well as 2500 men from the British forces. If General Ike could make available two or three thousand American engineers now stationed in England, the damage could be tidied much more readily.

General Ike immediately cabled Major General Harry Vaughn, U. S. Base Commander in England, instructions to help and declared that U. S. troops would consider it an honor to participate in this work. The only question would be one of availability of the proper type of troops. He thanked the Prime Minister for bringing the matter to his personal attention.

The Prime Minister then announced the loan of American troops to help with the repair of bomb damage and the news was warmly cheered in the House of Commons. They are already on the job.

The Dams

PARIS, THURSDAY, DECEMBER 14, 1944

General Ike had flown from his Advance CP for conferences in London, where he saw the Prime Minister.

Following his return, he wrote to General Marshall that the British, particularly Field Marshal Sir Alan F. Brooke, seemed disturbed by dispersion of our strength during the past week. General Ike had explained that the flooded conditions in the lower Rhine Valley prevented any further offensive action in that region at the moment, and that we had supported Montgomery's northern thrust with everything we could possibly maintain. Field Marshal Brooke appeared to understand the situation better than he had before.

The Supreme Commander also explained to the Chief of the Imperial General Staff that in the planned attack toward Bonn and Cologne, General Bradley had used all of the divisions he could possibly employ on that narrow front. The attack is held up for the time being not by lack of strength but because the Roer River is at flood level and there are three dams a short way up the river controlled by the Germans. He had told the CIGS that Bradley is now engaged in a subsidiary operation to capture the dams, and that all the new strength now coming in is being directed to the left flank of Bradley's Army Group, where it can support the northern attack for the Ruhr.

A Bet, a Wedding, and Five Stars

PARIS, SATURDAY, DECEMBER 16, 1944

Monty sent Ike a letter by air courier under yesterday's date that now that he has issued his orders for the next big operation—the large-scale attack from Nijmegen southeast to clear the west bank of the Rhine far enough to give elbow room for the ultimate crossing north of the Ruhr—he would like to have General Ike's assent to spending Christmas with his son in England. Monty included with his letter a reminder of a bet of five pounds he had made with General Ike that the war would not end by Christmas, 1944. The bet was made October 11, 1943, in Italy. In Monty's own handwriting, he noted: "For payment, I think, at Christmas."

General Ike replied that he envied Monty's opportunity to spend Christmas with his son, and said that Monty would receive his five pounds in his Christmas stocking but not until Christmas Day, for, after all, Ike said, he still has nine days. Ike chided Monty that at least he had to admit we had gone a long way toward the defeat of Germany since the bet was made fourteen months ago.

He assured Monty every possible arrangement was being made to strengthen the left of the 12th Army Group so that Monty could concentrate full attack so that both Bradley's and his attacks would be mutually supporting.

Mickey and Pearlie's wedding took place today. It was a sweet ceremony, but everyone shivered. I sat there in my bridge coat—the heaviest I own—and despite that and my long heavy GI underwear, wool muffler, socks, and gloves, I still shivered. General Ike sat just ahead of me in his blouse.

After the wedding, the party went to the Supreme Commander's house, where the bride was kissed by the Supreme Commander.

I saw General Ike again briefly during the evening at a reception at the WAC House at Versailles. He left early, as General Bradley was spending the night with him. They are discussing the problem of getting reinforcements for our divisions to replace losses.

Amongst other activities of a busy day, the Supreme Commander and his Chief of Staff had been formally presented the previously awarded Polish Medal of Honor, the Virtuti Militari, by General Kopanski, the Polish Chief of Staff. The presentation was made on behalf of the President of Poland, Wladyslaw Raczkiewicz.

Another incident of the day was the news that his nomination as General of the Army, with its five stars, has been sent by the President to the Senate. The man who always cautioned his family not to expect him to be promoted has risen from lieutenant colonel to a five-star general in three years, three months, and sixteen days—six promotions, one about every six months. He had been a major for sixteen years.

He won't put on the stars until the nomination is confirmed.

PARIS, SUNDAY, DECEMBER 17, 1944
Wes Gallagher left a note in my office today which said in part:

Thought you might like to know that Ike's recent trips to the front, coupled with the recent U. S. activity, appear to have completely silenced that "best general in the British Army" business.

Low- and High-Level Views of the Ardennes Counteroffensive

PARIS, FRIDAY, DECEMBER 22, 1944
Lieutenant Colonel Ralph, Major Brown, and I returned to Paris about 7 this evening. We unloaded our gear at the Express Building and found that SHAEF had issued an order requiring that all Allied enlisted personnel and officers must be off the streets by 8, because of the scare about German paratroopers operating in connection with the Ardennes offensive.

Ralph, Brownie, and I left Paris last Monday, December 18, and stopped first at Verdun to see Colonel Francis V. Fitzgerald. He gave us our first real news of the German counterattack in the Ardennes. In the war room there were red arrows indicating the depth of the penetration through our lines, and there was an atmosphere around the 12th Army Group headquarters which reminded me of the Kasserine. Fitz said that the teleprinter line from the First Army press camp at Spa had been in and out, but now seemed definitely out, indicating it had been cut. The Germans had dropped many paratroopers behind our lines, many in American uniforms, and other enemy troops were infiltrated in captured jeeps. Road blocks had been established to check all movements. We had been stopped a half-dozen times driving up from Paris. The MPs are using a slick system of questions. One MP asked me my native state. I told him "Iowa." This partially satisfied him. But to make absolutely certain I wasn't a German, he asked me the name of the large river that forms Iowa's eastern boundary. Fortunately, he found my knowledge of geography adequate, and we were permitted to pass.

On the more serious side, Fitz said that Bradley's tactical headquarters at Luxembourg might have to be moved, as the enemy was getting close. Brownie immediately started worrying about the safety of Radio Luxembourg, and particularly the short-wave transmitter, which he hopes to have operating to the States by Christmas.

We would like to have driven toward the battle front, but our business was with the Southern Group of Armies and, besides, I didn't think the commanding officers would appreciate kibitzers getting in the way when they had a red-hot battle on their hands. We got as far as Nancy that night.

I had a breakfast date with General Patton at 7:45 the next morning, but my jeep was held up by heavy road movement, and we were five minutes late. General Patton had eaten and gone to his headquarters, but had left his aide, Major Stiller, an old friend from African days, to eat with me and then to take me to the office. Stiller said that General Patton had been to Luxembourg the previous day and it looked as if many divisions of the Third Army would be wheeled northward to attack the Germans in the south flank of their penetration. Patton had received a call from Bradley that he was to attend the meeting at Verdun with General Ike today, and had gone to the office early to consult with his staff. I waited a while for General Patton to finish, and ultimately he strode down the corridor past the door of his aide's office. I called out, "Hello, General." He replied, "Hi, Butch." That was my interview.

From the staff I heard of Patton's comment when he learned of the German push. "Fine," he said. "We should open up and let 'em get all the way to Paris. Then we'll saw 'em off at the base."

Third Army officers welcomed this venture of the Germans from the Siegfried Line, and relished the idea of Patton and his Third Army in the role of saviors of the situation.

We drove to Saarebourg, seeing many signs of battle along the way, such as burned-out tanks, dead animals, and black crosses marking German graves, and spent some time with Brigadier General Tristram Tupper, Public Relations Officer for the 6th Army Group. There have been many complaints from the French that news from the First French Army, which is under the 6th Army Group, has to be sent to Paris by train courier, as there are no radio-transmission facilities at the French press camp, nor have any frequencies been found for transmission. Tupper asked me to see what I could do for the French.

We continued toward the Rhine to Saverne, where the American press camp serving Patch's Seventh Army had been set up in a schoolhouse, recently occupied by DPs.* An old associate of broadcasting days, Lieutenant Colonel Frank Pellegrin, is the PRO. We attended the evening briefing for correspondents, and I heard a junior briefing officer of G-2 of the Seventh Army criticize before the correspondents the tactics which had left the Colmar pocket on the west side of the Rhine as a thorn in the side of our forces. It was, however, off the record, and such frankness seemed to be taken as a matter of right.

Pellegrin went with us to Strasbourg, where I paid my respects to the acting commander of the 3rd Division, Brigadier General Robert N. Young. We were luncheon guests of Lieutenant Colonel John Heintges,† CO of the 7th Infantry Regiment of the 3rd Division. Heintges said the new VT fuse had been tried and found to be one of the answers to the business of killing Germans with artillery fire. It is most effective if set to explode about fifteen yards above the ground, thus throwing fragments into slit trenches. We were taken to an island in the Rhine alongside Strasbourg to see some shooting. There was desultory heavy machine-gun fire, principally from our side, from which we could see pillboxes and other strong points on the opposite bank. From several of them smoke curled, indicating the Germans were trying to keep warm as well as alive. A young Irish lieutenant, of the 1st Battalion of A Company, led us to an observation post in a grain elevator. We had to climb up narrow stairs and ladders for eleven stories.

There were three GIs directing mortar fire by telephone from their vantage point. On the opposite side of the Rhine was a brown building with a cupola with a red tile roof which we could see plainly through

---

* Displaced persons.

† Subsequently, I was told by General Young that Heintges is a son of a German officer who was killed in the last war. Young Heintges came to America and was graduated from West Point. His regiment was given the mission to take Berchtesgaden, and Heintges personally led his troops up the mountain to Hitler's Eagle's Nest and captured it.

the glasses, as it was only about 500 yards away. The observers suspected the enemy was directing its fire from the cupola and had just given directions over the telephone for the mortar crew below to shoot at it. There were three or four near misses. The directions were corrected and soon the cupola was directly hit.

Our energetic lieutenant thought this kind of fighting very quiet indeed and gave his thanks that they were not fighting in the forests. He said forest fighting was the worst kind the 3rd Division had ever experienced. Shell holes in the woods are practically useless, and afforded little protection from artillery shells, which detonate when they strike trees.

My blue naval uniform attracted attention, and some GIs asked me if I was reconnoitering a naval operation to help the Army cross the Rhine.

We made Vittel late that evening and next morning consulted with signal officers of the group, under Brigadier General Lenzer, another veteran from the Mediterranean, whom we found most co-operative in our efforts to speed movement of press and broadcast material. Ran into another friend, Major H. I. Leyshon, PRO for the Tactical Air Force supporting the 6th Army Group. He has only the feeblest kind of communication back to Paris, but has all sorts of aerial activity to report. He thinks I can do wonders for him, because I once got him a telephone when he was assigned at the Scribe. I visited the war room and found the Germans still advancing in the Ardennes, but learned that Devers' group was taking over a major part of the Third Army's front, while Patton was quickly moving divisions toward Luxembourg in an effort to pinch off the Germans on the south flank.

We drove to Luxeuil to see the French press camp, of which Commandant Baron was the PRO. His story of inadequate communications really was touching. The First French Army has fought valiantly to help liberate the country, yet the correspondents, particularly French, seeking to tell all France and the world about the Army's accomplishments, have to rely primarily on train service to Paris to get their stories delivered.

We returned to Vittel that evening and spent the night, and set out for Paris next day. We were stopped perhaps a dozen times during the day by MPs checking our identification. One MP said that a German paratrooper had just been stumbled over in a pile of snow by one of the search parties.

At the mess I met three friends who had just returned from Bastogne, where they had unwittingly driven into the battle. They were Lee Dayton and two Red Cross girls, Margaret Morin and Mollie Ford, who had been delivering Christmas packages to Red Cross personnel. At Aywaille, in Belgium, they had spent a night in a hotel with rooms facing the main street, over which American convoys of trucks pounded toward the battle throughout the night. In the early dawn a convoy stopped and a deep Southern voice had been heard to call out, "Men, douse your lights. From here on go as quietly as possible. We are getting close to the active battle area."

A Negro voice came out of the darkness: "My friends, ah hate wah, Sistie hates wah, Buzzie hates wah—we all hate wah. Ah'll never send you' boys ovahseas. But we ah ovahseas, and we ah goin' ovah de top." Amidst nervous laughter from darkened trucks, the voice trailed apologetically off into the song *Franklin D. Roosevelt Jones* as the convoy moved on.

Dayton said that he had heard on his trip that Field Marshal Montgomery had been given command of the U. S. First and Ninth Armies because of the seriousness of the Ardennes battle. There was also a story going around at the Scribe of a well-known and seasoned correspondent who had returned from the battle and had said that he was going to keep right on going until he got to the States because the Germans were coming through to Paris just as they did in 1940. There had been a forty-eight-hour blackout on information at the PRD briefing room. The correspondents were angry, and the home publics, being far from the scene of action, were obviously frightened.

The News Blackout on the German Gamble

PARIS, SATURDAY, DECEMBER 23, 1944

I had a busy day. George Lyon was in my office early this morning to tell me his side of his denunciation that "SHAEF is stupid," as quoted in the papers with respect to the forty-eight-hour blackout. Said it was the manner in which the announcement had been made rather than the content. He thought the correspondents were annoyed because they were talked down to rather than frankly told the reason for the arbitrary delay in giving them the news. He planned to return to the States and was suspicious that someone had ordered Air Transport Command not to give him a seat, although he had his orders from the PRD. George suspected that PRD was afraid he will talk to the press when he gets home, beyond the curb of SHAEF censors. I investigated this and found he was in error and through Colonel Plummer, who is in charge of ATC in Paris, got him booked on a plane leaving tomorrow.

I went out to Versailles and saw Ike today. He is a prisoner of our security police and is thoroughly but helplessly irritated by the restriction on his moves. There are all sorts of guards, some with machine guns, around the house, and he has to travel to and from the office led and at times followed by an armed guard in a jeep. He got some satisfaction yesterday in slipping out for a walk around the yard in deep snow, in the eyes of the security officers quite the most dangerous thing for him to do, but he had the satisfaction of doing something he wanted to do. I told him he now knows how it must feel to be President and be guarded day and night by ever-watchful secret-service men.

The restriction is caused by information from Intelligence officers of Hodges' First Army, who cross-examined a German officer captured at Liége the night of December 19. He was one of a group of English-speaking Krauts* who had infiltrated through Allied lines in American uniform, driving an American jeep and carrying American identification papers. The leader of this group, which specializes in kidnaping and assassination of high personages, is a character named Skorzeny, who, reputedly, rescued Mussolini. He is said to have passed through our lines with about sixty of his men and had the mission of killing the Supreme Commander. One of their rendezvous points is said to be the Café de la Paix in Paris, just around the corner from the Scribe. There German sympathizers and agents are supposed to meet Skorzeny's gang and to furnish information about General Ike's abode, movement, and security guard. The men were described as completely ruthless and prepared to sacrifice their lives to carry out their mission. All personnel speak fluent English. Similar attacks on other high officers have been given to other infiltrators, numbering about 150. Some units might have with them in their vehicle a German officer in uniform and, if questioned, would tell a false story that they were taking an important German prisoner to higher headquarters in the rear. They carry capsules of acid to be thrown in the faces of MPs or others to facilitate escape. Skorzeny's group may be in staff cars, civilian cars, command and reconnaissance cars, as well as jeeps.

Already about 150 parachutists wearing American uniforms or civilian clothes have landed in the U. S. First Army's area. Many of them have been captured, but some are still at large. Those in uniform are not wearing dog tags, but all carry explosives and have a new type of hand grenade discharged from a pistol.

Our security officers are always supercautious, and with this alarming information, I can readily understand why they have thrown a cordon around the Supreme Commander, yet he is thoroughly disgusted at the whole procedure and seemed pleased to have someone to talk with like me, seemingly from the outside world.

* Shows I've recently been with GIs who were in Italy and Africa.

Ike's office was serene. Outside, through the high French windows, the snow was falling, and the setting seemed appropriate for the approaching Christmas. I had already visited some of the staff at the Trianon next door and found everyone calm and going about his business as usual.

Ike was as calm as he ever is, and, except for the irritation caused by his confinement, was cheerful and optimistic. I told him of the wild rumors I had picked up both in my travels and in Paris and attributed some of these to the enforced forty-eight-hour delay of news. He said that his first knowledge that the blackout had been imposed was in the headline in the *Stars and Stripes*. I told him I thought the staff had mechanically followed the pattern successfully used on our offensives when blackouts were ordered to avoid giving the enemy information as to progress or direction of our spearheads, and that now the staff, perhaps, had failed to realize that with the tables reversed, great alarm was being caused, particularly at home, because the blackout was interpreted as a SHAEF device to withhold bad news and, consequently, imaginations of mothers and fathers and sweethearts were running wild. Ike felt this was something the public simply would have to stand for a few days and by now the home fronts must have developed sufficient confidence in his command to be patient until the complete news could be released. He agreed, however, that at some appropriate time the blackout could be lifted and further that we would issue a complete factual report, to be prepared by G-3, just as we had done after the Kasserine.

Once an action has been taken by his staff, Ike ordinarily supports it, and he did not change this one. After all, he felt, there was good reasoning behind the delay, as there was heavy movement of divisions toward the flanks and head of the bulge and this, of course, should not be disclosed. The G-2s argued that there was reason to believe that the German High Command did not know the location of their own front line, nor the progress of their armored thrusts. Any information we give out through PRD is on BBC within an hour, and intelligence reports indicate that the German headquarters frequently fix the pins in their war maps from the BBC reports. In addition, as our units in the Ardennes were withdrawn, insofar as they could be, the fact they had withdrawn was kept secret for forty-eight hours, and Ike assumed that therein lay the reason for the staff's selection of forty-eight hours as the period for the delay of news. However, he didn't share the belief that the German headquarters didn't know the location of their lines.

Over all, he felt that the situation was well in hand; that there was no need for alarm; that he and his senior commanders had taken prompt steps to meet what he figured was the Germans' dying thrust, and if we would be patient and the Lord would give us some good flying weather, all would be well and we would probably emerge with a tactical victory. He added that it is easier and less costly to us to kill Germans when they are attacking than when they are holed up in concrete fortifications in the Siegfried Line, and the more we can kill in their present offensive, the fewer we will have to dig out pillbox by pillbox.

As to the command of the First and Ninth U. S. Armies having been given to Field Marshal Montgomery, I suggested that since the news was all over the place, an announcement should be authorized to prevent further speculation. London papers were vaguely hinting at Monty's new responsibility and inferring that when the Americans got in trouble, Monty had come to the rescue. Ike felt that such inferences were deplorable from the standpoint of Allied relationships, but his decision to give Monty temporary command of the two American armies was dictated by the exigencies of the battle. If we were to be so generous as to tell the German High Command that Monty commanded on the northern flank of the bulge and Bradley on the southern, the Germans, being familiar with Monty's and Bradley's different types of fighting, would be greatly pleased to have the information and could better plan their tactics. The command arrangement could be announced later, but not now.

"I Want Only Cheerful Faces"

I learned from Colonel Jim Gault, who had accompanied the General and Air Chief Marshal Tedder to the meeting at Verdun on Tuesday (for which I had seen Patton hurrying to prepare to attend at Nancy), that, in addition, Generals Bradley and Devers, and the principal staff officers from SHAEF, 6th and 12th Army Groups, and the Third Army were present. Jim said that Ike opened the conference, saying, "I want only cheerful faces."

It had been decided that the whole front south of the Moselle would go strictly on the defensive and would give up all penetrations across the Saar River. Devers was to take over most of the present Third Army front, freeing Patton to move north with six divisions and temporarily to take over the VIII Corps. Patton was to organize a major counterattack with target date of December 23 or 24. Our weakest spot was in the direction of Namur, where the enemy was expected to attack with armor at Monschau to broaden its penetration and might attack with less strength from the region of Trier. The enemy might try also to attack north of the Ninth Army, but Montgomery had reserves capable of dealing with the Germans there. The general plan was to plug the holes in the north and to launch a co-ordinated attack from the south.

General Ike, Tedder, and Jim had returned to the Versailles headquarters. At 11 that night, Beetle phoned Ike that the G-2s now figured that the whole German effort was toward Namur and that at the current rate of progress the Boche might well be there in forty-eight hours. As a result of the enemy's offensive and his paratroop operations in the areas of Malmédy and Spa, Hodges' signal facilities had been disrupted, which left the SHAEF G-2s a bit confused as to what was happening.

In view of the situation, General Ike had agreed that Field Marshal Montgomery temporarily should take over command of the First and Ninth north of the break-through and instructed Beetle to send a message to him to that effect.

The battle of the Ardennes started a week ago today. Events leading up to the German offensive, and the action taken to defeat it, were discussed by the Supreme Commander. To him it had been clear that the Germans, beginning early in November after their succession of defeats of the summer and fall, were succeeding in their efforts hurriedly to form Volkssturm divisions. It had been apparent that unless the Allied forces quickly could attack the Siegfried Line, the Germans could add to their strength and make our advance through the line more difficult the longer we were forced by long supply lines to delay the attacks.

It was also clear that we would have to reach and hold the western bank of the Lower Rhine as far as Bonn before we could make a deep penetration into Germany. It had been considered desirable but not necessarily mandatory that we should also be up to the Rhine in the Frankfurt area.

It had not been possible for Monty's Army Group, due to limitations in strength, to join the attacks in the early stages. Consequently, the burden was borne by Bradley's 12th Army Group, supported by Devers' 6th Army Group from the south. Owing to the limited amount of frontage over which our attacks could be made, Bradley had felt that his concentrations on the north to assist Monty's forces to reach the Rhine had to be moderate in size. His intentions and his orders from the Supreme Commander were to keep the attack going at full strength while Patton prepared and launched his Third Army advance to the Rhine. In Patton's area, the enemy was badly stretched and Bradley had believed the Saar Valley could be captured with expenditure of little force. Once the Siegfried was reached by Patton, rapid exploitation could be expected behind and beyond the Siegfried.

Because of shortage of ammunition and insufficient replacements to keep all units up to strength, Patton's army had been allotted only a small proportion of incoming ammunition and received none of the replacements. Our attacks always were based on use of the ground-air team, and, although France in winter was normally a difficult area for flying, it was felt that with only average weather, our strength would be sufficient to accomplish our purposes.

Unfortunately, the worst period of weather of any of General Ike's campaigns grounded our planes much of the time and likewise made conditions difficult for the ground forces. On the north, the Roer River, which had been expected to be a relatively minor obstacle, became a major one. The dams backed up floods and rains and, since they were in enemy hands, the Germans, by releasing the water, could destroy any strong Allied force that crossed the Roer. Bombing had failed to knock out the dams, and Bradley had to stop his main attack in the north until he could maneuver through bad country to capture the dam sites.

With the fields muddy, tanks could operate only along the roads, and thus all maneuver became difficult. The enforced delay of the general attack planned in the north made Bradley desirous of continuing the Third Army attacks in the Saar area, particularly as Devers' 6th Army Group had been successful and Patch's Seventh Army had closed in on Patton's right in position to support Patton's effort to breach the Siegfried.

Throughout November, the situation at the front was carefully reviewed daily and the Supreme Commander had conferred with Monty, the British Chiefs of Staff, and the commanders on the American front. It had become clear from these conferences that more strength must be shifted to the north and that all incoming formations must be assigned to the U. S. First and Ninth Armies. General Ike had even attempted to bring three new divisions coming through Marseille to the Aachen area, but had to revoke his order when he found that all portions of these divisions could not come in until late January or February.

On the 6th Army Group front, where operations had begun auspiciously, the Colmar pocket west of the Rhine became a troublesome snag. The Germans in that pocket absorbed the strength of the entire First French Army and had prevented it from covering the Rhine from Switzerland to the Siegfried, and, in addition, a sizable American formation was required to help the French deal with the pocket.

When our attacks in the Aachen area and those in the south began to slow down, German Panzer formations were withdrawing from the line and their places taken by Volkssturm divisions. All Allied Intelligence services had tried assiduously to trace the Panzer formations and to learn their locations and intentions, but without definite success. An attack through the Ardennes was considered a possibility, particularly as American troops there were stretched thinly to provide additional troops for attack in the north. It still was not deemed highly probable that the enemy would try to come through the Ardennes with a major attack in winter. However, that is what the Germans did.

"Chins Up"

General Bradley had been conferring with General Ike at this headquarters on replacements when word was received that some penetrations had occurred and, sensing that this was more than a mere local attack, General Ike counseled Bradley to move the 10th Armored Division from the south and the 7th Armored Division from the north on both flanks of the attack. Bradley immediately ordered these moves and the next morning returned to his headquarters to keep a grip on the situation. It had become clear that day that the Germans were making an all-out effort to drive a wedge through our forces and to throw our campaign into disorder. General Ike immediately ordered cessation of all attacks and the collection of every possible reserve to strike the Germans on both flanks.

During the week, except for a few hours on one or two days, our air was practically grounded, although fighter bombers did excellent work when they could. However, the bad weather prevented reconnaissance by air, and, consequently, the Germans benefited from our temporary blindness. During that period our northern shoulder of the bulge was bolstered and, on the south, Patton had quickly carried out his orders to prepare for attack from the southern shoulder. The Germans were still moving straight west, and General Ike gave Bradley every engineer regiment, antiaircraft unit, and other odds and ends that could be made available to help protect the Meuse bridges.

General Ike had assigned to Bradley the 82nd and 101st American Airborne Divisions from the SHAEF reserve, and the 11th Armored was readied in the Rheims area to protect the center and to meet the head-on attack on the Meuse, if necessary. The 17th U. S. Airborne was ordered over from England, but weather was so bad the move was slow getting started. When it arrives, it is to join with the 11th Armored to help secure the line on the Meuse.

It had been apparent to General Ike that Bradley's left was badly separated from his right, and that his own tactical headquarters at Luxembourg tended to limit his command possibilities to the area south of the bulge. Consequently, all forces north of the penetration had been placed under the operational command of Monty, with a boundary of Givet, on the Meuse, to Prüm.

The 101st Airborne was having a time of it in the Bastogne area, and Bradley had hurried Patton's attack to the northward from the Arlon-Luxembourg area.

From 10 Downing Street came a personal phone call from the Prime Minister to the Supreme Commander, informing him that he was releasing a statement to the press as "a mark of confidence in you." The British government was calling out for Army service an additional quarter million men.

General Ike appreciated the gravity of the difficult decision the Prime Minister had made, and spoke of his gratitude for this additional evidence of the unshakable resolution of the Prime Minister and the British people in prosecuting the war.

General Ike had issued an order of the day to every member of the AEF:

> The enemy is making his supreme effort to break out of the desperate plight into which you forced him by your brilliant victories of the summer and fall. He is fighting savagely to take back all that you have won and is using every treacherous trick to deceive and kill you. He is gambling everything, but already, in this battle, your unparalleled gallantry has done much to foil his plans. In the face of your proven bravery and fortitude, he will completely fail.
> But we cannot be content with his mere repulse.
> By rushing out from his fixed defenses the enemy has given us the chance to turn his great gamble into his worst defeat. So I call upon every man, of all the Allies, to rise now to new heights of courage, of resolution, and of effort. Let everyone hold before him a single thought—to destroy the enemy on the ground, in the air, everywhere—destroy him! United in this determination and with unshakable faith in the cause for which we fight, we will, with God's help, go forward to our greatest victory.

He had also sent messages to General Hodges and Simpson, commending them and their respective armies for their performance, which had been in "magnificent style." The watchword, he told them, is "Chins Up."

Scott-Bailey, who has been assigned as the PRD contact with SHAEF G-2 and G-3 to obtain current and advance information about operations, came to see me at my office after my visit at Versailles today, and we compared notes. Both of us are at work spreading the word through our briefing officers and direct to correspondents, when possible, that there is no need for alarm.

I also saw T. J. today. He told me a story of his driver, Corporal Conrad. T. J. was being driven from his office at Versailles to his quarters, when the car was stopped at a road block. The MP proceeded to ask Conrad the new line of questions.

"Which state are you from?"

"Missouri."

"What's the capital?"

"St. Louis."

"O.K.," said the MP. "Drive on."

SHAEF Gets Direct Contact with Uncle Joe, at Last

PARIS, CHRISTMAS DAY, 1944

General Ike's most cheering present was the knowledge coming from General Marshall that the President had sent a message to Stalin of the Supreme Commander's desire to send a qualified staff officer to Moscow to exchange information essential to our mutual efforts. The President has assured Stalin that the Ardennes situation is not bad, but the time has arrived to discuss the next moves. The Combined Chiefs also cabled approval of the mission.

When Churchill was in Moscow last October, Stalin had suggested the possibility of outflanking the Germans by our troops passing through Switzerland, and also to the withdrawal of some of the Allied forces from Italy, with a view toward transferring them to the Balkans, where they could join up with the Red Armies near Vienna.

Christmas is not a holiday for General Ike. The fighting was intense in the bulge, and at Bastogne the 101st Airborne was putting up an epic fight. They were receiving supplies and ammunition by aircraft and gliders and so far have repelled all enemy attacks.

The 4th Armored Division of Patton's Army is now only two and a half miles away.

Stars and Stripes headlines this morning, reflecting news released by SHAEF after thirty-six-hour blackout (a drop from the forty-eight), read: "Yanks Stop Nazi Attack, Unleash Biggest Air Blow. Bulge Stabilized; Columns Halted 29 Miles from Sedan—5500 Planes Rock Enemy."

PARIS, TUESDAY, DECEMBER 26, 1944

Monty reported continuing heavy enemy pressure on the "west" flank of the First U. S. Army. He and Bradley had conferred, but Monty could not at present take the offensive and the initiative could not be wrested from the Germans until Monty had more troops.

Premier Stalin had replied promptly to the President and had agreed to meet General Ike's emissaries.

Air Chief Marshal Tedder, accompanied by the G-3, Major General "Red" Bull, and the Deputy G-2, Brigadier General Betts, are to be sent.

DECEMBER, 1944: *Allies advanced on all fronts in early part of month, with American Third battering its way across Saar River to gates of Sauerlautern. Seventh took Haguenau; First approached battered Düren. Battle of the Bulge opened with sudden German drive on fifty-mile front from Monschau to Trier. Ordered by Hitler, drive was designed to seize vast supply dumps at Charleroi, Namur, and port of Antwerp. Achieving surprise, German drive pushed Americans back in Belgium and Luxembourg, inflicting great damage and causing thousands of casualties. Support from thousands of planes and hundreds of tanks stopped German advances after nine days, allowed Allied troops to regain initiative, drive Germans back after destroying thousands of Nazi troops, tanks, and planes. Third and Seventh Armies halted drive. Patton started new offensive between Bastogne and Saint-Hubert. Widespread air activity blasted oil refineries, railyards, bridges, U-boat yards, and airplane factories all over enemy-controlled territory. On Leyte U. S. troops advanced in face of Jap suicide attacks, landed behind Jap lines near Ormoc in surprise move which destroyed enemy convoy with 4000 Jap soldiers. MacArthur landed on Mindoro, pounded Clark Field from air, further limiting dwindling Jap air power in Philippines. Jap losses in Leyte-Samar campaign reported as 113,221 killed against 2623 American dead. Superforts hit Tokyo, Nagoya, Kyushu, and Nomura. India-based Superforts bombed Rangoon and Bangkok rail targets. 14th Air Force twice hit Tsinan airfield in Shantung. Russians continued bloody drive to Budapest. King George of Greece acquiesced in a regency. (The Bulge was Hitler's great gamble, and when it failed, even he must have known the end of Nazi tyranny was near.*
—H.C.B.)

Monty Falls in Line

PARIS, MONDAY, JANUARY 1, 1945

The Supreme Commander went by train for a conference with Field Marshal Montgomery at his tactical headquarters last Wednesday. Major General de Guingand and General Whiteley joined the train at Brussels. Heavy fog and ice on the roads prevented motoring.

After discussing the current battle, the Field Marshal sought to continue control by himself of all forces to be engaged in the northern thrust toward the Ruhr. Monty suggested that for best results he should be given operational control over Bradley's Army Group. He is convinced that all available offensive power should be assigned to the northern line of advance to the Ruhr and that a sound setup for command required that one man direct and control the whole tactical battle. He declared that if there is not one-man control of the battle command we would fail again.

General Ike had informed Monty that he could not agree that one Army Group commander should fight his own battle and give orders to another Army Group commander. The plan for the advance to the Ruhr envisioned the placement of one complete U. S. Army under Montgomery's command, which General Ike considered militarily necessary and believed also that it reflected his confidence in the Field Marshal. The Supreme Commander knew that because of Montgomery's loyalty as a soldier and his readiness to devote himself to tasks assigned him, he would carry on. Frank and friendly counsel by the Field Marshal was appreciated, but General Ike was disturbed by Monty's predictions of failure unless his exact recommendations of command were met. General Ike hoped there was not being developed an unbridgeable gulf of convictions between them that would require settlement by the Combined Chiefs, for the debate and confusion which would follow would damage the good will and devotion to the common cause which have made this Allied force unique in history.

Monty responded, sympathetic with the great burden of responsibility which the Supreme Commander was forced to bear, and said that whatever the decision, he can be relied upon completely.

Lieutenant General Simpson had sent a message to the Supreme Commander that his Ninth Army was operating smoothly and cheerfully under command of the Field Marshal and that good relations prevailed between "Bimbo" Dempsey, commanding the British Second Army, and this feeling prevailed throughout their respective staffs and the lower echelons of their armies. In the Ninth Army, he said, "Our chins are up."

The rumblings in the press, particularly in London, have now grown to a roar of demand that there be a British deputy commander for all of General Ike's ground forces. The implication is clearly given that General Ike, as much as he is respected, has undertaken too much of a task himself. General Marshall was quick to notice this criticism and cabled Ike advising him against any such arrangement. On the American side of the Atlantic, General Marshall said, "You are doing a grand job and go on and give them hell."

Smoothing Out the Bulge—and de Gaulle

PARIS, FRIDAY, JANUARY 5, 1945

Because of his need of troops to smooth out the bulge, as well as to build up for the big northern push against the Ruhr, General Ike had decided to order withdrawal of forces in Devers' 6th Army Group from the Alsace

plain to the more easily defended Vosges Mountains. When General de
Gaulle heard of this, he feared there would be such a reaction in France
that his government might fall. Consequently, he issued orders direct to
the First French Army forbidding withdrawal without a fight. General Ike
had assured de Gaulle that his proposed withdrawal would assure permanent rather than merely temporary retention of Strasbourg and the plain.
He pointed to the effort being exerted to keep U.S. divisions up to strength
and urged that de Gaulle take the most drastic action to restore the
strength of the French infantry divisions.

In view of the strong representations as to the probability of turmoil
in France if much of Alsace-Lorraine were lost, General Ike modified his
order because, from a purely military standpoint, he could not afford to
have his lines of supply and his vast rear areas endangered by civil unrest,
which would accompany a revolt against de Gaulle's government.

PARIS, SATURDAY, JANUARY 6, 1945

I played poker with Spaatz and his gang and did all right. In any event,
the company is always good and the conversation exhilarating. I frequently
find myself, even though a naval officer, carrying the argument in behalf
of the ground forces. I have to seek an armistice when I have exhausted
all of the arguments for land, sea, and air co-operation which, from time to
time, I have heard General Ike advance.

Monty's C-47 was badly damaged when the Luftwaffe attacked Belgian
and Dutch airfields. General Ike is sending another one up which had
been fixed up for himself.

PARIS, MONDAY, JANUARY 8, 1945

General Marshall had been concerned about the problem of replacements
on which much attention had been given in the States and, with Ike's
consent, was sending General Gasser to investigate the situation in the
ETO. Meantime Ike had ordered an immediate comb-out of all the able-
bodied men in the rear areas. Able-bodied soldiers will be retrained and
sent into combat.

There are more than 100,000 Negroes performing useful service in
Com Zone, but the Supreme Commander felt he should not deny the
Negro volunteer a chance to serve in battle. Negroes are to be given the
opportunity to volunteer and, if the number of volunteers is greater than
those needed by existing Negro combat units, they will be organized into
separate battalions for front-line duty.

During the week the Germans have struck again—this time in the Saar, where they have made limited advances and Devers' group has made tactical withdrawals. The Germans are trying their damnedest to keep us off balance, to prevent our getting set to launch our main offensive.

Ike Prepares to Hit Back

PARIS, TUESDAY, JANUARY 9, 1945

The British Chiefs of Staff are proposing to the Combined Chiefs that General Ike be called upon for a report as to his plan of campaign following the elimination of the bulge. Representatives of the British Chiefs have discussed with General Marshall the advisability of a single commander for ground operations and the opinion has been expressed that General Ike has too many other pressing duties of supply, of political complexity, etc., and that, therefore, a more concentrated direction of ground operations is required.

British Chiefs are concerned that General Ike will have insufficient strength, after keeping up pressure on the enemy during the winter, to clear him back all along the Rhine and then to launch, probably not before May, 1945, strong converging attacks; first in the north by Monty's Army Group and Simpson's Ninth Army, and the other toward Frankfurt by the 12th Army Group, intended to continue in the area of Kassel, there to join up with the northern thrust and pinch out the Ruhr. The British Chiefs consider that overwhelming strength must be allotted to one major thrust and prefer that strength allotted in the north.

The Combined Chiefs probably will ask the Supreme Commander for a report by January 28 on the progress of his operations, the effect of the German counteroffensive, and his detailed appreciation and plan of operation for the remainder of the winter and spring.

The British Chiefs desire a directive to be issued by the Combined Chiefs which would point out to General Ike that the best results would be achieved if one man were given operational control and co-ordination of all ground forces for the main thrust.

General Marshall asked for the Supreme Commander's views and added his own opinion that the British proposal stems from the Prime Minister's recent visit to France and of Field Marshal Montgomery's evident pressure to get a larger command.

General Marshall cabled that the delay of the expected offensive on the Russian front seems to have been caused by unseasonable thaw, which prevented the movement of heavy equipment.

While I was in Ike's office today, he talked on the telephone with the Prime Minister, who was seeking to obtain a better Allied balance of news in the British press.

General Ike had sought to find a peg on which the press might draw attention to the fine work of General Bradley, much of which has been submerged by assignment to the Field Marshal of the two American Armies. He awarded a Bronze Star to General Bradley, the citation of which praised General Bradley for his important part in the battle.

The Prime Minister followed the award of the Bronze Star by publicly congratulating General Bradley.

PARIS, WEDNESDAY, JANUARY 10, 1945

The Supreme Commander got off a personal review of the campaign to date to General Marshall and outlined his future plans.

He felt it was completely appropriate and even desirable that the Combined Chiefs of Staff review the strategy in this theater. From his standpoint, the issues at stake are so great and the consequences of victory or defeat so vital that there should be achieved the greatest degree of conviction as to the line of action that should now be pursued.

He made clear that without exception all have agreed from the beginning that the main invasion into Germany, when it becomes possible, should be by the north flank with thirty-five divisions, the maximum that can be maintained in that area. There will be other crossings of the Rhine, depending somewhat on our good fortune, and certainly there will be a subsidiary attack south of the Ruhr.

If a separate commander for ground operations is set up, there would be duplication in personnel and communications. Any such officer necessarily would have to determine priority and allocation of divisions, supplies, and to decide upon broad battle strategy, all of which are the functions of the Supreme Commander and his headquarters. A ground commander-in-chief would have to exercise command through three Army Group commanders, just as is true now. If there were two ground commanders, assuming the long front might be divided along the Moselle, eventually some forty-five to fifty American divisions and fourteen British Empire and Allied divisions would be under the commander in the north. This would leave the southern commander with principally American but some French divisions largely in a defensive role. In view of the composition of the Allied force and the personalities involved, General Ike did not believe that the proposal for either a single ground commander or two of them would work well. He did not believe that any single individual could or should exercise a greater measure of control over group commanders who are in direct command in their respective areas than is now being applied, and felt that, although the organization for command may not be ideal, it is the most practical one.

General Ike has consistently sought to eliminate purely nationalistic considerations when these conflict with military requirements, but he could not see how a commander-in-chief of ground forces would provide any better co-ordination or better direction of battle than is possible at present. However, he was open to suggestions and direction from the Combined Chiefs, for, after all, they are his bosses.

PARIS, THURSDAY, JANUARY 11, 1945

Monty has sent a letter to General Bradley, now that the battle of the bulge is drawing to a close, anticipating that the U. S. First and Ninth Armies soon will be returning to Bradley's command, saying what a great honor it has been for the Field Marshal to command American troops and how well they have done. He had found Hodges and Simpson a great pleasure to work with and said that the corps commanders, particularly Gerow, Collins, and Ridgway, had been magnificent.

PARIS, FRIDAY, JANUARY 12, 1945

My communications job at PRD is now ending; at least the exploitation stage of getting facilities is about over, and I am trying to shake loose by turning my job over to a professional, Lieutenant Colonel Ralph. General Allen still insists I should then take over the Division's Planning Branch. This, at least, will give me more free time to spend with General Ike and his staff.

I have a notice from Admiral Kirk's headquarters that I am now the Navy's senior officer attached to SHAEF, but I haven't had time to inquire as to my duties. We released an announcement today that Steve Early is being loaned to us by the President for temporary duty. I asked for him, with General Allen's concurrence, some weeks ago because he can be helpful in advising PRD about its briefing of correspondents. He has probably given out more news in twelve years than has any other American.

Scott-Bailey brought back from Switzerland a story to illustrate his progress at getting the Swiss to interpret their neutrality rules sufficiently leniently to permit Radio Swiss to relay our press and broadcast material.

He said this story was current in Switzerland and was told him by a Swiss official to describe their slowness, particularly on questions of neutrality. A Swiss girl had been pregnant four months before she thought of the word "No."

"Is Your Travel Really Necessary?"

PARIS, SATURDAY, JANUARY 13, 1945

Had lunch with Ike today. He had heard of my debate at Spaatz's Wednesday evening when the air officers entangled me in a furious argument about the relative bravery of air versus ground personnel. The main point was that when the Air Force sends 1000 heavy bombers and 800 fighters to bomb Berlin, not a one voluntarily turns away from the battle, even though 100 might be shot down. Yet, in a recent attack, supported by fighter bombers, the thrust stopped when forty tanks had been knocked out of action for one cause or another—mines, enemy shell fire, etc. I had argued the cause of the ground forces as intelligently and heatedly as I could until my opponents began picking on the vulnerability of the battleship to air attack, and then I was really over my head.

Tedder, Bull, and Betts finally reached Moscow after thirteen days of misadventures with aircraft and bad weather. Today we had news that the Russians had begun their winter offensive in Poland. I saw the Deputy Chief of Staff, General Morgan, and he was chuckling over a reply just received from Tedder. He had reached Moscow just as the Russians had started their big offensive. When news that the Russians had started the offensive reached Morgan, and none whatsoever had arrived from the Air Chief Marshal, Morgan had sent a "wireless" to Tedder quoting the slogan widely used in England to curtail use of congested transportation facilities.

"Is your travel really necessary?"

To this Tedder had replied, "No."

PARIS, TUESDAY, JANUARY 16, 1945

Monty has reported to General Ike that the task given him in the Ardennes is now finished, as Hodges' First and Patton's Third Armies have joined up at Houffalize and are advancing to the east. Monty felt it could be said that a tactical victory had been achieved within the salient and he was returning the First Army to Bradley's command as ordered by General Ike. The Ninth stays under Monty's command for operational orders, but all administrative matters, such as supply and replacements, remain as heretofore Bradley's responsibility.

PARIS, WEDNESDAY, JANUARY 17, 1945

General Ike now feels that at last every commander, including his military superiors, understands what he means when he says we must secure a decent line on which to station defensive forces if we are to permit the greatest possible concentration for our forthcoming offensives. He still plugs away on his belief, consistently held, that the German forces west of the Rhine must be substantially defeated and we must make certain that the German is not free behind his strong defensive Siegfried Line to organize sudden powerful thrusts into our lines.

He has directed General Devers to clean out the Colmar pocket and to get a line on the Rhine south of the Siegfried Line. When this is accomplished, the whole Alsace-Lorraine plain can be turned over to the French forces, allowing Patch's Seventh Army to take over the line up to the Moselle, thus permitting greater strength to be allotted farther north.

Monty has fixed February 10 as the tentative target date for his operation to close up to the Rhine in the north and, as he has had some weeks of strenuous activity, he is returning to England for a few days of rest.

PARIS, FRIDAY, JANUARY 19, 1945

The Russian offensive has been headlined each morning by *Stars and Stripes.*

Monty and Bradley have had a conference and reached agreement on all points for their operations to the Rhine.

In an effort to pour oil on troubled Allied waters, we had both Beetle and his British deputy, General Morgan, for press conferences at the Scribe. General Morgan spoke feelingly about the teamwork of the Allied Command, praised General Ike to the skies, and said we simply must stick together.

Someone had hit Beetle with a question that he answered before he thought. "Was there any direct contact between SHAEF and Moscow?" Beetle told of the delegation headed by Tedder—off the record.

General Ike was worried about this disclosure, for fear it eventually might be printed. He says that one reason the Russians don't like to exchange information with their Western Allies is that we talk too much.

The Supreme Commander growled at me today because of a story about him in yesterday's *Stars and Stripes*. Oddly enough, I hadn't seen it, but later found this:

At SHAEF last week, an appeal was made to headquarters men for contributions of type O blood, needed immediately at the front.

A couple of days later, volunteers were lined up in the dispensary. No one paid much attention at first as an officer walked into the room. He lay down on a litter and a nurse bustled over to wrap a tourniquet around his arm.

A soldier on the next litter looked over idly, looked back, then did an astonished double-take. The guy next to him was General Eisenhower.

"It was just like any other GI," said T/4 Conrad J. Segrin, one of the dispensary's medics. "He wasn't a special case at all. Ike came in, they took his blood, he got a cup of coffee and he left. Just like that."

There was a private in the waiting line who saw the Supreme Commander on his way out. He turned to the man beside him and said, "Hey, that'd be the blood to get. Maybe I could make General with it."

Ike overheard him, turned around and grinned. "If you do," he said, "I hope you don't inherit my bad disposition."

A Kind Word About SHAEF PRD

PARIS, MONDAY, JANUARY 22, 1945

Caacie had a litter of six pups, one of which died. I won a bet of two dollars from Ike,* both of which he autographed—one to Caacie and one to Telek. Moaney is feeding one of the pups with an eye dropper every two hours, day and night, despite the prediction of the veterinarian that it could not live. The other four appear healthy.

Charles Collingwood of CBS, knowing that PRD has seldom had a kind word said for itself by the many correspondents it attempts to serve, sent me a script of a piece which he is doing today by the usual shortwave channel from the Scribe to New York, for relay to the network. As this is one of the few kind things ever said about PRD, I quote:

There are more war correspondents credited to the Supreme Headquarters of the Allied Expeditionary Force than to any other command in the world. At the moment more than a thousand correspondents hold identification cards with the special SHAEF stamp. Of these perhaps 700 are in the theater at present. Most of them are at the front with various armies, but on any day between 150 and 200 are in Paris. These are the correspondents who cover the war as seen from SHAEF.

There are so many of us here that the situation lacks some of the intimacy you find at smaller commands. SHAEF correspondents don't live at SHAEF

* I took the optimistic side. I would get a dollar for every pup over four and Ike a dollar for each one under four.

itself; most of them have never even been there. There are so many of us that instead of us going to SHAEF, SHAEF comes to us. No correspondent just drops in for a chat with General Eisenhower, except to pay his respects. When the Supreme Commander has something to say he comes to Paris to see us. Once when he came he was recognized by the Paris populace and there was a first-class mob scene outside the hotel where the correspondents live and work. General Eisenhower was almost smothered by thousands of people who suddenly turned up out of the busy Paris streets. People got pushed through plate-glass windows, the General got kissed by numerous excited women of all ages, and, in the end, it took a flying wedge of high-ranking generals running interference to get him out.

This hotel where the correspondents all live and where General Eisenhower and his staff officers sometimes come to see us is in the Hôtel Scribe. Before the war the Scribe was just a normal big hotel—much like any other modern hotel in a big city. Today it is like no other hotel in the world . . . the whole place has been turned upside down to serve as a base of operations for the SHAEF correspondents. There are rows of desks and typewriters in the lobby great, clacking telegraphic machines have been installed, offices have been set up, radio studios put in . . . where the ballroom used to be there is the conference room with the huge maps by which we follow the war. . . . And everywhere there are correspondents, good ones and bad ones, famous ones and unknowns, normal ones and psychopathic cases. . . . They speak all languages and are of all colors and descriptions. In theory they are all supposed to be covering the war, but Paris is a great magnet and many seem to be here just because they want to be in Paris. This is a great trial to the Public Relations Officers who are supposed to provide facilities for war coverage. They call the nonworking correspondents the "lunatic fringe." There are no neutrals, but any one of the United Nations can have its correspondents accredited to SHAEF, and most of them have. There are Russians, Brazilians, Chinese, Dutch, Czechs, Poles, French, British, Americans . . . and all united in a desire to inform the people whose attention we have what is going on in the area commanded by SHAEF.

Here at the Scribe, we find out. Every day there are three press conferences—there's one coming up half an hour from now. Before these conferences the two briefing officers, one British and one American,* telephone each of the Army Groups for the latest news. By the time we get it the news is generally about six hours from the time it happened, which is pretty good going. The briefing officers keep up their own war room, which, as far as the Western Front goes, is probably the most up to date in the world. It is often ahead of the big SHAEF war room, because they are not so much interested in last-minute happenings as they are in the broad picture.

Both censorship and cable offices are right in the hotel, so it's only a matter of minutes from the time the correspondents rush out of the conference until the news is flashed all over the world.

It takes a staff of 250 Public Relations Officers and men to keep everything going. Like everything else about SHAEF, this is an Allied operation and there are Americans, British, Canadians, and French, all working together

---

* Major A. M. Burnett-Stuart, British; Major James F. Hughes, Jr., American.

in harmony, playing no favorites. To a considerable extent this is also true of the correspondents who for SHAEF try to give the picture of the whole Western Front, no matter whose country's army is doing the fighting. . . .

Parable

PARIS, TUESDAY, JANUARY 23, 1945

I have a French friend who was in the resistance movement. He managed to get from Paris through the German lines in Normandy during the early days of the invasion. He carried the plan of the Free French for dealing with the collaborators in pro-Nazi newspapers in France, and for the creation in its place of a free press. He is Jacques Fano. He has been to see me several times to get information about the Supreme Commander for an article in *Carrefour*, a weekly. He says the French readers have a lively interest in the Allied Commander, but little is known about the man in France. He is quite correct.

Recently I took him with me to Versailles and introduced him. He told General Ike that current Franco-American relations are best illustrated by the story of the voyage of M. Perrichon, which apparently most French people know. He later wrote:

A man had a daughter to be married. Two suitors are in the running. During a walk, one of them saves the life of the father of his sweetheart. The father promises him eternal gratitude. But several days later the other suitor, who is cleverer, acts in such a way that M. Perrichon is able to save his life. M. Perrichon thinks himself a hero and delightedly gives his daughter to the suitor, whom he thinks he has saved from death.

For how could M. Perrichon bear to have the first suitor for his son-in-law, he to whom he owed such an immense debt of gratitude?

PARIS, WEDNESDAY, JANUARY 24, 1945

Leon Henderson is here and is wearing a tremendous fur coat. We were having cocktails at the Scribe bar while I was waiting to attend a moose-meat dinner being given by John M. O'Connell, Jr., of the *Bangor* (Maine) *News*. Leon stepped into an adjoining dining room and met my host, who thought I had brought in the moose alive. O'Connell, who is a Yankee Will Rogers, gave me some moose meat to take to General Ike.

Ran into Charlie Collingwood, and I thanked him for doing the nice piece about PRD. He said I shouldn't get too excited about it because the communications, for which I was responsible, had failed and he had been unable to get through to New York. Atmospherics, I trust.

Heart-to-Heart Talk with de Gaulle

SHAEF MAIN, SATURDAY, JANUARY 27, 1945

Jim Gault phoned me that General Ike wanted me to come to dinner Thursday night because Harry Hopkins would be there, and the General thought I would like to see him.

I arrived early, inspected the pups, whose eyes aren't open yet, and settled down to catch up on the news on the top level. I find that much of the "news" I hear at the PRD level is not quite so authoritative and certainly not as exclusive as that available from the Supreme Commander himself.

I had not seen Harry since December, 1943, when he returned with the presidential party from the Cairo conference. This was in Tunisia. That meeting was personally pleasant but financially unprofitable. In the meantime there had been Ike's ascension to his new post as Supreme Commander, decided at Cairo, the successful cross-Channel invasion under his direction, and the spectacular sweep across France only to overrun the supply capabilities, which forced a winter campaign.

General Ike had gone to see General de Gaulle yesterday and they had had a heart-to-heart talk. There had come to General Ike's attention a story that something he is reported to have said has been construed as a criticism of the effort of the French Army to clear out the Colmar pocket. The misinterpretation had grown out of a conversation of the Supreme Commander with General Juin, Chief of Staff to de Gaulle.

General Ike had told de Gaulle that in talking with General Juin he had intended to stress the necessity of impressing every single man, from the commanding general to the enlisted men in the First French Army, with the critical need of clearing the pocket.

General de Gaulle said there was no thought of attributing to General Eisenhower any critical comment, but the French General wanted to know if there was an impression that the First French Army was not carrying the load expected of it. General Ike declared that he wanted to see the First French Army execute its offensive with the same punch that had characterized its action in Italy, in the landings in southern France, and in its heroic drive through the Belfort gap.

General de Gaulle had called attention to the lack of trained and equipped French replacements and reminded the Supreme Commander that the combat troops were tired and that the enemy was proving very tenacious. Artillery support for the French was not as strong as it needed to be and, with the limited supply of ammunition, the density of artillery fire that was needed could not be maintained. Bad weather had limited the support of the Air Force.

General Ike had replied that he knew the French forces had been asked to do a great deal, but he was doing everything he could to help. He was, in fact, moving an American division from the Ardennes sector to reinforce Devers' 6th Army Group in order to strengthen our forces in Alsace. This division had been in operation since July and also was tired.

The French leader declared that everything possible would be done to win the battle.

General de Gaulle also called attention to the need of railway rolling stock in France and predicted that when we reached Germany we would find very little railway equipment available. General de Gaulle said that his Minister of Transport had just returned from the United States and had arranged for 27,000 railway cars and a proportionate number of locomotives for the French, but the impression had been gained there that General Eisenhower had not given his agreement to the use of shipping space, which he controlled, to bring the rolling stock to France.

General Ike had replied that he was keenly aware of the problem and had not only given his assent to the shipments, but had urgently requested a greater number of railway cars and locomotives than that quoted by General de Gaulle.

They shook hands and agreed that the eye-to-eye discussion had created a better understanding.

How to Address the House of Commons

Hopkins arrived. After pleasant greetings he told of his visit in London, where he had spent three nights with the Prime Minister. The night before, the Prime Minister had given a fatherly lecture to Mr. Eden on the art and science of making a speech to the House of Commons. Mr. Eden had accepted the lecture as son from father. In the course of the admonition the Prime Minister, according to Harry, had told Eden never slyly to peek at his notes. They should be flagrantly waved in the face of the MPs each time he made a point. Then he should proceed to the next. He should obviously study his notes, taking as much time as necessary—"two or three minutes, if you feel like it." He added that the speaker should not lounge or lean against "the box," which is the rostrum, but rather should stand well behind it and pace his remarks with forward and backward steps. The Prime Minister said he had had special glasses made which permitted him to see his notes five feet away. He advised Eden to patronize the same oculist. Neither should the box be tapped lightly with the hand, as this distracts the attention of the audience. If the box is to be touched at all it should be vigorously pounded with the fist at an appropriate moment. Added theatrical effect could be obtained if Mr. Eden then would scowl at the audience.

I have used, above, the word "fatherly" to describe the Prime Minister's attitude because after Harry had amusingly mimicked the Prime Minister I inquired as to Mr. Churchill's attitude. Hopkins assured me that it was one of kindness, consideration, and good humor.

This led to Ike's telling of some of his encounters with the Prime Minister, for whom the Supreme Commander expressed a real affection, but when the Prime Minister has an idea in mind, he presents it from all angles and pulls all the stops.

Ambassador Caffery arrived and we sat down to dinner.

In the discussion it developed that when de Gaulle visited Stalin at Moscow a couple of months ago—a visit widely heralded in the French press as most successful—the Russians had treated the French as a defeated nation. It has seemed to me that Britain and America are treating the French as a spoiled child who is just getting over the mumps. The more done for the patient, the more carping and picayunish he becomes. Perhaps it's because the patient is getting well.

The meeting of the Combined Chiefs of Staff is to take place in Malta, starting about the twenty-ninth, and the President is on his way by cruiser and is touching at Gibraltar on the twenty-eighth. This information was developed when Harry tipped off Ike that he was certain the Prime Minister would ask the President, probably by wireless aboard the cruiser, to insist that Ike, as well as Alexander, be present at the Malta meeting. Ike had emphasized that he had his hands full with a long front with not only defensive action to manage, but an impending offensive to get under way. He wouldn't feel easy until Devers got the situation around Strasbourg in hand and was chafing at the delay. He couldn't possibly leave his command at this time and had arranged for a delegation from SHAEF, including Beetle and the G-3, "Pinky" Bull, and Air Marshal Robb to attend.

Harry had said that he would be pleased to communicate to the President Ike's desire not to attend, but the President, because of radio silence of his ship, would probably not reply until he reached Gibraltar. In any event, the trip would upset Ike's plan because he was already committed to confer with General Marshall at Marseille on the twenty-seventh and later expected to go to the forward area to see Monty and Bradley.

We were just finishing our coffee when Beetle arrived, fresh from a couple of days in bed because of a cold. He arrived in something of the manner of the Marines, for he hadn't been there long when he took over the conversation and had the situation well in hand.

Hopkins told me that he wanted a couple of hours' visit with me, and so I saw him at the guest château in Saint-Cloud, called the "Brown House," yesterday afternoon. Harry is going first to Rome to see His Holiness, the Pope, and then to Malta. He told me he had been sent ahead by the President to do certain chores, including preliminary discussions with the Prime Minister and especially to deal with de Gaulle, whose pride has been hurt because France, and particularly he, has not so far been invited to the forthcoming conferences (and won't be, I was told later by Harry).

Harry said that the big issue at Malta will be the Pacific versus the European war. It will develop between General Marshall, whose heart is in completing the war against Germany first and with all possible support, and Admiral King, who, in the tradition of the Navy, has his heart in the Pacific. Harry thought the British would agree to making the Italian campaign merely defensive and thus releasing some divisions to our front. He thought the British would agree to two or three, but we would need more. Harry said that he was thoroughly convinced that Ike needed more divisions and that he personally was throwing his lot with Ike and would speak to the President at the earliest opportunity to comb the armed services for more men, as well as to allocate more men and matériel to this theater. He thought we had bases in the Caribbean, in Iceland, in the Pacific and elsewhere from which up to five, ten, or fifteen thousand men could be spared. He thought Ike had acted wisely in bringing General Lear to the theater to handle the manpower problem. Ike had conducted the campaign beautifully, had the complete support of all people at home, official and unofficial. Harry felt we could count on Stalin throwing Russia into the fight against Japan once the Germans were licked. Thus we should do more on the Western Front and supply the men to do it because, as he saw the problem, by so doing we would really hasten the end of the war in Japan.

Harry spoke also of his concern about postwar management in Germany. He said that the military would do its usual good job of policing, "getting the water turned on," stopping the sniping, and in general restoring law and order, but that, after all, the conduct of affairs in Germany should be by men who are of the liberal school. He was fearful that officers with previous connections with big corporations, particularly those having previous business connections with the Germans, might be more interested in reviving commercial life than would be desirable.

Harry had not yet seen de Gaulle but had sought an appointment. He said he was going to try to bring de Gaulle and Roosevelt closer together.

On the personal side he said that Steve Early was accompanying the President to Malta. After that Early is to spend several weeks in France as special representative of Secretary Stimson, but on the invitation of the director of our Public Relations Division. That Early could be of assistance in improving our Public Relations setup Harry had no doubt and said further that contrary to his facetious remarks of the night before, when he had said that Early's assignment here would be construed as a presidential investigation of lousy SHAEF Public Relations, he really wasn't worried on the score and expected Steve's high standing as a professional newspaperman to produce good results. He said he had already been told by correspondents in London of their great satisfaction that Early was coming and of their belief that he would contribute the benefit of his experience to our public-relations problems.

Ike and Jim left by train last night for Marseille, where General Marshall and party are to be met.

In my circle, i.e., Public Relations Division, particularly communications, we are beset by rumors such as "The Russians are ninety-four miles from Berlin" and fifteen minutes later, another "ninety-one miles," to which my secretary, Corporal Thora McClary, adds she has just heard "nine miles." All this is most distressing when two aircraft given the Communications Branch by General Spaatz are waiting at Burtonwood in England for installation of equipment which has taken weeks to get approved through SHAEF and Com Zone and, once approved, has been found to include items in short supply because of losses in Ardennes. Now my lieutenant who is to fly equipment and himself to Burtonwood to supervise an installation, which will require two weeks, is weatherbound in Paris. All of our plans stress the use of these aircraft for first coverage of Berlin. If they are not ready, our names will be mud.* On the other hand, SHAEF itself does not know from the Russians how many of our correspondents will be permitted into the Russian area. Our minimum requirement for the correspondents and PRD staff is thirtynine.

The story of Ike's mission to Moscow, headed by Air Chief Marshal Tedder, and including Bull and G-2 Betts, was disclosed to the correspondents about three weeks ago by Beetle with a severe injunction of secrecy. However, the inevitable happened and one of our correspondents returning from France to the U. S. has broken the story.

---

* To the reader who asks himself, "Who cares?" I guess the answer is, "We did."

Marshall Backs Ike, as Usual

PARIS, SUNDAY, JANUARY 28, 1945

General Ike returned today from seeing General Marshall and party at Château Valmante, near Marseille, where they conferred most of yesterday.

General Marshall is firmly against appointment of a ground commander-in-chief, the topic that is expected to be considered by the Combined Chiefs at their meeting starting tomorrow in Malta. Beetle is attending it, and both General Ike and General Marshall feel it would be unwise for the Supreme Commander to leave the battle at this juncture.

With the creation of the five-star generals, General Marshall has a number of promotions to be made to four stars and he is embarrassed because if one individual is promoted, some other deserving officer may interpret the act as a direct slap in the face. There are numerous lieutenant generals who by their action and service are in line for promotion. Insofar as General Ike's command is concerned, he wants Bradley and Spaatz promoted first.

I had stopped at General Ike's house en route to the WAC House to see the pups. The little one had died and Moaney was heartbroken. When I saw General Ike I was about to ask him if he would agree to our giving one of the remaining pups to Moaney, when he interposed that he had already spoken to Moaney and said he had told him he would undertake to use his influence with me. The Supreme Commander's influence is persuasive and Moaney shall have his pup, with our heartfelt gratitude.

Everyone is getting overexcited about the Russian push,* in my judgment. Each morning I G-2 the situation from the Paris edition of the *New York Herald Tribune* and *Stars and Stripes*, which are delivered to me at my room. I do not think the Russians will make Berlin in this plunge. The whole supply problem will catch up with them. This was repeatedly demonstrated in the desert, again in the rush for Tunisia, and, most recently, in our enforced holdup of our armies after their rapid dash across France. The Russians and Germans have demonstrated it in times past, and when the Germans invaded Russia, the Russians fell back to lengthen the German supply line and to save their armies. The fact that large numbers of German prisoners have not been taken by the Russians in their current drive indicates that the Germans are withdrawing rather than standing to fight. The old temper of the Germans—strengthened by Nazi training and inspired by the usual fervor that highly prevails when

_____
* I was right, for once.

the sacred soil of one's native land is invaded—will cause terrific resistance for months.

Warning from Uncle Joe

PARIS, MONDAY, JANUARY 29, 1945

Air Chief Marshal Tedder and Generals Bull and Betts returned from their "Mission to Moscow." Marshal Stalin had co-operated in every way. They found him pleased that the Soviet offensive was developing satisfactorily, but he, too, complained about unfavorable weather. Stalin foresaw that with the Russians pressing from the east and the eased position of the Allies, now that the bulge has been smoothed, the Germans will be forced to divide their reserves. From both sides the Germans are to be pressed until the two great forces meet somewhere in Germany. In their current drive Stalin figures his armies will have to stop at the Oder River and await build-up of supplies before pushing on.

One new factor in the Russian offensive discussed by Stalin was the presence of German saboteurs and spies in areas recently overrun by the Russians. Stalin placed this problem on a par with that of supply and sent a warning to General Ike to look out for spies as we move into Germany.

Ambassador Averell Harriman had been helpful and sent word to General Ike that further information would be available from Stalin as to future plans of the Russians.

At last a direct contact has been made with Stalin so that the two great forces closing in on Hitler can act with proper intelligence.

Plans for Crossing the Rhine

PARIS, TUESDAY, JANUARY 30, 1945

The British Chiefs of Staff have interpreted General Ike's plans as meaning that after closing to the Rhine in the north, he will make no attempt to force a crossing of the river even in the north until all the area west of the Rhine has been swept clear of the Germans.

General Ike has told Beetle to tell the Combined Chiefs for him that the Rhine crossings will be made in the north just as soon as the operation is feasible and without waiting to close to the Rhine throughout its length. Furthermore, General Ike will close to the Rhine in the north with maximum strength just as soon as the situation in the south allows him to collect necessary forces without incurring unreasonable risks.

Apparently, the issue has not been raised at the Malta meeting relative to a ground commander-in-chief. The new directive from the Combined Chiefs will require that General Ike immediately carry out a series of operations north of the Moselle, with the view of destroying the enemy and crossing the Rhine north of Düsseldorf. Efforts then are to be directed to eliminate other enemy forces west of the Rhine which still constitute an obstacle and a potential threat to subsequent crossing of the Rhine.

JANUARY, 1945: _First and Third U. S. Armies slowly pushed Germans out of Ardennes bulge and regained initiative lost in surprise December attack. Incessant and heavy air attacks supported Allied counterattack, destroying thousands of conveyances, 127 tanks and armored cars. Allied offensive penetrated deep into Siegfried Line. Germans lost 241 planes in sorties over France, Belgium, and Netherlands. Crescendo of Allied air attacks continued, with thousands of heavy bombers saturating rail and production centers in Germany and Austria. Germans took Esztergom in desperate drive to hold Budapest. In Poland Soviet forces approached Warsaw, took Cracow; Prussian drive of Russians captured Tilsit; Reds invaded Pomerania. Norwegian troops joined Russians east of Finnmark, captured Nazi air base at Banak. Conquest of Philippines moved forward with MacArthur's invasion of Luzon, following heavy bombing of Manila, Clark, and Batangas airfields; preliminary naval action in Subic Bay and Lingayen Gulf cost Japs four warships and thirty-one other vessels; by month's end Yanks approached Manila, took Olongapo. Air raids over Okinawa and Formosa downed 331 planes; eighty-three ships damaged or destroyed in two days. Pacific fleet and carrier planes hit Jap convoys and installations in French Indo-China area, sank forty-one ships, damaged twenty-eight, destroyed 112 planes at cost of sixteen planes. Third Fleet planes raided Swatow, Amoy, and Hong Kong. B-29s hit Kobe-Osaka area, bombed Nagoya, Iwo Jima, Tokyo, and Saigon with slight losses. Kobo fell to British in Burma. Indian and British troops took Akyab. Chinese captured Mues in Burma, to open Ledo-Burma Road. Hungary surrendered unconditionally and declared war against Axis. Roosevelt inaugurated for fourth term. (We prayed for good weather so we could make full use of our great superiority of air power.—H.C.B.)_

"You Don't Have to Stay Down There Forever"

PARIS, FRIDAY, FEBRUARY 2, 1945

I formally completed my career as Chief of the Communications Branch of the PRD today, lying flat on my back in bed. Colonel Ralph, who was promoted as scheduled, has taken over and I am taking Navy pills, consisting of aspirin, codeine, and sulfa.

We have had snow heavier than I ever saw in Washington, and it was followed by sleet and rain.

I had gone out to see Harry Hopkins at the Brown House to impress on him the need of the President personally obtaining approval of Stalin at the forthcoming conference at Yalta for permission for our accredited correspondents to go into the Russian zone when we get to Berlin, or wherever we join up. Harry promised to do this and saw the weight of my argument that there would be many recriminations, particularly in the liberal press of America and Britain, if correspondents were barred passage through the Russian lines to gather news.

Hopkins had been visited by a number of French leaders, including some of de Gaulle's ministers. Harry had observed that having been schooled in the resistance movement they were not only realistic, as is characteristic of the French, but are tough and blunt in their statements and do not use the usual diplomatic language expected from ministers.

In preparation for my assumption of my new temporary position as Chief of the Planning Branch of the Public Relations Division, my first plan is to plan myself out of the position and to make Colonel Scott-Bailey the Chief. He is now serving the branch as executive officer. Then I can be completely free to rejoin General Ike, who said the other night again, "You don't have to stay down there forever."

G-3 Appraises Ardennes

PARIS, MONDAY, FEBRUARY 5, 1945

SHAEF G-3 has prepared for the PRD to make public a summary of the German offensive in the Ardennes. It recites Hitler's order of the day: "If the Panzer Grenadiers fail now, they will have had the last word from their Führer." Rundstedt apparently saw the effort in its true light, for he said, "This is an all-out gamble."

Hitler planned to reach the Meuse in two days and Antwerp in three weeks, and he thought he would cut off thirty-eight Allied divisions, as well as deny the Allies the use of the vital port at Antwerp.

In December and January the enemy casualties in the west, where the principal fighting was in the Ardennes, amounted to 220,000, of which 110,000 were prisoners of war. In the two months, the Germans lost 1450 tanks and assault guns, as well as thousands of motor vehicles of all kinds.

Hitler's vaunted Ardennes offensive is described by G-3 as a complete defeat for the enemy and, summarizing, it is pointed out that the Germans have lost since June 6, 860,000 prisoners of war to this Allied force, and their killed and long-term wounded number well over 400,000. This represents almost 110 divisions. They have lost in tanks and assault guns enough to refit fifteen Panzer divisions twice over. It is stated that Allied ground losses are but a fraction of this, but our casualties are not given because the governments require that these announcements must be made by the War Department and the War Office.

With former Corporal, now Sergeant, McClary, I moved into the Planning Branch today. I think it will be a dull job and that most of the real planning has been done by our provision of mobile communications facilities to accompany the armies wherever and whenever they advance.

Monty and the Canadians Strike

PARIS, FRIDAY, FEBRUARY 9, 1945

General Ike is planning to use Negro volunteers by platoons. General Patton already has done this, and the results are good. When sufficient infantry platoons are available, General Ike hopes to make them into independent battalions.

Stars and Stripes this morning reports that the Canadians have struck in Holland in the northern tip of the Western Front. They attacked southeast of Nijmegen, between the Maas and Rhine Rivers, the beginning of the operation VERITABLE—intended to clear enough of the Rhine to give elbow room for the large-scale crossing planned by Monty. Today's report says that artillery barrage, lasting for eleven hours, had blasted German defenses. This is a typical Monty attack. Waves of 1500 planes were in support. The attack is on a five-mile front in a sector that has been quiet for months.

News of the "Big Three" meeting in Yalta has appeared in print, but the place is described as "Somewhere in the Black Sea Area."

Had a letter from Mother today. She opened with, "It's nice about General Eisenhower's fifth star. The price of eggs is 60 cents."

PART SIX

The Destruction of German Might

FEBRUARY TO MAY, 1945

Roer Dam Controlled

PARIS, SUNDAY, FEBRUARY 11, 1945

The battle for the Roer River dams, which began three months ago, ended yesterday when the First U. S. Army gained control of Schwammanuel Dam. The GIs found it intact, although the gates below it were blown up by the Germans, thus raising the Roer River three feet at Düren.

General Fred Anderson, deputy to Spaatz, has said in my presence that if the ground forces didn't take Germany by June, the Germans' present rate of production of jet and rocket planes would make it impossible for our great armadas of 1000 bombers, with 800 escorts, to continue to bomb Germany without such heavy losses that would make the bombings too expensive in lives and planes to continue.

Some of the correspondents, mostly American, but here and there a British one, have come to me recently to get information about General Ike's real role as a commander. He has been mentioned so frequently as "Chairman of the Board" during the flurry of criticism in the London papers that I lose no opportunity to tell all the correspondents who come to see me that he is master and director of the grand strategy.

PARIS, WEDNESDAY, FEBRUARY 14, 1945

Today is Valentine's Day, and my principal Valentine was William Fine, Red Cross Field Director with the U. S. 36th Infantry Division, who has just arrived in Paris for a rest after many months with that division, in Italy, southern France, and, most recently, during the German counter-attack in Alsace-Lorraine. Bill Fine is a fatherly soul to whom GIs, who are tired and battle-weary, tell their troubles. He thinks this and other divisions have had too little rest. Many soldiers believe they are being driven until they are killed. He thought perhaps I could do something about it. I told the story to General Ike and arranged for Fine to see General Lear.

Our Debating Society

PARIS, THURSDAY, FEBRUARY 15, 1945

The Planning Branch is practically a debating society. We have plans on paper and in discussion stage for numerous projects, especially Jackplane, the radio-equipped aircraft to be flown to any newsworthy scene. There is one for a big paratroop operation over the Rhine in Monty's sector and another one for a possible drop in the Frankfurt area. Plans have been in moth balls for months for the coverage of the possible surrender of Jersey and Guernsey. There have been numerous meetings with the French about Bordeaux, where a strong German garrison still is holding out on the mouth of the Gironde, preventing use of that port. This operation, to be conducted by the French, has been postponed several times, principally because the French forces were tied down by the Colmar pocket and sufficient forces could not be spared. The French have made available a large château for the press at Cognac, with all that name implies. There are plans for coverage of our entry into Berlin and even for a paratroop drop on the important port of Kiel.

I am spending about every day at General Ike's office and frequently lunch with him at the house. The pups are doing beautifully. They are learning to walk, mostly backward to date.

Steve Early is due here next week after the Yalta conference is concluded.

Perhaps the first American businessman to arrive in Paris is George O. Tiffany, lawyer for the Nestle's Company, which has extensive manufacturing interests in Spain, France, and Switzerland. Unlike accredited correspondents, he has to find his own billet and eat in French restaurants, although he is here on semiofficial business in which the Department of Commerce is interested.* I have arranged for him to eat occasionally at the Scribe mess and he has finally found a room. The Embassy staff assumed no responsibility.

My Volkswagen

Yesterday I was presented a German *Volkswagen*, something of the equivalent of our jeep, but it has only a two-cylinder air-cooled engine located in the rear. It was given to me by Lieutenant Colonel Rivkin, PRO for Ordnance, who some time ago sought my help to get a statement from General Ike as to the quality of our American tanks. I told him the best way to get such a statement was to have one drafted and approved by the Staff of Com Z, and then presented to General Eisenhower by General John C. H. Lee, or his Chief of Staff, Major General Roy Lord. Then, I told him, General Ike would be in the position of knowing that it had been through the mill with the staff and had been carefully considered. If I were to stick such a statement under his nose, he would immediately ask, "Has the staff approved this?" and I would have to say, "No, sir." The paper then would have to be sent to the staff and there would be delay. Rivkin followed this procedure and soon got his statement approved. The *Volkswagen* is the payoff.

Today we drove it to the American Express Building during the lunch hour. I left the office to see it and found that it has good tires, including a spare, consumes very little gas, and carries five passengers. It has a canvas top with side guards, a compartment, and there even is a sofa pillow, left there by its German owner. Rivkin's story accompanying the presentation is that General Patton personally shot and captured the German general who had it. Patton had instructed that the blood be washed off and the car should be sent to me.

---

* I have retained this thoroughly unimportant paragraph because I was so sorry for Mr. Tiffany, who was the guinea pig for American businessmen coming to France.

All members of my Planning Branch and numerous other kibitzers from PRD gathered to see my prize. There was even a photographer waiting to shoot me as I drove off in the *Volkswagen*, but it wouldn't start. Rivkin took over, tried in vain to start it, and then all of us pushed it up and down Rue Scribe, with passers-by stopping to enjoy the show. Finally, along came a French jeep, made in America, of course, with a sign, "Adolf Hitler Street," on it, and gave the *Volkswagen* a free push, with Rivkin driving. This combination circled the Opera House twice, messing up the traffic on the Avenue de l'Opéra, and finally came to rest back where it had started. But the engine still refused to run. Suddenly, while Rivkin was tinkering with the ignition switch, the motor started with a roar.

I drove it to Versailles today and find it runs very well, but shimmies on a rough road. It rides like a lumber wagon. There are no spare parts and I am not particularly in need of the *Volkswagen*, as I have use of a staff car. However, it will be used by members of the Planning Branch and others of PRD, as transportation always is short.

Steve Early Checks In

PARIS, TUESDAY, FEBRUARY 20, 1945

I saw the Supreme Commander today and enjoyed some very fine Smithfield ham sent him by some admirer at home.

Monty, who had returned from his leave in England early in the month, has reported that his attacks southeast between the Maas and Rhine are going well, and that the enemy will find it increasingly difficult to stand up to the pressure. Monty hopes to draw all available enemy reserves into that battle, so that the second punch, which is to be launched February 23 by Simpson's Ninth U. S. Army under his operational command, supported by Hodges' First Army under Bradley's command, will have an easier task and will advance all the quicker.

General Ike said that the Germans had handled the Roer dams in the one way that was most detrimental to us. They had not blown up the dams completely but had jammed the floodgates in a manner to create flood conditions throughout the length of the Roer and to prolong the period of the flood as long as possible. As soon as the floods subside, General Ike hopes we can really take a smack at the Germans that they will always remember.

On the diplomatic front, there were signs that General de Gaulle and the French in general were showing a bit of pique because de Gaulle was not invited to the Crimean conference. The French now want three divisions released from the front line to assist in development of new divisions and also to parade France's reviving military strength through the countryside. The French press expresses dissatisfaction with the Allies, including the Supreme Command, for failing to bring in more foodstuffs and rolling stock and lack of political deference to their government.

Nevertheless, Ike was in a jubilant mood and rubbed his coins as he talked about the prospect for favorable weather and release, so far as he was concerned, from the terrible strain of waiting for action to begin. He gets terribly impatient during such periods as he has just undergone, but occasionally takes some cheer from the fact that the Germans are in a much worse position and, consequently, he never loses his basic optimism.

So far this month, General Ike has had two conferences with the Field Marshal, who has emphatically stated that military plans and operations are developing soundly and has repeatedly spoken of his complete loyalty to the Supreme Commander and of his belief in the soundness of the SHAEF command system.

The manpower problem is of not only official but of personal concern to the Supreme Commander. He is going tonight with Lieutenant General Ben Lear to visit bases, replacement depots, and hospitals. This is his last chance, he feels, to make an extended inspection in the rear areas, as henceforth his forward headquarters will be at Rheims and his personal attention and presence will be required with combat commanders up front.

Steve Early arrived in a C-54, from Algiers, at Orly today, and I met him. He had just left the presidential party. "Pa" Watson had suffered a heart attack, and Steve was greatly worried about him. He thought the President would have a sad trip on the cruiser back to Washington.

Almost the first business question I asked Steve was whether Harry Hopkins had gotten the President to speak to Stalin about getting correspondents into the Russian-occupied area in Germany.

Steve said, "Yes, I have a very particular message for you from Harry. He said just before I left him at Algiers that I should tell you he forgot to mention the matter to the President."

I wondered if perhaps this was Harry's diplomatic cover-up of a presidential failure.

Steve brought six bottles of vodka given to him personally by Uncle Joe.

Steve was booked to stay at the Ritz in the Aga Khan suite. I took him there; he glanced around and said it was a very poor address for him. He asked to go to my hotel, so we are both living modestly at the Raphaël.

"Magnificent Performance"

SHAEF FORWARD (RHEIMS), MONDAY, FEBRUARY 26, 1945
Steve and I had dinner with Ike on Friday evening, February 23, at the
Brown House, his former house having been given up and the household
staff moved to Rheims. We talked until midnight. On his inspection trip
with General Lear, Ike's visit had been to some battalions of limited-
assignment personnel, practically all of whom had been wounded and
many psychoneurotic. Many of the men appeared to be thoroughly beaten
and rarely smiled. He said he was not satisfied with the type of instruction
and rehabilitation given these men and had told General Lear to go into
the problem immediately.

Steve told the Supreme Commander a story about Patton, which, he
said, was being widely repeated at home. It seems that the War Department had found that Patton's colorful and profane phrases made his
daily situation reports too florid. Consequently, the War Department had
instructed General Patton to write his reports in less colorful and more
official language. Patton complied. His first report was a model of such
military literature, but below his signature was a postscript: "I peed in
the Rhine today."

Steve was delighted to see the General. There was a fine woodfire burning, much to Steve's satisfaction because he has found the Raphaël quite
the coldest place he has ever lived. He practically sits on my 400-watt
electric heater, which gives off about as much comfort as a flatiron.

Steve has been observing the operations of the Public Relations Division in Paris. His presence was announced at a press conference on the
twenty-third by General Allen, and Steve made a short statement to the
effect that he was here on invitation to study our operations, based on his
training as a newspaperman and his experience in handling government
news. The reaction of the correspondents was excellent. Many stayed after
the conference to meet him or to renew old acquaintance.

From Wednesday until Saturday he listened to numerous briefings,
this phase of our activity being most subject to criticism. He also saw our
Communications Center in the Scribe and followed a story from the time
it was filed, through the copy room, through censorship, and to the commercial transmitter which sends it to New York—all taking only seventeen
minutes from start to receipt in New York.*

I took Steve yesterday (Sunday) from Paris to the neighborhood of
Saint-Valery, southwest of Dieppe, to the area in which newly arrived

* I still think this was damn good.

troops are held until called to join an army. Steve was anxious to see his son, Lieutenant Stephen Early, Jr., commanding a mortar platoon in Company M of the 259th Infantry of the 65th Division.

I have overlooked Ike's press conference held at 2:30, Saturday, February 24, at the Scribe. It was his first press conference since November and one which had been tentatively set two or three times, only to be postponed because of calls to the field or want of timeliness. By Saturday, however, the big push of the Ninth and First Armies was under way, and reports indicated satisfactory progress. Ike talked for perhaps an hour, giving a general statement, first, of development since he had last talked to them, and then of the current offensive.

Knowing something of the background of certain situations which Ike discussed in reply to questions, I marveled at the way he turned possibilities for error into diplomatic but honest answers. One question had to do with Montgomery, which he covered by explaining the meaning of operational command. I think this satisfied the correspondents, but we would have had less Anglo-American difficulty if such an explanation had been made either by Ike or by the Public Relations Officer weeks ago.

The correspondents were struck by Ike's appearance of fitness. One asked his weight. Ike said he did not know, as he hadn't weighed recently; he only judged his weight by the tightness of his belt and lately had felt a tightening.

He drew a laugh when he said he had not been afraid during the breakthrough until two weeks later, when he read the American newspapers.

When the conference finished, Ike motioned in my direction to follow him, which I did quickly. When I caught up with him in the correspondents' workroom, he said he wanted Steve. By the time I got Steve out of the crowd—there being perhaps 200 in the room—Ike had had to hurry along because the growing throng was crowding his departure from the Scribe. He said he had wanted to know from Steve what he thought of the press conference, but he would find out later, as he knew we would stop at Rheims on our forthcoming trip. Later, when I got through the crowd to Steve, I told him the question. He deliberated and said:

"It was the most magnificent performance of any man at a press conference that I have ever seen. He knows his facts, he speaks freely and frankly, and he has a sense of humor, he has poise, and he has command."

FEBRUARY, 1945: *U. S. First Army breached Siegfried Line near Aachen, joined Ninth in drive on Cologne. British took Cleve and Goch after heavy bombing, severe fighting. German Roer River defenses crumbled in Allied drive toward Rhine. U. S. First Army crossed Erft River, last obstacle before*

*Cologne; Düren fell; Canadians took Uedem as Yanks captured Bitburg.
Berlin was hard hit by ever-augmented air raids; other heavy Allied raids
pounded away at strategic targets. Reds crossed Oder River, took Liegnitz,
Steinau, approached to within forty-nine miles of Berlin. Dresden, astride
path of Russian advance, was principal target of 8000 Allied bombers in raid
which pounded nine other targets. General Bradley resumed command of
U. S. First Army. Philippine developments hurtled forward as Eighth landed
at Nasugbu. 1st Cavalry and 37th Division smashed into Manila, moved to
Corregidor, entered historic Bataan. Biri, Verde, and Capul Islands captured.
Fighting on Iwo Jima continued bitter as Marines took Mt. Surabachi and
half of central airfields. B-29s repeatedly hit Tokyo and other Honshu targets.
Pacific Fleet carrier planes destroyed 158 Jap planes, two trains, radar and
airfield equipment, sank or damaged thirty-two Jap ships in two attacks on
Tokyo. American Rangers and Filipino guerrillas rescued 513 prisoners from
infamous Cabantuan prison camp on Luzon. British naval units smashed Jap
oil resources at Palembang. "Big Three" meeting at Yalta announced decision
to split Germany into three parts; to control her until her armies are demobilized; to levy payment in kind for war damage. France invited to take zone
and join commission. Egyptian Prime Minister assassinated after declaring
war against Axis. Osmena resumed governmental functions in Philippines.
(Up and down the line and in the rear areas we watched and cheered as the
Red Army drew closer and closer to Berlin.—H.C.B.)*

Steve Gets Around

PARIS, SATURDAY, MARCH 3, 1945

We spent Monday night with General Ike at his new quarters in Rheims.
This is a handsome château in the heart of the town and is owned by one
of the champagne kings.

I found that the Prime Minister had advanced the idea of making Air
Marshal Tedder second in command in the Air Ministry, and, as the
Deputy Supreme Commander was a British spot in the SHAEF organization, hoped to move Field Marshal Alexander into it. It was obvious to
me that this move, if consummated after the campaign in some of the
British press for a ground commander-in-chief, immediately would be
misinterpreted. The idea had been discussed and General Ike was perfectly willing to accept Alexander, not as Ground Commander, but as a
true deputy to the Supreme Commander, in which position he would take
part in all SHAEF operations—land, sea, and air. I feel strongly that if this
appointment were made now, the interpretation placed on it in the press
would be very bad, indeed, for Allied relations. Some of the British press
would say, "I told you so," and inevitably there would be inference that

Ike had failed. Some inferences would be counterattacked in the American press, and a merry war of words would ensue.

General Ike had not thought of the reaction in quite that way. His admiration and respect for Alexander are such that he would not want him placed in a position which would make him unhappy or create any bad feelings whatsoever. If Alexander were appointed, General Ike would simply make clear to the press the nature of his duties.

I found the pups growing rapidly. General Ike has a red ribbon around the neck of one of the males, which he calls "Lopear" because one ear hasn't yet perked up to its proper level. He thinks this is the one he will want for himself. Without the ribbon he can scarcely distinguish one from the other. He was complaining again that no one around the house had the heart to housebreak the dogs, and now that there are four, not even a formal court-martial could prove wrongdoing of any of them.

At Verdun, we checked in with Colonel Fitzgerald and, in contrast with the bad news about the Ardennes which I received from Fitz during my last visit, now there was much good news to report. The U. S. First Army was closing in on Cologne. Patton's Third Army was getting set for a race to the Rhine north of the Moselle, and the Canadians and British had squeezed the Germans from the north with a tight bridgehead at Wesel-Beirsdort, and a tremendous victory was in the making.

We stopped at the Argonne-Meuse cemetery near Romaine, where Steve found the names of some of his buddies of the 80th Division, which had fought in this area in the last war.

At Luxembourg, we spent the evening visiting with a score or more of American and British correspondents, all of whom had questions to ask Steve about Yalta and the American home front. Finally Steve asked:

"What do you hear from your home office?"

"Blivets—nothing but blivets," was the reply.

"What the hell is a blivet?" Early asked.

The answer came in a chorus: "A blivet is a one-pound bag filled with two pounds of horse manure."

We stopped at General Patton's headquarters and had a delightful talk with him. He was chafing that he and his troops had not yet been turned completely loose to finish their push. For the moment, his orders called for defensive action, and under his interpretation of these orders, he felt he should not advance more than ten miles a day. He said that one of the finest actions of military history had occurred in the crossing of the Saar River by the 80th Division. This interested Steve, so with a guide we set out to find the headquarters of the 80th. The division's crossing had been made when the river was still partly in flood, with a current of fifteen miles an hour. On the opposite side were high hills studded with German pill-boxes—part of the Siegfried Line. On the American side was a level plain over which any movement was exposed to the observation and fire of the Germans in their fortifications. We talked to some of the officers and lads who had made the crossing, and none of them was quite sure how it had been done. Steve began to be impressed that there was some fighting in this war and that all of it had not occurred in World War I.

We found the division's headquarters a couple of miles west of Bitburg, which the division and its running mate, the 4th Armored Division, commanded by Major General Hugh J. Gaffey, were then attacking. We lunched as guests of Major General Horace McBride. General McBride said that there was no fraternization amongst his combat troops. Recently a German girl was caught sniping and had been quickly shot by the GIs, and all who have heard about the girl want nothing to do with German women.*

We returned through Echternach to Bastogne on one of the principal roads used by the Germans to advance when they attacked in the Ardennes. There were many signs of battle, with innumerable burned-out German tanks. Bastogne had been badly battered, as might be expected. The Belgian residents were trying to get relocated in what remained of their homes.

We spent the night at Spa, but most of the correspondents were forward, covering the First Army's attack on Cologne. Thursday we drove through Aachen, where we lunched with American officers of the Military Government for the city, and drove on to Jülich, which had been pulverized to prepare for the Ninth Army's crossing of the Roer at that point. In a heavy rain we finished the day at Ninth Army's press camp at Maastricht.

Friday we drove to Namur. We were taken to visit a fighter outfit with Thunderbolts, commanded by Colonel Stecker. He had just returned from a mission in support of one of our advancing columns whose tanks were waiting outside a German town until the air could deal with several German tanks hidden behind and under residences. His mission was to bomb some fifteen houses on the right side of the main street entering the town. He said that shortly after he dropped his bombs, he saw our tanks moving. At a briefing, we heard numerous pilots, just back from missions, telling their stories. There were cloud and rain over most of the front, but at one cleared space on the east bank of the Rhine, there was a train and supply depot. One pilot said there were so many of our planes in the hole in the cloud that he had to wait for his turn to dive into the target with his bombs.

* They said.

The next morning Steve and I met General Ike at Bradley's headquarters. He had been up in the forward areas and his cheerful attitude told us even before the morning briefing that the news was good. He had conferred with the Field Marshal at his tactical headquarters and also had seen Simpson. Over the radio we heard that an important decision was taken in a conference with Montgomery, but, actually, the battle preparatory to crossing the Rhine north of Düsseldorf was developing according to the decisions and plans made a long time ago.

The Ninth Army had taken Krefeld, the largest city on the Cologne plain, ten miles northwest of Düsseldorf and only two miles from the Rhine. It was a race to see who first would reach the Rhine.

The Supreme Commander was going to confer with General Gerow, now commanding the Fifteenth Army, whose job is primarily one of training new and refitting divisions. His headquarters are at Château d'Ardennes, near Dinant, and then Ike was driving on to Rheims, where the Prime Minister, Field Marshal Brooke, and party were expected to arrive on Monday.

Steve was getting the itch to get back to Paris because he had to meet General "Honk" Allen, who was taking him on a visit to press camps in Devers' group.

We made Paris that night after a quick roadside lunch of a can of hot corned beef, which I have learned to leave on the manifold of the engine as we drive, so we can do some of our cooking en route. Steve and I chuckled over odd names on jeeps—one shared by a chaplain and medical officer was called *Body and Soul*.

The Scribe was feverish with good news.

Remagen—"Get Right Across!"

SHAEF FORWARD (RHEIMS), SUNDAY, MARCH 11, 1945

Now and then my curiosity to know what's going on, aided perhaps by the fact that I miss the guy, prompts me to tell Corporal Street to head the Chevy toward Rheims, frequently without advance notice. It was after 5 Wednesday when I had finished at the office and by 7:30 I was at Ike's house in Rheims. He had several of the airborne commanders, including Generals Matthew B. Ridgway, Maxwell D. Taylor, and Gavin, as guests. They all looked superbly fit and keen in every way. The airborne units have been alerted for the big operation to help Monty cross the Rhine, but as other drops are under consideration, they are straining at the leash, never knowing from day to day just what their next show will be.

We had just sat down at dinner and Ike had said he didn't particularly care for the soup when Henry Clay answered the phone in the next room. It was for the Supreme Commander, who excused himself, and we soon heard his voice saying:

"Brad, that's wonderful."

There was a pause and then he continued:

"Sure, get right on across with everything you've got. It's the best break we've had. . . .

"To hell with the planners. Sure, go on, Brad, and I'll give you everything we got to get to hold that bridgehead. We'll make good use of it even if the terrain isn't too good. . . .

"It's wonderful! Congratulations."

While Ike was talking, the airborne generals were all ears, as indeed was I. General Ridgway said:

"Butch, couldn't you get us in on this show? It sounds good."

When Ike sat down again at the head of the table, he said:

"Hodges got a bridge at Remagen and already has troops across."

Bradley had wanted to be sure it was O.K. to exploit, and as usual they were in quick and complete agreement.*

I told Ike of the interest of the airborne generals to get in on the show. He replied that they were out of luck on this one, but there was still plenty of work to do elsewhere.

Now that it looked as if we might have a break at Remagen of exactly the kind Ike had been praying for, I told him that correspondents are asking when and how we will cover Berlin. I asked him if he planned to take the city. He said that the capture of Berlin in itself would not lead to a general collapse of the Nazi regime, but the loss of the Ruhr would have more serious repercussions on the Germans' will to resist, because of its far-greater effect on Germany's capacity to continue the war.

In the Middle

Last night we had a grand time. Tooey brought over his guitar and we had three enlisted WACs who do amateur entertaining. Two played the piano and banged out all the old tunes and some new ones. Tooey accompanied Ike, and the singing was so good that everyone got into it. Ike led the basso profundos and really got into the whole swing of things again—the first evening I've seen him really enjoy since the Lord knows

---

*We were so excited, listening, that it was difficult for me to record Ike's exact words. However, the words I used are pretty close to the original.

when. He is back at the office today, running the war with a new zip.

Steve was taken by General Allen to visit some press camps in the Southern Group during the week and returned to Paris last night. I am returning there this afternoon.

I have been "in the middle" between the officers and staff of the *Stars and Stripes*, who feel they are oppressed by brass hats and have asked me to present their case to the Supreme Commander. It seems incongruous that in a war for the Four Freedoms, which is taking all of his time and thought, the Supreme Commander should have to stop to give attention to the preservation of freedom for his Army newspaper. Yet that is what he is doing and he is drafting certain letters intended to protect the editor of *Stars and Stripes* from intervention by the so-called brass.

Last week, while Ike was on his trip up front, he had flown in an L-5 from a small field, about nine miles from Cologne, to Namur, where Steve and I had found him. The take-off was in a snowstorm, but just as the plane was airborne, a German artillery shell struck about 100 yards away. I had read about this in *Stars and Stripes*, but General Ike was displeased that the story had appeared. He said that such stories make the GIs feel that the only reason he goes up front is to get his name in the paper.

General Deane, head of the American Military Mission to Moscow, has radioed that among American prisoners of war released by the Russians in their great advance is our friend and my brother aide, Lieutenant Craig Campbell, who had been captured in Tunisia during the battle of the Kasserine.

"Come On and Deal"

PARIS, TUESDAY, MARCH 13, 1945

Steve had a grand trip with General Allen but nearly froze to death in an L-5. Colonel George Warden, our chief censor, was in the party, and Steve has developed a great liking for him.

We had dinner last night with General Spaatz and he had both of us at poker. We were engrossed in the game when Major Sally Bagby, Tooey's aide, came in. She said she had just heard over the radio part of a list of promotions to full general but had only caught those of Clark and Bradley. I knew that Tooey had been strongly recommended by Ike, so, of course, I couldn't say anything. The game went on quietly, each of us wondering. Then Sally returned and said she had heard on the Allied Forces Network that Bradley's aide was quoted as saying, "It's a well-deserved promotion." This gave all of us a chuckle, for what aide would say anything else. Then Sally went off to work the telephone, calling everyone who might have the complete list. She even called London. Presently she returned and said:

"General, sir, I just want to say that it is a well-deserved promotion."

We all congratulated Tooey, who immediately sent for champagne and turned to me and said:

"Come on and deal."

The game went on with the new four-star General contributing just as we ordinary people did.

But the Army Has So Many Divisions

PARIS, WEDNESDAY, MARCH 14, 1945

General Marshall has been pressing to get more publicity for divisions and their commanders. One of the troubles is size; there are so many divisions and so much news to write that each division can't be singly or especially publicized as are the Marines, who have only a few divisions in action, but who are making great news at Iwo Jima.

General Ike has sent a memo to Generals Bradley and Devers, with a copy to me at PRD:

Much of the publicity with respect to the achievement of U. S. ground units in this theater has been impersonal and generalized in character. Many opportunities have been lost to publicize forcefully the extraordinary achievements of particular commanders and units in specified situations. An exception to this rule was the account of the action of the 101st Airborne Division at Bastogne. Yet, in many instances other units have performed in equally gallant fashion—and under almost equally spectacular conditions.

There lies a danger in making distinctions among a number of units where all are doing well; moreover, I realize that this is a matter that cannot be handled through strictly official channels. It is not the function of Public Relations Officers to write stories. But by skillful briefing and particularly by interesting a few good reporters in an area in which some unusual action is taking or has taken place, commanders and units could be made to live before the American public rather than to exist as mere numerical designations.

To return to the example of the 101st Airborne Division: little has been said of the exploits of the 4th Armored, or of the 35th and other units in battling their way forward under appalling conditions to join up with the Bastogne position.

The action of the 3rd U. S. Division and the remainder of the 21st Corps in the Colmar pocket might have been more strikingly portrayed to the people at home. In the recent advance to the Rhine, the names of Collins, Gillem, and McLain have been mentioned in news stories only casually, whereas I believe that, with a little prompting, reporters would have made these men stand out more clearly for the public. The same applies with respect to the other Corps and Division Commanders engaged in the recent offensive.

Our problem is much more difficult than it is in the British service and press because we do not have the historical names of regiments and the concentrated interest based on geographical recruiting at home. Moreover, in seeking to present to the American people more vivid accounts of the accomplishments of American soldiers, we must be careful, as always, that there is no implication of disparagement of our Allies. These matters may not seem very weighty when you are engaged in operational problems of the greatest magnitude. I do not want to be interpreted as saying that we are fighting this war for headlines, but proper publicity does have an effect on our troop efficiency. A personalized presentation of the achievements of units of this great force would result in a greater appreciation at home and this, in turn, would have a beneficial result on the morale of every organization. Moreover, it will have an enduring effect on the future of American defense forces and I hope that you and your staffs and your subordinate commanders will give to the matter some imaginative thought.

General Marshall has frequently communicated with me on this general subject. He is vitally interested in it, not only because of its postwar effects but because of its influence on his current problems of manpower, equipment, deployment, and so on.

D. D. E.

To give further effect to his efforts, the Supreme Commander also has sent a memo to the PRD. Colonel George Warden, our chief censor, who is one of the fairest men I have met and whose liberal ideas would not be expected to be found in a censor, has an objection to General Ike's implication that the censors make the policy as to what must be "stopped" or may be "passed." He points out, and rightly, that G-2 makes the policy and the censors merely apply it. The Supreme Commander has used the term "censorship" to include the whole process of prevention of voluntarily telling the enemy the things he'd like to know.* Dated March 10, General Ike's instruction reads:

This memorandum is to remind you again of my attitude toward censorship, as explained personally to press correspondents dating back to before D-Day:

Censorship is intended to be applied only as demanded by the requirements of military security. The term "blackout" is a misnomer and should never be used by briefers. Enforced delays in the transmission of news should be prescribed only when the enemy can gain probable advantage through immediate publication. Such necessity will undoubtedly arise with greatest frequency

---

* In the midst of the final drive, with countless vital matters on his mind, General Ike still found time to try to cut red tape so that the people at home could get the full story. I think that's important and am therefore retaining this memorandum.

with respect to radio transmissions, which are always intercepted by the enemy. Normally, in such cases it is considered feasible to give appropriate explanation to correspondents because the circumstances should be so obvious that no reasonable argument could arise.

Correspondents should be encouraged, rather than discouraged, to mention by numerical designation and by name of the commander the identity of units actually in the line, when these have obviously been previously identified by the enemy. As a rule it would appear that after a unit has been in the line forty-eight hours there is little need for pretending the enemy is ignorant of its presence.

It must be remembered that censorship denies to the fighting soldier the immediate opportunity to see that his services and exploits are recognized and appreciated. The soldier likes to read about his unit and about his local commander. In this connection, there should be a rather standard procedure in referring to formations, particularly formations as large as armies. My own belief is that a good standard practice would be to refer to each army by both the name of the commander and the numerical designation, such as, for example, "Hodges' First Army."

I have no intention of interfering with the prerogatives of subordinate commanders, who are of course authorized to withhold, temporarily, any information, when they believe such procedure will facilitate tactical success. I desire, however, that subordinate headquarters be informed of the policies that apply in SHAEF PRD, so that misunderstandings will not arise. Moreover, this memorandum has nothing to do with normal censorship procedure that is supposed to eliminate glaring inaccuracies or statements damaging to Allied progress. I merely want to point out that trepidation should not lead us into the mistake of a constant use of negative methods, not only to the irritation of the correspondents and of the public, but frequently to the damage of the morale of our own troops.

The freest possible flow of news is not only in keeping with our traditions; it is the best way to keep the public accurately informed and working in support of the war effort. The saving of lives and military success are normally the only sound reasons for interference.

D. D. E.

First Presidential Citation for a Division

PARIS, THURSDAY, MARCH 15, 1945

Steve and I drove to Rheims today and joined with General Ike's party at the Ecole Professionnelle to drive to the headquarters of the 101st Airborne Division, about fifteen miles away, where Ike presented the Presidential Citation.

Every time the Supreme Commander has seen this division he has as usual asked for soldiers from Kansas. He first saw the 101st the night before

D-Day, and I was in his party. He asked time and again if there were any lads from Kansas present and, oddly, he found only two or three. He again saw the division after the drop, when it had returned to England, and again there seemed to be a shortage of Kansans. But on today's occasion, Major General Maxwell D. Taylor had a formation of about 200 Kansas paratroopers for Ike to review. They were strapping fellows. Ike inspected the formation, which then marched in review. At its head was th^r American flag and the official flag of the state of Kansas. Ike got a great kick out of it.

After a bountiful lunch with desserts of pie and ice cream, we drove to a near-by large open field where the entire division was drawn up by regiment for review. It was a glorious sight. Steve * and I were on the reviewing platform. The U. S. Army Band failed to catch the cue to begin playing. General Taylor ordered over the loudspeaker:

"Will the Army Band play *The Star-Spangled Banner?*"

General Ike made a spirited talk and, as usual, had no notes but had thought out his remarks. He closed with:

"Good luck and God be with you."

As he had been given command of another division, Major General Anthony C. McAuliffe was absent from the review. Temporarily commanding the 101st, he had fashioned a typically American terse answer to German demands for surrender on the fourth day of the siege when he replied "Nuts" to the enemy commander's ultimatum.

Monty's large-scale crossing of the Rhine is set for March 24. Two airborne divisions of the First Allied Airborne Army will participate. The Supreme Commander has given instructions that a firm bridgehead over the Rhine be taken north of the Ruhr as a basis for further operations to isolate the Ruhr.

Three Stripes vs. Three Stars

PARIS, FRIDAY, MARCH 16, 1945

Will Lang, of *Time*, came to see me at the Express Building today to deliver a message from Sergeant Bill Mauldin, the cartoonist of *Stars and Stripes* in the Mediterranean, whose stuff in recent weeks has been running in *Stars and Stripes* in France.

A couple of weeks ago, Sergeant Bill Estoff, whose current job is to

---

* One of the war correspondents, Vincent Sheean, not recognizing the Secretary to the President, passed the word that he was the Mayor of Rheims, and some correspondents so reported.

select news from the Paris edition and send it by the quickest means possible, usually jeep, to other editions circulated in the area of Devers' 6th Army Group, had brought Mauldin to see me about a crisis in his life. General Patton had written a letter to *Stars and Stripes*, saying that if Mauldin's cartoons continued to be carried, the paper would be barred from circulation in the Third Army area. Patton objected to the unkempt appearance of GIs as portrayed by Mauldin in his characters Willie and Joe, who are slovenly, dirty, and unshaven. Mauldin, who had been wounded in combat, thought his characters faithfully represented GIs in the front line, although his experience has been largely in Sicily and Italy.

I told Mauldin that both he and Patton were trying to win the war and, with this common denominator, they ought to be able to settle their differences. Wouldn't Mauldin like to talk it out with Patton eye-to eye? Mauldin quaked, but said he would think it over. He came back later and said he had mustered up his courage and if I'd make the appointment, he would go to Third Army headquarters and see old Blood and Guts himself.

I immediately put in a phone call to Lucky, Patton's headquarters, and surprisingly found that Patton was spending the day at Com Z headquarters, checking into his supply problem. I located him in the office of Major General Everett Hughes. His first answer to my suggestion was:

"That fellow's a bad influence on the Army and if he comes into Third Army area, I'll throw him in jail for thirty days."

I explained to him that they both had ideas for winning the war and that Mauldin's stuff was popular with the GIs and, in addition, he had a long string of papers carrying his cartoons in the States. If General Patton could explain his objections to Mauldin in person, perhaps there could be a meeting of their minds leading to delousing of the characters. General Patton thought this was a reasonable approach and said to send Mauldin along and he would see him at Third Army headquarters.

Mauldin, of course, heard my end of the conversation. I told him that when he went to Patton's office to make certain that his uniform was neat and tidy and that he was in proper dress for the Third Army area, where helmets are mandatory. He must stand at attention and salute smartly. If he did less, the interview was doomed to failure.

Now Will Lang reported that he saw Mauldin after the interview and since Bill was returning to Rome, he wanted Lang to report to me; the gist of which was that Mauldin was convinced he had not changed General Patton's mind and he was certain Patton hadn't changed his. So far as I was concerned, it was simply a case of "no hits, no runs, one error" on my part.

Lang asked if he could write a story for *Time*, and I said I had no objection, provided he wrote the story just as it happened and didn't embellish it with too much color.

PARIS, SATURDAY, MARCH 17, 1945

Late yesterday, General Gay, Chief of Staff to Patton, phoned me from the front to say that Steve's son had been wounded. The 65th Division had been in a relatively quiet front northwest of Saarbrücken, getting battle experience.

Buddy had already been moved to a field hospital at Thionville. The speed with which wounded are evacuated was illustrated by our experience in trying to track Buddy down. He had been operated on at a field hospital near Thionville, then flown with other wounded men to Liége and from Liége to a hospital north of Bristol, in England. The medicos were prompt and efficient in giving us information.

Steve flew to England today to see his son.

PARIS, SUNDAY, MARCH 18, 1945

While waiting at Orly to meet Steve today, I had two and a half hours of misery, seeing our lads on stretchers being carried off Air Transport planes.* One had most of his face shot away, and I can't get him out of my mind. They were moved in ambulances to the First General Hospital.

Steve had seen Buddy and found him a bit woozy from dope but otherwise in good spirit. A small party of Germans had infiltrated the line and Buddy and his gang intercepted them. There was a fight in the darkness; Buddy got off some hand grenades but caught a bullet, from a burp gun, in the upper calf of his leg. Small bones are broken, but not the main one. His greatest worry, Steve said, is that he may not get back to his division. He had been in the front line eight days.

PARIS, WEDNESDAY, MARCH 21, 1945

Steve left today. It's been grand having him, but now I can go back to work. He refused a private office set aside for him by General Allen and

---

* Quent Reynolds wrote, rightly, "The Wounded Don't Cry." I could add that, if they can, they whistle.

instead made his headquarters at a small pine table in my office and has been with me thirty days. He frequently had callers and so did I, and between the two sets of friends, we have had practically a continuous bull session.

He has made at least one contribution that I think will help greatly in our press relations. Henceforth, whenever security requires that news be delayed, the correspondents are to be given sufficient quotable information to write a story so not only they but the public at home will know, in general, the reasons for the delay. We are also going to try to avoid the use of the term "blackout."

Steve said that one of the most pleasant incidents of his stay had been his visit to *Stars and Stripes*, which operates in the *Herald Tribune* plant. He was escorted by Brigadier General Oscar Solbert, head of Special Services, under which *S & S* fits into our sprawling organization, and Lieutenant Colonel Arthur Goodfriend, the ingenious editor-in-chief. The staff had assembled and Steve reminisced a bit about the old *Stars and Stripes* in World War I. His talk was received so enthusiastically that when he departed, he saw some hastily improvised signs reading, "Early for President."

Patton Slips Around Right End

PARIS, SATURDAY, MARCH 24, 1945

At the Scribe this morning correspondents were chuckling that with Monty's obvious preparation for crossing the Rhine in the north, about which there have been numerous stories of smoke screens to hide activities of his troops and the massing of strength in that area, Patton had slipped around right end. *He was across the Rhine.* His Third Army troops had quietly crossed in small boats in the darkness of Thursday night. With our Remagen bridgehead enlarged and Patton across farther up the Rhine, Monty crossing the river today with great strength, Hitler's hordes should be seeing the beginning of something more than "the beginning of the end."

I drove up to Rheims today, but Ike was at the front, watching Ninth Army's part in Monty's big show. I saw scores of our aircraft returning from the big drop in Monty's area. There must have been heavy flak, as some seemed to limp at steadily declining altitudes. Fortunately, their home fields are mostly in the plain around the Rheims area.

I found that General Ike had notified the Combined Chiefs that the recent victories west of the Rhine have resulted, as planned, in destruction of a large proportion of the enemy forces on the Western Front. He didn't wish to appear overoptimistic, but he told his bosses that he was convinced that the present situation presents opportunities for which all have struggled and which now must be seized boldly. The dash and daring of Bradley's armies got us two bridgeheads cheaply and these can be consolidated and exploited rapidly to support a major thrust which will assist Monty's operation in the north.

General Ike expressed his personal belief that the enemy strength on the Western Front is becoming so stretched that our penetrations and advances soon will be limited only by our maintenance. In the north, he has all the strength that can be effectively maintained east of the Rhine for several weeks. He reported that he is directing vigorous action on all sectors and that he intends to follow up every success with the utmost speed.

The Joint Intelligence Committee feel that Hitler's strategy is now purely one of resisting to the bitter end and of doing all he can to create dissension among the Allies. They also call attention to a marked increase in U-boat activity. During the past five or six weeks, U-boats have had considerable success against our sea supply line, and there are indications that our losses of ships will become more severe. The Germans have a new method of recharging storage batteries on their U-boats without coming to the surface. This makes all the more difficult our efforts by sea and air to catch them.

I returned from Rheims by way of Châlons-sur-Marne, as I hadn't seen the place. En route I picked up three paratroopers of the 101st Airborne Division who were on forty-eight-hour leave en route to Meaux, which they had found more interesting for their purpose and less expensive than Paris.

By way of making conversation, I told them I understood that the finest airborne outfit is the 82nd, knowing the keen rivalry between the two. One of the lads said:

"Oh, yes, the 82nd is a very fine outfit—of course, we're the 101st."

I then asked if it were true that the 101st was saved at Bastogne by the heroic efforts of the 4th Armored. The reply:

"Oh, yes, they got into the fighting, too. They're a swell outfit."

One of the paratroopers in the front seat turned around and looked me over very carefully. My naval uniform frequently attracts attention of soldiers, and I happened to have on one with three dull stripes and one bright one.

"By the way," he said, "you've just been promoted, haven't you?"

He had me: from then on, we were real friends. As usual I said nothing of my association with General Ike. I asked if they had been present at the presentation of the citation to their division. They had. I asked if the Supreme Commander had made a speech.

"Oh, yes, he made a good one, but I hate to hear him end his speech with 'Good luck and God be with you.' "

I asked why.

"Because every time he's made a speech to us and said, 'God be with you,' he's sent us off on a tough job."

We Get to Be a Model

PARIS, MONDAY, MARCH 26, 1945

Just as I was about to get out of the planning job and to get Lieutenant Colonel Scott-Bailey to take over, the fact that he is especially popular with the Americans has attracted the attention of the British War Office, which plans to send him to Washington to be attached to the Embassy as the military adviser to the British Information Service. I regret losing him, as his experience has been invaluable. Now I am trying to teach him to stop saying, with respect to America, "out there" and instead to say "over there."

News is very good just now, and despite Ike's feeling there will be long guerrilla warfare after the German armies are beaten, I am beginning to be optimistic again—I'm hunching that Patton will get to Berlin first. We have been thinking the Russians will beat us in, but I have told the boys to dust off our Berlin plans.

We have had a delightful spell of weather for the past week and the number of air sorties flown each day is astronomical. . . . Paris is coming abloom and, like Washington in spring, is charming. . . . Gladys Hall sent me a copy of Paul Porter's first speech to the broadcasters after becoming Chairman of the FCC. It's the best-humored speech by a government official I've seen in many a day and it also is filled with ideas of good government and proper relations between the Commission and the industry. . . . Lieutenant Colonel Orla St. Clair, of the Signals Division in the War Department, has been in to see me. He first was opposed to assignment of additional frequencies for our press and broadcast operations from the battle fronts, but now has not only changed his mind in our favor but told me the War Department is using our setup of commercial mobile transmitters as a model for coming large-scale operations in the Pacific. . . . General Ike has agreed to have a press conference at the Scribe tomorrow.

General Ike Reports the War to Date

PARIS, WEDNESDAY, MARCH 28, 1945

The press conference was a peach. Colonel Dupuy gave me a transcript, which I will include because General Ike reviews the campaign to date in a way that no one can excel:

GENERAL EISENHOWER: Today, so far as I'm concerned, the conference is on the record, the only stipulation being that if you find it desirable to use any direct quotes, that you can check them with General Allen because I'm very apt, in the enthusiasm of expounding an idea, of being guilty of grammatical mistakes, not to mention other types.

Today I have brought with me also the Deputy Supreme Commander [Tedder] and after the conclusion of this conference he will be as available as I for answering questions.

It seemed to me a rather appropriate time to hold a press conference because we have reached the end of one phase of this campaign and we are entering upon another. The Rhine has been symbolic not only in Germanic history and song, but it is a definite geographical and military feature that any military plan must take into consideration when you are trying to advance across it, either way.

It seemed to me that one of the things we could do today is to go back and review the plan of campaign that was initiated with the breaking out of the bridgehead at Avranches last August and continue down to see where we are today. By bringing up the highlights of those various incidents that occurred along the way there will be suggested to you questions that you might want answered, and I think the time has come when we can afford to give you, so far as there was any reason behind them, the reasons for things that have happened which may have been a bit puzzling to

you and possibly to our publics, maybe even to professional men and soldiers.

As we broke out of the bridgehead you will recall that very shortly thereafter the operation started through Marseille and we had two forces, one approaching through southern France from the Upper Rhone Valley and the other driving across France toward the northeast. Immediately there became two possibilities that could be pursued: One, to allow the German to hold the line of the Siegfried except in a chosen point of penetration, say the north, and to ignore him in his West Wall except where we might try to drive through into Germany and defeat him with such forces as could be brought to bear in the heart of his country. The other plan was to join our converging armies and to use to the utmost the forces coming from the south to defeat the German west of the Rhine as an essential preliminary to the second phase; that is, what you hope to be the final phase of the operation against Germany on the Western Front.

There was a considerable difference of opinion as to which of these was correct. If concentration and speed were the only things to be considered, possibly the one idea of allowing the German to remain where he pleased west of the Rhine would have been a good one. But there was this to remember: as long as you allowed the German to remain west of the Rhine you had always the threat of his counterattack against your line of communications. Moreover, you had this knowledge: if you could not whip the German west of the Rhine, how would you whip him behind that great obstacle? And finally, if you penetrated his forces west of the Rhine only at one point and from there on attempted to drive straight on into the heart of his country, you'd give him advance notice of where you were going and he could concentrate all the forces he still had to defeat that thrust. Consequently, I held from the beginning an opinion that was shared by many but opposed by some that the first thing we must do is to defeat the German decisively west of the Rhine.

I think as long ago as a conference with you people in London before we moved over here I told you my hope and prayer was that the Germans stood and fought west of the Rhine. Only a few weeks ago I told you it was my purpose, so far as was humanly possible, to destroy the German forces west of the Rhine and I expected to do it. Now, you will recall that questions after that conference brought out this point, that by "destruction" I didn't hope to kill or capture every German then in the armies west of the Rhine but that I did expect to destroy his military organization and might west of that river and I did expect to knock off a very large proportion of his forces.

Now, to do that, the first thing necessary was to create an exposed flank. You could not possibly attack frontally all along that great line and use your force to the best advantage. So it was started on February 8 by the attack of the 21st Army Group southward between the Maas and the Rhine. We expected and hoped then and were ready to attack with the Ninth Army and the left of the First Army in support of that attack on February 10. We had an amusing thought at headquarters about that time because we had read in the papers that Rundstedt's attack of December would make it impossible for us to attack in force up to three and possibly six months after his attack had been polished off. Now, I remember the article

that said we were going to be immobile for that long and it said "experienced war correspondents on the front." In justice to you men, I never saw any single article printed from this theater where any pressman living with soldiers thought any such thing. But that is what the headlines said. In any event, we were completely ready for that attack to jump off on the tenth. As you know, the conditions on the Roer with the ability of the German to flood the Roer River held the rest of that attack up until February 23. I'll confess to you now that those were the two most anxious weeks I have spent in this campaign. To be all ready and to be held up by a combination of natural and artificial causes over which we had no control was a very bad time for me.

Now, the plan was laid out one-two-three. One—for the forces in the north to break through as far as Düsseldorf and create an exposed flank, and then for Bradley's forces to turn south against that exposed flank and, in combination with the forces still on the front, complete the destruction of the Germans west of the Rhine. You know the history. I think we had a press conference since Field Marshal Montgomery's early operations were carried on to completion and after, at least, the Ninth Army attack had started. General Bradley, in preparation for his part, attacked with his left in support of the Ninth Army on its right with the VII Corps. Very skillfully and secretly he got another corps all ready to follow along behind that VII Corps. The second that the VII Corps had advanced across the Erft and uncovered the right flank of the Germans left in the Eifel he turned south with a force that must have been very much stronger than the German expected. By his dislocation of that front he made it possible for General Patton, who, you remember, in the meantime, had been conducting a series of local attacks, to attract strength down there but, equally important, to get a nice jump-off position to throw his forces forward to Coblenz, on the Rhine. That movement had also been precalculated by General Bradley so that the Third Army now thrusting forward along the north bank of the Moselle was on the exposed flank of all the Germans left in the Saar. In the meantime, General Devers' forces had been built up until that army was very, very considerably stronger than any normal army. So he was able to conduct a very strong attack against the prepared defenses, so strong that he could pin them down while General Patton, attacking with the XX Corps from the direction of Trier and with his XII Corps through the mouth of the Moselle southward, was able to destroy the remaining German forces in that area. There's no use going over statistics in great detail, but there have been a quarter of a million Germans captured since March 1, and, without making any allowances at all for their killed and wounded, you see what a quarter of a million Germans left today on the east side of the Rhine would mean to our operations.

Now, as to that series of operations between March 1 and March 27. By the way, I thought they'd finish by March 15, but I'm always optimistic. The success of those operations was due to the extraordinary preparation and skill and drive General Bradley's armies, coupled with the tremendous power of General Devers' thrust—the Seventh Army under General Patch, and to which were attached also a French group called the Group Monsaberg, on the right—were able to put in from the south. Remember that the difficult fighting took place in the north. There you couldn't hope to destroy everything you ran into because Montgomery's forces not only had the Siegfried Line to break through on a narrow front but the Germans had brought up reinforcements so that many of those troops could retire in fairly good order across the Rhine. From Wesel southwards

there could be no retreat in good order. To prove that, when we got the bridgehead at Remagen, four divisions were constantly making progress against the remainder of the eleven German divisions, so that the actual destruction of those forces was accomplished about as completely as you could ever hope them to be when they had such a broad base through which to retreat—not through a neck like the Falaise gap. Through that whole operation again was exemplified the idea that there is no air war and there is no ground war. There is just one thing— there is a ground-air or air-ground, whichever word you prefer to use. But it's one. Even when the bomber goes as deep as Posen, what is it going after? It's going after the enemy ability to make war—not just to make war against the airplane in the air, but to make war specifically against troops on the ground and against troops at sea. It's all one war, ground, air, and navy. In recent stages the Navy hasn't appeared too prominently, at least in numbers. But never forget that it's the Navy that always makes possible these operations through the protection of our sea lines of communication, through bringing in supplies, maintenance, reinforcements, and so on, so that the growing forces we have here are all here because the Navy made safe their passage. But the ground-air team is one in which there is no such word in my dictionary as air "support" for ground or vice versa. It's a ground-air war. It works together to the only sane application of tactical force on the battlefield.

Now, I have read in the papers that there is some criticism that we did not destroy the Rhine bridges. Naturally, we would have liked the Rhine bridges destroyed. We weren't silly enough to think the Germans weren't going to destroy them if they could. But when you are operating through the types of conditions that we have been—our bombers have been forced to operate day after day through heavy cloud—to destroy a thing like a bridge would require an air strength that you couldn't afford to devote to bridges alone. There were too many targets of tremendous value to us; chiefly, in establishing what we call a line of interdiction—an area in which the enemy cannot move, or at least he can't move into it and he can't move out of it. We have been busy at it and the air has been tremendously successful. Coupled with that, they have had to carry on operations against enemy oil, airplane, and tank production and things of that kind that are directly supporting this battle on our front.

Another thing that is a point worthy to be noted in this campaign is this: since we did it one-two-three from north to south, immediately one was completed we started to prepare for the attack across the Rhine in the north. There we knew the resistance would be heaviest because it was closest to that extraordinary region, the Ruhr. We knew it would be heaviest there. So, there, deliberate plans were made. Army, Navy, and airborne troops —everybody was brought to bear on that with all the strength it was considered necessary to use. Troops to the south thereof as they were finishing up their jobs had one order—over and above everything else—that any time they got a chance to jump a bridge over the Rhine or, failing to get a bridge, jump a bridgehead with little boats or swimming or any other way they could get across, to do it and do it quickly. We were sure it would be done because we were certain we could destroy the forces west of the Rhine. General Hodges made a fine dash down onto the Remagen bridgehead—in spite of the fact that the bridge fell later, it rendered tremendous dividends to the Allied cause. General Patton dashed to the Rhine and was enabled to go right on across because the crucifixion of the German force had taken place on this side of the river. That's the thing that has made

possible their present swift advances. I can't tell you where they are right this minute. It's been three or four hours since I left my headquarters. But they are going very rapidly.

In this whole thing possibly I have used the personal pronoun more often than usual this afternoon. I don't mean to belittle in any way the one thing I have always expressed to you: that it's teamwork that wins wars, and that's Allied teamwork and teamwork among the services. The achievement that this Allied force has won is an achievement that is directly traceable to perfection in Allied co-operation, flowing primarily, as far as this force is concerned, from our two great governments, but also remember that the French are contributing very markedly. They are holding all the Rhine in the Alsace area and they have battled their way forward with the rest of us. The two larger forces worked together in Africa, and I am more or less accustomed to speaking of them together. Starting with the governments, flowing on down through my principal subordinates, there's no one that hasn't practiced this very principle and been imbued with it in carrying out his own job, which is the co-operation of air, ground, and sea, of all countries. They do it without stopping to think about personal glory or even, let's say, the glory of his own particular nationality. That is the thing in which I believe and which I know to be the basic cause of the success that has been so far achieved.

I would not have you people think I am writing off this war. No one knows yet what the German can do within his own country and it's certain that he's trying to do everything he possibly can. But it is equally certain that he has suffered defeats since June 6 that he could not afford. He's not in the position today to do what he could have if the great victories this Allied force has achieved had not been so achieved.

I think that I should say a word about the Services of Supply. Since last June 6 the Services of Supply of all countries involved have been faced with problems unprecedented. They have performed marvelously. So much so that they are doing things today that I am quite certain staff colleges of ten years ago would have said absolutely could not be done. I know that is true.

I think that brings us up to date and as usual I am ready to answer questions.

QUESTION: Do you consider that the main German defensive line in the West has now definitely been broken?

ANSWER: I know their main defensive line has been broken. I know that. But it doesn't mean that all our troubles are over, because we have many logistic and maintenance problems that will be just as difficult as any we have ever met up to now.

QUESTION: Do you think it's possible for them to establish another co-ordinated defensive line in view of what has happened?

ANSWER: They need more strength than they have on the West now.

QUESTION: When you were here before, you spoke of the fact you didn't often get a weather break. Do you think you have had one?

ANSWER: Yes.

QUESTION: Have you changed your opinion of when things are really going to crack?

ANSWER: I don't recall the exact words I may have used then, but I would—at any particular moment. I would say the German as a military force on the Western Front, and not considering anything else he might bring to bear, is a whipped enemy. But that doesn't mean there cannot be a front formed somewhere at that point where our maintenance becomes stretched to the limit and where his means can be brought to bear to better effect. To give you an example of what I mean: In the

fall of 1941, how many of you right here thought that the Russians could hold out another four weeks? But by retreating and retreating the Russians finally got to the point where the German armies could go no farther and the Russians could begin to rehabilitate their own forces. I'm not saying that any force, with the maintenance facilities we have now and with the obstacles we have to cover, can rush right square to Berlin. I don't say that for a minute and I don't want you people by any manner or means to report me as coming here and exulting and overoptimistic and ready to start waving flags and ringing bells. We have accomplished a great preliminary portion of our job, and if the German can bring no more to bear he can't make a front for long.

QUESTION: Last time you were here you said if the Germans couldn't hold the Ruhr that the organized resistance would probably fold up quickly.

ANSWER: As I recall, I said that if the German lost Silesia and the Saar and the Ruhr—of which the Ruhr was most important—that the power of Germany to continue war, short of some new invention that doesn't need heavy industries, could not be prolonged over a long period.

QUESTION: What I am trying to get at— if they did form another line in the West, wouldn't that line have to be back of the Ruhr? Wouldn't they have lost those industries?

ANSWER: I should say so.

QUESTION: General, you said earlier we have ended one phase and are entering another. Could you give us a quotable phrase defining the one ended and also the one to come?

ANSWER: What I meant to make clear was that the Rhine was a tremendous military and geographical feature. When you have driven the German out of all the country west of the Rhine—either destroyed him or driven

him out—that is, from the soldier's
standpoint, the completion of one
phase and the beginning of another. In
other words, I mean to say, without
any apology, and, it's owing to my
troops to say, that the winning of the
victory of the elimination of the German west of the Rhine is one of the
great victories of this war or any other
war.

QUESTION: Would you say from the way
the prisoners are rolling in that the
majority of the German Army is giving
up now, that they don't want to fight
any more?

ANSWER: They give up under conditions
they deem a bit hopeless. If you come
at them at the front and they have got
a chance in their steel and concrete
pillboxes to shoot their machine guns
they still do it. But as their manpower
gets thinner and thinner, our penetrations surround them. Then the prisoners come in more frequently than they
did at one time. Not all of them, after
all, are SS troops, nor do all of them,
like Raemck at Brest, fight to the bitter end.

QUESTION: Do you have any idea with
whom we are going to negotiate unconditional surrender?

ANSWER: This is my honest opinion—
there will be no negotiated unconditional surrender. It will be an imposed
unconditional surrender. I believe that
the Allied Armies and the Russians
from the East have to take over everything, and that will be unconditional
surrender.

QUESTION: Under what German personalities will it be imposed? Will surrender be broadcast on the air generally?
Will there be any government through
which they can communicate?

ANSWER: This is a military conference
today, not political. But I should say
this: our experience to date leads to
the view that you have got to take
each locality, go in and establish an

order over it that can prevail until
finally that time comes when our governments can decide what must be
done. The first thing is to establish
order, and we are going to have to do
that with force of arms.

QUESTION: To what extent did the previous Russian offensive make our rapid
advance possible?

ANSWER: The Russians attacked on January 12. By that time Rundstedt was
in complete retreat out of his bulge,
had given up the effort, and was going
out as fast as he could. When they
saw the weight of the Russian blows
they got out the battered remnants of
the Sixth Panzer Army and rushed it to
the East. With that gone, we were
certain we'd succeed in all of the plan
that we had laid out for this west-of-
the-Rhine offensive. One of the advantages of cleaning out the German all
the way west of the Rhine was that it
exposed him everywhere. He couldn't
tell where we were going to attack. Any
bridge or bridgehead we could seize
anywhere was a threat to him. While
we prepared methodically and with a
lot of power to get ready to cross in
that area close to the Ruhr, after we
had once driven him out then he was
very much more extended. Had he not
been forced to take out the Sixth
Panzer Army our task would have been
more difficult definitely. So there is no
question about the two attacks each
having a good effect upon the other.

QUESTION: Do you attach any importance to the civilians attacking American troops in the Third Army sector?

ANSWER: I can tell you what I have told all
my Army Commanders, for which I take
full responsibility, that resistance of
that kind will be dealt with sternly and
on the spot. I will not tolerate civilians,
people out of uniform bearing arms,
firing on our troops.

QUESTION: How far do you think we shall
have to go before it is necessary for the

Germans to pull out of northern Holland?

ANSWER: We have gone a long way and they haven't pulled out of Saint-Nazaire.

QUESTION: They are not firing V-bombs from Saint-Nazaire.

ANSWER: That's true. But I should say this, that if he follows his usual practices he will hang on to those places that are ports and try to fortify himself in there, well knowing that no commander can easily afford to detach troops from his principal efforts and go back and do something which in my own mind I can do later. Sometimes those things are important enough to go back and do if you either need a port or they are firing V-bombs. I believe if you cut off all the lines of communications that let his V-bombs go into Holland to be fired that soon there will be none. I haven't talked to Air Chief Marshal on this but I don't believe the Germans have big stocks of V-bombs lying ready at any sites.

MARSHAL TEDDER: I'm quite sure you are right.

GENERAL EISENHOWER: The cutting of the communications would stop that effort soon.

QUESTION: Why has the German kept the Channel Islands and these other places? What is his object?

ANSWER: To some extent they were cut off. You see, he was using secondary troops in many of these parts and they didn't have mobility. The RAF and the Eighth Air Force had been operating on his oil, his communications, and his motor transport for a long time. He could not afford to give to every garrisoning division that mobility which is necessary to conduct a war of maneuver. We have profited by it all the time. He saw he couldn't get his troops out and the next best thing was to keep them there and annoy us by being a festering sore and working on us as long

as he possibly could. I think it is partly because he couldn't get them out and partly because he saw it was a very good way to annoy us.

QUESTION: Do you see a possibility that on a future date you will be able to issue to us a clean-cut announcement that at such and such a time organized resistance in Germany has been broken?

ANSWER: I can say that there will be a day to come that I can say that for the Western Front.

QUESTION: How is nonfraternization working out?

ANSWER: There is fraternization and it would be silly to deny it, but the general conduct of our troops all the way from the extreme left flank to the extreme right in public has been almost exemplary as far as I am concerned. Just within the past few days I have been from almost one flank to the other and I am amazed with the way the soldiers go about their business and pay no attention to civilians. I would be the last one to deny that soldiers don't get in the back door and get Rhine wine and whatever else they are after, but I do say that the thing so far while the battle is going on has been well observed by our soldiers.

Incidentally, there is one point that has been discussed in the American press far more than in the British and French press. It involves comparisons of equipment. Some very broad statements have been made that seventy-five per cent of the equipment used by the Allies is definitely inferior to the equipment used by the Germans. Of course, that is silly. But it's perfectly true that when the Tiger and the Panther tanks appeared upon the battlefield there came against us a tank that in a tank-to-tank duel was capable of knocking ours out, particularly at extreme ranges. Also there is one other item of equipment in which they have comparatively held the

edge—their bazookas are more penetrating. Remember this: when the British Eighth Army was fighting its way
back across the desert the Sherman
tank was the greatest tank on the battlefield, by all odds. The German began
to try to find something with which
he could stop it. He developed a tank
which in many of its characteristics is
a defensive tank. Nevertheless, it's a
very fine piece of mechanism. Then
our people started to get something to
beat that. Our effort, of course, is not
to fight his tanks with our tanks. If
we possibly can we fight his tanks with
our antitank weapons while our tanks
go on to rip up his infantry and try to
encircle and defeat him. That can't
always happen. If you make a penetration the German will meet you with
his most mobile weapons. New tanks
have appeared on the battlefield and
so far both British and Americans are
handling themselves well; I should say
definitely that if this war unfortunately
lasts a number of weeks longer there
will be items of ours on the battlefield
that will lick that fellow head to head
in a duel. You see, once we started to
produce Sherman tanks—and with
mass-production methods used in the
United States and England, you
couldn't stop production and start on a
new one overnight—the question facing the armament people was, "Shall
we go on and produce a pretty good
tank in great numbers or stop and not
have anything in an effort to get something that head on could beat the
Panther or Tiger?" It's my opinion
that our people in the rear, both producing countries, have pursued the very
best policy, which was to produce a
good tank in numbers. In that way we
could always overwhelm the other fellow if necessary, while our home fronts
went about the business of producing
an even better tank individually than
the best the Germans had.

QUESTION: In the tactical operation we
are in now isn't the Sherman quite
good?
ANSWER: Once you break through and
are not meeting the other fellow's tank
I think every tank commander would
rather have the Sherman. They would
rather have our new light tank, the
M-24, than anything else. The tank
sergeant and the tank lieutenant when
he talks about the quality of tanks he
means, "When I meet the fellow in a
village street." In that circumstance
we would be idle to say that the Sherman can meet the Panther or Tiger on
equal terms. That is as it has been up
to date.
QUESTION: As a point of historical interest, may I ask whether the attack
one-two-three from the north was in
the plan of battle of the Rhine from
the start or whether you modified that,
say, from the experience of the Rundstedt break-through?
ANSWER: You put your finger on it. The
general conception was there as early as
August. Now, you will recall that when
we started that process we tried to pick
a place by penetrating the line so we
could get at his exposed flanks. You
remember that following the September thrust at Arnhem the 21st Army
Group was very busy taking Antwerp
and tidying up that whole flank. They
were not available to start in from the
north, so the First Army and the Ninth
Army started in to attack. The weather
got in the way, the weather and floods
on the Roer. We said we would attack
in the Saar and Patton kept attacking
and driving the German back. We were
determined to break through in one of
these places to get a flank. About in
December Rundstedt, when he came
through, created a situation that
brought our strength away from the
Saar and some of it away from that
area in which we had been attacking
on the Roer. With Rundstedt defeated

we knew we were in a good position. There was no change in plan. 21st Army Group was ready to start an attack that had been planned early last fall. Now we could start it exactly as it should have been started in the beginning. When the Ninth Army broke through and exposed that flank we were absolutely certain of what we could do from there on.

QUESTION: Has the crossing of the Rhine gone more quickly and at less cost to us than expected?

ANSWER: The 69th Division on the first day of their crossing lost fifteen killed and the 30th lost sixteen killed. Yes. We could not expect in that extreme northern angle—with the restricted places and tremendous fortifications— we could not expect to destroy the fellow in the north like farther south, where we had room for maneuver, where we could pierce his lines and surround him. He got a lot of the paratroop army out. The paratroop army was reinforced by the Fifteenth Panzer and 116th Panzer. I expected greater losses.

QUESTION: Do you think there is anything left in the West beyond what we are engaging now or meeting now?

ANSWER: A few odd units that are not engaged, but there is no power in the West within the area . . . let's have this off the record. I'll put it this way: there is no power of the German forces in the West that is in the area that our maintenance will allow us to operate that can withstand our forces.

QUESTION: Do you anticipate a switch of forces from the East to the West?

ANSWER: I cannot tell. I am sure that the Russians will never allow it if conditions will let them attack. Now, if the German should figure that the deep frost they have in that country renders the ground unsuitable for deep thrusts for some weeks he might try his old

game. I'll tell you this, if he does it again, all I ask for is good weather because our air will take care of it.

QUESTION: Do you think they might bring some troops up from Italy for that last stand in southern Germany?

ANSWER: If they do, our troops in Italy will be on their heels so fast they won't know what's happened to them. We have a big air force down there, too.

QUESTION: Is there time now for the Germans to bring forces from Russia or Italy to form a new line in the West?

ANSWER: As I pointed out before, if they keep their forces together and bring up reinforcements, when we get to the end of our maintenance possibilities they could put up a battle. You mustn't expect, in spite of the marvelous performance by the Engineers all along this river, that we can throw railway bridges across in a matter of two or three days. Caesar did it in two or three days, but his bridges didn't have to carry railroads.

By the way, in the Seventh Army there is a Colonel Mason Young, Engineer, and, under promises of enough champagne or something else for his men, not for himself, he got a bridge over the Rhine in ten hours and eleven minutes—a treadway bridge. As far as I know, that is a pretty good record.

QUESTION: Do you know where he's from? *

ANSWER: No.

QUESTION: Is our advance out of Normandy and Brittany and across France up to Metz and Nancy about the same measure of our maintenance capability?

ANSWER: Not the same conditions, because, you see, in the weeks we spent in the bridgehead from June 6 to July 25 we built up a terrific maintenance and supply. But that was on this side of the obstacle of the Channel. Now the main-

* A meticulous reporter.

tenance we have built up is on the wrong side of the obstacle. Not quite the same thing, you see.

QUESTION: What is the extent of the maintenance area—how far beyond the Rhine?

ANSWER; I think that our Com Zone and —I forget what you call it—the supply administration in the British forces— will be able to support by truck one hundred and fifty miles from the nearest railheads. I would ask you not to quote that figure.

QUESTION: What is the extent of co-operation between your armies on the Western Front and the Russians?

ANSWER: You mean the strength of the armies? The forces under my command today—this is not to be repeated—is about four million six hundred thousand persons. Now, just what the Russian has I don't know. That is, again, off the record.

QUESTION: Do you know if the weather on the Russian side's impeding operations?

ANSWER: I think it's more the ground than the weather. I saw a Russian general about three days ago and he told me that the conditions, unless they were vastly different from any other year, would be pretty bad for the next several weeks. You couldn't maneuver except on the roads. He did hold out this one point, that the roads in eastern Germany and western Poland are better than they were in eastern Poland and in Russia. So it might be that the Russians can still operate.

QUESTION: Do you expect the end in the west without any very great battle?

ANSWER: No. I think we will have some darn tough fighting. Whether it could be classed as a battle, where we can again bring into play all our forces in a well-co-ordinated attack—I would scarcely expect that. But there will be some very tough battling, particularly in the north.

QUESTION: Who do you think will be into Berlin first, the Russians or us?

ANSWER: Well, I think mileage alone ought to make them do it. After all, they are thirty-three miles and we are two hundred and fifty. I wouldn't want to make any prediction. They have a shorter race to run, although they are faced by the bulk of the German forces.

QUESTION: How far do you think the Germans could fall back eastwards before they would actually disintegrate?

ANSWER: They will have no intention of going off like a covey of quail. What they will try to do is pick some line toward which they can pivot. If you are of the school who believe they are going to defend the south of Germany I would expect them to fight delaying actions in the south while swinging rapidly from the north, possibly on both flanks. If you feel that their access to the sea is desperately important to them, then they will hang on desperately in the north. I certainly believe that they can't hope in the West to hold their line throughout and they will not attempt just to retire gradually on an even basis all the way. They won't do that.

QUESTION: What is your school of thought?

ANSWER: This is what I think, and it's not based on military reason—it's based on what the German has done in this war. I believe, as far as he is able, he's going to stand and fight where he can. At this stage it doesn't make sense, but there is nothing else he can do. When we once demonstrated with the attack of 21st Army Group and the Ninth Army that we could break through the defense west of the Rhine and he was exposed, any sensible soldier would have gone back to the Rhine and given us the Saar and stood there and said, "Now try to come across." They simply seem to want to stand and fight where they are. Starting on March 1, if they had gotten out the bulk of their force they would have been better off.

QUESTION: What is your opinion of the activity of the Luftwaffe?

ANSWER: My air man told me this morning that in one area they ran into two airplanes and in another area two airplanes. Among other things, you see, the Air Force always has the job of keeping the other air force out of the skies, and one of the best ways is constantly to drench his airdromes. We know we make it difficult for him to get off his fields for three or four days at a time and when the time is ripe we do it again. Once when you have the superiority we have it's very difficult for the other fellow to operate. I don't mean to say that he can't some morning come from the center of Germany and make a raid like that in Belgium on Christmas Day. But look what he paid for it. He paid fully half of the forces sent out. So the Luftwaffe itself if let alone and allowed to recuperate would again be an important factor, but not when you see the way our boys are watching them.

QUESTION: How would you assess the German Ardennes offensive?

ANSWER: The costliest mistake they have made since the decision to stand in the beachhead, particularly after we broke through at Avranches and they "obstinated," as the Prime Minister says, in their counterattacks from Mortain to Avranches.

QUESTION: I wonder whether you or the Air Chief Marshal could say how soon it will be before Allied aircraft are operating from airfields to the east of the Rhine?

ANSWER (TEDDER): We will be using fields there tomorrow morning.

QUESTION: Would you say that that decision, the one to fight west of the Rhine, was influenced by Hitler or by the German General Staff?

ANSWER: I think it was Hitler. I am guessing because I must confess that many times in this war I have been wrong in trying to evaluate that German mind, if it is a mind. When it looks logical for him to do something he does something else. But you people who were with me in Tunisia, after April 20, when he was trying to pour stuff into Tunisia, the air boys shot down twenty of their 120-men transports. Fantastic, but he tried to do it.

QUESTION: Each case is followed by the removal of an officer.

ANSWER: Probably removed because he wasn't successful. After all, a man like Hitler has to have a goat.

QUESTION: Would you say there is anything in the present operations that supports a very widely held theory that the Germans in the last resort would hold the Russians and let the Western Allies through?

ANSWER: Of course, again, if the Germans were reasoning like normal human beings they would realize the whole history of the United States and Great Britain is to be generous toward a defeated enemy. We observe all the laws of the Geneva Convention. Yet he gathered up his only mobile reserves when he knew the Russian was going to attack and came over and did his best to defeat us in the Ardennes. I don't know whom he considers his worst enemy in this war.

AIR CHIEF MARSHAL: I agree. I think he's irrational.

QUESTION: Do you think, General, that the Germans are quite disturbed that we put airborne forces down so close to the Rhine in this operation?

ANSWER: They may have been. They have been deceived in the strength of the Sixth Army Group, the strength of the French and Seventh Armies in the south. They were deceived on that. They thought their troops were free to maneuver. They were deceived on that as to the strength of the XII Corps attack as it came down from the mouth of the Moselle; they were deceived as to the strength of the XX Corps. They didn't know we had packed six divisions in the attack. They were probably deceived as to where that airborne attack was coming down. It came down on their artillery positions and before they knew it their defenses were captured.

QUESTION: Does that suggest a breakdown in their Intelligence?

ANSWER: To some extent. I should say their Intelligence and their calculations, both of them.

I know I have mentioned some names here today, and just for fear I might have omitted someone, I'd like to express to you for your own information, not for quotation, but so you understand me thoroughly, that there never has been a commander in history who has been blessed with better lieutenants than I. You can start on the north and you can go right down through to the south and there's not a commander I'd change. You can go into the Air Forces, and there's no one that I would trade. The same thing applies to the sea and all the way through. While it's my responsibility to determine, let's say, sketch in the rough outline of the great picture we are trying to paint, each man has been given his job and he's the one whose skill and devotion to duty fill in the picture. Now, as I say, I just think I

may have mentioned some names today. I want to say I don't make comparisons among my commanders anywhere. So far as I'm concerned they are all the ones I want. That is very earnest and not to be quoted. It's just for you people to think about as you write. I'll even go so far today as to praise people to their faces. Such trouble as I have ever had in press relations in this war have never sprung certainly, with very, very minor exceptions, from within our own group here. My troubles usually come from the headline writers at home. I have had certain of you people come to me and complain as much about them as I have myself. I think we have had a very fine team up to this stage and it's because of my confidence in that team, and that includes you people, that we are going through with this thing to a real victory.

QUESTION: May we hope to see you before the victory party?

ANSWER: Actually, last time I told the PRO I thought I'd never come back here again. We began to figure out ways and that we could perhaps put you on a train and bring you someplace eastward, but there's a lot of you people. It's a little awkward. I don't know whether the PRO has thought of moving his installations further eastward before final victory. I'll say this: when that day comes I'll meet you somewhere if you will come to the party.

Any of you want to put the Air Chief Marshal on the rack? No? Then goodby and good luck till I see you again.

After the conference, we stopped at a small projection room on the Champs-Elysées for a private preview of the official film eventually to be issued about operations from D-Day to some appropriate time when the picture can be ended. The date for ending has been advanced from time to time as the campaign has progressed and now may be delayed until Germany gives up. This is the picture that Lieutenant Colonel Harlan

Miller and Wing Commander Nickolls interviewed the General about
months ago to get his views as to strategy.*

Brigadier William Turner, Deputy Director of PRD, is in charge of
film activities. He had our people immediately concerned with production
of the picture on hand to meet the General. After the film, which I
thought extraordinarily good, General Ike made some suggestions. General Bradley had been omitted, which he thought should be corrected,
and insufficient attention had been paid to the landings in southern
France. Couldn't these be illustrated by animated charts? He made a few
other minor suggestions, all of which were noted by the Brigadier's
staff.

We had a pleasant bull session last night at the Raphaël. Ike's stopping
over with me was in the nature of an experiment, I having told him he
could stay there without attracting attention, and this proved to be correct.
Although Pierre, the obliging manager of the Raphaël, assigned the Supreme Commander the "ambassador's suite" on the fourth floor, I had
arranged for use of a small bedroom opening off my living room and it
was here the Supreme Commander slept.

We didn't talk much about the war, but he told me about his recent
trip to the front, where he had watched from a church tower his Allied
armies of British, Canadian, and American troops start the major crossing
of the Rhine. He had slipped off on this trip with only Mickey, who served
as aide, orderly, driver, and confidant. In this crossing he had another
combination of land, sea, and air forces. He had gotten a great kick out
of seeing the LCVPs of the U. S. and Royal Navies carrying infantry
across the river. The landing craft had been trucked overland for the
naval operation. The air had "done its stuff," not only in the usual
ground-support fashion, but with paratroopers and gliders. He had stayed
up most of the night to see the preliminary bombardment by 1250 guns.
He said this was an especially interesting sight because all the guns were
spread out on a plain. The flashes from one end of the line to the other
were all plainly visible.

MARCH, 1945: *Allied armies, continuing swift advance in Germany, took
München-Gladbach, Rheydt, Neuss, Krefeld, Cologne, Coblenz; swept deep
into Germany against dwindling resistance after trapping five or six German
divisions between Coblenz and Remagen. American First Army seized intact
Remagen Bridge across Rhine, established vital bridgehead. One thousand
U. S. tanks routed 80,000 Germans in battle within Saar-Moselle-Rhine*

---

* The True Glory.

triangle. Incessant heavy bombing blanketed Germany from east to west fronts, destroying production centers, supply dumps, and communications. Red Army offensives rolled forward with capture of Stargard, Lauenburg, Kolberg, Neustadt, Gdynia, Danzig, reaching Baltic on one side and Austrian border on the other. Huge stockpiling operations were rushed to prepare for final drive against Germany. U. S. Fifth in Italy took control of roads from Bologna to Pistoia and Florence. Philippine invasions continued successfully; by month's end Yanks were twelve miles from Baguio on Luzon, had taken capital of Negros, controlled most of Mindanao; MacArthur reported 90,000 Japs destroyed on Luzon. Bombers raided Formosa, B-29s plastered Tokyo, Kobe, and Nagoya. Carrier planes and naval forces attacked Kure and Kobe and Jap convoys off Ryukyus, hitting seventeen warships and six carriers, sinking and damaging thirteen freighters, while destroying 417 planes. U. S. fleet continued its nine-day-old attack upon Okinawa. Mandalay and Myittha fell to British. (General Ike was setting the stage for the historic double envelopment.—H.C.B.)

PARIS, SUNDAY, APRIL 1, 1945

Ike was immensely pleased that the campaign west of the Rhine, which he and his commanders had planned last summer and which he had insisted was necessary preliminary to a deep penetration east of the Rhine, had been executed so closely in accordance with the conception.*

One thing that had given him special pleasure was that Field Marshal Sir Alan Brooke, who had once argued heatedly against the plan, had generously told him on the banks of the Rhine, as the crossing was in progress, that he, General Ike, was right and that his current plans and operations are well calculated to meet the current situation.

The news was so good that General Ike felt a tremendous relief. The great defeats, in some cases complete destruction, inflicted by our troops on the Germans west of the Rhine have left the Germans so badly depleted in strength they can scarcely muster enough manpower to cause any serious trouble east of the Rhine.

The victories west of the Rhine, he felt, made possible the bold and relatively easy advances that both Hodges' First and Patton's Third Armies are now making toward Kassel. General Ike didn't wish to sound boastful, but he was like a football coach whose team had just won a big victory and he couldn't help talking about the accomplishments of his players.

---

* When we reached the Rhine the VGDIPs, the VIPIs (very important personages indeed), the VIPs, and the GIs observed the ceremony which later caused the day to become known as P-Day.

SHAEF FORWARD (RHEIMS), MONDAY, APRIL 2, 1945

Just as I was leaving the American Express this morning, Lieutenant Colonel Thor Smith handed me the latest air-mail edition of *Time* and said I would be interested in the article about Patton and Mauldin. I certainly am. Will Lang's story was rewritten in New York, for the piece now says that Butcher "ordered" Patton and Mauldin to get together. I hope I see Patton before he sees the magazine.

Ike was in an expansive mood today and, as usual, tossed bouquets of credit in all directions.

Monty had done a fine job crossing the Rhine and always could be relied upon to hold what he took, but in our latest spectacular successes, in which elements of the U. S. First Army had advanced northward almost to Paderborn, Hodges, Ike thought, had been the spearhead and the scintillating star. Before that, Hodges' drive southeast from Cologne and the capture of Remagen bridge had excited the admiration of the Supreme Commander, who felt that the First Army's assignment had been perhaps the most difficult of any U. S. formation.

General Ike said he would like very much to see Hodges get credit in the United States for his great work, but as an Allied Commander, he is always embarrassed himself, or might create embarrassment to others, if he publicly singles out any one commander on the whole front for particular commendation.

Not only Hodges' but Bradley's magnificent contribution in this campaign, General Ike advised, should be painted in more brilliant colors. Bradley has never held back and never has "paused to regroup" when he saw an opportunity to advance. General Ike praised his energy, common sense, tactical skill, and complete loyalty, and said that these qualities made Bradley a great lieutenant on whom he had always relied with greatest confidence.

In praising Hodges and Bradley, the Supreme Commander did not want to be misunderstood as deprecating the accomplishments of other Army commanders, because all, he felt, have performed in the finest fashion. Patton, being colorful and audacious, drew the headlines in the American press, while Monty, likewise colorful and always "good copy," led the parade of black type in England. Simpson had performed most creditably, and Devers and Patch have played their roles superbly. However, Ike was trying to place in proper perspective the contribution of Hodges and Bradley, who, he felt, seemingly are overlooked by correspondents and headline writers at home.

A Nibble from Kesselring

PARIS, THURSDAY, APRIL 5, 1945

General Alexander has had a nibble from intermediaries who say the Germans want to quit in Italy. After some preliminary talks, he notified the Combined Chiefs; told them the development of the intrigue, and appraised the approach as apparently sincere. The Russians evidently were not notified and had protested.

The story at SHAEF isn't too clear to me, as we only have a part of the story, but it seems that while so-called agents of Kesselring were approaching Alexander's staff, other German agents were feeding information to the Russians that the Western Allies were about to make a separate peace. The inference is that the Germans were thus seeking a separate peace with the Russians. Stalin bluntly told the story to the President and the Prime Minister and the President has sent a hot wire to Stalin asking, in effect, what kind of ally do you think we are? The upshot is that if there are any other approaches from German emissaries seeking peace, we are to notify the Russians immediately, so they can have a responsible representative present at any and all discussions.

Around the Ruhr Pocket

PARIS, SUNDAY, APRIL 8, 1945

Corporal Street got us to Luxembourg last Monday night, where Scott-Bailey, Pinkley, and I stayed at the Alfa Hotel. On Tuesday we lunched at Captain Jack Reading's press camp in a château near the city. Jack took us to see General Bradley, who, as always, was kind and courteous. He sat us down in front of his operations map and described the progress of the battle. He said that the Allies now could go anyplace any time in western Germany because the Reich is undergoing mass destruction. He said that if Kesselring, who, we hear, now commands the ground forces in front of us, reports the true situation, he must inform the German High Command that the Wehrmacht can no longer hold any line.

I was amused at General Bradley when he replied to my question as to when and where his tactical and main headquarters would move forward, this being important to PRD plans. He said he had intended to move to Bad Ems. In peacetime, it is a popular watering place, just east of Coblenz. But the Air Force, not being privy to his plans, unfortunately had bombed all the good buildings.

From Luxembourg, we drove northeast through Bitburg, Prüm, Blankenheim, Euskirchen, and Bonn, en route to Bad Godesberg to spend the night at the First Army press camp. Euskirchen is a principal railroad and road center with scores of high smokestacks. It is one of the centers on which Tooey's heavy bombers had made a "blanket call" to help First Army to the Rhine. As we approached the city, we could see so many smokestacks that we wondered how efficient had been the bombing, but when we reached the industrial area, we found the factories mangled, burning, and torn. Oddly, the smokestacks did not appear affected, although their bases were surrounded by wrecked buildings.

At Bad Godesberg, we found the correspondents and public-relations officers had moved forward to be closer to the front, but we were put up at their former press camp in a hotel which, in happier days for the Germans, had had Hitler as one of its distinguished guests.

As there was no mess in the hotel, we prepared to have our chow on C rations in our room. Scott-Bailey had heard there was a wine cellar, which, upon investigation, we found had been thoroughly scrounged by previous visitors. In a murky, damp corner, I found a bottle that looked attractive. In the room Scott opened it and, being something of a judge of wine, said he would tell us which year of Moselle it might be. He put the bottle to his lips, took a good swig, and nearly exploded. He had lost his voice. The "wine" was mentholated spirit—cooking alcohol. When Scott recovered we poured some in a metal ash tray, lit the stuff, and it burned long enough to heat water in a mess cup to make Nescafé. We liberated some linen tablecloths.

It was a moonlight night, which by itself made the Rhine and the high hills on either side beautiful to see. Great floodlights swept the river to detect saboteurs or rafts bearing explosives, floating downstream, intended to strike our pontoon bridges. In the beam of one light, a white church and spire glistened on the opposite bank. It looked like a scene on an old-fashioned sparkling Christmas card.

Scott-Bailey achieved his objective when we crossed the Rhine Wednesday morning on a pontoon bridge a few hundred yards downstream from the famous Remagen bridge, with its center span, now hanging from its stone piers, twisted and crumpled. General Bradley told us that at the time the bridge fell, it had not been used for five days, as pontoon bridges already were in service. Engineers with their welding torches were working feverishly to bolster its steel beams, which, Bradley said, had stood up under enemy shelling and bombings only by virtue of its safety factor. Another twenty-four hours and it would have stood for generations. Now it was a monument to bravery, not only of those who daringly raced across it to gain the bridgehead, but to the engineers who fell to their death when the span collapsed.

Landing craft and other small boats of the U. S. Navy were plying up and down across the river, which seemed as peaceful as the Navy training base at the Great Lakes.

As we turned eastward from the river over the hills on a narrow road to the *Autobahn* we could see many signs of fighting. The Germans had dug in in many places and there were the usual burned-out tanks and abandoned fieldpieces, not to mention trucks, deserted foxholes, wearing apparel, and, here and there, a black cross. These signs of battle, particularly burned-out vehicles, which one sees on many roads in France, Belgium, Luxembourg, and Germany, have become commonplace.

Reaching the *Autobahn*, the first I'd seen, I found it a two-lane super-highway with a grass parkway in the center. There were numerous bridges or underpasses to cross it and, as we sped southward toward Frankfurt, we saw that the Germans had blown up most of the overpasses. These fell on the *Autobahn*, but the engineers with bulldozers had cleared at least one-way passage. There were some detours or, as Scott-Bailey called them, diversions, because bridges of the *Autobahn* itself had been blown up and, because of work of higher priority, had not been repaired by our engineers.

Frankfurt was all the RAF and the 8th Air Force said it was, but seeing is most convincing. While Street changed a tire, we wandered into a factory building. There were two main workrooms, each perhaps 200 feet long and 100 wide. The building was severely damaged and machinery had been removed, but the thing that interested me most was a cement blockhouse in the wall between the two large workrooms. In it one guard with a gun could watch the workers, no doubt slaves, in both rooms.

I asked General Patton if he had seen the latest issue of *Time*. He hadn't. So I read to him the part where I was reported as having "ordered" him, a three-star general, to make peace with a three-stripe GI. Fortunately, he enjoyed my discomfiture at the misquotation, but when I read him the last paragraph, which said that Mauldin felt he had not convinced General Patton and was certain that Patton hadn't convinced him, that was too much. In his high-pitched voice, he said:

"Why, if that little s.o.b. ever comes in the Third Army area again, I'll throw him in jail."

Patton went on to say that, in the last war, the British Army had been hurt by the cartoons of Bairnsfather, originator of the famous "Better 'Ole," and the effect of Mauldin's characterization of American soldiers was likewise adversely affecting the discipline of the GIs. Such disrespect for military discipline should not be encouraged, particularly in *Stars and Stripes*. He concluded the topic abruptly with a statement that he was certain I couldn't change his mind and he assumed that he couldn't change mine.

We checked our road map against the latest at Third Army and found we could drive to Paderborn, where we could turn west and follow the main supply route of the Ninth Army until we recrossed the Rhine at Wesel. The official map showed a corridor of perhaps ten miles between the Ruhr pocket and a patch of enemy about Korbach, in First Army territory, which may or may not be clear. We were trying to reach the First Army's press camp, which we understood was at Marsberg. This we found, on the map, located about fifteen miles south of Paderborn. We were cautioned as we left Patton's headquarters that there had been some sniping along the road. In fact, Major General Hobart R. Gay, Patton's Chief of Staff, had been taking a quiet walk in a field near his caravan the night before and had been sniped at but not hit. Patton had ordered burned the two houses closest to the shooting.

The Germans were making a desperate attempt to get out of the Ruhr pocket and were fighting toward the east. Following our map carefully, we stayed in the corridor that showed clear of the enemy. I recalled that Ed Beattie and Wright Bryan had been captured near Chaumont last fall because of faulty road information.

We passed some batteries of American artillery along the road as we passed into Frankenberg, and I figured we must be four or five miles from the Ruhr front. But in the town we saw at the main crossroad two bodies of GIs and a couple of dead horses, which were convincing signs that the town recently had been under enemy artillery fire. Crews of tanks waiting on the road seemed alert, but we passed on, having checked our map to make certain we were on the proper road.

We were approaching the next town, Winterberg, which we could see down the valley was under shell fire. Buildings were burning and there were sounds of small-arms fire. Rounding a bend, we found three American tanks knocked out and the road blocked with other tanks waiting for our artillery to complete its preparation for their plunge into the town when the disabled tanks were removed. We decided we had gone far enough on this road, and Street managed to turn and head back.

While he turned, I talked to a tank crew and found there was a lively fight in progress and that the road had been under enemy fire—and that the small bridge we had just crossed had been a principal target. In crossing that bridge, we had squeezed past a still-burning Tiger.

We retreated with dignity and without wasting time. As we again approached the bridge in question, we met infantrymen slogging up to the battle on either side of the road. Street, a one-time machine-gunner, commented:

"First time I ever got ahead of the God-damned infantry in a staff car."

Checking in at the first battalion headquarters, Pinkley and I obtained a new route through Korbach which had just been reported clear of the enemy. We were told that someone in Korbach could give us a road clear of the enemy to our objective—Marsberg. We found an American major, who was looking· after civilian affairs and awaiting arrival of a Military Government team. While in his office, the janitor of the building entered the room, unconsciously saluted, and said: "Heil Hitler."

At Marsberg, we found that the First Army's press camp was at Marburg —a town through which we had passed about lunchtime. Fortunately, we were at the headquarters of General J. Lawton Collins, VII Corps, whom I had last seen in the Cherbourg Peninsula. General Collins made us welcome, gave us a fine dinner, and put us up for the night.

We set out the next morning for the Ninth Army press camp near Gladbach, where we arrived midafternoon. We had passed through Paderborn, which is a city, I judge, about the size of Cedar Rapids, Iowa. The RAF had paid the city a lasting call about three days previously to assist the Ninth Army's advance. Now it was in complete shambles. Bulldozers had pushed one-way passages through for motor supply trucks moving east and empties moving west. The press camp of Ninth Army was in a château, but most of the correspondents were forward with corps and divisions. Their copy was being flown back by liaison planes, which dropped it in weighted bags, hoping to hit the château, but occasionally tossing one into the near-by canal. Here Press Wireless transmitted the stories to New York. Forward communications by wire or radio were practically nil because of the rapid advance.

One of Pinkley's correspondents had interviewed the Archbishop of Münster that day. The Archbishop supposedly had been anti-Hitler. He described himself as a true German. He blamed the war on the Versailles Treaty. He said the British and Americans, particularly the latter, had permitted Germany to suffer from economic conditions and thus had fomented the unrest which led to the assumption of power by Hitler.

It sounded to me like the same old beer-hall propaganda line. I got a copy of the interview to show to General Ike.

We continued to Wesel that afternoon but, unfortunately, took a short cut, described as passable, over which we finally were dragged a distance of two miles by American bulldozers manned by two GIs. We crossed the Rhine over a one-way bridge recently completed by the engineers and, on the western side, found the car bogged down in the heavy ruts made by continual pounding of convoys of two-and-a-half-ton trucks. One of these hooked a chain on us and again we were dragged over three miles of muddy road, with the car's bottom scraping the earth. When we finally were pulled to the hard-surfaced road, the motor ran, but shrieked from the contact of the flywheel with the aluminum casing. Our gasoline tank had been punctured. We had two five-gallon cans of gasoline and by midnight reached Venlo, on the Dutch border, where we were given rooms for the night in a hotel operated by an American supply outfit.

Saturday we made Rheims in time for lunch, Virgil being a guest of T. J. at his mess and I going along with General Ike. He was disturbed by the attitude of the Archbishop, but interpreted it as a sign that all Germans, whether known to be friendly to Hitler or not, would require much education to correct their belief of modern history as taught by Goebbels.

I found that General Ike intended that the next principal move would be to push Bradley's 12th Army Group straight eastward from Kassel to the Leipzig area to split the Germans on the Western Front. When the Russian drive reaches the Dresden-Leipzig area and joins up with the Americans, the division of the Germans will be complete.

Monty's 21st Army Group, strengthened by one American corps, is to clean up the Germans on the northern coast and to push on to Lübeck, on the Baltic Sea, in an effort to prevent the Germans from making a desperate stand in Denmark and Norway.

Devers' 6th Army Group, with Patton's Third Army on its left flank, is to move southeast toward the southern redoubt.

I told the Supreme Commander that I had heard comment from the correspondents, officers, and GIs that they wanted to keep going until they got to Berlin. This desire is rampant. General Ike said that it was much more important militarily to divide the Germans and to prevent them from continuing to fight in Denmark and Norway or in the southern redoubt. He was apprehensive that if Hitler and his small group of Nazi leaders could hole in around Berchtesgaden, they could by radio continue to assert command over outlying garrisons and thus continue the war. The taking of Berlin would be a mere show; what he wanted to do was to end the war as quickly and economically in lives as possible.

Pinkley and I returned to Paris last evening, the Chevy still screeching.

It Wasn't de Gaulle

PARIS, TUESDAY, APRIL 10, 1945

I was at the Express Building, trying to catch up on my planning, when General Ike phoned me from Rheims and asked what I was doing.

I told him nothing much. He said he thought he would come down to spend the night. "Suits me fine," I said. He'd leave the airfield near Rheims in twenty minutes and I could meet him at Orly.

It took me almost as long to drive to Orly as the Supreme Commander needed to fly from Rheims. I told Corporal Street we were going to get the Supreme Commander and take him to the Raphaël.

"You mean we're going to get General Eisenhower in this car?"

Our Chevy had been turned in for repairs and we had been given temporary use of a Ford.

En route to Orly, the Boulevard des Italiens was crowded with people waiting to see someone important. This is the street along which I would have to return with General Ike.

When I reached Orly, I found a French guard with arms stacked, waiting for a VIP. I soon found it was a VGDIP—General de Gaulle himself, whose plane was due to arrive about the same time as that of the Supreme Commander.

In the control office, I arranged to have Major Hansen radioed to taxi the General's plane to the far side of the apron. I found that capable Tex Lee had phoned the secretariat at SHAEF Main at Versailles to have a car standing by for the crew. It was a handsome Packard.

General Ike and the faithful Mickey, with an overnight bag, stepped from the plane to the Ford, and we left Orly by a side exit. We still had to traverse the streets where crowds were lined to greet de Gaulle. The Ford has a large window in the rear, and I was apprehensive lest the Supreme Commander be recognized. But we traveled the entire distance across the city, up the Champs-Elysées to the Raphaël, and not a soul paid him the slightest attention.

Sergeants John Schwartz and Marty Snyder provided a good Army dinner in my room. There wasn't much bothering the General, except that he wanted to get away from the routine of his life at Rheims. At the moment, the only abnormal pressure on him is to combat the desire of those who wish him to rush our forces to Berlin. It may be that for political and psychological reasons, his bosses may direct and alter his plans, but unless he can take Berlin cheaply, without substantially altering his plans to clean up the northern and southern flanks, he will not do so.

Three Stripes Lick Three Stars

PARIS, WEDNESDAY, APRIL 11, 1945

At last things seem happy at *Stars and Stripes*. Today, I had a letter from Lieutenant Colonel Arthur Goodfriend, the editor-in-chief, saying that "Thanks to you, the *S & S* is at long last 'liberated.'" His thanks really are to General Ike, who has taken an intense personal interest in seeing that the staff of *Stars and Stripes* is not pestered by the brass.

To make certain that those above Colonel Goodfriend understood his policy, the Supreme Commander had written the same day to General Oscar Solbert, Chief of Special Services, ETOUSA, a letter which would protect him when he, too, sought to shield the editorial staff. This was followed by a subsequent letter to the Deputy Theater Commander, Lieutenant General Ben Lear, to whom he wrote in part:

A great deal of pressure has been brought on me in the past to abolish such things as Mauldin's cartoons, the "B" Bag, etc. You will make sure that the responsible officer knows he is not to interfere in matters of this kind. If he believes that any specific violation of good sense or good judgment has occurred, he may bring it to my personal attention.

It looks to me as if General Patton may now admit he has lost the battle of Mauldin.

One Man's Story

PARIS, THURSDAY, APRIL 12, 1945

Drove Craig Campbell up to Rheims today, which gave two hours for me to hear his story. Craig said that many of his brother prisoners thought the Russians had not treated them well during the long trip from Poland to Odessa, where they were taken over to Naples by a British ship, but he thought that the Russians had done admirably well in view of their shortages of transportation, food, clothing, and billets.

Craig had joined General Ike's personal staff in Third Army in Texas as a stenographer, and his ability to take shorthand had been put to use in the camp. Over a small secret radio receiver, he listened to BBC and supplied material for a daily clandestine news bulletin.

Lots had been drawn to select personnel who could try to escape. He happened to be among one small group privileged to try. Through the bottom of a latrine, at the end of a barracks, they had stealthily dug a tunnel, hoping to burrow under the barbed-wire enclosure to freedom.

They were about halfway to their goal when the soft soil through which they were digging collapsed and the ranking American officer forbade additional effort. The dirt had been hidden in empty Red Cross boxes in the garret of the barracks. The Germans ultimately discovered the attempt and thereafter detonated heavy charges of explosives around the camp to crush the walls of any other tunnels.

A Hushed Voice

PARIS, FRIDAY, APRIL 13, 1945

I had gone to bed early and was sound asleep when the phone rang last night. It was Bill Estoff, of *Stars and Stripes*. He said in a hushed voice: "Have you heard that Roosevelt died?"

I, of course, hadn't. I was shocked. Bill wanted a statement from General Eisenhower. I told him he could locate General Ike at Third Army headquarters with General Patton, but I doubted if he would wish to issue a statement so quickly and probably would first send a personal message to the family.

Then I immediately tried to get through to make certain Ike had the news, but all lines were engaged.

This morning at the American Express, Whitie, the French elevator man, said plaintively in his halting English:

"I'm so sorry you've lost your President. He was a friend of France."

Everyone from the highest officers to the GIs seemed overwhelmed by the loss of our country's great war leader.

PARIS, SUNDAY, APRIL 15, 1945

General Allen has agreed to release me as Chief of the Planning Branch. Group Captain J. P. Graham will take over the job, having done a large portion of the work, anyway. I am being labeled "Liaison between PRD and the Supreme Commander," which permits me to spend more time with him and also to keep PRD informed of his future plans.

The Prime Wants Ike to Take Berlin

PARIS, WEDNESDAY, APRIL 18, 1945

Drove to Rheims yesterday morning to fly with General Ike to London, where he had an engagement to see the Prime Minister. Ike had just returned from his visit in the forward area with the First and Third Armies. He had taken time to see the collection of German treasures in a salt mine.

I reminded him that once at Gibraltar, he and Wayne Clark had talked of absconding with American expense money if TORCH proved unsuccessful. He said there was plenty of expense money in the German cache, but the gold bars were too heavy to carry. He knew. He'd tried to lift one.

He had gone to one of the German internment camps near Gotha and had seen the horrible treatment given the inmates. He said that their condition beggared description. He had interviewed several through an interpreter and said that their stories of starvation, cruelty, and bestiality were so overpowering that he felt sick. In one room he had seen twenty to thirty naked men killed by starvation. Patton had refused to enter. Said he would upchuck if he did, but Ike said he had forced himself to see the bodies, as he wanted to be able to have firsthand evidence to combat anyone in the future who would say that stories of the atrocities were "propaganda." I told him I thought we should give responsible people at home an opportunity to see the ghastly scenes for themselves. He is planning to ask the War Department to select a group of editors and publishers to visit the camps.

The Supreme Commander is proud of his troops; they and their commanders, he thinks, have developed a "veteran" quality. He doubts if any military organization has ever existed that can reshuffle and regroup on a large scale and still continue offensives without a single pause better than Bradley and his 12th Army Group staff.

Patton is still unpredictable, but remains a great fighting leader in pursuit and exploitation. I told Ike of the flurry at PRD amongst the censors because General Patton had arbitrarily fired one of them for passing stories that we had captured some of the German loot and of an expedition Patton had ordered to liberate some American prisoners. General Ike said he had had this chapter and verse while he was visiting Patton, and had made clear to "Georgie" that he had no right to relieve a SHAEF censor, over whom he has no authority, anyway. Because of Patton's attitude, I knew that three or four correspondents had written bitter articles about him. Unfortunately, they appeared as examples of "Army blundering." Ike had taken Patton's hide off. But I think Patton must have as many hides as a cat has lives, for this is at least the fourth time that General Ike has skinned his champion end runner.

General Ike loaned me his plane, with Major Larry Hansen piloting, to fly from the Bovingdon airfield near London to Bristol, where I visited Buddy Early at the 74th General Hospital—about a thirty-minute drive north of the city. Buddy's wound is healing satisfactorily and his doctor told me that with good luck eventually Buddy would not even limp. He is anxious to get back to his division, which is going great guns in Germany, but the wounded are being returned to the States. Buddy eventually hopes to catch up with the 65th in the Pacific.

I had a date with General Ike to meet him at Telegraph Cottage at 6 o'clock to ride with him to 10 Downing. The sergeant driver, sent by always obliging Captain G. L. Tolhurst, of PRD Rear, to take me from Bovingdon to the cottage, got lost and we were two hours making the drive. I have made the trip a few times and should have known the way, but I didn't mind getting lost because of the beauty of the English countryside. I noticed, too, the people's faces. Once they seemed haunted; now they are smiling and cheerful. Flying bombs are a thing of the past and even the rockets have subsided. The English citizens unconsciously show their relief.

Of course, I missed going with Ike, but he returned before midnight. The Prime Minister wants him to take Berlin and Ike sees no military sense in it.

This morning I drove with him to the annex of 10 Downing, where he had a further meeting with the Prime Minister and the British Chiefs of Staff. I sat in the war room, visiting with Captain Pim, who had been given a bottle of champagne by the Supreme Commander to celebrate V-E Day when it comes.

When the meeting finished, the Prime Minister walked with General Ike to the car. They were as homey as neighbors on adjoining Iowa farms. As we drove back to Telegraph Cottage, Ike said that the Prime Minister always walked to the car with him, sometimes in his bathrobe. Ike has grown very fond of Churchill and, although they occasionally differ on military questions, they are the best of friends.

Ike had given the Prime Minister and the British Chiefs a fill-in on his operations in Germany, but one of the questions requiring decision, not by Ike but by the home governments, arose from a request from the French that they be given a larger zone of occupation. They wanted some area east and most of the territory west of the Rhine.

With respect to the insistence that our forces capture Berlin, Ike still thinks it more important that we clean up the important jobs on our flanks. The main job in the north is to get to Lübeck and then clear all the areas north and west of there. The other is the so-called "redoubt." In view of the relative situation of the Russians and ourselves at this time, it would be foolish to rush to Berlin. We could get our forces all coiled to spring for Berlin, and in all probability the Russians would already have it. He prefers that the center of his long line stand fast on the Elbe.

Another point discussed was the propriety of the Supreme Commander dealing directly with the Russians. Direct communications had been established between the Supreme Commander and the Chief of Staff of the Red Army in Moscow, Antonov, by Air Chief Marshal Tedder during his mission there, but a question involving boundaries of areas to be occupied had gone beyond the sphere of military headquarters. The British wanted communications with the Russians to flow from SHAEF through the Combined Chiefs to Moscow rather than direct. As the two ground forces draw together, there will be many details to be arranged with the Russians and General Ike needs direct contact with them, so he stood pat insofar as communications were needed on purely military matters.

I told Ike that some of the correspondents had asked me to get him to give them another talk. He said he thought he had already talked enough. I then suggested that Beetle could supply the information the writers wanted, which was an over-all picture of the campaign to date. He had no objection.

The Chief of Staff Reviews the Campaign to Date

PARIS, SATURDAY, APRIL 21, 1945

I dined with Beetle and Ike last night at Beetle's house in Versailles. It is modernistic and from the outside looks like a long box. Inside it is strictly utilitarian. It is laid out something like a Pullman car, with compartments on one side and an aisle alongside.

We reminisced about old times, and Beetle laughed when I recalled the time I was flying with him from Tunis to Algiers in dirty weather. We were flying in heavy rain, which we had been unable to avoid over either the sea or the mountains. We had tried both. The pilot, who was fresh from combat, had gone down low over the water and had flirted with a convoy of ships, some of which carried barrage balloons. It looked as if we couldn't land at Algiers but would have to go on to Oran or back to Tunis. I was standing behind the pilot, as if I could be of any help, and Beetle was sitting in the only seat, just behind me. He reached up, touched me on the shoulder, and said:

"Tell the pilot he doesn't have to go through just because there's a major general aboard."

Beetle thought that one of his worse trips, which really is saying something because Beetle always has excitement whenever he travels. He said, though, he wasn't as bad as Wavell, who has probably had more forced landings than any other high-ranking general in the war. Beetle said that Wavell's luck is so abominable that some of his staff try to avoid flying with him.

General Ike spent the day at SHAEF Main at Versailles and flew back to Rheims this afternoon. SHAEF Main and Forward are to be moved to the east, possibly to Frankfurt, provided enough buildings can be found which haven't been bombed.

Beetle had his press conference this afternoon and did a bang-up job. He is darned near as good as Ike in a press conference. He speaks without notes and is informal. The correspondents like him. Colonel Dupuy gave me a transcript, which I'm taking the liberty of running in a cut version:

GENERAL SMITH: Gentlemen, what I have to say to you today is in part going to be an anticlimax, because it's a review of the campaign, all of which is on the record, and thereafter we will deal in futures.

I did want to review the campaign which has just ended, the Battle of the Ruhr, taking up from where I left when I last spoke to you about the battle in the Ardennes. There are some very interesting facts about this campaign. The most interesting of all is that of all the campaigns I have known of or studied, it has followed most exactly the pattern of the commander who planned it. It has proceeded according to schedule in every single phase except one, and that I will cover when we come to it.

General Eisenhower planned his battle before the Ardennes fighting actually began. As a matter of fact, we were engaged in the regrouping for the first phase of this battle when the German breakthrough in the Ardennes took place. That slightly delayed the operation but, as I told you before, our counterattack in the Ardennes had only gotten under way when we about completed the regrouping for the first phase of the battle to destroy the German forces west of the Rhine. General Eisenhower had announced his intention of doing that months ago.

THE FOUR PHASES OF THE CAMPAIGN

He had planned his campaign actually in four phases. The main points of the operation were a series of three battles, or three phases of one big battle, which would, he believed, destroy the enemy forces west of the Rhine; then an attack across the Rhine to cut off the Ruhr. His original directive, given to him as Commander-in-Chief of the Allied Armies, told him to strike the heart of Germany. I think some of you who have heard me before have heard me say that when we examined this directive and examined our problem we decided that Germany had two hearts—one, Berlin; the other, the Ruhr—and that we had selected as our target the Ruhr, which was the industrial heart of Germany.

The first phase of the battles west of the Rhine was to have been initiated on the eighth, as you all know, and it did take place with General Montgomery's attack on February 8, which was to have been followed immediately by a crossing of the Roer by the Ninth Army under Field Marshal Montgomery's command, with a pincers movement from south to northeast, closing on the Erft River and investing the Cologne area. Now, in that one particular did the development of the battle depart from General Eisenhower's plan. He had believed that the Germans would defend Cologne, the Cologne area, this side of an all-out effort into cleaning out that densely populated built-up area. As it actually developed, our progress was so rapid that we were able to close the Rhine north of the Cologne-Bonn area and thereby saved at least four or five divisions.

You all know because of the flooded condition of the Roer the Ninth Army attack had to be postponed and it actually took place on February 23. In the meantime, the operation of 21st Army Group had attracted most of the German armored strength to their own front; consequently, the attack of the Ninth Army proceeded with great rapidity. We closed the Erft, and then were able without any serious loss and without much delay to penetrate, clear out Cologne and close up the Rhine. That gave us the crossing points north of Cologne-Bonn which were the minimum necessary to make the main effort which we had planned for north of the Ruhr.

DOUBLE ENVELOPMENT

Now, at that time there were two schools of thought among our masters as to further operations. General Eisenhower felt very strongly that the sound way to proceed with the campaign was to close the Rhine along its entire length. Among the Combined Chiefs of Staff there was a considerable difference of opinion. A number of them believed that the attack north of the Ruhr should be pressed with all the forces at our command and that we should take the defensive along the rest of the front. General Eisenhower did not agree with that because he considered that it was absolutely essential that there should be a strong secondary effort from the Frankfurt area, with the idea of executing a double envelopment and pinching out the Ruhr, which he had no intention of stopping to clean out if there was really desperate resistance.

I presented the views of the Supreme Commander at Malta, and after a couple of days of debate his ideas were accepted and he was allowed to proceed without further detailed instructions to carry them out.

In the meantime, the second phase of the operation, the reduction of the Eifel, was under way. It was carried out by the 12th U. S. Army Group, to whose command the Ninth Army reverted.

As soon as that was completed, the third phase of the operation, which involved an attack through the Siegfried Line by General Devers' 6th Army Group, was initiated. In the meantime, we had had an unexpected piece of success when we seized the Remagen bridge. Now the Remagen bridge did not last long, but it was worth its weight in gold during the time it was there. General Eisenhower was called up during the middle of the night and told that we had captured a bridge across the Rhine at Remagen, and within an hour he had, to a certain extent, to change his plans. It was a rather difficult decision to make and he made it without consulting the Combined Chiefs of Staff and actually on the spur of the moment. He authorized not less than five divisions to hold the bridgehead while the rest of the attack went on, the eruption of the Remagen bridgehead to be exploited after we had closed the rest of the river Rhine.

THE GERMAN MISTAKES

General Devers attacked through the Siegfried Line. That progressed rather slowly as expected because of the nature of the obstacles. In the meantime, General Patton, by a quick thrust, had arrived in the Coblenz area. The Germans here completely failed to estimate the next move. Having a bridgehead at Remagen, they naturally expected that Patton would also cross the Rhine, extend the Remagen bridgehead, and that we would erupt from there. Instead of that, instead of allowing General Patton to cross the Rhine, General Eisenhower directed him to turn south, cross the Moselle west of the Rhine, seize the high plateau at the confluence of the Moselle and the Rhine, and then attack, continuous attack from the south deep into the rear areas of the German army group which was opposing General Devers. I think that was the second critical point in the campaign, the decision to exploit across the Moselle and complete the closing of the Rhine, rather than to do the obvious thing and stretch the Remagen bridgehead. We knew we could hold it. We had enough troops in there to hold it, and that expedited the reduction of the Saar.

The third mistake the Germans made was to expect us to unfold the Remagen bridgehead north along the Rhine and they assembled their troops accordingly, their main forces being between Remagen and the Ruhr from the south. Instead of that, General Eisenhower's intention was to roll the bridgehead down toward the Frankfurt area so that the crossing of the Seventh Army would not have to be a crossing against opposition and, as you know, this is what he did.

Phase four occurred when the First and Third Armies made their junction in the Giessen-Weimar area. We then had Frankfurt, the good terrain around it, and a corridor stretching up toward Kassel. In the meantime, as you know, in accordance with their plan, 21st Army Group with the Ninth Army under command had made a power crossing of the Rhine north of the Ruhr. That was actually our main effort, and had the other effort failed it was the one we would have depended on to drive toward Berlin in the northern plain; but we were looking for something more than that. General Eisenhower has always had in mind the classic double envelopment on a large scale. The situation in which we found ourselves, the ability to economize divisions due to the fact that we were along the Rhine on its entire length, thus having a barrier between us and the German which made it impossible for him to stage any large-scale counterattack, put us in the favorable position that the Germans had previously occupied when they were behind the Siegfried Line. We were, therefore, able to increase the strength of the secondary effort through Frankfurt to about double what we had expected to use and drive straight for Kassel and for a juncture with the Ninth Army.

When that was completed, the largest double envelopment in military history was completed. You know the rapidity with which the maneuver was made. It left us with the whole of one German army group, plus two corps from another, cut off in the Ruhr. We had not expected that mass to stay there and fight, and I still don't understand why they did it; but they repeated the error which they made in Normandy. I think you may find the reason lies in the disbelief of the average German general in any sort of large-scale withdrawal. They do not think it can be carried out effectively. They may be right in that, but certainly against an operation of the kind they were faced with it's equally fatal to stand and fight. We estimated that there were between 150,000 to 200,000 troops in the Ruhr pocket. As you now know, when it was finally reduced two days ago there were over 300,000 in there. We completely destroyed an entire German army group with two additional corps, some twenty-one divisions. That would not have been possible if it hadn't been for the close co-operation and careful work of the Air Forces, which rendered the mobility of the army groups in the Ruhr pocket to almost nothing. It was practically impossible for them to move by day and practically impossible for them to switch ammunition and gasoline. The Ruhr had been cut off from the outside long before our double envelopment was completed. We have studied the double envelopment from Cannae down through Tannenberg, but never have seen anything like this before. I suppose it's the ideal of every military commander someday to execute a maneuver of this kind. Nobody ever expects to, and now it's been done. The result was that the German forces on our front which might have opposed our further advance were completely eliminated.

The only strength they had left was in the south facing General Devers. They gradually withdrew, as you know, to the triangular form of front before the so-called "national redoubt," but opposed to the First, Third, and Ninth Armies it was almost nothing.

The river Elbe was our objective after reducing the Ruhr, and the drive to the Elbe proceeded with very little opposition. During that phase of the operation it became increasingly apparent to us, from our various sources of intelligence, that Berlin, the second heart of Germany, had ceased to have much military significance. We were aware from various reports through neutral countries and otherwise that much of the German government had moved from Berlin. It had a psychological value, but nothing like the importance that it had when it was the center of German communications and the center of German government. That factor weighed very heavily with General Eisenhower in planning his future operations, about which I will now talk for a moment: and this is off the record.

THE GERMAN SOUTHERN REDOUBT

Now, what I have said has been very pedantic, I know. Now let's get down to cases and talk about two or three things that I will ask you, caution you must be kept very secret. This so-called "national redoubt" is something we don't know an awful lot about. We do know that the Germans have, as they could, shifted men and matériel and supplies down there into the area south of the Sudetenland and the Bavarian Alps, and so forth. Just what we will find down there we don't know. We are beginning to think it will be a lot more than we will expect. You have seen the underground installations around Mosbach and at Schweinfurt, where we have been just bombing the hell out of the ballbearing plants up there and doing a marvelous job of hitting buildings, and finding eighty-five per cent were underground, beautifully underground. We may find when we get down there a great deal more underground than anticipated, I am thinking we will. One thing to remember —as long as Hitler or any of his representatives are standing on a rock around Salzburg, proclaiming they are free Germans and broadcasting to all isolated fortress areas holding out that everything is going to come out all right, they are going to hold out. Our target now, if we are going to bring this war to an end and bring it to an end in a hell of a hurry, is this national redoubt, and we are organizing our strength in that direction. General Devers and General Bradley; in other words, the Third and Seventh Armies, will attack tomorrow morning. We hope that we will drive a deep wedge into that place, that we will prevent any further organization, and that we will so disrupt it that the thing will end up reasonably quickly. Once that is done, I cannot see the isolated garrisons around the periphery of northwestern Europe holding out and fighting with any grim bloodthirsty determination for any length of time. That is our estimate of the situation. Also we have an objective on the north, because we may ultimately have, by a major operation of war, to reduce the German garrisons in Norway and Denmark and other places. That is why I say that the center, that is, the so-called "thrust on Berlin," from a purely military standpoint has ceased to be of any great importance to us. Berlin is going to fall, anyway. We don't care who fights their way into Berlin. We will get up there. Same thing was true in Vienna. We had a telegram from the Russians the other day saying, "Hurry up and send a control group into Vienna." They were waiting for them and we didn't have a control group to send in. That is the reason and the answer to a number of questions which a number of you have been asking why we haven't pushed like hell toward Berlin. From a purely military standpoint it doesn't have much significance any more—not anything comparable to that of the so-called national redoubt and a jumping-off place from which later we can operate in Norway if we have to, and we have oriented our strength in that direction.

So that everything I have said so far is on the record except this question of futures. That is a very brief review of what has been done—the way General Eisenhower made his plan, the way the battle was carried out, and the way we expect to operate in winding up this thing.

I am vulnerable. Fire away.

QUESTION: The fact we stopped at the Elbe, was that in part due to arrangement with the Russians that we would come as far as the Elbe?

ANSWER: No. Our only arrangement with the Russians was to select the area in which we expected to join hands with them. In our correspondence some time ago—well, I should say about seven or eight weeks ago—we agreed with the Russians that we would join in the Leipzig-Dresden area.

QUESTION: Have the Russians indicated whether they wanted us to come on to Dresden or not?

ANSWER: The extent of our co-ordination was that we would meet in the general area, Leipzig-Dresden. That is what our plans were for.

QUESTION: Have you asked them subsequently to come beyond Leipzig?

ANSWER: No. Our only arrangement— and this is all off the record—when we join up, the boundary for subsequent operations will be arranged by mutual co-operation with the adjacent army commander.

QUESTION: We haven't joined up yet?

ANSWER: I have a report we have, but it's not confirmed that reconnaissance elements had contacted each other.

QUESTION: What could you tell us about the co-ordination of the command after the hookup is made?

ANSWER: Going to have to be the same thing. Certainly the Russians are not going to place their forces under our

command, nor will we place ours under theirs.

QUESTION: No Supreme-Supreme Commander then?

ANSWER: No. Fortunately, the stage of operations at that time will not be so critical, I trust, that that will be necessary. The only thing we can do is arrive at the simplest sort of solution; that is to say, the two adjacent armies will arrange boundaries in accordance with the tactical situation with mutual agreement.

QUESTION: The Russians won't participate in the reduction of the national redoubt?

ANSWER: I have no doubt they will. They are as anxious as we are to clear it.

QUESTION: Will the Russians participate in Norway?

ANSWER: I don't know. Our discussions with the Russians for reasons have been limited to very simple fundamental factors which must be solved, and the more complex questions that will arise later can only be arranged when we have direct contact.

QUESTION: Do you anticipate it will be a very difficult job reducing the national redoubt?

ANSWER: Personally, I don't. A month's fighting and then guerrilla warfare for an indeterminate time. That is not to be quoted. I don't know. That is only a guess.

QUESTION: Do you know where the German leaders are now?

ANSWER: No, I don't. It's only a wild guess—I'd say Hitler is probably at Berchtesgaden. I should imagine that. That is nothing but my own wild guess. There is nothing to indicate where he is.

QUESTION: In this phase of the war, how is command exercised by the Germans? Is the party controlling the Army more and more?

ANSWER: We don't know too much about it. We know that the party gradually has exercised more and more control over the Army, even going into distribution of ammunition, and that the SS had put representatives in all Wehrmacht units, etc. So that I should say they are so scrambled up now it's impossible to draw a line of demarcation to say—this is the Wehrmacht; this is the SS; this is controlled by the German Staff; or this is party-controlled—because I think that everybody who had any real ideas on the independence of the Wehrmacht has been pretty well scrubbed or else they have taken hostages in the shape of families or don't dare do anything.

QUESTION: What about the German military command? What is the staff work and military decisions like?

ANSWER: Technical work?

QUESTION: Yes.

ANSWER: Just as good as always. Very high order.

QUESTION: Are they carrying out this pretty complicated maneuver of swinging down into the national redoubt pretty well?

ANSWER: Of course, they are having a hell of a time. They are being bombed and their communications cut off.

QUESTION: Is it true that the roads in the national redoubt, that secondary roads will not carry armor?

ANSWER: I don't know of any road that won't carry armor.

QUESTION: The bridges?

ANSWER: I should think they would. If they don't, a bridge that only needs strengthening is a very quick job for the engineers. Our engineers are becoming very skillful, you know. You have seen recent samples of their work. The speed with which they do these things is phenomenal. The rate of construction of the railroad bridge across the Wesel is one of the great engineering feats of the campaign.

QUESTION: Is the Third Army going to participate in the new southeast phase,

and, if not, is the 6th Army Group to be enlarged in any way?

ANSWER: Third Army will attack.

QUESTION: Will the French First be in on this show?

ANSWER: Yes. They are swinging toward the south. The attack tomorrow will be made by the Third on the north, the Seventh striking in the direction of Munich, and the First French rather swinging down into the Black Forest area down in through here. You see, they have a pretty good start now, enveloping Stuttgart, and they will carry on toward the Swiss border. The role of the 6th Army Group after having arrived in the Munich area really becomes one of flank protection then.

QUESTION: What are our chances for moving into Berlin?

ANSWER: That is something we can't say. We are very much extended now and we have jobs on both flanks. Depends on how fast they go and on our supply situation which, I may tell you, is very, very strained. If it weren't for air supply we couldn't do this thing right now, not until about fifteen days from now, because the developments are that in order to carry out its mission on the north 21st Army Group will need practically the entire capacity of the Wesel bridge. We are going to reinforce it with an American corps. It will need practically the entire capacity of the Wesel bridge. We are building other bridges over the Rhine. Another one will be done up in the north in about fifteen to twenty days, but it's very doubtful if our supply situation will permit us to do what we want to do unless we had air transport, and we are gambling a little bit on the weather, although, as I think I have told you before, I never believe what the supply man tells us. He always has twenty-five per cent reserve in his hip pocket.

QUESTION: Aren't they going all-out for Hamburg?

ANSWER: Oh, yes. Pretty near there now.

QUESTION: Can you estimate what is likely to happen in Holland? How long do you think they can hang out there?

ANSWER: God only knows. That is causing us a great deal of concern because the food situation in Holland is very strained. If the Germans in Holland want to make an all-out defense of that fortress—it's been declared a fortress area by the Germans, northwestern Holland—and we undertook to reduce the fortress it would mean that in addition to the sufferings of the Dutch from starvation and flooding we would probably hammer it flat. That is why I am hopeful about what may result if we can act quickly in the so-called "redoubt" area. We may find that when we have cut the head from the snake the tail won't wiggle very long.

QUESTION: What could possibly be gained by announcing victory day? What advantage could there be in it?

ANSWER: This is off the record. I will be perfectly honest with you. There is a hell of a lot of pressure for the Pacific, you know, at home and the demands for redeployment of units will become intense. Politically, the head of every government likes to be able to announce a victory as soon as he possibly can. It means then that he can revoke all sorts of unpleasant regulations and offer all sorts of hope for prompt return of a certain number of men. The British program is for the return immediately of seventy thousand industrial workers, etc. It means they can start horse racing, let night clubs open. Canada wants all men back except 35,000 token force. They want it ended. They are a long way off and don't believe you too much.

QUESTION: The announcement, the formal announcement of the end, is weeks if not months ahead?

ANSWER: I trust so.

QUESTION: When General Eisenhower was here before he said he expected to issue proclamation of the end of organized resistance on the Western Front. I take it that idea has now been abandoned?

ANSWER: He does not himself expect to issue a proclamation. As a matter of fact, off the record, his recommendation is that it be done by our governments on concurrence of the two Commanders-in-Chief, Russian and Allied.

QUESTION: There will be a statement, but it will be from the government in Washington?

ANSWER: Undoubtedly, I don't anticipate any form of formal surrender by the German government.

QUESTION: Before the collapse of the national redoubt?

ANSWER: Won't be until afterwards. General Eisenhower himself does not expect to issue a proclamation. His recommendation is that it be done on a governmental level after consulting the two Commanders and at a time when they are prepared to say organized resistance is ended, that we are now prepared to accept the situation of victory.

QUESTION: Any indication of what the Russians may be doing as far as Berlin is concerned while this south movement is on?

ANSWER: They said they'd make a secondary effort toward Berlin.

QUESTION: Secondary?

ANSWER: When you consider the number of divisions the Russians dispose, a secondary effort would be a damn strong thing. Now you are asking my personal opinion—they will make a hell of an effort and take the place.

QUESTION: The redoubt area will be largely American?

ANSWER: I think it will be both if we join up in the Dresden-Leipzig area. My estimate would be that we find the German Army split with something like forty or forty-five divisions in the north and possibly 100 to 125 in the south.

QUESTION: Will the German troops in Italy act as a natural reserve for this redoubt if they want to withdraw?

ANSWER: Yes.

QUESTION: Can they get material back through the Brenner?

ANSWER: Not very much, I trust.

QUESTION: Who do you think is the top German general? Who do you think they have got left as the best general now?

ANSWER: I don't know. Of the ones they have got left, if he were allowed full complete authority—after all, Kesselring is pretty good, you know. Kesselring is a damn good man professionally. He's got a very good chief of staff. His chief of staff on the West Wall was formerly his chief of staff, then Rundstedt's chief of staff, and now Kesselring's. He's a very good man and a thoroughly trained professional soldier. I know very little about the caliber of the commanders on the Russian front. But I think, taken by and large, that of the ones we have had to deal with so far probably Kesselring is the best.

QUESTION: General, are the British booked for Berlin or going to the northeast?

ANSWER: Any time we go into Berlin it will be on an Allied basis, I will assure you of that.

QUESTION: Anything about von Papen?

ANSWER: I can tell you a good deal about him, although I haven't seen him. This is off the record. We thought that von Papen might have put himself in the way of capture, that he might have certain proposals to make. Well, we know that in the past the Germans have had the habit of trying to make overtures to us and at the same time reporting to the Russians that we were engaged in a little private negotiation. We were extremely leary when we picked von Papen up. This is why there was a hold-up on censorship for a while. Our masters told us not to release it until we had informed the Russians. We held it up until we informed the Russians. As soon as they acknowledged it we released the fact he was captured. That may happen again from time to time, too. I am going to ask for your sympathetic tolerance if we capture a fellow of some importance and you know about it and yet we won't let you publish it. It will probably be for the same reason. We must be extremely careful how to proceed with anything like consideration of a proposal unless we have got the Russians in on it. That is why we wouldn't let you publish von Papen's capture right away. However, it develops that he has no proposals to make. He was there in a private capacity. Although our personal opinion is he really did put himself in the way of capture in the hope we would offer something. Which so far we have no inclination to do.

QUESTION: Do you think the Germans may use gas in the redoubt?

ANSWER: No. Too late now. In order to use gas effectively, unless they have some gas we don't know about, you have to have either a preponderance of artillery or else have a large air force to spread it. In other words, you have to have mechanical means of distribution and disseminating gas where it will do the most good. The Germans have neither. Our artillery and air preponderance is so great that within a few hours after the Germans would fire a gas shell or drop a gas bomb we could reply on a ratio of about I should say twenty to one. If they were going to use gas the time would have been when we were concentrating in the Normandy beachhead.

Incidentally, von Papen made two rather interesting remarks. I read the transcript of his interview. He was asked by one of the Russian officers, I believe, when he made up his mind that Germany knew the turning point of the war had come. He said when the Allies landed in northwestern Europe. "That's your opinion," they told him.. "When do you think the German General Staff and the German High Command and German people generally realized when the war was lost?" He said, "When the Allies crossed the Rhine." I think he gave the wrong answer both times. I think the answer was supposed to have been "Stalingrad."

QUESTION: Do our plans call for a full-scale march on Berlin? From our side before the Russians?

ANSWER: I'll put it this way. We are not going to try to race the Russians to any point. We are fighting the battle, except for the joining up for carrying out our part of the agreement in joining up in the Leipzig-Dresden area, which apparently the Russians are following pretty scrupulously because they said they'd make their main thrust that way and they have done it. Marshal Stalin has never failed to keep any commitment he's made with us since this thing began. Except for that, we are conducting our operations still just as though we were the only army on the front. At the moment, except politically and psychologically, Berlin has lost a great deal of its significance. Of course, you mustn't publish that, because the Germans probably expect us to make an attack on Berlin. I don't know. At the moment we have other more important things to do. There isn't any place along this front that we are going to try to rush to at the cost of lives and material in order to get there before the Russians do, unless our masters tell us differently. We are handling it as a strictly military campaign. I think that is all we can do, don't you? After all, General Eisenhower has these lives entrusted to him and he will fight this

campaign as economically as he can. Britain has lost a lot of men. We have lost more, and it's his job to accomplish his mission as quickly and as economically as he possibly can without regard to political factors unless otherwise instructed by his government. In that case, of course, we will proceed as directed.

QUESTION: It would be invaluable if we could say on the record that it's being conducted strictly on military lines.

ANSWER: Yes, but don't say we are going to attack Berlin.

QUESTION: When you talk about "masters" whom do you mean?

ANSWER: The Combined Chiefs of Staff. They are responsible to the heads of our two governments. They are swayed by considerations of which we know nothing whatever.

QUESTION: Any chance of an airborne operation on this redoubt, say at Berchtesgaden?

ANSWER: We are keeping airborne divisions available. We will have all sorts of airborne operations.

QUESTION: How far west have the Russians actually gone in the area where we are to join?

ANSWER: As far as I know, the report I got this morning was that reconnaissance elements had made contact about halfway between Leipzig and Dresden and somewhat north thereof. But that hasn't been confirmed. I haven't been around the war room since I came down last night.

QUESTION: So the juncture is practically at hand?

ANSWER: Matter of hours.

QUESTION: Do you have any objection to us using that unconfirmed report?

ANSWER: I think the Germans gave it out, so soon you can quote them.

QUESTION: Any report on what the Germans have in the way of new weapons?

ANSWER: We get constant rumors, but nothing that would give us any really definite information. They are always threatening things and there may be something to them.

QUESTION: Is there any indication or feeling in high military places that President Roosevelt's death has stiffened German resistance in any way? Their will to resist?

ANSWER: I don't know. I should imagine that they would consider it, possibly, a break for them, or would have considered any change a break for them. They are hoping for anything. They are in the position of a man who is just hoping for anything, thinking maybe this change will produce friction, or maybe this will cause a change of policy. They don't know but they just hope. I am sorry to say I have got to leave. I have got time possibly for one more question.

QUESTION: Any change in policy in handling German prisoners since we have picked up some of our own?

ANSWER: There is going to be. We have got a lot of mines to be cleared up all through France and Belgium and places like that. An awful lot of work to be done pretty soon when we've got all our prisoners back. General Eisenhower is having all these poor wretched people who were killed buried by civilians. As a matter of fact, we always intended

having a lot of this work done by German prisoners. We have been very circumspect because, as you know, they are perfectly ruthless with ours. We shall stay within the limits of the Geneva Convention.

QUESTION: What about food for the civilians burying the dead?

ANSWER: They feed themselves.

QUESTION: Do you want to explain a bit more about that?

ANSWER: Every day we will draft burying parties from near-by towns. They can bring a piece of bread or lunch and come out and do a day's work and come back—if they can still stomach their food. Some of you ought to, by all means, go up and look at those places. Don't fail to do it. The next bad one we uncover go up and look.

QUESTION: Are the civilians able to eat lunch after they bury the bodies?

ANSWER: I don't know. They told me that some of our generals are making civilians come in and look, and they all cover up their faces and won't look. Sometimes their hands have to be removed by force and pulled down and made to look.

QUESTION: And they say they didn't know about it?

ANSWER: Yes—they all didn't know about it.

PARIS, SUNDAY, APRIL 22, 1945

Drove to Rheims today. Had lunch with the General and spent several hours around the headquarters.

Our troops continue to find German concentration camps for political prisoners. Conditions of indescribable horror are reported. It is probably true that the Nazis collected the liberal, or at least the non-Nazi, brains of Europe and methodically squeezed the life out of them by hard labor and inhuman treatment. General Ike has cabled General Marshall suggesting that about a dozen leaders of Congress and a dozen prominent editors and publishers might profit if they could see some of these camps. He has also suggested to the Prime Minister that British MPs and editors would be welcome.

Ike Really Hits His Stride

PARIS, WEDNESDAY, APRIL 25, 1945

General Ike made a quick trip to Paris late yesterday. I barely had time to get to Orly to meet him after he phoned from Rheims that he was coming. Street and I met him, and the Supreme Commander again passed unnoticed, although we created excitement amongst the staff at the Army Hospital where we stopped for an hour. He really had come to see his classmate, Major General John B. Wogan, who had been seriously wounded in the neck. He had been commanding the 13th Armored Division, now deep in Germany. Ike was pleased to find that his old friend soon would be sufficiently improved to be moved to the States.

Ike brought only a musette bag. He spent the night with me at the Raphaël and this morning had some of the Com Z staff in for consultation. Major General Everett Hughes came in for dinner last night and we had the usual bull session but got to bed early.

Ike is showing signs of "cabin" fever, the close association with his staff making him want to find some fresh faces and topics of conversation other than of the war. He's in swell health and, like the long-distance runner he is, now really is hitting his stride in the final stretch run.

PARIS, FRIDAY, APRIL 27, 1945

Was àt Rheims yesterday. Sat in with the editors and publishers when Ike talked to them. They had seen the Buchenwald concentration camp and had interviewed liberated American prisoners of war who were being flown to Paris. The Supreme Commander and the editors compared notes on their visits to the "hell camps," and Ike said he hoped every American newspaper would print the story of German bestiality in detail.

The editors were interested in knowing the manner in which the end of the war would be declared. Ike said there would be no V-E proclamation as long as any major German forces face the Allies.

"V-E Day is going to be a day of relief for a lot of soldiers and their families," he told them. "I don't believe we should have that relief until we are sure that our men are not losing their lives trying to defeat large numbers of enemy forces which may be dug in somewhere."

Ike praised all of his field commanders and said they were the "best anywhere." Duke Shoop is here with the editors. I brought him back to Paris with me. He knows President Truman well and says he hasn't done anything wrong to date and thinks he will be a fine President. Worships General Marshall, and rightly. As Duke represents the *Kansas City Star*, anything General Ike does is news for Kansas readers. Duke had a nice talk on the side with the Supreme Commander and was singing his praises. Said Ike would be President one day, but I said General Ike would have no part of it. All he wants now is to sit by a quiet stream and fish—he doesn't give a damn whether he catches anything.

Plans for V-E Day

PARIS, SUNDAY, APRIL 29, 1945

Spent the night with General Ike at Rheims. We were making plans for V-E Day and he has to make some recordings and movies for the grand finale. We talked about these things last night.

All the pups are fine and growing like weeds. Telek has been sick, holds his head sideways, and occasionally runs in circles. The vet had diagnosed his illness as tonsillitis, brain tumor, or just fleas. Caacie is more sprightly than I've ever seen her.

Sergeant Farr's wife had a baby just nine months after he had a week's leave at home last summer. Mickey has news that he is to be a father as well. It's a happy household, certainly on the sergeant level.

APRIL, 1945: *President Roosevelt died suddenly of a cerebral hemorrhage; Harry S. Truman sworn in as President. Tenth Army, under General Buckner, landed on west coast of Okinawa, pushed across to east coast near Tobara. Japs lost 150 planes attacking invasion fleet off Okinawa. Marines on Okinawa rapidly advanced to northern tip of island as Japs concentrated opposition in southern portion of island. Jap Kamikaze attacks against naval units and supply ships became a serious menace. Yank offensive on Mindanao moved steadily ahead, with Americans taking Padada airfield along Davao Gulf. Japs lost 308,180 men in Philippines against U. S. casualties of 31,132. Jap cabinet resigned after Russia denounced Russo-Jap neutrality pact. Fifth Fleet hit Jap fleet fifty miles from Kyushu, sinking six warships, two cruisers, and three destroyers. B-29s hit Tokyo and Nagoya; other bombers hit Hong Kong. Nimitz and MacArthur named to head Navy and Army forces against Japan. All Allied armies rolled forward against dwindling German opposition. Reds entered Berlin, linked up with Yanks on Elbe River. U.S. Seventh took Munich and infamous Dachau concentration camp; Third crossed Austrian border. Planes continued heavy pounding of German targets, with special attention to submarine pens at Kiel. British and American armies in Italy in final victory offensive scored gains on all fronts as Milan, Bergamo, and Genoa fell. Italian partisans captured and killed Mussolini and shabby followers. United Nations conference opened at San Francisco. (It seemed to me every GI wanted to keep going to Berlin and resented being ordered to stop at the Elbe.—H.C.B.)*

The Cracks Widen

PARIS, TUESDAY, MAY 1, 1945

Went up to Rheims again today. Things are really getting on. The First Army has linked up with the Russians at Torgau, on the Elbe. Rumors of peace are sweeping Allied capitals. Moscow has announced that Himmler had offered to surrender unconditionally to the United States and Britain, but his proposal has been rejected because it did not include Russia.

General Ike is working on redeployment. Hodges and his First Army staff are to go to the Pacific as soon as possible after the fighting is finished. Patton once had a commitment from the late President, who promised to let him go to the Pacific. Don't know what will happen to him now. He's always said he wanted to die fighting.

Major General Stephen G. Henry, G-1 of the War Department, has been over to discuss redeployment. General Ike is in complete accord with the idea of getting our high-point men started home with a rush. The GIs who fought in Africa, Italy, and in the current campaign won't have to fight any more, thank the Lord. He has authorized Spaatz to withdraw two transport groups to operate on one of our air links to the United States, to speed the flow. Ike felt it was like parting with life's blood to give up air lift now because of the appalling size of the relief problem on the Continent. All kinds of transportation are needed to deal with displaced persons, prisoners of war, distribution of food, and emergency supply missions. Heavy bombers could be used for these jobs, but there are not sufficient large fields in Germany to accommodate them and many of the fields are still unusable because of our bombings. Furthermore, the Germans built airfields with very light surfacing and our heavy bombers break through the runways and soon render the fields unfit for any other type of aircraft.

General Ike has sent a message to the German commander in Holland, telling him of our plans to drop supplies to the starving Dutch, whose condition is terribly serious. The German commander was told that if he attempted to interfere, every one of his officers and men responsible for the interference would be treated as violators of the laws of war. The German commander designated the dropping grounds and agreed to meet SHAEF's representatives so arrangements can be made for more adequate relief.

The Supreme Commander has had another French problem on his hands. For reasons of pride, the French First Army, under General Delattre de Tassigny, declined to evacuate Stuttgart, which is needed as a link in the supply and communication system supporting current operations of Patch's Seventh Army. Under the circumstances, General Ike accepted the situation, as he was unwilling to take any action at this late date in the war which would weaken the bonds of friendship between the two countries.

Mussolini's end is deserved but ghastly. Democracies may treat their ex-leaders carelessly and frequently without respect, but the way Mussolini and his mistress were executed and publicly displayed in the square at Milan should be a warning to all future would-be dictators. The pictures are revolting.

Ike's Postwar Plans

PARIS, THURSDAY, MAY 3, 1945

The psychological boys were quick on the trigger. They suggested that General Ike issue a statement to give the German people in the world facts to disabuse their minds that Hitler died a hero. The Supreme Commander authorized the issuance of a statement.

General Ike sent his plane for me last evening and, with Caacie, we went to Rheims in style. I had Caacie plucked in a French shop which specializes in trimming poodles into fantastic shapes. Caacie was a sight. The General was disgusted. Telek and the four pups were elated. They chased and bedeviled her for an hour. Jim's description was most appropriate: "She looks like a Parisian lady of the street in a black satin dress."

Ike and Jim had just returned from the office when I arrived and were talking about the surrender of the Germans in Italy. Berlin also had been taken by the Russians, but the news didn't seem surprising. I was pleased, though, when I learned that the Italian campaign had ended so gloriously for Alexander and Clark and everyone who fought in that blind alley.

General Ike had been working on his broadcast and newsreel speech for V-E Day. He had drafted it and redrafted it three times, with Telek and the pups vying for attention and, as usual, having no respect for the dignity of the Supreme Commander. He read his script. Jim Gault made a suggestion here and there, and I made one or two, but it needed little change. He didn't have to learn it for the recording, but for the movie he would have a few paragraphs to give from memory. This, I knew, would not be difficult, for once he had dictated and reworked a piece, even though it's a couple of thousand words, he can repeat its thought immediately, almost word for word.

The speech having been read, criticized, and reread, we relaxed and talked.

Ike still has as his No. 1 plan his often expressed desire to sit on the bank of a quiet stream and fish. I told him he seemed slated to be Chief of Staff and reminded him that General Marshall had pointedly hinted to this assignment as a probability. Ike thought he might be of greater use to his country if he could resign, not merely retire, from the Army and write and speak in support of proper military preparedness of the United States. He wants to be in a position to speak freely without even the trace of restriction that might be present if he were simply a retired rather than a resigned officer. He insists that America and Britain should continue to work together in peace as they have in war. America, he thinks, has much to gain by remaining friendly to Britain because, among other reasons, the British statesmen have the foresight to maintain air and sea bases. In America, there will be a revolt against spending, curtailment of appropriations will become popular with members of Congress, and the armed services are likely to go through the same withering process as after the last war. There is much streamlining that can be done to the land, sea, and air establishments of the United States and he is convinced the country would be best served if we had the same type of unity of command of these services in peacetime as has been demonstrated to be so effective in the war. Even West Point and Annapolis might well be merged into one national institution and thus avoid the rivalries inherent in the system of competition between the two. All young men should be taught how to defend themselves and their country. A year of military service for young men would contribute to their education and the discipline would be good for them.

I added that I thought the advocates of universal training were missing a bet. Why couldn't those drawn for universal training be given at least six months of their year's service with the occupational forces overseas? Most young men like adventure, I pointed out, and service with our troops in Germany and Japan would broaden their perspectives. I mentioned, too, that President Truman had been quoted as advocating that all members of Congress should travel abroad.* I agreed with the President. This would give our Representatives and Senators a chance to take a look at the United States from distant shores and perhaps gain a better perspective of our country of destiny.

So the talk ran until late in the evening, Ike being interrupted a couple of times by phone calls from Monty and Bradley, who had good news to report and questions to ask. If Monty had a large surrender he should accept it as a battlefield surrender in the name of the Supreme Com-

---

* A misquotation, I regret.

mander. The evening ended with my reminder to Ike that he had frequently talked about getting out of the Army, but when and if the President says to him, "You are to be the Chief of Staff of the United States Army," there is no doubt in my mind that he will respond to the call of duty. Ike growled, called for Mickey to take Telek out, and ambled up the stairs to bed, with the manuscript which would be his Western tonight.

Rheims

SHAEF FORWARD (RHEIMS), FRIDAY, MAY 4, 1945
I spent some time this morning answering questions of a French writer who is undertaking to write a book about the Supreme Commander for boys from ten to eighteen. I'm afraid I wasn't very helpful, as my mind was elsewhere.

At lunch, at the Chatham, with General Allen, Brigadier Turner, Colonel Dupuy, Lieutenant Colonel Ralph, Lieutenant Colonel Pawley, and Group Captain Pat Graham, I had an uneasy feeling that somewhere something was happening that I was missing. I wanted to get to Rheims. I stopped at the office to tell Sergeant McClary I was off again and in the corridor was stopped by Lieutenant Colonel Duncan-Clark, the American censor, who said he had just received a phone call from 21st Army Group, guardedly saying:

"We've got everything in hand, the correspondents are all set, and it looks as if everything will go off as scheduled."

Clark said it was a mystery to him; did I know anything about it? I imagined it was about a surrender ceremony and, on checking by phone with Colonel Gault at Rheims, got enough information to confirm my suspicion.

Corporal Street and I were in Rheims in two hours. The atmosphere at SHAEF Forward was tense. Ike was waiting for a phone call from Monty. At 6:55 he said he thought he might just as well go home and wait there. WAC Lieutenant Kay Summersby, his personal secretary, said: "Why don't you wait just another five minutes? The call may come."

At 7 o'clock it came.

"Fine. Fine. That's fine, Monty," * Ike said, as Kay and I eavesdropped in his office. Ike told Monty if the Germans had authority of Doenitz to stop all the fighting to send them to Rheims. Details are to be worked out between the Chiefs of Staff, Beetle and Freddie de Guingand.

---

* Freddie de Guingand, Monty's Chief of Staff, had been on the phone during the day with Beetle, worried because his chief wouldn't permit ranking representatives of sea and air forces in Monty's command to take part in the surrender ceremony.

Then he was ready to go home to dinner. As we walked down the private stairway from the Supreme Commander's office on the second floor (called the first by the British) and through the large entrance hall, Telek and the General played their usual game, Telek running ahead about thirty feet, skidding to a stop, and rushing back to the General, barking the joy that only a dog can sense so quickly. The solemn RAF guard and the American MPs stood stiffly at attention. But they grinned as they saluted.

Before dinner there was a call from Beetle that the Germans were being flown from Monty's headquarters to Rheims and would arrive about 11 Saturday morning, weather permitting. The question was whether they would have authority to surrender all the German land, sea, and air forces, not only to the Western Allies but to Russia. Monty had indicated that the Germans wanted more time but thought they had the authority.

Other news came in and as a result of it, and to keep an Allied balance in the flow of news, we spent an hour drafting and redrafting a statement which I phoned to Colonel Dupuy, at PRD in Paris, for release that night.

I asked Ike if he himself would sign the instrument of surrender if the Germans had authority to give up all the German forces to both the Russians and to us. Ike said he wouldn't even see them until after they had signed. He didn't want to bargain—that he was going to tell them through his staff what to do and would see them only after they had signed on the dotted line. The principals in the drama would be Beetle and Ken Strong, who had negotiated with General Castellano at Lisbon. Beetle subsequently had signed the Italian surrender in Sicily, after the then Allied Commander had wisely declined to accept my urgent suggestion that he sign it himself. Now I would not press the same subject.

I was, however, worried about press, radio, and movie coverage of the event, but the Supreme Commander had all in his mind he ought to bear and damned if I was going to bother him with this problem at this late hour. If the Germans come simply to negotiate, the correspondents can't be in on this anyway, so there was little I could tell General Allen (whom I was keeping informed by telephone at every opportunity), except that news was in the making, but I would keep in touch and let him know as soon as possible when and if correspondents could be sent to cover the historic moment.

General Allen, however, is sending two former newsmen to cover the development, with a view toward writing a blow-by-blow description for use of the correspondents when the story may be released. They are Lieutenant Colonel Burroughs Matthews and Lieutenant Colonel Pawley, both qualified reporters. They can get into headquarters and correspondents can't. They will also have the assistance of the *Stars and Stripes* pool reporter, Charles Kiley.

Ike went to bed, and I worked the telephone a while longer and made a few notes. Jim and I had a nightcap and I'm going to bed. I'm glad I played my hunch.

The Germans Arrive

SHAEF FORWARD (RHEIMS), SATURDAY, MAY 5, 1945
By the time I was dressed this morning, Ike had been on the telephone with Beetle. There might be a change in plans. The weather was bad—the plane bringing the Germans might not get to Rheims. It might be necessary to take General Ike's train, standing by at Rheims, to an intermediate point near an airfield where the weather was sufficiently clear to permit a landing. München-Gladbach was discussed.

We breakfasted quickly. Was at the office by 8:45. I found Pawley and Matthews waiting, briefed them on the overnight messages and latest dope I could pick up from G-2 and G-3. It looked a bit as if the actual signing could take place today, but it might be on a train.

I asked Ike if correspondents could go on the train, and he said that if there was actually to be a surrender and not merely a negotiation, I could "lay them in the aisles" if necessary.

With this carte blanche, I felt free to call for the correspondents whenever it became determined that the German mission wasn't merely to negotiate but had authority and would sign. After all, they still can kick up a fuss and fighting can go on to the bitterest end. There is no telling how stubborn and stupid they will be.

Pawley, Matthews, and Kiley have agreed on assignments to cover all contingencies—Kiley to go to the airport in event the weather lets the plane through; Matthews is to keep watch at the office of Lieutenant Colonel J. B. Moore, secretary of the General Staff, where messages flow in and out and where news of changes in plans may be first obtained, and Pawley is to keep in touch with G-2 and G-3. I don't have to write, but can fill them in from time to time on news I pick up from the Supreme Commander or the Chief of Staff.

From the secretariat, we learned that the German party consists of Admiral Hans Georg von Friedeburg, who now is said to be Commander-in-Chief of the German Navy, succeeding Admiral Doenitz, and former commander of the German Submarine Service, and Colonel Fritz Poleck, of the Oberkommando Wehrmacht, which is the German equivalent of the U. S. War Department or the British War Office.

About 11, Kiley called from the airfield and said the weather was still bad and that if the plane was coming in there, it was overdue.

About noon I learned from the secretariat that the plane carrying the Germans had landed near Brussels, the party would have lunch there and would drive to Rheims, reaching our headquarters, so there would be no news at the airfield today.

Now that we know the Germans definitely are coming to our headquarters, the war room has been designated as the place for the ceremony, when, as, and if. I have talked with General "Pinky" Bull, G-3, about arrangements and he has agreed to a plan, and has got it confirmed by Beetle, that if negotiations take place in the war room, we may bring in correspondents in time for any signature. Photographs may be taken when the Germans enter the room and again as they leave, but if any conversations are to take place before the Germans have indicated their assent to sign, then all photographers, radio men, and correspondents must clear the room. This seemed a bit awkward and would create confusion. Beetle solved the problem by saying that all preliminary discussions will take place in his office and unless the Germans agree and are authorized to sign, they will not be taken into the war room.

Lunch was quiet, Ike being contemplative as to the dilemma he would be in if the Russians refused to accept the surrender. He has messages from Antonov, Chief of Staff of the Red Army, communicated through the Military Mission to Moscow, headed by General Deane, which seemed to give him authority but which are not absolutely clear. In any event, the Russians will be represented at our surrender and Ike will not accept any terms from the Germans which are not equally applicable to the Russians.

I have been using the office set aside for VIPs, that of Tex Lee and Jim Gault being too crowded, as well as too noisy from the seemingly ever-ringing telephones. I was crowded out of my office this afternoon when the two Russian representatives arrived. They were Major General Ivan Susloparov, an artillery officer who normally is head of the Russian Mission to France, and his round-headed interpreter, Colonel Ivan Zenkovitch, who has a shiny bald head without a hair on it.

The sound and picture people arrived and I got them cleared past the guard into the war room and arranged to let them come and go, which was something of a triumph. The war room, where Ike generally has met with his top commanders and staff each morning at 9, is now strewn with cables, camera equipment, and batteries of klieg lights. The photographers generally take command wherever they go into action and they had pushed a huge table, normally in the center of the room, to a far corner to permit more coverage for their lenses. The room is about thirty feet square and has pale blue walls covered with battle maps showing the disposition of the forces on all fronts. There are charts showing the current day's air operations, casualty lists, records of supplies landed, railway and communications systems, and today's, tomorrow's, and the next day's weather—a series of charts that I have noticed always draws first attention of those entering the room. On one wall there was a thermometer, mounted on a background of swastikas, showing the mounting millions of German prisoners in Allied hands.

I was running around like crazy, taking care of phone calls from Paris, the needs of the photographers, and questions from Pawley, Matthews, and Kiley. On the one hand, I seemed to be an aide of the Supreme Commander and, on the other, the representative of the world-press, radio, and movie interests.

Shortly after 5 o'clock, I saw that Sergeants Chick and Serafin were craning their necks out the window, and, sure enough, the Germans were arriving. They were met by Brigadier E. J. Foord, of G-2, and Lieutenant Colonel K. A. S. Morrice, Assistant Secretary of the General Staff, both of whom had spent the day waiting to perform their duty, after having stayed at the airfield until noon. Both were British officers and they saluted smartly, the two Germans responding promptly and precisely, but I noticed the Germans didn't use the Nazi salute. Scores of our personnel quietly watched the proceeding.

They were brought to an office on our floor, two or three doors down and across the corridor to one I usually occupy. Pawley said the German Admiral was humming softly as he washed up and changed his collar, but Colonel Poleck appeared nervous.

I was standing in Beetle's outer office with a number of high-ranking officers when Ken Strong brought Admiral Friedeburg down the corridor. As the Admiral came face to face with the group, he stopped. He didn't salute, but he came to attention and passed on with Strong into Beetle's office. In the group were General Tooey Spaatz; Lieutenant General Morgan; Admiral Sir Harold Burrough, Commander of the Allied Naval Forces; Major General "Pinkie" Bull, G-3; Air Marshal Sir J. M. Robb, Chief of SHAEF's Air Staff; Brigadier Foord; Colonel R. G. H. Phillimore, who drafted the surrender terms, and, serenely at her desk, WAC Major Ruth M. Briggs, Beetle's secretary.

Ruth was the sole guard at Beetle's door while the conference took place. It lasted only about twenty minutes, and when it broke up, we learned that Friedeburg wasn't authorized to surrender. He could parley but could not enter commitments. The two Germans were authorized to communicate with Doenitz, but, unfortunately, they had not brought a code or arranged for frequencies for radio communication between Rheims and Flensburg, the new but, no doubt, temporary capital of Germany. Beetle had given him the terms of the Supreme Commander, which called for unconditional surrender. All German forces, aircraft, and surface ships were to remain at their present positions, and not allowed to scatter. The German War Department, the OKW, must guarantee to enforce and execute all orders issued by the Allied Command. Furthermore, the surrender terms had to apply to the Russians. Friedeburg emphasized the inability of the German High Command to send messages to its outlying forces. Communications were torn by our bombings and many German units were in flight. He indicated that at least forty-eight hours would be needed before he could sign and spoke feelingly of the hardships of the German civilian population. Beetle replied toughly that the Germans still are our enemies and would remain so until the surrender. But after they capitulate, they would be treated in accordance with the normal dictates of humanity. Beetle told Friedeburg either he would have to receive full authority from Doenitz to make complete and unconditional surrender in all theaters or Doenitz should send to Rheims his Chief of the OKW and the Commanders-in-Chief of the German Army, Navy, and Air Forces, with necessary authority to make a complete surrender. If, Beetle continued, the new German government did not promptly agree to surrender, it would be charged with guilt of continuance of hostilities.

The Admiral took the terms back to the office assigned him and called for whisky.

I was in the office of the Secretary, Lieutenant Colonel J. B. Moore, when Ken Strong relayed Friedeburg's request for refreshment. I hoped official reporters didn't learn of this request, or, at least, that it was fulfilled, because I had a vision of a bad reaction at home, in the Bible belt, but to the British general it seemed just a normal part of the process of negotiation.

While Beetle was delivering the terms to Friedeburg, the brass that had assembled in Beetle's outer office had moved to the war room and was joined by Susloparov.

The movie cameras were in focus, the lights lit, and all was in readiness in case the Germans were ready. Beetle walked in, blinded by the glare, and told the story to the assembled officials. There was nothing now to do but wait until Friedeburg heard from Doenitz.

Friedeburg got off his message to Doenitz. It had to be sent in SHAEF code to the Second British Army Headquarters, the nearest to Flensburg. Second Army was to decipher the message and send it by courier to Flensburg. This would take time.

Beetle brought Ike up to date on events, and, as there was nothing further to do at the moment, General Ike, escorted by the faithful Telek, left the building. I stayed behind to catch up on some of the notes of the day and to deal with the seemingly innumerable inquiries. I told Ike, as he went out, that if he had occasion to go to the war room, he would find it looked more like a Hollywood stage setting. He didn't give a damn so long as he got the formal and complete surrender.

During the day, surrender of three more German armies to General Devers' 6th Army Group had been announced.

At dinner Ike said the reason the Germans were stalling for time was to let Germans escape from Czechoslovakia, where they are being overrun by the Russians. It seems German high officials had sent their wives and children to Czechoslovakia to avoid our heavy bombings of German cities. Now that area, once regarded safe, is one in which there is great fear. Ike also detects a scheme of the Germans to get the Western Allies to accept a surrender and thus create a schism with the Russians. In the German mind, he thought, there is the desperate hope that we might yet succumb to Goebbels' old propaganda about the Bolsheviks. Once the Supreme Commander has the proper German representatives with suitable authority to act, he does not propose to let them dilly-dally. Furthermore, he wants the German Army to know this time that it has been completely and decisively beaten in the field, so there will not be the cry that was heard after World War I that it was the German home front that caved in and not the Army. General Ike wants to seal the Allied victory so completely that no one in Germany, civilian, soldier, airman, or sailor, will fail to appreciate the fact that the "superrace" has had the hell beaten out of it. He doesn't want our kids to be left an inheritance of World War III.

I asked Ike if he didn't think the French might well have a representative present for the signing, this being their country, and we are having the Russians present. He agreed and said that the omission was a complete oversight and sent word to Beetle to invite someone from the de Gaulle government to be on hand to sign as a witness. General Smith, as Chief of Staff of Supreme Headquarters, would, of course, sign representing both Britain and the United States.

It had been a long day, so all of us retired early.

The Germans Stall

SHAEF FORWARD (RHEIMS), SUNDAY, MAY 6, 1945
Admiral Friedeburg and Colonel Poleck had spent the night under guard
in the small villa for officers visiting SHAEF. It is a seven-room house at
3 Rue Godenot. Kiley had the names of all the MPs, the household staff,
and all the details that a good reporter should get. Said the Germans had
dined at 11 last night on tomato juice, pork chops, mashed potatoes, carrots and peas, fruit, coffee, and red wine. Admiral Friedeburg had commented on the fine linen and remarked that the owner of the house must
be "rich." The Germans listened to the radio in their sitting room until
after midnight and then retired.

After Ike got to bed last night the Prime Minister phoned for news, as
he had frequently during Saturday.

Secretary of the General Staff Lieutenant Colonel J. B. Moore told me
with a chuckle that General Ike had wandered through the office just
before 9 o'clock, soon returned, and made the passing comment:

"The damned war room looks like a Hollywood setting."

Shortly before noon, while I was working on my notes, Matthews and
Pawley poked their faces in the door. They said in a whisper that the Chief
of Staff had come to the office where they were working and said:

"Who represents the PRD here?"

They had replied, somewhat timidly, that they guessed they did.

"Then whoever's responsible for all that Hollywood equipment in the
war room must get it out immediately. This isn't going to be a show.
There's going to be a surrender. Get it out immediately."

My heart fell. I was practically sick. I was responsible for authorizing
the installation, not only on the word of the Supreme Commander that
if the surrender were on a train we could lay the correspondents in the
aisle, but also on the authority "through channels" of General Bull, G-3,
who discussed the arrangements at my request with the Chief of Staff
himself and had thereupon given me approval. Surmising that probably
Beetle's tummy was bothering him, I told Pawley and Matthews to sit
tight until I could reconnoiter. I suspected that Moore had told Beetle
of Ike's passing comment. The Chief of Staff, I guessed, had erroneously
construed the remark as a hint from his boss.

During lunch at the house, I told Ike of my dilemma and he said that all
he knew about it was that Beetle had come to his office during the forenoon and said that the war room had been made into a Hollywood stage
and that he didn't like it. Ike had merely said it was Beetle's show and he

could do as he liked. He had told the Chief of Staff to handle the negotiations and the signing, if any, and the Chief of Staff said he didn't want any publicity and that was the answer. But so far as the Supreme Commander was concerned, he had no objection but really desired that the public, through press, radio, and movies, should be given as much information as possible, since, after all, it was their war.

General Ike was pretty well whipped down from the tension of waiting and interruptions to his sleep caused by the Prime Minister and others telephoning him, so he decided to take a nap. I went back to the office to work out my problem.

When I reached there I found that Friedeburg had received a reply from Doenitz that the Chief of Staff of the German Army, General Gustav Jodl, who had succeeded General Guderian in the job, was flying to Rheims and would have authority to sign. Jodl was accompanied by his aide, Major G. C. Wilhelm Oxenius, and the two were in custody of Major General de Guingand, Monty's Chief of Staff.

To me this meant the end of our long vigil soon would be reached. I went to Beetle's office to clear the matter of the war room vs. Hollywood setting and found that he, too, was taking a nap and would not be at the office until 5 o'clock, in time to deal with Jodl. Meantime, Ruth Briggs couldn't disturb him.

I phoned General Allen's Executive Officer, Lieutenant Colonel Ben Crosby, in Paris; told him in guarded terms what was up and, despite Beetle's flare-up, I thought we could handle a pool of from fifteen to twenty correspondents who would be representative of world coverage. They should be flown up immediately, and I gave him the number of a room on the ground floor out of Beetle's sight where the correspondents could be held in seclusion and briefed by Matthews, Pawley, Kiley, and others so they would be fully prepared to cover the big story when, as, and if. Crosby said the correspondents would be on their way by air within an hour, and I arranged to have them met at Rheims and transported to the Ecole Professionnelle.

If I had a dozen horns to my dilemma before, now I had a dozen dozen. I had done some G-2ing on my own and arrived at the conclusion that Beetle's immediate staff had told him of General Ike's comment after seeing the war room and that Beetle had taken this as a firm indication that the Supreme Commander disliked what promised to be a showy performance; consequently, he had gone to his boss and disowned it. I was in the middle.

When the Chief of Staff arrived about 5, I went in and talked it out. The nap had improved his disposition; he was gracious, understanding, and co-operative. I told him it was the responsibility of the PRD to arrange for the world to know of the historic proceedings and that it was not just his show. He agreed but didn't like the idea of so many microphones on the table. I compromised on this immediately, as I knew Brownie could get a reasonably good pickup with one microphone for radio and movies. Beetle agreed. I heaved a sigh of relief, told him of the sweat I had been in, and he said:

"Your sweat? What do you think the rest of us are doing?"

Beetle didn't even seem to mind when I told him there were perhaps about twenty real live, ferocious correspondents lurking in a room just below his office.

He merely said: "Now that they're here, do the best you can for them." Just as I was leaving the office, he said:

"Ike asked me to make you superintendent of the fountain pens. Take these two and make sure they are used at the signing and that no one steals them."

"Aye, aye, sir," I said, as I examined the pens, one of which Beetle said was pure gold and the other gold-plated. I knew they had been sent to General Ike by an old friend he met in the Philippines many years ago, Kenneth Parker, who months ago had requested that when and if the peace was signed, these pens be used. However, he had made the stipulation that one be sent to him.

About this time there was much scurrying around the corridors. Jodl and his aide were arriving. He strode arrogantly from the car into the headquarters building, expressionless. An MP saluted and the German Chief of Staff returned the salute and, like Friedeburg, did not give the Nazi gesture. He was taken to the same office previously used by Friedeburg, where the latter, with Colonel Poleck, was sitting. Pawley, who practically had his ear to the keyhole, reported that when the Admiral opened the door to admit Jodl, there was no salute, but Jodl exclaimed, "Ah-ha." The door closed, but soon the Admiral came out, asked for coffee and a map of Europe. Jodl could be seen marching up and down.

Shortly after 6, Jodl and Friedeburg were taken by Ken Strong into Beetle's office, where again Strong was the interpreter. They stayed in nearly an hour and a half, when Beetle and Ken left and went to General Ike's office. As he left, Beetle told Ruth Briggs to send for Susloparov. General de Gaulle had sent General Sevez, representing General Juin, the Chief of Staff, who was away from Paris.

I had gone below to see the correspondents, found General Allen had the situation well in hand but was in a stew because other correspondents, particularly the "specials," were clamoring to be present. I didn't blame them for trying, but the seventeen selected by PRD in Paris were regarded as representative and would give world coverage. I felt it was an appropriate time for me to climb back into the ivory tower and again be a dignified aide to the Supreme Commander. I was ready to abdicate any PRD tasks to the director thereof. General Allen was ready to take over, but I didn't envy him his job. I made the mistake of showing the General the pens to be used in signing the surrender and he asked me to display them to the correspondents and also to hold them for the photographs.

Beetle and Ken were with General Ike about twenty minutes when Strong reappeared, but at the time I reached General Ike's office, Beetle and Strong had finished the progress of negotiations with Jodl and Friedeburg. They had gone into a huddle with Susloparov, who, so far, had not been in contact with the Germans at all. Ken Strong had told me there would be at least three hours' delay while Jodl, who brought a code, could make a signal to Doenitz.

Strong was just going in to talk further with the Germans as I went into General Ike's office to see if he wasn't tired enough to go home. We were invited to a reception at the WAC House and General Ike was not inclined to attend until I told him Susloparov and Sevez had been invited and had accepted. He thought he would stop for a few minutes and then go home to dinner.

General Ike told me to hang on to the fountain pens for dear life because he had promised to send one to his old friend Parker, and had in mind giving the solid-gold one to the President. I asked him how he would take care of the Prime Minister, for, after all, he is an Allied Commander.

"Oh, Lord, I hadn't thought of that."

Just then the phone rang. It was Ken Strong—the Germans again had insisted on forty-eight more hours. Without hesitation, Ike said:

"You tell them that forty-eight hours from midnight tonight, I will close my lines on the Western Front so no more Germans can get through. Whether they sign or not—no matter how much time they take." The Germans, of course, were frightened of the Russians and were seeking to surrender to French, American, and British forces. General Ike went on to make clear that the forty-eight hours would start running at midnight.

With this ultimatum, he left the office.

Surrender!

About 1:30 this morning I was called to the phone. It was Ruth Briggs. She said, "The big party is on," that General Ike already had arrived, and

that I, as custodian of the fountain pens, should hurry over to the headquarters.

"How could the war be ended without the pens?" she gibed. I found
Corporal Street, still in the kitchen, spinning yarns. He drove me to the
schoolhouse in record time.

At the front door there was a hornet's nest of correspondents waiting
to get into the school building. If I had good sense, or had seen them
first, I would have driven around the schoolhouse into the courtyard and
sneaked into the offices the back way. They had driven up from Paris on
the chance that they would be permitted to cover the ceremony, despite
the fact that a pool of seventeen already was on hand for the job. I
respected their enterprise, but from the standpoint of scores of correspondents who had stayed in Paris and not driven to Rheims on the
understanding that they would not be allowed into the ceremony, there
wasn't much that could be done for them, despite my normal desire to be
as helpful as possible. Standing on the steps, I hurriedly briefed them on
events of the two days and told them I would immediately seek General
Allen and get him to deal with them direct.

I found General Allen with General Bull, trying to work out details of
the procedure for complying with the order of the Combined Chiefs of
Staff that announcement of the end of the campaign was to be made
simultaneously at a later date by the governments at Washington, Moscow, and London. I gave General Allen the message, but the harassed
General could do little about it.

I was about to miss the big show myself, so hurried around to the war
room, where I found the Russian officers, General Spaatz, General Morgan, Admiral Burrough, Air Marshal Robb, and General Sevez already
gathered and waiting. General Bull followed me in.

Beetle arrived, looked over the seating arrangements, spoke briefly as
to procedure. He didn't seem to notice the one lonely microphone upon
which the whole world was dependent. He blinked in the floodlights, but
I felt that now with the proper pool of seventeen correspondents assembled quietly but attentively in the rear, he would not call off the proceedings.

General Jodl, Admiral Friedeburg, the two principals, arrived, escorted
by General Strong and Brigadier Foord. General Strong placed the documents for signature in front of General Smith, before whom I laid the
solid-gold fountain pen. Beetle spoke briefly to the Germans, which was
interpreted for them by Strong. It was merely that the surrender documents awaited signature. Were they ready and prepared to sign? Jodl
indicated assent with a slight nod. I already had before him the gold-

plated pen. Jodl had two documents to sign, so when he finished the first, I retrieved the gold-plated pen and substituted my own—one given me by Charlie Daly in Algiers. With this he signed the second document.

Generals Smith, Susloparov, and Sevez then signed both documents. At the conclusion of the signing, General Jodl stood at attention, addressed General Smith, and said, in English:

"I want to say a word."

Then he lapsed into German, later interpreted as:

"General! With this signature the German people and German armed forces are, for better or worse, delivered into the victor's hands. In this war, which has lasted more than five years, both have achieved and suffered more than perhaps any other people in the world. In this hour I can only express the hope that the victor will treat them with generosity."

The official time of the signature on the surrender document was 2:41 A.M. British Double Summer Time.

I had three pens, and Ike, if he chose, could now send the gold ones to the President and Prime Minister, and mine to Mr. Parker. The only trouble was that mine is a Sheaffer.

The delegates arose and the Germans were taken to the room assigned them and the remainder went to General Ike's office. He sternly asked the Germans if they fully understood the terms and whether they were prepared to execute them. This was interpreted by General Strong. The answer was made in the affirmative; the Germans bowed stiffly and left the room.

The photographers wanted more pictures. General Ike called all of us to surround him. Someone asked that he hold the fountain pens. He displayed them in a "V for Victory," the pictures were snapped, and congratulations said all round.

But Ike's work wasn't finished. He still had to make a short newsreel and radio recording. Taking the Air Chief Marshal with him to the war room, so both Allies would be shown together, General Ike spoke briefly "from the cuff." He had to make one retake after I butted in. He had used the word "armistice" and I was apprehensive that this term, which to me connoted all the laxity and unpreparedness of the period between the two wars, was a bad one to use. Growling and scowling at me, he substituted "surrender."

As we walked back to General Ike's office, Tedder poked me in the ribs and said with a twinkle in his eyes that General Ike could make the best speech in the world and I should mind my own damned business.

Anyway, it wasn't an armistice; it was a complete and unconditional surrender, and that's what we've been fighting for.

From time to time, we had joked as to the kind of heroic language that the Supreme Commander might use to tell the Combined Chiefs that the surrender had been achieved: "We have met the enemy and they are ours"; or "Don't give up the ship, we've just begun to fight." But the Supreme Commander dictated a cable to the Combined Chiefs simply:

"The mission of this Allied force was fulfilled at 0241 local time, May 7, 1945."

Now the problem was the timing of the release of the news. I told Ike about the correspondents at the front door—that the news was all over and that when the correspondents who actually saw and are writing about the surrender reach Paris in the morning, the story is likely to leak, no matter what precautions are taken or what admonitions are given to prevent it. General Bull came in with the orders to be sent to all the Allied forces in the field, telling them hostilities would cease as of one minute after midnight, Tuesday-Wednesday, May 8/9. This was Double British Summer Time. The orders were to go out in the clear. I called attention to the fact that they would be intercepted by every monitoring service and the news would be out. I suggested that we let the correspondents begin filing their stories as of 7 o'clock in the morning and hold the first "cease firing" order until that time and let it go in the clear. However, to a soldier an order is an order and General Ike had his instructions from the Combined Chiefs requiring that the announcement be made by the heads of the governments at a time to be fixed later. He stood by the order but instructed that the "cease fire" dispatches be sent in code.

It was nearly 5 o'clock when we hit the hay.

SHAEF FORWARD (RHEIMS), MONDAY EVENING, MAY 7, 1945

I am going to Berlin tomorrow. A lot of things have happened to me in this war, but this trip really has me keyed up. Ike isn't going. Instead he is sending Air Chief Marshal Tedder, his deputy, who, he feels, is a happy choice because there will be a British signature on the document.

I got up about 9 this morning, bathed, shaved, and dressed, poked my nose in Ike's bedroom and found him still in bed, but he had been awake for some time, taking and making phone calls. He was dealing with General Bull about arrangements for the final ratification with the Russians. He had been reading a Western, the current hair-raiser being *Cartridge Carnival.*

Ike got off a message to Antonov through the Military Mission in Moscow, emphasizing that SHAEF has scrupulously adhered to the understanding with the Russians that there would be no separate truce on this front. Ike wanted Antonov to know that although a brief instrument of unconditional military surrender (copy of which had been furnished Antonov) had been signed at Rheims before receipt of a request from the Russians to have the signing in Berlin, the Germans had signed a second agreement committing themselves to execute a formal ratification with the signatures of the Chief of the High Command and Commanders-in-Chief of the land, sea, and air forces.

On advice of some of his staff, who have had experience meeting with the Russians, General Ike has decided not to go to Berlin. In fact, the war was ended by the signing at Rheims last night and the desire of the Russians for a formal ceremony is interpreted by Ike's staff as an encore, insisted on for purposes of showmanship for the Russian people. The Prime Minister had already registered his objection, so Ike reluctantly gave way. Actually, this is one party he'd really like to be in on. He'd like to see Berlin and he'd like to meet the Russians.

While I was in Ike's bedroom, General Morgan phoned to break the bad news about the leak. When Kennedy's story started to roll in America, the OWI put it on short-wave transmission, which Radio Luxembourg, operated by SHAEF PWD, automatically rebroadcast. This gave credence to the story, as writers and broadcasters at home could get a new angle to their unconfirmed story by quoting Radio Luxembourg. The Germans themselves, desperate to get the surrender order to their own forces, had broadcast an official announcement from Radio Flensburg. Ike was burned up, but there was nothing he could do about the premature announcement except growl at me, and then philosophically accept the circumstances of the alliance which required his official silence until the news could be announced in Moscow, London, and Washington. If it had been merely a matter of co-ordinating London and Washington, this would have been relatively easy, but the Russians normally are suspicious, so we simply have to adhere to our agreement with them. PRD in Paris has stood pat and I'm glad I'm not there. The correspondents have had a mass meeting, demanding that punitive measures be taken against Ed Kennedy and the Associated Press. General Allen suspended the AP as an organization and then found that his authority applied only to the individual correspondent, not to the organization. He suspended Ed Kennedy and Bob Bunnelle, chief of the AP bureau in London, pending complete investigation.*

---

* Ultimately Kennedy's accreditation to SHAEF was withdrawn and he was sent home. Bunnelle was exonerated.

Ike's immediate worry was that the premature release might cause the loss of American, British, and French lives.

He seemed tired and weary. The last four days have taken more out of him than have the past eleven months of the campaign. Yet he is gratified to the point of exhilaration that so far as hostilities are concerned, the Russians and we are in complete understanding and the meeting at Berlin should be marked by cordiality. General Marshall has cabled him about plans to bring various groups of officers and enlisted men to America for celebrations in various cities. He cabled General Marshall that he would like to make each party as large as possible because he felt the public soon would get tired of repetition of the same type of celebration. So far as he personally was concerned, he would rather avoid the receptions and spend his time fishing.

This afternoon the radio waves were hot with efforts of Colonel Frank McCarthy, Secretary of the General Staff of the War Department in Washington, seeking to obtain agreement from Stalin, Churchill, and Truman as to a new release time.

Word came from the Russians this evening that the party is on tomorrow in Berlin and our special flight of C-47s will leave from the airfield near Rheims at 8:15 A.M.

The message from the Russians greatly relieved Ike's mind of the anxiety that he has felt, due to the danger of misunderstanding. His worry has been intensified by the Germans' skillful use of propaganda inspired by their desire to surrender to the Western Allies instead of to the Russians. It is evident to him that the Germans in the East are being paid back in the same coin that they used in their Russian campaign in 1941-42. Consequently, the Germans are completely terrified, collectively and individually, of Russian vengeance.

Ed Kennedy's premature release of the surrender story has caused the damnedest snafu I've ever experienced. It's not only snafu but tarfu and fumtu. I've learned the hard way it is much easier to start a war than to stop one. I thought the signing would mean a letup in work, but instead just the reverse has happened.

Berlin

PARIS, THURSDAY, MAY 10, 1945

I returned from Berlin yesterday morning, landing at Orly. The sun was shining brightly, but I was in a fog. Have spent eighteen hours in bed. I accompanied the pool of correspondents, Brigadier Bill Turner, and Colonel Dupuy.

As we were to be in Berlin such a short time, and as SHAEF could not on short notice get us approval to fly our radio-equipped aircraft into the Russian area, the two C-47s were left behind. It was considered best all around simply to fly the correspondents back to Paris, where they could write their stories and prepare their broadcasts, and have them cleared by the censors for release at whatever time finally was set by the three governments.

To sign for the Western Allies were Air Chief Marshal Tedder and, as witnesses, General Tooey Spaatz and General Delattre de Tassigny. They were accompanied by numerous assistants, including Major General Ken Strong, of G-2, and Major General "Pinky" Bull, of G-3.

The German delegation which had signed at Rheims—Jodl, Friedeburg, and party, were in one of the C-47s.

We got off from the Rheims airfield at 8:25, flying in a V formation. We were to rendezvous with Russian fighter-escorts over a German airfield at Stendal, on the American side of the Elbe. The Russian fighter-escort not being in sight, our planes landed. It was a sod field, and bumpy. Presently the RAF C-47 from the 21st Army Group arrived with Field Marshal Keitel; Admiral Friedeburg; Vice-Admiral Leopold Buerkner, Chief Adjutant to Keitel; Oberst Karl Boehm-Tettel Bach, aide to Keitel; Korpswetter Kapitän Salmon, Political Adviser to Admiral Friedeburg; General Oberst Stumpf; and Major Stange, aide to Stumpf. Keitel wore the Blood Ribbon, the highest Nazi decoration. The Germans, particularly Keitel, remained aloof, coldly and militarily correct.

While waiting for the Russian escort and the Germans, we sauntered around the field, where perhaps 150 German planes, mostly fighters, were in various stages of disrepair. I spoke to an American lieutenant colonel in charge. He said that more than 25,000 German prisoners had come in the day before and were constantly streaming across the Elbe to what they thought was the relative safety of the American lines. German arms were piled high in a near-by hangar, and the American officers and men vied in showing their trophies, such as German cameras, glasses, and weapons. My lieutenant-colonel friend, whose name I did not get, gave me a German air rifle which he said has the power of a .22. I reached in a pile of swords and pulled one out. It bore the name "Eisenhauer." I took it along as a souvenir for Ike.

We had arrived promptly according to our time schedule on Double British Summer Time. This, however, was an hour earlier than the time on which the Russians were operating—Central European Time.

The Russian escort planes flashed into view exactly on schedule on their time. We took off immediately and arrived over Berlin in a half-hour. Berlin was cloaked in haze and smoke—many buildings still smoldering from the battle—and the sight was awesome. We had heard for months how badly Berlin was beaten up, and everything we had heard was illustrated by the incredible destruction we could see. Hardly a building seemed not to have been hit.

As our plane circled Tempelhof, I was with the pilot. I heard a radio instruction from the Russians on the ground telling the pilot of the plane carrying the Germans to keep his passengers aboard until further notice. We landed. Our planes drew up in line, on a huge cement apron, marked with rusted fragments of antiaircraft shells. There was a three-company guard of honor with a band and three color-bearers with flags of the United States, Russia, and Britain.

Our party made its way to the scene of action, not in a military manner but more like a large, curious family ambling along the midway of a county fair. The band played *God Save the King, The Star-Spangled Banner*, and the Russian national anthem, and all of us stood at attention and saluted.

With formalities over, we were assigned to waiting cars for the drive to Zhukov's headquarters in a German Army Engineering College at Karlshorst, a suburb on the northeastern side of the city. Most of the cars had been confiscated from the Germans, with their identification tags written in Russian numerals. There were about thirty cars.

As Tempelhof is on the southern outskirts of Berlin, we hoped we would see considerable of the city, but our route took us around the outskirts between the suburbs and the city proper.

When we left Tempelhof, smoke poured from one of the large, four-story, yellow-brick, semicircular buildings. Much of our route was under an elevated railway. About every six blocks we passed through a road block. I had heard about these. The Germans placed two streetcars side by side and filled in between them and the buildings on either side with rubble from bombed buildings. The Russians had merely dug away enough debris for a car barely to squeeze through. Dust was thick. There were no other cars on the street and no streetcars were running. Neither were any German citizens allowed on our route, they having been warned to keep clear. On either side were houses showing all manner of destruction, some from fire, others from direct hits. There were few windows intact. Some of the damage looked old, some seemed fresh from the recent fighting.

I was amused by the Russian girls in uniform. We had heard a great deal about the use of women in the Russian Army, that they manned antiaircraft batteries just behind the front line, that they were first-class shots, many of them expert snipers, and, in general, had borne the hardships and lived close to the actual battle just like their men. The girls wore a three-quarter-length tunic, tightly belted at the waist, with shoulder straps crossing from each shoulder to the waist, accentuating their figures. They wore straight skirts and each had black boots about ten inches high.

On our route girls were serving as traffic policemen. Each had two flags, one red and one yellow. With the yellow flag in her left hand, she warned nonexistent cross traffic with a vigorous wave, then with her right she waved to the next car approaching in our caravan, indicating the coast was clear and to keep coming. As the car reached her, she quickly put both the yellow and red flags in her left hand and with her right smartly saluted. The vigorous rigmarole was repeated for each car. The caravan was moving about twenty-five miles an hour. This meant the girls were very busy indeed. They seemed to enjoy the humor of the situation, for as we passed they smiled broadly as they hurriedly saluted.

The Russians had planned that the French, British, and Americans would be separated by nationalities in different houses, but Air Chief Marshal Tedder, thoroughly Allied, explained to the conducting officer that SHAEF didn't separate its nationalities into compartments, that all lived and worked together. I found myself assigned to a cottage with Tedder and Spaatz, but no one paid much attention to assignments or even confinement to the cottages. Apparently there were no important factories in the Karlshorst area, for here there were no signs of bomb damage. The Russians had managed to get the public utilities in this area started and our cottage had electricity and running water.

We loitered in the front yard, looked at the Russians, whose uniforms were strictly utilitarian, all wearing tunics, tightly belted at the middle, and black boots. There was one Russian girl who stood on the corner opposite, calmly surveying these creatures of the Western world. She reminded me of Milton Caniff's Dragon Lady. She was tall and beautiful —a fact to which the Russian soldiers seemed to pay no attention. They were, in fact, more interested in us, and as they passed up and down the sidewalks, we were kept busy returning their salutes.

Tedder went off to make his formal call on Marshal Zhukov, where pleasantries were exchanged. The ceremony, expected to be finished in two hours, would have to be delayed. There would be a first meeting at 2:30 and a second at 4:30. Tex Lee and Jim Gault presented the SHAEF shield, in General Eisenhower's name, to the Russian Marshal.

Then came a long period of waiting, with many in our party wanting to see the bomb damage in the heart of Berlin. This was particularly true of the air officers, Tedder and Spaatz. The Russians, however, said time was required to lay on such a trip, as security guards had to be placed along the route. The Russians didn't want to spoil the party by letting some of their distinguished guests get sniped at. There were delayed-action bombs left by the Germans, too, and we could hear rumbles of detonations in the distance.

At the cottage a Russian girl in uniform efficiently laid out a buffet luncheon. Her roundish, almost Oriental face was scrubbed so clean it shone. She was smiling, courteous, and solicitous of our wants. We helped ourselves to sandwiches of thick white bread, both black and pink caviar, ham and fish. There was butter, but it must have been American Lend-Lease because it stuck to the roof of my mouth, like the butter we got in Africa which we always thought contained paraffin as a preservative. There was good Rhine wine, some red wine, a sweet wine like Passover, and cognac. All of us were hungry as well as thirsty, and as we seemed to have nothing to do but wait, the maid was kept busy between the kitchen and the living room.

There was a good German radio in the living room, which I found in working order, and at 3 o'clock, our time, I fished around and had the good fortune to hear in quick succession on different stations, Churchill from London, Truman from Washington, and de Gaulle from Paris, all proclaiming V-E Day.

The Russian maid, to whom I could speak only in sign language, made vigorous motions indicating "no." She wouldn't believe the war was over until she heard it officially over the Moscow radio.

General Deane, head of the American Military Mission to Moscow, had arrived in a C-54 direct from Moscow. He joined our group and said that American and British ships lying in the harbor at Odessa had celebrated the end of the war on Monday. They had put on a display of antiaircraft fire. The Russians immediately protested, said the war wasn't over, and that there should be no such celebrations until Moscow gave the word.

With Turner and Dupuy, I had reconnoitered the room where the ratification was to take place. It was about sixty feet long and forty feet wide, two stories in height, with a small balcony along one side. The building was plain and made of concrete. There were perhaps fifty Russian reporters and photographers. I found one who spoke English. He represented what he called "Inform Bureau," which I understood to be the equivalent of the OWI or the MOI. I found him writing rapidly in longhand an account of proceedings to date.

He stopped long enough to help me with a problem, important in my mind. PRD was under great pressure from the correspondents to get formal permission from the Russians to cross the lines to get stories.

Through SHAEF we had made repeated signals to the Military Mission in Moscow, asking for reciprocal arrangements, but we had received no satisfaction. I hoped that by putting the question direct to Zhukov we might work out local arrangements for coverage of Berlin without waiting on Moscow. My friend from the Inform Bureau introduced me to the chief representative of the Russian Tass agency and interpreted my request. The Tass man said he would present my plea, but probably the question could not be answered locally even by Zhukov, as Moscow would have to be consulted for authority.

I asked my English-speaking acquaintance how war news was covered by the Russians. He said all their correspondents are soldiers or officers of the Red Army. I knew that American correspondents assigned to Russia ordinarily were confined to Moscow and got their news by reading the Russian newspapers or from official statements by Soviet officials. The soldier-correspondents of the Red Army were "on their own" so far as censorship was concerned. There were no censors with the armies. The correspondents sent their copy to Moscow. They were instructed and trained to write stories without violation of military security and, I took it, of the official party "line." I asked what happened if a correspondent violated instructions. My friend simply shrugged his shoulders.

Returning the half block to the cottage, I found that most of our party was waiting in a caravan of cars to go to Tempelhof to get their handbags, as the delay in the proceedings indicated an overnight stay. They already had waited a half-hour and another hour elapsed before the Russian officer in charge obtained authority from higher up to make the trip. I found a place in a car with Tex O'Reilly, of the *New York Herald Tribune,* and we passed over the same route, but which now had been opened to civilian traffic. We saw hundreds of displaced persons moving slowly toward us. Many were walking, carrying all sorts of baggage; some were pushing handcarts, and here and there was a horse-drawn vehicle loaded with baggage, women, and children until it creaked. They were a disheveled and forlorn lot. Some carried flags, and I noticed Dutch, Belgian, Italian, and French amongst them.

I had seen hordes of displaced persons in my travels and each time I felt dejected by their pathetic appearance. No one can see them plodding along, undernourished, and shabbily and scantily clothed, many without shoes, returning to their homes, without realizing the awfulness of war, especially as practiced by the Germans, who ruthlessly enslaved millions.

We saw long queues of German civilians with buckets, dishpans, clothes boilers, and anything that would hold water, waiting for a turn at public pumps. There seemed to be absolutely no fight left in them.

Russian soldiers were busy adding French flags to the numerous displays of Russian, British, and American emblems we had noticed on the first trip. Apparently, the French had been overlooked.

While we were at Tempelhof, getting our overnight gear, we heard several heavy detonations in the distance; finally, a whopper in one of the buildings adjoining the field. Soon there was heavy smoke with licks of flame, undoubtedly from a delayed-action bomb.

Back at the cottage, we found there would be further delay before the signing and that dinner was to follow the ratification.

We stood around on one foot and the other in the administration building, where the ceremony eventually was to take place, and everyone was growing tired and weary. I was delighted that General Ike hadn't come because I could imagine him fuming with impatience. Tedder was philosophically sweating out the situation, filling, refilling, and puffing his pipe, while Ken Strong dealt with the Russians on the detailed wording.

I found myself dealing with an American sergeant looking for some chow. The Russian girl in my cottage fixed him some food and, as he ate, he told me his problem. He was one of a small crew sent with our party by SHAEF Signals to establish radio communication from Berlin to Rheims. We didn't have our own transmitter; we had to use one of the Russians'. A set of four frequencies, suitable for daylight and darkness, had been assigned, but he had been pounding the key for hours without getting a response from Rheims.

Both Tedder and Bull had been anxious to get a message back to General Ike, and the sergeant was frantic. I went with him to the mobile van, parked near the administration building, as I, too, wanted to get a message through to General Ike and to General Allen. By this time the Russian signalmen had nearly completed erection of another antenna beamed on Rheims, and there was a good prospect that as soon as the sun went down, we could raise a reply from SHAEF.

The Russians had brought out cheese and German beer in quantities. It wasn't the kind of German beer one hears about. It was like near beer. The drafters, who were working on the redraft of the ceremonial surrender terms, had drafted General Ike's secretary, Warrant Officer Nana Rae, to help them, she having thoughtfully brought a typewriter. Russian photographers bobbed up from everywhere, all the rank in our party being photographed from every possible angle. The process of redrafting was going on in a goldfish bowl. Correspondents came in and out; a heavily set Russian commissar drifted in and out of the discussion, he always wearing his hat. Zhukov wasn't there. The commissar would carry each question to Zhukov in another building for a decision.

Finally, all the points had been covered—the Russians, French, British, and Americans satisfied. We moved into the conference room, which had across one end a long table, obviously the head, from which spurred three similarly long tables—one for the press and two for the official party. Under the balcony, at one side, was a short table, about ten feet in length, for the Germans. My seat was at the long table with my back to that of the Germans, only six feet away. By turning I could have a close-up view.

At the head table, Zhukov took his place in the center, Tedder on his right, Spaatz on Zhukov's left, and Tassigny at the left of Tooey. On Tedder's right was the Russian commissar, the party representative (whose name, I had by then learned, was Vyshinsky), in civilian clothes. In the rear were batteries of klieg lights for the movies and stills. If Beetle thought our modest arrangements in our war room looked like Hollywood, we now were looking at something that was super-Hollywood. From the original fifty Russian photographers and correspondents whom I had seen early in the day, the number had grown to what seemed a hundred.

As we found our seats, the cameras ground and Zhukov rose and called the assembly to order. In front of him were two microphones. Zhukov seemed stern. His chest was covered with medals, as, indeed, were those of most of the Russians. The Russian guard brought in the Germans. Turning around in my chair, I had the kind of view of Keitel and his compatriots that a photographer must get of Kate Smith as he snaps her stepping down Pullman steps, only what I saw wasn't a cheerful, smiling, friendly face. It was one of arrogance and defiance. Keitel stepped to his table, raised his Field Marshal's baton as a salute, and sat down. Stumpf, the highest-ranking officer of the Luftwaffe that the Germans could find, was on his right and Admiral Friedeburg at his left. Under the Admiral's eyes were deep black circles. He looked morose. Stumpf made no particular impression on me. Keitel surveyed the room as he might have looked over the terrain of a battlefield. Here was the living Prussianism of which I had heard so much. His attitude contrasted sharply with that of the German civilians I had seen during the day, all of whom appeared completely whipped and cowed.

Tedder arose, paper in hand, and in his thin voice, which seemed appropriately harsh, asked if the Germans accepted the terms of surrender, copy of which had been handed them. He spoke in English and an interpreter translated his remarks, first in Russian and then in German. Keitel replied that he accepted the terms as written in the paper, which he held up, and his reply in German was translated back to Russian and English.

Keitel was told to come forward and sign. There were several copies, but he signed each quickly, firmly, and with an attitude of disdain. We couldn't actually see him sign because he was immediately surrounded by a horde of photographers and some reporters. One Russian sound-reel man, who carried his heavy camera and tripod on his shoulder, had an advance man who broke into the throng, shouldering other photographers and reporters right and left, to make room for his principal. This got him a sock in the jaw, to which he responded in kind, adding a light touch to our entertainment but not to the dignity of the affair. I wished for Beetle.

When Keitel returned to his seat, Friedeburg and Stumpf walked to the head table and signed. Zhukov and Tedder then signed as representatives of the Allies, with Spaatz and Tassigny signing as witnesses.

While this was going on, Keitel was arguing vehemently with the American interpreter, Reinhardt, who absorbed the argument, but it failed to move him. I later learned that Keitel was insisting that more time was necessary to get messages to all sections of their battle fronts, their communications having been badly disrupted. Keitel's arrogant dissent from the text he had already read and signed came too late, for there was no appeal and hostilities formally would cease within a few minutes.

When the Allies finished signing, Zhukov stood up and barked an order that the Germans should depart. Keitel rose promptly, followed by the others, snapped to attention, saluted with his baton, pivoted, and strode from the room.

After they left, the whole party broke up and wandered into the adjoining rooms, where, under many klieg lights, the cameramen continued their field day. It seems every Russian has liberated a camera. There must have been thousands of snapshots taken and there seemed to be no limit to the number of professional and amateur photographers permitted. The Western Allies had three.

Meanwhile girls in uniform were arranging the same tables for the inevitable ceremonial banquet. We took the same seats at about 1:30. I noticed my napkin. It was a torn piece of bedsheet and to me was a reminder of the hardship of the Russians. I tucked it into my pocket as a souvenir for Beverly.

Stalin's Secret Weapon

Across from me was a Russian general, who immediately got my eye. He pointed to the row of glasses in front of each of us and a forest of bottles —vodka, white and red wine, and champagne. He followed this with another sign indicating that in due course I, and others like me, would be under the table, which he demonstrated by a wide sweep of his hand and an appropriate grimace. I knew that vodka was the Russian secret weapon at such affairs, and I told myself to be careful.*

Soon Zhukov arose and proposed a toast to Premier Stalin, interpreted sentence by sentence by a Russian lieutenant standing beside him. As Zhukov raised his glass we all stood. I was cagey. I took a sip of wine, but my Russian friend across the table went "bottoms up" with vodka. I looked away.

Then Zhukov proposed a toast to General Eisenhower. I took an old letter from my pocket and immediately wrote down his words as the interpreter gave them:

General of the Army Eisenhower has given the most magnificent performance of any general of the current time. His great strides in the West helped me in the East. I raise my glass to the greatest military strategist of our time —General Eisenhower.

After having seen General Ike described in print so frequently as the "Chairman of the Board," which I always felt was a means of damning with faint praise his proven ability as a military strategist, I was delighted that the great Russian Marshal had spoken as flowingly and, to me, appropriately about my boss. I filled my glass with vodka. I looked my Russian friend straight in the eye and together we went "bottoms up." The Russian general filled his glass again and turned to Tex Lee, sitting two seats from me, who likewise was pleased with Zhukov's compliment to our boss. The Russian downed another glass of vodka, but Tex, the rascal, I saw, had only wine and just took a sip. The Russian frowned in despair, looked at me. I filled my glass again with vodka and "down the hatch." To hell with being cagey.

From that time on the party swirled with toasts and the effect thereof. There were toasts from Stalin to the "late and great" President Roosevelt, who had been such a great friend of Russia; to the indomitable Prime Minister, Mr. Churchill, and to the new President of the United States, Mr. Truman.

From where I sat, Zhukov, Tedder, Spaatz, and Delattre de Tassigny seemed to be popping up like jacks-in-the-box—offering toast after toast, barely giving me time to sit down and fill my glass and repeat. By now I was a vodka man and my Russian friend seemed my great admirer. Then came Vyshinsky, the political speaker. He seemed to start with the beginning of the Revolution and was coming on down through the years when

---

* Unfortunately, I didn't listen to myself.

I decided, having heard many political speeches in my Washington days, I could miss part of this one.

I wanted to get off a signal to General Ike, so I visited my American sergeant at the mobile transmitter just outside the building. I found that darkness had brought success to him and all was well. I wrote a signal to General Ike—no doubt punctuated with vodka—advising him of my version of the official ratification, that the banquet was on, and that the Russians were very fine people, indeed. I also sent a message to PRD in Paris to have transportation at Orly for the correspondents about 9 the next morning, as they would be flown back direct to do their stories and broadcasts from Paris. I also asked that Corporal Street be on hand with my car.

This seemed to complete my duty. I waited while the sergeant tapped off the messages, ciphering of my two now being unnecessary as the war was over. A great desire to sleep came over me. Remembering the room in the cottage, of which I had carefully obtained the key, I went back, undressed, and crawled in bed for the remaining few hours. I had had the banquet and vice versa.

I found myself standing with Tex O'Reilly on the apron of Orly airfield, near Paris, wondering what had become of Corporal Street. There was a bus for the correspondents to take them direct to the Scribe. While I searched for Street, the bus pulled away. Colonel Plummer gave me a French taxi and Tex accompanied me. Little was said. We were both out on our feet. I was more fortunate than Tex. He still had to write his story, but I could go right to bed. I had vague misgivings that something awful had happened and that I had created some disturbance of which I should be ashamed. I asked Tex if I had done all right, and he said:

"Oh, you've nothing to worry about. Anyone would have done what you did. After all, there were three generals carried out of the party."

I couldn't muster courage to inquire further, but if I had done anything to disgrace General Ike or the Allies, I had a vision that I would be court-martialed for "conduct unbecoming an officer" and promptly sent home by General Ike on "a slow boat, unescorted."

From my room, I phoned Jim Gault, who was back at his desk in Rheims, the SHAEF party having landed about 8:30. Jim said my conduct had been disgraceful. He had personally spoken to a half-dozen officers in my behalf and asked them to say nothing about it. I asked him what I had done. He said he would tell me when he saw me—that he didn't like to say anything more over the telephone.

I got General Ike on the wire. I told him I had done something awful;

that I didn't know at the moment exactly what it was, but if it had been at all disgraceful, I wanted him not only to know about it but I wanted to apologize.

Ike said: "I don't know what you did, but if it is as bad as you think it is, I thoroughly disapprove."

This was the end of the conversation, and if I hadn't been dogtired, I couldn't have slept eighteen hours, but I awakened with more than a hangover. I had the disquieting feeling that I had committed some terrible indiscretion, yet I didn't know what it was. I could see black and blue spots, some in long streaks, on my body, and my right hand was sore. It felt as if my little finger was broken. Every bone in my body seemed to ache.

In addition, I had left my overnight bag, my Navy raincoat, with a broken identification tag in the pocket and a half bottle of Johnny Walker, in the cottage in Karlshorst.

I haven't the courage to go to the office today, but hope to be able to face the PRD gang, particularly Brigadier Turner and Colonel Dupuy, my Berlin compatriots, at the regular 9 o'clock meeting in the morning.

Blackout

PARIS, FRIDAY, MAY 11, 1945

Everyone seemed quiet and respectful at the morning meeting. From the PRD standpoint, the arrangements for correspondents had worked satisfactorily, and Lieutenant Colonel Ben Crosby unnecessarily apologized because there had been a slight snafu in relaying that portion of my message applying to Corporal Street. No one, in fact, seemed particularly brilliant, as V-E celebrations in Paris had started on Monday and have continued since.

After the meeting, I went to Brigadier Turner to G-2 my personal situation. It wasn't good. He said that after the banquet broke up, about sunrise, and the caravan of cars had been formed to take our party through the center of Berlin en route to Tempelhof, I was missing. A search found me quietly and safely in bed in the cottage, but shaking and even cold water didn't awaken me. Thereupon he had struck me sharply with his stick and when I awakened, "I came out swinging." I had endeavored to commit a thoroughly un-Allied act by striking my British friend and coworker, but Colonel Dupuy had thrown his arms around me and prevented the landing of any blows. The kindly Brigadier said I had then quieted, quickly dressed, and accompanied them to the caravan of cars, where someone erroneously told me to get into a certain car which soon I was told to get out of because it was reserved for the Germans. He thought this had annoyed me and that certain attempts at fisticuffs had ensued, but it was all a part of the celebration and no harm had been done. He brightened my miserable load only a little when he told me he didn't think we had actually drunk vodka. He thought it was Lend-Lease alcohol, flavored as vodka; the same liquid fire Russian soldiers carry into battle in five-gallon tins and drink straight without chasers. Consumption of any quantity of the stuff was like TNT. He had learned from wise British diplomats, accustomed to such banquets, that vodka should be followed immediately with beer and the two interspersed throughout a bout. This was valuable intelligence, but a bit too late.

He reminded me that I had been discreet enough to leave the party and go to bed, whereas certain high-ranking officers of all nationalities had done their duty until they had fallen at their posts and had to be carried out. I wasn't quite sure whether this was a compliment or a reprimand.

I then saw Colonel Dupuy and he corroborated the Brigadier's story— but added another episode. When we reached Tempelhof, I, apparently, had been seized by the desire to take home a suitable trophy of the occasion. There were four flags—Russian, British, French, and American— on poles, guarded by a Russian sentry. I had left our party, assembled at the waiting plane, marched to the sentry, and inquired if I might have one of the flags. The sentry indicated "no" with his gun, which I seemed to understand, and just then Lieutenant Colonel J. B. Moore deployed in my direction, took me by the arm, and steered me back to the plane.

Everyone in the plane had fallen asleep and, so far as he knew, no one in the party aroused until the C-47 had pulled up on the apron at Orly. Colonel Dupuy likewise accepted my apology. The mystery of the long black-and-blue marks cleared as I realized I had been awakened by the Brigadier's stick.

Tex O'Reilly came in to see me. He said it was too bad we didn't get the flags.

I asked him why the "we."

"Well," he replied, "while we were waiting to take off from Tempelhof, you decided you wanted a flag. You marched to the flagpoles and I followed you. At thirty paces from the first pole, you stopped, came to attention, and saluted. Then you proceeded to the sentry and made signs to him. I was right behind you and as I noticed that you had stopped thirty paces from the flagpole, I stopped too and likewise saluted. I figured you knew the protocol, so I followed it."

So far as PRD business was concerned, I found that General Allen had battled out the Ed Kennedy episode, the aftermath of which I had fortunately escaped. Kennedy's action was a problem for the press itself.

General Allen remarked that his days of command of a combat team in an armored division in Italy were much more pleasant than those of the PRD; he was trying to get out of the job and hoped to be assigned to an armored division going to the Pacific.

So far as I was concerned, I was browned-off at the war, the PRD, and, most of all, myself. I told Corporal Street to be ready for a trip to Saint-Malo over Saturday and Sunday. I had landed there in 1923 while on a cattleboat junket to Europe, and I want to see the lovely place again.

PART SEVEN

"This War Was a Holy War"

MAY TO JULY, 1945

I Take a Call With Misgiving

PARIS, MONDAY, MAY 14, 1945

Returned from Saint-Malo late yesterday and feel much better, although Ike's stern words, "thoroughly disapprove," still lurk in my mind. The part of the old city within the walls of Saint-Malo had been ruthlessly destroyed by the Germans, who had arbitrarily set fire to most of the whole city. The Breton French were kind and pleasant to me, as I was told they were to all Americans. French architects of the national government already had arrived and were carefully marking each stone of the historic buildings with a view toward rebuilding the city.

The big news of the day, however, is not my escapist journey, but a telephone call from General Ike. I took it with misgiving and soon found that what he wanted was not to send me home but to have me take charge of PRD as long as he stayed in Europe. I told him I would do anything he wanted, and he said to see him at Rheims on Thursday.

I still have pending the letter of Secretary Forrestal indicating that he has a job for me to do in the Pacific, and, while I have said yes to Ike, now that the war is over in Europe, I'm not too keen about staying here. In addition, with the war over, the Allies are no longer motivated by the singleness of purpose—that is, to win the war—which has heretofore dominated all our thoughts and actions. General Ike and his entire command are in for a rough time. Correspondents filing stories from Europe to America are bound to find keen competition for space with the exciting accounts of action in the Pacific. Consequently, only critical stories of General Ike and his policies in handling displaced persons, repatriated prisoners, and the occupation of Germany will find space. In other words, the open season is here—each of the Allies will tend to revert to his nationalistic interest and all our operations constitute game to be shot at by correspondents and Congressional committees.

I hope General Ike doesn't have to stay too long. Governing his part of Germany will be very difficult, and although his military reputation will stand high in history, his standing in the near future is likely to slump.

The Possum

The Supreme Commander and I arrived at the same decision relative to my taking the PRD job, but our routes were different. He had thought over the matter further and figured that since nearly every public-relations officer eventually "broke his pick" and that although I had managed to get through the war thus far without being too much maligned for my efforts, after a few months I probably would be in the correspondents' doghouse. As for General Allen, he had served his sentence as PRO and was entitled as a regular officer again to have a combat command, and General Ike intended to assign him to an armored division going to the Pacific. My reasoning was that a regular Army officer should run PRD and that a naval officer probably ought to get back to the Navy or return to civilian life.

Ike said that if I hadn't voluntarily told him about my escapade in Berlin, he never would have known it. The possum.

I found that General Ike was flooded with congratulatory messages and invitations to be the recipient of the freedom of cities of a number of British centers, but most important was from London, where he would be required to make a speech at Guildhall, June 12. He already was thinking of what he should say.

"GI Stands for General Ike"

PARIS, MONDAY, MAY 21, 1945

The European war is over, but Ike's troubles certainly aren't. I drove up to Rheims this morning and took with me my ex-Navy boss, Rear Admiral Joseph Redman, Director of Naval Communications, and Paul A. Porter, Chairman of the Federal Communications Commission, who are with the Senatorial party investigating the feasibility of creating a unified American world-wide signal setup. Their main party was flying from Orly to Rheims for an appointment with General Ike, and I invited the Admiral and Paul to drive with me because I wanted a chance to visit with them.

When we reached Ike's office, the remainder of the delegation hadn't arrived. I reported in to Ike, and the first thing he told me was that he had had a hell of a kick from the War Department, which reported that a story had been carried in the States that some 50,000 Americans, repatriated from German prison camps, were being held at an American camp in France under conditions worse than they had experienced while prisoners of the Germans. Said he wanted to visit the camp immediately and hoped to find time to do it today, but the conference with the Senators would take some time and what did I think of taking them with him?

"It's the worst spot of trouble I've got, and if the Senators are interested in seeing the worst, I might as well take them with me and let them see firsthand," he said.

Those who elected to make the trip were Senators Burton K. Wheeler, Democrat of Montana; Albert W. Hawkes, Republican of New Jersey; E. W. McFarland, Democrat of Arizona; and Homer Capehart, Republican of Indiana, as well as Major General F. E. Stoner, of the Signal Corps, War Department; Paul; and myself.

"Lucky Strike" is a tent camp near Le Havre, sprawling on and around an airfield formerly used by the Germans. We landed on a strip in the camp area. Less than an hour of advance notice had been given those in charge of the camp that the Supreme Commander was coming, but Brigadier General Egmont Koenig, commanding officer of the Normandy Bay Section, under General John C. H. Lee, was present. As the General's C-47 pulled to a stop, there drew alongside a large black sedan, followed by a half-dozen jeeps. Some of the Senators started to get in the black sedan, but when they saw General Ike jump into a jeep, they immediately followed suit.

Ike's first interest in making an inspection of this kind is to see for himself how the boys are fed, so he directed that we first visit the messes. Someone had broadcast at home that sometimes the repatriates got only one meal a day. It was time for noon chow, so we got in line with mess kits and had a good meal.

General Ike started the walk of a mile and a half to the C-47. By this time news of his presence had spread throughout the camp, and he walked slowly through a narrow lane of thousands of Americans, talking briefly to every fourth or fifth man. The caravan of jeeps followed, having difficulty getting through the crowd. Senator Capehart stood in the leading jeep and, from time to time, shouted:

"Anyone here from Indiana?"

I meandered along in the wake of General Ike, amused by the enthusiastic comment of those to whom he had spoken or who had overheard his conversations. One corporal, who needed a haircut, his face drawn and sallow, I heard say:

"GI sure stands for General Ike."

One of the Senators said to me:

"I hope that fellow never decides to run against me in my state. He's got what it takes. I can see now why the GIs worship him. He speaks their language, he isn't high hat like you expect from brass, and he knows their problems and they know it."

Our party boarded the plane while General Ike conferred privately and earnestly with General Koenig. He was giving suggestions. He was pleased that the Red Cross girls had arrived and had organized clubs and recreation facilities. He knew the problem facing General Koenig; he gave him several suggestions and made a parting request:

"Get a lot of barbers in here right away. Get at least forty. All these men will feel better if they get haircuts."

General Ike on the Russians

PARIS, FRIDAY, MAY 25, 1945

General Ike flew down from Rheims Tuesday afternoon. Corporal Street and I met him in the Plymouth at Orly. Mickey came along with a bag, as the General expected to stay two or three days while Tex Lee and Jim Gault supervise the move of the household and office equipment to the new headquarters at Frankfurt, Germany.

General Wayne Clark arrived from Italy and also stopped at the Raphaël. He is spearheading one of the home-coming groups.

General Ike had numerous callers, so he occupied the ambassador's suite. Ambassador Harriman, and his daughter, Kathy, arrived for lunch. The Ambassador thinks Ike should visit Moscow because the Russians have such a high regard for him.* If this trip is made before we go home, Ike has invited me to accompany him. I would like to see Moscow.

General Ike didn't stir from the Raphaël, but conducted his business in the apartment, seeing a long string of officers, including General Lee, of Com Z, General Tom Larkin, who has supplanted Brigadier General Roy Lord as Chief of Staff to Lee. General Ike has given Lord the direct responsibility of assembling and shipping troops home and to the Pacific. It all comes under the general title of redeployment, and the center for initial assembly is in the Rheims area.

Last night, the General and I had an old-fashioned bull session that lasted until too late this morning. We talked about Russia. Ike said he felt that the American and British relationship with Russia was about at the same stage of arms-length dealing that marked the early contacts between Americans and the British when we first got into the war. As we dealt with each other, we learned the British ways and they learned ours. A common understanding developed and eventually we became Allies in spirit as well as on paper. Now the Russians, who have had relatively little contact, even during the war, with the Americans and British, do not understand us, nor do we them. The more contact we have with the Russians, the more they will understand us and the greater will be the co-operation. The Russians are blunt and forthright in their dealings, and any evasiveness arouses their suspicions. It should be possible to work with Russia if we will follow the same pattern of friendly co-operation that has resulted in the great record of Allied unity demonstrated first by AFHQ and subsequently by SHAEF. Only now, in peace, the motive for co-operation is the betterment of the lot in life of the common man. If we can create singleness of purpose on this theme, as we did to win the war, then peace should be assured.

Farewell to Telegraph Cottage

PARIS, WEDNESDAY, MAY 30, 1945

Jim Gault, in the General's plane, flew down from Frankfurt Monday, picked me up at Orly, and we flew on to London, where we were to close Telegraph Cottage.

I lunched with Joe Davies and his party at Claridge's. The former Am-

---

* This was demonstrated when General Ike visited Moscow and Leningrad with Zhukov after the Potsdam Conference. Subsequently, British papers referred to him as "America's best commercial traveler."

bassador to Russia had been sent to London to confer with the Prime
Minister and others in the British government about problems which re-
quire settlement in the forthcoming meeting of Churchill, Stalin, and
Truman.

Harry Hopkins had been sent by President Truman to Moscow and he
was to explore the same problems with Stalin. Davies and he were both
to report directly to the President so he would be informed of views of
both victorious partners before he went into the meeting. The President
had been explicit in his direction that nothing should be done which
would give the Russians the idea that the British and Americans were
ganging up on them.

MAY, 1945: *Unconditional German surrender of May 7 was preceded by
Russian capture of Berlin, widespread surrender of German field armies, including German forces of 1,000,000 in Italy, Austria, and the Tirol, all German forces in Netherlands, Denmark, and northwestern Germany. German
First, Nineteenth, and Twenty-fourth Armies surrendered to U. S. Seventh
and French First Armies. Reds in Czechoslovakia continued to battle German
troops refusing to surrender. Russian tanks wiped out guerrilla bands continuing to fight in Prague after surrender order. Von Ribbentrop, Göring,
Kesselring, Doenitz, Jodl, and three hundred other Nazi leaders captured.
Himmler committed suicide. War Department announced point system for
demobilization of soldiers. Fighting on Okinawa grew more intense as 100,000
Yanks pushed desperate Japs back. On Luzon organized resistance ended in
the Cagayan when Yanks trapped bulk of Jap troops at Santa Fe. Superforts
pounded Tokyo, Nagoya, Yokohama, and Osaka. Carrier planes hit industrial
targets and airfields in Kyushu and Shikoku. Chinese advanced, took Nanning
in Kwangsi Province. Mountbatten announced successful end of Burma campaign. Aussies took Tarakan city and airfield on Borneo. Churchill government resigned; new elections set for July 15. Chiang Kai-shek resigned as
Premier in favor of Dr. T. V. Soong. (We were hurrying troops from Europe
to the Pacific.—H.C.B.)*

FRANKFURT-AM-MAIN, SATURDAY, JUNE 2, 1945

Ike feels lost in his big office. It was the board room and once had a
huge table in the shape of a horseshoe. This has been removed. He has
a desk at one end, and when I walked in today, I told him I thought his
surroundings fitted the descriptions I had read of Mussolini's office.

In back of the building there is a large chromium fish pond with water
lilies and goldfish. Above this pool, at the far end near the snack bar and
officers' club, there is a large gray bronze statue of a seated female nude.
In an effort to make the gal somewhat more interesting, enterprising GIs
one evening polished her right nipple. Now it shines brassily. Officers and

GIs pose for photographs with the statue, either with their arms around her, or half sitting in her lap, or decorously standing two or three feet in front of her knee.

General Ike has spent a day and a night on the Riviera, where he attended a dinner-reunion of West Point classmates. The Riviera has been made into a rest camp for thousands of GIs and officers, and Ike was relating to me that the GIs, who have the run of Nice, seem much better behaved than some of the officers at Cannes.

While flying back from the Riviera, General Ike had drafted in longhand the text of the talk he has to give June 12 at the Guildhall when he receives the Freedom of the City of London. He had had it typed and read it to Jim and me this evening. Its theme is magnificent. It reflects modesty and humility.

I suggested that it would be a mistake to read it, not only because he would have to put on his spectacles, but a prepared speech read on such an occasion loses the effect of spontaneity. His only recourse is to learn it. He glowered at the thought, and I went to bed.

FRANKFURT-AM-MAIN, MONDAY, JUNE 4, 1945

General Ike has drafted and redrafted his Guildhall speech and has read it out loud two or three times to Jim and me. Each time he finds opportunity to improve it.

But the principal piece of business before him is his forthcoming trip to Berlin to sign the quadripartite agreements with the Russians, British, and French. He is to fly there in the morning with a small party. PRD in Paris had flown to Frankfurt today several correspondents, broadcasters, and cameramen, to cover the story. At last the two radio-equipped C-47s are to be used. They will be flown to Tempelhof in the morning and set up to transmit copy and broadcasts quickly to Paris for relay to the U. S., U. K., and the rest of the world.

I am expected to accompany General Ike, but I have given my place to Frank Page, who will get a great kick out of visiting Berlin, and, besides, the Russians have my identification tag.

"The Highest"

FRANKFURT-AM-MAIN, TUESDAY, JUNE 5, 1945

The signing at Berlin, after a considerable delay, has been accomplished, and Ike kept his pledge to himself to get back to Frankfurt the same day.

He and Monty had gone together to pay their respects to Field Marshal

Zhukov. General Ike presented Zhukov with the highest decoration America gives to foreigners, the Chief Commander grade of the Legion of Merit. Zhukov gratefully thanked Ike and said that Russia wished to show its appreciation of General Eisenhower's leadership by giving him an appropriate decoration. Ike chuckled as he told the story. He said that Vyshinsky, who was with Zhukov, had, when Zhukov said "appropriate decoration," whispered, "the highest," and Zhukov hastily added, "the highest." Zhukov had continued that, unfortunately, he could not present the decoration immediately, as he had to await approval from Moscow. When approval is obtained, he would like to visit General Eisenhower in his headquarters to present the decoration. The Russian Marshal told Monty that he would like to visit his headquarters, too, to present him the same decoration. Monty immediately had replied that he would like to have the presentation to him made in company with General Eisenhower because he had fought much of the war under the Allied Supreme Commander and he wanted to take his decoration in his presence.

After the courtesy call, General Ike had returned to the house set aside for him, expecting to be called any moment for the official ceremony. Time dragged; finally, it was discovered that the Russians were disturbed because of a provision in the agreement which required them to seek and confine any Japanese nationals in the German territory under Russian control. As the Russians were not at war with Japan, Moscow had asked for deletion of the few words.

Ike immediately sent word "take them out." This settled the problem and soon the actual formality was concluded. Zhukov was amazed that General Ike could modify the quadripartite agreement in the name of Britain and America without consulting the home governments. Zhukov seemed greatly impressed by the latitude of judgment allowed the Supreme Commander.

Zhukov had been insistent at their first meeting of the day and again at the signing that General Ike stay for the banquet in the evening. General Ike didn't want to stay, said he had business in Frankfurt, had planned to return the same day, and would have to depart from Tempelhof in time to reach Frankfurt before darkness. Zhukov was insistent. General Ike was adamant. Both were friendly but positive. General Ike finally assented to stopping at the banquet hall for fifteen minutes, where he drank toasts to President Truman, Prime Minister Churchill, and Premier Stalin.

It had been something of a contest of stubbornness between the two men, but the circumstances had been friendly and General Ike departed with a promise from Zhukov to visit him at Frankfurt on Sunday, June 10.

Just a Junket

FRANKFURT-AM-MAIN, SATURDAY, JUNE 9, 1945

Frank Page and I returned late today. We had been to Heidelberg, Munich, Innsbruck, through the Brenner Pass into Italy, back through the pass and on to Berchtesgaden, through Munich, Nuremberg, where we saw the huge Sportpalast made famous by Hitler's tirades, and back to Frankfurt.

We picked up Major Quirk, PRO of Third Army, at Bad Wies. While Frank and Corporal Street waited in the car, Quirk and I climbed up to the Eagle's Nest, policed by paratroopers of the 101st Division.

The climb made me dizzy, but, fortunately, Hitler had several rest benches along the way. The last turn of the narrow trail is on a spur of the mountain, from which I could look straight down for what I guessed was 5000 feet, if I had chosen to look, but I took the inside track. At the entrance to the Eagle's Nest, the paratrooper on guard was calmly walking up and down a wall one foot wide, two feet high from our side, but 5000 feet straight down from the far side. I marveled at his nonchalance. He complained that other troops preceding the 101st at Berchtesgaden had been unfair. They had collected so many souvenirs that now the Eagle's Nest was carefully guarded to prevent any further pilfering.

Inside I found a single paratrooper writing a letter home in the huge dining room. He was seated at a table that had twelve seats at each side and two at each end. The main living room was oval-shaped, with large windows through which the snow-capped peaks of the Bavarian Alps showed majestically in the twilight.

After seeing the Eagle's Nest, Quirk and I agreed that Hitler was crazy.

We descended and inspected Hitler's chalet halfway down the mountain, where I collected a few pieces of marble from Hitler's fireplace—one especially for Niles Trammell, to whom I am still indebted for his attempt to supply me with *langouste* in Africa. Although the Eagle's Nest had not been hit by bombs, Hitler's house, Göring's adjoining chalet, a large greenhouse, and SS barracks showed the effect of the RAF raid of several weeks before.

Hitler's house had been badly burned, but as it was constructed of brick, stone, and concrete, most of the main structure was still intact. In Hitler's kitchen, which I noticed had electric ranges, three large brass cooking utensils on the stove still contained decaying food. One of them held French-fried potatoes, another carrots, and the third what looked like soup, indicating the kitchen help had quickly abandoned their post when the bombers came.

Zhukov is arriving tomorrow, and Ike has laid on an aerial show with all of the planes available. Unfortunately, many of the heavy bombers already have gone back to the States.

"We Are Going to Have Peace if We Have to Fight for It"

FRANKFURT-AM-MAIN, SUNDAY, JUNE 10, 1945

Marshal Zhukov and his party arrived in two planes from Berlin this morning. Monty flew in, too, and both he and Ike received their decorations in Ike's office.

The Supreme Commander wished the presentation to be as simple and private as possible, but Charles Kiley, *Stars and Stripes* pool reporter, was permitted to witness the ceremony. I was there, and it was very simple. The decoration is the Order of Victory. It was presented first to General Ike and then to Field Marshal Montgomery. The decoration is magnificent. It is square; the base is of platinum covered with diamonds and rubies.*

After the brief ceremony in Ike's office, he and Zhukov had a good deal to talk about with respect to their occupational problems. In the course of it, something came up about the Japs, and Zhukov shrugged his shoulders in an attitude of disdain. I heard the interpreter relaying Zhukov's remark to General Ike. It was to the effect that "he had destroyed the Sixth Japanese Army in ten days," apparently referring to the Japanese attack on the Mongolian Republic in May, 1939. He didn't think the Japs would be tough for the Red Army and, from his attitude, indicated a desire to get at them.

After the presentation and private conference, the party walked to the veranda of the near-by large and handsomely equipped recreation center and mess hall, with its several dining rooms, for a luncheon. On the veranda we watched 1700 American and British fighters and medium and heavy bombers roar over Frankfurt in a flying welcome. As the planes passed over, General Ike described the types to Zhukov.

There were numerous toasts and glasses were raised to various aspects of the Allied victory.

---

* I found in a *Reader's Digest* story that it was worth $100,000 and later mentioned this fact to Ike. This evening he took a good look at it and thought the estimate too high. Counting up the diamonds and estimating their size, he figured the cost was in the neighborhood of $18,000. His estimate is based on realism and does not diminish his pride in receiving the decoration, and all it stands for, from the Russians.

MARSHAL ZHUKOV:

I want to raise a glass to General of the Army Eisenhower, due to whose abilities and talents the Allied armies attained their great and brilliant successes. I, as a military man, as a soldier, watched with amazement the brilliant successes of General Eisenhower. They were brilliantly planned, thought out, and most of all, brilliantly carried out. We watched massed uses of aviation, use of massed artillery and tanks, and we watched naval operations on a large scale—the infantry—and all this had to be united by one man, organized on the front lines and organized in depth as well—the blows of the enemy were pretty deep—one had to anticipate everything, calculate well, and guarantee everything in the operations which were carried out; the genius and talent of the American General, son of the American people, showed itself. Our Soviet officers and generals are watching and studying all the operations that General Eisenhower has conducted. I personally, and the forces under my command, have the deepest respect for General Eisenhower, and I am expressing the hope that in the future work of the four Allied Commanders in the Control Council, that we will be just as unified in our future work. If we had good co-operation in time of war, I am sure that the same co-operation that was shown before will show itself in peace. I raise my glass to General Eisenhower—to his health, his success, and his future work.

GENERAL EISENHOWER:

I raise my glass primarily to speak a word of admiration on behalf of the Allied forces for Marshal Zhukov, but I am going to wander a bit afield before I arrive at my final toast. Marshal Zhukov has praised me in extravagant terms, my job and my performance of my job in this war. It seems a fitting occasion to me to point out that I have had the advice of the most skillful soldiers and skillful diplomats that two great countries could produce. Soldiers, sailors, airmen, and diplomats, realizing that only in unity is there strength, have subordinated themselves to my commands with perfect loyalty, regardless of the claims made upon them from within their own countries. To those men I owe an immeasurable debt of gratitude. Those people have worked at my side in adversity and in prosperity and have never once deviated by one inch from the instructions laid down. I cannot name names today for the simple reason there have been so many who have performed so loyally that it would be an injustice to some if I named a single soldier; but I know those men intimately and I know what they want. They want peace. They want the opportunity for our peoples to live a little better next year. All of us who are right-thinking want the common man of all United Nations to have the opportunities that we fought to preserve for him. They want the opportunities that will let all nations that have been engaged in this war go forward together to greater prosperity—not for us, sitting around this table, but for the masses that we represent. That means peace. Speaking for the Allied forces, we are going to have peace if we have to fight for it.

On two occasions now I have had the great honor of meeting high officials of the Soviet Union. It is my feeling that in this basic desire of all of us, they are one with us. Regardless of the methods by which we arrive at that goal, that is what we are struggling for. I cannot speak for any other individual; in fact, while I am expressing here what is in my heart and mind, I am speaking for no one except Ike Eisenhower, but I believe that there is not a single man around this table that would not give back all the honors, all the publicity, and everything else that this war has brought to him if he could have avoided the misery and suffering and debt that have been brought to the populations by reason of this war. Yet this war was a holy war, more than any other in history this war has been an array of the forces of evil against those of righteousness. It had to have its leaders, and it had to be won—no matter what the sacrifices, no matter what the suffering to populations, to materials, to our wealth—oil, steel, industry—no matter what the cost was, the war had to be won. In Europe it has been won. To no one man do the United Nations owe a greater debt than to Marshal Zhukov.

As our honored guest today he has come down and very courteously conferred certain honors of the Soviet Union upon members of the Allied forces. But Marshal Zhukov, a modest man, probably underrates the standing that he holds in our hearts and minds. One day, when all of us here at this board are gathered to our fathers, there is certain to be another order of the Soviet Union. It will be the Order of Zhukov, and that order will be prized by every man who admires courage, vision, fortitude, and determination in a soldier. Gentlemen, I deem it a very great honor to ask you to rise and drink to Marshal Zhukov.

General Ike accompanied the Marshal and his party to the airfield and, with formal ceremonies and a band, said farewell. General Ike's first step had been taken toward understanding the Russians and getting them to understand us.

We are off tomorrow for London, where General Ike has the big reception Tuesday. He recited his address a couple of times and now has it down pat. I told him tonight he would have to be prepared for interruptions because inevitably he would find in his British audience a number of "heah-heahs." In fact, I manufactured a few during his second recitation, and although he glowered, he managed to finish creditably.

A Modest Yank at King George's Court

PARIS, WEDNESDAY, JUNE 13, 1945

The ceremony in London was magnificent. It was modest, touching, friendly, and all the other adjectives that could be used to describe the heartfelt feeling of the British for General Ike and his for their great moral and physical war record. His speech at Guildhall brought tears to the eyes of many, including the Prime Minister's. Even mine.

This morning's London *Express* printed the address under a big heading:

General Eisenhower Speaks in Immortal Words
of His Men and the Meaning of Their Work

THE HUMILITY OF A GREAT SOLDIER

In a box in the center of the spread of the text of his speech was Lincoln's Gettysburg Address, obviously intended favorably to compare the two.

Ike's only departure from the text, as I had heard him give it several times, was at the outset when, after having received the sword of the Duke of Wellington as a token of the Sword of Honor (not yet complete), he turned to the Lord Mayor, Sir Frank Alexander, and said calmly something to the effect that if he didn't know he was amongst friends, he doubted if he could ever make his speech. Sure enough, he got several "heah-heahs" which only added to the dignity and impressiveness of the occasion in bomb-scarred and burned Guildhall, in which the history of liberty-loving people has been made and confirmed for centuries.

Before the ceremony started in the morning, General Ike sought to compose his thoughts by taking a quiet walk all by himself in Hyde Park. I didn't know where he had gone and was waiting in my assigned seat in a car in the caravan outside on Park Lane, at the Dorchester entrance, when up turned the Supreme Commander, accompanied by two bobbies. They had rescued him from a crowd which had gathered when he stopped to satisfy the request of someone for an autograph. A helpful bobby had advised him to move on, as he was certain to be surrounded by a crowd, but General Ike had continued to be accommodating and soon had signed pound notes, ten-shilling notes, and all sorts of pieces of paper. In fifteen minutes the word had spread and GIs came in taxis from everywhere. Finally, the bobby got him free of the crowd as Ike said:

"Listen, folks, I've got to get back and make a speech."

On the way back to the Dorchester, a British general saluted and greeted him with the remark:

"Good morning, sir. I see you are being brought home by the police."

At Mansion House, where he was the guest of honor at luncheon, a crowd estimated at 30,000 had gathered in the street below. General Ike, with the Prime Minister and Mrs. Churchill in the background, stood on a balcony and spoke to the crowd extemporaneously. His words came as naturally as if he had rehearsed them for a week:

"Whether you know it or not, I am now a Londoner myself. I have as much right to be down in the crowd yelling as you have."

The Prime Minister had then spoken briefly. He stated that General Eisenhower "had shown the capacity for making great nations march together more truly united than they have ever been before."

I stood behind a pillar, and for the second time in the day, a great lump had arisen in my throat.

At luncheon, the Prime Minister spoke briefly. He said:

I am quite sure that the influence he will wield in the world will be one of always bringing our countries together in the much more difficult task of peace in the same way he has brought them together in the grim and awful cataclysm of war.

Further, Mr. Churchill cited the "terribleness" of General Ike's having to decide whether to go through with the invasion of France a year ago, despite adverse weather, and said:

"Not only did he take the risk and arrive at the fence, but he cleared it in magnificent style."

A call had come that Queen Mary was in town and would be happy if General Ike would call on her. In addition to all that had been printed about the Queen Mother, General Ike had heard innumerable stories of her kind personality and quickly accepted the opportunity. He found her everything he expected.

Then he had tea with the King and Queen at Buckingham Palace, where the King gave him the Order of Merit, the only British military decoration the monarch can bestow without recommendation or approval of his government. Foch and Joffre were both honorary OMs after the last war, but Ike was the first American soldier ever to be given this honor.

He had already received the highest military honor of the British government—the GCB—personally presented by the King at Algiers.

De Gaulle as a Host

PARIS, FRIDAY, JUNE 15, 1945

General Ike flew in to Orly from Frankfurt yesterday to receive the homage generously extended him by the French. I was at Orly a bit early. The French had a formal military reception with a band assembled on the apron to which General Ike's plane was to be taxied. Air Chief Marshal Tedder's plane arrived first, however, and when he "dismounted" the leader of the band apparently thought this was the Supreme Commander himself and started playing the numbers already rehearsed for General Ike. There was *The Star-Spangled Banner* and the *Marseillaise*, but no *God Save the King*.

General Ike arrived a few minutes later, and I heard the same tunes again, excellently rendered. He quickly inspected the guard of honor. General Joseph P. Koenig, Military Governor of Paris, escorted the General in an open car to the Arc de Triomphe, and in a few minutes General de Gaulle arrived. There was a presentation of the Compagnon de la

Libération. De Gaulle stooped slightly to perform the traditional ceremony of kissing Ike on both cheeks, and I remembered how the Supreme Commander had ordered me to kill, if possible, all photographs of his being kissed on both cheeks by General Giraud after the clean-up in Tunisia, when he was given Giraud's Grand Cordon of the Legion of Honor.

Beetle was formally presented with the Grand Cross of the Legion of Honor, with the similar French custom. As a matter of fact, Beetle had already received the Grand Cross, but it had come by mail. Beetle's receipt of the decoration in mail-order fashion was simply a slip-up of some new French employee, and when proper authorities heard about it, appropriate apologies were made and hence Beetle received it with due acclaim in the shadow of the Arc de Triomphe today.

General Ike then placed a wreath on the Tomb of the Unknown Soldier. Taps were sounded during a period of silence. He signed the guest book and then took his position beside General de Gaulle to receive the review of the French troops.

From the Arc de Triomphe, General Koenig conducted General Ike down the Champs-Elysées and across the Alexander III Bridge to the Invalides, to pay his respects at the tomb of Napoleon and at the mausoleum of Marshal Foch.

He was then received by Monsieur le Troquer, President of the Municipal Council of Paris, who took him on a tour of the city, whose streets were lined with cheering Frenchmen.

At the Hôtel de Ville, the City Hall, General Ike spoke appropriately of the great contribution of the French to the successful conclusion of the war, but to me the most interesting part of it was the delayed action of the applause. Ike, of course, spoke in English and few in the audience understood him. His remarks were interpreted by Lieutenant Colonel Dostert, interpreter since Algerian days, who didn't merely interpret but seemed to put himself in General Ike's skin and added gesticulations for emphasis. As he made the several points in the speech, the audience applauded in hearty volume. General Ike at first appeared somewhat startled and smiled sheepishly in acknowledgment. Few present knew that General Ike, after a year of study, didn't understand French well enough to know which statement of his the French were applauding. Anyway, it was a good speech, both times.

There was a state dinner that night given by General de Gaulle, which I attended. There had been a bit of a to-do about the dinner because General de Gaulle was angry with the British and, therefore, didn't invite any of them, although I, as an intermediary, had instructions that

General Ike was accepting the honor from the French as an Allied Commander. General Ike had been careful to have Air Chief Marshal Tedder
and General Morgan, the Deputy Chief of Staff, present at the ceremony at the Arc. He had wanted the dinner likewise to be Allied, but,
after all, it was General de Gaulle's and General Ike was only a guest.
De Gaulle wanted the dinner as an honor to the Americans alone. He
had a mad on against the British—the mess in Syria temporarily had
strained relations. Tedder and Morgan were, however, invited to attend
the presentation of the Napoleonic sword, which General Ike was to
carry back to America as a token of the friendship and esteem of the
French people. This presentation occurred immediately prior to the
dinner and in a room adjacent to the dining room. Tedder and Morgan
would then have to excuse themselves as the other guests marched into
dinner. This was a deplorable dilemma and caused unending telephone conversations from Paris to Frankfurt, Frankfurt to England
and back, until finally the decision was reached to make the best of the
situation. Tedder and Morgan graciously had a prior engagement for
dinner.

I knew that General de Gaulle had worked on the written text of his
speech until just before the presentation of the sword, only a few minutes
prior to the dinner, but when he arose, he spoke without notes and I
was told by one of my English-speaking French friends that he had
followed his outline almost exactly. In these circumstances, I found General de Gaulle sincere, friendly, and not merely pleasant, but most hospitable. He spoke of the traditional friendship of the two countries, the
great service of America in this war, and the effort of the French to retrieve victory from defeat. General Ike responded briefly in kind.

The dinner was, of course, in the usual French style of numerous
courses, with an assortment of excellent wines, including champagne.
As my French friend and I waited for the high rank to leave the room
first, I commented about the fine steaks we had enjoyed.

"Oh, yes, but we had to get them through the black market."

We returned to the Raphaël, had a short bull session, and called it a
day and a night, as General Ike had to be present at the Scribe at 9:30
this morning for a farewell press conference. I thought it was satisfactory
but not spectacular, perhaps because most of the topics covered were
things I had heard him talk about and therefore they did not seem new.
I then drove out to Orly with the General, who was flying back to Frankfurt. When I returned to my office, I had a query from Colonel Dupuy,
who said the Associated Press wanted to transmit to the United States
the complete text of the Supreme Commander's remarks. As there was

no military security involved, I said O.K., but I was surprised that there should be so much interest.

General Ike is finishing up some last-minute business at headquarters. We are starting for America tomorrow morning. Ike will start from Frankfurt, but his C-54 will stop briefly at Orly to take me aboard. We are due in Washington at 11 A.M. EWT, Monday, June 18, and will have a twenty-four-hour layover at Bermuda. This will give General Ike a rest which he badly needs before undergoing the ordeal of addressing a Joint Session of Congress and the several talks he will have to deliver informally at the daily succession of ceremonies at Washington, New York, West Point, Kansas City, and Abilene.

Homeward Bound

BERMUDA, SUNDAY, JUNE 17, 1945

The C-54 President Truman sent for Ike—*The Sacred Cow*—arrived here this morning after a quick, smooth, and uneventful flight from Paris.

After three years of travel in war zones, I felt virtually no emotion about our homeward flight. It was the Supreme Commander's sixth transatlantic flight, as it was mine. We had traveled hither and yon from little to big events and now even a transatlantic flight was commonplace.

Of more concern to me was the morning's *Stars and Stripes*, which had on the first page an editorial headed, "Adieu to a Great GI." He read it with a smile.

I also showed General Ike *The New York Times* of June 16, which the pilot, Hank Myers, had brought over. In "Topics of the Times" there was a complimentary summary of the General's reply to Zhukov, at Frankfurt. In it was a sentence reading:

Another gifted member of the Eisenhower personnel who had obviously subordinated himself to his Chief with perfect loyalty is the man who writes General Eisenhower's speeches for him.

Ike growled. He had no ghost writer—why should anyone think he had? *

This hasn't been a pleasure trip for the Supreme Commander. He was faced with an exacting task. He has to address a Joint Session of the House and Senate, enough to disturb the peace of mind of any man.

---

* Since coming home I have run into this idea several times; it seems that almost everyone thinks a successful speaker has a ghost writer. General Ike is his own ghost, only he seldom writes a speech, just thinks his thoughts in advance, gets his ideas in order, and then has the ability to deliver them.

He has been working on the text, the only address face to face with an audience that he will have read since I have been with him. This fact itself bothers him. Sergeant Sue Serafin, one of the WACs who has faithfully served him since Algiers, has been taking his dictation and typing and retyping his speech. As we crossed the ocean she worked most of the night. Ike slept less than two hours. We reached Bermuda before dawn.

General Ike sent for me around noon. I got his message while at the Officers' Club, where I was trying to find some white shoes to complete a white uniform so I could appear properly dressed for the ceremony in Washington.

Officers and enlisted men of our party were selecting their summer uniforms, flown here by arrangement of the War Department with a large clothier. General Ike had brought his old summer clothes, which he had last worn in Africa and, therefore, had to do no last-minute shopping.

When I arrived at the Governor's Mansion, Ike asked me what I was up to. I told him I was getting properly dressed.

"What do you mean, properly dressed? You look all right now."

I had on my slate-gray uniform.

"Admiral Kirk is wearing white and he is my senior. I should follow suit," I replied.

"Who are you working for—the Navy or me?"

"You, sir."

"Then wear your grays. That's the best-looking uniform the Navy ever had, and if anybody says anything to you about it, tell them you're under my orders."

"Aye, aye, sir," I replied—much relieved.

Admiral and Lady Glennie had a beach party in a small cove at Admiralty House. General Ike and party enjoyed a swim, broken only by the arrival of Beetle on an Army launch, proudly displaying a dozen fish. General Ike told me that I can drop off from his party after the ceremony at West Point.

"Stand Up So They Can See You"

NEW YORK CITY, THURSDAY, JUNE 21, 1945

Monday, Tuesday, and Wednesday were three of the most hectic days of my life and they certainly were in General Ike's. He still has Kansas City and Abilene. I had merely had to ride in the party. He has had to make speeches, all of them extemporaneous except the one to Congress, which he read too fast, but which the newspapers universally acclaimed as masterful.

"Hank" Myers did a snake dance from the coast across the Chesapeake to avoid being early. In three years, I had never seen General Ike late for an appointment with troops. In all the trips I had taken with him, I don't recall once when he kept soldiers waiting for him to review them.

In the pilot's cabin, a broadcast was switched on and I heard the familiar lucid tones of Bob Trout, describing from the airport our arrival. I went back to tell Ike to listen and found he already had the earphones on. "Boy, this *is* something," he grinned.

At 11:07 we were on the ground. Ike stepped down the portable stairway and was greeted by Mamie, and from then on it was a photographer's paradise. I finally managed to squeeze down the steps and found Ruth and Beverly standing out of range of cameras and the mobs. It was a joyous home-coming and mere words cannot adequately describe the story.

I still had duties to perform, so further home-coming greetings were interrupted. I was assigned to ride in the command car with General Marshall and General Ike to the Pentagon. There was such a crowd I had to stay close to the driver or lose my seat. Finally, when all our passengers from our flight had found their assigned places in the caravan, we moved off.

There were perhaps 20,000 or 30,000 people at the airport and additional thousands lined the drive to the Pentagon. They yelled for Ike, and I could hear General Marshall in the back seat, saying:

"Stand up so they can see you."

The idea of standing in an open car to take or acknowledge the cheers hadn't occurred to Ike, but he stood up, found his balance unsteady in the rumbling command car, and clutched my shoulder.

General Marshall spoke sternly to the driver:

"Drive slowly. Avoid fast starts and stops. Be careful when you shift gear."

Cars with photographers, cameras mounted on the top, dashed crazily in and out of the caravan like rubber-bumpered scooters at Glen Echo Amusement Park.

Under the direct orders of the Chief of Staff of the United States Army, the corporal driving the car tried his best to give General Ike a smooth ride, but his efforts were simply impossible, considering the nature of the C & R and the necessary stopping and starting to avoid the dashing camera cars.

"Dammit," General Marshall said to me. "Why don't you make the driver go smoother?"

"Aye, aye, sir," I replied, trying to keep my shoulder firm so the Supreme Commander could have his customary support from the Navy and retain dignity suitable to the Army.

At the Pentagon, crowded with cheering men and women of the War Department, Secretary Stimson officially welcomed the Supreme Commander. General Ike responded warmly, praising their part in the great teamwork that had won the war.

After the brief Pentagon ceremony, General Marshall, having done his duty, dropped out of the parade, his place in No. 1 car being taken by Beetle and mine by Brigadier General Robert Young, in charge of the military details of the ceremony. I dropped back to the second command car and relaxed.

Mickey was beside the driver, excited not only by the occasion but at the prospect of soon seeing again his bride, Pearlie, who was at her home in Minnesota. Next to me sat a veteran of the 3rd Division, Colonel Woodward W. Stromberg.

I was in my old home town and I could now enjoy the parade. It was wonderful. The streets of Washington, even without people on them, would have been good to see, but with the thousands of friendly faces —even though they may forget us all in a week—made the drive from the Pentagon past the Lincoln Memorial, down Constitution Avenue, up Fifteenth Street, and down Pennsylvania Avenue to the Capitol one that only few in the history of our country have had the privilege of sharing.

General Ike was standing, waving like a prize fighter. His friendliness radiated through the crowds and, following in the refrain, I could hear numerous comments. "He waved at me." "Isn't he handsome?" "He's marvelous."

Driving past Thirteenth and Pennsylvania Avenue, I waved to the eighth floor of the Earle Building, where I knew the old Columbia gang would be watching out the window, but I could scarcely see them for the trees.

We saw a sign, "Welcome Home, Butch." Mickey turned to me and said:

"Who is this guy Eisenhower?"

As a broadcaster, I had covered numerous events from inaugurations to committee hearings, but I never heard such long and sincere applause as that which followed General Ike's speech to Congress.

After the luncheon at the Statler, Mamie and Ike went to the White

House, where President Truman gave the General his second oak-leaf cluster to his Distinguished Service Medal. Then General of the Army Ike and Mamie drove to Walter Reed Hospital to pay their respects to General of the Army John J. Pershing, who greeted them warmly.

I had gone from the luncheon to the Pentagon, where General Ike was to have a press conference at 4:30. Before an auditorium packed with correspondents, General Ike paid tribute to GIs, spoke of the magnitude of our problem in Europe, mentioned redeployment, displaced persons, and the required reformation of Germany. He advised the nation not to slacken until she had Japan defeated. To obtain this defeat with minimum casualties means hitting the Japs with our greatest strength.

A brief respite at the Wardman Park, and General Ike and I were on our way to the White House, where President Truman entertained the stag party of fifty-three officers and enlisted men at a dinner as simple and homey as a community supper in Missouri. There were no speeches and we left the White House by 9:30. It had been General Ike's first opportunity to visit with the new President, although he had seen him briefly that afternoon. What he saw and heard, he liked.

Headlines for a Hero

General Ike and I had to get an early start to the airport for the flight to New York for the celebration on Tuesday. My thirteen-year-old daughter got my breakfast, then hurriedly dressed to ride to the airport with us —probably the fastest ride in her career. She forgot her own breakfast. All was well, though, as she was heard to remark:

"I figured it wouldn't do me any harm at all to be seen with Uncle Ike."

General Ike has been the subject of blazing headlines, millions of words of copy, innumerable cartoons, the commentators have vied for the most complimentary references, and columnists and editorial writers have nominated him for a variety of jobs, including Supreme Command of the Pacific, Secretary of State, Secretary of War, Chief of Staff, and almost any other position which occurred to them.

Headlines in Washington said: Oh, God, It's Swell to Be Home— Mrs. Ike Gets in a Quick Kiss and Steps Happily to Side Lines. . . . Ike Sees Keys as Symbol of GI Treatment. . . . Congress Pays Ike Its Greatest Ovation in 25 Years. . . . Pays High Tribute to Yanks in Report to Congress. . . . General Ike's Combat Comrades Welcome Him Home.

. . . I Have No Fear of My Soldiers and the Future. . . . President Honors Ike. . . . Truman Host to Ike's Party at Simple White House Dinner. . . . Nearly a Million Welcome Ike. . . . Like Any GI He Wants Furlough. . . . Eisenhower Calls for End of Germans' General Staff. . . . Ike's Bugler Blasts Statler. . . . Two Early Risers—Ike and Harry.*

On Tuesday in New York: Welcome to Eisenhower Is City's Greatest. . . . 30,000 Pupils Out to Welcome Hero. . . . Financial District Roars Its Tribute. . . . Garment District Cheers Vie with Times Square Roar. . . . Harlem's 500,000 Turn Out for Ike. . . . Brooklyn Proudly Joins City's Welcome. . . . Wounded GIs at Reception Hail Their Ike. . . . Ike Grins and the City's Millions Let Go. . . . He Calls for Strong U. S. to Maintain Peace. . . . We Have Met the General and He Is Ours. . . . Ike Wins Easy at Polo Grounds. . . . Eisenhower Hailed at Waldorf by 1600 Who Pay $18 a Plate. . . . Commissioner Valentine Estimates Crowd at 4 Million. . . . Inspector John J. O'Connell Says 6 Million. . . . City May Break Even on Eisenhower. . . . Professor, University of Kansas, says: "Sense of Humor Keeps Kansas Populated." . . . "My God," murmured a GI, "Five Stars and Human, Too."

From West Point: West Point Welcomes Ike. . . . 17 Guns Salute Allied Chief. . . . Future Generals Pass in Review. . . . Guns Roar Salute. . . . General Tells Cadets Army, Navy, Air Forces Must Be United. . . . Ike Leaves Group to Talk to Wounded Soldier on Crutches. . . . Eisenhower Cadet Again as He Visits West Point.

Noncontroversial Subject

WASHINGTON, TUESDAY, JUNE 26, 1945

After formal and informal celebrations at Rheims, Berlin, London, Paris, Washington, and New York, I dropped off the Eisenhower express at West Point, leaving him to roar on to Kansas City and Abilene. We met again in Washington yesterday. He was completely fatigued and looked forward to a holiday at White Sulphur Springs.

He was tired and was limping from a fall at the railway station at Topeka, where he got off the train to greet a group of Purple Heart soldiers. He said the train started off without him and when he ran to jump on the steps, he missed and banged his knee. It was painful but not serious.

He told me of some of his experiences in Abilene, where, as one head-

* Truman.

line described it, "Abilene's 6000 Shoot Works for Mrs. Eisenhower's Son," and another, "Ike Deploys Mother Past Surging Crowd."

He had stood on a railway platform as a train bearing troops headed for the Pacific passed slowly, and shook as many hands as he could reach. As one GI gave him a firm clasp, he yelled:

"I won't wash that hand until I get Tojo."

A story he enjoyed telling me was on his lawyer brother, Edgar, of Tacoma. After the picturesque festivities in Abilene, the brothers—Earl, an engineer of Charleroi, Pennsylvania; Milton, President of Kansas State College; and Arthur, a banker of Kansas City; Edgar, and Ike—sat down for a reunion. Ike said they talked till well past midnight and covered many subjects. There were some heated arguments.

The next day, Ike said, a reporter asked Milton what the brothers had discussed. Milton didn't know quite what to answer, so he told the reporter to wait and he would check. He then sought out Ike and received the advice simply to say that it was a family affair and of no public consequence. Milton found the reporter and when he undertook to give him the official reply, the reporter thanked him but said he already had the story from Edgar.

Milton got Edgar in a secluded place and said:

"What did you tell that reporter?"

"Oh," said Edgar, "I didn't tell him anything much—certainly nothing controversial."

"Well, what was it?" Milton queried, adding, "Ike said to say it was just a family affair."

"I told him we had a long talk and now all of us agree on one point because Dwight convinced us," Edgar said. "I said it was the first time in our lives that after an argument we agreed, for you know I'm a lawyer and pretty hard to convince."

"But what did we agree on?" asked Milton.

"Nothing controversial—just universal military training."

Ike felt he had won a considerable victory in winning his hard-boiled brothers to his point of view, but laughed at Edgar's idea of a noncontroversial subject.

JUNE, 1945: *Bloody campaign on Okinawa ended with 90,401 Jap dead against 6990 Americans killed and missing in eighty-two-day campaign. Lieutenant General Buckner, killed on Okinawa, replaced by General Stilwell. Australians made unopposed landing at Lotong. Luzon campaign ended after five months, nineteen days. B-29s raided Nagoya, Osaka, Kobe, Akashi, Honshu, and Sasebo. Australians captured Brunei and Beaufort on Borneo.*

Chinese liberated Tsinkong, Juian, and Linchau airfield. De Gaulle complied
with British order to cease firing in Syria and Lebanon. Disorders within
France mounted as returned prisoners demonstrated and factions hurled
charges of political maneuvering. Pétain, on trial for treason, asserted he had
concluded a pact with Great Britain before signing Nazi terms; Churchill
denied Pétain charge. American, British, Russian, and French commanders
assumed full control of Germany, found to be devastated by incessant bombing, industries and cities reduced to rubble, people without shelter, food, or
transport. American Third, Seventh, and Fifteenth Armies announced as occupation troops. United Nations conference admitted Denmark, closed meeting
in San Francisco. Stettinius resigned as Secretary of State. (We followed the
accounts of the debates during the San Francisco meeting with the fervid
hope that here at last might be the real mechanism to avoid another world
war. There already had been two in my generation.—H.C.B.)

Three Years to the Day

WASHINGTON, TUESDAY, JULY 10, 1945.

General Ike, Mamie, and John returned from White Sulphur yesterday,
Ike buoyantly refreshed by his rest. He had tried trout fishing with a fly
and had been beaten by both Mamie and John, who used worms. He
had played golf and had ridden horseback. With hundreds of wounded
men he had seen a preview of the Ernie Pyle movie, *The Story of GI Joe,*
which I had laid on from Washington.

He had sent a memorandum to Admiral King releasing me from his
personal staff. It was dated July 3—three years to the day of my reporting
for duty at General Ike's headquarters at 20 Grosvenor Square in London.

I talked with Ike last night about writing a book. I said I could do the
human-interest and personality story from the diary. He agreed and
immediately began outlining to me the problem of writing a book. He
once had written one—a guidebook of the battle fronts of France for the
Battle Monuments Commission. He said he struggled against a deadline
and found himself still sending copy to the printer at the last minute.

"It's a whale of a job," he said, as he advised me to make an outline to
a limit of words for each section and chapter, and to plan on writing so
many words a day—10,000 words on Africa, 1000 on Pantelleria, 5000 on
Sicily, another 10,000 on Italy, and 50,000 on OVERLORD—that would
do it.*

Flying across the Atlantic, he had taken time out from working on his
speech to polish the draft of a foreword for a book, *These Names Made*

---

* Maybe he could do it this way, but I couldn't.

News, by Wing Commander E. G. Ogilvie, of PRD, who had asked me to try to get the Supreme Commander to do it. Ogilvie had collected a selection of the best war stories by SHAEF accredited correspondents.

I asked him if he would like to do a foreword for my effort.

"Well," Ike said, "if I were to do a foreword for your book, I think I would have to say that I lived with the fellow for three years and I didn't even know he could read or write.

"But," he cautioned, "whether you can write or not, tell the story in your own way, and don't let anyone change it."

I went to the National Airport to say good-by this morning. Mamie was taking one of the few flights of her career—as far as Stewart Field, near West Point—and had the promise of Larry Hansen that he would fly low and smoothly. She, Ike, and John were going to Hyde Park, where the feted Supreme Commander would lay a wreath on the tomb of the Well-Known Soldier, Franklin Delano Roosevelt. Mamie would return to Washington by train; General Ike would fly the northern route back to his troubles as occupational commander in Germany.

In saying good-by, General Ike's last words to me as he boarded the plane were:

"Don't make any mistakes in a hurry."

I am flying to California by Navy Air Transport tonight to see my mother.

"Aren't You Awake Yet?"

SONORA, THURSDAY, JULY 12, 1945

After nearly twenty-four hours of flying, I reached Mother's house at Shaw's Flat, near Sonora, last night in time for a late supper. I awakened this morning in a peaceful and quiet surrounding, which fits my name for her cottage, "Shangri-La."

Still very tired, half awake, half asleep, I lay quietly in the comfortable bed, my thoughts turning backward over the past three years—blackouts in the Dorchester . . . the rhododendrons and cuckoos at Telegraph Cottage . . . the missing directive for TORCH . . . the days at Gibraltar . . . Giraud . . . Darlan . . . de Gaulle . . . the plaintive peals of church bells in Algiers . . . mosquito netting in tents . . . the PM . . . surrender of the Italian fleet . . . the Palace in Caserta . . . the olive groves in Italy . . . Kasserine . . . flying bombs . . . dashes for the air-raid shelter . . . the grinding cinders at the Portsmouth camp . . . musty sandbag dugouts . . . D-Day . . . the apple orchard . . . the

rockets and flying bombs again . . . Paris . . . kilocycles and kilowatts
. . . correspondents and crackpots . . . press camps and Spam . . .
Versailles . . . cows, dogs, pups, kittens . . . Ardennes . . . grand
strategy . . . Ike's fortitude and humor . . . the burden he carried . . .
Remagen . . . double envelopment . . . a chairman, but the strategist
—the great strategist . . . fountain pens, silly . . . Berlin . . . Eagle's
Nest . . . GIs . . . homeless, wandering Jews and Poles . . . Paris in
springtime . . . Scribe and its headaches . . . Arc de Triomphe . . .
Guildhall . . . Hyde Park orators . . . FDR's death . . . Ernie Pyle's
death . . . Hitler's death . . . Mussolini and his mistress, gruesome
. . . moral for dictators . . . *Victory* . . . Keitel's arrogance . . . Ikus
Africanus . . . *Stars and Stripes* . . . cheering crowds . . . Navy, Army,
Air . . . singleness of purpose . . . Mother's vine shades the window
beautifully . . . this place is so restful . . . peace. . . .

In the midst of this panorama of thoughts came a knock on the door.
Mother said:

"Aren't you awake yet?"—entering as she called.

"Yes, I am," I said. "I've been enjoying your room, the sun on the vines.
It's peaceful here. The war seems only a dream."

"I'm glad you like it," she said. She smiled and her brow furrowed a
little. "You know, son, there's something I've been wanting to ask you."

"What, Mother?" I said.

"My neighbors and I have seen you several times in pictures and movies
with General Eisenhower. You're always away back in the background.
Why didn't you get up front?"

INDEX

Dupuy, Col. R. Ernest
(*cont.*)
    671, 701, 708, 779, 806,
    821, 822, 836, 840, 847,
    848, 866
Düren, 438, 736, 757, 764
Durlacher, Commander L.
    G., 353
Durno, Capt. George, 234
Du Santon, 179, 180, 198
Düsseldorf, 127, 754, 767,
    780
Duzzerville, 187

E

Eagle, 52, 53
Eagle's Nest, 859, 876
Eaker, Maj. Gen. Ira C., 9,
    62, 122, 123, 157, 238-
    239, 242, 287, 463, 507,
    508, 549, 565, 629, 648
Early, Helen, 466
Early, Stephen, 5, 23, 24-
    25, 26, 27, 28, 29, 30, 31,
    32, 94, 234, 277, 278,
    280, 303, 445, 466, 741,
    751, 759, 761, 762-763,
    764-767, 769, 772, 773,
    775-776
Early, Lieutenant Stephen,
    Jr., 763, 775, 803-804
East Prussia, 438, 714
Echternach, 766
Eddy, Major General Man-
    ton S., 102, 128, 285, 291
Eden, Anthony, 96, 225,
    319, 321, 322, 417, 439,
    441, 551, 698, 748, 749
Edwards, Major General
    Idwal H., 293
Egan, Lieutenant Com-
    mander R. C., 358, 359
Egypt, 39, 75, 148,161,170
Eifel, 780, 807
18th Army Group,273,274
8th Air Force, 99,379,398,
    496, 502, 503, 532, 586,
    613, 620, 785
Eighth Army (British),
    160, 161, 169, 198, 236,
    240, 243, 244, 253, 258,
    261, 268, 271, 273, 276,
    280, 283, 285, 286, 289,
    294, 299, 306, 307, 362,

365, 368, 369, 375, 377,
    380, 384, 385, 387, 390,
    420, 421, 422, 423, 426,
    429, 450, 453, 484, 506,
    515, 698, 786
VIII Corps, 604, 730
8th Infantry Division, 487
80th Div. (U.S.), 765-766
82nd Airborne Division,
    402, 404, 407, 418, 552,
    585, 638, 639, 642, 675,
    678, 685, 733, 777
Eisenhower, Arthur, 873
Eisenhower, General
    Dwight D., headquarters
    in London, 3, 5-6,7; made
    Commanding General,
    ETO, 4; on the "social
    front," 6; on staff, 6-7;
    visit to Mountbatten's es-
    tate, 7-8; speech at Wash-
    ington Club, 8; at Fourth
    of July reception, 9; on
    SLEDGEHAMMER, 11; pre-
    fers cross-Channel inva-
    sion, 12; on publicity, 14,
    41,42, 250, 504-505,770-
    772; advocates American
    soldiers living in British
    homes, 14; promoted, 15,
    259-260; at airborne dem-
    onstration, 15-16; conver-
    sations with King George,
    17-18, 151, 158, 331-333,
    472, 550; health of, 18,
    208, 209, 234, 235, 655-
    656,658-659; on offensive
    operations in 1942, 18-
    19, 22-23, 24, 25-26, 27-
    28; on convoys to Russia,
    19; and the press, 19-21,
    59, 116, 120, 486-487,
    574, 608-609, 684-685,
    702-704, 708, 763; on
    censorship, 19, 20, 64,
    614-615, 657; and public
    relations, 22, 27; disap-
    pointed at decision
    against second front, 29;
    on ROUNDUP, 30, 43, 136;
    to be Supreme Com-
    mander of TORCH, 32, 33-
    34, 36; and American Red
    Cross, 34, 35; plans

TORCH, 36-40, 42-172;
    meets King Haakon, 44;
    plans ruses, 46; concern
    about anti-British senti-
    ment,48; on Anglo-Amer-
    ican co-operation, 48,274,
    315, 342-343, 388-389,
    581-582, 606-607, 654;
    on Navy, 49-51; made Al-
    lied Commander-in-Chief
    of AEF, 53; and Negro
    troops, 55-56, 756; on
    Dieppe raid, 67-68; asks
    for civil administrator for
    North Africa, 68; sum-
    marizes chances for suc-
    cess of TORCH, 69-71;
    conferences with Church-
    ill, 74, 75, 76, 77-78, 79,
    80, 94, 95-96, 102, 118,
    119, 125, 133, 140, 157,
    255, 257, 315-320, 322-
    323, 457-458, 465, 485,
    497, 498, 511, 524, 535,
    546, 559, 570, 576, 588,
    589, 601, 607-608, 616-
    617, 623, 625, 631-632,
    634-635, 638, 639, 644,
    652,721,804; on daylight
    precision bombing, 90;
    conversations with new
    C/S, General Smith, 90-
    94; on Axis prisoners, 101-
    102, 310; and Murphy
    discuss French political
    situation in North Africa,
    106-110; and Franco, 111-
    112; visit to Bomber
    Command, 122-123; and
    naval command for
    TORCH, 126, 129-130; and
    Telek, 137,140,143, 480;
    and Allied command,
    137-138; to assume mili-
    tary command of Gibral-
    tar, 143; arranges Clark's
    rendezvous with French,
    145-146; and Giraud,
    146, 161, 163, 164, 165,
    166, 167, 168, 170, 171,
    173, 174, 177, 178, 179,
    182, 184, 190, 191-193,
    223, 224, 226, 229-230,
    232-233, 263, 300-301,

Juin, General Alphonse, 109, 175, 191, 228, 236, 244, 245, 312, 321, 434, 540, 747, 830
Jülich, 766
Jullouville, 659
JUPITER (invasion of Norway), 125

K

Kaimaing, 555
Kassel, 739, 792, 799, 808
Kasserine Pass, 266, 267, 268, 270, 271, 272, 276, 304, 387, 729, 769
Kaunas, 655
Kavieng, 498, 510
Kegelman, Captain Charles C., 9, 16
Keitel, Field Marshal Wilhelm, 837, 843, 844, 876
Kelly, Jack, 10, 15
Kennedy, Ed, 403, 835, 836, 849
Kenner, Major General Albert W., 645, 659
Kesselring, General Albert, 550, 794, 813, 856
Kesten, Paul, 715
Kharkov, 251, 270
Khartoum, 443
Kherson, 510
Kiangsi, 80
Kiel, 483, 624, 758, 817
Kiev, 450, 464
Kiley, Charles, 823, 824, 825, 828, 829, 860
King, Admiral Ernest J., 4, 11, 22, 24, 25, 27, 28, 29, 30, 31, 32, 49, 82, 91, 92, 94, 124, 126, 230, 233, 237, 238, 239, 241, 246, 247, 249, 251, 270, 300, 340, 431, 443, 445, 446, 511, 535, 544, 575, 576, 578, 585, 589-590, 607, 613, 636, 639, 678, 750, 874
King, Mackenzie, 367
Kirk, Admiral Alan G., 49, 264, 340, 361, 514, 533, 561, 568, 571, 572-573, 578, 741, 868

Kirkpatrick, Commander Charles C., 578
Kirkpatrick, Helen, 10, 188, 336, 380
Kiska, 127, 294, 320, 339, 400
Kittredge, Commander Tracy D., 320, 321
Klauber, Edward, 467, 670
Klauser, General, 300
Kluge, Field Marshal von, 665
Knickerbocker, H. R., 395, 396, 597
Knox, Franklin, 4, 425-426, 427, 532, 533, 555
Kobe, 754, 792, 873
Kobo, 754
Koeltz, General Louis M., 107
Koenig, Brigadier General Egmont, 853, 854
Koenig, General Pierre Joseph, 526, 591, 660, 864, 865
Koesfeld, 438
Kokoda, 209
Kolberg, 792
Kolman, Sergeant, 205
Kolombangara, 270, 439
Kopanski, General, 723
Korbach, 797, 798
Korosten, 450
Krefeld, 767, 791
Krichev, 426
Krock, Arthur, 236
Kronke, Private, 166
Krueger, Lieutenant General Walter, 41, 270
Krum, Colonel Morrow, 149, 159, 297
Krupp, 709
Kuh, Frederick, 64
Kula Gulf, 375
Kure, 792
Kurile Islands, 426, 677, 698
Kusaie Island, 485, 510
Kuter, Major General Laurence S., 578
Kwajalein, 498
Kwangsi, 856
Kweilin, 677
Kweiping, 698

Kyushu, 595, 655, 698, 736, 817, 856

L

Laboratoire Matériel Téléphonique, 687
Lack, Colonel, 593
Laconia, 195
Lae, 426
La Falconara, 450
La Haye-du-Puits, 608,630
La Marsa, 363
Lambe, Captain Charles E., 36, 37, 38, 42, 43, 238
Lampedusa, 311, 322, 330, 333, 339
land forces for OVERLORD, 502
landing craft, for ANVIL, 524, 594; for HUSKY, 275, 297; for OVERLORD, 472, 487, 488, 491, 500, 501-502; for TORCH, 53,61,62
Landis, James M., 427
Lang, Will, 773, 774, 775, 793
Largo, 129
Larkin, Brigadier General Thomas B., 119, 133, 855
Larminat, General de, 320
La Senis, 158
Lauenburg, 792
Laval, 635
Laval, Pierre, 197, 209
Lavitrona, Cardinal, 377
Lawford, 573
Lawrence, Colonel Jock, 313, 651, 654, 659
Lawrence, Lance-Corporal Richard, 26, 27
Leahy, Admiral William D., 11, 45, 123, 233, 455
Lear, Lieutenant General Ben, 750, 758, 761, 762, 801
Leathers, Frederick James, Baron, 611
Lebanon, 874
Lechfeld, 532
Le Clerc, General Jacques, 338, 513, 524, 653
Ledo, 754
Lee, Clark, 403, 409, 438, 579

ABOUT THE AUTHOR

When Harry Butcher was returned to the U. S. Navy by General Eisenhower, the General wrote the following letter to Admiral King:

My dear Admiral King:

Now that the various homecoming ceremonies have been concluded, and in conformity with my previous agreement with you, I now release back to the Navy Department, Captain Harry C. Butcher, USNR, who has served me as aide and staff officer for three years.

For his services, Captain Butcher has been awarded by the War Department, with concurrence of the Navy, the Legion of Merit, the Bronze Star, and stars denoting participation in seven campaigns in the North African and European Theatres of Operations.

I am grateful to you and the Navy for the use of his services which have been conscientious and loyal. His presence on my personal staff has been a symbol of the cooperation of the Army and Navy in all our campaigns.

Harry Butcher met the then Major Eisenhower in Washington in 1926 and became his close friend in subsequent years. At the time of the meeting, Butcher was managing editor of The Fertilizer Review, *published by the National Fertilizer Association. He held this job through 1929 and has not stopped hearing about it ever since. He got into it as a logical development of his graduation from Iowa State College in 1924 with a degree in Agricultural Journalism.*

In 1929, Captain Butcher joined the Columbia Broadcasting System and opened its Washington office. When the war started in Europe in 1939, Butcher was commissioned as a Lt. Commander in the Naval Reserve. He was a vice-president of CBS at the time of his volunteering for enlistment in the Navy in 1942. Two months later, General Eisenhower requested his services as Naval Aide.

In addition to the decorations mentioned in General Eisenhower's letter above, Captain Butcher was decorated by the Sultan of French Morocco with the Order of Ouissam Alaouite. He is an honorary Deacon in Elder Michaux's Church of God (colored) in Washington.

Captain Butcher is 44, is a low nineties golfer (his short game being excellent, particularly on the first tee when making bets), a low seventies cigar smoker, and is well over a hundred in his poker game.

He reports that, after having kept his day-by-day diary for three years, having worked on it for six months preparing it for book publication, and having read proof on ten articles abstracted from it by the Saturday Evening Post, *his most enjoyable hobby is not writing a book.*

June 6, 1944 — May 7, 1945

Scale in miles (approximate)

0   100   200

⊳ Gen. Eisenhower's Headquarters
⟹ Allied Attack
German Attack

Will

Liverpool   Manchester   Hull

WALES   Birmingham   Norwich

Oxford   High Wycombe   Ipswich

Cardiff   Bristol   ENGLAND   Newbury   ⊳ London   Thames

Salisbury

Exeter   Southampton   Southwick   Dover   Dunkirk

Weymouth   Bournemouth   Brighton   Calais   Lille

Falmouth   Plymouth   Portsmouth   Boulogne

Slapton Sands   Dartmouth

Amsterdam
The Hague
Rotterdam   Arnhem

Flushing
Ostend   NETHERLAND

Antwerp   BELGIUM   Brussels   Liége   Aach   Mo

Spa
Bastogne

Abbeville   Sedan

Dieppe   Compiegne   Rheims   Verdun   Me

Le Havre   Rouen   ⊳

Cherbourg   Tournières   Bayeux   Meaux

Guernsey   St. Lô   Caen   Argentan   Versailles   ⊳ Paris

Jersey   Falaise   Chartres

St. Brieuc   St. Malo   Avranches   Alencon

Brest   Granville

Rennes   Laval   Le Mans

Lorient   Orléans   C   N   E

St. Nazaire   Angers   Tours   Bourges   Dijon

Nantes

Loire   Vichy

Limoges   Clermont-Ferrand   Lyon

Bordeaux   Grenob

F   R   A   Valence

Garonne   Rhone   Nimes

Toulouse   Arles

Montpellier   Marseille

SPA   Carcassonne